THE VICTORIA HISTORY
OF THE
COUNTIES OF ENGLAND

———

A HISTORY OF
MIDDLESEX

VOLUME XI

THE VICTORIA HISTORY
OF THE
COUNTIES OF ENGLAND

EDITED BY C. R. J. CURRIE

THE UNIVERSITY OF LONDON
INSTITUTE OF
HISTORICAL RESEARCH

Oxford University Press, Great Clarendon Street, Oxford OX2 6DP
Oxford New York
Athens Auckland Bangkok Bogotá
Buenos Aires Calcutta Cape Town Chennai
Dar es Salaam Delhi Florence Hong Kong
Istanbul Karachi Kuala Lumpur
Madrid Melbourne Mexico City Mumbai
Nairobi Paris São Paolo Singapore
Taipei Tokyo Toronto Warsaw

and associated companies in
Berlin Ibadan

Oxford is a registered trade mark of Oxford University Press

Published in the United States
by Oxford University Press Inc., New York

British Library Cataloguing in Publication Data
Data available

ISBN 0 19 722791 0

Printed by H Charlesworth & Co Ltd
Huddersfield, England

INSCRIBED TO THE

MEMORY OF HER LATE MAJESTY

QUEEN VICTORIA

WHO GRACIOUSLY GAVE THE TITLE TO

AND ACCEPTED THE DEDICATION

OF THIS HISTORY

A HISTORY OF THE COUNTY OF MIDDLESEX

EDITED BY T. F. T. BAKER

VOLUME XI

EARLY STEPNEY WITH BETHNAL GREEN

PUBLISHED FOR

THE INSTITUTE OF HISTORICAL RESEARCH

BY

OXFORD UNIVERSITY PRESS

1998

CONTENTS OF VOLUME ELEVEN

LIST OF CONTENTS

LIST OF ILLUSTRATIONS

For permission to reproduce material in their possession, thanks are rendered to: the British Museum; City of London, Guildhall Library; Docklands Light Railway Ltd; Hunting Aerofilms Ltd.; Mr. Nathaniel Kornbluth; London Metropolitan Archives (formerly G.L.R.O.), Photograph Collection; the Mercers' Company; the National Monuments Record (N.M.R.) of the Royal Commission on Historical Monuments (England); London Borough of Tower Hamlets, Local History Library and Archives (T.H.L.H.L.); the *Morning Star*; the Victoria and Albert Museum.

Plates between pages 138 and 139

LIST OF ILLUSTRATIONS

LIST OF MAPS AND OTHER TEXT FIGURES

All maps were drawn by K. J. Wass of the Department of Geography, University College, London, from drafts prepared by T. F. T. Baker, Diane K. Bolton, and Patricia E. C. Croot. Figure 26 was drawn by Pamela Studd. For permission to reproduce material in their possession, thanks are rendered to: the British Library; the Bodleian Library, University of Oxford; City of London, Guildhall Library; London Metropolitan Archives (formerly G.L.R.O.); the Trustees of Lambeth Palace Library; the Mercers' Company; the National Monuments Record (N.M.R.) of the Royal Commission on Historical Monuments (England); London Borough of Tower Hamlets, Local History Library and Archives (T.H.L.H.L.).

LIST OF MAPS AND OTHER TEXT FIGURES

EDITORIAL NOTE

The present volume is the fourth to have been compiled for the Middlesex V.C.H. Committee formed in 1979 to complete the Middlesex History. The University of London gratefully acknowledges the help of the Committee, which has continued under the chairmanship of Dr. David Avery until 1998 and thereafter of Dr. Alan Clinton, with Mr. Roy Harrison succeeding Dr. K. A. Bailey as Treasurer in 1997. The University also records its gratitude for the continued generosity of the City of Westminster and the London Boroughs of Kensington and Chelsea, Islington, and Hackney in supporting the Committee's work. Changes in the funding and structure of the Committee in the early 1990s are recorded in the Editorial Note to volume X. Thanks are once more offered to those who contributed to the Middlesex V.C.H. appeal from 1990, including the Corporation of London, the Marc Fitch Fund, the British Academy, the Pilgrim Trust, the Goldsmith's Company, the Mercer's Company, Camden History Society, Mr. Graham Bird, the late Mr. S. E. Piesse, and others giving privately. Their help was essential to the completion of this volume.

No changes in the editorial staff have occurred since the publication of volume X, but in 1996 Mrs. Jenny Free retired after long service as secretary.

Those who have provided information for the volume or commented on parts of the text are named in the footnotes, and they are sincerely thanked for their help.

The structure and aims of the Victoria County History as a whole are set out in the *General Introduction* (1970) and its *Supplement* (1990). The contents of the first seven volumes of the Middlesex History are listed and indexed in outline in a booklet, *The Middlesex Victoria History Council*, which also describes the work of the precursor of the present Middlesex Victoria County History Committee.

CLASSES OF DOCUMENTS
IN THE PUBLIC RECORD OFFICE
USED IN THIS VOLUME
WITH THEIR CLASS NUMBERS

Chancery

		Proceedings
C	1	Early
C	2	Series I
C	3	Series II
C	5	Six Clerks Series, Bridges
C	6	Collins
C	7	Hamilton
C	8	Mitford
C	9	Reynardson
C	10	Whittington
C	11	1714–58
C	47	Miscellanea
C	54	Close Rolls
C	62	Liberate Rolls
C	66	Patent Rolls
C	78	Decree Rolls
C	93	Proceedings of Commissioners of Charitable Uses, Inquisitions, and Decrees
C	103	Masters' Exhibits, Blunt
C	104	Tinney
C	107	Senior
C	110	Horne
C	131	Extents for Debts
		Inquisitions Post Mortem
C	133	Series I, Edw. I
C	134	Edw. II
C	135	Edw. III
C	136	Ric. II
C	138	Hen. V
C	139	Hen. VI
C	141	Ric. III
C	142	Series II
C	143	Inquisitions ad quod damnum
C	145	Miscellaneous Inquisitions
C	146	Ancient Deeds, Series C
C	260	Chancery Files (Tower and Roll Chapel), Recorda

Court of Common Pleas

CP	25(1)	Feet of Fines, Series I
CP	25(2)	Series II
CP	40	Plea Rolls
CP	43	Recovery Rolls

Exchequer, Treasury of Receipt

E	36	Books
E	40	Ancient Deeds, Series A

Exchequer, King's Remembrancer

E	101	Accounts, Various
E	134	Depositions taken by Commission
E	145	Extents (Excise)
E	150	Inquisitions Post Mortem, Series II
E	164	Miscellaneous Books, Series I
E	178	Special Commissions of Inquiry
E	179	Subsidy Rolls, etc.
E	210	Ancient Deeds, Series D
E	212	Series DS
E	214	Modern Deeds

Exchequer, Augmentation Office

E	317	Parliamentary Surveys
E	318	Particulars for Grants of Crown Lands
E	326	Ancient Deeds, Series B

Exchequer, Lord Treasurer's Remembrancer's and Pipe Offices

E	352	Chancellor's Rolls (Pipe Office)
E	372	Pipe Rolls (Pipe Office)

Ministry of Education

ED	3	Educational Returns, London
ED	4	Transfer Files, London
ED	7	Public Elementary Schools, Preliminary Statements
ED	14	London General Files
ED	20	Higher Elementary School Files
ED	21	Public Elementary School Files
ED	32	Special School Files

Home Office

HO	45	Registered Papers
HO	107	Population Returns
HO	129	Ecclesiastical Returns

Board of Inland Revenue

IR	29	Tithe Apportionments
IR	30	Tithe Maps

Justices Itinerant, Assize and Gaol Delivery Justices, etc.

JUST	1	Eyre Rolls, Assize Rolls, etc.

CLASSES OF DOCUMENTS IN THE PUBLIC RECORD OFFICE

Ministry of Agriculture, Fisheries, and Food

MAF 20   Manor Files
MAF 68   Agricultural Returns: Parish Summaries

Prerogative Court of Canterbury

PROB 3–4   Inventories
PROB 11   Registered Copies of Wills proved in P.C.C.
PROB 32   Exhibits with Inventories

Office of the Registrar General

RG 9   Census Returns, 1861
RG 10   1871
RG 11   1881
RG 31   Registers of Places of Worship

Court of Requests

REQ 2   Proceedings

Special Collections

SC 5   Hundred Rolls
SC 6   Ministers' and Receivers' Accounts
SC 11   Rentals and Surveys (rolls)
SC 12   Rentals and Surveys (portfolios)

State Paper Office

SP 1   State Papers, Hen. VIII, General Series
State Papers, Domestic
SP 12   Eliz. I
SP 16   Chas. I
SP 23   Committee for Compounding with Delinquents
SP 29   State Papers, Domestic, Chas. II

Court of Wards and Liveries

WARD 5   Feodaries' Surveys
WARD 7   Inquisitions Post Mortem

SELECT LIST OF
CLASSES OF DOCUMENTS IN THE
LONDON METROPOLITAN ARCHIVES
(FORMERLY GREATER LONDON RECORD OFFICE)
USED IN THIS VOLUME
WITH THEIR CLASS NUMBERS

A/CSC	Corporation of the Sons of the Clergy, records
AR/BA	London County Council Architect's Department, Building Surveyors' returns
C72	Bethnal Green Borough Council, records
C93	Stepney Borough Council, records
CL	London County Council Clerk's Department, records
E/PHI	Spencer Phillips Estate, Stepney, records
M79/LH	Hackney Manorial Records, Lordshold
M93	Stepney and Hackney Manorial Records
MBO/DS	Metropolitan Buildings Office, District Surveyors' Returns
MBW	Metropolitan Board of Works, records
MR/B/C	District Surveyors' Certificates
MR/B/R	Building Certificates Registers
MR/LV	Licensed Victuallers' Lists
MR/PLT	Land Tax Assessments
MR/RR	Enrolment Registration and Deposit, Recusancy
MR/TH	Hearth Tax Assessments
P72	Bethnal Green, parish records
P93	Stepney, parish records
SBL	School Board for London, records
TA	Tithe Awards
THCS	Tower Hamlets Commissioners of Sewers, records

NOTE ON ABBREVIATIONS

Among the abbreviations and short titles used the following may require elucidation, in addition to those noted in the Victoria History's *Handbook for Editors and Authors* (1970):

Archit. of Lond.	E. Jones and C. Woodward, *A Guide to the Architecture of London* (1983)
B.L.	British Library (used in references to documents transferred from the British Museum)
BNC	Brasenose College, Oxford
Bacon, *Atlas of Lond.* (1910)	*New Large-Scale Atlas of London and Suburbs*, ed. G. W. Bacon (1910)
Beaven, *Aldermen*	A. Beaven, *The Aldermen of the City of London temp. Henry III to 1912* (2 vols. 1908–13)
Booth, *Life and Labour*	C. Booth, *Life and Labour of the People in London* (17 vols. revised edn. 1902–3). Survey begun 1886
Booth's Map (1889)	*Charles Booth's Descriptive Map of London Poverty, 1889* (London Topographical Society 1984)
C.C.C.	Council for the Care of Churches (formerly Council for Places of Worship).
C.L.R.O.	Corporation of London Record Office
Calamy Revised	*Calamy Revised*, ed. A. G. Matthews (1934)
Cal. Mdx. Sess. Bks.	Calendar of Sessions Books, 1638–1752, at G.L.R.O.
Cal. Mdx. Sess. Rec.	Calendar of Sessions Records, 1607–12, at G.L.R.O.
Cheke's Reg.	Mercers' Company of London, Register of lands compiled by John Cheke 1578–9
Clarke, *Lond. Chs.*	B. F. L. Clarke, *Parish Churches of London* (1966)
Colvin, *Brit. Architects*	H. Colvin, *Biographical Dictionary of British Architects, 1600–1840* (1978)
Cruchley's New Plan (1826, 1829)	[G. F.] *Cruchley's New Plan of London and Its Environs* (1826, 1829)
E.L.A.	*East London Advertiser*
Endowed Chars. Lond. (1897)	*Endowed Charities* (County of London), I, H.C. 394 (1897), lxvi (2)
Endowed Chars Lond. (1904)	*Endowed Charities* (County of London), H.C. 334–I (1904), lxxii
Freshfield, *Communion Plate*	E. Freshfield, *Communion Plate of the Parish Churches in the County of London* (1895)
Ft. of F. Lond. & Mdx.	*Calendar to the Feet of Fines for London and Middlesex*, ed. W. J. Hardy and W. Page (2 vols. 1892–3)
G.L.C.	Greater London Council
G.L.R.O.	Greater London Record Office (from 1997 London Metropolitan Archives). Contains the collection of the former Middlesex Record Office (M.R.O.)
G.R.O.	General Register Office (later Office for National Statistics, Birkdale)
Gascoyne, *Map*	J. Gascoyne, *Map of Stepney Par.* (1703)
Gavin, *San. Ramblings*	H. Gavin, *Sanitary Ramblings. Illustrations of Bethnal Green* (1848)
Guildhall MSS.	City of London, Guildhall Library. Contains registers of wills of the commissary court of London (London division) (MS. 9171), bishops' registers (MS. 9531), diocesan administrative records (MSS. 9532–9560), and registers of nonconformist meeting houses (MS. 9580)
Gunnis, *Sculptors*	R. Gunnis, *Dictionary of British Sculptors, 1660–1851* (1951)
H.B.M.C. Lond.	Historic Buildings and Monuments Commission, London Division
Hennessy, *Novum Rep.*	G. Hennessy, *Novum Repertorium Ecclesiasticum Parochiale Londinense* (1894)
Hist. Lond. Transport	T. C. Barker and M. Robbins, *History of London Transport* (2 vols. 1975)
Hist. Mon. Com. E. Lond.	Royal Commission on Historical Monuments of England, *Inventory of the Historical Monuments in London*, v, *East London* (H.M.S.O. 1930)
Horwood, *Plan* (1792–5)	R. Horwood, *Plan of the Cities of London and Westminster, the Borough of Southwark, and Parts Adjoining* (1792–5, facsimile edn. 1966).
Hug. Soc.	Huguenot Society of London

I.L.E.A.	Inner London Education Authority.
L.B.	London Borough
L.C.C.	London County Council
L.C.C. *Lond. Statistics*	L.C.C. *London Statistics* (26 vols. 1905–6 to 1936–8, beginning with vol. xvi). Followed by ibid. new series (2 vols. 1945–54 and 1947–56) and by further new series from 1957
L.C.C. *Names of Streets*	L.C.C. *List of the Streets and Places within the County of London* (1901 and later edns.)
Langley & Belch's New Map	E. Langley and W. Belch, *Langley & Belch's New Map of London* (1812, facsimile edn. 1972)
List of Bldgs.	Department of the Environment, *21st List of Buildings of Historic Interest* (1975 and amendments to 1991)
Lysons, *Environs*	D. Lysons, *The Environs of London* (4 vols. 1792–6 and Supplement 1811)
M.B.	Metropolitan Borough
M.B.W.	Metropolitan Board of Works
M.L.R.	Middlesex Land Registry. The enrolments, indexes, and registers are at G.L.R.O.
Mackeson's Guide	C. Mackeson, *A Guide to the Churches of London and Its Suburbs* (1866 and later edns.)
Mdx. County Rec.	*Middlesex County Records* [1550–1688], ed. J. C. Jeaffreson (4 vols. 1886–92)
Mdx. County Rec. Sess. Bks. 1689–1709	*Middlesex County Records, Calendar of the Sessions Books 1689–1709*, ed. W. J. Hardy (1905)
Mdx. Sess. Rec.	*Calendar to the Sessions Records* [1612–18], ed. W. le Hardy (4 vols. 1935–41)
Mems. Stepney Par.	*Memorials of Stepney Parish*, ed. G. W. Hill and W. H. Frere (1890–1)
Middleton, *View*	J. Middleton, *View of the Agriculture of Middlesex* (1798)
Mudie-Smith, *Rel. Life*	R. Mudie-Smith, *The Religious Life of London* (1904). Census taken 1903
N.M.R.	Royal Commission on Historical Monuments of England, National Monuments Record
New Lond. Life and Labour	H. Llewellyn Smith and others, *New Survey of London Life and Labour* (9 vols. 1930–5). Survey undertaken 1928
Newcourt, *Rep.*	R. Newcourt, *Repertorium Ecclesiasticum Parochiale Londinense* (2 vols. 1708–10)
Norden, *Spec. Brit.*	J. Norden, *Speculum Britanniae: Middlesex* (facsimile edn. 1971)
Old O.S. Map	Old Ordnance Survey Maps: the Godfrey edition (from 1983) (reduced facsimile reproductions of 1: 2,500 maps *c.* 1866–1914)
P.L.A.	Port of London Authority
P.N. Mdx. (E.P.N.S.)	*Place-Names of Middlesex* (English Place-Name Society, vol. xviii, 1942)
Pevsner, *Lond.* ii	N. Pevsner, *Buildings of England: London except the Cities of London and Westminster* (1952)
Plan of Mercers' est.	Mercers' Company of London, Plan of the Colet estate in 1615
Rawcliffe, 'Margaret Stodeye'	C. Rawcliffe, 'Margaret Stodeye, Lady Philpot (d. 1431)', in *Medieval London Widows, 1800–50*, ed. C.M. Barron and A.F. Sutton (1994)
Regency A to Z	*The A to Z of Regency London*, intro. P. Laxton (1985)
Rep. on Bridges in Mdx.	*Report of the Committee of Magistrates Appointed to make Enquiry respecting the Public Bridges in the County of Middlesex* (1826). Copy at G.L.R.O.
Rep. Com. Eccl. Revenues	*Report of the Commissioners Appointed to Inquire into the Ecclesiastical Revenues of England and Wales* [67], H.C. (1835), xxii
Rocque, *Map of Lond.* (1741–5)	J. Rocque, *Exact survey of the cities of London, Westminster, and the borough of Southwark, and the country near ten miles around* (1746, facsimile edn. 1971)
Stanford, *Map of Lond.* (1862–5)	*Stanford's Library Map of London and Its Suburbs* (1862 edn. with additions to 1865)
Stow, *Survey* (1720)	J. Stow, *Survey of London*, ed. J. Strype, 2 vols. (1720)
T.H.L.H.L.	Tower Hamlets Local History Library
T.L.M.A.S.	Transactions of the London and Middlesex Archaeological Society (1856 to date). Consecutive numbers are used for the whole series, although vols. vii–xvii (1905–54) appeared as N.S. i–xi

NOTE ON ABBREVIATIONS

Vestry mins [Bethnal Green]	T.H.L.H.L. (1747–1900)
Vestry mins. [Stepney]	G.L.R.O. P 93/DUN. Minutes for 1580–1662 pub. in *Mems. Stepney Par.*
Walford, *Lond.*	E. Walford, *Old and New London*, v (*c.* 1878)
Walker Revised	*Walker Revised*, ed. A. G. Matthews (1948)

OSSULSTONE HUNDRED

(continued)

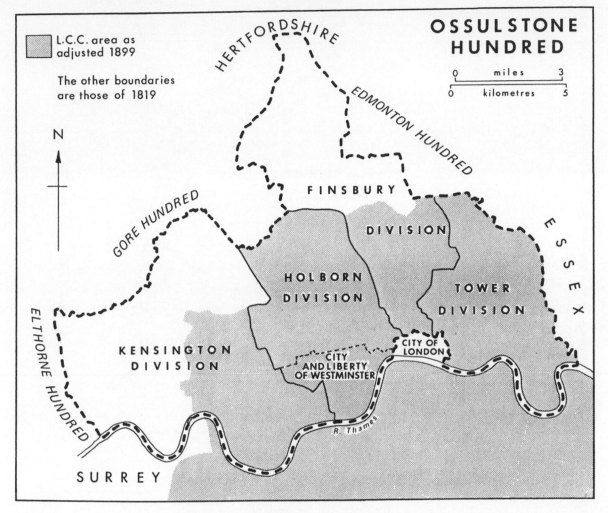

FIG. I

TOWER DIVISION

EARLY STEPNEY

STEPNEY covered almost all the area between the suburbs of the City of London and the river Lea, the eastern boundary of Middlesex, until the early 14th century when the first of several daughter parishes was created. Partly built up in the Middle Ages and great in size, it served many economic functions, with contrasting social conditions, over a long period. A maritime parish with the associated activities and docks, Stepney was also closely involved in London's economy, especially in housing the latter's industries. The western part provided the first English home for generations of immigrants, while farther east it was largely suburban in character.[1]

The parochial jurisdiction devolved from the much larger vill of Stepney belonging to the bishop of London and covering east, north-east, and part of north London.[2]

[1] For Bethnal Green, below. Histories of the other daughter parishes are reserved for a later volume. The article was written in 1991–5.
[2] Below, manors.

I

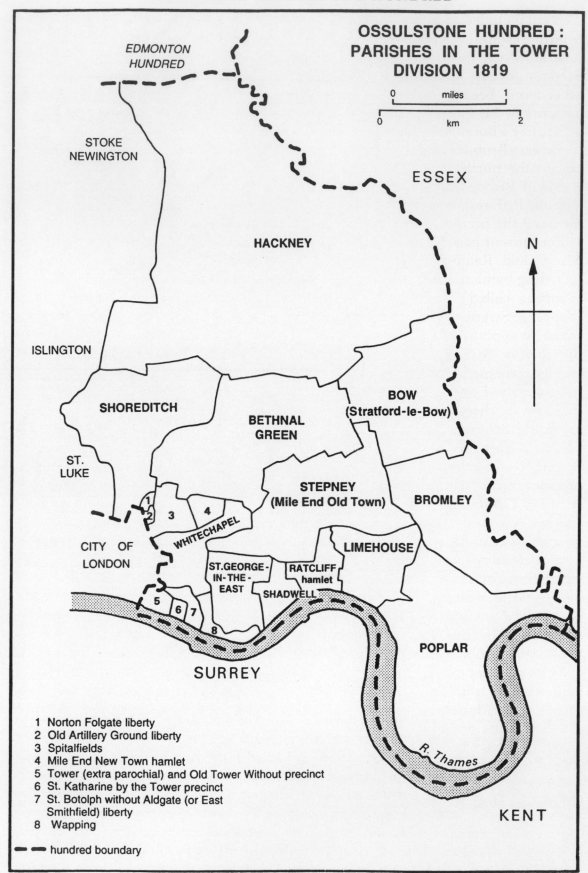

FIG. 2

The vill included Hackney, and probably at one time also Bromley, a parish created from an estate in 'Stepney' claimed unsuccessfully by the bishop in 1086.[3] The date at which the three achieved separate parochial status is not known: since Stepney gave its name to the vill it is assumed it was a Saxon *parochia*,[4] but on the other hand, because of its closeness to London it may have remained part of the *parochia* of St. Paul's until relatively late.

Stepney's boundaries were first delineated in 1703:[5] to the south was the Thames, to the east Bromley and, across the Lea, West Ham (Essex), to the north Hackney, and to the north-west Shoreditch. To the west the City of London's suburban wards of Bishopsgate Without and Portsoken formed the parishes of St. Botolph without Bishopsgate and St. Botolph without Aldgate respectively; the second also included the precinct of St. Katharine by the Tower and East Smithfield.

The ancient parish included the hamlets of Mile End Old Town, Mile End New Town, and Ratcliff, which remained part of St. Dunstan's, Stepney, and the following hamlets which became separate parishes: Whitechapel, including part of Wapping called Wapping-Whitechapel which became the parish of St. John, Wapping; Stratford Bow, including Old Ford; Shadwell; the major part of Wapping called Wapping-Stepney, which became the parish of St. George-in-the-East; Spitalfields; Bethnal Green; Limehouse; Poplar, which included the Isle of Dogs and its settlements of Blackwall, Millwall, and Cubitt Town.

Under the London Government Act, 1899, the separate parishes were brought together in three M.B.s: Bethnal Green, coterminous with its parish; Poplar, including Stratford Bow and Bromley; and Stepney, including all the remaining parishes, East Smithfield, and the small liberties along the western boundary of Stepney — the liberty of the Tower, by the river, Holy Trinity (formerly the precinct of the Minoresses' abbey of St. Clare), just north of the Tower, and Old Artillery Ground and Norton Folgate, both near Bishopsgate.[6]

Stepney's land boundaries were not natural: that with Bromley followed the bounds of an estate given with the foundation of St. Leonard's priory, and a small area of meadow on the east side of the Lea lay in Stepney. Part of the boundary with Shoreditch followed a highway from Shoreditch church to Cambridge Heath; most of the western boundary presumably represented the limits reached by Londoners' jurisdiction. The boundary with Hackney cut across fields in 1703, suggesting that it was laid down when that part of the manorial demesne was unassarted, probably woodland, and before any man-made features were available.[7]

At its greatest extent Stepney parish covered *c.* 4,150 a. (1,679.5 ha.), including land wrested from the Thames.[8] By 1320 it had lost *c.* 211 a. to form the parish of St. Mary Matfelon or Whitechapel,[9] whose boundaries seem to have followed those of fields or estates, apart possibly from the line along Back Church Lane, which may have been the medieval Chapel Street. The new parish took the western side of Stepney extending from the property and waste lining the north side of the Colchester road southward to the Thames, with an extension eastward along the Colchester road and the waste on either side as far as Mile End, probably to share

3   *V.C.H. Mdx.* i. 128.
4   *Minster and Parish Chs.: The Local Church in Transition 950–1200*, ed. J. Blair (Oxford Univ. Cttee. for Archaeol., Monograph no. 17, 1988), 41, 43 n.
5   Gascoyne, *Map*.

6   63 & 64 Vic. c. 14; below, fig. 3.
7   As happened with the southern boundary of Hampstead: *V.C.H. Mdx.* ix. 2.
8   Acreages in 1801: *V.C.H. Mdx.* ii. 114.
9   Guildhall Add. MS. 9. Fig. includes *c.* 20 a. taken from Thames in 16th cent.

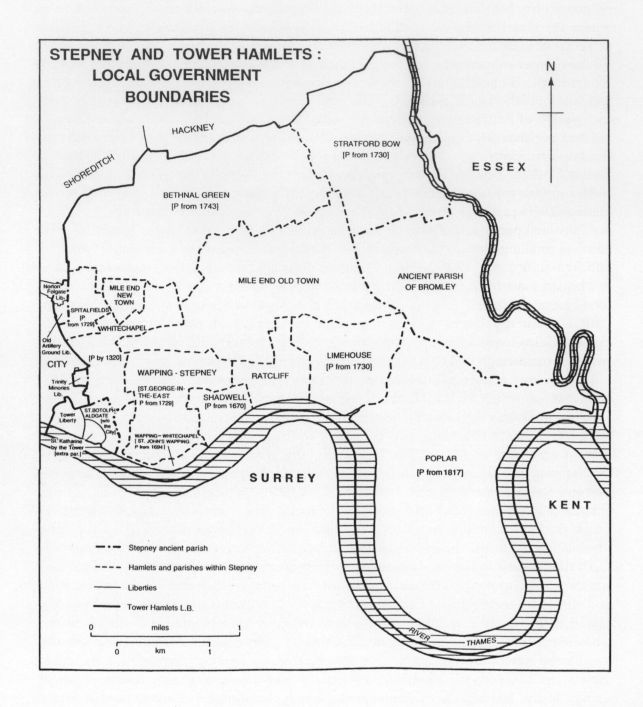

STEPNEY AND TOWER HAMLETS :
LOCAL GOVERNMENT
BOUNDARIES

FIG. 3

responsibility for that important highway. Whitechapel may have ended at the river where the Crash mills stood, but by the 16th century it included a narrow tongue of reclaimed land running eastward between Wapping's medieval river wall and the low-water mark and known as Wapping-Whitechapel; it almost completely cut off from the Thames the rest of Wapping, which remained part of Stepney and was distinguished as Wapping-Stepney.[10] Wapping-Whitechapel became the separate parish of St. John, Wapping, in 1694.[11]

Later parishes were formed from the hamlets whose boundaries had been settled by the late 17th century.[12] St. Paul, Shadwell (68 a.), was created by an Act in 1670.[13] Christ Church, Spitalfields (73 a.), and St. George-in-the-East (formerly Wapping-Stepney) (244 a.) followed in 1729, St. Mary, Stratford Bow (565 a.), and St. Anne, Limehouse (244 a.), in 1730, and St. Matthew, Bethnal Green (755 a.) in 1743.[14] The last new civil parish was All Saints, Poplar (1,158 a.), in 1817.[15] There remained three hamlets totalling 830 a. (335.9 ha.) in the parish of St. Dunstan, Stepney: Mile End Old Town (677 a.), Mile End New Town (42 a.), and Ratcliff (111 a.).

Though most of the ancient parish lies on River Terrace high flood plain gravel on top of London Clay, the area north-west of a line from the north-west corner of Victoria Park to the south-west corner of Bethnal Green parish consists of brickearth, patches of which also overlie the gravel elsewhere.[16] The gravel ends just short of the Lea, which runs through a valley of alluvium lying over London Clay, which provided an important area of meadows and grazing.[17] In the south part of the parish the gravel ends at a line which runs from the northern half of St. Katharine's docks, north of the London docks, to the junction of Cable Street and Butcher Row, then continues to the southern end of West India Dock Road, along Poplar High Street, and then to the north-west corner of the East India docks. The edge of the gravel formed a steep bank in Wapping and Shadwell, called the Linches from the 12th century; it had been the site of a Roman road and was later that of Ratcliff Highway.[18] Along the Thames an alluvial belt, joining the alluvium of the Lea valley, includes the whole of the Isle of Dogs, the land around the Limehouse basin, and the southern parts of St. George-in-the-East and Whitechapel, lying on London Clay or on Woolwich and Reading Beds.

All the parish, save the western part of Bethnal Green and a patch near the west end of Commercial Road, lies at less than 15 m. above sea level; the riverside and the south-east parts lie at less than 10 m.[19] Deposits since Roman times have added to the Neolithic alluvium along the Thames, where much of the land may have been submerged at high tide as late as the 2nd century A.D.[20] By the 12th century those areas were known as marshes, the most important being Walmarsh or Wapping marsh, in St. George-in-the-East and Whitechapel, and Stepney marsh or Poplar marsh, in the Isle of Dogs.[21] The extent of the alluvial marsh may explain why a landing-place, the *Stybba's hythe* which evolved as 'Stepney', gave its name to a large area of Middlesex:[22] the only place on the north bank below London

[10] Below, settlement and bldg.

[11] St. John, Wapping: 5 & 6 Wm. & Mary, c. 20 (Private); map of med. par.

[12] Below, local govt., and also to be treated in a later volume. Acreages from *V.C.H. Mdx.* ii. 114.

[13] 22 Car. II, c. 14 (Private).

[14] 2 Geo. II, c. 10, c. 30; 3 Geo. II, c. 3, c. 17; 16 Geo. II, c. 28 (all Local and Personal).

[15] 57 Geo. III, c. 34 (Local and Personal).

[16] Para. based on Geol. Survey Map 6", drift, Lond. V. NE. SE., VI. NW. SW (1919 and 1920 edns.); ibid. 1/50,000,

sheet 256 (1994 edn.).

[17] Below, econ. hist.

[18] Below, communications; manors.

[19] O.S. Maps 1/10,000, TQ 38 SW. (1979 edn. B); TQ 38 SE. (1982 edn. B).   [20] *V.C.H. Mdx.* i. 6, 8.

[21] Detailed hist. reserved for later volume. There was also marsh in the north-west of the parish, where several springs arose, called Haresmarsh in 1335: Guildhall MS. 25403/2; below, Bethnal Green.

[22] *P.N. Mdx.* (E.P.N.S.), 149–50; below, settlement and building.

where the river approaches the gravel ridge to make landing feasible is at Ratcliff Cross, where Butcher Row meets Ratcliff Highway, and in the 1st century A.D. the bank may even have been farther north, possibly as far as Cable Street.[23]

The marshes provided sites for medieval tidal mills.[24] By the early 13th century embanking and drainage had created much cultivated land: arable adjoined the river wall at Wapping that gave its name to Walmarsh.[25] An inquiry in 1324 on the area between St. Katharine's marsh and the vill of Shadwell (that is, Walmarsh) found that an unknown lord of Stepney in 'ancient time' had recovered about 100 a. with banks and ditches; when they had fallen into disrepair he had granted 42½ a. to freemen and the rest to his bondmen, all of whom held by the service of maintaining the river walls and sewers under the supervision of two wall-reeves answerable to the manor court. The measure had worked well, except when bad weather or exceptionally high tides had left the tenants in need of financial help.[26] A tenement near Limehouse called the Mote had a similar obligation to repair river walls.[27]

The high tidal range made necessary repeated reclamation work until adequate embanking was carried out in the 16th century. The Crown often appointed commissions to inspect and repair stretches of riverbank from the City eastward, occasionally well into Essex. The earliest commission known was in 1297–8; another was named in 1324 after major flooding, and they later became frequent, with nine between 1354 and 1381, and five between 1395 and 1407. In 1395–6 the lord lost rents from submerged land and the manor paid expenses for attending the inquiries at Whitechapel into repair of walls.[28] In 1429 ordinances were to be made for Stepney and Walmarsh similar to the laws and customs of Romney marsh, in order to obtain labourers and make quick repairs. A similar commission was appointed in 1447 for land as far north as the parish churches of Bromley, Stepney, and Whitechapel, but floods in 1448 led to an inquiry into the cause. Further commissions were held in 1455, 1467, 1474, and 1480.[29] The large number of freeholders, whom the manor court could not easily coerce, probably accounted for presentations in the king's courts, as in 1369–70, when landholders were summoned to repair their stretches of wall.[30]

Flooding in Stepney or Poplar marsh hastened the transition from arable to pasture in the 15th century and saw the abandonment of a settlement at the south end of the Isle of Dogs.[31] In 1448 a major breach in the wall on the south-west of the marsh through neglect by the freeholder John Harpur, presumably as lord of the manor of Pomfret, was said to have allowed the flooding of c. 1,000 a.[32] Sixteen years later 400 a. of Stepney manor were still flooded, causing loss of revenue to the bishop, of 7 tenements and 9 cottages to his tenants, and of land on other manors.[33]

More permanent solutions were found in the 16th century: after the whole of Wapping marsh had been flooded, building was encouraged on top of the wall c. 1570, the site of the roads called Greenbank and Wapping Wall, and gradual enwharving on the river side helped to contain the tides.[34] Statutory commissions

23 Cf. for the City: M. Biddle, D.M. Hudson, C.M. Heighway, *Future of Lond.'s Past* (Rescue Publ. no. 4, Worcester 1973), maps 2 and 4.

24 Below, econ. hist. (mills).

25 B.L. Cott. MS. Tib. C. v, ff. 156–8; P.R.O., E 40/1801; below, econ. hist. (agric.); manors (St. Thos. of Acre; Holy Trinity).

26 *Abbrev. Plac.* (Rec. Com.), 352–3; W. Dugdale, *Hist. of Imbanking and Draining* (1722), 69–70.

27 Below, manors (Huscarl). 28 Guildhall MS. 25403/5.

29 Dugdale, *Hist. Imbanking*, 69–72.

30 *Pub. Wks. in Med. Law*, ii (Selden Soc. xl), 40–1.

31 Below, econ. hist. (agric.).

32 Dugdale, *Hist. Imbanking*, 72.

33 P.R.O., SC 6/1140/24; below, manors. Chapel also ceased to be used: below, churches.

34 B.L. Lansd. MS. 38, f. 21.

for sewers in the 16th and 17th centuries for all the areas around London provided closer supervision and spread the financial burden more widely.[35]

A watercourse, probably rising near Spitalfields, ran south-eastward through Haresmarsh to Mile End, crossing the Colchester road near the junction with Cambridge Heath Road, passing north of the parish church, and curving round into Poplar to enter the Thames at Limehouse dock. It may have given the name to Brokestreet, near the church, by the 14th century.[36] In 1703 it crossed the Colchester road by a bridge, known as Stonebridge in 1731.[37] The stream was gradually culverted and by the late 18th century, when it was known as the Black Ditch, was clearly distinguished only between Rhodeswell Road and the Thames. Long straight stretches suggest that its course had already been modified.[38]

Other watercourses may have been small streams running into the Thames but later dug out for drainage. The 13th-century Cropats ditch near Cropats well, south of Hachestreet (later Cable Street),[39] was possibly the stream that ran along Nightingale Lane to the Crash mills. Although a 16th-century plan shows it running from East Smithfield, it was more likely to have risen in Wellclose Square.[40] Another stream rose in the gravel near Shadwell well, by the site of St. Paul's Shadwell, and was still known to residents in 1684.[41] A stream c. 12 ft. wide that existed by the 12th century formerly skirted the road at the eastern junction of Butcher Row with White Horse and Cable streets. It probably flowed from north-east to south-west, but has not been traced to the Thames.[42]

In the 20th century a concealed stream arose at the junction of Devons Road and Weston Street, in Bromley, and ran erratically southward to cross Poplar High Street and then turn eastward through the workhouse to Poplar dock. The only other known 20th-century stream (also concealed) rose at the junction of West and South Tenter streets in Goodman's Fields, in Whitechapel, and ran south to the Thames at Tower Bridge.[43]

COMMUNICATIONS

ROADS. Roman and pre-Roman roads are still largely conjectural.[44] An Iron-Age route linking the Trinobantes' capital at Colchester with a Thames crossing is thought to have run through Stepney and been rebuilt by the Romans. It forded the Lea and continued west of Stepney along the line of Old Street.[45] Despite the discovery of a section of Roman road, unaligned, at the junction of Green Street (renamed Roman Road) and Cambridge Road in 1938,[46] the most likely route to Old Street is that of Hackney Road, the parish boundary and therefore probably ancient.[47]

The ford is assumed to have lain at Old Ford opposite Iceland wharf, where Roman tiling was found in 1905.[48] It is also assumed to have been the crossing-point for the road to Colchester from London by way of Aldgate,[49] since a three-track highway, built soon after the Claudian invasion, has been uncovered a few hundred yards to the west. The south track may have remained in use until soon after 400 A.D.[50] Extrapolation in a straight line suggests that it was the Aldgate–Colchester road,[51] although it would have run only a few hundred yards south of the road at Green Street.[52]

There is little evidence from 1703 for the route,[53] nor as to when or why it was changed

[35] I. Darlington, *Lond. Commrs. of Sewers and Their Records* (1970); recs. covering parts of Stepney from 1629 in G.L.R.O.
[36] *P.N. Mdx.* (E.P.N.S.), 155; below, communications.
[37] Gascoyne, *Map*; G.L.R.O., M93/280.
[38] G.L.R.O., M93/1, p. 49, precept for culvert, 1654; Gascoyne, *Map*; N. J. Barton, *Lost Rivers of Lond.* (1982), 47.
[39] B.L. Cott. MS. Tib. C. v, f. 159.
[40] Barton, *Lost Rivers*, 47.
[41] *Trial between Thos. Neale and Lady Theodosia Ivie, 4 June 1684, for part of Shadwell* (1696), evidence for Dean of St. Paul's and Neale; Bodl., Gough Maps 17, f. 26.
[42] *T.L.M.A.S.* xxviii. 215–51.
[43] Geol. Survey Map 6", drift, Lond. V. SE., VI. NW. SW. (1919, 1920 edns.).

[44] I. D. Margary, *Rom. Rds. in Britain* (1967), 53, 56. Later writers, esp. after excavation in 1970s (below), have been more decided: e.g. W.F. Grimes, *Excavation of Rom. and Medieval Lond.* (1968), 45 and map; A. Vince, *Saxon Lond.: An Archaeol. Investigation* (1990), 119–20.
[45] Margary, *Rom. Rds.* 53. [46] *Jnl. Rom. Studies*, xxix. 217.
[47] *Survey of Lond.* viii. 3; below, Bethnal Green, communications.
[48] *Proc. Soc. Antiq.* [2nd ser.], xxiii. 230–6.
[49] Margary, *Rom. Rds.* 56.
[50] *T.L.M.A.S.* xxiii. 42–54, 101–47; xxxv. 25–36.
[51] Ibid. xxiii, plans facing pp. 46, 62.
[52] R. Merrifield, *Lond.: City of the Roms.* (1983), 123–7, also doubted whether the modern A11–A12 had been an imperial route. [53] Gascoyne, *Map*.

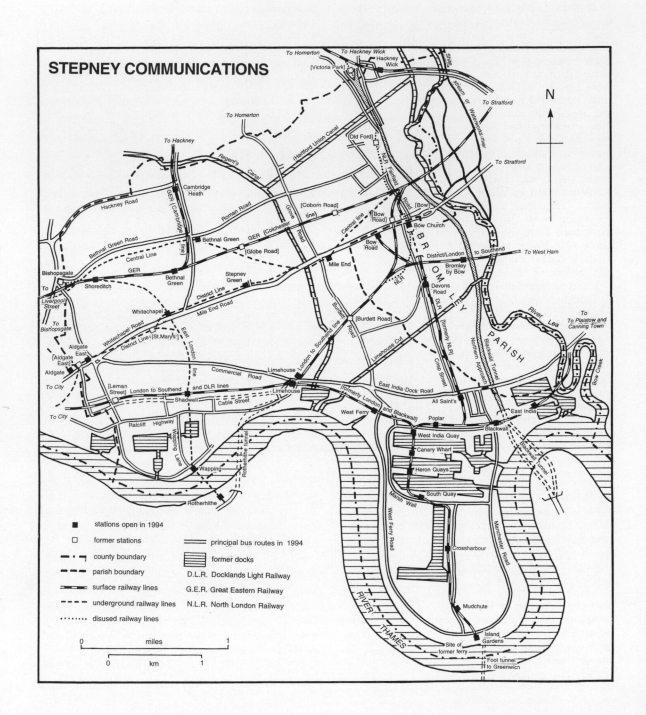

STEPNEY COMMUNICATIONS

Legend:
- ■ stations open in 1994
- □ former stations
- ═══ principal bus routes in 1994
- ▦ former docks
- –·–·– county boundary
- – – – parish boundary
- ▬▬▬ surface railway lines
- – – – underground railway lines
- ········ disused railway lines

D.L.R. Docklands Light Railway
G.E.R. Great Eastern Railway
N.L.R. North London Railway

0 ———— miles ———— 1
0 ———— km ———— 1

FIG. 4

to its later line, to cross the Lea at Stratford Bow. In 1302 it was found that the bridges at Bow had been built at the instruction (between 1100 and 1118) of Maud, wife of Henry I, to replace a dangerous ford which the jurors assumed to have been at Old Ford, a name recorded in 1230.[54] The road itself was not mentioned; it may have been realigned when the bridges were built, although if it still ran to Old Ford the bridges would probably have been built there. Excavations near Old Ford have found no evidence for the use of that road after the early 5th century.[55] The modern road forms part of the northern boundary of Bromley parish, created from a manor in existence by 1066, and so is likely to have been in use by then. Its straightness between Aldgate and the junction with the Romford road in West Ham indicates a Roman origin. The name Stratford given to the settlements on both the Middlesex and Essex sides (Stratford Langthorn), in conjunction with the name *Old* Ford, suggests the existence of two fords and of a metalled road in use with a ford well before the bridge.[56]

Further signs of the antiquity of the modern Colchester road, with stretches known as Aldgate High Street, Whitechapel High Street, Whitechapel Road, Mile End Road, and Bow Road, date from the Middle Ages. Like the Cambridge road from Mile End to Hackney, and the road from Mile End to Stepney church, the Colchester road ran between wide bands of manorial waste that possibly stretched from Aldgate bars into the hamlet of Stratford Bow. Free and copyhold messuages along the edge of the waste where it adjoined the cultivated fields suggest that the road pre-dated the fields. The antiquity of the part nearest Aldgate was confirmed by Roman metalling found below Aldgate High Street,[57] and the medieval name for Whitechapel High Street was *Algatestrete*.[58]

Other main routes are also uncertain before the 13th century. London's wall of 200 A.D. may have had a gate, St. Peter's gate, to a road along the gravel ridge to a signal station on the south side of Ratcliff Highway at the junction with Gravel (later Old Gravel, then Wapping) Lane. Romano-British burials took place farther east near the junction of Ratcliff Highway and Love Lane, whence the road may have continued as far as Ratcliff Cross to a likely landing-place.[59] A Roman road running south-east, across the site of the Minoresses' convent, was aligned on Hart Street in the City and thus probably older than the wall; its destination is not known[60] but may have been the signal station.

From c. 1200 the evidence for south-western Stepney is firmer. Slightly north of the Tower a postern gate was made in the wall, from which two roads ran eastward. That called Hachestreet by 1250[61] had become Heggestreet or Hoggestreet in the 14th century, Hog Lane by 1542,[62] and Rosemary Lane by 1637.[63] It reached White Horse Street, Ratcliff, probably by the 13th century and certainly by c. 1577.[64] The part through Wapping was known as Cable Street by 1703,[65] and that nearest to Ratcliff as Brook Street by 1652.[66]

South-east of the postern was the settlement of East Smithfield, where a road ran parallel to Hachestreet. Called the 'vicum de Shadwell' in 1272[67] or Shadwell Street, later Ratcliff Highway, it lay almost on the southern edge of the firm gravel, and from its name and nearby remains was probably of Roman origin. It existed by the early 13th century and probably in the 11th, as it gave access to Shadwell and Wapping mills,[68] and in 1362 was referred to as the highway between the *Redclyf* and the Tower of London.[69] Wapping mill was probably reached by the road running south from Ratcliff Highway and later known as Wapping Lane. Since the holder of the mill paid a service to the bishop of London c. 1270 for a way from Wapping to Stepney, it was not an ancient right of way.[70]

Other main routes led off the Colchester road. The later Cambridge Heath Road left it a mile from Aldgate pump and ran northward to Hackney; Bethnal green and Cambridge Heath were parts of the waste along its length.[71] The junction became known as Mile End and later marked the eastern extremity of Whitechapel parish.

A little to the east of Mile End a road branched off towards the parish church. In 1725 an ancient highway called Mile End Green leading from the hamlet of Ratcliff to the City,[72] it was later renamed Stepney Green. It continued through Ratcliff linking Stepney church, White Horse Street, and Butcher Row to Ratcliff Cross and the river, and probably was at least as old as the church. Late 14th-century settlements along it were called Churchstreet (west of the churchyard), Spilmanstreet, Clevestreet, and Redclyff.[73] Brokestreet, near the church but unlocated, may have been the lane on the east side of the churchyard, or the road beside a stream north of the church (later Ben Jonson Road) leading towards Rogueswell common.[74] By 1577 the road south of the churchyard was called White Horse or White Hart Street, after the White Hart near the junction with Rose Lane.[75]

[54] *Abbrev. Plac.* (Rec. Com.), 316–17; *P.N. Mdx.* (E.P.N.S.), 136.
[55] *T.L.M.A.S.* xxiii. 101–47.
[56] H. L. Smith, *Hist. E. Lond.* (1939), 188.
[57] Merrifield, *Lond.* 123.
[58] Demesne 'behind Algatestrete' in 1362 lay near Brick Lane: P.R.O., SC 6/1139/18.
[59] Biddle, Hudson, Heighway, *Future of Lond.'s Past*; *V.C.H. Mdx.* i. 67; above, intro.
[60] *Brit. Atlas of Historic Towns*, ed. M. D. Lobel, iii (1989), Rom. map.
[61] P.R.O., E 40/2543–4, dated from internal evidence.
[62] Lobel, *Brit. Atlas of Historic Towns*.
[63] P.R.O., WARD 5/27, bdl. 1 (Sir John Gore).
[64] Ibid. MPF 282.   [65] Gascoyne, *Map*.
[66] G.L.R.O., M93/157, p. 26. Apparently unconnected with 15th-cent. Brokestreet (below).
[67] B.L. Cott. MS. Tib. C. v, f. 159, dated from P.R.O., CP 25/1/147/24, no. 501.
[68] Below, settlement and bldg.; econ. hist. (mills).
[69] *Cal. Pat.* 1361–4, 153.
[70] B.L. Cott. MS. Tib. C. v, f. 162; below, manors (St. Thomas Acre).
[71] Below, Bethnal Green, communications.
[72] Cal. Mdx. Sess. Bks. xiii. 57, 149, 199, 242.
[73] P.R.O., SC 12/11/31, f. 1.
[74] Ibid. f. 7v.; SC 6/1139/22; C 66/527, m. 11.
[75] Cheke's Reg., ff. 190–1.

Opposite the White Hart a road ran north-west to join Whitechapel Road by the church there. In the 18th century it was known as White Horse Lane,[76] having been known in 1459 as the path or road from the church of St. Mary Matfelon to Ratcliff.[77] Three roads ran eastward from Ratcliff to Limehouse, Poplar, and Blackwall by the late 16th century. The most northerly, Salmon's Lane in 1652, was a public highway to Ballscross in 1454 and the road from Stepney church to Limehouse in 1577.[78] Another, Rose Lane in 1703, was the highway from the White Hart to Poplar in 1484 and the Back Lane from Limehouse to White Horse Street in 1652.[79] Both Salmon and Rose lanes, referred to as routes to Blackwall in 1615,[80] joined a lane from Ballscross to Limehouse, known in the 14th century as Forby Street or Forby Lane and in 1652 as Three Colt Street or Forbes Street.[81] The southernmost route ran eastward from Ratcliff Cross to Limehouse, and may have been the highway between Ratcliff and Limehouse mentioned in 1440.[82] It was lined with waste which was let for building by Lord Wentworth in the late 16th century, that on the south side being valuable for riverside wharves. In 1652 it was called Limehouse Street, and in the 1740s the Narrow Street, later the Narrow Way.[83]

From Limehouse the route to Blackwall lay along Poplar High Street, another area of medieval settlement.[84] Roads ran from the street northward to Bow bridge and Bromley, and southward to a ferry at the southern end of the Isle of Dogs. These routes were probably that of Edward I from Pomfret manor in the Isle of Dogs to Stratford Bow, and of James I from his favourite palace at Theobalds (Herts.) to Greenwich.[85] In 1652 the road to the ferry was known as Chapel Lane.[86]

The medieval road pattern changed little until the 19th century. Mile End Road, as an important highway to Essex, required much mending: John Hadley, a prominent local landowner, left £10 towards repairs in 1409.[87] The parish was reported as neglectful of its highways in 1637.[88] In 1696 it was stated that the road had been improved 30 years earlier under pressure from the Lieutenant of the Tower, by timbers covered with earth and gravel with a higher row of large gravel packed into the middle to throw water off into the ditches on each side.[89] Despite building on the waste, the Colchester road and its two offshoots retained wide carriageways and open ground either side, which still gave them a distinctive character in 1994.

The London–Harwich road was turnpiked between Whitechapel and Shenfield (Essex) under Acts of 1722 and 1737, with each hamlet contributing proportionately.[90] The only turnpike gate in Stepney until the 1820s, Mile End Gate, allegedly was erected in 1714,[91] but presumably was built in connexion with tolls for mending the road under the Acts. It stood just west of the junction with Cambridge Road and was long survived by its name, in 1994 that of a bus terminal. In 1809 a parliamentary committee reported that the whole road should be paved in the centre but that any unbuilt verges should be left for driven animals.[92]

Roads were improved for access to the East and West India docks in the 19th century. White Horse Lane became Commercial Road East, authorized in 1802, which continued eastward to join East India Dock Road by 1825.[93] Minor improvements to main routes throughout the parish were made by the M.B.W. after 1855.[94] More significant was the East Cross route, a motorway completed in 1979 linking Hackney Wick with the Blackwall tunnel,[95] which absorbed parts of several local roads in Stratford Bow and Bromley and created a barrier down the middle of both parishes. In the 1980s roads to and within the Isle of Dogs were altered to improve access and allow new building around the docks.[96]

Transport from Blackwall to the City was heavy in 1825, with 29 short-stage coaches making 72 return journeys a day, including coaches run by the West India Docks Co. to carry passengers and samples of goods. Bow and Bromley was the terminus for two coaches making five return journeys a day.[97] In 1838–9 licensed services again reflected the importance of the docks. From Blackwall four short-stage coaches and one omnibus ran to the City, 23 omnibuses ran to Piccadilly, 10 to Sloane Street, and five to Edgware Road. There were also nine short-stage coaches running from the East or West India docks to the City. Other services ran along the Mile End Road: seven omnibuses ran from Bow to Oxford Street and Hyde Park Corner. From Mile End Gate, 27 omnibuses ran to Chelsea, 10 to Bond Street and Oxford Street, 8 to Notting Hill, 2 to Hammersmith and 1 to Fulham. From Whitechapel church three omnibuses ran to Hammersmith Gate, and one to Chelsea. Four operators each ran a short-stage coach from south of the Thames (Brixton Hill, Herne Hill, Sydenham) to Bow church. The

76 Rocque, *Plan of Lond. & Westm.*
77 P.R.O., C 146/4128.
78 Mercers' Co., Bk. of Evidences of Dean Colet, f. 128v.; Cheke's Reg., f. 191.
79 Mercers' Co., Bk. of Evidences, f. 127; G.L.R.O., M93/437.   80 Plan of Mercers' est.
81 G.L.R.O., M93/437; below, settlement and building.
82 *Cal. Pat.* 1436–41, 432.
83 G.L.R.O., M93/437; Rocque, *Plan of Lond. & Westm.*
84 Below, settlement and bldg.
85 *Itin. of Edw. I*, ii. 88; Smith, *Hist. E. Lond.* 191.
86 G.L.R.O., M93/436, p. 14.
87 P.R.O., PROB 11/2A (P.C.C. 20 Marche).
88 *Cal. S.P. Dom.* 1637, 128.
89 A. S. Turberville, *English Men and Manners in 18th Cent.*

(1964), 151, cited in M. J. Power, 'Urban Development of E. Lond., 1550 to 1700' (Lond. Univ. Ph.D. thesis, 1971), 13.
90 8 Geo. I, c. 30; 10 Geo. II, c. 36; G.L.R.O., P93/DUN/328, pp. 271, 273, 357; W. Albert, *Turnpike Rd. System in Eng. 1663–1840* (1972), 40.
91 *Abstract of Ret. of Turnpike Gates in Boros. of Tower Hamlets*, H.C. 243 (1849), xlvi. 365.
92 *Lond. Topog. Rec.* viii. 25–6.
93 *Survey of Lond.* Vol. xliii, Poplar, Blackwall and the Isle of Dogs (1994), 12.
94 P. J. Edwards, Hist. *Lond. Street Improvements, 1855–1897* (1898), passim. Local improvements reserved for treatment under the separate hamlets.
95 *V.C.H. Mdx.* x. 7.   96 *Survey of Lond.* xliii. 12–13.
97 *Hist. Lond. Transport*, i. 5, 391.

parish was also served by vehicles starting in Romford or in Hackney.[98]

The North Metropolitan Tramways Co. opened a service along Mile End Road between Whitechapel church and Bow church in 1870, offering cheap early-morning fares for workmen. The line carried over a million passengers in the first six months and was extended into Essex and westward to Aldgate High Street in 1871. The company opened a line from the East India docks to Aldgate in 1872, and one from South Hackney along Burdett Road to Limehouse in 1879, with a spur to West India docks in 1885. In addition to early-morning fares, it introduced all-day 1d. fares in 1891 on special trams from Aldgate to Poplar and Stratford.[99]

WATER TRANSPORT AND TUNNELS.

The ferry from the southern end of the Isle of Dogs to Greenwich, a perquisite of the lord of the manor of Pomfret, was included in the sale of that manor in 1302.[1] After division of the manor the ferry apparently passed with the third belonging to the Heryng family and later to Thomas Appleton, who leased the ferry for 7 years in 1422 to Thomas Woodward of East Greenwich and his wife Emmote for 6s. 8d. a year, the lessees to maintain it and its wharf, to take sufficient care of men and women crossing, and also to allow the lessor and his household and horses to cross free of charge. It was leased again for 7 years from 1430 to Robert Cheseman of Eltham (Kent) and John Lalleford of East Greenwich, for 26s. 8d a year.[2] It was still part of that third of Pomfret in 1444,[3] but it was almost certainly the ferry belonging to the manorial demesne of Stepney in the 17th century, possibly acquired in the late 15th century when the area was flooded and Pomfret may have escheated to the lord of Stepney manor.[4] As Potters ferry in 1652 it ran from the south end of Chapel Lane to East Greenwich and was valued at £21 a year net, although in 1642 it had been valued at only £11. It was leased in 1626 for 31 years at 20s. a year to Nowell Warner, who was not to take more than 2d. for a horse and man or 1d. for a person alone, and was to convey the lord's carriages freely to any landing place in Greenwich; the lessee also had to repair the nearby banks and wall.[5]

A ferry at Blackwall in the mid 16th century[6] may have carried passengers to and from ships. Boats were hired in the 16th century for travel between Stepney and London, or between Ratcliff and Greenwich, and warrants from the Privy Council in the 1540s include boathire from London to Blackwall.[7]

In the late 16th century the City Corporation unsuccessfully sought an Act to build canals to link the Lea near Hackney with the City, or Bromley with Limehouse.[8] In 1770 the Limehouse cut was built from the Lea to the Thames at Limehouse dock, allowing goods traffic on the Lea to bypass the long meanders near its mouth, where it was known as Bow creek, and the Isle of Dogs. The Regent's canal, opened in 1820, ran roughly north–south through the middle of Stepney to the Limehouse basin or Regent's canal dock, which was substantially increased in size c. 1852 and again in the 1870s. In 1905 the canal carried over a million tons of goods including nearly a quarter of a million tons of sea-borne coal, for canalside gasworks, and timber; long-distance traffic to the Midlands having declined, most of the traffic was local. A direct link with the Lea navigation was provided in 1830 by the Hertford Union canal, built by Sir George Duckett, but tolls prevented it from taking traffic from Bow creek and Thames-side wharves and it was unused by 1848.[9]

Tunnelling began with the Thames tunnel, designed by Marc Brunel, whose young son Isambard was resident engineer. Intended for wheeled traffic, it was built with difficulty between Wapping and Rotherhithe from 1825 to 1843, and finally opened only for pedestrians.[10] It was bought by the East London Railway in 1865 and became a railway tunnel, which still carried the East London line in 1994.[11] The Blackwall tunnel was opened in 1897 and the Rotherhithe tunnel in 1908, both for road traffic, and the Greenwich tunnel, for pedestrians, in 1902.[12] An additional tunnel at Blackwall was opened in 1967[13] and thereafter generally used for the southbound traffic.

RAILWAYS.

Railways through the western half of the parish, which had been largely built over, ran on viaducts. The railways had little effect on growth there, apart from increasing the number of warehouses and depots, but probably stimulated residential building farther east.

The London & Blackwall Cable Railway opened its line between Stepney and the City, from Blackwall to a temporary station in the Minories in 1840 and to a new terminus at Fenchurch Street in 1841.[14] The service was intended to tempt travellers away from the river, as it nearly halved the distance by water from London to Blackwall, where they caught the steamboats for Gravesend, but most users of the railway lived or worked around Blackwall or intermediate stations, Cannon Street Road, Shadwell, Stepney, Limehouse, West India Docks, and Poplar. The trains were hauled by cables with a service every 15 minutes, but the

98 *Hist. London Transport,* i. 393–403.
99 Ibid. 273.
1 Hist. MSS. Com. 69, *Middleton,* p. 110.
2 Nottingham Univ. Libr., Mi D 3614; 3615.
3 Guildhall MS. 9171/5, f. 12.
4 Below, manors (Pomfret).
5 G.L.R.O., M93/436, p. 14; B.L. Add. MS. 22253, f. 16.
6 *Mdx. County Rec.* i. 61–2.
7 *L. & P. Hen. VIII,* iii (1), p. 49; xiv (2), p. 328; *Acts of P.C.* 1542–7, 369.

8 *Lond. Jnl.* v. 218–27; viii. 90–1.
9 C. Hadfield, *Canals of E. Midlands* (1966), 131, 134–5, 234–5, 237–8. Below, plate 6.
10 Below, plate 5.
11 *Hist. Lond. Transport,* i. 133; *D.N.B.* svv. Brunel, Marc I.; *and* Isambard K.; below.
12 *Hist. Lond. Transport,* i. 371–2.
13 Datestone.
14 Two paras. based on *Hist. Lond. Transport,* i. 48–50; E. Course, *Lond. Rlys.* (1962), 117–22, 124.

operating system was such that a passenger boarding a train at an intermediate station could leave it only at a terminus. After eight years the service was improved by the introduction of steam locomotives.

A branch line was opened in 1849 from the Blackwall line near Stepney station to a station at Bow operated jointly with the Eastern Counties Railway (Great Eastern Railway from 1862), and from 1866 the railway was leased and operated by the G.E.R. Intermediate stations were opened at Burdett Road in 1871 and Leman Street in 1877. The Bow branch's freight trains to the docks from the east needed to reverse on the Blackwall line until the construction of a spur between Salmon's Lane and Limehouse junctions. The North Greenwich branch line from Millwall junction to the south end of the Isle of Dogs was added in 1871. Six goods depots were built along the line near the City by four railway companies and the Port of London Authority.

In 1850 the East & West India Docks & Birmingham Junction Railway (later the North London Railway) linked its line with the Eastern Counties and the London & Blackwall via Bow, using Fenchurch Street as its City terminus until it opened Broad Street in 1865. The final section of the N.L.R. between Bow and Poplar was opened in 1852, but a passenger service began only in 1866 when the N.L.R. opened Poplar station in East India Dock Road.[15]

The Eastern Counties ran trains to Romford from a temporary terminus at Mile End in Cambridge Road (Devonshire Street) in 1839.[16] Its permanent terminus was opened in 1840 at Shoreditch, renamed Bishopsgate in 1847, and the line was extended to Colchester in 1843. Stations were opened at Mile End (near the temporary terminus) in 1843 and Coborn Road (Bow) in 1865.

The G.E.R. opened a line through Hackney to Enfield and Chingford in 1872, later extended to Cambridge, which branched off the Romford line at Bethnal Green junction; Mile End station was replaced in 1872 by Bethnal Green station which served both lines; a station was opened at Cambridge Heath on the Enfield line, and at Globe Road on the Romford line in 1884. Bishopsgate (low level) station on the new line was built for passengers and the old terminus reserved for goods. A new pasenger terminus was opened at Liverpool Street in 1874.

The East London Railway Co. was formed in 1865 to purchase the Thames tunnel,[17] and a railway was opened through it in 1869 between Wapping & Shadwell station by the Thames at Wapping Lane and the Brighton and the South Eastern lines at New Cross (Surr.).[18] Despite difficulties in tunnelling through the gravel under the London docks, an extension northward to Liverpool Street station linking the East London railway with the G.E.R.'s main line was opened in 1876, with new stations at Shoreditch (in Pedley Street on the Bethnal Green/Mile End New Town boundary), Whitechapel (opposite the London Hospital), Shadwell (where it crossed the Blackwall railway), and the renamed Wapping station. From 1884 the line was linked with the Metropolitan & District line, with regular services from Whitechapel to New Cross. The East London was acquired by the Southern in 1925, but working arrangements remained the same.

In the 20th century competition from improved roads and Underground lines led to a contraction of inner suburban passenger services. The G.E.R. found it more profitable to use its lines in Stepney for freight and traffic from the outer suburbs and closed three inner suburban stations in 1916: Bishopsgate (low level), Globe Road, and Coborn Road. Coborn Road was reopened in 1919 but closed finally in 1946, as were the platforms on the Romford line at Bethnal Green. Passenger services into Fenchurch Street on the Blackwall line east of Limehouse and on the North Greenwich branch ended in 1926. Burdett Road, Shadwell, and Leman Street closed in 1941. The G.E.R.'s lines were electrified between 1949 and 1960, and the area continued to be served by Bethnal Green and Cambridge Heath stations on the Liverpool Street to Cambridge line, and Limehouse on the Fenchurch Street to Southend line.[19] The East London Railway was acquired by the new London Transport Executive in 1948. In 1994 Shoreditch station was open only for peak hours, but the other stations continued to connect the area with Rotherhithe, Surrey Docks (renamed Surrey Quays and serving a large shopping centre from the 1980s), and New Cross.

In 1878 the scheme by the Metropolitan and the Metropolitan District Railway companies to complete the Circle line included connections from north and south of Aldgate station to run eastward and join the East London line south of Whitechapel station. The joint company opened stations in 1884 at Aldgate East on Whitechapel High Street just inside Whitechapel parish, and St. Mary's or Whitechapel (St. Mary's) in Whitechapel Road opposite St. Mary Street. The District also built its own terminus in 1884 beside the East London's Whitechapel station, called Whitechapel (Mile End).

The District Railway and the London, Tilbury & Southend (L.T.S.) Railway built an Underground line from the District's station at Whitechapel to the L.T.S.'s line at Campbell Road junction (Bow), opened in 1902 with stations at Stepney Green (in Mile End Road at Globe Road), Mile End (in Mile End Road near Burdett Road), and Bow Road. The new line was intended to relieve the L.T.S.'s service into Fenchurch Street and carried heavy traffic, mostly from Essex rather than Bow and Stepney.[20] Whitechapel (Mile End) was renamed Whitechapel in 1901 and reconstructed in 1902. In 1938 Aldgate East was rebuilt east of its original site and St. Mary's was closed.[21]

[15] *Hist. Lond. Transport*, i. 51; Course, Lond. Rlys. 120–1, 132.
[16] *Hist. Lond. Transport*, i. 50.
[17] Above.
[18] Para. based on *Hist. Lond. Transport*, i. 133, 227, 229;

ii. 255, 341; A. E. Bennett and H. V. Borley, *Lond. Transport Rlys.* (1963), 22–5.
[19] *Hist. Lond. Transport*, i. 50, 53.
[20] Ibid. ii. 76.
[21] Bennett and Borley, *Lond. Transport Rlys.* 25, 20.

The Underground Railway's Central line from Liverpool Street to Stratford (Essex) was opened by the London Passenger Transport Board in 1946, with stations at Bethnal Green and Mile End (connected with the existing District line station).[22]

The Docklands Light Railway was constructed in the 1980s by the London Docklands Development Corporation to serve new offices on the Isle of Dogs, largely using the embanking, viaducts, and stations of the former Blackwall railway. Its City terminus was initially at Fenchurch Street, later at Tower Gateway close to Tower Hill, but an extension to Bank Underground station was opened in 1991. The line from the City to the Isle of Dogs had stations at Shadwell connecting with the East London line,

Limehouse (formerly Stepney East) connecting with the Fenchurch Street to Southend line, and Westferry, and an extension northward to Stratford (Essex), using the former N.L.R. line, had stations at Poplar, All Saints, Devons Road, and Bow Church connecting with the District line. Five other intermediate stations on the line in the Isle of Dogs ending at Island Gardens were common to both lines.[23] An extension east to the Royal Victoria Docks (London City airport) and Beckton (Essex), with stations at Poplar, Blackwall, and East India, was built in 1994, despite doubts about the future of the line following a decline in use. Rail links for the Isle of Dogs were to be increased with an extension of the Jubilee line through south London approved in 1994.

SETTLEMENT AND BUILDING TO *c.* 1700

IN the 8th century B.C. there were huts and pits in Mile End Old Town, west of the site of the parish church.[24] Burials took place in the 1st and 2nd centuries A.D. in Spitalfields and between the Minories and Back Church Lane, Whitechapel,[25] and in the 3rd century farther from London in Shadwell north of Ratcliff Highway and west of Love Lane.[26] A Roman signal station at the junction of Ratcliff Highway and Wapping Lane may have had a small garrison in the late 3rd century, but the site was not occupied again until the 17th.[27] At Old Ford, between Old Ford Road and the railway at Morville Road, a settlement apparently occupied by the later 3rd century included burials, and along the south side of the Roman road, between the modern Lefevre and Armagh roads, pebbled yards and possibly a tile-kiln were part of an area used for commerce and the slaughter of cattle.[28] The settlement was abandoned, as was the road, in the first decade of the 5th century, and the site was not settled again until the 19th.[29]

The inclusion in the Domesday vill of Stepney of a wide area north and east of London prevents any estimate of the population of the parish from the numbers of husbandmen. Saxon and early medieval archaeological levels were largely destroyed by medieval gravel-quarrying. No post-Roman occupation has been shown on surviving levels near the City before the late 11th or 12th centuries,[30] nor by the few excavations farther east until *c.* 1300.[31]

Evidence for Saxon settlement is etymological. The first reference to Stepney is to men of the bishop of London's estate (vill) of *Stybbanhythe c.* 1000,[32] recording a hithe or landing-place either on the Thames or the Lea. Since the place-names Old Ford and Stratford

are associated with the Lea, while the name Stepney has always been linked with the southwest quarter of the parish, the hithe was probably on the gravel at Ratcliff Cross, one of the few sites below London Bridge suitable for landing before the marshes were embanked and wharfed.[33] The landing-place was most likely the site of the earliest settlement, and probably the most noteworthy feature in the area, since by 1086 its name was given to the bishop's extensive vill and manor, which probably predated the parishes.[34] By the 13th century the name was usually a variation of Stubanee or Stibanhe; later Stubbanheth became usual, gradually giving way to Stepney in the 16th and 17th centuries.[35] The manor was formally known as Stebunheath *alias* Stepney from the 18th century, and Stebunheath was the place-name included in a barony created in 1906.[36]

Bethnal Green may also suggest Anglo-Saxon settlement.[37] Wapping was formerly thought to record a settlement linked to a personal name *Waeppa*;[38] more recently, however, it has been thought to derive from *wapol*, a marsh, as the area was almost entirely marshland, where early settlement was unlikely, and no such personal name has been found.[39]

Early evidence for Stepney's scattered settlements is thin. Freehold land transactions, recorded in the 12th century and numerous in the 13th, rarely included buildings until the 14th century, suggesting that settlement before 1300 was light;[40] records of customary land transactions, however, have not survived. The vigorous land market indicates economic importance but, as many of the parties were Londoners, may not necessarily indicate a rising local population. Landholders included Salomon of Stepney from

22 Ibid. 13, 20.   23 Below, plate 7.
24 *T.L.M.A.S.* xxxiii. 324–44.   25 *V.C.H. Mdx.* i. 74.
26 Ibid.; W. Maitland, *Hist. Lond.* ii (1756), 1380.
27 *T.L.M.A.S.* xxvi. 278–80.
28 Ibid. xxiv. 135–45; *V.C.H. Mdx.* i. 73.
29 *T.L.M.A.S.* xxiii. 42–54, 101–47.
30 A. Vince, *Saxon Lond.: Archaeol. Investigation* (1990), 13.
31 Below.
32 Robertson, *Anglo-Saxon Charters*, 144; *P.N. Mdx.*

(E.P.N.S.), 149–50. 'Hithe' was commonly used for landing-places on the Thames between 8th and early 11th cent.: *Lond. Jnl.* xv (2). 107.
33 Above, Intro.   34 Below, manors (Stepney).
35 First known use of 'Stepney' dated 1516: Guildhall MS. 9171/9, f. 1.   36 Below, manors (Stepney).
37 Below, Bethnal Green, settlement to 1836.
38 *P.N. Mdx.* (E.P.N.S.), 152.   39 *Med. Arch.* x. 27.
40 Based on extant feet of finnes and charters.

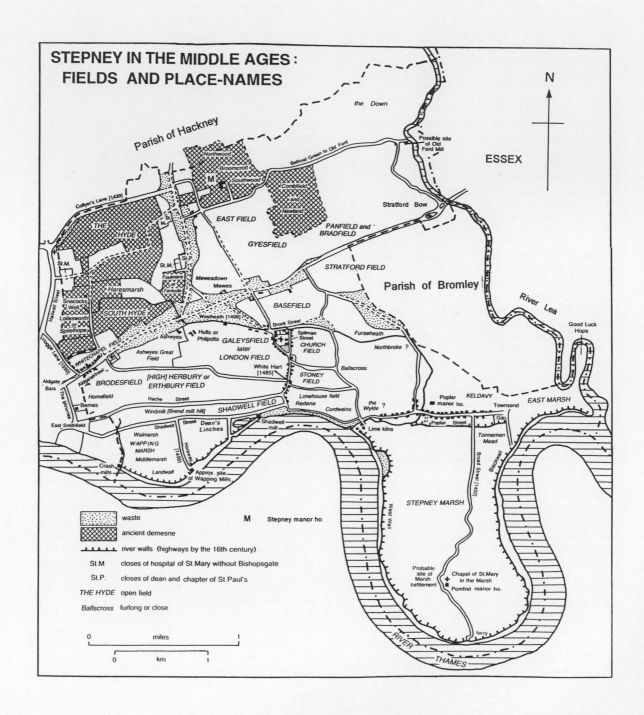

STEPNEY IN THE MIDDLE AGES:
FIELDS AND PLACE-NAMES

FIG. 5

the 1140s, and Bernard of Stepney in 1178. Be-twccn 1163 and 1187 Ralph the clerk, of Stepney, was granted a house in Stepney which had assarted land to the west and south, with land his father Elfsus had held there.[41] By the mid 13th century several Londoners had Stebbenheth as a cognomen, including the prominent citizen and fishmonger John de Stebbenheth (d. 1281).[42]

Mills, of great economic significance to Stepney and the only buildings noted in 1066, were tidal and, until the 16th or 17th centuries, isolated among the riverside marshes. The bishop and his tenants had seven mills in the vill in 1086, including some of those standing later on the Lea and the Thames.[43] Sathewell or Shadwell mill existed before 1198, with a messuage by 1223; its holder Brice of Stepney (d. c. 1216) was also 'of Shadwell', where he may have lived.[44] Wapping mill was named in 1218,[45] Old Ford mill in 1230,[46] and the Cressemills or Crash mills on the Thames on the boundary between Whitechapel and St. Botolph Aldgate in 1233.[47]

In addition to mills in Old Ford and Stratford Bow, an early building near the Lea was the convent of St. Leonard's, founded between 1086 and 1122, which stood slightly south of the main road and Bow bridge in what became the parish of Bromley.[48]

The location and size of early medieval settlements have largely to be inferred. A survey of c. 1400 distinguished customary tenements owing smokepennies, helpennies, and suit of court, from other messuages and cottages, especially those lining the Colchester road at Whitechapel and Stratford, which owed only a small money-rent and which were therefore probably more recent.[49] Receipts by the bishop of 34s. 2d. for aid and wardpenny from Stepney in 1228, and 100s. 9d. for helpenny and wardpenny at Stepney in 1243,[50] make it likely that tenements owing such dues existed by the early 13th century. No tenements held for smokepennies are listed along the highway at Algatestreet (Whitechapel), which was probably open waste until the 13th century, and much of the free land nearby belonged to messuages in St. Botolph Aldgate in the 12th century and later.[51] A free messuage formerly belonging to Emma de la Milaunde may indicate some settlement at Mile End by the mid 13th century;[52] evidence for customary tenements there is lacking.

The bishop's manor house of Stepney and Hackney existed by 1207,[53] apparently isolated in his woods near the Hackney boundary. Not far away, however, beside the highway from Mile End to Hackney lay Bethnal green, where settlement is suggested by mention of a Reimund of Blithenhal before 1216 and of a house at 'Blithehale' in the mid 13th century.[54]

Stepney church stood roughly midway between the Thames and the Colchester road by 1180,[55] and may imply a parsonage and possibly other residents nearby. Excavations in Stepney High Street opposite the church showed no trace of habitation between 700 B.C. and c. 1300,[56] but two customary cottages owing smokepennies lay on the west side of the churchyard, in Churchstreet, possibly a sign of building on land that was later part of the cemetery. Dues were also owed by a tenement in Spilmanstreet and by at least 6 tenements in Clevestreet running south from the church, but by none in Ratcliff ('Redecleve').[57] A limited excavation near Ratcliff Cross revealed no settlement before the 15th century.[58]

There were 3 tenements owing smokepennies at Forbystreet, east of Ratcliff; by 1335 the 'limehostes' or kilns stood nearby, later giving the name Limehouse to the whole area.[59] A little to the east, however, Poplar had many more early tenements: c. 30 along the high street and to the north of it (Northstreet), 9 at Westwall or nearby, and 11 at Newbiggin.[60] In 1200 it included the estate that became the manor of Poplar, with a capital messuage, 6 free tenants, and 5 customary tenants.[61] William of Pontefract had a house in Stepney, presumably the later manor house of Pomfret at the southern end of the Isle of Dogs, where he built a chapel between 1163 and 1180. Complaints about diminished dues at the parish church suggest that the chapel was used by local residents, possibly Pomfret's customary tenants.[62] There were also three early customary tenements of Stepney manor in the marsh.[63]

The presence of the bishops and embarkations to the continent brought important visitors. Edward I often stayed in Stepney,[64] and held a parliament there in 1299.[65] To Stow's statement that it met at the house of Henry le Waleys (d. 1301),[66] mayor of London and a prominent royal servant,[67] later writers have added that the house was on Stepney Green (a 19th-century name) and that Edward paid other visits there.[68] No contemporary records associated Henry le Waleys with Stepney, although his son Augustine of Uxbridge had property in the parish in 1315.[69]

41 Below, manors.
42 G. A. Williams, *Medieval Lond.: From Commune to Capital* (1963), 336–7.
43 Below, econ. hist. (mills).
44 Guildhall MS. 25516, f. 38, dated from internal evidence; P.R.O., CP 25/1/146/6, no. 46; below, manors (Shadwell).
45 B.L. Cott. MS. Tib. C. v, f. 152.
46 *Cur. Reg. R.* xiv. 68.   47 P.R.O., E 40/14033.
48 *V.C.H. Mdx.* i. 156; below, econ. hist. (mills).
49 P.R.O., SC 12/11/31: Mile End with Bethnal Green is missing.   50 P.R.O., E 372/72, m. 10d.; E 352/36, m. 5.
51 e.g. below, manors (Bernes).   52 P.R.O., C 146/1993.
53 Hist. MSS. Com. 8, *9th Rep. I, Dean and Chapter of St. Paul's*, p. 491.
54 P.R.O., E 40/7317; C 146/799.   55 Below, churches.

56 *T.L.M.A.S.* xxxiii. 324–44.
57 P.R.O., SC 12/11/31. Rent for several in Clevestreet missing.   58 *T.L.M.A.S.* xxviii. 215–30.
59 P.R.O., SC 12/11/31; below, econ. hist. (ind.).
60 P.R.O., SC 12/11/31.   61 Below, manors (Poplar).
62 Below, manors (Pomfret); churches.
63 P.R.O., SC 12/11/31.
64 *Itin. Edw. I, passim.* What follows gives an outline of growth throughout Stepney; more detailed treatment is reserved for accounts of individual hamlets.
65 *Bull. Inst. Hist. Res.* v. 147.
66 J. Stow, *Annals* (1631), 207; the statement is unsupported.
67 Williams, *Medieval Lond.* 333–5.
68 e.g. *E. Lond. Antiquities*, 6–7
69 *Cal. Pat.* 1313–17, 248.

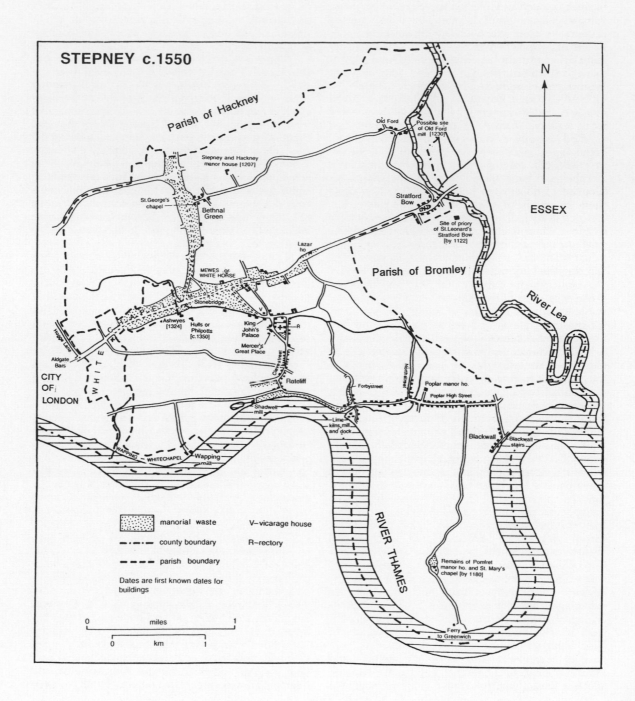

STEPNEY c.1550

Parish of Hackney

Old Ford
Possible site of Old Ford mill [1230]
Stepney and Hackney manor house [1207]

St.George's chapel
Bethnal Green

Stratford Bow

ESSEX

Site of priory of St.Leonard's Stratford Bow [by 1122]

Lazar ho.

MEWES or WHITE HORSE

Parish of Bromley

River Lea

Stonebridge

Ashwyes [1324]
Hulls or Philpotts [c.1350]
King John's Palace
Mercer's Great Place

Aldgate Bars

CITY OF LONDON

Ratcliff
Forbystreet
Poplar manor ho.
Poplar High Street

Shadwell mill

Lime kilns, mill, and dock

Blackwall
Blackwall stairs

WAPPING WHITECHAPEL Wapping mill

N

RIVER THAMES

Remains of Pomfret manor ho. and St. Mary's chapel [by 1180]

Ferry to Greenwich

manorial waste
county boundary
parish boundary

V – vicarage house
R – rectory

Dates are first known dates for buildings

0   miles   1
0   km   1

FIG. 6

Henry's house has been identified with several buildings, such as Colet's Great Place and King John's Palace, which were substantially 15th-century or later. More likely is the 17th-century Red Bull opposite the west end of the church and perhaps medieval: fine pottery dated c. 1270 to 1350 from south-west France, with which le Waleys had close links, was excavated beside the inn's likely site.[70] Edward I also visited Shadwell in 1291, and Pomfret in 1302, about the time a royal servant, John Abel, acquired it.[71]

The extensive waste known as Mile End green along the Colchester road also acquired prominence, chiefly as an assembly place of Londoners. In 1299 a London carpenter was accused of holding a 'parliament' of carpenters there to oppose a City ordinance.[72] Insurgents camped at Mile End during the Peasants' Revolt in 1381, when Richard II rode out to hear their grievances,[73] and during Jack Cade's rebellion in 1450.[74] In the 16th century it was used for training the City militia,[75] and in the 1640s a fort was built on the Whitechapel boundary.[76] The green was gradually reduced, particularly from the late 16th century, by grants of small parcels for building.[77]

Residents' names in the late 13th century included Ateclive, possibly connected with Ratcliff, and Atewell,[78] but it is not known where they lived. From c. 1300 messuages without land, and 'shops' (workshops), were conveyed,[79] and from the mid 14th century not only freehold but customary lands changed hands frequently. Almost all the freeholders also held customary land. Prominent citizens and courtiers acquired substantial estates, with residences dateable only from the 14th century but perhaps older.[80] The lay subsidy of 1334 indicates either a large or a wealthy population: Stepney's payment, specifically including Stratford and probably also Whitechapel which is not mentioned elsewhere, was the highest in Middlesex and nearly twice Westminster's, although the rate and distribution of the taxation are not known and Westminster's figure may have excluded payments for its extensive ecclesiastical lands.[81] A population of 1,005 aged over 16 is indicated by the poll-tax return of 1377 for Stepney, Stratford, Haliwell-street (Shoreditch High Street), and Whitechapel.[82] Such figures suggest that most people lived near the City (Haliwellstreet, Whitechapel), or near the Thames (Stepney) and the Lea (Stratford). By 1320 records for

Stepney no longer included Whitechapel, which had become a parish,[83] although it still appeared in Stepney's manorial records.

When, by 1282, the white chapel by Aldgate was built on the roadside waste between Aldgate bars and Mile End,[84] the road west of it was presumably already lined on both sides with the dwellings which were there in 1400, owing money rents to Stepney manor. No dwellings are indicated, however, in the southern part of Whitechapel parish.[85] Similarly Wapping and Shadwell, apart from their mills and associated buildings, were still fields.

Whitechapel's boundary seems to have been drawn up to exclude all the buildings then at Mile End, where the green was so wide that buildings stood well back from the road. On the south side of the highway immediately east of the Whitechapel boundary stood Hulls manor house by the mid 14th century; Ashwyes manor house, recorded in 1324, stood close by. On the north side east of Cambridge Heath Road and opposite the road to Stepney church stood Mewes, possibly by 1330.[86] Two or three tenements, including that of Sir John Cobham, who held the manor of Cobhams (in existence in 1368), stood on the south side of Mile End green north-west of the church,[87] and others may have stood on the east side of the road leading to the church. Another group of messuages and gardens lay on the south side of Mile End Road east of White Horse Lane by 1325 and included workshops by 1364.[88]

Both free and copyhold messuages also stood on the north side of Stepney churchyard, some inhabited by prominent landowners.[89] The rectory house stood at the east end of the church by c. 1390.[90] In addition to the early customary tenements, there were 13 tenements and cottages in Clevestreet and cottages covering 1 a. at Ratcliff by c. 1400.[91] A road laid at the junction of Cable Street and Butcher Row in the 14th or 15th centuries was metalled and so perhaps was connected with shipbuilding at Ratcliff,[92] where by the 1350s timber was brought for vessels for the king; a ship was built at Limehouse for the duke of Bedford in 1421.[93]

Settlements in 1348–9 were Mile End, Stratford, Old Ford, Algatestreet (the early name for Whitechapel High Street), Marsh (in the Isle of Dogs, probably at Pomfret and the chapel at the southern end), and Poplar.[94] Forbylane and Lymestreet (Forbystreet, the nucleus of settlement in Limehouse), Clevestreet (the nucleus of

[70] D.N.B.; T.L.M.A.S. xxxiii. 324–44; G.L.R.O., M93/157, p. 39.
[71] Below.
[72] Cal. Early Mayor's Ct. Rolls 1298–1307, ed. A. H. Thomas (1924), 25.
[73] V.C.H. Mdx. ii. 23–4; Cal. Pat. 1381–85, 237.
[74] V.C.H. Mdx. ii. 25–6.
[75] L. & P. Hen. VIII, xiv (1), p. 439; B.L. Royal MS. 18 A. lxvi, f. 17v.; Acts of P.C. 1577–78, 222.
[76] Below, manors (Hulls).
[77] Below, manors (Stepney). Details reserved for growth of individual hamlets.
[78] London Eyre 1276 (Lond. Rec. Soc. xii), nos. 245, 564.
[79] Ft. of F. Lond. & Mdx. i. 70, 87, and passim.
[80] Below, manors.

[81] Lay Subs. of 1334, ed. R. E. Glasscock (1975), 191.
[82] P.R.O., E 179/141/23, m. 5; i.e. payment of £14 5s. divided by 4d. a head.   [83] Below, local govt. (par. govt.).
[84] P.N. Mdx. (E.P.N.S.), 153.
[85] Guildhall MS. 25422; P.R.O., SC 12/11/31.
[86] Below, manors (Philpots; Ashewys; Mewes).
[87] P.R.O., SC 12/11/31.
[88] Below, manors (Savoy).
[89] e.g. 'Garlik': Cal. Fine R. 1437–45, 37; P.R.O., C 66/527, m. 11; Chedworth's ho.: below, manors (Cobhams).
[90] Guildhall MS. 25422.
[91] P.R.O., SC 12/11/31. Below, plate 1.
[92] T.L.M.A.S. xxviii. 215–30.
[93] Below, econ. hist. (ind.).
[94] P.R.O., SC 2/191/60; roll is incomplete.

Ratcliff), and Blethenale (later Bethnal green) were mentioned in 1405.[95] Transactions apparently concerning existing or former dwellings specified only Stepney, Algatestreet, Stratford, and Haliwellstreet in 1348–9, but specified Limehouse (Lymhostes), Old Ford, Ratcliff (Redeclyve), and Mile End in 1383.[96]

Although the dean and chapter's manor of Shadwell had several tenants owing quitrents, the land around the mill, which later formed the parish of Shadwell, was held in demesne, and the mill and messuage were the only buildings there c. 1400. The house, where Edward I stayed in 1291,[97] had a hall, chamber, solar, offices and outbuildings in 1334.[98]

At the southern end of Forbystreet lay the dock, the limekilns in use by 1335, and a mill for grinding the chalk.[99] By 1400 in addition to the 3 early customary tenements there stood another tenement, 6 cottages, and 5 limekilns held for money rent.[1]

Poplar street and some adjoining lanes were lined with at least 50 tenements and cottages by 1400. Such dense settlement was perhaps due to the anchorage at Blackwall, used by travellers and for military embarkations.[2] Poplar manor house on the north side of Poplar High Street, probably the capital messuage of 1200, was a residence of Sir John Pulteney, who was lord by 1339; the Black Prince used it as a residence during the 1350s and Sir Nicholas Lovayne in the 1360s.[3] The customary tenements at Westwall and Newbiggin, beside a few other unlocated tenements, also lay in Poplar and the Isle of Dogs. At the south end of the isle 12 customary tenants of Pomfret in 1322 probably lived near the manor house, where a settlement existed until it was flooded in the mid 15th century. Stepney manor had a newly built hamstall there with its earlier customary tenements.[4]

In 1443 the pledges in Stepney manor came from Marsh, Poplar, Clevestreet and Brookstreet, Lymestreet and Forbylane, Mile End, Brochenale (Bethnal green), Stratford, Old Ford, Algatestreet, and Haliwellstreet, in each of which the assize of bread or of ale had been broken.[5] Up to that time Stepney, after the exclusion of Whitechapel, seems to have had a small population for its size, despite interest in acquiring land there. In particular, the long and piecemeal rebuilding of the church does not suggest a rich community.[6]

Courtiers' and citizens' residences multiplied in the 15th and early 16th centuries. South-west of the church the copyhold cottage which became the Mercers' Great Place was built in the mid 15th century by a London citizen and improved by Sir

Henry Colet (d. 1505) and afterwards by Thomas Cromwell.[7] King John's Palace (Worcester House) had a imposing gateway of the early 16th century and this, or another house to the north-west, may have been Fenne's great place, let to Lord Darcy in the 1520s.[8] Three messuages and gardens on the south side of Mile End Road were bought for Henry VIII and granted to Sir John Neville, being rebuilt as his residence.[9]

By the late 16th century many copyholders were knights and gentry.[10] It was less the influx of wealthy outsiders, however, than the growth of shipbuilding and the victualling trades that led to a more general rise in wealth and in population. The parish of Stepney had 1,720 communicants in 1548,[11] most of whom probably inhabited the riverside areas of Poplar and Ratcliff: in the 1650s, after considerable growth in Ratcliff and Shadwell, c. 40 per cent of the incumbent's income from Easter dues and small tithes still came from Poplar and Blackwall.[12] Estimated numbers in 1670s were c. 260 for Mile End, c. 550 for Spitalfields, 500 for Poplar, 2,000 for Ratcliff, and 2,000 for Wapping. No figures were given for Limehouse (possibly included with Ratcliff), Bethnal Green (possibly with Mile End), or Stratford Bow, but the rest form some guide to the distribution of settlement.[13] The parish church was often short of space from the late 16th century.[14]

Increasing population was associated with silk-weaving in Spitalfields, mainly by immigrants from the late 16th century, and with maritime industries.[15] The latter had the strongest influence on the character of Stepney; Stow remarked on the growth of riverside building during his lifetime.[16] Although large ships were built at Limehouse and in the 17th century at the East India Co.'s dock at Blackwall, Stepney's ship builders worked mainly on small vessels and refits. Both royal and merchant ships were fitted out and victualled at Ratcliff in the 16th century, and later at Blackwall, involving a wide range of trades from butchery to rope-making, besides such specialized crafts as instrument-making.[17]

Several merchant seamen were among the parish vestrymen by the late 16th century.[18] Mariners such as William Borough (d. 1599) and John Vassall (d. 1625) were responsible for voyages of discovery,[19] while local seamen had travelled to the Far East by the early 17th century,[20] presumably contributing to the social unrest and religious nonconformity that became widespread in the parish.[21]

Disturbances and seditious rumours were often reported, perhaps because loose talk encouraged informers or because the government was worried by lack of control in a crowded

95 Guildhall MS. 25370.   96 Ibid. MS. 10312/136.
    97 *Itin. of Edw. I*, ii. 88.   98 Guildhall MS. 25403/2.
    99 Below, econ. hist. (ind.).   1 P.R.O., SC 12/11/31.
2 Ibid.   3 Below, manors (Poplar).
4 Above; below, manors (Pomfret); P.R.O., SC 12/11/31.
5 P.R.O., SC 2/191/62.
6 Below, churches.   7 Below, manors (Mercers).
8 B.L. Add. MS. 36070, f. 170; below, manors (Fenne); plate 8.
9 Below, manors (Savoy).   10 B.L. Eg. Rolls 2080–81.
11 *Lond. and Mdx. Chantry Cert.* (Lond. Rec. Soc. xvi), 72.
12 Below, churches (value of benefice).

13 *Compton Census*, ed. Whiteman, 65.
14 Below, churches.
15 Detailed treatment reserved for individual hamlets.
16 J. Stow, *Survey* (1633), 461. Below, plate 2.
17 P. Earle, *Making of the Eng. Middle Class* (1989), 24; *L. & P. Hen. VIII*, iii (2), p. 995; iv. p. 762; *Cal. S.P. Dom.* 1635–6, 526; 1664–5, 29, 31, 202, 417; 1672–3, 556; *Mdx. County Rec.* iv. 208; below, econ. hist. (ind.).
18 *Mems. Stepney Par. passim.*
19 *D.N.B.* s.v. Borough, Wm.; Vassall, Jn.
20 e.g. Guildhall MS. 9171/22, *passim*, for seamen who died on E. India Co. voyages.   21 Below, churches.

maritime area. Examples of sedition confirmed official fears during most national crises, at the succession of Mary I, during the Protectorate, soon after the Restoration, and in the 1680s.[22] Many 'plots' in the late 17th century were connected with or blamed on nonconformist meetings; the extent of nonconformity after 1660 led to repression in Stepney more severe than anywhere else around London.[23]

Both masters and mariners in Stepney petitioned for exemption from taxation and musters, because they bore more of the cost of providing ships than other Londoners.[24] Fitting out royal ships led to impressment within the riverside hamlets in 1630, 1634–5, 1653, and 1672, and met resistance by masters of merchant ships. In 1634 owners and masters were ordered to deliver names, and from East Smithfield to Blackwall constables were to collect the names of all seamen, for delivery to Trinity House.[25] Unpaid seamen discharged from the navy rioted in 1626.[26] They were to be billetted in 1628 in the riverside hamlets until money could be found, but guards were needed to prevent disorder.[27] Seamen from Ratcliff, Limehouse, and Blackwall took part in disturbances in Southwark in 1640, in a mutiny downriver in 1648, and in a riot in Wapping and Tower Hill in 1653.[28] Apprentices also rioted, demolishing four houses at Wapping in 1617.[29]

Maritime importance brought peculiar problems. There was a high risk of plague off ships, as in 1602, and Stepney suffered particularly severely in 1624–6 and 1665.[30] Throughout the 17th century mariners were captured by Algerian pirates: 140 men from Stepney were taken from 22 merchant ships in 1670.[31] Kidnapping in the riverside hamlets was particularly prevalent 1657–63 and 1675–84, when men, women, or children were lured on board ships and sold in Barbados or Virginia.[32]

MANORS AND ESTATES

THE manor of *STEBUNHEATH* or *STEPNEY* devolved from the bishop of London's Domesday manor or vill of Stepney, which in 1066 and 1086 covered most of north and east Ossulstone, and was part of a larger block of land around London thought to have been the foundation grant of the see of London, probably acquired by the bishopric *c.* 604 and certainly before *c.* 1000.[33] The Domesday manor was assessed at 32 hides and included most of Stepney parish as constituted in the 13th century, Hackney, a small part of Shoreditch, and large parts of Islington, Hornsey, and Clerkenwell; the 14 hides held in demesne later formed the demesnes of Stepney, Hackney, Harringay, Muswell, and possibly Brownswood manors.[34] By 1086 the bishop, having acquired overlordship of a holding belonging to the canons of St. Paul's in 1066, had ten chief tenants and claimed, although unsuccessfully, the two remaining holdings in 'Stepney'.[35]

Of the Domesday tenants, Hugh de Berners held 5 hides in 1086, divided between Sired, canon of St. Paul's, and the canons as demesne in 1066 and identified as the Islington manors of Barnsbury and probably Canonbury; Hugh also held 1 virgate and a mill, probably at East Smithfield (parish of St. Botolph Aldgate), which Doding had held of the bishop in 1066.[36] Hugh also seems at one time to have held the 4 hides of Robert Fafiton claimed by the bishop, which have been identified with the Hackney manor of Kingshold, but may partly may have lain at Mile End.[37] The 5 hides held by the wife of Brien, part of the bishop's demesne in 1066, are thought to have included lands in Clerkenwell and Stepney granted to the priory of St. Mary, Clerkenwell, and to the Knights Hospitallers in the 12th century.[38] William de Ver's hide probably lay in Hackney where the estate paying Ver's fine at the view in 1384 was held by John Shoreditch.[39] William the chamberlain's 1¾ hide may have become the manor of Topsfield (Hornsey).[40] The 3½ hides held by Robert son of Roscelin of the king, but claimed by the bishop, probably later formed part of the manor of Bromley.[41] The other Domesday estates held of the bishop have not yet been identified.

Other freehold estates were granted out of the manor in the 12th century. In the 1220s Bishop Eustace de Fauconberg recovered overlordship of several holdings including those of Ralph the clerk, Robert le Cutiller, Maurice of Harlow, canon of St. Paul's, and a mill held by Hugh le Fraunceys.[42]

In the 14th century the manors that had devolved out of the bishop's Domesday demesne and some Domesday and later tenants in chief paid sums towards the common fine of 64s. at

[22] *Acts of P.C.* 1552–4, 384; 1554–6, 27; *Cal. S.P. Dom.* 1660–1, 270, 409; 1661–2, 74, 98, 161, 511, 530, 569; 1664–5, 35, 246; *Mdx. County Rec.* iv. 160, 201, 210, 212, 284, 296.
[23] Below, prot. nonconf.   [24] *Acts of P.C.* 1588, 40.
[25] *Cal. S.P. Dom.* 1629–31, 340; 1633–4, 541; 1634–5, 575; 1652–3, 544; 1671–2, 584.
[26] *Mdx. County Rec.* iii. 161.
[27] *Cal. S.P. Dom.* 1627–8, 561, 568.
[28] Ibid. 1640, 171; 1648–9, 200; 1652–3, 369; *Mdx. County Rec.* iii. 225.   [29] *Cal. S.P. Dom.* 1611–18, 442.
[30] Hist. MSS. Com. 9, *Hatfield Ho.*, xii, p. 438; below, churches.
[31] Hist. MSS. Com. 7, *8th Rep. I*, p. 241b; *Cal. S.P. Dom.* 1670, 294.   [32] e.g. *Mdx. County Rec.* iii. 262, 266, 302, 271, 315, 335; iv. 65, 78, 94, 147, 232–3.

[33] P. J. Taylor, 'Estates of Bishopric of Lond. from 7th to early 16th cent.' (Lond. Univ. Ph.D. thesis, 1976), 18–19, 431; *Hist. Research*, lxiii. 17–18.
[34] *V.C.H. Mdx.* vi. 140, 144–5; ibid. x. 75.
[35] *V.C.H. Mdx.* i. 120–2. One was in later par. of Bromley.
[36] *V.C.H. Mdx.* viii. 51, 54; below, econ. hist. (mills).
[37] *V.C.H. Mdx.* x. 77; below (Mewes). Fafiton's holding and part of Berners holding were both held by Canon Sired T.R.E.
[38] Taylor, 'Estates of Bishopric of Lond.', 59–60; *Hist. Research*, lxiii. 17–28.
[39] Taylor, 'Estates of Bishopric of Lond.', 109–10; *V.C.H. Mdx.* x. 81.   [40] *V.C.H. Mdx.* vi. 142.
[41] Taylor, 'Estates of Bishopric of Lond.', 59.
[42] Below (Ralph); P.R.O., CP 25/1/146/7, nos. 52, 54; below, econ. hist. (mills).

the Stepney view of frankpledge: the bishop's manors of Stepney, Hackney, and Haringey, the priories of St. Mary, Clerkenwell, St. John of Jerusalem, St. Bartholomew, Smithfield, and the men of Islington (Barnsbury), of the rector of Hackney, of the dean of St. Paul's (Shadwell), of the estate once Richard Pomfret's, of William de Ver, of Daniel or Rumbolds (possibly Grumbold in Hackney and Cobhams or Rumbolds in Stepney), of John of Bedfont (manor of Poplar), and of Edmund Trentemars (manor of Bernes).[43]

In 1353 the bishop himself answered for only ½ knight's fee in the vill of Stepney,[44] and by 1395 he had apparently been relieved of most services for his estate there.[45] The bishops held Stepney until 1550; grants of the manor by the Crown during vacancies of the see included one to the Treasurer, the bishop of Carlisle, in 1228.[46]

By the 14th century the bishop's demesne in Haringey was administered on its own. Stepney and Hackney, however, continued to share a manor house, were accounted for together until the 15th century, and were valued together until they acquired separate lords in the 1660s. The location of customary holdings, however, always distinguished between Stepney and Hackney by the 14th century, when Stepney manor included free and customary holdings in all the hamlets of Stepney parish and in Whitechapel parish, others in Shoreditch on both sides of Haliwell-street (later Shoreditch High Street),[47] and freehold in East Smithfield.[48]

In 1550 Nicholas Ridley surrendered the manors of Stepney and Hackney to the king, who immediately granted them to the Lord Chamberlain Sir Thomas Wentworth, Baron Wentworth (d. 1551). The grant included the marshes of Stepney, waters, fishing, wastes, mills, and the liberties, including free warren and view of frankpledge, that the bishops had enjoyed.[49] The manors passed to Wentworth's son Thomas, Lord Wentworth (d. 1584), governor of Calais, who suffered forfeiture in 1558 but was restored in 1559 and protected by an Act against any claims of the bishop or the chapter of St. Paul's.[50] Stepney was conveyed to Lord Burghley, who may have held the courts, in 1581 on the marriage of Wentworth's eldest son William (d. 1582) to Burghley's daughter Elizabeth,

but returned to the Wentworths on her death without children in 1583.[51]

Stepney and Hackney passed to the surviving son Henry, Lord Wentworth (d. 1593), and to his widow Anne for life.[52] In 1615 Anne and her second husband Sir William Pope, Bt., surrendered her interest to her son Thomas, Lord Wentworth, then aged 24.[53] He was created earl of Cleveland in 1626.[54]

Cleveland and his son Thomas, Lord Wentworth, were prominent at court and incurred heavy debts.[55] The earl began to secure loans on his estates in the 1620s, and in 1632 created mortgages by 99-year leases of Stepney manor to Richard Cartwright and of Hackney to Sir Thomas Trevor. In 1634 the leases were bought for Paul, Viscount Bayning (d. 1638), and to secure further loans Cleveland conveyed the reversion of both manors to Bayning's trustees Henry, Viscount Newarke (later marquess of Dorchester), and Sir Thomas Glemham.[56]

By the 1640s Cleveland's hope of clearing his debts through an advantageous marriage for his son had failed,[57] and the value of land he put up for sale was not enough to clear the mortgages and convey an unencumbered title.[58] In 1640 he sought an Act for the sale of all his estates, but a Bill, which received two readings in 1641, did not become law.[59] Meanwhile Bayning's trustees, Sir Thomas and Dr. Henry Glemham, were ordered to take possession of the manors, and they held the courts from 1641. The equity of redemption was reserved to Cleveland and his heirs.[60]

In 1643 Bayning's trustees sold the mortgage leases of Stepney and Hackney manors to Richard Walcot and Richard Wallop in trust for William Smyth (or Smith), of the Middle Temple, and others.[61] The trustees retained the reversion and apparently kept possession, since the Glemhams held a court in 1643 after the sale,[62] but Frances, Lady Weld, another of Cleveland's creditors, had gained possession by 1647,[63] and she was referred to as lady of the manor and held courts until 1652.[64]

In 1650 the estates of the royalist Cleveland and his son were sequestered. Bayning's trustees tried to compound for the reversion of the manors to recover their debt, but Lady Weld was initially left in possession.[65] In 1651 the

43 P.R.O., SC 2/191/60, 62; Guildhall MSS. 10312/136; 25370.
44 *Feud. Aids*, iii. 376. 45 B.L. Add. MS. 15555, f. 39v.
46 *Cal. Pat.* 1225-43, 232-3.
47 P.R.O., SC 2/191/60, 62; SC 12/11/31; *Survey of Lond.* viii. 3, 5, 10-12, 15.
48 Below (Poplar).
49 *Cal. Pat.* 1549-51, 404; B.L. Add. MS. 12505, f. 249.
50 W. L. Rutton, *Three Branches of Fam. of Wentworth* (1891), 47; B.L. Add. MS. 15555, f. 40.
51 P.R.O., SP 12/152, no. 49; ibid. CP 25/2/172/24 Eliz./Trin.; *Cal. S.P. Dom.* 1581-90, 21; Rutton, *Fam. of Wentworth*, 49. Only ct. rolls to survive for this period are 1581-2: B.L. Eg. rolls 2080-1.
52 B.L. Add. MS. 15555, f. 40.
53 P.R.O., CP 25/2/13 Jas.I/Mich.
54 Complete Peerage, xii (2), 497-8.
55 *D.N.B.*
56 B.L. Add. MS. 15555, f. 28; Eg. MS. 3006, f. 6. Possession of the mans. remained with Cleveland. His only property outside Stepney and Hackney was in Beds., notably Toddington manor where he lived.

57 Ibid. Eg. MS. 3006, ff. 26-7; P.R.O., SP 16/408, no. 61; SP 16/540, no. 153.
58 His debts amounted to over £100,000: B.L. Eg. Ch. 646; M. J. Power, 'Urban Development of E. Lond. 1550 to 1700' (Lond. Univ. Ph.D. thesis, 1971), 91.
59 Hist. MSS. Com. 3, *4th Rep.*, H.L. pp. 30, 33-5, 61; B.L. Eg. MS. 3006, ff. 12-15.
60 B.L. Eg. MS. 3006, ff. 62-70, 204; Eg. Ch. 646; T.H.L.H.L., TH/3710.
61 B.L. Add. MS. 15555, f. 28; G.L.R.O., M79/LH/100. The following acct. amends that given by Dr. J. Thirsk in *Econ. H.R.* 2nd ser. v. 195-9. Thanks are due to Dr. Thirsk for the loan of notes concerning Stepney. Material on Stepney in *Hist. Parl., Commons*, 1660-90, iii. 445, is incorrect.
62 B.L. Eg. MS. 3006, f. 70. However, Wallop and Smyth as mortgagees granted a 31-year lease of some demesne in Feb. 1648: G.L.R.O., M93/439, f. 3.
63 Hist. MSS. Com. 5, *6th Rep.*, H.L. p. 156b; *L.J.* viii. 696.
64 G.L.R.O., M93/209; P.R.O., C 54/3811, no. 31; below.
65 It was stated, however, that she did not yet have possession of Hackney which had been extended for another debt.

Middlesex estates were sequestered from her for having disobeyed the Committee of Compounding regarding the accounts, although she was still collecting rents in 1652. William Northey was appointed to keep the courts on behalf of the committee, and by 1653 all the earl's estates had been let to his creditors, even though the interest on the debts greatly exceeded the revenues.[66] In 1651 Smyth and his partners mortgaged to Dr. Henry Glemham demesne in Hackney, the Dusthill in Limehouse, marshes in Poplar, and land in Bethnal Green near Shoreditch church in order to pay the balance owed for their purchase of the mortgage leases in 1643; presumably to help the partners sell land and so pay what they owed, Bayning's trustees conveyed to William Smyth's brother John the reversion of the manors bought from Cleveland in 1634.[67]

In 1653 William Smyth, Clement Oxenbridge, Edward Gittings, and William Potter sold the mortgage leases to Richard Blackwell,[68] who assigned back to them Hackney manor and parts of Stepney including the quitrents, wastes, most demesne in Bethnal Green, some wood and trees, and specified rents in hand, as security for payment of debts owed to Glemham, Smyth and others.[69] The trustees for sale of forfeited lands conveyed the equity of redemption and all Cleveland's other rights to John Smyth and Joseph Drew in trust for Blackwell, William Smyth, and Gittings, for the payment of Cleveland's debts.[70] William Northey held courts and managed the manors on behalf of the interested parties.[71]

In 1658 Oxenbridge and Potter assigned their interests to William Smyth and Gittings,[72] who with others were appointed as commissioners to sell the manors to pay Blackwell's debts, including that to the state. Blackwell assigned the mortgage leases for this purpose, and the commissioners made several sales of land.[73] In 1660 the Smyths, Gittings, Blackwell, and Drew sold to William Hobson and others both the reversion and the equity of redemption of Stepney manor, excluding land recently sold, the rectory and advowsons of Stepney and Whitechapel, and the offices of steward and bailiff.[74] Hobson was lord in 1660,[75] and his executors or trustees had possession in 1665.[76]

Cleveland regained his equity of redemption,

and obtained two Private Acts in 1660 and 1661 for the sale of nearly all his lands in order to pay off his debts.[77] He was allowed seven years in which to redeem the mortgages. The Exchequer was to assess the debts, and in 1663 ordered that purchasers who had redeemed the mortgage leases and reversions on parcels of the manors should also pay to Cleveland 21 years' value for land and 13 years' for houses held in possession for his equity of redemption.[78] In 1664 Cleveland and his son authorized two Chancery masters to settle with some of their creditors, including William Robinson, who would not relinquish the manor house (Bishops Hall estate) in Bethnal Green until he had been reimbursed for mortgages he held on land in Hackney.[79]

The sale of Stepney and Hackney was hindered by new claimants to the manor, who had acquired Blackwell's debt to the state (now owed to the Crown), and in 1666 Cleveland obtained another Act to extend the time for the redemption of the mortgages by four years.[80]

In 1658 Cleveland settled on Philadelphia wife of his son Thomas, Lord Wentworth, an annual income secured by a lease to trustees of lands including Stepney manor. Thomas died in 1665 leaving a daughter, Henrietta Maria.[81] On Cleveland's death in 1667 control of his estates passed to Philadelphia and the equity of redemption to Henrietta Maria, de jure Baroness Wentworth.[82] William Smyth, created baronet in 1661,[83] had joined with Cleveland and Philadelphia in making conveyances, perhaps as principal creditor or as Philadelphia's lawyer or as joint guardian with the latter of Henrietta Maria.[84]

Philadelphia, having obtained a pension from the Crown in 1665,[85] redeemed some of the encumbrances on her jointure, presumably on Stepney manor,[86] but did not recover Hackney manor, which was settled in fee on the heirs of William Hobson in 1663.[87] The manors passed separately from 1669, when Hobson's executors conveyed the reversion of Stepney to Philadelphia's trustees, but as free and copyhold lands sold before 1659 were specifically excluded, the manor now contained hardly any demesne. Smyth and the other trustees for settling Blackwell's debts assigned the remainder of the mortgage lease of Stepney to Philadelphia.[88] From December 1669 courts were held in her

66   Cal. Cttee. for Compounding, iii (2), 2156–9.
67   G.L.R.O., M79/LH/97; P.R.O., C 8/116/76; C 54/3585, no. 13.
68   G.L.R.O., M79/LH/99; Earl of Cleveland's Bill [c. 1665].
69   G.L.R.O., M79/LH/100.
70   P.R.O., SP 23/18, p. 910; C 54/3805, no. 29. Smyth did not own the manors and did not sell off the entire estate as stated in Econ. H.R. 2nd ser. v. 196–7. He acted in partnership with others, and they never had simultaneous control of the mortgages, reversion, and equity of redemption. Smyth's sales of his own land, purchased from Cleveland in 1640, have been confused with the partners' activities and sales as commissioners to redeem Blackwell's debts. His description as a land jobber seems unjustified.
71   P.R.O., C 54/3805, no. 24. Good court records date from 1654: G.L.R.O., M93.
72   G.L.R.O., M79/LH/102.
73   P.R.O., C 54/3989, no. 9; below.
74   P.R.O., C 54/4038, no. 14. Hobson also bought the mortgage and reversion of the Hackney land mortgaged to

Glemham. For Hackney see V.C.H. Mdx. x. 75.
75   P.R.O., C 78/610, no. 2.
76   Jnl. Mod. Hist. xxvi. 323.
77   Below; Northants. R.O., Sotheby MSS., box X 1074, folder item xi, copy of printed Act 12–13 Car. II; Earl of Cleveland's Bill [c. 1665].
78   T.H.L.H.L., TH/3712; Jnl. Mod. Hist. xxvi. 323.
79   T.H.L.H.L., TH/3712; below; below, Bethnal Green, ests.
80   P.R.O., SP 29/176, ff. 35–40; Cal. S.P. Dom. 1664–5, 177, 290, 409; 1665–6, 73; Hist. MSS. Com. 8, 9th Rep. II, H.L. p. 32b; Northants. R.O., X 1074, folder item xi.
81   P.R.O., C 7/594(pt. 2)/132.
82   Complete Peerage, xii (2), 498.
83   G.E.C. Baronetage, iii. 191.
84   According to the extremely unreliable A. Fea, The Loyal Wentworths (1928), 65.
85   P.R.O., C 7/594(pt.2)/132.
86   Ibid.; C 78/1630, no. 1.
87   G.L.R.O., M79/LH/104; V.C.H. Mdx. x. 75.
88   B.L. Add. MS. 15555, f. 28v.

name, sometimes with her daughter's or Smyth's.[89]

Philadelphia made further mortgages of Stepney between 1674 and 1683. In 1684 she assigned the estate to her daughter's trustees, reserving her own jointure, and her daughter settled Stepney manor on herself for life with remainder to her mother.[90] Henrietta Maria, mistress of James, duke of Monmouth, died unmarried in 1686.[91] Philadelphia retained Stepney manor, resisting claims to it by Cleveland's daughter Anne (d. 1697), wife of John, Baron Lovelace, and heir to the Wentworth barony.[92]

In 1695 Philadelphia sold the manor, still mortgaged and described as 4 messuages, 20 cottages, 200 a. of pasture, and all rights and royalties including common of pasture, views of frankpledge, courts leet and baron, and other franchises as before except fishing, with the advowsons of the churches of Stepney and Whitechapel, to trustees for William Herbert, known as Lord Montgomery.[93]

In 1710 Lord Montgomery sold Stepney to Windsor Sandys, who paid off the mortgages and was lord in 1715 and 1718. In 1720 Sandys held the manor in trust for John Eyre, who had inherited the lands of his brother Henry Eyre in 1719 and sold the manor in 1720 to John Wicker the younger, and a mortgagee. Wicker was lord with S. Blunt 1722–9 and alone 1731–54.[94] He or his son of the same name alienated the manor in 1754 to his brother-in-law George Colebrooke,[95] who inherited a baronetcy in 1761.[96]

Sir George Colebrooke was bankrupted in 1773; a settlement was made in 1775 of the manor, which consisted of the lordship, quitrents, perquisites of court and royalties, and the remaining waste from Mile End Road to the parish church.[97] Further settlements were made in 1777 and 1785 under the bankruptcy commission.[98] In 1791 settlement of all Sir George's estates in tail male provided for sales from the manor of Stepney to pay debts.[99] A limited grant seems to have been made, as by 1795 the beneficial interest in the lordship belonged to Jonathan Eade for the lifetime of Sir George. The reversion belonged to Colebrooke's eldest son George, who with Eade enfranchised copyholds in 1807 and 1809.[1]

George predeceased Sir George in 1809, having devised Stepney to those of his children who reached 21 years. Sir George Colebrooke's estates passed in 1809 to his next surviving son Sir James, but Stepney later passed to Belinda, George's only surviving child, and on her marriage to Sir Charles Joshua Smith in 1823 was settled on her husband, herself and their issue with remainder as devised in her will.[2] Under that will the manor passed to her uncle Henry Thomas Colebrooke (d. 1837), who left it to his son Thomas Edward Colebrooke (d. 1890), who inherited the baronetcy in 1838. Under a settlement of 1887 it passed to his son Sir Edward Arthur Colebrooke,[3] created Baron Colebrooke of Stebunheath (d. 1939), who left only female heirs, whereupon the barony became extinct.[4]

In 1926 the remaining copyholds were converted into freeholds under the Law of Property Act, 1922. They remained subject to such manorial incidents as quitrents, fines on change of ownership, and the lord's right to timber, until 1 January 1936.[5]

MANOR HOUSE. The manor house of Stepney and Hackney was one of the residences of the bishops of London. Bishop William dated a grant at Stepney in 1207, and Bishop Roger Niger died there in 1241.[6] After the death of Bishop Gravesend in 1303 his household at Stepney was kept on for a month, and 13 stablemen were employed for longer to look after 22 horses.[7] Bishop Baldock, Chancellor in 1307, sealed royal writs at Stepney[8] and left ornaments and books from his study there to St. Paul's in 1313.[9] The bishops' itineraries between 1306 and 1337 show that they regularly paid several visits a year.[10]

In 1336 52½ a. of hay and grass were used for the bishop's horses when at Stepney, and although most of the demesne was farmed out between 1339 and 1362, meadow was retained to supply hay for the manor house.[11] Bishop Sudbury regularly stayed at Stepney between 1362 and 1375.[12] Thereafter, although officials' horses still received hay, it is not clear whether the bishop himself resided.[13] In 1408–9 the manor buildings were not let because they were reserved for his use, and hay was again provided,[14] but in 1418 the bishop was dispensed from maintaining residences in Middlesex other than his palace in London and manor house at Fulham. Stepney was used as before in 1424[15] and a close near the house was partly occupied by the bishop's stock in 1439, but no hay was then supplied and the bishop's household apparently did not stay thereafter.[16]

89 G.L.R.O., cal. of M93.
90 B.L. Add. MS. 15555, ff. 29–v., 43v.–45v.; P.R.O., C 78/1630, no. 1.
91 B.L. Add. MS. 38847, f. 123; D.N.B.
92 P.R.O., C 7/594(pt.2)/132; C 78/1630, no. 1; B.L. Add. Chs. 13736–8; Complete Peerage, xii (2), 497–8.
93 P.R.O., CP 25/2/854/7Wm.III/Trin.; B.L. Add. MS. 15555, ff. 46–7v.
94 B.L. Add. MS. 15555, ff. 50–1; G.L.R.O., cal. of M93.
95 Lysons, Environs, iii. 419.
96 G.E.C. Baronetage, v. 116.
97 V.C.H. Mdx. viii. 56; G.L.R.O., M93/442–3.
98 G.L.R.O., M93/444–6.   99 Ibid. M93/448.
1 Lysons, Environs, iii. 420; P.R.O., CP 43/896, m. 2; BNC, MS. Stepney 57-H.
2 G.L.R.O., M93/450–1; Stebunheath otherwise Stepney (1894), in G.L.R.O. Libr.

3 P.R.O., MAF 20/167, file 2596.
4 L. G. Pine, New Extinct Peerage (1972), 80.
5 G.L.R.O., M93/435.
6 Hist. MSS. Com. 8, 9th Rep. I, Dean and Chapter of St. Paul's, p. 491; D.N.B.
7 Acct. of Exors. of Ric. Bp. of Lond. 1303 (Camd. Soc. N.S. x), p. xviii.   8 Cal. Pat. 1301–7, 519.
9 Hist. MSS. Com. 8, 9th Rep. I, pp. 29a, 46b.
10 Reg. Baldock (Cant. & York Soc.), 78, 126, 147, 257, 317–20; Cal. Pat. 1334–8, 92.
11 Guildhall MS. 25403/2; P.R.O., SC 6/1139/18.
12 Reg. Sudbury (Cant. & York Soc.), i, passim.
13 e.g. P.R.O., SC 6/1139/21–2 (1399, 1402). The surviving accts. are for vacancies of the see.
14 P.R.O., SC 6/1139/23.
15 Taylor, 'Estates of Bishopric of Lond.', 303.
16 P.R.O., SC 6/1139/24.

Wages for a janitor and keeper of the manor house were paid for 23 weeks in 1362–3, possibly when the bishop or his officials were absent,[17] and by 1384 wages were paid to keepers for the whole year;[18] they managed the demesne and repaired the house. The post was confirmed by the bishop by 1439[19] and a keeper was still employed in 1517.[20] A bailiff managed the farms by 1457 and his deputy accounted for the revenue of the manor. Bailiffs were prominent landowners: William Pecche in 1457–8, Thomas Raymond in 1458–9, John Norris in 1460–1, William Haydore in 1461–2, and William Chedworth in 1464–5.[21]

The manor house included a chapel by 1243.[22] An ambulatory between the lord's chamber and the clerks', the thatched stair to the solar, the chapel roof, and the gardener's house were repaired in 1336. The site also included separate thatched granges for barley, wheat, and rye.[23] Repairs in 1363 involved large supplies of lime, sand, and gravel from within the manor; tiling was done on the kitchen, the bakery, the bishop's chamber, a chamber outside the 'Breshour'(?) and one beyond the gate, and the long stable, and daubing and plastering were done to the hay grange.[24] A dovecot, great garden, and kitchen garden existed in 1383, when 3,000 reeds were bundled for thatching manorial buildings, the furnace or oven was mended, and a new window made for the steward's chamber.[25] In 1402 shinglers with scaffolding worked on the main hall, using shingles from the manor of Haringey; glass was bought for the chapel windows, and other work was done to the laundry, buttery, great door, and carriage house, besides daubing the walls of the lord's chambers. The kitchen had a well.[26] In 1416 the great stable roof was mended and the windows of the great chamber were given new glass.[27]

The manor house was called Bishopswood in 1465.[28] The woods nearby were Bishopshall woods in 1538, and the site was generally called Bishopshall (or Bishops Hall) in 1548 and thereafter; confusingly, that name was sometimes also applied to the manor.[29] The supposition in 1642 that the house had been inhabited by Edmund Bonner (bishop 1539–49 and 1553–9)[30] led to the site being called Bonner Hall in the late 18th and the 19th century, which name has survived in later streets.[31]

The house and manorial buildings with the office of keeper were included in leases of de-

mesne to William Goddard for 30 years in 1538 and to Thomas Parsons alias Fairbrother for 80 years from 1568; the bishop reserved the right to reside for 3 months each year on giving Goddard 14 days' notice.[32] Goddard was reeve of the manors of Stepney and Hackney in 1539,[33] and although he lived mainly in Shoreditch he had goods and animals at Bishopshall at his death in 1548.[34] His widow had sold the lease by 1550 to Sir Ralph Warren,[35] who may have resided. The lease was later held by Thomas Wilson, brewer, and this or a sublease by 1582 by John Fuller, resident at his death in 1592 when his interest passed to his widow Jane, later wife of Sir Thomas Mansell.[36] In 1640 the earl of Cleveland claimed that the manor house was not unworthy of his rank. In 1642 Bishops Hall, with outbuildings and 3 a., had last been let to Sir Basil Brook,[37] but the parliamentary surveyors found it uninhabitable in 1652; built mostly of brick, it had only the walls standing with a little timber and tiles, the materials being valued at £104 after the expense of demolition.[38]

The Wentworths did not occupy the manor house, and of these later lords of the manor only Philadelphia, Lady Wentworth, and her daughter Henrietta Maria are known to have lived in Stepney. A copyhold capital messuage and 5 houses nearby were surrendered in 1679 by George Ayres apparently to trustees for Lady Wentworth. Referred to as her dwelling, it lay north-east of the parish church in the hamlet of Ratcliff, on the site of the later Durham Row. The 5 houses were demolished to create her garden, which adjoined the rectory grounds on the south. The house, possibly rebuilt, seems to have been on the north side of the site and was a substantial two-storeyed brick building with attics and a frontage of 10 bays, enclosed with a brick wall.[39] Evidently it was where the duke of Monmouth stayed with Philadelphia and Henrietta Maria in 1684. Both mother and daughter died there, the mother having 11 servants at her death besides goods, cattle, and grain.[40]

SALES OF DEMESNE. Most of the demesne was sold in parcels by the earl of Cleveland and his creditors from the 1630s to 1660s, though the freehold of Lollesworth or Spitelhope (43 a.), leased to the hospital of St. Mary without Bishopsgate, was apparently sold between 1550 and the 1560s.[41] A messuage and several fields in the Isle of Dogs, sold to Sir Edward Yate,

17 Ibid. SC 6/1139/18.
18 Guildhall MSS. 25403/3, 7.
19 P.R.O., SC 6/1139/24.
20 Guildhall MSS. 10123/1–2.
21 P.R.O., SC 6/1140/24.
22 Ibid. C 62/19, m. 5.
23 Guildhall MS. 25403/2.
24 P.R.O., SC 6/1139/18.
25 Guildhall MS. 25403/3.
26 P.R.O., SC 6/1139/22.
27 Guildhall MS. 25403/7.
28 P.R.O., SC 6/1140/24.
29 e.g. ibid. C 1/728/11; Guildhall MS. 9531/12, f. 115.
30 B.L. Add. MS. 22253, f. 6d. Although the bp. retained the right to occupy the ho. there is no evidence that he exercised it.
31 Below, Bethnal Green, building 1837–75; ests.

(Bishop's Hall).
32 G.L.R.O., M93/208; below, econ. hist. (agric.).
33 P.R.O., SP 1/153, f. 172d.
34 Ibid. PROB 11/32 (P.C.C. 5 Populwell), f. 36.
35 G.L.R.O., M79/LH/128/1/1.
36 P.R.O., SP 12/152, no. 49; ibid. PROB 11/79 (P.C.C. 46 Harington), f. 355; below, charities (almshos.). For later occupiers, below, Bethnal Green, the East.
37 B.L. Eg. MS. 3006, f. 12; Add. MS. 22253, f. 6d.
38 G.L.R.O., M93/158, f. 1. Later hist. of site treated below, Bethnal Green, the East; ests.
39 G.L.R.O., M93/132, ff. 139, 282; BNC, MS. Stepney 17; below, plate 9.
40 B.L. Add. MS. 38847, f. 123; P.R.O., C 107/16, pt. 1, acct. of rents, etc., 1696; PROB 32/66, nos. 1, 59; Fea, *Loyal Wentworths*, 172–3.
41 *Survey of Lond.* xxvii. 96.

Bt., *c.* 1627, may have been the former manor of Pomfret which escheated to the lord in the 15th century.[42]

The freehold of four messuages, brickworks, a storehouse in the Shipyard with closes called the Shipyard and Dock, and six other messuages at Limehouse, occupied by John Graves, shipwright, and his tenants, was bought by William Graves in 1637.[43] The property lay beside the Dusthill, and there seems to have been confusion with the purchasers of the latter during the 1650s.[44]

The freehold of the Dusthill, divided into several tenements, with a mansion and ground called Shipyard or Hope, and 8 parcels of marsh in Poplar totalling 75¼ a., was sold to William Lambe, Clement Stoner, and Francis March in 1638 in trust for John March. Although March's heirs paid a fine to discharge sequestration on this property in 1653,[45] the mortgage on the manor still applied, and the Dusthill and marshland, occupied by Francis March, were still encumbered in 1660.[46] The Dusthill was not listed among lands excluded from sale in 1661, but its absence from later manorial records means it was almost certainly sold off in fee at that time.[47]

The freehold of part of 18 a. of demesne in Spitalfields south of Lollesworth, bounded by Wentworth Street, Petticoat or Artillery Lane, and Bell Lane, with 69 houses and appurtenances, including the Red Cock and the White Cock with a bowling alley, was sold in 1639 and 1640 to Henry Montagu, earl of Manchester.[48] In 1643 Edward, earl of Manchester, and George and Sidney Montagu gave a bond to pay off a small part of Cleveland's mortgage debt,[49] probably their purchase of the 1634 reversion of 43 a. of nursery, garden, and pasture lying east of Brick Lane and covering the southern half of the later Mile End New Town, and sold to James Ravenscroft by 1642.[50] On the same date William Smyth, Richard Wallop, and others conveyed all their interest in both the houses sold to Lord Manchester and the 43 a., presumably the 99-year mortgage term which they had bought earlier that year, to Edward Montagu of Boughton, William Montagu, and Maurice Tresham, for a nominal sum.[51] The Montagus' land was not included in Cleveland's sequestration since they had already bought his equity of redemption, and the Act of 1661 confirmed both parcels to George and Sidney Montagu.[52]

The freehold of the rest of the 18 a. south of Lollesworth, between Lord Manchester's purchase and Brick Lane, with 112 houses in Wentworth Street, Bell Lane, and Rose Lane, and tenter grounds for drying cloth, was sold to William Smyth in 1640, with 7 a. of demesne in Limehouse called Cordwains (originally customary land which had escheated in the 14th century), which included a ropeworks and new houses in Cordwell and Green Dragon alleys. Both parcels were subject to the 99-year mortgage lease.[53]

Seven closes totalling 62 a., including 14 a. dug for brickmaking, in the north part of Bishopsfields (between Shoreditch and Cambridge Heath Road), and 43 a. in the south part including a nursery, were sold to James Ravenscroft in 1640.[54] Ravenscroft apparently sold the 43 a. to the Montagues, and all of the rest to William Smyth in 1643.[55]

In 1641 Cleveland covenanted to convey unspecified land in Bishopsfields to William Smyth and Dr. Hugh Barker;[56] it was later shown to have included closes of 14 a. and 16 a.[57] Despite the sales to Ravenscroft, Smyth, and Barker, the closes in the northern part of Bishopsfields were included in the survey of Cleveland's manor in 1652, possibly because it was not clear which ones had been sold.[58]

Five closes of *c.* 60 a. in the north-west corner of the parish near Shoreditch church were included in a mortgage in 1651 to Henry Glemham by Smyth and Wallop. Not having been redeemed, the 99-year mortgage term and reversion in the closes was conveyed by Glemham to Charles Constable and Thomas Jennings in 1660. In 1663 the closes apparently belonged to Richard Blackwell and the 99-year mortgage lease was held by two of his creditors, Humphrey Blake and Clement Oxenbridge.[59] The land may be that of which the freehold was sold to Blake's successors in 1681, although this only amounted to *c.* 40 a.[60]

The equity of redemption of the manor house and its closes and woods totalling 93 a., known subsequently as the Bishop's Hall estate, was sold by the trustees for sale of forfeited lands in 1653, and bought for Mary, widow of Gen. Deane; she sold the equity in 1654 to William Robinson.[61] The estate was also subject to the 99-year mortgage lease and the reversion, as well as to a 21-year lease in possession from 1648; in 1652 William Smyth was said to have all three interests.[62] Later events are not clear, but in 1664 the Wentworths claimed that Robinson had received Bishop's Hall in satisfaction of a mortgage he had bought up on Hackney.[63]

The equity of redemption of land in Mile End

42 Guildhall MS. 17199; P.R.O., C 7/390/51.
43 B.L. Add. MS. 22253, f. 10d.; *Cal. Cttee. for Compounding*, iii (2), 2160.
44 Detailed treatment reserved for Limehouse. See also below, econ. hist. (ind.).
45 *Cal. Cttee. for Compounding*, iii (2), 2159.
46 G.L.R.O., M93/252; P.R.O., C 54/4053, no. 31.
47 Further treatment reserved for Limehouse.
48 P.R.O., C 54/3194, no. 2; C 54/3195, no. 26; below, econ. hist. (agric.).
49 P.R.O., C 6/149/50.
50 Below.
51 P.R.O., C 54/3307, no. 32. Ravenscroft sold the rest of his land to Smyth on the same day: below.

52 Schedule to 1661 Act; later hist. in *Survey of Lond.* xxvii.
53 G.L.R.O., M93/206; B.L. Add. MS. 22253, ff. 3–4.
54 B.L. Eg. Ch. 646; Add. MS. 22253, ff. 4v.–5; P.R.O., C 3/422/36; Schedule to 1661 Act; Lambeth MS. 2731/2.
55 Above; Lambeth MSS. 2731/2–3.
56 G.L.R.O., M93/158, ff. 13–14; 1661 Act.
57 Lambeth MS. 2731/3.
58 G.L.R.O., M93/158, ff. 13–14.
59 *Cal. S.P. Dom.* 1663–4, 46.
60 Below, Bethnal Green, ests.
61 Ibid.
62 G.L.R.O., M93/158, f. 7.
63 T.H.L.H.L., TH/3712.

leased to Hilary Mempris, who had bought the mortgage and reversion, was bought by his brother and heir Thomas,[64] and the equity of Sutlepen's (Sickle Pen-) fields and Six Acre Close were granted to Edmund Denton to pay a debt of Cleveland's, and conveyed to John Smyth.[65]

The equity of redemption of the rest of Stepney and Hackney was conveyed to John Smyth and Joseph Drew in trust for Richard Blackwell, William Smyth, and Edward Gittings. They, with their partners in the purchase of the mortgage leases,[66] thus made sales of demesne from 1654, mainly of small parcels of waste leased for 500 years in the 1580s, which went to the lessees or occupiers.[67] Further sales were made from 1658 by the commissioners enpowered to pay Blackwell's debts.[68]

The sales of the 99-year mortgage terms, the reversion, and Cleveland's equity, regained in 1660, in parcels of the demesne were confirmed after the Exchequer had decided the creditors' claims. Most of the sales were finally settled 1669–72 after several purchasers had sued for assurance that the equity of redemption of their parcels would be conveyed to them.[69] What little demesne remained after 1660 may have included Broomfields, 92 a. near the manor house, conveyed or confirmed by Philadelphia, Lady Wentworth, Smyth, and others in 1669.[70]

OTHER MANORS AND ESTATES. William of Pontefract, the bishop of London's steward at Stortford in the 1180s–90s, held ⅓ knight's fee of the bishop in 1166.[71] Between 1163 and 1179 the rector complained that William had built a chapel on his estate in Stepney.[72] William witnessed a grant in Stepney marsh in 1204–5,[73] and may have died by 1216, when livery of his land was granted to Thomas Esturmy.[74] Thomas of St. Paul, who had claimed the ⅓ knight's fee in Stepney, quitclaimed it in 1241 to Richard, son of William of Pontefract, and his heirs.[75] Sir Richard of Pontefract (also Pomfret) held the land in the 13th century,[76] and witnessed deeds to land in Stepney from the 1230s until c. 1260.[77] Men belonging to the land once of Richard of Pontefract paid 2s. at the view in 1349, which sum was thereafter owed by the tenement of Pomfret,[78] and the family gave its name to the manor of PONTEFRACT, POMFRET, or POUNTFREIT. In 1283 Alice of Pontefract,

Sir Richard's daughter, granted a messuage and 2 a. in the fields of Stepney to Nicholas de Castello, to whom Ralph de Herun and his wife Joan, Alice's sister, granted a messuage and its appurtenances in Stepney. Other land of Sir Richard adjoined these properties.[79]

In 1302 Nicholas's son John de Castello (or John atte Castle) and his wife Joan granted and quitclaimed the manor of Pountfreit with its lands, liberties including reliefs, escheats, freemen and villeins, all appurtenances of the river ferry, together with the advowson of the chapel of Pountfreit and rents from East Greenwich, to Sir John Abel, royal servant and guardian of the queen's lands,[80] and Edward I visited Pomfret later that year.[81] Abel paid £300 for the manor, which was settled on the issue of Abel and his wife Margery.[82] However, Joan widow of John de Castello still held in her own right a messuage and 2 a. in the south marsh of Stepney, adjoining Abel's land, in 1311 when she granted and quitclaimed it to John son and heir of John Bacheler, citizen and fishmonger of London.[83] In 1303 Nicholas de Castello quitclaimed to Abel all right in 2s. 4d. annual rent paid by Richard son of Roger Waryn of Ketteringham from the tenements purchased from the Heruns and Alice of Pontefract,[84] and in 1305–6 John de Castello for himself, his wife, and his children acquitted Abel of the purchase money.[85] In 1322 Abel's manor of Pomfret on the Thames, held of the bishop for a ¼ knight's fee and consisting of garden, 80 a. of arable, a windmill, and 12 bond tenants, valued at £8 11s. 4d., passed to his daughters Joan, Margaret, and Catherine.[86] Catherine and her husband John Chicche in 1333 granted her third to Joan and her husband Sir William Vaughan,[87] who still held two-thirds in 1357.[88] Their son Sir Thomas Vaughan died in 1361 seized of the two thirds, now held of the bishop for service of 16d. a year and suit at Stortford, leaving an infant son Hamo.[89] The bishopric being vacant, the estate was let by the Crown for 53s. 4d. and in 1365 the king granted the wardship of Hamo to Richard of Sutton,[90] whose widow surrendered it in 1372, whereupon it was granted to Sir Thomas Vaughan's widow Alesia and her husband John Burton.[91] Sir Hamo Vaughan died in 1394 without issue, a daughter Eleanor having predeceased him. Pomfret presumably passed with West Tilbury (Essex) and Henshurst (Kent) to coheirs, who may have included his executors William Burton, Thomas

64 P.R.O., SP 23/18, p. 917; C 54/3806, no. 52.
65 Ibid. C 54/3807, no. 41.   66 Above.
67 e.g. P.R.O., C 54/3806, no. 25; C 54/3811, no. 31; C 54/3815, no. 36; C 54/3908, no. 1; T.H.L.H.L., TH/2382.
68 G.L.R.O., M93/223–39; M93/215; E/PHI/46A.
69 Above.   70 Below, Bethnal Green, ests.
71 Red Bk. Exch. (Rolls Ser.), i. 187; Taylor, 'Estates of Bishopric of Lond.', 124–5.
72 Charters of Gilb. Foliot, ed. A. Morey and C. N. L. Brooke (1967), 316.
73 P.R.O., E 40/2601.
74 Rott. Litt. Claus. (Rec. Com.), i. 254.
75 Cur. Reg. R. xvi. 55, 197; P.R.O., CP 25/1/146/12, no. 192. Thos. was not the bp.
76 Testa de Nevill (Rec. Com.), 360.
77 B.L. Cott. MS. Tib. C. v, ff. 153, 158v.; P.R.O., E 40/2580; E 40/2634.

78 P.R.O., SC 2/191/60; SC 2/1140/24; Guildhall MS. 10312/136.
79 Nottingham Univ. Libr., Middleton MSS., Mi D 4841–2.
80 Ibid. Mi D 3604–7; E. Foss, Judges of Eng. iii (1851), 210–11.
81 Itinerary of Edw. I, ii. 88.
82 P.R.O., CP 25/1/148/36, no. 297. Abel had sons by another marriage.
83 Nottingham Univ. Libr., Mi D 4844.
84 Ibid. Mi D 4843.   85 Ibid. Mi D 3608.
86 P.R.O., C 134/75, m. 10.
87 Ibid. CP 25/1/150/56, no. 85.
88 Ibid. CP 25/1/287/45, no. 540.
89 Ibid. C 135/167, no. 9.
90 Cal. Fine R. 1356–68, 314–15.
91 Cal. Close, 1369–74, 416; Cal. Fine R. 1369–77, 189.

Skinner, a kinsman, and Roger Bokelton.[92] Hamo's heirs owed 4s. 6d. and suit at Stepney c. 1400 for a manor called Pomfret in the marsh.[93]

After the death of Thomas Skinner of Shrewsbury, the two thirds passed by 1412 to Sir Baldwin Strange, Hugh Dorset, Richard Mitton, and Philip Bokelton as coheirs of Vaughan, though the manor was apparently in the possession of the holder of the remaining third, from whom Strange received 12s. 2d. rent.[94] Strange and Dorset each held a third of the two-thirds in right of their wives. Bokelton with his sisters Catherine and Margaret, the wife of Richard Mitton, shared another third of two-thirds. Margaret, widow of Sir Baldwin Strange, died seized of her portion in 1419, and although the see of London was not vacant, the king granted the wardship of her daughter and heir Elizabeth to John, duke of Bedford, who granted it to Maud, widow of Sir Roger Salvayn. Maud farmed the wardship to John Harpur and Hugh Dorset for rent which she granted in 1422 to John Thoralby and Thomas Holden. In 1431 Elizabeth, aged 14, was the wife of Robert Molyneux.[95] Dorset granted his portion after the death of his wife Joan to Harpur in 1435.[96] Shares of the remaining third of two- thirds passed in 1420 from Margaret, widow of Sir Richard Mitton, to her son William, and from Philip Bokelton to his sister Catherine, wife of John Falk of Hereford. The total value of the manor was given as 60s. and each moiety was 6s. 8d.[97] John and Catherine in 1423 conveyed their moiety of a third of two-thirds in trust for John Harpur, to whom their son Nicholas quitclaimed in 1437.[98] William Mitton conveyed his moiety in trust in 1436 and quitclaimed to Harpur in 1437.[99] In 1447, therefore, part of the two-thirds was held by Harpur and the other part by Elizabeth and Robert Molyneux. John Harpur of Rushall and his wife Eleanor settled their share on John's heirs in 1458.[1]

John Abel's third daughter Margaret (d. 1355), widow of Sir Walter Heryng, leased her third of Pomfret in 1342 to Thomas Lambard, citizen of London, for his lifetime, for a rent to Margaret and her heirs of 8 marks a year for the first 8 years, and £10 a year thereafter.[2] Margaret apparently released all her right in her portion to Lambard in 1344,[3] and on his death in 1361 it had been taken into the king's hands,[4] but Margaret's son and heir Raymond Heryng was apparently trying to recover the third from the

Crown against his aunts in 1365.[5] Thomas Appleton held a third of Pomfret, presumably the Heryng third, in right of his wife Anne in 1412 when Sir Baldwin Strange gave him an acquittance for 12s. 2d. being Strange's share of the rent of the remaining two thirds.[6] Appleton was holding the third in 1422 when he let the ferry for 7 years, but in 1430 the estate was in the possession of William and Robert Aleyn, who with William Rotheley let the ferry again.[7] In 1436 William Aleyn and his wife Anne settled Pomfret with land in Essex on Robert Aleyn, with a warranty against the heirs of Anne.[8] This third was held by Richard and William Appulby for the use of Elizabeth Holden, widow of Thomas Holden, by 1443 when they granted it with the ferry to several feoffees including Robert Aleyn. Because of a suit between the Appulbys and John Filoll of Dorset, Elizabeth agreed with Filoll in 1444 to enfeoff those designated by Filoll and to deliver the deeds of her third of Pomfret to him,[9] but in her will shortly afterwards she left a payment from the property to Richard Appulby for life, after which her third of Pomfret together with the ferry and lands in Essex was then to be sold by her daughter Elizabeth, wife of Sir John Burcestre.[10]

The flooding of much of the Isle of Dogs in 1448 was attributed to neglect of the river walls on the south-west by the freeholder, John Harpur, presumably as part of Pomfret.[11] Several tenants of the bishop and of Poplar manor lost their holdings, still flooded in 1465,[12] and it is likely that all the tenants of Pomfret did so also.[13] The fact that the ferry belonged to one portion of the manor, and was described as running between that third and Greenwich,[14] suggests that the manor may have been physically divided by the 15th century. One or both portions may have escheated to the bishop as lord of Stepney, since in the early 17th century the ferry was part of the demesne of Stepney and let on the same terms as in the 15th century.[15] Pomfret may have formed part of the land let by the bishop after reclamation in the late 15th century; it probably included parcels near the chapel-house and the ferry which were acquired by Sir Edward Yate, Bt., from the lord of Stepney in the early 17th century.[16]

Between 1163 and 1187 Bishop Gilbert Foliot granted to his vassal *RALPH THE CLERK*, of Stepney, and his heirs the land that Ralph's father Elfsus (Aelfsus) had held, together with a quarter of the meadow called Sunewineshamme

92 Guildhall MS. 9171/1, f. 314.
93 P.R.O., SC 12/11/31.
94 Nottingham Univ. Libr., Mi D 3613.
95 P.R.O., C 139/53, no. 10; Cal. Close, 1422–9, 50--1.
96 Cal. Close, 1435–41, 124.
97 P.R.O., C 138/44, no. 8; C 138/47, no. 48.
98 Ibid. CP 25/1/291/65, no. 8; Cal. Close, 1435–41, 120.
99 P.R.O., CP 25/1/292/68, no. 181; Cal. Close, 1435--41, 128.
1 P.R.O., CP 25/1/293/73, no. 429.
2 Nottingham Univ. Libr., Mi D 3610.
3 Ibid. Mi D 3611 (fragment only).
4 P.R.O., C 135/209, no. 16. There are discrepancies in all the inqs.
5 Nottingham Univ. Libr., Mi D 3612.

6 Ibid. Mi D 3613.
7 Ibid. Mi D 3614, 3615; above, communications.
8 P.R.O., CP 25/1/292/68, no. 188.
9 Nottingham Univ. Libr., Mi D 3616, 3617.
10 Guildhall MS. 9171/5, f. 12. Burcestre held Ewell or Tilehouse manor (q.v.).
11 Dugdale, Hist. Imbanking, 72.
12 P.R.O., SC 2/1140/24.
13 A Pomfret copyholder's complaint of dispossession cannot be dated: P.R.O., C 1/73/67.
14 Nottingham Univ. Libr., Mi D 3616.
15 Above, communications.
16 Above, manors (Stepney); below, econ. hist. (agric.). Details of later ests. in Isle of Dogs reserved for treatment under Poplar.

and 2½ a. of assarted land west and south of a house which the bishop had granted to Ralph, and its appurtenances, for 9s. 1d. a year; Ralph was to defend the king for ½ hide.[17] The grant was confirmed in 1196 × 1198.[18]

Grants of land were witnessed by Ralph in 1204–5 for Stepney marsh[19] and by his son Robert in 1216 for Walmarsh (Wapping-Stepney). Robert also confirmed a grant by his father of freehold land in Whitechapel or Wapping-Stepney.[20] That some of Ralph's land lay in Wapping-Stepney and Shadwell was confirmed by the inclusion of a copy of the bishop's charter to Ralph in the cartulary of the manor of Shadwell.[21]

Bishop Eustace of Fauconberg's attempts from 1224 to recover land which had belonged to Bishop Gilbert included proceedings against eight tenants of Robert concerning a virgate, a messuage, and 44½ a. in Stepney, and ½ virgate in Hackney. Three Hackney tenants were required to answer, as Stepney and Hackney were considered to be in the same manor.[22] The land was eventually granted back to Robert's brother and heir Ralph in 1226 to hold of the bishop for 16s. 3½d. and 1 lb. of cumin.[23] Robert's widow Maud claimed dower in 1224 from 50½ a. in Stepney and 1 a. in Hackney, for which tenants who included Simon Blund and Terricus of Aldgate granted a third of their holdings.[24] By 1228–9 Martin of Pattishall, dean of St. Paul's, held 2 a. in Stepney from Ralph son of Ralph, for which he paid 12d. which was also granted to him; Walter son of Salomon of Stepney quitclaimed the 12d. to the dean. Ralph's quitclaim to Dean Geoffrey de Lucy (1231 × 41) of three houses and rent which had once belonged to Ralph's father, free of all services except that owed to the bishop,[25] was his family's last known connexion with Stepney.

BERNARD OF STEPNEY, who owed the king 10 marks in Middlesex and 15 marks in Essex in 1178 for the marriage of his daughter,[26] presumably held land in Stepney. In an exchange of 1200 Robert son of Bernard granted Henry of Bedfont Bernard's capital messuage, the vinery, land called *winhiard* (probably vineyard), and land in ten other fields, with the services totalling 30s. from five tenants including Maud daughter of Bernard, and the services and tenements of five other tenants including Walter son of Bernard; Henry paid 40s., and was to pay 6d. a year to Robert and his heirs. That estate became the manor of Poplar (q.v.). Robert received 80 a. from Henry and retained to his use the messuage that had belonged to Edmund son of Alfred, and 16 a. in seven parcels.[27]

Rodland the brother of Maud daughter of Bernard gave William de Clovilla 9 a. at Shadfliet (Schadflet) in Stepney marsh and held by Ralph of the marsh; by 1204 Maud received 4s. a year for the land, and in 1204–5 William granted the land to Brice of Shadwell (q.v.) for the 4s. to Maud and 4s. to himself. Between 1204 and 1221 William granted the 8s. rent to the canons of Holy Trinity Aldgate; they were to pay 4s. to the chief lord (Maud), who confirmed the grant between 1218 and 1221.[28] They also paid a quitrent from Shadfliet to Hamo of Bedfont.[29] There may have been a link between Bernard of Stepney and the later Bernard or Barnard family.

SALOMON OF STEPNEY witnessed charters of the bishop of London in 1141 × 1150 and of the abbot of Westminster in 1138 × 1157, and the bishop's confirmation to Ralph the clerk in 1196 × 1198,[30] and paid a relief of 10s. in the bishopric in 1187–8.[31] Salomon son of Walter of Stepney held a tenement and a virgate of land in Stepney from Lettice de Munteny, who granted his service to the priory of St. Mary, Clerkenwell, in 1193 × 1196.[32]

In 1203 Salomon claimed 10 a. in Stepney against Walter son of Adam,[33] and in 1204–5 Salomon and his son Daniel witnessed a grant for Stepney marsh.[34] Salomon also held land in Walmarsh (Wapping-Stepney),[35] and in 1219 Terricus of Aldgate and his brothers held 1 a. in Stepney from John son of Salomon.[36]

Salomon's daughter Catherine married Brice of Shadwell, who thereby may have obtained Shadwell mill.[37] In 1222 Brice's nephew and heir Benet of Maneton claimed that Catherine had only dower in the mill, while she and her husband Adam le Despenser claimed it as her inheritance from Salomon. Her brother Daniel stated that Brice had agreed, in default of issue by Catherine, that all the lands held in fee of Salomon would go to Salomon's heirs. When the allegation was disproved, Daniel surrendered his claim as Salomon's heir and quitclaimed Brice's estate to the bishop, who had bought it, in return for 10 a. of Brice's near Bethnal green, which later passed to the hospital of St. Mary without Bishopsgate.[38] Daniel also granted to Benet for 1 mark a year all the land that Edwyn *passavant'* had held of Salomon in the east marsh of Stepney, as Brice had held it, and all the meadow Daniel had in Careswyesham.[39]

Daniel granted to Holy Trinity Aldgate a quitrent of 2s. from a tenement held of him by Odo *parmentarius* in the vill of Stepney; it was quitclaimed to the canons in 1222 × 1230 by his sister Alice daughter of Salomon of Stepney,

17 *Charters of Gilb. Foliot*, 438.
18 Guildhall MS. 25122/146.   19 P.R.O., E 40/2601.
20 Ibid. E 40/7233; E 40/1801.
21 Guildhall MS. 25516, f. 38.
22 *Cur. Reg. R.* xi. 353, 371, 519, 580; xii. 121.
23 P.R.O., CP 25/1/146/7, no. 60.
24 *Cur. Reg. R.* xi. 457; xii. 242.
25 Guildhall MS. 25516, f. 38d.
26 *Pipe R.* 1178 (P.R.S. xxvii), 35, 130.
27 P.R.O., CP 25/1/146/2, no. 9.
28 Ibid. E 40/2601; E 40/2593; E 40/2589. Shadfliet-bridge lay in Poplar c. 1380.

29 P.R.O., E 40/2592.
30 *Med. Miscellany for D.M. Stenton* (P.R.S. N.S. xxxvi), 61, 102; Guildhall MS. 25122/146; above (Ralph).
31 *Pipe R.* 1188 (P.R.S. xxxvii), 12.
32 *Cart. of St. Mary Clerkenwell* (Camd. 3rd ser. lxxi), pp. 40, 44, 56–7.
33 *Cur. Reg. R.* ii. 174, 233, 245.
34 P.R.O., E 40/2601.   35 Ibid. E 40/1801.
36 *Cur. Reg. R.* viii. 138.   37 Below (Shadwell).
38 Guildhall MS. 25516, ff. 38d.–39; below (St. Mary Bishopsgate).
39 Guildhall MS. 25516, f. 38d.

who added 2s. from a tenement which Odo held of her.[40] Alice also granted 10½ a. in Golfreland, in Stepney or Hackney, to St. Mary without Bishopsgate.[41] Walter son of Salomon quitclaimed a rent granted to Dean Martin of Pattishall 1228 × 1229.[42]

Daniel's estates apparently passed to his sisters Alice, wife of John of Wittenham, and Martine(?), wife of Richard Grumbald, as they granted to Bishop Eustace (d. 1228) the 1 mark a year that had belonged to Daniel, 9 a. which the bishop had demised to him, two tenements on the north side of the bishop's woods in Stepney, and the land on the south side used for a road.[43] The men of Daniel's estate paid a fine of 2s. at the view in 1349. Since that fine was paid by the men of 'Danyels now Grymbaldes' in 1384,[44] some or all of the land of the Grumbald family may have been Salomon's, possibly including Grumbolds in Hackney and Cobhams or Rumbalds in Stepney.[45] Richard's son Walter Grumbald granted to Hugh son of Hugh Belebarbe his villein William of Aston and 13 a. for a service of 8s. a year; the land later passed to Adam Francis (Fraunceys) and became part of Hackney Wick manor.[46] Walter also granted all his land in Hackney and 5s. rent from Stepney to the hospital of St. Mary without Bishopsgate, to which in 1249 he quitclaimed 11½ a. in Stepney and Hackney.[47]

Brice of Shadwell (also of Stepney and of Hecham) acquired in the late 12th century an estate known by 1261 as the manor of SHADWELL.[48] It included 12d. rent from land called the Linches[49] acquired from Robert le Messag'; meadow in Broadmead and Lochamme acquired from Reginald of Cornhill for ½ mark a year; the rent and service owed by John son of Edrich from a virgate in the east marsh of Stepney, from Lettice de Munteny for 1 lb. of cumin a year; two 2 linches on the north side of Walmarsh, from St. Thomas à Becket's nephew Theobald of Helles for 2s. a year; Swetyngfeld and land in Summerleas from Angeline widow of Alexander of Stepney and her son Thomas and 2½ a. in Summerleas, from Thomas son of Alexander of Stepney, both for 12d. a year; land on the Linches called Mayesling, from Adam son of Liefing (or Lyving) and from Salomon son of Siward, both for 12d.; and 2 a. in Woluresesland from William son of Eylwake for 12d.[50] From his father-in-law Brice may have acquired the mill at Shadwell, later claimed by Salomon's heirs, and possibly other land.[51]

Bishop Richard (1189×1198) confirmed to Brice,

his sergeant, all acquisitions including the mill of Shadwell in the vill of Stepney, and granted to him 6 a. in a marsh called the Wylde (near Limehouse) and ¼ a. in the chief field called Northhyde (near Shoreditch church), paying 2s. 1d. a year for all services. Bishop William of Ste.-Mère-Eglise (1199 × 1224) also confirmed the lands.[52]

In 1200 Jeremy of Stepney or Stratford, son of Orgar, sued Brice as holder of 6 a. in Stepney.[53] Brice probably died by 1216 when the king granted livery of all his lands in Stepney to the value of 12 marks to Robert Turneboet'.[54] Shadwell passed to Brice's nephew Benet of Maneton, to whom the bishop confirmed it, reserving annual services of 4s. for ½ virgate that had belonged to Reymund son of Aluric, beside four other rents of 2s. or less for land bought from Daniel heir of Lyving de fonte, Almanus son of Edward de Brok, and Salomon and Adam, and for 2 a. between land formerly Reymund's and the way to the bishop's field at Blithenhale (Bethnal Green).[55] Benet also received land from Daniel son of Salomon of Stepney, for 1 mark a year, and agreed with Brice's widow Catherine for her dower. William Dolund granted Benet 7½ a. in the south marsh and William Picton's son Richard granted him all William's land sold in the court of Bishop William with the king's licence.[56]

Although Benet had established his claim to Shadwell mill,[57] he nonetheless quitclaimed it in 1223 to Daniel in return for which Daniel conveyed it to Bishop Eustace of Fauconberg (1221 × 1228), who was buying Brice's estate from Benet for 60 marks and who compensated Daniel.[58] The estate, with land and rent later acquired from Daniel's sisters and their husbands,[59] was left by the bishop in 1228 to the dean and chapter of St. Paul's, who were to pay 10 marks for various purposes.[60] In 1235 Richard of Hecham surrendered to them all his right, presumably as heir of Brice or Benet, in 60 a., a messuage, and a mill in Stepney.[61]

The dean and chapter continued to add to their estate. By 1228–9 Dean Martin of Pattishall had received 12d. rent from Ralph son of Ralph the clerk and his wife. In 1231 × 1241 Ralph son of Ralph quitclaimed further property to Dean Geoffrey de Lucy.[62] In 1244 Robert of Aleford (possibly Old Ford) granted £5 13s. 10d. rent and 16 a. in Stepney and Hackney,[63] which may have been included in the manor of Shadwell. Dean Henry de Cornhill (1243 × 1254) was granted 4d. annual rent by William Scot of Stratford

40 P.R.O., E 40/2623.
41 B.L. Cott. MS. Nero. C. iii, f. 225v.
42 Guildhall MS. 25516, f. 38d.
43 Ibid.
44 P.R.O., SC 2/191/60; Guildhall MS. 10312/136.
45 V.C.H. Mdx. x. 79; below (Cobhams).
46 Cal. of Carts. of John Pyel and Adam Fraunceys (Camd. 5th ser. ii), p. 204; V.C.H. Mdx. x. 80–1.
47 B.L. Cott. MS. Nero. C. iii, f. 225v.; P.R.O., CP 25/1/147/16, no. 292.
48 Guildhall MS. 25516, f. 39.
49 A linch was a ridge of higher ground or a terrace: O.E.D.; the Linches in Stepney lay along Ratcliff Highway.
50 Guildhall MS. 25516, f. 38.

51 Above (Salomon).
52 Guildhall MS. 25516, f. 38.
53 Cur. Reg. R. i. 362; ii. 25.
54 Rot. Litt. Claus. (Rec. Com.), i. 256.
55 Guildhall MS. 25516, f. 38d.
56 Ibid.
57 Cur. Reg. R. x. 323; above (Salomon).
58 P.R.O., CP 25/1/146/6, no. 46; Guildhall MS. 25516, f. 38d.; below (St. Mary Bishopsgate).
59 Guildhall MS. 25516, f. 38d.; above (Salomon).
60 Guildhall MS. 25516, f. 39.
61 P.R.O., CP 25/1/146/9, no. 125.
62 Guildhall MS. 25516, ff. 38d.–39; above (Ralph).
63 P.R.O., CP 25/1/147/14, no. 226.

from land that been Brice's, and 3s. rent by Pentecost son and heir of Alan the draper, owed for a tenement in Stepney called Blienhale (Bethnal Green), part of the dean's fee and formerly Brice's.[64] Dean Robert (possibly de Barton, 1257 × 1261) was quitclaimed 11s. a year from a tenement belonging to the manor of Shadwell, for a clove of garlic or a rose, by Walter Trentemars. Dean John de Chishull (1268 × 1274) was quitclaimed the rights of Adam Scray in a messuage and service in south marsh.[65]

Before 1285 Shadwell had 51 tenants holding by a money rent; they included Stephen Aswy, Ralph de Munchensy, Ralph Crepyn, the vicar of Stepney, the prioress of St. Helen's, and other freeholders in Stepney. Nothing was received from the farm of the mill. The manor had 40 a. of arable in Stepney marsh and 34½ a. in the upper fields (near the church, the gate of the manor, the bishop's windmill and the chapel of Matfelon), 15 a. of meadow, some of it at Old Ford, and another 9 a. held by Walter son of Alan Cole for ½ mark.[66]

The canons were exempted from purveyance from Shadwell in 1314 and 1316, and were granted free warren in their demesne there in 1316.[67] The dean was inhibited from holding a plea in his court when his tenants took a case to the king's court, presumably concerning free land.[68]

Edward I stayed at Shadwell in 1291, when the only recorded buildings were those of the manor house near the mill.[69] In 1334 the hall and adjoining chamber were worth nothing, windows, doors, stairs and solars had been removed, and the domestic offices and stable were in ruins. Other buildings were also decayed, as were the great grange next to the gate, the mill with its tidal ditches and watergate, and the river defences. The manor had been farmed out to Richard, the bishop's beadle, for the term of the dean's life.[70]

In 1649 the dean and chapter's estate in Whitechapel, Stepney, and Hackney consisted of four houses on the north side of Whitechapel Street, 4½ a. of meadow on the west side of Bethnal green, which had been arable in 1576, a nearby close of c. 4 a. of meadow and two parcels in Hackney marsh totalling 9½ a.[71] At Stratford Bow the dean held Brodow Mead containing 6 a.[72] In Shadwell the dean and chapter held 18 a. called Ropemakers field bordered by Ratcliff Highway, north by the later White Horse Lane, east by Cut Throat Lane, and west by Maiden

Lane; Hilly Lynch south of Ratcliff Highway and west of Foxes Lane, with tenements; and part of Shadwell from Foxes Lane to Cock Hill and from Ratcliff Highway to the Thames, mostly built up.[73] Apparently they no longer had land in Limehouse or Poplar. A house west of the site of the mill had a cellar, four rooms on the ground floor, four on the first, and four garrets. It might have been a remnant of the manor house, being the only building with a garden and orchard; one of the larger of Shadwell's many inns is another possibility. The manor was mostly let on long leases to Thomas Neale.[74]

The Trentemars family held free land of the bishop in Stepney and Hackney in the 12th and 13th centuries, for which its tenants paid 12d. towards the common fine. The men of Edmund Trentemars still owed that sum in 1349 and 1384, but John Cornwaleys, who held most of the estate, paid it in 1405.[75] The Trentemars land passed in at least two parts during the 14th century.

The major part of the Trentemars estate formed the later reputed manor of *BERNES* or *BARNES*, the principal tenement and curtilage being called Bernes in 1395. It was held in the 12th century of the *Cnihtenagild* for a quitrent of 7s. 5d., which was granted to the priory of Holy Trinity Aldgate with the rest of the soke, and lay in the parish of St. Botolph Aldgate, stretching eastward from the Minories on the site of the later Goodman's Yard to join the Trentemars land held of the bishop in the parish of Whitechapel.[76] The family had another tenement in St. Botolph Aldgate, on the north side of Algatestreet, held of Holy Trinity, and one in East Smithfield in 1308 held of an unknown lord.[77] Osbert Trentemars paid the quitrent from the principal tenement in the 12th century. Later payers were Susan Trentemars, Geoffrey son of Susan, Walter Trentemars, and in 1307 Edmund Trentemars.[78] Geoffrey son of Osbert, possibly the same family, was granted 40 a. in Stepney by Andrew Plundit in 1198.[79]

The land in Whitechapel that adjoined the tenement in the Minories, probably the later Homefield, was held by Geoffrey son of Susan 1222 × c. 1230, Geoffrey Trentemars 1222 × 1248,[80] and Walter Trentemars 1222 × 1248.[81] Walter witnessed deeds for Stepney until the 1260s.[82]

In 1248 St. Helen's priory obtained 6½ a. in Stepney of the fee of the dean of St. Paul's, who held Shadwell, by a writ of novel disseisin against Walter Trentemars,[83] and this was probably the property held by St. Helen's at the

64 Guildhall MS. 25516, f. 39.
65 Ibid.; Guildhall MS. 25501, f. 61[a].
66 Guildhall MS. 25516, ff. 39v.–40. One of the tenants had died by 1285.
67 *Cal. Pat.* 1313–17, 190, 459; *Cal. Chart. R.* 1300--26, 305.
68 *Cal. Chanc. R. Var.* 154.
69 *Itin. of Edw. I*, ii. 88; *Cal. Fine R.* 1272–1307, 299.
70 Guildhall MS. 25164.
71 Ibid. 25121/1711; T.H.L.H.L., TH/7022.
72 Guildhall MS. 11816, ff. 211–12.
73 Ibid. ff. 66–210. See *Lond. Jnl.* iv (1), 29–46, for analysis of survey and bldg.
74 Guildhall MS. 11816, f. 140. Later hist. reserved for

treatment under Shadwell.
75 P.R.O., SC 2/191/60, m. 16; Guildhall MSS. 10312/136; 25370.
76 Thanks are due to the Centre for Metropolitan Hist. for use of notes on St. Botolph Aldgate.
77 *Cart. of Holy Trinity Aldgate* (Lond. Rec. Soc. vii), 171, 183.
78 Ibid. 182–3.
79 P.R.O., CP 25/1/146/1, no. 5.
80 *Cart. of Holy Trinity*, 182.
81 Ibid. 180. It later became Goodman's Fields.
82 *Cart. of Holy Trinity*, 170, 177, 185; P.R.O., E 40/2579; E 40/2580.
83 Guildhall MS. 25501, f. 44.

Dissolution.[84] Walter Trentemars quitclaimed to Dean Robert (probably de Barton 1257 × 1261) a rent of 11s. from a tenement which had been included in Shadwell.[85]

In 1261 John le Waleys granted to Walter Trentemars 20 a. in Stepney, most likely the Trentemars family's later holding in Galeysfield or Waleysfield.[86] In 1263 Edmund son of Walter Trentemars was granted land and houses held by his father, and in 1303 Edmund son of Walter held the land adjoining the tenement.[87] Edmund Trentemars also held land east of Cambridge Road to the south of Bishopswood (near the boundary between Bethnal Green and Mile End), including Gyesfield.[88] In 1313 Edmund Trentemars, citizen, settled 7 a. in 'Gundesfield' (possibly Gyesfield) on his son Edmund.[89] After the elder Edmund's death his land near Old Ford and customary land including part of Gyesfield passed separately from Bernes, probably to the second Edmund, a younger son.[90]

Edmund senior's son and heir Walter was holding the land adjoining Bernes by 1315,[91] when he and his wife Lettice settled a carucate and 30s. rent in Stepney on themselves.[92] In 1320 Walter granted to Agnes, widow of Richard de Dunlegh of Southwark, property in St. Botolph Aldgate and Stepney, with the reversion of portions held for life by his mother Joan.[93] Shortly afterwards he granted to Simon of Abingdon, citizen and draper, and his heirs 12 a. in Gyesfield on the north side of the highway to Bishopsgrove, with the reversion of the adjoining 6 a. held as dower by Joan. In 1324 Simon's widow Eve, with her husband John of Causton, quitclaimed the 12 a. to Alice, Walter's daughter and heiress.[94] The land granted to Agnes Dunlegh also apparently returned to Trentemars; in 1328 Joan widow of Edmund Trentemars claimed 42 a. land and a third of a garden and 2 a. meadow in Stepney, and Beatrice Trentemars claimed 35s. 8d. rent in Stepney, all formerly granted to Agnes Dunlegh by Walter.[95]

Alice Trentemars and her husband William Haunsard in 1343 settled a messuage, 97 a., £4 rent in Stepney on themselves with remainder to William's father and namesake,[96] who granted his reversionary interest to his daughter Joan and her husband Henry Vanner, citizen and vintner. The estate comprised the tenement with adjoining curtilage in St. Botolph Aldgate, 40 a. in Homefield, 20 a. in Waleysfield, 20 a. in Gyesfield, 6 a. in Longmead, all arable, and 10 a. of meadow in Poplar and 2 a. at Old Ford on the Lea.[97] William Haunsard the younger died in 1349, leaving goods in the Trentemars tenement to his wife Alice, who probably married John Mokking by 1354.[98]

William Haunsard the elder had acquired 13 a. near the Crash mills in 1330 from Richard, son and heir of Richard of Gloucester, alderman, a kinsman of Walter Crepyn;[99] the mills lay on St. Botolph Aldgate's boundary with Whitechapel, a parish so narrow there that the land may have lain in either parish or in Stepney. In 1338 Haunsard or his son acquired a garden in the Minories on the north side of the Bernes tenement,[1] whose holder thereafter paid the quitrent to Holy Trinity. A messuage in Whitechapel, acquired in 1331 from Nicholas Eliot and his wife Margery,[2] may have been the one which Haunsard held north of Algatestreet.[3] He also acquired 18 a. in Collesfield in 1331 and 4a. in Old Ford called Bolemad in 1332, both from Edmund Crepyn, whose widow Mary in 1344 surrendered to Haunsard all her right in Crepyn's property in Stepney, Whitechapel and elsewhere.[4]

Haunsard granted Collesfield to John de Brendwood in 1340, and Bolemad to Joan and Henry Vanner in 1348.[5] He may also have granted the 22 a. in Stepney which the Vanners granted to Nicholas atte Wyke and John de Benyngfeld, feoffees for Adam Fraunceys, in 1352, as the property included 18 a. called 'Harinsardesfeld' (Haunsardsfield) next to Gyescroft.[6] The Vanners also granted 20 a. in Stepney to John Marreys.[7] After Vanner's death in 1354, John Mokkinge and his wife Alice settled the Bernes messuage with 98 a. and £4 rent in Stepney on Joan Vanner for life, with remainder to Vanner's son and namesake.[8] All the lands and rents in St. Botolph Aldgate, Old Ford, Poplar, and elsewhere in Stepney were similarly settled.[9] Joan paid the quitrent in 1356, as did her husband Thomas Cornwaleys of London in 1359.[10] Henry Vanner the younger, citizen and vintner, in 1368 granted them both a life interest in all the property in St. Botolph and Stepney which Joan held for life.[11] Although he held land in Stepney by marriage to Margery, daughter and coheiress of John Stodeye,[12] Bernes was still in his mother's possession when Henry made his will in 1395. He left the reversion of his mother's estate, described as the tenement 'le Bernes', with lands in Algatestreet and in Stepney, Whitechapel, and St. Botolph Aldgate, to his halfbrother John Cornwaleys and his issue, with remainders to his brother William Vanner or to Joan and her heirs.[13]

84 Below (St. Helen's).
85 Guildhall MS. 25516, f. 39.
86 P.R.O., CP 25/1/147/21, no. 419.
87 Cart. of Holy Trinity, 171, 187.
88 P.R.O., C 146/2771.
89 Guildhall Add. MS. 7.
90 Below.
91 Cart. of Holy Trinity, 181.
92 P.R.O., CP 25/1/149/45, no. 172.
93 Guildhall Add. MS. 8.
94 Ibid. 10–11.   95 P.R.O., CP 40/275, m. 161d.
96 Ibid. CP 25/1/150/59, no. 169.
97 Guildhall Add. MS. 24.
98 C.L.R.O., HR 77(213); below.
99 Guildhall Add. MS. 14.

1 C.M.H., notes on St. Botolph Aldgate, property no. 8.
2 P.R.O., CP 25/1/150/55, no. 51.
3 Cal. Close, 1429–35, 65.
4 Cart. of Adam Fraunceys, 214; Guildhall Add. MSS. 16, 22.
5 Cart. of Adam Fraunceys, 215; Guildhall Add. MS. 23.
6 P.R.O., CP 25/1/150/64, no. 290; Cart. of Adam Fraunceys, 217; below.
7 P.R.O., CP 25/1/150/64, no. 297.
8 Ibid. CP 25/1/150/66, no. 326.
9 Guildhall Add. MS. 25.
10 Cart. of Holy Trinity, 183.
11 Guildhall Add. MS. 30; Cal. Close, 1369–74, 186.
12 Below (Stodeye).
13 Guildhall MS. 9171/1, ff. 331v.–32v.

Vanner's will did not mention his copyholds of Stepney manor, which seem to have passed to John Cornwaleys and were probably included in the Bernes estate, since some field names were the same. John Cornwaleys c. 1390 held copyholds of 5 a., possibly north of Whitechapel Road, and 8 a. south of Whitechapel formerly of Thomas Cornwaleys, and owed a free rent of 33s. 2d. and suit of court at Stepney for Homefield, part of Bernes.[14] In 1401–2 c. 11 a. in Walmarsh (in Wapping) late of Henry Vanner were in the lord's hands after disagreement between William Vanner and John Cornwaleys, but by 1408–9 46 a. customary land of John had been confiscated for refusal to serve as beadle for Stepney.[15] In 1426 the bishop leased the arable for 100 years to Roger Pynchepole, whose lease was eventually assigned to Thomas Cornwaleys in 1464.[16]

In 1417 possession of Bernes was given to John Cornwaleys, citizen,[17] whose feoffees in 1430 settled the manor in St. Botolph, Stepney, and Whitechapel on him and his heirs.[18] In 1431 the prior of Holy Trinity brought an action against John, presumably to obtain the quitrent,[19] and between 1431 and 1443 Thomas Cornwaleys sued the tenant of Bernes for waste.[20]

When Bernes was leased by Thomas Cornwaleys for eleven years in 1472, it was described as a great messuage in St. Botolph, with Homefield of 50 a. in Stepney (recte Whitechapel) and tenements north and south of the great gate by the highway.[21] Thomas's son John settled Bernes on himself and his heirs in 1489.[22] Sir John Cornwallis paid the quitrent in 1538–9, when the occupant was a tenant.[23]

In 1560 Sir Thomas Cornwallis apparently conveyed the manor to William Bromefield, with eight messuages and eight cottages, with gardens, an orchard, a dovecot, 110 a., and 9s. rent and appurtenances in St. Botolph, Whitechapel, St. Katharine near London, and Stepney.[24] In 1594 Catherine Bromefield, widow, and William and Arthur Bromefield conveyed to Thomas Goodman the manor of Barnes with 54 messuages, 72 gardens, 20 cottages, 1 windmill, and 70 a. in St. Botolph Aldgate, Whitechapel, and Stepney.[25] Goodman died in 1606 seized of 11 tenements and 16 gardens in St. Botolph Bishopsgate, held of the king for 1/100th knight's service and valued at £3 a year, and a messuage, 22 tenements, 12 cottages, 5 stables, 1 mill, 45 gardens, and 42 a. pasture in St. Botolph Aldgate, Whitechapel, and Stepney, valued at £11 and held partly of the mayor and corporation of London for an annual quitrent of 9s. 5d., and

partly of the manor of Stepney for service of 18s. 8d. In 1598 he had settled 9 tenements of the latter, valued at 40s., on his daughter Elizabeth, her husband Walter Halliley, and their eldest son, and in 1602 he had settled most of the rest on Mary Watts, wife of his son William Goodman, and their issue, and the remainder on himself and his wife Beatrice for life, with remainder to his son William.[26] Most of the estate was sold in 1628 by William Goodman and his wife Alice and Alan Carey and his wife Anne to Sir John Leman (d. 1632),[27] who settled 10 messuages, 40 cottages and 40 a. pasture called Goodman's Fields, described as part of the manor and capital messuage anciently called Barnes, on his nephew William Leman, citizen and fishmonger.[28] It was settled by William Leman the elder in 1655 on the marriage of his son William.[29]

The tenement called Bernes was a substantial building in 1472 with a great gate to the Minories, a dovecot, and a chamber over the hall with two rooms adjacent called 'les withdraughtes'.[30]

Another portion of the *TRENTEMARS* estate in Stepney probably descended through Edmund Trentemars the younger to augment the manor of Hackney Wick. In 1361 Edmund's widow Maud and her husband William de Gloucester of London, and John son and heir of Edmund Trentemars, leased 16 a. in parcels in Old Ford to Adam Fraunceys, to whom John shortly afterwards released the freehold. Fraunceys granted it with other land, including Hackney Wick, to feoffees, to whom John Trentemars quitclaimed in 1375,[31] apparently ending his family's connexion with Stepney.

Fraunceys in 1352 acquired Collesfield, which had passed from John de Brendwood to Michael Mynot in 1343 with land in Hackney and Tottenham, and then in 1347 to Walter Turk.[32] The major part of Fraunceys's estate came from the Belebarbe family. Hugh Belebarbe held land in Stepney c. 1200, and he or his son Hugh witnessed grants in Wapping, the Isle of Dogs, and by the Lea until the 1260s. Amongst other acquisitions was William of Aston, a villein, and 13 a. which Walter son of Richard Grumbald granted to Hugh son of Hugh Belebarbe to hold for 8s. a year.[33] Hugh was succeeded in the late 13th century by John and Robert Belebarbe.[34] In 1316 Robert Belebarbe the elder granted two messuages and 90 a. in Stepney and Hackney to Simon of Abingdon, which became part of the manor of Wick,[35] and 24 a. in Stepney to Walter Crepyn.[36]

[14] Guildhall MS. 25422.

[15] P.R.O., SC 6/1139/22–23. Some copyholds may have been part of Stodeye's land (q.v.).

[16] Guildhall Add. MSS. 43–4, 46.   [17] Ibid. 41.

[18] C.L.R.O., HR 158(30).

[19] Ibid. HPL 55, m. 3.

[20] P.R.O., C 1/9/349b.

[21] Guildhall Add. MS. 47.

[22] Ibid. 49–50.

[23] *Cart. of Holy Trinity*, 183.

[24] P.R.O., CP 25/2/171/2&3 Eliz./Mich.

[25] Ibid. CP 25/2/262/36 Eliz./Trin.

[26] Ibid. C 142/294, no. 88.

[27] P.R.O., CP 25/2/526/4 Chas.I/Trin.

[28] Ibid. C 142/482, no. 45; C 54/17040, no. 8.

[29] Ibid. C 110/114; CP 25/2/617/1655/Trin.

[30] Guildhall Add. MS. 47. Later hist. reserved for Whitechapel.

[31] *Cart. of Adam Fraunceys*, 217; *Cal. Close*, 1374–7, 200.

[32] *Cart. of Adam Fraunceys*, 215; B.L. Add. Ch. 40513; above, and below (Crepyn).

[33] *Cart. of Adam Fraunceys*, 203–5; P.R.O., E 40/1801; E 40/7233; E 40/2580; E 40/2916; E 40/2634; B.L. Cott. MS. Tib. C. v, ff. 153, 156v.

[34] B.L. Add. Ch. 24069; Cott. Tib. C. v, ff. 155, 158-v.; P.R.O., E 40/2636; C 146/409.

[35] P.R.O., CP 25/1/149/46, no. 192; *V.C.H. Mdx.* x. 80.

[36] P.R.O., CP 25/1/149/46, no. 188; below (Crepyn).

Frednceys also acquired lands of Robert Bar-nard, who had been granted the moiety of a messuage and 108 a. in Stepney in 1294 by John Westheye and his wife Aubrey, which included a messuage in Old Ford and were Aubrey's inheritance. Barnard's lands had passed by 1323 to his daughter and heir Agnes and by 1346 to Isabel wife of Roger Osekyn who conveyed them to Frednceys in 1359.[37]

Frednceys's feoffees granted all his lands with Hackney Wick to his widow Agnes, with succes-sive remainders in tail to his children Maud and Adam. Maud married (as her third husband) John Montagu, earl of Salisbury, who was hold-ing in her right in 1399 when his lands were forfeited and granted to his widow.[38] Agnes, succeeded by the countess of Salisbury, owed the bishop a service of 13s. 4d. and fealty for Brodesfield and Gyesfield, whose names suggest they had been part of the Trentemars lands, and 4s. 8d. for part of the tenement and land formerly of Agnes Bernard. Although listed with the free rents, they were later granted by copy.[39] All the land seems to have descended with Hackney Wick and was probably not distinguished in descriptions of that manor. Its history may explain why Wick was said to be held partly of the bishop in 1400.

Maud, countess of Salisbury, died in 1424 seized of 40 a. in Brodfield in Stepney, 18 a. in Gyesfield, and an annexed piece once Agnes Bernard's. Alice, countess of Salisbury, held it at her death but it was in the hands of the lord unclaimed in 1464. In 1509–10 Sir John Risley, lord of Hackney Wick, and Sir Henry Wyatt were admitted to the copyhold, possibly as feoffees.[40] As the copyhold was later held by the Bowyer family, it seems that it was sold by Margaret, countess of Salisbury, and her son with the manor in 1538 to William Bowyer, later lord mayor of London.[41]

Sir William Bowyer's will was proved in 1544, but years of litigation followed, apparently re-solved in 1566 in favour of Francis, infant son of John Bowyer of Histon (Cambs.). However, land that was probably part of his copyhold was said to belong to the heirs of Thomas Bowyer in 1550,[42] and in 1564 a John Bowyer was admitted to copyholds which included 55 a. in Panfield, Bradfield, and Gyesfield, which he surrendered in 1569 to Edward Partridge of London.[43]

A Thomas Bowyer granted 11 a. called Poorefield in Stepney and Hackney to John Jones, citizen and girdler, in 1640. It passed to James Jones, administrator in 1664 of the goods of his deceased infant son, and he sold it to George Hockenhill.[44]

In 1673 Nicholas Cooke the elder of East Greenwich left to his daughter Elizabeth and her husband William Buckeridge with remainder to her son, three parcels containing 13 a. in the tenure of Richard Hopper, which seem to have been Gyesfield. He also left annuities from 28 a. at Mile End, where the land presumably passed to his son Nicholas Cooke.[45] In 1703 Buckeridge held 13 a. on the northern boundary of Mile End Old Town adjoining demesne of Stepney called Broomfields; Hopper had been holding the land adjoining the latter in 1652.[46] Gyesfield passed to the Corporation of the Sons of the Clergy by 1849.[47]

Two a. formerly part of Panfield or Bradfield were included in 45 a. in Stepney belonging to Thomas Gouge, clerk, and let in 1672 to John Preston,[48] who occupied 45 a. at the eastern end of Mile End Old Town belonging to Dr. 'Gouch' in 1703.[49] The Gouge estate derived partly from Elizabeth Culverwell, who in 1589 bequeathed to her daughter Elizabeth, wife of Thomas Gouge of Stratford Bow, two messuages in Stepney converted into one, and the Queen's Head at Mile End with 7 a. of free land; another daughter Cecilia, wife of Laurence Chaterton, was left seven other messuages in Stepney.[50] In 1661 Thomas Gouge, clerk, and his wife Anne settled 13 messuages, 17 gardens, 6 barns, and 70 a. in Stratford Bow on themselves and their sons William, Thomas, Edward, and Nicholas.[51] In 1849 c. 22 a. of the former Gouge estate in Mile End was still not built on and belonged to Sir Charles Morgan, Bt.[52]

The manor of *HUSCARL* derived from land probably by Roger Huscarl 1196 × 1198, when he witnessed the bishop of London's grant to Ralph the clerk.[53] Roger owed Robert son of Bernard a service of 12d., which was granted to Henry of Bedfont in 1200 as part of the later manor of Poplar,[54] and was involved in several actions re-garding free land in Stepney. He claimed ½ virgate and a messuage from Robert son of Terricus in 1200, warranted 5 a. which John son of Baldwin held of him in 1205, and claimed 7 a. in Walmarsh (Wapping) from Peter son of Oger in 1212.[55] In 1219 he was found not to have disseised William Blund and his wife Lettice of a free tenement[56] and reached agreement with Maud widow of Robert son of Chedric over her dower.[57]

In 1230 Roger's son William Huscarl claimed ½ a. from Terricus of Aldgate, which Roger had claimed, but the land was found to belong to St. Paul's.[58] William also released to Gilbert son of Emma de la Milaunde (Mile End) and his heirs a messuage and 2 a., for 2s. a year,[59] and witnessed deeds until 1250.[60]

37 *Cart. of Adam Frednceys*, 209, 211.
38 *V.C.H. Mdx.* x. 80.
39 Guildhall MS. 25422; P.R.O., SC 12/11/31.
40 P.R.O., SC 2/191/63, m. 1d.
41 *V.C.H. Mdx.* x. 80, for descent.
42 G.L.R.O., M79/LH/128/1/1, p. 2.
43 Ibid. A/CSC/997A.
44 T.H.L.H.L., TH/626–7.
45 G.L.R.O., A/CSC/997B.
46 Gascoyne, *Plan of Mile End Old Town*; G.L.R.O., M93/158.
47 P.R.O., IR 29/21/51; G.L.R.O., A/CSC/997C–E; later hist. reserved for Mile End Old Town.

48 T.H.L.H.L., TH/2207.
49 Gascoyne, *Plan of Mile End Old Town*.
50 Guildhall MS. 9171/17, ff. 262–3.
51 T.H.L.H.L., TH/4230/5.
52 P.R.O., IR 29/21/51. Detailed hist. reserved for Mile End Old Town and Stratford Bow.
53 Guildhall MS. 25122/146.
54 P.R.O., CP 25/1/146/2, no. 9.
55 *Cur. Reg. R.* i. 145; iii. 204, 328; vi. 282, 392.
56 Ibid. viii, p. xi.   57 P.R.O., CP 25/1/146/5, no. 24.
58 *Cur. Reg. R.* xiii. 528; xiv. 8.
59 P.R.O., C 146/1993 (n.d.).
60 Ibid. E 40/2580; E 40/2634.

Ralph Huscarl witnessed a grant c. 1270,[61] received 6s. a year from Aline de Ba in 1273-4, and in 1278-9 held 16 marks of land in Stepney.[62] In 1290 Hugh of Cressingham, possibly a feoffee, settled land in Somerset and the manor of Stepney Huscarl on John Huscarl and his wife Alexandra, with remainder to their son Humphrey and his heirs.[63]

Humphrey Huscarl of Bruton (Som.) granted a messuage, 70 a. in Stepney and Hackney, 10s. rent, and the reversion of 5 a. held by John de Pulteney to Geoffrey Aleyn, citizen and fishmonger, and his wife Maud for life.[64] The property was among that settled in reversion by Humphrey in 1348 on his son and heir Nicholas and his issue, to be held for a red rose.[65] Nicholas in 1356 confirmed his father's grant to Maud and for twelve years after her death to her husband Thomas Gatyn.[66]

By c. 1380 the free tenement and land late of Humphrey Huscarl was held by Adam Chaungeour (Adam of St. Ives), merchant, of the bishop for 18s. 7d. and suit of court.[67] Adam also acquired the Mote in 1371 and other property in Stepney,[68] and by 1380 had granted 12 a. to John Hadley.[69] In 1393 his Stepney estate included a messuage called Huscarles with 81 a., two cottages next to it, a cottage and curtilage on the N. side of the churchyard, and, among other property, a messuage called the Mote with a garden and 46 a. in the marsh. Adam also had rents of assize from tenements in Stepney, besides small properties in Bromley, Hackney, and East Smithfield.[70] His heirs held 92½ a. c. 1400, of which 45 a. were free, 33 a. including 5 a. late Thomas Gatyn's were claimed as free, and 12½ a. were customary. He had also held a customary tenement and curtilage called (Ca?)tesplace paying a helpenny and smokepenny.[71]

Adam's estate in Stepney passed to John Seymour and his wife Joan, and by 1401-2 the customary land had escheated after unlicensed alienation. It included 52 a. of cotland and 34 a. of meadow, an allowance being made for free lands which could not be distrained upon and included 50 a. called Huscarles.[72] In 1407 William Waryn and his wife Joan, daughter of Nicholas Huscarl's brother Ralph, claimed the manor of Stepney Huskarl from the Seymours, apparently without success.[73]

In 1413 the manor was settled in trust by Walter Green and his wife Alice.[74] It is not clear which of the family's properties were part of Huscarls. Walter resided in Poplar in 1421 and

acquired a messuage in Mile End from Ralph Holand in 1437.[75] The garden on the north side of Stepney churchyard that had belonged to Adam of St. Ives was Walter's in 1438.[76] He, or possibly his son Walter, married Elizabeth daughter of Robert Warner (d. 1439),[77] and Robert son of Walter later claimed that Warner had been seized of the manor of Poplar, probably meaning a free tenement held of that manor, which was conveyed to Walter Green and his heirs.[78] William Sellewood, cousin and heir of Humphrey Huscarl, quitclaimed all his right in Humphrey's lands in Stepney to Thomas and Walter Green and others in 1439. Eleanor Huscarl, daughter and heir of John, quitclaimed to other feoffees in 1444.[79]

In 1454 Walter Green held land in Churchfield on the east side of the highway to Stepney church (White Horse Street), perhaps part of Huscarl.[80] He also held the Mote formerly of Adam Chaungeour, which afterwards passed to Edmund Ratcliff.[81] Walter apparently died by 1460×1465, when his son Robert alleged dispossession of a feoffee by a freeholder of Poplar,[82] and Walter's widow Elizabeth died in 1473, followed soon after by Robert, whose widow Cecily married John Acton but died in 1480. The family held the manor of Cowley Peachey, which passed to Robert's son Edward and in 1493 to Edward's sister Cecily, wife of William Burbage.[83] In the 1490s Burbage and John Green owed rent of 12d. to the manor of Poplar for ground in Eastmarsh beside Leamouth.[84] Cecily Burbage, widow, was in default of suit of court in Poplar in 1497[85] and seems to have married William Craythorn with whom she settled Cowley Peachey, including appurtenances in Stepney and Whitechapel, in trust in 1498. Craythorn was a member of the homage of Poplar in 1499.[86]

Some 16th-century transactions in Stepney and Poplar also concerned the Greens' estate. Lands were conveyed by William Green in 1539, by Robert Green in 1541 and, called Leymouth in Eastmarsh, in 1546, and by Roger Green in 1553.[87]

William COLE probably held land in Stepney in 1196×1198.[88] In 1206 Edmund son of Gerard of Old Ford quitclaimed to him his right in lands in the vill which Algar his (presumably Cole's) father had held of the bishop of London.[89] William witnessed grants in Stepney in the early 13th century,[90] and agreed with Brice of Stepney to lease Summerleas.[91]

In 1237 William de Blancmuster and Alice his

61 B.L. Cott. MS. Tib. C. v, f. 158v.
62 P.R.O., C 133/4, no. 5; ibid. SC 5/Mdx/1, m. 1.
63 Ibid. C 54/107, m. 17d.
64 Cal. Close, 1354-60, 306-7.
65 P.R.O., C 260/153, no. 26.
66 Cal. Close, 1354-60, 306-7.
67 Guildhall MS. 25422.
68 Cal. Close, 1369-74, 321; above (Crepyn).
69 P.R.O., C 146/2777; below (Hadley).
70 P.R.O., C 131/43, no. 10.   71 Ibid. SC 12/11/31.
72 Ibid. SC 6/1139/22.   73 Ibid. CP 40/585, m. 417.
74 Ibid. CP 25/1/291/63, no. 5.
75 Reg. Chichele, ii. 254; P.R.O., CP 25/1/152/91, no. 78.
76 P.R.O., C 146/483.   77 V.C.H. Mdx. iii. 173.
78 P.R.O., C 1/27/82.

79 Cal. Close, 1435-41, 254; 1441-7, 230.
80 Mercers' Co., Bk. of Evidences of Dean Colet, f. 128v.
81 P.R.O., SC 11/453; above (Crepyn).
82 P.R.O., C 1/27/82; SC 2/191/48.
83 V.C.H. Mdx. iii. 173.
84 P.R.O., SC 11/453. Dated from internal evidence.
85 P.R.O., SC 2/191/50.
86 Ibid. CP 25/1/294/80/13 Hen.VII/East.; SC 2/191/50.
87 Ibid. CP 25/2/27/183/31 Hen.VIII/Trin.; CP 25/2/27/184/33 Hen.VIII/Mich.; CP 25/2/27/186/38 Hen.VIII/Mich.; CP 25/2/74/629/1 Mary/Mich.
88 Guildhall MS. 25122/146.
89 Pipe R. 1206 (P.R.S. N.S. xx), 59.
90 P.R.O., E 40/2601; E 40/1801; E 40/2589.
91 Guildhall MS. 25516, f. 38d.; above (Shadwell).

wife granted a virgate in Stepney to Roger son of William Cole and his heirs, to hold of the chief lords as the grantors had done.[92] Roger witnessed grants in Stepney between c. 1218 and 1250,[93] including one in 1250 by Anketun or Asketin Cole, of unknown relationship. Soon after he became bishop of London in 1244, Fulk Basset confirmed to Roger Cole all the lands held of Fulk and his predecessors, seemingly referring to the Basset estates, henceforth to be held for a quitrent of 6s. 8d.[94]

In 1247 two tenants, Robert le Coner and Richard Aynolf, obtained confirmation of their land held from Asketin for annual quitrents.[95] In 1250 Asketin son of Robert Cole granted to Fulk Basset, for 80 marks, all his lands and rents in Stepney and Hackney. They were specified as on the Down between the land of Robert of Wick on the north and Old Ford on the south, arable called Onaker and 2 a. called Smythesfield, meadow in Bokkemad and meadows called Barnhamme and Rissemad, and five annual quitrents of money and one rent of a lb. of cumin. The meadow and most of the arable was by the Lea near Old Ford. There was no reference to the church in the grant, which was therefore probably to Fulk and his personal heirs, and may have been of land held of the Bassets.[96] Asketin also granted to the hospital of St. Thomas Acre a quitrent he received from it for a watercourse they held, probably at Wapping.[97] In 1275 Asketin's widow Eldreda claimed dower in a third of a messuage and 40 a. in Stepney from John de Bathonia, who held it of the Basset heiress Aline, daughter of Fulk's brother Philip and wife of Roger Bigod, earl of Norfolk (d. 1306).[98]

Alan Cole as a landholder in the 1260s witnessed grants in Walmarsh and along the Lea.[99] He was charged with making gold at Stepney but found innocent in 1269.[1] In 1285 Amice widow of Alan Cole claimed a messuage and 52 a. in Stepney as dower from William de Lude, prebendary of St. Paul's.[2] In the late 13th century Shadwell manor was said to include 9 a. once held by Walter son of Alan Cole, but the canons did not know where the land was.[3] Walter witnessed a grant in Stepney in 1287–8.[4]

Robert the grandson and heir of Asketin Cole stated in 1286 that he had been dispossessed of a free tenement which the bishop claimed to be held in villeinage. It was found that Asketin had died in possession, that Robert had held it for 16 years, and that the tenement was of the fee of Crevequer.[5] In 1289 Robert granted to Adam de Stratton, clerk, 1 a. in Stepney on the east

bank of the Lea to hold for a rose.[6] Robert was hanged as a felon c. 1294 and c. 3 a. were delivered to Alexander Cole in 1295, as Robert had held them of him.[7] Collesfield and Colleshach may have been part of the family's estate: in the 14th century they became part of Hackney Wick, the deeds of which included the confirmation of Roger Cole's lands.[8]

A family called Hulles or Helles held land in Stepney in the 12th century, giving its name to the manor of *HULLS* or *MILE END*. Before 1216 Theobald of Helles granted two lynches that had belonged to Agnes, sister of St. Thomas à Becket, to Brice of Stepney; they formed part of the manor of Shadwell (q.v.).[9] In 1225 Theobald's widow Alice claimed dower from 60 a. in Stepney, which she received from Theobald's son Thomas.[10] As Hulls lay next to Ashwyes manor in the 14th century, a plea by Stephen Aswy against Alan de Hull of Kent in 1273–4 may indicate a connexion between the two estates.[11]

In 1321 William, son of John of Helles of Kent, released all his right in lands in West Ham, Stepney, and London which John de Ramesey had demised to Richard of Hackney (de Hakeney), alderman, citizen and woolmonger (d. 1343).[12] In 1330 a messuage was said to have been held of Richard, who held the manor of Helles, since 1319.[13] Richard acquired a further 6 a. in Stepney in 1331.[14] His lands in London, probably including Stepney, passed to his wife Alice (d. 1349) for life,[15] and his eldest son Niel (Nigellus de Hakeney) settled the Stepney property on himself and his wife and their issue in 1349. It consisted of a messuage formerly of Robert le Forster in Stepney, with houses and gardens and 4 a. within its close, 69 a. divided between Basesfield on the east side of the messuage, Cloutesfield, and Hungerdown, in Stepney and Hackney, and 5½ a. in Bernamesmede (or Barnhammesmead) next to Stratford Bow.[16]

Sir John Philpot (d. 1384), mayor of London, acquired some or all of Richard of Hackney's lands including Helles. A claim against Philpot's heir was made by Richard's daughter Isabel in 1390,[17] and Philpot held meadow in Old Ford that had formerly belonged to Niel of Hackney's heirs.[18] Sir John's estate at Mile End was known as Hulls, and Hakeneye hedge lay there along the footpath from Whitechapel to Stepney church in 1615.[19] In 1365 Sir John and his first wife Joan received custody of a messuage and land in Stepney and Hackney which had belonged to John Marreys the elder and been

92 P.R.O., CP 25/1/146/1, no. 153.
93 B.L. Cott. MS. Tib. C. v, f. 153; P.R.O., E 40/2580; C 146/1993.
94 *Cart. of Adam Fraunceys*, 204.
95 P.R.O., CP 25/1/147/15, nos. 257, 259.
96 Ibid. E 40/2634.
97 B.L. Cott. MS. Tib. C. v, f. 155v.
98 P.R.O., CP 40/9, rot. 55.   99 Ibid. E40/7828.
1 *Cal. Close*, 1268–72, 23.
2 P.R.O., CP 40/60, m. 110d.
3 Guildhall MS. 25516, f. 40.
4 P.R.O., C 146/1483.
5 Ibid. CP 40/63, rot. 14.
6 Ibid. E 40/2636.

7 Ibid. C 145/55, no. 14; *Cal. Close*, 1288–96, 437.
8 *Cart. of Adam Fraunceys*, 204; above (Bernes and Trentemars).
9 Guildhall MS. 25516, f. 38.
10 *Cur. Reg. R.* xii. 309, 494; xiii. 66, 159; xiv. 302.
11 P.R.O., JUST 1/538, m. 7.
12 *Abbrev. Plac.* (Rec. Com.), 338.
13 P.R.O., E 145/112, no. 16.
14 Ibid. CP 25/1/150/54, no. 48.
15 *Cal. of Wills in Ct. of Husting*, i. 467–8, 625–6.
16 P.R.O., C 54/186, m. 7d.
17 *Yr. Bk. 13 Ric. II* (Ames Foundation), 124.
18 P.R.O., C 146/3410.
19 *D.N.B.*; Plan of Mercers' est.

seized by the Crown for debt.[20] In 1373 they were quitclaimed a parcel on the north side of Hachestreet, which they had bought from Robert Greyland.[21] A grant of 1375 by Sir John at Hale and his wife Ellen of a messuage, 169 a., and rent in Stepney, Hackney, and Stratford Bow, may have marked the acquisition of Hulls.[22] Philpot may also have acquired some land in Stepney and Whitechapel, besides the manor of Hoxton and property in the City, through his third wife Margaret Birlingham, daughter and coheir of John Stodeye (d. 1376).[23]

Sir John Philpot or his heirs held freely from the bishop for quitrents the tenement and 60 a. called Hulls, 28 a. once of Robert de Bine(?), and 20 a. land once of Hugh Gilnest. He also held customary land in Galeysfield, south of Mile End Road, and to the south, and 6 a. of free land near Limehouse c. 1400.[24] All the estates passed to Philpot's widow for life; Hulls was then to pass to Sir John at Hale's son, John at Hale of Dorset, who was to marry Philpot's daughter Margaret. Stodeye's lands in the City were left to Margaret and her heirs, and Hoxton was left to Philpot's son Thomas, with remainder to another son Edward.[25] Philpot's widow Margaret married first John Fitznichol (d. 1391) and then Adam Bamme (d. 1397), mayor of London,[26] who exchanged 4½ a. near Whitechapel Road with John Hadley,[27] and Margaret's lands in Stepney were valued at 13s. 4d. in 1412.[28] John and Margaret at Hale apparently had no issue, since the widowed Margaret granted Hale's Dorset estates in remainder to Sir John Philpot's heirs, and after Lady Philpot's death in 1431, the Philpot estates including Hulls passed to John, son of Sir John Philpot's son John (d. 1415).[29] In 1433 John exchanged the manor of Gillingham (Kent) with Richard son of Adam Bamme for the manor of Twyford,[30] and he may have been the John Philpot who died in 1484, seized of the manor of Mile End (Hulls) which he had settled on his son John (d. 1502); it was valued at £5 and held of the bishop of London for fealty and 17s.[31]

The manor passed to his son Sir Peter (d. 1540), who was granted livery in 1510.[32] He left it to his son Henry as his son and heir, with remainder to another son Thomas, but an inquisition in 1542 decided that Thomas was the heir,[33] and on the grounds of his lunacy the Crown seized the land, consisting of 6 a. at Limehouse in the tenure of Richard Driver, the manor of Mile End held by six tenants, and 15 a. next to Bethnal green in the tenure of John Moane.[34] It was later fraudulently claimed that Thomas had made a lease of a messuage and 52 a. at Mile End.[35] Henry died in 1567 leaving his brother Thomas as his heir, and the latter died in 1586 leaving a son Sir George (d. 1624).[36] By c. 1590 Henry Freeman and Henry Smyth were lessees to George at Mile End,[37] and in 1591 another tenant, Arthur Webster, left the lease of Hulls farm to his son-in-law Christopher Pate.[38] Pate was said (erroneously) to have been seized in fee of two messuages and 60 a. at Mile End green c. 1617, and the premises were held by George and Thomas Lawrence in 1621.[39]

Pate's lease probably included the manor house, as Sir George occupied a new house to the north-east.[40] When settled in 1607, the estate consisted of five messuages, one the capital messuage called Hulls otherwise Philpots, five gardens, 350 a., and 10s. rent in Hackney, Stepney, and Stratford Bow, 1 a. on the north and east sides of Hulls with a new capital messuage, and 20 smaller messuages and 60 a. in Mile End, Bethnal Green, Old Ford, Whitechapel, and Limehouse.[41] It passed from Sir George's son Sir John (d. c. 1637) to the latter's son Henry with some life interest to another son William.[42] Henry Philpot of Thruxton (Hants) sold Sir George's mansion with 1 a. on the south side of Mile End green to Nicholas Cooke, citizen and innholder, in 1637.[43]

Hercules King and his wife Mary granted to William Philpot in 1644 a third of a messuage and other property in Stepney, Hackney, and Old Ford, with warranty against the heirs of Mary, who was presumably holding it as dower.[44] Henry Philpot was fined as a royalist on lands which included the old Hulls manor house in 1644, when its value was abated because part of the farm had been taken to build a fort for the defence of London.[45] In 1647 the remainder of his fine was in the hands of Mr. Austen of Hoxton, who owed money to Philpot on the sale of his land.[46] Since Robert Austen of St. Martin-in-the-Fields in 1692 mortgaged the mansion house and farm called Hulls or Philpots with c. 65 a. in Stepney and Old Ford,[47] it seems his family bought most of Philpot's land in Stepney including Hulls. In 1703 Mr. Austen owned six parcels in Mile End Old Town south of Hulls totalling 48½ a.[48]

The Philpots' connexion with Stepney seems to have ended in 1654 when Henry made con-

20 P.R.O., C 66/272, m. 20.
21 Cal. Close, 1369–74, 582.
22 P.R.O., CP 25/1/151/74, no. 526. There was a later family connexion between Philpot and Hale in Dorset.
23 Below (Stodeye); V.C.H. Mdx. x. 82–4.
24 Guildhall MS. 25422; P.R.O., SC 12/11/31. For Bine, below (Bathonia).
25 C.L.R.O., HR 118(30).
26 Rawcliffe, 'Margaret Stodeye', 91–3.
27 P.R.O., SC 12/11/31; Hadley was married to another Stodeye heir.
28 Beaven, Aldermen, i. 174; Feud. Aids, vi. 489.
29 Cal. Close, 1429–35, 171; Rawcliffe, 'Margaret Stodeye', 97.
30 V.C.H. Mdx. vii. 174; D.N.B.
31 P.R.O., C 141/6, no. 26.   32 Ibid. E 40/12856.
33 Ibid. C 142/64, no. 152.

34 Ibid. SC 6/Hen.VIII/6128.
35 Ibid. C 3/228/18.
36 Ibid. C 142/191, no. 85; C 142/213, no. 84. Neither inq. mentions property in Mdx.
37 Ibid. C 3/228/18.
38 Guildhall MS. 9171/17, f. 436v.
39 P.R.O., C 142/644, no. 11.
40 Plan of Mercers' est.
41 P.R.O., C 142/402, no. 129; WARD 5/26, bundle 4.
42 Ibid. C 142/611, no. 129; T.H.L.H.L., TH/35.
43 Herts. R.O., Martin-Leake MS. 83795.
44 P.R.O., CP 25/2/458/20 Chas.I/Mich.
45 Ibid. SP 19/95, no. 1; SP 19/5, pp. 108, 123, 229.
46 Ibid. SP 19/5, p. 265.
47 T.H.L.H.L., TH/1340.
48 Gascoyne, Map of Mile End Old Town. Later hist. reserved for Mile End Old Town.

veyances of 17 messuages and 12 cottages and of six cottages nearby in Limehouse.[49] He also conveyed a smith's shop at Limehouse in reversion after the death of his brother William.[50]

FIG. 7. SIR GEORGE PHILPOT'S HOUSE IN 1615

Sir George Philpot's new house was shown in 1615 as a substantial building with two wings and a central dome. In 1672 it included a great gate from the green, a hall with the throwsters' arms painted on the shutters by an owner in the 1650s, a cellar, two storeys with garrets, and gardens with fruit trees.[51]

John le Ghyepe or Yepe, also known as John le Waterlader, of East Smithfield, acquired 3½ a. in Crepenne and Walmarsh, in Whitechapel and Wapping-Stepney, from Ralph the clerk, whose son Robert confirmed the grant before 1216.[52] The land was probably that conveyed by five separate holders in Landmarsh (in Walmarsh) and next to the stream called Cropet and lying between Hachestreet and the lower road.[53] Between 1222 and 1239 John conveyed to the priory of *HOLY TRINITY ALDGATE* land and buildings in the parish of St. Botolph Aldgate and the 3½ a. in Stepney, reserving quitrents to the five grantors or their heirs,[54] two of whom confirmed John's gift.[55]

Holy Trinity also acquired, from William de Clovilla, before 1221 8s. rent which Brice of Stepney and Ralph his nephew (*nepos*) paid for Shadfliet in Stepney marsh; Maud daughter of Bernard confirmed the grant.[56] Between 1222 and 1243 Hamo of Bedfont granted the canons the annual quitrent of 12d. which they paid him for Shadfliet, in return for 1½d. a year.[57] Between 1244 and 1250 John son of Robert de Tessunt (or Teffunt) granted them 10 a. in Stepney marsh, in return for 1d. a year, 10s. to the heirs of Alan le Baud, and the sheriff's aid; Christine

de Monasterio, who held the land for life, paid them 10s. 1½d.[58] This was probably the land once Christine Mainard's that Holy Trinity quitclaimed to Walter Trentemars and his heirs in 1261 × 1264.[59]

Between 1222 and 1250 Holy Trinity confirmed the sale to John *Uvenus* by Aubrey son of Baldwin of 2 a. held of it in Northcroft, thought to be in Stepney; John was to hold the land freely for 2s. a year and suit of court.[60] In 1310 Salomon de Ripple was paying 4s. a year to the priory for a messuage and 2 a. 1 r. next to the tenement of the chapel of St. Mary Matfelon outside Aldgate;[61] the quitrent of 4s. paid by John Stodeye c. 1374 seems to have been that property.[62]

Records of the priory's estate in St. Botolph Aldgate do not mention Stepney. Its land in Wapping and Whitechapel may have been managed with the manor of Bromley, which it held until the Dissolution.[63]

In the mid 13th century the hospital of *ST. MARY WITHOUT BISHOPSGATE*, whose precinct bordered the west side of Stepney, received 10 a. formerly part of Brice of Shadwell's estate which had been granted by Bishop Eustace de Fauconberg to Daniel of Stepney. It consisted of 8½ a. next to the way from Colmrichehath (Cambridge Heath) towards Twentyacres and 1½ a. in Bothelelcroft, all held by Daniel of the bishop for 1 lb. of incense or 3d. and later of the dean and chapter's manor of Shadwell.[64] The land was given to the hospital by Roger, vicar of Stepney;[65] it was probably the 10 a. quitclaimed to him by Richard of Hecham in 1235[66] and possibly the 11½ a. in Stepney and Hackney which Daniel of Stepney's nephew Walter Grumbald confirmed to the hospital in 1249.[67] In 1387–8 the two parcels lay west of the later Cambridge Heath Road and were held to farm for 16s. 4d.[68]

The hospital also acquired Snecockswell, east of its precinct in a demesne field called Lollesworth. The bishop granted the well in 1278, with licence to pipe the water to the infirmary and other offices.[69] Grants in Hackney, Stepney, and Shoreditch included 4 messuages and 24 a. from John Blanche and Nicholas of Shoreditch in 1349,[70] a messuage, 3 shops, and 28 a. from Robert Game in 1362,[71] and a messuage and 80 a. held of Stepney manor for 19s. 2d. a year, which Roger of Winchcomb and others were licensed to alienate in 1376.[72]

At the Dissolution the hospital's holdings included 2 a. in Bethnal Green leased to John Maxfield, probably the smaller part of Roger's grant, which passed with lands in Hackney to

49 T.H.L.H.L., TH/37–38, 51.   50 Ibid. TH/35.
51 Herts. R.O., Martin-Leake MSS. 83786, 83795; deeds contain further details of the interiors.
52 P.R.O., E 40/1801.
53 Ibid. E 40/7316–19; E 40/7233; E 40/2544.
54 Ibid. E 40/2544.   55 Ibid. E 40/2543; E 40/2545.
56 Ibid. E 40/2593; E 40/2589; above (Bernard).
57 Ibid. E 40/2592.
58 Ibid. CP 25/1/147/13, no. 221; E 40/2579–80.
59 Ibid. E 40/2916; above (Trentemars).
60 Ibid. E 40/2566.
61 Ibid. E 40/2610.
62 Ibid. E 164/18, f. 26; below (Stodeye).

63 *Cart. of Holy Trinity*, 200–1. Some land in Poplar manor was held of Bromley: below (Poplar).
64 Above (Shadwell); P.R.O., CP 25/1/146/6, no. 46.
65 Guildhall MS. 25121/1710.
66 P.R.O., CP 25/1/146/10, no. 128; Ric. also quitclaimed Shadwell to the dean and chapter.
67 P.R.O., CP 25/1/147/16, no. 292. Grumbald also gave the hospital 5s. rent from land in Stepney: B.L. Cott. MS. Nero C. iii, f. 225v.
68 Guildhall MS. 25121/1710.
69 Ibid. 25121/1708.   70 *Cal. Pat.* 1348–50, 363.
71 P.R.O., CP 25/1/151/69, no. 401.
72 Ibid. C 143/388, no. 7; *Cal. Pat.* 1374–7, 388.

John Pope in 1545,[73] and a 9-a. close in the tenure of Thomas Nosterfield, which was accounted for with Burganes lands in Shoreditch and Hackney in 1539–40 and was probably sold with them to Sir Ralph Warren in 1544.[74] A barn, garden, and 3 a. on the north side of Cock Lane near Shoreditch, with land of William Holwaye on the north and west and land of Christopher Austen on the east, was let for 99 years in 1538. It was retained by the Crown and accounted for as part of Hickmans lands, with which the freehold was granted at fee farm to Thomas Emerson and William Bennett in 1607.[75] The freehold and reserved rent of the hospital's site, with the right to bring water from 'Simcock's' well, was granted to Stephen Vaughan, king's servant, and his wife Margery in 1542.[76]

A common fine paid at the view in 1349 by the men of John of Bedfont[77] was paid in 1405 and 1443 by men of the abbey of the Tower (St. Mary Graces), which held the manor of *POPLAR*.[78] In 1464–5 the fine for the abbey's tenement called Bedfonts was sixteen years in arrears.[79] The manor had probably been part of the estate of Bernard of Stepney,[80] whose son Robert in 1200 exchanged the capital messuage, vinery, lands, and money and other services with Henry of Bedfont.[81] In 1220 Henry of Bedfont's son Hamo acknowledged that one of the tenants, Robert son of Robert de Pinkeny, and his heirs held freely for 10s. a year;[82] presumably the other tenants of 1200 holding for a money service were also free. Hamo witnessed the confirmation by another tenant, Maud daughter of Bernard son of Robert, of her tenant's grant of Shadfliet to Holy Trinity Aldgate and by 1243 he had granted Holy Trinity the quitrent for that land.[83]

Hamo son of Hamo of Bedfont witnessed grants in Stepney in 1250 and in Wapping in the 1260s, in one case with Roger of Bedfont, and near the Lea.[84] Roger acquired land in Stepney through his wife Edith in 1270 and was involved in transactions there as late as 1289,[85] but the Poplar estate apparently passed to John of Bedfont, who in 1284 confirmed to Nicholas of Winchester and his heirs 70 a. and 60s. rent in Stepney.[86] Nicholas died by 1293 leaving most of his property to his son John,[87] who in 1313 confirmed a messuage and 74 a. in Stepney, Edmonton, and Hackney to Stephen of Abingdon, alderman;[88] Stephen held land in Poplar in 1328.[89]

The manor was held for life by Sir John Pulteney, mayor of London, in 1339, when it was granted to him and his heirs with other property by Sir Philip de Columber in return for £80 a year for life, of which £20 was to be drawn from Poplar. It is not clear how the two families, who had dealings over property in Kent, came to be connected with Poplar,[90] though Pulteney held a messuage and 50 a. in Stepney, confirmed to him in 1334 by Alan at Conduit.[91] Pulteney settled Poplar on himself, his wife Margaret, and their issue,[92] and in 1347 he granted it, with two watermills (the Crash mills) and 10 marks of rent in East Smithfield, to Humphrey de Bohun (d. 1361), earl of Hereford and Essex, for life on payment of one rose a year. The earl granted the property back for £80 a year[93] and at Pulteney's death in 1349 held only the mills and rent in East Smithfield; the issues of Poplar manor, held of the bishop and valued at £20, were granted to Margaret Pulteney.[94]

Between 1354 and 1358 the Black Prince stayed on the manor of Poplar, usually for a few days during the summer, and in 1358 he had planks of beech sent there. He also occupied Pulteney's Inn in the City from 1354 until 1359, when he ordered its surrender to Sir Nicholas Lovayne who had married Pulteney's widow.[95] Poplar was not among Pulteney's lands held by his widow in 1366,[96] so was probably surrendered to Pulteney's son.

Sir John's son and heir Sir William Pulteney was of age by 1362, when he and his wife Margaret settled the manor of Poplar with its three messuages, four tofts, watermills and fulling mill, 329 a., and rents, in Stepney, East Ham, Stratford, Edmonton, Hackney, Bromley, and Old Ford, on themselves and their issue with remainders to Guy Lovayne (probably father of Sir Nicholas). The Crash mills and the rent in East Smithfield were included as appurtenances of Poplar.[97]

The manor was among property leased by Sir William Pulteney and his wife Margaret to Sir Nicholas Lovayne in 1364[98] and reverted to Guy Lovayne's heirs when Sir William died, leaving as heir his cousin Robert Owen alias Pulteney, in 1367.[99] Margaret Lovayne probably died soon afterwards, as Sir Nicholas married Margaret, daughter of John de Vere, earl of Oxford, and widow of Sir Henry Beaumont, between 1369 and 1375.[1] Poplar was settled with other property in 1374 on Sir Nicholas Lovayne, Sir John Pekbrugge and his wife Margaret, and others, to

73 P.R.O., C 66/765, m. 31.
74 Ibid. C 66/775, m. 38; C 66/780, m. 17. For later hist. of the two parcels, below, Bethnal Green, ests.
75 P.R.O., E 318/7/233; ibid. SP 14/12, no. 22; ibid. E 308/3/21.   76 *L. & P. Hen. VIII*, xvii, p. 637.
77 P.R.O., SC 2/191/60, f. 16.
78 Guildhall MS. 25370; P.R.O., SC 2/191/62.
79 P.R.O., SC 6/1140/24.   80 Above (Bernard).
81 P.R.O., CP 25/1/146/2, no. 9. *Ft. of F. Lond. & Mdx.* i. 5, is inaccurate.
82 *Cur. Reg. R.* ix. 44; P.R.O., CP 25/1/146/6, no. 29.
83 P.R.O., E 40/2592–3; E 40/2589.
84 Ibid. E 40/2634; E 40/2916; E 40/7828; C 146/1993; B.L. Cott. MS. Tib. C. v, ff. 156–7.
85 P.R.O., E 40/2636; ibid. C 146/2771; ibid. CP 25/1/147/24, nos. 480, 502.
86 Ibid. CP 25/1/148/26, no. 123.
87 C.L.R.O., HR 22(64).
88 P.R.O., CP 25/1/149/43, no. 103.
89 Ibid. CP 40/273, m. 15d.
90 Ibid. CP 25/1/287/40, no. 278.
91 Ibid. CP 25/1/150/56, no. 97.
92 Ibid. CP 25/1/287/42, no. 390; CP 25/1/287/40, no. 291.
93 Ibid. CP 25/1/150/62, no. 237; ibid. C 135/95, no. 13; ibid. C 54/181, m. 29d.
94 Ibid. C 135/95, no. 13; Cal. Close, 1349–54, 49.
95 *Register of Edw. the Black Prince*, iii. 244 and *passim*; iv. 323.   96 P.R.O., C 131/15, no. 17.
97 Ibid. C 54/200, m. 20d.; ibid. CP 25/1/288/47, nos. 64, 627.   98 *Cal. Close, 1364–8*, 53.
99 P.R.O., C 135/195, no. 3.; D.N.B.
1 *Complete Peerage*, s.v. Devereux.

whom Robert Owen quitclaimed in 1375.[2] Apparently Sir William Pulteney's widow Margaret had married Pekbrugge, as in the 1380s they were holding Poplar for her lifetime.[3] In 1375 Sir Nicholas Lovayne died, dating his will at Poplar, and his widow Margaret married John, later Lord, Devereux (d. 1393).[4]

Margaret Pekbrugge's property was settled on her male issue shortly before her death in 1387, with remainders to Lord Devereux and his wife for the lifetime of Margaret Devereux, then to Sir Nicholas Lovayne's male heirs, or in default to William of Wykeham, bishop of Winchester, and Lovayne's other executors;[5] Devereux was holding the manor in 1390, when he was in Calais on the king's service.[6] The bishop of Winchester and others were licensed in 1395 to alienate the reversion of the manor of Poplar to the abbey of St. Mary Graces; in 1392 the manor had been valued at £20 and held of Stepney manor for 37s. and fealty, of Holy Trinity Aldgate of their manor of Bromley (Bromley Hall) for 12s. 2d., of the priory of St. Leonard's Stratford of their manor of Bromley for 6s. and suit of court, and for 12d. to John Hadley.[7] Margaret Devereux died in 1398,[8] and the abbey was in possession by 1405.[9] In 1418–19 Thomas Erneys alias Lefflete, a kinsman of Sir William Pulteney, released all his right to St. Mary Graces,[10] which retained the manor until 1538.

The abbey held a court for Poplar, which was managed separately from the Crash mills.[11] In 1454 there were at least 25 free and customary tenants, wholly or partially relieved of their rent because of flooding. In 1455 William Chedworth and William Marowe, freeholders with large estates in Stepney, bought two of the flooded holdings.[12] Free and customary holdings lay in Northstreet, Eaststreet in Poplar, Sandhill in the marsh, by Leamouth, Longmede, Stokswellstreet, Alstonesland, Bromleystreet, on the south side of Poplar High Street, near the Wylde and the Dusthill in Limehouse, and elsewhere.[13] The manor of Poplar was valued at £60 15s. 10½d. in 1535, and the abbey paid quitrents to the bishop of London for the manor of Poplar and Lions Garden in East Smithfield, to the 'abbess' of Stratford for Bromley marsh, and to the manor of Bromley Hall for Bromley marsh.[14] Demesne in 1539 included a tenement in Poplar, and land in Poplar, the Isle of Dogs, Bromley, Balls Cross probably in Limehouse, near Bow Road and in Stratford Bow, Woolwich marsh (Kent), and 33 a. in the marshes of Old Ford, Hackney, Edmonton, and Bromley. Eleven customary tenants included Sir Thomas Spert and prominent Londoners.[15]

After the Dissolution the manor was retained by the Crown, being among the estates assigned to Charles I before his accession and later to the City of London as part of the Royal Contract Estates. Parcels of the demesnes were leased out for 21 years by Henry VIII to Thomas Jolles and others. In 1627 the rents of customary tenants amounted to 47s. 6d. and free rents to £36 15s. 10d. The copyhold was said to be of inheritance with arbitrary fines, but so many leases of the demesne had been granted in reversion that holdings in the demisable lands could not be identified.[16]

The manor house was presumably the residence of the Black Prince and Sir Nicholas Lovayne, and stood south of the later East India Dock Road east of Wade Street, approached by a lane from Poplar High Street.[17] It included a dovecot in 1513,[18] and was granted away separately from the lordship and the rest of the manor by the Crown, apparently before 1539.[19] The house and grounds were granted by the duke of Northumberland to William Carden, whose widow Bridget owned it in 1553, when it was occupied by a tenant.[20] In 1558 Bridget conveyed the manor house with six messuages, a dovecot, gardens, orchards, and 185 a. in Poplar, Stratford Bow, and Stepney, to Sir Francis Jobson,[21] apparently in trust as she later sold the property to John Hampton of London, who conveyed it to Thomas Fanshawe, Queen's Remembrancer.[22] In 1583 the estate was described as the site of the manor, with two messuages, two cottages, a dovecot, barns, gardens and an orchard, and 116 a. in Poplar, Stepney, and Stratford Bow, and in 1593 Fanshawe conveyed it to Edward Elliott and his heirs.[23] Elliott was succeeded in 1606 by his two daughters Elizabeth, widow of Sir Francis Cherry, and Alice, wife of Thomas Gerrard,[24] and in 1610 Sir Thomas Hunt and his wife Elizabeth, presumably Elizabeth Cherry or her heir, were given livery of a moiety of the manor site.[25] In 1620 Alice's son Edward Gerrard and Elizabeth Hunt, widow, conveyed the site to John Williams, goldsmith of London, possibly on behalf of his debtor David Bourne, who had paid Edward Gerrard £1,600 for it.[26]

The dean and chapter of St. Paul's granted their mills at Wapping with adjoining land and river walls, and the right to grind all the corn for their common bakehouse, to Terricus son of Edrich of Aldgate and his heirs in 1218, to hold

2 *Cal. Close, 1374–7*, 107–8, 201.
3 *Year Bk. 12 Ric. II* (Ames Foundation), 190–2.
4 *Complete Peerage*, s.v. Devereux.
5 P.R.O., CP 25/1/289/55, no. 165.
6 *Cal. Close, 1389–92*, 183.
7 *Cal. Pat. 1391–6*, 643; P.R.O., C 143/418, no. 12; ibid. CP 25/1/151/81, no. 160.
8 *Complete Peerage*, s.v. Devereux.
9 Guildhall MS. 25370.   10 P.R.O., C 54/268, m. 15.
11 Ct. rolls exist for 1423–58, 1479–81, 1496–1508, 1512–14, 1535, 1543: P.R.O., SC 2/191/48–53.
12 P.R.O., SC 2/191/48; below (Cobhams; Marowe).
13 P.R.O., SC 2/191/48–53, *passim*.
14 *Valor Eccl.* (Rec. Com.), i. 398–9.
15 P.R.O., SC 6/Hen.VIII/2396, m. 49 and d.

16 C.L.R.O., Royal Contract Estates, Rentals Box 3.2.
17 *Survey of Lond.* xliii, *Poplar, Blackwall and Isle of Dogs* (1994), 156.
18 P.R.O., SC 2/191/52.
19 It was not accounted for in ibid. SC 6/Hen.VIII/2396, m. 49 and d.
20 Ibid. STAC 4/10/57; *Survey of Lond.* xliii. 156–7.
21 P.R.O., CP 25/2/74/630/4&5 P&M/East.
22 Ibid. C 142/308, no. 133.
23 Ibid. CP 25/2/172/25&26 Eliz./Mich.; CP 25/2/172/35 Eliz./East.
24 Ibid. C 142/308, no. 133.
25 Ibid. C 60/457, no. 45.
26 Ibid. CP 25/2/324/17 Jas.I/East.; C 3/391/28. Later hist. of site and ests. reserved for Poplar.

freely for 5 marks.[27] In 1231 the chapter sued for arrears, but agreed that the mills should be held for 4 marks a year in return for surrendering the right to grind the chapter's corn.[28] Terricus then granted a moiety to his brother Adam, but by 1239 they had sold the property to the college or hospital of *ST. THOMAS OF ACRE*, the hospital to pay the rent to the chapter and 1 lb. of pepper to Terricus and his heirs.[29] In 1239 Terricus's widow Florence claimed a third of the mills as dower.[30]

In 1269 the hospital granted the mills and a way from Wapping to Stepney to Richard of Ewell in exchange for houses in Ironmonger Lane (City), Richard to pay the rent to the chapter for the mills and 18*d*. to the bishop for the way. After a dispute with the hospital, Richard in 1274–5 granted his tenement and mills and other appurtenances at Wapping for a chantry. His widow Aubrey recovered a third as dower and in 1286 his son Richard granted two thirds of the property, with the reversion of Aubrey's third, back to the hospital for the chantry.[31]

In the late 13th century William May, citizen and woolmonger, granted to the hospital 10 a. in Walmarsh, Wapping, in 5 parcels, to hold for 16½*d*. a year, for which they paid him 21 lb. of silver.[32] The hospital also acquired 5 a. arable in Stratford Bow and 4 a. nearby in the parish of Bromley,[33] and other additions to their estate included grants by Asketin Cole of a quitrent which the hospital paid for a watercourse, by Walter Crepyn of a hope and wall in Walmarsh, and by Benet son of William of Aldgate of the 1 lb. of pepper owed to the heirs of Terricus.[34] In 1324 the hospital held 10 a. of the free land in Walmarsh granted by the bishop for the upkeep of the river wall when the area was drained.[35]

The estate passed to the Crown at the Dissolution. In the 1540s it consisted of a capital messuage with 6 a. called marshland and the mill house with wharf and dock, in Whitechapel, and several parcels of Thames wall between the dock and the common wall, all let to Robert Wyott in 1537 for 99 years, a house and land let to John Kydman, and a tenement and wharf let to William Furner or Farnes;[36] both Wyott's and Kydman's holdings included a brewhouse in 1544.[37] In 1562 the freehold of Wyott's property was conveyed by John Stepkyn alias Typkyn to Thomas Smythe,[38] who died in 1575 seized of

Wapping House, a mill house, 2 a. called the wharf and the dock, and 6a. of meadow, in Wapping, Stepney, and Whitechapel.[39]

The priory of *ST. HELEN*, Bishopsgate, claimed in 1230 to hold a moiety of Old Ford mill by charter of William le Blund of Stepney and his wife Lettice; the mill was the inheritance of Lettice.[40] In 1248 the priory obtained from Walter Trentemars 6½ a. in Stepney belonging to the fee of the dean of St. Paul's (Shadwell manor),[41] and in the late 13th century the prioress paid a rent of 7*s*. 9*d*. to the dean's manor of Shadwell.[42] The priory also held 12 a. freehold in Haresmarsh of the bishop of London for a quitrent of 6*s*. in 1350.[43]

At the Dissolution the priory had a tenement, garden, 3 closes, and two other parcels, all in Whitechapel and apparently representing the 6½ a. They had been leased in 1537 for 40 years and were granted in fee by the Crown to Rowland Goodman, citizen and fishmonger, in 1543;[44] a messuage, garden, and 4 a. passed to his son Thomas in 1545.[45] In 1619 the estate lay between property lining the south side of Whitechapel Street and land in the manor of Bernes.[46]

The 12 a. in Haresmarsh, leased in 1536 for 60 years,[47] was granted by the Crown in 1545 to John Pope,[48] who sold it to Richard Pelter, citizen and brewer (d. 1578), who left it to his daughter Blanche, wife of Morgan Richards, citizen and skinner, and her male heirs.[49] In 1615 William Richards of Hampshire sold the 12 a., called Great Haresmarsh, to Thomas Bate, citizen and armourer,[50] who by his will of 1615 left the land to his wife Jane and then to her son Francis Turvill and his heirs. After Bate's death Jane released her right to Turvill, who mortgaged the land and died in Spain without issue. Jane had married Thomas Lawes of Edmonton *c*. 1620, who redeemed the mortgage and took possession, concealing Turvill's death. Turvill's niece Susan and her husband John Godowne in 1647 brought an action against Sarah Richardson, widow of Charles Richardson to whom Lawes had made a conveyance, and her son Thomas.[51] The 12 a., occupied by Geoffrey Brown in 1645 when the chief lord was unknown,[52] were held by the Godownes in 1652.[53]

Ralph Eswy (Aswy, Ashwye) (d. 1247), mayor of London, probably held land in Stepney, as his son Thomas, prebendary of St. Paul's, confirmed the grant to Bishop Fulk Basset by

27 B.L. Cott. MS. Tib. C. v, f. 152.
28 *Bracton's Note Bk*. ed. Maitland, ii. 379–80; Guildhall MS. 25501, f. 34v.; P.R.O., CP 25/1/146/8, no. 85; *Early Charters of St. Paul's* (Camd. 3rd ser. lviii), 256–7.
29 B.L. Cott. MS. Tib. C. v, ff. 153–4v.; Guildhall MS. 25501, f. 34v.
30 *Cur. Reg. R*. xvi. 153.
31 B.L. Cott. MS. Tib. C. v, ff. 160v., 161v.–2; J. Watney, *Hosp. of St. Thos. of Acon* (1892), 259; below (Ewell).
32 B.L. Cott. MS. Tib. C. v, f. 155.
33 P.R.O., C 3/289/37.
34 B.L. Cott. MS. Tib. C. v, ff. 155v.–156.
35 *Abbrev. Plac*. (Rec. Com.), 352–3.
36 P.R.O., SC 6/Hen.VIII/2396, m. 8d.
37 *L. & P. Hen. VIII*, xix (2), p. 77.
38 P.R.O., CP 25/2/171/4 Eliz./Trin.

39 Ibid. C 142/175, no. 87. Later hist. of site reserved for Wapping.   40 *Cur. Reg. R*. xiv. 68.
41 Guildhall MS. 25501, f. 44.
42 Ibid. 25516, f.39v.
43 P.R.O., SC 6/1258/2.
44 Ibid. E 318/11/489.
45 Ibid. C 142/85, no. 7.
46 Ibid. WARD 5/26, bdl. 7.
47 Ibid. SC 6/Hen.VIII/2396, m. 23d.
48 *L. & P. Hen. VIII*, xx (1), p. 123.
49 C.L.R.O., HR 262(1); *Lond. Inq. p.m*. iii (Brit. Rec. Soc. xxxvi), 10.
50 P.R.O., CP 43/131, rot. 10–11; C 78/582, no. 8.
51 Ibid. C 78/582, no. 8.
52 Ibid. C 142/787, no. 74.
53 G.L.R.O., M93/158, ff. 11–12. Later hist. reserved for Bethnal Green, ests. (Grt. Haresmarsh) (below).

another son Adrian of all his property there in 1250–1.[54] Sir Stephen Aswy, alderman and son of Ralph's son Ralph, in 1273–4 claimed services and arrears of rent from Alan de Hull for his free tenement and 75 a. in Stepney,[55] and in 1293 quitclaimed land in East Smithfield (St. Botolph Aldgate) which had belonged to his father Ralph.[56] He also owed a rent of 13s. 7d. to the manor of Shadwell in the late 13th century, probably for the estate later known as the manor of *ASHWYES*.[57]

Sir Stephen Ashwye apparently mortgaged all his estate in Stepney except his watermills to John de Triple, citizen, and Sir Geoffrey de Scrope and their heirs in 1324.[58] Henry, Lord Scrope of Masham, granted it in 1377 to John Hadley, citizen and pepperer (grocer), who made many acquisitions in Stepney, notably through his second wife Thomasia.[59] In 1380 Hadley and his first wife Margery granted a cottage next to his other land on the east side of a highway, probably Forbylane,[60] and in 1405 he leased a parcel on the south side of the highway from Forbylane to Poplar.[61]

By will of 1405 Hadley left his lands to Thomasia for life and then to their issue, and in default the manor of Ashwyes or Mile End to John Pecche, the son of his daughter Joan; presumably Hadley's two daughters were from his first marriage.[62] The lands were to be delivered to his heirs in 1410, although Ashwyes was not specified.[63] A dispute over Ashwyes between Sir John Pecche and Sir William Wolf, the husband of Hadley's daughter Catherine, was settled in 1429,[64] whereupon feoffees in 1431 vested it in the Wolfs for their lives with remainder to Pecche.[65]

Catherine Wolf died in 1446 seized *inter alia* of 17 messuages in Whitechapel held of the bishop and the dean and chapter[66] and valued at 20s. a year, which may have included the Ashwyes land held of Shadwell manor. All Hadley's estates passed to Sir John Pecche's son Sir William Pecche, who in 1459 sold his lands in Stepney except Ashwyes with its manor house, garden and curtilage, and its adjoining great field of 50 a. in Stepney and Whitechapel, which lay next to and between the lands of John Philpot on the east, and was bounded on the north by the highway, and on the south by Philpot's lands and the way from Whitechapel church to Ratcliff.[67] Ashwyes, with 25 messuages, 5 tofts, 30 gardens, and 52 a. in Stepney and Whitechapel, was vested in Sir Thomas Urswick and others, for unknown purposes, in 1471.[68]

The estate was apparently that called Red Lion farm from the 16th century. In 1567 the buildings included the Red Lion inn then owned or tenanted by John Brayne, citizen and grocer, who contracted for the erection of galleries, a stage and a turret in order to put on a play at the inn.[69]

The estate consisted of a messuage called the Red Lion and 26 a. in Whitechapel and Stepney when held by Humphrey Millward at his death in 1609. It passed to his son John, then in 1610 to John's sister Mary, wife of Thomas Hayes, and in 1612 was found to be held from the dean of St. Paul's of his manor of Shadwell for fealty and 13s. 4d.[70] Hayes' estate was shown in 1703 as *c.* 36 a. straddling the boundary of Whitechapel and Mile End Old Town,[71] but by 1713 it had passed in moieties to Ann and Katharine the daughters of Arthur Bailey. Both moieties were bought by the London Hospital, in 1755 and 1772 respectively. The Red Lion was almost certainly the site of the manor house, and stood on the south side of Mile End green, on the boundary between Stepney and Whitechapel.[72]

In the mid 13th century Fulk Basset, bishop of London, had land and rents in Stepney in his own right, possibly part of the Basset estates which he inherited in 1241. Part of the Stepney land was held by the Cole family (q.v.), and in 1250 a grant of land and rent was made to Fulk by Asketin Cole. At about the same time Fulk received lands and tenements in Stepney from Adrian Eswy (or Aswy), confirmed to Fulk and his heirs by Adrian's brother Thomas.[73] Fulk died in 1259 and the Basset estates passed to Sir Philip Basset, justiciar, and on his death in 1271 to his daughter Aline and her second husband Roger Bigod, earl of Norfolk.[74] Part of the Stepney land was held by Philip's niece Aline, wife of Henry de Ba or *BATHONIA*, judge of the Common Pleas, and in 1259 her son John de Bathonia conveyed 3 messuages, 62 a., 16s. 4d. rent and appurtenances in Finsbury and Stepney, with the manor of Uplambourn (Berks.), all part of Aline's estate, to Nicholas of Yattendon and his wife Alice for their lives, with remainder to John and his heirs.[75] Nicholas married Aline de Bathonia as her second husband,[76] and although Henry de Bathonia is said not to have died until 1260,[77] it seems likely that the grant was connected with this marriage. Aline died *c.* 1274 seized of a messuage and 27 a. in Stepney held of the bishop of London for 42d. p.a., a messuage and 2 a. land held of the heirs of her uncle Sir Philip Basset for 12d. p.a.,

---

54 P.R.O., E 40/2602; below (Bathonia); also grants in Ironmonger Lane: Watney, *Hosp. of St. Thos. Acon*, *passim*.

55 P.R.O., JUST 1/538, m. 7; above (Hulls).

56 P.R.O., JUST 1/543, m. 10.

57 Guildhall MS. 25516, f. 39v.; below.

58 *Abbrev. Plac.* (Rec. Com.), 347. The mills were the Landmills in Stratford Bow: below, econ. hist. (mills).

59 P.R.O., C 54/217, m. 20d.; below (Cobhams), (Stodeye).

60 P.R.O., C 146/364.   61 Ibid. C 146/2725.

62 Ibid. PROB 11/2A (P.C.C. 20 Marche).

63 *Cal. Close*, 1409–13, 50.   64 Ibid. 1422–9, 472.

65 P.R.O., CP 25/1/152/90, no. 54.

66 Ibid. C 139/122, no. 38.   67 Ibid. C 146/4128.

68 Ibid. C 54/323, m. 5d.

69 W. Ingram, *The Business of Playing*, 103–13; *Rec. of Carpenters' Co.* iii. 95–6; *Shakespeare Quarterly*, 34 (1983), 306–10. Thanks are due to Prof. Ingram for these refs.

70 P.R.O., C 142/307, no. 74; C 142/326, no. 29.

71 Gascoyne, *Map of Mile End Old Town* (1703).

72 London Hosp. Archives, LH/D/1/12–34; Plan of Lond. Hosp. est., 1783. Later hist. of est. reserved for Mile End Old Town.

73 P.R.O., E 40/2602; above (Ashwyes).

74 *D.N.B.*; Dugdale, *Baronage*, i. 383.

75 P.R.O., CP 25/1/283/17, no. 454.

76 Ibid. C 133/4, no. 17 (Norfolk).   77 *D.N.B.*

3 a. held of Ralph Huscarl for 6s. p.a., and rents of assize in Stepney, which passed to her heir Sir John de Bathonia.[78] The property has not been located, although land of John de Ba on the south side of a highway was recorded.[79] John died c. 1291, when 45 a. and rents from free tenants, all held of the bishop of London, passed to his daughter Joan, wife of John de Bohun.[80] Sir John Philpot c. 1380 held 28 a. land once of Robert de Bine (possibly Bohun), which was not part of Hulls, for the same amount of quitrent that Aline and John had owed to the bishop.[81]

Richard of *EWELL*, royal agent and alderman of London,[82] acquired land which included freehold in Wapping granted out by a bishop for the upkeep of the river wall when the land was drained.[83] The land lay near Wapping mills and the way from Wapping to Stepney, which Richard received by exchange with the hospital of St. Thomas of Acre in 1269.[84] Other acquisitions in the vill of Stepney and Hackney were from William son of William son of (?)Keynes and from Walter Tovy. In Walmarsh, Wapping, he acquired 7 a. once of William Leman and his son-in-law Sir Roger de Samford from John le Rous, and 4 a. in six parcels from Jordan, sergeant of St. Paul's. Richard also acquired from William May the meadow beside the Thames which May had been granted by Jordan[85] and in 1272 exchanged 7 a. with May for three parcels between Hachestreet and Shadwell street (later Ratcliff Highway).[86]

Richard died c. 1280 apparently leaving a widow Aubrey, since she recovered a third of the property which he had granted to St. Thomas of Acre for a chantry. Aubrey had married Ralph de Munchensy by 1283.[87] Richard's son and namesake confirmed the grant of the whole property to the hospital in 1286.[88]

The younger Richard, who was involved in a dispute over property in London in 1282 and served abroad in 1286,[89] apparently died before 1292, when Eleanor of Ewell made a grant of the Stepney property;[90] he was probably the Sir Richard of Ewell whose nuncupative will was enrolled in 1291, mentioning only property in the City.[91] Eleanor (d. 1349), who figured in several transactions from 1292 and was more likely the daughter of the elder Richard, shared the Ewell estates, in Stepney, Kelvedon (Essex), Ashwell (Herts.), and elsewhere with her sister Agnes,[92] wife of Sir John Neyrnuit of Fleet Marston (Bucks.),[93]

and apparently with two other sisters, Maud, wife of Stephen of Cambridge, and Margery (d. 1305), wife of John Gisors (II) (d. 1296):[94] in the 14th century the Neyrnuit, Cambridge, and Gisors families all held parts of Ewell.

In 1292 Eleanor granted to her nephew Richard, son of John Neyrnuit, the reversion of a messuage, 120 a., and a mill in Stepney, held for life by Aubrey de Munchensy (d. 1307–8).[95] In 1332 Richard's brother Thomas granted two thirds of the property to his brother Sir John Neyrnuit the younger,[96] who in 1340 settled it on his sons John and Thomas. The other third may have been held by his brother William, since he apparently held a third of Ashwell.[97] Sir John's son, a third Sir John Neyrnuit, was alive in 1383 but died without issue and was eventually succeeded by the daughters of his brother Thomas, Margaret, wife of John Hervey of Thurleigh (Beds.), and Elizabeth, wife of John Hertishorne.[98] Sir John Neyrnuit owed the quitrent of 26s. 9d. and suit to Stepney manor for Ewell c. 1400, when holders or tenants of Ewell also held 64 a., mainly molond, in Stepney manor and shared with St. Mary Graces and St. Thomas of Acre 70½ a. cotland in Walmarsh; an acre belonging to Ewell was inclosed into the cemetery of St. Mary Graces.[99] In 1471 John Hervey the elder granted the manor of Ewell called the Tilehouse and all his property in Stepney and neighbouring parishes to feoffees.[1] His interest may have passed to John Rooke, who in 1494 left his manor of Ewell alias the Tilehouse in the parish of Whitechapel to be sold,[2] since a John Rooke the elder had witnessed Hervey's grant.

In 1324 John Gisors, John Peyroun (possibly a misrendering of Neyrnuit), and Maud of Cambridge jointly held 32 a. of Walmarsh granted to freeholders, presumably part of Ewell's estate.[3] John Gisors, son of John and Margery, did not mention Stepney in his will in 1351, but a later settlement included a sixth of a messuage and 140 a. in Stepney, Hackney, and Shoreditch which had been his.[4] A moiety of the sixth was conveyed in 1378 by his granddaughter Margaret and her husband Sir William Burcestre,[5] to whom in 1385 the feoffees of another Gisors heir, Francus Nicole (d. 1379–80), quitclaimed all right in a sixth of the property.[6] In 1366 John, son of Stephen of Cambridge, licensed John Wendover to dig clay for tiles on land of the manor of Ewell;[7] Wendover was probably the

78 P.R.O., C 133/4, no. 5.
79 B.L. Add. Ch. 24069.
80 P.R.O., C 133/59, no. 11.
81 Guildhall MS. 25422 (partially illegible).
82 *Cal. Pat.* 1247–58, 221; *Cal. Chart. R.* 1226–57, 422; Williams, *Medieval Lond.* 70.
83 *Abbrev. Plac.* (Rec. Com.), 352–3.
84 B.L. Cott. MS. Tib. C. v, ff. 160v.–2; above (St. Thos. of Acre).
85 B.L. Cott. MS. Tib. C. v, ff. 157–58v.
86 Ibid. f. 163; P.R.O., CP 25/1/147/24, no. 501.
87 *Cal. Close*, 1279–88, 29, 207; *Cal. Chart. R.* 1257–1300, 256; P.R.O., CP 25/1/148/30, no. 147; *Misc. Geneal. et Heraldica*, x. 5; above (St. Thos. of Acre).
88 B.L. Cott. Tib. C. v, f. 160v.; P.R.O., CP 25/1/148/30, no. 147; above (St. Thos. of Acre).
89 *Cal. Pat.* 1281–92, 46, 267, 272.
90 Below; *Cal. Pat.* 1281–92, 417–18.
91 *Cal. of Wills in Ct. of Husting*, i. 100.

92 *Feet of Fines for Essex*, ii. 73, 122; *V.C.H. Bucks.* iii. 408; *Cal. Anct. D.* ii, C. 1509.
93 *Cal. Close*, 1381–5, 417.
94 They put in claims against a grant by Eleanor in Ashwell: *Feet of Fines for Essex*, ii. 73; Eleanor left 20 marks to Margery's son John Gisors (III), who held land in Ashwell: C.L.R.O., HR 78(248); HR 114(7).
95 P.R.O., CP 25/1/148/32, no. 197.
96 Ibid. CP 25/1/150/55, no. 65.
97 Ibid. CP 25/1/287/40, no. 280; *V.C.H. Herts.* iii. 203.
98 *Cal. Close*, 1381–5, 412; *V.C.H. Bucks.* iii. 408; *V.C.H. Herts.* iii. 203.
99 P.R.O., SC 12/11/31.   1 *Cal. Close*, 1468–76, 197.
2 P.R.O., PROB 11/10 (P.C.C. 19 Vox).
3 *Abbrev. Plac.* (Rec. Com.), 352–3.
4 C.L.R.O., HR 114(7).
5 P.R.O., CP 25/1/289/54, no. 125.
6 C.L.R.O., HR 114(7).
7 B.L. Cott. MS. Tib. C. v, f. 160.

man of that name who was a son-in-law and executor of John Gisors (III).[8] In 1383–4 the holder of the tenement late John Wendover's was in default of suit of court in Stepney.[9] No further trace of the Cambridge interest has been found.

Margaret Burcestre died in 1393 and Sir William in 1407, leaving a widow Margaret and son John, a minor; feoffees conveyed the reversion of Burcestre's moiety of the manor of Ewell to John in 1422.[10] In 1417 Tilehouse meadow, once of Sir William, lay near the Thames and land of St. Thomas of Acre and John Cornwaleys.[11] Ewell was settled on Sir John Burcestre in 1462 but soon afterwards conveyed to the use of John Lewknor,[12] whose widow Jane in 1472 quitclaimed her right to Roger Coppeley and others, presumably feoffees.[13]

A quitrent of 27s. 1d. from Tilehouse was paid to Lord Wentworth by John Stepkyn, and later by Thomas Pennington. In 1589 a barn called Tilehouse was said to have lain in Whitechapel, but no other details were known. Some land of the manor was distrained by Wentworth for 6s. 8d. quitrent due for Ewell, and other lands were let to the Smyth family by Pennington, whose son Thomas, of Chigwell, bought 28 a. from Stepkyn and in 1589 sued Stepkyn's widow and her husband William Chester.[14] In 1635 Thomas Pennington of Chigwell held land in Stepney leased in parcels for £107 10s. a year.[15]

Ralph *CREPYN*, also called Ralph of Aldgate, clerk in the service of the mayor of London, bought lands from John Baud between 1281 and 1286 including 14 a. in Hackney and 14 a. in Stepney in which Alice de Pinkeny had dower; in 1286 all Ralph's lands were taken temporarily into the king's hands.[16] In 1303 Ralph granted to his son Walter Crepyn or Walter of Gloucester, citizen, 2 messuages, 2 mills, 175 a., 30 a. of wood, and 4 marks rent in Stepney, Hackney, and elsewhere for £10 a year.[17] Walter also acquired in Stepney a messuage and shop from Robert de Lynton of Stratford Bow in 1314, a messuage, 5 shops, and 14 a. from Nicholas Meau in 1315, 24 a. from Robert Belebarbe the elder of Stepney in 1316, and 3 a. from Thomas le Moyne of Abingdon in 1318.[18] He witnessed a grant in Old Ford in 1322,[19] but by 1331 his land had passed through his son Ralph to Ralph's brother and heir Edmund Crepyn.

Edmund granted land in Collesfield to William Haunsard, probably the elder, in 1331 and released a rent in Hackney to John de Brendwood in 1341; both properties became part of

the manor of Hackney Wick.[20] He also granted Bolemad, inherited from his brother, to William Haunsard in 1332 and his widow Mary quitclaimed all claim on Haunsard's acquisitions in 1344.[21] Edmund's estate was or included a manor, since he granted suit of court owed to him by John Morice for a tenement at Bethnal Green.[22]

A messuage in Stepney called the *MOTE*, with dovecots and other appurtenances, which had been held by Edmund, was quitclaimed in 1371 by Oliver son and heir of John son of Robert de Ingham to Adam of St. Ives.[23] In 1393 the Mote, with a garden and 46 a. in the marsh, was in ruins and the land was charged with the repair of a Thames wall, also decayed, and with a large rent to the chief lord.[24] It passed to John Seymour but had escheated to the bishop by 1402, when the quitrent for the land formerly of Edmund Crepyn was remitted.[25]

The Mote was acquired by Walter Green, with other lands of Adam, but may later have passed separately to Edmund Ratcliff and then Hugh Ratcliff, who in the 1490s held a piece of ground of that name for 1d. due to the manor of Poplar. Edmund Ratcliff also acquired other property in Poplar manor,[26] for which the quitrents of 9s. 6d. had been in arrears for 10 years in 1496. In 1513 Edmund's son Hugh and widow Alice were in default of suit of court.[27] Alice, daughter and coheir of Hugh Ratcliff (d. 1531), of the Middle Temple, married Ralph Shakerley and was succeeded by her daughter Anne (d. 1615), who married Sir Paul Tracy, Bt., and bore ten sons and ten daughters.[28] Seven of the sons were admitted in 1617 to copyhold in Stepney, which may have been part of the Ratcliff property and the Mote. It included 4 a. in Stratford field (Mile End Old Town), 6 a. called Balls Cross, later Ballscroft in Ratcliff (Limehouse hamlet), 2 tenements and a garden in Three Colt Street, Limehouse, and a cottage on the north side of Stepney churchyard (in Ratcliff). The tenements and cottage passed to one of the sons, Vicessimus, and then to his son Paul, who surrendered to John Jennings of Ratcliff in 1635. The 4 a. and 6 a. passed to George Tracy, citizen and mercer, the son of Paul, another of the sons, and then to George's sister Elizabeth, wife of John Geary, who was admitted in 1670.[29] The family had other property in Stepney, as in 1663 Paul's eldest surviving son and namesake was living at Mile End.[30]

Before 1285 Philip Lynde granted to John *MORICE* of Stepney 3 a. between a highway (possibly Cambridge Heath Road) and the

[8] C.L.R.O., HR 78(248); D. J. Keene and V. Harding, *Cheapside Gazetteer*, St. Mary Colechurch par., property 105/10.
[9] Guildhall MS. 10312/136.
[10] *Cheapside Gaz.* 105/10; P.R.O., PROB 11/2A (P.C.C. 14 Marche), f. 108–v.; *Cal. Close, 1422–9*, 71.
[11] B.L. Cott. MS. Tib. C. v, f. 161; above (Bernes) for Cornwaleys.   [12] *Cal. Close, 1461–8*, 383–5.
[13] Ibid. 1468–76, 240.
[14] P.R.O., E 134/31&32 Eliz./Mich.14.
[15] Ibid. SP 16/310, no. 6. [16] Ibid. C 145/44, no. 21.
[17] Ibid. CP 25/1/148/36, no. 298.
[18] Ibid. CP 25/1/149/44, no. 133; CP 25/1/149/45, no. 173; CP 25/1/149/46, no. 188; CP 25/1/149/48, no. 242.
[19] P.R.O., C 146/1234.

[20] *Cart. of Adam Fraunceys*, 214–15.
[21] Guildhall Add. MSS. 16, 22; above (Bernes). Cf. P.R.O., C 146/41.
[22] P.R.O., C 146/1939; below (Morice).
[23] *Cal. Close, 1369–74*, 321. Adam also held Huscarls (q.v.).
[24] P.R.O., C 131/43, no. 10.
[25] Ibid. SC 6/1139/22.
[26] Ibid. SC 11/453: dated from internal evidence; above (Huscarls).   [27] P.R.O., SC 2/191/50, 52.
[28] *Visitation of Mdx. 1663*, 64; *Complete Baronetage*, i. 42.
[29] G.L.R.O., M93/157, p. 42; M93/1, pp. 125–6; B.L. Eg. MS. 3006, f. 34; T.H.L.H.L., TH/390, 237–8.
[30] *Visitation of Mdx.* 64.

bishop's wood, to hold freely for a quitrent of 3s.[31] In 1287–8 a messuage with houses on it and land in the vill, acquired from John son of Robert le Spenser, was granted by Morice to Robert of Kington, clerk, for life for 20s. a year, John retaining the right to share the dwelling with Robert.[32] Morice's grant of a messuage and 5 a. in Stepney to his son Walter was confirmed by another son John c. 1300.[33] Walter Morice acquired parcels in 1313 from John Cotekyn, in 1314 from Christine daughter of William May, and in 1322 from Robert son of Robert Gratefig.[34] In 1321 he was released by Gillian, widow of Henry Box, from any actions regarding her dower.[35] Walter also acquired land in Hackney.[36] An agreement which he made in 1332 with John of Stepney (de Stebbenheth) suggests that he may have married Margery, widow of another John of Stepney.[37]

Walter's brother John was probably the John Morice who had died by 1340, when Edmund Crepyn granted the 3s. 11d. quitrent and suit of court from Morice's tenement at Blithenhale (Bethnal Green) to John de Colewell, citizen and mercer.[38] Colewell had married Morice's widow Alice or Amice by 1347 when John Morice's son John surrendered his interest to them.[39] In 1351 Colewell's widow held property which was the inheritance of Margery wife of Richard de Waleton, which Richard and Margery granted to Thomas Morice with the rest of the estate;[40] Margery's title was unexplained.

Thomas, perhaps Walter's son, was a citizen of London by 1346. He paid rent in 1335 to Robert of Colebrook for land leased to Walter, in 1346 acquired a messuage, 3 shops, 3 a., and 3s. rent in Stepney from John, son of John Heved,[41] and in 1348 seems to have held meadow in Old Ford that had been John of Stepney's in 1332.[42] His estate in Stepney and Hackney was later known as the manor of *COBHAMS* or *RUMBOLDS*, and may have derived from the estate of Salomon of Stepney (q.v.). Thomas Morice (d. 1368) referred to his son Thomas of Cobham, possibly meaning son-in-law;[43] Reynold Cobham later referred to Thomas Morice as his grandfather. In 1369 Thomas of Cobham, of Rundale (Kent), and his wife Maud settled lands including 14 messuages, 186 a., 20s. rent in Stepney, Bromley, 'Hamme' (possibly W. Ham), and Hackney, and meadow in Stratford Langthorn (Essex), on themselves and their issue or the heirs of Maud.[44]

In 1388 Sir Thomas Cobham held land in Bethnal Green west of Cambridge Heath Road[45] and c. 1400 Sir John Cobham held over 20 parcels of customary land totalling 51 a., of which at least 14 a. had been Thomas Morice's. Among the quitrents owed to Stepney manor was 53s. 4d. for a tenement on the heath at Mile End, Whetecroft, and other lands, which was owed for Cobhams in 1446.[46]

In 1404 Reynold Cobham, possibly Sir John's brother, exchanged the land of his grandfather Thomas Morice with John Hadley and his wife Thomasia for land in Kent.[47] Hadley already held Ashwyes and acquired more land through Thomasia, coheiress of John Stodeye and an heir general of John Gisors.[48] Hadley held about 66 a. c. 1400, mostly free, near Whitechapel and Shadwell and in the Isle of Dogs; 22 a. in Whitechapel field formerly of Henry Vanner were probably the Stodeye land. An area east of Whitechapel church was later known as the garden of John Hadley.[49]

Hadley left his Middlesex lands to Thomasia for life and to any issue; in default Ashwyes was to remain to his grandson John Pecche and Cobhams to Giles Augentem.[50] In 1410 the estate included a manor called Cobhams in Stepney held by grant of Reynold Cobham and his wife Elizabeth, lands in Whitechapel once of John Stodeye, and others granted by Richard Litlington. Hadley's daughter Catherine, wife of William Winkfield or Wingfield, had obtained possession of part of his land.[51]

In 1415 the Wingfields granted a moiety of 40 messuages, 183 a., and rents in Stepney, Hackney, Stratford Langthorn, and Whitechapel to feoffees.[52] Catherine's second husband Sir William Wolf made an agreement with Sir John Pecche[53] and had land in the Isle of Dogs of an unspecified manor in 1434.[54] Catherine died in 1446, seized of the manor called Cobhams, held of the bishop of London and valued at 10 marks a year, and also of 17 messuages in Whitechapel, held of the bishop and of the dean and chapter of St. Paul's. Her heir Sir William Pecche, grandson of her sister Joan,[55] in 1459 confirmed the sale of all his Stepney property except Ashwyes to William Chedworth,[56] who as 'lord of the place of Stepenhyth' in 1451 had been granted an indult for a portable altar.[57] Chedworth may have been lessee of the manor house and in 1464–5 was bailiff of the manor.[58] His purchases included flooded freehold lands in the Isle of Dogs formerly of John Wotton in 1455,[59] the estate of Robert Clopton in Whitechapel, Stepney, and Hackney in 1460,[60] and a freehold messuage on the north side of Stepney churchyard in 1461.[61] He and his son William granted his Middlesex property to feoffees in 1462,

31 P.R.O., C 146/2771.
32 Ibid. C 146/1483.
33 Ibid. C 146/2378.
34 Ibid. C 146/1100; C 146/2106; CP 25/1/149/50, no. 295.
35 Ibid. C 146/2683.
36 *Cart. of Adam Fraunceys*, 218.
37 P.R.O., CP 25/1/150/55, no. 73.
38 Ibid. C 146/2886.
39 Ibid. C 54/182, m. 17d.
40 Ibid. CP 25/1/150/64, no. 286.
41 Ibid. C 146/1939; C 146/1264.
42 Guildhall Add. MSS. 16, 23.
43 *Cal. of Wills in Ct. of Husting*, ii (1), 107–8.
44 P.R.O., CP 25/1/288/48, no. 696.
45 Guildhall MS. 25121/1710.

46 P.R.O., SC 12/11/31 (excludes Bethnal Green); ibid. C 139/122, no. 38.   47 Ibid. C 146/4735.
48 Above (Ashwyes; Ewell); below (Stodeye).
49 P.R.O., SC 12/11/31; C 66/723, m. 14.
50 Ibid. PROB 11/2A (P.C.C. 20 Marche).
51 *Cal. Close, 1409–13*, 50.
52 P.R.O., CP 25/1/291/63, no. 30.
53 Above (Ashwyes).   54 P.R.O., SC 2/191/48.
55 Ibid. C 139/122, no. 38; *Cal. Close, 1441–7*, 327.
56 P.R.O., C 146/5038.   57 *Cal. Papal Reg.* x. 524.
58 P.R.O., SC 6/1140/24.
59 Ibid. SC 2/191/48.   60 Below (Clopton).
61 P.R.O., C 146/1148; C 146/483; C 146/2976; C 146/2843; ibid. CP 25/1/152/91, no. 97. Chedworth granted waste in 1475: C 146/118.

receiving it back from another son John Chedworth, archdeacon of Lincoln, in 1470.[62]

In 1481 'Rumbolds or Cobhams' was conveyed as 4 messuages, 2 gardens, 280 a. and 30s. rent in Stepney and Hackney, with other land presumably the Clopton estate.[63] The elder William's wife Joan, jointly seized with him in all their lands, was empowered to sell by his will of 1482. In 1486 she left land to feoffees to provide sums for her daughters Elizabeth and Joan, and then to be conveyed to her surviving son Nicholas Chedworth and his heirs. Her dwelling house was to go to Nicholas for life, then to his sister Anne Crosby for life and Joan's heirs.[64] Nicholas was presented at Poplar manor court for hunting and hawking in 1481 and was in default for his tenement in 1497, but attended in 1499.[65] Trustees to whom Joan had surrendered Stepney copyholds[66] granted freeholds of 30 a. of land and 340 a. of marsh to lawyers probably acting for Nicholas.[67] The copyhold, however, was in the hands of the lord unclaimed in 1509, and Joan's daughters were admitted in 1510.[68]

Cobhams passed to Nicholas's three sisters or their heirs, Elizabeth, wife of John Audley, Margaret Carew, widow, and Thomas, son of Joan and William Marowe; Anne Crosby had probably died childless. When disputed with George Conghurst and his wife Margaret, widow of Nicholas Chedworth, between 1518 and 1529, Cobhams was held in trust for Elizabeth and Margaret and after their deaths and that of John Audley, it would remain to their heirs and those of Joan Marowe.[69]

Thomas Marowe's third share of Rumbolds passed in 1538 to his son Thomas and was merged in the Marowe estate.[70] Edward Saunders, his wife Margaret, and Thomas Carewe in 1554 conveyed a moiety of the manor to John Drayner;[71] the share, if only a third, was of an apparently reduced estate. Carewe also conveyed 20 a. in Stepney and Hackney to Edward and Richard Broke in 1556.[72] John Drayner or Dragoner of Hoxton[73] was a citizen and clothier when fined in 1561 for hedging and ditching Stebbenhithe close.[74] His son Thomas was probably in possession c. 1593.[75] Rumbolds and 14 a. used with the manor were settled in 1605 on Thomas Drayner,[76] who in 1615 held several contiguous fields from Mile End green south to the later Commercial Road.[77] In 1621 he died seized of the manor, held of the manor of Stepney and valued at £3, and of property in Hoxton where he lived. Rumbolds passed to his

wife Margaret for life, and then, probably in 1634, to Elizabeth, daughter of his sister's son Sir Roger Halton.[78] The conveyance in 1686 of Rumbolds with 6 messuages, 2 barns, a stable, 5 gardens, and 22 a. to Arthur Bailey, was probably the sale by the Halton heirs.[79] In 1703 Bailey held fields of nearly 20 a. which Drayner had held in 1615, besides 16 a. north of Mile End Road;[80] he also acquired much other land in Mile End, Bethnal Green, Old Ford, Poplar, Limehouse, and Wapping-Stepney. By 1713 Rumbolds and the other land had passed to his daughter Katharine Bailey (d. 1727), wife of Thomas Heath, and then to her eldest son Bailey Heath (d. 1760). All the lands were sold in lots in 1772.[81]

John of Stepney (de *STEBBENHETH*), clerk, who acquired land in Stepney from 1317, may have been a kinsman of John of Stepney the younger (d. by 1326), himself the nephew of the prominent Londoner John of Stepney the elder (d. 1281–2).[82] John the clerk was granted parcels by John le Rede and by Andrew of Ludlow in 1317, by John de Taleworth in 1319 and 1324,[83] and by Agnes, widow of Robert Bernard, in 1322 and 1324.[84] A John of Stepney who made a grant in 1327[85] may have been the man of that name who with his wife Catherine made an agreement in 1332 with Walter Morice regarding a messuage, 5 shops, 144 a., and 2s. rent in Stepney. John had granted two thirds of the property to Walter, who granted it back, together with 34 a. of his own land which Margery widow of John of Stepney held for life and which was to remain to John's son Edmund.[86] In 1352 Walter Turk and Thomas Morice held some of John of Stepney's land.[87] In 1368 Walter, son of John and grandson of John of Stepney and Catherine, quitclaimed land in Old Ford to William of Tuddenham, with all reversions to which John and Catherine had been entitled.[88]

Thomas, Lord *WAKE* (d. 1349), forfeited in 1330 a so-called manor in Stepney consisting of a messuage held of Richard of Hackney of the manor of Hulls and 17 a. held of the bishop of London, valued in all at 10s. Wake had leased it in 1319 to John of Eynsham, citizen and pelterer, to whom the Crown gave possession in 1330.[89] The freehold was restored to Wake, who also held land of the king, who licensed him in 1331 to exchange 24 a. with the bishop,[90] and he may have held additional customary land, as did later holders of his estate. In 1349 the capital mes

[62] P.R.O., C 146/2842; C 146/4664. John (d. 1471) was R. of Stepney and asked to be buried in the ch.: PROB 11/6 (P.C.C. 3 Wattys).
[63] P.R.O., C 146/4610.
[64] Ibid. C 146/9571; C 146/9547.
[65] Ibid. SC 2/191/49–50.
[66] Ibid. SC 2/191/63, m. 1.
[67] Ibid. CP 25/1/152/100/11 Hen.VII/Trin.
[68] Ibid. SC 2/191/63, mm. 1–2.
[69] Ibid. C 1/459/6.
[70] Ibid. C 142/61, no. 115; below (Marowe).
[71] P.R.O., CP 25/1/74/629/1&2 P&M/Mich.
[72] Ibid. CP 25/2/74/630/3&4 P&M/Mich.
[73] *Mdx. Pedigrees* (Harl. Soc. lxv), 63.
[74] *Mdx. County Rec.* i. 38.
[75] *Mdx. Pedigrees*, 63.
[76] P.R.O., C 142/509, no. 34.

[77] Plan of Mercers' est.
[78] B.L. Harl. MS. 757, f. 105v.; *Mdx. Pedigrees*, 63.
[79] P.R.O., CP 25/2/786/1&2 Jas.II/Hil.
[80] Gascoyne, *Map of Mile End Old Town*.
[81] Lond. Hosp. Archives, LH/D/1/23, 1/31. Later hist. reserved for Mile End Old Town.
[82] Williams, *Medieval Lond.* 336–7; *Cal. of Wills in Ct. of Husting*, i. 56; C.L.R.O., Bridge Ho. deeds F. 64.
[83] P.R.O., CP 25/1/149/47, no. 210a; CP 25/1/149/48, no. 223; CP 25/1/149/49, no. 256; CP 25/1/149/51, no. 314.
[84] Ibid. C 146/1234; CP 25/1/149/51, no. 319.
[85] Ibid. E 326/13420.
[86] Ibid. CP 25/1/150/55, no. 73; above (Morice; Cobhams).
[87] B.L. Add. Ch. 40513.
[88] *Cal. Close, 1364–8*, 477.
[89] *D.N.B.*; P.R.O., C 145/112, no. 16; *Cal. Close, 1330–3*, 57.
[90] P.R.O., C 66/174, m. 4.

suage and 20 a. freehold were all said to be held of the bishop. Wake's heir was his sister Margaret, countess of Kent,[91] although his widow Blanche received a tenement and land as dower in 1349,[92] which passed in 1381 to Margaret's daughter Joan, *de jure* countess of Kent and Baroness Wake, wife of Edward the Black Prince.[93]

Joan's eldest son Thomas Holland, earl of Kent (d. 1397), held the estate in 1383–4, before her death.[94] Apparently larger than Wake's holding, in 1397 it consisted of a messuage, toft, and 105 a. valued at £6,[95] which probably included customary land; *c.* 1400 it included 51 a. of molond (customary land), and at Mile End a tenement called Beneyns, a toft called Sherwood, and a free tenement once of Nicholas Heved.[96] The estate passed to Thomas Holland's son Thomas, earl of Kent and duke of Surrey, on whose execution in 1400 it was described in two groups of inquisitions. A messuage called *MEWES* place at Mile End,[97] granted in 1400 to the king's servant Louis Recoches,[98] seems to have been the principal building and may have been named from the Meau family recorded in Stepney between 1315 and 1346. A messuage, one hide and a bordell of ½ hide and ½ virgate in Stepney, with common of pasture for 60 pigs in the forest of Havering, held in chief by the service of a greyhound's leash,[99] resembled the estate that Roger the sheriff held of Robert Fafiton in 1086,[1] but since no estate of that size has been identified, the description was presumably formal. It denoted the 2 messuages, 92 a. at Mile End, and common of pasture for 60 pigs, which Kent had received from his mother and had granted to John Cassous in 1398.

Cassous, possibly in 1402, granted the lands at Mile End, which included Mewes with two gardens and 12 a., for £95 a year, to George Bennet and John Potter, citizens and cordwainers, who were pardoned in 1405 for having entered without licence;[2] Heved's tenement was also called Bennetts in 1582, when it was a copyhold.[3] Cassous died seized, but 10 a. called Mewesdown in the lord's hands had been let by 1438–9 to Sir John Robesard,[4] a customary tenant of Stepney in 1443.[5] Robesard granted his interest to Humphrey, duke of Gloucester, but in 1447 Cassous' son John was confirmed in possession of the estate which his father had received in 1398.[6] In 1451 he acquired a messuage and 28 a. from the heir of John Potter,[7] and in 1461 he granted the freehold Mewes to Sir James Pickering and his wife Margaret,[8] presumably with the copyhold since they held

Beneyns and the other customary land that the earl of Kent had held *c.* 1400. Sir James and his wife died before 1503, when those copyholds passed in moieties to Christopher and Edward Pickering, Sir James's descendants by his first and second wives. On Edward's death in 1509 Christopher claimed that sons by the first wife should take precedence and was admitted to the whole property with James, Thomas, and William, his brothers.[9] The freehold evidently passed to him, as in 1517 Sir Christopher Pickering died seized of a messuage called Mewesdown and its land, valued at 30s. a year, leaving his infant daughter Anne as heir.[10] Anne married, as her second husband, Sir Henry Knevet (d. 1548) and in 1541 they held the copyhold Mewes tenement and 61 a. which they let for 21 years at £5 13s. 4d. Shortly after Knevet's death a Thomas Pickering and his two brothers, probably sons of Christopher's brother Thomas, claimed equal shares in the copyhold with Anne, and were apparently granted Mewes and 34 a. by the homage of Stepney.[11] Anne (d. 1582) and her third husband John Vaughan conveyed 15 a. freehold in Stepney to Thomas Pickering in 1550, possibly part of a settlement between them.[12] In 1562, however, the Vaughans claimed that Thomas Pickering had made conveyances of a freehold house, barn, stable, and 50 a. at Mile End which belonged to Anne.[13]

Thomas Pickering made a settlement of Beneyns and his other copyholds in 1582, and provided for the sale of most of his lands by will proved 1584.[14] By 1598, after the death of his widow Margaret,[15] the copyhold belonged to William Lee and the freehold Mewes to the navigator William Borough. On Borough's marriage to his second wife Jane, widow of Thomas, Lord Wentworth, in 1589,[16] Henry, Lord Wentworth, granted them a 500-year lease of 2 a. of waste between Borough's and Lee's lands on the north and Mile End Road.[17] In 1590 the Boroughs leased a parcel of the waste to Richard Lea for 450 years; it passed to Sir Stephen Powle and was the site of a mansion called the Gatehouse and other buildings belonging to the Pert family in 1625, and attached to a copyhold messuage, garden and orchard enfranchised by Powle in 1617.[18] The rest of the 2 a. belonged to the Mewes estate in 1652 under Borough's lease.[19] Borough settled his farm called Mewes or the White Horse on his widow for life.[20] His heir was his daughter Mary, wife of Adrian Moore, who owed a quitrent to Stepney for unspecified property in 1641.[21] Some or all of

91 *Cal. Inq. p.m.* ix, p. 201.
92 P.R.O., C 54/185, m. 1.
93 Ibid. C 136/17, no. 3.
94 Guildhall MS. 25403/3.
95 P.R.O., C 136/92, no. 30.
96 Ibid. SC 12/11/31.   97 *Cal. Inq. Misc.* vii, p. 45.
98 *Cal. Pat.* 1399–1401, 228.
99 P.R.O., C 137/44, no. 38.
1 Below, econ. hist. (agric.); Lysons, *Environs*, iii. 426.
2 P.R.O., CP 25/1/151/82, no. 22; *Cal. Close*, 1402–5, 465–6; *Cal. Pat.* 1405–8, 20.
3 B.L. Eg. Roll 2081.   4 P.R.O., SC 6/1139/24.
5 Ibid. SC 2/191/62.   6 *Cal. Pat.* 1446–52, 85.
7 P.R.O., CP 25/1/152/94, no. 154.
8 Ibid. CP 25/1/152/95, no. 196A.

9 Ibid. SC 2/191/63, m. 2; *Visitation of Yorks.* (Harl. Soc. xvi), 250–1.   10 P.R.O., E 150/475/7.
11 Ibid. REQ 2/17/92
12 Ibid. CP 25/2/61/474/4 Ed.VI/East.
13 Ibid. C 3/185/20.
14 B.L. Eg. Roll 2081; P.R.O., PROB 11/67 (P.C.C. 35 Watson), f. 276.
15 Guildhall MS. 9171/17, f. 216.
16 P.R.O., CP 25/2/172/24 Eliz./Hil.; B.L. Harl. MS. 6994, f. 193; below (Soldier).
17 G.L.R.O., M93/178.   18 B.L. Add. Chs. 71638–40.
19 G.L.R.O., M93/439, f. 7.
20 P.R.O., PROB 11/92 (P.C.C. 89 Lewyn), ff. 229–30.
21 *Mdx. Pedigrees* (Harl. Soc. lxv), 168; B.L. Eg. MS. 3006, f. 205.

Pickering's estate belonged in 1642 to Margaret Perkins and William Clarke and his wife Elizabeth, who let to Thomas Grimley the inn called the White Horse otherwise the Mewes, Pond field, and four adjoining closes, including Mewesdown and some of the copyhold.[22] Grimley was still the occupier in 1652.[23] In 1654 Elizabeth Clarke's cousin and heir surrendered his right in the property to William Clarke's nominee.[24]

The White Horse and c. 51 a. of its land let to Grimley was purchased by Thomas Hodgkins, and settled in 1678 on Hodgkins's grandson Michael, passing to the latter's daughter Anne and her husband Edward Fenwick, and then to their son Michael.[25] In 1703 the White Horse was called the Three Colts, and the land to its north belonged to Perkins (12½ a.) and Fenwick (45 a.) and was let to Edward Elderton.[26]

As Bennetts stood near Lord Kent's gate (Mewes tenement) c. 1400,[27] they probably shared one site in the 17th century. The White Horse in 1642 had a great hall with a cellar, a great parlour, five chambers, garrets, and domestic offices, besides a great barn and other outbuildings around a large courtyard. In 1728 a three-storeyed brick house stood on the south side of an ancient timber building with a back addition of brick; the timber building, containing the great hall, had itself been divided, and to the north were the outbuildings and courtyard with the water supply.[28] It is not clear whether Beneyns or Sherwood still descended with Mewes in the 17th century.

In 1349 Richard of Croydon, citizen, quitclaimed to Nicholas of Wick and his wife Idonea, and to one de Mordon, a messuage with houses on it, shops, lands, and rents in Whitechapel and Stepney.[29] Mordon was probably William de Mordon, executed in 1363, whose 11 a. in Stepney and 1 a. in Hackney had been held of the bishop of London and occupied since 1349 by Idonea, widow of Nicholas of Wick, who had married John Gosebourne.[30] Nicholas also bought 4 a. in Eastmarsh from Henry Vanner.[31] In 1362 Gosebourne made a settlement of 3 messuages and 11½ a. freehold in Stepney, Bromley, and Whitechapel.[32] He held at least 86 a. of customary land by 1400, spread throughout the parish, besides several cottages in Algatestreet, and property at Stratford and Mile End, and paid part of the rent for land which John Hadley had bought from Henry Vanner.[33] He also rented escheated customary land in 1383–4 and 1395–6 and 25 a. of Stepney demesne in Southhyde in 1398–9 and 1401–2.[34]

Gosebourne's estate was bought by Robert *CLOPTON*, alderman of London, from John Burgoyne and others, who were involved in other sales to Robert Cristendom (below), possibly as feoffees of Sir Guy de Allesley. Lands and tenements in Whitechapel, Stepney, and Hackney, with 12 a. of wood in Berkingclay (Essex), had been conveyed for the use of Allesley's wife Agnes to Roger Hungarton and others, who demised some property to Cristendom and the rest in 1424 to Thomas Burgh and others, who were to pay Hungarton £20 a year for Agnes, by then a widow.[35] Thomas's brother John Burgh was sued for part of the £20 in 1432–3.[36] In 1428 the tenant of John, Richard, and Robert de Burgh was licensed to use towards repairs an old barn on the west side of Crommesplace with a *garnarium* annexed to it.[37] In 1436 John Burgh quitclaimed his right as Thomas's heir to Hungarton's other devisees, who sold the estate to Clopton.[38] In 1460 it was conveyed to Clopton's daughter Alice by his surviving feoffee Thomas Burgoyne, who by grant of Alice reserved to himself two tenements in Algatestreet, on the east side of the Minoresses' tenement.[39] Alice and her husband Henry Chichele in 1460 conveyed all the lands to William Chedworth, to whom Thomas Chichele, archdeacon of Canterbury, quitclaimed all his right.[40]

Chedworth, who held Cobhams and other property in Stepney, settled 10 messuages, a dovecot, 2 gardens, 160 a., and 2s. rent in Whitechapel, Stepney, and Hackney, and an acre of wood in Berkingclay in 1462 and again in 1481.[41] They passed to his widow Joan and then to her son Nicholas and to his sisters with Chedworth's other property.[42]

The amount of land granted to Robert Cristendom before 1424 is not known. In 1438–9 quitrents of 3s. 7d. in the manor of Stepney were deducted from rents due from him for 4 a. in Stratford Bow and an acre in Stratford field (in Mile End and Stratford), because the land was held of the dean of St. Paul's, probably of Shadwell manor.[43] It was presumably sold in accordance with Cristendom's will written before 1443.[44]

John *STODEYE*, citizen and vintner, had lands in Stepney, Whitechapel, and Hackney, perhaps partly acquired through his wife Joan, whose mother was an heir of John Gisors.[45] Having been granted a messuage and 16 a. in Whitechapel and Stepney by John Berland and his wife Margaret in 1358,[46] and 10½ a. by John Chauser in 1363,[47] he bought the manor of Hoxton (in Shoreditch and Hackney) in 1372.[48]

22 B.L. Eg. MS. 3006, f. 199.
23 G.L.R.O., M93/439, ff. 4–5, 7.
24 P.R.O., C 54/3807, no. 24.
25 T.H.L.H.L., TH/1382 (ref. supplied by Isobel Watson); Herts. R.O., Martin-Leake MS. 83812.
26 Gascoyne, *Map of Mile End Old Town*. Later hist. reserved for Mile End Old Town.
27 P.R.O., SC 12/11/31.
28 B.L. Eg. MS. 3006, f. 199; Herts. R.O., MS. 83812: schedule contains much detail about the fittings.
29 P.R.O., C 146/5734.
30 *Cal. Inq. Misc.* iii, p. 190.
31 P.R.O., SC 12/11/31.
32 Ibid. CP 25/1/150/68, no. 394.

33 Guildhall MS. 25422; P.R.O., SC 12/11/31.
34 Guildhall MSS. 25403/3; 25403/5; P.R.O., SC 6/1139/21–2.
35 P.R.O., C 146/6017; C 1/12/189.
36 Ibid. C 1/12/189.   37 Ibid. C 146/5089.
38 Ibid. C 146/2869; C 146/892; C 146/373.
39 Ibid. C 146/549.   40 Ibid. C 146/482; C 146/284.
41 Ibid. C 146/2842; C 146/4664; C 146/4610.
42 Above (Cobhams).
43 P.R.O., SC 6/1139/24.
44 Ibid. C 54/293, m. 13d.
45 Above (Ewell).   46 P.R.O., CP 25/1/150/67, no. 358.
47 Ibid. CP 25/1/151/69, no. 402.
48 *V.C.H. Mdx.* x. 83.

He also owed a quitrent to Holy Trinity Aldgate,[49] probably that owed by Salomon de Ripple in 1310.[50] By will dated 1376 Stodeye left the bulk of his property to be divided equally between his four daughters and their husbands: Idonea and Nicholas Brembre, Margaret and John Philpot, Margery and Henry Vanner, and Joan, who later married Thomas Goodlake.[51] Brembre's share was conveyed shortly before his execution in 1388 to his brothers-in-law, John Fitznichol and Henry Vanner;[52] Idonea apparently had no issue. Sir John Philpot, by a codicil to his will of 1381 proved in 1389, left his share of Stodeye's property in London to his daughter Margaret, and Hoxton to his son Thomas.[53] Vanner paid the quitrent to Holy Trinity[54] and settled his share in 1394.[55] His will of 1395 left Stodeye's property in Stepney, Whitechapel, and a City parish to his wife Margery and her heirs, while property in two other City parishes was left to Thomas and John Birlingham, Margaret Philpot's sons by an earlier marriage.[56] In 1404, however, feoffees granted half of the Birlinghams' share to Margaret Philpot and the other half to the daughters of Joan Goodlake: Thomasia wife of John Hadley, Margaret wife of John St. Jermyn, and Idonea wife of Thomas Grey.[57] Margery Vanner, whose land was not mentioned, may have died about that time, leaving her sisters as coheirs. It is not certain what part of Hadley's estate had been Stodeye's lands. Other lands may have been subsumed into Hulls and Ewell.[58]

In 1380 William Acton granted to William Badby 7 messuages, 3 tofts, a dovecot, and 142 a. in Stepney.[59] Richard Marlowe, citizen and ironmonger, paid quitrent to the bishop for a free tenement and 50 a. late of William Badby c. 1400, held lands in Stepney valued at £13 6s. 8d. in 1412,[60] and granted the manor of OLD FORD called Marlaw or Badby manor to feoffees in 1420.[61] By will proved in 1422 it was left to his wife Agnes and then to his son Thomas, with remainder to John Lenyng the younger.[62] Sir John Manningham, who resided in Old Ford before 1475,[63] settled the manor in 1493, as did William Manningham. It was described as 14 messuages and gardens, 8 tofts, and 372 a. including 2 a. wood in Old Ford, Stepney, Hackney, and Stratford Bow.[64] Sir John Shaa (d. 1503), one of the grantees, left the manor, valued at £20, to his wife Margaret and then his son Edmund, with remainders to his younger sons

Reginald and Thomas.[65] Edmund Shaa having been declared a lunatic in 1527,[66] it was held in 1532 by Thomas. The manor was presumably the subject of grants by him in 1542 of messuages and land in Stepney and in Old Ford to Thomas, Lord Audley of Walden (d. 1544), the Lord Chancellor,[67] whose family held it in the 17th century.[68]

William *MAROWE*, mayor of London and perhaps son of Stephen Marowe of Stepney,[69] in 1455 bought a flooded freehold in the manor of Poplar from Robert Peny.[70] At his death c. 1465 he left his free and copyhold lands at Poplar and Limehouse to his wife Catherine and then to his eldest son William,[71] who was one of the lessees of Stepney marsh in 1488.[72] Richard Broke in 1486 conveyed to William Marowe and Thomas Marowe, probably his brother, a messuage in Poplar.[73] William, who in 1497 owed ten years' quitrent to Poplar for ½ a. next to Leamouth,[74] increased his property in Stepney through marriage to Joan, daughter and coheir of William Chedworth.[75] In the 1490s his holdings in Poplar included freehold and leasehold of Chedworth's, 3 a. formerly of Robert Peny, ground leased by the abbey of St. Mary Graces to William's father, and a great messuage and other customary lands.[76]

William Marowe c. 1499 left an infant son Thomas as heir, having ordered the sale of all his wood unless it should disfigure his 'place of Poplar'.[77] In 1500 the ½ a. at Leamouth was seized because Thomas had not been admitted; it lay in a 9-acre close belonging to Joan Marowe, widow, which may have been Chedworth's.[78] In 1501 all Marowe's property held of Poplar was seized, as it was held without licence,[79] but in 1513 it was held on behalf of Thomas, still a minor.[80]

Thomas Marowe joined with his mother's sisters between 1518 and 1529 to obtain the deeds of Cobhams from Nicholas Chedworth's widow.[81] He died in 1538 seized of a capital messuage at Poplar, two tenements with a wharf in the vill of Limehouse, and a third part of Rumbolds or Cobhams and other property, all held of Stepney manor and inherited by his son Thomas.[82] By 1545 the elder or younger Thomas had sold property to Roger Starky, citizen and mercer, including 17 a. of St. Katharine's marsh near the Tower of London.[83] A grant by Thomas Marowe and his wife Alice to John Warley of two messuages and 155 a. in 1553 may have been of Alice's inheritance.[84]

49 P.R.O., E 164/18, f. 26.
50 Ibid. E 40/2610; above (Holy Trinity).
51 *Cal. of Wills in Ct. of Husting*, ii. 191–2.
52 *Genealogist*, N.S. iv. 104; Rawcliffe, 'Margaret Stodeye', 90–1.
53 C.L.R.O., HR 118(30).
54 P.R.O., E 36/162.   55 Guildhall MS. 10065.
56 C.L.R.O., HR 126(76).
57 Guildhall MS. 10065.
58 Above (Hulls; Ewell; Cobhams).
59 P.R.O., CP 25/1/151/76, no. 34.
60 Ibid. SC 12/11/31; *Feud. Aids*, vi. 491.
61 P.R.O., CP 25/1/291/64, no. 97.
62 Ibid. PROB 11/2B (P.C.C. 50 Marche).
63 *Cal. Inq. p.m. Hen. VII*, ii, p. 552; *Cal. Pat.* 1467–77, 570.
64 P.R.O., CP 25/1/152/100, nos. 41–2.
65 *Cal. Inq. p.m. Hen. VII*, ii, pp. 552–3.
66 P.R.O., E 150/482/3.

67 Ibid. CP 25/2/52/377/34 Hen.VIII/Mich.
68 Detailed treatment reserved for Stratford Bow.
69 S. Thrupp, *Merchant Class of Med. Eng.* 355; Beaven, *Aldermen*, ii. 10.
70 P.R.O., SC 2/191/48.
71 Ibid. PROB 11/5 (P.C.C. 9, 11 Godyn).
72 Above, Stepney manor.
73 P.R.O., CP 25/1/152/100/1 Hen.VII/Trin.
74 Ibid. SC 2/191/50.   75 Above (Cobhams).
76 P.R.O., SC 11/453 (damaged).
77 *Cal. of Wills in Ct. of Husting*, ii (2), 606.
78 Above (Cobhams).   79 P.R.O., SC 2/191/50.
80 Ibid. SC 2/191/52.
81 Ibid. C 1/459/6; above (Cobhams).
82 P.R.O., C 142/61, no. 115.
83 Ibid. PROB 11/30 (P.C.C. 41 Pynnyng), ff. 319d.– 20.
84 Ibid. CP 25/1/74/629/1 Mary/Hil. Later hist. reserved for Poplar.

In 1466 Hugh Kingston conveyed a freehold messuage, garden, and 2 a. which had formerly belonged to Robert Sutton, citizen and draper, to John FENNE (d. 1474), merchant of the Staple of Calais,[85] who also acquired copyhold from Kingston and others (below). By will dated 1474 Fenne left his free and copyhold lands in Stepney and his dwelling in London to his wife Elizabeth and then to his son John,[86] but Fenne's four children were all under age and the two youngest, Hugh and Margaret, were in the guardianship of Elizabeth wife of William Stonor by 1477, and Elizabeth received rents from Stepney in 1476-77.[87] Several copyholds held by John and Hugh Fenne were surrendered by Hugh to Stonor's feoffees, but copyholds held solely by John Fenne, including a garden with 15 a. in crofts purchased from one Poole, and a cottage with a curtilage in Bethnal Green with 4 a. land, were to go to John's next heir. Arrangements were being made to let Stonor's place at Stepney to Lady Somerset.[88] John the younger, also later a merchant of the Staple of Calais, came of age in 1482 and in 1486 settled the property acquired from Kingston and a barn with an adjoining garden, which included a house called his great place at Stepney.[89] In 1495 John sold the barn and garden to Richard Algor, girdler of London, for £7.[90] Presumably it was the same John, son of John Fenne, who in 1497 surrendered copyholds to Henry Colet: 28 a. of arable in London field, of which 15 a. had once belonged to Hugh Kingston, and 15½ a. of arable in two crofts abutting Mile End green. One Robert Fenne had surrendered 3 r. in London field to Colet in 1488.[91]

In 1516 John, as John Atfenne of Stepney, who also had a copyhold dwelling at Mile End, let his freehold called his great messuage or place, with orchard, garden and waters, to Thomas, Lord Darcy (d. 1537), and Sir George Darcy for 20 years.[92] Lord Darcy was resident in 1519,[93] was appointed with Sir John Neville to search for suspected persons in Stepney in 1519 and 1525,[94] and was still there in 1531 when fire damaged the house.[95] In 1518–19 Darcy's goods included hangings bought from the earl of Kent at Stepney.[96]

By will dated 1524 John Fenne left his lands and tenements at Stepney to his wife Anne and then to his son Hugh, who was to surrender to John's daughter Christian and her heirs his (copyhold) dwelling house with freehold ground enclosed on the moat side; if he did not, the great place was to go to Christian.[97] By 1529 she had

married Thomas Hodgson and brought an action against Hugh, who confirmed his surrender of the copyhold messuage.[98] In 1525 he agreed to surrender to the Mercers' Company a strip on the west of its property.[99] Before 1549 overseers of the will of John Fenne, presumably his father, sold copyholds to William Billingsley; they later became the Mempris estate.[1]

Hugh's heir was his daughter Anne, wife of Henry Walter, who made a settlement in 1558 of their freehold messuage with four gardens, three orchards, and 8 a.,[2] and a conveyance to John Brock in 1568.[3] Walter also held considerable copyhold. In 1637 Henry Walter, probably a descendant, settled on himself and his son Henry all his Stepney copyholds, which were valued at £80 in 1641.[4]

Reference to a moat suggests that the great place may have been on the south-west side of Stepney Green, where old sites with a common stream in front of them included King's John's Palace and Lord Morley's house, although the most likely was the property to the north-west, belonging to Richard Loxame in 1577, surrounded on three sides by copyhold granted to Colet by Fenne,[5] and which may have been the messuage conveyed to Brock. Fenne's land presumably included c. 11 a. west of the Mercers' Great Place, which were held by Walter in 1615[6] and by Rolliston, with c. 23 a. north-east of Rogueswell common, in 1703.[7] Robert Rolliston was allowed to inclose waste in front of his dwelling house near Stepney church in 1654.[8]

Sir Henry Colet (d. 1505), mayor of London,[9] in 1482 acquired 3 a. of copyhold with buildings next to Stepney church. The land, in Curteysfield and without buildings when held by Robert Browning's heirs in 1410, was surrendered to John Crosse, citizen, in 1450, had a cottage on it when he settled it in 1471, and a cottage and curtilage in 1478. Colet received it from Thomas Foster and John Foster of London, possibly feoffees, and used it as a residence, later known as the Great Place. Between 1487 and 1497 he acquired, mainly from other Londoners, 10 cottages and 2 tenements in Clevestreet (later White Horse Street), Ratcliff, 6 cottages in Algatestreet, and 72 a. in various fields. The largest acquisition, south of Mile End Road, was from John, son of John Fenne.[10] Colet, who was buried in Stepney church,[11] was succeeded in the copyholds by his widow Christine and surviving son John (d. 1519), dean of St. Paul's. In 1518 they vested them in the MERCERS' COMPANY for the maintenance

85 P.R.O., CP 25/1/152/96, no. 21.
86 Ibid. PROB 11/6 (P.C.C. 17 Wattys).
87 Stonor Letters and Papers, I (Camd. 3rd ser. xxix), pp. xxix–xxx; P.R.O., C 47/37/9, no. 24.
88 Stonor Letters and Papers, II (Camd. 3rd ser. xxx), pp. 25–6.
89 P.R.O., E 210/5898; C 1/415/46.
90 Ibid. E 210/10299; E 210/15874; below (Savoy).
91 Below (Mercers).
92 P.R.O., E 210/9774.
93 L. & P. Hen. VIII, iii (1), p. 218; xii (2), p. 64; P.R.O., SP 1/29, pp. 40–4; SP 1/122, pp. 1–103; SP 1/51, pp. 279–87.
94 L. & P. Hen. VIII, iii (1), p. 126; iv (1), p. 473.
95 P.R.O., SP 1/122, f. 98.
96 Ibid. SP 1/21, m. 2.
97 Guildhall MS. 9171/10, f. 40v.
98 P.R.O., C 1/415/46.
99 Acts of Ct. of Mercers' Co. 1453-1527 (1936), 692.
1 P.R.O., C 78/5, no. 24; below (Mempris).
2 Guildhall MS. 9171/14, f. 33v.; P.R.O., CP 25/2/74/630/4&5 P&M/Trin.
3 P.R.O., CP 25/2/171/10 Eliz./Trin.
4 B.L. Eg. MS. 3006, ff. 41v., 209v., 232v.
5 Cheke's Reg., f. 189.   6 Plan of Mercers' est.
7 Gascoyne, Survey of Mile End Old Town.
8 G.L.R.O., M93/1, p. 12.
9 D.N.B. Para. based on Mercers' Co. Archives, Book of Evidences of Dean Colet, ff. 124–30.
10 Above (Fenne).
11 P.R.O., PROB 11/14 (P.C.C. 41 Holgrave).

of St. Paul's school, which John had founded in 1512, the company to pay a fine to Stepney manor of £3 6s. 8d. for its entire holding every five years.[12] Christine occupied the house until her death in 1523.[13]

At John Colet's suggestion, the company in 1516 had bought copyholds from William Browne the elder,[14] including a house at the north-west corner of White Horse Street and the Back Lane to Whitechapel.[15] After arbitration, Thomas, Lord Wentworth, enfranchised the whole estate in 1570 in return for £200.[16] It remained with the Mercers into the 20th century and was developed for building by them.[17] A plan drawn for the Mercers in 1615, the earliest known map of Stepney,[18] shows boundaries that had changed little by 1703.[19] The largest block of land lay in Mile End Old Town from Mile End Road south to Commercial Road, separated from Colet's house and nearby property in Ratcliff by Cobhams manor. Another block, including most of the cottages, lined the east side of White Horse Street in Ratcliff and stretched into Limehouse hamlet. Further parcels lay in Wapping-Stepney and Shadwell, but the six tenements in Algatestreet (later Whitechapel High Street) were not shown.

Sir Henry Colet's residence lay south-west of the church and in Ratcliff. In the 16th century the Mercers described it as their great mansion place and in the 18th century it was called the Great Place, leading to suggestions that it had been a seat before Colet's time.[20] It is clear, however, that building on the site was first carried out under John Crosse's ownership between 1450 and 1471.[21] The Mercers took possession of the Great Place in 1523 and allowed Sir John Aleyn, mayor of London, to occupy it for life, in return for repairs and for finishing the altar in their chapel in Mercers' Hall.[22] They later leased two closes in Stepney to Aleyn,[23] who seems to have left by 1533 when Thomas Cromwell secured a 50-year lease of the mansion and a tenement and other land nearby.[24] Cromwell carried out building work, although reference in the 1790s to 'an ancient wooden mansion' indicated half-timbering rather than brick.[25] The lease was forfeited to the Crown in 1540 and granted in 1542 to Cromwell's nephew Sir Richard Williams, gentleman of the Privy

Chamber, who had taken the surname Cromwell.[26] It was left in trust for Sir Richard's younger son Francis in 1544-5[27] and evidently was sold, as John Harington paid the rent between 1550 and 1571[28] and by 1577 had been succeeded by Simon Throckmorton.[29]

In 1325 John Cotekyn, citizen of London, held messuages and a garden on the south side of Mile End Road, just east of White Horse Lane.[30] One tenement passed to his daughter Alice and her husband John Mitcham, and then to William Mousbroun (Mucebron) in 1358 and to William Spir of Old Ford in 1363. Spir granted 4 shops and gardens there to John Wolward, smith, in 1364.[31] A messuage and garden on the east side of the tenement, belonging to John de Buntingford, carpenter, in 1342, passed to Alice daughter of Philip de Buntingford of London, carpenter, and her husband John Wellington in 1345, and then eventually to William Potter of Mile End and his wife Cecily.[32] They granted it to John Smyth of Mile End who in 1357 granted it to John Bogays, potter, of Mile End.[33] In 1359 William Potter granted to Bogays a plot of land with houses on it with a frontage of 25 ft. on Mile End Road and extending south for 7 virgates, which lay next to Bogays's messuage and was possibly part of the same property.[34] Bogays conveyed this plot to his son John and his issue in 1367, but by 1384 a messuage and garden, 3 shops and 1 a. land, all lying on the south side of Mile End Road, had passed to John's sister and heir Felicia.[35] In 1387 John Smyth's widow Margery quitclaimed her right in Smyth's property at Mile End to Felicia and her husband John Frebarn.[36]

The estate passed between feoffees, and by 1406 included another 1 a. acquired from John Gosebourne and his wife Margery. The beneficial owners after Frebarn are not clear but probably included John Bythewater, citizen and baker, who was granted the property in 1435.[37] In 1455 John Bythewater and his wife Joan granted the Bogays estate to Richard Pleystowe, citizen and cooper, and his feoffees,[38] and in 1475 Pleystowe sold it for £40 to John Pryour, citizen and cooper.[39] In 1480 Pryour and his feoffees demised the estate to Thomas Ewen and others as security for a loan of £50,[40] and in 1482 they sold it to Richard Algor or Algar, citizen and

12 *Acts of Ct. of Mercers' Co. 1453–1527* (1936), 454; *D.N.B.*
13 *E. Lond. Papers*, vi. 90.   14 Ibid.; *Acts of Ct.* 440–1.
15 Plan of Mercers' est.; Cheke's Reg., ff. 189, 210 (undated rental 1550x1571).
16 *E. Lond. Papers*, vi. 90.
17 Ibid. ix. 3–25.
18 Original at Mercers' Hall; copies in T.H.L.H.L., B.L. maps.
19 Gascoyne, *Map*.
20 The Fenne fam. (q.v.) also had a 'great place' in Stepney, and the Mercers acquired another in Lond., also let to John Aleyn: *Acts of Ct.* 694–5, 765; Mercers' Co. Archives, MS. Acts of Ct. 1527–60, f. 44.
21 Mercers' Co. Archives, Bk. of Evidences, ff. 124v., 129v.
22 *Acts of Ct.* 674.
23 Mercers' Co. Archives, MS. Acts of Ct. 1453–1527, f. 6d. Rent not as in *Acts of Ct.* 765.
24 Ibid. MS. Acts of Ct. 1527–60, ff. 70v., 72.
25 *L. & P. Hen. VIII*, ix, p. 19; Lysons, *Environs*, iii. 428.
26 *L. & P. Hen. VIII*, ix, p. 50; xii (2), p. 577; xvii, p. 258.

27 P.R.O., PROB 11/31 (P.C.C. 20 Alen), f. 156. Copy, with inventory and accts. inc. goods at Stepney, in B.L. Add. MS. 34393.
28 Cheke's Reg., f. 210. Presumably the writer and agent of Henry VIII, who lived at Stepney and was father of Sir John Harington (d. 1612), poet: *D.N.B.*
29 Cheke's Reg., f. 188v. Later hist. of ho. reserved for Ratcliff
30 P.R.O., E 210/6154.
31 Ibid. E 210/5872; E 210/6336; E 212/94; E 210/9576.
32 Ibid. E 210/5849; CP 25/1/150/62, no. 235; E 212/5; E 210/5746; E 210/6327.
33 Ibid. E 212/91; E 210/6324.
34 Cal. entry under ibid. E 212/78, but doc. mis-filed.
35 P.R.O., E 210/5747; E 210/5875.
36 Ibid. E 210/6299.
37 Ibid. E 210/5840; E 210/5897; E 212/33; E 210/5782; E 210/5877; E 210/6158; E 210/5894; E 210/5895; E 210/5798.
38 Ibid. E 210/6329; E 210/10296.
39 Ibid. E 210/10296; E 210/5856; C 1/60/169; *Cal. Close, 1476–85*, 77.
40 P.R.O., E 210/10302.

girdler.[41] In 1495 Algor bought from John Fenne a barn with a garden which lay on the W. and N. of his lands.[42]

In 1514 Richard's son and heir, James Algor, citizen and grocer, settled all his freehold estate at Mile End on himself and his wife Margaret and their issue,[43] but sold it for £140 in 1517, described as 3 messuages, with 3 gardens, and 3 a. at Mile End, to William White and William Gibbons, leathersellers of London, who immediately conveyed the estate to Sir John Neville (d. 1541) and others for the use of Henry VIII.[44] Neville was probably resident in Stepney when he was appointed to search for suspected persons there in 1519 and 1525,[45] and in 1523 the king granted the property, now a principal messuage with 3 other cottages, to Neville and his wife Elizabeth with remainder to their heirs, to hold for fealty and rent.[46] In 1557 Queen Mary gave the reserved rent to the refounded *HOSPITAL OF THE SAVOY*,[47] to which Francis Neville gave the estate in return for a 60 years' lease,[48] but he surrendered all his interest in 1560. The Master of the Savoy granted a 500-year lease to John Swift of London, who demolished a 'fair brick place' in order to sell the materials,[49] leased part of the property to William Hickes, a silk-weaver,[50] and sold the main lease to William Lambe, citizen and clothworker, in 1563.[51] Lambe assigned it in 1576 to the Corporation of London for the benefit of Christ's Hospital, to take effect after his death; £6 a year was to be paid to the Clothworkers' Company while the income from the property was £12 or more.[52]

Lambe and Christ's Hospital let the property in two parcels for 99 years in 1578. The great messuage, with an adjoining tenement on the west and two others on the east, and a close of ground of c. 2½ a., were granted to John Smith, citizen and mercer, subject to underleases to Hickes and others.[53] Two messuages and gardens at Mile End were granted to William Tilley, citizen and clothworker.[54]

In 1586 the Savoy sought to dispossess Smith, alleging that Swift's lease had been granted without the consent of the chaplains, who had anyway made a 200-year lease in 1559 to Richard Berwick and Edward Cosen.[55] Christ's Hospital, the Clothworkers' Company, Lambe's executors, and the two tenants, Smith and the holder of Tilley's lease, agreed in 1588 to buy the 200-year lease making annual payments to the Savoy, which made a further claim in 1594, apparently because of non-payment. The surrender of the leases both of 1559 and 1578 was ordered in 1600 but apparently later forgotten by Christ's Hospital until 1733 and by the Clothworkers' Company until 1759.[56]

The hospital of the Savoy was dissolved in 1702, when its estate at Mile End passed to the Crown having been leased in 1692 to Mary Johnson, the tenant in 1707.[57] The property was shown in 1703 as Johnson's close, with the buildings along the highway to the west.[58] In 1734 William Pryor Johnson petitioned for a lease of 4 a. at Mile End which had passed to his late son Edward Johnson, governor of St. Helena[59] and presumably the 'Justice Johnson' who was said in 1735 to have formerly occupied the mansion house. By then the house had been neglected, as the inhabitants of Mile End Old Town asked for the removal of lewd persons who haunted it.[60] The Crown received no rent between 1728 and 1746, although from 1741 the executors of Mary Johnson were held responsible for payment.

In 1733 Christ's Hospital realized that it had received no rent from Mile End since 1599.[61] The mansion was a den of thieves, and the rest of the estate was inhabited by beggars; a corn chandler at Mile End received the rents and had stripped the great house of materials, while another man had built two houses and a coach house which his family occupied. The absence of the Crown's leaseholder seems to have allowed Christ's Hospital to obtain the rents from the subtenants. Overlooking the decree of 1600 and thinking that the estate was part of the first Savoy's lands granted to Christ's Hospital by Edward VI, the governors in 1736 persuaded the occupiers, presumably the 'lewd persons', to become their own tenants. The property consisted of the Magpie alehouse with an adjoining house and close, four neighbouring houses, garden ground, and the Great House, which had been sublet in two parts. Christ's Hospital, sued presumably by the Crown or its leaseholder, was advised in 1761 that it had no title from William Lambe. The Clothworkers' Company, having found a record of the 500-year lease which would have come into effect after the end of the 200-year lease, approached Christ's Hospital in 1759 and presumably then learnt that its rights had ended in 1600.

The Crown leased the estate in 1752 to Robert Evans for 50 years. Mary Evans, who obtained a further lease, paid rent from c. 1779 and the Revd. Robert Evans from 1811 until 1816,[62] when the survey made then may have preceded a sale. The site then stretched for c. 500 ft. eastward from the Jews' hospital on the south side of Mile End Road; it contained three terraced houses between the hospital and a freehold house, both perhaps once part of the estate, and nos. 1 to 23 Crown Row; behind Crown Row were a nursery ground and the hospital garden.[63]

41 Ibid. E 210/5893; E 210/5340.
42 Ibid. E 210/10299.
43 Ibid. E 210/5800; E 210/5891.
44 Ibid. E 40/2386; E 40/2398; E 40/2596; E 40/2632; E 40/2702; *Hist. Parl., Commons, 1509–58,* iii. 9.
45 *L. & P. Hen. VIII,* iii (1), p. 126; iv (1), p. 473.
46 P.R.O., C 66/642, m. 21.   47 *Cal. Pat.* 1557–8, 362.
48 Guildhall MS. 13430, nos. 1, 4.
49 P.R.O., E 134/28 Eliz./Trin. 1.
50 Ibid.; Guildhall MS. 13431, no. 8.
51 Guildhall MSS. 13430, nos. 3, 4; 13434.
52 Ibid. 13430, no. 5; 13434.

53 Ibid. MS. 13431, no. 8.
54 Ibid. no. 9.
55 P.R.O., E 134/28 Eliz./Trin. 1; Guildhall MS. 13434.
56 Guildhall MS. 13434.
57 B.L. Add. MS. 11599, p. 104; P.R.O., LR 2/314.
58 Gascoyne, *Map of Mile End Old Town.*
59 *Cal. Treas. Bks. & Papers,* 1731–4, 449, 596.
60 Ibid. 1735–8, 91.
61 Two paras. based on Guildhall MS. 13434.
62 P.R.O., LR 2/314.
63 B.M., Crace Colln. maps, portf. XVI, no. 21.

Elizabeth (d. 1591), widow of Robert, Baron Rich (d. 1581), was a copyholder in 1582,[64] probably as the daughter of George Baldry (d. c. 1539).[65] In 1595 her kinsman Edmund Style and son-in-law Thomas Cannock surrendered to her son Sir Edwin Rich a customary messuage, with appurtenances including a small grove (grovett), on Westheath at Mile End. Edwin surrendered it in 1596 to Isabel, dowager countess of Rutland (d. 1606), to remain to her grandson William Cecil, Lord Roos, or to William Borough if Roos should be under age. Borough's executor was admitted in 1606,[66] and William, Lord Roos (d. 1618), in 1611, but he surrendered it to his uncle Richard Cecil, who in 1612 surrendered it to Nicholas Diggons of Limehouse, mariner.[67] Diggons was a party to the copyholders' agreement with Lord Wentworth in 1617.[68] His son Joseph Diggons of Liss (Hants) paid the quitrent c. 1641[69] and left his copyholds to CLARE HALL, Cambridge, which forfeited it on his death in 1658 because surrender to a corporation was not permitted. After a petition the property, described as a messuage, tenement, 2 new tenements, a garden, and 4½ a., was granted to the college for a fine of £100, with licence to let for up to 99 years.[70]

The property passed to successive trustees of Clare Hall, and in 1721 contained a messuage, 10 tenements and land.[71] Adjoining parcels were added to the estate. On enfranchisement in 1857 it consisted of Clare Hall Row, Clare Hall Court, and Clare Hall Cottages, and land containing in all 7 a. at Stepney Green, which might profitably be let for building.[72] Part not built on in 1868 lay between Diggons Street and Oley Place.[73] The capital messuage was probably the mansion let as apartments in 1795, when the ceiling of an upper room, possibly once a gallery, had the coat of arms of Baldry impaling Ford. It may also have been the building called Agent Nurse's house in 1703.[74]

William Billingsley, citizen and haberdasher (d. c. 1553), bought from the overseers of the will of John Fenne a copyhold messuage and 2 tenements, a garden, an orchard, and 30 a. at Mile End.[75] He was confirmed in possession in 1549 but ordered to sell a piece of the orchard to Henry Barnes, who claimed Billingsley bought the property on his behalf.[76] The estate probably passed to William's youngest son Henry Billingsley, mayor of London,[77] who in 1578 was granted the trees in front of his property in Mile End. By 1652 that property consisted of freehold houses belonging to Hilary

MEMPRIS, citizen and haberdasher; probably it had been enfranchised after 1617, although Mempris does not seem to have owned the 30 a.[78] He lived on Mile End green, but perhaps not on Billingsley's estate, as he had other property there. In 1630 he paid £1,500 for a capital messuage formerly occupied by Lord Morley (d. 1622) on the south-west side of the green, and other houses, one of them on the north side of Mile End Road next to the house later occupied by Mempris's brother; all had been enfranchised in 1621.[79]

Mempris also acquired 4 a. of copyhold in 1635, surrendered a tenement on Mile End green in 1636, and leased out a copyhold tenement with two garden plots in 1642.[80] Henry Clowes surrendered 4 a. on the north side of Mile End Road to him in 1642.[81] Mempris took a 99-year lease of three parcels of demesne totalling 12 a. on the north side of Mile End Road in 1638, acquiring the manorial mortgage term on those and 5 a. nearby called Longmead in 1643. The freehold of these parcels was conveyed to Isaac Mempris, son of Hillary's brother Thomas, and Longmead was bought from the trustees selling the Wentworth's family right to the equity of redemption.[82] Hillary died in 1652[83] and his brother Thomas inherited his freehold and was admitted in 1653 to the copyhold messuages at Mile End green.[84] Thomas died between 1655 and 1658 leaving most of his property to his wife Elizabeth and then all to be divided among his seven children. It comprised the mansion where he lived, with 5 or 6 neighbouring houses, at Mile End green, all copyhold, over 30 a. of freehold land, and freehold houses in Three Colt Yard (Three Colt Court in 1703), and elsewhere in Mile End, and others in London.[85]

Henry Barnes, citizen and grocer, after a dispute in 1549, obtained part of an orchard from William Billingsley.[86] At his death shortly after 1557, Barnes held a cottage and curtilage on the north side of Mile End Road, divided into two and called the EAST HOUSE, a garden with an entry underneath the gallery, a croft of c. 5 a., and other parcels at Mile End. By will dated 1557, that land was devised to Edward Barnes, who died without issue, and passed to Henry's surviving daughters Agnes, wife of Michael Wendover, and Elizabeth, wife of Thomas Baynard or Barnard.[87] Other property passed to Henry's son William, who in 1566 devised to his sisters lands in Uxbridge and elsewhere.[88] In 1568 Agnes and Elizabeth conveyed lands in West Middlesex and Stepney to William Pinchbeck,[89] who also acquired some or all of Barnes's

64 B.L. Eg. Roll 2081.   65 Complete Peerage, s.v. Rich.
66 Clare Coll. Archives, safe A: 4/1 (1606). Material from Clare Coll. supplied by Isobel Watson.
67 Ibid. deedbox 6:11 (1611, 1612); sale A: 4/1 (1611).
68 Below, econ. hist. (agric.).
69 B.L. Eg. MS. 3006, f. 209d.
70 G.L.R.O., M93/2, pp. 187, 283.
71 Ibid. M93/24, p. 271.   72 Ch. Com. file 12552.
73 P.R.O., C 54/16958, no. 6. Later hist. reserved for Mile End Old Town.
74 Lysons, Environs, iii. 428; Gascoyne, Plan of Mile End Old Town.
75 P.R.O., C 78/5, no. 24; above (Fenne).
76 P.R.O., C 78/5, no. 24; below (Soldier).

77 Beaven, Aldermen, ii. 42; Visitation of Lond. 1568, 69–70.
78 G.L.R.O., M93/439, f. 22; above, Stepney manor.
79 Herts. R.O., Martin-Leake MSS. 83806–7.
80 B.L. Eg. MS. 3006, ff. 34v., 39, 189.
81 Ibid. f. 181; above (Soldier).
82 G.L.R.O., M93/439, ff. 1–4.
83 Herts. R.O., Martin-Leake MS. 83807.
84 G.L.R.O., M93/132, f. 42.
85 P.R.O., PROB 11/272, f. 4 (pp. 27–9); Herts. R.O., Martin-Leake MSS. 83806–7. Later hist. reserved for Mile End Old Town.
86 Above (Mempris).   87 P.R.O., C 3/22/8.
88 Ibid. PROB 11/48 (P.C.C. 20 Crymes), f. 304.
89 Ibid. CP 25/2/171/10&11 Eliz./Mich.

copyhold and by 1582 for an unexplained cause had forfeited two customary cottages and curtilages recently made into three mansions on the west side of his East House.

Lord Wentworth settled the forfeited property for his wife Jane's dower.[90] In 1581 a copyhold tenement and a 5-a. close on the north side of Mile End Road had been vested in the same feoffees,[91] who included two of Jane's relatives;[92] that property, which became known by the sign of the *SOLDIER*, was probably also held on her behalf. In 1600, after the death of her second husband William Borough, Jane made a settlement of all her property, and in her will of 1608, when living in Stepney, she left her copyhold to her nephew John Harlstone and his wife Jane, who also held a lease of 3 a. at Mile End for Jane Wentworth's use. The will received probate in 1616.[93]

Robert Harlstone held houses and lands in Mile End valued at £40 c. 1641.[94] In 1642 he granted a copyhold messuage, orchard, gardens, three cottages, and close of 5 a. to Henry Clowes, who surrendered 4 a. to Hilary Mempris.[95] Clowes leased the orchard and garden in 1653 to George Higgins, gardener, who covenanted to build a house and surrender it after the 31-year lease with 200 good fruit trees.[96] In 1655 Clowes surrendered some of his copyhold to Elizabeth Cage, including that leased to Higgins and described as a tenement called by the sign of the Soldier with a cottage and orchard on the north side of Mile End Road.[97] A neighbouring copyhold was conveyed in 1656 to Thomas Manwaring.[98] Lessees of the Soldier sublet a plot to Sephardic Jews for a burial ground in 1657. After the death of Elizabeth Cage's son Cornelius, who had been admitted in 1669, the Jews bought the copyhold and were admitted in 1677, taking possession of the whole tenement when Higgins's lease expired in 1684; they let the buildings near the road and used all the rest for burials, securing enfranchisement in 1736.[99]

ECONOMIC HISTORY

AGRICULTURE TO *c.* 1550. The bishop's manor was assessed at 32 hides and valued at £48 in 1086, only £2 less than in 1066.[1] He held 24¼ hides in demesne in 1066, with 4 tenants holding 10 hides and 2 mills; by 1086 the demesne had been reduced to 14 hides by further subinfeudations and the bishop had 10 chief tenants holding 20¼ hides and 3 mills. It is not clear how much of the demesne, the tenants', or the villeins' land lay in Stepney parish.[2] Other land was granted out by the bishops, probably after 1086, to hold by suit and a money service, and some was assarted; the grant to Ralph the clerk in the late 12th century included 2½ a. assarted land near his house.[3]

By the 14th century the larger freehold estates had generally been built up by accumulating parcels, some as small as half-acre strips. They reveal an active land market from an early date[4] and some, therefore, were not solely held of the bishop: Poplar manor comprised freeholds held of Stepney and of the manors of Bromley belonging respectively to St. Leonard's priory, Stratford, and to Holy Trinity, Aldgate.[5] Where freeholders also held customary land of Stepney it seems sometimes to have been enfranchised and absorbed into the freehold estate, as on Philpot's manor of Hulls. Often, however, free and customary land continued to pass separately but to the same heir by means of surrenders to feoffees and later to the use of wills, bypassing inheritance custom.[6]

CUSTOMARY TENURE AND WORKS. Of the 60 husbandmen in 1086, 7 held ½ hide each, 44 held 1 virgate each, and 9 held ½ virgate each. The 46 cottars occupying 1 hide for 30s. were, from the size of the rent and the proximity of London, probably craftsmen or market gardeners.[7]

Labour services had been commuted on *c.* 1,056 a. by 1362–3.[8] An incomplete rental, probably *c.* 1381, of the commuted service on each parcel of land, indicates 160 customary tenants, 146 with full and legible entries. It is not clear how many tenants lived in Stepney; some were citizens of London and others were also freeholders.[9] Any standard size for customary holdings had disappeared, the largest amount held by one person being 38½ a. and the smallest a plot. Frequent identification of strips of land by the names of previous holders, who were nonetheless still living, shows that few holdings passed intact, that there was a vigorous market for strips of 1 r. upwards, and that the same process of accumulation occurred as for freehold land.[10] Strips were also acquired to build up unified holdings in place of scattered parcels.[11]

Partible inheritance was customary, with land passing first to all sons, then to daughters, and then to next of kin of equal degree.[12] Some holdings, with or without a dwelling, were heriotable, but no heriot was taken if there were no animals.[13] In 1348–9 holdings were being surrendered to the use of the holder for life, to the use of another and their issue, or outright to

90 B.L. Eg. Roll 2081. 91 Ibid. 2080.
92 Guildhall MS. 9171/22, f. 524.
93 B.L. Harl. MS. 6994, f. 193; above (Mewes); Guildhall MS. 9171/22, f. 524. 94 B.L. Eg. MS. 3006, f. 231.
95 Ibid. f. 181; above (Mempris).
96 *Jewish Hist. Soc. Trans.* xix. 169 (lessee given as Sigins).
97 G.L.R.O., M93/1, p. 67. 98 Ibid. pp. 125–6.
99 *Jewish Hist. Soc. Trans.* xix. 169–70, 173, 175, 177; G.L.R.O., M93/282. Later hist. reserved for Mile End Old Town.
1 Two paras. based on *V.C.H. Mdx.* i. 120–1, 128.
2 Above, Stepney manor.
3 Guildhall MS. 25122/146; above, manors (Ralph).
4 Above, manors (e.g. Shadwell; St. Thos. Acre; Holy Trinity).

5 Above, manors (Poplar) 6 Above, manors (Hulls); below.
7 *V.C.H. Mdx.* i. 120; cf. *Agrarian Hist. Eng. and Wales, II, 1042–1350,* ed. H. E. Hallam (1988), 60. Possibly in Haliwellstreet or Algatestreet, which both lay partly within the manor.
8 P.R.O., SC 6/1139/18.
9 Guildhall MS. 25422. Defective; dated by Guildhall to 1404 vacancy of see, but internal evidence and field survey (P.R.O., SC 12/11/31) suggest previous vacancy.
10 Guildhall MS. 25422; above.
11 e.g. Mercers' est.; below.
12 P.R.O., SC 2/191/60, *passim.* 13 Ibid. m. 12d.

another and their heirs. The fine payable was not a standard rate per acre, but its terms were not recorded. Mortgages occur in 1383,[14] and licenses to let for 21 years and surrenders to uses of will in 1582.[15]

Disagreements over customs led to payments by a group of copyholders to Henry, Lord Wentworth, in 1588 and by others, headed by Sir John Jolles, to his son, Thomas, later earl of Cleveland, for an agreement set out in a Chancery decree in 1617 and confirmed by Act 1623–4.[16] Under the agreement the lord could levy only specified fines, customs, or services, and could not grant away any copyhold, although he could grant the freehold to the holder. It was confirmed that enfranchised copyholders would continue to have common of pasture in the wastes and that the inheritance custom, as before, accorded no rights to the spouse surviving a holder; fines on admittance were fixed at 16d. an acre, 13s. 4d. for customary messuages with their courtyards and gardens, 10s. for a dwelling called a tenement with courtyards and gardens, 20d. for a cottage that could not be let for more than £3 a year and 10s. if let for more, and 16d. for buildings not used as dwellings. Surrenders for a marriage jointure paid half the fine. Holders could let for up to 31 years and 4 months without licence or fine; copyholders could dig up their copyhold ground at will and fell timber for their own profit; they were also allowed waste without forfeiture, whereas tenants for life or years committing waste could be fined by the homage. Copyholders could demolish and rebuild and dig gravel on the waste for building or repairs. Coheirs in dispute might request a precept for seven tenants to make a partition. Only the 343 copyholders (and their successors) that had contributed to the composition and were party to the agreement had the benefit of it.[17]

Tallage, paid in 1228, and *maritagium*, paid in 1318,[18] were not recorded later. A distinction in 1348–9 between copyholders who were free men and those who were *nativi* showed no practical effects,[19] and was no longer apparent by 1384.[20] Citizens of London were among those labelled as free men and were holding customary land in 1348, possibly before the commutation of labour services.[21] If cotmen, hidemen, schirmen, and molmen mentioned in the early 14th century had once been distinct classes of peasantry, works by then were attached to specific strips of arable and not to holdings or tenants; later in the century most tenants held more than one category of land.[22] It was perhaps unusual for labour services to survive in the 14th century so near London, but they were the only service paid for land. Some customary tenements were held for smokepennies, romepennies or helpennies, and some, including limekilns and other buildings, for a small money rent.[23]

Before commutation labour services fell into two categories.[24] The first were the week-works owed by cotmen and schirmen. Schirmen's works comprised 2,652 works from customary tenants holding a total of 8½ virgates of land, with each virgate owing 6 works a week, and 312 works from tenants holding a total of 2 virgates, each virgate owing 3 works a week; 4 virgates of the first group were accounted for in Hackney in 1362–3.[25] Cotmen's comprised 2,860 works from tenants holding 11 virgates (5 works a virgate a week), and 624 works from tenants holding 3 virgates (4 works a virgate a week); 52 works came from tenants holding half a virgate of ferthingland (1 work a week); and 260 works from tenants holding 1 virgate of boundyngland or bultingland (5 works a week), a total of 3,796 works. There was some confusion over the acreage of a virgate, but the accounts generally settled on 20 a. in 1362–3.[26] Allowances on all those works were made for serving a manorial office, for the weeks of Christmas, Easter, and Pentecost and for feasts falling on a Friday, for performing specific boonworks (below), and carriage inside and outside the manor. In 1335–6 allowances were also made for the schirmen's works on 6 virgates let for a money rent, possibly indicating commutation. In 1335–6 the lord used only 873 works, to hoe and thresh (380 works), make drainage furrows, purify rye seed of weeds, bundle straw, and carry to the bishop's castle at Stortford and to Newgate. After allowances he sold 2,129, either to the tenant owing the works or to a third party.

The second category of works comprised specific services owed by molmen and hidemen besides cotmen and schirmen: *nedherths* and *benherths*, which were ploughing services (1 *nedherth* ploughed 1 a.),[27] *wodelodes* and *timberlodes*, carrying services, *nedreps*, a reaping service, and *falcones* or mowing (1 work mowed 1 a.). The 6 virgates let or commuted owed for each virgate 4 *nedherths*, 2 *benherths*, 4 *wodelodes*, 2 *timberlodes*, 1 mowing work, and 4 *nedreps*. In 1335-6 the lord was entitled to 94 *nedherths*, of which 65 were owed by schirmen and cotmen and 29 by hidemen; he used 8 and sold 60⅔ at 6d. each. *Benherths* totalled 167½, from schirmen, molmen, and hidemen, and over 152 were sold for 6d. each. Of *wodelodes*, 97 were owed by cotmen and schirmen and 233 by molmen and hidemen, and 301½ were sold at 4d. each. Of *timberlodes*, 48½ came from cotmen and schirmen and 116½ from molmen and hidemen, and 150¾ were sold at 6d. Of mowing works, 24½ were done by cotmen and schirmen and 7 by molmen and hidemen; the lord used 22. Forty-two *nedreps* were owed by schirmen in the harvest and 32 by molmen and hidemen.

The linking of works to strips may have arisen from partible inheritance, but the resulting complexity of holdings was probably not the reason for commutation, since the payments for the

14 Guildhall MS. 10312/136.   15 B.L. Eg. Roll 2081.
16 P.R.O., C 78/211, no. 9; 21 Jas. I, c. 6 (Priv. Act).
17 *Customs and Privileges of Manors of Stepney and Hackney* (1736), 113–23.
18 P.R.O., E 372/72, m. 10d.; Guildhall MS. 25369/1.
19 P.R.O., SC 2/191/60. 20 Guildhall MS. 10312/136.
21 P.R.O., SC 2/191/60, m. 4d., refers to 3 a. rendering service of 1/2 virgate schirland.
22 Guildhall MS. 25422.   23 P.R.O., SC 12/11/31.
24 Based on only full accts. before commutation, in 1335–6: Guildhall MS. 25403/2.
25 P.R.O., SC 6/1139/18.
26 Ibid.
27 Guildhall MS. 25403/1.

commuted services were equally complex, specifying sums as precise as fractions of a farthing.[28] More likely a diminishing need for works led to commutation: 70 *timberlodes* and 6 *wodelodes* were sold in 1313, and 73 *wodelodes*, 37 *timberlodes*, 35 shirman's works, and 450½ cotman's works were sold in 1318; few of the works were used in 1335–6.[29] Most of the demesne having been let, all the labour services were commuted by 1362–3, at rates of between 4*d.* and 2*s.* an acre according to type of land to reflect the number of works each type owed.[30] Some of the rates may have changed slightly later in the 14th century,[31] and the very different total acreage given *c.* 1400 perhaps included Hackney,[32] but thereafter the rates remained fixed and therefore increasingly favourable for the customary tenants.

The bishop's income from his tenants up to and including 1402–3 was *c.* £33 from rents of assize for free and customary tenants and *c.* £58 for the commuted works. In 1408–9 he received *c.* £66 for rents and services together. The approximate income varied little thereafter, an inexplicable loss to the bishop.[33]

DEMESNE PRODUCTION. The bishop had 3 ploughteams on his demesne throughout the vill in 1086, compared with 22 held by the husbandmen, and in 1066 he had only had 6½ teams, suggesting little interest by him in demesne farming here.[34] That much of his 14-hide demesne consisted of the extensive meadow, pasture, and woods (possibly all the woodland for 500 pigs plus a surplus) listed in 1086 is made likely by the fact that in Stepney little wood belonged to medieval freeholders.[35] The demesne arable at first was probably concentrated between Bethnal green and Shoreditch High Street, overlapping into Hackney and on the south reaching Whitechapel Road, but lying mostly in the later hamlet of Bethnal Green. The demesne around the manor house, possibly as far west as Cambridge Heath and Bethnal green, was probably still woodland in 1086 and had been partially cleared by 1318.[36] Little is known of the exploitation of the demesne before the 14th century. Although both Harringay and Hackney probably had separate collectors within the manors by the 13th century, their accounts were often included in those for Stepney, which also contained totals for other manors.[37]

Rents of assize were received from an unknown number of tenants, and the 44 hens and 500 eggs sold in 1229 were received as rent; cumin, ploughshares, capons, and hens were customary rents in 1273. Other receipts were for tallage, aid and wardpenny, pleas and perquisites of court, sheriff's aid, pannage, a heriot, fugitive's chattels, and mills in 1229; helpenny and wardpenny in 1264; and for aid and recognitions of customary tenants in 1273. Other items included sales of 86 sheep in 1243 and cheese in 1264, when payments of barley and 13*s.* 6*d.* were made for guarding vines at Stepney.

In the early 14th century, as in the 13th, the mills, the fishery on the Lea, and escheated customary holdings were farmed out, but most of the rest of the demesne was managed directly.[38] It was used primarily to support the bishop's household, rather than to produce perishable products for the London market; there was also some coordination with other episcopal manors, principally Bencham. The main product at Stepney was grain, and in 1336 stock from the granary was used to sow 108 a. of wheat, 140 a. of rye, 124 a. of barley, 19½ a. of vetch, and 71 a. of oats, of which 8 a. of oats and 21 a. of rye were sown in Hackney.[39] No maslin was sown but wheat and rye were mixed and, with barley and oats, used for servants' liveries and animal feed. Unknown quantities of grain, with 10 quarters of vetch, were sold.[40] Similar crops were produced in 1303, 1318, and 1339. A distinction between old and new crops was applied to the contents of the granary in 1339, when long-term storage indicated a lack of interest in their commercial value.

The livestock consisted mainly of working animals, sheep bought in, and a few breeding pigs. In 1336 and 1339 six plough-horses, 14 stots, and 16 oxen were kept from year to year, with replacements bought when needed, and numbers in 1303 were similar. Other cattle acquired during the year, mainly as heriots, were disposed of; 30 cows from Bencham were grazed in Stepney on the stubble in 1335–6 but were not included in the stock at the end of the account. A flock of 43 wethers in 1335 was supplemented by 14 from Orsett (Essex); disposals, including 14 eaten by the bishop's household, left 37 at the end of the account. After Pentecost 108 yearling lambs were sent from Bencham, and remained at the end of the account; 140 of the bishop's sheep were grazed on the stubble. Wool from 39 sheep was delivered to Richard of Hackney, a woolmonger. Pigs in 1336 formed a small breeding herd of 1 boar and 2 sows, with 26 adult pigs, 31 under a year, and 33 under six months at the start of the

28 Ibid. 25422.
29 Ibid. 25403/1–2.
30 P.R.O., SC 6/1139/18.
31 Guildhall MSS. 25422; 25403/3.
32 Field survey of 1,335 a., besides probably at least 200 a. for a missing digit in the total of schirland; the beginning, concerning the N. part of Stepney, is missing: P.R.O., SC 12/11/31.
33 Guildhall MS. 25403/6; P.R.O., SC 6/1139/23.
34 *V.C.H. Mdx.* i. 120; *Agrarian Hist. Eng. and Wales,* II, 102, and cf. 90 for other rates.
35 *V.C.H. Mdx.* i. 120; below, woods.
36 Below, woods.
37 This and foll. paras. based on P.R.O., E 372/72, m.

10d. (for 1228–9); E 352/36, m. 5 (1242–3); E 352/57, [m. 13d.] (1263–4); E 352/66, m. 6 (1272–3).
38 The following is based on the serjeant's accts. for 1335–6, partly illegible but the only accts. for a full year while the Stepney demesne was managed directly by the bishop. They are supplemented by executors' accts. for Dec. 1303 and Mar. 1339, and by the reeve's acct. for Aug. to Nov. 1318: *Acct. of Exors. of Ric., Bp. of Lond. 1303* (Camd. Soc. N.S. x), 94–6; Guildhall MSS. 25403/1 (1318); 25403/2 (1335–6); P.R.O., E 154/1/47 (1339). All are vacancy accts.
39 Reading for wheat is uncertain: its acreage greatly exceeded rye in the other accts.
40 72 of total receipts covers totals for the illegible arrears and for sales of corn.

account: the household used 33 of the youngest and 26 adults, most of the latter killed in the autumn. Twenty pigs and 45 piglets had been sold in 1303, besides 19 flitches of bacon.

Birds for the table in 1303 included geese, cranes, cygnets, and peacocks. In 1336 a flock of 62 geese was increased to 138 during the year, and 62 were eaten. The 9 hens and 1 cock were augmented by 42 received as rent at Christmas; 29 were eaten, a few were sold and the remaining 10 farmed out for 5s. The bishop still had a cock and 10 hens in 1339. He also received 450 eggs at Easter as rent and 55 more were bought in 1335–6; all were used by the household except for 25 given to the beadle. The only other important product from the manor was a rent of 300 sacks of lime from the kilns.[41] Pannage was usually sold,[42] 8 a. of vetch were sold growing for 56s. in 1335–6, while straw in stack fetched only 20s. because some was needed for the 30 cows from Bencham and the lord's horses. Straw in the field fetched only 33s. because 38 a. were ploughed in specifically to improve the soil and 8 a. bundled for thatching. Grazing on the stubble fetched only 13s. because part was used for the bishop's sheep. The gardens produced nothing in 1336 because the trees had not 'sprouted' (presumably fruit had not set), and the herbage fetched only 6s. 8d., one garden having been closed off and replanted.

Demesne meadow in the 14th century was probably the same as in 1550, when it lay in several places along the Lea from Mill fields in Hackney to Old Ford marsh in Stepney, with a small adjoining piece in West Ham (Essex).[43] In 1336 the bishop had 96 a. of meadow in demesne: hay was made on 82½ a. and mostly used for his horses. Another 13½ a. were sold in grass for 78s. Kechenfeld, near the manor house, was grazed in 1336 for the third year running by plough animals, as were Northwood and Southwood, the headlands in Combfield, and the fallow fields. Grazing on headlands around the winter corn was let for 15s. 6d. a parcel, but headlands around spring corn fetched only 11s., because Broomcroft, sown with oats, had no headland. By the 14th century demesne income also included rents for grazing on the earthen walls along the river banks, such as Nasflete and Blackwall, and for 'hopes' or enclosures of reeds such as Goodluckhope near Leamouth. Information on grazing sales in 1318 is not complete, but grazing at the *quabba* by the Lea in Hackney and in the Wylde near Limehouse were let in 1318 up to Michaelmas. Farm of a garden brought in 15d. for the 5 weeks up to Michaelmas, but nothing thereafter.

Three carters, 3 herdsmen, 3 drivers (ploughmen), a dairy maid, a shepherd, a swineherd, and a man to look after the animals for the six winter months, received money wages and corn liveries in 1336; liveries were also paid to a man chasing off birds and a man looking after the 30 cows from Bencham. The lord also used some

of the labour services owed by his customary tenants.[44] Harvesting on the demesne was mainly done by the customary tenants owing weekworks: 498 man-days were done by Stepney tenants and 358 by Hackney tenants. Forty tenants from Stepney and 30 from Hackney carried the reaped corn, 32 men loaded and 8 stacked. During the harvest wages were also paid to another two stackers, to the beadles for Stepney and Hackney and their two grooms, and to the bishop's servants as overseers.

Threshing was largely paid for as piece-work, and most ploughing was presumably done by the wage labourers, as little was done by customary labour: the bishop used only 33 of c. 260 ploughing services he was entitled to in 1318, and only 8 in 1335–6. Similarly, only a third of his hay was mown and carried by customary labour, and most of the lifting, carrying, and the second mowing were paid for by piece-work. Smithy work on the ploughs was done by a customary tenant holding by that service, and some weekworks were used in carriage and other tasks for the bishop,[45] but most works were sold. The cost of labour services may have contributed to their decline: the 37 ploughs from Stepney and 39¼ ploughs from Hackney working the bishop's fields during the winter each received 4d. in 1318, while in 1335–6 every man performing labour services during the harvest received ½d. in bread and ¼d. in cheese each day, amounting to 62s. 9½d. that year.

FARM OF THE DEMESNE. Between 1339 and 1362 the bishop ceased to grow crops, and let all his land except some meadow.[46] In 1362–3 385 a. in the arable fields were let in 32 parcels ranging from 2 a. to 30 a., two parcels for 6 years and the rest apparently by the year. Most of the land was let at 2s. 6d. an acre, although 45 a. fetched 3s., 82 a. fetched 2s., and 13 a. were let at 1s. Usually the tenants were local free and customary tenants, such as William Potter, the older and younger John Reyson, Salamon Walthey the beadle, and John Shoreditch of Hackney.[47]

Closes, probably former woodland which had been sown in 1336, were let as grazing in 1362. They included Combfield (52 a.) and Newland (30 a.), let together for 6 years at 40s. to Adam Chaungeour (Adam of St. Ives), citizen and merchant, holder of Huscarl manor, and Broomcroft and Northwood, let for 6 years. Of the demesne meadow, 20 a. were let for between 6s. 8d. and 8s. an acre; another 8¾ a. were let with Bullivant mill and 1½ a. with Crachlegh mill. Mowing for the bishop's own use at the manor house continued on 49½ a. using wage labour.[48] Between 1408 and 1439 hay ceased to be made for the bishop, although his animals grazed for part of the year in the kitchen garden and a garden called Derehawe. Grazing had ceased by 1465, when the closes next to the house and the grange were all let.[49]

Rents for the demesne arable and from arable

41 Below, ind.   42 Below, woods.
43 P.R.O., SC 6/1139/18; G.L.R.O., M79/LH/128/1/1.
44 Above.   45 Above.
46 P.R.O., E 154/1/47; ibid. SC 6/1139/18.

47 Ibid. SC 6/1139/18.
48 Ibid. SC 6/1139/18. Another 18½ a. were accounted for under Hackney man.
49 P.R.O., SC 6/1139/23–24; SC 6/1140/24.

on escheated holdings had fallen by 1383–4.[50] About £100, a very high amount, was in arrears and the rents for farms of land had been reduced or could not be fully collected. The farm of land, meadow, and pasture fetched some £20 less than in 1363 and although eventually increased by leasing for industrial use, leasing for agricultural use was not to be so profitable again. The farm of land in 1384 included fields let as pastures in 1362–3. Combfield and Newland were still let to Adam of St. Ives but as arable and at 45s. for the two, of which only 33s. 4d. had been collected; Adam also rented Southwood and Kechenfeld. Broomcroft and Northwood were let for the same amount as in 1362, but most of the other demesne parcels fetched about 6d. less an acre than in 1362. Lollesworth or Spitelshot was let as 43 a. to Sir John Philpot at 18d. an acre (only 12d. an acre collected), instead of three or more smaller parcels as in the 1360s, although the total number of parcels had risen to 38 with the subdivisions of some furlongs. Possibly it had proved difficult to find enough substantial tenants.

Low rents continued into the 15th century, except for Lollesworth, now let to the hospital of St. Mary without Bishopsgate at 1s. an acre in 1402 and 2s. in 1409. Typical rates were for land in the Hyde, which fetched 2s. 6d. in 1363 and only 1s. 4d. in 1465. Between 1439 and 1465, however, c. 160 a. of the demesne in that area were amalgamated, with the result that 30 parcels became 14, ranging from 4 a. to 30 a. Another change was in land use: in Southhyde, near Whitechapel Road, three parcels possibly totalling c. 18 a. were let for brickmaking at a total rent of £10 17s. 4d., helping to restore the income from the demesne to the level of 1362–3.[51]

Land in the marsh cut for hay fetched the highest rents, although they too fell. Two meadows along the Lea fetched 8s. and 6s. 8d. an acre respectively in 1362–3 but were 5s. and 6s. in 1383–4. Rent for the Wylde at Limehouse remained the same in 1383–4,[52] but had fallen slightly by 1395–6. Most rents for meadow had recovered slightly by 1398–9 and reached 7s. by 1401–2, but were only about 4s. an acre in 1464–5.[53] Pasture used solely for grazing fetched very little throughout the 14th and 15th centuries, despite the proximity of London.

Manorial income also came from escheated customary holdings: these were usually let from year to year until granted out again, but by the late 15th century some remained with the lord. They were surveyed in 1550 as part of the demesne, which then comprised 315¾ a. west of Cambridge Heath Road, enclosed into large parcels, and 195½ a. including the woods to the east around the manor house, a total of 511¼ a. accounting for the 14th-century demesne fields of 467 a., with c. 50 a. for woodland not given acreages in the medieval accounts. By 1550, however, there had been added, mostly from escheats, 41 a. in and near Eastfield, 17 a. south of Mile End Road, 30½ a. in Hackney excluding land by the Lea, and 90 a. unlocated.[54] Despite its fall in revenue from the late 14th century, Stepney generally made the third highest annual contribution to the bishop's temporal income after two Essex manors, and except in one account it always exceeded Fulham. An average of figures from 13 accounts between 1386 and c. 1480 shows Stepney providing just over 11 per cent of the bishopric's temporal income.[55]

Management by piecemeal or short-term leasing ended between 1518 and 1538 when the manor house and most of the demesne were divided between two leases granted for long terms. Small parts of the demesne had already been granted on long leases: in 1466 Richard Heyward, citizen and mercer, had been leased a messuage called the Bakehouse, a building called the stable and a 'hope' and wall at Limehouse with 1 r. of land nearby, for 99 years.[56] A lease of Spitelhope or Lollesworth (43 a.) to the hospital of St. Mary without Bishopsgate from 1498 for 99 years was sold to Robert Lorde in 1538 and held by Mr. Polsted in 1550; the freehold had been sold by the 1560s.[57] A 21-year lease from Bishop Tunstall of the manor and land around the manor house to Thomas Pilkington apparently became void on Tunstal's translation to Durham in 1530.[58]

In 1538 a 30-year lease known as the Bishopshall lease was made of the manor house and 97½ a. around it including Bishopswood, 92 a. called Broomfields, 26 a. in Eastfield, 47 a. in closes north and south of Mile End Road including Cordwains in Limehouse, Pawne farm and other meadow in Hackney totalling 67¾ a., together with parcage and poundage of the manor. The lessee was William Goddard of Shoreditch, merchant of the Staple of Calais, who at his death in 1548 also held the Bishopsfields lease, expiring in 1562, of the demesne fields between Shoreditch and Cambridge Heath Road, containing 268¾ a., with another 81 a. probably nearby.[59] Under his will[60] the Bishopshall lease had been sold by 1550, to Sir Ralph Warren, while the Bishopsfields lease was held by Goddard's widow and her husband Erasmus Leveningham. The rest of the demesne, comprising holdings of 11 a. and 40 a. meadow by the Lea in Hackney, the dusthills in Limehouse, Goodluckhope and other beds of reeds and

[50] Only 8 full accts. survive between 1362–3 and 1517–18: 2 others are defective and 2 have only totals. The following have been used for this section: Guildhall MS. 25403/3 (1383–4); P.R.O., SC 6/1139/20 (1391–2); SC 6/1139/21 (1398–9); SC 6/1139/22 (1401–2); SC 6/1139/23 (1408–9); SC 6/1139/24 (1438–9); SC 6/1140/24 (1464–5).
[51] Below, ind.
[52] P.R.O., SC 6/1139/18; Guildhall MS. 25403/3.
[53] Guildhall MS. 25403/5; P.R.O., SC 6/1139/21–22; SC 6/1140/24.

[54] G.L.R.O., M79/LH/128/1/1, correcting transcript in Robinson, *Hackney*, i. 325–43, which has errors and omissions.
[55] Based on figs. in Taylor, 'Estates of Bishopric of Lond.', 408.
[56] P.R.O., PROB 11/5 (P.C.C. 23 Godyn).
[57] B.L. Add. Chs. 209–210; G.L.R.O., M79/LH/128/1/1; above, manors (Stepney).
[58] P.R.O., C 1/728/11–13; below, local govt. (man. govt.).
[59] G.L.R.O., M93/206; M79/LH/128/1/1.
[60] P.R.O., PROB 11/32 (P.C.C. 5 Populwell), f. 36.

osiers, three holdings totalling 472 a. in Stepney marsh, and 164 a. called the demesne of Hackney, were all let for terms expiring between 1563 and 1590. In 1550 only the two tileyards were still let on annual tenancies.[61]

A second lease of Bishopshall, for 80 years from 1568 at the same rent, was granted by the bishop in 1546 to Thomas Parsons alias Fairbrother.[62] Parsons assigned his interest to Thomas Wilson in 1564. By c. 1582 John Fuller held a lease for years of Bishopshall,[63] which he left to his wife in 1592:[64] it may, however, have been only a sublease, as a Bishopshall lease was sold by Wilson's widow Susan to Philip Wilson and was thereafter assigned to Simon Jackson and his wife Elizabeth and Thomas Coleman and his wife Margaret; its assignment by the latter to William Smyth in 1643 was part of the sales to pay the earl of Cleveland's debts. A 21-year lease from 1648, granted by the earl in 1636 to Philip Wilson, was also surrendered to Smyth in 1643.[65]

A reversion of the Bishopsfields lease was granted in 1547 by the bishop to Thomas Parsons and William Mountjoy for 90 years from 1562 at a revised rent.[66] The lease was held by John Heath in 1582[67] and by Lady Bennet in 1638–9 and 1642, when some parcels sublet to the earl of Manchester and Mr. Smith (probably William Smyth) had been built on.[68]

By 1514–15 the bishop received income, £21 7s. 3d. in 1535, from leases of Stepney marsh, which was accounted for separately from the manor.[69] That land, in the Isle of Dogs, had been flooded in 1448 and drained by Bishop Thomas Kemp (1448–89) c. 1488. Kemp held 282 a. as part of the manor, a further 115 a. for 94 years and formerly belonging to his free tenants, and 85 a. conveyed by the abbot of St. Mary Graces and others. The bishop let the 115 a. in 1488 for 40 years to William Marowe, of Stepney, and seven others of Stepney, London, and Greenwich. When their land was again flooded, before 1524, the lessees enclosed and recovered it. As part of the bishop's personal estate, the remainder of the 94-year term was sold by his executors in 1521 to William Goddard, together with the rent due for the residue of the 40 years, and in 1524 Goddard sold his interest to John Botulph of London.[70] The rent agreed in 1488 was unchanged in 1550.[71] In 1588 it was said that in 1512 the abbot of St. Mary Graces had let c. 8 a. of flooded land for 80 years to Bishop Richard Fitzjames, who had let it with c. 130 a. called the Isle of Dogs, Saunders nase, and the drunken dock to Thomas Knight, brewer, of London for 80 years.[72] The acreages were probably higher, as Knight may have been holding all of the bishop's 282 a. in Stepney marsh by 1517–18.[73] After Knight's death c. 1559, the lease was surrendered to the lord.[74]

Another 75 a. adjoining the marsh was let to Thomas Samme and John Etgose by 1517–18; the lease had 34 years to run in 1550.[75] The Wete marsh, 40 a. reclaimed by Kemp, was let by St. Mary Graces c. 1529, having been flooded again.[76]

TENANTS' PRODUCTION. In 1086 the husbandmen in the vill held arable for 22 ploughteams, all under cultivation, with meadow to support all the teams and pasture for the cattle of the vill with a surplus valued at 15s. By the 14th century, though a little arable belonging to free and customary tenants lay among the demesne north of Whitechapel Road, most lay in open fields covering the rest of the parish except where watercourses were bordered by meadow.[77] Reclaimed land such as Walmarsh (including furlongs called Landmarsh, Middlemarsh and Southcroft), Stepney marsh (including furlongs called Summerleas, Hedwynesfield, Tunamcroft, Newland, and Stowland), and East marsh were open-field arable c. 1200.[78] A marsh called the Wylde, where 6 a. of arable were granted by the bishop in the 1190s, was probably the Wylde near Limehouse that was meadow and pasture in the 14th century.[79]

Individuals' holdings were very irregularly spread between different fields c. 1380.[80] Land of freehold estates and customary tenants lay intermixed in small strips in the open fields c. 1400, although there were some closes and blocks of strips.[81] The consolidation of strips was a gradual process, through purchases and exchanges, as was the piecemeal enclosure of parcels. In 1331 the Crown licensed a freeholder to exchange 24 a. with the bishop,[82] and in 1380 two prominent freeholders, John Hadley and Adam of St. Ives, exchanged 12 a.[83] Sir Henry Colet purchased copyhold parcels, some already in closes within the open fields, from several holders in the late 15th century to form an estate of three large blocks.[84] Such practices eventually created the field pattern shown in the first plan of the parish in 1703.[85]

Field names from c. 1200 do not indicate any unified system of communal management or of rotation within the manor or parish. The only reference to grazing on the stubble concerned

[61] G.L.R.O., M79/LH/128/1/1; above, Stepney manor; below, ind.   [62] P.R.O., C 3/453/41.
[63] B.L. Eg. MS. 3006, ff. 1–2; P.R.O., SP 12/152, no. 49.
[64] P.R.O., PROB 11/79 (P.C.C. 46 Harington), f. 355.
[65] G.L.R.O., M93/208; M93/158, f. 7.
[66] Ibid. M93/158, f. 13.
[67] P.R.O., SP 12/152, no. 49.
[68] Ibid. SP 16/540, no. 153; B.L. Add. MS. 22253, f. 1–3d.; above, manors (Stepney).
[69] Taylor, 'Estates of Bishopric of Lond.', 408; Valor Eccl. (Rec. Com.), i. 356.
[70] P.R.O., SP 1/32, pp. 1–9.
[71] G.L.R.O., M79/LH/128/1/1.
[72] P.R.O., C 3/230/60.
[73] Guildhall MS. 10123/2: given as Ric. Knyght;

G.L.R.O., M79/LH/128/1/1.
[74] P.R.O., C 3/230/60; C 142/204, no. 155(2).
[75] Guildhall MS. 10123/2; G.L.R.O., M79/LH/128/1/1.
[76] L. & P. Hen. VIII, iv (3), p. 2366; xv, pp. 560–1.
[77] See fig. 5.
[78] Dugdale, Hist. Imbanking, 69–70; P.R.O., E 40/2601; E 40/2543–5; E 40/7317–19; E 40/7233; B.L. Cott. MS. Tib. C. v, f. 158; Guildhall MS. 25516, f. 40.
[79] Above.
[80] Guildhall MS. 25422.
[81] P.R.O., SC 12/11/31.
[82] Cal. Pat. 1330–4, 52.
[83] P.R.O., C 146/2777.
[84] Above, manors (Mercers').
[85] Gascoyne, Map.

the demesne and the lord's stock,[86] probably because extensive pasture on the waste and the meadows reduced the need for communal grazing on the arable.

Arable farming was probably dominant throughout the Middle Ages for both free and customary landholders. Evidence, however, is sparse: only 4 out of c. 120 commissary court wills between 1374 and 1500 mention agricultural produce or stock.[87] More frequent references to land do not indicate who was working it or how. The 80 a. demesne arable of Pomfret manor in the Isle of Dogs, which was owed harvest works in 1323, had by 1362 been abandoned to sheep grazing, but perhaps only because the manor house was no longer occupied.[88] Tenants living in the Marsh continued to cultivate arable until the floods of the mid 15th century: the will of William Potter of the marsh in 1380 mentioned 2 a. of wheat, 2 oxen, 1 horse, and 2 plough-teams in 1380.[89] Tenants of Stepney, Poplar, and Pomfret lost their holdings in the floods, which allowed a radical changed in land ownership and use: after the Isle of Dogs was reclaimed in 1488 pasturing became the dominant agriculture there.[90]

In 1364 Walter Page had freehold, leasehold, and customary land in Stepney, of which 7 a. were sown with wheat, 7 a. with barley, 8¾ a. with tares, and 14 a. sown with mixed wheat and barley; 2 a. were meadow and 3 a. fallow.[91] In 1383 c. 5 a. of pasture in northern Poplar were let to a Londoner, who in 1385 sublet it at a rent which suggests that it was mown for hay, rather than used merely for grazing.[92] Adam of St. Ives in 1393 had c. 50 a. of wheat, 23 a. of barley, and 16 a. of beans, peas, and vetches on 126 a. of arable in northern Poplar and Limehouse, but had only 16 a. of pasture and 5 a. of meadow. When the land was let in 1401–2 the meadow and pasture were let for between 2s. 6d. and 3s. an acre.[93]

Gardens at the manor house probably produced only top fruit as they were being grazed by stock; the fruit was valued at 4s. in 1362–3, and ½ a. formerly customary arable was let by the lord as garden for 4s.[94] Freehold messuages in Mile End Road east of White Horse Lane included a garden in 1325.[95] In 1383–4 the farm of a garden in Haliwellstreet once held by Gilbert at Stone was let for a reduced rent of 6s. 8d. to John Sperhankes, whose garden was in the hands of the lord in 1401–2 and let for the same rent to Richard Loxley, spicer of London.[96]

Another garden in Haliwellstreet was granted to Adam Kareswell in 1385 for a new customary rent.[97] The abbey of St. Mary Graces paid an unchanged rent for Champeneys garden, near Wapping, c. 1380 and c. 1400, as did the abbey of St. Osyth (Essex) for a garden next to Whitechapel church.[98] John Hadley also had a garden near the latter, part of his freehold estates,[99] and in 1464–5 2 a. of demesne in Southhyde north of Whitechapel Road were let as a garden.[1] Three gardens lay at the east end of Poplar street c. 1400, held by customary tenants of Stepney manor.[2]

MEDIEVAL MILLS.[3] In 1086 the bishop held in demesne four mills which rendered £4 15s. 8d. In addition a mill on the Thames which had been held by Doding in 1066 was held by Hugh de Berners, a mill on the Lea which had been built since 1066 was held by Edmund son of Algot', and an unlocated mill worth 20s. was held by Alwin son of Brihtmar, as in 1066.[4]

In 1228–9 the bishop received, besides issues from the mill of Hackney, rent for a fulling mill and a water mill in Stepney. In 1243 five mills paid him rent, including one held for a rent of assize and one held at fee farm by Ralph Alwy' (possibly for Aswy), and in 1264 three mills were held at farm.[5] In 1313 only rents from a water mill and a windmill were recorded.[6]

In the 14th century the bishop had two demesne water mills. Bolyfan (Bullivant) mill was let in 1318, 1335–6,[7] 1362–3,[8] and, as a fulling mill, in 1383–4 and 1391–2.[9] It was let on different terms by 1395–6 and was being repaired in 1401–2.[10] In 1438–9 rent was recorded from a fishery at the mill and meadows near it but not from the mill itself.[11] The mill presumably stood on the watercourse in Bow and Hackney called Bullivant river in 1550, possibly where it joined the Lea on the parish boundary.[12]

Crachehegh or Crachegg fulling mill paid rent to the bishop in 1318 and was repaired. In 1335–6 only part of the rent was received, because of disrepair, and a new waterwheel was put in.[13] The mill was not mentioned in 1362–3 and presumably had been alienated or abandoned; in 1550 a parcel of meadow, probably in Hackney, was called Crathe's mill.[14]

Land at the windmill in 1272 was bounded by the later Ratcliff Highway and Cable Street, in Wapping-Stepney, probably the bishop's

86 Above.
87 Guildhall MSS. 9171/1, ff. 36v. (1376), 71 (1380), 160 (1388); 9171/2, f. 26 (1403).
88 Above, manors (Pomfret).
89 Guildhall MS. 9171/1, f. 71.   90 Above.
91 P.R.O., C 145/190, no. 11.
92 *Year Bk. 12 Ric. II* (Ames Foundation), 190–2.
93 P.R.O., C 131/43, no. 10; ibid. SC 6/1139/22.
94 Guildhall MS. 25403/2; P.R.O., SC 6/1139/18.
95 Above, manors (Savoy).
96 Guildhall MS. 25403/3; P.R.O., SC 6/1139/22, SC 6/1139/24.
97 P.R.O., SC 6/1139/21.
98 Guildhall MS. 25422; P.R.O., SC 12/11/31.
99 Above, manors (Cobhams).

1 P.R.O., SC 6/1140/24.
2 Ibid. SC 12/11/31, f. 16v.
3 Later hist. of most mills or sites reserved for treatment under ests. or ind. in individual hamlets.
4 *V.C.H. Mdx.* i. 120–1; below.
5 P.R.O., E 372/72, m. 10d.; E 352/36, m. 5; E 352/57, [m. 13d.].   6 Guildhall MS. 25426.
7 Guildhall MSS. 25403/1–2.
8 P.R.O., SC 6/1139/18.
9 Guildhall MS. 25403/3; P.R.O., SC 6/1139/20.
10 Guildhall MS. 25403/5; P.R.O., SC 6/1139/21–2.
11 P.R.O., SC 6/1139/24; below, fisheries.
12 G.L.R.O., M79/LH/128/1/1.
13 Guildhall MSS. 25403/1–2.
14 P.R.O., SC 6/1139/18; G.L.R.O., M79/LH/128/1/1.

windmill that lay next to land in the upper fields of Shadwell manor in the late 13th century.[15] The bishop's windmill was let in 1313 but in 1318 it was in ruins and without a miller.[16] In 1335–6 the windmill was let and part of the mill was renewed.[17] It was again in ruins and could not be let in 1362–3, and was so recorded thereafter until last mentioned in 1395–6.[18] In 1386 an acre between two highways in Wapping-Stepney lay next to Brendmill (Burnt mill) hill, whose name survived in 1427[19] and may have been that of the ruined windmill. Another windmill seems to have stood in the demesne fields (north of the Colchester road) where a furlong was called Windmillshot in 1318,[20] and a close was called Millfield in 1362.[21]

Pomfret manor had a windmill in 1322, valued at 1 mark.[22] Simon Oliver conveyed a freehold windmill in Stepney to Richard of Croydon, citizen and fishmonger, before 1349.[23]

The mill held by Doding in 1066 and Hugh de Berners in 1086 may have stood in the parish of St. Botolph Aldgate, where Dudding pond lay and where Sir Ralph de Berners held two mills in 1274–5. It was taken into the site for the hospital of St. Katharine.[24]

In 1218 St. Paul's granted Wapping mill with the right to grind corn for the common bakehouse of the chapter to Terricus (Theodoricus) son of Edrich of Aldgate and his heirs to hold freely for 5 marks a year,[25] which was reduced in 1231 to 4 marks a year in return for surrendering the right to grind the chapter's corn.[26] Terricus then granted a moiety to his brother Adam but by 1239 they had sold the mills to the hospital of St. Thomas of Acre, which was to pay the rent to the dean and chapter and 1 lb. of pepper to Terricus and his heirs.[27] In July 1239 Terricus's widow Florence claimed a third of the mills as dower.[28]

In 1269 the hospital granted their mills at Wapping to Richard of Ewell and his wife Maud, but in 1274–5 Richard of Ewell granted the property back to the hospital to endow a chantry. Richard's widow Aubrey and her husband Ralph de Munchensy recovered a third as dower, and Richard's son Richard of Ewell confirmed the

grant to the hospital in 1286.[29] The property continued in the possession of the hospital until the Dissolution when it passed to the Crown. The mill house had a wharf and dock adjoining in 1537, and seems to have been used as a brewhouse, as was another house on the property.[30]

Despite the grant to the hospital, one mill at Wapping was granted with the manor of Ewell, both held for life by Aubrey wife of Ralph de Munchensy, by Eleanor daughter of Richard de Ewell to her nephew Richard son of John Neyrnuit in 1292. This mill continued in the Neyrnuit family until c. 1400, but may have passed to the hospital, as its later history is unknown.[31]

Shadwell mill was among purchases confirmed between 1189 and 1198 by Bishop Richard Fitzneal to Brice of Stepney,[32] who had probably obtained the mill on his marriage to Catherine, daughter of Salomon of Stepney. Brice's estate passed to his nephew Benet of Maneton, who in 1222 as Benet of Stepney sought to recover the mill from Brice's widow Catherine and her husband Adam le Despenser. At about that time Benet sold the estate and mill to Bishop Eustace of Fauconberg (d. 1228), to whom in 1223 Catherine's brother Daniel quitclaimed the mill.[33] The bishop left Shadwell, including the mill, to the dean and chapter of St. Paul's. A rental of before 1285 gave no income from the farm of the mill.[34] When Shadwell manor was farmed to Richard the bishop's beadle in 1334, the mill was in ruins and the watercourse dried up.[35] In 1652 the mill existed but was out of use. It lay by the Thames among extensive tidal channels.[36]

The Cressemills or Crash mills on the Thames near East Smithfield existed by 1233, when a judgement divided the tithes from the mills and its adjoining premises between the churches of Stepney and St. Botolph Aldgate.[37] John Elylond and his wife Clemence granted rent from the Crash mills in 1265.[38] The mills were acquired by Sir John Pulteney, lord of Poplar manor; he granted them with the manor in 1347 to Humphrey de Bohun, earl of Hereford and Essex, who leased them back for 50 years. The mills were held of the bishop for fealty only.[39]

15 B.L. Cott. MS. Tib. C. v, f. 159v.; Guildhall MS. 25516, f. 40.
16 Guildhall MSS. 25426; 25403/1.
17 Ibid. 25403/2.
18 P.R.O., SC 6/1139/18, 20; Guildhall MSS. 25403/3, 5.
19 P.R.O., C 146/2665; B.L. Cott. MS. Tib. C. v, f. 161v.
20 Guildhall MS. 25403/1.
21 P.R.O., SC 6/1139/18; see fig. 5.
22 P.R.O., C 134/75, no. 10.
23 Ibid. C 146/5734.
24 V.C.H. Mdx. i. 120; Cart. of Holy Trinity Aldgate (Lond. Rec. Soc. vii), 167, 195; Rot. Hund. i. 413.
25 B.L. Cott. MS. Tib. C. v, f. 152; above, manors (St. Thos. of Acre).
26 Bracton's Note Bk. ed. Maitland, ii. 379–80; Guildhall MS. 25501, f. 34v.; P.R.O., CP 25/1/146/8, no. 85; Early Charters of Cath. Ch. of St. Paul (Camden 3rd ser. lviii), pp. 256–7.

27 B.L. Cott. MS. Tib. C. v, ff. 153–54v.; Guildhall MS. 25501, f. 34v.
28 Cur Reg. R. xvi. 153.
29 B.L. Cott. MS. Tib. C. v, ff. 160v.–62; V.C.H. Lond. i. 49; above, manors (St. Thos. of Acre).
30 P.R.O., SC 6/Hen. VIII/2396, m. 8d.; L. & P. Hen. VIII, xix (2), p. 77.
31 Above, manors (Ewell).
32 Guildhall MS. 25516, f. 38; above, manors (Shadwell).
33 Above, manors (Salomon; Shadwell).
34 Guildhall MS. 255126, f. 40.
35 Ibid. 25164.
36 Bodl. Gough Maps 17, f. 26, and Trial between Thos. Neale and Lady Theodosia Ivie (1696) have plans of Shadwell showing the watercourses.
37 P.R.O., E 40/14033.
38 Ibid. CP 25/1/147/22, no. 439.
39 Ibid. C 54/181, m. 29d.; ibid. C 135/95, no. 13. Pulteney also held Algodsmill: below.

They were settled by Pulteney's son Sir William in 1362[40] and passed with Poplar manor to the abbey of St. Mary Graces, which kept them until the Dissolution.[41] In 1535 the mills were farmed out for a rent of flour.[42] In the 1530s the site, between Nightingale Lane and Wapping marsh, included the newly-built Katharine Wheel and a wharf, six other tenements and a garden, the Swan's Nest or Hermitage with a wharf, two gardens and a pond, and Crashmills meadow; the mills themselves were not mentioned.[43]

On the Lea the mill held by Edmund son of Algot' in 1086[44] was evidently the fuller's water mill called Algodsmill. Abandoned because of lack of water, it was restored by Sir John Pulteney by means of a trench from the river. It was part of the estates held by Humphrey de Bohun, earl of Hereford and Essex, in 1355[45] and was presumably the fulling mill among the appurtenances of Poplar manor settled by Sir William Pulteney.[46] It passed to St. Mary Graces[47] but was not specified among the abbey's property in the 1530s.[48]

Old Ford mill was granted by Lettice, wife of William le Blund of Stepney, to the priory of St. Helen, Bishopsgate. In 1230 William confirmed that after her death a moiety that they held would revert to St. Helen's.[49] Its later history is uncertain, as is that of a water mill at Old Ford belonging to the priory of St. Bartholomew, West Smithfield, which obstructed the Lea in 1355.[50] John Henley, clerk, leased a water mill at Old Ford to Adam Smale, baker of Stratford Bow, who blocked the Lea adjoining the mill with turves and water-gates, flooding neighbouring meadows in 1394.[51] It is possible that these are all the same mill.

In 1287 a water mill at Stratford Bow called Rothleys mill was released by John son of Sir William de Chishull to Ralph Crepyn of Aldgate.[52] In 1303 Ralph granted to Walter of Gloucester, his son, 2 mills and other property in Stepney, Hackney, Stratford, and elsewhere.[53]

The Land mills were evidently the water mills which belonged to Sir Stephen Ashewy and were excluded from his release of the rest of his Stepney estate in 1324.[54] In 1412 two water mills in Stratford Bow called Land mills were quit-claimed by Henry, Lord Scrope of Masham, to John Lynne of Stratford Bow,[55] who in 1391 had been described as a baker.[56] By 1579 the mills formed a capital messuage called the Land Mills, held by Henry Alington in right of his wife Anne, widow of Richard Elkyn.[57] Early in the 17th century Monks mead, formerly belonging to the dean and chapter of Westminster, was claimed as part of the Land mills.[58]

A third of two mills in Stratford Bow was granted in 1353 by William of Causton, citizen and mercer, and his wife Christian to William of Tuddenham, citizen and mercer, and his wife Christine, being Christian's dower.[59] The mill was used for grinding corn in 1360.[60]

Westminster abbey is said to have purchased a mill in Stratford (Essex) from Robert Alleyn, citizen and fishmonger, in 1364–5, and the reversion of a mill and 12 a. from him in 1375–6. In 1392 Robert Alleyn and his wife Maud were granted a corrody in return for the mill at Stratford,[61] perhaps the mill with 35 a. in Stepney and Stratford Bow granted by Alleyn to feoffees in 1371 and quitclaimed to him and Maud in 1379.[62] An estate in Stepney which was assigned to the abbey's chamberlain in 1381 has been identified as the mill at Stratford (Essex) given by Ailnod of London.[63] The abbey's mill or mills may have been in the part of Stepney manor that lay in West Ham (Essex). Two water mills and land in Stepney, granted in 1520 by Lancelot Lyle and his wife Alice to William Knight, lay partly in Essex and so presumably on the Lea.[64]

Unlocated mills included one claimed by the bishop in 1228 from Hugh le Fraunceys, whose grant by a previous bishop had not received the assent of the chapter.[65] If he succeeded the bishop, who was establishing overlordship, probably made a new grant to Franceys.[66] In 1233 Henry Bucointe successfully claimed from Peter son of Roger two mills and appurtenances in Stepney.[67]

Robert de Mordon bought a mill from Edmund Crepyn in 1334. It was regained by Robert's daughter Mary in 1348 after the death of his brother William, who had taken possession illegally. In 1348 it was held with 5 a. of the dean and chapter of St. Paul's by fealty and a small rent, and was in bad condition.[68]

40 P.R.O., C 54/200, m. 20d.
41 Above, manors (Poplar).
42 *Valor Eccl.* (Rec. Com.), i. 398–9.
43 P.R.O., SC 12/11/13; ibid. SC 6/Hen. VIII/2396, m. 42; ibid. C 66/723, m. 2; *Plan, c. 1590, of area lying E. of St. Katharine's Hosp. (now Dock)* (Lond. Topog. Soc. Publ. no. 61).
44 *V.C.H. Mdx.* i. 121.
45 *Cal. Inq. Misc.* iii, p. 70; above.
46 P.R.O., C 54/200, m. 20d.; ibid. CP 25/1/288/47, no. 627.
47 *Cal. Close 1374–7*, 107–8; P.R.O., C 54/268, m. 15; above, manors (Poplar).
48 P.R.O., SC 6/Hen. VIII/2396, m. 49.
49 *Cur. Reg. R.* xiv. 68.
50 *Cal. Inq. Misc.* iii, p. 71.
51 *Public Works in Med. Law,* ii (Selden Soc. xl), p. 44.
52 *Abbrev. Plac.* (Rec. Com.), 212.
53 P.R.O., CP 25/1/148/36, no. 298.
54 Above, manors (Ashwyes).

55 *Cal. Close 1409–13*, 417–18.
56 *Cal. Anct. D.* vi, C 4915.
57 P.R.O., C 142/268, no. 125. Later hist. reserved for Stratford Bow.
58 P.R.O., C 78/203, no. 10; below for Westm. abbey's mill.
59 P.R.O., CP 25/1/150/65, no. 309.
60 *Munimenta Gildhallae Londoniensis,* iii, *Liber Albus,* 421.
61 B. F. Harvey, *Westm. Abbey and its Estates in the Middle Ages* (1977), 424.
62 P.R.O., CP 25/1/151/72, no. 485; *Cal. Close, 1377–81,* 243.
63 J. A. Robinson, *Gilb. Crispin, Abbot of Westm.* (1911), 45; *V.C.H. Essex,* vi. 89.
64 P.R.O., CP 25/2/51/362/12 Hen.VIII/East.
65 *Cur. Reg. R.* xiii. 123.
66 Above, agric.
67 *Cur. Reg. R.* xv. 81; P.R.O., CP 25/1/146/10, no. 127.
68 *Cal. Inq. Misc.* iii, p. 3.

WOODS. In 1086 the bishop's extensive demesne woods fed 500 pigs and were worth 40s.; his tenants' woods were probably not in what became Stepney parish.[69] The indeterminate boundary with Hackney near the manor house and the nature of nearby closes in the 14th century suggest that woodland stretched eastward from Bethnal green in 1086 and had been divided, enclosed, and partly cleared by 1318. Such closes may have included Combfield, Newland, Woodland, and Redding: although sometimes used for crops, they differed from the other arable in having no subdivisions; all, except for Redding, were let as whole units and not subdivided.[70] Mention of the bishop's woods east of Bethnal green before 1285 suggests that the woodland may have reached farther south, over the area later called Broomfields.[71]

In 1291 the bishop was granted free warren, probably as a preliminary to emparking, and in 1292 his petition to enclose two woods near his manor house for deer and other game was seen as a threat by Londoners to their traditional hunting rights.[72] By 1335 the woods around the manor house were used for grazing.[73] In 1363 the grazing in Southwood was let with 22 a. called Kechenfeld nearby, while Northwood was let with Broomcroft, which separated the two woods, as a pasture for 6 years.[74] The acreage of the woods probably did not exceed 50 a. by this time: they were included in 97 a. let with the manor house in 1550,[75] but all the former demesne to the east amounted to only 48 a. in 1703.[76] In 1539 the manor was said to include 26 a. of woodland, with little timber left on it.[77]

FISHERIES. The bishop received rent for the farm of a fishery in 1263–4.[78] His fishery at Bullivant was let in 1313, for 1 mark a year, and in 1318.[79] The rent remained 13s. 4d. in 1335–6 and 1362–3,[80] but from 1383 to 1399 that sum was accounted for by the beadle of Hackney and from 1402 it was not recorded.[81] By 1439, however, a new farm of £1 18s. 4d. was accounted for under Stepney for a fishery at Bullivant mill, let to the widow of Richard Colliers with ½ a. at Algoryshyde.[82] In 1464–5 £2 6s. 8d. was received for the fishery at Bullivant mill with Lockacre and the hopes containing ½ a., let to Laurence Fanne. The bishop also received 40s. for all the fishing and fowling in Stepney marsh, which had been flooded 15 years previously, together with

a moiety of the reeds, let for 10 years to Richard Daniel and Thomas Shipman.[83] The fishery at Bullivant mill was later let to Sir John Shaa and by 1518 to Sir John Raynesford at the same rent as in 1464–5.[84] In 1550 it was included in the Bishopshall lease.[85] The royalty of fishing on the Lea was valued at £5 in 1642 and 1652.[86]

INDUSTRY TO c. 1550. Bakers supplied London by the early 13th century, paying city tolls for carrying bread from Bromley and Stepney;[87] in 1356 the City imposed a higher toll on carts carrying wheat or flour from Stratford Bow than on other carts.[88] Some millers at Stratford may also have been bakers: John Lynne, holder of Land mills, was so described in 1391.[89]

By the 15th century bakers and brewers of Ratcliff and Limehouse probably also helped to victual ships. Together with men in the lime, brick, and ironwork industries (below), they were often among Stepney's leading inhabitants, with substantial landholdings and financial and family connections with Londoners. Roger Clerk, baker, rented grazing along the river wall at Limehouse in 1391–2,[90] and bakers at Limehouse made wills in 1430 (Simon Cok), 1455 (William Canon), and 1472 (John Austyn), as did Thomas Aubrey of Stepney in 1440.[91] Early 16th-century bakers from Limehouse, Ratcliff, and Stratford Bow supplied royal ships refitting in the Thames.[92]

Brewers making wills included Vincent Syward of Limehouse in 1419 and William Brigge of Stepney, who had pledged his goods as security to citizens of London, in 1449.[93] John Debenham of Limehouse was mentioned in 1430 and 1450, William Peste of Stepney in 1456, and Thomas Mott of in 1449, possibly the Thomas Mote of Ratcliff who died in 1461.[94] John Allardson of Ratcliff, who paid a subsidy as an alien in the 1450s, pledged goods in 1461, and Thomas Mason of Stepney, with two others, was granted the goods of a London cooper as security in 1475.[95] William Potter, priest and member of a Poplar family, left a brewhouse to Nicholas Salle or Sawlle of Stepney and his wife Alice with land in Ratcliff in 1487; in 1496 Salle left a brewery called the Cherker and a brewery at Newbrigge, besides land in Poplar and Ratcliff.[96]

In 1549 meat for the king's ships at Ratcliff was supplied from 1,017 oxen brought there

69 V.C.H. Mdx. i. 120.
70 Guildhall MSS. 25403/1–2; P.R.O., SC 6/1139/18, 20–1.
71 P.R.O., C 146/2771; above, manors (Trentemars).
72 Taylor, 'Estates of Bishopric of Lond.' 180–1.
73 Guildhall MS. 25403/2.
74 P.R.O., SC 6/1139/18.
75 G.L.R.O., M79/LH/128/1/1.
76 Fig. 5; Gascoyne, Map.
77 P.R.O., SP 1/153, f. 172d. Later hist. of site of the manorial woods treated below, Bethnal Green, ests.
78 P.R.O., E 352/57 [m. 13d.].
79 Guildhall MSS. 25426; 25403/1.
80 Ibid. 25403/2; P.R.O., SC 6/1139/18.
81 Guildhall MSS. 25403/3, 5; P.R.O., SC 6/1139/21–2.
82 P.R.O., SC 6/1139/24.   83 Ibid. SC 6/1140/24.
84 Guildhall MS. 10123/2, f. 40d.

85 G.L.R.O., M79/LH/128/1/1; above, agric.
86 B.L. Add. MS. 22253, f. 16; G.L.R.O., M93/157.
87 Munimenta Gildhallae Londoniensis, i, Liber Albus, 232.
88 McDonnell, Med. Lond. Suburbs, 77, where refs. should be treated with caution.
89 Cal. Anct. D. vi, C 4915; above, mills.
90 P.R.O., SC 6/1139/20.
91 Guildhall MSS. 9171/3, f. 269; 9171/5, f. 168v.; 9171/6, f. 128v.; P.R.O., PROB 11/3 (P.C.C. 28 Luffenham).
92 P.R.O., E 36/11.
93 Guildhall MSS. 9171/3, f. 33v.; 9171/4, f. 252; Cal. Close, 1447–54, 29.
94 Guildhall MSS. 9171/3, f. 269; 9171/4, f. 254; 9171/5, ff. 86, 189, 352v.; Cal. Close, 1447–54, 67.
95 Cal. Close, 1461–8, 62; 1468–76, 417; P.R.O., E 179/235/57.
96 Guildhall MSS. 9171/7, f. 104; 9171/8, f. 117v.

from outside London. The miller of Ratcliff (probably of Shadwell mill) let a close near the slaughterhouse to hold the animals, and men and buildings were hired for the slaughter and salting. Although the scale of the operation exceeded Ratcliff's own resources, some local facilities already existed for such provisioning.[97]

Lime used on the manor for building repairs in 1335 came from the 300 sacks received by the bishop each year as render for the limekilns near the later Limehouse dock.[98] In 1362–3 the manor received only 25 sacks and bought 42 more.[99] In 1398–9 the manor received 50 sacks of lime from the kiln of one tenant, and 25 each from the kilns of another four.[1] The same renders were paid in 1401–2 and 1408–9.[2] Money rents of 8d. or less were also paid c. 1400 for the kilns of four tenants.[3] The tenants of the limekilns included in the 14th century members of the Dike, Golding, atte Hatch, and Kent families, and William Edwin and Thomas Warris, who made wills in 1404 and 1443 respectively.[4] Several also held customary land or leased demesne in Limehouse, including Peter atte Hatch (d. 1405), who was beadle of Stepney in 1391–2.[5] In 1464–5 the five kilns rendered 25 sacks each and all the lime was sold.[6] The same render was due in 1517–18, when two kilns formerly in the tenure of Edmund Ratcliff were unlet.[7]

Richard Etgose or Etgoos, yeoman, had at his death in 1503 an extensive limeburning operation at Limehouse and Greenhithe (Kent). In 1491 he had taken a 99-year lease of the Dusthill, with a hope enclosed from the marsh, where he built a new house and had a chalk kiln, a wharf, and a chalk boat called the *Katharine*. He also had four tenements adjoining his dwelling with a tanhouse, a beerhouse, and 28 a. of marsh, besides four copyhold tenements and a wharf and garden which he had rebuilt into six or eight tenements, another kiln at Greenhithe, a little arable, and 32 a. in the marsh let to butchers.[8] The property all passed to his eldest son John, also a brickmaker, and then to John's eldest child Elizabeth and her husband Richard Driver (d. 1549). Driver left his limekiln and other property to his younger son George.[9] The property seems to have included two kilns and two wharves that had belonged to St. Bartholomew's hospital and had been granted to the mayor and corporation of London in

1547;[10] those kilns may have derived from a messuage by the limekiln in Stepney, late of John Elmeshale, clerk, in 1399.[11]

In 1524 Richard Driver, John Etgose, and another limeburner were accused of trying to fix the price of lime sold in London. A new rate was agreed but in 1526 they refused the prices which the City set.[12] John Crow supplied 6 loads of lime to Henry VIII.[13] Other limeburners at Limehouse included Richard Deacon, who made a will in 1563, William Becket (fl. 1566), and William Harman (fl. 1593).[14]

A licence to dig clay for tiles was granted in 1366 by John, son and heir of Stephen of Cambridge, holder of a moiety of Ewell manor, to John Wendover, citizen, possibly the holder of the other moiety. By c. 1400 the manor was sometimes also called Tilehouse, and in 1401–2 the holder was summoned for not cleaning ditches at the tilehouse.[15] Brickmaking seems to have been concentrated in Whitechapel. Between 1401 and 1409 ½ a. of demesne in Southhyde near Whitechapel Lane, north of Whitechapel Road, was let for a 'lompette', presumably for making tiles or bricks, at a very high rent,[16] and the Whitechapel Lane of 1409 may have been that called Brick Lane by 1485.[17] In 1438–9 the demesne fields between Shoreditch and Cambridge Heath Road included both 'lompettes' and 'tilehouseland',[18] and by 1465 all but 2 a. of 25 a. in Southhyde were let for brickmaking to John Caunton, John Kendall, and Henry Etwell, the first of whom described himself as a brickmaker in his will proved in 1476.[19] Nicholas Fakys, brickmaker of Whitechapel, made bequests of bricks in his will c. 1454.[20] The lease of 18 a. in Spitalfield to Thomas Rooke at a high rent in 1464–5 suggests that this may also have been for brickmaking. Rooke's property passed to his son-in-law John Brampston or Bramston (d. 1504), who moved to Whitechapel and bequeathed 10,000 bricks each to the London Charterhouse, St. Bartholomew's priory, Smithfield, and his son Hugh.[21] Hugh (d. by 1539) was also a brickmaker and in 1509–10 held a 'brickplace' on the south side of Spitalfield.[22] Hugh's eldest son John was a mercer, but the family continued to live in Whitechapel and also held considerable copyhold property in Whitechapel and Stepney. In 1550 the garden of John Bramston lay east of Brick Lane near its junction with Whitechapel

97 P.R.O., E 101/62/38.
98 Guildhall MS. 25403/2.
99 P.R.O., SC 6/1139/18.
1 Ibid. SC 6/1139/21
2 Ibid. SC 6/1139/22–3.
3 Ibid. SC 12/11/31.
4 Guildhall MSS. 9171/2, f. 53v.; 9171/4, f. 139v.
5 P.R.O., SC 6/1139/18, 24; SC 12/11/31; ibid. C 146/364; Guildhall MS. 25422.
6 P.R.O., SC 6/1140/24.
7 Guildhall MS. 10123/2.
8 P.R.O., PROB 11/14 (P.C.C. 2 Holgrave); G.L.R.O., M79/LH/128/1/1. .pa
9 P.R.O., PROB 11/32 (P.C.C. 38 Populwell), f. 293. He also had brickmaking interests: below.
10 L. & P. Hen. VIII, xxi (2), p. 415.
11 Cal. Fine R. 1391–9, 301.
12 McDonnell, Med. Lond. Suburbs, 111–12.

13 Lond. Topog. Rec. xix. 113.
14 Guildhall MS. 9171/15, f. 165; Mdx. County Rec. i. 57, 218.
15 B.L. Cott. MS. Tib. C. v, f. 160; P.R.O., SC 12/11/31; SC 6/1139/22; above, manors (Ewell).
16 P.R.O., SC 6/1139/23.
17 Guildhall MS. 9171/7, f. 23v.
18 P.R.O., SC 6/1139/24.
19 Ibid. SC 6/1140/24; Guildhall MS. 9171/6, f. 188v.
20 Guildhall MS. 9171/5, f. 136.
21 Autobiog. of Sir John Bramston (Camden Soc. 1st ser. xxxii), pp. xvii–xix; P.R.O., PROB 11/14 (P.C.C. 17 Holgrave), f. 133v.
22 Ibid. PROB 11/28 (P.C.C. 1 Alenger); SC 2/191/63, m. 1d.

Road. He also held one of the two tileyards in Stepney manor, the other being held by John Hall, of another Whitechapel brickmaking family; both lay on the east side of Brick Lane and were let annually.[23]

In 1511 part of Cordwainers mead in Limehouse was let for brickmaking to John Etgose for 10 years at an increased rent, with the obligation to maintain the river walls around the meadow between Limehouse and Ratcliff.[24] It may have been the brickplace that Richard Driver left with all the bricks and profits to his wife Elizabeth in 1549.[25]

Shipbuilding at Ratcliff was recorded in 1354, when timber was brought for the king's ships, and 1356, when 50 ship's carpenters of Norfolk and Suffolk were impressed to work on ships and barges;[26] presumably small boats and merchant ships were already being built there. A galley of Edward III at Ratcliff, with tackle and utensils from other vessels, was ordered to be sold in 1380.[27] In 1421 a ship was built for John, duke of Bedford, at the limekilns in Stepney.[28] In 1485 George Cely, merchant of the Staple of Calais, had his ship the *Margaret Cely* brought to Blackwall and bought nails and bread for her from Ratcliff tradesmen.[29] From 1512 several royal ships were fitted out at Blackwall and Wapping, including the *Mary Rose*,[30] for which a dock was made at Blackwall. Local smiths, ironmongers, and carpenters supplied materials.[31] Four workshops and gardens at Mile End

were granted to John Wolward, smith, in 1364.[32] Other smiths included John Fotheringay of Poplar, who made a will in 1412, John Hudson of Ratcliff, recorded in 1466 and 1468,[33] Christopher Saunderson of Poplar, William Brett of Stepney, and John Ernest of Mile End, who made wills in 1479, 1481, and 1519 respectively. William Ivy of Limehouse was overseer of a will in 1537.[34]

Stepney residents involved in maritime trade included a shipman who owed a large sum in 1423 for beer, probably for his crew, to another resident,[35] and John Norfolk, merchant, who with others was licensed in 1452 to collect merchandise in Denmark, Norway, and Iceland.[36] John Warde of London, vintner, formerly of Portsmouth and then Ratcliff, victualled Calais in 1478. Lightermen were mentioned in 1479.[37]

John Bogays, a potter living at Mile End *c.* 1360, had considerable property there including 3 workshops.[38] Other craftsmen included Walter Colt, brasier of Mile End, in 1434, and William Shelfield, arrowsmith of Stepney, in 1444,[39] William Saber of Stepney, white tawer (1457),[40] John Pole (1454), Edmund Walsh (1456), and John Bothe (1466), all tailors of Stepney,[41] Richard Laurence, fuller, and John Yardley, tailor (both 1454), and William Lynston, tailor (1461), all of Stratford Bow.[42] John Bowle of Southwark had an oil mill in Stepney in 1495.[43] Henry Basse, barber of Ratcliff, made a will in 1500.[44]

LOCAL GOVERNMENT

MANORIAL GOVERNMENT. Pre-Conquest rights confirmed to the bishop and the chapter of St. Paul's in 1199 included exemption from all gelds, pleas, and suit of shire, the right to hold view of frankpledge, and profits from waste and forest jurisdiction in the bishop's own lands. He and his men were also quit of all tolls and customs.[45] In 1294 the bishop claimed view of frankpledge, the assize of bread and of ale, infangthief, outfangthief, felons' goods, waifs, strays, tumbril, pillory, and gallows for all the manors belonging to his Stepney view.[46] In 1395 the king confirmed the exemptions from exactions by the Exchequer and also waste,

felons' and fugitives' goods, and other royalties and privileges.[47] Felons were hanged on the bishop's gallows in Stepney.[48] A whale beached at Stepney in 1309 was claimed by both the bishop and the chapter of St. Paul's, who had a manor by the river.[49] The rights conveyed with the manor in 1695 were specified as fairs, ferries, weights and measures, assize of wine and beer, sac, soc, tolls, dues, stallage, picage, pontage, treasure trove, returns and issue of all writs and mandates, gaol and prison.[50] By the late 16th century, however, the court leet no longer handled criminal cases, and the prison was used only for debtors. Customs, dues, picage, and

23 *Autobiog. of Bramston*, p. xvii; *D.N.B.*; B.L. Eg. Roll 2081; G.L.R.O., M79/LH/128/1/1; Guildhall MS. 9171/10, f. 263 (Chris. Halle). Bramston est. reserved for Whitechapel.
24 Guildhall MS. 10123/2.
25 P.R.O., PROB 11/32 (P.C.C. 38 Populwell), f. 293; above.
26 *Cal. Pat.* 1354–8, 117, 447.
27 Ibid. 1377–81, 543–4.   28 Ibid. 1416–22, 327.
29 *Cely Papers* (Camden 3rd ser. i), 179–80.
30 Sunk off Portsmouth and now in mus. there: W.L. Clowes, *Royal Navy: Hist.* i (1897), 420.
31 P.R.O., E 36/11.
32 Ibid. E 210/9576.
33 Guildhall MS. 9171/2, f. 232; *Cal. Close*, 1461–8, 332; *Cal. Pat.* 1467–77, 78.
34 Guildhall MSS. 9171/6, ff. 250, 316v.; 9171/9, f. 100v.; 9171/10, f. 307v.

35 McDonnell, *Med. Lond. Suburbs.* 104.
36 *Cal. Close*, 1447–54, 341.
37 *Cal. Pat.* 1476–85, 139, 156.
38 P.R.O., E 210/6324; E 210/5875; above, manors (Savoy).
39 Guildhall MSS. 9171/3, f. 391; 9171/4, f. 146v.
40 *Cal. Close*, 1454–61, 257.
41 Ibid. 1454–61, 33; Guildhall MS. 9171/5, f. 189; *Cal. Fine R.* 1461–71, 188.
42 *Cal. Pat.* 1452–61, 136; 1461–7, 53.
43 P.R.O., PROB 11/10 (P.C.C. 27 Vox).
44 Guildhall MS. 9171/8, f. 240v.
45 Taylor, 'Estates of Bishopric of Lond.', 140–2, 146.
46 *Plac. de Quo Warr.* (Rec. Com.), 475–6.
47 B.L. Add. MS. 15555, f. 39v.
48 *Eyre of Lond. 1321* (Selden Soc. lxxxvi), p. 212.
49 *Cal. Inq. Misc.* ii, p. 16.
50 P.R.O., CP 25/2/854/7 Wm. III/Trin.

stallage were attached to the market and fair established in 1664, and sold with them in the 18th century.[51]

Courts were held by 1228,[52] and records survive for 1318, 1348–9, 1361, 1383–4, 1402–3, 1405, 1443, 1509–10, 1581–2, and 1640–3.[53] A complete series of court books, many indexed, runs from 1654 until the abolition of copyhold in 1925.[54] Perquisites and pleas brought in 52s. 6d. during six months in 1228.[55] In 1362–3 they amounted to £40 3s. for five courts and the common fine of 64s. paid at the view of frankpledge,[56] but they varied from £22 13s. 5d. in 1391--2, to £45 4s. 11d. in 1398–9.[57] Much less was received in 1438–9 and 1464–5 from the view and two courts, apparently because Hackney was accounted for separately; most of the common fines from the view were several years in arrears in 1464–5.[58] Perquisites amounted to £20 6s. 7d. in 1517–18, again from a view and two courts,[59] and were valued at an average of £20 a year in the 1580s, when the common fine was still apparently paid by the same manors as in the 14th century.[60] In 1642 fines for copies were reckoned to yield £213 a year, payments at the court leet £50, waifs £60, and green wax £66, in addition to the leet fine,[61] while in 1652 fines and amercements at the courts, reliefs, waifs, strays, parcage, poundage, fowling (fishing was valued separately), and other royalties except return of writs were estimated at £463,[62] nearly four times the value of the quit-rents and reserved rents on the demesne. Sales of the demesne had left perquisites of court as the most valuable part of the lordship.

Medieval courts presumably met at the manor house, probably still the meeting place in the early 16th century when bishops reserved the right to occupy the house for three months a year. The manor house was in ruins in 1652,[63] and courts were held in Whitechapel in 1655,[64] near Whitechapel church in 1677,[65] and at the New Court House on Mile End green, probably the court of record, in 1702.[66] Special courts were often held in taverns near the property being conveyed[67] and by the 19th century were often no more than meetings in the steward's office in the City. From the 1890s the general courts at Easter and in November were held at the Rising Sun, Green Street, Bethnal Green.[68]

The view of frankpledge was usually held on Hock day, the second Tuesday after Easter, as in 1349, although occasionally on another day in the second week after Easter;[69] it was fixed on Hock day in the customal of 1587.[70] The view reflected the extent of the bishop's Domesday manor, as it included men from the bishop's manors of Stepney, Hackney, and Harringay, and 11 other manors in Stepney, Hackney, Clerkenwell, and Islington, who each contributed to the common fine of 64s.: 20s. from Stepney, 16s. from Hackney, 5s. from Islington, 4s. each from Harringay and St. John of Jerusalem, 3s. 6d. from the St. Paul's manor of Shadwell; the rest paid 2s. or less. The view was always followed by a general court for Stepney and Hackney which dealt mainly with court leet business, and three or four other courts baron were held between September and April. The view was still held in 1582, when the inhabitants of Islington were in default of suit and payment of their contribution to the common fine, but by 1655 was simply called the leet and included only Stepney and Hackney residents; the common fine or poll money was paid only by tenants resident in those manors.[71] In 1581–2 general courts were held in December and April (after the view), and courts baron in May and July; transactions also took place out of court, and this and courts convened for individual transactions were common from 1654.[72] Under the confirmations of customs of 1587 and 1617 copyholders had to attend two general courts, one on Hock day and the other near the feast of St. Andrew, and up to 18 courts baron.[73]

Business at the view in 1349 concerned the assize of bread and of ale, defective ditches, and escheated holdings, but only for Stepney and Hackney. Each of the main settlements in Stepney presented its own offenders: Mile End, Stratford, Old Ford, Algatestreet (Whitechapel High Street), Haliwellstreet (Shoreditch High Street), Marsh (Isle of Dogs), and Poplar, were mentioned in the incomplete roll of 1348–9; Forby Lane (Limehouse), Clevestreet (Ratcliff), and Blethenale (Bethnal Green) occur in 1405. These areas were referred to as hamlets as early as c. 1400.[74] Business at the general courts concerned pleas between the bishop's tenants, for land, debt, and loss of service (rent) from their own tenants, besides land transfers for both customary and free tenants; encroachments on common land were also mentioned. By the late 16th century the general court after the view dealt with public nuisances: false weights and measures, adulteration, encroachments on pub-

[51] Ibid. C 66/3065, no. 1; CP 25/2/945/3 Anne/Trin.; CP 25/2/1037/10 Geo. I/Mich.; CP 25/2/1037/11 Geo.I/Hil.; CP 25/2/1037/13 Geo.I/East. Mkt. and fair reserved for treatment under Ratcliff; Mile End Old Town.
[52] P.R.O., E 372/72, m. 10d.
[53] Ibid. SC 2/191/60–63; Guildhall MSS. 10312/136; 25369/1–2; 25370; B.L. Eg. Rolls 2080–1; Eg. MS. 3006, ff. 57–204.
[54] G.L.R.O., M93/1 sqq.
[55] P.R.O., E 372/72, m. 10d.
[56] Ibid. SC 6/1139/18.
[57] From the 5 surviving accts.: ibid. SC 6/1139/19– 23.
[58] P.R.O., SC 6/1139/24; SC 6/1140/24.
[59] Ibid. SC 6/1139/24; SC 6/1140/24; Guildhall MS. 10123/2.
[60] B.L. Lansd. MS. 109, f. 150; Eg. Roll 2081.
[61] Ibid. Add. MS. 22253, f. 16.
[62] G.L.R.O., M93/157.
[63] Above, Stepney manor; G.L.R.O., M93/208; M93/158, f. 1.
[64] G.L.R.O., M93/1, p. 53.
[65] T.H.L.H.L., TH/3711.
[66] G.L.R.O., M93/20, p. 36.
[67] Ibid. M93, ct. bks. passim.
[68] Smith, Hist. E. Lond. 61, 65–6; H. G. C. Allgood, Hist. Bethnal Green (1894), 127.
[69] Two paras. based on extant ct. rolls: above n. 53.
[70] G.L.R.O., E/PHI/444.
[71] Ibid. M93/1; M93/157.
[72] Ibid. M93/1 sqq, passim.
[73] Ibid. E/PHI/444; Customs and Privileges of Manors of Stepney and Hackney (1736), article 3; above, econ. hist. (agric.).
[74] P.R.O., SC 12/11/31, f. 22.

lic ways, and offensive trades. Presentments in 1655 concerned defective paving and sewers, keeping pigs, uncovered and dangerous cellars, fouling the streets, and fraudulent sales.[75] As the only sanction was another presentment at the next court, courts were largely ineffective, particularly in densely built-up areas.[76]

Each of the main settlements was represented by two chief pledges in the 14th century, except Bethnal Green and Old Ford with one each, known as headboroughs by the 17th century; most if not all had one or two aletasters in 1349, and possibly their own constable, as did Mile End in 1385 and Limehouse in 1387.[77] By 1611 a constable was chosen by each hamlet to be sworn in at the court leet, and quarter sessions was prevented from removing a constable so chosen.[78] In 1640 officers were elected for 10 districts: Whitechapel, Spitalfields with Artillery Lane and Wentworth Street, Mile End, Ratcliff, Limehouse, Bethnal Green, Haliwell street, Stratford Bow, Wapping, and Blackwall and Poplar. Each had one constable, one aletaster (except Wapping with two), and two headboroughs (except Ratcliff with eight, and Whitechapel and Wapping with four each).[79] Between 1640 and 1655, in response to changes in population, Whitechapel was allotted five headboroughs with another two for Rosemary Lane,[80] and headboroughs seem to have served specific streets.[81] The leet still elected officers from names supplied by the town meeting of each hamlet at the end of the 18th century,[82] although on occasion the justices refused confirmation; in 1725 they ordered the constable in Mile End Old Town to submit to the leet a list of men who were not infirm.[83] In the 17th century the constables and headboroughs often received orders direct from the justices, particularly about conventicles.[84]

In 1335–6 wood from the manor was used for a new pillory at Stratford,[85] and in 1464–5 a decayed pillory and a cuckingstool were rebuilt.[86] The Privy Council in 1554 delivered offenders to the bailiff for punishment in the pillory and cuckingstool.[87] Gallows at Wapping, on the foreshore which belonged to the Crown, were for maritime felons; they were built or rebuilt in 1584.[88] The Ducking Pond, Ratcliff, was mentioned c. 1638,[89] and another at Mile End Gate, on the border of Whitechapel and Bethnal Green, where it was let for 99 years in

1715, though it seems to have been called the brick pond in 1642.[90] Pillories stood near the court house at Mile End (probably in Whitechapel parish), at Spitalfields market, and at Ratcliff Cross in the 1680s; possibly each hamlet had one, used for punishments set by the justices.[91] A cage stood in Ratcliff Highway in 1641.[92]

A bailiff of Stepney was recorded in 1283.[93] A reeve and separate beadles for Stepney and Hackney were given remittance of their rent and labour services in 1318,[94] but later there seems to have been a single official for each manor, called either reeve or beadle. Remittances were again granted in 1335–6,[95] and after services had been commuted were replaced by a wage, as in 1362–3 when a beadle, bailiff, and keeper of the manor were paid.[96] The beadle received 2d. a day (60s. 10d. a year) from 1383, as did the keeper in 1401.[97] A tenant who refused to serve as beadle forfeited his customary land.[98] A bailiff for the bishop's liberty of Middlesex was established c. 1400 and superseded Stepney's reeve in accounting for the soke of Cornhill, amercements from royal courts, strays, felons' goods, and rebuilding of the gallows; by 1439 he also received the socage rents in Stepney.[99] By 1458, when all the demesne had been let, Stepney's bailiff managed the farms and his deputy accounted for the revenue of the manor, while the beadle and the keeper were paid as before.[1] In 1517–18 there were a bailiff, a deputy who also collected the rents of Stepney marsh, and a paid keeper, but apparently no beadle.[2]

The keepership was leased c. 1530 to Thomas Pilkington for life, with the fee of 2d. a day, unspecified livery, and parcage and poundage (pawnage), which included 1d. for every impounded horse, ox, or cow not belonging to a manorial tenant, with a separate rate for every score of sheep.[3] The leases of Bishopshall to William Goddard and Thomas Parsons from 1538 to 1648 included the parcage, pawnage, and custody of the manor place.[4] Goddard, as reeve in 1539, received a fee of £3 6s. 8d. and livery.[5] John Colet, dean of St. Paul's, was said to have been reeve of Stepney in 1520 and may therefore have held the same lease.[6] In 1587 the homage presented 2 candidates for the reeveship to the lord each year, and the man chosen received £3 6s. 8d. and cloth for a coat.[7] In 1617 the reeve was to be chosen from tenants with lands worth

75 G.L.R.O., M93/1, pp. 53–4.
76 Smith, *Hist. E. Lond.* 66–8.
77 P.R.O., SC 2/191/60; ibid. JUST 2/96, f. 5v.; B.L. Eg. MS. 3006, f. 57–7v.; *Cal. Pat.* 1385–9, 322.
78 Edw. Bulstrode, *Reports* (1657), i. 174.
79 B.L. Eg. MS. 3006, ff. 57–8, 61.
80 G.L.R.O., M93/1, p. 54.
81 *Mdx. County Rec.* iii. 252.
82 T.H.L.H.L., 351.11 (pamphlet), 'St. Dunstan, Stepney, extracts of vestry mins. 1778 [*recte* 1798]– 1871' (TS. copy of mins. of Mile End Old Town vestry), pp. 3–4.
83 Cal. Mdx. Sess. Bks. xiii. 231.
84 *Mdx. County Rec.* iii. 13–14; iv. 16, 240–1.
85 Guildhall MS. 25403/2.
86 P.R.O., SC 6/1140/24.
87 *Acts of P.C.* 1554–6, 27.
88 B.L. Add. MS. 12505, f. 214.
89 *Cal. S.P. Dom.* 1638–9, 262.

90 G.L.R.O., M93/272; below, Bethnal Green, econ. hist. (ind.).
91 *Mdx. County Rec.* iv. 210, 241.
92 *N. & Q.* 8th ser. x. 4.
93 *Reg. Pecham* (Cant. & York Soc.), 215.
94 Guildhall MS. 25403/1.
95 Ibid. 25403/2.
96 P.R.O., SC 6/1139/18.
97 Guildhall MS. 25403/3; P.R.O., SC 6/1139/21–2; SC 11/813.
98 e.g. Guildhall Add. MS. 43.
99 Taylor, 'Estates of Bishopric of Lond.', 164–5, 167.
1 P.R.O., SC 6/1140/24.
2 Guildhall MS. 10123/1–2.
3 P.R.O., C 1/728/11–12 (defective).
4 G.L.R.O., M93/208; above, econ. hist. (agric.).
5 P.R.O., SP 1/153, f. 172d.
6 *L. & P. Hen. VIII*, iii, p. 286.
7 G.L.R.O., E/PHI/444.

at least £16 a year; a tenant refusing to act was fined £10.[8]

In 1587 and 1617 1d. poundage was paid for the animals of copyholders or their tenants, and 4d. for non-copyholders.[9] In 1617 tenants from each hamlet were chosen at the general court to drive the commons and impound strays; profits of poundage after expenses paid for scouring common ditches.[10] The lady of the manor in 1669 enclosed waste on the north side of Mile End Road just east of the junction with Cambridge Heath Road to build a new pound and house for the keeper.[11] In 1731 the lord of the manor leased the pound with its fees and the office of poundkeeper for 71 years to a bricklayer and a carpenter, who were also to replace 5 houses on the site with 3 new ones.[12]

Prior to 1579 the lord of the manor was trying to gain possession of the court rolls from a steward whom he had removed for levying excessive fines and nominating members of the homage.[13] The steward's fees were fixed as part of the confirmation of customs in 1617.[14] The stewardship of Stepney and Hackney was sold for life in the 17th century.[15] In 1639 Robert Dixon sold his stewardship for £600 to Timothy Stampe, who paid £50 to the lord of the manor.[16] Stampe was confirmed in the stewardship for life by the House of Lords in 1641 but forfeited it as a royalist in 1646.[17] In 1650 Thomas Pennington, a landholder in Wapping, claimed that Cleveland had in 1631 granted him the office of bailiff (presumably meaning that of steward) of Stepney and Hackney in reversion after Dixon, who had died in 1648.[18] In 1652, however, William Northey, a lawyer and landowner of Stratford Bow, was appointed to keep the courts of both manors and, after the sale of Cleveland's rights in 1653, was granted the stewardship on the terms by which his predecessors had held it.[19] Stampe was later restored to the stewardship and was serving in 1665, but Northey was again steward by 1669.[20] In 1679 a reversionary grant was made to Edward Northey.[21]

The office of bailiff of Whitechapel was granted to one Maddox in 1660.[22] Described as that of chief bailiff, together with the bailiwick of Stepney manor and Whitechapel liberty and the custody of the gaol, it was granted for five years or life in 1681 to Paul Pawley. He also had a lease of the fines called green wax and profits of the court leet and Green Goose fair (in Stratford Bow) at a peppercorn rent.[23] Presumably the bailiwick originated in rights formerly exercised by the steward of Stepney.

A manorial prison, whose site measured 23 ft. by 94 ft. in 1608, stood on the north side of Aldgate or Whitechapel High Street. It had an unsavoury reputation, and was mentioned by John Taylor the 'water poet' in 1623.[24] As 'Lord Wentworth's gaol or prison', with a great garden behind it, it was presumably still used for debtors in 1597 when Thomas Andrews, who held it by copy, leased it to Robert Harrison for 14 years. Andrews surrendered the prison, then in the possession of Robert Dickson, in 1608 to Daniel Godfrey (d. 1620), whose brother Cornelius (d. 1640) left it in remainder to Godfrey Helden. In 1641 Helden was admitted to the customary tenement, then called the Prison House, which his widow Frances held in 1656. Called the Old Prison House in 1696, it remained with Helden's heirs until 1719.[25]

A prison connected with the court of record (below) used either the old manorial prison or a new building. In 1712, when known as Whitechapel prison, it contained 'a great number' of debtors; the gaoler's fees were settled by the justices in 1729 and 1733.[26]

The royal court of record for the liberty of Stepney and Hackney was established in 1664 following petitions by the Wentworths, as lords of the manor, and the inhabitants of Stepney. Cleveland had petitioned in 1624 for a court to settle small debts, which residents were said to forego rather than seek to recover at Westminster Hall, and the court could settle actions of up to £5 in value. At the Wentworths' request the court was granted to Sir William Smyth, possibly in recompense for money which they still owed him.[27] In 1667 the privileges of the court were extended like those of the Marshalsea[28] and the court was formally instituted from 1668. The court house was probably the one recorded at Mile End in 1683, and called the New Court House on Mile End green (probably in Whitechapel on the site of Whitechapel station, where Court Street once lay) in 1702; it was rebuilt in 1804.[29] Although Smyth already held the profits by royal patent, Lady Wentworth in 1694 conveyed to him the court and its profits with 20 buildings and 10 a. of pasture in Stepney and Whitechapel.[30] All those premises were conveyed by Smyth's son and other executors to Francis Wright in 1703 and, presumably in confirmation, by Sir Henry Johnson and Martha, Baroness Wentworth, to two of the executors in 1704.[31]

The court was one of those that parliament proposed to regulate in 1690–1.[32] Its procedure

8 *Customs and Privileges*, articles 40, 43.
9 G.L.R.O., E/PHI/444; *Customs and Privileges*, article 55.
10 *Customs and Privileges*, articles 60, 62.
11 G.L.R.O., M93/6, f. 197-7v.; marked on Gascoyne, *Map of Mile End Old Town*.
12 G.L.R.O., M93/280.   13 P.R.O., C 3/190/8.
14 *Customs and Privileges*, article 66.
15 P.R.O., C 54/3805, no. 24.
16 B.L. Eg. MS. 3006, f. 8.
17 P.R.O., SP 23/119, f. 267.
18 *Cal. Cttee. for Compounding*, iii (2), p. 2156.
19 P.R.O., C 54/3805, no. 24.
20 G.L.R.O., M93/5; M93/6, f. 197.
21 BNC, MS. Stepney 1.
22 P.R.O., C 54/4038, no. 14.

23 BNC, MS. Stepney 1.
24 Smith, *Hist. E. Lond.* 69 ('Praise and Vertue of a Jayle and Jaylers', 1623).   25 P.R.O., C 107/285.
26 Cal. Mdx. Sess. Bks. x. 114; xv. 21–2; xvi. 47.
27 P.R.O., PC 2/57, ff. 116v., 118v.; *Cal. S.P. Dom.* 1663–4, 376, 509; 1664–5, 14, 22; Hist. MSS. Com. 23, *12th Rep. I, Cowper*, p. 171.
28 *Cal. S.P. Dom.* 1666–7, 548, 560.
29 Datestone illus. in 19th-cent. drawing: P.L.A. MSS., Portfolio 'Stepney Church'; *Mdx. County Rec.* iv. 210; G.L.R.O., M93/20, p. 36.
30 P.R.O., CP 25/2/853/6 W&M/Trin.
31 Ibid. CP 25/2/945/2 Anne/Trin.; CP 25/2/945/3 Anne/Trin.
32 Hist. MSS. Com. 17, *13th Rep. V, H.L.*, pp. 24–5.

grew cumbersome and in 1750 it lost the right to try actions for debts under 40s. to a new court of requests for the Tower Hamlets. An Act of 1781 reduced fees in the older court, dividing them between the patentee, a steward, and four attorneys, and defined the procedures. The court continued to deal with debts of £2–5 until such courts were abolished in the 19th century.[33]

PARISH GOVERNMENT (STEPNEY). Whitechapel had become a separate parish by 1320.[34] The rest of Stepney was apparently divided into districts or hamlets for parish government; the inhabitants of Stratford Bow, with their own chapel, were allowed in 1497 to compound for church rates and excused from serving parish offices.[35] The four remaining hamlets (Ratcliff, Limehouse, Mile End with Bethnal Green, and Poplar) provided the lights in the parish church in 1532, an arrangement that may explain references to the ward light of Bethnal Green in 1520 and the ward of Mile End in 1522.[36] Obligations such as the collection of church dues were probably carried out through the same districts, recorded as Stepney's administrative divisions from 1580 until increased population led to subdivision in the mid 17th century. By the early 17th century each hamlet had its own officers acting under the parish vestry, collected dues, and relieved its own poor.[37]

Parish government may have been reorganized in 1580, when a change was made in the rating of pews and vestry orders were recorded.[38] The vestry was open until 1589, when, after complaints about lack of repairs to the church and provision for the poor because rates were not paid, the chief parishioners decided on a select vestry for which each of the four hamlets chose eight representatives in addition to the vicar and churchwardens. The number was increased to 10 each in 1598,[39] and thereafter new vestrymen seem to have been co-opted.[40] Vestry meetings had become open again by the 1640s, until disorders led to a return in 1655 to a select vestry, with 20 representatives from Ratcliff (divided equally between Ratcliff and Shadwell by 1657) and 10 from each of the other three hamlets; 12 members and 2 churchwardens formed a quorum, and the vicar's presence and approbation were required as before.[41] The select vestry was not accepted by all the leading inhabitants until it was endorsed by the bishop in 1662; he nominated 44 inhabitants (12 from Mile End, Bethnal Green and Spitalfields, 8 each from Ratcliff, Shadwell, Limehouse, and Poplar), who with the vicar had powers to co-opt future members.[42]

After Shadwell became a separate parish in 1670[43] 8 vestrymen were appointed for Wapping instead. In 1679 the bishop granted a revised constitution, but withdrew it when it caused serious disagreements within the parish. However, it was decided that from 1681 as vestrymen died the numbers were to be reduced to 8 each from Ratcliff and Limehouse, and 7 each from Spitalfields, Mile End with Bethnal Green, Poplar with Blackwell, and Wapping; two candidates chosen at the hamlet meetings, also called inhabitants' or town meetings, were to be presented for each vestryman.[44]

The incumbent continued in the 18th century to claim a right of veto at the parish vestry meetings, to which church matters were referred by the hamlets.[45] The creation of new parishes reduced the size of Stepney vestry to 24 by 1730, and in 1735 it was increased again to 32: 4 vestrymen from Mile End New Town, and 7 each from Mile End Old Town, Bethnal Green, Ratcliff, and Poplar.[46] Bethnal Green was omitted after it too became a separate parish in 1743. The select vestry continued until complaints by excluded parishioners in 1776 led to a lawsuit, and at a public meeting of the whole parish in 1778 the select vestry was dissolved, and replaced by open vestries.[47] Meetings were infrequent, about one a year in the 1790s, by which time they were concerned mainly with church repairs and quarrels with the rector.[48]

Vestry meetings were held in the church and in the church house in the churchyard by the 1580s.[49] From 1619 the vestry met in the 'new vestry house',[50] which presumably had been erected with money said in 1620 to have been collected towards the rebuilding of a house in the churchyard for the meetings.[51] Repairs were needed in 1655 and estimates were obtained for a new brick house, 50 ft. by 20 ft., but it may not have been built.[52] Further repairs were made in 1685, but the vestry house which apparently stood on the west side of the churchyard in 1696 was demolished in 1697 and the materials sold. The rectory house east of the church was taken on lease in its place, and by 1706 the curate occupied the house, with the use of the great room reserved for vestry meetings.[53] A new vestry house had been built by 1763 when the

33 Stepney and Hackney Manor Cts. Act, 21 Geo. III, c. 73; Smith, *Hist. E. Lond.* 69.
34 Referred to as par. of St. Mary Matfelon without the bar at Aldgate: Guildhall Add. MS. 9.
35 Guildhall MS. 9531/12, ff. 58–60. Thereafter Bow was autonomous in local govt.; like Whitechapel, it is reserved for treatment elsewhere.
36 Guildhall MSS. 9171/9, f. 162v.; 9171/10, ff. 137v., 180.
37 Below.
38 Vestry mins. from 1580 are in G.L.R.O., P93/DUN. Mins. for 1580–1662 (P93/DUN/327) are published as *Mems. Stepney Par.*; *Mems. Stepney Par.* 1, 3–4.
39 *Mems. Stepney Par.* 18, 27.
40 Smith, *Hist. E. Lond.* 106.
41 *Mems. Stepney Par.* 202–4, 235.
42 Ibid. 232, 242–3.
43 Act for Endowment of Ch. at Shadwell, 22 Car. II, c. 14 (Priv. Act); *Endowed Chars. Lond.* (1897), 599.
44 Smith, *Hist. E. Lond.* 109–10; G.L.R.O., P93/DUN/328, p. 105.
45 Ibid. 111; T.H.L.H.L., 351.11 (pamphlet), p. 24.
46 G.L.R.O., P93/DUN/328, pp. 334–5.
47 'Vestry mins. 1778–1871', p. 1; G.L.R.O., P93/DUN/237, p. 1.
48 G.L.R.O., P93/DUN/237, *passim*; Smith, *Hist. E. Lond.* 120.
49 *Mems. Stepney Par.* 1, 3.
50 Ibid. 85, 95.
51 Ibid. 89.
52 Ibid. 212–13, 215.
53 G.L.R.O., P93/DUN/328, pp. 141, 179–80, 186–7, 221.

old rectory was demolished. A parish room was built over the south porch of the church in 1847 and a hexagonal vestry added beside the priest's vestry in 1872.[54]

Although Stepney in 1534 and 1542 apparently had only two churchwardens,[55] in the 1580s each of the four hamlets put forward one churchwarden, with two or more former officers chosen annually as auditors: in 1586 each hamlet chose four auditors, except Poplar which chose three.[56] Churchwardens apparently served for two years; Mile End and Poplar wardens were chosen in 1589, and those for Ratcliff and Limehouse in 1590. A sidesman was chosen for each hamlet in 1590.[57] By 1606 all four wardens were appointed together, apparently still for two years, and two of them hired substitutes to serve.[58] The vestry appointed a parish clerk, to collect Easter dues and write the churchwardens' accounts, and a sexton.[59]

By 1641 Ratcliff, which then also included the later parishes of Shadwell and St. George-in-the-East, was so populous that two men were chosen to perform the duties of the hamlet's churchwarden; one man was responsible for Stepney (presumably the area around the church), White Horse Street, Brook Street, Ratcliff Wall, and Ratcliff Street; the other for Wapping, which included upper and lower Shadwell, Ratcliff Highway, Foxes Lane, Wapping Wall, Prusons Island, King Street Wapping, Knockfergus, New Gravel Lane, and Old Gravel Lane.[60] By 1645 Ratcliff had been divided into Ratcliff and Shadwell, each with a churchwarden and auditors,[61] In 1656 an upper and a lower churchwarden were chosen for each of the 5 hamlets.[62] Spitalfields had its own churchwarden from 1662, making a total of six,[63] Wapping, often known as Wapping-Stepney, was substituted for Shadwell after 1670, and Bethnal Green had its own churchwarden from 1685.[64] Mile End New Town in 1689 successfully petitioned the justices for its own watchhouse, since it claimed to derive no benefit from Mile End's watch; in 1690 the New Town, having greatly increased, became a separate hamlet by agreement with Mile End, and had its own churchwarden from 1691.[65]

In 1703 the eight hamlets were surveyed and mapped at the parish's expense.[66] The hamlet meetings by the late 17th century had taken over almost all parish administration, except matters concerning the church, and formed the basis for local government not only in the new parishes but also in the four hamlets which remained within St. Dunstan's Stepney, where increased

powers through Local Acts were obtained by the hamlets, not the parish.[67] Hamlet divisions overrode even new parochial organization: the incorporation of part of Ratcliff into the new parish of St. Anne's Limehouse in 1730 affected only the payment of church dues, other rates and the choice of officers remaining in 1795 with the rest of Ratcliff, which was still in the parish of St. Dunstan's Stepney.[68] In the 18th century the hamlets also chose their own constables and other manorial officers for presentation to the court leet.[69] In the 19th century the separate town meetings were called vestries for the purposes of local administration; the churchwardens and overseers continued to make and collect local rates.[70]

Parish income was obtained in 1580 from pew rents, later known as pewage money, set by the churchwardens and collected quarterly. Additional income, for building galleries, paying the lecturer, and other extraordinary needs, was obtained by levying an extra year's or half year's pewage on each pewholder, as in 1580, 1584, 1598, 1602, and 1605.[71] As no reference exists to a church rate levied on land, pewage apparently was the only rating then in use. In 1601 each parishioner without a pew was to pay 8d. 'according to the ancient custom of this parish', besides the usual quarterly due. The refusal of many residents without pews to pay the extra dues contributed to the vestry's decision to build galleries and thus increase income.[72] Until 1637 money raised by pewage also furnished contributions towards maimed soldiers, hospitals, and similar works of relief, thereafter met by voluntary collections.[73] Pewage was still the basis for regular repairs in 1659–60, when the parish clerk was ordered to record the sums raised, presumably in a book of rates that the justices were asked to confirm in 1662.[74]

As income could not be increased without increasing the rate of pewage on rich and poor alike, new methods of raising revenue were introduced. A landscot and assessment of all inhabitants and outdwellers occupying land was first mentioned in 1617, and one year's pewage for repairs and building in 1621 was supplemented by the imposition of a groat (4d.) on all tenants of non-resident landlords.[75] It was recognized that much of Stepney's wealth was not based on land: although a general assessment was made of landholders in 1632 at the rate of 6d. an acre, they were to pay a quarter of their poor rate assessment if that yielded more. Inhabitants not occupying land also paid one quarter of their poor rate assessment.[76] Later

54 Smith, *Hist. E. Lond.* 111; below, churches.
55 Guildhall MS. 9531/12, f. 260B; *L. & P. Hen. VIII*, vi, p. 43.
56 *Mems. Stepney Par.* 3–4, 13.
57 Ibid. 17, 22.
58 Ibid. 54.
59 Ibid. 6–7, 13.
60 Ibid. 171.
61 Ibid. 182.
62 Ibid. 217.
63 Ibid. 242.
64 G.L.R.O., P93/DUN/328, pp. 48, 142.
65 Cal. Mdx. Sess. Bks. viii. 108–9; P.R.O., C 6/270/73; G.L.R.O., P93/DUN/328, p. 160.
66 G.L.R.O., P93/DUN/328, pp. 203, 210; Gascoyne,

Map.
67 P.R.O., C 6/270/73; 'Vestry mins. 1778–1871', p. 3; below, Bethnal Green, local govt.
68 Lysons, *Environs*, iii. 236.
69 'Vestry mins. 1778–1871', pp. 3–4.
70 *2nd Rep. Sel. Cttee on Met. Local Govt.* H.C. 452, p. 502 (1866), xiii.
71 *Mems. Stepney Par.* 1, 3, 10, 44, 50.
72 Ibid. 33, 38.
73 Ibid. 159.
74 Ibid. 135, 229, 241.
75 Ibid. 77, 95.
76 Ibid. 136–7.

that year all occupiers of land were ordered to pay 6*d*. an acre, while non-occupiers were to be assessed according to their personal estates: Ratcliff's assessment amounted to £40, Limehouse's to £20, Mile End's to £12, and Poplar's to £9.[77] The combined land rate and assessments were again used for repairs in 1634 and 1656, although on occasion a voluntary contribution could be paid instead of the assessed sum.[78] Another assessment divided the sum required between the four hamlets in the proportions used to distribute a collection for the poor, whereby Ratcliff and Shadwell paid three eighths, Limehouse a quarter, Mile End with Bethnal Green and Spitalfields a quarter, and Poplar and Blackwall one eighth;[79] it was presumably left to each hamlet to decide how to raise the amount. These proportionate levies were used in 1664 and thereafter to the end of the 17th century, with Wapping substituted for Shadwell after 1670, but pewage was no longer mentioned after 1660.[80] In 1733, however, it was ordered that money for repairs or payment of debts should be raised in future by a levy according to the Land Tax quota: Ratcliff £15, Mile End Old Town £263, Mile End New Town £93, Bethnal Green £369, Poplar £255.[81] Smaller sums, for parish debts, repayment of loans, rent for the vestry house, were found after 1662 from the fees for burials and the use of the parish palls.[82]

Funds for the poor in the late 16th century came from regular church collections and from legacies, rents for rooms in the church house, and fines (1*s*. in 1602) for non-attendance by vestrymen.[83] They also benefited from paschal money, when each communicant paid 1*d*. at Easter towards the bread and wine. The vestry usually leased out the right to that sum to the vicar for 40*s*. a year (£4 from 1581 and £6 13*s*. 4*d*. in 1633), used for the poor, and during disagreements with him in 1605 itself collected the money.[84] In 1606 money collected and disbursed for poor relief was to be recorded in two separate books and kept in a chest with keys for the vicar and each of the four wardens, following criticism of earlier methods.[85] In 1615 money from collections at the communion table was distributed between the hamlets: three eighths to Ratcliff, a quarter each to Limehouse and Mile End with Bethnal Green, and an eighth to Poplar, the hamlets presumably being responsible for relieving their own poor; from 1649 Ratcliff's share was split equally between Ratcliff and Shadwell.[86] In 1681 it was ordered that a poor-man's box should be fixed by each door of the church, and in all taverns, victualling and other public houses in the parish.[87] A poor rate was mentioned in 1619 and 1632: the basis of the rate was not explained, although it was evidently not a rate per acre.[88] Overseers for the poor were mentioned in 1650, and collectors for the poor in 1654,[89] but in 1681 the churchwardens were also overseers and ordered to account for the money for the poor. In 1684 the churchwardens were required to meet to adjust the rates for poor relief in each hamlet, and join in a petition to the justices for their assistance with poor relief.[90] Spitalfields had five supervisors of the poor in 1684, and Bethnal Green had at least one.[91]

Rooms in the church house were let by the vestry to widows and other needy people, for rents paid for the use of the poor, or occasionally for nothing to curates, clerks or sextons as part of their remuneration.[92] In 1626 rooms over the new vestry house held by the curate, clerk, and sexton, were to be taken after their deaths for the benefit of the poor.[93] In 1657, however, damage was caused by water running down from the rooms, whereupon the occupants were ordered to move.[94] The parish had the management of Fuller's almshouses by 1641, of Cook's from 1673, and of Bowry's built in 1744.[95] In 1683 the vestry granted liberty to all charitably disposed persons to build houses for the parish's poor on the plot of land on the edge of the churchyard they had recently bought from Mrs. Bissaker, though there is no indication that anyone did so.[96]

Stock of £100 given for setting the poor to work was so inadequate for their numbers in 1654 that the churchwardens used it for apprenticing instead;[97] nothing further is known of it. In 1655 Stepney was among the parishes receiving money from the duty on seacoal to assist the poor: £400 was to be distributed by the vicar and two justices, to the annoyance of the vestry, which appointed three representatives to be consulted. By 1658 nearly 800 families and paupers had been relieved and the vestry, after requesting an account, registered approval.[98] In 1659 it was decided that pensioners of the parish should wear pewter badges with the name of their division.[99] By 1700 all poor relief was probably managed by the hamlets: in 1694 Ratcliff applied independently for an assessment.[1]

Public services were also largely provided by and for individual hamlets by the 17th century. The vestry allowed fire buckets belonging to the church in 1639 to be used elsewhere in the hamlets, with any loss being met by the hamlets contributing proportionally.[2] The parish clerk

77 Ibid. 139.
78 Ibid. 147, 216.
79 Ibid. 153, 195.
80 G.L.R.O., P93/DUN/328, pp. 23, 47, 140.
81 Ibid. p. 314.
82 Ibid. *passim*.
83 Ibid. 44, 52, 54, 78.
84 *Mems. Stepney Par.* 4–5, 12, 15, 47, 49, 52.
85 Ibid. 54. No poor relief recs. survive.
86 Ibid. 72, 200.
87 G.L.R.O., P93/DUN/328, p. 118.
88 *Mems. Stepney Par.* 84, 136–7.
89 Ibid. 72, 92, 196, 199–200.

90 G.L.R.O., P93/DUN/328, pp. 117, 139–40.
91 *Mdx. County Rec.* iii. 364; iv. 240–2; G.L.R.O., P93/DUN/328, p. 142; below, Bethnal Green, local govt. (manorial and early par. govt.).
92 *Mems. Stepney Par. passim*.
93 Ibid. 110.
94 Ibid. 221.
95 Below, charities.
96 G.L.R.O., P93/DUN/328, p. 129; below, churches.
97 *Mems. Stepney Par.* 199.
98 Ibid. 214, 216, 223, 225.
99 Ibid. 228.   1 *V.C.H. Mdx.* ii. 95.
2 *Mems. Stepney Par.* 167.

was ordered to prepare a petition to the justices for a watch and watchhouse for Stepney in 1662,[3] but some hamlets already had watchhouses: Bethnal Green had one in 1652,[4] possibly provided through the manorial court leet. The vestry ordered £3 a year to be paid to the watchmen in the churchyard to ring the great bell for half an hour morning and evening throughout the year in 1684.[5] The vestry also ordered that from 1665 two or more women were to be appointed in each hamlet as searchers of the dead.[6] In 1685 the vestry ordered that fines from tipplers were to be used to maintain a house of correction which they wanted for the parish, as it was troublesome and sometimes dangerous for peace officers to take malefactors to the county's house at Clerkenwell.[7]

CHURCHES

THE church of Stepney, which existed by 1154,[8] served the whole parish until the foundation of chapels of ease and private chapels from the 12th century and of independent parishes from the 14th (below). The suggestion in 1708 of an additional dedication led writers to assume the church was a Saxon foundation, rededicated to St. Dunstan after his canonization in 1029.[9] A groundless statement that Matthew Paris attributed the foundation to Dunstan[10] has often been repeated,[11] but the dedication to him may date from the Church's revived interest in him after 1093.[12]

The rectory was in the gift of the bishop of London until 1550. In 1380 the bishop was licensed by the king to appropriate the benefice with the advowsons of the vicarage and Whitechapel.[13] His successor was granted the appropriation by the pope for the bishop's term in office, and in 1391 in perpetuity on the rector's death, when a vicarage was to be endowed.[14] However, since the bishop continued to collate to the rectory, it may not in fact have been appropriated.[15]

In 1550 Nicholas Ridley relinquished the benefice with the manor to the king, who granted them to Thomas, Lord Wentworth.[16] The advowson remained with the Wentworths until 1695 but, as a result of leases of the rectory,[17] was often exercised by others in the 16th and 17th centuries. Sir Richard Williams alias Cromwell, who had inherited a grant of the next presentation made in 1538 to his uncle, Thomas Cromwell,[18] presented in 1544, Thomas Parsons and William Mongay or Mountjoy in 1558, and Thomas Preston in 1562. The bishop collated to the rectory in 1564 on the deprivation of Nicholas Aspinall.[19] The Crown presented in 1668–9, because of deprivation for simony,[20] and Philadelphia, Lady Wentworth, in 1681.[21]

In 1695 the freehold of the rectory and the advowsons of Stepney and Whitechapel were sold with the manor to trustees for William Herbert, Lord Montgomery.[22] Montgomery sold them in 1708 to Brasenose College, Oxford,[23] which also bought an outstanding grant of the next presentation to the vicarage, besides leases of the rectory and glebe.[24] The purchase was confirmed by an Act of 1710,[25] made necessary by uncertainty about Montgomery's title and the dependence of the patronage of Whitechapel on the rectory of Stepney. The Act secured payments from the benefice to support two scholars at the college, which had been the reason for the purchase, and provided for the amalgamation of the rectory and vicarage of Stepney, the vicar John Wright to become rector. It also confirmed to the college right of presentation to the chapel at Bow and to any new churches or chapels.[26] The advowson remained with Brasenose until exchanged in 1864 with the bishop of London, with whom it has remained.[27]

A vicar, Roger, was mentioned in 1233, although the first recorded institution was in 1326.[28] Presentations were made by the rector until 1534, except in 1456 and 1499 when the bishop presented,[29] and thereafter often by farmers of the rectory or grantees. They were made by the king in 1534 by grant of Sir Richard Layton and in 1540 on the vicar's attainder, by the farmer of the rectory Sir Richard Williams or his executors from 1544 to 1555, by the Crown in 1577 and 1603, by Nicholas Woodroffe and others in 1587, by the instituted rector, who presented himself, in 1593, by the farmers William Freeman[30] in 1598 and 1605 and Robert Dixon in 1634, and by D. Herbert and others in 1641. The earl of Cleveland presented in 1660 and his grantee Alexander Frazier in 1662.[31] The Crown presented in 1660 and 1661 due to lapse,

3 Ibid. 241.   4 Below, Bethnal Green, pub. svces.
5 G.L.R.O., P93/DUN/328, p. 137.
6 Ibid. p. 24.
7 Ibid. p. 143; below, Bethnal Green, pub. svces. Other pub. svces. are reserved for treatment under hamlets.
8 Charters of Gilb. Foliot, 150.
9 e.g. J. Paterson, Pietas Londiniensis (1714), 76; below (par. ch.).
10 Mackeson's Guide (1872), 29, but not in earlier edns.
11 e.g. N. & Q. 4th ser. xi. 355, 370; W. C. Pepys and E. Godman, Church of St. Dunstan, Stepney (L.C.C. Survey, monograph vi, 1905), 7; T. F. Bumpus, Ancient Lond. Chs. (1927), 217–18; P. Wyld, Stepney Story (1952), 5; G. Barnes, Stepney Chs. (1967), 45.
12 R. W. Southern, St. Anselm and his Biographers (1963), 253.
13 Cal. Pat. 1377–81, 499; P.R.O., C 143/395, no. 2.
14 Cal. Papal Reg. iv. 410.
15 Hennessy, Novum Rep. 410.

16 Newcourt, Rep. i. 737.   17 Below.
18 L. & P. Hen. VIII, xvii, p. 258.
19 Hennessy, Novum Rep. 410; Guildhall MS. 9531/13, f. 134v.
20 Cal. S.P.Dom. 1668–9, 114, 121, 148.
21 Hennessy, Novum Rep. 410.
22 B.L. MS. 15555, f. 46; P.R.O., CP 25/2/854/7 Wm. III/Trin.
23 BNC, MS. Stepney 26.
24 Ibid. MSS. Stepney 28, 30, 33.
25 9 Anne, c. 16 (Priv. Act).
26 BNC, MSS. Stepney 25, 38, 46.
27 Lond. Gaz. 12 July 1864, p. 3487.
28 P.R.O., E 40/14033; Reg. Baldock, Segrave, Newport, and Gravesend (Cant. & York Soc.), 277.
29 Rest of para. based on Hennessy, Novum Rep. 411.
30 Guildhall MS. 9537/5, f. 20.
31 P.R.O., Institution Books. Frazier was a relative and feoffee of Philadelphia Wentworth.

and again in 1668 because of deprivation for simony. The last presentation before the amalgamation of the rectory and vicarage was by Thomas Wright in 1679.

The Act of 1710 allowed Brasenose to divide the amalgamated benefice after the death of John Wright, and present two of its Fellows as joint rectors, known as the portionist of Ratcliff Stepney and of Spitalfields Stepney respectively. They were to hold the benefice in common, officiating in alternate months. After payment of £106 a year to Brasenose, all income was shared equally, although Ratcliff paid the first fruits of the former rectory and Spitalfields those of the former vicarage.[32]

The value of the rectory was £40 in 1291, when only three other benefices in the archdeaconries of London, Middlesex, and Essex were worth more,[33] and also in 1535.[34] The bishop was said to give £40 to the parsonage in 1539,[35] but the reason is not clear. The rector received £50 a year in 1548,[36] and in the late 1640s the rectorial tithes were said to be worth £100,[37] at which sum Philadelphia, Lady Wentworth, valued the rectory in 1670.[38]

The vicarage was valued at £8 in 1291,[39] and £33 6s. 8d. in 1535,[40] which last amount the vicar received in 1548.[41] The vestry granted him the paschal money, 1d. a year paid by each communicant for bread and wine in addition to the offerings to the vicar, for 40s. c. 1556, increasing his payment to £4 a year in 1581 and £6 13s. 4d. in 1634, as a greater population made it more valuable.[42] Fees for marriages, churchings, and burials were agreed with the chief inhabitants c. 1613.[43] In 1650 the vicar's income came from an annual due of 3d. from each communicant, fees, and small tithes of 6d. for a cow and 1d. for a cock or hen: it was said to total only c. £75 because few paid the due and most christenings took place at home. In addition, parliament had ordered that the income from Poplar and Blackwall, amounting to £32, should be made over to support the minister at Stratford Bow chapel.[44] Before the amalgamation of the benefices, the Exchequer decreed that the vicar was entitled to 3s. 6d. for every garden, 20d. for every sow in pig, Easter dues of 3d. for every person aged over 16 except hired servants, besides a modus on vegetables, and 6d. for every cow.[45]

In 1729 Spitalfields became a separate parish under an Act which allotted annual payments from it of £50 to the portionists and £16 to the clerk of St. Dunstan's in respect of fees lost; small tithes were abolished and great tithes reserved to Brasenose.[46] Similarly, the Acts creating the parishes of St. George-in-the-East, St. Mary, Stratford Bow, and St. Anne, Limehouse, authorized payments of £50, £10, and £25 respectively to each portionist, and £13 from Wapping and £5 from Limehouse to the clerk.[47] With the creation of Bethnal Green parish in 1743 the payments came to an end: the portionist of Spitalfields became the first rector of St. Matthew, Bethnal Green, and the portionist of Ratcliff, Dr. Robert Leyborne, became sole rector of St. Dunstan's; the Bethnal Green clerk was to pay £12 a year to St. Dunstan's and the great tithes were again reserved to Brasenose.[48]

Income was greatly reduced by the creation of new parishes: the fees and Easter dues for Spitalfields, Wapping-Stepney, and Limehouse had yielded £523 c. 1698.[49] The net income of the rectory was only £150 in 1759, whereupon Brasenose reduced its reserved payment to £40, as permitted under the Act of 1710 after it had recouped the cost of purchasing the benefice.[50] The gradual impoverishment of a once rich benefice was not apparent from official valuations of £600 gross in the 1780s[51] and £1,318 in 1831:[52] the second figure included £700 in surplice fees, which fluctuated widely, and Easter dues and tithes, which were hard to collect and in decline.[53]

The rector received all the great tithes, in the form of a composition for each acre of wheat and rye (5s.), other grain (4s.), hay (2s. 6d.) and pasture (4d.), and for each milch cow (6d.).[54] Their value dwindled as pasture replaced arable and building replaced pasture, amounting in 1810 to c. £230, less £70 for expenses and the poor rate for Bow; on commutation in 1849 only 218½ a. remained tithable, producing a rent charge of £50.[55] Fixed payments, paid from 1803 to compensate for the loss of tithe caused by building roads, docks, and canals, provided a fifth of the income in 1850.[56]

In 1842 the new rector complained that Brasenose had estimated his income, excluding Easter dues, at £1,125 a year, whereas the fees amounted to only £435 a year and the income from all sources to £701. After paying nearly £70 to the college (the £40 reserved, £10 10s. rent for an addition to the glebe bought by the college in 1831, and an annual charge for the land tax redeemed on behalf of the incumbent in 1801), besides £250 to two curates, he was left with only £381. He claimed that one curate

32 BNC, MS. Stepney 46, copy of 9 Anne, c. 16 (Priv. Act).
33 *Tax. Eccl.* (Rec. Com.), 17–23.
34 *Valor Eccl.* (Rec. Com.), i. 433.
35 P.R.O., SP 1/153, f. 172d.
36 *Lond. Rec. Soc.* xvi. 72.
37 P.R.O., SP 16/520, no. 29.
38 *Cal. S.P. Dom.* 1670, 53.
39 *Tax. Eccl.* (Rec. Com.), 17.
40 *Valor Eccl.* (Rec. Com.), i. 434.
41 *Lond. Rec. Soc.* xvi. 72.
42 *Mems. Stepney Par.* 4–5, 145.
43 Guildhall MS. 9531/13, pt. 2, ff. 399d.–400.
44 *Home Counties Mag.* iii. 221–2.
45 BNC, MS. Stepney 181, letter from Dan. Vawdrey,

16 Sept. 1842.
46 2 Geo. II, c. 10.
47 2 Geo. II, c. 30; 3 Geo. II, c. 3; 3 Geo. II, c. 17.
48 BNC, MS. Stepney 60, citing Act 16 Geo. II, c. 28.
49 Ibid. MS. Stepney 19.
50 Brasenose Quatercentenary Monographs, vol. i, monograph vi (Oxf. Hist. Soc. lii), 50; BNC, MSS. Stepney 46, 59, 60.
51 Guildhall MS. 9557, f. 24.
52 Rep. Com. Eccl. Revenues, 672.
53 Ch. Com. file NB 23/426B, pt. 1.
54 BNC, MS. Stepney 66.
55 Ibid. MS. Stepney 57–I; P.R.O., IR 29/21/51.
56 BNC, MSS. Stepney 57–B; Stepney 181, statement of income Dec. 1850.

was wholly occupied in collecting trifling fees and attending to certain duties which seemed to be almost peculiar to Stepney.[57]

In 1850 the income was £963 a year, including £493 in fees, £204 in tithe compensations from docks and roads, £100 in chancel pew rents, £40 in Easter dues, and £90 in tithes. Leasing of the glebe in 1865 produced £200 a year in ground rent. In 1896 the income was only £522 (including the ground rent, £172 tithe corn-rents, £50 in lieu of pew rents, and £80 in fees); outgoings included £67 10s. to Brasenose and left only £305 net.[58] The bishop sought to augment it in 1914 from the revenues of St. Martin-in-the-Fields, and in 1934, when £55 a year was added, he asked that Stepney, as the mother church of East London, should have first claim on any unexpected increase in revenue from a City church in his gift.[59] Payments to Brasenose continued after its surrender of the patronage, and puzzled and irritated every new incumbent.[60] The charge for the land tax was paid off by Queen Anne's Bounty in 1932;[61] the sums of £40 and £10 10s. were still payable in 1946,[62] although they were probably redeemed before the benefice was reorganized in 1951.

RECTORY AND VICARAGE HOUSES. The gate of the rectory lay opposite Churchfield on the east side of the church c. 1380, as in the 17th century.[63] A lease of the rectory for 80 years made to Thomas Cromwell was inherited by his nephew Sir Richard Williams,[64] one of whose executors, the rector Gabriel Donne, was allowed by his fellow executors to occupy the parsonage house in 1545 as long as he kept it repaired and performed Sir Richard's will.[65] The house had an orchard, garden, and yard enclosed by a mud wall in 1610,[66] and was shown in 1615 as a substantial building east of the church, with a large barn to the south.[67] It was farmed with the rest of the rectory in the early 17th century, and later leased to Lord Cleveland;[68] the conveyance of the house by Cleveland's creditors in 1660 probably concerned his leasehold interest.[69] It was again leased with the glebe by the rector to Edward Northey and Samuel Knowles in 1691.[70] The house, an adjoining dwelling, and pasture, was then sublet to the vicar and other trustees for 99 years or the three lives in the head lease, its use to be decided by the vestry. A brick wall on the north side of the parsonage, dividing it from the former house of Lady Wentworth, was to be rebuilt.[71]

A vicarage house in 1610 had a garden, orchard and c. 3 a. adjoining;[72] in 1650 only the house and orchard were mentioned.[73] It lay on the west side of White Horse Lane near the later Stepney Green in 1703,[74] and was occupied by the vicar John Wright, who continued there when he also became rector in 1710. Under the Act of 1710, after Wright's death the portionist of Spitalfields was to have the vicarage until the parishioners could buy another house for him, while the portionist of Ratcliff would occupy the parsonage house after the end of the 1691 lease.[75]

After 1743 two houses were no longer necessary. In 1763 Brasenose petitioned to demolish the rectory house, described as three or four cottages and other mean buildings, all ruinous, and spend the money from their materials on the vicarage house.[76] In 1795 only the brick wall around the old rectory house survived[77] and in 1854 its site of c. ¼ a. became part of the churchyard.[78] The rector, Dr. Ralph Cawley, built a new house in 1763–4 largely at his own expense, at the corner of White Horse Lane facing the road leading to the church, the old vicarage also being demolished and its site thrown into the grounds.[79] In 1843 a new rectory was built in White Horse Lane behind the old one, which had become dilapidated, darkened by trees, and a hindrance to building on the glebe.[80] The rectory house in the late 19th century contained parish and club rooms, which were converted into a flat for curates in 1923 with grants from the City Parochial Charities Fund.[81] Sold to the London Diocesan Fund in 1987,[82] the building was converted in 1989 into nine leasehold flats called the Rosery.[83]

MEDIEVAL CHURCH LIFE. Henry, canon of St. Paul's, held the living 1163 × c. 1179, although an earlier rector may have been John of Canterbury, who disputed Stepney and other benefices with the bishop in 1154. In the Middle Ages the rectory, a valuable sinecure after the vicarage was established, was held by prominent churchmen.[84] John of Silverstone, canon of St. Paul's, rector 1294–9, bequeathed a rent charge for a chantry in St. Dunstan's.[85]

57 Ibid. MS. Stepney 181, letter from Vawdrey 16 Sept. 1842.
58 Ibid. MS. Stepney 181, statement of income Dec. 1850; letter from rector 3 Oct. 1896; Ch. Com. file 32074.
59 Ch. Com. file 83022, reps. of estates cttee.
60 BNC, MS. Stepney 181, letters 26 Sept. 1881; 16 Oct. 1896; ibid. 182, letters Apr. 1909, 29 Sept. 1920; Ch. Com. file NB 23/426 (QAB), letters 1934–5; letter 13 Mar. 1946, from BNC's agent to rector.
61 Ch. Com. file K 10287.
62 Last ref. in ibid. file NB 23/426.
63 Guildhall MS. 25422.
64 L. & P. Hen. VIII, xvii, p. 258.
65 B.L. Add. Ch. 39372; P.R.O., PROB 11/31 (P.C.C. 20 Alen), f. 156.
66 Guildhall MS. 9628/box 5, file 3.
67 Plan of Mercers' est.
68 P.R.O., C 8/145/52.
69 G.L.R.O., M93/253, 254.
70 BNC, MS. Stepney 12.

71 Ibid. MS. Stepney 17.
72 Guildhall MS. 9628/box 5, file 3.
73 Home Counties Mag. iii. 221–2.
74 Gascoyne, Map of Mile End Old Town.
75 BNC, MS. Stepney 46, copy of 9 Anne, c. 16 (Priv. Act). Apparently no other ho. was bought.
76 BNC, MS. Stepney 64.
77 Lysons, Environs, iii. 440.
78 BNC, MS. Stepney 182, letter from Vawdrey, 11 May 1844; Ch. Com. file 20848; below (par. ch.).
79 Brasenose Quat. Monographs, i, mon. iv. 37; Lysons, Environs, iii. 440.
80 BNC, MS. Stepney 181, letters from Vawdrey, 19 Sept. 1842, 27 Oct. 1843.
81 Ch. Com. file 83022.
82 Ibid. deed 659699.   83 Advert. by agent.
84 Charters of Gilb. Foliot, 150, 316; inf. below supplements list of rectors in Hennessy, Novum Rep. 409–10.
85 P.R.O., C 145/207, no. 13; Le Neve, Fasti, 1066–1300, St. Paul's, Lond. 47.

Stephen of Gravesend (d. 1338), nephew of Richard of Gravesend, bishop of London, and a prebendary of St. Paul's, was rector in 1303, in 1306 when given leave of absence for study, and in 1311; he himself became bishop of London in 1318.[86] Stephen Segrave (d. 1333), rector from 1315 and later archbishop of Armagh, was succeeded by Richard of Baldock, who was rector in 1324[87] and 1326.[88] In 1325, however, the pope provided the Frenchman Gaucelin Jean Deuza, cardinal and later bishop of Alba, to the rectory, and he held it until his death in 1348.[89] Richard of Saham, ambassador, petitioned the pope for the rectory in 1348, and received dispensation to hold it with another benefice.[90] His successor Robert Crull, rector 1368–1406, went to Ireland on royal service in 1391 and 1393.[91] Both John of Silverstone and Richard of Saham sometimes resided in Stepney,[92] and the bishops' possession of a residence led to use of the church for such functions as ordinations, including one by the archbishop of Canterbury in 1303.[93]

Vicars included John atte Lee, who in 1352 was also parson of St. Margaret, Friday Street (Lond.),[94] and John Frere, who was also rector of St. Swithun's (Lond.) at his death c. 1408.[95] John Colet, vicar from 1499 or later until 1505, became dean of St. Paul's and founded St. Paul's school.[96]

Chaplains assisted or substituted for the incumbents. William, chaplain of Stepney, witnessed charters 1189 × 1199,[97] and other parish chaplains, usually named, were mentioned from 1374.[98] In addition to the rector and vicar, a celebrant and a clerk paid the poll tax in 1381.[99] Wills indicated more than one chaplain in 1377 and generally at least two clerks.[1]

A chapel was built in the later 12th century by William of Pontefract during the absence of the rector, who claimed loss of income. William appealed to the pope, with whom the archbishop of Canterbury discussed the case 1163 × c. 1179.[2] The advowson of the chapel of Pountfreyt was part of the perquisites of the estate formerly belonging to the Pontefract family when it was sold in 1302.[3] It is therefore likely that the chapel of St. Mary in the marsh, first mentioned in 1380,[4] was the Pontefracts' chapel. It has been identified with remains visible near the southern end of the Isle of Dogs in 1857,[5] probably also the site of the manor house of Pomfret

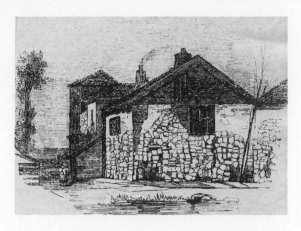

FIG. 8. OLD CHAPEL IN THE ISLE OF DOGS IN 1857

which was in ruins in 1362.[6] Several testators between 1380 and 1447, many living 'in the marsh', mentioned the chapel, with its high altar, east window, and image of St. Mary, and also the chaplains and clerks.[7] The chapel was probably abandoned during the flood of 1448 which destroyed the settlement in the Isle of Dogs:[8] the last reference was in an undated will proved in 1447, at about the time of the first bequests to the fraternity of the Blessed Virgin Mary in the parish church (below), which may therefore have taken the chapel's place in local devotion.[9]

The white chapel stood by 1282 outside the bars at Aldgate[10] and by 1320 served the new parish of St. Mary Matfelon, Whitechapel, whose vicarage was in the gift of the rector of Stepney.[11] In 1311 the inhabitants of Stratford Bow and Old Ford received permission to build a chapel in the highway near Stratford bridge (Bow bridge) because of difficulties in reaching Stepney church.[12] Inhabitants could be buried at Stratford Bow and by 1497 were withholding contributions to the parish church. Having been cited by the other hamlets before the bishop's commissary court, they were ordered to attend Stepney church twice a year and pay 24s. a year towards repairs and other dues, but were excused from serving as officers.[13] Thereafter Stratford Bow, whose annual payment never increased, was usually treated as a separate parish. There was also a

86   D.N.B. s.v. Ric. de Gravesend; Reg. Baldock, 23, 147; Le Neve, Fasti, 1300–1541, St. Paul's, Lond. 1, 28, 68.
87   Cal. Pat. 1324–7, 43, 163, 202.
88   Reg. Baldock, 277.
89   Cal. Papal Reg. ii. 244; Reg. Baldock, 292; C. Eubel, Hierarchia Catholica Medii Aevi, I (1913 edn.), 15; Cal. Papal Pets. i. 138. Hennessy, Novum Rep. 409–10, wrongly lists Gaucelin and Gamaliel, bp. of Alba, as different men.
90   Cal. Papal Pets. i. 138; Cal. Papal Reg. iii. 303.
91   Cal. Pat. 1367–70, 108; 1388–92, 395; 1391–6, 259.
92   Sel. Canterbury Cases (Selden Soc. xcv), intro. pp. 31–33: Silverstone was official sede vacante 1292–4; Cal. Pat. 1348–50, 389.
93   Reg. Winchelsey (Cant. & York Soc.), ii. 959.
94   Hennessy, Novum Rep. 411; Cal. Pat. 1350–4, 304.
95   Cal. Pat. 1405–8, 403. List of vicars in Hennessy, Novum Rep. 411, should be amended: Nic. Dene was V. 1375–9, succ. by Gilb. of Drayton, V. 1379–?86: Lond. Rec. Soc. xiii. 78, 86; Cal. Close, 1377–81, 462.   96   D.N.B.
97   Cal. Doc. France, ed. Round, 152–3.

98   In wills, e.g. Guildhall MSS. 9171/1, ff. 11, 38v., 49v., 50, 160, 257, 306v., 402, 436; 9171/2, passim.
99   Lond. Rec. Soc. xiii. 36.
1   e.g. Guildhall MS. 9171/1, ff. 49v., 102.
2   Charters of Gilb. Foliot, 316.
3   Nottingham Univ. Libr., Middleton MSS., Mi D 3605; above, manors (Pomfret).
4   Guildhall MS. 9171/1, f. 71.
5   Fig. 8.
6   P.R.O., C 135/167, no. 9; N. & Q. 9th ser. ix. 121; above, manors (Pomfret).
7   Guildhall MSS. 9171/1, ff. 71, 253, 270, 292, 323, 405; 9171/2, ff. 26, 51v., 54v., 110, 316v.; 9171/3, ff. 34v., 130, 234v., 299, 310, 317v., 366v., 379, 508; 9171/4, ff. 34v.
8   Above, Intro.
9   Guildhall MS. 9171/4. ff. 206v., 216v.
10   P.N. Mdx. (E.P.N.S.), 153.
11   Guildhall Add. MS. 9; Reg. Baldock, 292.
12   Reg. Baldock, 147.
13   Guildhall MS. 9531/12, ff. 58–60.

chapel of St. Katharine on Bow bridge itself in 1344.[14]

Permission to have a portable altar was granted in 1435 to the vicar Nicholas Norton and in 1451 to a local landowner, William Chedworth.[15] Among other indications of increased religious activity from the mid 15th century were bequests to the fraternity of the Blessed Virgin Mary from 1446,[16] extensive rebuilding in the church including a new south aisle with a chapel to St. Mary in the 1460s, and bequests for the statues and altars of five other saints.[17] The fraternity continued in the 16th century, and bequests to the fraternity of Our Lady and St. Anne were especially common in the 1520s.[18] St. George's chapel, which stood on the waste at Bethnal green and received 20s. from the king in 1512, may have been a hermitage.[19]

Amy or Anne Stephyn (possibly Stepkyn) left a house in Blackwall in 1460 to provide a chantry.[20] Richard Etgoos of Limehouse in 1503 required his executors to continue payments of 20s. a year for 10 years for a priest in St. Dunstan's if three neighbours continued likewise; alternatively, a chantry priest was to be paid 9 marks a year for two years. Thomas Taylor, priest, received a bequest from Richard's widow Alice in 1504.[21] The sole obit recorded in 1548 was supported by a tenement in Forby Street, Limehouse.[22]

CHURCH LIFE IN THE 16TH AND 17TH CENTURIES. Prominent 16th-century vicars included Richard Pace (d. 1536), 1519–27, dean of St. Paul's and frequently an envoy overseas, who was buried in Stepney church.[23] His successor Richard Sampson (d. 1554), a member of Cardinal Wolsey's household who held other preferments, resigned in 1534 on receiving the rectory of Hackney, and became successively bishop of Chichester and of Coventry and Lichfield.[24] Miles Willan, canon of Windsor, was presented by the king in 1534 but was deprived that year, probably for not reporting treasonable words.[25] Simon Heynes (d. 1552), vicar 1535–7, rector of Fulham and canon of Windsor, went on an embassy and was later dean of Exeter.[26] William Jerome, vicar 1537–40, preached at court but was executed as a Lutheran in 1540 at the time of Thomas Cromwell's fall.[27] Anthony Anderson (d. 1593), vicar 1587–93, the theological writer and preacher, held other livings,[28] and George Goldman, vicar 1605–34, became archdeacon of Essex.[29]

Several leading residents clashed with Henry More, vicar 1545–54 and formerly the last abbot of St. Mary Graces, when he tried to prevent protestant preaching, and More was taken up before Archbishop Cranmer by Edward Underhill (d. 1562), the 'hot gospeller' who had come to live in Limehouse. Underhill was imprisoned under Mary, as was a protestant neighbour Thomas Ivey, the high constable, and moved away from Stepney to avoid More and others, including one whom he called the spy for Stepney parish.[30] Marian protestants met in Stepney, as elsewhere around London, in a group numbering from 20 to 200 and including Frenchmen and Dutchmen; locations included Church's house by the river in Wapping (Whitechapel), the King's Head, Ratcliff, and the Swan, Limehouse.[31]

Separatist meetings continued in the parish and included both mariners exposed to new ideas abroad and religious refugees; some congregations formed nonconformist churches in the late 17th century.[32] Brownists or Barrowists led by Francis Johnson in the 1580s and 1590s used many of the same meeting places as the Marian protestants; members included three shipwrights from Wapping, and the house of one Lewes in Stepney was also used for meetings.[33] John Penry (d. 1593), printer of the Martin Marprelate tracts, joined the congregation in 1592 when it was meeting near Stepney; his recognition by the vicar led to his arrest at Ratcliff and execution.[34] Richard Lacy, tailor, buried in Stepney churchyard in 1608, was described on his grave as a 'stubborn Brownist'; although he was not otherwise recorded among the separatists, his surname occurred among them in the 1560s and 1580s.[35] The first Arminian or General Baptist church in England was formed in 1612 in Spitalfields, where Thomas Helwys settled on his return from Amsterdam.[36] It continued under John Murton and may have been the group meeting in 1626.[37]

The former playwright Stephen Gosson (d. 1624) was appointed lecturer in 1585, preaching every Wednesday and catechizing on Sunday, and was paid £20 a year from a special rate and £10 by the rector; he became rector of Great Wigborough (Essex) in 1591.[38] Subsequent lecturers also acted as curates.[39] Other signs of the inhabitants' desire to control religious matters were the keeping of a permanent record of vestry orders from 1580, the setting and granting of the paschal money to each vicar, and readiness to proceed against a vicar who did not pay the set fee for it.[40]

Some of the Stepney residents prosecuted for absence from the parish church, attending conventicles in private houses, and being rebaptized[41]

[14] Cal. Pat. 1343–5, 352.
[15] Cal. Papal Reg. viii. 572; x. 524. Chedworth was bailiff of Stepney 1465: above, Stepney manor; Cobhams.
[16] Guildhall MS. 9171/4, f. 206v., and passim.
[17] Below.
[18] e.g. Guildhall MS. 9171/10, ff. 52v., 60, 73v., 90v., 93, 123, 137, 180, 187.
[19] Guildhall MS. 9531/12, f. 115; L. & P. Hen. VIII, ii (2), p. 1453; below, Bethnal Green, churches.
[20] Guildhall MS. 9171/5, f. 306.
[21] P.R.O., PROB 11/14 (P.C.C. 2 Holgrave, wills of Ric. and Alice Etgoos).
[22] P.R.O., E 318/30/1712; Lond. Rec. Soc. xvi. 72.
[23] D.N.B.   [24] Ibid.
[25] L. & P. Hen. VIII, vii, pp. 312, 614.   [26] D.N.B.
[27] L. & P. Hen. VIII, xiv (2), p. 305; J. J. Scarisbrick,

Henry VIII (1971), 490–5.
[28] D.N.B.
[29] Le Neve, Fasti, 1541–1857, St. Paul's, Lond. 9.
[30] D.N.B.; Tudor Tracts, ed. A. F. Pollard (1903), 170–98.
[31] C. Burrage, Early Eng. Dissenters (1912), i. 70–2.
[32] Congs. which continued after 1660 are treated below, prot. nonconf., and under respective hamlets.
[33] Burrage, Early Eng. Dissenters, i. 145–9.   [34] D.N.B.
[35] Lysons, Environs, iii. 451; Burrage, Early Eng. Dissenters, ii. 10, 12, 19.
[36] M. R. Watts, The Dissenters (1978), 49.
[37] A. C. Underwood, Hist. of English Baptists (1947), 49–50.
[38] D.N.B.; Mems. Stepney Par. 10.
[39] e.g. Mems. Stepney Par. 38 n.
[40] Ibid. passim; above.
[41] Cal. S.P. Dom. 1635–6, 98, 468.

may have been members of the first Calvinistic or Particular Baptist church in England, formed in Wapping in 1633 by seceders from John Lathrop's Independent church which met in and around the City. In 1638 they were meeting in a building between Old Gravel Lane and Broad Street in Wapping-Stepney, probably the Meeting House Alley where they were still worshipping in 1669.[42]

A second lectureship was established after a petition in 1641, when the House of Commons ordered that the parishioners could pay for Sunday morning and afternoon lectures and that the week-day lecture, then held on Thursday, be continued. Stepney's petition also resulted in an order that parishioners elsewhere, who lacked such provision, could set up lectures and maintain a preacher.[43] The morning and afternoon preachers were respectively Jeremy Burroughs (d. 1646) and William Greenhill (d. 1671), noted Independents to whom the Commons gave the permanent management of preaching on the fast-days.[44]

The petition for the second lectureship was lodged a month after the arrival of a new vicar, William Stampe. Both he and his curate, Edward Edgworth, provoked ill feeling in 1642 by opposing the Long Parliament: a parishioner from Limehouse said she would rather hear a cart-wheel creak or a dog bark than hear the curate preach, while one from Stepney made wild speeches against both men and the Book of Common Prayer.[45] Divine service, taken by the curate, was interrupted on the day that 'tumults' took place in the churchyard, when four men enlisting volunteers to serve parliament were dragged off to a justice, apparently Timothy Stampe, by the constable and the vicar. They, another constable, and Timothy Stampe, were summoned before the Commons as delinquents, and an impeachment was drawn up against both Stampes, who escaped to Oxford.[46] William Stampe was replaced as vicar by Joshua Hoyle (d. 1654).[47]

An Independent church, formed in Mile End in 1644 under William Greenhill, maintained a separate organization while Greenhill was vicar, 1654–60. Many parishioners joined and moved between sects both inside and outside the parish, and remained dissenters after 1662.[48] The vestry failed to buy the advowson of the vicarage from the mortgagees in 1660,[49] and that year Greenhill was replaced by Dr. Emanuel Utye, chaplain to Charles I and II.[50] Utye, however, agreed that the vestry might appoint an orthodox lecturer for Sundays and Thursdays at a fee of £100 raised by the parish.[51]

NEW CHAPELS AND REDUCTION OF THE PARISH. Although proposals in 1641–2 and 1650 to divide Stepney into four parishes were not carried out,[52] chapels were founded to serve populous outlying areas. At Poplar, after a petition in 1642, the East India Co. gave a site and later £200 towards the building of a chapel, completed in 1654; the first chaplain was appointed by William Greenhill.[53] Shadwell chapel was built in 1656 by Mr. Neale, lessee of the dean and chapter's estate; its first minister was Matthew Mead, nominated by Greenhill, ejected at the Restoration, and later Greenhill's successor as minister of the Independents' Stepney meeting.[54] An Act in 1669 made the chapel the parish church of St. Paul, Shadwell.[55] St. George's chapel on Bethnal green was perhaps not in public use in 1547 when the bishop granted it with its adjoining house and garden to Sir Ralph Warren and his wife Joan for 99 years,[56] but it was used by inhabitants of the hamlet in 1652, who heard three sermons a week there and, having repaired it, wanted to acquire it in trust for their permanent use.[57] By 1716, however, it had fallen into decay.[58] A proprietary chapel for Spitalfields was opened in 1692 by Sir George Wheler on his estate, south of White Lion Street fronting the later Church Passage.[59]

The report which preceded the Act of 1711 for Building Fifty New Churches stated that the population of Stepney (by then excluding Shadwell) had increased to 86,000, served only by St. Dunstan's, the chapels at Bow and Poplar, and Wheler's chapel. The commissioners empowered under the Act spent nearly £107,000 on the parish.[60] Their new churches were St. Anne's, Limehouse, built 1712–24, St. George-in-the-East, 1715–23, and Christ Church, Spitalfields, 1723–9, serving the three parishes created from the hamlets of Limehouse, Wapping-Stepney, and Spitalfields respectively. At Stratford Bow a parish was delineated and in 1719 the chapel was consecrated by the bishop, but separation from St. Dunstan's was delayed until an Act of 1730 provided an endowment from public funds.[61]

Bethnal Green in 1716 petitioned for a church, which might also serve Mile End New Town. A site was bought in 1725, but it was not until 1743 that an Act made the hamlet of Bethnal Green a separate parish, for which St. Matthew's church was built in 1743–6.[62] Mile End New Town, except for a small portion given to Spitalfields,[63] was left with Mile End Old Town, Ratcliff, and Poplar, in the truncated parish of St. Dunstan's, Stepney. Poplar became a separate ecclesiastical and civil parish in 1817 with a new church, All Saints.[64]

42 Burrage, *Early Eng. Dissenters*, i. 326; E. F. Kevan, *Lond.'s Oldest Bapt. Ch.* [1933]. Later hist. reserved for Wapping.
43 *C.J.* ii. 281; W. A. Shaw, *Hist. of Eng. Ch.* ii (1900), 183, 300.
44 *D.N.B.* s.v. Burroughs; Greenhill; *C.J.* ii. 686, 744.
45 *Mdx. County Rec.* iii. 174.
46 *C.J.* ii, 690, 728, 768; *Walker Revised*, 58.   47 *D.N.B.*
48 Ibid. s.v. Greenhill; A. T. Jones, *Notes on Early Days of Stepney Mtg.* [1887], 17, 22; below, prot. nonconf.
49 *Mems. Stepney Par.* 232.
50 *Cal. S.P. Dom.* 1660–1, 552.
51 *Mems. Stepney Par.* 232–4.
52 *C.J.* ii. 165, 180, 461; Lysons, *Environs*, iii. 448.
53 B.L. Lansd. MS. 814, ff. 26–8.

54 Below, prot. nonconf.   55 Smith, *Hist. E. Lond.* 96–8; Clarke, *Lond. Chs.* 153. Later hist. of Poplar and Shadwell chapels reserved for treatment under those hamlets.
56 Guildhall MS. 9531/12, f. 115–v.
57 G.L.R.O., M93/158, f. 24; below, Bethnal Green, parish church; below, for possible chapel in par. ch.
58 Barnes, *Stepney Chs.* 15.
59 *T.L.M.A.S.* viii. 454, 461–2.
60 Barnes, *Stepney Chs.* 18, 23, 30.
61 Ibid. 26; 3 Geo. II, c. 3.
62 Barnes, *Stepney Chs.* 25; Clarke, *Lond. Chs.* 153; below, Bethnal Green, parish church.
63 Barnes, *Stepney Chs.* 26.
64 57 Geo. III, c. 34 (Local and Personal).

CHURCH LIFE IN THE 18TH AND 19TH CENTURIES. In the 18th century incumbents, assisted by one or two curates, were mainly fellows of Brasenose; Ralph Cawley, 1759–71, later became its principal. Two services were held on Sunday and communion once a month and on the great festivals; the children were catechized in Lent.[65] At the general catechizing in 1805 children of all backgrounds, notably those from the workhouse, showed good understanding; catechizing continued once a month and sermons were adapted to the needs of the young.[66] Margaretta Brown by will proved 1830 left £1,400 stock, from which the rector was to have £20 a year for monthly prayers and lessons on a weekday, followed by a catechism; the clerk and sexton received small sums and the rest was to buy bibles and prayerbooks. In 1894 services every Thursday were attended by c. 600 children from Stepney Parochial, Red Coat, and Infant schools. The charity was still operating in 1986.[67]

In the early 19th century the work of the Church was hampered by Stepney's worsening social conditions and the rectors' financial problems.[68] Richard Sandbach, 1785–9, left many debts, the settlement of which depended on a suit for the recovery of tithes, and Thomas Barneby, 1815–42, let much of the income dwindle for want of collecting small dues.[69] Not only financial problems but possibly religious differences as well led Daniel Vawdrey, 1842–7, to describe his incumbency as a time of constant warfare; thankful to leave, he waited until 'proper wardens' were in place, in order to spare his successor the usual 'odious struggle'.[70] Richard Lee, 1847–69, found the afternoon lectureship in abeyance, until in 1851 the vestry chose a lecturer. The bishop refused to license him, and a public meeting asserted the rights of protestants against Tractarianism. The lecturer's first sermon was disrupted, and the rector was said to have opposed the parish's right of appointment.[71] Several writs for debt were issued against Lee, including one by Brasenose College, besides a writ for damages probably for cancelling a building contract for the glebe. As a result he lived abroad from 1853 until 1858 or later,[72] and the living was sequestered from 1853 to 1868, to the detriment of local religious life. Lee also sold off gravestones, and the stock held in his name for Hester Welch's charity for bread for the poor in Mile End Old Town.[73]

After Poplar became a separate parish, Step-ney's three remaining hamlets had a population of 35,000 but Anglican church provision for only 1,500. Subscriptions were raised for a chapel of ease to seat 1,340, two-thirds free; it was begun in 1818 and, with aid from the church building commissioners, consecrated in 1823. It later became the district church of St. Philip the Apostle, Newark Street, Mile End Old Town.[74] The average attendance at St. Dunstan's in 1851 was 1,500 in the morning, 130 in the afternoon, and 1,200 in the evening;[75] in 1886 it was 847 in the morning, and 1,466 in the evening,[76] and in 1902 it was 416 in the morning and 462 in the evening.[77]

Despite efforts by all denominations, including mission services in the street, in 1870 Mile End Road and all its alleys revealed Sabbath desecration: food shops were full, photographers were at work, and most goods could readily be bought.[78] Few inhabitants were attracted by ordinary Anglican services, while the large congregations at High Church services came mainly from outside the area, later declining as such services were provided elsewhere.[79]

Many attempts to improve morality in the East End in the late 19th century took the form of social welfare and did not increase church attendance. The Alfred Head Curacy fund, founded by Head's family in 1881, provided the interest on £4,000 for a curate in Mile End Old Town or Ratcliff, the trustees to decide on the church and the duration of the support and the incumbent to nominate the curate. Head's widow Ellen bequeathed an additional £1,000 in 1888, and in 1895 the fund paid £150 a year to a curate at St. Dunstan's.[80] The bishop of London's concern for the East End resulted in north and east London coming under a suffragan from 1879, entitled bishop of Stepney from 1895, who exercised the bishop of London's rights of patronage.[81]

Missionary interest from the 1880s coincided with Jewish immigration from eastern Europe, which prompted Christian families to move away. By 1900 some parishes were entirely Jewish, while in others the population was reduced by slum clearance.[82] Anglican church attendances started to fall in the 1880s (Table), as did those of nonconformists. Increases were shown by Roman Catholics, with high Irish immigration centred on Wapping, and by Jews, whose attendance figures for 1902 probably excluded large numbers in small and unrecorded *chevra*.[83]

65 Guildhall MSS. 9550; 9557, f. 24; *Brasenose Quat. Monographs*, i, mon. iv. 37.
66 *Gent. Mag.* lxxv (2), 608.
67 *Endowed Chars. Lond.* (1897) 72–3, 591, 637–8; Char. Com. file 312290.
68 Above; B. I. Coleman, 'Anglican Ch. Extension and Related Movements c. 1800–1860 with special ref. to Lond.' (Camb. Univ. Ph.D. thesis, 1968), 3.
69 BNC, MS. Bursar Estates 111, I, letter 27 Nov. 1791; MS. Stepney 182, letter from J. M. White, 10 Feb. 1846; above.
70 BNC, MSS. Stepney 182, letters from Vawdrey, 24 Dec. 1846, 1 Feb. 1847.
71 P.L.A. MSS., Portfolio 'Stepney Ch.', copy of notice 7 Apr. 1851; T.H.L.H.L., cuttings 221 Par. Ch., *Illus. Lond. News*, 28 June 1851.
72 BNC, MS. Stepney 181, letters from rector of Poplar, 31 Jan. 1853, and from R. Lee, 7 Nov. 1856, 28

Dec. 1857.
73 Guildhall MS. 19224/233; P.L.A. MSS., Portfolio 'Stepney Ch.', cutting *Illus. Lond. News*. 7 Feb. 1857; T.H.L.H.L., cuttings 221, *Tower Hamlets Indep.* 3 Feb. 1872; *Endowed Chars. Lond.* (1897) 592, 703–4.
74 Guildhall MS. 19224/233, new chapel 1823. Hist. of dist. chs. reserved for treatment under hamlets.
75 P.R.O., HO 129/24, 2/1/5.
76 *Brit. Weekly*, 12 Nov. 1886, p. 4.
77 Mudie-Smith, *Rel. Life*, 49.
78 J. E. Ritchie, *Rel. Life of Lond.* (1870), 206–7.
79 Barnes, Stepney Chs. 41.
80 P.R.O., C 54/18513, m. 31; Endowed Chars. Lond. (1897) 670–1.
81 V.C.H. Mdx. i. 141
82 Clarke, Lond. Chs. 154.
83 Below, Rom. Cathm.; prot. nonconf.

RELIGIOUS ATTENDANCE 1851, 1886, AND 1902

IN MILE END OLD TOWN, MILE END NEW TOWN, AND RATCLIFF

	1851	1886	1902
Population	81,997	137,193 (1881)	140,896 (1901)
Church of England			
attendance	11,815	8,799	6,583
no. of congregations	7	15	16
Church of Scotland			
attendance	910	43	0
no. of congregations	1	1	0
Nonconformist			
attendance	5,319	11,314	7,753
no. of congregations	10	19	20
Roman Catholic			
attendance	2,650	1,756	3,238
no. of congregations	1	3	3
Jewish			
attendance	0	(not known)	2,437
no. of congregations	0		7

Note: Figures for missions, foreign churches, and undenominational services are excluded

Sources. Attendance figures and number of congregations 1851 from P.R.O., HO 129/22 and 24; 1886 from *Brit. Weekly,* 12 Nov.1886, p. 4; 1902 from Mudie-Smith, *Rel. Life,* 49, 55; population figures from *Census.*

The religious census of 1902 showed the Church of England, supposedly strongest in poor districts because of its High Church clergy, to be weaker than expected. Since attendance apparently conferred less status in East London than in West London,[84] all churches tried to attract people through more informal missions. St. Dunstan's in 1906 ran St. Faith's mission church, a mission house at no. 54 Beaumont Square, and missions and bible classes in halls or rooms in Old Church Road, Grosvenor Street, Dongola Street, Clive Street, the parish room, St. Faith's hall, and Red Coat school hall.[85]

The closure of churches began in 1911 in the Spitalfields and Whitechapel area, but despite the destruction of many churches in the Second World War, population changes left a surplus of church buildings,[86] and most of those that remained, including the parish church, were reorganized in 1951 under a measure of 1944 with bombed and surplus churches being demolished.[87] A survey in 1975 showed falling attendances by all denominations in the East End. Most churches were barely half full and lack of funds was forcing many to close or hold their services in small side rooms.[88] A report in 1974 identified the main problems as the lack of local church leaders, most being middle-class outsiders, and the old, expensive buildings or 'plant'; it examined the possible establishment of a Mission Area, where special ecclesiastical laws would assist progress, and recommended the appointment of a mission worker and courses for the clergy.[89]

The deanery of Tower Hamlets, with 22 parishes, was part of the bishopric of Stepney, considered in 1985 the poorest in London and among the Urban Priority Areas identified in the report of the Archbishop of Canterbury's commission on the role of the Church in inner-city areas.[90] Although the report recognized that the old buildings gave the Church a visual presence and were often the only fixed landmarks amidst rapid changes, preservation was difficult as churches continued to close.[91] Of the 16 churches which had served the hamlets of Mile End Old Town, Mile End New Town, and Ratcliff, only the parish church of St. Dunstan and a rebuilt district church were still open as parish churches in 1994.

THE PARISH CHURCH. The church had been dedicated to *ST. DUNSTAN* by

84 Mudie-Smith, *Rel. Life,* 25.
85 Nat. Soc., file on St. Dunstan and St. Faith, Rep. on Par. 1906–7.
86 Hist. of individual chs. reserved for treatment under hamlets.
87 Lond. Gaz. 17 July 1951, p. 3879; Ch. Com. file NB

23/426B, pt. 2.   88 *Evening Standard,* 21 Jan. 1975.
89 T.H.L.H.L., 270, Rep. of Bp. of Stepney's Com. *Mission for Ch. in E. Lond.* (1974).
90 *Faith in the City: A Call for Action by Ch. and Nation* (1985).
91 *Spectator,* 8 Mar. 1986, pp. 9–12.

FIG. 9. THE PARISH CHURCH IN 1755

1302[92] and was rededicated to *ST. DUN-STAN and ALL SAINTS* in 1952,[93] in recognition of a suggestion made in 1708, but never substantiated, that the church might also have been dedicated to All Saints.[94] The existing church, mostly 15th-century but much restored, was refaced with Kentish rag and knapped flint with stone dressings in the Perpendicular style by Newman & Billing in 1872.[95] It has a chancel without aisles, a two-storeyed north vestry with a hexagonal annexe, an aisled and clerestoried nave, north and south porches, and a west tower opening into the nave at its lowest stage.

Before major rebuilding in the 15th century, the church had a chancel in the same position as the later one. The elliptical-headed doorway in its north wall, which led to the vestry, and the heavily restored 13th-century sedilia in the south wall are probably the oldest parts to survive. The shafts of the east window are from a 14th-century window which was rebuilt in the 15th century, as was the south window of the chancel.[96] A nave of unknown length had a north aisle probably by the early 14th century, the date of the second window from its east end.

A squint, preserved in 1994, looked through to the high altar and the aisle may have had a chapel for the altar to St. Katharine, which existed by 1395.[97] The nave may have had a clerestory on the north side, as the windows are smaller than those usual in the 15th century, but the absence of a clerestory in the arcade east of the 15th-century choir screen suggests either that the screen was already there or that the whole clerestory dated from the rebuilding of the nave; traces of a string course east of the screen well below the roof level of 1905 probably mark that of the earlier church.[98]

The building or rebuilding of the nave, aisles, and tower has been dated to the early 15th century,[99] although wills from the 1370s point to work spread over much of the 15th century. Bequests towards construction (*fabricium*), as opposed to repair, were made in 1374–83, 1393–4, 1415, 1429–39, and 1449.[1] Construction of a new bell-tower, contemplated in 1419, was under way in 1425–6 and 1433,[2] and work on the nave in 1451 and 1455.[3] A south aisle, contemplated in 1461 and 1462,[4] had been built by 1467 when work was under way on the new chapel of St. Mary at its east end, where the height of walls

92 Guildhall MS. 25127, no. 2008.
93 *Crockford* added 'All Saints' between 1892 and 1907 edns.
94 Newcourt, *Rep.* i. 738; above.
95 Barnes, Stepney Chs. 46; below, plate 11.
96 Pepys and Godman, Ch. of St. Dunstan, 15–16.
97 *Cal. of Wills in Ct. of Husting*, ii (1), 318.
98 Pepys and Godman, *Ch. of St. Dunstan*, 14–15.

99 Clarke, *Lond. Chs.* 154.
1 Guildhall MSS. 9171/1, ff. 11, 36v., 71, 160, 270, 323; 9171/2, f. 316v.; 9171/3, ff. 234v., 317v., 361, 426, 379, 508; 9171/4, ff. 34v., 262.
2 Ibid. 9171/3, ff. 33v., 34v., 149v., 154, 313.
3 Ibid. 9171/5, ff. 34, 160v.
4 Ibid. f. 352v.; P.R.O., PROB 11/5 (P.C.C. 12 Godyn), f. 96.

FIG. 10. THE PARISH CHURCH IN 1815

east of the rood-loft stairs was raised and the two windows were enlarged.[5] Unspecified new work was mentioned in 1469.[6]

The rood loft was under construction in 1474, but a parishioner left 2d. a week for nearly three years towards the work in 1481, and another made his loan into a gift in 1483.[7] Presumably it was at this time that an external stair turret to the loft, still visible in 1994, was built against the south aisle.

In 1615 the nave had a high pitched roof, and the chancel a flat roof, but by 1795 the chancel had been given a pitched roof, perhaps during repairs in 1656. Both aisle walls seem to have been heightened, partly in brick, between 1615, when the clerestory windows were apparently visible well above the roof of the south aisle, and 1795, when they were hidden by the south aisle.[8] An embattled parapet along the nave was removed in the early 19th century.[9]

The vestry was repaired in 1449,[10] and was probably single-storeyed, because in 1619 the vestry roof was to be altered to allow two windows to be unblocked to improve lighting in the church.[11] The door to the vestry from the chancel was blocked at an unknown date, and a new entrance made from the north aisle. An organ loft was built over the vestry in 1872, when the hexagonal parish vestry was added.[12]

A clock was installed in the tower in 1583,[13] presumably depicted c. 1658.[14] By 1703 the spire had apparently been replaced with the octagonal cupola above an open arcaded stage on a louvred base that was illustrated in 1795 and 1809.[15]

Requests for burial before the west door in 1477 and in the churchyard before the south door in 1540 may suggest that those doors were then unporched.[16] By 1582 a west porch sheltered the recently laid gravestone of Thomas Pickering and his wife.[17] In 1610 a west porch in 'Tuscan style' against the tower was paid for and in 1619 repairs were made to timbered and glazed north and south porches. Two porches were rebuilt in 1684. The north and south and probably the west porch were removed in 1806–8. A south porch with a parish room over it was built in 1847, although the west door remained the main entrance. New north and south porches were built in 1872.[18]

A fire in 1901 damaged the vestries and some of the roofs, the church was restored by J.E.K.

5 Guildhall MS. 9171/6, f. 10v.; Pepys and Godman, *Ch. of St. Dunstan*, 14. They date the chapel to early 15th century. Drawing of 1615 shows different heights of two halves of S. aisle wall.
6 Guildhall MS. 9171/6, f. 45.
7 Ibid. ff. 154, 324v., 369v.
8 Plan of Mercers' est.; Lysons, *Environs*, iii, facing p. 428; Pepys and Godman, *Ch. of St. Dunstan*, 13–14. Below, plate 10.   9 *N. & Q.* 2nd ser. xi. 434.
10 Guildhall MS. 9171/5, f. 1v.
11 *Mems. Stepney Par.* 86.
12 T.H.L.H.L., cuttings 221, *E. Lond. Advertiser*, 24 May

1968; Pepys and Godman, *Ch. of St. Dunstan*, 15, plate 3.
13 *Mems. Stepney Par.* 8.
14 *An Exact Delineation of the Cities of London and Westminster and the Suburbs* by Wm. Faithorne, 1658 (Lond. Top. Soc. 1905). The drawing of the ch. is not very accurate.
15 Gascoyne, *Map*; Pepys and Godman, *Ch. of St. Dunstan*, 12–13.
16 Guildhall MSS. 9171/6, f. 211v.; 9171/11, f. 43.
17 P.R.O., PROB 11/67 (P.C.C. 35 Watson), f. 276; Guildhall MS. 9171/17, f. 216.
18 Pepys and Godman, *Ch. of St. Dunstan*, 14–16.

and J.P. Cutts and rededicated in 1902. War damage, notably in 1945, led to restoration by A. Wontner Smith 1946–52, when the upper stage of the tower was rebuilt, the side aisles were reroofed, and the west door was widened.[19]

Lights for St. Mary were mentioned in 1374 and 1428,[20] but after the chapel of St. Mary was built, the altar, statue, and lights of St. Mary were mentioned very frequently. Besides the altar to St. Katharine, recorded in 1395, 1487, and 1518,[21] the image of St. Anne was mentioned from 1449 and an altar of St. Anne in 1488.[22] Bequests were made for gilding the tabernacle of St. Nicholas in 1500 and for the 'painting of St. Nicholas' in 1501.[23] 'The making of St. George' was considered in 1500, money was bequeathed for an image of the saint in 1518 and 1525, and St. George's chapel in the parish church was mentioned in 1520 and 1540.[24] There were also images of St. Margaret in 1518 and of St. John the Baptist in 1524, besides a Trinity chapel in 1524.[25] Lights were provided by each hamlet, bequests being made in 1520 to the ward light of Bethnal Green[26] and in 1532 to those provided by Poplar, Limehouse, Ratcliff, and Mile End and Bethnal Green.[27] In 1522 torches from a funeral were left to Mile End ward.[28]

A gallery was built in 1580 on the south side of the nave, seven alterations increased the seating between 1601 and 1636, and a gallery was paid for by the Coopers' Company in 1656 for its school.[29] The church was described as a very old, dark, and too small in 1714.[30] It was reseated in 1806,[31] and again in 1847 to a design of Benjamin Ferrey, when short rows of free seats were inserted in the central aisle and, with a gallery on three sides, the church seated 1,600 with 330 free.[32] In 1851, however, the accommodation was recorded as 1,800, of which 400 were free.[33] New fittings were provided in 1885 by Basil Champneys, who shortened the north and south galleries and lowered the ground around the church.[34] The galleries were taken down and the church reseated in 1899[35] by J. E. K. and J. P. Cutts, who removed plaster from the walls, and repositioned some monuments.[36] A new east window by Hugh Easton was dedicated in 1949 and one in the north aisle in 1951. Alterations in 1967–8 included the formation of a priest's vestry in the organ loft of 1872, a parish room in the hexagonal vestry, and of a baptistery by moving the font from the west end of the nave to the north aisle.[37]

An organ was presented in 1525 but removed in 1585. A new organ, by Renatus Harris the elder, was being paid for in 1679. The organ loft was over the west entrance in 1847. The organ was sold in 1872 to Drury Lane theatre and a new organ by Bryceson was installed in the case of 1679 over the vestry, but was burnt in 1901.[38]

Money was left to repair the bells in 1474.[39] The tenor bell was bought in 1540 from the former Holy Trinity priory, Aldgate, where it had been renewed in 1386. In 1600 the peal numbered five; the fifth or great bell, needing repair in 1570, was recast in 1599 by Lawrence Wright of Houndsditch, and again in 1619; the fourth bell was recast in 1600.[40] There were six bells in 1708, eight during the 18th century, and ten from 1806 when the peal was recast by Thomas Mears. When retuned in 1952, the peal was considered among the best in London.[41]

A rood of Barnack stone[42] with the cross and figures in low relief, which was outside over the south door by 1795, is behind the high altar and has been attributed both to the late 12th century[43] and to the early 11th.[44] Shafts on the font are thought to be Norman[45] and a panel of the Annunciation in the chancel wall is 14th-century.[46]

A silver chalice was bought in 1433,[47] perhaps stolen with other plate in 1530.[48] In 1656 the parish owned two silver and gilt bowls with covers, two pewter flagons, a pewter basin, and a brass basin.[49] In 1895 plate included a silver flagon of 1675 given by Mary Masters and another bought in 1687, two cups of 1559 and 1631 and two patens of 1631 and 1713, all silver gilt, a large silver paten and foot of 1686 bought in 1687, and a fine silver gilt spoon of 1692. A beadle's silver headed staff was inscribed '1784' and another was inscribed 'Hamlet of Ratcliff 1752'.[50] The registers begin in 1568.[51]

Many monuments existing in 1714 were removed during 19th-century restorations.[52] In 1994 survivors included the table tomb of Sir Henry Colet (d. 1505) and the painted marble memorial to Robert Clarke (d. 1610), both on the north side of the chancel, and on the south the memorial to

[19] Ibid. 14; T.H.L.H.L., cuttings 221, *E. Lond. Advertiser*, 24 May 1968.
[20] Guildhall MSS. 9171/1, f. 11; 9171/3, f. 460v.
[21] Ibid. 9171/7, f. 104; 9171/9, f. 93; *Cal. of Wills in Ct. of Husting*, ii (1), 318.
[22] Guildhall MSS. 9171/4, f. 262; 9171/7, f. 137v.
[23] Ibid. 9171/6, ff. 231, 251.
[24] Ibid. 9171/8, f. 231; 9171/9, ff. 100v., 162v.; 9171/10, f. 66v.; P.R.O., PROB 11/28 (P.C.C. 28 Alenger, will of Morice Parry), f. 180.
[25] Guildhall MSS. 9171/9, f. 93; 9171/10, f. 40v., 93.
[26] Ibid. 9171/9, f. 162v.   [27] Ibid. 9171/10, f. 180.
[28] Ibid. f. 137v.   [29] *Mems. Stepney Par.* passim.
[30] Paterson, *Pietas Lond.* 76.   [31] *N. & Q.* 2nd ser. xi. 434.
[32] Clarke, *Lond. Chs.* 154; Guildhall MS. 19224/223.
[33] P.R.O., HO 129/24, 2/1/5.
[34] Pepys and Godman, *Ch. of St. Dunstan*, 17.
[35] Misprinted 1889 in Clarke.
[36] T.H.L.H.L., cuttings 221 Par. Ch., 7 Jan. 1900. Below, plate 4.
[37] Barnes, *Stepney Chs.* 47; T.H.L.H.L., cuttings 221, *E. Lond. Advertiser*, 24 May 1968.
[38] *Mems. Stepney Par.* 11; T.H.L.H.L., cuttings

221, article in *Co-Partnership Herald*, 21 Apr. 1935, 37–44, and Feb. 1936, pp. 277–85; *D.N.B.* s.v. Harris, Renatus.
[39] Guildhall MS. 9171/6, f. 154.
[40] *Mems. Stepney Par.* 33–4, 37, 42, 84; Guildhall MS. 9171/16, f. 11v.; Lysons, *Environs*, iii. 428 n.
[41] E. Hatton, New View of Lond. (1708), 218; *V.C.H. Mdx.* ii. 167; T.H.L.H.L., cuttings 221, *Manchester Guardian*, 1 Nov. 1952.
[42] Inf. from rector. Below, plate 3.
[43] Pepys and Godman, *Ch. of St. Dunstan*, 14.
[44] Clarke, *Lond. Chs.* 154.
[45] C.C.C., Clarke MSS., i, f. 51.
[46] Clarke, *Lond. Chs.* 154.
[47] Guildhall MS. 9171/3, ff. 365v., 426.
[48] *L. & P. Hen. VIII*, v, p. 365.
[49] *Mems. Stepney Par.* 227.
[50] Freshfield, *Communion Plate*, 13–14.
[51] In 1994 regs. were in G.L.R.O., P93/DUN. The earliest have been published.
[52] Listed in Lysons, *Environs*, iii. 429–31. Full descriptions of major monuments in Pepys and Godman, *Ch. of St. Dunstan*, 20–39.

Sir Thomas Spert (d. 1541), erected in 1723 by Trinity House which he founded, and a marble monument to Benjamin Kenton (d. 1800), by Richard Westmacott the younger.[53]

The churchyard was enlarged to cope with plague burials in 1626: the vestry used burial fees to take a lease of *c*. 1 a. of waste on the south side of the churchyard from the lord of the manor; a pond was filled in, a wall built,[54] and in 1655 the freehold was bought from the parliamentary trustees.[55] During the plague of 1665, however, the manor court authorized the enclosure of *c*. 1 ¼ a. of waste on the north side of Whitechapel Road near Stonebridge as a additional burial ground.[56] In 1671 the vestry raised funds to take into the churchyard waste on the south side; in the 1680s the churchyard was enlarged with a plot of land acquired from Mrs. Bissaker, probably north or west of the church, and in 1696 with the site of the demolished vestry house on the west side of the

church.[57] Grave-diggers were ordered to collect old bones and deposit them in a charnel house in 1685.[58] In 1683 tavern doors opening into the churchyard were to be blocked off because of tippling and bottles being thrown.[59] Drinking, prostitutes, and grave-robbers who sold bones to local butchers, led the parish in 1845 to seek closure of some paths crossing the churchyard. The rector agreed in 1845 to add the site of the old parsonage to the churchyard;[60] burials in the main part ceased in 1854, and the additional piece was consecrated in 1855 and used until 1856.[61] Earth excavated for building the underground railway was also added. The churchyard became a public garden in 1886 and was managed by the L.C.C. from 1937. Covering *c*. 7 a. in 1935, it was thought to be the largest in London. Graves include those of naval and merchant marine officers, many of distinction, and Matthew Mead (d. 1699), the nonconformist divine, is commemorated.[62]

ROMAN CATHOLICISM TO *c*. 1700

STEPNEY'S maritime role probably accounted for many reports of papists. In 1594 Thomas Leeds was said to keep a priest in Thorne House, Wapping, and his friend Nicholas Wolfe to have a hiding-place and altar in Washington House nearby.[63] A seaman called Hill who lived at the Green Dragon, Ratcliff, was reported to bring many seminary priests into England.[64] The Jesuit Henry Garnett had a house in Spitalfields in 1597[65] and a Jesuit called Stansby or Drury was in Poplar in 1605.[66]

Papists reported in the 17th century were connected with foreign textile workers in and around Spitalfields or with Irish immigration into the riverside hamlets in the 1630s.[67] Recusants in 1678 included 30 from Spitalfields, 15 from Bethnal Green, and 9 from Wapping-Stepney.[68] In 1680 35 were listed for Spitalfields, 15 for Stepney and Spitalfields, 20 for Bethnal Green, 18 for Stepney, 14 for Stepney and Wapping-Stepney, and 3 for

Poplar; in Spitalfields and Bethnal Green most were apparently foreign.[69] Individuals summonsed in 1678–9 included two weavers of Spitalfields with foreign surnames, a victualler of Mile End, and a framework-knitter and a weaver of Bethnal Green. Three foreign tapestry-workers of Bethnal Green stood surety for 16 suspected papists, mostly with foreign surnames; a carver and a sculptor of Blackwall were also suspected.[70] John Potter of Poplar, accused in 1681 of harbouring papists, claimed that one was his Italian servant and that two who had escaped were visitors from Holland.[71] In 1690 a house in Spitalfields was to be searched for articles used in several London chapels.[72] The curate of Stepney had thought that there were no papists in 1706 but found eight, in Wapping, Bethnal Green, Mile End New Town, and Spitalfields.[73] In 1714 about 60 names were reported, in Ratcliff, Wapping, Spitalfields, and Mile End New Town.[74]

PROTESTANT NONCONFORMITY TO 1689

SOME separatist congregations of the early 17th century[75] registered their meetings after 1660, including the Particular Baptists, founded in 1633 in Wapping-Stepney, where in 1669 their meeting house in Meeting House Alley, restored 'as in Cromwell's time', was shared with Independents and was attended by 300,[76] and the Independents' Stepney Meeting, founded in 1644 at Mile End, which registered William Greenhill's house near the parish church in 1669.[77]

Craftsmen and mariners from Wapping, Shadwell, Ratcliff, and Spitalfields attended meetings in 1661 at John Adams's house in Spittle Yard and other sites.[78] Quakers were meeting in the parish by 1664[79] and possibly in 1662–3 when conventicles of *c*. 50 or 100 were broken up;[80] in 1669 it was reported that while the Five Mile Act was being enforced only Quaker meetings were much in evidence.[81] Quakers met in 1664 at the houses of William

53 Clarke, *Lond. Chs.* 154.
54 Pepys and Godman, *Ch. of St. Dunstan,* 40; *Mems. Stepney Par.* 110–11, 113, 116–18, 120; G.L.R.O., M93/204.   55 P.R.O., C 54/3858, no. 19.
56 G.L.R.O., M93/5, ff. 100d.–101d.
57 Ibid. P93/DUN/328, pp. 47, 97, 126, 129, 180.
58 Ibid. p. 141.   59 Ibid. p. 137.
60 Ch. Com. file 20848.   61 Guildhall MS. 19224/233.
62 Ibid; Barnes, *Stepney Chs.* 47. Many of those buried are listed in Lysons, *Environs,* iii. 434–9; tombs described in Pepys and Godman, *Ch. of St. Dunstan,* 43–7.
63 *Cal. S.P. Dom.* 1591–4, 510.
64 Ibid. 511.   65 *D.N.B.*
66 *Cal. S.P. Dom.* 1603–10, 264.
67 *Recusant Hist.* x. 124.
68 Hist. MSS. Com. 17, *11th Rep. II, H.L.,* p. 59.

69 G.L.R.O., MR/RR 3.
70 *Mdx. County Rec.* iv. 101–2, 115, 118–19, 129.
71 Hist. MSS. Com. 17, *11th Rep. II, H.L.,* pp. 148– 9.
72 *Cal. S.P. Dom.* 1689–90, 538.
73 Guildhall MS. 9800, file 2.
74 G.L.R.O., MR/RR 22/8; list largely illegible. Details of individual congs. reserved for treatment under hamlets.   75 Above, churches.
76 Burrage, *Early Eng. Dissenters,* i. 326; *Orig. Rec. of Early Nonconf.* ed. G. L. Turner, i. 89.
77 *Early Nonconf.* ed. Turner, i (1911), 89.
78 *Mdx. County Rec.* iii. 311–13.
79 J. Besse, *Collection of Sufferings of People called Quakers,* i (1753), 361–478.
80 *Mdx. County Rec.* iii. 321–2, 325, 330, 332.
81 *Early Nonconf.* ed. Turner, i. 90.

Beane in Stepney, of Capt. James Brock, of Peter Burdett in Westbury Street, Spitalfields, and of Sibyl Heaman in Limehouse, and at another building. From the numbers arrested, the Quaker meetings at Beane's and Burdett's houses, both of which led to permanent meeting houses, were of similar size and exceeded only by the City meeting at Bull and Mouth Yard.[82]

In 1669 Stepney was reported to have several buildings fitted up as meeting houses, besides conventicles in private houses.[83] Presbyterians had fitted up a warehouse near Ratcliff Cross, where 200 were said to meet, and a purpose-built house in Spitalfields, where 800 met under Dr. Samuel Annesley; they also had a chapel in Broad Street, Wapping-Stepney, from 1668.[84] Quakers had a purpose-built brick house in Schoolhouse Lane, Ratcliff (Brook Street), for 500, and a meeting place for 500 in Westbury Street. Baptists met at the houses of Thomas Launder, a rich butcher, in Limehouse, where the congregation was 100, and of Mr. Cherry in Poplar, where Launder was the preacher; in Wapping they had a purpose-built house in Artichoke Lane, with a congregation of 200, as well as the old meeting house in Meeting House Alley. In addition to the congregation who shared the Meeting House Alley building with the Baptists and the Stepney Meeting at Greenhill's house, Independents also met in Rose Lane, Spitalfields, at a house fitted up at Bethnal Green, and at a new brick house in Red Maid Lane, Wapping, with a congregation of 300. The Baptists and Independents were said to assemble daily at one or other of their meeting houses, and to baptize many of the children of the parish.

In addition to the fixed meetings there were itinerant groups meeting in private houses, individuals who moved between sects, and Sunday walkers drawn by curiosity. The women and persons of low rank who in 1669 were reported to make up most meetings presumably included the many prosperous trades- and craftsmen who were summonsed. It was said that meetings had increased greatly since the Five Mile Act was no longer enforced but that greater resolution would soon reconcile most dissenters, especially Independents and Presbyterians, to the Anglican church, whose services they had attended until recently. Since the death of Sir William Ryder and Major Manly, 'who kept this parish in good order', there had been no resident justice.[85]

In 1666 the Secretary of State was informed about six Stepney meeting houses, including those at Spitalfields and Wapping,[86] and in 1670, perhaps as a result of the report on conventicles of 1669, the lieutenant of the Tower Hamlets, Sir John Robinson, was ordered to keep watch on sectarians. Robinson, who thought that dissenters were losing heart, wanted to compel owners of meeting houses to put them to other uses.[87] Despite the Declaration of Indulgence in 1672, many meetings were refused licences, and many others may have chosen to avoid drawing attention to themselves by applying. Licences were issued for the houses of Samuel Annesley and T. Danson in Spitalfields (both Presbyterian), of Richard Loton (Congregationalist) and Mr. Gould (Presbyterian) in Spittle Yard, of Richard Ward (Congregationalist) in Bethnal Green, of Joseph Farnworth in Buky Street and another in Globe Alley, both Wapping (Presbyterian), for a house by the Hermitage, near Wapping (Congregationalist); and the house of W. Polter in Bell Lane, Stepney (Baptist).[88]

Between 1661 and 1689 more conventiclers were summonsed from Stepney than anywhere else in Middlesex. Arrests reflected not only the strength of Dissent but also the availability of troops under the lieutenant of the Tower Hamlets and his troops, whereas elsewhere in Middlesex, except in Westminster, justices had to rely on the local constables.[89] The lieutenancy also reported meetings and destroyed meeting houses: in 1670 soldiers took away furniture from the Ratcliff Quaker meeting, and soon after demolished the house, removing 12 loads of materials.[90] In 1682 the lieutenant, Sir William Smyth, used troops to smash the fittings in the Independents' Stepney meeting house.[91] While many conventiclers arrested in Stepney were not residents, parishioners were themselves arrested farther afield. Only after the Toleration Act of 1689 did residents make up the majority of members of dissenting churches within the parish.[92]

Quaker meetings at Beane's house were broken up on 20 successive Sundays in 1664–5, when attendances ranged from 14 to 134 and the numbers convicted from 4 to 34. From 1664 inhabitants convicted for a third time were transported, their goods being seized by the constables and headboroughs to pay for conveying them to the ships. In Middlesex only St. Sepulchre's parish had more transportees than Stepney in 1665.[93]

Sympathy, if not support, for dissenters, was shown in 1665 by a Stepney yeoman and five craftsmen of Limehouse, one of them a Baptist, who were fined for refusing to help the constable take conventiclers from Sibyl Heaman's house to Newgate. In 1683 a headborough of Stepney and the surveyor of the poor of Limehouse neglected to distrain conventiclers' goods,[94] and in 1685 another headborough was fined for warning a Quaker about a warrant.[95]

In 1682, when persecution resumed, Matthew Mead, minister of Stepney Meeting, William (probably the same as Hercules) Collins, of Old Gravel Lane, Wapping-Stepney, and Samuel

81 *Early Nonconf.* ed. Turner, i. 90.
82 Besse, *Sufferings*, i, *passim*.
83 Two paras. based on *Early Nonconf.* ed. Turner, i. 88–90.
84 T.H.L.H.L., pamphlets 222.5, *John Knox Church, Stepney Way.*
85 *Early Nonconf.* ed. Turner, i. 88–90.
86 *Cal. S.P. Dom.* 1665–6, 412.
87 Ibid. 1670, 237, 267–8, 310.

88 F. Bate, *Declaration of Indulgence*, App. xxxvii, xxxviii, xxxix.
89 *Lond. Jnl.* xiii. 108; below.
90 Besse, *Sufferings*, i. 416, 428.
91 Hist. MSS. Com. 2, *3rd Rep., Legh*, p. 269.
92 *Mdx. County Rec.* iii, *passim*.
93 Ibid.; Besse, *Sufferings*, i, *passim*.
94 *Mdx. County Rec.* iii. 370; iv. 201–2.
95 Besse, *Sufferings*, i. 478.

Annesley, were each convicted several times of teaching at conventicles in their homes and at meeting houses. Also convicted in 1682 were preachers in Wapping-Stepney (Independent and Baptist), Limehouse (Quaker), Ratcliff (Quaker). While Hercules Collins was imprisoned his Baptists met in private houses from 1683 to 1688.[96] Convictions in 1683 for meetings in Stepney, Spitalfields, and Bethnal Green,[97] were followed by others until 1686 for conventicles in private houses, mainly in the Spitalfields area.[98] In 1686 20 out of 70 such convictions at quarter sessions were of people who lived in Stepney.[99]

CHARITIES FOR THE POOR

THE Charity Commissioners in the 1890s apportioned all the charities which had been established before partition of the ancient parish among its relevant subdivisions. Neither Whitechapel (including St. John's, Wapping), whose separation predated the charities, nor Stratford Bow, for practical purposes autonomous since 1497, was entitled to a share;[1] before Shadwell's separation only Gibson's almshouses and schools and Fuller's almshouses had been established. By the 20th century all the charities managed by the parish had been divided among the benefiting hamlets or parishes, most or which drew up schemes to administer several charities together.

The following account gives the early history of each charity founded for the ancient parish and indicates how the charity was later divided amongst the hamlets; details of its later application and the collective schemes are reserved for the accounts of those hamlets.

ALMSHOUSE CHARITIES. The Ratcliff charity originated in almshouses and a school built in 1531 by Nicholas Gibson (d. 1540), citizen and sheriff of London, on part of his copyhold land on the north side of Broad Street and the east side of the later Schoolhouse Lane.[2] In 1552 his widow Avice, then widow of Sir Anthony Knyvett, settled Gibson's copyhold estate on the Coopers' Company of London in trust to maintain the school and almshouses. The profits were to support seven poor people from Stepney and seven members of the Coopers' Company or their widows in the almshouses, each inmate to receive £1 6s. 8d. a year.[3] Avice also granted London property for the same uses to John Chorley, who left it to the company in 1553.[4] The copyhold in Ratcliff was enfranchised in 1774.[5] Property in London was also given by Henry Cloker in 1573, to provide 1s. a year to each inmate and money for the school, and by Peter Thelloe in 1599, to maintain the school and almshouses. Richard Young left £50 for coals in 1665, and Henry Strode left £500 in 1703 to increase the pensions.[6] Six more almshouses, for coopers, were built beside the existing ones in 1613 with money left by Tobias Wood, and thereafter the original almshouses were used only for women.[7] Stepney parish vestry brought a suit against the Coopers' Company regarding their administration of the almshouses and school in 1684.[8] New almshouses were built by the company in 1694 (below).[9]

In 1818 the whole income of the charity was £595 and most of the expenditure of £562 was on the almshouses, where c. 1830 the schoolmaster seems to have acted as unofficial warden for the company.[10] An additional house was built in 1826, allowing the number of Stepney widows to be increased to eight. The payment to each almswoman was raised from £8 to £10 in 1814 and to £15 in 1826. Income was £1,057 and expenditure £663 in 1837. Allowances were again raised in 1846, 1860, and 1876.[11]

The Ratcliff charity was combined with Prisca Coborn's school charity under a Scheme of 1891. The almshouse branch received £1,400 a year instead of sums from Cloker's and Thelloe's gifts; with property in the City and in Woolwich, and £1,027 in stock, its total income was £1,822 a year. In 1894 the almswomen, eight from Stepney and eight coopers' widows, each received £26 a year besides coal, 10s. at Christmas, and medical attendance; six former coopers were supported by Wood's gift. Out-pensions were paid from 1854; in 1894 ten pensioners received £20 a year, ten received £15, and ten received £10, half of each group being resident in Stepney.[12]

The almshouses were closed and the inmates given pensions in 1894, when the whole site was cleared and let by the Coopers' Company. In 1936 c. 60 people received pensions.[13] In 1964-5 the income of £2,518 relieved 9 poor of the company (£1,007) and 19 poor of Stepney (£739). In 1972-3 the income was £3,853 and the payments were £1,570. A Scheme of 1976 for what had been renamed the Ratcliff Pension charity allotted 29/52nds of the income to relieve members of the Coopers' Company and the remainder to residents of Stepney parish as it had existed in 1897. The assets of the charity

96 *Mdx. County Rec.* iv. 182-6; Kevan, *Lond.'s Oldest Bapt. Ch.* 44-5, 66.
97 *Mdx. County Rec.* iv. 201-2, 230.
98 Ibid. iv. 235, 238, 242, 247, 249, 252-6, 258-9, 262, 288-9.
99 Ibid. iv. 301-2. Later hist. of individual chs. reserved for treatment under hamlets.
1 *Endowed Chars. Lond.* (1897), 600.
2 *Lond. Topog. Rec.* xvii. 5. For the sch.: *V.C.H. Mdx.* i. 291-4.
3 P.R.O., PROB 11/28 (P.C.C. 12 Alenger), f. 93v.; *Endowed Chars. Lond.* (1897), 559, 584.

4 *Endowed Chars. Lond.* (1897), 603; *Cal. of Wills in Ct. of Husting,* 2 (ii), 654.
5 W. Foster, *The Ratcliffe Charity 1536-1936* (1936),8.
6 *Endowed Chars. Lond.* (1897), 584-5.
7 Foster, *Ratcliffe Char.* 12.
8 G.L.R.O., P93/DUN/328, pp. 132, 137.
9 *V.C.H. Mdx.* i. 291.
10 Ibid. 292.
11 Foster, *Ratcliffe Char.* 23-4, 31; *Endowed Chars. Lond.* (1897), 587.
12 *Endowed Chars. Lond.* (1897), 610, 619.
13 Foster, *Ratcliffe Char.* 32.

consisted of 46 per cent of the net sale or rents of property in Schoolhouse Lane, Ratcliff, belonging to the Coopers and Coborn Educational Fund, the right to £1,400 a year from that fund, and £21,987 stock.[14]

The almshouses of 1694 stood slightly north of the older buildings, forming with the school three sides of a narrow courtyard off Schoolhouse Lane; to the north were garden plots for the almswomen. After a fire at Ratcliff the almshouses were rebuilt in 1795–6, a little farther north and on a similar plan. The central block had a chapel, served from St. James's, Ratcliff, and attended by the almswomen twice a week. The chapel was flanked by two-storeyed houses, including lodgings for the schoolmaster and schoolmistress; the wings, after the addition of 1826, each contained four houses. The main part of the school, vacated under the reorganization of 1891, was behind the north wing.[15]

John Fuller by will proved 1592 directed his wife to build almshouses in Stepney for 12 single men aged 50 years or more and in Shoreditch for 12 widows. The almshouses were to be managed by the Mercers' Company and each set was to be supported by a rent charge of £50 a year from lands in Lincolnshire.[16] The almshouses had been built by 1623, when Fuller's widow and her husband Sir Thomas Mansell settled the lands on her for life, the rent charge to be paid by her husband's two sons.[17] Stepney vestry apparently managed the almshouses by 1641, having asked the company in 1639 to accept responsibility or relinquish it to the parish. Receipts in 1641 were £88 and disbursements £44 to the churchwardens of Shoreditch for the women's almshouses, £37 13s. to the almsmen, and £4 18s. for a lawsuit.[18] Since no residential qualifications had been laid down, in 1662 the six westernmost rooms were reserved for men from Ratcliff, Shadwell, and Poplar, and the other six for Limehouse, Mile End, Bethnal Green, and Spitalfields.[19] The rent charge was finally settled on the almshouses in 1687 by George Kemeys, the landowner, after a Chancery suit.[20]

In 1837 inmates were chosen by the churchwardens but no longer came from Shadwell. Ratcliff, Poplar, Limehouse, and Spitalfields each appointed two inmates; Mile End Old Town, Mile End New Town, St. George-in-the-East, and Bethnal Green each appointed one. Married men were admitted and their widows allowed to stay. Each hamlet paid for the repairs of its room. The churchwarden of Christ Church (Spitalfields) received £50 a year from the managing solicitors, from which he paid £4 to each inmate, keeping £2 for himself. Despite a Chancery Order, the charity had not

apparently been incorporated. In 1864 the property and rent charge were vested in the Official Trustee, and the several churchwardens were appointed trustees. The almshouses were sold in 1865, after new ones had been built at Harrow Green, Leyton (Essex). There was no fund for repairs in 1894, when the rent charge provided £3 15s. 3d. for each inmate.[21] Pensions were paid from the charity between 1922 and 1950.

Fuller's (men's) almshouses, presumably those built by 1623, stood in 1652 on former waste given to the parish by the earl of Cleveland on the north side of Mile End Road, east of Cambridge Heath Road and bounded south and west by Mile End green. They consisted of 12 brick dwellings, with a wall in front and small gardens behind,[22] and probably formed the building shown in 1703.[23] The same buildings may have survived in 1837 in Eagle Street, called Spread Eagle Place in 1864.[24]

Capt. James Cook and his widow Dame Alice Row left money for four almshouses, providing eight rooms for seamen of Stepney and their widows, which were built on land leased to the churchwardens by Thomas Grimley in 1673; this may be the waste that Grimley was asked by the vestry to procure from the lady of the manor in 1671.[25] The hamlet of Mile End Old Town repaired the decayed buildings c. 1815 and put one person into each room, normally a seaman's widow who lived rent free. Although given for the benefit of Stepney as a whole, in 1837 the charity was in practice confined to Mile End Old Town. Coals at Christmas were provided under the will of Thomas Daplyn, proved 1845, from the interest on £50 stock after repair of his tomb. In 1871 the charity also received £20, invested in stock, for a neighbour's use of the almshouse wall as a party wall.

After the almshouses' site had been leased for building (below), a Scheme in 1885 for the Cook, Row, and Daplyn charities furnished pensions to up to eight seamen or their widows, resident in Stepney for at least 5 years and not receiving poor relief. The income was £90 a year from the builder, besides £1 19s. 4d. interest on stock. In 1894 eight women received 4s. a week with extra during winter, and the charity was regarded as exclusively for Mile End Old Town.[26] In 1976 the charity received rents of £3,000 a year and held c. £16,000 in stock and c. £20,000 on deposit. From 1977 the income was administered under Mile End Old Town's Scheme for Stepney Relief in Need Charity.[27]

The almshouses in 1845 stood on the north side of Mile End Road opposite York Place, in 1871 called no. 391 Mile End Road. They were dilapidated in 1880 and taken on a 70-year building lease by Abraham Barnett, who built

[14] Char. Com. file 234613.
[15] Foster, *Ratcliffe Char.* 17; Rocque, *Map of Lond.* (1741–5), sheet 6; *Endowed Chars. Lond.* (1897), 610, 619. Below, plate 12.
[16] P.R.O., PROB 11/79 (P.C.C. 46 Harington), f. 355.
[17] *32nd Rep. Com. Char.* II, H.C. 140, pp. 503–5 (1837–8), xxvi; W. K. Jordan, *Chars. of Lond. 1480–1660* (1960), 145.
[18] *Mems. Stepney Par.* 168, 175.
[19] Ibid. 241.

[20] *32nd Rep. Com. Char.* II, H.C. 140, pp. 503–5 (1837–8), xxvi.
[21] *Endowed Chars. Lond.* (1897), 587–8, 628–30.
[22] G.L.R.O., M93/439, f. 5.
[23] Gascoyne, *Map of Mile End Old Town* (1703). Below, plate 14.
[24] *Endowed Chars. Lond.* (1897), 587.
[25] G.L.R.O., P93/DUN/328, p. 52.
[26] *Endowed Chars. Lond.* (1897), 593, 638–40.
[27] Char. Com. files 250130, 250131.

six houses (nos. 1–6 Barnett Market or nos. 391A-F Mile End Road) on the site.[28]

John Pemel by will dated 1681 left £1,200 to the Drapers' Company to buy land, using the rents to pay for a single-storeyed almshouse in Mile End and £4 a year to each of the eight almspeople, besides coals and gowns with the company's badge; the residue was for repairs and sick relief. Four rooms were for widows of freemen of the company and four for widows of Stepney seamen. Land was bought in Southwark and the City in 1694 and the almshouses were completed in 1698, situated near Stonebridge (Mile End Gate), the four easternmost rooms being used for widows nominated by the eight Stepney hamlets in turn. Rents produced £52 12s. a year in 1861. Money from the sale of the almshouses in 1863 provided new ones in Bromley (Mdx.) and then in Tottenham (below). Additional land in Tottenham produced a rental income of £130 16s. in 1892, when four of the almshouses were still appropriated to Stepney, although the rotation of nominations had been abandoned in 1884. In 1894 each of the four widows received £25 4s. and 2 tons of coal a year, with medical care.[29]

Pemel's almshouses were called the Drapers' Almshouses in 1813, lying on the north side of Whitechapel Road in the parish of Bethnal Green.[30] They were sold in 1863 for £5,133 in money and stock, spent partly on those built in Bromley on land held by the Drapers' Company for Sir John Jolles's and Edmanson's almshouse charities, which were compensated. The Bromley site was taken for the N.L.R. in 1867 and Elmslea in Bruce Grove, Tottenham, was bought with 50 a., where new buildings for Pemel's, Jolles's, and Edmanson's charities were later known as the Sailmakers' almshouses.[31]

Mary Bowry, by will proved 1728, left the residue of her property to buy land between Stepney church and Bow and to build as many almshouses as possible for mariners or their widows, to be nominated by the minister and churchwardens after the death of her trustees. Under a Chancery order of 1740 land was bought in 1742[32] and eight almshouses were built in 1744[33] for which each parish or hamlet nominated an inmate. Stock purchased for a maintenance fund was valued at £2,555 in 1810. The inmates received £5 a month between them until 1836, later increased by 12s. a month to each. Repairs to each house were defrayed by its respective hamlet. By 1894 the almshouses had been sold and the whole income was distributed as pensions of £21 12s. with £2 for coal to each of the eight widows.[34] In 1939 the charity was divided and each hamlet or parish received c. £763 in stock, the income to be paid as before in pensions to poor seamen or their widows.[35]

Bowry's almshouses stood in the parish of Bromley on the south side of Bow Road, next to the Drapers' Company's almshouses (Jolles and Edmanson charities).[36]

APPRENTICING CHARITIES. William Curtis by will proved 1670 left a rent charge of £60 from which £24 was to apprentice eight boys and eight girls in alternate years, two to come from Poplar, one from Mile End, two from Limehouse, and three from Ratcliff and Shadwell; the remainder was to be distributed among the poor (below).[37] In the ten years to 1894 no suitable apprentices were found in Mile End and only four in Ratcliff, all apprenticed to watermen. Between 1891 and 1893 the whole income was distributed among the poor.[38] The later history of this charity is uncertain.

Samuel Butler by will proved 1837 created an accumulating fund for charity schools of 23 parishes, including St. Dunstan's, Stepney. Chancery in 1844 declared the gift legal, but the sinking fund was found impractical in 1852 and Schemes of 1853 and 1875 provided scholarships and apprenticeships for boys and girls. In the five years to 1894 seven scholarships worth £8 each were awarded to pupils at Stepney Parochial and Ratcliff Charity schools. Thereafter the scholarships were held at a secondary or technical school.[39]

Penelope Vicars by will dated 1732 left £200 for placing out children and other poor in Stepney. It was mentioned with her similar gift to the poor of Davenham (Ches.) in 1837 but the Stepney charity apparently had lapsed by 1894.[40]

DISTRIBUTIVE CHARITIES. John Matthew, citizen and merchant tailor, by will proved 1569 left 40s. a year to the poor of Stepney, with 3s. 4d. to the churchwardens for distributing it. Payment was received in 1586 but had lapsed by 1786.[41]

William Curtis by will proved 1670 left £24 of the residue of his rent charge after apprenticing (above), in the first year to relieve debtors in prison and thereafter for annual distribution among 48 poor: 12 in Poplar, 6 in Mile End, 12 in Limehouse, and 18 in Ratcliff and Shadwell. A further £8 was to be distributed in bread to the aged poor of Poplar. £1 to be used for a sermon, and £3 for a dinner for the trustees. By 1894 the capital produced £55 a year and the apprenticing share was spent on the poor, distributed in gifts of 10s. to women in Mile End Old Town, Mile End New Town, Ratcliff, Shadwell, Limehouse, and Poplar, in addition to prison charities.[42]

Richard Underhill by will dated 1671 left £60 to buy land, the income to pay for bread and an

28 *Endowed Chars. Lond.* (1897), 593, 638–40.
29 Ibid. 582–3, 595, 625–8.
30 Horwood, *Plan* (1813 edn. in *Regency A to Z* (1985)). Below, plate 15.
31 *Endowed Chars. Lond.* (1897), 583, 595, 625–8; *V.C.H. Mdx.* v. 320.
32 G.L.R.O., P93/DUN/341.
33 On datestone: *Endowed Chars. Lond.* (1897), 271.
34 *Endowed Chars. Lond.* (1897), 270–2, 632.

35 Char. Com. files 250132; below, Bethnal Green, charities.
36 G.L.R.O., P93/DUN/341; Horwood, *Plan* (1813 edn. in *A to Z of Regency Lond.*). Below, plate 13.
37 B.L. Add. Ch. 13730; below, distributive charities.
38 *Endowed Chars. Lond.* (1897), 273, 632.
39 Ibid. 33, 643–4.   40 Ibid. 704.
41 Ibid. 592; *Mems. Stepney Par.* 14–15, 249–50.
42 *Endowed Chars. Lond.* (1897), 273, 632.

annual sermon. His gift was mentioned in 1786–8 but nothing was known of it in 1837.[43]

Prisca Coborn by will dated 1701 left a manor and 250 a. in White Roding (Essex) in trust to relieve seamen's widows in Stepney. From 1733 half the income went to St. Dunstan's and the other half was divided among the new parishes of St. George-in-the-East (5s. 6d. in the £), Spitalfields (2s. 6d.), and Limehouse (1s.). After the creation of more new parishes, Stepney's half was divided in 1737–6 between Ratcliff (8s. in the £), Poplar (5s. 6d.), Mile End Old Town (3s.), Mile End New Town (1s. 6d.), and Bethnal Green (2s.). In 1894 the average net income of £110 was divided among the eight parishes or hamlets in the same proportions.[44]

Dame Sarah Pritchard by will dated 1707 left the income of £32 from £800 held by the Orphans' Fund of the City of London, for several parishes including Stepney, where £2 10s. was to be paid at Christmas to ten single women. Stock was bought in 1812 and Stepney received c. £2 17s. 8d. a year,[45] paid from 1824 to 1837 to the churchwarden of Ratcliff and distributed usually within the three remaining hamlets of St. Dunstan's: in Mile End New Town it was distributed in sums of 2s. to poor widows not receiving parochial relief, in Ratcliff among the most needy aged persons, and in Mile End Old Town it was put into the hamlet's common fund. In 1871, however, the parish was ordered to appoint trustees to receive the sum, then £3, and in 1894 all eight hamlets of Stepney (excluding Shadwell) received 6s. 3d. each.[46]

Robert Radford[47] by will dated 1750 left the interest on £100 to provide bread for the poor of Stepney. In 1837 Ratcliff, Mile End Old Town, Mile End New Town, and Poplar each received 15s. and distributed it independently. In 1894 £110 stock yielded £2 15s., divided evenly between the four hamlets. Each hamlet received £2.76p in 1976–7.

Susanna Wilson by will dated 1784 left the income from £50 for repair of her tomb, the residue for bread to be distributed by the churchwardens of Stepney. In 1837 £67 stock yielded £2 0 8d., divided equally between Mile End Old Town, Mile End New Town, and Ratcliff. The income was £1 17s. 4d. in 1894 and £1.68p for each hamlet in 1976–7.

Elizabeth Gordon by will dated 1790 left the interest on £100 stock for bread every Sunday. Until 1833 the money went into the church rate account but was spent fully on bread in the four hamlets. In 1837 Mile End Old Town's share was put into its common fund. In 1894 £110 stock yielded £2 15s., divided unequally according to the number of loaves previously distributed; the Charity Commissioners requested an equal distribution or one according to population. In 1976–7 each hamlet received £2.76p.

Dorothy Smith by will dated 1792 left the interest on £250 stock, from which £5 was to provide flannel petticoats for ten industrious women in Stepney and £2 10s. was for roasting beef for 20 women. The income was divided between Mile End Old Town, New Town, Ratciff, and Poplar, which distributed it independently. In 1837 Poplar had not received a share for four years but was to do so in future. In 1894 £275 stock yielded £6 17s. 4d. divided between the four hamlets. Each received £6.88p in 1976–7.

Capt. Timothy Mangles by will proved 1800 gave £100 in stock to Trinity House Corporation, the interest for the poor of Stepney. Stock bought with arrears of interest in 1825 increased the endowment to £257, yielding £7 1s. 4d. Bakers were invited to tender for bread distributed once a year at Trinity almshouses. In 1893 the 377 recipients were seamen or their widows and daughters residing in Stepney and recommended by local clergy; Poplar received no benefit.

Nicholas Undeutsch by will dated 1812 left £3 a year for the poor not receiving alms, which was secured by the purchase of £100 stock. The gift was added to Gordon's charity until 1834, but thereafter the income was divided between Mile End Old Town, New Town, and Ratcliff. In 1894 £100 stock yielded £2 15s. In 1976–7 each hamlet received £2.76p.

---

43 Ibid. 592.
44 Ibid. 588–9, 633–4.
45 *14th Rep. Com. Char.* H.C. 382, p. 256 (1826), xii.
46 *Endowed Chars. Lond.* (1897), 589–90, 636.
47 Rest of section based on ibid. 590–1, 636–7, 641, 702; Char. Com. files.

BETHNAL GREEN

BETHNAL GREEN was known as the scene of the legend of the Blind Beggar and later as the archetypal East End slum, the green lying *c.* 2½ miles (4 km.) north-east of St. Paul's cathedral.[1] A hamlet of Stepney until 1743, when it became a separate parish, it contained 755 a.[2] and was bounded by Shoreditch on the west and north, Hackney on the north, Stratford-at-Bow on the east, and Mile End and Spitalfields on the south. Hackney Road, possibly ancient, formed part of the northern boundary and the common sewer part of the southern.[3] Perambulations of the parish boundaries were supposed to be triennial[4] but in practice they were much less frequent[5] and disputes occurred as building encroached: with Christ Church, Spitalfields, over Wheeler Street in 1769[6] and with Hackney over Cambridge Heath in 1732, 1779, 1788, and 1826.[7] Tower Hamlets sewer commissioners defined the northern boundary in 1854.[8] Adjustments to all the borders when Bethnal Green became a metropolitan borough in 1900 left an overall acreage of *c.* 760 (307.5 ha.). The main effect was to make Cambridge Road the eastern boundary from Mile End Road to the railway line and to make the railway the southern boundary from Globe to Grove roads.[9] The metropolitan borough became part of the London Borough of Tower Hamlets in 1965.[10]

Bethnal Green is covered by River Terrace gravels on London Clay. North-west of a wavy line from Bishopsgate station to the Hackney border at Grove Street lies Taplow Gravel; south-east lies Higher Flood Plain gravel. The 15m. contour runs through the Taplow Gravel. Most of the parish is flat, with a slight incline to the south.[11]

The common sewer, which marked Bethnal Green's southern boundary from Brick Lane to Mile End Gate,[12] may have originated as a natural stream. The flat ground, in spite of its underlying gravel, was frequently marshy. Haresmarsh[13] and Foulmere[14] covered much of the south and there was a causeway probably on the site of Dog Row.[15] Rushes feature in place-names on both sides of Cambridge Heath.[16] A field in the north-west in 1652 was 'usually drowned with water'.[17] It was then being worked for bricks and the extraction of brickearth and gravel left the landscape pitted with holes, adding by 1848 'filthy, pestilential lakes'[18] to the natural ponds, like that on the green by St. George's chapel.[19]

[1] J. Dugdale, *New Brit. Traveller* (1819), iii. 473.
[2] *Census* (1831).
[3] Gascoyne, *Map*; Lysons, *Environs*, ii. 27. For Hackney Rd., below, communications.
[4] Vestry mins. 1782–1813, p. 31.
[5] Ibid. 1820–3, p. 157. The perambulation in 1821 was the first since 1814.
[6] Vestry mins. 1747–81, p. 277.
[7] Ibid. 1823–8, 29 Mar., 7 Sept. 1826; *The Times*, 16 June 1788, 3a; 12 Sept. 1788, 2d; *V.C.H. Mdx.* x. 3.
[8] G.L.R.O., MCS/498/719.
[9] Ibid. CL/LOC/2/10; *Census* (1901).
[10] Below, local govt. (local govt. after 1965).
[11] Geol. Surv. Map 6", drift, Lond. sheet V. NE. (1920 edn.); ibid. 1/50,000, sheet 256 (1994 edn.); *V.C.H. Mdx.* i,

map facing p. 2; T.H.L.H.L., Map no. 1885.
[12] Gascoyne, *Map*.
[13] P.R.O., SC 6/1139/18 (1362–4).
[14] Guildhall MS. 25121/1710 (1388).
[15] B.L. Eg. Ch. 2081.
[16] Rush croft or land and Rush (Russia) Lane to E.: Guildhall MS. 25422 (1404); B.L. Eg. MS. 3006, f.1 (1546); survey of 1550 in W. Robinson, *Hist. Hackney*, i (1842), 325; Rush mead and meadow to W.: Lambeth Pal. Libr., MS. 2731/2 (1640); G.L.R.O., M93/158, f.8 (1652).
[17] G.L.R.O., M93/158, f.9.
[18] Gavin, *San. Ramblings*, 87.
[19] Gascoyne, *Map*; Survey of Bethnal Green (1706) (T.H.L.H.L., Map no. 301).

COMMUNICATIONS

ROADS. A pre-Roman road following a route from Oxford Street and Old Street to Old Ford and Essex crossed Bethnal Green, probably in part along the line of Hackney Road and Old Ford Lane (later Road).[20] Hackney Road, part of the parish boundary, was referred to in 1587 as the highway from Shoreditch to Mare Street[21] and, as Collier's Lane, dated from 1439 or earlier.[22] An Iron-Age coin was found in Victoria Park.[23] The king's way from Bethnal Green to Old Ford, identifiable from abutments as Old Ford Lane, was mentioned c. 1549[24] and was probably from the Middle Ages the route to Bishop's Hall. Its eastern section was straightened in 1844 when Victoria Park was created.[25]

The Romans are thought to have built a more direct road to Colchester from London Bridge via Old Ford. Remnants of a Roman road or roads have been uncovered at Old Ford and at the junction of Cambridge Heath Road and Roman Road, although the road at that junction may have been one running north to Clapton.[26] The name Roman Road, existing earlier in Bow, was not applied to the eastern route from Bethnal Green until modern times. If it denoted the pre-Roman route[27] or the Roman road from London bridge, it seems to have fallen out of use.[28] In 1703 the western portion was marked as 'Driftway' with a path to the east, called 'footway to Clay Hall' in 1760.[29] The road was first depicted in its entirety in the 1740s[30] and named Green Street by 1790.[31] It gained importance after the development of Globe Town and Victoria Park districts and was widened by 1887 under an Act of 1883.[32] It was widened again in the 1960s.[33]

The main north–south route from London, Ermine Street, lay slightly west of Bethnal Green parish. Another route, passing through the centre of Bethnal Green as a broad stretch of waste, was mentioned in the 1580s as the highway from Mile End to Cambridge Heath and Hackney.[34] The name was changed from Cambridge to Cambridge Heath Road in 1938.[35] The road was widened in 1862, c. 1905, and 1926.[36] Grove Street, which by the 16th century

had given its name to a hamlet in Hackney,[37] extended to Old Ford Lane by 1701.[38] As New Grove Road it was extended southward to Mile End Road under an agreement of 1803.[39]

By c. 1549 Brick Lane led northward from Spitalfields to meet 'the way . . . from Bishop's Hall to Halliwell Street'.[40] The western part of that way was called Cock Lane by 1538[41] and the rest, which probably existed in 1223[42] and which was called Rogue Lane by 1642[43] and Whores Lane in 1717,[44] became Old Bethnal Green Road after a more direct route of it south, Bethnal Green Road, was made by an Act of 1756 on the line of a bridleway.[45] The western section was called Church Street after the church was built in 1743 but entry to Shoreditch was only through a narrow passageway until the Act of 1756.[46] By 1872 the western approach was again inadequate, since it was the main route from the developing Victoria Park district to the City and Finsbury. Replacing the 18th-century road with a 60-ft. wide road farther south was also seen as a means of clearing slums in south-western Bethnal Green. The M.B.W. obtained an Act in 1872 and opened the new road, called Bethnal Green Road throughout, in 1879.[47]

Lanes that became the eastern end of Old Bethnal Green Road and of Three Colts Lane, and which both led from Cambridge Road, existed in 1388 as New Lane and Water Lane respectively.[48] Globe Road, probably the 'lane from Bethnal Green to Mile End', an abutment of Eastfield in 1581,[49] was called Thieving Lane c. 1600 and in 1703.[50] Other early roads were Beny Lane (1388)[51] and Barnard's Lane (1581, probably Bernareys 1404),[52] both probably back lanes east of the green, Rush (later Russia) Lane to the east of Cambridge Heath (1550),[53] and Crabtree Lane leading from Hackney Road in the west (1582).[54]

Leases of waste along Cambridge Road in the 16th century included covenants to keep the footway well gravelled[55] and in 1654 Bethnal Green's highway surveyors were ordered to fill up a gravel pit which they had made in the green.[56] In the 18th century they took their

20 I. D. Margary, *Rom. Rds. in Britain* (1967), 54.
21 G.L.R.O., M93/201.
22 P.R.O., SC 6/1139/24.
23 G. Black, *Archaeol. of Tower Hamlets* [1977], unpag.
24 Survey in Robinson, *Hist. Hackney*, i. 326.
25 *Illus. Lond. News*, 9 Nov. 1844, 301.
26 Margary, *Rom. Rds.* 54, 56, 246; Black, *Archaeol. of Tower Hamlets*; *V.C.H. Mdx.* i. 66–7.
27 Margary, *Rom. Rds.* 57 and later writers assume that Green St. (Roman Rd.) rather than Old Ford Rd. was the earlier road.
28 Not shown e.g. on T.H.L.H.L., TH/2350.
29 T.H.L.H.L., Map no. 301.
30 Rocque, *Map of Lond.* (1741–5).
31 P.R.O., C 104/173.
32 46 & 47 Vic. c. 178; P. J. Edwards, *Hist. Lond. Street Improvements, 1855–97* (1898), 87; G.L.R.O., MBW 2459/8.
33 G.L.R.O., CL/HIG/2/163.
34 P.R.O., M.P.F. 282; B.L. Eg. Roll 3080; G.L.R.O.,M93/170.
35 L.C.C. *Names of Streets* (1955).
36 G.L.R.O., MBW 2459/1; L.C.C. *Lond. Statistics*, xvi. 335; *Tower Hamlets in Photos. 1914–1939* (Tower Hamlets

L.B., 1980), 14.
37 *V.C.H. Mdx.* x. 59.
38 G.L.R.O., M93/19, ff. 302–3.
39 T.H.L.H.L., TH/7828; *Langley & Belch's New Map*.
40 Survey in Robinson, *Hist. Hackney*, i. 336.
41 *P.N. Mdx.* (E.P.N.S.), 84.
42 As an abutment of what became Burgoynes est.: P.R.O., CP 25/1/146/6/46; below, estates.
43 B.L. Add. MS. 22253.
44 M.L.R. 1717/6/64.
45 Act for making road, 29 Geo. II, c. 43.
46 Rocque, *Plan of Lond.* (1746).
47 *Lond. Gaz.* 29 Nov. 1870, p. 5444; Edwards, *Lond. Street Improvements*, 47 and plan XI.
48 Guildhall MS. 25121/1710.
49 B.L. Eg. Roll 3080.
50 *P.N. Mdx.* (E.P.N.S.), 84; Gascoyne, *Map.*
51 Guildhall MS. 9171/1, f. 160.
52 Ibid. MS. 25422; B.L. Eg. Roll 3080.
53 Survey in Robinson, *Hist. Hackney*, i. 325, where it is misread as Bush.
54 B.L. Eg. Ch. 2081.   55 G.L.R.O., M93/158, f. 18.
56 Cal. Mdx. Sess. Bks. ii. 97.

gravel from the Sotheby estate at Cambridge Heath.[57] Bethnal Green was rated with other Stepney hamlets in 1671 to repair the highways and causeways 'in great decay'.[58] In 1696 it petitioned that Spitalfields, being small but populous, should contribute towards Bethnal Green's highways,[59] and in 1655 it sought the repair of Brick and Cock lanes.[60] By 1671 it was generally accepted that roads built up on both sides should be paved.[61] Paving with stone and gravel was the responsibility of the houses lining the roads, Thomas Street being singled out in 1734.[62] Once Bethnal Green became a separate parish, the vestry prosecuted defaulting householders.[63] In 1772 it opposed an attempt by Spitalfields to obtain an Act to pave and clean streets in its own and neighbouring parishes, including Brick Lane.[64] An Act was passed in 1793, however, for streets in the south-west, most built-up, corner of Bethnal Green[65] and was extended in 1843, when it was to be put into effect by commissioners for paving and lighting.[66] By 1848, of more than 400 roads in Bethnal Green, only 14 per cent were classed as granite roadways and 40 per cent had paved footpaths, both still concentrated in the south-west.[67] By 1905 there were 40 miles of streets in the borough.[68] Some of the narrow, cobbled streets, probably late 18th- and early 19th-century remained in 1988.

The route from Essex to Smithfield market passed from Mile End along Cambridge Road to Cambridge Heath and thence along Hackney Road to Shoreditch, bringing 'vast numbers of cattle and many heavy carriages' which left the roads beyond the ability of Bethnal Green to keep in repair.[69] In 1738 an Act included the route among those administered by the new Hackney turnpike trustees.[70] To the existing turnpike gate in Mile End, at the junction with Dog Row, they added one at Cambridge Heath, at the junction with Hackney Road.[71] There was another at the western end of Hackney Road by 1822.[72] The trust's term and powers were extended in 1753, 1756, 1782, 1802, when tolls were adjusted to cope with the increasing traffic of carts loaded with bricks, and 1821.[73] In 1788, however, the Cambridge Road was still dangerous, with the pathways broken and 'heaps

of filth . . . every 10 or 20 yards'.[74] A second turnpike trust was set up by Act in 1756 for the new west–east route along Church Street and Bethnal Green Road.[75] The trustees had erected a gate in the middle of the road by 1760.[76] Acts in 1767 and 1805 extended their powers and increased tolls on brick-carrying waggons.[77] In 1826 an Act replaced the trusts with the metropolitan turnpike roads commissioners, whose responsibilities from the start included Hackney and Cambridge roads.[78] Control of Bethnal Green Road lay with the parish, which removed the tollgate in 1827, until 1833 when it was assumed by the commissioners.[79] Other tollgates were closed when the commissioners were abolished in 1863[80] and responsibility for all roads passed to the local authorities and M.B.W.

The only bridges were those made after the Regent's canal, opened in 1820, had been constructed through the eastern part of the parish, where it was crossed by Old Ford Road, Green Street (Old Ford Footpath bridge), and Bonner's Hall footpath.[81] A cast iron bridge was built in Green Street in 1866.[82] As Twig Folly bridge, it was widened a century later.[83]

Two coachmen petitioned, apparently unsuccessfully, in 1688 for permission to run a service from London to Bethnal Green.[84] In 1838 the nearest omnibus service ran from Mile End gate.[85] In 1856 18 omnibuses ran between Chelsea and Bethnal Green.[86] There were 274 buses a day along Bethnal Green Road by 1870 and 48 a day along Green Street by 1882.[87]

The North Metropolitan Tramways Co. opened a route along Grove Road to Old Ford Road in 1872 but closed it in 1873 when it opened routes along the old turnpike roads from Mile End along Cambridge Road to Stamford Hill, and along Hackney Road.[88] In 1879 it opened lines from Bethnal Green across Victoria Park to Hackney.[89] In 1893 the Cambridge Road route was called the Museum line, along which red trams ran from Aldgate.[90] Attempts in the 1870s and 1880s by the North Metropolitan and East London Tramways cos. to open a route along Bethnal Green Road[91] were apparently unsuccessful but the Victoria Park line, with yellow trams running between South Hackney and the docks, was opened along Grove Road in 1879.[92] The

57 Northants. R.O., X 1074 (xiii); X 1077, Notebk. 1716–24.
58 Cal. Mdx. Sess. Bks. iv. 130.
59 Mdx. County Rec. Sess. Bks. 1689–1709, 150–1.
60 Cal. Mdx. Sess. Bks. ii. 121, 126.
61 Wren Soc. xviii. 17–18, 25.
62 Cal. Mdx. Sess. Bks. xvi. 82.
63 Vestry mins. 1747–81, p. 126.
64 Ibid. p. 299.
65 Ibid. pp. 137, 141, 155; 33 Geo. III, c. 88.
66 6 & 7 Vic. c. 134 (Local and Personal).
67 Gavin, San. Ramblings, 81 and tables of streets.
68 L.C.C. Lond. Statistics, xvi. 323.
69 C.J. xxii. 774; xxiii. 145.
70 Act for repairing road from Shoreditch ch., 11 Geo. II, c. 29; V.C.H. Mdx. x. 5.
71 G. F. Vale and S. Snaith, Bygone Bethnal Green (1948), 12; B.M., Crace Colln., Portf. xxxiii. 55, 103; below, plate 22.
72 Vestry mins. 1820–3, p. 219.
73 26 Geo. II, c. 55; 29 Geo. II, c. 41; 22 Geo. III, c. 115; 42 Geo. III, c. 16 (Local and Personal); 54 Geo. III, c. 233 (Local and Personal); 1 & 2 Geo. IV, c. 112 (Local and Personal).
74 The Times, 12 Sept. 1788, 2d.
75 Act for making road from east side of . . . Bethnal

Green, 29 Geo. II, c. 43.
76 Map of Bethnal Green (T.H.L.H.L., Map no.301).
77 7 Geo. III, c. 105; 45 Geo. III, c. 6 (Local and Personal).
78 7 Geo. IV, c. 142; Rep. of Sel. Cttee. on Metropolis Turnpike Trusts, H.C. 355, p. 5 (1825), v.
79 G.L.R.O., MR/UTT/A/4; vestry mins. 22 Sept. 1827; 23 Sept. 1833.   80 26 & 27 Vic. c. 78.
81 Rep. on Bridges in Mdx. 119; G.L.R.O., M93/159; M. Denney, Lond.'s Waterways (1977), 71, 73.
82 Edwards, Lond. Street Improvements, 144; G.L.R.O., MBW 2459/2.
83 G.L.R.O., CL/HIG/2/163.
84 Cal. Treas. Bks. 1685–9, 1819.
85 Hist. Lond. Transport, i. 393–403.
86 Ibid. i. 404–5.
87 Edwards, Lond. Street Improvements, 47, 87.
88 Hist. Lond. Transport, i. 185.
89 V.C.H. Mdx. x. 8–9.
90 East End News, 17 Jan. 1893 (T.H.L.H.L., files 386).
91 G.L.R.O., MR/UP 1228, 1397, 1445, 1501.
92 Hist. Lond. Transport, i. 259; E.E. News, 1 Jan. 1892 (T.H.L.H.L. files 386).

L.C.C. ran electric trams over the existing routes, along Hackney Road from 1907, Cambridge Road from 1910, and Grove Road from 1921.[93]

The London General Omnibus Co. ran a motorbus from Victoria station to Old Ford along Bethnal Green Road and Green Street in 1911[94] and by 1930 buses ran on the same routes as trams.[95] The Empress Omnibus garage was built at Cambridge Heath in 1925 and a coach station in Knottisford Street in 1936.[96] In 1939 the London Passenger Transport Board introduced trolleybuses along Cambridge, Hackney, and Grove roads.[97] Although less frequent, motorbuses ran along the same routes in 1958 as in 1938.[98] Services had been reduced by 1987, when 6,070 people travelled to work from Globe Town neighbourhood and 10,230 from Bethnal Green neighbourhood; they used ten bus services within the former borough, along Hackney, Cambridge Heath, Bethnal Green, and Roman roads.[99]

RAILWAYS. In 1839 the Eastern Counties (later the Great Eastern) Railway, created to build a line from London to Norwich,[1] opened the first section from Romford to a station (Devonshire Street) south of Victoria cemetery, just outside the Bethnal Green boundary.[2] In 1840 the line was extended through south-western Bethnal Green to a station on the border called Shoreditch, in 1846 renamed Bishopsgate (high level). Brick Lane goods station opened south of St. John Street,[3] was enlarged under an Act of 1854, and expanded and moved eastward until by c. 1865 it occupied a large site west of Carlisle Street.[4] In 1843 Devonshire Street was replaced by a passenger station to the west, next to Cambridge Road but called Mile End.[5] In 1872 that was replaced by a passenger station to the west called Bethnal Green or Bethnal Green Junction, from which the G.E.R. opened a northward branch parallel with Cambridge Road through Cambridge Heath station to Hackney Downs, where it divided. At the western end Bishopsgate (low level) station opened in 1872 and the line was extended to a new terminus in Liverpool Street in 1874. Bishopsgate (high level) station was closed to passengers in 1875. Another passenger station on the main G.E.R. line opened at Globe Road in 1884.[6]

The East London Railway, having opened a line to Wapping from New Cross in 1869, extended it northward to Liverpool Street in 1876 through Whitechapel and Shoreditch station (which was within Bethnal Green approximately on the site of the first Brick Lane goods station, which had shifted to the east and was called Spitalfields Goods station). There was a passenger service from Brighton to Liverpool Street until 1885 when Shoreditch became the London terminus. The G.E.R. ran a service on the line from Liverpool Street to New Cross until 1914, when passenger services passed to the Metropolitan. A partly built freight link between the Great Eastern and East London lines between Whitechapel and Bethnal Green was abandoned for lack of money, a hoist at Spitalfields goods station being used to bridge the difference in level between the two lines.[7]

Bishopsgate (low level), Globe Road, and Cambridge Heath stations closed in 1916, although the last reopened in 1919.[8] The East London line was electrified in 1913,[9] whereas on the G.E.R. lines the 'most intensive steam-operated suburban service in the world' was inaugurated in 1920, with 24 trains an hour between Liverpool Street and Bethnal Green.[10] Some platforms at Bethnal Green station were closed in 1946[11] and as freight traffic declined the Spitalfields hoist ceased to be used after 1955,[12] Bishopsgate (high level) station for goods was replaced by Liverpool Street after a fire in 1964, and Spitalfields goods station closed in 1967.[13]

The Underground railway was late in coming to Bethnal Green. Under an Act of 1936[14] the London Passenger Transport Board acquired a site on the green for a station on the planned eastward extension of the Central line but its opening was delayed by the war. The station was being used as an air-raid shelter in 1943 when 173 people died in a disastrous accident. It opened as Bethnal Green station in 1946 on the line from Liverpool Street to Stratford.[15]

There were plans in 1989 for an East–West Crossrail to link British Rail at the City and West End. The eastern end was planned to run in a tunnel from Liverpool Street under Spitalfields and the southern part of Bethnal Green and then alongside the existing G.E.R. line to Stratford.[16] A final decision to build had still not been made in 1991.

93 *Hist. Lond. Transport,* ii. 100–1; L.C.C. *Municipal Map* (1913, 1930).
94 *Hist. Lond. Transport,* i. 169.
95 L.C.C. *Municipal Map* (1930).
96 G.L.R.O., AR/BA/4/423, no. 3; 628, no. 4.
97 1 Ed. VIII & 1 Geo. VI, c. 90, pt. 2; *Hist. Lond. Transport,* ii. 300-1.
98 G. M. L. Simpson, 'Comparative study of contemporary and pre-war geog. of E. End of Lond.' (Lond. Univ. M.A. thesis, 1959), 197–9.
99 G. O. Grey, *Recent Pub. Transport Bus Changes* (Feb. 1987, Tower Hamlets, L.B., Planning Dept.) (T.H.L.H.L., pamphlet 386, LP 6792); *Central Lond. Local Bus Map* (Spring 1987).
1 6 & 7 Wm. IV, c. 106.
2 A. Leonard, *Chronology of Passenger Stations in Gtr. Lond.* (pamphlet, 1980).
3 Ibid.; Map (1843) in Gavin, *San. Ramblings.*
4 17 & 18 Vic. c. 153 (Local and Personal); Stanford, *Map of Lond.* (1862-5).

5 Stanford, *Map of Lond.* (1862–5); Leonard, *Passenger Stas.*
6 Leonard, *Passenger Stas.*; *Hist. Lond. Transport,* i. 133; H. V. Borley, *Chronology of Lond.'s Rlys.* (1982), 16, 44–45.
7 E. Lee, *E. Lond. Line and the Thames Tunnel* (Lond. Transport pamphlet, 1976), 13, 16, 19, 22, 24; O.S. Map 1/2,500, Mdx. XVII. 11 (1894-6 edn.).
8 C. R. Clinker, *Clinker's Reg. of Closed Passenger Stations and Goods Depots 1830-1977* (1978).
9 Lee, *E. Lond. Line,* 22.
10 *Hist. Lond. Transport,* ii. 257.
11 Borley, *Chronology of Lond.'s Rlys.* 45 n.
12 Lee, *E. Lond. Line,* 24.
13 *Clinker's Reg. of Closed Stas.*
14 26 Geo. V. & 1 Edw. VIII, c. 131, s. 56.
15 L. Menear, *Lond.'s Underground Stations* (1983), 98–9; Borley, *Chronology of Lond.'s Rlys.* 44; H. P. Clunn, *The Face of Lond.* (1951), 291.
16 T.H.L.H.L., file 385, Crossrail.

SETTLEMENT AND BUILDING

SETTLEMENT AND BUILDING TO 1836.
Early archaeological finds are scanty and may
not denote settlement: an Iron-Age coin near a
possible road through Victoria Park[17] and a
Roman coffin from New Corfield Street (formerly Camden Gardens), probably part of a
cemetery at Spitalfields.[18] Saxon beads from
Brick Lane may have been associated with a
settlement in Whitechapel.[19] The place-name
Blithehale or Blythenhale, the earliest form of
Bethnal Green, is from the Anglo-Saxon *healh*,
'angle, nook, or corner' and *blithe*, 'happy,
blithe', or a personal name Blitha. Cambridge
Heath (Camprichesheth), unconnected with
Cambridge, likewise may derive from an Anglo-
Saxon personal name.[20] The area was once
marshland and forest which, as Bishopswood,
lingered in the east until the 16th century.[21]
Settlement's dependence upon water suggests
that the 'happy corner' was cleared next to the
natural spring, St. Winifred's well, in Conduit
field at the northern end of the green.[22]

A settlement at Bethnal Green was recorded
in the 12th and 13th centuries.[23] The green was
the village common[24] and the medieval houses,
mostly cottages which gave rise to copyhold
tenements, clustered around it, chiefly on the
north and east. The excellence of the soil when
cleared of trees may explain why much of the
demesne of Stepney manor lay in Bethnal
Green.[25] Apart from Bishop's Hall, perhaps
built as a hunting lodge,[26] there is no evidence
of medieval settlement outside the green.

Although peasant holdings predominated,
there were freehold estates, including parts of
holdings which extended beyond Bethnal
Green,[27] and a few residents of higher status
from the 12th century.[28] Sir Thomas Cobham
was a landowner in 1388, as was John Potter (d.
1388),[29] who lived in a 'mansion'[30] and whose
family remained until 1520 or later.[31] By the
16th century Bethnal Green provided country
retreats for London merchants, lawyers, and
courtiers. They were especially associated with
two houses on the east side of the green: the
Corner House (Pyott's) and Kirby's Castle.[32]
Among other inhabitants were Edward Grey,
Lord Powis (1533– 1544/9),[33] the lord mayor Sir
Richard Gresham (d. 1549) and his widow Isabel
(d. 1565),[34] Sir John Gates (d. 1553), chancellor
of the duchy of Lancaster,[35] Alice (d. 1554),
widow of Peter Sterkye, draper,[36] William
Dawkes (d. 1555), mercer,[37] William Palmer
(d. 1627), haberdasher,[38] Thomas Parmiter,
merchant tailor (c. 1650),[39] and John Harwood,
merchant (1666).[40] Robert Catesby (d. 1605),
the Gunpowder conspirator, was associated with
a house owned by Lady Gray 'in an out-place'
in Bethnal Green.[41] The vegetarian religious
eccentric Roger Crab (d. 1680) spent his last
years in Bethnal Green as a hermit.[42] Those
holding property included John Pyke, goldsmith
(1526),[43] Sir William Cordell, master of the Rolls
(1564),[44] William Baynes (d. 1595), mercer,[45]
William Rider, haberdasher (1581),[46] George
Barrows, merchant tailor (c. 1615),[47] Richard
Hunt, mercer (1652),[48] and Samuel Bartlett,
assay master to the Mint and churchwarden for
Bethnal Green (1670).[49] Early 17th-century
Bethnal Green had a proportionally larger middle class than any of the Stepney hamlets except
Mile End.[50]

Bethnal Green emerged from obscurity as the
setting for a ballad which was dramatized in 1600
and later embellished. The story of a blinded
soldier named Montford, rescued by a woman
with whom he lived as a beggar on the green,
may relate to a man who lived in the 15th
century, although an 18th-century editor identified him with Simon de Montfort's son Henry,
reputedly slain at the battle of Evesham in
1265.[51] The play of 1600 displays a knowledge
of local topography[52] and by the 17th century
the legend was well established with an inn, the

17 Above, this article (communications); Inner Lond.
Archaeol. Unit, *Archaeol. Surv. of Tower Hamlets: Gaz.* May
1975 (T.H.L.H.L. file 570); *Problems of Iron Age in S.
Britain*, ed. S. S. Frere (Council for Brit. Archaeology,
1961), 223.
18 *V.C.H. Mdx.* i. 68; *Illus. Lond. News*, 5 Apr. 1862;
Gent. Mag. ccii(1), 614.
19 *Archaeol. Surv.*; Black, *Archaeol. of Tower Hamlets*,
unpag.
20 *P.N. Mdx.* (E.P.N.S.), 83; Ekwall, *Eng. Place-Names*,
(1960), 40, 212.
21 B.L. Eg. MS. 3006, f. 1.
22 John Gretton, quoted in D. Hughson, *Lond., Brit.
Metropolis* (1811), iv. 444–5; Parish Map 1760 (T.H.L.H.L.
Map no. 301); below, pub. svces.
23 Guildhall MS. 25516, ff. 38–39; P.R.O., E 40/7317;
ibid. C 146/799.
24 'Territorium ac communiam' in 1547: Guildhall MS.
9531/12, f. 123.
25 Above, Stepney, manor.
26 *Memorials of Lond. and Lond. Life, 1276–1416*, ed. H.
T. Riley (1868), 28.
27 e.g. below, estates (Burgoyns); above, Stepney, manors
(Cobhams).
28 P.R.O., E 40/7317.
29 Guildhall MS. 25121/1710.
30 Ibid. 9171/1, f. 160.
31 Ibid. 9171/9, f. 162v.; MSS. 25370, 25422.

32 Below, estates (Pyotts; Kirby's Castle). For other hos.,
below, the Green.
33 P.R.O., PROB 11/34 (P.C.C. 17 Bucke), f. 127v.;
Mont. Collns. lxvii. 117–58; lxix. 93–4.
34 *D.N.B.*; P.R.O., PROB 11/48 (P.C.C. 16 Morrison),
ff. 121v.–5.
35 *D.N.B.* s.v. Gates; Wingfield, Sir Ant.
36 Guildhall MS. 9171/13, f. 13v.
37 P.R.O., PROB 11/37 (P.C.C. 31 More), ff. 235v.–7.
38 Ibid. PROB 11/151 (P.C.C. 7 Skynner), ff. 51v.–2.
39 Ibid. C 7/323/121.
40 Ibid. C 7/543/135.
41 Ibid. E 214/602; Hist. MSS. Com. 9, *Salisbury XVIII*,
pp. 336–7.
42 *D.N.B.*; *Mdx. & Herts. N. & Q.* i. 160–3.
43 Guildhall MS. 10123/2.
44 P.R.O., E 179/142/193.
45 Guildhall MS. 9171/18, f. 259v.
46 B.L. Eg. Roll 2080.
47 P.R.O., C 3/327/26.
48 Ibid. C 8/312/5.
49 G.L.R.O., M93/166; *Mems. Stepney Par.* 230 and n.
50 M. J. Power, 'Urban Development of E. Lond. 1550–
1700' (Lond. Univ. Ph. D. thesis, 1971), 176–9.
51 For the legend and its sources, A. J. Robinson and D.
H. B. Chesshyre, *The Green* (1986), 31–5.
52 e.g. Broomfield : G. F. Vale, *Old Bethnal Green* (1934),
69; below, estates (Broomfields).

Blind Beggar of Bethnal Green (1654),[53] the identification of a fine house within a stone wall (presumably Kirby's Castle) with the beggar's dwelling,[54] and the figure of the beggar on a medallion attached to the beadle's staff (1690).[55]

New settlements grew up from the 16th century, usually as encroachments from neighbouring districts: at Collier's Row next to Shoreditch, at Dog Row, next to Mile End, and in the south-west adjoining Spitalfields. The process started on roadside waste and from the mid 17th century continued on both freeholds and copyholds, although the ability to grant long leases made it easier to build on freehold. In the 1650s sales of the demesne created several freehold estates. Only the smallest parcels were bought by local men, most purchasers being London merchants who leased out the land for farming or gardening until the time was ripe to let or, more rarely, sell to builders.[56] The timing was usually determined by proximity to existing settlement and to main roads, whose frontages were built up before new roads were constructed behind. Most development took place in isolation, producing a street pattern explicable only by the boundaries of individual estates. Building was small-scale, especially at first, and often by men described as bricklayers, plasterers and, probably most numerous, carpenters. Many old houses were said to be weatherboarded and half timbered,[57] although brick was the main material. The bricks were usually made locally, creating a pitted landscape, and builders often lived where they were working. A few, like James Waddilove and William Causdell[58] and John May Evans and William Timmins,[59] built on a larger scale on several estates. In parish politics Timmins supported Joseph Merceron, who was notorious for corruption.[60] Another successful builder was David Wilmot, who started as a labourer,[61] took long leases from 1761,[62] and entered local politics in 1764,[63] resigning most of his building interests to John Wilmot, presumably his son, from the 1770s.[64] Wilmot became an enemy of Merceron and may have set him an example; he was accused in 1788 of issuing summonses for non-payment of rack rents while paying only half rent on his own houses.[65]

Most of the new houses, with frontages of only 13–19 ft., were built for the predominantly weaving population which spread from Spitalfields. Some weavers were masters and reasonably well-off, like Thomas Norton (d. 1683), whose house had five rooms,[66] James Church (d. 1686),[67] and Thomas Jones, with property around the green 1688–1720.[68] William Lee (d. 1720), a dyer, had a house with eleven rooms[69] and Thomas Price (d. 1745) had a leasehold house in Virginia Row, two houses in Edmonton, and money lent out as mortgage.[70] Cottages with broad first-floor windows, for poorer weavers, survived on the Red Cow and Willetts estates until the 1950s.[71]

The poor were seen to be displacing the 'better sort of people' in 1743.[72] Kirby's Castle had probably ceased to house people of substance by 1700 and had become a lunatic asylum by 1726, while the Corner House, although rebuilt after its occupation by a rich merchant at the end of the 17th century, had less important residents than before.[73] Benjamin Godfrey (d. 1758), a Quaker medical doctor who leased the Austen estate, lived in Castle Street.[74] William Caslon, the type-founder, died at his home in Bethnal Green in 1766.[75] Gentry and a few rich Jews still lived around the green in the 18th and early 19th century, when a great imbalance in wealth caused acute problems in local government.[76]

Huguenot immigration was a striking feature of the late 17th and 18th century. An alien, Hans Spyer, had been listed under Bethnal Green in 1455[77] and another, Peter or Petrus Flower (Flowerkin) who lived there in the 1580s and 1590s,[78] apparently left a family, associated with Anchor Street in 1694, which remained until the 1720s or later.[79] Two 'picture drawers' from Antwerp and a Walloon weaver lived in Bethnal Green in 1635.[80] Five names of possible Huguenot origin were among the 215 assessed for hearth tax in 1664.[81] The main influx, however, came after the Revocation of the Edict of Nantes in 1685: in 1694 some 100 out of 520 people assessed for Bethnal Green were apparently Huguenot, most of them in the south-west, where they had spread from Spitalfields.[82] The Huguenots, who were mainly silkworkers, weavers, throwsters, and dyers from Normandy

53 G.L.R.O., M93/132, f. 1; below, the Green.
54 *Jnl. of Wm. Schellink's Travels in Eng. 1661–3*, ed. M. Exwood and H. L. Lehmann (Camden 5th ser. 1), 59; Pepys noted an allegation that outhos., rather than Kirby's Castle, had been built by the beggar: *Diary of Sam. Pepys*, ed. R. Latham and W. Matthews, iv (1971), 200; below, estates (Kirby's Castle).
55 Freshfield, *Communion Plate*, plate III.
56 Below, s.v. localities and estates.
57 *Builder*, 28 Jan. 1871, 69.
58 Below, Cambridge Heath; Hackney Rd.
59 Below, the Centre; the East.
60 Vestry mins. 1813–21, p. 7; BNC, Bethnal Green 3, letter by vicar, 12 Mar. 1823; below, local govt. (par. govt. 1743–1836).
61 *The Times*, 30 Sept. 1788, 1b.
62 G.L.R.O., BRA 898/126; M.L.R. 1762/7/176; below, Dog Row; the Centre; Cambridge Heath.
63 Vestry mins. 1747–81, pp. 224, 269, 300; G.L.R.O., MR/B/R2, no. 37.
64 M.L.R. 1774/7/205; T.H.L.H.L., TH/5849.
65 *The Times*, 27 Sept. 1788, 3c; below, local govt. (par. govt. 1743–1836).
66 P.R.O., PROB 4/14493.

67 Below, econ. hist. (ind.).
68 P.R.O., PROB 11/412 (P.C.C. 207 Fane), f. 179; G.L.R.O., M93/132, f. 441.
69 P.R.O., PROB 3/20/119; C.L.R.O., Assess. Box 43, MS. 22; M.L.R. 1772/2/91.
70 T.H.L.H.L., TH/361.
71 P.R.O., PROB 11/381 (P.C.C. 115 Cann), ff. 58–9; Pevsner, *Lond.* ii. 70; *Survey of Lond.* xxvii. 275.
72 *C.J.* xxiv. 369.
73 Below, the Green; estates (Pyotts; Kirby's Castle).
74 P.R.O., PROB 11/841 (P.C.C. 331 Hutton), ff. 284–5; T.H.L.H.L., BG/256, 260; G.L.R.O., M93/34, pp. 445–6.
75 Lysons, *Environs*, ii. 32; *D.N.B.*
76 Below, local govt.
77 P.R.O., E 179/235/57.
78 *Rets. of Aliens in Lond.* 1523–1625, ii. 433; iii. 34 (*Proc. Hug. Soc.* x); M.L.R. 1842/4/923.
79 C.L.R.O., Assess. Box 43, MS. 22; Lambeth Pal. Libr., MS. 2712, ff. 182–3, 193.
80 I. Scouloudi, *Rets. of Strangers in Metropolis 1593, 1627, 1635, 1639* (Hug. Soc., Quarto. ser. lvii). 259, 274, 347.
81 G.L.R.O., MR/TH/4, m. 92.
82 C.L.R.O., Assess. Box 43, MS. 22.

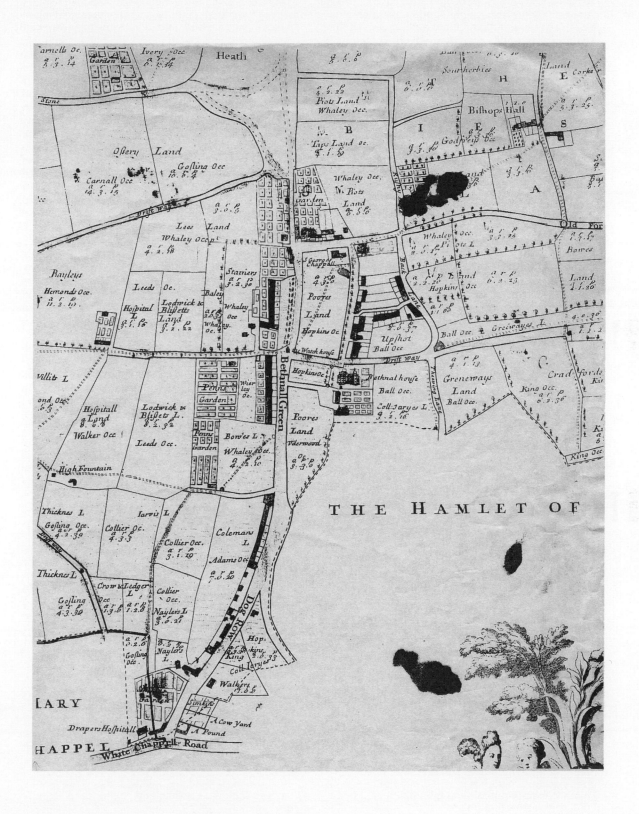

Fig. 11. BETHNAL GREEN AND DOG ROW IN 1703

and Picardy, had their own church, St. Jean or St. John in St. John Street, and their own charities, friendly societies, and clubs.[83] They were gradually assimilated, 14 out of 103 petitioners for an Anglican church in Bethnal Green in 1727 being recognizably Huguenot and another two Sephardi Jews.[84] Anglicization, such as that from 1813 to 1819 of a surname from Lhereux to Happy,[85] sometimes disguised French ancestry. Descendants of Huguenots nonetheless were long associated with silkweaving in Bethnal Green; George Dorée (d. 1916), a velvet weaver, was one of the last.[86] Although numerous and economically important, and including names like Renvoize and Merceron prominent in local affairs, Huguenots left little trace on the topography. They were rarely landlords and virtually never builders who might have been commemorated in street names. Depression in the silk trade could provoke widespread unrest. The area had a tradition of political and religious disaffection,[87] with a strong anti-papist sentiment which attracted the Huguenots. In 1642 the mob attacked the house of the courtier Sir Balthazar Gerbier (d. 1667), himself the son of Huguenot refugees who had settled in Holland, because it was thought to harbour priests.[88] A search in 1678 for an unlicensed printing press discovered only a silkweaver's loom[89] but in 1683 a local group, led by Maj. Chamberlain and Edward Proby, former overseer and lessee of the Corner House, was found to be arming against papists.[90] Sporadic disturbances arising from the vicissitudes of the silk industry continued until conditions improved after the passing of the first Spitalfields Act in 1773.[91] Latent unrest persisted, to be exploited by Joseph Merceron, until weaving was again depressed by the repeal of the Acts in 1824, stimulating religious and political radicalism and crime.[92]

The fortunes of the silk industry influenced the pace and type of building. The population grew from c. 8,496 in 1711[93] to c. 15,000 in 1743[94] but many families, of which there were 1,416 in 1711,[95] had no home of their own. An exaggerated statement in 1738 that there were 800 houses with 7–10 families each[96] probably showed that many buildings had been subdivided. The decision to make Bethnal Green a separate parish in 1743 was opposed by builders who had lately taken long leases of 'a great number of houses' and spent large sums converting them to tenements. Most houses let at less than £10 a year consisted of two or three tenements[97] and the builders, like the plasterer and haberdasher who took a lease of 62 houses on the Byde estate in 1745[98] or lessees on the Carter estate in Hare Marsh in the mid 18th century,[99] crammed courtyard dwellings on existing gardens. Throughout the 1750s and 1760s the vestry tried, generally unsuccessfully, to prise more rates out of the tenemented houses[1] and it was said in 1763 that a third of all houses were leased to a few people who let them to journeymen weavers and the like, either in separate apartments or furnished lodgings.[2] In 1743 with 1,800 houses there was an average of 8.3 persons to a house.[3] Improving conditions during the period of the Spitalfields Acts (1773–1824) were shown by averages of 1.5 family or 6.2 persons to a house in 1801 and of 1.3 family and 5.8, 5.6, and 5.7 persons respectively in 1811, 1821, and 1831.[4]

Until the late 17th century Bethnal Green was the smallest and least significant of Stepney's hamlets, often coupled with, and inferior to, Mile End.[5] In 1663 and 1664 Bethnal Green was assessed at £37 and £15 and Mile End at £67 and £26 [6] In 1664 there were 215 houses listed for hearth tax under the single heading Bethnal Green. Nearly 60 per cent of them were small, assessed for one or two hearths, while there were only four large houses, assessed for 11, 12, 14, and 16 hearths respectively; the largest was Kirby's Castle, Bishop's Hall apparently being omitted.[7] By 1674 there were 280 houses, listed under Bethnal Green, Back Lane, Shoreditch Side, and Collier Row. Eight had more than 11 hearths and one house, presumably Bishop's Hall, had 30. Houses of 3 to 10 hearths had increased to form nearly 60 per cent of the whole.[8] By 1685 Bethnal Green was assessed at £1 14s. 6d. and Mile End at only £1 9s. 3d. [9] In 1694 assessments were listed under Bethnal Green, Bishop's Hall and Grove Street, Dog Row, Brick Lane, St. John Street, Carter's Rents, George Street, Ass Park, Anchor Street, York Street, Cock Lane, Club Row, Castle Street, and Virginia Row.[10]

In 1703 buildings covered some 210 a. out of a total of 760 a.[11] Settlement clustered around the green and reached south along Cambridge

83 *Reg. of ch. of St. Jean Spitalfields* (Hug. Soc. xxxix), pp. xi–xv; *Case Bk. of La Maison de Charité de Spittlefields 1739–41* (Hug. Soc., Quarto ser. lv); R. D. Gwynne, *Huguenot Heritage* (1985), 171; *E. Lond. Papers*, xiii(2), 72–88.
84 Lambeth Pal. Libr., MS. 2712, f. 193.
85 Gwynne, *Huguenot Heritage*, 183.
86 A. Plummer, *Lond. Weavers' Co.* 1600–1970 (1972), 369.
87 Above, Stepney, settlement and bldg.
88 *D.N.B.*; Vale, *Old Bethnal Green*, 49. For Gerbier's ho., below, the Green.
89 *Cal. S. P. Dom.* 1678, p. 70.
90 Cal. Mdx. Sess. Bks. vii. 13; G.L.R.O., o/113/1; Power, 'Urban Development of E. Lond.' 262.
91 Below, econ. hist. (ind.).
92 F. H. W. Sheppard, *Lond. 1808–1870: The Infernal Wen* (1971), 26, 166–8; below, local govt.; social; prot. nonconf.
93 *C.J.* xvi. 542.
94 Ibid. xxiv. 369.
95 Ibid. xvi. 542.
96 Ibid. xxiii. 145.
97 Ibid. xxiv. 448.
98 M.L.R. 1745/1/98.
99 Ibid. 1752/1/592–8; 1755/2/507; 1761/4/141; 1763/2/306.
1 Act for cleansing streets etc., 24 Geo. II, c. 26; Vestry mins. 1747–81, p. 109.
2 Act for Maintaining the Poor, 3 Geo. III, c. 40; *C.J.* xxix. 425, 446.
3 *C.J.* xxiv. 369.
4 *Census*, 1801–31.
5 e.g. in the vestry: *Mems. Stepney Par.* i, p. x.
6 Cal. Mdx. Sess. Bks. iii. 157; *Mdx. County Rec.* iii. 337.
7 G.L.R.O., MR/TH/4, mm. 92-3d.
8 Ibid. TH/46.
9 Cal. Mdx. Sess. Bks. vii. 89.
10 C.L.R.O., Assess. Box 43, MS. 22.
11 Lysons, *Environs*, ii. 27–8.

Road towards separate ribbon development in Dog Row. In the west it had spread from Shoreditch to Virginia Row and in the south-west from Spitalfields to Cock Lane and Nichol Street and on the east side of Brick Lane to Hare Street.[12] The demographic balance had probably already shifted from the green towards the west, which offered the most suitable site for a church in 1724, when c. 200 houses had been built in the last five years.[13] In 1732 there were 71 streets and courts, of which five were around the green, two at Dog Row, and the rest in the west and south-west.[14] By 1734 Bethnal Green was the largest of all the hamlets with a quota of £369 of the land tax, compared with £356 for Mile End, Old and New Towns.[15] When the church came to be built in 1743 it was sited at the eastern end of the most built up area.[16] Building then reached north to New Nichol Street, with only a garden separating it from development on the Austen estate and in Virginia Row.[17] The estimated number of houses rose from 1,800 in 1743[18] to 2,000 in 1774[19] and 2,400 in 1778.[20]

Probably aided by the Spitalfields Acts, the pace of building quickened and more estates were developed. By 1795 c. 3,500 houses, many built within the last three years, covered 250 a.[21] Building had spread eastward on both sides of Church Street and Bethnal Green Road and on several estates on either side. It included new settlements in Hackney Road and Cambridge Heath and in the hitherto empty area east of the green, especially along Green Street.[22] There were 3,586 inhabited houses in 1801, 5,715 in 1811, when the increase was 'especially in the part of the parish adjoining Hackney', 8,095 in 1821, and 10,877 in 1831.[23] By 1812 ribbon development was complete along the Cambridge Road and Bethnal Green Road and virtually complete along Hackney Road and Green Street as far as the canal.[24] By 1826 there was little open space between the settlements except in the north-east, the heart of Bishops' Hall estate, and in the east, at Broomfields.[25]

THE GREEN: BETHNAL GREEN VILLAGE.[26] The earliest area of settlement was probably around the green, particularly in the north-east near St. Winifred's well and St.

George's chapel, the area possibly identifiable with the original 'bright or Blitha's corner' (Blithehale).[27] The village was defined on the east by Rushy (Russia) Lane and the Back Lane (Globe Road), which separated it from the demesne lands and open fields. Besides medieval cottages around Barnard's Lane (Old Ford Road),[28] St. George's chapel stood by 1512 in an inclosure on the green at the western corner of the lane and what later became Victoria Park Square.[29] There were added, by the 16th century and probably earlier, a few larger houses, the retreats of courtiers or merchants from London. The Corner House, the capital messuage of Pyott's estate, stood by 1538 on the eastern corner of Barnard's Lane opposite the chapel; it was later rebuilt and extended.[30] By c. 1550 Sir John Gresham's house, rebuilt as Kirby's Castle in the 1570s, adjoined the green just south of Green Street.[31] The estate included a farmhouse which had dwindled to a cottage by 1577.[32]

Most of the green itself was preserved by the purchase in 1678, by Thomas Rider and other owners and occupiers of neighbouring houses, of 11 a. of waste east of Cambridge Heath Road and ½ a. to its west to prevent any new building. It was let out as three closes of farmland,[33] and in 1690 was settled in trust for the poor.[34] The purchase apparently succeeded in keeping humble building at bay while encouraging gentry, several of whom were said in 1688 to have come to live there since the inclosure.[35]

Though from the late 16th century piecemeal development began to fill in the empty plots around the green, eventually extending back from it in all directions, even in the 18th century, while much of the rest of Bethnal Green was being covered with small houses for weavers, the area around the green remained socially superior. Contemporary descriptions and illustrations suggest that Gascoyne in 1703 confused two houses at the northern end of the green, the capital houses respectively of the Dickens and Pyotts estates. The large, winged house depicted at the northern corner of Cambridge Heath Road and Old Ford Road should probably have been shown on the site of the Corner House at the north-east corner of Old Ford Road and Victoria Park Square, while the smaller three-gabled house depicted there[36] was probably Lyons Hall, demolished c. 1794.[37]

12 Gascoyne, *Map*.
13 Lambeth Pal. Libr. MS. 2712, ff. 182–8, 192.
14 Co. of Par. Clerks, *New Remarks of Lond.* (1732), 197–8.
15 G.L.R.O., P93/DUN/328, p. 314.
16 Act to make hamlet of Bethnal Green a separate par. 16 Geo. II, c. 28.   17 Rocque, *Plan of Lond.* (1746).
18 *C.J.* xxiv. 369. There were c. 1,787 hos. on rate bks. in 1751: T.H.L.H.L., B. Gr. /256.
19 *Ambulator* (1774), 13–14.
20 Lambeth Pal. Libr., Fulham Papers, Lowth 5, ff. 386–9.
21 Lysons, *Environs*, ii. 27–8, 34.
22 Horwood, *Plan* (1792–9).
23 *Census*, 1801–31; Lysons, *Environs*, Suppl. 102.
24 *Langley & Belch's New Map*.
25 *Cruchley's New Plan*(1826).
26 Where possible, in this section Bethnal Green refers to the par., the Green to the primary settlement.
27 *P.N. Mdx.* (E.P.N.S.), 83.
28 P.R.O. C 142/743, no. 17 (1643). The names 'late Ric. Reason's', 'le Homestall adjoining le tenement of Wm. Reymond',

Eastwell and Hedgate, suggest a much earlier date. The Reason (Reyson) fam. fl. 1391–1421: P.R.O., SC 6/1139/20; Guildhall MS. 9171/3, f. 85v. Reymund and his s. Adam fl. c. 1200: P.R.O., E 40/7317; Guildhall MS. 25516, f. 38v.
29 Netteswell Ho. occupies part of the site; below, parish church.
30 Below, estates (Pyotts); Gascoyne, *Map*.
31 Below, estates (Kirby's Castle).
32 T.H.L.H.L., TH 2328.
33 Deed quoted in H. G. C. Allgood, *Hist. Bethnal Green* (1894), 293 sqq. Of the contributors, Thos. Rider was owner of Kirby's Castle, Rog. Gillingham owned Dickens est. (G.L.R.O., M93/132, ff. 36,46, 72, 173), and Wm. Northey was manorial steward and owned former demesne land in Old Ford: T.H.L.H.L., TH/3711, 3717.
34 Below, charities (distributive chars.).
35 *Cal. Treas. Bks.* 1685–9, 1819.
36 Gascoyne, *Map*, version in B.M., Crace Colln., Portf. xvi. 33.
37 Lysons, *Environs*, ii (1), p. 32 (grangerized copy in Guildhall Libr.).

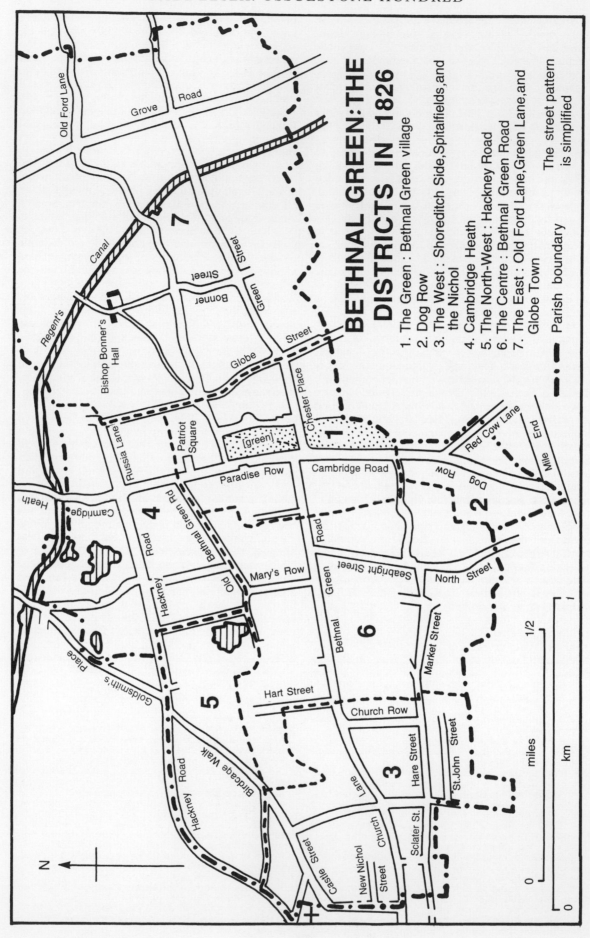

BETHNAL GREEN: THE
DISTRICTS IN 1826

1. The Green : Bethnal Green village
2. Dog Row
3. The West : Shoreditch Side, Spitalfields, and
   the Nichol
4. Cambridge Heath
5. The North-West : Hackney Road
6. The Centre : Bethnal Green Road
7. The East : Old Ford Lane, Green Lane, and
   Globe Town

The street pattern
   is simplified

———— Parish boundary

FIG. 12

In 1751 there were some 65 houses around the green on the eastern side of Cambridge Heath Road and 93 on the western side. Those on the western side were overwhelmingly small houses, 84 per cent being rated at £5 or less a year, compared with 53 per cent on the eastern side; 11 per cent were rated at £6–£10 compared with 33 per cent on the east. There were two houses on the west rated at £11–£15 compared with five on the east, and only one large house on the west, rated at £16 compared with one house rated at £16 and two at £30 on the east.[38]

The following paragraphs trace the piecemeal expansion of settlement round the green beginning at its northern end. North of the green and the later Old Ford Road were copyhold houses belonging to the Dickens family, probably by 1614, on a site bounded west by Cambridge Heath Road, north and east by Conduit Close.[39] In 1637 Nicholas Dickens (d. 1653), a London haberdasher, built a house on the green south of his copyhold property[40] and by 1661 the estate contained two tenements and five cottages.[41] In 1763 it had a large house on the corner site, a house with a large garden north of it, and five houses running eastward from the corner house along the north side of Old Ford Road.[42] The Dickens estate experienced the first extensive building: Aaron Eele, of Mile End New Town and Daniel Bowyer of Whitechapel were building in Patriot Square in 1792–4[43] and, joining it to the west where it fronted Cambridge Road, Patriot Row was built about the same time.[44] Among those buying the new houses were an employee of East India House, a Whitechapel brandy merchant, a Covent Garden coal merchant, and a City gentleman.[45]

East of the Dickens estate lay Conduit close, part of Pyotts. In 1643 that estate included several cottages, tenements, and tofts which were probably old[46] and in 1734 six ruinous wooden houses stood north of Old Ford Road.[47] One was the Hampshire Hog, probably the Hog and Pye licensed in 1722.[48] The others perhaps included three old houses on the estate leased to the Revd. John Lawrence and Roderick Patcheco, one of the Jews living in the vicinity who gave rise to the name Jews' Walk for the western end of Old Ford Lane. When Pyotts was

broken up and sold in 1753, the houses were bought and pulled down by Anthony Natt.[49] He replaced them with a three-storeyed terrace (originally 10–12, renumbered in 1875 as nos. 17–21 (odd) Old Ford Road),[50] still there in 1988. The Hampshire Hog continued to be licensed until 1775, perhaps not in its old building.[51]

Natt (d. 1756), a carpenter who had built on Nichol and Carter estates in the 1720s and 1730s,[52] bought what was described as the chapel house in 1748 and shortly afterwards built two houses adjoining it to the west.[53] In 1772 his son Anthony Natt, rector of Netteswell (Essex), bought the freehold from the lord of the manor[54] and in 1790 employed Ruby, a carpenter, to replace the two houses with four, forming the Terrace, Old Ford Road.[55]

On the east side of the green and south of the Corner House, at least by the 17th century and probably earlier, several houses faced the green, with their tofts and crofts stretching to Back Lane. By 1703 a lane (later Victoria Park Square) ran from Old Ford Road to Green Street in front of the houses.[56] Three houses were built on the ground next to the Corner House, probably fronting Victoria Park Square, c. 1736.[57] The Corner House itself was renamed Aldgate House after 1753, later occupied by prominent Jews, and demolished in 1806.[58]

On the site later occupied by nos. 21–23 Victoria Park Square stood, possibly by 1621, the Wheatsheaf, in 1662 two cottages associated with another tenement as part of John Stonier's estate.[59] Two houses were associated with Markhams by 1654:[60] the Blind Beggar at the southern end and, possibly on the site of no. 18, the house then occupied by Edward Pratt and in 1659 perhaps by one of the joint owners, Waldrof Lodowick, a London merchant.[61] South of the Blind Beggar, between it and Green Street, were two tenements and a cottage by 1647:[62] they were four tenements by 1683,[63] held with 4 a. stretching eastward to Back Lane.[64] North of the Blind Beggar were, by 1668, a tenement and three cottages,[65] which by 1688 had become six tenements.[66] Nearby houses in 1688 included five tenements associated with Eastfields[67] in 1657 and a messuage and three tenements belonging to Hawes in 1659.[68] Both estates passed through

38 T.H.L.H.L., BG 256. Three empty hos. in the E. and 4 in the W. were not rated.
39 G.L.R.O., M93/158, ff. 23–24; M93/35, p. 491; *Mems. Stepney Par.* 67.
40 G.L.R.O., M93/158, ff. 23–24; B.L. Eg. MS. 3006, f. 47; P.R.O., PROB 11/230 (P.C.C. 296 Brent), ff. 219–21v.
41 G.L.R.O., M93/132, f. 33.
42 Ibid. M93/35, pp. 490–5.
43 T.H.L.H.L., TH/2273, 7949; M.L.R. 1794/3/287, 759.
44 Horwood, *Plan* (1792–9).
45 M.L.R. 1794/3/287, 759; T.H.L.H.L., TH/2273, 7949.
46 P.R.O., C 142/743, no. 17; below, estates (Pyotts).
47 G.L.R.O., O/113/1.
48 Ibid. MR/LV3/101, ff. 8v.–9.
49 M.L.R. 1753/3/371; Robinson and Chesshyre, *The Green*, 17–18.
50 Robinson and Chesshyre, *The Green*, 19; *Bricks and Mortar. Some Important Bldgs. in Tower Hamlets*, ed. H. Ward, D. Keeling, H. Cooke, B. Nurse and B. Jackson, no. 15.
51 G.L.R.O., MR/LV8/68b; Robinson and Chesshyre, *The Green*, 18.

52 G.L.R.O., THCS 130; M.L.R. 1754/3/333.
53 G.L.R.O., M93/142, 167; Robinson and Chesshyre, *The Green*, 19.
54 M.L.R. 1772/4/102; G.L.R.O., M93/138.
55 G.L.R.O., MR/B/R4; Horwood, *Plan.* (1792–9).
56 Gascoyne, *Map*.
57 G.L.R.O., O/113/1; Horwood, *Plan* (1792–9).
58 Below, estates (Pyotts); Judaism; below, plate 18.
59 G.L.R.O., M93/13, ff. 35, 37. For Stonier, below, estates (Cambridge Heath).
60 G.L.R.O., M93/132, f. 1; below, estates (Markhams). For the Blind Beggar, Horwood, *Plan* (1792–9).
61 G.L.R.O., M93/132, f. 23.
62 Ibid. ff. 98–9.
63 Ibid. M93/12, p. 236.
64 Ibid. M93/35, p. 440; M93/142; M93/167; M.L.R. 1772/5/132. Identifiable with Upscher's (Upshot) est.: Gascoyne, *Map*.
65 G.L.R.O., M93/132, f. 68. Somewhere on the site later nos. 6–16: M93/69, p. 629.
66 Ibid. M93/132, ff. 88, 137, 221; M93/142.
67 Ibid. M93/132, f. 17; below, estates (Eastfields).
68 G.L.R.O., M93/132, f. 22; M93/142.

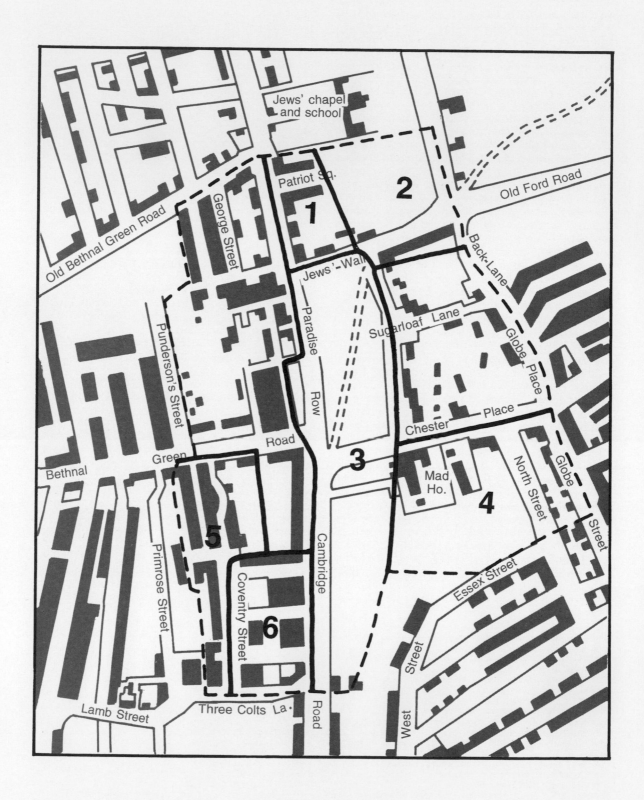

FIG. 13. BETHNAL GREEN VILLAGE: PRINCIPAL ESTATES

1 Dickens, 2 Pyott, 3 Poor's Lands, 4 Kirby's Castle, 5 Penn, 6 St. Paul's. The boundary is that of the district in 1826

the hands of the Grunwins before they were divided at the beginning of the 18th century.[69] In 1692 James Grunwin, a merchant tailor, leased to Peter Causton, another London merchant, a house with nine rooms, a banqueting house which was probably separate, a summer house, and a two-seated latrine.[70] The house may have been that occupied by Robert Edmunds, assessed for 4 hearths in 1664,[71] which, together with cottages, occupied the site later known as nos. 19[72] and 20 Victoria Park Square[73] and passed to the Goulds.[74] A Jew, Jacob Cohendezevedo, occupied it before 1769.[75] The rest of the property was sold in 1701 to Joseph Blissett,[76] who from 1693 accumulated fractions of Markhams[77] which by 1687 included a house called the Sugar Loaf.[78] Blissett may have built nos. 16–18, a brick and tiled range of two storeys with cellars and attics and pilastered doorways of c. 1700.[79]

Sugar Loaf Walk, which joined Victoria Park Square to Back Lane by 1703,[80] probably marked the boundary of Blissett's and Gould's estates. Goulds, to the north, was split up in 1769. Cohendezevedo's house passed to Peter Mestear, who built another in the garden and enfranchised both in 1772.[81] In 1779 Mestear acquired, on the south side of Sugar Loaf Walk, from Blissetts four houses[82] which had existed by 1744[83] and were probably those depicted in the alley in 1703.[84] An old garden of Goulds was bought by David Horne, a peruke maker, who had bought two houses on the neighbouring Stonier estate in 1757.[85] He built a new house and obtained the enfranchisement of all three houses, probably on the site of no. 21, in 1772.[86] Further south three houses were built 'near the Blind Beggar' in 1788.[87]

Two or more tenements in Back Lane in 1653 had become six wooden cottages by 1674.[88] They were split into two estates in 1720,[89] the northern three with an added one becoming nos. 11–14.[90] The southern three had been replaced by two partly brick houses by 1734[91] and there were another two by 1766.[92]

South of Green Street Kirby's Castle had wealthy occupants throughout the 17th century.[93] From 1726 the house, by then misleadingly called the Blind Beggar's House, was a private

lunatic asylum.[94] It was extended and by 1777 was called the White House.[95] In 1685 the owner James Alpha agreed to build a two-storeyed and garretted house for John How, lessee of the former home farmhouse, then a cottage.[96] By 1698 the old farmhouse had been replaced by five brick tenements fronting the green south of Kirby's Castle, a terrace of four small houses, and almost on the southern border a detached house with 14 rooms, a brewhouse, and coach house, occupied in 1703 by the estate's owner Col. Joseph Jorey.[97] Jorey's house was by 1760 a workhouse[98] and, of the terrace of four houses, one had been pulled down by 1802 and the others converted into two, owned by the widow of the 'keeper of lunatics'.[99]

The western side of the green apparently had no settlement before the 16th century. Shortly before 1581 John Soda, a London grocer, built a house on the waste west of Cambridge Heath Road, slightly south of Cambridge Heath,[1] for which his widow Joan obtained a 500-year lease from Henry, Lord Wentworth, in 1585.[2] It remained the most northerly of the houses on the west side of the green in the 17th century, and in 1652 was a 'great messuage' with an adjoining tenement, courtyards, gardens, and 1 a. of pasture containing fruit trees and 32 elms.[3] Called the City of Nineveh in 1713, when William Coleman owned it,[4] it may have been the winged house depicted in 1703 opposite Old Ford Road or a smaller house to the north.[5] In 1722 William Spering's daughters conveyed at least part of Coleman's estate to George Colson, a London carpenter.[6] Colson probably built George Street, which ran southward from Old Bethnal Green Road, parallel with Cambridge Heath Road, where in 1726 he leased building plots fronting east onto it.[7] In 1740 he leased to a butcher a shop 'lately built' and ground called 'the Grove'.[8] By 1750 nine houses stood near the watchhouse, seven fronting east and two south on 'the Grove near Bethnal Green'.[9] The Grove may have been the belt of trees depicted running north alongside Cambridge Heath Road from the watchhouse in 1703. A row of houses already existed there in 1703, possibly the northern part of the later-named Paradise Row.[10] The group

69 Ibid. M93/132, ff. 51, 155, 174–5, 227, 303, 399.
70 Guildhall MS. 7588.
71 G.L.R.O., MR/TH/4, m. 92.
72 Ibid. M93/38, p. 389; M93/41, p. 21; M93/48, p. 396; M93/63, p. 20; M93/82, p. 604.
73 Ibid. M93/60, p. 16; M93/86, pp. 559–65.
74 Guildhall MS. 7588.
75 G.L.R.O., M93/38, p. 9.
76 Ibid. M93/132, f. 303.
77 Below, estates (Markhams).
78 Northants. R. O., X 1077. (corresp. of Jas. Sotheby and s. 1650–87); G.L.R.O., MR/LV3/101, ff. 8v.–9; ibid. M93/30, p. 371.
79 Hist. Mon. Com. E. Lond. 9.
80 Gascoyne, Map.
81 G.L.R.O., M93/38, pp. 22, 305; M.L.R. 1772/5/142.
82 G.L.R.O., M93/37, pp. 172–3; M93/40, p. 467.
83 Ibid. M93/30, p. 371.
84 Gascoyne, Map.
85 G.L.R.O., M93/34, p. 89.
86 Ibid. M93/38, p. 23; M.L.R. 1772/3/196–7.
87 G.L.R.O., MR/B/R4, nos. 195–7.
88 Ibid. M93/132, ff. 110–11.
89 Ibid. f. 441.
90 Ibid. M93/59, p. 58; M93/64, pp. 654–5.
91 Ibid. M93/27, p. 441.
92 Ibid. M93/41, p. 2.
93 Below, estates (Kirby's Castle).
94 M.L.R. 1727/4/12; Robinson and Chesshyre, The Green, 11 sqq.; below, pub. svces. (medical svces.).
95 Robinson and Chesshyre, The Green, 11; Rocque, Plan of Lond. (1746); Horwood, Plan (1792–9).
96 P.R.O., C 7/1/2; C 7/2/68.
97 G.L.R.O., M93/132, ff. 197, 286; M93/32, ff. 83–5; Gascoyne, Map; P.R.O., PROB 3/25/4.
98 T.H.L.H.L., Par. Map (no. 301); below, local govt. (par. govt. 1743–1836).
99 G.L.R.O., M93/48, pp. 317–18; Robinson and Chesshyre, The Green, 11 sqq.
1 B.L. Eg. Roll 2080.
2 G.L.R.O., M93/158, f. 22.
3 Ibid. M93/158, f. 22; M93/142.
4 M.L.R. 1713/2/18.
5 Gascoyne, Map.
6 T.H.L.H.L., TH/1666–7.
7 Ibid. 1668.
8 Ibid. 1669.
9 Ibid. 1670.   10 Gascoyne, Map.

of very small houses opposite Old Ford Road, Little George Street and Peacock Court or Place, apparently existed by the mid 18th century,[11] possibly earlier as the Peacock inn was there by 1730.[12] By the end of the century Paradise Row extended to Bethnal Green Road and Hollybush Place had been built to the west.[13] Another three houses were 'nearly finished' at nos. 7–9 Paradise Row in 1814.[14] From 1788 no. 3 Paradise Row housed Daniel Mendoza, the Jewish boxer.[15] In 1783 Capt. Jonathan Punderson was building Punderson's Place and Gardens on the narrow 2-acre strip running north from Bethnal Green Road to the west of Stainer's estate,[16] which had belonged to Nicholas Dickens.[17]

Other pieces of waste south of Soda's were granted as copyhold to London butchers in 1581.[18] They were probably the two parcels of waste which were leased by Thomas, Lord Wentworth, in 1614 for 50 years after the death of Lady Anne Wentworth (d. 1625), with a covenant to maintain buildings. By 1652 they contained three cottages and farm buildings, all built by the lessee, Timothy Rushbrook.[19] The property was sold in 1654 to John Spering, a local man[20] who let out one house in 1666 to John Harwood and in 1669 to Robert Hudson.[21] A second house, to the east of the first, was leased or sold shortly before 1667. In 1671 Spering left 1 a., a house in his own possession, one occupied by Hudson, two tenements, and cottages.[22]

Also west of the green William Sebright (d. 1620) occupied a house separated from St. Paul's estate to the south by 1½ a. of attached land. In 1625 Ellis Crisp, alderman, held the freehold. Dame Hester Pye, probably his widow, and his son Sir Nicholas Crisp leased the house and 2 a., and a further ½ a. of exotic trees beyond a little lane, to Balthazer Gerbier,[23] who opened his academy in the house.[24] Gerbier had started his English career when presented to James I by the Dutch ambassador Noel de Caron, who had earlier lived in Bethnal Green.[25] In 1655 Crisp sold his property to Robert Stainer,[26] who was assessed for as many as 12 hearths in 1664[27] and 15 in 1671.[28] He was dead by 1678 when his land contained one or more houses west of the green. By 1703 there were two houses there,

with east of them a terrace of houses and gardens fronting the Poor's Land.[29]

From 1620 Walter Cooke, Master of Trinity House (d. c. 1656)[30] held 3 a. south of the lane which became Bethnal Green Road. By 1686 the land was used as a nursery by Matthew Penn,[31] who had a house at its northern end by 1696.[32] On the adjoining estate to the east terraced houses fronting Cambridge Road ran southward from the lane by 1703.[33] On the corner of the lane and Cambridge Road the Salmon and Ball stood in 1733.[34] The Green Man existed by 1750 in the middle of the terrace.[35] By 1764 five houses fronted Bethnal Green Road.[36]

As in other districts, the Napoleonic era saw piecemeal building make way for the development of whole estates. East of the green the 4 a. between Victoria Park Square and Back Lane had been fragmented by 1797[37] and houses were being built in 1807 in Chester Place on the north side of Green Street, partly by Thomas Seares, a local bricklayer.[38] Thurlow Street existed by 1809,[39] as by 1826 did houses behind Chester Place in Helen's Place and the beginnings of Bernham or Burnham Square in the corner between Globe Street (Back Lane) and Sugar Loaf Walk.[40] Joseph Merceron accumulated property to the north between 1810 and 1833 but did not build.[41] On Peter Mestear's estate, centred on Sugar Loaf Walk, the White Hart brewery had been built by 1819.[42] At the northwest corner of Victoria Park Square and Old Ford Road Aldgate House was replaced by 1811 by Ebenezer or Park chapel and small tenements,[43] which by 1813 covered the whole frontage on Old Ford Road as far as Back Lane and Gretton Place.[44]

At the northern end of the green the houses at the end of Old Ford Road, on the Dickens estate, were rebuilt in the early 19th century as plain, three-storeyed houses in what was called Jews' Walk or North Side.[45] Pyotts to the east was leased for building in the 1820s when Bates Place fronting Old Ford Road, the west side of Russia Lane, and the new Providence Place were built.[46]

At the southern end the Kirby's Castle estate, occupying the whole area south of Green Street and west of Globe Road, was split up in 1809. Houses were soon built, some by Charles Pike,

[11] Rocque, *Map of Lond.* (1741–5); Horwood, *Plan* (1792–9).
[12] G.L.R.O., MR/LV5/26, pp. 14–15.
[13] Horwood, *Plan* (1792–9).
[14] T.H.L.H.L., TH/7792.
[15] *Jewish Hist. Soc. Trans.* xxx. 79.
[16] Gascoyne, *Map*; G.L.R.O., MR/B/R/3 (1784), 84–7; M.L.R. 1794/3/503; Horwood, *Plan* (1792–9); Vestry mins. 1782–1813, p. 99.
[17] G.L.R.O., M93/157, f. 53.
[18] Hen. Baker and Wm. Andrews: B.L. Eg. Roll 2080.
[19] G.L.R.O., M93/158, f. 21.
[20] P.R.O., C 54/3806/11.
[21] Ibid. C 7/543/135.
[22] Ibid. PROB 11/335 (P.C.C. 29 Duke), ff. 227v.–30v.
[23] Ibid. WARD 7/74/150; ibid. C 8/100/159; C 9/13/54.
[24] Below, educ. (private schs.).
[25] *Proc. Hug. Soc.* x. 327–8. For Caron, below, estates (Kirby's Castle).
[26] P.R.O., CP 25/2/575.
[27] G.L.R.O., MR/TH/4, m. 92.
[28] Ibid. MR/TH/16, f. 22; cf. ibid. M93/142.

[29] Ibid. A/PLC/1/1–2; ibid. A/PLC/VI/2, nos. 1,8; H. Allgood, *Hist. Bethnal Green*, 294; Gascoyne, *Map*, espec. version in B.M., Crace Colln., Portf. xvi. 33.
[30] *Mems. Stepney Par.* 98.
[31] P.R.O., C 110/83; G.L.R.O., M93/132, ff. 7, 99, 117, 200.
[32] M.L.R. 1716/1/26–27; 1718/3/25; Gascoyne, *Map*.
[33] Gascoyne, *Map*; Horwood, *Plan* (1792–9).
[34] Robinson and Chesshyre, *The Green*, 28.
[35] G.L.R.O., MR/LV6/79, pp. 3–5.
[36] P.R.O., C 110/83.
[37] G.L.R.O., M93/97, p. 107; M93/57, p. 13.
[38] Ibid. MR/B/C3/1807, no. 565; M.L.R. 1807/6/729.
[39] G.L.R.O., Acc. 240/26.
[40] *Cruchley's New Plan* (1826).
[41] G.L.R.O., M93/52, pp. 228–9, 287; M93/54, pp. 243 sqq.; M93/60, p. 16; M93/63, p. 504; M93/86, pp. 559–65; M93/96, p. 104.
[42] P.R.O., C 110/164.
[43] Below, estates (Pyotts).
[44] M.L.R. 1813/7/785; *Cruchley's New Plan.* (1826).
[45] T.H.L.H.L., TH/4554–5, 7956.
[46] P.R.O., C 54/12480.

on the west side of Globe Road and fronting the new James or North Street and Cornwall Street.[47] A factory existed by 1817.[48] Kirby's Castle (the White House) remained an asylum; the Red House, a house designed for the insane, had been built to the south of it by 1831.[49]

St. John's church was built on the green at the junction of Cambridge Road and Green Street in 1828.[50]

On the west side of Cambridge Road the St. Paul's estate, bounded south by Three Colts Lane and long held on leases for lives by the Boon family, was 'in the hands of' Blake and Mead in 1809.[51] Thomas Blewett Mead, a Shoreditch victualler, was involved in leasing new houses in Bath, Parliament, and Coventry streets and Cambridge Road in 1811 and 1813;[52] Blake was probably James Blake, an auctioneer from Bishopsgate Without and a developer of Nag's Head Field near Hackney Road in 1807–8.[53] Part of the St. Paul's estate was acquired c. 1818 by John C. Severne, who gave his name to Severne or Abingdon Street.[54] Building was complete by 1826. There were 207 houses and one public house, the Queen Adelaide, on the estate in 1836.[55]

The Penn's Garden estate, a strip of 3 a. west of St. Paul's estate from the south side of Bethnal Green Road to Three Colts Lane, passed to the Lucas family in 1789. In 1811 Joseph Lucas leased it to Ann Potts [56] who granted 56-year leases of plots to local builders, among them William Timmins, John Pitt, and Francis Fuller.[57] By 1822 there were, besides the 17th-century farmhouse fronting Bethnal Green Road, 106 houses in Lucas, Potts, Pitt, and Fox streets.[58] By 1836 there were 25 houses and the Lord Wellington on the southern part of the estate, on the north side of Three Colts Lane and in Primrose Street.[59] On the north side of Bethnal Green Road, Hollybush Gardens existed between Hollybush Place and Punderson's Gardens by 1818[60] and contained four houses by 1836.[61] Rebuilding included the construction by John Litchfield of five houses on the site of old wooden houses, possibly George Colson's, on the north side of George Street, once called Nineveh Corner, after 1824.[62]

By 1836 Bethnal Green village had c. 289 houses, a public house, a brewery, and a factory on the east side of Cambridge Road and 401 houses and seven public houses on the west side.[63]

DOG ROW. In the 1570s a broad area of waste stretched from Mile End to Bethnal green, through which the later Cambridge Heath Road ran from north to south.[64] In 1582 Thomas, Lord Wentworth, made three grants of waste on the west side of the road, initially as copyhold but converted to 500-year leases in 1585. The plots were 30–57 ft. with frontages from north to south of 120 ft., 120 ft., and 450 ft. respectively. Between 1582 and 1585 one house had been built on the first plot and two houses on the second. In 1585 Henry, Lord Wentworth, leased for 500 years another plot to the south, measuring 495 ft. by 66 ft. The southernmost plot, abutting Mile End green and including a house, was leased out for 40 years by Thomas, Lord Wentworth, in 1621. By 1652 there were 39 houses or cottages[65] in what by 1649 was called Dog Row.[66] By 1671 there were 46.[67] In 1652 at least 16 buildings were of brick and the southernmost one had six rooms, although most of the others were very small.[68] In 1671 two houses in Dog Row were assessed for 5 hearths, three for 3 hearths, 33 for 2 hearths, and eight for only one hearth.[69] The 39 dwellings of 1652 included two public houses, the Dun Cow and the White Bear, and farm buildings were associated with 11. Some of the tenements had sheds,[70] possibly the dog kennels which gave their name to the road, and which survived, blocked up and stuccoed, on the front of nos. 65–76 Cambridge Road c. 1930.[71]

Building was on a small scale, the five leases being held in 1652 by 11 intermediate tenants who had probably built most of the dwellings, which they sublet.[72] Another two houses were built on the northernmost plot between 1659 and 1665 and two more between 1677 and 1679.[73] Sales of wastehold in the Interregnum[74] were usually to the existing intermediate tenants, most of them local inhabitants. Other tenants and purchasers were a London goldsmith, [75] a Kentish 'esquire'[76] and a yeoman of the Minories (Peter Smith).[77] It was probably the latter's son William Smith, a London merchant, who engaged a bricklayer and carpenter to replace decayed houses with three new houses c. 1679.[78]

47 G.L.R.O., M93/53, pp. 217–23; M93/54, pp. 76, 129; M93/55, p. 403.
48 Ibid. 56, p. 128.
49 Robinson and Chesshyre, The Green, 11–16; below, building 1837–1875; pub. svces. (medical svces.).
50 Below, list of churches.
51 T.H.L.H.L., TH/7499.
52 M.L.R. 1812/2/239–40; 1812/2/369–70; 1813/7/512.
53 Below, the North-West, Hackney Road.
54 T.H.L.H.L., TH/7499.
55 G.L.R.O., THCS 447.
56 P.R.O., C 54/13855, mm. 52–66.
57 Ibid.; M.L.R. 1813/7/545–6; 1813/9/224.
58 G.L.R.O., M93/58, p. 222.
59 T.H.L.H.L., TH/7499.
60 P.R.O., C 54/9753, m. 36.
61 G.L.R.O., THCS 446.
62 M.L.R. 1842/6/718.
63 G.L.R.O., THCS 446–7.

64 P.R.O., M.P.F. 282; above (communications).
65 G.L.R.O., M93/158, ff. 15–19; 170; B.L. Eg. Roll 2081.
66 P.R.O., PROB 11/209 (P.C.C. 140 Fairfax), f. 177–v. (will of Thos. Whitberd).
67 G.L.R.O., MR/TH/16, m. 26.
68 Ibid. M93/158, ff. 15–19.
69 Ibid. MR/TH/16, m. 26.
70 Ibid. M93/158, ff. 15–19.
71 Hist. Mon. Com. E. Lond. 9, where the hos. are dated late 17th.-cent.
72 G.L.R.O., M93/158, ff. 15–19.
73 Ibid. M93/163.
74 For sales, below, estates.
75 P.R.O., C 54/3858, no. 14.
76 G.L.R.O., M93/166. Petty had been a tenant since 1613/4: P.R.O., C 54/3805, no. 29.
77 G.L.R.O., M93/166.
78 He was dissatisfied with the quality of the work and materials: P.R.O., C 5/557/81.

In 1671 Lady Wentworth and Sir William Smyth granted another plot, to the south of the existing wastehold plots, for 99 years to Henry Meacock, blacksmith of Mile End. A house there, occupied with *c.* 3 a. of garden by Walter Simkins in 1703, passed in 1709 to Capt. Robert Fisher, who founded almshouses on the site in 1711.[79]

In 1673 Lady Wentworth was licensed to build on West Heath, the waste named by 1475[80] on either side of Mile End Road, which included the portion in Bethnal Green around the southern part of Dog Row. Sir Christopher Wren, as surveyor for the licence, depicted the plague burial ground on the west side of Dog Row, and 'ancient houses' on the east, at the junction with Mile End Road. By 1703 houses fronted Mile End Road on both sides of the junction, as projected by Wren. Those on the west lay within Bethnal Green.[81]

Houses on the east side of Dog Row were part of property owned by Sir William Smyth of Stepney, Bt., who leased a brick house and 1 a. in 1678 to Abraham Neale for 200 years[82] and another house and ground in 1689 to Matthew Walker, cowkeeper.[83] By 1703 there were four buildings, the most northerly in the fork between Dog Row and Red Cow Lane, the most southerly, Walker's, opposite what was to become Darling Row; between were two smaller buildings, one of them probably Neale's house.[84] Smyth's property and Neale's house passed to Joseph Jorey, whose estate consisted in 1728 of four brick houses, farm buildings, and *c.* 6 a.[85] Neale's 1 a. passed to the Leeds family.[86]

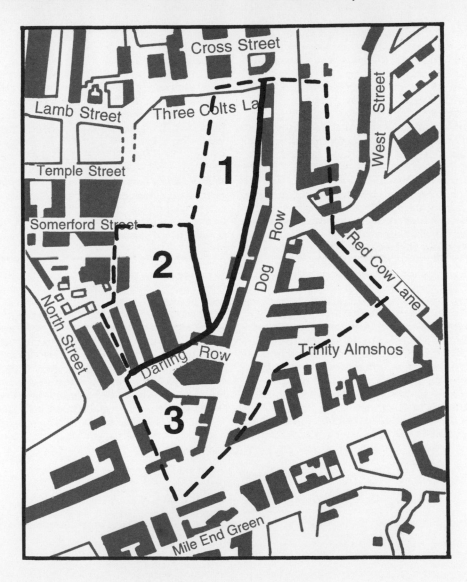

FIG. 14. DOG ROW: PRINCIPAL ESTATES

1 Fulmore Close, 2 Naylor, 3 Simkins Gardens

79 M.L.R. 1711/5/53–5; 1713/3/172; T.H.L.H.L., TH/204; Lysons, *Environs*, ii. 36; Gascoyne, *Map*; Rocque, *Plan of Lond.* (1746). For the gdn., below, econ. hist. (mkt. gdns.).
80 P.R.O., C 146/118.
81 Lysons, *Environs*, iii. 446–8; Gascoyne, *Map*.

82 G.L.R.O., C93/1541.
83 Ibid. 1535.
84 Gascoyne, *Map*.
85 M.L.R. 1728/2/235; G.L.R.O., C93/1541.
86 T.H.L.H.L., TH/6313; below, estates (Cambridge Heath); econ. hist. (agric.).

In 1695 Trinity House founded almshouses to the south of Smyth's and Neale's estates, just outside Bethnal Green.[87] Thereafter it acquired additional sites within Bethnal Green: waste ground next to Fisher's almshouses in 1723,[88] two almshouses built by William Ogborne nearby in 1725,[89] Fisher's almshouses by 1732,[90] and Walker's farm buildings, which adjoined Trinity almshouses, in 1805.[91] Capt. Fisher's almshouses, still there in 1838, had gone by 1850.[92]

There appears to have been little change in Dog Row during the early 18th century, with three farms on the eastern side and probably one, at the entry to fields (called Mile End Corner at the end of the century and later Darling Row) on the west. A terrace replaced some of the scattered houses farther north on the west side.[93]

In 1765 David Wilmot took a lease of ground on the east side of Cambridge Road, before it branched into Dog Row and Red Cow Lane, where he built several houses within a year.[94] In 1775–6 at least five houses were built opposite them by Plaw, a bricklayer, in Queen's (or Charlotte) Row,[95] which by 1783 formed a complete terrace.[96] Beardwood or Barwood, a builder, erected 16 houses in Dog Row in 1766–81,[97] and another 4 in 1783,[98] Galton built 5 there in 1788–9,[99] and Dodd and Wyers two each in 1802.[1] One Lara built 4 houses 'near Dog Row' in 1783,[2] possibly at what was called Mile End Corner in the 1790s.[3] Purim Place on the east side of Dog Row was built opposite, south of Walker's estate, c. 1783.[4] Griffin's Place, brick cottages encroaching on the waste, existed nearby when the Corporation of Trinity House purchased Walker's farm in 1805. The Corporation granted a 70-year building lease to Plunkett, a timber merchant who built third-rate houses there.[5]

The dairy farms north of Trinity House's estate, on the east side of Dog Row, mostly farmed by John Johnson, were given over to the builders, John Jenkins of Whitechapel and Thomas Oliver of Thomas Street, from 1808 to 1813. Houses were built fronting west on Dog Lane, east on Red Cow Lane, and in new streets (John, originally Johnson, and Thomas streets).[6] Building also spread on the west side of Dog Lane behind the waste holdings fronting the main road. Darling Row (formerly Mile End Corner), perhaps named after Sir Robert Darling, a local official of 1769,[7] and Lisbon Street (existing by 1811)[8] ran westward to join North Street and Collingwood Street ran northward. William Green, a Spitalfields builder, and John Reynolds and John Dible, both local men, were responsible for much of the building there between c. 1810 and 1825.[9] In 1818 Green bought 6 a. of Fulmore Close to the north,[10] on which he built Northampton Street by 1828[11] and Norfolk and Suffolk streets by 1836. By 1836 there were nearly 500 houses in Dog Row district: 80 houses and two public houses fronted the main road on the west, with 249, three public houses, a brewery, a factory, and a slaughter house in the streets behind; 73 houses and two public houses fronted the main road on the east, with 92 houses behind.[12]

THE WEST: SHOREDITCH SIDE, SPITALFIELDS, AND THE NICHOL.

Waste alongside Collier's (Crabtree) Lane had been granted out by 1518[13] and was inhabited by 1597.[14] A reference in 1603 to 'late builded houses' on the waste, originally a laystall, 'beyond Shoreditch church towards Hackney'[15] was possibly the first mention of Collier's Row, the name given to houses fronting Hackney Road south and north of Collier's Lane. Collier's Row was a recognized locality in 1625.[16] Houses south of the lane were mortgaged with demesne land in 1629.[17] The row housed weavers, brickmakers, a glover, a cooper, a mariner, a sawyer, and a labourer in the 1640s[18] and in 1652 consisted of 23 mostly dilapidated cottages on waste near Shoreditch church, running north-eastward from the Half Moon next to Shoreditch High Street.[19] There were only 19 houses in Collier's Row in 1663.[20] About that time land north of Collier's Lane was leased to brickmakers and six houses, including a farm on the corner, had been built in the northward extension of Collier's Row by 1674.[21] By 1703 building in Collier's Row lined the eastern side of Hackney Road from Shoreditch church to beyond Crabtree Lane.[22]

87 Lysons, *Environs*, iii. 483.
88 G.L.R.O., C93/1530–1.
89 Ibid. 1533–4.
90 Co. of Par. Clerks, *New Remarks of Lond.* (1732), 196. Datestone 1733: P.L.A. MSS., Portfolio 'Stepney', watercolour by R. B. Schnebbelie, 1816.
91 G.L.R.O., C93/1538–43.
92 *Pigot & Co.'s Lond. Dir.* (1838); *P.O. Dir. Lond.* (1850).
93 Gascoyne, *Map*; Rocque, *Plan of Lond.* (1746).
94 M.L.R. 1766/1/220; 1766/7/416.
95 G.L.R.O., MR/B/R/2, nos. 633, 680, 765; M93/143.
96 *Bowles's New Pocket Plan of Lond. and Westm.* (1783).
97 G.L.R.O., MR/B/R/3 (1777–84), nos. 363–6; (1781), nos. 144–9, 151–2; (1784), nos. 25–8.
98 Ibid. (1784), nos. 78–81.
99 Ibid. R/4 (1788), nos. 47, 123.
1 Ibid. R/5 (1802), nos. 101–2.
2 Ibid. R/3 (1784), nos. 67–8, 70–1.
3 Horwood, *Plan* (1792–9).
4 Below, Judaism.
5 G.L.R.O., C93/1545.
6 Ibid. Acc. 1621/8; M.L.R. 1808/8/230, 703; 1812/2/295,

602; 1813/7/54; T.H.L.H.L., TH/2316, 3192.
7 Vestry mins. 1747–81, p. 278.
8 Then home of Thos. Oliver: M.L.R. 1811/5/823.
9 M.L.R. 1813/9/242; G.L.R.O. M93/145, ff. 3–6; T.H.L.H.L., TH/2305–8.
10 G.L.R.O., M93/57, p. 37.
11 T.H.L.H.L., TH/2293.
12 G.L.R.O., THCS 447.
13 Guildhall MS. 10123/2.
14 *Marriage Regs. of St. Dunstan's Stepney*, ed. T. Colyer-Fergusson (1898), i. 37.
15 J. Stow, *Survey of Lond.* ed. C. L. Kingsford (1908), ii. 74. Laystall marked on map of 1680: P.R.O., C 103/157.
16 *Mems. Stepney Par.* 107–8.
17 G.L.R.O., M93/158, ff. 26–7.
18 *Marriage Regs. of St. Dunstan's*, ii. 2–3, 5–8, 19, 25, 27, 30–1.
19 G.L.R.O., M93/93, ff. 25–6; P.R.O., E 317/Mdx./13.
20 *Cal. S. P. Dom.* 1670, Addenda 1666–70, 68.
21 P.R.O., C 103/157.
22 Gascoyne, *Map*; named in Stow, *Survey* (1720), map between pp. 48 and 49.

Stepney Rents, which housed artisans and servants in the early 1640s,[23] lay behind Collier's Row,[24] being probably named from its position within Stepney before the boundary with Shoreditch changed between 1682 and 1703.[25] In the 1670s c. 30–50 houses were assessed for a district called Shoreditch Side and 47–54 for another entitled Shoreditch Church, which in 1674 was called Collier Row.[26]

Spitalfields, officially the parish of Christ Church created out of Stepney in 1729, was often taken by contemporaries, particularly in connexion with silkweaving, to include the adjoining built up area to the north in what after 1743 was Bethnal Green parish. Clay was being dug for bricks in Brick Lane in 1550[27] and a century later streets were being laid out on the Wheler estate as building advanced northward to Bethnal Green along Brick Lane and Wheler Street.[28] The freehold, former demesne, estate of Hare Marsh was acquired by the Carter family in 1653 and John Carter (d. 1687), who inherited it in 1661,[29] claimed to have designed and managed building there.[30] The estate thrust deep into Spitalfields and presumably was developed from the south, until in 1669 Carter leased parcels in Hare Street, at the northern end, to a London carpenter, Josias Hill, who had built houses there by 1671.[31] Carter in 1671 stated that most houses in Hare Marsh had existed long before a proclamation of 1667 for restraining new buildings. Christopher Wren, then surveyor to the Crown, supported Carter's petition for a licence to finish the building and pave the roads, then impassable in winter.[32]

Carter leased plots, usually for 70 years, both to builders such as John Welsh, a Shoreditch bricklayer, in 1677 and to London merchants, including Joshua Green in 1670 and John Williams in 1676, who presumably sub-contracted.[33] The houses were narrow, on a 17-ft. frontage, and tall, one at least consisting of a single room on each of five storeys, including cellar and attic.[34] Most of the streets were built up by 1682.[35] Ram Alley, where Carter himself had a house, existed by 1687, as possibly did Fleet Street,[36] which was certainly there two years later.[37] The western part of Spicer Street, named after Richard Spicer, a local carpenter[38] to whom Carter left £100[39] and who was involved in leasing and presumably building on the estate,[40] existed in 1682 as George Street.[41]

The south-west corner of Bethnal Green, into which Wheeler Street ran, belonged to the Byde family and in the 1640s and 1650s was known as Preston's garden.[42] In 1669 Sir Thomas Byde leased to Edward Adams a house, possibly assessed in the 1670s for six hearths,[43] and 3 a., where 119 houses stood by 1713. Bounded north by Cock Lane, west by York Street, and east by Club Row, they included Anchor Street and Patience Street (Ass Park) and several courts[44] and probably existed by the 1680s.[45]

The rest of the area bordering Shoreditch, between Collier's Row and Stepney Rents in the north and the Byde estate in the south, belonged in the mid 17th century to the copyhold estates of the Austen and Snow families[46] or the freehold estate of the Nichols. In 1675 36 houses had recently replaced a three-storeyed brick farmhouse containing a great hall, a four-bayed cowhouse, two other tenements, and a barn, all near Shoreditch church on the Austen estate.[47] By 1703 Austin and Castle streets contained[48] 81 tenements and 17 cottages, most of which had been built by 1682.[49] Castle Street was named by 1685 after a fortification erected in the Civil War.[50] Some early 18th-century brick and tiled houses, with two storeys and attics, survived at nos. 15–33 Austin Street in 1930.[51]

Most of the ground south of Castle Street served as gardens in 1680 when John Nichol (or Nicoll) of Gray's Inn leased 4¾ a. bounded west and south by Cock Lane to Jon Richardson, a London mason, for 180 years, with permission to dig for bricks.[52] Nichol, member of a family associated with Bethnal Green by 1659,[53] had already built seven houses.[54] Richardson subleased, usually in plots giving a frontage of 16–20 ft. with a depth of 60 ft. for each house. Sublessees

23 *Marriage Regs. of St. Dunstan's*, ii. 2, 15, 20, 30.
24 Rocque, *Plan of Lond.* (1746).
25 Cf. Morgan, *Surv. of Lond. and Westm.* (1682) and Gascoyne, *Map*.
26 T.H.L.H.L., MR/TH/110, 16 mm. 24, 26.
27 Survey quoted in Robinson, *Hist. Hackney*, i. 341.
28 *Survey of Lond.* xxvii. 97–9.
29 Below, estates (Hare Marsh).
30 P.R.O., PROB 11/387 (P.C.C. 75 Foot), ff. 242v.–5.
31 Guildhall MS. 9968. Hill was building in Spitalfields Mkt. at about same time: *Survey of Lond.* xxvii. 128.
32 *Wren Soc.* xviii. 7, 17–18, 25.
33 Guildhall MS. 9968; P.R.O., C 107/70; T.H.L.H.L., TH/118; M.L.R. 1713/3/140; 1713/4/134; 1714/1/193; 1714/2/92.
34 Four hos. in St. John St. were 16 ft. × 17½ ft.: Guildhall MS. 9968; M.L.R. 1713/3/140.
35 Morgan, *Surv. of Lond. and Westm.* The map does not show E. part of estate.
36 Carter's will mentioned property in Fleet Street, perhaps in London rather than Bethnal Green: P.R.O., PROB 11/387 (P.C.C. 75 Foot), ff. 242v.–5.
37 G.L.R.O., A/PLC/VI/2, no. 26.

38 Spicer was assessed for 4 hearths in 1674: G.L.R.O., MR/TH/46.
39 P.R.O., PROB 11/387 (P.C.C. 75 Foot), ff. 242v.–5.
40 Guildhall MS. 9968; T.H.L.H.L., TH/118.
41 Not the N.–S. George St. of 1703: Morgan, *Surv. of Lond. and Westm.*; Gascoyne, *Map*. Presumably named after Carter's brother Geo.
42 G.L.R.O., BRA/685/1/80; M93/158, f. 12.
43 P.R.O., E 179/143/407, s.v. Shoreditch Side.
44 M.L.R. 1713/1/179; 1745/1/98; C.L.R.O., Assess. Box 43, MS. 22.
45 Morgan, *Surv. of Lond. and Westm.*; Gascoyne, *Map*; cf. King's Head Ct.: P.R.O., PROB 11/396 (P.C.C. 98 ENT), ff. 60v.– 61. For Ass Park and Lt. York St. in 1689: G.L.R.O., A/PLC/VI/2, no. 26.
46 Below, estates (Austin; Snow).
47 G.L.R.O., M93/9, p. 42; M.L.R. 1736/5/536.
48 G.L.R.O., M93/20, p. 126.
49 Morgan, *Surv. of Lond. and Westm.*
50 H. L. Smith, *Hist. of E. Lond.* (1939), 283; P.R.O., PROB 11/381 (P.C.C. 115 Cann), ff. 58–9.
51 Hist. Mon. Com. *E. Lond.* 9.
52 M.L.R. 1709/2/126–8.
53 G.L.R.O., M93/3, p. 6.
54 M.L.R. 1709/2/126–8.

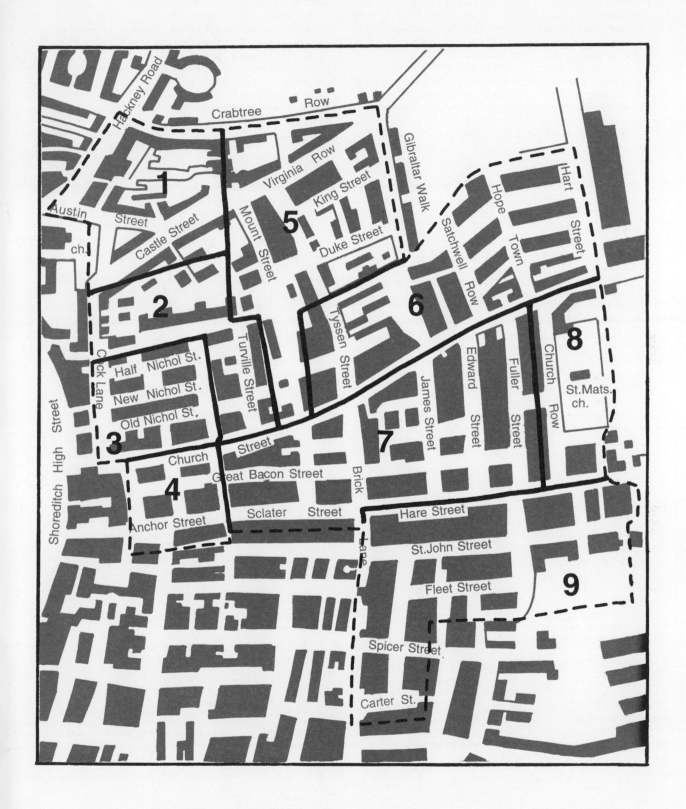

FIG. 15. THE WEST: PRINCIPAL ESTATES

1 Austen, 2 Snow, 3 Nichol, 4 Byde, 5 Fitch, 6 Tyssen, 7 Red Cow, 8 Willett (Wood close), 9 Hare Marsh

included Thomas Clarke, a London salter (1680), who built a house fronting Cock Lane,[55] Joseph Devonshire, a London carpenter (1682), who built one in Nichol Street,[56] and Thomas Hartshorne, a Stepney brickmaker (1685), who built houses on the north side of Nichol Street.[57] Henry Sleymaker (d. 1693), a London mason, who was a sublessee from 1682[58] and had built at least one house in Nichol Street in 1684, was probably related to Edward Sleymaker, who was building in Brick Lane in 1671.[59] Robert Tregoult, sublessee from 1683,[60] paid a lot 'for his houses' in the assessment of 1694.[61] Joseph Hayward, tiler of London, built a 'good brick house' on a plot between Cock Lane and Nichol Street which he took in 1688. In 1706 and 1708 he took three plots with a total frontage of 360 ft. (enough for 20 houses) from Richardson's son Thomas, a London clothworker. One large plot was at the eastern end of the estate, next to Turville's lands.[62] All the roads on John Nichol's estate were named after him, although he was directly responsible for only a few houses. Nichol (by 1723 Old Nichol)[63] Street existed by 1683,[64] New Nichol Street was 'new intended' in 1708,[65] and Nichol Row, existing by 1703, and Half Nichol Street were listed in 1732.[66]

The freehold former demesne lands later called Fitches, north and east of the Austen, Snow, and Nichol estates,[67] were conveyed in a chain of six subleases, several holders of which carried out small-scale building. In 1685 the third in the chain built 9 houses and the fifth laid out £500 in new building. The fourth, who claimed a lease dating from 1673 and who had been to Virginia with Sir John Berry,[68] may have given the name 'Virginia Row'. First recorded in 1694,[69] the road, an eastward extension of Castle Street, had houses by 1682.[70] Where the estate thrust southward to New Cock Lane (later Church Street and subsequently Bethnal Green Road), Rose (later Mount) Street was built by 1725.[71]

To the east, fronting New Cock Lane (Church Street), was a long but narrow estate connected with the Tyssens.[72] The Satchwell (Satchell) family, which leased nearby demesne in 1654[73] and was assessed under Shoreditch Side,[74] leased the eastern part of the estate by 1657[75] and was presumably responsible for Satchwell's garden and the buildings called Satchwell Rents at the eastern end of the estate by 1689.[76]

Except on the Snow estate, where two houses in Cock Lane disappeared between 1666 and 1693,[77] building took place on all estates bordering Spitalfields and Shoreditch southward from Crabtree Lane during the later 17th century. It spread steadily eastward and northward during the early 18th.

The freehold, former demesne, Red Cow estate lay south of Church Street, between Bydes to the west and Hare Marsh and Willetts.[78] In 1652 a house called the Red Cow and farm buildings stood at the north-east corner of Brick Lane and Church Street (then called Rogue Lane) and a new brick house to the south.[79] The Red Cow disappeared between 1682 and 1703 when the estate, then called Slaughter's (Sclater's) land, contained a few isolated buildings at the north-west corner of Brick and Cock lanes, on the east side of Brick Lane and Club Row, on the north side of Hare Street, and as the beginning of Sclater Lane.[80] Sclater Lane, linking Anchor Street on Byde's estate with Hare Street on Carter's, had apparently been completed by 1711[81] and paved by 1723.[82] Three houses were built in 1717 in Club Row.[83]

From 1718 Thomas Bacon (formerly Sclater) developed the Red Cow estate, leasing out usually small parcels for 61 years to carpenters of London[84] and others.[85] The estate consisted of Swanfield to the west and Harefield (or Crossfield) to the east of Brick Lane. Building began in Swanfield with Sclater Street in the south,[86] reaching Swan and Bacon streets by 1720.[87] Portions of Harefield were leased out from 1723 and laid out with James Street in 1723,[88] Thomas Street in 1724,[89] Fuller Street in 1725,[90] and Edward and Oakey streets by 1732.[91] Most building took place in the south and west parts bordering Brick Lane and Hare Street, leaving a large area of pasture in the north-east in 1746.[92] By 1751 there were c. 295 houses on the estate.[93] Numbers 3–9 (odd)

55 M.L.R. 1712/5/38.
56 Ibid. 1729/3/376.
57 Ibid. 1728/3/199.
58 Ibid. 1728/6/134; Guildhall MS. 9052/30, f. 63; 24, f. 69.
59 Wren Soc. xviii. 13.
60 M.L.R. 1716/3/9.
61 C.L.R.O., Assess. Box 43, MS. 22.
62 Presumably E. of Nichol Row: P.R.O., C 110/83.
63 G.L.R.O., THCS 250.
64 Guildhall MSS. 854, 919.
65 P.R.O., C 110/83.
66 Co. of Par. Clerks, New Remarks of Lond. (1732), 197–8; Gascoyne, Map.
67 Below, estates, demesne nos. 40–1.
68 P.R.O., C 7/581/142; ibid. PROB 11/330 (P.C.C. 98 Coke), ff. 328–9v.
69 C.L.R.O., Assess. Box 43, MS. 22.
70 Morgan, Surv. of Lond. and Westm.
71 Co. of Par. Clerks, New Remarks of Lond. (1732), 198; Rocque, Plan of Lond. (1746); Builder, 28 Jan. 1871, 69.
72 Below, estates (Tyssen).
73 P.R.O., C 54/3817, pt. 47, no. 10.
74 G.L.R.O., MR/TH/4, m. 92; MR/TH/110; MR/TH/16, m. 24; MR/TH/46.
75 P.R.O., C 103/157.
76 Gascoyne, Map.
77 G.L.R.O., M93/132, pp. 55, 251.
78 Below, estates (Red Cow).
79 G.L.R.O., M93/158, f. 11.
80 Morgan, Surv. of Lond. and Westm.; Gascoyne, Map.
81 Lambeth Pal. Libr., MS. 2750/16.
82 Cal. Mdx. Sess. Bks. xiii. 57.
83 T.H.L.H.L., TH/8111.
84 M.L.R. 1719/6/270–1; 1728/2/124–5, 181, 446; 1745/2/255–6; 1761/4/35; 1765/5/555; 1771/3/126. One, Edw. Grange, was also active in Spitalfields: Survey of Lond. xxvii. 89, 184.
85 M.L.R. 1728/2/181; 1752/3/488; 1754/2/299; 1771/1/20; 1771/3/126; 1772/2/84.
86 Lease of 1718: M.L.R. 1728/2/446; 1719: ibid. 1754/2/299.
87 Leases of 1720: M.L.R. 1728/2/124–5. Tablet dated 1723 in Bacon St.: Builder, 28 Jan. 1871, 69.
88 M.L.R. 1765/5/555.
89 Ibid. 1752/3/488; 1772/2/84.
90 Ibid. 1771/3/126.
91 Co. of Par. Clerks, New Remarks of Lond. (1732), 198.
92 Rocque, Plan of Lond. (1746).
93 T.H.L.H.L., BG/256.

Hare Street and 1–4 Hare Court, all near Brick Lane, survived in 1930 as three- or four-storeyed brick and tiled houses with some exposed ceiling beams.[94]

East of Harefield, bricks were being made in the 6-acre Wood Close in 1652 by Abraham Carnell.[95] In 1670 Thomas Willett leased the land to Carnell (d. c. 1679), with two houses which were pulled down after c. 1681. By 1703 building covered the whole of the frontage on the north side of Hare Street; Silver or Willett Street and Wood Street, with houses at their southern end, led north from Hare Street, and there were at least two houses and three cottages at the northern end of the field fronting Bethnal Green Road (Rogue Lane). Damage was reported c. 1705 from a great storm, presumably that of 1703.[96] By 1741 there were 56 houses on the estate, some of them probably built by William Farmer, a Brick Lane carpenter.[97] The building of the church in the centre of the field blocked further development north except on the west side of Silver Street (later Church Row).[98]

On Hare Marsh to the south building spread eastward to Weaver Street and Fleet Street Hill (Little Fleet Street in 1732) in the 1720s and 1730s.[99] One of the builders was Anthony Natt.[1] By 1751 there were c. 400 houses in Hare Marsh and 157 on the neighbouring Byde estate.[2] In addition parts of Hare Marsh east of Brick Lane were acquired before 1749 by Truman's brewery.[3]

On the north side of Bethnal Green Road (New Cock Lane) building leases on the divided Snow estate,[4] usually for 61 years, were granted by George Turville to Edward Yates, carpenter,[5] and to Robert Howard, joiner, both of London,[6] and others from 1723.[7] Bordering the Nichol estate, they built Turville Street north from Bethnal Green Road and New Turville Street east from New Cock Lane.[8] Turville's estate was said to contain 43 houses by 1736.[9]

On the neighbouring Fitch's estate David Dobbins[10] and John Wells[11] took leases to build brick houses with frontages of 16ft. They were built in Virginia Row and its southward extension, called New Virginia Row in 1732,[12] Virginia Street c. 1780,[13] and Turk Street by the 1790s.[14] Public houses included the Virginia Planter and Two Loggerheads in Virginia Row

in 1722[15] and the Turk's Head from 1750.[16] Virginia Row ran westward into Castle Street, part of the Austen estate which by 1740 had 112 cottages and tenements.[17]

Apart from Satchwell Rents at its eastern end, the Tyssen estate contained only Jamaica House, near the watchhouse at the top of Brick lane, until Samuel Tyssen leased plots from 1724. Leases, usually for 80 years, were made to Samuel Vevers[18] and John Rippin, both Spitalfields bricklayers, and Samuel Cohell,[19] William Breedon,[20] and William Farmer,[21] all carpenters, the last an inhabitant of Brick Lane who built on other Bethnal Green estates. Breedon's houses, and perhaps others', were of brick and timber, mostly with 16- or 17-ft. frontages on Church Street or a new 30-ft. wide street (Tyssen Street), which ran northward from Jamaica House to Virginia Row, its southern end existing by 1728.[22] By 1732 it was crossed by Shacklewell Street,[23] named after the Tyssens' seat in Hackney. Along Bethnal Green Road building proceeded from the west, with plots being leased to Farmer in 1732 and 1734,[24] to Matthew Wright, 'gentleman',[25] and to John Wolveridge, a plasterer, both local men in 1735.[26] The Gibraltar public house, named in 1750,[27] probably existed much earlier 'in the fields' at the northern edge of the estate.[28] By 1751 there were c. 524 houses in the area to the north of Bethnal Green Road and 931 to the south.[29]

The opening of the church and reconstruction of Bethnal Green Road (Church Street and New Cock Lane) in the 1740s led to more building, notably on the remaining farmland or garden ground. Fresh activity started on the Red Cow estate in 1769 when Thomas Sclater King granted leases to Thomas Green, a Petticoat Lane baker, of land fronting Church Street and the northern part of Edward Street and other plots on James Street and the new Granby Street.[30] Green applied for building licences in 'New' James Street, presumably at the northern end, in 1770.[31] Henry Busby, who acquired an interest in the estate in 1770, granted leases to John Price, a Petticoat Lane builder, in 1770[32] and to Jonathan Gee, a Bethnal Green carpenter, in 1771.[33] Price was building in James and Granby streets in 1771–2[34] and Gee had built at

94 Hist. Mon. Com. E. Lond. 9.
95 Below, estates (Willetts, demesne no. 49); G.L.R.O., M93/158, f. 11.
96 P.R.O., C 5/227/14; C 5/593/96; Gascoyne, Map.
97 M.L.R. 1771/3/127.
98 Rocque, Plan of Lond. (1746); Horwood, Plan (1792–9).
99 M.L.R. 1725/6/110–1; 1730/3/276; 1752/1/570.
1 Ibid. 1754/3/333; above, the Green.
2 T.H.L.H.L., BG/256.
3 Survey of Lond. xxvii. 116–18.
4 Below, estates (Snow).
5 M.L.R. 1759/4/126.
6 Ibid. 1728/5/10–11.
7 Ibid. 1724/6/318; 1728/2/17; 1752/3/726; 1767/6/85; 1772/1/34.
8 Rocque, Plan of Lond. (1746); Horwood, Plan (1792–9).
9 M.L.R. 1736/4/472.
10 Ibid. 1752/3/726; 1767/6/85.
11 P.R.O., C 107/172.
12 Co. of Clerks, New Remarks of Lond. (1732).
13 B.M., Crace Colln., Portf. xvi. 34.
14 Horwood, Plan (1792–9).

15 G.L.R.O., MR/LV3/101, ff. 8v.–9.
16 Ibid. MR/LV6/79, pp. 3–5.
17 T.H.L.H.L., TH/2309.
18 M.L.R. 1724/1/448; 1745/3/53; 1769/6/377.
19 Ibid. 1754/2/608.
20 Ibid. 1728/5/79; 1759/2/460.
21 Ibid. 1771/3/126.
22 Ibid. 1728/5/79.
23 Co. of Par. Clerks, New Remarks of Lond. (1732), 198; B.M., Crace Colln., Portf. xvi. 34.
24 M.L.R. 1808/5/780.
25 Ibid. 1735/1/391.
26 Ibid. 1735/1/392.
27 G.L.R.O., MR/LV6/79, pp. 3–5.
28 M.L.R. 1792/6/108; Gascoyne, Map; Rocque, Plan of Lond. (1746).
29 T.H.L.H.L., BG/256.
30 Ibid. TH/7970–1.
31 G.L.R.O., MR/B/R/2, no. 37.
32 T.H.L.H.L., TH/7972.
33 Ibid. TH/7975.
34 G.L.R.O., MR/B/R/2, nos. 94, 105, 281.

least five 'good brick houses' in Oakey Street by 1773.[35] Work continued into the 1790s under several other builders, including John May Evans and William Timmins,[36] until by 1799 the built-up area had advanced eastward to James Street.[37] By 1809 there were 467 houses on the estate, 274 of them east of Brick Lane.[38] The remaining spaces were soon filled[39] and by 1826 there were some 725 houses on the estate.[40]

Except in the south-east of Hare Marsh, streets already covered all the other estates south of Bethnal Green Road. Development, which continued patchily, was either rebuilding or the cramming of new courts into gardens of existing houses. Such, for example, were four houses built in Fleet Street by Samuel Ward in 1767,[41] Cheeseman Court by 1775,[42] Carter's Rents by Kilner in 1791,[43] all in Hare Marsh, and two houses built in Ass Park by William Ellington in 1770[44] and six in Anchor Street by Vine in 1775,[45] both on Bydes. Truman's brewery built a vat house fronting Carter Street c. 1805 and an engineer's house and stables fronting Brick Lane in 1831–6.[46] By 1836 there were 1,606 houses on all the estates south of Bethnal Green Road.[47]

Most building in the late 18th and early 19th centuries, however, was on the northern side of Bethnal Green Road. The Tyssens granted leases to Samuel Coombes, a Spitalfields carpenter, for an 'intended street',[48] probably 'Coomb' or Prince's Street, in 1766 [49] and a similar lease to John Wilcox for a plot on the west side of Virginia Street in 1768.[50] Truman's brewery had built storehouses between Tyssen and Shacklewell streets by 1775.[51] In 1792 leases were granted to Henry Vine, an Islington builder, of ground in Gibraltar Field near Shacklewell Street[52] and to Edward Clark, broker of Spitalfields, of ground together with the Gibraltar and 23 houses in Satchwell Rents.[53] By 1813 there were 49 houses on the plot.[54]

In 1769 the Tyssens leased 6 a. at the eastern end of the estate to William Atkins, a Bethnal Green gardener who laid out £200 in building a house.[55] Atkins leased out a plot next Bethnal Green Road to Robert Gavill, bricklayer of Mile End New Town, in 1770,[56] when Richard

Atkins, whose father had taken part of the 6 a. in 1769, subleased a plot with a frontage to the main road of 472 ft.[57] Norwell Place and Thorold Square had been built there by 1794.[58] The rest of the 6 a., east of Satchwell Rents and north of Thorold Square and Bethnal Green Road, was built up by John Gadenne, carpenter of Satchwell Rents, who subleased houses in the new streets: New Tyssen Street, Union Street (or Hope Town), and City Garden Place by 1808,[59] and Hart Street or Lane, George, Charlotte, and Tyrell streets by 1812.[60] By 1836 there were some 475 houses on the Tyssen estate.[61]

There was building to the north around Crabtree Row, where eleven brick houses stood on former garden ground by 1779[62] and others were built in 1788, 1790, and 1807, by John Lealand, Eccles, and Watson respectively.[63] John Godfrey, a Bethnal Green carpenter, was building north of Castle Street in 1772;[64] New Castle Street to the south and Sweetapple Court to the south of (Old) Castle Street existed by 1775.[65] The court was probably named from Joseph Sweetapple (fl. 1770)[66] and the nearby Cooper's Gardens, although not recorded until later,[67] from Thomas Cooper, occupier of the 2 a. between Castle Street and Hackney Road in 1779.[68] By 1800 there were c. 235 houses on the Austen estate.[69]

The unbuilt part of Fitches, south of Virginia Row with a portion east of Crabtree Lane (Gascoigne Place), was offered for building, probably in the late 1770s; anyone who took a 61-year lease and put up six houses was offered ground for a seventh freehold.[70] Among builders who sought certificates from 1777 to 1789 for houses around Virginia Row and Street and near the Loggerheads were William Tayler, Warn, Hide, Chidgey, King, and Thomas Southcomb.[71] James Green, a Spitalfields bricklayer, may have built 34 houses leased from William Gascoigne in 1779.[72] Prince's and King streets existed by 1787, with houses recently built by Samuel Lazonby, licensee of the Virginia Planter.[73] William Rider, bricklayer of Brick Lane, had lately built two houses on the west

35 T.H.L.H.L., TH/2887–8.
36 G.L.R.O., MR/B/R/3 (1777), nos. 383–4; (1781), nos. 112–3, 153–4; R/4 (1788), nos. 214–6; (1792), no. 280.
37 Horwood, *Plan.* (1792–9).
38 Act for Partition by will of Hen. Busby, 49 Geo. III, c. 110 (Priv. Act), schedules.
39 *Langley & Belch's New Map.*
40 G.L.R.O., THCS 446.
41 Ibid. MR/B/C 3/1767/36.
42 T.H.L.H.L., BG/264.
43 G.L.R.O., MR/B/R/4 (1792), no. 271.
44 Ibid. R/2, nos. 55–6.
45 Ibid. no. 641.
46 *Survey of Lond.* xxvii. 119, 121–2.
47 G.L.R.O., THCS 446.
48 M.L.R. 1766/6/183–4; 1766/7/236; 1808/5/780.
49 B.M., Crace Colln., Portf. xvi. 34; Horwood, *Plan* (1792–9).
50 M.L.R. 1808/5/780.
51 T.H.L.H.L., BG/264; B.M., Crace Colln., Portf. xvi. 34.
52 M.L.R. 1792/7/766.
53 Ibid. 1792/6/108.
54 Ibid. 1813/7/139.
55 P.R.O., C 110/174C.

56 Ibid. C 110/174E.
57 M.L.R. 1792/4/213–14.
58 T.H.L.H.L., BG/261; Horwood, *Plan.* (1792–9).
59 M.L.R. 1808/4/471; 1808/5/549; 1808/8/97–8, 392. Hope Town may commemorate the Hope Bldg. Soc. which had land nearby: M.L.R. 1842/4/258, 688.
60 *Langley & Belch's New Map.*
61 G.L.R.O., THCS 446.
62 M.L.R. 1779/3/431.
63 G.L.R.O., MR/B/R4 (1789), no. 105; (1790), no. 296; B/C3/1807, nos. 216, 223.
64 Ibid. MR/B/R2, nos. 264–70; M.L.R. 1779/3/582.
65 T.H.L.H.L., BG/264.
66 Vestry mins. 1747–81, p. 283.
67 G.L.R.O., MR/PLT 5065. Marked on Horwood, *Plan* (1790–2).
68 M.L.R. 1779/2/149.
69 G.L.R.O., MR/PLT 5025.
70 B.M., Crace Colln., Portf. xvi. 34.
71 G.L.R.O., MR/B/R/3 (1777–84), nos. 381–2; (1781), nos. 127–32, 137, 139–41, 150, 158; R/4 (1787), nos. 155, 160–3, 196–8, 261–2; (1788), nos. 25–7; (1789), no. 240.
72 M.L.R. 1779/3/173.
73 Ibid. 1787/7/202.

side of Gibraltar Walk in 1790.[74] Houses extended southward along Turk Street and on the west side of Gibraltar or Lord's Walk[75] by 1800, when there were c. 145 on the estate.[76] Benjamin Wire, a former cowkeeper, took a lease from Peter Gascoigne in 1806 and built west of Prince's Street by 1808.[77] By 1812 the building line had reached Duke Street.[78]

The western part of Fitches, named Friar's Mount probably after James Fryer who farmed it in the 1720s,[79] was apparently sold to Sanderson Turner Sturtevant, a local tallow chandler,[80] who was leasing out ground on the west side of Turk Street by 1804.[81] John Gadenne was building on the west side of Mount Street in 1807.[82] Mount Street, from Rose Street to Virginia Row, existed by 1806,[83] Nelson and Collingwood streets running west from it by 1807,[84] and Peter Street and Lenham Court, at the southern end of the estate, by 1810, when there were 115 houses on Sturtevant's land.[85] Some of the summer houses in Weatherhead's Gardens south of Crabtree Row had been converted to dwellings by 1820.[86]

Kemp's Garden on the Snow estate was taken for building at about the same time. Mead built nine houses in Mead Street in 1806[87] and others were under construction in Charlotte and Half Nichol streets in 1807 and 1808.[88] By 1810 'Kemps land', then including Trafalgar and Christopher streets, contained 83 houses.[89] Probably included with Mead Street, of which it was a western extension, was Vincent Street, where houses were going up in 1807.[90] At least 22 houses were built in Old Nichol Street in 1801-2, probably on the sites of 17th-century ones and mostly by Matravers.[91] By 1827 there were 237 houses on the 5-a. Nichol estate.[92] Between 1812 and 1826 Nelson and Collingwood streets extended westward across the remaining land,[93] and by 1836 the entire area was built up. There were over 2,000 houses north of Bethnal Green Road and 3,609 in the whole western district.[94]

CAMBRIDGE HEATH was an area of gravel spanning the Hackney boundary, between marshland to the east and west which is included in the district described below. The heath was waste of Stepney manor and used as common pasture in 1275 when at least one 'ancient' house stood there.[95] John Slater, merchant tailor of London, was leased a piece of waste 24 rods by 11 rods on the west side of the heath, abutting Hackney Road to the north, for 99 years in 1587.[96] No building followed, as it did under similar leases of land farther south, and the lease had apparently lapsed by 1652.[97] There were no buildings on or near the heath on the Bethnal Green side of the boundary in 1703 or 1720.[98]

In 1722 the trustees of Parmiter's charity purchased 4½ a. of waste on the west side of Cambridge Road, on either side of Hackney Road.[99] One house had been built at each end of the estate by 1760,[1] three houses in all by 1775.[2] In 1724 waste on the west side adjoining the sewer was leased for 99 years to Thomas Thorne, a Bethnal Green carpenter who built a house there.[3] Several cottages had been built, probably by Thomas King, glazier and plumber of Hackney, on waste 20 p. by 24 p. on 'the sweep following the road' by 1729.[4] There was no building on the adjoining freehold and copyhold estates, although it was contemplated on Sotheby's land.[5]

More sustained activity began in 1786, when Parmiter's charity leased the whole estate to Wilmot, who built six houses and sold his term in 1790 to William Lovell, who built five more. In 1791 the trustees granted two leases to Lovell, one with 11 houses and five recently built by him, the other north of Hackney Road with 10 houses 'now building'.[6] By the late 1790s Howard's and Heath places and the Hare public house fronted Hackney and Cambridge roads[7] and by 1800 Cambridge Place formed the north-western boundary of the estate.[8] Between 1788 and 1791 applications were made to build 18 houses at Cambridge Heath;[9] although not in the names of Wilmot or Lovell, most were probably for building on their land. Five houses, however, built in 1788 by Lealand (Leland) were to the north and were claimed by the parish authorities of both

74 Ibid. 1790/3/479.
75 Horwood, *Plan.* (1792–9).
76 G.L.R.O., MR/PLT 5025.
77 M.L.R. 1806/2/447; 1808/5/115.
78 *Langley and Belch's New Map.*
79 M.L.R. 1728/5/10.
80 T.H.L.H.L., TH/654; G.L.R.O., MR/PLT 5025, 5045.
81 M.L.R. 1804/3/164.
82 Ibid. 1807/7/244, 781.
83 Ibid. 1807/6/242.
84 Ibid. 1807/1/587; 1807/6/625.
85 G.L.R.O., MR/PLT 5045.
86 Ibid. MR/PLT 5067; Gavin, *San. Ramblings*, 12; O.S. Map 1/2,500, Lond. XXVII (1877 edn.).
87 G.L.R.O., MR/B/R/6 (1806), no. 119.
88 M.L.R. 1807/6/682; 1808/3/171.
89 G.L.R.O., MR/PLT 5045.
90 Ibid. MR/B/C3/1807, nos. 122, 225, 528, 565; M.L.R. 1807/6/353.
91 G.L.R.O., MR/B/R/5 (1801), nos. 3, 29; (1802), nos. 42–3, 103.
92 Ibid. O/102/3, with map.

93 *Langley and Belch's New Map; Cruchley's New Plan* (1826).
94 G.L.R.O., THCS 446–7.
95 *Rot. Hund.* i. 413, 426.
96 G.L.R.O., M93/201.
97 Ibid. 158, f. 22. The most northerly lease then was of waste S. of Old Bethnal Green Rd.
98 Gascoyne, *Map*; Stow, *Survey* (1720), map between pp. 46 & 47.
99 *1st Rep. Com. Char. for Educ. of Poor*, H.C. 83, pp. 196–7, App. pp. 322–5 (1819), x–A.
1 Parish Map (1760) (T.H.L.H.L., Map no. 301).
2 G.L.R.O., M93/143.
3 Ibid. 277.
4 M.L.R. 1729/5/392.
5 Northants. R.O., X 1075 (22).
6 *1st Rep. Com. Char. for Educ. of Poor*, 196–7, 322–5.
7 Horwood, *Plan* (1792–9).
8 G.L.R.O., MR/PLT 5024; *Langley and Belch's New Map.*
9 G.L.R.O., MR/B/R4 (1788), nos. 207–11; (1789), nos. 55–7; (1791), nos. 216, 226; (1792), no. 263.

Bethnal Green and Hackney.[10] In 1808 the southern portion of Parmiter's estate was leased to James Waddilove and William Causdell (Cansdell), builders of Hackney Road, for 77 years. They had constructed Suffolk Place and Felix Street by 1812 and Clare Street and Barossa and Felix places by 1819, when the estate was rated at more than £1,800 a year.[11]

Durham Place, fronting Hackney Road on the Rush Mead, was being built in 1789.[12] In 1792 roads were planned to the south: Elizabeth, Lausanne (Claremont), and Durham streets. Builders who took 99-year leases included James Nicoll from Marylebone and William Selby from Hanover Square (Westm.).[13] Three parcels were sold and five leases granted between 1793 and 1808.[14] Bond's Place had been built by 1810, under an agreement of 1807 with Benjamin Bond of Hackney.[15] Temple Street formed the eastern boundary of Rush Mead by 1821,[16] with houses on its west side by 1826. Building extended south with Catherine and Charles streets[17] by 1836, when there were 266 houses on the estate.[18]

Andrew Pritchard, 'tilemaker of Hackney Road' in 1789,[19] had interests in the area from the 1770s[20] and had bought Bullocks on the north side of Hackney Road by 1792 when he contracted with William Olley, a Woolwich bricklayer, to build houses in Hackney Road next to a factory.[21] The houses, called Matthew's Place, had been built by 1800.[22] Oxford House existed by 1808,[23] Ann's Place (later Pritchard's Road) forming the western boundary by 1819,[24] and the Oval, with 36 cottages and a chapel, on the eastern boundary by 1836.[25] Much of the estate, however, was occupied by a fishpond until the mid 19th century.

Chambers, the most northerly estate on the east side of Cambridge Road, was taken for building from 1802, when William Ditchman of Hackney Road was leased a strip on the west fronting Cambridge Road and another on the east. He built houses fronting the road by 1804,[26] Newmarket Terrace in Russia Lane in 1805,[27] and houses in new roads at the northern end of Cambridge Road, Norfolk or Martha and John (in Hackney) streets, soon afterwards.[28] John Scott, an Islington brickmaker, was let the central portion of the estate in 1808, building Prospect Place in Russia Lane and houses in a new road

running north from it, called West Street and later Potter's Row after Thomas Potter, his sublessee.[29] Lark Row, at the eastern boundary of Chambers, had 10 houses by 1812.[30]

In 1807 the Leeds family agreed with Joseph Brown of Durham Place to develop the Cambridge Heath estate between Rush Mead and Parmiter's estate. In 1808 Brown engaged James Waddilove and William Causdell to build 30 houses.[31] They were employed at the same time on Parmiter's estate, with which a joint layout was apparently made. By 1812 Cambridge Circus existed on the eastern boundary of the Leeds's land[32] and by 1821 Hope and Minerva streets ran from Hackney Road to Old Bethnal Green Road, while other streets (Bellona or Matilda, Centre, and the extension from Parmiter's of Felix Street) existed in the south-east. Philadelphia and Minerva places faced Hackney Road and there was a continuous frontage on Old Bethnal Green Road, although most of the centre of the estate was still empty. About a third of the estate was available for building in 1831.[33]

On the eastern side of Cambridge Road, the 5-a. field belonging to Bishop's Hall was leased in 1811 to the London Society for Promoting Christianity among the Jews, which built the Episcopal Jews' chapel and associated buildings, called Palestine Place by 1836.[34] To the north and south were portions of Pyotts, that to the south developed in the 1790s as Patriot Square[35] and that to the north granted in 80-year building leases between 1819 and 1824 to John Spencer, William Bradshaw, Samuel Ridge, and Joseph Whiltenbury.[36] Prospect Place or Row had been built fronting Russia Lane and Grosvenor Terrace fronting Cambridge Road by 1826,[37] and Gloucester Street between Cambridge Road and the north–south section of Russia Lane by 1836.[38]

There remained Sebright's estate, in the north-west. Aware of its 'increasing and improving neighbourhood', the trustees in 1813 obtained an Act to grant long building leases.[39] In 1821 they leased a large part north of Hackney Road to Joseph Teale of Shoreditch,[40] who was responsible for the building of Sebright Street by 1822,[41] Sebright Place, Gloucester Street and Place and Hill Street by 1826,[42] and Wolverley and Teale streets by 1836. By then

[10] *The Times*, 29 May 1788, 3c; 16 June 1788, 3a; 12 Sept. 1788, 2d; 18 Sept. 1788, 1c.
[11] G.L.R.O., THCS 305; *1st. Rep. Com. Char. Educ. of Poor*, 197, 325.
[12] G.L.R.O., MR/B/R/4 (1790), no. 110.
[13] Ibid. Acc. 240/25; M.L.R. 1794/3/74.
[14] T.H.L.H.L., TH/7713.
[15] Ibid. TH/7694-5.
[16] Ibid. TH/5043.
[17] M.L.R. 1842/2/143.
[18] G.L.R.O., THCS 447; map (1843) in Gavin, *San. Ramblings* (1848).
[19] G.L.R.O., MR/FR/1789/J81.
[20] Below, Hackney Rd.
[21] i.e. Hayes or Haynes factory: M.L.R. 1792/8/164; 1794/3/107.
[22] Horwood, *Plan* (1792-9); G.L.R.O., MR/PLT 5024.
[23] M.L.R. 1808/8/357.
[24] T.H.L.H.L., TH/3406; *Cruchley's New Plan* (1826); M.L.R. 1842/2/986.
[25] P.R.O., C 54/13106, mm. 30-34; G.L.R.O., THCS 447.

[26] M.L.R. 1804/2/369-73, 569; 1808/5/460, 743.
[27] Ibid. 1805/3/328; 1842/5/254.
[28] Ibid. 1804/3/711; 1807/6/687; 1808/5/743; *Langley and Belch's New Map*.
[29] M.L.R. 1808/5/743-4; *Cruchley's New Plan*. (1826).
[30] G.L.R.O., THCS/305.
[31] T.H.L.H.L., TH/5043.
[32] G.L.R.O., THCS 305; *Langley and Belch's New Map*.
[33] T.H.L.H.L., TH/5043; M.L.R. 1842/3/715.
[34] M.L.R. 1812/2/317; G.L.R.O., THCS 447; below, list of churches (Episcopal Jews' chap.).
[35] Above, the Green.
[36] P.R.O., C 54/12480, mm. 37 sqq.
[37] *Cruchley's New Plan* (1826).
[38] G.L.R.O., THCS 447.
[39] *Act to enable trustees . . . of Wm. Seabright in Bethnal Green to grant bldg. leases*, 53 Geo. III, c. 202 (Local and Personal).
[40] G.L.R.O., Acc. 1416/39-50. For the portion of the charity's est. S. of Bethnal Green Rd., below, the Centre.
[41] T.H.L.H.L., TH/3390.
[42] *Cruchley's New Plan*. (1826).

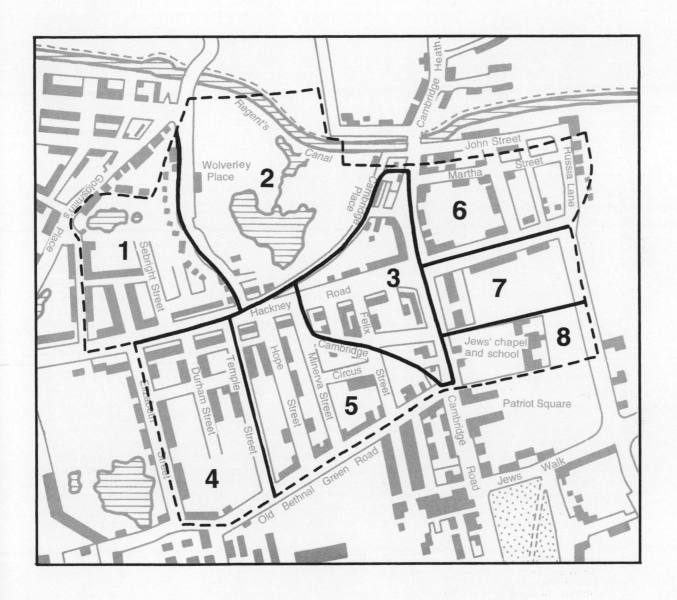

FIG. 16. CAMBRIDGE HEATH: PRINCIPAL ESTATES

1 Sebright, 2 Bullock, 3 Parmiter, 4 Rush Mead, 5 Cambridge Heath, 6 Chambers, 7 Pyott, 8 Bishop's Hall

there were some 250 houses on Sebrights north of Hackney Road.[43]

By 1836 there were 1,276 houses in the area, all but 231 on the west side of Cambridge Road.[44]

THE NORTH-WEST: HACKNEY ROAD.

Despite its antiquity, Hackney Road was, on its southern, Bethnal Green side,[45] almost devoid of buildings until well after 1700. The land belonged to freehold estates created from demesne land: Milkhouse Bridge in the west, where a farmhouse was apparently built between 1682 and 1703[46] slightly north of the junction with Crabtree Lane, the Barnet charities in the centre with, in 1679, a house and outbuildings at the eastern end of Crabtree Lane at the junction with a field way (later Gibraltar Walk) and a path (later Birdcage Walk),[47] and Sickle Penfield to the east. Most of the western part of Milkhouse Bridge was garden ground in 1703. The Nag's Head inn fronted Hackney Road at the eastern end of the estate and was occupied c. 1706–12 by Edward Carnell, a cowkeeper who in 1710–12 was described as brickmaster,[48] although in 1720 there was no building nearby except for a few cottages at the Crabtree Row end.[49] The inn's licensee in 1722 and 1730 was John Pritchard,[50] whose family was in possession, probably as lessees, of Carnell's interests, which included Sickle Penfield, by 1751.[51] The family may have been responsible for a small settlement around the Nag's Head and for a few cottages at the northern end of Birdcage Walk by the mid 18th century.[52]

Development later quickened. Between 1786 and 1789 26 houses were built, mostly by Baker at Greengate north of Crabtree Row, including Crescent Place and Somerset Buildings.[53] In 1789 John Allport (d. 1807), lessee of the western part of Milkhouse Bridge which he ran as a nursery, bought 6½ a. where in 1797 the Middlesex chapel was built fronting the curve of Hackney Road.[54] Houses were being built nearby in 1807[55] and Middlesex Terrace existed by 1826.[56] In 1822 the Allport family made an agreement with John Poole, who built behind the chapel in Chapel, King, Queen, and Charles (later Hassard) streets.[57]

To the east Andrew Pritchard, in 1789 a tilemaker of Hackney Road,[58] built 11 houses near the Nag's Head in 1789–91[59] and bought part of Milkhouse Bridge in 1790,[60] when John Pritchard, similarly described, took a 99-year lease of ground and five houses on the east side of 'the pathway from Spitalfields to the Nag's Head'.[61] The pathway was presumably Birdcage Walk, named after the public house which by 1760 had replaced the 17th-century farmhouse on the southern boundary of Barnet hospital estate.[62] Seven houses were built in Birdcage Walk in 1787–8,[63] partly by the licensee Samuel Lazonby.[64] Most were at the northern end, forming a settlement with Edith Gardens, Nag's Yard, and fronting Hackney Road near the Nag's Head by 1800.[65]

At the southern end of Milkhouse Bridge, north of Crabtree Row and east of Crescent Place, Nova Scotia Gardens existed by c. 1779[66] perhaps only as gardens or allotments. Crude, probably wooden, cottages which may have originated as sheds existed by 1800[67] and became notorious as the home in 1830–1 of John Bishop and Thomas Williams, the Resurrectionists, who murdered an Italian boy there.[68]

In 1807 Nag's Head Field, 8 a. of Milkhouse Bridge between Allport's and Pritchard's estates, was leased for 80 years to James Waddilove and John Crispin of Cambridge Heath and Charles Fichet of Hackney. Thirty-eight houses had already been built, mostly two-storeyed and fronting Coldharbour (or Coleharbour) Street at the western end.[69] The ground was staked out, presumably in building plots, around London Terrace fronting Hackney Road and a group of new streets: Coldharbour, Caroline, Henrietta, and Nelson streets, all projecting south from Hackney Road, and Bath Street, parallel with it. The three men jointly granted building leases before partitioning the ground in October 1808.[70] Among the builders, whose work was well advanced by the end of 1808 and apparently complete by 1812,[71] were Thomas Merrett, of St. Luke, Middlesex,[72] Isaac Clapson, carpenter of Henrietta Street, [73] Claxton Catchfield[74] and William Causdell,[75] of Hackney Road, and Joseph Foulkes, of London Terrace.[76] James Blake, a Bishopsgate Street auctioneer, had a large area[77] which he in turn leased out in plots

43 G.L.R.O., THCS 447.   44 Ibid.
45 For its eastern end, which included estates N. of the road, above, Cambridge Heath.
46 Morgan, *Survey of Lond. and Westm.*; Gascoyne, *Map*.
47 Map accompanying deed, 1679, Jesus Hosp. Char., Barnet.
48 G.L.R.O., MR/FB2, ff. 143, 260, 388; FB3.
49 Stow, *Survey* (1720), map between pp. 46 and 47.
50 G.L.R.O., MR/LV/3/101, ff. 8v.–9; 5/26, pp. 14–15. Pritchard was licensed in 1716 for an unspecified house: ibid. 3/2, ff. 4–5.
51 T.H.L.H.L., BG/256.
52 Rocque, *Map of Lond.* (1741–5); Parish Map (1760).
53 G.L.R.O., MR/B/R4 (1787), nos. 210–11; (1788), nos. 223–31; (1789), nos. 102–4, 107–9, 111–13, 115–16, 119; (1790), 100–1.
54 M.L.R. 1789/5/364; *Home Counties Mag.* xi. 293–8. The nursery bldgs. were on the N., Shoreditch, side of Hackney Rd.: Horwood, *Plan* (1792–9).
55 M.L.R. 1807/4/706.
56 *Cruchley's New Plan* (1826).
57 *Home Counties Mag.* xi. 293–8; T.H.L.H.L., TH/7700.
58 G.L.R.O., MR/FR/1789/J81.

59 Ibid. MR/B/R4 (1790), no. 113; (1792), no. 276.
60 Ibid. Acc. 157/1.
61 M.L.R. 1790/3/139.
62 G.L.R.O., MR/LV/7/49, pp. 3–4; Horwood, *Plan* (1792–9); for farmho., above.
63 G.L.R.O., MR/B/R4 (1787), nos. 231–5; (1789), no. 48.
64 Ibid. MR/LV/9/136, pp. 25–7.
65 Horwood, *Plan* (1792–9).
66 B.M., Crace Colln., Portf. xvi. 34.
67 G.L.R.O., MR/PLT 5025.
68 Lysons, *Environs*, ii (pt. 1), p. 38 (grangerized copy in Guildhall libr.); *The Times*, 3 Dec. 1831, 3a.
69 M.L.R. 1808/2/175.
70 Ibid. 1808/8/90, 692.
71 *Langley and Belch's New Map* (1812).
72 M.L.R. 1808/8/90, 138, 692.
73 Ibid. 1808/3/161.
74 Ibid. 1808/3/273, 654; 1808/8/366.
75 Ibid. 1808/3/274, 660; 1808/4/328; 1808/5/290–1, 442; 1813/7/77.
76 Ibid. 1808/3/272; 1808/5/627.
77 Ibid. 1808/4/239; 1808/8/692.

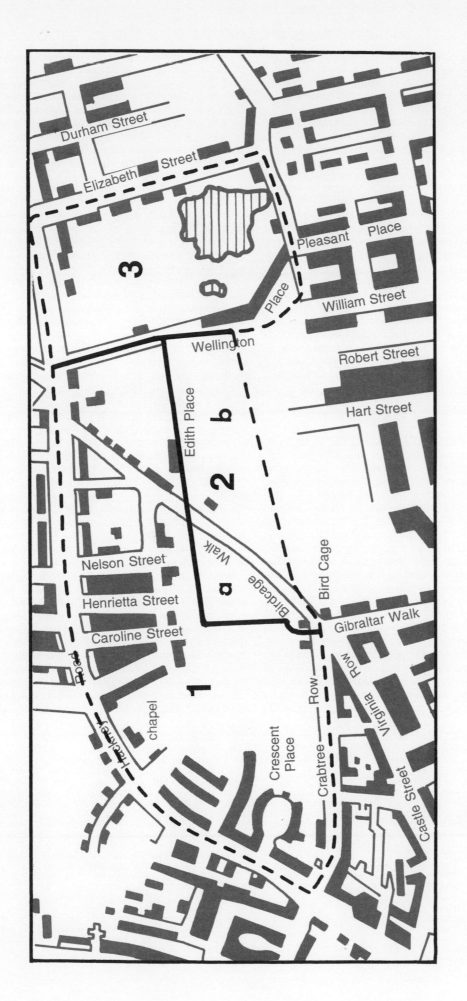

Fig. 17. The North-west: principal estates

1 Milkhouse Bridge, 2 Barnet: a Chancel b Jesus Hospital, 3 Sickle Penfield

to two carpenters, Robert Scott, of Hackney Road, and William Brailey, of Bishopsgate, and a bricklayer, John Gardiner, of Holborn.[78] Queen Street formed a westward continuation of Bath Street by 1823.[79]

Ten houses built in Hackney Road in 1786–9[80] may have included some new ones on Sickle Penfield assigned to Thomas Darling, a Southwark carpenter, in 1795.[81] The estate joined Rush Mead and there was building on the west side of Elizabeth Street, the boundary, and in Wellington Place at its south-western side by 1826[82] and in Warner Place by 1828.[83] The Barnet charity lands remained virtually empty until the 19th century, one building fronting Birdcage Walk being added at the northern end of the Jesus Hospital charity estate by 1760[84] and another opposite the Bird Cage at the southern end of the Chancel estate by the 1790s.[85] Willow Walk at the northern part of Jesus Hospital estate had at least one house by 1807,[86] 11 houses by 1820,[87] and 21 by 1836.[88] The Chancel lands on the west side of Birdcage Walk were built up in the 1830s, with Barnet, James, and Ravenscroft streets.[89] There were 855 houses in the area in 1836, with space for more in the south and east.[90]

THE CENTRE: BETHNAL GREEN ROAD.

The area between the green and Dog Row on the east, Spitalfields and Shoreditch Side on the west, and Hackney Road and Cambridge Heath on the north remained farmland until the later 18th century. Its only house c. 1650 was one built by John Godowne at the north-west of Great Haresmarsh before 1646,[91] at the eastern end of Hare Street in 1703.[92] By 1687 another house with farm buildings in the westernmost of the two fields forming Turney Field estate was occupied by Anthony Wells, who made bricks there, possibly for the neighbouring Satchwell Rents. By 1696 3 ft. of topsoil had been stripped from the field and the house was in ruins,[93] although it may have been shown in the south-west corner of the field in 1703.[94]

One building stood in the centre of Willetts in 1703[95] and three houses in the same field, possibly at its northern end, by 1713.[96] Godowne's house had become two by 1712.[97] Buildings in Saffron

Close on the north side of Bethnal Green Road, in 1713 four boarded houses on the west side and four brick houses at its south-east corner, one the George inn,[98] apparently existed by 1703.[99] In 1746 the western houses were absorbed by the extensive Coates's Farm but the George and its neighbours formed a small settlement with a few buildings on the south side of the new Church Street (Bethnal Green Road), probably the Willett houses of 1713.[1]

The new east–west road was the chief stimulus to building. On Markhams in 1766 the Blissett family granted a 93-year lease of 9 a. south of Bethnal Green Road to David Wilmot, who was to spend £4,000 in four years. One of the first buildings was the Lord Camden public house; Camden Row fronted Bethnal Green Road and Wilmot Street ran south from it by 1770.[2] Among Wilmot's sublessees was John Price, a London plasterer who built 20 houses in Wilmot Street in 1771.[3] By 1777 there were 67 houses on the estate.[4]

In 1772 Philip James May, parish and vestry clerk, bought Saffron Close on behalf of David Wilmot.[5] From 1777 houses were built fronting Bethnal Green Road and behind in Wilmot Square and Grove.[6] A big house for Wilmot himself in the north, called Wilmot's Folly,[7] was possibly the 'house and other structure' built in 1787 in a new bowling green in Wilmot Square.[8] In 1808 it was known as the Abbey,[9] from which Abbey Place, in existence by 1806,[10] was named. In 1791 William Pollard of Islington built 16 houses in Saffron Close,[11] most presumably in Pollard Row (formerly May's Lane) at the western border of the estate.[12] A Southwark surveyor, William Fellowes, and a City plumber, John Shillitoe, initiated the main development on the estate, a plan for 90 houses in two sizes featuring grotesque animated keystones, financed by monthly subscription and leased to ballotted subscribers. The scheme, which was associated with the White Hart in Bethnal Green Road, was only partially successful and James Pollard, who presumably succeeded William, was bankrupt by 1798.[13] The ground was already mortgaged in the early 1790s when William Pollard granted leases to other builders, Thomas Harrison, brickmaker of St. Pancras,[14] and James Naish, carpenter of Shadwell.[15] Ann Street ran parallel with Bethnal

78 M.L.R. 1808/3/687, 688, 689.
79 Ibid. 1824/2/126.
80 G.L.R.O., MR/B/R4 (1787), nos. 207–9, 248, 256; (1788), nos. 24, 28–9; (1789), no. 231.
81 T.H.L.H.L., TH/2352.
82 Cruchley's New Plan. (1826).
83 M.L.R. 1842/5/283.
84 T.H.L.H.L., Map no. 301 (Parish Map).
85 Horwood, Plan (1792–9).
86 M.L.R. 1807/6/196.
87 G.L.R.O., MR/PLT 5067.
88 T.H.L.H.L., THCS 447.
89 M.L.R. 1830/6/616; 1833/6/73.
90 G.L.R.O., THCS 447; Cruchley's New Plan. (1826).
91 P.R.O., C 9/25/65. It stood on the edge of Willetts: G.L.R.O., M93/158, f. 10 (no. 47).
92 Gascoyne, Map.
93 P.R.O., C 5/184/99; C 8/358/197.
94 Gascoyne, Map.
95 Ibid.
96 Lambeth Pal. Libr., MS 2731/9.
97 M.L.R. 1712/1/138.

98 Lond. Hosp. Archives LH/D/1/23.
99 Gascoyne, Map.
1 Rocque, Plan of Lond. (1746).
2 T.H.L.H.L., TH/5849; C. Bowles, Traveller's Guide through Lond. (1770).
3 T.H.L.H.L., TH/5849; G.L.R.O., MR/B/R 2. no. 218.
4 G.L.R.O., M93/40, pp. 231–2.
5 T.H.L.H.L., TH/2277.
6 G.L.R.O., MR/B/R 3 (1781), 102–9, 125–6, 160–1, 166–8, 179; (1784), 48, 88; R 4 (1787), 229; (1788), 9–12, 20–3.
7 Bowles's Plan of Lond. and Westm. (1799).
8 G.L.R.O., MR/B/R4 (1788), 18–19.
9 M.L.R. 1808/4/492.
10 Ibid. 1808/4/215.
11 G.L.R.O., MR/B/R4 (1791), 218; (1792), 272, 278, 281; Horwood, Plan (1792–9).
12 M.L.R. 1794/3/125, 447, 612.
13 I. Watson, Gentlemen in the Building Line (1989), 30–1; V.C.H. Mdx. x. 61.
14 M.L.R. 1794/3/125.
15 Ibid. 1794/3/447.

Green Road by 1792[16] and linked Pollard Row with Mary's Row, which formed the eastern border of the estate by 1794.[17] There were c. 200 houses on the estate by 1800.[18]

In 1788 much of Willetts (George and Gravel fields) south of Bethnal Green Road was divided into lots, most of which were leased for 99 years to John May Evans, a Surrey builder, and William Timmins, a local brickmaker.[19] They immediately built along the main road,[20] including Shepherd's Place or Row,[21] and in the streets running south from it, named from the estate's owners: White, Thomas, and Charles streets.[22] Houses 'in the back ground'[23] were probably in the narrow street parallel with Bethnal Green Road, called White's[24] or Thomas Passage[25] or Granby's Row. Abbey Street, at the west end of the development, existed as Benal Abbey Street in 1788.[26] Part of the land was still a brickfield in 1803.[27]

In 1794 Samuel Scott, owner of Thickness estate, had a house in a brickfield opposite a house in the Jewish burial ground at the southern end of the district, next to Ducking Pond Lane.[28] Three houses had been built there by 1801 when he had leased ground to Isaac Bird, coachmaster of Whitechapel.[29] By 1809, when he was 'builder' or 'brickmaster', Bird had built along North Street (formerly Ducking Pond Lane) and on a new side road, Pleasant Row.[30]

Building began on Jarvis's, the estate to the east, in 1812 when two parallel streets were planned to run the length of the estate from Three Colts Lane: Hinton Street, to join the northern part of Collingwood Street, and Tapp Street to the west. Westover (Temple) Street was to link them in the middle of the estate. Sir George Ivison Tapps in 1812 agreed with Edward Bumford, engraver of Islington, for building south of Temple Street[31] and thereafter granted several leases to Bumford and his brother (or son) John, who started from the south with Somerford Street and Trafalgar Place. Their sublessees William Miller and Richard Leavitt were the builders in Somerford Street.[32] Building had reached Temple Street by 1826[33] and there were nearly 100 houses on the estate by 1836[34] although half of it, east of Hinton Street, was still open.

In 1818 Bumford agreed with the Pope family

for ground to the west, where he built Winchester (or Market) Street as an extension from Hare Street and Carlisle, Great Manchester, Nottingham, and Arundel (or Albion) streets running south from it. In 1825 the Popes agreed to grant the rest of the estate (Great Haresmarsh) to the south and west, Bumford to spend £7,000 on 56 houses with frontages of 14–21 ft.[35] Artillery (or Anglesea) Street was 'new intended' in 1826.[36] The southern and eastern parts of the estate were leased to George Selby, who in 1828–9 was involved with Edward Bumford, by then a 'surveyor', in leasing houses in Albion, Anglesea, Wellington (the southern extension of Nottingham Street), and Selby (at the southern border) streets. The whole area was called Waterloo Town.[37]

Building meanwhile continued on Willetts, extending southward in streets named after the White family and places associated with it: Hereford, by 1823,[38] and Derbyshire, Manchester (after 1864 Menotti), Cheshire, Sale (Ches.), Mapes (Willesden), Ramsey, and Hague,[39] all by 1826.[40] In 1836 there were 785 houses on the estate, all but 79 in the central area.[41]

In 1807 John Warde of Squerryes Court, Westerham (Kent) leased the whole of his Turney estate, 21 a. west of Saffron Close, to Daniel Gosset of Edmonton for 61 years. A few houses had been built fronting Bethnal Green Road between c. 1799 and 1807[42] and Gosset had built another 10 in 1813[43] and the parallel Ward's Row by 1812.[44] John Henry Berry, carpenter of Hackney, had been engaged by Gosset to build along Gibraltar Walk, the western boundary, by 1811;[45] houses fronted the eastern boundary, Pollard Row, by 1812 when Squirries Street, not yet named, also apparently existed.[46] Robert, William, and South (later Florida) streets had been added by 1826[47] and King Street and Wellington Street (Row) in the north of the estate and Orange Street in the west by 1836. Gosset Street, the westward extension of King Street, probably existed as Daniel Street by 1836, when there were 486 houses on the estate.[48]

The remaining frontage on Bethnal Green Road belonged to Markhams or to Sebrights. Some houses may have been built on the northern portion of Markhams, fronting south on the main road, between c. 1799 and 1812[49] but

16 Ibid. 1794/3/125.
17 T.H.L.H.L., BG/261.
18 G.L.R.O., MR/PLT 5024.
19 BNC, Bethnal Green 1; T.H.L.H.L., TH/1160–1; M.L.R. 1788/7/265–8.
20 G.L.R.O., MR/B/R4 (1789), nos. 61, 63, 122, 236; (1790), nos. 112, 114, 295, 297, 304; (1791), no. 210; (1792), nos. 255, 262.
21 Jas. Shepherd had hos. there: M.L.R. 1808/8/146; T.H.L.H.L., BG/261; Horwood, Plan (1792–9).
22 M.L.R. 1788/7/265–8; G.L.R.O., MR/B/R4 (1789), no. 234; (1791), nos. 44–45.
23 G.L.R.O., MR/B/R4 (1789), nos. 232, 235, 239, 242; (1791), no. 41.
24 T.H.L.H.L., TH/160.
25 Stanford, Map of Lond. (1862–5 edn).
26 M.L.R. 1788/7/268; Horwood, Plan (1792–9).
27 BNC, Bethnal Green 1.
28 T.H.L.H.L., BG/261.
29 M.L.R. 1802/3/549.
30 Ibid. 1812/2/581; 1813/9/219; P.R.O., C 107/124.
31 M.L.R. 1812/3/423.

32 Ibid. 1812/6/134; 1813/3/286; 1813/7/114, 143.
33 Cruchley's New Plan (1826).
34 G.L.R.O., THCS 446.
35 T.H.L.H.L., TH/2344.
36 Vestry mins. 1823–8, 7 Mar. 1826.
37 M.L.R. 1828/5/157, 171; 1828/10/214; 1829/1/657; map (1843) in Gavin, San. Ramblings.
38 BNC, Bethnal Green 1.
39 Maiden name of Frances, who married Thos. White in 1787: BNC, Bethnal Green 1.
40 Cruchley's New Plan (1826).
41 G.L.R.O., THCS 446. For the 79, above, the West.
42 M.L.R. 1807/7/96; Horwood, Plan (1792–9).
43 G.L.R.O., B/C3/1813.
44 M.L.R. 1842/5/281.
45 Ibid. 1842/1/251.
46 Langley and Belch's New Map.
47 Cruchley's New Plan (1826).
48 G.L.R.O., THCS 446–7; map (1843) in Gavin, San. Ramblings (1848).
49 Horwood, Plan (1792–9); Langley and Belch's New Map (1812).

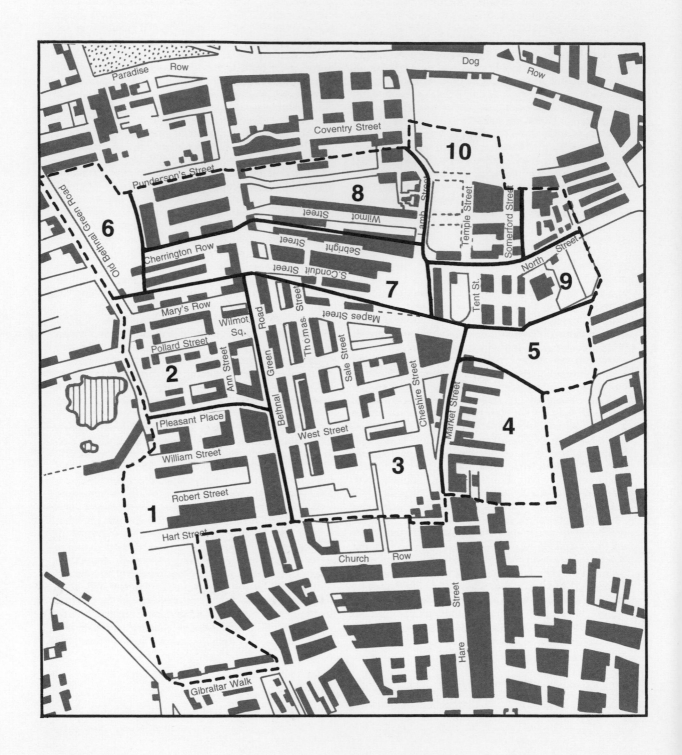

FIG. 18. THE CENTRE: PRINCIPAL ESTATES

1 Turney, 2 Saffron Close, 3 Willett, 4 Great Haresmarsh, 5 Acres Land, 6 Burgoyn
7 Sebright, 8 Markham, 9 Thickness, 10 Jarvis

others, together with one of the streets running northward, Camden Street, were built after 1820 by William Miller of Bethnal Green Road.[50] By 1826 building was well advanced in Camden Street and the other new streets, Blisset (later New York) and Grove streets.[51] Cambridge Street had been added by 1836, when Markhams contained c. 143 houses north of Bethnal Green Road.[52]

For the neighbouring Sebrights an Act to grant building leases was obtained in 1813. Apart from 10 a. at Cambridge Heath, the estate consisted of 3½ a. north and 8½ a. south of Bethnal Green Road.[53] Joseph Teale, who was largely responsible for building north of Hackney Road, was also the chief developer on both sides of Bethnal Green Road. On the 3½ a. William Hewitt, a local builder, had already built four houses fronting the main road and six in a new road, another Wolverley Street, by 1822, when Teale leased the ground to Seaman Ives of Norfolk Street, New Road, who financed the operation.[54] A parallel road, North Conduit Street, existed by 1823.[55] Teale had built 12 houses south of Bethnal Green Road by 1822 when he took a 99-year lease, with instructions to complete six more in Sebright Street and 22 in South Conduit Street by 1826.[56] He apparently exceeded the quota by 1826 and Teale Street existed at the south of the estate by 1829.[57] By 1836 Sebrights contained 90 houses north and 182 south of Bethnal Green Road.[58]

By 1836 there were 1,163 houses north of Bethnal Green Road and 1,976 to the south.[59] The only empty areas were the Burgoyn estate in the north, abutting Old Bethnal Green Road, and c.10 a. on the southern borders.[60]

THE EAST: OLD FORD LANE, GREEN STREET, AND GLOBE TOWN.

For centuries the area east of the green was virtually empty of houses. It is unlikely that any owners occupied Bishop's or Bonner's Hall after Bishop Bonner. Lessees like John Fuller (d. 1592), wealthy Londoner and so-called judge,[61] lived there, as did Sir Hugh Platt in 1594.[62] Some people described as 'of Bishop's Hall' from 1592 to 1640 may have been servants but the presence of silkweavers and bricklayers by 1612 suggests that the house was tenemented.[63]

By 1642 the site contained five additional houses, one of them an alehouse created out of two houses.[64] The old dining room had been pulled down by Bishop Richard FitzJames (1506–22)[65] and by 1652 the brick manor house had been 'torn to pieces', with only the walls still standing. The outhouses and offices had been converted into four timber cottages; a fifth cottage stood apart, probably on the east side of the lane to the manor house.[66] A sketch map of 1648 depicting a small plain building of two storeys, with large chimneys on either side, may not have been intended as an accurate representation of Bishop's Hall.[67] In 1655 the mansion house was taken down and the materials were used to build four new houses[68] as a single structure with two wings, three storeys, and attics with dormer windows. Substantial rebuilding may have taken place between 1671 when Thomas Walton, who taught at Bishop's Hall in 1673, was assessed for 10 hearths at an empty house, and 1674 when his assessment was for 30 hearths.[69] By 1741 three or four wooden houses, possibly those mentioned in 1652, joined the main building on the west. The most easterly, next to the lane, was a public house,[70] probably the Three Golden Lions of 1750.[71] A large sum was laid out in repairs and new building on the farm to the east of the lane in 1721.[72] Thereafter there was little change before the creation of Victoria Park in the 1840s.[73]

The only other dwellings in 1703 were a group on the boundary at Grove Street, where they formed part of the Hackney hamlet of that name, and single buildings in Rushy (Russia) Lane and the driftway (later Green Street).[74] The Rushy Lane cottage probably originated as a wasteholt property, in existence by 1648[75] and by 1741 an inn, the Blue Anchor, which gave an alternative name to the lane.[76] Between 1760 and the 1790s another building stood to the south, at the junction with Old Ford Lane; it was called Globe Hall in 1826, when Globe Cottage had been built to the north.[77] The Green Lane buildings had apparently disappeared by 1750.[78]

In 1790 Charles Digby, whose copyhold estate of Eastfields had been enfranchised, sold most of it to John May Evans, William Timmins, and Martin Wilson, an Aldgate brewer who provided the finance for the building of what became Globe Town.[79] Evans and Timmins began

50 G.L.R.O., C/72/379.
51 *Cruchley's New Plan* (1826).
52 G.L.R.O., THCS 446.
53 *Act to enable trustees of Wm. Seabright to grant building leases*, 53 Geo. III, c. 202 (Local and Personal). For the 10 a., above, Cambridge Heath.
54 T.H.L.H.L., TH/2318.
55 P.R.O., C 104/176. *Cruchley's New Plan* (1826) marks only 'Cherrington Row' between Markhams and Saffron Close.
56 G.L.R.O., P72/AND/27.
57 *Cruchley's New Plan*. (1826, 1829).
58 G.L.R.O., THCS 446.
59 Ibid. THCS 446–7.
60 Map (1843) in Gavin, *San. Ramblings* (1848).
61 'One of the judges in the Sheriff's court of London': J. Stow, *Survey of Lond.* ed. Kingsford, i. 115; P.R.O., REQ 2/63/24; PROB 11/79 (P.C.C. 46 Harrington), f. 355; Allgood, *Hist. Bethnal Green*, 210.
62 H. Platte, *The Jewell House of Art and Nature*, 52 and frontispiece; above, Kirby's Castle; below, econ. hist. (agric.).
63 *Marriage Regs. of St. Dunstan's*, i. 28, 39, 57, 62, 84,

92, 140, 180, 265; ii. 7.
64 B.L. Add. MS. 22253.
65 Leland, *Itin.* ed. Toulmin Smith, iv. 117.
66 G.L.R.O., M93/158, f. 1.
67 Northants. R.O., X 1123 (13), Bps. Hall 1647–1742.
68 Ibid. X 1075 (23), Accts.
69 *Calamy Revised*, 509; G.L.R.O., MR/TH/16, f. 22; MR/TH/46; below, prot. nonconf.; below, plate 17.
70 G.L.R.O., MA/DCP/72B; B.M., Crace Colln., Portf. xxxiii, nos. 57–58.
71 G.L.R.O., MR/LV6/79, pp. 3–5.
72 Northants. R.O., X 1074 (xiii); X 1075 (23).
73 *Cruchley's New Plan* (1826).
74 Gascoyne, *Map*; *V.C.H. Mdx.* x. 59.
75 See plan in Northants. R.O., X 1123 (13), assignment (1648).
76 G.L.R.O., MA/DCP/72B.
77 Par. map of Bethnal Green (1760); Horwood, *Plan* (1792–9); *Cruchley's New Plan*. (1826).
78 Rocque, *Map of Lond.* (1741–5).
79 T.H.L.H.L., TH/2324; P.R.O., C 104/173. For the portions around the green, above, the Green.

building at the western end of the estate on either side of Green Street, bounded on the west by Globe Street and Back Lane. In 1790 and 1791 they applied to build 92 houses in Globe Lane (Street), Digby Street, 'in the square' at the back of Digby Street, Green Street, and North Place.[80] They sold plots to other builders. James Price of Mile End Old Town, for example, bought a plot in Globe Street in February 1790 and immediately applied to build 8 small houses.[81] Other builders were William Willcox of Poplar,[82] Edward Smith of Oxford Street,[83] and William Lovell of Shoreditch.[84] Lovell Street, together with Bully Rag Row or Digby Walk, existed by 1792.[85] Evans and Timmins were also active on Cradfords estate where Green Place and West Street were being laid out in 1791.[86] They sold four houses in the road later known as Bullard's Place to Richard Bullard, mercer of St. Giles-in-the-Fields, in 1792,[87] when they had also built four in North Street nearby.[88] Although most houses were built by Evans and Timmins themselves,[89] they granted a 99-year lease of land between West and North streets to Edward Holdsworth, carpenter of Bethnal Green.[90] By 1800 there were c. 90 dwellings, many of them small cottages, in the area then designated Green Place.[91]

Opposite, on the north side of Green Street, houses had been built in Bonner Street and Pleasant Row by 1800[92] and spread eastward during the next decade. Evans was no longer associated with Timmins and Wilson by 1806 when they conveyed ground in what by then was called Globe Town.[93] Jefferys, Cross, Sidney (or Sydney), Norton, and Type streets had been built there by 1808,[94] partly by Timmins but also by others such as Henry Hawkes[95] and John Caton[96] both of St. George-in-the-East, and Samuel Cotterell, of Stepney.[97]

Development quickened on neighbouring estates at about the same time. On the south side of Green Street, east of Timmins's land, Smarts Street by 1808 had houses built by another carpenter from St. George-in-the-East, Samuel Maryon,[98] and adjoining streets to the east and south existed by 1812: East Street, Surat and Hampden places, and Twig Street and Twig Folly.[99] North of Green Street there were houses on the south side of John Street, north of Pleasant Row, by early 1808, when Samuel

Ridge, then described as farmer, enfranchised 7 a. north of John Street and Timmins's Globe Town, bounded north by Old Ford Lane and west by Bishop's Street.[1] He had built many houses there, in John, Bishop's, and King streets by 1822.[2] Building took place on the neighbouring Pyotts from 1818, starting near the green and spreading east of Globe Street (Back Lane) by 1820, when 17 houses in Grosvenor Place and 14 in Park Street were leased to William Bradshaw. Several plots, usually with houses, were leased for 80 years during the 1820s. Ridge took a lease of part of the estate near the green in 1818 and two leases of plots south of Old Ford Lane in 1823. While continuing to farm from Bonner's Hall, he was by then described as a brickmaker[3] and by 1825 he had built houses in George's Place fronting Old Ford Lane.[4] He was let 2 a. adjoining the canal from the Sotheby estate in 1822, where his houses fronted Green Street by 1823, and bought land from Timmins's widow. When Ridge died in 1839 his freehold and leasehold property south of Old Ford Lane stretched from Globe Street to the canal and contained 75 houses.[5]

The two largest estates, Bishop's Hall and Broomfields, saw little development. East of the canal a few cottages, King's Arms Row, stood on the south side of Old Ford Lane by 1799.[6] In 1803 Sir Thomas Coxhead, owner of Broomfields, had made an agreement with Henry Stevens and James Butt, brickmakers of Mile End, for a new road (New Grove Road) with houses fronting it at the eastern end of the parish. Only a few had been built on either side of the Mile End boundary when Coxhead died in 1811, after which his successors abandoned the enterprise.[7]

The second phase of building on Cradford estate in the 1820s and 1830s involved William Walter Gretton and John Butler, all their names being given to new roads as development spread westward to meet the already built up Eastfield estate. Also involved in the development was William Mudd, carpenter of Hackney Road,[8] and the Union Building Society, which gave its name to Union Row (later Morpeth Street), where its members leased houses in 1834.[9] By 1836 there were over 370 houses on Cradfords, part of a total of 1,088 houses in the eastern area, 550 to the north and 538 to the south of Green Street.[10]

80 G.L.R.O., MR/B/R4 (1790), nos. 116–7, 301; (1791), nos. 38, 40, 42, 47, 211–5, 217, 220, 230; (1792), nos. 253, 256–61, 279.
81 Ibid. (1790), nos. 118, 120; M.L.R. 1792/4/259–60. The whole plot was only 30 ft. by 107 ft.
82 T.H.L.H.L., TH/664.
83 Ibid. 2321, 2324.
84 P.R.O., C 104/173.
85 M.L.R. 1792/1/390; Horwood, *Plan.* (1792–9).
86 M.L.R. 1792/4/168–9.
87 Ibid. 1792/5/497.
88 Ibid. 1792/6/91.
89 Ibid. 1792/6/465–7, 678; 1792/7/568.
90 Ibid. 1792/6/92.
91 G.L.R.O., MR/PLT 5024.
92 Horwood, *Plan.* (1792–9); G.L.R.O., MR/PLT 5024.
93 M.L.R. 1813/7/100.
94 Ibid. 1813/3/186; 1813/4/21; 1813/7/71, 100; T.H.L.H.L., TH/5138.

95 M.L.R. 1808/3/765; 1808/5/594.
96 T.H.L.H.L., TH/5138.
97 M.L.R. 1808/3/764.
98 Ibid. 1808/8/238.
99 G.L.R.O., THCS/305; *Langley & Belch's New Map*.
1 M.L.R. 1808/3/186.
2 Ibid. 1822/5/577–9.
3 P.R.O., C 54/12480, mm. 37 sqq.; T.H.L.H.L., TH/2854.
4 T.H.L.H.L., TH/2842.
5 Ibid. 2849, 2867; G.L.R.O., MA/DCP/72c.
6 Horwood, *Plan* (1792–9); *Langley & Belch's New Map*.
7 G.L.R.O., BRA/641/40; *Langley & Belch's New Map. Cruchley's New Plan* (1826).
8 *Cruchley's New Plan.* (1826); M.L.R. 1832/3/95–7; 1835/4/483–5.
9 M.L.R. 1836/6/768; 1836/7/272.
10 G.L.R.O., THCS 447.

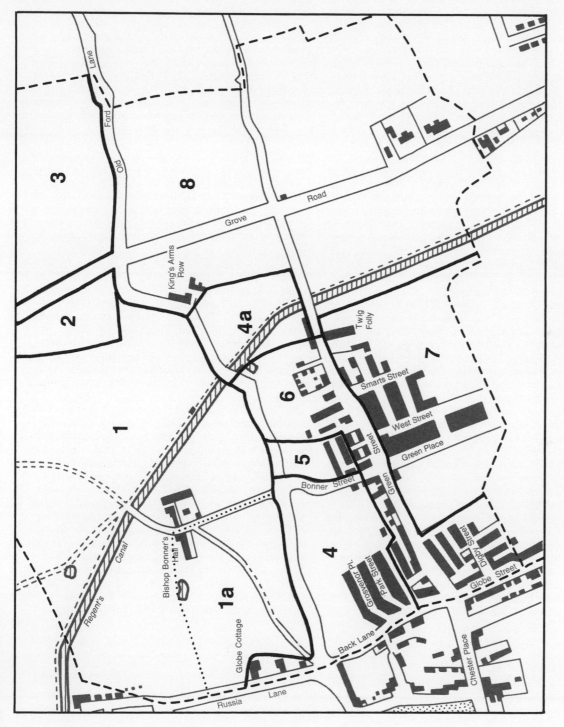

Fig. 19. The East: principal estates

1 Bishop's Hall, 1a Robinson's Charity, 2 Cass, 3 Goosefields, 4 Pyott, 4a Pyott Sotheby, 5 ? St. Paul's (Bowes 2), 6 Eastfield, 7 Cradford, 8 Broomfields

BUILDING AND SOCIAL CONDITIONS FROM 1837 TO 1875.[11] At Victoria's accession tradesmen's houses lined all the main roads in the west: Cambridge, Bethnal Green, and Hackney roads, Brick Lane, and Sclater Street. Similar houses occupied the Nag's Head Field settlement off Hackney Road and the eastern part of the green, Patriot Square, Jews' Walk, and Victoria Park Square. All other housing was classified as occupied by weavers and labourers.[12]

During the next 40 years building overwhelmed all the empty land and intensified on existing estates. Rebuilding was usually to a greater density. Between 1851 and 1859, for example, James Latham constructed 12 houses on the site of one at the corner of Swan and Great Bacon streets.[13] Railways, built in 1840 and 1872,[14] formed barriers between districts, helped to spread industry, and displaced people into already crowded streets and courts. Density rose from 6.3 persons a house in 1841 to 7.5 in 1871.[15] Life expectancy was low. Of 1,632 deaths in 1839, 1,258 (77 per cent) were of 'mechanics, servants, and labourers', who had an expectancy of 16 years, 273 of tradesmen, with an expectancy of 26, and 101 of gentry and professional people, with an expectancy of 45.[16] Huguenot influence was diluted by outsiders from other parts of London. Over 80 per cent of Bethnal Green's population in 1851 and 1861 had been born in London.[17] Although Bethnal Green was still the main silkweaving parish, the industry was in decline and weavers were under-employed. Occupations such as tailoring, furniture making, and costermongering replaced it but none was prosperous, sweated labour was prevalent, and the population was caught in a downward spiral of poverty. A modern analysis has placed Bethnal Green as the second poorest London parish in 1841, the poorest by 1871.[18]

From 1837 to 1842 inclusive 548 houses were built, the great majority classed as fourth-rate.[19] There were 11,983 houses in 1838,[20] 12,358 in 1841, 13,819 in 1851, 15,358 in 1861 and 16,430 in 1871.[21]

In 1837–8 waste was being covered by houses,[22] many of them in 1842 'more huts than houses, built in swamps, at a cheap rent', to be let for as much as possible to weekly tenants.[23] In the worst areas garden sheds became dwellings and gardens (*recte* allotments) became Gardens; George and Gale's Gardens west of Cambridge Road, where at least 21 houses were built between 1846 and 1854, were 'lamentable' in 1848. A similar process took place in Punderson's and Hollybush places and gardens and was beginning in Whisker's gardens near Bonner Lane. On Markhams north of Lamb Street (later part of Three Colts Lane), Lamb Gardens, Place, and Row consisted of narrow lanes and converted garden sheds.[24]

Buildings encroached on the grounds of larger, usually older, houses around the green. On its east side William South built Falcon Place between 1836 and 1842[25] and White Hart Place was built near Sugar Loaf Walk by 1844.[26] South of Sugar Loaf Walk building continued in the existing places and squares and in Chester Street, which ran through the centre of the area by 1850 when James Catling of James Street was building there.[27] At the northern end of the green Peel Grove ran north from Old Ford Road by 1842, when one house was 'lately built' by Edward Blacktop, carpenter of Felix Street.[28]

The green continued to decline socially. In 1858 the incumbent of St. John's commented that soon there would be no residents of easy means left.[29] Institutions increasingly replaced them. In 1853 Henry Merceron leased out no. 21 Victoria Park Square as a store for the Queen's Own Light Infantry Regiment of the Tower Hamlets militia. The site stretched to Globe Street[30] and by the 1860s included a barracks.[31] Of Anthony Natt's houses on the north side of Old Ford Road, no. 12 (after 1875 no. 21) became a home for reformed prostitutes, run by the Guardian Society for the Preservation of Public Morals, in 1840 and no. 10 (after 1875 no. 17) housed the Maritime Penitent Female Refuge in 1842–3.[32]

In 1872 Bethnal Green Museum opened at the northern part of the green on part of the Poor's Lands. An iron structure nicknamed 'the Brompton Boilers', it had been built by C. D. Young & Co. in 1855–6 as the original museum in South Kensington. When replaced by permanent buildings in 1867 the iron structure was re-erected in Bethnal Green behind a brick façade with terracotta panels by James William Wild. The site had been purchased with the intention of diffusing 'a knowledge of science and art among the poorer classes' and for its first three years the museum housed the Wallace Collection. Later it specialized as a museum of childhood.[33]

At the southern end of the green there were

---

[11] Section based on Dist. Surveyors' Returns, G.L.R.O., MBO/DS/12A–H (1845–52); MR/B/C (1853–5); MBW 1621, 1628, 1636, 1643, 1651(2) (1871–5).
[12] *Rep. from Poor Law Commrs. on San. Condition of Labouring Pop.* H.L. (1842), xxvi, map facing p. 160. The map wrongly places housing on the green on W. side of Vic. Pk. Sq.
[13] G.L.R.O., BRA 898/125.
[14] Above, communications.
[15] *Census,* 1841–71 (inhabited hos. only).
[16] *Rep. Com. San. Condition of Labouring Pop.* 159.
[17] G. Stedman Jones, 'Social Consequences of Casual Labour Problem in Lond. 1860–90, with ref. to E. End' (Oxford Univ. D. Phil. thesis, 1970), 197, 207.
[18] *Lond. Jnl.* xi. 118–19.
[19] G.L.R.O., MR/B/SR/5.
[20] *Rep. from Asst. Commrs. on Handloom Weavers,* pt. II, H.C. (43–I), p. 54 (1840), xxiii.
[21] *Census,* 1841–71 (inc. uninhabited and 'building' hos.).
[22] *Rep. Sel. Cttee. on Educ.* H.C. 589, p. 609 (1837–8), vi.
[23] Quoted in E. E. Gauldie, *Cruel Habitations: Hist. of Working Class Housing, 1780–1918* (1974), 91.
[24] Gavin, *San. Ramblings,* 11–12, 17–19, 32; below, econ. hist. (mkt. gdns.).
[25] M.L.R. 1842/2/512.
[26] G.L.R.O., M93/67, p. 250.
[27] T.H.L.H.L., TH/7076.
[28] M.L.R. 1842/7/24.
[29] Guildhall MS. 9561, no. 22.
[30] G.L.R.O., Acc. 295/1.
[31] Stanford, *Map of Lond.* (1862–5).
[32] Robinson and Chesshyre, *The Green,* 19–20.
[33] *The Times,* 22 June 1872, 5c; 25 June 1872, 5a; G. Stamp and C. Amery, *Victorian Bldgs. of Lond. 1837–87* (1980), 46–8; *Archit. of Lond.* 372.

additions to Bethnal House, the asylum; the Red House was extended in 1841, and the White House was rebuilt in 1843-4.[34] Factories existed by 1838 east of the asylum and west of the green, behind Paradise Row.[35] J.& J. Colman of Norwich acquired no. 7 Old Ford Road for a starch factory in 1860[36] and later took over the neighbouring houses, building warehouses by the mid 1870s.[37] Other warehouses were built between 1871 and 1874 behind Victoria Park Square, Sugar Loaf Walk, Patriot Square, and Peel Grove.

Burgoyn's estate, 8½ a. fronting Old Bethnal Green Road west of the green, was nursery land in 1842, when the Church acquired the eastern 3½ a., primarily for St. Jude's church and school but with the roads later named St. Jude's Street and Place and Treadway Street already planned.[38] Houses were built from 1849 by Hallett of Abbey Street, J. Tully of Kingsland Road, and R. Borton of 103 Bethnal Green Road.[39] In 1845 the western portion was leased to Islip Odell, a building promoter,[40] but it was George Clarkson, a Pentonville surveyor and lessee from 1857, who developed it, employing William Riley of Hoxton to build Canrobert, Clarkson, and probably Middleton streets,[41] all completed by the mid 1860s.[42]

Another area empty in 1838 lay west of Dog Row. On Fullmore Close, Essex (later Buckhurst) and Bedford (by 1858 Newport)[43] streets existed by 1841.[44] Oxford Street joined Dog Row (Cambridge Road) to Essex Street by 1851.[45] Nearly 70 houses were built in Essex, Suffolk, and Norfolk streets between 1845 and 1854, mostly by James Lucas for Samuel Emsley. Lucas and Emsley were also involved in developing Jarvis's, the neighbouring estate to the west. Somerford Street was extended eastward as New Somerford Street by 1841, when a plot to the north was leased to Emsley,[46] and Cudworth and Barnsley streets were built there by 1851.[47] Between 1845 and 1855 well over 100 houses were added to the estate, 37 in Tapp Street and the rest in the new streets. Other builders were Hugh O'Donnell, Thomas Hatchell, and Flick, who was also active in 1855 in Lamb's Fields, notorious for its filthy ditch. There was small-scale building on neighbouring estates. Tolly, who worked on several, in 1845 was building in St. Andrew's Street on Sebrights, where by 1864 building was complete and South Conduit Street was renamed Viaduct Street.[48]

William Henry Teale, a Shoreditch auctioneer whose father had developed much of Sebrights, subleased the portion north of Hackney Road to Thomas Holland, an Essex builder, in 1842.[49] To the east John Preedy, William Simpson, and Henry Bradbury, all local builders, and Charles Southby Shaw, of Hackney,[50] were active on the Pritchards' estate, Bullocks, where between 1845 and 1855 some 15 houses were built in the existing Pritchard's Road (formerly Ann's Place) and the Oval, and over 100 in the new Emma Street, Marian Street and Square, Ada Place, and Wharf Road. The gasholders of the Imperial Gas Co. replaced the large pond in the centre of the estate, probably by 1856.[51]

South of Hackney Road on the southern part of Cambridge Heath estate, still open in 1838,[52] at least 25 houses were built between 1846 and 1854 and all frontages had been filled by the early 1860s.[53] On Sickle Penfield 24 houses were built in Warner Place, four in Adelphi Terrace in the north, and eight in Wellington Place in the south between 1845 and 1853. Around St. Peter's church, in the centre from 1840 with an adjoining school from 1851, 35 houses were built in St. Peter's Street, Terrace, Square, and Place between 1852 and 1855. Nelson Street, replacing a large pond, completed the development by 1865.[54] To the west Ion Square existed by 1845 on the portion of Milkhouse Bridge purchased by Pritchard,[55] with 38 new houses by 1848,[56] and 63 houses were built on the triangular plot between Ion Square and Birdcage Walk which had been conveyed in 1840 by Joel Emmanuel for alms-houses.[57] On the rest of Milkhouse Bridge, behind the curve of Hackney Road, 18 houses were built in 1851-2 in Charles Street as it extended south to Crabtree Row and Birdcage Walk. Houses added to the Barnet Chancel estate completed building there by the mid 1840s; some, as on the adjoining Jesus Hospital estate, originated as summerhouses.[58] Barnet Grove crossed the centre of the hospital estate by 1845, with at least 31 houses by 1846.[59] The long narrow Willow Walk existed in the north, Bourne's or Baker's Arms Gardens in the east by 1848,[60] and Cross Street by 1851.[61] To the south over 80 houses were built, many by William Palfrey of Kingsland and a few by George Huxtable of Friar's Mount, on Turney estate between 1845 and 1855. Most were in Gosset Street, the new Daniel Street[62] running south from it, and Montague Street, the northern

34 Robinson and Chesshyre, *The Green*, 16; G.L.R.O., MBO/DS/12 A-B, E; below, pub. svces. (medical svces.).
35 *Rep. Com. San. Condition of Labouring Pop.* map facing p. 160.
36 Robinson and Chesshyre, *The Green*, 20.
37 G.L.R.O., M93/134; O.S. Map 1/2,500, Lond. XXVIII (1873 edn.).
38 T.H.L.H.L., TH/2313; M.L.R. 1842/4/317.
39 P.R.O., HO 107/1541/21/3/22, f. 661, pp. 22-34.
40 T.H.L.H.L., TH/2314; *V.C.H. Mdx.* x. 31; below, econ. hist. (ind.).
41 M.L.R. 1857/14/724; G.L.R.O., C/72/88, 366.
42 Stanford, *Map of Lond.* (1862-5).
43 P.R.O., C 54/15164, mm. 18-19.
44 M.L.R. 1842/2/369.
45 P.R.O., HO 107/1540/21/2/11, f. 307, p. 53.
46 M.L.R. 1842/1/130.
47 P.R.O., HO 107/1540/21/2/14, pp. 19, 45.

48 Stanford, *Map of Lond.* (1862-5); L.C.C. *List of Streets* (1901).
49 G.L.R.O., Acc. 1416/39-54; above, the Centre.
50 G.L.R.O., C/72/386; T.H.L.H.L., TH/6547, 6557.
51 G.L.R.O., O/126/7; map in Gavin, *San. Ramblings*; Stanford, *Map of Lond.* (1862-5).
52 T.H.L.H.L., TH/5043; *Rep. Com. San. Condition of Labouring Pop.* map facing p. 160.
53 Stanford, *Map of Lond.* (1862-5).   54 Ibid.
55 G.L.R.O., Acc. 157/1. Ion was apparently a Pritchard family name: T.H.L.H.L., TH/6559.
56 Gavin, *San. Ramblings*, 62.
57 P.R.O., C 54/19859, mm. 37-40.
58 Gavin, *San. Ramblings*, 60-1 and map.
59 G.L.R.O., THCS 520.
60 Gavin, *San. Ramblings*, 61, 64; G.L.R.O., THCS 520.
61 P.R.O., HO 107/1539/21/1/21, f. 455, pp. 35-7.
62 Probably not the Daniel St. of 1836, above.

extension of Hope Town or Union Street (the whole after 1864 called Turin Street).[63]

More than 50 houses were built between 1845 and 1855 on each of three estates in the west, north of Church Street: Austens (mainly by Thomas Gadbury),[64] Fitches, and Tyssens. The only new road was Victoria Street on Austens but many houses were listed under previously built-up streets, like 36 in Virginia Row, denoting either replacements or courts behind. Later rebuilding on Tyssens by Samuel James, a local builder, produced nearly 150 houses between 1872 and 1875, mostly in Tyrrell, George, and Charlotte streets and in the new Thorold Street, constructed across Thorold Square in 1872.[65]

South of Church Street between 1845 and 1855 some 70 houses were built on Red Cow estate, 45 in Hare Marsh, and 56 in Willetts, mostly in Abbey and White streets, which had been extended southward to Cheshire Street by 1838.[66] By 1846 some 100 houses had been added to Great Haresmarsh[67] which, after the eastward extension of Weaver Street as a second Carter Street by 1848, was separated from the built-up Hare Marsh only by a goods shed.[68]

The most striking development was in the east on the two largest estates, Bishop's Hall and Broomfields. The Sotheby family in 1840 conveyed a site on the east side of the access lane to Bishop's Hall (Bonner Lane, later St. James's Road or Avenue) for a church, St. James the Less,[69] and soon surrendered land on the north-west of the estate for a workhouse.[70] Negotiations started in 1841 with the Commissioners of Woods, who were seeking land for a public park.[71] An Act of 1842 enabled them to purchase[72] and in 1844 the Sotheby family and the trustees of Robinson's charity agreed to sell.[73] Victoria Park, opened in 1845, consisted of 53 a. of Sothebys, that part of Bishop's Hall north of Old Ford Road and east of the Regent's canal, the whole of the Cass and Goosefields estates in Bethnal Green, and other estates in Hackney and Bow. The commissioners also purchased adjoining land south of Old Ford Road and the whole of Robinson's charity land, usually called Bonner's Fields, where they planned access roads to the park and spacious housing. Sotheby was left with some 12½ a. of Bishop's Hall west of the canal, bordering Bonner's Fields on the east and north.[74]

Sotheby and the commissioners' architect James Pennethorne drew up a joint plan for building north of Old Ford Road and west of the canal. Pennethorne was presumably responsible for the layout of four roads enclosing the square of Bonner's Fields: the existing Old Ford Road, Bishop's Road (from 1937 Bishop's Way), an eastern extension of Russia Lane, the existing Russia Lane, and in the east St. James's Road (from 1937 St. James's Avenue) along the lane to the manor house (which, with its attendant buildings, was demolished). The fields were quartered by Bonner Road, running north-west, and Approach Road (originally called Victoria Park Road), running north-east to enter the park. Pennethorne planned Approach Road as a grand way from the park across the green to join Cambridge and Bethnal Green roads near St. John's church but several submissions failed to gain approval and the road stopped at Old Ford Road. Sewardstone Road, wholly on Sotheby's land, ran parallel with the canal from Old Ford Road.[75] Additions by the mid 1850s included, in the south-east, Bandon Road, and, on Sotheby's land in the north-west, Waterloo and Albert roads, and on the commissioners' land in the south-west, Robinson Road.[76]

Sotheby leased plots at the north-west corner, on each side of Bonner Road, to William Drew and Edward Rayner in 1845, and adjoining plots to the east to William Bayst, a local butcher, and Walter Carson in 1846.[77] The Prince of Wales public house had been built on Drew's portion by 1848.[78] Much of Rayner's ground had passed by 1847 to George Furby, a Whitechapel ironmonger, who with Bayst employed Higgs, a builder from Bacon Street, in Bishop's and Bonner roads in the 1840s. Houses had also been built on Rayner's ground in Bonner Road and Russia Lane by 1847.[79] Single plots were sometimes taken.[80] A larger area, probably all the land east of St. James's Road, was taken by William Hosford, whose architects W. G. & E. Habershon may have been connected with Matthew Habershon,[81] a Bishop's Hall resident in 1842.[82] In the early 1850s houses were built in St. James's and Bandon roads; William Bowen, William Walsham, and John Abbott were among those who built Bedford Terrace in Old Ford Road.[83] By 1857 building on Sothebys estate consisted of the north side of Old Ford Road, the east side of St. James's Road to Bandon Road, a few houses north of the church, much of the north side and some of the south-west of Bishop's Road, and blocks in Russia Lane and Bonner Road.[84] In 1858–9 Ezekiel Wadley, a local builder, was working in Sewardstone

[63] L.C.C. *List of Streets* (1901); Gavin, *San. Ramblings*, 54 and map; Old O.S. Map Lond. 51 (1872).
[64] G.L.R.O., M93/73, pp. 335, 346.
[65] L.C.C. *List of Streets* (1901); Old O.S. Map Lond. 51 (1872, 1893).
[66] Rep. Com. San. Condition of Labouring Pop. map facing p. 160.
[67] Cf. G.L.R.O., THCS 446, 520.
[68] Gavin, *San. Ramblings*, 40; Stanford, *Map of Lond.* (1862–5).
[69] Guildhall MS. 19224/297; M.L.R. 1842/2/368; below, list of churches.
[70] G.L.R.O., MR/UTJ/1; below, local govt. (local govt. 1836–1900).
[71] G.L.R.O., Victoria Pk. Papers, vol. 1.
[72] 5 & 6 Vic. c. 20.

[73] G.L.R.O., Victoria Pk. Papers, vol. 1, letters 9 Feb., 10 June 1844.
[74] Ibid. map 1844; P.R.O., MPE 1365, IR 30/21/40; G.L.R.O., TA 1; C. Poulsen, *Victoria Park* (1976), 34, 38; below, estates (Bishop's Hall).
[75] G.L.R.O., MA/DCP/73; MR/UP 340, 349, 371.
[76] P.R.O., LRRO 1/2111.
[77] G.L.R.O., MA/DCP/73.
[78] M.L.R. 1848/5/280.
[79] G.L.R.O., C/72/295.
[80] Ibid. 53.
[81] Ibid. MA/DCP/84.
[82] 5 & 6 Vic. c. 20, schedule.
[83] G.L.R.O., C/72/153, 439, 451, 479; M.L.R. 1851/7/574–8.
[84] P.R.O., LRRO 1/2111.

Road[85] and Thomas Fleming from Mile End and Joseph Charles Morgan from Cambridge Heath were building in Brighton Terrace on the south side of Bishop's Road.[86] William Turner, a south Hackney builder, built Park House at the northern end of St. James's Road in 1858[87] and Charles Terrace on the north side of Bishop's Road in 1861.[88] Building was complete on Sotheby's Bishop's Hall by the mid 1860s.[89] In 1868 the family of George Lansbury (1859–1940) came to live in Albert Road; the future Labour leader attended St. James the Less National school, the Primitive Methodist chapel in Bonner Lane, and freethinkers' meetings in Victoria Park.[90]

The commissioners' estate was developed more slowly. Pennethorne in 1845 had proposed ornamental gardens west of St. James's Road, with detached houses around the entrance to the park.[91] The whole of Bonner's Fields was divided into 37 lots.[92] One, off Old Ford Road, was let in 1851 for workshops[93] and in 1853 five, on either side of Robinson Road, were to be leased to James Thomas Stephenson.[94] In 1855 the area conceived as gardens and later numbered lot 37 was leased for the London Chest hospital. Pennethorne's original plan was cancelled in early 1857.[95] His Tudor lodge for the park's superintendent was built by the main gate in 1845[96] but terraces such as Arran Terrace were substituted for the other detached houses. Terraces by 1857 lined the southern side of Bishop's Road (Gore Terrace), Bonner Road (Denmark Terrace on the north and Prince's, Church, and Buckingham terraces on the south), the south side of Robinson Road (Barton Terrace), and the north side of Old Ford Road (Saunders and Albany terraces).[97] J. Saunders agreed to build four houses a year from 1866 to 1868 on two lots fronting Approach Road.[98] Wesleyans in 1867 acquired two lots at the northern junction of Approach and Bonner roads, where a chapel opened in 1868.[99] To the west, a lot comprising nos. 1–6 Denmark Terrace and workshops behind, which was leased with the adjoining plot on Sotheby's land by George Holgate in 1861–4 and 1868, was taken for the Methodist orphanage, which opened in 1871.[1] Congregationalists built a chapel at the south corner of Approach and Bonner roads in 1869 and the adjoining Victoria hall in 1870.[2] Parmiter's charity in 1871 bought plots to the south, and rear for its school, opened in 1887.[3]

John Robson, builder of Antill Road, built 9 houses in Bishop's Road and 10 in Approach Road between 1871 and 1874. As in other districts warehouses were built in the 1870s behind older frontages. Although by the 1850s roads (Gore Place or Road and Morpeth Road) were planned by the commissioners north of the park, linked to development in Hackney,[4] they were not built on until the 1870s; 53 houses were built in Gore Road between 1871 and 1875. The historian J. R. Green (d. 1883) lived successively in Approach Road and Bonner Road (Prince's Terrace) in 1865, when he became incumbent of St. Philip's, Stepney.[5]

South of the park, the commissioners had building land between Old Ford Road and Duckett's canal. Bisected by Grove Road, it had been taken from Pyotts and Broomfields. Pennethorne had planned an imposing entry to the park along Grove Road, with plots of 70-ft. frontage and mews to the east. Plots at the entrance were granted on long leases between 1858 and 1860;[6] a few houses were detached but most, built between c. 1865 and c. 1875, were terraced, Lansmere in the west and Victoria in the east.[7] Royal Victor Place ran behind the houses, next to Duckett's canal, by 1871 and houses and factories were soon built there.

Eastward, on the estate John Ridge inherited from his father in 1839,[8] terraces were built fronting northward on Old Ford Road from 1845: George's Place and Adelphi Terrace west of the junction with Bonner Lane, and Park Terrace to the east.[9] Abraham Keymer, landlord of the City of Paris, the only old building in the area, built some houses in 1850–1,[10] but most were put up by professional builders like Joseph Higgs, John Perry, John Litchfield,[11] and especially Robert Wright, who lived in Wharf Cottage, Park Terrace.[12] Building spread south in 1850–1 to Wellington (after 1879 Cyprus) Street and Place, west of Bonner Lane, to Cranbrook Street and Place by 1851, and Alma Road (formerly Street and Place) in the east from 1855. Wright was active in most streets, building double-fronted houses with windows running along the whole of the upper floor for weavers[13] who predominated in 1851.[14]

East of Ridge's estate a 10-a. field, originally Pyotts, from the 18th century was owned by the Sotheby family.[15] It was broken up by the Regent's and Duckett's canals and lost its northern part to the Commissioners of Woods.[16] The portion east of the Regent's canal was leased to

85 T.H.L.H.L., TH/7895.
86 Ibid. 5301; G.L.R.O., C/72/285.
87 G.L.R.O., C/72/170.
88 T.H.L.H.L., TH/7253.
89 Stanford, *Map of Lond.* (1862–5).
90 R. Postgate, *Life of Geo. Lansbury* (1951), 6, 8–9; *D.N.B.*; Bethnal Green M.B. *Official Guide* (1950), 66.
91 G.L.R.O., MA/DCP/73; Poulsen, *Victoria Pk.* 34.
92 P.R.O., LRRO 1/2111, 2116.
93 Ibid. 2116.   94 Ibid. 2068.
95 Ibid. 2111, 2116.
96 Poulsen, *Victoria Pk.* 37.
97 P.R.O., LRRO 1/2116.
98 Ibid. 2081.
99 Ibid.; below, prot. nonconf. (Meths.).
 1 P.R.O., C 54/17989, mm. 43–9; LRRO 1/2081; below, educ. (pub. schs., Bonner Rd. Home).
 2 P.R.O., LRRO 1/2081; below, prot. nonconf. (Congs.).

 3 P.R.O., LRRO 1/2116; Bacon, *Atlas of Lond.* (1910); below, educ. (pub. schs., Parmiter's).
 4 P.R.O., LRRO 1/2116.
 5 G. H. Cunningham, *Lond.: Comprehensive Survey* (1931), 15, 58; *D.N.B.*
 6 P.R.O., LRRO 1/2115–6, 2085; G.L.R.O., MR/UP 346.
 7 Stanford, *Map of Lond.* (1862–5); O.S. Map 1/2,500, Lond. XXVIII (1873 edn.).
 8 T.H.L.H.L., TH/2849.   9 Ibid. 2867.
10 M.L.R. 1851/7/951.
11 Ibid. 1850/5/763, 939; 1850/8/562, 749, 818; 1851/7/952.
12 Ibid. 1851/7/748; P.R.O., HO 107/1540/21/2/1, p. 12.
13 *Proc. Hug. Soc.* x. 339; below, plate 25.
14 P.R.O., HO 107/1540/21/2/1, p. 12.
15 Guildhall MS. 19224/297.
16 M.L.R. 1828/1/327, 676; G.L.R.O., TA 1; P.R.O., IR 30/21/40.

the Gardner family which farmed it and built barges to carry bricks.[17] Gardner's wharf was built in 1854 and Gardner's Road by 1859,[18] when Sotheby leased ground north of Bridge (later Roman) Road to Samuel Charles Aubrey, a Hackney surveyor who built some houses before assigning the lease in 1860 to Joseph Ashwell (d. 1876).[19] Land to the north was leased to Henry Harrison, a Westminster contractor, in 1864[20] and Ashwell and Wennington streets existed there by the mid 1860s, as did Havelock Hill and Nelson Place west of the canal.[21]

Broomfields covered the whole area east of Grove Road and south of Duckett's canal, that south of Roman Road between the Regent's canal and Grove Road, and a strip west of the canal. The only buildings before the creation of Victoria Park were John Gardner's farmhouse on the west side of Grove Road next Duckett's canal, King's Arms Row in Old Ford Road, a tollhouse, and the substantial Park House and Grove House on the south-east side of Grove Road,[22] occupied respectively in 1851 by a 'lady' and a brick merchant.[23] King's Arms Row was demolished when Old Ford Road was straightened in 1844.[24]

The owners of Broomfields, the Marsh family, chose to sell rather than lease. In the early 1850s the area west of Grove Road was divided into plots, the purchasers including William Palmer of Essex, Higgs, Tayler, and W. S. Bowen, who from 1852 built in Bridge and Grove roads, Totty, Lessada, and Palm streets.[25] Victoria works had been built on the west side of the Regent's canal by 1854[26] and, south of Palm Street, Hamilton Road by the early 1860s[27] and Cordova Road in 1866.[28] Streets were laid out on Sixteen Acre field, east of Grove Road between Old Ford Road and Roman (originally Claremont and later Esmond) Road, by 1857, when it was to be sold to the Revd. George Townshend Driffield, rector of Bow, and others, presumably as trustees. They found difficulty in raising the money, the Marshes acting as mortgagees, and in 1865 conveyed the land to the London & Suburban Land & Building Co.[29] Thomas Rogers, a London solicitor, was involved from 1857 in building in Esmond, Kenilworth, Vivian (formerly Woodstock), Auckland (formerly Blenheim, from 1937 Zealand), Ellesmere, and Chisenhale roads.[30] Sydney Terrace on the east side of Grove Road was leased in 1864 to Henry Lawrence Hammack, surveyor, of Bow Road. The builders were probably James and Josiah Goodman. Adjoining side roads, Thoydon and Gernon roads, existed in 1864[31] and were soon

built up, as were Alma (later Maidhurst or Medhurst Road) and Shaftesbury terraces to the south.[32] By 1871 building had reached east to Medway Road, which crossed into Bow, and south to Antill Road, which had been driven westward from Bow to Grove Road. West of Grove Road the remaining space, north of the railway, was covered with Belhaven and Burnside streets. William Harris of Limehouse, William Willis of Antill Road, William Bruty, William Ward of Mile End, Noah Smith of Ellesmere Road, and the Goodmans of Twig Folly bridge between them built over 330 houses on Broomfields between 1871 and 1875, mainly in the new roads on the east and south borders of the estate and parish.

Meanwhile the state of London's East End, and of Bethnal Green in particular, had caught the national attention. In 1837 James Phillips Kay, the assistant Poor Law Commissioner, commented on the distress of the Spitalfields weavers, most of whom lived in Bethnal Green, and on their feeble physical condition.[33] In 1838 Dr. Southwood Smith, Benthamite and friend of Edwin Chadwick, reported on the link between the environment and disease, especially 'typhus' (probably typhoid or paratyphoid fever) allegedly caused by stagnant water, refuse, and leaking privies in Lamb's Fields and around Virginia Row.[34] A survey of the weaving districts in 1838 and published in 1840[35] remarked that nowhere else in London were there so many low-rented houses, 93 per cent of Bethnal Green's total of 11,983 being rated at under £20; only 15 houses were rated at over £50 and 18 at £40–50. Most houses built since 1800 were two-storeyed with no foundations, small and damp, of the cheapest timber and half-burnt bricks with badly pitched roofs, 'erected by speculative builders of the most scampy class'. Landlords negotiated with the builders, 'frequently men of no property', and advanced materials in return for an exorbitant ground rent. Property was sold in summer, when defects were less visible, to purchasers or mortgagees who, when they found that ground rent, repairs, and taxes were greater than the rent obtained, abandoned it to the ground landlord. Unmade roads turned to mud or dust by builders' carts, lack of sewerage, and overcrowding, together with the unhealthy effects of the weaving industry, produced a stunted and sickly population.

Bishop Blomfield of London, who had served with Chadwick on the Poor Law Commission in the 1830s,[36] decided to concentrate new churches in Bethnal Green and in his appeal in 1839

[17] G.L.R.O., TA 1; G. F. Vale and S. Snaith, *Bygone Bethnal Green* (1948), 49.
[18] G.L.R.O., C/72/668.
[19] Ibid. 531.
[20] Ibid. 1–2, 25–8.
[21] Stanford, *Map of Lond.* (1862–5); T.H.L.H.L., TH/2867.
[22] P.R.O., IR 30/21/40; G.L.R.O., TA 1; 5 & 6 Vic. c. 20, schedule.
[23] P.R.O., HO 107/1540/21/2/7, p. 33.
[24] *Illus. Lond. News*, 9 Nov. 1844, 301.
[25] G.L.R.O., C/72/103, 524.
[26] E. Ruff & Co. *Map of Lond. . . . to 1854* (P.R.O., MR/1480).
[27] Stanford, *Map of Lond.* (1862–5).

[28] L.C.C. *List of Streets* (1901).
[29] T.H.L.H.L., TH/7828; M.L.R. 1857/14/713.
[30] T.H.L.H.L., TH/4728, 5818, 6413, 7052, 7254, 8341/1; M.L.R. 1857/14/715–23.
[31] T.H.L.H.L., TH/3411–3, 3419.
[32] Stanford, *Map of Lond.* (1862–5).
[33] *Poor Law Com. 3rd Rep.* H.C. 546, p. 84 (1837), app. B.
[34] *Poor Law Com. 4th Rep.* H.C. 147, pp. 62 sqq. (1837–8), xxviii, app. A. Typhus, spread by lice, was not separately distinguished from typhoid and similar enteric fevers until the later 19th cent.
[35] *Rep. Asst. Com. Handloom Weavers*, pt. II, pp. 53 sqq.
[36] *Rep. on San. Condition of Labouring Pop. of Gt. Britain by Edwin Chadwick, 1842*, ed. M. W. Flinn (1965), 45.

alluded to the misery of its population, which included many driven out of other parts of London by 'improvements'.[37] According to one of the new incumbents, before the appeal as little was known in London's West End of 'this most destitute parish as the wilds of Australia or the islands of the South Seas'.[38] As a result of the bishop's sermons before the lord mayor and in wealthier parishes, Bethnal Green's problems were reported from 1839 in *The Times*,[39] the *London City Mission Magazine*, and other publications. Chadwick's report in 1842 reaffirmed the link between the environment and disease.[40] The incumbent of St. Philip's, the church serving the Nichol, quoted by Engels, in 1844 had found that conditions were far worse than in a northern industrial parish, that population density was 8.6 people to a (small) house, and that there were 1,400 houses in an area less than 400 yards square.[41]

The most detailed report on Bethnal Green was published in 1848 by Dr. Hector Gavin,[42] health inspector and lecturer at Charing Cross hospital, who hoped to enlist the rich in 'the great work of sanitary improvement and social amelioration'. He wrote before development around Victoria Park, when the 'most respectable' area was Hackney Road. The rest of the parish, including the area on either side of Green Street, was 'filthy', 'appalling', and 'disgusting'. The older districts bordering Spitalfields contained paved streets and larger houses but the former were broken up and the latter overcrowded. Elsewhere roads were unmade, often mere alleys, houses small and without foundations, subdivided and often around unpaved courts. An almost total lack of drainage and sewerage was made worse by the ponds formed by the excavation of brickearth. Pigs and cows in back yards, noxious trades like boiling tripe, melting tallow, or preparing cat's meat, and slaughter houses, dustheaps, and 'lakes of putrefying night soil' added to the filth. Henry Mayhew was then visiting Bethnal Green for the articles first published in the *Morning Chronicle* in 1851, which later became his great work.[43] He added descriptions of tailors, costermongers, shoemakers, dustmen, sawyers, carpenters, and cabinet makers to the already prolific literature on silkweavers. In 1861 John Hollingshead, special correspondent of the *Morning Post*, published *Ragged London* with detailed desriptions of Shoreditch Side and the Nichol, which had grown even more squalid in the last 20 years as old houses decayed and traditional trades became masks for thieves and prostitutes.

Reaction varied. Anglican and nonconformist clergy, with London City missioners active in Bethnal Green since 1838, were shocked chiefly by immorality, even if they did not assert as bluntly as the rector that it was the main cause of the prevailing misery. Many, especially in the 1840s, agreed with the bishop on the need for religion and education. The ten churches with their National schools, mostly Gothic buildings standing out among the wretched houses, offered both, while the clergy's articulate leadership compensated for the flight of the middle class. By 1858, however, it was clear that they had not found the panacea: the inhabitants of all districts were overwhelmingly 'labouring poor', and churchmen were pessimistic.[44]

Despite failing to move the landlords and parish authorities, Chadwick and Gavin stimulated individual philanthropy. It provided soup kitchens, orphanages, medical and other needs, co-ordinated after 1869 by the Charity Organisation Society,[45] and began to address the housing problem with plans to replace slums by model housing.

When Baroness Burdett-Coutts accepted Charles Dickens's suggestion of rebuilding an area of the East End,[46] he advised her in January 1852 to consult Southwood Smith. By March a site had been prepared at Nova Scotia Gardens,[47] north of Crabtree Row, described by Gavin as a space formed by the 'erasement' (probably to make room for St. Thomas's church) of a vast number of vile dwellings.[48] Dickens made Bethnal Green the home of Nancy in *Oliver Twist* (1838). Nova Scotia Gardens was probably the dust heap described in *Our Mutual Friend* (1864-5); when bought by the baroness in 1857, it was a 'huge mountain of refuse' with a row of small houses on one side and the new church and schools on the other. The total lack of drainage, the stench, and disease were vividly portrayed.[49] Dickens advised the building of large houses, to which services could be supplied.[50] Henry Darbishire, later architect to the Peabody Trust, designed the model dwellings which were called Columbia Square after the bishopric of British Columbia, founded by the baroness in 1857. The first of the four five-storeyed blocks set around a square opened in 1859 and the last in 1862.[51] In a vaguely Gothic but rather 'flat and monotonous' style, they provided some 180

37 B.L. Add. MS. 40427, f. 396; BNC, Second Ser. [Tower], 148; below, church extension.

38 Revd. G. Alstone in 1844, quoted in F. Engels, *Condition of Working Class in Eng.* ed. W. O. Henderson and W. H. Chaloner (1958), 35-6.

39 *The Times*, 18 July 1839, 5d; 7 Nov. 1839, 3c; 31 Dec. 1839, 5c; 24 Mar. 1840, 6d; 12 May 1840, 5e sqq.

40 *Rep. Com. San. Condition of Labouring Pop.* 159-60 and map.

41 Engels, *Condition of Working Class*, 35-6.

42 Gavin, *San. Ramblings*.

43 H. Mayhew, *Lond. Labour and Lond. Poor* (1861), i-iv, extra vol.; *D.N.B.*; see also *The Unknown Mayhew*, ed. E. P. Thompson and E. Yeo (1971).

44 Lambeth Pal. Libr., Fulham Papers, Tait 440/6-18; below, church; prot. nonconf.

45 K. J. Heasman, 'Influence of Evangelicals upon Voluntary Charitable Institutions in Second Half of 19th cent.' (Lond. Univ. Ph.D. thesis, 1959).

46 E. Healey, *Lady Unknown. Life of Angela Burdett-Coutts* (1978), 119.

47 *Letters from Chas. Dickens to Angela Burdett Coutts, 1841-65*, ed. E. Johnson (1953), 18, 192, 197.

48 Gavin, *San. Ramblings*, 87.

49 *Builder*, xv. 225-6.

50 *Letters from Chas. Dickens*, 198.

51 C. Burdett Patterson, *Angela Burdett-Coutts and the Victorians* (1953), 206; J. N. Tarn, *Working-Class Housing in 19th-cent. Britain* (1971), 15.

FIG. 20. NOVA SCOTIA GARDENS IN 1857

sets of rooms, which housed more than 1,000 people by 1869, and a top storey with reading rooms and washing facilities.[52] In 1864 Darbishire began the magnificent Columbia Market buildings in the style of a French Gothic cathedral on 2 a. to the west. Opened in 1869, they included dwellings for shopkeepers.[53] The scheme involved Crabtree Row being widened and the new Westminster Street (later Baroness Road) driven from Queen's Place through Greengate Gardens to Hackney Road.[54] Alfred Ewin, a local builder, applied to build 18 houses there in 1871 and W. H. Hall erected Charlotte Buildings, between Nichol Row and Turville Street, for 140 people by 1872.[55]

Companies, partly philanthropic and partly commercial, began building in the 1860s.[56] The Improved Industrial Dwellings Co., which had been founded by Sydney Waterlow in 1863, purchased the 9 a. of Markhams south of Bethnal Green Road in 1868. It replaced the old property with five-storeyed blocks in Wilmot Street and new streets,[57] Corfield (replacing the narrow Camden Gardens), Ainsley, and Finnis streets. The first blocks, in the north, opened

in 1869. Homes for 72 families had been completed by 1871 and for another 130 by 1873 and 90 by 1875. The School Board for London purchased ½ a. between Wilmot and Finnis streets in 1873 and work began on 21 blocks (for 210 families) in the rest of Finnis Street in 1875 and on 12 blocks for 295 families in Corfield Road in 1878. The estate, later called Waterlow, complete by 1890 and the largest built by the company, was grim and canyon-like in appearance.

In 1868 the company acquired the 9-a. estate of the Barnet Jesus Hospital charity, where the alleys made way for terraces of 'breakfast-parlour houses', mostly two- but some four-storeyed, with back gardens, in streets named after visitors to the hospital: Baxendale, Wimbolt, Elwin, Durant, and Quilter.[58] In 1871 the company built five blocks called Leopold Buildings on the south side of Crabtree Row (later Columbia Road) for 112 families.[59]

BUILDING AND SOCIAL CONDITIONS FROM 1876 TO 1914.[60] The population reached its peak, 129,727, in 1901.[61] Mobility

[52] *Illus. Lond. News*, 8 Mar. 1862, 251, 256; *All the Year Round*, 7 June 1862, 301; *The Times*, 29 Apr. 1869, 5e.
[53] *The Times*, 29 June 1869, 5e; *Guildhall Miscellany*, ii. 353–66.
[54] G.L.R.O., MR/UP 828; Old O.S. Map Lond. 51 (1872).
[55] C. Gatliff, *On Improved Dwellings* (1875) (B.L. Maps 30 a 29); Old O.S. Map Lond. 51 (1872).
[56] Para. based on J. N. Tarn, *Five per cent Philanthropy* (1973), 54–5; *T.L.M.A.S*, xxii. 43, 48, 52–4.
[57] *Pace* Tarn, Corfield St. was new in 1870 and Ainsley St. in 1871: L.C.C. *List of Streets* (1901); Old O.S. Map

Lond. 51 (1872).
[58] *Bldg. News*, 2 Oct. 1868, 668; inf. from clerk to visitors, Jesus Hosp. Char. 1992; Old O.S. Map Lond. 51 (1872).
[59] *Builder*, 19 Aug. 1871, 654; Tarn, *Five per cent Philanthropy*, 56; Old O.S. Map Lond. 51 (1872); below, plate 37.
[60] Section based on Dist. Surveyors' Returns, G.L.R.O., MBW 1659, 1667, 1675–6, 1684, 1692, 1702, 1711, 1721, 1729, 1739, 1748, 1757, 1766 (1876–88); AR/BA/4/4, 13, 22, 31, 40, 46, 55, 63, 71, 80, 89, 99, 108, 117, 125, 133, 142, 150, 162, 176, 190, 206, 221, 235, 251, 269 (1889–1914).
[61] *Census*, 1871–1911.

FIG. 21. COLUMBIA MARKET IN 1869

was such that a school inspector in the 1880s calculated that, of 1,204 families on his books, 530 (44 per cent) had moved within the year.[62] Those who prospered left the area[63] but most remained continually on the move within the East End. Emigration rose from 1,088 in the decade 1851–61 to 15,233 in 1871–81 and 21,546 in 1901–11, when it produced a net loss of population,[64] but mostly was more than balanced by a natural increase and by immigration. Although there was a high death rate (26.5 per 1,000 in 1883, 25 in 1899, 19.5 in 1904, and 16.1 in 1912),[65] especially for children,[66] there was an even higher birth rate, 40.1 per 1,000 in 1887, 34.9, compared with a London average of 27.9, in 1904, and 30.7 in 1912,[67] largely due to child-bearing at an early age. In 1891 only Whitechapel and Spitalfields had more women married under 25[68] and the failure to get married was always shocking missioners. In 1881, of the 16.5 per cent of Bethnal Green's population who were not London born, the largest category, especially in Green ward, came from Essex and the next from Middlesex.[69] As the native Londoners, 'for the most part noticeably undersized',[70] died out, they were replenished by people from the country.[71]

A typical family in many ways was that of Arthur Harding, a criminal.[72] Descended on his father's side from Cornishmen who settled in the Borough and then in Spitalfields and on his mother's from Norfolk farm labourers who moved to Hoxton c. 1875, he was born in 1886 in a rented room in a three-storeyed tenement in Boundary Street on the borders of the Nichol. His father kept a public house and was later a cabinet maker. His mother worked in a rag factory, until she was crippled in an accident, and then as a matchbox maker. When the Nichol was cleared in the 1890s the family moved to Hoxton, then to Bacon Street, in 1902 to Queen's Buildings in Gosset Street, and in 1904 to Gibraltar Buildings, a tenement block in Gibraltar Gardens.

In 1881 only 872 people in Bethnal Green were Irish and 925 foreign-born. Foreign immigrants formed 0.7 per cent of the population in 1861, 1871, and 1881, 3.6 per cent in 1901, and 6.1 per cent in 1911. Mostly born in Germany, Poland, and, from the 1880s, Russia,[73] they were usually poor Jews who had fled pogroms and whose concentration made them much more prominent than their numbers merited. They spread, as had the Huguenots, from Spitalfields and Whitechapel. In the late 1880s the area of the Byde, Red Cow, and Hare Marsh estates had 'many Polish Jews'.[74] By 1899 Jews formed at least 95 per cent of the population south of Hare Street and 75–95 per cent in Brick Lane and the Boundary Street estate (the former Nichol), but

62 Booth, *Life and Labour*, i(1), 27.
63 *The Times*, 16 Feb. 1914, 9f.
64 Susan King, 'Formation and development of slums: East Lond. in second half of 19th cent.' (Lond. Univ. Ph.D. thesis, 1981), 218–19.
65 Ibid. 74; *Lond. City Mission Mag.* lxiv. 206;L.C.C. *Lond. Statistics*, xvi. 33; xxiv. 100.
66 182 per 1,000 children under 1 yr. in 1883: King, op. cit. 74.
67 *The Times*, 7 Nov. 1887, 4c; L.C.C. *Lond. Statistics*, xvi. 31; xxiv. 97.
68 Booth, *Life and Labour*, final vol. 19, 22.
69 Ibid. i(3), 112–13, 116–17.
70 *The Times*, 16 Feb. 1914, 9f.
71 Booth, *Life and Labour*, i(3), 64–66.
72 Based on R. Samuel, *East End Underworld. Chapters in Life of A. Harding* (1981).
73 *Census*, 1901–11; King, op. cit. 223, 227. The figures refer only to those born abroad, not to the Jews' perceived numbers.
74 Booth, *Life and Labour*, i(2), App. 24.

less than 25 per cent and often less than 5 per cent in most of Bethnal Green.[75] Wood Close school near Hare Street had so small an attendance on Jewish fast and feast days that it applied to the L.C.C. to become a Jewish school.[76] The ghetto, 'full of synagogues, backroom factories, and little grocery stores reeking of pickled herring, garlic sausage, and onion bread',[77] was occupied by exotic-looking people speaking a strange language. Among those raised in that culture were the Grades who arrived from Russia in 1912. After two years in rented rooms in the northern part of Brick Lane, they moved to the Boundary Street estate and Louis (later Baron Grade) and Bernard (later Baron Delfont) attended Rochelle Street school, where Yiddish was spoken by 90 per cent of the pupils.[78] Sweating, overcrowding, and high rents were associated with Jews, as victims and sometimes as perpetrators. Some Jews were middle-class, for example Woolf Goldstein who lived in Vivian Road on the Broomfields estate,[79] and invested in property which they rackrented. Anti-Jewish feeling, fuelled by the resentment of slum dwellers expelled in clearances, exploded in a revolt against landlords in 1898. It was supported by the liberal Jewish establishment of the United Synagogue, including Sir Samuel Montagu and the Rothschilds who perceived the danger of the unassimilated alien. Besides opposing the sweating system and rackrenting, they founded the Four Per Cent Industrial Dwellings Co. to provide homes for Jewish artisans.[80] One benefit from Jewish settlement, acknowledged by its opponents the missioners, was the decline in drunkenness and, possibly because of that, in infant mortality.[81]

The influx of Jews aggravated poverty and overcrowding. By 1901 there was an overall density in Bethnal Green of 170 people to an acre. The number of houses reached 17,283 in 1881 and 17,354 in 1891, a density of 23 houses to an acre, after which numbers appeared to decrease, to 14,848 in 1901 and 13,649 in 1911, because tenement blocks were counted as single dwellings. There were 28,209 tenements in 1901 and 27,693 in 1911, compared with 10,975 'ordinary houses'. Most people (76 per cent in 1901 and 79 per cent in 1911) lived in tenements of fewer than five rooms and nearly a third of those in two rooms.[82] In the 1880s there were old houses where the upper room, once used for weaving, had been partitioned into two or three rooms for two families, with another family on each floor.[83] Overcrowding was made worse by the loss of gardens to workshops and warehouses, although sanitation improved.

Overcrowding was caused by poverty, since the poor could not afford more space and needed to stay near their work, whether or not they moved within the area. In the late 1880s the largest category of the population, 39.86 per cent., was 'comfortable', with standard earnings, mostly artisans in the furniture trade or regular labourers. Although St. George-in-the-East possessed the poorest district, Bethnal Green had the highest proportion, 44.6 per cent, of poor and very poor, mostly casual labourers and people under-employed in the furniture and dress trades. Only 4.2 per cent were classed as middle-class, small manufacturers and shopkeepers in Cambridge Road, the east side of the green, Bethnal Green Road, Green Street, and the eastern part of Hackney Road.[84] 'Comfortable artisans and clerks' lived near Victoria Park and a similar 'fairly comfortable' population in the more recent Broomfields houses. Elsewhere a mixture of old, crowded houses and workshops was general. There was very great poverty in the large old weavers' houses bordering Spitalfields but the worst area was the Nichol, dilapidated and with 'several bad characters'.[85]

The Nichol's average death rate for 1886–8 was 40 per 1,000, compared with 22.8 for Bethnal Green as a whole and 18.4 for London.[86] Houses were built with 'billy-sweet', a mortar including street dirt which never dried out, and were often more than a foot below street level in alleys less than 28 ft. wide.[87] If houses had been closed as unfit for human habitation,[88] they stood empty and the inhabitants crowded into the rest. When the area was surveyed for clearance in 1891, there were 730 houses of which 43 were empty; 5,719 people lived there, 2,265 of them in 506 two-roomed dwellings, 2,118 in 752 one-roomed dwellings, 1,183 in 211 three-roomed dwellings, and 153 in two common lodgings. Very few weavers were left, most of those in work being labourers, hawkers, furniture makers, general dealers, shoemakers, washerwomen, sawyers, and costermongers. Many were criminals, one street containing 64 people who had been in prison.[89] A warren of alleys and courts, the Nichol was a haven for rival gangs, vividly described by Arthur Morrison. Arthur Osborne Jay, the incumbent of Holy Trinity, read Morrison's *Tales of Mean Streets* (1894), and invited him to the parish. Morrison made several visits to the Nichol, then being transformed into the Boundary Street estate but of which enough remained to provide a setting for his novel *A Child of the Jago*, published in 1896. He made use of the old street plan, substituting the names Jago for Nichol, Honey for Mead, and Edge for Boundary.[90]

Jay himself,[91] a colourful and controversial

[75] C. Russell and H. S. Lewis, *Jews in Lond.* (1900), map. For Boundary Street est., below, this section.
[76] *E. Lond. Rec.* iii. 30.
[77] E. Litvinoff, *Journey through a Small Planet* (1972), 9, 29.
[78] H. Davies, *The Grades* (1981), 11, 17, 19.
[79] T.H.L.H.L., TH/5287.
[80] *The Jewish East End 1840–1939*, ed. A. Newman (1981), 205, 208–13.
[81] *Lond. City Mission Mag.* lxxviii. 11.
[82] *Census*, 1881–1911; King, op. cit. 311–19.
[83] Booth, *Life and Labour*, i(1), 71.

[84] Ibid. 37, 76–7; *Booth's Map* (1889).
[85] Booth, *Life and Labour*, i(2), App. 24–25.
[86] L.C.C. *Housing of Working Classes in Lond. 1855–1912* (1913), 36.
[87] L.C.C. *Opening of Boundary Str. Area* (1900), 5.
[88] *The Times*, 11 Mar. 1891, 3f.
[89] L.C.C. *Housing Question in Lond.* [1900], 191–2; 54 & 55 Vic. c. 60 (Local Act).
[90] A. Morrison, *A Child of the Jago* (1982); *E. Lond. Papers*, ii(1), 39–47.
[91] Below, churches, Holy Trinity.

local figure, published several books on the area and its problems in the 1890s.[92] It was during the 1880s and 1890s that Bethnal Green assumed its symbolic importance as the heart of the East End, the land of the outcast, attracting writers and social reformers[93] such as Charles Booth[94] and Sir Walter Besant with its streets 'full of costermongers' barrows and its mingled odours of unwashed garments and fried fish'.[95] The scene was later recalled by a Huguenot descendant who spent his childhood near Old Ford Road in the 1870s and 1880s: the constant movement of women with bundles of match boxes, men with baskets of boots or rolls of cloth, barrows with furniture, hawkers with all kinds of food, pawnbrokers, pie shops, cows in the streets, drunkards, pigeon lofts and caged birds and rabbits and, until they disappeared under workshops, the gardens whose plants were sold in the streets on Sundays.[96]

Except on the remaining south-east corner of Broomfields, where Palmer and Ward built 179 houses in 1882–4[97], and the nursery in Russia Lane, where Thomas Quinn built 10 blocks of model dwellings (Quinn Square) in 1882–3, development after 1875 was on occupied sites. Slum property collapsed and other houses were replaced, especially when long leases fell in,[98] to increase profits and sometimes to benefit the inhabitants. Warehouses and workshops multiplied, often as solid rear extensions to houses, and many blocks of 'industrial', 'model', or 'artisans' dwellings, essentially tenements in the form of flats, replaced the terraces.[99]

Most building was small-scale. Among the major projects was work on the Red Cow estate by Christopher Forrest of Victoria Park Square, who built 40 houses in Edward Street between 1877 and 1881 and 12 in Busby and Granby streets in 1881 and 1886. In 1884 he was also building model dwellings in Boundary Street and 22 houses in Cambridge Road and Punderson's Gardens. Forrest was a vestryman, guardian, and trustee of the Poor's Land, which in 1889 he tried to free for new parochial buildings, presumably with an interest in the building potential.[1] On Turney estate George Cannon built over 90 houses between Pollard Row and Squirries Street, including the new North Street, in 1883–4 and B. Wire of Church Row, whose family had been building in Bethnal Green since the 1800s,[2] erected 10 houses in Brady's Buildings on the east side of Hart Lane in 1891. Between 1891 and 1894 52 houses were rebuilt in Hart Lane (renamed Barnet Grove in 1897).[3] All the houses in Daniel Street, also part of Turneys, were replaced by 12 on the east side in 1895 and a board school on the west in 1900.

Henry Winkley of Homerton was the main builder in 1886–7 of over 60 houses in Felix and Clare streets and Cambridge Circus on Parmiter's estate, where leases were falling in.[4] He also built 18 houses in Derbyshire Street in 1888 on Willetts, where Frederick Higgs built 14 houses in 1887. Balaam Bros. built 20 houses in Mape, Cheshire, and Menotti streets, also on Willetts, in 1888–9. Charles Winkley, Henry's brother,[5] rebuilt in Rush Mead: 37 houses, 33 shops and workshops and at least 8 warehouses in Temple, Canrobert, and Catherine (after 1938 Winkley) streets from 1899 to 1901 and 18 warehouses in Teesdale (before 1875 Durham) Street in 1904.

On Fitches William Jones of Tufnell Park built 17 houses in Mount Street in 1884 and Jackson and Todd built a factory in 1887.[6] Between Prince's Place, Gosset, and Prince's (Chambord) streets, six model dwellings (Queen's Buildings) were erected in 1884 and another two in 1887, designed to house 200 people.[7] Another 21 houses were built in Chambord Street in 1893–4 and 10 in 1913; 14 were added in Mount Street in 1893–4.

Davis Bros. of Bishopsgate, probably a Jewish firm,[8] built 11 houses in Brick Lane in 1899 and most of the 32 houses erected in Boreham Street on Snow's estate (next to Fitches) in 1899–1900. A more ambitious project was on Saffron Close where in George and Middle walks, south of Old Bethnal Green Road, cottages inhabited c. 1880 by 'respectable mechanics' had been condemned by 1898, when they were occupied by those driven out by clearance schemes, mostly costermongers and casual labourers.[9] In 1901 Davis Bros. replaced the cottages with Teesdale Street, continuing the street of that name north of Old Bethnal Green Road, where they built 95 houses. They also replaced the houses in Blythe Street, which had gardens, with 50 new houses, three-storeyed, red-brick in front and stock-brick behind, containing workshops for cabinet makers and tailors on the top storey. The estate became a Jewish enclave.[10]

Teesdale Street was an example of how the old pattern of alleys and gardens was simplified when streets ignored estate boundaries to form thoroughfares between main roads. Also on Saffron Close, Mansford Street had been put out to tender in 1877[11] as a through road linking Elizabeth (renamed Rushmead in 1876

92 P. J. Keating, *Working Classes in Victorian Fiction* (1971), 178.
93 Ibid. 105, 107, 109, 111. For the reaction of the Church and the Univ. Settlement movement, below, church.
94 Booth, *Life and Labour*: above.
95 W. Besant, *Survey of Lond.* ix. 614–15.
96 *E. Lond. Rec.* iv. 30–5.
97 Medhurst, Arbery, Strahan, and Medway rds.
98 *The Times*, 20 Oct. 1887, 3*d*; 8 Nov. 1887, 12*b*.
99 Booth, *Life and Labour*, i(1), 31.
1 H. G. C. Allgood, *Hist. Bethnal Green* (1894), 312.
2 M.L.R. 1806/2/447; 1808/5/115; G.L.R.O., MR/B/C, Mar. 1855.
3 L.C.C. *List of Streets* (1901); below, plate 35.

4 *The Times*, 20 Oct. 1887, 3*d*.
5 For the Winkley bros. of Hackney, see I. Watson, *Gentlemen in the Bldg. Line* (1989), 43, 99.
6 *Builder*, 3 Sept. 1887, 352. For developments on N. part of est., below.
7 *Town Planning Rev.*, xlvii. 165.
8 Israel Davis was leased the estate in 1903: T.H.L.H.L., TH/6948.
9 *Lond. City Mission Mag.* lxiii. 69–70.
10 Samuel, *E. End Underworld*, 96; G. M. L. Simpson, 'Comparative study of contemporary and pre-war geography of East End of Lond.' (Lond. Univ. M.A. thesis, 1959), 135–6; Old O.S. Maps Lond. 51 (1893, 1914).
11 *Builder*, 15 Dec. 1877, 1260.

and Mansford in 1881)[12] Street on Rush Mead with Bethnal Green Road and, in the process, destroying Wilmot Grove and Square and Abbey Place. Most of the ground was allotted in 99-year leases in 1878, 8 houses were built in 1879, 4 in 1883, a chapel in 1881, a board school in 1883, and model dwellings on the east side from 1880 to 1889. From south to north, probably the order in which they were built, they were named Wilmot House, Mansford Buildings, and Toye's Buildings, after the builder Samuel Toye.[13]

About the same time the alleys and courts on Fitches in the triangle formed by Crabtree Row, Gascoigne Place, and Virginia Row, in 1871 in a 'wretched condition',[14] were replaced by Fountain Street in the east and the broad Herat Street, which ran from Crabtree Row (renamed Columbia Road in 1874) to link with Turk Street. The name Brick Lane was extended to include Tyssen Street in 1882, Turk Street in 1883, and Herat Street in 1855,[15] thereby linking Whitechapel Road with Columbia Market. Some 80 houses were built on the triangular site on Fitches between 1879 and 1888, many by A. Ewin.

Other houses included 23 built in Darling Row 1878–80, mostly by Charles Firne of Mile End Road, 29 in Key (formerly John) Street east of Dog Row 1880–4, 12, mostly by George Chambers, in Peel Grove 1883–4, 18 by John Peppiatt in Ramsey Street in 1884, 17 in Victoria Street and Cooper's Gardens on Austens in 1885–7, and 16 in Bonner and Mace streets, south of Old Ford Road, in 1892 by A. W. Price. Privately built model dwellings included four by J. H. Johnson in Pereira Street in 1884, a small block for M. & A. Davis, designed by C. A. Legg in Half Nicholl Street in 1885,[16] three in Lisbon Street in 1887, three for the G.E.R. Co. between the railway and Winchester Street in 1890,[17] and two in Brick Lane in 1904. Small houses on Jarvis's estate were replaced 1903–6 by Barnsley and Somerford houses, eight joined blocks between Somerford, Tapp, Barnsley, and Collingwood streets, built by Frank Dolly for A. Davis.[18]

Most blocks of flats were built by the philanthropic companies. The East End Dwellings Co.[19] was founded in 1884 to house the very poor while realizing some profit. The M.B.W. having cleared the north side of Green Street between Victoria Park Square and Globe Road under the Metropolitan Street Improvements Act of 1883, making 111 people homeless, the company was leased a central plot where in 1888 it opened the four-storeyed Museum House, for 166 people.[20] Meadows Dwellings, two parallel four-storeyed blocks on the west side of Mansford Street,

opened in 1894, featuring a new staircase access plan.[21] The architects were Davis & Emmanuel, who were responsible for the company's most ambitious scheme, Ravenscroft, completed in 1897 under a 99-year lease from Barnet Chancel charity[22] for most of its 2-a. estate, where 194 tenements were constructed in a five-storeyed red-brick building in an Italianate style; a more ornamental roof-line with octagonal towers and cupolas relieved a continuous frontage to Ravenscroft Street, Columbia Road, and Hassard Street. In 1900 the five-storeyed Mendip Houses in a baroque style and four-storeyed Shepton Houses, 'most uninspired',[23] opened on part of Pyotts east of Globe Road, between Gauber (or Gawber) Street and Kirkwall (once North) Place. The company then turned to the heart of the green, north of Sugar Loaf Walk, which finally took on the surrounding working-class character after the Mercerons in 1900 leased the plot stretching from nos. 22 and 23 Victoria Park Square to Globe Road.[24] The flamboyant red- and yellow-brick Merceron Houses and Montfort House, designed by Ernest Emmanuel with a Georgian porch and internal staircase, had been completed by 1901, as had Gretton Houses, five-storeyed parallel blocks with terracotta decoration, to the north. In 1905 the company opened the larger but similar Evesham House, fronting Old Ford Road, and in 1906 a terrace designed by Henry Davis on the site of weavers' cottages in Globe Road opposite Merceron Houses.

The Guinness Trust, founded in 1889, acquired a triangular site on the east side of Columbia Road (formerly Birdcage Walk), north of the Barnet Charity estate, in 1890. It replaced 63 houses with six blocks of mostly two-roomed tenements designed by Joseph & Smithem, completed in 1901.[25] The Four Per Cent Industrial Dwellings Co., founded in 1885, built the six-storeyed Mocatta House next to the Jews' burial ground in Brady (once North) Street in 1905.[26] The Sutton Dwellings Trust, founded by W. R. Sutton (d. 1901), head of a firm of carriers, to house the poorest class, acquired an acre on the west side of James Street (once North and later Sceptre Road), formerly part of Kirby's Castle estate. Having cleared 'one of the worst slums', the company applied to build in 1907. The first of eight five-storeyed red-brick blocks containing 160 tenements, each with its own sanitation, opened in 1909.[27] The Peabody Trust, although dating from 1862, did not come to Bethnal Green until 1910, when seven plain five-storeyed blocks containing 140 flats opened on a site bounded by Cambridge Crescent or Circus, Minerva, Felix, and Centre

[12] L.C.C. *List of Streets* (1901); *Lond. Dir.* (1880, 1881).
[13] Old O.S. Maps Lond. 51 (1872, 1893); T.H.L.H.L., TH/4741–2.
[14] *Builder*, 28 Jan. 1871, 69.
[15] L.C.C. *List of Streets* (1901); *Lond. Dir.* (1884, 1885).
[16] *Builder*, 21 Feb. 1885, 289.
[17] Old O.S. Maps Lond. 51 (1872, 1893).
[18] Ibid. (1893, 1914).
[19] Based on J. E. Connor and B. J. Critchley, *The Red Cliffs of Stepney. Hist. of Bldgs. erected by East End Dwellings Co. 1885–1949* (1984).
[20] *Ann. Rep. of M.B.W.* H.C. 157, p. 105 (1887), lxxi;

ibid. H.C. 159, p. 13 (1888), lxxxvii; ibid. H.C. 326, p. 141 (1889), lxvi; G.L.R.O., MBW 2459/8.
[21] Tarn, *Five Per Cent Philanthropy*, 102.
[22] Inf. from chairman of Barnet Chancel est. (1992).
[23] Connor and Critchley, *Red Cliffs of Stepney*, 18.
[24] G.L.R.O., M93/86, pp. 559–65.
[25] Tarn, *Five Per Cent Philanthropy*, 105; Old O.S. Maps Lond. 51 (1872, 1893).
[26] Plaque on bldg.; G.L.R.O., AR/BA/4/142, no. 5. Tarn, *Five Per Cent Philanthropy*, 103, gives the date as 1890.
[27] *The Times*, 9 Feb. 1909, 10b; 13 Feb. 1909, 8c.

streets on the Cambridge Heath estate.[28] An eighth block was built in 1915.

The Bethnal Green House Property Association was formed of local tradesmen who, on a small scale, emulated the big companies in improving conditions while taking a modest return. They replaced ruinous property, often cottages in culs-de-sac, with three-storeyed tenements in more open settings. In 1880 they employed J. H. Johnson of Limehouse to build 35 houses designed by A. & C. Harston in Gale's Gardens, 'heretofore a most insanitary area'.[29]

Bethnal Green vestry preferred to restrict its improvements to widening roads, Patriot Square and George Street in 1879 and Hollybush Gardens in 1883, for which it received contributions from the M.B.W.[30] Probably as part of the widening 15 houses and model dwellings were built in Hollybush Gardens in 1884–5.

It was to improve access from the City and Finsbury to Bethnal Green Museum and Victoria Park that the vestry in 1870 sought major changes to Bethnal Green Road (Church Street),[31] which, where it joined Shoreditch High Street, was less than 30 ft. wide. An Act of 1872[32], in addition to changes in Shoreditch, provided for a broad thoroughfare from the existing road at Gibraltar Walk to Anchor and Sclater streets, where it joined Shoreditch High Street. Work began in Bethnal Green in 1878 and the new road, completed in 1879, displaced 800 people where it crossed Red Cow and Byde estates.[33] The surplus land on each side was leased for 80 years in building plots, the M.B.W.'s architect to approve the plans.[34] All the plots had been taken by 1884,[35] including two large plots on the north side of Bethnal Green Road reserved for 'dwellings for the labouring classes'.[36] One, bounded by York (later Ebor), Little York (Whitby), and Little Anchor (Chance) streets, was where Huntingdon Buildings were opened in 1879 by the Improved Industrial Dwellings Co.[37] The other, behind the main road frontage between Tyssen Street (Brick Lane) and Shacklewell Street, was auctioned in 1882 to Henry Foskett, who erected model dwellings (Linden Buildings). [38]

Neither the vestry nor the M.B.W. were anxious to tackle the worst slum, the Nichol. In 1883 the board dismissed as 'too small' an appeal by Shoreditch's medical officer of health to deal with Boundary Street involving only 29 houses[39]

and as too big a scheme by Bethnal Green's medical officer to demolish all the houses in the Nichol under the Artisans' Dwelling Act. Instead the board decided to apply the Torrens Act requiring owners to repair and render the premises 'tolerably comfortable'.[40] At a government inquiry in 1887 the Nichol buildings were said to be in a fair condition but in 1890 they were declared a slum and the new L.C.C. answered another appeal from the medical officers with its first ambitious plan to rebuild the Nichol and Snow estates, together with a small piece on the Shoreditch side of Boundary Street (once Cock Lane), an area of some 15 a.[41] Demolition began in 1891 of the 730 dwellings holding 5,719 people, 144 of whom were housed in cottage dwellings built on land in Goldsmith's Row [42] purchased by the L.C.C. in 1892. Owen Fleming designed the Boundary Street scheme for the Nichol, which retained only Boundary Street in the west and Mount Street in the east, both to be widened to 40 ft. Old Nichol Street to the south was to be widened, extended to Mount Street, and renamed Calvin Street.[43] Other streets, 50-ft. wide, whose names recalled Huguenot associations, radiated from an ornamental space called Arnold Circus. One of them, Calvert Avenue, 60-ft. wide, led directly to Shoreditch High Street. T. Blashill, one of the L.C.C.'s architects, designed 21 and Rowland Plumbe two of 23 blocks containing between 10 and 85 tenements each, named after places along the Thames. A total of 1,069 tenements, mostly two- or three-roomed, accommodated 5,524 persons and set 'new aesthetic standards for housing the working classes'.[44] The scheme included a laundry, 188 shops, and 77 workshops, and preserved churches and schools. Building began in the east in 1893 and was completed for opening by the Prince of Wales in 1900. There were then 5,380 tenants, a density of 359 people to an acre compared with 381 in the Old Nichol.

Twelve public houses were cleared away, giving the new, 'dry' estate a respectability lacking in the area for well over a century. Its tenants were, with few exceptions, not the original ones whose preference for small houses had been ignored[45] and who could not afford the rent of 3s. a room even if they could stomach the enforced sobriety. The newcomers were clerks, policemen, cigarmakers, nurses, and many Jews. Former inhabitants moved into old property

[28] Tarn, *Five Per Cent Philanthropy*, 43, 45; J. E. Connor and B. J. Critchley, *Palaces for the Poor* (1984), 21–2, illus. betw. pp. 14 and 15.
[29] *Builder*, 14 Aug. 1880, 218.
[30] P. J. Edwards, *L.C.C. Hist. of Lond. Street Improvements, 1855–97* (1898), 144; *Ann. Rep. of M.B.W.* H.C. 246, p. 49 (1875), lxiv; ibid. H.C. 212, p. 20 (1880 Sess. 2), lxii; ibid. H.C. 186, p. 67 (1884), lxviii.
[31] *Builder*, 28 Jan. 1871, 69.
[32] Metropolitan Street Improvements Act, 35 & 36 Vic. c. 163.
[33] Edwards, *Lond. Street Improvements*, 47.
[34] *Ann. Rep. of M.B.W.* H.C. 212, p. 97 (1880 Sess. 2), lxii.
[35] Ibid. H.C. 186, p. 11 (1884–5), lxvii.
[36] Ibid. H.C. 230, p. 20 (1878–9), lxi.
[37] Not 1869, as in Connor and Critchley, *Palaces for the Poor*, 25, illus. between pp. 14 and 15; G.L.R.O., MBW 2557/5; Old O.S. Map Lond. 51 (1893).

[38] G.L.R.O., MBW 2557/6; *Ann. Rep. of M.B.W.* H.C. 188, p. 98 (1882), lix; *Builder*, 4 Feb. 1882, 148; O.S. Map 1/2,500, TQ. 3382 (1964 edn.).
[39] *Ann. Rep. of M.B.W.* H.C. 169, p. 16 (1883), lix; H.C. 186, p. 14 (1884), lxviii.
[40] *The Times*, 3 Nov. 1883, 10f.
[41] Section based on R. V. Steffel, 'Boundary St. est.', *Town Planning Rev.* xlvii. 161–73; L.C.C. *Opening of Boundary Str. Area* (1900); L.C.C. *Housing Question in Lond.* [1900], 190– 210.
[42] Goldsmith's Row, off N. side of Hackney Rd., was in Shoreditch until 1900 when its S. portion formed the boundary with Bethnal Green.
[43] Name reverted to Old Nichol Street, presumably under one of several modifications of the plan in the 1890s: L.C.C. *Housing of Working Classes in Lond. 1855–1912* (1913), 36; Old O.S. Map Lond. 51 (1914).
[44] Steffel, op. cit. 167; below, plate 33.
[45] *The Times*, 9 Dec. 1890, 9d.

nearby, spreading, if diluting, the squalor of the Nichol eastward.[46] It was recognized that statutory clearances often aggravated overcrowding,[47] since owners merely closed buildings and the evicted tenants camped out in backyards.[48] Demolitions, as part of sanitary or street improvements, or for schools or 'business premises', far outnumbered replacements. Between 1902 and 1913, for example, 1,656 working-class rooms were demolished, only 859 of them to provide sites for working-class dwellings.[49] One ex-vestryman declared in 1898 that local authorities should house the poor[50] but in 1911 the only municipal housing was the 23 blocks of the L.C.C.'s Boundary Street estate, out of a total of 322 blocks of 4,716 flats and 13,327 other dwellings.[51]

The L.C.C. planned redevelopment under a housing Act of 1890 and the first Town Planning Act of 1909.[52] The case for clearance around Brady (formerly North) Street near Whitechapel was made in 1904 and again in 1912, when Bethnal Green's medical officer stressed its overcrowding (430 people to an acre) and high death rate (24.74 per 1,000 compared with a borough average of 16.71). The Local Government Board in 1914 ordered the L.C.C. to deal with at least part of the area under the Act of 1890, but work was delayed by the war.[53]

BUILDING AND SOCIAL CONDITIONS FROM 1915 TO 1945.[54] The population continued its decline, both because the birth rate fell to 22.1 per 1,000 in 1925 and 13.3 in 1937–8 and because emigration was much greater than immigration.[55] Between 1911 and 1921 a natural increase of 14,871 and a migration loss of 25,816, left a net decrease of 8.5 per cent; in the next decade the increase of 8.5 per cent was offset by a loss of 16.2 per cent.[56] People moving to outer suburbs were replaced at a much lower rate after the 1905 Aliens Act. Inhabitants born in continental Europe, mostly Jews, numbered 6,255 (6 per cent) in 1921 and 5,276 (5 per cent) in 1931. The proportion of London-born inhabitants, 87 per cent in 1921 and 85 per cent in 1931, remained amongst the highest in the capital and would have included some Jews.[57] There were c. 13,000 Jews in Bethnal Green in 1930, about 12 per cent of its population.[58]

Anti-semitism, which had died down, flared up during the First World War when suspicion

of aliens was coupled with resentment over the failure of Jewish refugees to distinguish between conscription under the Tsars and 'doing their bit' for England. Bethnal Green had the highest record for voluntary enlistment in London and it was felt that immigrants were making money by taking the volunteers' jobs. The manufacture of military uniforms was in the hands of Jews who were thereby exempted from military service.[59] In 1917 there was a fight between more than 2,000 Jews and gentiles in the Jewish enclave of Blythe and Teesdale streets.[60] In 1919 returning troops, finding the street markets taken over by aliens, petitioned for a market exclusively for ex-servicemen.[61] Anti-semitism was reflected on the left in opposition by the M.B. to Jews becoming tenants of its new Lenin estate in 1927.[62] It developed most virulently in the 1930s among the right-wing Mosleyites, drawn from costermongers and cabinet makers, thrown out of work by Jewish-owned factories, and local criminals hoping for trouble.[63]

The New Survey of c. 1930 classed 80 per cent of the population as skilled and unskilled artisans, compared with Booth's 51 per cent. At the ends of the social scale, only 2 per cent was middle-class and 18 per cent poor. The middle class still lived mostly along the main roads, but there had been deterioration in the east which c. 1930 included the lowest category, 'degraded and semi-criminal', around Quinn Square and Russia Lane. Almost all the areas built up in the early 19th century were poor, with some of the worst slums along the canal and railways, especially west of Cambridge Heath Road.[64]

Although overcrowding, in terms of people to an acre, fell from 168 in 1911 to 142 in 1931[65] and, in terms of people living more than two to a room, from 33 per cent to 28 per cent respectively, a minority (6,600 in 1921 and 7,322 in 1931) still lived more than three to a room. Conditions were as bad as ever in that there were more families to a dwelling (1.54) in 1931 than in 1921 (1.51) because families were smaller, their size having shrunk from 4.48 in 1911 to 4.14 in 1921 and 3.79 in 1931.[66] In 1933, when seeking government help, a local M.P. stated that 43 per cent of the population was overcrowded, 17 per cent below the poverty line, and 23 per cent of the male population unemployed.[67]

The period saw greater activity by the local authorities, under the pre-war Acts and further

46 Booth, Life and Labour, iii(2), 67–8, 71.
47 Ann. Rep. of M.B.W. H.C. 246, p. 49 (1875), lxiv.
48 Lond. City Mission Mag. lxiv. 206.
49 L.C.C. Lond. Statistics, xxv. 166.
50 Lond. City Mission Mag. lxiii. 67.
51 L.C.C. Lond. Statistics, xxiv. 46.
52 Tarn, Five Per Cent Philanthropy, 123, 176, 179–80.
53 L.C.C. Housing [1920], 12–13, 27; H. Quigley and I. Goldie, Housing and Slum Clearance in Lond. (1934), 210.
54 Section based on Dist. Surveyors' Returns, G.L.R.O., AR/BA/4/284, 297, 309, 319, 331, 346, 361, 377, 391, 406, 423, 437, 451, 466, 500, 539, 561, 585, 606, 628, 650, 672, 694 (1915–39).
55 L.C.C. Lond. Statistics, xxx. 42; xxxix. 38.
56 Census, 1911–31.
57 Ibid.; New Lond. Life and Lab. i. 83; iii. 345.
58 Jewish E. End, ed. Newman, 37.
59 Vicar of St. Jas. the Gt., quoted in Morning Post, 1918

(G.L.R.O., P72/JSG/118).
60 J. Bush, Behind the Lines: E. Lond. Lab. 1914–19 (1984), 181.
61 The Times, 26 Sept. 1919, 7c.
62 Ibid. 10 Sept. 1927, 9d.
63 J. A. Gillespie, 'Economic and Political Change in E. End of Lond. during 1920s' (Cambridge Univ. Ph.D. thesis, 1984), 269; J. Pearson, The Profession of Violence: Rise and Fall of the Kray Twins (1984), 32; below, local govt.
64 New Lond. Life and Lab. iii. 138, 147, 149, 151; iv, Maps, sheet 1; R. Barnes, Coronation Cups and Jam Jars (1976), 22, 98.
65 A suggested density of 186 in 1938 was probably exaggerated: J. H. Forshaw and P. Abercrombie, County of Lond. Plan (1943), 83.
66 New Lond. Life and Lab. iii, 236, 251; Census, 1911–31.
67 The Times, 14 Feb. 1933, 7g.

housing Acts of 1925, 1930, and 1935.[68] In 1917 there were five condemned areas, the most notorious being Brady Street.[69] A speech by the mayor at a meeting over housing conditions in 1919 led to the involvement of Queen Mary.[70] In 1922 the L.C.C. proposed to clear over 7 a., displacing 1,875 people and replacing the 310 old houses (393 tenements) with accommodation there for 1,600, to be provided by the L.C.C., the M.B., housing companies, and others; the rest were to be housed elsewhere.[71]

The L.C.C., having resolved to improve part of Sebrights under the Housing Act of 1925, agreed in 1930 to buy large sections west of Pritchard's Road and south of the Shoreditch border.[72] The scheme, called Teale Street, was drawn up in 1931 under the Act of 1930 to provide for 727 people on 5 a., displacing 843 people from 143 houses (196 tenements). Work was delayed by lack of finance until 1933 when the L.C.C., after an appeal by the Minister of Health,[73] drew up a scheme for nearly 3½ a. of Nag's Head Field, displacing 903 people from 172 houses (215 tenements). Housing for 206 people was to be provided on the site by others, the L.C.C. merely issuing clearance orders.[74]

In 1934 the L.C.C. designated four more clearance areas: Potts Street, just over 2½ a. displacing 709 people in 134 houses and providing for 676, Hollybush Gardens, displacing 115 people in 18 houses (29 tenements) on less than ½ a., Ada Place and Pritchard's Road, displacing 368 in 61 houses (83 tenements) on 2 a., and Delta Street, displacing 95 in 18 houses (29 tenements) on 1 a. The M.B. had listed 11 insanitary areas for demolition in 1934 but the L.C.C. considered them too small for council housing[75] and in 1935 the programme was hampered by a lack of sites for rehousing.[76] Pedley Street, just over 1½ a. housing 353 people in 85 houses (96 tenements), was declared a clearance area in 1935. Areas declared in 1936 were Darling Row, 146 houses (258 tenements) housing 981 people on just over 4 a., and James Street, 91 houses (101 tenements) occupied by 402 people on 2½ a.[77]

In 1936, under an Act of 1935 which provided for redevelopment on a much larger scale, the L.C.C. drew up a plan for 46 a. around Cambridge Heath Road from the Hackney border to Old Bethnal Green Road and Bethnal Green hospital, bounded west by Pritchard's Road and Temple Street and east by Lark Row and Russia Lane. The area contained 1,210 properties, made up of 693 working-class houses, 183 flats in Peabody

Buildings, 134 houses over shops, 59 factories, 54 commercial premises, a school, a church, 12 public houses, empty buildings, and a population of 5,471. Of the working-class dwellings, 583 were overcrowded or unfit. The L.C.C. planned improved streets and new blocks of flats and zoning to separate industry and business premises from housing, although the latter was to be built by private enterprise. It was thought that 4,700 would be rehoused. Under the same Act the L.C.C. acquired 20 a. of Hackney marsh for those residents who could not be rehoused in Bethnal Green.[78]

Seven clearance areas were announced in 1937. Three, Minerva Street with 1,364 people in 272 houses (362 tenements) on over 8 a., Emma Street with 585 people in 94 houses (159 tenements) on 3 a., and Vyner Street, 572 people in 125 houses (166 tenements) on 3½ a., all lay within the 34-a. redevelopment area. The other areas were Tent Street, with 505 people in 80 houses (123 tenements) on nearly 2 a., Cooper's Gardens with 424 people in 99 houses (123 tenements) on just over 2 a., Punderson's Gardens, 1,245 people in 226 houses (339 tenements) on nearly 5½ a., and Lansdell Place, with 432 people in 78 houses (109 tenements) on 2½ a. Herald (formerly Abingdon) Street, 2½ a. with 89 houses (122 tenements) for 467 people, was declared a clearance area in 1938.[79] The L.C.C. also decided to clear Turin Street[80] and in 1939 was planning to dislodge 1,706 people from 10 a. around Squirries Street.[81]

Apart from bricking up some weavers' windows and rebuilding factories, building had virtually ceased during the First World War, at the end of which there was a housing shortage. Clearance was always hampered by the need first to rehouse the dispossessed. Generally the L.C.C. built on the larger and the M.B. on the smaller sites. The L.C.C. produced four type-plans in 1934 and erected mainly five-storeyed blocks[82] in brick in a neo-Georgian style.

The first post-war L.C.C. housing[83] was the Collingwood estate, on 5 a. of the cleared Brady Street site between Brady and Collingwood streets. Work began on the first block in 1922, which opened in 1923, on the second in 1924, the third in 1925,[84] and by the end of 1927, together with Codrington House fronting Scott Street on the west side of Brady Street, the four blocks provided 185 flats for 1,126 people. Rowley Bros. built Harvey and Blackwood houses at the southern end of the site fronting Merceron Road. Rutherford House, fronting

[68] 15 & 16 Geo. V, c. 14; 20 & 21 Geo. V, c. 39; 25 & 26 Geo. V, c. 40. Inf. on clearance areas from L.C.C. *Lond. Housing* (1937), 263–6; L.C.C. *Lond. Statistics*, xxxix. 134.

[69] *The Times*, 15 Sept. 1917, 3b.

[70] Ibid. 15 Feb. 1919, 16f; 24 Feb. 2a; 15 Mar. 12c; 18 Mar. 10d; 19 Mar. 8c.

[71] L.C.C. *Lond. Statistics*, xxx. 111.

[72] T.H.L.H.L., TH/8351, box 1 (Agreement, 1930).

[73] L.C.C. *The Lond. County Council, 1938*, 116.

[74] L.C.C. *Ann. Rep.* (1935), ii. 33.

[75] *Hackney Gaz.* 4 July 1934 (T.H.L.H.L. Bethnal Green Cuttings, Housing 1915–53).

[76] L.C.C. *Ann. Rep.* (1935), ii. 26.

[77] L.C.C. *Lond. Statistics*, xli. 138–9.

[78] L.C.C. *Lond. Housing* (1937), 26–9, map; *The Times*, 1 March 1937, 11a; 26 Apr., 16d; L.C.C. *Ann. Rep.* (1936), ii. 36–37; G.L.R.O., LCC/CL/TP/1/27.

[79] L.C.C. *Lond. Statistics*, xli. 139–40; *The Times*, 8 Mar. 1938, 21f.

[80] L.C.C. *E. End Housing* (1963), 20.

[81] *The Times*, 13 Mar. 1939, 11a.

[82] L.C.C. *The Lond. County Council, 1938*, 116, 121, 127.

[83] Inf. on L.C.C. ests. from L.C.C. *Lond. Housing* (1937), 258–9; L.C.C. *Housing Ests.* (1939), map in G.L.R.O.; L.C.C. *E. End Housing* (1963), 30 sqq.; L.C.C. *Lond. Statistics*, xli. 150–4.

[84] The blocks were Bullen, Pellew, and Fremantle hos.

Brady Street, completed the scheme in 1930, providing a total of 272 dwellings for 1,600 people.[85]

As part of the Teale Street scheme, the L.C.C. began building Dinmont estate in 1934 on 4¼ a. west of Pritchard's Road. Four blocks, each containing c. 60 flats, had opened by 1938 for 1,076 people.

Hollybush House, 90 flats for 400 people on 1½ a. between Hollybush Gardens and the railway, opened in 1936. In 1934 the L.C.C. made a compulsory purchase order on Penn estate, 2 a. south of Bethnal Green Road around Pott Street.[86] Building began in 1936 and 110 dwellings, called Horwood estate after the earliest of three blocks, opened in 1937 to house 511 people.[87]

In 1935 the L.C.C. decided to take over the site of Waterloo House, the former workhouse, and also acquired the adjoining properties in Lark Row and Lyte Street, giving it 5¾ a. north of Bishop's Way (Road). In 1936 R. J. Rowley began building the first of four blocks, which was opened in 1937 as Waterloo estate;[88] of 312 flats planned, 152 had been completed and 107 were under construction in 1939. In 1936 the L.C.C. began the first of two blocks (Ada and Pritchard houses) on a 1½-acre site, Ada Place, off Pritchard's Road at the northern tip of the borough, within the 36-a. redevelopment area. Called Pritchard's, the estate opened with 77 dwellings in 1938. A small block of 8 dwellings opened at the junction of Brady and Scott streets by 1936, another 1¼ a. between Scott and Tent streets was cleared in 1937, and work began on Northesk House, containing 61 dwellings, in 1938.[89] The last two developments were later classified as part of Collingwood estate.

By the beginning of the Second World War the L.C.C. had built or were building 2,170 flats and planned another 1,830 mostly on new sites throughout the borough, the largest being Minerva Street (375) within the redevelopment area, Turin Street (640), Darling Row (198), and James Street (188).

Meanwhile political changes had led the M.B.[90] to undertake rehousing.[91] Its first estate, called simply Bethnal Green estate, was in the heart of the borough on the site of Kirby's Castle. Privacy had been threatened at Bethnal House asylum (Kirby's Castle) by the construction of Sutton Dwellings and in 1920 the asylum moved to Salisbury. The M.B. purchased the site in 1921, demolished the old house, retained the Cottage, and between 1922 and 1924 built four-storeyed brick blocks named after poets (Burns, Milton, Moore, Morris, Shelley, Swinburne, and Whitman), containing 137 flats.[92]

The second estate, called Lenin by the Communist-Socialist council, opened in 1927 on a corner between Cambridge Heath Road and Parmiter Street. Containing 32 flats in a four-storeyed brick block by the borough architect E. C. P. Monson, who designed most of the subsequent pre-war estates, and described as the 'best in the East End', it provided free electric light and was considered extravagant.[93] In 1928 the name was changed by the new Liberal-Progressive council to Cambridge Heath estate.[94]

Weaver House in Pedley Street, part of the Hare Marsh estate, opened in 1929 with 16 flats. The M.B. had applied to build two blocks in Diss Street, off Hackney Road, in 1922 but the Vaughan estate, containing 20 flats, did not open until 1931. In 1932 the red-brick and concrete Hadrian estate, containing 83 flats, opened south of Hackney Road on what had been Sickle Penfield and work began on Claredale estate, a little to the east on Rush Mead, where a single block of 73 flats opened in 1933.[95] In 1935 the foundation stone was laid of Digby estate, a five-storeyed brick building containing 55 flats east of Globe Road, which opened in 1936.[96] Another 5-storeyed block, Delta estate, north of Gosset Street on Turney estate, which had been proclaimed a clearance area by the L.C.C., was started in 1936 and opened in 1937 with 35 flats.[97] Although started in 1934, the 5-storeyed block of Butler estate, 40 flats fronting Digby Street east of Bacton Street and Digby estate, did not open until 1938.[98] The last pre-war council estate was Burnham, two 5-storeyed blocks containing 80 flats between Globe Road and Burnham Street, started in 1937 and opened in 1939.[99] Bethnal Green M.B. by then had built 601 flats.

The only non-municipal building on a large scale was on Nag's Head Field, declared a clearance area in 1933. The Nag's Head Housing Society then started building flats, north of Shipton Street and west of Ropley Street, which were completed in 1937. A second phase, to the west and bounded by Ravenscroft Street, started in 1939.[1]

The Bethnal Green and East London Housing Association was formed in 1926 by an Industrial Housing Fellowship Group. It was supported by the Poplar Ruridecanal Conference and

85 L.C.C. Housing 1928–30 (1931), 59.
86 Bethnal Green News, 14 July 1934 (T.H.L.H.L., Bethnal Green Cuttings, Housing 1915.53).
87 The other blocks were Norden and Newcourt hos.
88 The Times, 2 Mar. 1936, 11e; L.C.C. Ann. Rep. (1935), ii. 45.
89 Not Trent St. as in The Times, 15 Feb. 1937, 9c.
90 Below, local govt. (local govt. 1900–64).
91 Inf. on boro. council housing from Tower Hamlets L.B. Year Bk. (1981/2); Opening Programme of Reynolds Ho. 1953, containing list of M.B.'s housing schemes (T.H.L.H.L. 331.2B); Bethnal Green M.B. Official Guide (8th edn. c. 1950), 88–9.
92 Robinson and Chesshyre, The Green, 16; Programme for opening of Bethnal Green Est. 1922 (T.H.L.H.L., 331.2B).
93 Programme for Parmiter St. Rehousing Scheme, 1926

(T.H.L.H.L., 331.2B); Daily Mail, 24 Aug., 27 Aug. 1927 and Sunday Worker, 25 Sept. 1927 (T.H.L.H.L., Bethnal Green Cuttings, Housing, Cambridge Heath est.).
94 The Times, 3 Dec. 1928, 16c; 7 Dec. 1928, 10e.
95 Stone-laying programme, 1932 (T.H.L.H.L., 331.2B, Claredale est.).
96 Bethnal Green News, 19 Oct. 1935 and N.E. Bethnal Green Citizen, Aug. 1937 (T.H.L.H.L., Bethnal Green Cuttings, Housing, Digby est.).
97 Opening programme, 1937 (T.H.L.H.L. 331.2B).
98 Stone-laying programme, 1934 (T.H.L.H.L., 331.2B).
99 Stone-laying programme, 1937 (T.H.L.H.L., 331.2B, LC 939).
1 E. Lond. Observer, 18 Feb. 1939 (T.H.L.H.L., Bethnal Green Cuttings, Housing 1915–53).

Hackney Council of Social Services and opened its first block of 15 flats, the four-storeyed Queen Margaret Flats designed by Ian Hamilton, in St. Jude's Road. It also built in Hackney and Poplar and by 1934, when it acquired three houses in Bonner Road, had provided nearly 100 homes at low rents.[2] Philanthropic societies after the First World War provided only Mulberry House, built in 1934 by the East End Dwellings Co. fronting Victoria Park Square north of Montford House in an Art-Deco style.[3]

Private building included Coventry House, 10 flats in Coventry Street for Allen & Hanbury, tenements and workshops at the corner of Cheshire and Menotti streets,[4] a block on the site of nos. 34–40 Viaduct Street for Sebright estate, and a four-storeyed brick and concrete building on the site of nos. 107 and 109 Cambridge Road by S. Leapman, all in 1936, and 24 flats in Cheshire Street by New Era Estates in 1937. Louis de Soissons's application to build on the site of nos. 202–52 Hackney Road in 1938 was presumably frustrated by the war.[5]

Factories, often themselves 5-storeyed, were built between 1918 and 1939 but not individual houses, in spite of the unpopularity of flats. There were objections to most of the L.C.C.'s schemes, both because residents preferred houses with small gardens and because shopkeepers resented losing businesses and paying higher rates.[6]

Colville House on the Waterloo estate was completed by 1940.[7] Building otherwise ceased during the Second World War, when bombing had one beneficial effect in clearing slums. Some 80 tons of bombs fell in the borough, no part of it escaping damage; 555 people were killed and 400 seriously injured. They included 173 who died on 3rd March 1943 in Bethnal Green Underground station when anti-aircraft gunfire caused panic among those rushing down dimly lit stairs to shelter. Evacuation accelerated the decline in population, which in 1945 had fallen to 50,641.[8] Bombing affected 21,700 houses, including 2,233 which were destroyed, 893 made uninhabitable, and 2,457 seriously damaged.[9]

BUILDING AND SOCIAL CONDITIONS AFTER 1945.
The immediate problem after the war was to house those whose homes had been bombed. Longer-term objectives were to complete

and extend earlier clearance programmes in order to reduce the population density and separate industry from residential areas, as reaffirmed in the County of London Plan of 1943.[10] Some 5,000 people lived in temporary housing, including requisitioned properties and hutments or mobile homes, 'prefabs', of which the L.C.C.'s first in East London were in Florida and Squirries streets.[11] All but 15 of its 190 'prefabs' were in use in 1955, together with 309 requisitioned properties;[12] at least 48 mobile homes were still in use in 1966.[13] War damage had been repaired by 1953 and attention shifted to slum clearance; flats were to be allotted to those in cleared areas rather than by a waiting list. The L.C.C. and M.B. co-operated in drawing up five-year plans:[14] by 1954 there were 16,852 permanent homes of which 2,434 were unfit, 1,711 in the L.C.C.'s clearance areas and 675 in the M.B.'s, together with 48 individual houses.[15] The L.C.C. demolished 510 and the M.B. 550 between 1956 and 1960[16] and the M.B. demolished another 151 unfit and 46 other houses in 1961–2.[17] Most were replaced by municipal estates, although both councils also acquired sites scheduled for industry, business, or open space.[18] It was estimated that to find a site and build an estate took six years.[19]

The first estates were on sites scheduled for redevelopment before the war. Bethnal Green No. 1 Redevelopment Area was part of the L.C.C.'s 46-a. clearance area of 1936.[20] It was a 7¼-a. site[21] north of Old Bethnal Green Road consisting of 277 dwellings, mostly small two-storeyed houses accommodating c. 1,400 people, a few workshops, and shops. The L.C.C. had compulsorily purchased most of it and closed four streets in 1938. After bomb damage the L.C.C. in 1945 announced the scheme for the estate, named Minerva after the central street and consisting of 8 three- or four-storeyed blocks in pairs, named after characters in the Trojan war. It was based on plans by the former L.C.C. architect T. H. Forshaw, using one of the pre-war block types but experimenting with monolithic concrete to save materials and labour. Built by Holland & Hannen and Cubitts, the blocks were faced with concrete made from Portland stone salvaged from bombed buildings and had playgrounds on the roof. Begun in 1946 and officially opened in 1948, Minerva estate contained 261 flats for 950 people.[22]

[2] *The Times*, 16 Apr. 1929, 20; 17 Apr. 13c; 8 Oct., 13f; 4 Apr. 1931, 6a; 5 May, 18; 6 May, 11e; *E. Lond. Observer*, 23 Apr. 1932; *City and E. Lond. Observer*, 9 June 1934 (T.H.L.H.L., Bethnal Green Cuttings, Housing 1915–53).
[3] Connor and Critchley, *Red Cliffs of Stepney* (1984), 20.
[4] Possibly Barwell Ho.: O.S. Map 1/2,500, TQ 3482 (1966 edn.).
[5] Cf. O.S. Map 1/2,500, TQ. 3483 (1955 edn.).
[6] *Bethnal Green News*, 25 Sept. 1937; 2 Apr. 1938; *E. Lond. Observer*, 2 Oct. 1937; *Hackney Gaz.* 22 June 1938 (T.H.L.H.L., Bethnal Green Cuttings, Housing 1915–53).
[7] *P.O. Dir. Lond.* (1939, 1940).
[8] G. F. Vale, *Bethnal Green's Ordeal 1939–45*; *The Times*, 19 July 1944, 8a.
[9] Bethnal Green M.B. *Official Guide* (8th edn. c. 1950), 85.
[10] T. H. Forshaw and P. Abercrombie, *County of Lond. Plan* (1943), 83, 160–1.
[11] Bethnal Green M.B. *Official Guide* [1962], 37; L.C.C.

E. End Housing (1963), 28.
[12] L.C.C. *Lond. Statistics*, N.S. i. 107–8.
[13] G.L.C. *Mins.* (1966), 447.
[14] D. V. Donnion, V. Chapman and others, *Social Policy and Admin.* (1965), 47, 50–54.
[15] L.C.C. *Lond. Statistics*, N.S. i. 104–5, 112.
[16] Donnion, *Social Policy*, 55.
[17] L.C.C. *Statistics of Metrop. Boros.* (1960–1, 1961–2).
[18] e.g. Cheshire St.: *G.L.C. Mins.* (1977), 22–23.
[19] G.L.C. Housing Dept. *Ann. Rep.* (1969–70), 61.
[20] Above, building 1915–45.
[21] Inf. on L.C.C. and G.L.C. estates from L.C.C. *E. End Housing* (1963), 30; G.L.C. *Housing Svce. Handbk.* pt. II. *Index of Housing Ests., at Dec. 1974*; Tower Hamlets L.B. *Year Bk.* (1981/2).
[22] L.C.C. *Minerva Est. Bethnal Green Ceremonial Opening*, Apr. 1948; *The Times*, 31 July 1939, 9e; 3 Nov. 1945, 2b; map of air raid incidents in G. F. Vale, *Bethnal Green's Ordeal 1939– 45*.

A still larger scheme was revived for the so called Turin Street or Squirries Street site north of Bethnal Green Road.[23] Compulsory purchase had begun by 1939 and building began in 1945 on Avebury estate, which opened with 208 dwellings in 1948.[24] On 5½ a. to the east private architects, Howes & Jackman, designed red-brick four-storeyed blocks of 99 flats which opened as Teesdale estate in 1949.[25]

Between 1945 and 1951 the L.C.C. built 830 dwellings in Bethnal Green,[26] the others being added to existing estates: Collingwood, with 178 new flats in Grindall, Redmill, and Collingwood houses on the Darling Row site, and Dinmont, with 92 in Beechwood and Sebright houses to the west and Croft House to the north.[27]

The first post-war L.C.C. estate east of Cambridge Heath Road was Park View, opened in 1951 with 207 flats[28] on 7 a. bordered north-east by the canal and Victoria Park, west by St. James's Avenue, and south by Old Ford Road. Bandon Road disappeared as brick blocks replaced Victorian terraces; Mark House, with 60 flats, completed the estate of three 6-storeyed blocks by 1955.[29] During the mid 1950s 128 flats went up in blocks of 3–5 storeys west of the pre-war Wellington (formerly Waterloo) estate.[30]

From the mid 1950s the councils built increasingly tall blocks, encouraged by government grants and by the architects', though not the tenants', preference for a jagged skyline over the monotony of Victorian terraces and lower blocks.[31]

In 1957 the L.C.C. opened Hereford estate, 237 dwellings in blocks of up to 10 storeys on 6½ a. east of Hereford Street. It also began the compulsory purchase of 8½ a. east and north of Collingwood estate containing nearly 300 houses, 7 factories, and a cinema,[32] where by 1962 25 flats had been completed. Lysander House (60 flats) was added to Minerva estate, which had grown to 9½ a. and 354 flats. Other extensions by 1962 included 56 flats in Turin Street, 136 in Satchwell Road, and 340 in Squirries Street, mostly built in the late 1950s,[33] all part of Avebury estate which then covered 20 a., and another 130 flats completed on Teesdale estate. By the end of 1962 the L.C.C. had built 2,317 flats in Bethnal Green since 1945 and controlled a total of 4,213 flats on estates covering 80 a.

The post-war M.B. built to designs by four private firms which worked with its officers, while construction was divided between contractors and the surveyor's department.[34] The resulting flats possessed 'more sympathetic detailing' than contemporary L.C.C. estates.[35] Many were named after left-wing political personalities. Like the L.C.C., the M.B.[36] began with sites scheduled for clearance before the war or built individual blocks on bombed sites.

A site east of Sutton Dwellings, between Globe Road and James Street (renamed Sceptre Road in 1938), was scheduled in 1936.[37] Bombs demolished some of the 93 houses, a church, and several factories and in 1947 the foundation stone was laid of Rogers estate, named after Sgt. Maurice Rogers, a local winner of the V.C.; it opened as two 5-storeyed blocks containing 120 flats in 1949.[38]

In 1950 work began on two blocks off Grove Road, the 5-storeyed brick Bunsen House in Bunsen Street, designed by Donald Hamilton, Wakeford & Partners, with 20 flats, and Hooke House[39] in Thoydon Road, with 48; both blocks opened in 1951. Margaret Bondfield and Beatrice Webb houses, with 9 and 15 flats, opened nearby in Chisenhale Road in 1952 and 1953 respectively.

In 1953 Clarion House with 6 flats was opened in Roman Road, with larger blocks to the north and south: Reynolds House,[40] a 6-storeyed reinforced concrete block of 60 flats designed by Hamilton, Wakeford & Partners at the corner of Bishop's Way and Approach Road, and Stafford Cripps House, with 51 flats on the east side of Globe Road opposite Rogers estate, a site scheduled in 1937 for clearance by the L.C.C. as Lansdell Place.[41] Also in 1953 James Middleton House opened with 45 flats on the south side of Middleton Street, the first post-war municipal estate west of Cambridge Heath Road. Susan Lawrence House opened with 9 flats in Zealand Road near Chisenhale Road in 1954. The M.B. had provided 728 dwellings in the 10 years since 1945.[42]

In 1955 Pepys House opened with 38 flats in two blocks in Kirkwall Place off Globe Road, opposite the pre-war Mendip Houses, and William Fenn House with 16 flats in Shipton Street, near the Nag's Head estate.[43] Work began on the more ambitious Dorset estate, called

23 L.C.C. *Housing Ests.* (1939); *The Times*, 13 Mar. 1939, 11*a*.
24 Bethnal Green M.B. *Tenants' Handbk.* [1950].
25 G.L.R.O., L.C.C./HSG/PP/107.
26 K. Young and P. L. Garside, *Metropolitan Lond.* (1982), 265.
27 Croft Ho. lay in Shoreditch. Bethnal Green M.B. *Tenants' Handbk.* [1950]; Bethnal Green M.B. *Official Guide* (1950), 97; O.S. Map 1/2,500, TQ 3483 (1955 edn.).
28 Bethnal Green M.B. *Official Guide* (1950), 91.
29 *P.O. Dir. Lond.* (1954, 1955).
30 Bethnal Green M.B. *Official Guide* [c. 1962], 39. Colville Ho. (50 flats), built by 1940, apparently inc. in post-war total.
31 *Tower Hamlets News, N.S.* 5(2), June 1976, 6; G. M. L. Simpson, 'Comparative study of contemporary and pre-war geography of E. End of Lond'. (Lond. Univ. M.A. thesis, 1959), 66–7, 70.
32 *E. Lond. Advertizer*, 31 May 1957; *Hackney Gaz.* 7 Mar. 1958 (T.H.L.H.L., Bethnal Green Cuttings, Housing).
33 *P.O. Dir. Lond.* (1951–63); O.S. Map 1/2,500, TQ

3482 (1966 edn.).
34 Donnion, *Social Policy*, 51–52.
35 Pevsner, *Lond.* ii. 73.
36 M.B. estates based on Tower Hamlets L.B. *Year Bk.* (1981/2).
37 L.C.C. *Housing Ests.* (1939).
38 *Stone laying programme*, 1947; *Opening ceremony invitation*, 1949 (T.H.L.H.L., 331.2B, LC 1644); *Hackney Gaz.* 17 Oct. 1949 (T.H.L.H.L., Bethnal Green Cuttings, Housing 1915–53).
39 Named after chairman of housing cttee.:*Stone laying programmes*, 1950 (T.H.L.H.L., 331.2B); Bethnal Green M.B. *Official Guide* (1950), 87.
40 Named after G. W. M. Reynolds, radical founder of *Reynolds News: Opening Programme*, 1953 (T.H.L.H.L., 331.2B).
41 O.S. Map 1/2,500, TQ 3482 (1966 edn.); above, building 1915–45.
42 L.C.C. *Lond. Statistics*, N.S. i.
43 *E. Lond. Papers*, iv(1), 10.

after the Tolpuddle martyrs, on 3 a. around Arline Street, between Diss and Ravenscroft streets off Hackney Road. The original scheme included land to the north fronting Hackney Road, which proved too expensive. Designed by Skinner, Bailey & Lubetkin, the estate was the first to feature high-level blocks, with two 11-storeyed Y-shaped buildings (George Loveless and James Hammett houses) on the north, four 4-storeyed houses (James Brine House) to the south and two more (Robert Owen and Arthur Wade houses) on the south side of Baroness Road. The estate, completed by 1957 and officially opened with 266 flats in 1958,[44] marked a change in municipal housing, with the emphasis on height and reinforced concrete.[45]

Skinner, Bailey & Lubetkin also designed Lakeview estate on a narrow site east of Grove Road, between Old Ford Road and the former Hertford Union canal, where bombing had left only one villa. An 11-storeyed twin tower block of 60 flats was flanked by two 2-storeyed blocks, all the blocks being placed to avoid a northern façade. Built by direct council labour, the estate opened in 1958.[46]

Although Greenways estate[47] on the south side of Roman Road, north and west of Meath Gardens, was started in 1949,[48] it was not officially opened until 1959 and not listed among projects completed by 1955.[49] The original scheme by Yorke, Rosenberg & Mardall was for 341 flats in 5-storeyed blocks, two facing in Warley Street (the Usk Street site) and five north of Meath Gardens (Braemar and Moss Street sites). The eastern Warley Street block (Mary Macarthur House with 60 flats), the two Braemar Street blocks (Chater House with 37 flats and Ellen Wilkinson House with 70), and the westernmost Moss Street block (George Belt House) had been built c. 1950.[50] The second part of the scheme, designed in concrete by Fry, Drew, Drake & Lasdun, was begun in 1952 on 2½ a. to the west and north, partly on the abandoned site of the western Usk Street block. It consisted of the 8-storeyed Sulkin and Trevelyan houses with 24 maisonettes each and the 4-storeyed Jenkinson and Wedgwood houses with 20 maisonettes each. The 8-storeyed cluster blocks by Sir Denys Lasdun were innovative and intended to create a vertical street.[51] Extensions to Greenways were built on the site of St. Simon Zelotes (Jowitt House with 8 flats) and fronting Roman Road: Bevin (with 32 flats) in 1957 and Windsor (28 flats), Clynes (18 flats), Thorne (16 flats), and Sleigh (12 flats) houses by 1959, when

the completed Greenways estate had 515 flats. Sylvia Pankhurst House (12 flats) opened in Bullard's Place in 1962, although not originally considered part of the estate.

Lasdun and his partners designed another cluster block scheme for Claredale estate in 1957. Keeling House, 16-storeyed with 56 stacked maisonettes separated by bands of concrete and 8 bed-sitting rooms on the fifth floor, contrasted with the 6-storeyed Bradley and Connett houses (with 54 and 42 flats) in dark brick. The estate, opened in 1960 in a clearance area, stretched from the pre-war Claredale House to Old Bethnal Green Road, where Peachey Edwards House contained 20 flats for old people.[52]

The Approach Road scheme, opened in 1963, consisted of the 12-storeyed Thomas Hollywood House with 47 flats and the smaller James Campbell and Allen McAuliffe houses with 25 and 6 flats respectively.[53] By 1963 the M.B. had built 1,546 dwellings since the war.[54]

Council building, mainly of high-rise blocks and large estates, continued after the changes from L.C.C. to G.L.C. and from metropolitan to London borough in 1965. The whole of western Bethnal Green was scheduled for redevelopment under a 5-year plan for 1962–7, the southern part for industry, relieved by an open space called Weavers' Fields around Mapes Street, the northern part to be dominated by housing estates.[55]

A new L.C.C. estate, between Boundary and Avebury and called Newling after the street south of Gosset Street, opened in 1963 with 193 flats in blocks of 2–6 storeys.[56] It included Columbia Market on the north side of Columbia Road, which had belonged to the L.C.C. since 1915, had always been a white elephant, and after bombing had been used as a depot. Its Gothic architecture, making it probably the most striking building in Bethnal Green, might have been preserved by a proposal for a county college, but in the early 1960s such preservation was considered 'Quixotic'.[57]

Avebury estate was extended in 1963 by four small blocks west of the Turin Street site near Gibraltar Walk[58] and by Rapley Place, also west of Turin Street, between Lorden Walk and Dence House, where a 6-storeyed block of 18 flats and a 4-storeyed one of 15 were designed in brick by T. P. Bennett & Son of Bloomsbury Square.[59] Another extension was planned in 1967 to house 78 people on the site of St. James the Great's Vicarage in Bethnal Green Road.[60]

44 Ibid. 3–7; *Invitation to stone-laying, 1955* and *Invitation to opening ceremony, 1958* (T.H.L.H.L., 331.2B); *Hackney Gaz.* 26 Mar. 1958 (T.H.L.H.L., Bethnal Green Cuttings, Housing).
45 Donnion, *Social Policy*, 56–57.
46 *E. Lond. Papers*, iv(1), 7–9.
47 Named from 'Greenwayes *alias* Grunwin's Land', i.e. Eastfields: Gascoyne, *Map*. Most of the site, however, belonged to Cradfords: below, estates.
48 *Stone-laying programme, 1949* (T.H.L.H.L., 331.2B).
49 L.C.C. *Lond. Statistics*, N.S. i.
50 Bethnal Green M.B. *Tenants Handbk.* [1950].
51 *Municipal Rev.* Jan. 1954 (T.H.L.H.L., 331.2B, LC 2632); A. Service, *Architects of Lond.* (1973), 194; *Archit. of Lond.* 373–4; *The Times*, 13 Jan. 1958, 10d.

52 *Contract Jnl.* 21 Nov. 1957 (T.H.L.H.L., 331.2B); *Archit. of Lond.* 374; Bethnal Green M.B. *Official Guide* (1963), 40.
53 Bethnal Green M.B. *Official Guide* (1963), 40.
54 Ibid. 38–40. Fig. did not inc. Sylvia Pankhurst Ho. (above).
55 G.L.C. *Mins.* (1964–5), 466, 499.
56 Bethnal Green M.B. *Official Guide* (1963), 39; below, plate 36.
57 Bethnal Green M.B. *Official Guide* (1963), 39; *The Times*, 1 Apr. 1958, 6g; L.C.C. *E. End Housing* [1963], 20.
58 G.L.R.O., LCC/HSG/PP/4.
59 Ibid. 89.
60 G.L.C. *Mins.* (1967), 244.

In 1965 the L.C.C. began modernizing its oldest estate, Boundary Street, reducing the number of flats by adding new bathrooms and kitchens.[61] An adjoining area to the north had been scheduled for redevelopment before the war as Cooper's Gardens.[62] It served as an open space in the late 1950s,[63] was scheduled for an L.C.C. housing estate in 1962,[64] and opened in 1966 as Virginia estate, Casket Street, with 71 dwellings in blocks of 4 and 14 storeys on 1½ a.[65] In 1965 the G.L.C. acquired over 5 a. which it called the Virginia Road site, for 260 dwellings as an extension to Newling estate.[66] New housing was planned in 1968 in Cuff Place, west of Columbia Market, and Nelson Gardens, north of Cobden House on Avebury estate off Old Bethnal Green Road.[67]

Extensions were made to other L.C.C. estates. The Eastman Street area west of Brady Street, south of the pre-war Scott Street development, was cleared in 1958[68] and in 1965 the L.C.C. approved plans by Booth, Ledeboer & Pinckheard for a 5-storeyed block of 20 flats set at a right angle to a 6-storeyed block of 25 maisonettes.[69] The scheme, called Heathpool Court, opened in 1968/9 as part of Collingwood estate.[70] In the extension to the east six out of nine blocks had been completed in 1966, and two more, each of two storeys, for another 63 dwellings, had been proposed. In the same year the G.L.C. approved a 1-a. extension north of Headlam Street, between Buckhurst Street and Cambridge Heath Road, of 56 dwellings in 4- and 7-storeyed blocks.[71] In 1969 it also approved a scheme by Noel Moffett and Associates for 45 flats and maisonettes on 1 a. between Barnsley, Collingwood, and Tapp streets and decided to modernize, thereby reducing in number, some pre-war Collingwood flats.[72] Fronting Cambridge Heath Road, Sovereign House was built c. 1967 and Donegal House by 1970. Orion House, in Barnsley Street by 1974, may have existed by 1971 as Ashington House.[73]

In 1966 the G.L.C. approved a scheme by T. P. Bennett & Son for the 5-storeyed Argos House of 18 flats for the elderly in the south-west corner of Minerva estate[74] and in 1967 another by Pearlman Moiret Associates for a 4-storeyed block of 43 dwellings on 1 a. at Gale's Gardens between the railway and the pre-war Horwood estate.[75] In 1969 the G.L.C. decided to acquire

a factory in Hollybush Gardens, initially for firms displaced by redevelopment,[76] where by 1974 58 flats in 4-storeyed blocks had been added to the pre-war estate.

By 1974 the L.C.C. and G.L.C. had built 3,260 dwellings since 1945 on 108 a. in Bethnal Green, housing nearly 14,000 people.

The M.B. had cleared 14 a. between Old Ford and Roman roads, east of Bonner Street, by 1959 for its most ambitious estate, called Cranbrook after the central street. Terraced houses, workshops, and one large factory were replaced by a figure of eight called Mace Street, which echoed the diagonals of the street pattern to the north.[77] Large and small buildings, of concrete faced with grey brick, were to have an overall density of 136 persons to an acre and to house 600 families.[78] The first blocks opened at the southern end in 1963: the 5-storeyed Holman House, with 48 flats and 12 shops, and the low-rise Stubbs and Tate houses, with 16 and 14 dwellings for old people.[79] Cranbrook estate officially opened in 1964 with 530 dwellings contained in those blocks, in six more of 11–15 storeys named after towns twinned with Bethnal Green,[80] and five of 4 storeys named after demolished streets.[81] The estate, designed by Skinner, Bailey & Lubetkin and constructed by Wates (London), won an award from the Civic Trust. Elizabeth Frink's statue of the Blind Beggar of Bethnal Green was set in a garden in Market Square, surrounded by single-storeyed blocks for the elderly,[82] but was not widely appreciated and was damaged soon after its unveiling in 1959.[83]

In the 1960s the M.B. began to acquire property for refurbishment rather than demolition. In 1963 it purchased 20 of the 120 terraced blocks of Waterlow estate, which were modernized into 234 dwellings.[84] By the beginning of 1964 it owned c. 150 houses, including a three-storeyed Victorian terrace east of Lakeview estate in Old Ford Road, which it converted into flats.[85] The six-storeyed Mayfield House opened with 54 flats in 1964 on the east side of Cambridge Heath Road, south of the town hall.[86]

The new Tower Hamlets L.B. in 1965 announced a 10-year housing programme, initially to complete the schemes of the metropolitan boroughs.[87] In 1965 Tower Hamlets acquired the 19th-century Leopold Buildings (79 flats) in

61 Ibid. (1964–5), 423; (1966), 126; *Town Planning Rev.* xlvii. 171–2.
62 L.C.C. *Housing Ests.* (1939).
63 Simpson, 'Geog. of E. End of Lond.', 32.
64 L.C.C. *E. End Housing* (1963), 31.
65 Casket St. was parallel to Cooper's Gdns., both of which disappeared: O.S. Map 1/2,500, TQ 3382 (1964 edn.); *Tower Hamlets Street Plan* [1988].
66 G.L.C. *Mins.* (1964–5), 459.
67 G.L.C. *Housing Ests. and Sites* (1968).
68 *E. Lond. Advertizer*, 28 Feb. 1958 (T.H.L.H.L., Bethnal Green Cuttings, Housing).
69 G.L.R.O., LCC/HSG/PP/37; G.L.C. *Mins.* (1966), 449.
70 *P.O. Dir. Lond.* (1968, 1969).
71 G.L.C. *Mins.* (1966), 455, 542.
72 Ibid. (1969), 569, 577.
73 *P.O. Dir. Lond.* (1966, 1968, 1970, 1971, 1974).
74 G.L.C. *Mins.* (1966), 374.
75 Ibid. (1967), 613.

76 Ibid. (1969), 327.
77 *The Times*, 10 Apr. 1959, 6a; Tower Hamlets L.B. *Official Boro. Map* (1991); below, plate 34.
78 *E. Lond. Papers*, iv(1), 10–12.
79 Named after M.P. and councillors: *Bethnal Green Civic News*, no. 2, Apr. 1963; *Luncheon menu on completion of Cranbrook St. Scheme 1963*, (T.H.L.H.L., 321.2B).
80 Alzette, Modling, Offenbach, Puteaux, St. Gilles, and Velletri.
81 Ames, Doric, Harold, Longman, and Norton.
82 *The Times*, 11 Mar. 1965, 6; *Municipal Rev.*, May 1965, 274–5 (T.H.L.H.L. 331–2); A. Cunningham and H. Watton, *Glimpses of Globe Town* (1988), 37.
83 *The Times*, 26 Aug. 1959, 10b; 8 Sept. 3f; 18 Sept. 12d.
84 Ibid. 10 Oct. 1962, 2c; Tower Hamlets L.B. *Year Bk.* (1981/2).
85 *Bethnal Green Civic News*, no. 6, Feb. 1964 (T.H.L.H.L., 331.2B, Old Ford Rd.).
86 *Hackney Gaz.* 2 Oct. 1964 (T.H.L.H.L., 331–2).
87 *Tower Hamlets News*, i(2), July 1965, 9.

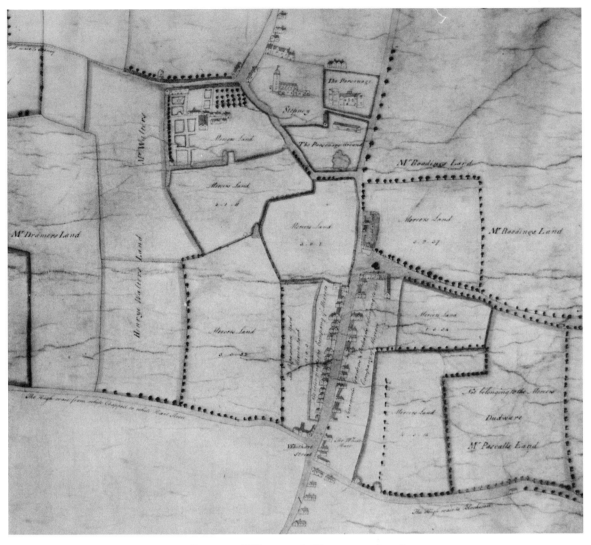

1. Stepney Village and Clevestreet in 1615

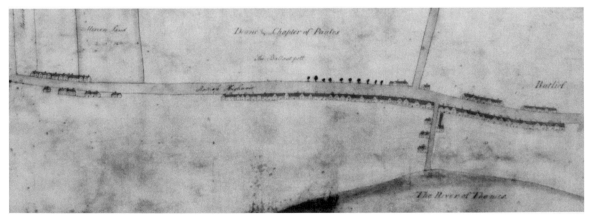

2. Ratcliff Highway in 1615

4. St. Dunstan's and All Saints' Parish Church

3. Anglo-Saxon panel in the parish church

5. Thames Tunnel: plan and section in 1827

6. The Regent's Canal in 1935

7. Docklands Light Railway at Heron Quays

8. King John's Gate in 1791

9. Lady Wentworth's house in 1834

10. St. Dunstan's Parish Church in 1794

11. St. Dunstan's and All Saints' Parish Church

12. Coopers' Almshouses in 1898

13. Bowry's Almshouses in 1857

14. Fuller's Almshouses c. 1850

15. Pemel's Almshouses c. 1850

18. Remains of Aldgate House in 1800

16. Cambridge Heath Road in 1819

17. Bonner's Hall in 1794

19. Netteswell House

20. Victoria Park Square, no. 17

21. Paradise Row, nos 1–11

22. Cambridge Heath turnpike in 1813

23. Kirby's Castle in 1794

24. Dog Row *c.* 1910

25. Cheshire Street in 1955

26. Sclater Street in 1955

27. Hackney Road, nos. 375–85

28. Cambridge Heath Road, nos. 208–10

29. Bishop's Way, nos 111–89 (odd)

30. Butler Street, rear of nos. 7–12

31. Anglesea Street, nos. 4–26

32. Boundary Street area before clearance *c.* 1890

33. Boundary Street estate in 1903

34. Cranbrook estate from the south-west. Roman Road is in the foreground

36. Newling estate

35. Brady Street Dwellings

37. Waterlow estate, model dwellings of 1869

38. Collingwood House, Collingwood estate

39. St. Matthew's Church in 1817

40. Palestine Place Chapel *c.* 1840

41. St. Barnabas's Church

42. St. Peter's Church

43. St. John the Baptist's Church

44. Brick Lane: street market in 1903

45. Brick Lane: demonstration in 1976

Columbia Road and opened five dwellings in Shipton Street and 7 in Cadell Close off Hackney Road; 25 dwellings opened on the east side of Ravenscroft Street as part of the same development in 1966, when the high-rise Sivill House opened with 76 flats in Columbia Road.

Bethnal Green M.B.'s slum clearance programme, intended to end in 1965, included an area between Hackney and Old Bethnal Green roads, bounded west and east by Warner Place and Mansford Road. It covered the pre-war Hadrian estate and the L.C.C. agreed to develop the southern part, which adjoined its Avebury estate,[88] leaving 3½ a. to the M.B., which planned 6-storeyed blocks with 176 dwellings.[89] Mary Janes and Sheppard houses, with 16 and 46 flats, opened in Warner Place in 1966 and Wyndham Deedes House,[90] with 38 flats in Hackney Road, and Blythenhale and George Vale[91] houses, with 54 and 22 flats in Mansford Street, in 1967. The estate was called St. Peter's after the church which alone had survived clearance.

In 1966 Keats House (22 flats) in Roman Road was added to Bethnal Green estate and, to the east, the 14-storeyed Bacton Tower (52 flats) opened at the junction of Roman and Globe roads. Designed by Yorke, Rosenberg & Mardall and built by Wates, Bacton Tower was the first fully industrialized block built for Tower Hamlets and featured ceramic tiles cast on the site.[92]

Council flats built by the L.B. in 1967 included 12 in Walter Street, 23 in Morpeth Street, 4 in Knottisford Street, 25 in Portman Place, all south of Roman Road in Globe Town, and 7 in Bonner Street and 8 in Mace Street, north of Roman Road on Cranbrook estate. In 1968 Tuscan House opened with 48 flats in Knottisford Street and 24 flats in Robinson Road and 40 in Russia Lane were added to Approach estate, replacing the notorious Quinn Square.[93]

The enthusiasm for high-rise building, at its height in 1966 when the L.B.'s architects were 'now working on tall blocks',[94] culminated in Bethnal Green in 1969 when the 22-storeyed Charles Dickens House opened with 130 flats in Mansford Street. The collapse of Ronan Point flats (West Ham, Essex) in 1968, however, proved to be a turning point, as both the G.L.C. and the L.B. switched to low-rise building or refurbishment.[95]

In 1969 Tower Hamlets approved schemes by its architect's department for two estates of compact cluster blocks, mostly four-storeyed with lower wings, which could be linked or grouped to give an informal appearance. They were built of brick with timber windows and had gardens, the emphasis being on privacy.[96]

Rowley Bros. of Tottenham, who had built some of the Roman Road flats, agreed to build 4-storeyed flats on 7½ a. around Lanfranc Road, between Roman, Arbery, Grove, and Medway roads. The site included Clarion and Hooke houses of the 1950s and a public house, everything else to make way for an estate to be completed in 1971. Twelve blocks with 269 dwellings were grouped amid landscaping and named after naval destroyers.[97] After Rowley Bros. went bankrupt in 1971 the estate was completed by F. G. Minter and J. & R. Rooff and opened between 1972 and 1975.[98]

The second scheme was for six blocks containing 66 dwellings on 2 a. west of Mansford Street, which included the nearly completed Charles Dickens House and was part of a clearance area where Mansford Buildings had been compulsorily purchased in 1965.[99] Whyatt (Builders), recently responsible for extensions to Greenways estate in Walter Street and Roman Road, agreed to complete the estate in 1971;[1] Southwood House opened with 21 flats in Florida Street in 1971 and Jeremy Bentham House with 30 in Pollard Street in 1972. A third stage,[2] announced in 1972, was for 97 dwellings in nine 4-storeyed blocks[3] on 2½ a. stretching east from Mansford Street to Canrobert Street. Teesdale, Blythe, and Wear streets were accordingly closed.[4] The nine blocks opened between 1975 and 1976. John Nettlefold House, with 14 dwellings, opened at no. 375 Bethnal Green Road in 1981.

In 1972 Tower Hamlets designated the area between Patriot Square, Bethnal Green hospital, and Cambridge Heath Road for redevelopment, where demolition and the closure of Peel Grove were to make room for 106 dwellings. Problems were feared from the existence of a 'plague pit', in reality the 19th-century Peel Grove cemetery.[5] The four 3-storeyed blocks, named after prominent inhabitants,[6] opened in 1977 and included houses for the elderly.[7] Another 3-storeyed estate opened in 1977 was Brierley Gardens, 96 dwellings on the site of Brierley and Royston streets.[8] Although Tower Hamlets had more than 1,000 houses planned, its building was ended by government restrictions in 1980.[9]

G.L.C. building continued in the late 1970s in

88 i.e. Nelson Gdns., below.
89 *Bethnal Green Civic News*, no. 4, 1963 (T.H.L.H.L., 331.2B).
90 Sir Wyndham Hen. Deedes (1883–1956), soldier, administrator, and local politician, lived at no. 17 Victoria Park Sq. 1923–39: Robinson and Chesshyre, *The Green*, 25; *D.N.B.*
91 Named after local historian.
92 *Tower Hamlets News*, 2(1), May 1966, 12, 15; 2(6), Mar. 1967, 74.
93 Ibid. 6(4), Mar. 1971, 3.
94 *Tower Hamlets News*, 2(1), May 1966, 15.
95 Ibid. 5(2), July 1969, 3; N.S. 5(2), June 1976, 6; G.L.C. Housing Dept. *Ann. Rep. 1968–9*, 7, 16.
96 *Tower Hamlets News*, 5(2), July 1969, 1.
97 Ardent, Crane, Daring, Diamond, Exmouth, Grenville, Hyperion, Imperial, Ivanhoe, Mohawk, Sturdy, and Wren.
98 *Tower Hamlets News*, N.S. 2(2), June 1973.

99 *The Times*, 7 May 1965, 17d; below.
1 *Tower Hamlets News*, 5(2), July 1969, 1; 6(4), Mar. 1971, 3.
2 The first was presumably Chas. Dickens Ho.
3 Adrian Boult, John Fielden, Gwilym Maries, Jos. Priestley, and Wm. Rathbone hos. were named in 1972. The others were Chas. Darwin, John Cartwright, Thos. Burt, and Wm. Channing hos.
4 *Tower Hamlets News*, N.S. i(4), Oct. 1972, 6.
5 Ibid. i(3), Aug. 1972; *E. Lond. Advertizer*, 21 July 1972 (T.H.L.H.L., 331.2B).
6 Ebenezer Mussel, Hugh Platt, Jas. Docherty, Wm. Caslon.
7 *Tower Hamlets News*, N.S. 6(6), Feb. 1978, 5; *East End*, 5 Aug. 1978 (T.H.L.H.L., 331.2B).
8 Plan on site.
9 *E. Lond. Advertizer*, 31 Oct. 1980 (T.H.L.H.L. Cuttings 331.2).

western Bethnal Green, north of Bethnal Green Road, between Boundary and Newling estates and south of Bethnal Green Road on a new estate around Granby Street. In 1971 Boundary Street estate's Streatley Buildings, on the east side of Swanfield Street, was demolished[10] and 1 a. to the south called Boreham Street, containing 49 houses, 19 workshops, a warehouse, and 10 shops, was about to be cleared.[11] It was scheduled for 30 dwellings in 1974, part of Virginia estate.[12] In 1976 the G.L.C. planned 181 dwellings for the estate, on 7 a. in 2- and 3-storeyed terraces with two 4-storeyed blocks of maisonettes fronting Chambord Street. The north-west corner, adjoining the existing Virginia estate at Casket Street, was to be temporarily retained for businesses and later replaced by housing.[13] By 1982 there were 252 dwellings on the estate.

In 1966 the G.L.C. was acquiring property, much of it industrial, around Granby Street under the Housing Act of 1957.[14] It was probably the Ronan Point disaster which brought a new sensitivity to the G.L.C.'s architectural department, which in 1971 was planning a low-rise estate and consulting local inhabitants.[15] Granby estate, between Chilton Street and St. Matthew's Row and incorporating Bentworth Court and Goldman Close in place of the old street pattern, opened in 1977 with 280 dwellings.[16]

By the early 1980s[17] the G.L.C. owned 5,865 flats in the former M.B., 4,439 of them built since the war. Tower Hamlets L.B. owned 4,785 dwellings, of which 4,166 had been built or acquired since the war. The G.L.C.'s flats were contained in 15 relatively compact estates of 1½ a.–23 a. in extent. The L.B.'s dwellings comprised 77 sites, some large and compact estates, some individual blocks on bombed sites, and some terraced houses bought by the council.

Consolidation by 1986[18] had produced 15 estates for the G.L.C. and 11 for the L.B. The G.L.C.'s were Boundary, Collingwood, Dinmont, Hollybush Gardens, Horwood, Waterloo, Pritchard, Minerva, Avebury, Teesdale, Park View, Hereford (which included Granby), Newling, Virginia, and Charlwood. Tower Hamlets' were Rogers,[19] Approach,[20] Weaver House, Dorset,[21] St. Peter's or Claredale,[22] Digby,[23] Lakeview or Lanfranc,[24] Mansford, Greenways,[25] Waterlow, and Cranbrook.[26]

The history of Bethnal Green since 1945 has been determined by the importance of the public sector. By the mid 1950s nearly one third of all housing stock, in 1961 over 40 per cent, was owned by the L.C.C. or M.B.[27] and by the late 1970s their successors owned more than three-quarters.[28] There was little private building for domestic purposes. The last block of Nag's Head estate, Shipton House, was built in 1947 and the estate was sold to the Peabody Trust in 1956.[29]

Slum clearance affected not only the housing rented out for private profit, still 55 per cent in 1961,[30] but the earlier blocks of flats erected on a semi-charitable basis by the trusts. All the property of the Improved Industrial Dwellings Co. was disposed of, having by the early 1960s become 'malodorous litter dens'.[31] The Waterlow estate had been taken over by Greencoat Properties and in 1963 by the M.B., which later also bought Leopold Buildings. Huntingdon Buildings were owned by the G.L.C. when closed in 1969; one block was demolished in the early 1970s and another in 1980,[32] the rest being improved to accommodate, by 1988, Huntingdon Industrial Units. The last of the Improved Industrial Dwellings Co.'s estates was Jesus Hospital charity estate. The G.L.C. bought a small piece in the south-west corner in 1970 and the central triangle, which became a public open space, in 1979. The rest of the estate was conveyed in 1980 to Structadene, a Hackney firm which refurbished the Victorian terraces.[33]

Of the East End Dwelling Co.'s properties, Meadows Dwellings closed in 1962 and were demolished by 1971 to make way for Mansford estate, while Ravenscroft was emptied in 1970 and demolished partly in 1982 and, after featuring as a home for fallen women in the film 'The Missionary', finally in 1984. Of the group between Victoria Park Square and Globe Road, the war-damaged Merceron Houses were replaced in 1949 while Westbrook House was built to the south c. 1950. Two blocks of Merceron and Gretton houses were demolished in 1982 and the rest, Merceron, Gretton, Evesham, Montford, Mulberry, and Westbrook houses, were taken over by

10 *Town Planning Rev.*, xlvii. 171–2.
11 G.L.C. *Mins.* (1971), 263.
12 G.L.C. *Housing Svce. Handbk.* pt. II. *Index of Housing Ests.* Dec. 1974.
13 G.L.C. *Architects Rev.* 2 (1976), 77–78.
14 G.L.C. *Mins.* (1966), 447.
15 Ibid. (1970), 721; *The Times*, 6 Oct. 1971, 5g.
16 G.L.C. *Mins.* (1977), 406; plan on site.
17 Based on Tower Hamlets L.B. *Year Bk.* (1981/2) but inc. hos. acquired but not listed.
18 Tower Hamlets L.B. *Official Boro. Map. Inf. Map no. 7.5. Housing Ests. Jan. 1986.* Key to map in ibid. *Guide to Housing Ests.* (Sept. 1981); Tower Hamlets L.B. Housing Dept. *Postal Index to Council-owned Dwellings* (Apr. 1967), all in T.H.L.H.L. And see map.
19 Inc. Bethnal Green, Burnham, and Brierley Gdns. ests. and Pepys Ho.
20 Inc. Cambridge Heath and Patriot Sq. ests., Mayfield Ho., Robinson Rd., Russia La., Reynolds Ho. and Approach Rd.
21 Inc. Vaughan est., Leopold Bldgs., Wm. Fenn and Sivill hos., Shipton St., and Cadell Close.

22 Inc. Delta and Hadrian ests.
23 Inc. Butler est., Bacton Tower, Stafford Cripps and Tuscan hos., hos. in Knottisford and Morpeth sts. and Portman Pl., and (formerly in Greenways est.) Bevin, Clynes, Sleigh, and Thorne hos.
24 Inc. Bunsen, Hooke, Marg. Bondfield, Beatrice Webb, Clarion, Sus. Lawrence hos. and hos. acquired in Chisenhale, Driffield, Ellesmere, Grove, Kenilworth, Medway, Old Ford, Vivian, and Zealand rds.
25 Inc. Sylvia Pankhurst Ho. and hos. in Walter St.
26 Inc. hos. in Bonner and Mace sts. and Old Ford Rd.
27 M. Young and P. Willmott, *Family and Kinship in E. Lond.* (1962), 41 and n.; *Census*, 1961.
28 *Tower Hamlets Boro. Plan* (1986), 34; *Tower Hamlets News*, 4(3), Oct. 1975, 5.
29 Inf. from Peabody Trust. 30 *Census*, 1961.
31 Connor and Critchley, *Palaces for the Poor*, 28.
32 Ibid. 29, illus. betw. pp. 14 and 15; G.L.R.O., CL/HIG/2/163.
33 Inf. from Clerk to the Visitors, Jesus Hosp. Char. and Structadene Ltd. (1993).

the G.L.C. as Victoria Park Square or Charlwood estate.[34]

The first of the model dwellings, Columbia Square flats, in 1957 were very damp. The M.B. bought them in 1961, demolished them in 1962,[35] and built Sivill House on the site. Other model dwellings which made way for council flats included Brady's Buildings in Barnet Grove (for Avebury estate), Queen's Buildings in Gosset Street (for Virginia estate), Barnsley and Somerford houses (for Collingwood estate), and Mansford and Toye's Buildings (for Mansford estate). Craven Buildings, a 'grim five-storey tenement block' of the late 19th century in Poyser Street near the railway, was in 1967 about to make way for a building for handicapped children.[36] Demolition proposed in 1963 for Linden Buildings in Shacklewell Street[37] had provided a public open space by 1973.[38]

The G.L.C. began to retreat from its leading role in local housing when Conservatives took over in 1967. Until stopped by the Labour government in 1968, it offered to sell its council houses to tenants and planned to transfer estates to the London boroughs, although it continued with a reduced building programme.[39] Meanwhile it began to turn to conservation, declaring in 1967 10 conservation areas in Tower Hamlets, one of which, Bethnal Green Gardens, was in the former Bethnal Green M.B.[40]

The Labour-dominated L.B. was slower to relinquish housing and refused to take over G.L.C. estates in 1969 largely for financial reasons.[41] From 1970 successive governments favoured modernizing the existing stock.[42] In 1977 when the G.L.C. reiterated its policy of encouraging home ownership and transferring estates to the boroughs,[43] Tower Hamlets devoted only 17 per cent of its total expenditure to housing. Its largest expense, 35 per cent, was on social services,[44] partly necessitated by its own earlier policies.

By the end of the 1970s the post-war objectives had been attained, population had been reduced by 44 per cent and railway land by 37 per cent, only to produce a 'dying inner city' with acute financial problems. A shrunken population, industry, and commerce had lowered income while capital expenditure on clearance and estate building was enormous. Much of the open space

was derelict land and the need was for investment in attracting business and in refurbishment rather than demolition.[45] In 1977 the G.L.C. possessed 39 per cent of all vacant land in Tower Hamlets, which it had acquired under clearance schemes but had no plans to redevelop; Tower Hamlets owned another 26 per cent.[46] By 1984 Tower Hamlets acknowledged its prime problem, exacerbated by the national recession, to be the lack of employment created by displacing firms for housing estates. In future it would prevent the conversion of industrial premises, create industrial improvement areas, as at the northern end of Brick Lane, and allow office developments, especially near Underground stations.[47] A Borough Plan, published in 1986 when unemployment in Tower Hamlets was the highest in London, listed sites scheduled for light industry: several fronting Hackney Road and others in Pritchard's Road, Shacklewell, Bacon, and Cheshire streets in the west and Coborn Road in the east.[48] When the plan was slightly modified in 1988 unemployment, at 18 per cent, was the second highest in London.[49]

Refurbishment applied both to council housing and to the few remaining old houses. General Improvement Areas were declared where all property was to be modernized, for example Driffield Road in 1975[50] and the Barnet Jesus Hospital estate in 1986.[51] From the mid 1970s Tower Hamlets assumed some of the G.L.C.'s responsibilities, taking over the western Bethnal Green comprehensive area in 1976.[52] In 1979, after discussions with the G.L.C. begun in 1977, a joint housing management committee was set up but in 1982 the L.B. withdrew, setting up its own housing directorate and management districts.[53]

The council's greatest challenge by the 1970s came from its own estates, in 1986 'cramped, unlovely and unloved'.[54] Not only did the older ones need refurbishment but the newer were plagued by vandalism, reported in tower blocks in 1974, or by defects as on the recently built Donegal and Sovereign houses on Collingwood estate in 1970 and in 69 per cent of flats on Lanfranc estate in 1978.[55] Among the most dilapidated in 1981 were Greenways and Claredale.[56] Rogers estate was rife with crime, its passages and walkways providing rat-runs for

34 Connor and Critchley, *Red Cliffs of Stepney* (1984), 22–4; (1987) 42–3; inf. from Globe Town neighbourhood; *P.O. Dir. Lond.* (1950, 1951).
35 *E. Lond. Advertizer*, 20 Sept. 1957; *The Estates Gaz.* 2 Sept. 1961 (T.H.L.H.L., Bethnal Green Cuttings, Housing); Connor and Critchley, *Palaces for the Poor*, 13–14.
36 *Tower Hamlets News*, 3(2), June 1967, 21.
37 G.L.R.O., CL/HIG/2/163.
38 *Tower Hamlets News*, N.S. 2(5), Dec. 1973.
39 G.L.C. Housing Dept. *Ann. Rep.* (1968–9), 16; (1969–70), 3; (1971–3), 8; *Whitaker's Almanack* (1970, 1974, 1982) s.v. G.L.C.
40 *Tower Hamlets News*, 5(3), Nov. 1969.
41 Ibid. 5(2), 1.
42 Ibid. 5(2), June 1976, 6.
43 G.L.C. *Mins.* (1977), 389.
44 *Tower Hamlets News*, 6(1), Apr. 1977, 5.
45 A. Coleman, 'Land Use in Tower Hamlets. Rep. for 2nd Land Utilization Survey'. (TS. in T.H.L.H.L., Pamphlet 720); Tower Hamlets L.B. Planning Dept. *Vacant Land in Tower Hamlets*, Oct. 1978 (T.H.L.H.L. pamphlets 720).

46 Tower Hamlets L.B. Planning Dept. *Vacant Land in Tower Hamlets*, Oct. 1978 (T.H.L.H.L. pamphlets 720); G.L.C. *Mins.* (1977), 22–3.
47 Tower Hamlets L.B. *Planning Handbk.* [1984].
48 *Tower Hamlets Boro. Plan*, 1986, p. 157.
49 Tower Hamlets L.B. *Proposed Draft Alterations to Boro. Plan Proposals*, 1988.
50 *Tower Hamlets News*, 4(3), Oct. 1975, 5.
51 *Tower Hamlets Boro. Plan*, 1986, p. 13.
52 G.L.C. *Mins.* (1976), 872. In 1976 Tower Hamlets accepted Brady St. Bldgs., just S. of the Bethnal Green boundary, which had been offered to the G.L.C. for conversion: *Tower Hamlets News*, 4(5), Feb. 1976.
53 *Tower Hamlets News*, 6(2), June 1977; ibid. June 1983; Tower Hamlets L.B. *Ann. Rep.* (1982/3), 13; Tower Hamlets L.B. *Official Boro. Map, Inf. Map no. 7.5. Housing Ests. Jan. 1986.*
54 *Tower Hamlets Boro. Plan*, 1986, p. 13.
55 G.L.C. *Mins.* (1970), 159; *Tower Hamlets News*, N.S. 3(4), Dec. 1974, 8; *E. End*, 8 Apr. 1978 (T.H.L.H.L. 331.2).
56 *E. Lond. Advertiser*, 2 Oct. 1981 (T.H.L.H.L. 331.2B).

BETHNAL GREEN: HOUSING ESTATES c. 1986

L.C.C. and G.L.C. ESTATES

 Pre-Second World War   Post-Second World War

1 Boundary Street 1895, 1a Boundary Street block demolished 1971, 2 Collingwood 1923, 2a Darling Row and other eastern extensions, 2b Eastman Street, 3 Dinmont 1934, 3a extension, 4 Hollybush Gardens 1936, 5 Horwood 1937, 5a Gales Gardens, 6 Wellington (Waterloo) 1937, 6a extensions, 7 Pritchard 1938, 8 Minerva 1948, 9 Avebury 1948 onwards, 10 Teesdale 1949, 11 Park View 1951, 12 Hereford 1957, 12a Granby Street, 13 Newling 1963 onwards, 14 Virginia 1966, 15 Victoria Park Square (Charlwood), acquired 1982

BETHNAL GREEN M. B. and TOWER HAMLETS L.B. ESTATES

 Pre-Second World War   Post-Second World War

1 Rogers, 1a Bethnal Green 1922, 1b Burnham 1939, 1c Rogers 1949, 1d Pepys House 1955, 1e Brierley Gardens 1977, 2 Approach, 2a Cambridge Heath (Lenin) 1927, 2b Reynolds House 1953, 2c Approach Road Scheme 1963, 2d Mayfield House 1964, 2e Patriot Square 1977, 3 Weaver House 1929, 4 Dorset, 4a Vaughan 1931, 4b Dorset 1958, 4c Leopold Buildings, acquired 1965, 4d Sir Graham Rowlandson House 1978/84, 5 St. Peters, 5a Hadrian 1932, 5b Claredale House 1933, 5c Delta 1937, 5d Claredale 1960, 5e Mary Janes and Shephard Houses 1966, 5f Barnet Grove, 6 Digby, 6a Digby 1936, 6b Butler 1938, 6c post-war extensions 1953–68, 7 Lakeview, 7a Bunsen House 1951, 7b Lanfranc 1974 (including Hooke House 1951), 7c Margaret Bondfield House 1952, 7d Beatrice Webb House 1953, 7e Susan Lawrence House 1954, 7f Lakeview 1958, 8 Mansford, 8a James Middleton House 1953, 8b Mansford 1969–81, 9 Greenways 1959, 10 Waterlow, acquired 1963, 11 Cranbrook 1964

COMPANY AND PRIVATE ESTATES

1 Improved Industrial Dwellings Co., 1a Jesus Hospital Barnet c. 1868, 1b Waterlow 1869, 1c Leopold Buildings 1871, 2 East End Dwellings Co., 2a Museum Buildings 1888, 2b Mendip and Shepton Houses 1900, 2c Evesham and Montford Houses 1901, 2d Mulberry House 1934, 3 Guinness Trust 1901, 4 Four Per Cent Industrial Dwellings Co., Mocatta House 1905, 5 Sutton Dwellings Trust 1909, 6 Peabody Trust 1910 (and see 8), 7 Bethnal Green And East London Housing Association Ltd., Queen Margaret Flats 1926, 8 Nag's Head 1933, acquired by Peabody Trust 1957, 9 Bates 1970.

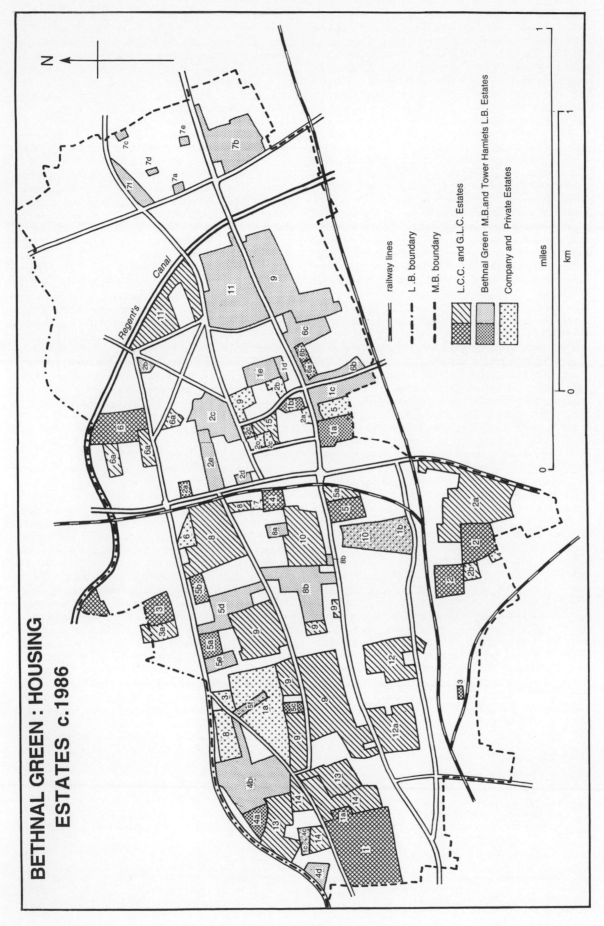

FIG. 22 BETHNAL GREEN HOUSING ESTATES c. 1986

criminals which recalled the 19th-century Nichol. In 1990 the author of the critical report of *c.* 1978 was invited to modify its design, add bungalows and gardens, reorientate entrances, and block passageways.[57] Disillusion with high-rise building culminated in 1993 with a demand for the demolition of Lasdun's Keeling House, a 'symbol of everything that was wrong with doctrinaire post-war planning'.[58] Although it became the country's only listed tower block in 1993, it was empty and again threatened with demolition in 1995.[59]

Modernization was attempted: Tower Hamlets announced plans for Butler estate in 1980 and renovated one block of Burnham in 1985 before funds ran out. Recourse was had to the private sector, especially after the G.L.C.'s abolition in 1986 when its estates passed to Tower Hamlets and were broken up by the Alliance into seven neighbourhoods with responsibility for housing. Three, Bethnal Green, Globe Town, and Bow, covered parts of the old M.B., although all contained districts outside it. Among further adjustments Lakeview, which fell within Bow neighbourhood, by 1993 was classified as part of Ranwell West estate.[60]

The new council policy, emphasizing local responsibility and reinforced by financial constraints, was to offer council housing to tenants for sale or in self-help schemes or encourage housing associations and trusts. At the end of the 1980s nearly 2,000 council tenants in Bethnal Green and Globe Town neighbourhoods were said to be buying their homes;[61] tenants on Burnham estate agreed in 1989 to renovate their own flats in a privately financed scheme.[62] Proposals in 1986 to privatize whole estates, including Bethnal Green, Boundary, Bacton Towers, Hadrian, and Waterlow, provoked tenants to form the Tower Hamlets Campaign Against Estates Sales.[63] At the end of 1986 Bethnal Green neighbourhood decided to sell Hadrian estate to five property developers.[64] In 1987 it agreed that Barretts should refurbish Waterlow estate, return 125 flats to the council to rent, and sell 105 cheaply to local people and 70 on the open market. Such projects and Structadene Ltd.'s refurbishment of 19th-century terraces on the Jesus Hospital estate led to attacks on gentrification. Protestors pointed to the many empty properties and the long official waiting list but offered no solution to the expense of renovation.[65]

In 1988 Tower Hamlets hoped for 'greater flexibility in the management of housing stock'[66] and adopted the proposal of the government, which had intervened through rate-capping, to involve

Housing Action Trusts, despite opposition by both council employees and many tenants. Boundary Street estate was one suggested by the government[67] but one of the first was Hadrian estate, which was handed over to Samuel Lewis Housing Trust and demolished in 1990.[68] The trust,[69] founded in 1901 by will of the eponymous London financier to provide rented accommodation, became in 1991 part of the Southern Housing Group with an office for the East Region in Bethnal Green Road. It absorbed earlier associations like the Elizabeth Bates Housing Society, which had been founded in 1955 to provide housing on the Elizabeth Bates Trust estate in Bethnal Green. The society refurbished the Victorian houses in Cyprus Street and built four mainly seven-storeyed blocks of flats (Kingswood, Malmesbury, Tytherton, and Brockweir) at the western end of the estate in the late 1960s. The society possessed approximately 315 units in Tower Hamlets when financial and staffing difficulties led to its merger with the Samuel Lewis Housing Trust in 1993. For Hadrian estate the Samuel Lewis Housing Trust contracted Laing Homes to complete by 1992 43 flats, maisonettes, and houses for homeless tenants, 65 per cent white and 35 per cent Bengali. Laing also worked from 1992 in Selby Street, on council and railway land on the southern borders of Bethnal Green and Spitalfields, where 116 houses and flats, designed by Feilden & Manson, were planned by a consortium of Samuel Lewis Housing Trust and three other housing associations, Toynbee, Spitalfields, and Newlon.

Housing associations assumed an increasing importance. At the end of the 1960s the G.L.C. had recognized their role in the improvement of older houses and had offered them loans.[70] Associations, however, owned under 4 per cent of Tower Hamlets' housing in 1974.[71] With more official encouragement their activities expanded, most still converting old property but others building their own estates. Among the chief was Circle Thirty Three, which had 460 properties in Tower Hamlets by 1992.[72] They included acquisitions in Driffield Road in 1979 and Baxendale Street in 1985, and new developments at Coll Sharp Court in the junction of Austin Street and Virginia Road in 1990 and Royston estate, west of Cranbrook, in 1992.[73] Bethnal Green and East London Housing Association, active in Bethnal Green since the 1920s, was registered as a charity in 1961[74] and amalgamated in 1993 with Victoria Park Housing Association. In 1988 redevelopment of

57 *Building*, 23 Nov. 1990 (T.H.L.H.L. 331.2B).
58 *Independent*, 27 Jan. 1993 (T.H.L.H.L., Cuttings 331.2).
59 *The Times*, 2 Nov. 1995, 7g.
60 Inf. from Bow neighbourhood.
61 *Right to Buy* (Leaflet, T.H.L.H.L., 331.2).
62 *Independent*, 4 Sept. 1989 (T.H.L.H.L., 331.2).
63 *Mtg. by Tower Hamlets Fed. of Tenants, Oxford Ho. 29 Oct.* [1986] (T.H.L.H.L., 331.2); *Spitalfields News*, Apr. 1987, 6.
64 *Morning Star*, 3 Dec. 1986 (T.H.L.H.L. Cuttings 331.2).
65 *Spitalfields News*, Apr. 1987, 6.
66 Tower Hamlets L.B. *Proposed Draft Alterations to*

Boro. Plan Proposals (1988), 10.
67 *News Line*, 20 July 1988; *Housing and Planning Rev.* 44(1), Feb./May 1989; leaflet by NALGO 1988 (T.H.L.H.L. 331.2).
68 *E. Lond. Advertizer*, 27 Apr. 1990 (T.H.L.H.L. 331.2).
69 Rest of para. based on inf. from Sam. Lewis Housing Trust Ltd.
70 G.L.C. Housing Dept. *Ann. Rep.* (1968–9), 7.
71 *Tower Hamlets News*, 4(3), Oct. 1975, 5.
72 Circle Thirty Three Housing Trust, *25th Anniv. Yearbk.* (1993); *V.C.H. Mdx.* x. 16. Name derived from 32 L.B. and City of Lond.
73 Inf. from Circle Thirty Three Housing Trust.
74 Char. Com. file no. 249131.

the site of Bethnal Green hospital was discussed[75] and in 1990 Victoria Park Housing Association bought the eastern part, bounded north by Parmiter Street and east by Russia Lane. Its mixed development, opened in 1993, included Ted Roberts House, named after the association's founder and vicar of St. James the Less (1961–78), with 30 flats for the elderly, Roger Dowley Court, comprising a day hospital on the ground floor and 32 shared flats, and, grouped around a new road, Huddleston Close with 40 houses, 12 shared flats, and two houses offering 'care in the community', for people with learning difficulties or mental illness. The architects were Baily Garner and the builders Willmott Dixon. Other properties of the association included Approach Road, opened in 1992 for people with mental health problems, and small developments in Bishop's Way and, for the elderly, in Globe Road.[76]

The western part of the hospital site was sold to Structadene, which built flats in a 3-storeyed yellow-brick block called Heritage Place, a supermarket, office units, and a doctor's clinic in 1993. The firm was also working in Old Ford Road.[77] Other private developments in the 1990s included 4-storeyed flats in a vaguely classical style, The Academy Court at the corner of Globe Road and Kirkwall Place, Jameson Court in Russia Lane, and City Walk, flats around a courtyard in St. Matthew's Row.[78] Other projects to attract middle-class buyers included the conversion of churches, like St. James the Great in Bethnal Green Road and the Methodist chapel in Hackney Road. In 1991 Tower Hamlets Environment Trust, which had been set up in 1979, was engaged in a 'Green Homes in Bethnal Green project', building 34 houses to new environmental specifications.[79] From c. 1990 Globe Town neighbourhood disposed of Cambridge Heath, Digby, and Bacton Tower estates, in addition to the portion of Burnham estate relinquished earlier.[80]

The appearance of Bethnal Green was transformed between 1945 and 1995. Endless streets of two-storeyed cottages of c. 1840–60[81] where the typical home was a 4-roomed house with a yard full of boxes of geraniums, rabbit hutches, pigeon lofts, 'dilapidated but cosy, damp but friendly',[82] made way for equally monotonous rows of 5-storeyed blocks or high- and low-rise estates whose intended landscaped grounds more often became empty or waste-strewn spaces. In 1945 poverty was such that 89 per cent of families were said to be without bathrooms.[83] By 1951 79 per cent were still without or sharing a bathroom; 37 per cent lacked a

W.C., 35 per cent piped water, 27 per cent a kitchen sink, and 4 per cent a cooking stove. By 1961 those lacking the first three facilities had fallen to 58, 29, and 7.6 per cent.[84] Overcrowding also lessened: where there had been 1.35 families for each dwelling in 1931, there were 1.24 in 1951 and 1.15 in 1961. Families becoming smaller, the density for each room averaged 1.35 in 1931, 0.92 in 1951, and 0.84 in 1961.[85] By the 1980s there were 'probably as many homes in the borough as there are households'.[86]

Bethnal Green could be presented in the early 1950s as 'some sort of Utopia.'[87] The streets, though crowded with stalls, were bearable because 'no one in Bethnal Green owns a motor-car'. Strong local loyalties and a respectable working class, which engaged in fanatical door-step-scrubbing in areas like Mace Street and Gibraltar Walk,[88] made for a stable society described in 1951 as orderly and safe.[89] Most people had been born in the borough, like their parents and probably grandparents, and lived near their relatives, the wife's mother in particular being the centre of family life. Most had private landlords and obtained tenancies through the mother's connexions and her influence with the rent collector. The unemployment and grinding labour of earlier periods were over, small workshops in the many buildings left empty by bombing and slum clearance offering a variety of jobs for men and part-time work for women. Both birth and death rates had fallen, leaving fewer widows and orphans, while television was beginning to weaken the power of the public house over the men. It was a homogeneous society, working-class and English although with some who still cherished their Huguenot ancestry.[90] Many Jews had dispersed during the war. In 1948 it was estimated that c. 10 per cent (6,000) of the population was Jewish, mostly in the west and south, but there too the numbers were decreasing. By c. 1955 the proportion was c. 8 per cent and the remaining Jews were indistinguishable from other East Enders. Immigration from the Commonwealth had not started. In 1954 it could be said that there was little colour prejudice because the non-European population was minute. There was little political or criminal violence.[91]

The 'changing face' of Bethnal Green excited comment by the end of the 1950s as the deeply conservative East Ender was deprived of his familiar streets. The growth of traffic led the council in 1959 to divert street trading to a new market off Roman Road, when it met the same kind of resistance as the earlier attempt to promote Columbia Market.[92] The number of

75 Tower Hamlets L.B. *Proposed Draft Alterations to Boro. Plan Proposals* (1988), 7.
76 Inf. from Bethnal Green & Victoria Park Housing Assoc.
77 Inf. from Structadene Ltd. 1993; brochure and board on site.
78 *Observer*, 9 Jan. 1994 (*Life* section, p. 67).
79 *Daily Telegraph*, 20 Apr. 1991 (*Weekend* section, p. VI).
80 Inf. from Globe Town neighbourhood.
81 Pevsner, *Lond.* ii. 71.
82 M. Young and P. Willmott, *Family and Kinship in E. Lond.* (1962), 38.
83 M. Rose, *E. End of Lond.* (1951), 263n.

84 *Census*, 1951–61. Later Census figs. relate only to Tower Hamlets as a whole.
85 *Census*, 1931–61; Young and Willmott, *Family and Kinship*, 23–4.
86 Tower Hamlets L.B. *Planning Handbk.* [1984], 17.
87 J. Platt, *Social Research in Bethnal Green* (1971), 139.
88 R. Sinclair, *E. Lond.* (1950), 342, 345, 347.
89 Rose, *E. End*, 269.
90 Young and Willmott, *Family and Kinship*, 21–22, 24, 35–37, 39, 41, 44, 54, 92, 95, 104, 109.
91 J. H. Robb, *Working Class Anti-Semite* (1954), 52–53, 159; Young and Willmott, *Family and Kinship*, 13.
92 *The Times*, 13 Jan. 1958, 10d; 10 Apr. 1959, 6a.

dwellings declined from 15,854 in 1951 to 14,649 in 1961, when they were contained in 5,729 buildings, 230 of them blocks of more than 10 dwellings.[93]

In accordance with council policy, slum clearance was accompanied by a fall in population and a contraction in industry. Between 1931 and 1955 nearly 11,000 families, more than 40,000 people, from Bethnal Green were rehoused on L.C.C. estates, many of them outside the borough, mainly in Essex. Those rehoused within Bethnal Green, whether by the L.C.C. or the M.B., were relocated without regard to family connexions.[94]

The break-up of the old social order and contraction of privately rented housing, coupled with the abolition of council housing waiting lists in the mid 1950s, increased the number of homeless. Their plight contributed to exploitation in a climate of commercialism and criminality,[95] culminating in the reign of the Kray brothers with their headquarters in Vallance Road and a celebrated murder in the Blind Beggar in Whitechapel Road in 1966.[96] Rent protests were common in the early 1960s. In 1960 Quiltotex Ltd. offered the tenants of Mansford Buildings a choice of eviction or tenancies at double the rent. The M.B., alleging neglect, threatened to compulsorily purchase the flats, which after a temporary compromise were replaced by Mansford estate.[97] Greencoat Properties took similar action on Waterlow estate in 1962. It was generally agreed that the estate was in disrepair and the controversy led directly to the purchase of part by the council in 1963.[98] In 1964, after touring Bethnal Green, the Liberal leader Joseph Grimond called for an open register of landlords and for the G.L.C. to assume direct responsibility for all housing.[99] By 1968-9 the G.L.C.'s tenants were withholding rent.[1]

Immigration further undermined the homogeneity of the early 1950s. Pakistanis (after 1974 Bangladeshis), like the Huguenots and Jews earlier, moved into Bethnal Green from the south,[2] settling around Cable Street and, after its clearance in 1963, around Brick Lane in privately rented, multi-occupied dwellings. As single men were joined by their families, their overcrowded living and working conditions in sweated labour in the clothing industry aroused the same hostility as their predecessors'. Fascism revived in Bethnal Green in 1958 and grew throughout the 1960s.

'Skinheads', themselves the product of weakened family ties, attacked Asians at the London Chest hospital and in Brick Lane in 1970.[3] Increasing activity by the National Front led to the formation of the Spitalfields Community and the Spitalfields Bengali action groups in 1974, the Spitalfields Project in 1975,[4] and an Anti-Racist Committee of Asians in East London in 1976, when a new police station opened in Brick Lane.[5] More than 3,000 people marched in protest through the Front's strongholds in Bethnal Green in 1977 and the murder of a Bengali in Whitechapel provoked demonstrations which included a march of 7,000 from Brick Lane to Downing Street in 1978 when the Front moved its headquarters from Bethnal Green to Shoreditch. In 1981 the Spitalfields Local Committee, a grant-making body funded by the council, was set up to defuse Bengali anger.[6]

Much racial violence was youthful vandalism, exploited for political ends. Another element was the Asians' claim to be offered only the oldest council housing; an analysis based on the 1971 census showed that, of a selected group of G.L.C. estates, the highest concentration of Asians was in Boundary Street and Collingwood and the lowest in Newling and Park View.[7] The G.L.C.'s plan to set aside certain blocks for Bengalis was attacked by both sides. Many flats were too small for the immigrants' families but in 1982 the Spitalfields Housing and Planning Rights Service showed that Collingwood and Boundary Street still had the most Asians while Wellington and Avebury had least. English-born East Enders, however, complained of new houses in Columbia Road that 'the whole row is Indian'. In the late 1980s the L.B. was accused of discrimination when it refused to continue paying for recently arrived Bangladeshi families on the grounds that they were voluntarily homeless.[8]

Ethnic minorities formed about a fifth of Tower Hamlets' population by 1981, mostly Bangladeshis and Pakistanis.[9] The immigrants moved into all parts although in 1988 they were mostly still in the west, in Bethnal Green neighbourhood where they formed 30 per cent of the population. Bangladeshis increased by over 200 per cent between 1981 and 1988 in Globe Town neighbourhood, where in 1986 they formed 10 per cent of the population with Pakistanis and New Commonwealth minorities forming another 7 per cent. The same categories comprised 12.6 per cent of the population in Bow neighbourhood in 1988.[10] Other immigrants

93 Census, 1951-61.
94 Young and Willmott, Family and Kinship, 41-42, 121; Simpson, Geog. of E. End of Lond.'
95 Donnion, Social Policy, 57.
96 J. Pearson, The Profession of Violence. Rise and Fall of the Kray Twins (1984), 216.
97 The Times, 30 Aug. 1960, 8c; 6 Sept., 5d; 7 Sept., 6c; 8 Sept., 3g; 4 Oct., 11c.
98 Ibid., 24 May 1962, 8e; 28 May, 8g; 7 June, 8d; 10 Oct., 12c; Connor and Critchley, Palaces for the Poor, 28.
99 The Times, 23 Mar. 1964, 8d.
1 G.L.C. Housing Dept. Ann. Rep. (1969-70), 3.
2 Two paras. based on K. Leech, Brick Lane 1978 (1980); D. Phillips, What Price equality? G.L.C. housing in

Tower Hamlets (G.L.C. Housing Research and Policy Rep. 9, 1986).
3 See also Tower Hamlets News, 5(7), June 1970, 1.
4 Ibid. N.S. 3(5), Feb. 1975, 8.
5 Spitalfields News, Oct. 1987, 3; above, plate 45.
6 Spitalfields News, Oct. 1987, 2.
7 Teesdale was the other est. in Bethnal Green: K. Dugmore, Social Characteristics of Tenants of 72 G.L.C. Housing Ests. (G.L.C. Research Memo. 1975), 21.
8 Spitalfields News, June 1987, 4; Guardian, 2 Sept. 1988 (T.H.L.H.L., 331.2); Tower Hamlets News, Oct. 1988.
9 Tower Hamlets Boro. Plan (1986), 36.
10 Tower Hamlets L.B. Proposed Draft Alterations to Boro. Plan Proposals, 1988, 6-7.

included refugee Vietnamese and Somalis, for whom an association was set up in 1983.[11]

By 1993 Bethnal Green was thoroughly cosmopolitan. The self-governing neighbourhoods and numerous associations tended to involve the whole community. Although partly funded by local and central government, they represented a movement away from paternalism, whether of largely middle-class bodies like the Church and the philanthropic companies or of the providers of municipal housing. Care was taken by housing associations constantly to consult local groups.

Housing associations and private firms were still building on relatively small sites. Much older property, including whole terraces, had been refurbished, although there were still run-down areas like Cambridge Heath Road and parts of Hackney Road. Road improvements included ramps to slow down traffic and there were many more open spaces. Industry, in old workshops or new industrial units, was mostly small-scale and confined to certain areas, notably in the north on either side of Cambridge Heath Road or in the south around Brick Lane. Bethnal Green was still predominantly working-class but recent gentrification was manifest in specialist shops in Columbia Road or a Buddhist vegetarian restaurant in Globe Road. A special feature was the art galleries and studios which were attracted by low rent and often opened in former industrial premises.[12]

The population, 22,310 in 1801, doubled to 45,676 by 1821 and again to 90,193 by 1851, reaching 120,104 by 1871 and its highest point, 129,727, in 1901. Thereafter it declined, to 108,194 in 1931, 58,353 in 1951, and 47,078 in 1961. After a further fall it started to rise again, by natural increase and immigration, from the 1980s.[13]

SOCIAL AND CULTURAL ACTIVITIES

THERE were four alehouses in 1552,[14] 74 in 1716,[15] 99 in 1730,[16] 84 in 1785,[17] and 105 in 1825.[18] There were 117 public houses and 100 beershops in 1834,[19] an average of one for 285 people. Although the numbers rose to 136 public houses and 121 beershops by 1905,[20] the increase in population gave an average of one licensed premise for 504 people. By the mid 1930s, with 94 public houses and 64 beershops,[21] the average was one for 684.

Between 1613 and 1616 indictments were brought against three victuallers or tipplers, one for taking in inmates and another (a spinster) for unlicensed tippling, against a brewer for overpricing,[22] and against another spinster for entertaining unknown men and musicians in the evening.[23] One of the oldest alehouses was probably the Cock, from which Cock Lane, recorded in 1538, took its name.[24] An alehouse stood at Bishop's Hall in 1642,[25] two (the Dun Cow and the White Bear) in Dog Row in 1652,[26] and one (the Half Moon) in Collier's Row in 1653.[27] Most early public houses were presumably around the green, including the Black Bull tavern, near Gerbier's house in 1642[28] and possibly identifiable with a timber victualling house on the west side of the green in 1652.[29] On the east side, fronting what was to become Victoria Park Square, were the Wheatsheaf before 1662 and possibly since 1621, on the site of nos. 21–3,[30] and the Blind Beggar at the southern end by 1654,[31] with the Sugar Loaf, from which the walk took its name, by 1687.[32] On the west side the Salmon and Ball, on the southern corner of Cambridge Road and Bethnal Green Road, mentioned from 1733,[33] assumed its central importance after the building of Bethnal Green Road in 1756.[34] It was outside the Salmon and Ball that rioters were hanged in 1771.[35] The Green Man, where manorial courts were sometimes held,[36] existed to the south by 1750.[37] Other houses which probably served travellers were the Nag's Head in Hackney Road by 1703[38] and the George, fronting Old Bethnal Green Road, then part of the west–east route through Bethnal Green, by 1722.[39]

Of the 82 alehouses in 1722,[40] 37 were in the south-west, south of Bethnal Green Road, including 7 in Brick Lane, 6 in Anchor and 6 in Hare Street, and 27 in the north-west, between Bethnal Green Road and Crabtree Lane, including 7 in Cock Lane and 6 in Castle Street. The King's Head at the northern end of Wheeler Street was mentioned in 1689.[41] Many alehouses

11 Spitalfields News, Nov. 1987, 3.
12 Thompson's Dir. (1991–2).
13 Census, 1901–81; Tower Hamlets L.B. Proposed Draft Alterations to Boro. Plan Proposals (1988), 6–7.
14 G.L.R.O., MR/LV/1.
15 Ibid. LV/3/2, ff. 4–5.
16 Ibid. 5/26, pp. 14–15.
17 Ibid. 9/136, pp. 25–27.
18 Ibid. 25/1, ff. 20–23.
19 Rep. Com. Poor Laws, H.C. 44, p. 111a (1834), ii, app. A, pt. 3.
20 L.C.C. Lond. Statistics, xvi. 207.
21 Ibid. xxxix. 198.
22 Mdx. Sess. Rec. N.S. i. 202; iii. 66, 143, 235.
23 Ibid. iii. 294.
24 P.N. Mdx. (E.P.N.S.), 84. The Cock, on the Bethnal Green side of the lane, was licensed in 1722 but not thereafter: G.L.R.O., MR/LV/3/101, ff. 8v.–9.
25 B.L. Add. MS. 22253.
26 G.L.R.O., M93/158, f. 16.
27 P.R.O., E 317/Mdx./13.
28 E. Lond. Papers, x(1), 24.
29 G.L.R.O., M93/158, f. 20.
30 Ibid. 13, ff. 35, 37; above, the Green.
31 G.L.R.O., M93/1; 3, p. 43; Horwood, Plan (1792–9).
32 Northants. R.O., X 1077 (corresp. of Jas. Sotheby and son, 1650–87).
33 Daily Jnl. 31 May 1733, quoted in Robinson and Chesshyre, The Green, 28.
34 29 Geo. II, c. 43; above, communications.
35 Cal. H.O. Papers, 1770–2, 401; above, settlement and building to 1836.
36 Robinson and Chesshyre, The Green, 28.
37 G.L.R.O., MR/LV/6/79, pp. 3–5.
38 Gascoyne, Map.
39 Then called 'George in the Fields': G.L.R.O., MR/LV/3/101, ff. 8v.–9.
40 Ibid.
41 P.R.O., PROB 11/396 (P.C.C. 98 Ent), ff. 60v.–61.

were not recorded before 1722, although names such as Anchor Street in 1682,[42] Ram Alley in 1687,[43] and Virginia Row in 1694[44] indicate that they were built in the late 17th century, at the same time as the surrounding weavers' houses. There were Huguenot names among the licensees of 1722 and alehouses were often called by their equivalent French names.[45] In 1726 more than 40 weavers sold 'geneva and other strong waters by retail'; by 1736 the number had risen to 90.[46] The 99 licensed victuallers of 1730 included 11 brandy sellers, all in the western part of Bethnal Green.[47] In 1834 much poor relief was said to be spent on gin.[48]

Public houses provided recreation and were meeting places for all kinds of societies, the earliest of them for Huguenots.[49] The society of Parisians, founded in 1687 for Parisian exiles living within 3 miles of Christ Church, Spitalfields, with rules dating from 1720, met once a month, and paid 1s. a month for sickness benefits of 8s. a week and £5 for funerals. Reconstituted as the Huguenot friendly benefit society, it met in 1882 at the Norfolk Arms in William Street and survived c. 1900.[50] The Bachelors benefit society was founded in 1697, met monthly at the King's Arms in Abbey Street in 1832, and survived until 1878.[51] The Norman society, founded in 1703, met fortnightly, paid 1s. a week towards beer and tobacco but forbade gambling and offered sick benefit of 7s. a week. It met at an alehouse in Spitalfields in 1800 but the Pitt's Head, Tyssen Street, was its headquarters at least from 1809 to 1843; it had 60 members c. 1900.[52] Also surviving c. 1900 was the society of Lintot (a Norman village), which was founded in Spitalfields in 1708, met at the Flower Pot in Brick Lane in 1800 and the Pitt's Head in 1831, and revised its rules in 1886.[53] The Friendly society was founded in 1720 for Huguenots aged between 21 and 31. The society of Protestant Refugees from High and Low Normandy, dating from 1764, had 20–30 members in 1826 who met at the Gibraltar in Gibraltar Walk, moving in the 1830s in turn to the Dolphin in Boundary Street (formerly Cock Lane), the Pitt's Head, and the Hope in Pollard Row. In 1857 it moved to the Norfolk Arms in Ivimey Street, which remained its headquarters, as of several other Huguenot societies, c. 1900. It survived at the end of the 1950s.[54] Other friendly societies probably of Huguenot origin were the Piccards and Wallons (sic), which met at the Panther in Hope Town in 1832,[55] and the Gift Fund of the Grand Council of the Knights of Burgundy, which met at the Knave of Clubs in Club Row in 1845.[56] Although founded for refugees from specific localities, most societies changed their rules to admit all of French descent, provided they were Protestants.

Huguenot culture, with its mathematical, history, recitation, musical, entomological, floricultural, and columbarian societies, survived into the 19th century.[57] As the middle classes moved away, there was a decline in the more intellectual interests but gardening and birds remained popular well into the 20th century. Two birdcages were among possessions listed in 1764,[58] shortly after the appearance of the Birdcage alehouse (probably formerly the King's Head),[59] from which Birdcage Walk took its name. The heyday of the weavers' societies was 1800–26, when bird fancying and breeding canaries were widespread.[60] Visitors mentioned aviaries c. 1841 and the matches between singing birds in the taverns around Hare Street c. 1874.[61] Wooden structures were built on roofs to house racing pigeons.[62] Bird-singing and racing were among the activities centred on public houses around Hague Street in 1884, usually held on Sundays.[63] The pigeon lofts survived, together with poultry and rabbits in back yards, into the 1950s.[64] One of the best poultry clubs in the country was said to have met at Bethnal Green men's institute in the 1930s.[65]

The one area of continuing intellectual interest to weavers and other craftsmen, especially shoemakers,[66] was that of radical politics and religion. Alehouses, headquarters in the 1760s of rioting weavers, organized along club lines as the Bold Defiance,[67] were 'the pivotal institution in plebeian social life' in the late 18th century. The Seven Stars in Fleet Street housed radical debating clubs from the late 1790s[68] and the Spencean society probably had a branch in Bethnal Green long before it was recorded in 1817.[69] The government's attempts at suppression largely depended on the tavern-keepers and licensing magistrates. Debating clubs enforced solidarity by recreation and fraternal rituals like linking hands and singing,[70] and the rector's complaint in 1816[71] against the alehouses associated with

42 W. Morgan, *Surv. of Lond. and Westm.* (1682).
43 P.R.O., PROB 11/387 (P.C.C. 75 Foot), ff. 242v.–5.
44 C.L.R.O., Assess. Box 43, MS. 22. The Virginia Planter probably named from a lessee of c. 1673: above, settlement and building to 1836; the West.
45 e.g. l'Ancre, Chien Noir, le Cigne Noir, le Boucher: *Case Bk. of La Maison de Charité de Spitalfields 1739–41* (Hug. Soc., Quarto ser.lv, 1981).
46 Cal. Mdx. Sess. Bks. xiii. 279; xvii. 6.
47 G.L.R.O., MR/LV/5/26, pp. 14–15.
48 *Rep. Com. Poor Laws*, H.C. 44, p. 111a (1834), ii, app. A, pt.3.
49 Para. based on W. C. Waller, 'Early Hug. Friendly Socs.' *Proc. Hug. Soc.* v. 201–32.
50 Guildhall MS. 9899.
51 G.L.R.O., MC/R1, no. 182; *E. Lond. Papers*, xiii (2), 79.
52 G.L.R.O., MC/R1, no. 113; R2, no. 1140.
53 Ibid. R1, no. 127.
54 Young and Willmott, *Family and Kinship* (1962), 114.
55 G.L.R.O., MC/R1, no. 209.
56 Ibid. R2, no. 1439.
57 *Rep. from Asst. Commrs. on Handloom Weavers*, pt. II

(43-I), H.C. pp. 216–17 (1840), xxiii; T. Kelly, *Geo. Birkbeck* (1957), 66.
58 P.R.O., PROB 3/60/36.
59 Lewis Gilbert was licensed for the King's Head in 1750 and for the Bird Cage in 1760, both in Virginia Row: G.L.R.O., MR/LV/6/79, pp. 3–5; 7/49, pp. 3–4.
60 Sheppard, *Lond. 1808–70*, 167.
61 Quoted in M. Rose, *East End of Lond.* (1951), 104.
62 *Lond. City Mission Mag.* xxxvii. 250; J. Hollingshead, *Ragged Lond. in 1861* (1861), 70.
63 *Lond. City Mission Mag.* xlix. 87.
64 Rose, *E. End of Lond.* 104.
65 Vale, *Old Bethnal Green*, 9–10.
66 M. Chase, *The People's Farm. Eng. Radical Agrarianism 1775–1840* (1988), 172; *Lond. City Mission Mag.* xix. 89.
67 Above, settlement and building to 1836.
68 *E.H.R.* cii. 309, 312.
69 Chase, *People's Farm*, 100.
70 *E.H.R.* cii. 314, 317.
71 *Rep. from Cttee. on State of Police in Metropolis*, H.C. 510, pp. 152–3 (1816), v.

Joseph Merceron may well have been based upon their subversive politics. He singled out the Seven Stars, leased by Merceron since 1788, and the Three Sugar Loaves in St. John Street as haunts of suspicious characters. Other alehouses which he wanted suppressed included the Sun in Sclater Street, where boys and girls at a 'cock and hen club . . . get drunk and debauch each other'. Merceron was also accused of collusion with dissenters; there were links between Dissent and radical politics, the spy Shegog, for example, being involved in both.[72] Independents met in 1808 at property in Mount Street belonging to the Lazarus Society.[73]

Merceron's alehouses[74] survived to become meeting places of many friendly societies, to which c. 3,000 people in Bethnal Green belonged by 1813–15.[75] Between 1831 and 1857 40 public houses were the meeting places of at least 41 friendly and 21 loan societies,[76] including the Sons of Prudence at the Red Cross in Hare Street in 1831, the Amicable Society of Master Tradesmen at the Hope in Pollard Row, the Friendly Artizans at the White Horse in Hare Street in 1831, and the Hackney Road Philanthropic at the Roebuck there in 1843. The Knave of Clubs in Club Row was the headquarters of five friendly and two loan societies. Only four friendly societies and 11 loan societies avoided public houses. Three of them, including the Honorable Sons of True Temperance and the Hand-in-Hand Teetotal Provident loan society, met in coffee houses in Bethnal Green Road in 1843 and 1848. Schoolrooms, too, accommodated the few benefit building societies which did not meet in public houses. Fifteen societies were registered between 1850 and 1863,[77] 11 of which met in public houses. At the end of the 1880s 5,445 people belonged to friendly societies in Bethnal Green, 3,280 of them to the Loyal United Friends, 841 to the Ancient Order of Foresters, and 802 to the Hearts of Oak. Only 27 were Sons of Temperance.[78]

There were several coffee houses, mostly in Bethnal Green Road and its western end, then called Church Street, in the late 1830s and 1840s[79] and in Bethnal Green and Hackney roads in the 1870s.[80] Although normally associated with evangelical Christianity, teetotalism had a branch belonging to the radical, often atheist, movement.[81] In 1848 freethinkers, who usually met outdoors in Bonner's Fields, leased a large house at no. 1 Warner Place, off Hackney Road, and built a temperance hall at the back, where

Charles Bradlaugh (d. 1891) lived and developed his ideas.[82]

An early mechanics' institute, the Eastern Literary and Scientific institution, opened in 1825 in the Bethnal Green part of Hackney Road. It survived until c. 1847[83] and was the headquarters of a benefit society in 1845[84] and a building society in 1846.[85] The Christian Soc. of Silkweavers existed in Thorold Square by 1851[86] and was recorded among charitable organizations in 1870.[87] Bethnal Green Working Men's Benevolent society, founded in 1859 to pay for medical aid, survived in 1901.[88]

Most workers' societies remained primarily concerned with radical politics and closely associated with alehouses. The British Association for Promoting Co-operative Knowledge, founded in 1829, which developed into the National Union of Working Classes, often met at the Blind Beggar.[89] Several Bethnal Green names appear among those of political radicals in the 1830s, including three members of the Radical club in 1838.[90] The prevalence of irreligion and the circulation of the *Poor Man's Guardian* was noted of Twig Folly district in 1833.[91] A group of the Prestonian society met in 1836 in Club Row,[92] probably at the Knave of Clubs. From 1837–41 groups like the East London Democratic Association operated from 'old alehouse haunts' and from chapels like Bowling Square chapel,[93] possibly Wilmot Square where Merceron's ally the Revd. Francis Platt lived.[94] The Association also met at the 'Trades' hall in Abbey Street, where in 1840 arms were found at a meeting of 600 people amid rumours of an uprising.[95] The probably small membership of the clubs acted as a leaven in the mob. About 5,000 people from Bethnal Green and its neighbourhood attended a demonstration demanding political rights in 1834.[96] Preston, founder of the Prestonian society, led a group from Bethnal Green in a plan to attack the Tower and Bank of England.[97] The parish was at the forefront of Chartist agitation in 1848, with 'monster meetings' cheering the French Republic in Bonner's Fields, Nova Scotia Gardens, and Cambridge Heath Road.[98] Socialists met in Trinity chapel in Peel Grove in 1851.[99] Throughout the 1850s, 1860s, and 1870s crowds from Bethnal Green flocked to radical speeches on Sundays in Bonner's Fields and to meetings held by a 'demagogue' and 'noted sceptic', probably Bradlaugh, in Shoreditch and at the Hall of Science in Old Street. There was

72 Below, prot. nonconf.; *E.H.R.* cii. 315.
73 Guildhall Libr., RG 31/3/692.
74 Listed in *Rep. Cttee. on Police in Metropolis*, 207.
75 *Poor Law Abstract 1818*, H.C. 82, pp. 264–5 (1818), xiii.
76 Para. based on regs. of socs.: G.L.R.O., MC/R1–2.
77 G.L.R.O., MC/R3.
78 Ibid. MC/R1–2; B. Lillywhite, *Lond. Coffee Hos.* (1963).
79 Booth, *Life and Lab.* i(1), 110.
80 *P.O. Dir. Lond.* (1879).
81 *E.H.R.* cv. 329.
82 H. B. Bonner, *Chas. Bradlaugh* (1894), i. 9–12, 20; C. M. Davies, *Heterodox Lond.* (1874), ii. 198–9.
83 T. Kelly, *Geo. Birkbeck* (1957), 313.
84 G.L.R.O., MC/R2, f.4, no. 70.

85 Ibid. no. 173.
86 P.R.O., HO 129/21/3/1/10.
87 G.L.R.O., A/FWA/C/B2/1.
88 *The Times*, 10 May 1901, 9f.
89 *Lond. Radicalism, 1830–43* (L.R.S. v), 142.
90 Ibid. 69, 120, 155.
91 *Rep. Sel. Cttee. on Educ.* H.C. 465, pp. 271–4 (1835), vii.
92 Chase, *People's Farm*, 107, 163.
93 *E.H.R.* cii. 331.
94 M.L.R. 1808/4/492. For bowling, below.
95 D. Goodway, *Lond. Chartism, 1838–48* (1982), 33.
96 *Lond. Radicalism, 1830–43*, 42.
97 Chase, *People's Farm*, 107, 163.
98 Goodway, *Lond. Chartism*, 79.
99 P.R.O., HO 129/21/3/1/10.

an 'infidel lecture hall' in the eastern part of Bethnal Green.[1]

Working men's clubs were opening in the 1860s: at Peel Grove in 1863, in St. Matthias's schoolroom in 1864,[2] and in New Nichol Street in 1865.[3] Bradlaugh was a major influence on the New Commonwealth club in Bethnal Green Road, a radical 'proprietary' club which existed by the 1870s. It was joined by Stewart Headlam, the curate of St. Matthew's, whose lecture on music halls in 1877 shocked conventional clerical opinion.[4] By 1934 the club had moved to nos. 272–6 Hackney Road,[5] formerly the Gladstone Working Men's club. Other radical clubs followed: the United Radical in Kay Street in 1884[6] and Bethnal Green radical at no. 143 Green Street in 1887.[7] The Borough of Bethnal Green club, in Abbey Street by 1889,[8] built a new working men's club at no. 44 Pollard Row in 1895.[9] Officially the Borough of Bethnal Green Liberal and Radical club and the chief Liberal club in the M.B., it was usually called the Borough of Bethnal Green Working Men's club[10] and was on the same site in the 1990s.[11] By 1889 other clubs included the Gladstone Radical in Baroness Road (which was housed at nos. 272–6 Hackney Road in 1912 and 1918 but had apparently closed by 1927),[12] the New Labour in Victoria Park Square, the Conservative Working Men's at no. 343 Bethnal Green Road, and three 'proprietary' clubs, the National Standard in Bethnal Green Road, the Cambridge in Cambridge Road, and the Oxford and Cambridge in Swan Street.[13] The British Brothers' League, founded in 1901 in reaction to Jewish immigration,[14] had a large, though short lived, membership in Bethnal Green.

Charitable, as distinct from self-help, societies, were mostly run by middle-class people from outside the parish.[15] Bethnal Green Philanthropic Pension society, founded in 1822, met at the Salmon and Ball in 1841[16] and at the Green Man in 1870. The East London General Pension Society was founded in 1824 and based in Bethnal Green Road in 1870, when it distributed weekly pensions of 2s. 6d. for men and 2s. for women. The Royal Adelaide Provident institution originated in a charity ball 'under very high patronage' held in 1837 to relieve the silkweavers. It was registered as a loan society in 1839, the intention being to persuade them to pay a subscription to insure against unemployment, but the weavers were hostile and the institution was overwhelmed by demand.[17] Other societies which were united into Bethnal Green Charity Organisation society in 1869[18] included such enterprises of Baroness Burdett-Coutts as the provision of district nurses and training girls for service and boys as shoeblacks, missions like Ashley's, organized as sewing classes by two ladies from Cambridge Heath or by the East End Mission, free dinners provided by Old Castle Street Mission, and services provided by Sisters of Charity working from Thomas Street.

The churches by the 1850s were running provident societies, lectures, classes, libraries, and clothing clubs. Their involvement in recreational pursuits provided an alternative to the radical and often atheistic culture of the public houses and secular working men's clubs. St. Philip's had a young men's association by 1861 but the fastest expansion came with the incumbency of Septimus Hansard, rector 1864–95, and Stewart Headlam, curate 1873–8, of St. Matthew's, who debated in the secular clubs and founded the Guild of St. Matthew's in 1877. Nonconformist activities, including men's clubs, were especially associated from the 1870s with the Baptist Shoreditch tabernacle, the Congregational Union and Victoria Park chapels, the Christian Memorial hall, and, from the late 1880s, the Unitarian Mansford Street chapel. Anglican activity increased from the 1880s. In 1888 St. Francis of Assisi mission opened with a clubroom. In 1889 Holy Trinity opened in the Nichol with a clubroom, gymnasium, and large hall and soon supported a vigorous social life, including a men's club with 500 members.[19] Six philanthropic and religious clubs listed in 1889[20] were associated with Anglicans. One, St. Bartholomew's club in Brady Street, was by c. 1891 among many activities run by that church, including tobacco sociables for men and meals, besides clubs and classes for boys, mothers, and young women.[21] St. Jude's institute, built in 1896, housed clubs, a choral society, a band of hope, and, from 1899, literary, cricket, and athletic clubs. St. Paul's institute was built in 1896 in Gosset Street, about the time that All Saints' mission opened in Vyner Street with a clubroom and gymnasium. Parochial buildings for St. James the Less, opened in Sewardstone Road in 1901, included a gymnasium, girls' and mens' clubs, billiard, reading, and drawing rooms, and a tennis court, bowling green, quoit beds, and bandstand.[22] By 1903 St. James was running cricket, football, rambling, and chess clubs and, by 1914, a women's hockey club.[23]

[1] *Lond. City Mission Mag.* xix. 95–97; xxvii. 55; xlii. 93.
[2] *Builder*, 12 Dec. 1863, 887; 6 Feb. 1864, 106.
[3] *Ragged Sch. Union Mag.* xvii (1865), 187.
[4] F. G. Bettany, *Stewart Headlam* (1926), 41, 43; below, parish church.
[5] *P.O. Dir. Lond.* (1934).
[6] G.L.R.O., MBW 1730, no. 27.
[7] Ibid. 1757, no. 26.
[8] Booth, *Life and Lab.* i(1), 105.
[9] G.L.R.O., AR/BA/4/55, no. 6.
[10] *P.O. Dir. Lond.* (1902); Samuel, *E. End Underworld*, 264.
[11] Thomson, *Dir. E. Lond.* (1991–2).
[12] *P.O. Dir. Lond.* (1905, 1912, 1918, 1927).

[13] Booth, *Life and Lab.* i(1), 105.
[14] *Lond. Jnl.* viii. 7.
[15] Para. based on G.L.R.O., A/FWA/C/B2/1.
[16] Ibid. Acc. 1844/A1/2.
[17] *Rep. Asst. Commrs. on Handloom Weavers*, pt. II (43-I), p. 257.
[18] Below, local govt. (local govt. 1836–1900).
[19] Below, list of churches; prot. nonconf.
[20] Booth, *Life and Lab.* i(1), 105.
[21] Lambeth Pal. Libr., Fulham Papers, F. Temple Papers.
[22] *Souvenir of opening of parochial bldgs.* (T.H.L.H.L., 225.5, pamphlet no. L.P. 4592).
[23] St. Jas. the Less, *Par. Mag.* July 1903, Feb. 1914 (T.H.L.H.L., 225.5).

FIG. 23. ST BARTHOLOMEW'S MISSION ACTIVITIES C. 1891

The most important religious institution was Oxford House,[24] which from its foundation in 1884 began organizing a boys' club and 'smoke and talk' facilities for men, together with a library and lectures. In 1886 it founded the Federation of Working Men's Clubs, to have no political aims but to promote clubs providing recreation, education, and 'non-intoxicant refreshment'. Oxford House itself founded several clubs. It housed a working men's club when in the former St. Andrew's National school until in 1894 it moved with the club into new buildings in Derbyshire Street. University club opened in Cambridge Road and moved to nos. 16 and 17 Victoria Park Square, where in 1887 it built Oxford hall in the rear.[25] By 1890 it had 1,000 members and housed a café, reading room, billiard room, hall, and three co-operative societies. It added a rifle range in 1910, when it was largely self-managed,[26] becoming formally independent of Oxford House in 1942. The Webbe institute for working boys opened in 1888 at no. 457 Bethnal Green Road and moved in 1889 to new buildings at the corner of Hare (later Cheshire) and Hereford streets, where it had more than 400 members by 1890. Financed by friends of H. B. Webbe, a New College man with cricketing connexions, it was run by Oxford House and provided a gymnasium, games, and a band. Repton club for a 'lower class of boy' opened in 1895 with 80 boys in Bethnal Green Road and was supported by Repton school. St. Anthony's opened in 1902 and changed its name in 1906 to Eastbourne club after the school which adopted it. Oxford House was leased the Excelsior baths,[27] which could be floored over for concerts given by its musical and dramatic association, in 1898 and published the monthly *Excelsior* from 1912.

St. Margaret's House from 1889 and St. Hilda's East from 1898 were the counterparts for women of Oxford House.[28] By 1902 St. John's girls' club had its own premises at no. 1 The Terrace, Old Ford Road.[29]

In the late 1880s missioners were complaining of the 'many evils' which the rapidly increasing working men's clubs seemed to foster.[30] Most clubs were for drinking and gambling and favoured a 'vague, unorganised Socialism'.[31] Two beer retailers applied in 1886 to build club rooms.[32] By the 1900s Oxford House was described as famous for its clubs and varied activities.[33]

Although contracted during both world wars, Oxford House's clubs flourished in the 1920s. By 1929 Oxford House had 200 members, University club 250, Repton club 150, and Webbe institute, partly supported by Berkhamsted and Chigwell schools, 275. Repton club had acquired premises in Devonshire Street just outside Bethnal Green and Repton Old Boys maintained a club at no. 16 Victoria Park Square, which also housed Eastbourne boys' club. Although the Excelsior had become a weekday cinema in 1921, the 150-member Oxford House Musical and Dramatic association continued to perform there on Sundays. A book and picture club, started in 1924 in co-operation with Bethnal Green public library, had 150 members. In 1924 a group of Cambridge graduates founded the Cambridge and Bethnal Green Jewish boys' club, which met in the former Blue Anchor in Chance Street.[34]

Bethnal Green men's institute was one of several established by the L.C.C. in 1920. Opened in Wolverley Street, by 1925 it had more than 900 members attending 50 classes for low fees in subjects ranging from art and photography to carpentry and metal work, a choir, an orchestra, a gymnastic club, and a dramatic society.[35] New premises opened at no. 229 Bethnal Green Road in 1928[36] and there were 3,500 members by 1939.[37]

By 1912 Bethnal Green Progressive club was at nos. 137–41 Globe Road and the Metropolitan Working Men's club was at no. 265 Cambridge Road, where it remained until 1939.[38] New Century Working Men's club existed in Mansford Street by 1918 but had gone by 1927, when Cambridge Temperance club existed at nos. 461–3 Hackney Road.[39]

During the 1920s Oxford House increasingly turned to politics and social questions, opening a day nursery in 1921 and providing sports facilities for the unemployed. By the mid 1930s Oxford House was an important centre of social work and there were said to be only 15 clubs of any kind in Bethnal Green,[40] although 16 were listed in 1934.[41] Five were associated with Oxford House, three were established political clubs (the New Commonwealth, the Borough of Bethnal Green Working Men's, and Bethnal Green Progressive), two others established clubs (the Metropolitan Working Men's and the Cambridge and Bethnal Green Jewish boys'), and the rest new: the Cambridge and Bethnal Green Old Boys' in Chance Street, the Bethnal Green Trade and Labour at no. 291 Cambridge Road, the London Unemployed Association in Green Street, the United Workers' club and institute in Austin Street, and Dew Drop Inn for Education and Joy in Vallance Road. The Labour club at no. 18 Victoria Park Square had become a British Legion club. Shortly afterwards the British Union of Fascists opened a branch,[42]

24 Three paras. based on *The Oxford Ho. in Bethnal Green, 1884–1948* (1948); M. Ashworth, *Oxford Ho. in Bethnal Green*; G.L.R.O., A/FWA/C/D164/1. And see below, Anglican missions, univ. settlements.
25 G.L.R.O., MBW 1757, no. 26.
26 Booth, *Life and Lab*. i(1), 95; G.L.R.O., AR/BA/4/206, no. 4.
27 T.H.L.H.L., TH/7056; below.
28 Below, Anglican missions, univ. settlements.
29 *P.O. Dir. Lond*. (1902).
30 *Lond. City Mission Mag*. lii. 227.
31 Booth, *Life and Lab*. i(1), 95, 99.
32 Ibid. iii(2), 86–7.

33 G.L.R.O., MBW 1748, no. 27; *P.O. Dir. Lond*. (1905).
34 Inf. from Mr. M. Meth (Hon. Appeals Sec., New Cambridge Boys' Club).
35 *The Times*, 7 Apr. 1925, 17d; *New Lond. Life and Lab*. ix. 97.
36 G.L.R.O., (LCC) CL/CER/3/7.
37 P. J. O. Self, *Voluntary Organisations in Bethnal Green* (1945), T.H.L.H.L. 372 (pamphlet).
38 *P.O. Dir. Lond*. (1912, 1934, 1942).
39 Ibid. (1918, 1927).
40 *New Lond. Life and Lab*. ix. 175.
41 *P.O. Dir. Lond*. (1934).
42 *Lond. Jnl*. viii. 12.

which claimed 4,000 members,[43] and there were also Young Communists. The attraction of the extremists led to a fall in membership of other clubs.[44] In 1938 the Cambridge and Bethnal Green Jewish boys' club, renamed the Cambridge and Bethnal Green boys' club, was reorganized to be interdenominational and played a part in dampening anti-Semitism.[45]

Most clubs contracted or closed during the Second World War and some, like Repton club, were bombed. The Webbe club moved into Oxford House which offered the vacated premises to the Cambridge and Bethnal Green boys' club.[46] Sir Oswald Mosley tried to revive Fascism in the late 1940s as the Union Movement, concentrating in the East End and holding meetings in Kerbela Street. In 1958 the East End branch of the National Labour party formed at a public house in Cheshire Street. It merged into the British National Party in 1960 with Cheshire Street and Brick Lane among its regular meeting places. When the National Front was formed by a further amalgamation in 1966, attention had shifted from Jews to more recent immigrants and during the 1970s, when a para-military group called Column 88 emerged, and again in the 1990s, there was active and often violent racism in Bethnal Green.[47]

Of the pre-war clubs, the North-East Labour Party opened at no. 349 Cambridge Heath Road and the Borough of Bethnal Green Working Men's club at its old premises. Several of Oxford House's clubs reopened, though with more emphasis on mixed clubs, local control, and community projects, including many for Asians.[48] Repton club, offering several sports besides dressmaking and art,[49] was voted in 1969 the top amateur boxing club in London.[50] The Cambridge and Bethnal Green club moved to Virginia Road school in 1945 where in 1955 it was renamed the New Cambridge boys' club as the trustees supported an existing club which became the Cambridge and Hackney Associated clubs.[51] New clubs included Pavilion Social in Vallance Road and Mann, Crossman & Paulin's in Cambridge Heath Road by 1959.[52] Bethnal Green institute survived as a major source for adult education for Bengalis.[53] By the 1980s and 1990s there were clubs associated with housing estates, for example Wellington and Hollybush, with the Bengali community, especially in the south-west,[54] and community centres for Globe Town in the former Oxford House club,

Eastbourne House, St. Hilda's East in Club Row, St. Matthew's in Wood Close, and Wessex in Wessex Street.[55] The Bethnal Green Society was registered as a charity in 1961 to provide centres with recreational facilities.[56] In 1971 the clubs were evicted from University House, which itself closed in 1988.[57] Praxis, a movement mainly concerned with refugees and immigrants, opened in 1985 as a project of Robert Kemble Christian Institute in Pott Street.[58] The New Cambridge boys' club closed in 1989 as the school premises were needed for the expanding Bengali population, although it continued as a grant-making body for youth clubs.[59]

In 1292 London citizens defended their traditional right to hunt within the woods of the bishop in Stepney, in practice near Bishop's Hall,[60] and in 1561 their right to shoot with bows in the common fields of Stepney and Bethnal Green was reaffirmed.[61] There was a bowling alley at Kirby's Castle in the 1590s[62] and a bowling green in Wilmot Square by 1787.[63] Most sport was much rougher: whipping a cock on Shrove Tuesday in 1656,[64] dog-fighting, hunting ducks, for which the weavers bred a special small spaniel called a splasher,[65] and chasing bullocks. A subscription was raised to pay drovers on their way to Smithfield for a bullock which was maddened with prods and peas in its ears and driven through the most populated part of the parish. In 1816 the rector saved two bullocks which had taken refuge in the churchyard but Joseph Merceron, as magistrate, refused to stop the practice and declared that in his youth (c. 1780) he was first in the chase.[66] The chief amusements in 1861 were said to be dog fights, rat matches, and 'drawing the badger',[67] although few badgers could be found in the parish. Dog- and cock-fighting in 1896 had been a recent feature of the bird fair.[68]

Gambling with cards and shuffleboard, especially on Sundays, were included in charges against disorderly alehouses in 1818.[69] Gambling at cards and skittles in beershops were the principal recreations around Virginia Row in 1875.[70] Among public houses which acquired skittle grounds were the Three Compasses in Sclater Street in 1870[71] and the Black Bull in Thomas Street in 1877.[72]

Daniel Mendoza (d. 1836) the pugilist patronized by the Prince Regent, wrote his *Art of Boxing* (1789) from his home in Paradise Row[73]

43   K. Leech, *Brick Lane 1978* (1980), 14.
44   Self, *Vol. Organisations*.
45   Inf. from Mr. M. Meth.   46   Ibid.
47   *Lond. Jnl.* viii. 14–18; Leech, *Brick Lane*, 14.
48   Self, *Vol. Organisations*; *E.L.A.* 6 Mar. 1987 (T.H.L.H.L., 360.3 files, University Ho.).
49   *Repton Club Jnl.* (1965–70) (T.H.L.H.L., 360.3).
50   *E.L.A.* 13 June 1969 (T.H.L.H.L., 360.3 files, University Ho.).
51   Inf. from Mr. M. Meth.
52   *P.O. Dir. Lond.* (1959).
53   Leech, *Brick Lane*, 21.
54   Char. Com. no. 273767; Leech, *Brick Lane*, 21.
55   *Thomson Dir. E. Lond.* (1991–2); Char. Com. no. 300506.
56   Char. Com. no. 303239.
57   *E. End News*, Nov. 1983; inf. from T.H.L.H.L.
58   Inf. from Praxis; below, prot. nonconf., Congregationalists.

59   Inf. from Mr. M. Meth; Char. Com. no. 303247.
60   P. J. Taylor, 'Estates of Bishopric of Lond. from 7th to early 16th cent.' (Lond. Univ. Ph.D. thesis, 1976), 180–1.
61   *V.C.H. Mdx.* ii. 284.
62   P.R.O., REQ 2/27/115.
63   G.L.R.O., MR/B/R4 (1788), nos. 18–19.
64   Attended by a multitude 'riotously assembled': *Mdx. County. Rec.* iii. 258.
65   *Rep. Asst. Commrs. on Handloom Weavers*, pt. II (43-I), 216–17.
66   *Rep. Cttee. on Police in Metropolis*, 151–2.
67   J. Hollingshead, *Ragged Lond. in 1861* (1861), 70.
68   *Lond. City Mission Mag.* lxi. 275.
69   *The Times*, 18 May 1818, 3c.
70   *Lond. City Mission Mag.* xl. 156.
71   G.L.R.O., MR/UP 953.
72   Ibid. MBW 1667, pt. 24.
73   Robinson and Chesshyre, *The Green*, 26.

and later another boxer, Jim Smith, lived in Old Nichol and attended Nichol Street board school.[74] Boxing remained one of the most popular sports, disapproved of by evangelicals. In 1898 the letting of Mansford Street baths for boxing, footracing, and 'balls of a very low order' was the 'curse of the district'.[75] It was the High Church and Christian Socialist Anglicans like Jay of Holy Trinity and the heads of Oxford House that recognized the value of boxing facilities.[76]

Apart from a cricket club established in Victoria Park in 1846, and other groups associated with the park,[77] there were no sports clubs other than those connected with the church and university clubs until recent times. Victoria Park provided artificial lakes for swimming, replaced in 1936 by an open-air swimming pool.[78] A private company applied in 1899 to build swimming baths, called the Excelsior, at the corner of Mansford and Florida streets.[79] There was an application to build swimming baths in Columbia Market in 1895,[80] Russian vapour baths existed in Brick Lane during the First World War,[81] and a municipal swimming bath opened in York hall in 1929.[82] Bethnal Green swimming club was formed in 1962 with support from the M.B.[83] There was a roller-skating rink in Victoria Park in 1951.[84]

The parish was required to raise 12 men for the navy in 1795 and men for the militia in 1796.[85] The Bethnal Green volunteers were portrayed by Rowlandson in 1798[86] and the parish joined with its neighbours in seeking relief from the burden of the militia in 1799.[87] A rate of 18d. in the £ to pay the volunteers was imposed in 1803 and details of the militia men were recorded in 1807.[88] In the late 1820s and early 1830s several Bethnal Green men served in the 1st and 2nd Royal Regiments of Tower Hamlets militia in place of people in Whitechapel.[89] In 1853 Henry Merceron leased no. 21 Victoria Park Square as a depot for the Queen's Own Light Infantry Regiment of Tower Hamlets militia.[90] Barracks had been built behind nos. 10–12 by 1870[91] and were occupied by 1879 by the 2nd Tower Hamlets Engineer Volunteers, who in 1895 built a drill hall to the south, adjoining University House.[92] The Volunteers, called the East London Royal Engineers by 1902 and the 1st Division London

Division Royal Engineers by 1912, occupied the premises until 1939.[93]

In 1834 penny plays exhibited opposite Hart's Lane tended to 'demoralize the lower order'.[94] Inhabitants in 1851 included a theatrical performer (Frederick Middleton, in Old Castle Street) and a comedian (William Jones, in Willow Walk).[95] One of the earliest alehouses licensed for music and dancing was the Falcon in Victoria Park Square which in 1839, under the direction of T. Wilson of the Pavilion theatre in Whitechapel Road, announced the opening of a concert room with a succession of singers and a weekly change of varieties.[96] The Salmon and Ball received its licence in 1840[97] and seven other alehouses in 1841.[98] In 1861 concerts, mostly of street 'nigger' singing, held in rooms over the bars, were among the chief amusements.[99] By 1870 31 public houses were licensed for music and dancing.[1] They included the Northampton Arms in Northampton Street (1849–89), with a hall for 100 people on the ground floor, the Red Cross at no. 25 Hare Street (1849–71), which opened the Apollo music hall accommodating 600, the Duke of Wellington at no. 52 Cyprus Street (1854–91), the Victoria at no. 21 Morpeth Road (1854–90), and the Black Dog at no. 101 Bethnal Green Road (1856–90), each with a concert room on the first floor. The Hare at no. 505 Cambridge Road (1858–89) contained a hall for 120 which was used as a music hall twice a week and at other times for billiards. Plays were performed at the Peacock at no. 325 Cambridge Road (1859–83) and weekly concerts on the first floor of the Earl of Ellesmere at no. 19 Chisenhale Road (1866–90). The Royal Victor at no. 234 Old Ford Road (1867–87 and 1891–1903) had a hall, reconstructed in 1890 for 300, which served as a music hall. The 18th-century Artichoke in Cambridge Road was licensed from 1856 and altered by 1875 into the Foresters' (or Royal Foresters') music hall. In 1893 it was reconstructed to hold 3,000 and had a stage said to be one of the finest in London,[2] where such artists as Dan Leno and Little Tich played before boisterous audiences on Monday, the costermongers' day-off.[3] The Sebright Arms north of Hackney Road was licensed from 1865, reconstructed for 704 in 1885,[4] and altered in 1918.[5] Called variously Sebright's Palace of Varieties, Belmont music hall, and Regent's theatre,[6] it

74 S. Maclure, *One Hundred Years of Lond. Educ. 1870–1970* (1970), 35.
75 *Lond. City Mission Mag.* lxiii. 70.
76 Above.
77 *Lillywhite's Guide to Cricketers* (1853); see *V.C.H. Mdx.* x. 69.
78 C. Poulsen, *Victoria Park* (1976), 56.
79 G.L.R.O., AR/BA/4/4, no. 27.
80 Ibid. 55, no. 6.
81 H. Blacker, *Just Like It Was* (1974), 16.
82 Below, pub. svces. (pub. baths).
83 *Tower Hamlets News*, 3(4), Oct. 1967, p. 47.
84 Rose, *E. End of Lond.* 243.
85 Vestry mins. 1782–1813, pp. 190, 209.
86 G. F. Vale and S. Snaith, *Bygone Bethnal Green* (1948), 55.
87 Vestry mins. 1782–1813, p. 233.
88 Ibid. pp. 289, 323.
89 T.H.L.H.L., TH/782, 785.
90 G.L.R.O., Acc. 295/1.

91 Ibid. MR/UP 955.
92 G.L.R.O., AR/BA/4/55, no. 5; (LCC) CL/LOC/2/10; *P.O. Dir. Lond.* (1900).
93 *P.O. Dir. Lond.* (1879, 1902, 1912, 1927, 1939, 1942).
94 Vestry mins., Easter Mon. 31 Mar. 1834.
95 P.R.O., HO 107/1539/21/1/8, p. 1 sqq.; 22, f. 479, p. 1 sqq.
96 G.L.R.O., MR/LMD/M&D 2/56; A. E. Wilson, *East End Entertainment* (1954), 211.
97 G.L.R.O., MR/LMD/M&D 2/12.
98 The Royal Standard, Prince of Wales, Crown, Birdcage, Woodman, Red Cross, and Northampton Arms: G.L.R.O., MR/LMD/M&D 4/73, 75–6, 97, 118, 129, 142.
99 Hollingshead, *Ragged Lond.* 70.
1 Based on G.L.R.O., MR/LMD and D. Howard, *Lond. Theatres and Music Halls 1850–1950* (1970).
2 Wilson, *E. End Entertainment*, 215–16.
3 Samuel, *E. End Underworld*, 41, 299, n. 13.
4 G.L.R.O., MBW 1739, no. 27.
5 Ibid. AR/BA/4/319, no. 5.
6 L.C.C. *Lond. Statistics*, xvi. 188.

opened twice nightly as a music hall and hosted one of Marie Lloyd's earliest appearances.[7]

The cinema made a sudden impact shortly before the First World War, with conversions of buildings, including music halls, and purpose-built 'picture theatres' or 'palaces'. The Foresters' music hall at no. 93 Cambridge Road became a cinema in 1910, was renamed the New Lyric in 1916, closed in 1917, reopened as the Foresters in 1925, closed in 1949, and reopened in 1949. It seated 1,000 when finally closed in 1960, whereupon the site was redeveloped.[8] Applications were made in 1910 and 1911 to convert Adelphi chapel at no. 354 Hackney Road into a cinema, which was named Hackney Grand Central[9] and lasted into the 1930s.[10]

An application to build a cinema in Cambridge Road was made in 1910[11] and again, by Bethnal Green Cinema Co., in 1913.[12] Called the Museum cinema after the nearby Bethnal Green Museum,[13] it was reconstructed for 802 people by Leslie H. Kemp in 1931, renamed the Odeon in 1950, closed in 1956, and replaced by Mayfield House.[14] A building belonging to Charles Spencer & Co. at no. 186 Grove Road was adapted in 1912 as cinema.[15] When enlarged in 1913 it belonged to Victoria Park Picture Theatre Co.,[16] which ran it in 1934, together with a cinema at nos. 62–6 Green Street (Roman Road).[17] It closed during the war.[18] The Green Street cinema, the Empire Picturedrome, had also opened in 1912,[19] was altered in 1926[20] and seated 650. It closed in 1959 when the site was redeveloped.[21]

Smart's Picture Palace was built at nos. 281–5 Bethnal Green Road in 1912[22] and altered in 1920.[23] It was run in 1927 by Attractive Cinema (Bethnal Green)[24] and reconstructed by George Coles as the Rex, seating 865, after 1934. It was renamed the Essoldo in 1949 and closed in 1964,

becoming a bingo club and later a warehouse.[25] Sebright's music hall at no. 28 Coate Street had been converted to a cinema by 1914.[26] It closed between 1927 and 1934 and flats were built on the site.[27] The Excelsior hall in Mansford Street was converted by Emden & Egan to a cinema in 1921.[28] After minor changes by Frank Matcham & Co. in 1926, it accommodated 800 people for weekday 'trade performances' in 1929. It was remodelled by Maple of London in 1939 and seated 661 when it closed in 1961. Asian films were shown there until it was demolished for a housing estate in 1969.[29]

Newspapers[30] printed just outside the borough were the *East London Advertiser*, the *East London Handbook and Diary*, and the *Eastern Post* in Mile End Road and the *East London Observer* in Whitechapel Road. Two were published in Bethnal Green. The *Bethnal Green Times* was founded in 1860 and renamed the *Eastern Argus* in 1882. It was a weekly owned in the 1900s by Seth Carlo, who printed it at no. 519 Cambridge Road. Vaguely Conservative and largely financed by advertising publicans,[31] it ceased publication between 1913 and 1917.[32] The *North Eastern Leader* was owned and edited by J. Forsaith, another local printer, member of the board of guardians and friend of the Liberal M.P., G. Howell.[33] The *East London Advertiser* moved from Mile End Road to no. 3 Paradise Row in 1978/9 and was still there in 1990.

A Yiddish paper connected to the Association of Jewish Socialists based in Whitechapel, *Arbeter Fraint*, was printed in Chance Street, Bethnal Green, in the 1890s and again for a few years after a gap in 1900–2.[34] Baruch Weinburg, a local printer, founded a Yiddish daily paper, *The Jewish Times*, printed first at his business in Bethnal Green Road and from 1915 at no. 175 and from 1937 at no. 73 Brick Lane.[35]

ESTATES

DEMESNE ESTATES. Bethnal Green lay wholly within Stepney manor.[36] In 1652 a parliamentary survey was made of the demesne lands, mostly within Bethnal Green, sequestrated from the royalist earl of Cleveland.[37] Trustees appointed by Act for the sale of

forfeited estates, who included William Robinson, conveyed in 1653 the former manor house, *BISHOP'S* or *BONNER'S HALL*, and 93 a. surrounding it between the Hackney border and Old Ford Lane,[38] to Mary, widow of Gen. or Adm. Richard Deane.[39] In 1654 she

7 Wilson, *E. End Entertainment*, 217–18; Bethnal Green M.B. *Official Guide* (1950), 65.
8 M. Webb, *Amber Valley Gazetteer of Gtr. Lond.'s Suburban Cinemas 1946–86* (1986), 95.
9 G.L.R.O., AR/BA/4/206, no. 5; 221, no. 5; *P.O. Dir. Lond.* (1934).
10 *P.O. Dir. Lond.* (1934, 1942).
11 G.L.R.O., AR/BA/4/206, no. 5.
12 Ibid. 251, no. 4.
13 Ibid. 284, no. 4.
14 Webb, *Amber Valley Gaz.* 11; above, building after 1945.
15 G.L.R.O., AR/BA/4/235, no. 4.
16 Ibid. 251, no. 4.
17 *P.O. Dir. Lond.* (1934).
18 Ibid. (1942, 1947).
19 G.L.R.O., AR/BA/4/235, no. 4.
20 Ibid. 437, no. 3.
21 Webb, *Amber Valley Gaz.* 10.
22 G.L.R.O., AR/BA/4/235, no. 5.
23 Ibid. 346, no. 5.
24 *P.O. Dir. Lond.* (1927).

25 Ibid. (1934); Webb, *Amber Valley Gaz.* 11.
26 Old O.S. Map Lond. 51 (1914).
27 T.H.L.H.L., TH/8351, box 2; Wilson, *E. End Entertainment*, 218; *P.O. Dir. Lond.* (1927, 1934).
28 G.L.R.O., AR/BA/4/346, no. 5; 361, no. 3.
29 Ibid. A/FWA/C/D164/1; Webb, *Amber Valley Gaz.* 10.
30 Two paras. based on *Willing's Press Guide* (1896 et seq.).
31 J. J. Bennett, 'East End Newspaper Opinion and Jewish Immigration, 1885–1905' (Sheffield Univ. M. Phil. thesis, 1979), 230).
32 *P.O. Dir. Lond.* (1913, 1917).
33 Bennet, 'E. End Newspaper Opinion', 248.
34 *E. Lond. Papers*, viii(2), 124.
35 *Spitalfields News*, June 1987, p. 5.
36 Above.
37 G.L.R.O., M93/158. The following estates are enumerated according to the survey.
38 i.e. nos. 1–15.
39 Northants. R. O., X 1123 (9), title deeds of Bps. Hall 1653–79.

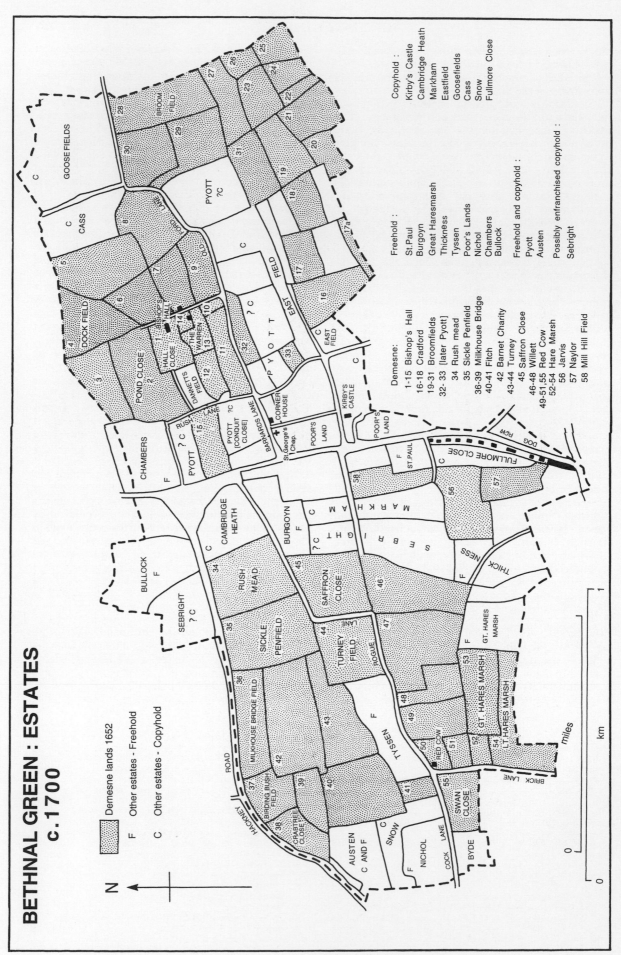

BETHNAL GREEN : ESTATES
c.1700

N

Demesne lands 1652

F Other estates - Freehold

C Other estates - Copyhold

Demesne:
1-15 Bishop's Hall
16-18 Cradford
19-31 Broomfields
32-33 [later Pyott]
34 Rush mead
35 Sickle Penfield
36-39 Milkhouse Bridge
40-41 Fitch
42 Barnet Charity
43-44 Turney
45 Saffron Close
46-48 Willett
49-51,55 Red Cow
52-54 Hare Marsh
56 Jarvis
57 Naylor
58 Mill Hill Field

Copyhold :
Kirby's Castle
Cambridge Heath
Markham
Eastfield
Goosefields
Cass
Snow
Fullmore Close

Freehold :
St.Paul
Burgoyn
Great Haresmarsh
Thickness
Tyssen
Poor's Lands
Nichol
Chambers
Bullock

Freehold and copyhold :
Pyott
Austen

Possibly enfranchised copyhold :
Sebright

FIG. 24

156

sold the estate to Robinson, a parliamentary major and former colleague of her husband.[40] Cleveland's daughter-in-law Philadelphia, Lady Wentworth, and her trustees later plausibly maintained that the conveyance of 1653 was only in trust for Robinson, who had induced Sir William Smyth and other mortgagees to assign the mortgage under threat.[41] In 1660 Robinson conveyed the estate to Samuel and Ellis Crisp, relatives of his wife, whose father Sir Nicholas Crisp had fought as a royalist under Cleveland.[42] The Wentworth estates were heavily encumbered and attempts by the earl and Lady Wentworth to recover them were accordingly inhibited. Mary Deane and Robinson contracted to pay off the debt on their portion and Lady Wentworth settled with Robinson's widow in 1672.[43] An attempt by a 'great creditor' of the earl of Cleveland on the Robinson title in 1677[44] failed and Bishop's Hall remained with Robinson's descendants.

By will proved 1667 Robinson left all his estates to his widow with remainder to their daughter Ann, except Bishop's Hall and 17 a. adjoining to the south, then leased to John Bumpstead for £30 a year, which were to be settled in trust for 'poor godly persons for ever'.[45] The trustees of what Robinson's widow described as a private charity allowed her to distribute the money,[46] as may have been done by her successors, who seem to have treated the site of the house as their own until well into the 18th century.[47] Trustees for Robinson's charity were appointed in 1711, however[48] and in 1842 they conveyed Bonner's Hall and Fields, 17 a., to the Commissioners of Woods to form part of Victoria Park.[49]

William Robinson's widow Ann married Francis Howell (d. 1680) c. 1670 and died in 1700.[50] In 1674 her daughter Ann (d. 1727) married James Sotheby (d. 1720), son of James Sotheby (d. 1685) of Hackney. In 1686 the younger James bought Dannetts field, 6 a. west of the former mansion house. Dannetts had been conveyed to trustees by Lord Wentworth in the 1630s, possibly in another mortgage, and sold to John

Byde in 1642 and to Thomas Hodgkins by Sir Thomas Byde in 1668. James and Ann Sotheby succeeded to Bishop's Hall in 1700 and the estate descended in the Sothebys of Sewardstone (Essex) through Ann's sons James (d.s.p. 1742) and William (d. 1766), to William's son and namesake (d. 1833), the younger William's son Adm. Charles (d. 1854), and his sons Charles William Hamilton (d.s.p. 1887) and Frederick Edward (d.s.p. 1909).[51] The eastern 10 a. portion of Pyotts were added in 1753.[52] Parts were sold for canals in 1814 and c. 1830[53] and more was sold to form the bulk of Victoria Park.[54] A branch of the Sothebys, descended from the second son of William (d. 1766), retained some freehold in 1925.[55]

Most of the remaining demesne lands were sold in parcels between 1653 and 1660. The Wentworths later confirmed the sale of their right to the freehold and most sales were finally settled in 1669–72.[56]

Some 16 a. between Mile End and what became Green Street (Roman Road) and 4½ a. next to Old Ford Lane and Back Lane[57] were sold to 'Lady Windham'.[58] The sale, not recorded among those made in the 1650s, was most probably to Barbara, wife of Sir Wadham Wyndham (d. 1668), justice of the King's Bench.[59] There seem to have been field boundary changes, probably as part of the final inclosure of Eastfield and involving exchanges with Pyotts and Eastfields estates.[60] By 1703 c. 22 a. south of what became Green Street were called Cradfords[61] and later Kings Field and Barwells after the occupiers of 1703.[62] The estate was apparently owned by John Gretton and his wife Sarah in 1768 when they granted a rent charge from it to Thomas W. Morgan and his daughter Elizabeth Mary.[63] The annuity was included in Elizabeth Mary's grant in 1813[64] and remained with her trust until it was sold to the L.C.C. c. 1900.[65] The Gretton family retained the freehold and during the 1830s William Walter Gretton was associated with John Butler of Grove House in developing the western part of the estate.[66] In 1840 Butler's son Charles Salisbury Butler of

40 Northants. R.O., X 1075 (23), Jas. Sotheby's notes; X 1077, correspond. of Wm. Robinson.
41 T.H.L.H.L., TH/3710.
42 Probably her uncle and his son: P.R.O., PROB 11/319 (P.C.C. 42 Mico), f. 334; Northants. R. O., X 1123 (9); X 1078 (2), Sir Thos. Crisp's will and notes; X 1078 (13), pedigree; Burke, *Ext. & Dorm. Baronetcies* (1838), s.v. Crispe.
43 Northants R.O., X 1123 (9); T.H.L.H.L., TH/2353, 3712, 3717. The Robinson title included a conveyance in fee and the 99-yr. lease of 1632. For the mortgages and other encumbrances in Stepney manor, above, Stepney, manor.
44 T.H.L.H.L., TH/3711.
45 P.R.O., PROB 11/325 (P.C.C. 137 Carr); copy in Northants. R. O., X 1078 (11).
46 Northants. R. O., X 1074 (bundle E, no. 4), papers from Ann Howell concerning the Poor's Land.
47 Ibid. X 1077, memo. 1724; X 1123 (13), lease of Bps. Hall 1742. Gascoyne's *Map* names the whole estate as 'Southerby's land'.
48 T.H.L.H.L., TH/225.
49 Act enabling purchase for Victoria Park, 5 & 6 Vic. c. 20; P.R.O.., IR 30/2/40; G.L.R.O., rm, rpp/TA 1; Victoria Pk. Papers, vol. i, 9 Feb. and 12 Feb. 1844, letters from solicitors of Robinson's char.
50 *Lond. Marriage Licences* (Index Libr. lxvi), ii. 18; Northants. R. O., X 1074 (C), will of Fras. Howell; X 1078

(1), will of Ann Howell; X 1123 (13), Bps. Hall 1647–1742.
51 Northants. R. O., X 1078 (10), certs. of marriage and burials; (32), pedigree of Sotheby.
52 M.L.R. 1753/3/364–5; below, Pyotts.
53 M.L.R. 1828/1/327; G.L.R.O., MA/DCP/72 c, d.
54 5 & 6 Vic. c. 20; G.L.R.O., Victoria Pk. Papers, vol. 1, 27 July 1842; 10 July 1844; above, building 1837–75.
55 T.H.L.H.L., TH/7895; Northants. R. O., X 1078 (32), pedigree of Sotheby.
56 P.R.O., C 54/3805, nos. 24, 29; 3989, no. 9; *Econ.H.R.* 2nd ser. v. 196–8; thanks are due to Dr. Joan Thirsk for lending her notes for the above article. For details, above, Stepney, manor.
57 i.e. demesne nos. 16–18, 32–33.
58 G.L.R.O., M93/158, ff. 4, 6.
59 *Complete Peerage*, s.v. Wyndham; H. A. Wyndham, *A Family Hist. 1410–1688* (1939); *1688–1837* (1950), *passim* and genealogies at end.
60 Below.   61 Gascoyne, *Map*.
62 M.L.R. 1840/4/603.
63 Ibid. 1779/1/153.
64 Below, Pyotts; P.R.O., C 54/12480, mm. 37 sqq.
65 Bates Trust Memo. & Plans 1906 (Gregory, Rowcliffe & Milners, solicitors to Mrs. E. M. Bates Trust).
66 M.L.R. 1832/3/95–6; 1835/1/365; 1835/4/483–5; 1836/6/768; 1836/7/272.

Upper Clapton (Hackney) apparently purchased the whole estate.[67] As the building plans collapsed, a private company sought to buy the undeveloped eastern portion in 1845 for a cemetery, although Butler resumed the freehold in 1853 when the company defaulted. In 1891 his son the Revd. John Banks Meek Butler of Sussex conveyed 11½ a. (Victoria Park cemetery) for the Metropolitan Public Gardens Association.[68]

BROOMFIELDS,[69] in the south-east corner of Bethnal Green, possibly incorporated closes known in the 14th century as Combfield and Newland but was mentioned by name c. 1439.[70] Described in 1538 as three closes containing 92 a. of arable and pasture,[71] it was mortgaged with the rest of Stepney manor for 99 years in 1632. In 1669 Philadelphia, Lady Wentworth, Sir William Smyth, and other trustees assigned the residue of the lease and sold the fee simple of Broomfields, then 82 a., to Arnold Browne, a Stepney mariner, who assigned it in 1676 to trustees for Sir Nathaniel Herne, alderman of London.[72] By will proved 1679 Sir Nathaniel left the estate to his eldest son Frederick,[73] who by will proved 1695 left it to his son Nathaniel, a minor.[74] Frederick's executors leased out Broomfields, by then 79 a. in 12 closes, in 1701[75] although Lady Herne, presumably Sir Nathaniel's widow, was considered the owner in 1694 and 1703.[76] The younger Nathaniel apparently died young and the estate passed, on the marriage in 1705 of his sister Judith to William Villiers, to the earls of Jersey.[77] In 1789 Judith's grandson George Bussy Villiers, earl of Jersey (d. 1805), sold the estate, then 78 a., to Thomas, later Sir Thomas, Coxhead,[78] who by will proved 1811 left all his estates, consisting of 17 houses and c. 100 a. in Bethnal Green and Mile End Old Town, to Thomas Coxhead Marsh, natural son of Sarah Marsh (and presumably of Coxhead). The estate passed in 1847 to T.C. Marsh's brother William Coxhead Marsh and William's son Thomas Coxhead Chisenhale Marsh.[79] In 1851 William had 55 a., after surrenders for the canals and Victoria Park in the 1830s and 1840s.[80] From 1857 William and Thomas sold building land to the Revd. George Driffield

and others[81] and in 1874 Thomas was considering selling land for a gasworks.[82]

RUSH MEAD, 15 a. between Hackney Road and Old Bethnal Green Road,[83] formed part of demesne lands sold by Lord Cleveland to James Ravenscroft in 1640[84] and which Sir William Smyth claimed had been sold to him by Ravenscroft in 1643. In 1652 Smyth sold the 99-year mortgage term and the reversion he acquired in 1651 to Florentine Tainturier of Blackfriars, a tailor, and his daughter Mary, who also acquired the equity of redemption in 1654.[85] By 1703 it was called Cuthberd's and owned by Ossery,[86] who had been assessed for 'Cuthberds' in 1694[87] and was probably John Ossery, oilman of Holborn, a freeholder in 1697.[88] By will proved 1732 Elizabeth Sheldon left Rush Mead to her son Cuthbert Sheldon, whose daughter Elizabeth married James Durham, guardsman, in 1779. They granted building leases from 1792[89] and Col. Durham was apparently the owner in 1831,[90] although the Sheffield family possessed at least part of the estate in 1876.[91]

One of the earl of Cleveland's creditors, Edmund Denton, William Smyth's brother-in-law, was assigned the equity of *SICKLE PEN-FIELD* and Six Acre Close,[92] together 13 a. west of Rush Mead, by the parliamentary trustees in 1653.[93] He conveyed it to John Smyth, William's brother, who sold it to Richard Knight of St. Giles without Cripplegate, armourer, in 1654.[94] The field was marked as Willett's land in 1679[95] but as Knight's land in 1703. Richard Knight's grandson Peter Knight, of Essex, took out several mortgages between 1711 and 1717 with Samuel Payne, gentleman, of Shoreditch, and Edward Carnell, sadler of London. Carnell's father occupied the estate,[96] from c. 1751 to c. 1794 called Carnell's land,[97] and Samuel Carnell was making leases there in 1795.[98]

MILKHOUSE BRIDGE and Birding Bush fields and Crabtree and Three Acre closes formed a 27-a. estate in the north-west.[99] A 99-year lease was assigned in 1651 by Thomas Dunstervile, haberdasher, to Edward Trussell and in 1654 by Trussell to Humphrey Blake.[1] In 1680 Blake's children Robert and Ann, wife of

67 Ibid. 1840/4/603; J. J. Sexby, *Municipal Pks. of Lond.* (1898), 571.
68 Guildhall MS. 21670/40; *Clergy List* (1891); Sexby, *Municipal Pks.* 571-2; below, pub. svces. (burial grds. (Vic. Pk. cem.) and parks and open spaces (Heath Gdns.)).
69 i.e. demesne nos. 19-31.
70 P.R.O., SC 6/1139/24; above, fig. 5.
71 G.L.R.O., M93/208.
72 Ibid. 166; T.H.L.H.L., TH/2425; P.R.O., C 10/90/7; C 54/3805, no. 29.
73 P.R.O., PROB 11/360 (P.C.C. 107 King).
74 Ibid. PROB 11/424 (P.C.C. 6 Irby).
75 T.H.L.H.L., TH/2350.
76 C. L. R. O., Box 43, MS. 22; Gascoyne, *Map*.
77 Burke, *Peerage, Baronetage & Knightage* (1970); family tree in G.L.R.O., catalogue to Jersey Colln., Acc. 510.
78 M.L.R. 1789/5/118-19.
79 T.H.L.H.L., TH/7828.
80 6 a. next the canal for the park: P.R.O., MPE 1365; IR 30/21/40; G.L.R.O., rm and rpp/TA 1; Vic. Pk. Papers, vol. 1, 22, 25 July 1841, 2 Apr. 1844.
81 T.H.L.H.L., TH/5818, 7254, 7828.
82 G.L.R.O., MR/UP 1098.

83 Demesne no. 34.
84 B.L. Add. MS. 22253, f. 40; P.R.O., C 3/422/36.
85 Lambeth Pal. Libr., MS. 2731/2; P.R.O., C 54/3813/6.
86 Gascoyne, *Map*.
87 C. L. R. O., Assess. Bk. 43, MS. 22.
88 G.L.R.O., MR/FBI, ff. 18, 85.
89 Ibid., Acc. 240/25; T.H.L.H.L., TH/7694-5, 7713.
90 G.L.R.O., MR/PLT 5096.
91 T.H.L.H.L., TH/7322.
92 Demesne no. 35. Called Knightsland in 1703: Gascoyne, *Map*.
93 P.R.O., C 54/3805, no. 29; *Cal. Cttee. for Compounding*, iii(2), 2167; *V.C.H. Bucks.* iv. 174.
94 P.R.O., C 54/3807, no. 41; 3817, no. 10.
95 Map, part of foundation deed (1679) *penes* Jesus Hosp. Char., Barnet (Herts.).
96 T.H.L.H.L., TH/2143; M.L.R. 1712/6/67; 1714/1/138; 1717/3/264.
97 T.H.L.H.L., BG/356, 261; Map no. 301.
98 Ibid. TH/2352.
99 Demesne nos. 36-9. Para based on *Home Counties. Mag.* xi. 293-8.
1 P.R.O., C 103/157.

Christopher Todd, sold the lease to James Smithsby, woollen draper of Westminster, who bought the freehold from the Wentworths in 1681. Smithsby was soon succeeded by his daughters Margaret, wife of Sir Francis Head, and Ann, wife of Sir Hans Hamilton, Bt., whose portion, the easternmost, was in 1703 'Hambletons land'.[2] Ann's daughter Ann (d. 1771), wife of James Campbell, left her moiety to Margaret's descendants. Margaret (d. 1732) was succeeded by her son Sir John Head (d. 1769), whose moiety passed to his widow Jane and then to the daughters of his sister Ann Egerton, Charlotte (d. 1770), wife of William Hammond, and Jemima, wife of Edward Brydges, who inherited Ann Campbell's portion. Some 6½ a. were sold to John Allport in 1789 but most of the estate was still held in fractions by members of the Hammond and Brydges families in 1848, when they gave the site for St. Thomas's church in Nova Scotia Gardens.[3]

Some 15–16 a. on the Shoreditch borders,[4] later divided by Virginia Row, were among lands sold by Cleveland to Ravenscroft in 1640 and by him to Sir William Smyth in 1643.[5] They were sold with other lands to Thomas Willett in 1653[6] and were still Willett's in 1669[7] but probably lost after 1672 when his widow had to raise portions for his children.[8] By 1694 Ann, widow of Sir Thomas Fytche, Bt., held at least part,[9] presumably the fields south of Virginia Row described as 'Lady FITCH'S land' in 1703.[10] Her son Sir Comport Fytche, Bt. (d. 1720), was listed as a freeholder in Bethnal Green from 1709 to 1719.[11] From 1723 to 1734 building leases, mostly for Virginia Row, were made by Richard Ordway, draper of London, and Thomas Coates, farmer of Bethnal Green.[12] William Gascoigne (or Gascoyne), probably son of the mapmaker, was the owner by 1780.[13] He left all his freeholds in Bethnal Green by will proved 1793 to provide for the education of his children and pass after his wife's death to his son William.[14] Harriet, née Gascoigne, wife of Thomas Smith Child was the owner in 1852.[15]

Among the lands bought by Ravenscroft in 1640 was a 14-a. field south of Milkhouse Bridge field,[16] which he conveyed to two charities in his native Chipping or High Barnet (Herts.) in 1679, when himself living in High Holborn.[17] Subsequently known as *BARNET CHARITY* estates, most of the field, 10¾ a. south-east of Birdcage Walk, was given to support Jesus Hospital, while the other 3¼ a. were to maintain the church and the tombs of Ravenscroft's parents (the Chancel charity). The charities retained the estates until the 20th century. Part of the portion belonging to Jesus Hospital was compulsorily purchased by the L.C.C. and the rest was sold in 1980.[18]

TURNEY or Comonfield was one of two closes,[19] 21 a. in all, south-east of Ravenscroft's, which by 1679 was held by Patient Ward[20] and in 1687 by John Ward, merchant of London.[21] Called Wards land in 1703,[22] it remained with the Warde family of Squerryes Court, Westerham (Kent), until 1920 when John Roberts O'Brien Warde sold it to William Parrish (d. 1925).[23]

To the east lay *SAFFRON CLOSE*, 12 a. bounded on two sides by Rogue Lane,[24] which William Smyth and others sold in 1655 to Isaac Joyce (d. 1676), clothworker of London.[25] In 1694 and 1703 it was owned by Mr. Bailey (presumably Arthur Bailey of Mile End Green, a Virginia merchant) and occupied by Hemmons or Hemonds.[26] It descended to Arthur's daughter Katharine (d. 1727) who in 1713 married Thomas Heath (d. 1741), East India merchant, and to her eldest son Bailey Heath (d. 1760). All the Heath estates were sold under a lunacy order in 1772. Philip James May purchased Saffron Close on behalf of David Wilmot, who sold parts for building.[27] Most of the estate was held in 1843 by Samuel Mills and on the death of John Remington Mills in 1865 was divided between his daughters, Florence Sophia and Marion Jane, later wife of Maj. George Malcolm Fox (d. 1918). The Fox family retained the freehold in 1955.[28]

A block of c. 36 a. south and west of Saffron Close[29] was among land sold by Smyth to Thomas Willett of London in 1653.[30] After Willett's death c. 1672 the estate, by 1703 called

---

[2] Gascoyne, *Map*.

[3] Wm. Osmond Hammond held 35/112 in fee and 14/112 in tail male, Lady Isabella Anne Brydges 39/112 as tenant for life, and J. G. W. Brydges and Charlotte Harrison each 12/112 in fee: Guildhall MS. 19224/658.

[4] Demesne nos. 40–1.

[5] Lambeth Pal. Libr., MS. 2731/2; P.R.O., C 3/422/36; B.L. Add. MS. 22253, ff. 4d–5. The parl. survey noted Smyth's claims under the 99-yr. mortgage but ignored Cleveland's conveyance in 1640 to Ravenscroft and his to Smyth in 1643, treating all those lands as still demesne in 1652: G.L.R.O., M93/158, ff. 13–14.

[6] Lambeth Pal. Libr., MS. 2731/3–4; P.R.O., C 54/3716, no. 13.

[7] P.R.O., PROB 11/330 (P.C.C. 98 Coke).

[8] Lambeth Pal. Libr., MS. 2731/9; below, this section.

[9] C. L. R. O., Assess. Box 43, MS. 22. For the Fytches see Burke, *Ext. & Dorm. Baronetcies* (1838), 212.

[10] Gascoyne, *Map*.

[11] G.L.R.O., MR/FB 2, f. 328; FB 3, f. 452.

[12] M.L.R. 1729/1/344; 1752/3/726; P.R.O., C 107/172.

[13] G.L.R.O., MR/PLT 4988; B.L., Crace Colln., Portf. xvi. 34.

[14] Wm. also bequeathed 'my late father's draughts and

surveys': P.R.O., PROB 11/1239 (P.C.C. 596 Dodwell), ff. 282–3v.   [15] P.R.O., C 54/14375, mm. 49–53.

[16] Demesne no. 42.

[17] Foundation deed (1679) *penes* Jesus Hosp., Barnet.

[18] Inf. from Clerk to the Visitors, Jesus Hosp. Char., Barnet (1992); *V.C.H. Herts.* ii. 334–5.

[19] Demesne nos. 43–4.

[20] Map, part of foundation deed (1679) *penes* Jesus Hosp., Barnet.

[21] P.R.O., C 5/184/99; C 8/358/197.

[22] Gascoyne, *Map*.

[23] G.L.R.O., MR/FB 1–3; T.H.L.H.L., TH/8276; BG/260; *The Times*, 20 Oct. 1887, 3d.; P.R.O., C 54/16454, mm. 20–25; G.L. Gower, *Parochial Hist. Westerham* (1883), 51–61.

[24] Demesne no. 45.

[25] P.R.O., C 54/3858, no. 32; ibid. PROB 11/353 (P.C.C. 6 Hale), f. 46v.

[26] C. L. R. O., Assess. Box 43, MS. 22; Gascoyne, *Map*.

[27] T.H.L.H.L., TH/2277, 6465–6; T. Wright, *Hist. Essex*, ii (1831), 159; Lond. Hosp. Archives, LH/D/1/23; and see Stepney, other manors (Rumbolds); above, the Centre.

[28] T.H.L.H.L., TH/4741–2.

[29] Demesne nos. 46–8.

[30] Lambeth Pal. Libr., MS. 2731/3–4; P.R.O., C 54/3716, nos. 13–14.

WILLETT'S[31] land, passed to his widow Martha (d. 1713) and to their surviving child Martha (d. *c.* 1716), widow of Richard Wightwick, merchant of London.[32] Martha's son Thomas Wightwick[33] was succeeded in 1722 by his sister Martha and her husband Charles White of the Inner Temple, who paid off a mortgage of 1713.[34] By Charles's will, proved 1754, the estate was left to his brother William, with remainder in tail male. A younger Charles, son of the testator's younger brother Thomas, bought out his cousins' interests in 1771 and his grandson John was in possession in 1823.[35] Some building had taken place by 1703[36] and Charles White negotiated 99-year building leases in 1789.[37]

Some 18½ a. south of Bethnal Green Road, on either side of Brick Lane and centred on the *RED COW* or Milkhouse,[38] were described by 1703 as Slaughter's Land.[39] Thomas Sclater or Slaughter of Gray's Inn and later of Catley (Cambs.) in 1711 offered Harefield or Crossfield, the land east of Brick Lane, as a site for a church[40] and in 1716 leased a plot next to Club Row, part of Swanfield, the land west of Brick Lane.[41] Negotiations for the church site collapsed because of 'some defect' in the title,[42] but Thomas (d. 1736), who adopted his wife's surname Bacon, continued in possession. He left his estates to Sarah (d. *c.* 1738), wife of his coachman Edward King and his putative mistress, with remainder to her sons Robert (d. 1749) and Thomas Sclater King (d. 1777).[43] In 1770 the estate was settled in trust on the marriage of T.S. King's daughter Elizabeth (d. 1778) to Henry Busby of Hanover Square,[44] the profits to provide an annuity for Martha King and the rest to be divided between T. S. King and Busby.[45] Busby (d. 1792) having left one third of the estate to his son Edward Sclater Busby and the rest to his four daughters as tenants in common, an Act of 1809 divided the estate into five.[46] It was further fragmented when the portion of one daughter, Margaret, wife of Edward Augustus Butcher, was divided among their six children in accordance with his will, proved 1838.[47]

Most of *HARE MARSH* in the south-west, in 1652 19 a. in three closes east of Brick Lane,[48] was acquired by Sir William Smyth in 1643.[49] In 1653 he sold it to Ansell Carter (d. 1661),[50] a London grocer, who left it to his sons George, who died shortly after his father,[51] and John, also grocers. John (d. 1687) administered one moiety for his brother's children and left the united estate to George's surviving son George, gentleman of Hackney, the holder in 1704.[52] Elizabeth Carter of Hackney, presumably George's daughter, made building leases from 1721 to 1745[53] and in 1740 sold the southernmost portion, south of Carter's Rents, to Joseph Cooper, glazier of London.[54] The rest, 18½ a. south of Hare Street, passed *c.* 1752 under her will to Charles Petley of Kent.[55] Charles Robert Carter Petley still owned what was called the Petley estate in 1887.[56]

Some 9 a. in two closes [57] abutting Markhams and Colemans copyhold were sold by Smyth and others to David Murray of St. Clement's, Middlesex, and his daughter Temperance in 1653[58] and in 1657 by Temperance, wife of Edmund Phillips, and her siblings to trustees for Mary Brett with remainder to William Lowe.[59] William died in or before 1681[60] and in 1703 the estate was called *JARVIS'S* land.[61] It passed to Lydia Jarvis (d.s.p. 1751), who married Peter Mews in 1719 and left property in Hampshire to Jarvis Clerke, son of her sister Agnes, whence it passed in 1778 to George Ivison Tapps, descendant of her sister Elizabeth.[62] The Bethnal Green property, however, may have been left to Elizabeth's family in 1751, when it was described as 'Tapp's land'.[63] It was owned in 1812 by George Ivison Tapps of Hinton House (Hants), created a baronet in 1791,[64] whose son Sir George William Tapps Gervis, Bt., leased it to developers in the 1840s.[65]

A 4-a. close on the borders with Mile End, occupied in 1652 by Jeremy Chalker,[66] and 2 a.

31 Spelt Willits: Gascoyne, *Map*.
32 Lambeth Pal. Libr., MS. 2731/9.
33 Ibid. 10.
34 Ibid. 13–14.
35 BNC, MS. B. Gr. I Ms. B. Gr. 1.
36 e.g. in Silver St. and Rogue Lane: Gascoyne, *Map*.
37 e.g. on S. side of Bethnal Green Rd.: T.H.L.H.L., TH/1160–1; Horwood, *Plan* (1792–9).
38 Demesne nos. 49–51, 55.
39 Gascoyne, *Map*.
40 Lambeth Pal. Libr., MS. 2750/16.
41 T.H.L.H.L., TH/8111.
42 Lambeth Pal. Libr., MS. 2712, f. 192; below, parish church.
43 *V.C.H. Cambs.* vi. 85; T.H.L.H.L., TH/304, 2894; M.L.R. 1728/2/446; 1765/5/320, 555.
44 T.H.L.H.L., TH/2885.
45 Ibid. 2886, 7972, 7975.
46 Ibid. 2896, 2906; Act for Partition by Will of Hen. Busby, 49 Geo. III, c. 110 (Local and Personal, not printed).
47 i.e. section E. of Brick Lane and N. of Busby St.: T.H.L.H.L., TH/2915.
48 Demesne nos. 52–4; Gt. and Lt. Hares Marsh and the Pingle: G.L.R.O., M93/158, ff. 11–12.
49 Lambeth Pal. Libr., MS. 2731/2.
50 P.R.O., C 54/3688, no. 13.
51 The wills of Ansell and Geo. were both proved 3 Sept.

1661: P.R.O., PROB 11/305 (P.C.C. 136 May), ff. 247-v.
52 Ibid. PROB 11/387 (P.C.C. 75 Foot), ff. 242v.-5; Guildhall MS. 9968; M.L.R. 1713/5/101.
53 e.g. M.L.R. 1725/6/110–1; 1730/3/276; 1752/1/570-2, 592–8; 1763/2/306.
54 G.L.R.O., o/188/1.
55 M.L.R. 1752/2/281-2.
56 G.L.R.O., MR/UP/1190; P.R.O., C 54/19352, mm. 14–16.
57 Demesne no. 56.
58 P.R.O., C 54/3943, no. 12.
59 Ibid. C 54/3943, no. 48. Temperance's siblings were Jane and Francis [? *recte* Frances].
60 Wm. Lowe, innholder (d. 1681), mentioned no land in Bethnal Green but requested burial in Holborn near his kinsman Wm. Lowe, 'lately deceased': P.R.O., PROB 11/365 (P.C.C. 46 North), f. 360v.
61 Gascoyne, *Map*.
62 *V.C.H. Hants*, v. 93.
63 T.H.L.H.L., BG/256. Lydia's will mentions no real estate: P.R.O., PROB 11/789 (P.C.C. 215), f. 121.
64 M.L.R. 1812/6/134.
65 Ibid. 1842/1/130; 1842/2/554; 1842/5/167; Burke, *Peerage & Baronetage* (1828) s.v. Tapps. Called Sir Geo. Wm. Gervis Tapps in Burke, *Land. Gent.* (1846), s.v. Fuller. For later hist. of fam., which changed its name to Tapps-Gervis-Meyrick, see *V.C.H. Hants*, v. 93.
66 Demesne no. 57.

of Mill Hill field farther north, fronting the Cambridge Road,[67] were both sold in 1654 to Laurence Chalker, a local cowkeeper.[68] Chalker sold Mill Hill field in 1654 to Thomas Coling (Coleing),[69] tenant in 1652 of a house in Dog Row,[70] and it later became Penn's nursery.[71] Chalker was in possession of the southern close in 1672[72] but by 1694 it was held by Thomas Blackett (d. 1701) who left it to his widow until his son Thomas was of age. Joshua *NAYLOR*, a London cheesemonger, whom Blackett's widow married within the year, gave his name to the estate which was occupied by Henry Collier in 1703. The younger Thomas Blackett and his sister, still minors, accused Naylor of defrauding them in 1704[73] but Blackett had apparently regained the estate by 1727.[74] For most of the 18th century it formed the core of the farm held by the Farmer family, possibly as lessees.[75]

OTHER ESTATES. The estate belonging to the dean and chapter of *ST. PAUL'S*,[76] deriving from the fee of Brice of Shadwell, consisted in 1649[77] of a close of 4½ a. west of the green, abutting south on a common way from the green to meadow, which was leased in 1638 to the dean's sister. Earlier the southern abutment was described as a lane from the green to Conduit close.[78] Another 5-a. close, occupied by Thomas Hart, lay to the west of demesne land in 1641.[79] One close was 'Bowes land', in 1703 west of Cambridge Road and north of what became Three Colts Lane.[80] Paul Bowes of the Middle Temple was among those interested in preserving the green in 1678.[81] In 1707 Martin Bowes conveyed copyhold land (also called Bowes Land in 1703)[82] in Old Ford Road to Charles Boon, which descended in the Boon family until 1765 or later.[83] The dean leased the close in Cambridge Road to Stephen Boon for life in 1775 and to Stephen's son Thomas, surgeon of Sunbury, in 1803.[84] Building began soon afterwards, since by 1809 the estate abutted on Parliament and Abingdon streets. It was apparently auctioned c. 1822.[85] The second close probably lay to the north, adjoining the first or beyond, next to Stainers land,[86] but it may have

been east of the green, in the area south of Old Ford Lane.

The 8½ a. west of Cambridge Road and south of Old Bethnal Green Road, part of the lands of St. Mary without Bishopsgate, was granted after the Dissolution to Sir Ralph Warren as part of *BURGOYNS* (Burganes),[87] a freehold estate centred in Shoreditch and named after Thomas Burgoyn, who held most of it, although not the Bethnal Green part, in 1472. Sir John Lee held it by 1652 and Thomas Lee and his son Baptist by 1717.[88] Baptist Lee (d. 1768) of Suffolk leased the Bethnal Green portion in 1758[89] and left the estate in trust for his niece's widower Nathaniel Acton (d. 1795) with remainder to Nathaniel's son Nathaniel Lee Acton (d. 1836). N. L. Acton was succeeded by his sisters Caroline (d.s.p. by 1838) and Harriot, wife of Sir William Middleton, Bt. In 1838 Harriot and her son Sir William Fowle Fowle Middleton, Bt., broke the entail and in 1842 sold 3½ a. to the bishop of London and William Cotton for the site of St. Jude's church.[90] In 1845 and 1858 Sir William (d. 1860) leased out the rest of the estate, previously a nursery, for building.[91]

The 12-a. portion of Haresmarsh east of that belonging to the demesne, sometimes called *GREAT HARESMARSH*, had belonged to St. Helen's Bishopsgate and was granted in 1545 to John Pope, whose successor was said to hold it of the Crown in free socage.[92] Following litigation in 1646, it was held in 1652 by John and Susan Godowne,[93] who initiated further litigation to eject the other party, the Richardsons, who still held the deeds. Sir John Clarke of Twickenham acquired the estate from Humphrey Turkey and Walter Carnaby and his wife Mary, possibly trustees, in 1664.[94] Sir John Clarke was in possession in 1694[95] of what by 1703 was 'Clarks Land', divided into a western garden and an eastern field.[96] Clarke (d. 1712) left the estate to his niece Judith, wife of Arthur Foresight, a London apothecary.[97] By 1745 it was in the hands of Sir Philip Hall,[98] who sold it in 1761 to Peter Bigot of Essex.[99] James Goden Bigot sold it in 1794 to Michael Pope of Finsbury Square,[1] whose descendants held it in 1842.[2]

Some 6 a., part of 30 a. of mainly demesne land

67 Ibid. no. 58.
68 P.R.O., C 54/3808, nos. 4, 9. T.H.L.H.L., TH/2267, 2382.
69 T.H.L.H.L., TH/40.
70 G.L.R.O., M93/158, f. 15.
71 Below, econ. hist. (mkt. gdns.).
72 T.H.L.H.L., TH/3717.
73 C.L.R.O., Assess. Box 43, MS. 22; P.R.O., C 5/592/66; Gascoyne, *Map*.
74 Lambeth Pal. Libr., MS. 2712, f. 193; M.L.R. 1767/3/446.
75 Below, econ. hist. (agric.).
76 For earlier hist., above, Stepney, estates.
77 Guildhall MS. 25121/1711.
78 Ibid. 1713. Markhams rather than Pyotts Conduit close: below, pub. svces. (water).
79 Guildhall MS. 25121/1714.
80 Gascoyne, *Map*.
81 G.L.R.O., A/PLC/IV/1; above, the Green.
82 Gascoyne, *Map*.
83 G.L.R.O., M93/36, p. 270; 132, f. 343.
84 T.H.L.H.L., TH/2338, 7499.
85 Ibid. 7499–50.
86 P.R.O., WARD 7/74/150; above, the Green. The

demesne abutment may have been Mill Hill field.
87 Based on *Survey of Lond.* viii. 36–37; G.L.R.O., M93/157, f. 53; P.R.O., SC 6/1108/18; *Valor Eccl.* (Rec. Com.), i. 401–2; *L. & P. Hen. VIII*, xix (2), 75. And see M. J. Power, 'Urban Development of E. Lond. 1550–1700' (Lond. Univ. Ph.D. thesis, 1971), 107; *V.C.H. Mdx.* x. 85.
88 M.L.R. 1717/6/64–5.
89 T.H.L.H.L., TH/2339; *V.C.H. Mdx.* x. 85.
90 G.L.R.O., C/72/187; Burke, *Peerage & Baronetage* (1828), s.v. Middleton.
91 G.L.R.O., C/72/88; T.H.L.H.L., TH/2313–4.
92 *L. & P. Hen. VIII*, xx(1), p. 123. For early hist., above, Stepney, estates.
93 G.L.R.O., M93/158, ff. 11v.–12; P.R.O., C 8/105/104; C 9/13/15, 25/65, 26/62; C 10/66/121.
94 P.R.O., C 103/157.
95 C.L.R.O., Assess. Box 43, MS. 22.
96 Gascoyne, *Map*.
97 M.L.R. 1712/1/138–41.
98 T.H.L.H.L., TH/371.
99 Ibid. 436–7.
1 M.L.R. 1794/3/661.
2 Ibid. 1842/2/252.

south of Rogue Lane, was from the mid 17th century and possibly earlier held by the *THICKNESS* family, which had held property in Whitechapel since the 1580s.[3] The Bethnal Green estate was freehold[4] and in 1703 formed 9½ a. in two fields,[5] later described as 'near the ducking pond'. Ralph Thickness (d. 1718) was succeeded by five daughters[6] and between 1755 and 1775 the estate passed to Samuel Scott, a brick merchant who leased other land nearby.[7] A Samuel Scott was listed as the holder in 1821–2 and 1835[8] and A. J. Scott in the 1880s.[9]

In 1652 John Stint (d. 1660) possessed an estate bounded south by the later Church Street or Bethnal Green Road and on the other sides by demesne land, later Fitches and Turneys.[10] It derived from a 12-a. freehold close in the Hyde which Thomas Wyndham's wife Elizabeth inherited from her cousin Robert Weston, a London mercer, and which the Wyndhams sold in 1529 to Thomas Armorer,[11] who held it in 1550.[12] By 1657 it had been divided into two fields with different lessees, one of them Robert Satchwell.[13] In 1709 the whole estate, presumably freehold, was in the hands of the *TYSSEN* family[14] from whom the Satchwells leased part in the 1760s.[15] The family was an offshoot of the Tyssens of Hackney, the Bethnal Green estate[16] passing from Francis Tyssen of Shacklewell (d. 1710)[17] to his fifth son Samuel (d. 1748) and to Samuel's widow Sarah (d. 1778) and their son William (d. 1788), then to William's widow Mary and their daughter Sarah and her husband John Tyrell (from 1809 Sir John Tyrell, Bt.).[18] From their son Sir John Tyssen Tyrell (d. 1877) it passed to trustees for John Lionel Tufnell, son of their daughter Eliza Isabella, who assumed the name Tyrell.[19]

In 1678 Thomas Rider and others bought 11½ a. of waste, later called the *POOR'S LANDS*,[20] mostly east of Cambridge Road, to prevent building and relieve the poor. The waste was inclosed into three closes, treated as freehold, which were leased out and the rents applied in charity. Trustees were appointed in 1689 but because of delay in enrolling the deed the process was repeated in 1690, usually quoted as the foundation date. They sold plots for St. John's church in 1825[21] and Vicarage in 1849, and for Bethnal Green Museum in 1868. Plans

in the 1880s to erect municipal buildings on the Poor's Land were defeated.[22] Under a Scheme of 1891, 2½ a. north of St. John's and 6½ a. south of Roman Road were conveyed to the L.C.C. for public gardens, which were opened in 1895.[23] In 1892 a small strip was sold to the Warburton trustees who ran the asylum bordering the Poor's Land, of which they had long been lessees.

The freehold *NICHOL* (Nicoll or Nicholl) estate, a compact 5 a. bounded west and south by Cock Lane (later Boundary Street and Bethnal Green Road respectively), was possibly the barn, garden, and 3 a. held by the hospital of St. Mary without Bishopsgate in 1538.[24] It took its name from John Nichol of Gray's Inn who leased, or possibly mortgaged, it for 180 years to Jon Richardson in 1680.[25] In 1725 his son John Nichol of Hendon sold the estate, which he called Nichol Street, to his wealthy cousin[26] John Nichol the elder (d. 1731)[27] of Colney Hatch. It passed through that John's son and namesake (d. 1747)[28] to the younger John's only child Margaret, who in 1753 married James Brydges, later duke of Chandos (d. 1789).[29] The estate descended with the rest of the Chandos lands[30] until 1827 when, crowded with 237 houses, it was put up for sale.[31] The Chandos estate still owned c. 50 houses in 1836[32] and Mary, Baroness Kinloss, who succeeded in 1889, was still one of the principal landowners when the whole area was purchased by the L.C.C. for the Boundary Street scheme of 1900.[33]

Two freehold estates at the northern end of Bethnal Green, east and west respectively of Cambridge Heath, may have derived from Cobhams (Rumbolds) manor.[34] In 1688 George Hockenhill paid 2s. 8d. rent for a freehold estate 'sometime Jones's', which by 1689 was held by Mr. Chambers, a scrivener in Lombard Street.[35] Chambers was the owner in 1694 and in 1703 when *CHAMBERS'S* land, occupied by William Hawkins, was 8 a. in two closes between Cambridge Heath and Bishop's Hall estate.[36] From John Chambers, a London draper, the estate descended by c. 1711 to his daughter Mary and her husband John Dorrill and to their son John Chambers Dorrill, who conveyed it in trust in 1795 for Michael Pope of Finsbury Square (d. by 1808).[37]

3 B.L. Add. MS. 22253; G.L.R.O., M93/158, f. 10.
4 G.L.R.O., M93/142, 143, 167.
5 Gascoyne, *Map*.
6 G.L.R.O., E/PH1/11.
7 Ibid. M93/142–3; BNC, MS.B.Gr.1.
8 G.L.R.O., M93/144, 145, ff. 3–6.
9 Ibid. 150.
10 G.L.R.O., M93/3, p. 75; 158 ff. 9–10.
11 P.R.O., CP 40/1102, f 2.
12 Survey in Robinson, *Hist. Hackney*, i. 336–8.
13 P.R.O., C 103/157.
14 G.L.R.O., MR/FB2, f. 328; M.L.R. 1724/1/448.
15 M.L.R. 1792/6/108.
16 For the descent, see Burke, *Land. Gent.* (1855), s.v. Tyssen; Burke, *Peerage & Baronetage* (1828), s.v. Tyrell; Walford, *County Families of U.K..* (1888), s.v. Tufnell. See also *V.C.H. Mdx.* x. 75, 77.
17 G.L.R.O., MR/FB 2, ff. 328, 388.
18 M.L.R. 1808/5/780.
19 G.L.R.O., C/72/265.
20 Based on Allgood, *Hist. Bethnal Green*, 290 sqq.; Robinson and Chesshyre, *The Green*, 5 sqq.; A. J. Robinson, 'The Poor's Land Min. Bks.' (TS. in T.H.L.H.L., Pamphlet 720.4); above, Bethnal Green village.

21 Guildhall MS. 19224/304; below, list of churches.
22 *The Times*, 21 Aug. 1889, 9f; 11 Sept. 12d; 25 Nov. 4f; 7 Dec. 10f; 6 Nov. 1890, 4f.
23 *Opening of Bethnal Green Gdns.* 3 June 1895 (G.L.R.O., LCC/CL/CER/3/1).
24 Above, Stepney, estates(St. Mary Bishopsgate).
25 M.L.R. 1709/2/126.
26 Sometimes referred to as uncle, making John Nichol of Gray's Inn and John Nichol of Hatton Gdn. brothers: G.L.R.O., Acc. 262/68/185, 198. Negotiations were conducted by Mary, wife of John of Hendon.
27 G.L.R.O., Acc. 262/68/185–98.
28 Ibid. 47/66.   29 Ibid. 51/2.
30 *V.C.H. Mdx.* vi. 17.
31 G.L.R.O. 0/102/3.   32 Ibid. 5.
33 *Complete Peerage*, vii. 312; *Town Planning Review*, xlvii (1976), 163; above, building 1876–1914.
34 e.g. 3a. between highway and bp.'s wood granted to John Morrice in 1285: above, Stepney, other manors.
35 G.L.R.O., M93/142.
36 C. L. R. O., Assess. Box 43, MS. 22; Gascoyne, *Map*.
37 Northants. R. O., X 1074 (xiii), abstract of leases of Bps. Hall; X 1123, parcel 3, 1684–1728; M.L.R. 1808/5/257.

Ownership was fragmented after the death of Pope's son Michael before 1848 but had been reunited in the hands of Maria Pope of Kensington Gardens by 1896.[38]

In 1694 Thomas Ivery was assessed for *BUL-LOCK'S* land, identifiable in 1703 as 12½ a. in two closes west of Cambridge Heath.[39] From 1747 to 1835 the estate was said to be freehold, held for 10s. by Thomas Plumer Byde.[40] The Pritchard family, rated for nearby property from the mid 18th century[41] and for Bullock's land, then called Clay Pitfield, in 1794[42] and probably in 1778,[43] may have originally been lessees but were presumably the owners for most of the 19th century. Successive Andrew Pritchards held the land,[44] and issued 99-year leases from the 1850s, until Clive Fleetwood Pritchard, eldest son of Andrew (fl. 1889) sold part or all of the estate to Bethnal Green M.B. in 1902–4.[45]

An estate,[46] mostly treated as copyhold but sometimes as freehold,[47] may have been a mixture of both;[48] from c. 1643 to 1775 it was held for £1 4s. or £1 4s. 1d. quitrent.[49] Part at least originated in a customary estate held in 1404 by John Reyson (d. 1421).[50] In 1538 the royal favourite Anthony Denny (d. 1549) of the Privy Chamber held a house and lands which he conveyed in 1544 to Sir Ralph Warren (d. 1553),[51] lord mayor of London, who acquired Burgoyns and was leased St. George's chapel for 99 years from 1547.[52] Successive holders were Sir Ralph's widow, his son Sir Richard (d. 1597) from 1572, and his grandsons, sons of his daughter Joan (d. 1586), wife of Sir Henry Cromwell. In 1601 they sold the estate, first described in full, to Richard Pyott (d. 1620), a London grocer and alderman. Thereafter commonly called *PYOTTS*, it consisted of a house at Bethnal green, 6 a. in two parcels nearby, 4½ a. at Cambridge Heath, Conduit close (7 a.), ¾ a. and 10 a. in parcels next Old Ford Lane, and 4 a. 'towards the spitle'.[53] Richard left the estate to his younger son William (d. 1643),[54] who by will proved 1645 left his copyholds in Bethnal Green to his wife Jane, with remainder to his brother John,[55] but in 1648–9 they were disputed between Jane and her second husband, John Christmas, and William's elder brother Richard, who claimed the remainder for his son William.[56] John Pyott (d. 1689), probably the son of the elder William's brother John, paid the quitrent in 1688[57] and in 1703 'Piots land' consisted of 38 a. east of Cam-

bridge Road in blocks near Cambridge Heath and south of Old Ford Lane.[58]

The estate presumably descended to the second John's sons John and then Robert (both d.s.p.), to be divided in 1734 between the children of his daughters Ann and Susan. Ann, wife of John Gubbs, had a daughter Jane (d. 1739) who married Henry Winteringham and had a daughter Martha, who died aged 16. Jane having left her moiety to Martha with remainder to her nearest relative of the name Pyott, her executors conveyed it to Richard Pyott (d.s.p. 1747), heir in the direct male line of the first Richard Pyott (d. 1620). He left his estates in trust for his wife Pyarea, but his father's siblings claimed as the nearest Pyotts.[59] John Pyott's other daughter Susan married William Cockram and had a son Sigismund, who left his moiety in 1741 to his wife Rebecca, with remainder to Henry Smith of St. Clement Danes. In 1746 Rebecca conveyed her interest to Smith in return for an annuity. The rights of all the Pyott siblings, Charles and his sisters Ann Righton, Blanch Hinckley, and Caroline Malie, were upheld in 1749, when a partition apparently assigned the estates in Bethnal Green to the Pyott heirs, with instructions for their sale. The Bethnal Green property consisted of a capital house, three new houses, two stables, and 30½ a.

The Pyott family drew rents from the estate until its sale in 1753. The 10 a. adjoining Broomfields in the east, being separate, were sold to William Sotheby and thereafter descended with Bishop's Hall.[60] Old buildings on 1 a. in the south-west corner of Conduit field were sold to Anthony Natt.[61] The rest, c. 21 a. which included the mansion, three other houses, and the rest of Conduit field, was sold to Ebenezer Mussell (d. 1764), lessee of the mansion.[62] Mussell paid the full quitrent in 1755[63] and left his portion to his second wife Sarah, as guardian for his infant son.[64] Both the son and Elizabeth, Mussell's daughter by his first wife, were apparently dead by 1768, when Sarah and her second husband John Gretton conveyed the land but not the house to Thomas Wilkins Morgan, with remainder to Elizabeth Mary Morgan, respectively Mussell's son-in-law and granddaughter.[65] Elizabeth Mary (d. 1835), who had married Ely Bates in 1788, was a widow by 1813 when she settled the estate on the Moravian Church. Thereafter the estate was administered

38   M.L.R. 1808/5/743; G.L.R.O., MR/UP 340; P.R.O., C 54/20115, mm. 25–30.
39   C. L. R. O., Assess. Box 43, MS. 22; Gascoyne, *Map*.
40   G.L.R.O., M93/142–5, 167.
41   T.H.L.H.L., BG/256.
42   Ibid. BG/261.
43   G.L.R.O., P93/DUN/201.
44   e.g. in 1850: P.R.O., C 54/18007, mm. 11–14.
45   T.H.L.H.L., Th/6547, 6552, 6557, 6559.
46   Based upon G.L.R.O., o/113/1.
47   e.g. in 1688 and 1755: G.L.R.O., M93/142, 167. The death of [Robt.] Pyott was presented in 1734 but there was no description of the est. and no one claimed as heir: G.L.R.O., M93/27, f. 432.
48   Ric. Pyott (d. 1620) referred to freehold and customary lands at Bethnal Green: P.R.O., PROB 11/135 (P.C.C. 5 Soame), ff. 41–43v.
49   P.R.O., C 142/743, no. 17; G.L.R.O., M93/142–3, 167.
50   i.e. 4 ½ a. molond at le Bery, identified as part of Wm. Pyott's est. in 1643. Reyson also held 8 ½ a. in 4 other

parcels: Guildhall MSS. 9171/3, f. 85v., 25422.
51   *L. & P. Hen. VIII*, xix, p. 13; *D.N.B.*
52   Below, parish church; *T.L.M.A.S.* xix. 113–14; *D.N.B.*
53   B.L. Add. Ch. 39410; P.R.O., C 142/248/42.
54   P.R.O., PROB 11/135 (P.C.C. 5 Soame), ff. 41–43; ibid. C 142/743/17; G.L.R.O., BRA 1/437/1.
55   P.R.O., PROB 11/193 (P.C.C. 65 Rivers), f. 63.
56   Ibid. C 6/115/99. And see ibid. C 5/404/90; C 6/116/182.
57   G.L.R.O., M93/142; P.R.O., PROB 11/396 (P.C.C. 102 Ent), f. 89v.
58   Gascoyne, *Map*.
59   G.L.R.O., M93/27, f. 432; P.R.O., C 11/1098/24; *V.C.H. Staffs.* xiv. 276.
60   M.L.R. 1753/3/364–5; above.
61   M.L.R. 1753/3/371–2.
62   Ibid. 1753/3/368–9.
63   G.L.R.O., M93/167.
64   P.R.O., PROB 11/903 (P.C.C. 396 Simpson).
65   M.L.R. 1779/1/152.

as the Elizabeth Mary Bates Trust. Sales of land, mostly in Conduit field and including the site of Globe board school, took place between 1815 and 1906. Much was sold to the East End Dwellings Co. in 1934 and most of the rest to the Elizabeth Mary Bates Housing Association before 1974 and to individual lessees from the 1970s.[66]

A house recorded in 1538 and 1601 was by 1622 'the great house called the Corner House'.[67] Leased in 1599 to Lady Katharine St. John[68] and occupied in 1622 by Richard Pyott's son-in-law Humfry Robinson, of the East India Co.,[69] it stood opposite St. George's chapel, in the angle between Old Ford Lane and what was later called Victoria Park Square.[70] The house had been 'newly built' in 1643[71] and was occupied in 1683 by Sir John Goldsborough,[72] a wealthy sea captain in the service of the East India Co., who died in India in 1693.[73] In 1694 the house, which was sublet, contained a great and little parlour, withdrawing room, hall, piazza, and numerous chambers with painted wainscots, tapestry, Indian chintz hangings and Dutch painted tiles.[74] The three-gabled building depicted in 1703 was perhaps a different house,[75] since the Corner House in the mid 18th century, when leased to 'Justice Mussell', had three storeys and two wings.[76] Mussell, an antiquarian, purchased the reliefs from the façade of Aldgate on its demolition in 1760 and rebuilt them into an addition to the house, which then became Aldgate House.[77] He also incorporated bricks from a wharf at Richborough Castle (Kent) into the paving of a courtyard.[78] The house was occupied by prominent Jews in 1765 and 1769,[79] pulled down in 1806, and replaced by Ebenezer chapel and some small tenements in 1811.[80]

William *SEBRIGHT*, town clerk of London in 1574, accumulated an estate around the City, which he left by will proved 1620 for the foundation of a grammar school in Wolverley (Worcs.), his birthplace.[81] The endowment included 12 a. in Markhams field in the centre of Bethnal Green and 8 a. on the northern borders. Although the will described the estate as held in free socage by deed of Lord Wentworth at 13s. 4d. a year,[82] rentals from 1688 to 1835 listed it as copyhold, albeit at the same rent; possibly it was early enfranchised copyhold.[83] In 1813

the trustees obtained an Act to grant 99-year building leases,[84] at whose expiry Wolverley Grammar school was said to have become the richest in the county.[85] A strip of land on the northern borders was sold to Bethnal Green and Shoreditch M.B.s in 1909 and sales to the L.C.C. were made in the 1930s under housing Acts: blocks between Pritchard's Road, Gillman Street, and Spencer Passage in 1930, between Teale, Kay, and Gillman streets and Garner Passage in 1934, and between Canrobert and Wolverley streets and Minto Place in 1939. The trustees retained many rents in 1952[86] but the remaining freehold, except for a few sites sold privately, was compulsorily purchased by the L.C.C. in the late 1950s and early 1960s.[87]

The copyhold estate called *KIRBY'S CASTLE* was built up by John Kirby or Kirkby (d. 1578). Its core was a house and 3½ a. held by Sir John Gresham, the most highly assessed person in Bethnal Green in 1545–6.[88] He conveyed the estate in 1553 to James Alton, whence it passed to John Cheyney, in 1556/7 to Robert Offley, in 1557/8 to Sir Thomas Offley, in 1559/60 to Cuthbert Tunstall, and in 1561 to Sir Thomas Grey, on whose death in 1570[89] the house and the lease of the adjoining farmhouse were sold to John Walsh (d. 1572), justice of the Common Pleas. Walsh's executors sold them to Kirby,[90] who acquired 2¾ a. called Stonerock[91] in 1575 and the farmhouse, by then a cottage, and 3 a. which he probably already held on lease, in 1577. The combined estate passed to his three daughters Ann, wife of Michael Lenton, Margaret, wife of William Thompson, and Elizabeth, wife of John Watson. Between 1589 and 1600 the Watsons acquired the other portions and in 1609 they sold the whole estate to William Palmer, whose sons Robert and William sold it in 1630 to William Dormer.[92] Dormer, a man of 'great fortune', died in 1652,[93] having recently settled it in remainder for three years on his two daughters, then on his son Barnard for 60 years, with remainder equally divided between his daughters and their heirs. The daughters, Ann Gill and Mary Deccombe, were admitted in 1652. Barnard, admitted in 1655, had conveyed his interest to Thomas Marsh by 1656 and, after controversy over the deeds, all

66 Trust deed 1813, Bates Trust memo. & Plans 1906, and other inf. supplied by Gregory, Rowcliffe & Milners; Robinson and Chesshyre, *The Green*, 24; inf. from Sam. Lewis Housing Trust Ltd.
67 *L. & P. Hen. VIII*, xix, p. 13; B.L. Add. Ch. 39410; G.L.R.O., BRA 1/437/1.
68 G.L.R.O., O/113/1; P.R.O., E 179/142/234.
69 G.L.R.O., BRA 1/437/1; P.R.O., PROB 11/135 (P.C.C. 5 Soame), ff. 41–43v.; Allgood, *Hist. Bethnal Green*, 227.
70 Robinson and Chesshyre, *The Green*, 17.
71 P.R.O., C 142/743/17.
72 G.L.R.O., M93/269.
73 P.R.O., PROB 11/430 (P.C.C. 12 Bond), f. 89v.; Hughson, *Lond., Brit. Metropolis*, iv. 444.
74 P.R.O., PROB 32/38/75–80.
75 B.L., Crace Colln. Portf. xvi. 33 (Gascoyne, *Map*; above, the Green.
76 G.L.R.O., O/113/1.
77 Lysons, *Environs*, ii. 32; ibid. ii (i), 32 (grangerized copy in Guildhall Libr.); Hughson, *Lond., Brit. Metropolis*, iv. 44 and illus. Above, plate 18.
78 *N. & Q.* 11th ser. vi. 90.

79 *Jewish Hist. Soc. Trans.* xxx. 78–9.
80 Robinson and Chesshyre, *The Green*, 24; Guildhall MS. 9580/3; Lysons, *Environs*, Suppl. 101.
81 *V.C.H. Worcs.* iii. 570; iv. 529–30; *Guildhall Miscellany*, iii. 61–2.
82 G.L.R.O., P 72/AND/27; *Act to enable trustees of Wm. Seabright to grant bldg. leases*, 53 Geo. III, c. 202 (Local and & Personal).
83 G.L.R.O., M93/142–3, 145, ff. 3–6.
84 53 Geo. III, c. 202 (Local and Personal).
85 *V.C.H. Worcs.* iii. 570, 573 (1913); iv. 473 (1924).
86 T.H.L.H.L., TH/8351, boxes 1–3.
87 Inf. from Clerk to Governors, Sebright's Educ. Foundation 1991.
88 P.R.O., E 179/141/138;/160, m. 12; *D.N.B.*
89 T.H.L.H.L., TH/2328.
90 P.R.O., PROB 11/52 (P.C.C. 34 Lyon); PROB 11/54 (P.C.C. 18 Daper); ibid. WARD 7/13/46; ibid. C 3/108/33; T.H.L.H.L., TH/2328.
91 Possibly the 2 ½ a. molond '*super Stonerok*' held by Thos. Gray in 1404: Guildhall MS. 25422.
92 T.H.L.H.L., TH/2328.
93 *P.C.C. Admins.* i (1649–54), 102.

the Dormer family interests were conveyed to Marsh by 1661.[94] Marsh conveyed the estate in 1661 to Sir William Rider (d. 1669), a hemp merchant, who left all his property to his wife Priscilla, with remainder to his eldest son Thomas.[95] In 1685 Thomas Rider surrendered the estate to James Alpha, who surrendered it to Col. Joseph Jorey (or Jorye) in 1698.[96] Jorey's niece Frances Foche, later wife of Martin Bladen, succeeded in 1726[97] and was followed in 1748 by her cousin and heir George Hodges. A dispute between Hodges and Mary Helden, named as devisee in Frances's will, was resolved in 1750 when Hodges took Jorey's other estate (Goosefields, below) and Mary Helden was admitted to Kirby's Castle. By will dated 1752 she left the estate to her daughter Mary, wife of Thomas Foster, with remainder to a kinsman John Notcutt, an Ipswich linen draper, who was admitted in 1770.[98] Under his will, proved 1778, the estate, with adjoining property in Mile End, was to be sold to provide for his children.[99] Trustees, admitted in 1779,[1] conveyed it to James Stratten in 1780.[2] The southern part was sold in 1787 to William and John Kilbinton[3] and Stony Rockfield had been split up for building by 1835.[4] Kirby's Castle was sold by Stratten's executors in 1800 to Thomas Warburton, who sold part to Samuel Preston Child in 1817. The rest descended to Thomas's son Dr. John Warburton (d. 1845) and then to John Abernethy Warburton (d. 1850), whose trustees obtained its enfranchisement in 1866.[5]

A house existed by 1547, when Sir John Gresham was granted waste to the west of it.[6] The 'mansion house' was inhabited by Sir Thomas Grey, who died there,[7] and by John Walsh.[8] It was rebuilt and in 1578 William Fleetwood, Recorder of London, referred to 'John Kirby that builded the fair house upon Bethnal Green'.[9] It was known as Kirby's Castle by 1592 when leased to Noel de Caron, who was accused by John Watson of destroying the garden, orchard, and 'fair walk' made of boards and plaster of Paris; de Caron was more interested in vegetables. Watson referred to a castle-like house, its turrets falling into decay.[10] The garden was presumably restored by Sir Hugh Platt (d. 1608), the horticulturalist, described in his son's epitaph of 1637 as 'of Kirby's Castle'.[11] Platt,

previously at Bishop's Hall, was a lessee but the owner Sir William Rider was resident in 1663, when Pepys found 'a fine place', which he considered 'the very house . . . built by the blind beggar of Bednall Green'.[12] Pepys was among those who stored valuables there during the Great Fire in 1666.[13] The house was assessed at 16 hearths, the largest in Bethnal Green, in 1664,[14] was known as Bethnal Green or Bethnal House by 1698,[15] and depicted in 1703 as having a tower and several gables.[16] It had been used as an asylum for many years in 1795, when two turrets at the end of the court wall were where the blind beggar was said to have deposited his gains.[17] A ramshackle building, it was characterized c. 1800 by numerous gables, tiled roofs, and some weatherboarding, although most was stuccoed, and was by then known as the White House.[18] Recent repairs in 1816 had uncovered painted panels and carved chimney pieces.[19] The Red House was added to the asylum before 1831 and another block in 1896. In 1920 the patients were moved to Salisbury and in 1921 the site was sold to the M.B., which demolished all the old buildings, only the 1896 block being converted into Bethnal Green library.[20]

John Hunt was admitted in 1621 to a copyhold estate which included a house at Bethnal Green and 10 a. of pasture near *CAMBRIDGE HEATH*,[21] probably the 10 a. in Rush croft surrendered by Roger Bramston to William Rider, haberdasher of London, in 1581.[22] Hunt's sons John and Nathaniel succeeded in 1662[23] and soon sold the estate to John Stonier (or Stonyer).[24] Ruth, wife of William Assiter (Ossiter) succeeded under Stonier's will in 1684[25] and her son John Assiter under her will in 1705.[26] The house, which in 1662 had become a tenement and two cottages, formerly one called the Wheatsheaf, was sold to Samuel Holland in 1707 and the 10 a. were sold to George Leeds in 1711.[27] Leeds was a cowkeeper at Dog Row and from at least 1694 leased other land in Bethnal Green.[28] He or his son in 1749 left a son George, a minor who succeeded in 1755 and obtained enfranchisement in 1774. By will dated 1785 George left all his estates to his widow Elizabeth, with remainder to his nephew

94 T.H.L.H.L., TH/2329; P.R.O., C 5/409/80–1; 432/25; C 8/131/163; 139/74; G.L.R.O., M93/132, ff. 6, 13, 30.
95 M93/132, ff. 32, 82; P.R.O., PROB 11/331 (P.C.C. 127 Coke).
96 G.L.R.O., M93/132, ff. 197, 286; M93/142; P.R.O., PROB 3/25/4.
97 G.L.R.O., M93/132, f. 492.
98 Ibid. C/93/1541; M93/38, pp. 149–50; 142, 167; 32, pp. 83–5.
99 Ibid. C/93/1541.
1 Ibid. M93/96B, p. 122.
2 Ibid. p. 136.
3 Ibid. C/93/1541.
4 Ibid. M93/145.
5 P.R.O., MAF 20/167 (file 2593); Robinson and Chesshyre, *The Green*, 11 sqq.
6 T.H.L.H.L., TH/2328.
7 P.R.O., PROB 11/52 (P.C.C. 34 Lyon); ibid. C 142/158/19.
8 Ibid. PROB 11/54 (P.C.C. 18 Daper).
9 B.L. Lansd. MS. 26, f. 191v., quoted in John Stow, *Survey of Lond.* ed. C. L. Kingsford (1908), ii. 299. Fleetwood described Kirby as one of several rich men that 'died of surfeit'.

10 P.R.O., REQ 2/27/115; 200/29; below, econ. hist. (mkt. gdns.).
11 Allgood, *Hist. Bethnal Green*, 212.
12 *Diary of Sam. Pepys*, ed. Latham and Matthews, iv. 200.
13 Ibid. vii. 272.
14 G.L.R.O., MR/TH 4, m. 92.
15 Ibid. M 93/132, f. 286.
16 B.L., Crace Colln. Portf. xvi. 33 (Gascoyne, *Map*).
17 Lysons, *Environs*. ii. 29.
18 Lysons, *Environs*, ii. 28 (grangerized copy in Guildhall Libr.); above, plate 23.
19 Brewer, *Beauties of Eng. and Wales*, x (4), 280.
20 Robinson and Chesshyre, *The Green*, 11–16; below, pub. svces. (libraries).
21 G.L.R.O., M93/132, f. 38.
22 B.L. Eg. Roll 2080.
23 G.L.R.O., M93/132, f. 35.
24 Ibid. f. 37.
25 Ibid. f. 186; M93/142.
26 Ibid. M93/132, f. 328.
27 Ibid. ff. 37, 339, 375.
28 C. L. R. O., Assess. Box 43, MS. 22; Gascoyne, *Map*.

Richard, who had succeeded by 1798[29] and concluded a a 99-year building lease with Joseph Brown of Durham Place, Hackney Road, in 1807. After Richard Leeds's death without issue in 1831, trustees sold most of the estate to John Joseph Tanner (d. 1873), who sold part to the Great Eastern Railway in 1871. The rest was put up for sale in 14 lots by Tanner's trustees in 1887.[30]

MARKHAMS, originally an open field west of the green, consisted of several closes before 1620, when the western part belonged to William Sebright.[31] The 12 a. to the east, together with the 'Blind Beggar', formed a copyhold estate, of which Patrick Roberts held a quarter from 1653,[32] Waldrof Lodowick and his wife Elizabeth half on the surrender of Matthew Kenrick, Elizabeth's father, from 1654,[33] and the daughters of Christopher Bowman a quarter from 1663.[34] Roberts surrendered his portion in 1658 to William Haynes, whence it passed in 1659 to William's son Joseph,[35] in 1669 to Bridget Haynes, and in 1672 to Joseph Blissett and his wife Sarah.[36] Bowman's daughters conveyed their quarter in 1675 to Thomas Coling and his wife Bridget, with remainder to Bridget's daughter Sarah and her husband Joseph Blissett.[37] Blissett's executors succeeded in 1708 and held on behalf of his descendants, successively named Joseph.[38] Lodowick, who probably died c. 1684, left his share to his wife, with remainder to his sons Charles and Thomas. Elizabeth Lodowick had apparently remarried by 1685 when she and David Clarkson were admitted for life.[39] David Clarkson's sons David, Matthew, and Robert were admitted in 1688[40] but by 1692 had surrendered their interests to Charles and Thomas Lodowick.[41] Thomas Lodowick conveyed part of his lands to Joseph Blissett in 1693[42] and Charles Lodowick and Elizabeth Clarkson, presumably his mother, surrendered part in 1700.[43] The rest, a moiety of Markhams, was left by Charles Lodowick by will dated 1723 to his son Charles, who conveyed it to his sister Elizabeth and her husband George Streatfield in 1734.[44] George, a London merchant tailor, conveyed it to Joseph Blissett in 1748.[45] The united estate remained with the Blisset(t) family until it was sold in lots after the death of the Revd. George Blisset of Hereford in 1889.[46] Development started with a building lease of 9 a. to David Wilmot in 1766.[47]

FULLMORE CLOSE, a long field next to Dog Row, originated in Foulmere, where strips of customary land were held in the 14th and 15th centuries.[48] By 1652, when called Mrs. Coleman's land,[49] it was an 8-a. copyhold. In 1656 it was divided between John and Robert (I) Coleman. John left his moiety to his widow Elizabeth, who was admitted in 1662. Elizabeth Dallock, probably their daughter, succeeded in 1690[50] and in 1694, when wife of Robert Allan, she conveyed it to Robert Coleman.[51] The other moiety was divided on Robert Coleman (I)'s death in 1665 between his sons Robert (II) and Stephen. Robert (II)'s son Robert (III) succeeded in 1672 to his father's 2 a.[52] which he settled in 1699 on himself and his wife Anne, with remainder to his son Robert (IV).[53] The whole estate was reunited by 1712, Robert (III) having purchased the first 4 a. in 1694 and Stephen Coleman's 2 a. in 1712.[54] Robert (IV), who had apparently succeeded by 1735 when he made a marriage settlement for his son John, died in 1745. Robert (IV)'s son Henry inherited his moiety (4 a.) and 2 a. of John's moiety as heir to his childless brother. The other 2 a., under the settlement of 1735, passed to John's widow Martha.[55] In 1755 Martha, by then Martha Banfield, conveyed her 2 a., at the northern end of the estate, to William Fortescue during her life[56] and between 1775 and 1821 they passed to Brown, the holder in 1835.[57] In 1750 Henry Coleman's widow Catherine was admitted to John's other 2 a. and in 1755 she and her husband Harry Drake conveyed them to Isaac Coxe,[58] who sold them in 1759 to Anthony Malpas (d. 1777).[59] His son Anthony conveyed them in 1778 to Edward Barnard,[60] who already held the southern 4 a. which had passed from Henry Coleman to John Nickleson in 1749,[61] from Nickleson's widow Sarah to Joshua Thomas in 1764,[62] and to Edward Barnard in 1767.[63] The combined 6 a. were sold in 1818 to William Green, builder, of Brick Lane,[64] and owned by Elizabeth Green in 1841.[65]

A copyhold estate of c. 24 a., mainly inclosed pieces of EASTFIELD,[66] was held in 1655 by William Pyott, who surrendered it to his father Richard Pyott of Streethay (Staffs.).[67] In 1658 Richard surrendered it to Francis Andrews and his wife Susanna,[68] whose daughter Susanna, wife of James Grunwin, succeeded under her mother's will in 1683.[69] Under Susanna Grunwin's

29 T.H.L.H.L., TH/6313; G.L.R.O., M93/31, p. 343.
30 T.H.L.H.L., TH/5043; G.L.R.O., C/72/136.
31 Above, s.v. Sebright.
32 G.L.R.O., M93/132, f. 20.
33 Ibid. M93/1.   34 Ibid. M93/132, f. 39.
35 Ibid. ff. 20, 22.   36 Ibid. ff. 76, 92.
37 Ibid. ff. 105, 117; P.R.O., C 103/157.
38 G.L.R.O., M93/132, f. 354; M93/30, pp. 369–70.
39 Ibid. M93/132, ff. 181, 188.
40 Ibid. f. 213.
41 Ibid. ff. 213, 225–6, 240.
42 Ibid. f. 253.   43 Ibid. f. 294.
44 Ibid. M93/27, pp. 139–42, 413.
45 Ibid. M93/31, p. 375.
46 Ibid. C/72/379.
47 T.H.L.H.L., TH/5849.
48 Guildhall MSS. 25121/1710; 25422.
49 G.L.R.O., M93/158, p. 12.
50 Ibid. M93/132, pp. 37, 229.   51 Ibid. pp. 258.
52 Ibid. pp. 52, 97.   53 Ibid. p. 292.

54 Ibid. p. 381.
55 Ibid. M93/30, pp. 396–401.
56 Ibid. M93/33, pp. 211 sqq., 237–9.
57 Ibid. 143–5.
58 Ibid. M93/32, p. 110; 33, p. 203.
59 Ibid. M93/34, p. 439.
60 Ibid. M93/40, pp. 185–6; M93/96B, p. 116.
61 Ibid. M93/94B, p. 137.
62 T.H.L.H.L., TH/2269.
63 G.L.R.O., M93/95B, p. 167.
64 Ibid. M93/57, p. 37.
65 M.L.R. 1842/2/369.
66 i.e. one close called Turnip field bounded by Thieving Lane (Globe Rd.) and Green St., with 5 closes called Eastfields to N. and E. Five tenements and 2 cotts. formed part of est.
67 Presumably respectively nephew and elder brother of Wm. Pyott (d. 1643): above, Pyotts; G.L.R.O., M93/1, p. 69;132, f. 17.
68 G.L.R.O., M93/132, f. 21.
69 Ibid. ff. 174–5.

will, James Grunwin was admitted in 1690 with remainder to Francis Grunwin,[70] who sold the estate in 1715 to John Walker, who sold it in 1718 to Sir Edward Gould and his wife Frances.[71] Under Sir Edward's will of 1724, the estate passed to his widow for life, with remainder in tail male. His great-nephew Edward Thorston Gould, who succeeded in 1769, sold the estate in 1771 to Charles Digby, father and son, of Mile End. They sought enfranchisement in 1772 and sold the land in parcels for building in 1790.[72]

In 1668 Ursula Cock or Cox acquired 24 a. of copyhold in four closes (*GOOSEFIELDS* and Burton field) on the north–eastern borders of Bethnal Green from Sir Thomas Byde of Ware Park (Herts.). All but 6 a. had been recently purchased by Byde from Robert and Ann Sweet; the 6 a. had been bought from John Meure or Meare.[73] Robert Haughton or Horton of Shoreditch, Ursula's nephew, succeeded under her will in 1687[74] and conveyed the estate in 1700 to Col. Joseph Jorey.[75] In 1703 the estate formed a single field called Hortons field.[76] It descended to Frances Foche and in 1748 to George Hodges.[77] In the settlement of 1750 Hodges secured Goosefields in return for surrendering his interest in Kirby's Castle.[78] In 1753 he conveyed Goosefields to Alexander Mackrabie and John Nightingale[79] who conveyed it in 1754 to Stephen Leach of Bread Street (Lond.).[80] In 1772, as two fields, it passed to Stephen's sons Thomas and Samuel, both linen drapers,[81] who obtained enfranchisement.[82] The estate was occupied by Richard Monksfield and probably owned by Robert Withers in 1780 and occupied by Thomas Hollingshead in 1794 and by Samuel Ridge in 1800, when the owner may have been Hobson.[83] William Hobson was the owner in 1831.[84] William Bradshaw had 15 a. c. 1840, when 7 a. in the north formed part of an estate mostly in Hackney, owned by the Polish and Portugese Jews. Both estates were absorbed into Victoria Park.[85]

Between Bishop's Hall and Goosefields lay some 10 a., part of the Cass estate in Hackney.[86]

Two small copyhold estates bordering Shoreditch were important in the building history of Bethnal Green. The *AUSTEN* estate existed by 1550 when John Austen's lands near Collier's Lane abutted the demesne.[87] In 1582

Richard Austen, monier of Hoxton, was licensed to lease land abutting south on Crabtree Lane.[88] Thomas Austen's land abutted demesne land in the area in 1652.[89] On Thomas's death in 1658 his copyholds, then a house, two cottages, and 4 a. of garden and pasture, were divided between his sons Thomas and Robert, both minors.[90] He left money to St. Leonard's, Shoreditch, which was used in 1671 and 1674 to purchase ½ a. next to the churchyard from the two sons.[91] In 1674 Robert surrendered the rest of his moiety to Thomas[92], who was licensed in 1675 to lease 3 a. bounded east and south by the estates of Thomas Willett (Fitches) and Snow (below) respectively.[93] Thomas Austen moved to South Mimms and by will proved 1701 left the copyhold estate to his eldest son (later Sir John Austen, Bt.) (d. 1742) and other lands to his younger son Thomas.[94] Austen's name was not recorded in 1703, probably because the land was either garden ground, leased since 1683 to John Sharp and Daniel Brown,[95] or built-up. In 1740 Sir John Austen settled the estate on himself for life, then successively on Mary Wright and Peter Storer.[96] Storer held it in 1751 and by will proved 1759 left it to his sister Martha, wife of William Baker.[97] Martha was succeeded in 1775 by her son Peter William Baker,[98] who paid a quitrent of 1s. 10d. for the copyholds in Castle and Austin streets and 4s. 10d. for 2 a. enfranchised, part of 6 a. (*recte* 4 a.).[99] In 1788 Baker conveyed the whole estate, including 112 houses in Austin and Castle streets, bounded by Shoreditch churchyard, Cock Lane and Kemp (Snow) and Gascoigne (Fitches) estates, to Benjamin Godfrey of Bishopsgate Street,[1] who had leased it since the death in 1758 of his uncle Dr. Benjamin Godfrey, the lessee since 1736.[2] Edward William Windus (d. 1832), admitted to the copyhold estate under Godfrey's will in 1813,[3] sold part for the enlargement of Shoreditch burial ground in 1824[4] and left the rest to his son Benjamin Godfrey Windus.[5] It was split up in 1863 among 6 or 7 people, of whom the chief were Edward Bird Wearing, Henry Frederick Wearing, and George Trist. Most of the Wearings' portion was enfranchised from 1873.[6] James Bishop, who acquired part of Trist's portion in 1880 and Edward Wearing's in 1883, enfranchised them in 1935 and 1931 respectively.[7]

70 Ibid. f. 227.   71 Ibid. ff. 399, 423.
72 T.H.L.H.L., TH/2324, 6535; P.R.O., C 104/173; M.L.R. 1772/3/171–2.
73 G.L.R.O., M93/132, f. 69.
74 Ibid. M93/14, pp. 210–11, 248–52.
75 Ibid. M93/132, p. 300.
76 Gascoyne, *Map*.
77 G.L.R.O., M93/132, f. 492; /142.
78 Ibid. M93/32, pp. 83–5; above, Kirby's Castle.
79 G.L.R.O., M93/32. p. 414.
80 Ibid. M93/33, p. 140.
81 Ibid. M93/38, pp. 472–3.
82 M.L.R. 1772/4/120.
83 T.H.L.H.L., BG/261; G.L.R.O., MR/PLT 4988, 5024.
84 *Starling's Map of Hackney* (1831).
85 G.L.R.O., Victoria Pk. Papers, vol. 1, 24 July 1841, list of freeholders; P.R.O., MPE 1365; *Act enabling purchase for Victoria Pk.* 5 & 6 Vic. c. 20.
86 *V.C.H. Mdx.* x. 87–8.
87 Survey in Robinson, *Hist. Hackney*, i. 337.
88 B.L. Eg. Roll 2081.

89 No. 38 abutted W. and S. on Austin's land, no. 40 abutted W. on it, and Collier's Row abutted 'the way leading to Mr. Austin's ground': G.L.R.O., M93/158, ff. 8–9, 25–6.
90 G.L.R.O., M93/3, pp. 18–19.
91 Ibid. M93/7, p. 168; 8, p. 133; *Survey of Lond.* viii. 121.
92 G.L.R.O., M93/8, pp. 134–5.
93 Ibid. M93/9, p. 42.
94 Ibid. M93/20, p. 126; *V.C.H. Mdx.* v. 284.
95 M.L.R. 1736/5/537; C. L. R. O., Assess. Box 43, MS. 22.
96 T.H.L.H.L., TH/2309.
97 G.L.R.O., M93/34, pp. 445–6.
98 Ibid. M93/39, p. 430.
99 Ibid. M93/143.
1 Ibid. M93/43, p. 375; M.L.R. 1788/4/260.
2 M.L.R. 1736/5/536–7; P.R.O., PROB 11/841 (PCC 331 Hutton), ff. 284–5.
3 G.L.R.O., M93/54, pp. 120–2.
4 Vestry mins. 1823–8, p. 151.
5 G.L.R.O., M93/141, p. 77.
6 Ibid. M93/73, pp. 329–46, 360, 381; 150.
7 Ibid. M93/79, p. 63; 168.

The *SNOW* copyhold estate, south of Austens, was held in 1652 by Mrs. Joan Noble[8] and possibly in 1640 by Thomas Noble, then headborough for Bethnal Green.[9] In 1664 she conveyed two tenements, 1 a. 1 r. adjoining their gardens, 1 a. (le Homestall), and a parcel of land (Pickfield) to Thomas and Elizabeth Snow.[10] On Thomas's death in 1665 Elizabeth inherited two tenements and 1 a. 1 r. 'lately made into a garden' near Halliwell Street and 3 a. 'in Stepney' converted to a garden and two tenements.[11] She conveyed the two tenements and 2 a. 1 r. near Halliwell Street in 1666 to Richard Turville and on her death in 1686 the 3 a. and three tenements were divided into three portions among her descendants.[12] The tenements had disappeared by 1693 when Turville was succeeded by his son George,[13] who was in turn succeeded in 1730 by his sons George (d. 1735), Lytrott (d. 1731), and William.[14] By 1735 when the Turville estate was reunited, it consisted of 9 tenements and 2 a. in Cock Lane.[15] William Turville conveyed it in 1741[16] to Ellen Turville (d. 1769), whose nephews William Halhead and John Caswell succeeded as tenants in common. In 1789 Nathaniel Brassey Halhead, Robert William Halhead, and John Halhead were admitted in trust under the will of William Halhead.[17] Part of the land, bounded west by Cock Lane, south by Nichol Street and north by the rest of Snow's estate[18], was repre-

sented by New Turville Street; part to the east was represented by Turville Street.[19]

The rest of Elizabeth Snow's estate was divided in 1686, one third each to her daughters Anne Harford and Elizabeth West, and one third between her grandsons Edward, John, and Thomas Kemp.[20] Anne sold her share in 1687 to Thomas Dawbane,[21] who was succeeded in 1720 by his son Thomas,[22] and Elizabeth left hers to James Dawbane in 1723.[23] The Kemp brothers' third was united in the hands of John Kemp in 1693,[24] whose sons Thomas and Matthew succeeded in 1754.[25] A quitrent of 2s. 4d. for a copyhold 'garden behind Shoreditch church' was paid in 1747 by Mrs. Kemp and in 1755 and 1775 by Kemp and Hill.[26] The estate, north of Turville's portion and south of Austens,[27] was presumably that depicted in 1703 as Kemp's garden.[28] Thomas Kemp ran it as a garden in 1789[29] and 1800[30] but 73 houses had been built there by 1810.[31] In 1814 Thomas and John Kemp sold the 3 a. to George Woolley of Hollywell Street[32] but the estate had presumably split up by 1821 when the quitrent was divided among George Woolley, who paid 1s. 4d., and Samuel Martin, William Atkinson, and John C. Hodgson, who each paid 4d.[33] G. J. Woolley owned the largest section in 1891, when the estate was included in the Boundary Street scheme.[34]

ECONOMIC HISTORY

AGRICULTURE. Possibly excepting parts of Eastfield, all open-field land had been inclosed by 1652.[35] Demesne land, nearly 400 a., then covered more than half Bethnal Green.[36] It had 20 occupiers, ten with less than 10 a. each, three with 11–20 a., two with 41–50 a., and one (Treadway, with 61 a.) with more than 50 a. When the demesne was divided and sold a few years later, only one 4-a. close was apparently bought by the occupier.[37] There were minor boundary changes and some division and recombination of fields both before and after 1703 but most fields remained unaltered until built upon.[38]

Farmers were almost all lessees, who usually leased land in adjacent blocks from more than one owner. In 1703, of the known occupiers of agricultural land (excluding gardens), nine had less than 10 a. each, three had 11–20 a. each,

seven had 21–30 a. each, two had 31–40 a. each, and Matthew Ball had 52 a. and John Preston had 83 a.[39]

The largest estate was Bishop's Hall, in 1652 *c*. 93 a. divided into 15 fields and occupied by six tenants, the largest of whom, Henry Rowe, had 40 a., mostly in the north-east.[40] Augmented by Dannetts field, there were still 15 fields, slightly regrouped, in 1703, probably held by five tenants.[41] Matthew Ball, 'husbandman of Stepney', who was leased 29 a. in the south-east of the estate from 1690,[42] was the largest and also took leases from other estates along Green Street. Richard Corker occupied 23 a. of Bishop's Hall in the north-east, together with 11 a. of the adjoining estate. In 1712 Ball 'ran away' when he could not pay his rent and in 1714 his son Thomas, who followed him at Bishop's Hall, also fled: Joseph Gosdin, tenant of part of

8 Ibid. M93/158, f. 9.
9 B.L. Eg. MS. 3006, f. 57v.
10 G.L.R.O., M93/132, f. 48.   11 Ibid. f. 52.
12 Ibid. ff. 55, 203.   13 Ibid. f. 251.
14 Ibid. M93/93B, pp. 119, 134.
15 Ibid. M93/28, p. 10.
16 Ibid. M93/94, p. 70.
17 Ibid. M93/37, p. 476; M93/97, p. 23.
18 M.L.R./752/3/726; 1759/4/126; 1772/1/34; Horwood, *Plan* (1792–9).
19 M.L.R. 1730/1/291; Horwood, *Plan* (1792–9).
20 G.L.R.O., M93/132, p. 203.
21 Ibid. p. 204.
22 Ibid. p. 435.
23 Ibid. p. 470.   24 Ibid. pp. 221, 247.
25 Ibid. M93/33, p. 75.
26 Ibid. M93/142–3, 167.
27 Ibid. M93/43, p. 375; M.L.R. 1752/3/726.

28 Gascoyne, *Map*.
29 G.L.R.O., MR/FR/1789/J81.
30 Ibid. PLT 2025; Horwood, *Plan* (1792–9).
31 G.L.R.O., MR/PLT 5045.
32 Ibid. M93/54, p. 289.
33 Ibid. M93/144, 145, ff. 3–6.
34 Ibid. M93/150; *The Times*, 11 Mar. 1891, 3f.
35 G.L.R.O., M93/158, ff. 1–31.
36 Total 760 a.: *Census*, 1831.
37 No. 57, sold to Laurence Chalker in 1654. Jeremy Chalker was occupier in 1652. Some purchasers are unknown: above, estates.
38 Gascoyne, *Map*; *Regency A–Z*. For determination of street patterns by ests.: above, settlement and building to 1836.
39 Gascoyne, *Map*.
40 G.L.R.O., M93/158, ff. 2–4.
41 Gascoyne, *Map*.
42 Northants. R. O., X 1074 (xiii), leases.

Bishop's Hall from 1706 and of 52 a. from 1711, took a lease for Ball's 29 a. in 1716, for the whole 81 a. in 1721, and for 13 a. of Norris's estate in Hackney at about the same time.[43]

Bishop's Hall farmhouse, after improvement in 1721, became the centre of a farm consisting of all Sotheby's lands[44] and, probably by 1769,[45] including the Robinson charity lands and, by 1778, at least part of neighbouring estates south of Old Ford Road.[46] The tenant in 1778 was Joseph Wilkinson,[47] who farmed over 100 a.[48] Samuel Ridge (d. 1839),[49] tenant by 1799,[50] paid land tax for nearly 118 a. in 1800, farming a block in the north-east corner of the parish on either side of Old Ford Road.[51] He and his sons were among the leading inhabitants, exploiting the land for farming, brickmaking, and building.[52]

Broomfields, the second largest estate with c. 80 a. in the south-east, changed from three closes in 1550[53] to 13, divided between one farm with 35½ a. in the south and another with 41½ a. in the north, in 1652.[54] In 1669 it was 82 a., 'late divided' into several closes with hedges, all with one occupier, John Preston.[55] Broomfields and an adjoining part of East-fields[56] were farmed from a farmhouse in Mile End Road which, together with 44 a. of Dr. Gouch's land in Mile End, formed a block from Mile End Road to Old Ford Lane in 1703.[57] By 1744 the estate was divided between two farms, 33½ a. in the north occupied by the Leeds family and 45 a. in the south.[58] The 12 fields had become 6 by 1760, 3 for each of the farms.[59] Both farms had been reunited by c. 1786[60] and were still together in 1794,[61] but the estate was again in two farms in 1800.[62] By 1836 50 a. were farmed by John Gardner,[63] who leased most as market gardens in 1846.[64]

The Leeds family farmed from one of several farmhouses in Dog Row; presumably it was a brick house on the east side, leased with 1 a. to Abraham Neale in 1678 and vested in George Leeds[65] probably by 1694, when he was leasing Markhams. He occupied 15½ a. in 1703[66] and enlarged the farm by purchase and lease in 1711 and 1729[67] By 1744 he or a namesake was rated for 84 a.[68] George Leeds's widow Mary was rated in 1751 for her property and for land leased from Pyotts, Eastfields, and Broomfields,[69] all except Cambridge Heath east of Cambridge Road and south of Old Ford Lane. Mary's son George succeeded in 1755 and by the 1770s occupied a total of nearly 100 a.,[70] although he was titheable only for 47 a. in 1778.[71] The estates passed to his widow c. 1785 and then to his nephew Richard, who lived elsewhere and let out his own estates by c. 1800.[72]

The southernmost farmhouse on the eastern side of Dog Row had been leased to Matthew Walker in 1689[73] and occupied by him in 1703.[74] John Johnson, the occupier in 1787, may have succeeded by 1760 when he was rated for land.[75] He paid tithes for c. 60 a. c. 1778, when he had apparently succeeded Leeds in Eastfields besides occupying part of neighbouring estates.[76] He followed Leeds on part of Broomfields[77] but by 1794 was rated for only 35 a.[78] He still paid land tax for Dog Row in 1820[79] but by then was interested chiefly in building.[80] A third farmhouse on the east side of Dog Row was the centre of a 21-a. farm in Bethnal Green and Mile End[81] which belonged from c. 1772 until 1789/94 to William Billett (Bilert).[82]

A 6-roomed brick house, with farm buildings, existing by 1621 and occupied in 1652 by Jeremy Chalker,[83] may have been that on the west side of Dog Row depicted in 1703 as north of Simkins Gardens and probably the centre of farmland belonging to Naylor's and Jarvis's estates, occupied by Henry Collier.[84] Collier enlarged the farm, which had passed to Daniel Farmer, poulterer, by 1751.[85] Daniel, still there in 1760,[86] had been succeeded by Ursula Farmer by 1775.[87] A Farmer

43 Ibid. memos.
44 Occasionally, as in 1742, excluding the 5 a. fronting Cambridge Rd. (no. 15): Northants. R. O., X 1123 (Box 13).
45 M.L.R. 1779/5/203.
46 Pyotts, Dickens's and Eastfields: G.L.R.O., P93/DUN/201.
47 T.H.L.H.L., BG/202; G.L.R.O., P93/DUN/200.
48 G.L.R.O., P93/DUN/201.
49 Ibid. M93/44, p. 192; 48, p. 27; 49, p. 130–1; T.H.L.H.L., TH 2849.
50 Guildhall MS. 19224/297.
51 G.L.R.O., MR/PLT 5024.
52 Poor Law Com. Rep. H.C. 44, App. III, pt. III, p. 111A (1834), ii; T.H.L.H.L., TH/2867. For brickmaking, below, industry; building, above, the East.
53 Robinson, Hist. Hackney, i. 326.
54 G.L.R.O., M93/158, f. 6.
55 T.H.L.H.L., TH/2425.
56 Ibid. 2350; C. L. R. O., Assess. Box 43, MS. 22; Guildhall MS. 7588.
57 Gascoyne, Map; Gascoyne, Map of Mile End Old Town (1703).
58 Ibid. 1789/5/118–19; T.H.L.H.L., BG/260.
59 T.H.L.H.L., Map no. 301; BG/202.
60 M.L.R. 1789/5/118–9.
61 T.H.L.H.L., BG/261.
62 G.L.R.O., MR/PLT 5024.
63 Ibid. THCS 447.
64 Ibid. TA 1.
65 T.H.L.H.L., TH/6313; G.L.R.O., C93/1541.

66 Gascoyne, Map, which does not identify Leeds's farmho.
67 Above, estates (Cambridge Heath); G.L.R.O., O/113/1. Both occupied in 1703 by Hopkins, who also occupied land in the fork between Dog Row and Red Cow Lane: Gascoyne, Map.
68 T.H.L.H.L., BG/260.
69 Ibid. 256.
70 Ibid. 202, 256; Map no. 301; T.H.L.H.L., TH/2324; P.R.O., C 54/12480, mm. 37 sqq., where date 1765 should read 1865.
71 G.L.R.O., P93/DUN/201.
72 T.H.L.H.L., TH/6313, 2268.
73 G.L.R.O., C93/1535.
74 Gascoyne, Map.
75 G.L.R.O., C93/1541; T.H.L.H.L., BG/202.
76 G.L.R.O., P93/DUN/201; MR/PLT 4988.
77 M.L.R. 1789/5/118–19.
78 T.H.L.H.L., BG/261.
79 G.L.R.O., MR/PLT 5065.
80 Above, Dog Row.
81 G.L.R.O., P93/DUN/201. Nos. 55–6, 61–2, 65, were in Mile End.
82 G.L.R.O., P93/DUN/200; MR/FR/1789/J 81; C93/1541. In 1794 Jas. Chambers held 'Billetts land': T.H.L.H.L., BG/1541.
83 G.L.R.O., M93/158, f. 15.
84 Gascoyne, Map.
85 T.H.L.H.L. BG/256; M.L.R. 1767/3/446.
86 T.H.L.H.L., BG/202.
87 Ibid. BG/264.

was rated for Naylor's estate in 1794[88] and Titus Farmer was assessed for land tax near Mile End Corner in 1800[89] but by then the farm had probably become gardens, soon to be built over.[90]

There were few other identifiable farms. The mid 18th-century Lord's Farm, probably small[91] and near the Gibraltar public house,[92] was named after Thomas Lord, who was rated in 1751 and 1760 for land held of two estates.[93] His field fronted Bethnal Green Road in 1756[94] but was probably soon built upon.

More important was Coates's Farm on Saffron Close, fronting in 1746 on Coates's Lane[95] (previously Rogue Lane, later May's Lane and Pollard Row), land occupied in 1703 by Edward Hemond as part of a 28½-a. holding to the south and west.[96] Members of the Coates family had been recorded in Bethnal Green in the 17th century[97] although not in 1703. Thomas Coates occupied part of the Tyssen estate before 1724,[98] when he occupied Fryes (or Fryers) field south of Virginia Row (on Fitchs),[99] and leased Bishop's Hall by 1728,[1] when he was probably the most important farmer in the hamlet. Coates's Farm was depicted under that name in 1773[2] but had long passed from his family, probably to James May, Thomas Coates's successor at Bishop's Hall.[3] May was rated for 68 a. in two parcels in 1744[4] and for land leased from three estates in 1751.[5] He still had Saffron Close in 1758[6] and Samuel May was rated for it in 1760.[7] May & Son were described as farmers in 1754[8] and Samuel May in 1772 was 'near the new church',[9] possibly at Coates's Farm.[10] By 1792 the farm had been built upon.[11]

Farming in the 16th and early 17th centuries was mixed, with evidence also of arable and of sheep, geese, and pigs.[12] At Bishop's Hall in 1594 Hugh Platte grew 5½-inch-long ears of barley on ground fertilized with waste ashes left over from soap-boiling.[13] Oats were mentioned in 1610[14] and 1660.[15] There was a shift towards grassland: St. Paul's close on the west side of Cambridge Road was arable in 1576 but meadow by 1649[16] and leases at Bishop's Hall in 1658 contained penalty clauses for ploughing.[17] Arable did not disappear entirely, however, especially in the east of the parish, and cowkeepers often possessed some besides pasture and meadow.

Almost all farmers werre described as cowkeepers, milk production for London being the chief local farming activity from the 17th century. Before the sale of the demesne lands, the Red Cow, also called the Milkhouse, had its cowhouse in Brick Lane in 1643[18] and Milkwives (1620)[19] or Milkhouse Bridge (1642)[20] in Hackney Road indicated dairying, as did the 15 cows and milkhouse belonging to a farm at the junction of Crabtree Lane and Hackney Road in 1684.[21] Cowkeepers in Dog Row[22] and elsewhere were mentioned from the 1670s to 1801.[23]

There were said to be several large-scale cowkeepers in the 17th and especially the early 18th centuries,[24] but few farmers at any time held more than 100 a. Joseph Gosdin, father and son, had a joint stock of 110 milch cows in 1723.[25] Assessments in 1775 included one of 80 cows for Joseph Wilkinson, one of 35, one of 28, and one of 24.[26] In 1794 there were 200 cows in the whole of Bethnal Green. Bought in calf from country breeders at about three years old, they were fed on turnips and meadow hay from October to May and on meadow hay for the summer.[27]

In 1763 John Preston and Richard Ware, farmers of parts of Broomfields and Bishop's Hall, protested that they held several closes of 'barren land' near Bethnal Green, valued at 25s. an acre a year, which had been rated at £4 or £5.[28] Matthew and Thomas Ball did not find farming profitable and Joseph Gosdin in 1716 was allowed a year's rent because the farm was 'out of heart'. Mortality among cows in 1714 affected Gosdin and Joseph Green, both in the north-eastern part of the parish. Gosdin put much effort into Bishop's Hall, on buildings, a well and pump for the cows, and draining and

88 Ibid. BG/261.
89 G.L.R.O., MR/PLT 5024.
90 Horwood, *Plan* (1792–9); *Regency A–Z*; above, Dog Row.
91 Lysons, *Environs*, ii. 35.
92 Gibraltar Walk was also called Lord's Walk: B.L., Crace Collh., Portf. xvi. 34.
93 T.H.L.H.L., BG/256, 202.
94 29 Geo. II, c. 43.
95 Rocque, *Plan of Lond.* (1746).
96 Gascoyne, *Map*. For Hemond, below, mkt. gdns.
97 Thos., assessed for 5 hearths in 1664: G.L.R.O., MR/TH 4, m. 92; Hen., for 100 stock and land near Carter's Rents in 1694: C.L.R.O. Assess. Box 43, MS. 22.
98 M.L.R. 1724/1/448.
99 Ibid. 1728/2/140; 1729/4/6.
1 Northants. R. O., X 1123 (3).
2 Watercolour reproduced in H. L. Smith, *Hist. E. Lond.* (1939), pl. 16.
3 Northants. R. O., X 1123 (Box 13).
4 T.H.L.H.L., BG/260.
5 Ibid. 256.
6 Ibid. TH/2339.
7 Ibid. BG/202.
8 P.R.O., PROB 3/53/23.
9 G.L.R.O., P93/DUN/200.
10 Rocque, *Plan of Lond.* (1746) marks 'May Farm' as the northernmost of the eastern Dog Row farms (probably Leeds's farm). It was still farther from the church and not

otherwise connected with the Mays, although Isaac May was assessed for St. Paul's est. on the W. side of Dog Row in 1751: T.H.L.H.L., BG/256.
11 M.L.R. 1794/3/125; above, the Centre.
12 P.R.O., REQ 2/27/115; *Mdx. County Rec.* i. 249; *Mdx. Sess. Rec.* N.S. i. 147; iii. 307.
13 H. Platte, *Jewell House of Art and Nature* (1594), frontispiece and p. 52.
14 Cal. Mdx. Sess. Bks. v. 26.
15 P.R.O., PROB 11/301 (P.C.C. 243 Nabbs), f. 259v.
16 T.H.L.H.L., TH/7022.
17 Northants. R. O., X 1074 (xiii).
18 G.L.R.O., BRA/685/1/80.
19 Ibid. P72/AND/27.
20 B.L. Add. MS. 22253.
21 P.R.O., C 103/157.
22 T.H.L.H.L., TH/2267; G.L.R.O., M93/166.
23 Northants. R. O., X 1123 (Box 13) and parcel 3; G.L.R.O., C 93/1535., 1538–40; ibid. MR/FB 2, ff. 143, 202; ibid. MR/FR/1789/J81; Guildhall MS. 7588; Cal. Mdx. Sess. Bks. xi. 18; T.H.L.H.L., TH/6313.
24 L. Martindale, 'Demography and Land Use in late 17th and 18th cents. in Mdx.' (Lond. Univ. Ph. D. thesis, 1968), 306, 313, 316, 321.
25 Northants. R. O., X 1074 (xiii), memo.
26 T.H.L.H.L., BG/264.
27 P. Foot, *Agric. of Mdx.* (1794), 80–3.
28 Cal. Mdx. Sess. Bks. iv. 200–1.

dunging fields.[29] When the field at Cambridge Heath (no. 15) was leased to Thomas Coates in 1729 he was permitted to sow 'the usual sort of crop', beans, peas, or turnips and 'garden things except potatoes'. The 5-a. field was to be given 15 loads of cow and horse dung once in two years and to be laid down to grass seven years before the expiry of the lease with 8 bushels of 'best rye grass' and 8 lb. of clover seed for each acre.[30]

In 1701 Broomfields consisted of mixed arable, meadow, and pasture, probably in the proportions of 13 a., 24 a., and 42 a. respectively.[31] In 1789 it had almost equal amounts, 27 a. being pasture, 31 a. arable, and an 18-a. field containing both.[32]

In 1772 of nearly 500 a. of farmland,[33] 107 a. (21.5 per cent) were arable (24 a. known to be ploughed, 2 a. to be wheat, and 5 a. oats),[34] 212¼ a. (42.5 per cent) were mowed, and 179½ a. (36 per cent) were for grazing.[35] Of 134 a. of identifiable mowed land, 40 a. belonged to Wilkinson, 33½ a. to Johnson, 19 a. to Samuel Scott, and 10¾ a. to William Billett.[36] Nearly 300 a. were listed for great tithes in 1778,[37] of which 77½ a. were arable, 134 a. mowed, and 87 a. grazing. The arable was mostly in the east: 31 a. belonging to Wilkinson, together with another 10½ a. on Cass's adjoining estate, and 23 a. of Broomfields farmed by Leeds. The arable included at least 20 a. of wheat, c. 17 a. of oats or barley, and 17 a. of beans and peas. There was some rotation, one field in the east, for example,[38] being mowed in 1779 and growing peas in 1780; another, Rush Mead, consisted of 14 a., half mowed, half grazing (fed) in 1779, and half wheat, half oats in 1780. By 1795, of c. 490 a. of farmland, 190 a. were arable, 160 a. grassland, and 140 a. market gardens. Land often produced one crop a year of corn and another of garden vegetables.[39] Crops in 1794 were 8½ a. of wheat, 7 a. of rye, and 9 a. of oats; for 1795 the figures respectively were 2 a., none, and 5 a.[40] Agriculture employed 16 families in 1801, 17 in 1811, and 50 in 1831.[41]

Only 200 a. yielded titheable produce in the seven years ending 1835, of which 20½ a. were arable, 2 a. meadow, and 97 a. pasture, the rest being brickfields, cemeteries, and buildings. Surveyed in 1846 for the Act extinguishing tithes, there were 172½ a., all in the east, comprising Victoria Park and the rest of Bishop's Hall and Robinson's Charity estate belonging to the Commissioners of Woods and Forests, the remaining Sotheby estate, Broomfields, and part of Ridge's estate, by then a brickfield. Apart from nearly 13 a. of brickfield and 45 a. of (mostly market-) garden ground, all the land was pasture.[42]

Victoria Park was rented out for pasturing sheep well into the 20th century[43] but other evidence, admittedly scanty, is of pasture used mainly for cattle. In the mid 18th century there were cattle in the fields bordering the churchyard[44] and the eccentric Baron Ephraim Lopez Pereira D'Aguilar later sent cows from Islington to graze on the west side of Cambridge Road.[45]

Cowkeeping was not dependent on pasture land. Like pigkeeping, which persisted into the 20th century, it needed so little space that cowhouses and styes were found in areas which had been built up. At least some of the vegetable crops were for fodder. Turnips, which were grown by Katharine Carter in a field 'back of Bethnal Green' in 1736,[46] were used for cattle, as presumably were most of the beans and peas and crops such as the mangel-wurzels grown by John Ridge in 1842.[47]

There were at least 30 cowmen or dairymen c. 1850,[48] most of them with cowyards in populous districts and presumably producing milk for local consumption rather than, as formerly, for the City. In 1848 one of the largest, in Wood Street, had 40–50 cows,[49] and William Brooks the older and younger ran a dairy in Russia Lane, south of the nursery.[50] Paradise Dairy, which had 16 cows and 20 pigs behind Paradise Row, was blamed for 'typhus'[51] and there were large cowsheds and pig styes in Punderson's Gardens.[52] There was a cowyard in Bacon Street,[53] where there were two dairies and cowhouses occupied by William Pettit in 1871.[54] There were 98 milk cows in Bethnal Green in 1866[55] and 408 cows and heifers in milk, kept by 37 people, in 1874, when only one person occupied land and there were 2½ a. of meadow or pasture.[56] By 1884 stock was kept by 32 people, who occupied no land, and there were 352 milk cows, 4 ducks, and 51 fowl.[57] In the late 19th century there were several cowkeepers, including the Royal Dairy, in Cambridge Road and cows were driven down the street and milked as needed.[58] In 1901 most of the 65 people employed in agriculture were commercial

[29] Northants. R. O., X 1074 (xiii), memos.; X 1075 (23), memo.
[30] Ibid. X 1075 (23).
[31] T.H.L.H.L., TH/2350. The deed contains a coloured map without a key.
[32] M.L.R. 1789/5/118–19.
[33] Based on great tithes payable to Stepney and therefore excluding mkt. gdns.: G.L.R.O., P93/DUN/200.
[34] The 24 a. belonged to Bps. Hall under Wilkinson, the wheat and oats to John Johnson.
[35] 'Fed' in original.
[36] Leeds was listed but with no details.
[37] G.L.R.O., P93/DUN/201.
[38] No. 96 (10 1/2 a.) S. of Old Ford Lane, W. of Broomfields. Nos. identifiable on par. map: T.H.L.H.L., map. no. 301.
[39] Lysons, Environs, ii. 28.
[40] P.R.O., HO 42/37, no. 84.
[41] Census, 1801–31. The figs. for 1821 (81) are inaccurate.
[42] G.L.R.O., TA 1.
[43] Poulsen, Victoria Pk. 71.
[44] Vestry mins. 1747–81, p. 126.
[45] Vale, Old Bethnal Green, 95–6.
[46] Justice in 18th-cent. Hackney, ed. R. Paley (L.R.S. xxviii), 36.
[47] G.L.R.O., Victoria Pk. Papers, vol. 1, 29 June 1842.
[48] Based on census 1851: P.R.O., HO 107/1539–42.
[49] Gavin, San. Ramblings, 36–7.
[50] G.L.R.O., MR/UP 340.
[51] Gavin, San. Ramblings, 7–8; above, building 1837–75.
[52] Gavin, San. Ramblings, 28.
[53] Ibid. 38.
[54] G.L.R.O., MR/UP 1011.
[55] P.R.O., MAF 68/43/15.
[56] Ibid. 364/1.
[57] Ibid. 934/1.
[58] E. Lond. Rec. iv. (1981), 33.

gardeners and nurserymen; cowkeepers were probably classified with other food dealers.[59] There were 40 in the 'agriculture' category in 1911.[60] Fifteen cowsheds and 344 milkshops existed in 1903[61] but cowsheds dwindled from 13 in 1913 to 8 in 1935[62] as clearances replaced them by retail dairies. By 1960 there were 95 dairies and milkshops.[63]

MARKET GARDENS AND NURSERIES. Gardening was carried on at Bishop's Hall from the Middle Ages[64] and by merchants and gentlemen in the 16th and 17th centuries, some of whom sent produce to the City.[65] From the 17th century and probably earlier substantial gardens were associated with the Corner House, Dickens's, Soda's and Crisp's houses[66] and, above all, with Kirby's Castle. In 1592 Kirby's Castle had at least 100 fruit trees and a garden with knots of hyssop and lavender and a quarter planted with roses and strawberries, hedged with privet and whitethorn. John Watson accused his tenant Noel de Caron, 'agent of the United Netherlands', of destroying the garden and leaving 'the dead roots of cabbages, collworth, carrots and such like' but Caron maintained that he had improved it by pruning, manuring with dung from London, and planting herbs, roses, gooseberries, vines, artichokes, 'myllions' and 'pompians'.[67] The house was later occupied by the horticulturalist Sir Hugh Platt (d. 1608), whose wine from grapes grown there was praised by the French ambassador.[68] In 1663 Pepys found 'the greatest quantity of strawberries I ever saw, and good'.[69] Before he moved to Kirby's Castle, Platt had leased Bishop's Hall which had a great orchard and garden in the mid 17th century.[70] James Sotheby (1727–42) planted 42 trees and shrubs at Bishop's Hall, white jasmine, red honeysuckle, grapes and 'double-flowered pomegranate' against the farmhouse and apricots, peaches, plums, cherries, and nectarines on the walls of the garden or orchard.[71]

To serve such gardens, to meet the Huguenots' demands for small plots with cut flowers and new vegetables,[72] and probably above all to supply London, commercial gardening developed. Five a. converted from Eastfield by 1581[73] may have been the 5-a. Turnip field, which was part of

Eastfield in the mid 17th century,[74] suggesting that the cultivation of root crops in common fields, described in parishes west of the City in 1635,[75] was also known in Bethnal Green.

The district was one of those suburbs where market gardening grew rapidly from the early 17th century to replace the Continent as the source of vegetables, fruit, and possibly flowers, for the capital.[76] Two gardeners from Bethnal Green were recorded in 1611,[77] one in 1631[78] and another in 1653.[79] Gardening was usually an intermediate stage between farming and housing and, like brickmaking, spread eastward from the area nearest the City. Most gardens were leased and subdivided, sometimes into hundreds of plots for Londoners and local weavers. They often had mud walls which were probably themselves planted in a system of intense cultivation as in modern China. Most gardens took their names from lessees, generally gardeners.

One of the earliest gardens was Preston's, 3 a. on the Byde estate in the south-west in 1643[80] and built over probably in the 1680s.[81] To the north the Nichol estate was apparently all garden ground, subdivided by the 1660s, the largest portion being the 'great garden' of 4 a. in the corner of Cock Lane, which was leased out successively to Thomas Dubber and John Askew. In 1680 the whole area was leased out to Jon Richardson, who was not a gardener[82] but gave his name to the estate.[83] He began building the Nichol on the southern part, leaving the northern as garden ground, worked by Peter and then John Povey into the 1720s.[84] Benjamin Wyersdale was a gardener there in 1753[85] and a small area survived in the 1790s.[86] 'Mrs. Noble's garden' existed on the eastern part of the neighbouring Snow's estate in 1652.[87] More of that estate had been converted to garden by 1665,[88] and the northern section was occupied in 1675 by Ralph Kemp, gardener,[89] whose descendants cultivated it until the end of the 18th century;[90] some remained in 1813.[91]

On Austens there was a garden, probably occupied by Isaac Bryan, in 1658.[92] In 1675 part of the garden ground was lost to Shoreditch churchyard and the rest was occupied by William Benbow, gardener.[93] Most of the southern ground disappeared under Castle and Austin

59 *Census*, 1901.
60 Ibid. 1911.
61 L.C.C. *Lond. Statistics*, xvi. 94.
62 Ibid. xxv. 120; xxx. 80; xxxix. 79.
63 L.C.C. *Statistics of Metrop. Boros.* (1960–1).
64 Above Stepney, econ. hist. (agric.).
65 *Econ. H.R.* 1st. ser. v (2), 53.
66 Above, the Green.
67 P.R.O., REQ 2/27/115. 'Collworth' was colewort, a synonym for any brassica in Culpeper.
68 *D.N.B.*
69 *Diary of Sam. Pepys*, ed. Latham and Matthews, iv. 200.
70 Northants. R. O., X 1123, Box Bp's. Hall 1647–1742, no. (13); G.L.R.O., M93/158, f. 2.
71 There were at least 8 varieties of plums, 4 of cherries, and 3 of apricots: Northants. R. O., X 1075 (23).
72 R. D. Gwynne, *Huguenot Heritage* (1985), 71.
73 B.L. Eg. R. 2080.
74 G.L.R.O., M93/132, f. 17.
75 *Ecom. H.R.* 1st. ser. v (2), 54.

76 Ibid. 51–2.
77 Cal. Mdx. Sess. Bks. ix. 29.
78 *Marriage Regs. of St. Dunstan's Stepney*, ed. Colyer-Fergusson, i. 201.
79 Cal. Mdx. Sess. Bks. ii. 54.
80 G.L.R.O., M93/158, f. 12; BRA/685/1/80.
81 Above, the West.
82 M.L.R. 1709/2/126–8; 1712/5/38. For Dubber in 1664 and 1671 and Askew in 1671 at 'Shoreditch Church': G.L.R.O., MR/TH/4, m. 92; TH/16, m. 24.
83 Gascoyne, *Map*.
84 M.L.R. 1719/5/211; 1728/2/17; 1752/3/726.
85 Ibid. 1753/2/495.
86 Horwood, *Plan of Lond.* (1792–9).
87 G.L.R.O., M93/158, f. 9.
88 Ibid. M93/132, f. 52.
89 M.L.R. 1736/5/536.
90 T.H.L.H.L., BG/261, 264. Above, estates (Snows).
91 *Regency A–Z* (Horwood, 1813 edn.).
92 G.L.R.O., M93/3, pp. 18–19.
93 Ibid. 9, p. 42.

streets, probably by 1682,[94] but in 1683, when Thomas Austen leased 1 a. of Benbow's garden to John Sharp, Daniel Brown occupied much of the estate to the north[95] and Sharp's and Brown's gardens filled most of the ground between Crabtree Lane and Virginia Row in 1703.[96] They were subdivided in the mid 18th century, one tenant in 1760 being Thomas Cooper, who gave his name to Cooper's Gardens.[97] North of Crabtree Lane gardens existed by 1680, designated Goodwell's in 1703.[98]

A secondary area of early market gardens was around the green, where on the west side of Cambridge Road a 'garden, stable and hayloft' of 1654[99] were occupied by Benjamin How, gardener, in 1686[1] and remained garden ground until the 1790s.[2] In 1685 John How leased 3 a. of Kirby's Castle[3] which he had converted from pasture by 1698, planting fruit trees.[4] It was still garden ground in 1813.[5] Other gardeners probably at the green were Robert Hill, who leased two orchards or garden plots in 1673,[6] and Edward Edes, who leased 2 a. in 1686.[7]

The most important of the central group was Penn's garden, 3 a. west of Cambridge Road and south of Bethnal Green Road, which originated between 1656 and 1660 as the nursery of Thomas Colinge.[8] It passed to Matthew Penn by 1686 and was run as a nursery by his widow and son, William. It was 'sometime the nursery' c. 1775, although Penn's house was occupied by a gardener in 1771[9] and most of the garden ground survived in 1813.[10]

Thirteen gardens were named in 1703:[11] Border's, Goodwell's, Brown's, Sharp's, Kemp's, Richardson's, Satchwell's, Austin's, Hambleton's, Simkins's, Penn's, Beasley's,[12] and Edger's. There were five unnamed gardens: Benjamin How's and Dickens's repectively west and east of Cambridge Road, Kirby's Castle, Bishop's Hall, and one to the east of Russia Lane.

Border's and Goodwell's adjoined on Milkhouse Bridge estate at the bend of Hackney Road.[13] A 6½-a. area fronting the road was leased to Richard Atkins, then to William Hopcroft (fl. 1758), and by 1789 to John Allport, seedsman, by which time the ground formed several parcels with summer houses.[14] It was on Goodwell's site that one of the most notorious

slums, Nova Scotia Gardens, grew out of plots and sheds.[15] The northern portion, however, mostly Border's, became part of Allport's large nursery, which existed by the 1790s on the Shoreditch side of Hackney Road,[16] although the family had possessed a small garden north of Virginia Row in 1751.[17] In 1807 Allport's widow and son John, who was listed with his father in 1802 as 'nursery and seedsmen',[18] began to sell land for building.[19] Although the firm retained extensive gardens into the next decade,[20] all had gone by 1832.[21]

Satchwell's garden, the eastern part of Tyssen's estate in 1703, consisted of 6 a. leased in 1769 to William Atkins, already the occupier. Part went for building but 3 a. were leased in 1772 to Richard Atkins, also a gardener,[22] who renewed his lease in 1792, when the garden had shrunk to 2 a.[23] Only a tiny part was left behind Norwell Place by 1813.[24]

Austin's garden, in 1703 opposite Satchwell's on Red Cow estate, was 1 a. occupied in 1711 by Jane Austin[25] and leased with much of the estate to Thomas Scott in 1713.[26] It was leased to William Atkins in 1768[27] but probably soon disappeared.

Hambleton's garden, 6 a. forming the western half of Great Haresmarsh, was in 1712 'in the possession of Hamilton, gardener, and of late years converted to gardens'.[28] By 1721 it was Bridgman's;[29] Thomas Bridgman, gardener, of St. John Street occupied it until his death between 1760 and 1765.[30] John Wolveridge (or Woolveridge), who had leased part of the neighbouring Hare Marsh since 1740,[31] in 1775 occupied extensive garden ground on the southern borders of Bethnal Green,[32] including 11¼ a., all that remained unbuilt, of Great Haresmarsh and the eastern portion of Hare Marsh.[33] It is not clear whether Wolveridge or his son Thomas were gardeners, as were their successors William Broad in 1805[34] and John Mandeno in 1818.[35]

Simkins's garden, at the southern tip of the parish, took its name from Walter Simkins (d. by 1726),[36] whose family had lived in Dog Row since the 1670s.[37] The garden remained behind the houses in Dog Row and Mile End Road until the 1790s but had gone by 1813.[38]

94 Ibid. 20, f. 126; above, the West.
95 M.L.R. 1736/5/537.
96 Gascoyne, Map (1703).
97 T.H.L.H.L., BG/256; 202; Regency A–Z.
98 P.R.O., C 103/157; Gascoyne Map.
99 G.L.R.O., M93/166.
1 M.L.R. 1719/2/237.
2 Horwood, Plan of Lond. (1792–9).
3 P.R.O., C 7/2/68.
4 Ibid. C 7/1/2.   5 Regency A–Z.
6 P.R.O., C 5/93/61.
7 Ibid. C 7/166/144.
8 G.L.R.O., M 93/3, p. 73; 1, pp. 230–1.
9 P.R.O., C 110/83.
10 Regency A–Z.
11 Gascoyne, Map, copy in B.L., Crace Colln. Portf. xvi. 33.
12 Hartley's on Gascoyne, Map of Stepney (1703).
13 See Estate map (fig.24), nos. 37, 39.
14 M.L.R. 1789/5/364; 1758/3/554.
15 Above, building 1837–75.
16 Horwood, Plan of Lond. (1792–9).
17 T.H.L.H.L., BG/256.
18 Holden's Triennial Dir. (1802–4).

19 M.L.R. 1807/6/4.
20 Ibid. 1808/2/175; Regency A–Z; Johnstone's Lond.Com. Dir. (1818).
21 Pigot & Co.'s Nat. Lond. & Provincial Com. Dir. (1832–4).
22 P.R.O., C 110/174C–I.
23 M.L.R. 1792/4/213.
24 Regency A–Z.
25 M.L.R. 1711/2/14.
26 Ibid. 1713/5/172.
27 P.R.O., C 110/174B.
28 M.L.R. 1712/1/138. Hamilton was lessee of the whole estate in 1694: C.L.R.O., Assess. Box 43, MS. 22.
29 M.L.R. 1730/3/276.
30 Ibid. 1766/3/98; vestry mins. 1747–81, p. 173; T.H.L.H.L., BG/202.
31 Survey of Lond. xxvii. 266.
32 T.H.L.H.L., BG/264.
33 M.L.R. 1794/3/661; Horwood, Plan (1792–9).
34 M.L.R. 1812/2/330.
35 Ibid. 1818/6/785.
36 T.H.L.H.L., TH/204, 2267.
37 G.L.R.O., MR/TH 16, m. 26; 46.
38 Horwood, Plan (1792–9); Regency A–Z.

Beasley's garden, at the opposite end of the parish, was occupied by Barth, a gardener, in 1792,[39] by which time it had expanded to cover all of Sebrights north of Hackney Road.[40] It survived in 1813 when an Act permitted building on the estate.[41] Edger's garden on the Cass estate, probably named after Joseph Edger, lessee in 1694,[42] formed part of Grove Street hamlet in Hackney.

The Dickens garden east of Cambridge Road was not commercial, but a cottage and garden belonging to the same estate were built on the east side of Russia Lane between 1696 and 1703.[43] The cottage became the Blue Anchor inn and the garden, for which the Brown family secured enfranchisement in 1881,[44] was a nursery until the 1870s or later,[45] run in 1848 by Henry Clarke.[46]

By the mid 18th century, despite some building, the total area of gardening had increased since 1703. Hambleton's garden, for example, had expanded to the east and south, and Simkins's, which was probably held by Richard Burchall from 1751 to 1775 or later, [47] to the estates to the north, Naylors and Fullmore Close,[48] while Samuel Marriott (or Merrett), gardener of Mile End New Town, who leased 4¾ a. of the Mile End portion of Hare Marsh in 1745,[49] was rated for a house and garden near Dog Row in 1751.[50] Garden ground was extensive on the east side of Dog Row, on both sides of Red Cow Lane (partly outside the parish), and on the southern part of the Poor's Lands.[51] The latter was occupied in 1765 by Benjamin Hopkins,[52] who paid rent in 1755 for a garden called Long Mead.[53] William Calder, gardener, of Stepney, leased 6 a. on the east side of Cambridge Road between Red Cow Lane and the Poor's Land in 1765[54] and took over from Hopkins on the Poor's Land in 1775. He was followed in 1784 by Alexander Duthie; Duthie's nursery, named after him and William Duthie, occupied the site until 1826 when it passed to Peter Duval and John Mears.[55] Joseph Wilkinson, primarily a cowkeeper at Bishop's Hall, had 15 a. of garden in 1775[56] and 6 a. south of Old Ford Road in 1778 for 'pears late strawberries'.[57]

Expansion on the west side of Cambridge Road by 1775 included John Smart's garden ground on Markhams west of Penn's garden. William Atkins was tithed in 1775 for 6 a. of Tyssens, 1 a. of Willetts and 3 a. of Turney estate,[58] most of which was garden ground by the 1790s. Gardening also spread eastward from Goodwell's to Barnet charity land on the north west and to Edith's Gardens on the south-east of Birdcage Walk, westward from Cambridge Road to Burgoyns, to part of Rush Mead fronting Old Bethnal Green Road and, in the eastern part of the parish, to Cradfords south of Green Street,[59] where the ground was rated in 1794 to Samuel Phillips, perhaps not himself the gardener.[60]

Market gardeners occupied over 28 per cent of Bethnal Green's agricultural land by 1795.[61] Gardens probably reached their greatest acreage c. 1800,[62] with large ones divided like allotments, each with its summer house, where weavers and citizens grew flowers and vegetables and dined on Sundays.[63] Among professional gardeners were James Chapman of Ann's Place, north of Hackney Road, in 1819[64] and William Gabell with ground in North Place, north of Green Street, in 1825.[65] The most important was the Mandeno family. John Mandeno, tithed for 3¼ a. on the western side of Cambridge Road in 1775,[66] or his son had a house in Bethnal Green Road in 1800.[67] In 1802 he acquired ground to the north, between Punderson's and Hollybush gardens, which he and his son John, both gardeners, retained until 1836.[68] He leased other gardens: the 11-a. Great Haresmarsh before 1818,[69] one of two market gardens on Goosefields in 1824,[70] and the 8½-a. Burgoyns in 1838, although he had worked it as a nursery since 1828.[71] The nursery adjoined the family home at no. 11 Hollybush Place. The elder Mandeno was dead by 1836, when the family relinquished its original garden,[72] and by 1842 part of Burgoyns had passed to the developer and the rest to John Byford, market gardener.[73] The younger Mandeno still had the Goosefields garden in 1843 but soon lost it to Victoria Park.[74] John Gardner, who leased from Broomfields, also lost land to the park, north of Duckett's canal,[75] but retained 37 a. of market garden in 1846.[76] Other gardeners included T. Cousins of Cambridge Row, Cambridge Heath, in 1844 and 1850,[77] Henry Bradbury of Emma Street in 1848,[78] and James Mead in Gale's Gardens in 1851.[79]

39 M.L.R. 1792/8/164.
40 Horwood, *Plan* (1792–9).
41 *Regency A–Z*; above, Cambridge Heath.
42 C. L. R. O., Assess. Box 43, MS. 22.
43 G.L.R.O., M93/132, f. 342; Northants. R. O., X 1123, Box (Bp's. Hall 1647–1742), no. 13; Gascoyne, *Map*.
44 G.L.R.O., M93/43, pp. 12, 115; 143; 469.
45 O.S. Map 1/2,500, Lond. XXVIII (1876 edn.).
46 G.L.R.O., MR/UP 340.
47 T.H.L.H.L., BG/202, 256, 264.
48 Rocque, *Plan of Lond.* (1746).
49 Marriott assigned it to Wm. Atkins in 1762: P.R.O., C 110/174A.
50 T.H.L.H.L., BG/256.
51 Rocque, *Plan of Lond.* (1746).
52 M.L.R. 1766/1/219.
53 G.L.R.O., M93/167.
54 M.L.R. 1766/1/219.
55 T.H.L.H.L. 261; Map no. 301; Lysons, *Environs*, ii. 36; *T.L.M.A.S.* xxvi. 294; G.L.R.O., A/PLC/IV/I.
56 T.H.L.H.L., BG/264.
57 G.L.R.O., P93/DUN/201.
58 T.H.L.H.L., BG/264.
59 Horwood, *Plan* (1792–9).
60 He also held grassland: T.H.L.H.L., BG/261.
61 Lysons, *Environs*, ii. 28.
62 Middleton, *View*, frontispiece map.
63 Gavin, *San. Ramblings*, 17.
64 T.H.L.H.L., TH/888.
65 Vestry mins. 1823–8, 23 Dec. 1825.
66 T.H.L.H.L., TH/264.
67 G.L.R.O., MR/PLT 5024.
68 Ibid. MAB 2590; THCS/305.
69 M.L.R. 1818/6/785.
70 The other was Jas. Byford's: 5 Geo. IV, c. 47 (Local and Personal), schedule.
71 G.L.R.O., C/72/187.
72 Ibid. MAB/2590; THCS 446.
73 Ibid. C/72/187; M.L.R. 1842/4/317.
74 G.L.R.O., Victoria Pk. Papers, vol. 1, 10 Nov. 1843.
75 5 & 6 Vic., c. 20, schedule.
76 G.L.R.O., TA 1.
77 *P.O. Dir. Lond.* (1844, 1850).
78 G.L.R.O., C/72/386.
79 P.R.O., HO 107/1541/21/3/3, f. 58.

Between 1795 and 1845 the parish lost *c.* 100 a. of garden ground, mostly to building or by degeneration into land used as rubbish dumps or by squatters.[80] As Bethnal Green lost its attraction for Londoners and as the local weavers grew poorer, plots were abandoned and the summer houses converted into insanitary dwellings. The process started in the earliest gardens and spread eastward. In 1848 the worst sites were Weatherhead's and Greengate gardens off Hackney Road and Gale's Gardens west of Cambridge Road, while George and Camden gardens nearby were deteriorating rapidly.[81] In 1838 Saunderson's gardens, 6 a. *c.* ¼ mile east of the green, were divided into 170 plots for vegetables, tulips, and dahlias. Some produce was sold, flowers for example in the market in Virginia Row.[82] By 1848 deterioration had reached the east, where in Whisker's gardens near Bonner Lane only 16–20 out of hundreds of summer houses had not been turned into dwellings.[83] By 1851 only 47 a. of market gardens and one garden tenant were left.[84] Except at the nursery in Russia Lane, the professional market gardeners and nurserymen had left for Hackney and more distant suburbs.

MILLS. The mill, presumably a windmill, which gave its name to Mill Hill field on the west side of Cambridge Road existed before 1404.[85] The millhouse was mentioned in 1626[86] although the mill may have ceased to function. By 1660 the site had become part of a nursery, later Penn's garden.[87]

There was a windmill in a field near Centre Street on Cambridge Heath estate in 1836.[88]

INDUSTRY. Manorial customs in 1550 forbade tenants or lessees to dig clay for bricks or tiles without the lord's agreement.[89] A century later 31-year leases of the demesne granted permission to dig for an extra £2 an acre, digging to cease for the last three or four years to allow the ground to recover.[90] In practice exhausted brickfields usually left hollowed-out areas which filled with water. Exploitation began in the south, where land was let for brickmaking in the 15th century and 'le bryk place' at the

Whitechapel end of Brick Lane existed by 1510[91] and was producing bricks by 1527.[92] Brick Lane was so called by 1550,[93] Lollesworth field, just outside the boundary in Spitalfields, was leased to Edward Hemmynge, a brickmaker in 1596,[94] while a former brickfield, then called the brick pond and later ducking pond, lay on the north side of Mile End Green in 1642.[95]

There was a brickmaker 'of Bethnal Green' in 1630[96] and one at Bishop's Hall in 1640[97] and there were several in Collier's Row in the 1640s and 1650s.[98] Most brickfields were on demesne land west of Cambridge Road, which was broken up into freehold estates in the 1650s. Relatively few brickmasters leased the fields, often in several places, and moved on as they exhausted the brickearth. Exploitation presumably started in the west and south, moving a little way ahead of the building. The Collier's Row brickmakers almost certainly worked east of Hackney Road and north of Bethnal Green Road. The Fourteen Acres (no. 40) was being dug in 1642,[99] when held by Michael Gisby (d. 1654), active as a builder in Spitalfields before 1638 and occupier in 1642 of a field south of Bethnal Green Road called Wood Close (no. 48),[1] which in 1643 was 'new digged for brick'.[2] The Fourteen Acres was exhausted by 1652, as were the adjoining Crabtree close (no. 38) next to Hackney Road and Three Acre Close (no. 39), both to the north. The brick kilns had moved to the east, to no. 42.[3] The adjoining field to the south (no. 43) was leased to a brickmaker, Anthony Wells, in 1687,[4] while west of the demesne estates John Nicoll leased his land with permission to dig for bricks in 1680,[5] so initiating the building of the Nichol.

Gisby was replaced by Abraham Carnell (or Cardnall), brickmaker of Mile End Green (d. *c.* 1679), who was leased Wood close in 1652 and 1670.[6] He was also leased Sickle Pen field (no. 35), which lay between Hackney Road and Old Bethnal Green Road and was held by his son and grandson, both called Edward, into the second decade of the 18th century.[7] Exhausted brickworkings at its south end were covered by the 1790s by a large pond,[8] advertized as the Wellington fishery in 1815[9] and, as Wellington pond, a 'filthy pond' in 1848.[10] Edward Carnell was described in 1710 and 1712 as brickmaster of

80 P. G. Atherall, 'Displacement of Mkt. Gardening around Lond. by Urban Growth 1745–1939' (Camb. Univ. Ph.D. thesis, 1975), 176.

81 Gavin, *San. Ramblings*, 12. Other gdns. were Lamb and Smart's off Three Colts La., Chapman's and Pain's near Sebright St., and Baker's Arms near Barnet Grove: ibid. 32–3, 56, 61.

82 *Rep. Asst. Com. Handloom Weavers*, pt. II, pp. 216, 218; below, markets.

83 Gavin, *San. Ramblings*, 10, 12,

84 Atherall, 'Displacement of Mkt. Gardening', 177.

85 Guildhall MS. 25422.

86 P.R.O., WARD 7/74/150.

87 G.L.R.O., M93/3, p. 73.

88 Ibid. THCS 447.

89 Robinson, *Hist. Hackney*, i. 344.

90 G.L.R.O., M93/158, f. 13.

91 *Survey of Lond.* xxvii. 96; above, Stepney, econ. hist. (ind.).

92 Guildhall MS. 10123/2.

93 Robinson, *Hist. Hackney*, i. 332.

94 *Survey of Lond.* xxvii. 96.

95 B.L. Add. MS. 22253.

96 *Marriage Regs. of St. Dunstan's, Stepney*, ed. T. Colyer-Fergusson (1898), i. 195.

97 Ibid. ii. 7.

98 Ibid. 8, 30, 81.

99 B.L. Add. MS. 22253. For field nos., above, fig. 24

1 Lambeth Pal. Libr., MS. 2731/2; *Mem. Stepney Par.*164 n; M. J. Power 'Urban Development of E. Lond. 1550–1700' (Lond.Univ. Ph.D. thesis, 1971), 25.

2 Lambeth Pal. Libr., MS. 2731/3; G.L.R.O., BRA 685/1/80.

3 G.L.R.O., M93/158, ff. 9, 13.

4 P.R.O., C 8/358/197.

5 M.L.R. 1709/2/126.

6 G.L.R.O., M93/158, f. 11; P.R.O., C 5/227/14; Lambeth Pal. Libr., MS. 2731/3.

7 T.H.L.H.L., TH/2143.

8 Horwood, *Plan* (1792–9).

9 *The Times*, quoted in Vale, *Old Bethnal Green*, 44.

10 Gavin, *San. Ramblings*, 87.

Nag's Head, which adjoined Sickle Pen field to the west.[11]

Another probable brickmaker was Edward Hemings or Hemonds,[12] assessed in 1694 for 'Mr. Balleys land and profits in brickearth'.[13] Presumably it was Saffron Close (no. 45), of which he was tenant in 1703, together with the adjoining 17 a. (nos. 46 and 47) of Willetts,[14] parts of which were plots staked out for bricks in 1711.[15]

The interests of both Carnell and Hemings passed to Thomas Scott, recorded as brickmaster or brickmaker from 1709 and as of Nag's Head in 1712–13.[16] He was the tenant of Willett's fields (nos. 46 and 47) by 1713[17] and of Wood Close (no. 48) by 1722.[18] Samuel Scott, probably Thomas's son, a brickmaker or brick merchant, leased 14 a. of Willetts (Hare Street and George fields, probably at least part of nos. 46 and 47) in 1768.[19] He also acquired Thickness estate to the south, adjoining the old brickfield at ducking pond, which he was exploiting for bricks in 1778.[20] In 1794, besides Thickness, which he owned, Scott was rated for six parcels, one of them Tilekilnfield (Chambers) on the east side of Cambridge Heath and several others along Hackney Road.[21] John Scott, brickmaker of Islington, leased Tilekilnfield, then called Clay Pits, in 1808.[22] It was probably one of the southern Scott brickfields which was referred to in 1826 as Spicer Street, the meeting place of ruffians.[23]

The Pritchard family, like the Carnells and Scotts, combined farming with brickmaking. Andrew Pritchard was rated for Carnell's land in 1751[24] and he or his son was 'tilemaker of Hackney Road' in 1789.[25] 'Mr. Prickard' had the Nag's Head brickfield and part of Bullocks estate north of Hackney Road by 1778.[26] Ponds left by brickmaking were apparent by the 1740s[27] and had grown enormously by 1826.[28] George field on Willetts was leased in 1788 to William Timmins, who in partnership with John May Evans did much local building and who still worked it as a brickfield in 1803.[29]

In 1795 Bethnal Green furnished bricks not only for local use but for general sale.[30] As building spread across the exhausted brickfields, extraction moved to the east. The right to dig brickearth was considered when leasing part of Bishop's Hall at Cambridge Heath in 1729.[31] Chambers, to the north, was being exploited by 1794[32] and Samuel Ridge began brickmaking at Bishop's Hall c. 1811. The Regent's canal facilitated the transport of bricks and of gravel, which was also excavated along its banks by Ridge. By 1841 the Bishop's Hall fields were nearly worked out and Ridge and his son John were planning to dig on a field which they had bought 'many years ago' beyond Bethnal Green's north-eastern boundary.[33] Digging in the area was ended by the opening of Victoria Park, with the former brickfields converted to lakes.[34] John Ridge was still listed as a brickmaker in 1844 and 1858, presumably on his family's large open brickfield south of Old Ford Road and east of the canal. It had apparently closed by 1863.[35]

Other brickfields in the mid 19th century included one on Sebrights, where a pond existed by 1826.[36] Rhodes, the occupier in 1813,[37] was presumably William Rhodes (d. 1843), who had a brick- and tileworks in Hackney Road in 1802 and 1840.[38] The pond, then being filled in, was in 1848 a deep hollow behind Teale Street, the result of excavation more than 20 years before.[39] In 1845 part of Burgoyns, the most conspicuously empty area west of Cambridge Road, was leased to Islip Odell, who could use the brickearth.[40] There was a brickfield there in 1846[41] and a brickmaker in the adjoining Punderson's Gardens in 1851. Other brickmakers in 1851 were in West Street north of Scott's brickfield near the ducking pond [42] and in Portland Place, White Street,[43] suggesting the survival of the Willetts brickfield, and there were colonies of brickmakers in the Nichol, Old Castle Street, and Weatherhead Gardens,[44] and in the east by the canal.[45] The latter probably worked for John Ridge and on 7 a. of Broomfields between Grove Road and the canal, which were occupied in 1846 by John Hatfield.[46] Edward Hatfield, described as a brick merchant in 1851 and brickmaker in 1855, lived in Grove House opposite the field.[47]

There were brickmakers in 1855 in William Street, Globefields (E. Bates & Co.), Old Ford Road (William Bird), Morpeth Street (William White), and Grove Road (James Thomas

[11] G.L.R.O., MR/FB2, f. 388; FB3.
[12] Possibly connected with Edw. Hemmynge (fl. 1596), above.
[13] C. L. R. O., Assess. Box 43, MS. 22.
[14] Gascoyne, *Map* (copy in B.M., Crace Colln., Portf. xvi. 33).
[15] M.L.R. 1711/2/14.
[16] G.L.R.O., MR/FB2, f. 328; FB3.
[17] Lambeth Pal. Libr., MS. 2731/9.
[18] Ibid. MS. 2731/13.
[19] BNC, Bethnal Green 1 (abstr. of title); G.L.R.O., P93/DUN/200.
[20] G.L.R.O., M93/142, 143; P93/DUN/201. Tell-tale ponds are on Horwood, *Plan*. (1792–9).
[21] Also Jarvis's: T.H.L.H.L., BG/261; Map no. 301.
[22] M.L.R. 1808/5/460, 743–4.
[23] *The Times*, 19 Sept. 1826, 3f; 20 Sept. 3f.
[24] T.H.L.H.L., BG/256.
[25] G.L.R.O., MR/FR/1789/J81.
[26] Ibid. P93/DUN/20; T.H.L.H.L., Map no. 301.
[27] Rocque, *Map of Lond.* (1741–5).
[28] *Cruchley's New Plan*. (1826).
[29] BNC, Bethnal Green 1 (abstr. of title).
[30] Lysons, *Environs*, ii. 28.

[31] Northants. R.O., X 1075 (23), Memos.
[32] Above.
[33] G.L.R.O., Victoria Pk. Papers, i, *passim*; P.R.O., MPE 1365.
[34] Extensive beds of clay used for brickmaking noted in 1831 edn. of Lewis, *Topog. Dict. Eng.* i. 152. No reference to brickmaking in 1849 edn.
[35] *P.O. Dir. Lond.* (1844, 1855, 1858, 1863); P.R.O., IR 30/21/40; G.L.R.O., TA 1; Gavin, *San. Ramblings*, 10.
[36] *Cruchley's New Plan*. (1826).
[37] 53 Geo. III, c. 202 (Local and Personal), schedule.
[38] *Holden's Triennial Dir. (1802–4); Robinson's Com. Dir.* (1840); *V.C.H. Mdx.* x. 88-9
[39] Gavin, *San. Ramblings*, 57.
[40] T.H.L.H.L., TH/2314.
[41] G.L.R.O., THCS 521.
[42] P.R.O., HO 107/1541/21/3/22, f. 661, p. 2; 8, f. 190, p. 1.
[43] Ibid. HO 107/1542/21/4/6, f. 117, p. 31.
[44] Ibid. HO 107/1539/21/1/1, p. 34; 7, p. 17; 8, p. 19; 11, p. 16.
[45] Ibid. HO 107/1540/21/2/1, p. 66; 2, p. 47; 6, p. 34.
[46] Ibid. IR 30/21/40; G.L.R.O., TA 1.
[47] P.R.O., HO 107/1540/21/2/7, f. 192, p. 33; *P.O. Dir. Lond.* (1855).

Hammack & Co.).[48] The latter, still listed in 1863,[49] leased the Grove Road site until 1874 when it was for sale, the last working brickfield in Bethnal Green.[50]

Brick merchants, using canal wharves, continued into the 20th century: Robert Wright (d. 1873) of Wharf Cottage, Old Ford Road, in 1863,[51] Thomas Wright, John Robson at Northumberland Wharf, Bishop's Road, and Doulton and Co. at Globe Wharf, Mile End Road and Crown Wharf, Globe Road, on the Hertford Union canal, in 1879.[52] The latter, with Harold Goodman at Cumberland Wharf off Green Street, still operated in 1902.[53]

Other industries were located in Bethnal Green because of its closeness to the London market, its plentiful labour, and the ease of canal transport, particularly from the docks. Most raw materials and finished goods, however were carted or taken by hand to warehouses and middlemen there or in neighbouring districts.

The dominant industry for nearly two centuries was silkweaving. Traditionally ascribed to the Huguenot influx into Spitalfields after the Revocation of the Edict of Nantes in 1685, it originated earlier, possibly in Jacobean mulberry-growing at Bishop's Hall.[54] Weavers were recorded in Bethnal Green from 1604[55] and silkweavers from 1612, the earliest at Bishop's Hall.[56] They were present in the western parts, in Collier's Row,[57] Stepney Rents,[58] Cock Lane,[59] and Brick Lane[60] by the 1640s. The Dolphin in Cock Lane, a well-known weavers' resort in the 18th century, may have been connected with the old Dolphin inn in Bishopsgate, a district settled by weavers in the 16th.[61]

The building which spread from Spitalfields in the 1660s and 1670s was mostly for weavers.[62] London weavers, like Solomon Bonner in Great Haresmarsh in 1675 and Miles White in Hare Street in 1680,[63] began to acquire property. By 1684 it was said of Bethnal Green that 'the people for the most part consist of weavers'.[64]

The early weavers included foreigners like Gerrard Vanton, a Walloon living in Bethnal Green in 1635.[65] The main influx of Huguenot silkweavers came later, when English masters welcomed cheap, skilled labourers during the dominance of French fashion, which depended on pattern rather than cut. The immigrants' skill in figured silk, brocades, and lustrings

brought a boom to the industry in the late 17th and early 18th centuries.[66] Silkweaving then was small-scale and paternalistic with masters and journeymen usually working in the master's house, itself set among the smaller journeymen's houses.[67] Although most immigrants were poor, a few brought capital or, with some English weavers, prospered to become masters. Master weavers included the Garretts, who had lived in Bethnal Green since the 1670s,[68] had property in Castle Street in 1694[69] and tenements in Weaver Street in the mid 18th century.[70] Others were John Rondeau (1694–1706) and, in the 1740s, Peter Triquet in St. John Street, James Sufflee and Abraham Jemmett in Fleet Street, Jonathan Pulley in New Cock Lane, William Grinsell in Turvey (? Turville) Street, Jonathan Hauchecorne of New Cock Lane and Isaac Dupree,[71] whose family had property in St. John Street and Carter's Rents in 1694.[72]

Bethnal Green, although not named, may have been a scene of the riots against mechanized silk looms in 1675.[73] In 1697 it petitioned against the import of materials from India and Persia, which had 'extinguished' weaving and its dependent trades.[74] In 1719-20 there were violent protests, with attacks on women wearing calico, and in 1721 legislation forbade its manufacture.[75]

The industry changed in the mid 18th century, partly because the most successful masters tended to leave for the land or liberal professions, being replaced by humbler journeymen, usually Englishmen.[76] The spread of more cramped houses for journeymen made Bethnal Green a less desirable residence, from which the departure of the 'better sort' by 1743 was leaving a population chiefly of journeymen and 'other inferior artificers belonging to the weaving trade'.[77] Giles Bigot (d. 1742), for example, whose family came from Poitou, moved to Spital Square in 1739. His son Peter, a master weaver, leased a building with five tenements and two back rooms at the corner of Swan and Bacon streets[78] but by 1761 when he bought Great Haresmarsh he had moved to Essex and apparently left the industry.[79] By 1788 there was said to be not one silk master or manufacturer resident in Bethnal Green, the weavers working in their homes, sometimes the tenemented houses of former masters, for employers in Spitalfields or the City.[80]

48 *P.O. Dir. Lond.* (1855).
49 Ibid. (1863).
50 Ibid. (1879); G.L.R.O., MR/UP 1098.
51 G.L.R.O., Acc. 128/10; *P.O. Dir. Lond.* (1863).
52 *P.O. Dir. Lond.* (1879).
53 Ibid. (1902).
54 Mulberry trees from the avenue to the hall survived into the 20th cent.: Bethnal Green Mus. *Cat. of Drawings and Prints relating to Hackney and Bethnal Green* (1925), 21.
55 Vale, *Old Bethnal Green*, 36; *Marriage Regs. of St. Dunstan's, Stepney*, i. 68, 78, 81–2, 148, 168, 178, 186; ii. 16.
56 *Marriage Regs.* i. 84, 92, 114, 121, 139, 181; *Mdx. Sess. Rec.* iii. 255.
57 *Marriage Regs.* ii. 2, 5–6, 31.
58 Ibid. 20.
59 Ibid. 8, 17, 25, 28. 60 Ibid. 20.
61 Vale, *Old Bethnal Green*, 37.
62 Above, the West.
63 Guildhall MS. 9968.
64 Vale, *Old Bethnal Green*, 36, quoting local pamphlet of procs. of J.P.s.
65 I. Scouladi, *Rets. of Strangers in Metropolis* (Hug. Soc.,

Quarto ser. lvii), 347.
66 R. D. Gwynne, *Huguenot Heritage* (1985), 66–68; F. Warner, *Silk Ind. of the U.K.* (1921), 57.
67 N. K. A. Rothstein, 'Silk Ind. in Lond. 1702–66' (Lond. Univ. M.A. thesis, 1961), 183.
68 P.R.O., E 179/143/407, p. 270.
69 C. L. R. O., Assess. Box 43, MS. 22.
70 Rothstein, 'Silk Ind. 1702–66', 59.
71 Ibid. 59–61; vestry mins. 1747–81, p. 14; Grinsell went bankrupt in 1750.
72 C. L. R. O., Assess. Box 43, MS. 22.
73 *Guildhall Studies in Lond. Hist.* i. (1973), 14 sqq.
74 *MSS. of H.L.* N.S. ii. 509–10.
75 *E. Lond. Papers*, vii (i), 3–21; I. Gilmour, *Riot, Risings and Revolution* (1992), 253.
76 Rothstein, 'Silk Ind. 1702–66', 216; *Proc. Hug. Soc. of Lond.* xx. 85–6.
77 *C.J.* xxiv. 369.
78 Rothstein, 'Silk Ind. 1702–66', 55, 59.
79 T.H.L.H.L., TH/436–7; above, estates (Gt. Haresmarsh).
80 *The Times*, 2 Oct. 1788, 1d. And see Lysons, *Environs*, ii. 28.

The rift between masters and men exacerbated the turbulence which followed the end of the Seven Years' War, with journeymen combining to sabotage those paying or accepting reduced wages. After riots in 1763, 1765, and 1766,[81] the single-handed weavers organized themselves as the Bold Defiance with their headquarters at the Dolphin in Cock Lane, raised a strike fund, and smashed engine looms. The military raided the Dolphin and two of the weavers' leaders, Doyle and Valline, were hanged before a great crowd near the Salmon and Ball.[82] Some 15 months later the mob murdered a witness against the hanged men. David Wilmot was the magistrate active in apprehending two culprits, whose execution in 1771 led troops to guard his house.[83] In 1773 weavers allied with coal heavers to press for lower food prices and help for the weaving industry but the Bethnal Green magistrates prevented assemblies which might have led to riot.[84] In 1773 a Spitalfields Act banned foreign silks and in 1792 and 1801 further Acts regulated prices and wages, whereupon the weavers' riots came to an end.[85]

The Act of 1773 brought some stability, although the industry remained vulnerable to changes in fashion and by c. 1800 expertise had declined as demand for elaborate materials dwindled.[86] The independent weaver more and more fell into the power of a middleman, the factor who procured woven material at the lowest possible price to supply wholesale dealers.[87] By 1816 the weavers were in greater distress than for many years.[88]

A related decline took place in the specialized occupations that had formed part of the early silk industry. Framework knitters, who produced stockings and gloves, were recorded in 1660,[89] 1671,[90] and 1685, when three worked at 'engines wherewith to make knitwork' belonging to a victualler,[91] and 1734, when there was a stocking-maker in Bacon Street.[92] In 1763 many knitters worked privately at home for the capital's shops, although none of the manufacturers lived in Bethnal Green.[93] Their occupation had ceased to be recorded by 1800.

Silk throwsters, who twisted the raw silk into thread, were recorded from 1631[94] and were often men of position: James Church (d. 1686) left money and property in the City and several counties.[95] In the 1720s John (d. 1732) and Matthew Oakey were men of substance in the western part of Bethnal Green; John, also styled a merchant, was a justice.[96] After c. 1760 the industry, by then usually called silkwinding, declined in status, being carried on in small factories or in the weaver's home, usually by his wife and children.[97] The Cranfields of Hare Street were throwsters, Jeremiah being described as a worsted thrower in 1817 although Isaac Cranfield & Sons were among London's very few surviving silk-throwing firms in 1832.[98] In 1851 there was a silkwinder, along with two silk manufacturers, in Paradise Row,[99] whose widow was still in business in 1863.[1] Other silkwinders in 1851 were William Engleburtt of Elizabeth Street off Hackney Road, with 15 employees, and another in Sebright Street, with 5.[2] Only two silkwinders were recorded in 1863 and none by 1879.[3]

The chief and longest lasting related industry was dyeing. A dyehouse stood on the east side of George Street near St. John Street, probably by 1694;[4] it lasted until Ham's Alley was built between 1783 and 1791.[5] William Lee (d. 1720), its first dyer, was in partnership with John Ham,[6] and a John Ham retained considerable property there in 1783.[7] A second dyehouse nearby belonged by 1751 to another prominent parishioner, Vincent Beverley (d. 1772),[8] whose successor John Beverley had a dyehouse in 1775.[9] One of the two dyehouses was occupied in 1818 by Powell.[10] John Wright had a dyehouse in Hare Street in 1775[11], perhaps that owned by the only identifiable Huguenot dyers, James Racine and Frank Jacques, whose dyehouse was variously described as in Hare Street or next to the French chapel in St. John Street from c. 1817–1846/50.[12] Other dyers included John Hilliard at no. 10 London Terrace, Hackney Road, and Thomas Stracey at no. 23 George Street, possibly a successor of Ham or Beverley, in 1817 and 1826–7, W. Tillett in South Conduit Street in 1826–7[13] and 1836, John Barker at no. 2 Winchester Street in 1826–7 and no. 5 Bacon Street and Spicer Street in 1832–4, Edmund

81 C. Bermant, *Point of Arrival* (1975), 34.
82 G. Rudé, *Hanoverian Lond.* (1971), 198–201; Gilmour, *Riot, Risings and Revolution*, 254; *Annual Reg.* 1768, pp. 57–60, 139, 157.
83 *Cal. H.O. Papers*, 1770–2, 273–4, 401.
84 Ibid. 1773–5, 39.
85 *E. Lond. Papers*, i (i), 5.
86 W. M. Jordan, 'Silk Ind. in Lond. 1760–1830' (Lond. Univ. M.A. thesis, 1931), 42–47, 60–66, 83–84, 93–116; above, settlement and building to 1836.
87 A. K. Sabin, *Silk Weavers of Spitalfields and Bethnal Green* (1931), 15–17.
88 Vestry mins. 1813–21, f. 66v.
89 P.R.O., PROB 11/297 (P.C.C. 1 Nabbs), f.6–v.
90 Ibid. PROB 11/337 (P.C.C. 143 Duke), ff. 327v.–8.
91 Ibid. PROB 11/381 (P.C.C. 115 Cann), ff. 58–59.
92 *Justice in 18th-cent. Hackney*, ed. R. Paley (Lond. Rec. Soc. xxviii), 119.
93 Mortimer, *Universal Director* (1763).
94 *Marriage Regs. of St. Dunstan's, Stepney*, i. 203.
95 P.R.O., PROB 11/384 (P.C.C. 93 Lloyd), ff. 121v.–22. He left wrought silk, mohair, and Spanish silk hose: PROB 4/4271.
96 M.L.R. 1723/1/14–15; 1771/3/126; *Justice in 18th-cent. Hackney*, p. xii.

97 Jordan, 'Silk Ind. 1760–1830', 12, 26; *Rep. Com. Poor Laws*, H.C. 44, p. 110a (1834), ii, app. A, pt. 3; *Rep. from Asst. Commrs. on Handloom Weavers*, pt. II (43–I), H.C. p. 234 (1840), xxiii.
98 *Johnstone's Lond. Com. Dir.* (1817); *Pigot's Com. Dir.* (1832–4).
99 Sam. Daniels: *P.O. Dir. Lond.* (1851); P.R.O., HO 107/1540/21/2/8, pp. 1 sqq.
1 *P.O. Dir. Lond.* (1863).
2 Ibid. (1851); P.R.O., HO 107/1540/21/3/9, p. 1; 17, p. 26.
3 *P.O. Dir. Lond.* (1863, 1879).
4 C. L. R. O., Assess. Box 43, MS. 22.
5 T.H.L.H.L., BG/258, 262.
6 P.R.O., PROB 3/20/119.
7 T.H.L.H.L., BG/256, 258.
8 Ibid. 256; Mortimer, *Universal Director* (1763); Lysons, *Environs*, ii. 33; M.L.R. 1772/2/91.
9 T.H.L.H.L., BG/264.
10 M.L.R. 1818/6/746.
11 T.H.L.H.L., BG/264.
12 *Johnstone's Lond. Com. Dir.* (1817); *Pigot's Lond. Dir.* (1826–7); *Pigot's Com. Dir.* (1832–4); G.L.R.O., MR/PLT 5061, 5065; THCS 446, 520; P.R.O., C 54/14139, mm. 41 sqq.
13 *Johnstone's Lond. Com. Dir.* (1817); *Pigot's Lond. Dir.* (1826–7).

Reynolds in Durham Place, Hackney Road, in 1832–4[14] and 1863, and James Elkins at no. 11 Weaver street in 1863 and 1879.[15]

An estimated 68 per cent of adult males were employed in clothing (59 per cent in silk) in 1770 and only 48 per cent (39 per cent in silk) in 1813.[16] The repeal of the Spitalfields Acts in 1824, which led to a steady drop in wages, and the treaty of 1860, which opened English markets to French silk, furthered the decline, as did fashion's favouring other fabrics over silk and the spread of cheap factory production elsewhere, notably in the north of England.[17] In 1838 nearly 11 per cent of the parish's population worked as silkweavers. Bethnal Green dominated the Spitalfields weaving industry, having 77 per cent of the looms and 82 per cent of the families employed.[18] The industry had spread to all parts of the parish although it was still densest in the south and west, where the finest goods were produced. Of a total of 7,847 working looms, 2,932 were in Church and 2,703 in Town ward. Besides the 7,847 people employed as weavers (4,232 men, 2,897 women, and the rest children and apprentices), there were 776 unemployed weavers and 189 who called themselves weavers but had had to part with their looms; 3,512 families were at work, most owning one or two looms. Nine per cent of the looms in Church ward and 5 per cent in Town ward produced Jacquard velvet or figured silk, compared with 4 per cent in Hackney Road and barely 3 per cent in Green ward. By far the largest output was of plain goods, ranging from 61 per cent in Church ward to 86 per cent in Hackney Road. Velvets, which made up the rest, in 1867 required 600 distinct operations to make 1".[19]

Only two wealthy silkmasters were said to live in Bethnal Green in 1834.[20] Although the industry in London remained overwhelmingly domestic, a few factories were opened.[21] There were Bethnal Green residents during most of the 19th century who called themselves silk manufacturers but most firms were small-scale and short lived. They included one in Elizabeth Street, off Hackney Road, in 1821,[22] five in 1832–4 (two in Pollard Row, and one each in Bethnal Green Road, Church Street, and Tyssen Street),[23] 10 in 1851,[24] 3 in 1863, and 5 in 1879.[25]

Charles Tripany in Sebright Street in 1851 employed 5 men[26] but references to a foreman or watchman in a silk factory, numerous in 1851,[27] imply that there were factories. One of the manufacturers of 1851 was John Warner, who lived in Northampton House, Elizabeth Terrace, off Hackney Road, with servants.[28] By 1872 Messrs. Warner & Ramm had built the East London silk mills in Hollybush Gardens,[29] where by 1876 nearly 100 in- and out-workers produced furniture silk.[30] In 1895 the firm, the last to leave the parish, acquired mills in Braintree (Essex) to which it soon transferred 60 silkweavers from Bethnal Green.[31]

After the collapse of the plain silk market after 1860, the East London industry concentrated on furniture silk and on handkerchiefs, ties, and scarves, such as those produced by Slater, Buckingham & Co. of Spitalfields at a factory in Lark Row, Cambridge Road, in 1876. Vavasseur, Carter & Collier made a variety of silks in the Nichol c. 1876–1902.[32] By the late 1880s 284 households were employed in silkweaving, forming 1 per cent of the population.[33] Only two manufacturers were listed in 1902[34] although the borough still had more silk workers than any other in London.[35] By 1914 114 weavers occupied 46 workshops, mostly in Cranbrook Street and Alma Road in the eastern part, but by 1931 there were only 11 elderly weavers.[36] Efforts to revive the industry in the 1930s failed[37] and it finally ended in 1940 when France could no longer supply the raw material.[38]

Craftsmen in the early 17th century included an ironyer (1613),[39] a wireworker (1636),[40] and makers of boxes (1621), clasps (1623), felt (1629),[41] sieves (1630), baskets (1633), spectacles (1634),[42] and gloves (1638 and 1641).[43] There was a tobacconist in Brick Lane and a collarmaker (Joseph Blissett, owner of Markhams) in 1707,[44] a perukemaker in 1762,[45] and a cardmaker in 1763.[46]

Brewing, besides serving the local market, included a share in one of the big commercial breweries. The Black Eagle brewery, founded in 1669, taken over by Joseph Truman before 1683, transformed into Truman, Hanbury, Buxton & Co. c. 1800,[47] and taken over by Maxwell Joseph before 1978,[48] lay on either side of Brick Lane, mostly in Spitalfields but including early

[14] *Pigot's Com. Dir.* (1832–4); G.L.R.O., THCS 446.
[15] *P.O. Dir. Lond.* (1863, 1879).
[16] Based on par. regs. and therefore excluding Jews and nonconf.: *E. Lond. Papers,* xiv (2), 93.
[17] Sabin, *Silk Weavers,* 14–17; A. Plummer, *Lond. Weavers Co. 1600–1970* (1972), 358–9, 368–9.
[18] Other dists. were Christ Ch. Spitalfields, Mile End New Town, and Shoreditch: *Rep. Asst. Commrs. on Handloom Weavers,* pt. II, pp. 219 sqq.; *Census,* 1841.
[19] *The Times,* 14 Feb. 1867, 5d.
[20] *Rep. Com. Poor Laws,* p. 112a.
[21] Warner, *Silk Ind.* 75–76.
[22] Thos. Cole: P.R.O., C 108/205.
[23] *Pigot's Com. Dir.* (1832–4).
[24] *P.O. Dir. Lond.* (1851); P.R.O., HO 107/1539/21/1/23, p. 29; 24, p. 4; HO 107/1540/21/2/8, p. 1; 9, p. 38; HO 107/1541/21/3/9, p. 1; HO 107/1542/21/4/19, p. 1.
[25] *P.O. Dir. Lond.* (1863, 1879).
[26] P.R.O., HO 1541/21/3/9, p. 1 sqq.
[27] Ibid. HO 107/1539/21/1/29, p. 28; HO 107/1541/21/3/7, p. 30; 9, p. 1; HO 107/1542/21/4/27, p. 9.
[28] Ibid. HO 107/1539/21/1/23, p. 29.
[29] Old O.S. Map Lond. 51 (1872).

[30] W. G. Crory, *E. Lond. Industries* (1876), 110, 113.
[31] Sabin, *Silk Weavers,* 18–19.
[32] Crory, *E. Lond. Inds.,* 21; *P.O. Dir. Lond.* (1879, 1902).
[33] Booth, *Life and Labour,* i (1), table IX.
[34] *P.O. Dir. Lond.* (1902).
[35] Booth, *Life and Labour,* ii (2), 374.
[36] Sabin, *Silk Weavers,* 19.
[37] *The Times,* 22 Nov. 1930, 9c; 2 Nov. 1931, 9a.
[38] H. Rees, 'N.E. Expansion of Lond. since 1770' (Lond. Univ. M.Sc. (Econ.) thesis, 1946), 32.
[39] *Mdx. Sess. Rec.* i. 147.
[40] *Marriage Regs. of St. Dunstan's, Stepney,* i. 242.
[41] Ibid. 126, 140, 187.
[42] Ibid. 192, 218, 226.
[43] Ibid. 264; ii. 16, 22.
[44] G.L.R.O., MR/FB 2, f. 202. Blissett was a Bethnal Green resident in 1706: ibid. f. 143.
[45] D. F. McKenzie, *Stationers' Co. Apprentices 1701–1800* (1978), 335.
[46] John Champain, possibly of Huguenot descent: T.H.L.H.L., TH/1149.
[47] *V.C.H. Mdx.* ii. 168–9; *Survey. of Lond.* xxvii. 116–18.
[48] K. Leech, *Brick Lane 1978,* 5.

19th-century buildings in Bethnal Green. Production rose from 60,140 barrels in 1760 to 600,000 in 1876[49] and by 1775 the firm had built storehouses and stabling on the corner of Tyssen and Shacklewell streets.[50]

There were two other breweries in 1751,[51] one in Garrett Street and a much larger one in Hare Street, which existed in 1775[52] and possibly, as Daniel Levesque's, in St. John Street, in 1817, when there was also an ale brewer in Austin Street.[53] By 1836, in addition to the Black Eagle, there were four: in Punderson's Place, Ann Street, Sugar Loaf Walk, and Whitechapel Road.[54] The Sugar Loaf Walk brewery, called the White Hart, existed in 1819.[55] The Whitechapel Road brewery, at the southern tip of Bethnal Green, was held by James Mann in 1836,[56] employed 158 men in 1851,[57] and was called the Albion brewery when a warehouse was built in 1872.[58] The owners Mann, Crossman & Paulin in 1937 applied, presumably unsuccessfully, to build a factory at the junction of Dinmont and Coate streets at the other end of Bethnal Green.[59] Their Albion brewery survived on its original site in 1988 but had closed by 1994.

The north side of Hackney Road by 1846 had a brewery in Gwynne's Place[60] and to the east by the early 1860s the Wiltshire brewery of Chandler & Co.,[61] which was rebuilt or extended in 1871 and 1893.[62] The south side had two breweries in 1872, almost opposite Wiltshire brewery and at the junction of Temple and Claremont streets.[63] The City of London brewery had a factory in Smarts Street by 1902.[64] There were at least five distillers in the western and southern districts in the 1740s.[65] John Liptrap had a distillery in Hollybush Gardens from 1812 until 1838 or later.[66]

Ropemaking, requiring a long strip of ground, was established partly to serve the shipping industry. Liberty to 'carry a ropewalk' was included in a lease of land north of Green Street in 1714.[67] A cordmaker was leased part of Turville estate in 1728,[68] near the rope ground in Shacklewell Street in 1820.[69] A rope walk on the north side of Sugar Loaf Walk by 1747[70] was leased in 1851 to John Elam, 'master rope and twine spinner', who employed 11 men;[71] it survived in the 1870s.[72] There was another rope walk on the east side of Dog Row c. 1801– 12[73] and a rope manufacturer at no. 50 Church Street in 1817.[74] Several rope walks around Barnet Grove in the mid 19th century[75] included one which in 1862 employed 24 men and 18 boys 'depraved drunkards'.[76] There were at least three rope walks in the early 1870s, in Sugar Loaf Walk, the southern part of Cambridge Road, and Peel Grove,[77] and one, at Usk Street, in 1894.[78]

Warehouses and factories began to appear in the late 18th century. There was a warehouse in Sweetapple Court on Austens in 1775.[79] A cotton factory established by Messrs. Paty and Burchall in St. John Street c. 1783 employed 200-300 workers by 1795[80] and was 'very extensive' in 1831 and 1849;[81] it had gone by 1851 although there were still cotton workers in the parish.[82] A factory was established at the end of Pollard Row by 1794 by Hegner, Ehrliholtzer & Co. to make flaxen pipe hose for fire engines, breweries, and ships. It employed only a few hands in 1795[83] but was 'large' in 1831 and apparently survived in 1849.[84] A floor-cloth factory existed by 1794 in St. Matthew's Place at the eastern end of Hackney Road;[85] owned from c. 1816 by Christopher Daniel Hayes, it had probably closed by 1851.[86] Hayes also had premises in Fenchurch Street and another floor-cloth manufacturer, Thomas and William Davis, had factories on the Shoreditch side of Hackney Road and at nos. 159 and 160 Whitechapel Road, next to Albion brewery, by 1842.[87] Both existed in 1879, as did floor-cloth factories in Globe Road, Cambridge Road, and on the south side of Hackney Road, but all had gone by 1902.[88]

In 1800 there were warehouses in Digby and Carter streets and a factory in Church Row[89] and in 1812 factories in Bond's Place near Mary's Row and in Church Street.[90] By 1817 there were at least seven warehouses in Bethnal Green Road alone[91] and manufacturers included a patent colour firm (Linschoten & Co.), a file maker

49 Crory, *E. Lond. Inds.* 55.
50 B.M., Crace Colln., Portf. xvi. 34; T.H.L.H.L., BG/264.
51 T.H.L.H.L., BG/256.
52 Ibid. BG/264. The brewer was Ben Clempson c. 1751–65, Wm. Moseley in 1775: ibid. 202; *Reg. of Ch. of St. Jean Spitalfields* (Hug. Soc. xxxix), pp. xii–xiii.
53 *Johnstone's Lond. Com. Dir.* (1817).
54 G.L.R.O., THCS 446–7.
55 P.R.O., C 110/164.
56 And see M.L.R. 1842/6/689.
57 P.R.O., HO 107/1540/21/2/12, p. 34.
58 G.L.R.O., MBW 1628 (23); Old O.S. Map Lond. 63 (1873).
59 G.L.R.O., AR/BA/4/650 (3).
60 Ibid. THCS 520.
61 Stanford, *Map of Lond.* (1862–5 edn.).
62 G.L.R.O., MBW 1621 (23); ibid. AR/BA/4/40 (24); ibid. Acc. 1844/B14/1/1.
63 Old O.S. Map Lond. 51 (1872).
64 G.L.R.O., AR/BA/4/117 (4).
65 Vestry mins. 1747–81, pp. 21, 24, 25.
66 G.L.R.O., THCS 305; MR/PLT 5065; map in *Rep. Com. San. Condition of Labouring Pop.* H.L. (1842), xxvi.
67 M.L.R. 1729/2/34.
68 Ibid. 1728/5/10.
69 G.L.R.O., MR/PLT 5065.
70 Ibid. M93/142.

71 Ibid. M93/86, pp. 559–65; P.R.O., HO 107/1540/21/2/118, p. 1.
72 O.S. Map 1/2,500, Lond. XXVIII (1873 edn.).
73 G.L.R.O., THCS 305; C/93/1553–6.
74 *Johnstone's Lond. Com. Dir.* (1817).
75 G.L.R.O., THCS 520; Gavin, *San. Ramblings*, 61.
76 *Lond. City Mission Mag.* xxvii. 42.
77 O.S. Map 1/2,500, Lond. XXVIII (1873 edn.).
78 Old O.S. Map Lond. 52 (1894).
79 T.H.L.H.L., BG/264.
80 Lysons, *Environs*, ii. 28.
81 Lewis, *Topog. Dict. Eng.* (1831), i. 152; ibid. (1849), i. 224–5; G.L.R.O., MR/PLT 5025.
82 P.R.O., HO 107/1539/21/1/1, p. 49; 2, p. 2; 5, p. 32; 6, p. 1.
83 T.H.L.H.L., BG/261; Lysons, *Environs*, ii. 28.
84 Lewis, *Topog. Dict. Eng.* (1831), i. 152; (1849), i. 224–5.
85 G.L.R.O., MR/PLT 5025; M.L.R. 1794/3/107.
86 G.L.R.O., MR/PLT 5057; *Pigot's Nat. Lond. & Provincial Com. Dir.* (1832–4); *P.O. Dir. Lond.* (1851). 'Late factory' in 1851: G.L.R.O., C 72/396.
87 M.L.R. 1842/6/689; *P.O. Dir. Lond.* (1851).
88 *P.O. Dir. Lond.* (1879, 1902).
89 G.L.R.O., MR/PLT 5024–5.
90 Ibid. THCS 305.
91 i.e. inc. western end, wrongly listed as Church St. Shoreditch in Dirs.

(William Rhodes), and a saltpetre refiner (John Vanneson or Van Heson) in Hackney Road, and a soda maker (Whitwell & Co.), two surgeon's lint manufacturers, and two 'orchill makers', Samuel Child and Dent & Child, at the green.[92] Orchil was a red or violet dye made from lichen. A factory, usually called Archall's or Archill,[93] was built, probably by Joseph Dent, on the eastern part of Kirby's Castle estate and conveyed by him in 1817 to Samuel Preston Child.[94] Child was there in 1851 but by 1855 the premises had passed to Burton & Garraway, 'merchants etc.'[95] William Burton & Sons had a peroxide factory there in 1911[96] and in 1934 were merchants and manufacturers of orchil, cudbear, extract of indigo, hydrogen peroxide, aluminia lakes and aniline dyes, sharing the premises with R. B. Brown & Co., dye manufacturers.[97] The site was bombed and later taken for Rogers estate.[98] A white lead works on the east side of Hollybush Gardens belonged to Edward Ball & Co. in 1817[99] and was still there in 1902.[1]

Factories employed only a minority of the workforce. Large numbers affected by the decline of silkweaving in the 1820s and 1830s were absorbed into home- or workshop-based industries. The chief manufactures, lacking the monopoly position of silk, were furniture, clothing, and shoemaking.

One cabinet maker and several weavers were among 14 people eligible for parish office in 1756.[2] William Blunt, formerly of St. Botolph's Bishopsgate, was a cabinet maker in Bethnal Green in 1772.[3] There was a timberyard in 1794[4] and one, associated with a carpenter and undertaker, at the north end of the green in 1800.[5] There were no cabinet makers, chairmakers, or upholsterers in 1811[6] but two timber merchants in Hackney Road, a cabinet and a chair maker in Dog Row, and a cabinet maker in Church Street in 1817.[7] The industry then developed rapidly, making cheap furniture with imported timber which from 1820 could be brought by the Regent's canal.[8] As the traditional cabinet makers, 'society men' based mostly in Clerkenwell, declined in status in the 1830s, Bethnal Green, with its competitive garret-masters, began to take over.[9] In the early 1830s it had two timber dealers, at least one timber merchant, five chair makers, and ten cabinet makers, all except one dealer to the west of Cambridge Road and most along Hackney Road.[10]

Numbers multiplied, to 26 cabinet making, chair making, and upholstering establishments by 1846, 84 by 1859, and 121 by 1872. Steam saw mills fostered the expansion[11] and by 1851[12] the industry had spread east of Cambridge Road to the canal, where there were timberyards at Twig Folly bridge[13] and the proprietor of a steam mill (Richard Tower) lived in Lark Row,[14] probably running the saw mill and yard near Sewardstone Road.[15] Production was still thickest, however, in the west, especially around the Nichol. Although cabinet and chair makers were the most numerous, there were many specialists to make other articles of furniture, frames, or boxes, besides carvers, workers in cane, ivory, bone, willow or veneer, and upholsterers, japanners, and french polishers. The industry was small-scale, in homes or workshops; a chair maker in Clarence Place who employed 8 men was exceptional and there was apparently only one furniture factory, in Hope Street.[16] There were still no large establishments in 1861, when 2,563 people worked in furniture making.[17] By 1872 nearly 700 addresses in Bethnal Green were connected with the industry, compared with 85 in Hackney and 659 in Shoreditch.

There were at least three saw mills and 16 timberyards in the early 1870s, of which 8 yards were in Bethnal Green Road and 4 in Gosset Street.[18] Saw mills were built in 1873 in Sewardstone Road and next to the railway at Cambridge Heath and in 1874 in Busby Street.[19] Numbers in the industry reached 4,326 in 1881 and 4,766 c. 1890, more than half of them described as cabinet makers and upholsterers.[20] Although Curtain Road in Shoreditch was the centre of the trade, Gosset Street was the manufacturing centre. When the 15 a. of the Nichol came to be cleared in 1890, its occupiers included 120 cabinet makers, 74 chair makers, and 24 woodcutters and sawyers.[21] The small workshop remained the standard unit of production, with yards and saw mills interspersed. Mills often let space and steam power to up to 20 specialist workers. Increasing mechanization brought cheaper products, carvers for example being replaced by machine mouldings.[22] A tendency towards larger premises gave rise to three with more than 100 employees by c. 1900,[23] but individuals continued to make and hawk single items. The intense competition and many small workshops which eluded inspection encouraged sweating, which

92 *Johnstone's Lond. Com. Dir.* (1817).
93 *Rep. Com. on San. Condition of Labouring Pop.*, map facing p. 160.
94 G.L.R.O., M93/56, p. 128.
95 *P.O. Dir. Lond.* (1851, 1855).
96 G.L.R.O., AR/BA/4/221, no. 4; O.S. Map 5 ft.; Lond. VII. 48 (1938 edn.).
97 *P.O. Dir. Lond.* (1934).
98 Above, building after 1945.
99 *Johnstone's Lond. Com. Dir.* (1817); *Com. on San. Condition of Labouring Pop.*, map facing p. 160.
1 *P.O. Dir. Lond.* (1879, 1902).
2 Jacob Fish: vestry mins. 1747–81, p. 120.
3 M.L.R. 1772/2/527.
4 T.H.L.H.L., BG/261.
5 G.L.R.O., MR/PLT 5024; THCS/305. The carpenter was Thos. Ruby: M.L.R. 1779/2/598.
6 J. L. Oliver, *Development and Structure of Furniture Ind.* (1966), 37.
7 *Johnstone's Lond. Com. Dir.* (1817).

8 Account based on Oliver, *Furniture Ind.*
9 H. Mayhew, *Lond. Lab. and Lond. Poor* (1861), iii. 221–7.
10 *Pigot's Lond. & Provincial Com. Dir.* (1832–4).
11 J. E. Martin, 'Location of Ind. in Inner NE. Lond.: a study in industrial geog.' (Lond. Univ. Ph.D. thesis, 1961), 223.
12 Based on P.R.O., HO 107/1539–42.
13 Ibid. HO 107/1540/21/2/2, p. 23.
14 Ibid. 22, p. 44.
15 O.S. Map 1/2,500, Lond. XXVIII (1873 edn.).
16 P.R.O., HO 107/1539/21/1/31, p. 3.
17 P. G. Hall, *Industries of Lond. since 1861* (1962), 76–7.
18 O.S. Map 1/2,500, Lond. XXVIII (1873 edn.); Old O.S. Maps Lond. 51 (1872); 63 (1873).
19 G.L.R.O., MBW 1636 (23), 1643 (23), 1667 (24).
20 Booth, *Life and Labour*, i(4), p. 159.
21 L.C.C. *Housing Question in Lond.* [1900], 191.
22 Ibid. 159–90; Martin, 'Location of Ind.', 207–28; J. E. Martin, *Gtr. Lond.* (1966), 10.
23 Martin, 'Location of Ind.', fig. 6.

was exacerbated by Jewish immigration. In 1888 Brick Lane was notorious for boy labour, many garret masters worked people until 11.30 p.m., and a larger factory near Bethnal Green Junction station, with 60–70 employees, worked them until 10.0 p.m.[24]

By 1901 7,874 men and 1,167 women (mostly french polishers) worked in the wood and furniture industry, 3,729 of them as cabinet makers. There were 7,632 men and 1,125 women workers in 1911,[25] when there were 377 cabinet or chair making and upholstery firms. Few firms were long lived, White Bros. in Church Street from 1831 to 1911 being an exception[26] and bankrupt ones being replaced, as little capital was needed to set up a workshop. After a slight decline during the First World War, the industry continued to expand, to 439 cabinet and chair making and upholstery establishments by 1939, the highest concentration in the country and employing 5,961 people in 968 factories.[27] The wholesaler or middleman gradually disappeared as retailers were supplied directly and some of the larger ones ran their own factories. Many hand-made furniture and french polishing workshops closed. The move towards larger premises was reinforced by the need for more space for electrically driven machinery. Larger firms were sited along the Regent's canal or its eastward branch, the Hertford Union, where rents were lower than in the west.[28] In 1938, in the northern area between the canal and Vyner Street, there were four firms with 10–25 employees and two with 26–99. To the east one firm had more than 100 employees, three had 26–99, and one had 10–25.[29] Companies seeking cheaper sites outside Bethnal Green included Beautility, which moved to Edmonton in the mid 1930s.[30]

Slum clearance and bombing reduced their numbers, as did the shortage of timber after 1945.[31] There was diversification into other materials like plastic.[32] Workers in the furniture industry fell from 4,040 in 1951[33] to 2,518 at 307 establishments by 1957.[34] Among firms which moved away were Jarman & Platt to Romford c. 1955,[35] and two in Palmer's Road, a saw mill in Kenilworth Road, and a cabinet firm at no. 293 Old Ford Road which had employed 150 before the war, by 1958.[36] Joseph Gardner (Hardwoods), timber merchants founded in Liverpool in 1748 who had opened a London branch c.

1870 and moved to Twig Folly Wharf in Roman Road in 1932, left between 1964 and 1975.[37] Emerald Furniture Co. moved away in 1969 when its factory, built c. 1890 in Hollybush Gardens, was acquired by the G.L.C.[38] Premises in workshop areas like Teesdale Street dwindled by 1958[39] and vanished in rebuilding later. Many small firms, however, continued into the 1990s in the traditional areas like Hackney Road.[40] There were at least 30 firms in 1991, some in new estates like Crown works in Temple Street or Parmiter Street industrial estate.[41]

The clothing industry arose from the second-hand trade which had existed around Houndsditch since the 16th century and spread eastward to focus on Petticoat Lane. By the early 19th century clothes were 'clobbered' or renovated and a market developed for cheap clothing, including uniforms.[42] There were a haberdasher and worsted manufacturer, a stay manufacturer, a hosier and glover, and a cotton and hosiery warehouse in Bethnal Green Road in 1817[43] and three tailors there, two in Hackney Road, and one each in Cambridge Road, Cambridge Heath, and Stepney Rents by the early 1830s.[44] In 1833 there were attempts to train unemployed weavers in the workhouse in skills which included the 'making of workmen's apparel'.[45] The tailor's condition, like the weaver's, was then beginning to decline, as work paid for daily by the master tailor on his premises gave way to piece work at home. The change, origin of the sweating system, was owed to middlemen who commissioned the work as cheaply as possible.[46]

Although less numerous than weavers or wood workers, clothing workers were in all districts by 1851.[47] The large number called tailors probably reflected their change in status, while there were also needlewomen, dressmakers, seamstresses,[48] and makers of individual garments: waistcoats, shirts, headgear, collars, stays and, more rarely, trousers and shawls. Specialized activities included making buttons and artificial flowers, and preparing ostrich feathers, while in East Street off Russia Lane Edward Thurgood employed 16 men to make elastic hat bands[49] and in Ravenscroft Street James Webb employed 12 to dress skins.[50] Fourteen trimming manufacturers[51] included Thomas Lester in Half Nichol Street with 15 employees[52] and John Lingwood in Fuller Street with 20.[53] There were also clothes

24 1st Rep. Sel. Cttee. of H.L. on Sweating System, H.C. 361, pp. 282, 289, 315 (1888), xx.
25 Census, 1901–11; New Lond. Life and Labour, ii. 210.
26 R. Samuel, E. End Underworld, 5.
27 Presumably inc. all operations with wood: J. H. Forshaw and P. Abercrombie, County of Lond. Plan (1943), 88.
28 New Lond. Life and Labour i. 213, 215; H. Rees, 'NE. Expansion of Lond. since 1770' (Lond. Univ. M.Sc.(Econ.) thesis, 1946), 49, fig. 7.
29 G. M. L. Simpson, 'Comparative study of contemporary and pre-war geog. of E. End of Lond.' (Lond. Univ. M.A. thesis, 1959), 129–31.
30 Hall, Inds. of Lond. 90.
31 R. Sinclair, East Lond. (1950), 55.
32 Simpson, 'Comparative Study', 134.
33 Hall, Inds. of Lond. 80–1.
34 Simpson, 'Comparative Study', 138–9.
35 Hall, Inds. of Lond. 90.
36 Simpson, 'Comparative Study', 134.
37 Leff and Blunden, Story of Tower Hamlets (1967), 127;

P.O. Dir. Lond. (1964, 1975).
38 G.L.C. Mins. (1969), 61.
39 Simpson, 'Comparative Study', 129.
40 e.g. Esspec Finishers Ltd., advertizing 'contemporary legs of all kinds', closed by 1988.
41 Thomson, Dir. E. Lond. (1991–2).
42 Martin, 'Location of Ind.' 95–96.
43 Johnstone's Lond. Com. Dir. (1817).
44 Pigot's Lond. & Provincial Com. Dir. (1832–4).
45 Vestry mins. 1831–3, p. 281.
46 The Unknown Mayhew, ed. E. P. Thompson and E. Yeo (1971), 181 sqq.
47 Para. based on census: P.R.O., HO 107/1539–42.
48 One seamstress in Old Ford Rd. employed 20: P.R.O., HO 107/1540/21/2/19, p. 53.
49 P.R.O. HO 107/1540/21/2/22, p. 38.
50 Ibid. HO 107/1539/21/1/17, p. 11.
51 P.O. Dir. Lond. (1851).
52 P.R.O., HO 107/1539/21/1/3, pp. 1 sqq.
53 Ibid. HO 107/1541/21/3/10, p. 18.

hawkers and dealers, a clothes shop in Austin Street, a rag shop keeper in Birdcage Walk, and rag merchants in Church Street and Giles Row.

Mechanization, following the introduction of the sewing machine to Britain in 1851 and the handsaw in 1858, hastened specialization and sweating. Middlemen, who arranged outlets for an agreed number of goods, contracted with the workshops or homeworkers, who often sub-contracted individual processes. Competition drove down prices while the skilled tailor was superseded by machines and cheap labour, increasingly women, children, and immigrants.[54] In 1861 1,276 people worked in tailoring, 1,401 on women's outerwear, and 904 on shirts and underwear, mostly along Bethnal Green Road, Hackney Road, in the Nichol, and the south-west.[55] In 1865 tailoring in the East End was mainly done by females because of the increased use of the sewing machine[56] and women were making trimmings for a third of the men's wage.[57] Although Jews worked in the clothing trade from the early 19th century, it was their influx in the 1880s which enormously expanded output in the small workshops of Whitechapel and Bethnal Green at the expense of the West End.[58] At the end of the 1880s most workshops were small, with cheap 'slop' coats the main product of the humblest, which often used top floors or backyard sheds. Although workshops existed throughout the parish, there were a group producing mixed garments east of the canal, two larger ones on each side of Bethnal Green Road, and makers of men's coats in Cambridge Road and around Brick Lane.[59] Bethnal Green's industry was only a fraction of Whitechapel's in 1889 but was spreading to the 'Jewish island' of Teesdale and Blythe streets.[60] By 1901 7,310 were employed in 'dress', including 3,206 tailors (71 per cent of them women) and 1,229 shirtmakers and seamstresses; another 2,123 worked in textile fabrics. In 1911 1,623 were employed in textiles and 12,382 (62 per cent of them women) in dress, which probably included shoemaking. Shoemakers were among the 10,181 employed in textiles and dress, the largest category of employment, in 1921.[61]

Strikes by the tailors' unions in 1889 reduced working hours to 12 a day[62] and by 1903 better factory inspection and compulsory registration of outworkers had improved conditions.[63] Out-working was nevertheless common in 1914 and in tailoring involved low pay and long hours, interspersed with long periods of unemployment;[64] fragmentation among nine clothing unions impeded militant action.[65] After the First World War Jewish firms led a shift from men's to

women's tailoring and towards production in larger factories.[66] Legislation guaranteeing minimum piece-prices had increased real wages, especially for women, by 1921. In 1929 there were 423 tailoring establishments, made up of 189 ready-made, 152 wholesale mantle, and 82 retail bespoke firms. In 1931 there were 41 clothing firms (33 of them tailors), which employed 662 outworkers (538 of them in tailoring),[67] and in 1938 the 5,402 people in 411 factories made clothing the largest employer after furniture making.[68] Small firms predominated: tailors with fewer than 10 people clustered in Teesdale and Blythe streets, south of Old Bethnal Green Road, in the south-west, and east of the green. There were a few large firms in gentlemen's tailoring, one in Bethnal Green Road with 400 employees making army clothing, one, London Co-operative Tailoring, employing 101 nearby. Silberston & Sons, long established in Cambridge Heath Road, specialized in uniforms for the Royal Horse Guards. Most firms were small, Jewish, short lived, and employed more women than men.[69]

By 1951 the borough's share of the London clothing industry had declined from 3.13 per cent in 1861 to 1.4 per cent; 2,207 people were employed in tailoring, 510 in women's outer-wear, and 82 in shirts and underwear.[70] Slum clearance, bombing, and attempts to separate industry from residential areas reduced the number of premises, especially the older ones used by small firms. In Teesdale and Blythe streets tailoring firms decreased from 26 in 1938 to 10 in 1958. Silberston survived in 1959 but by 1964 had been replaced by sportswear manu-facturers. A new firm with 140 employees had opened by 1958 to make coats.[71] Closures under development plans began to affect the larger firms and were made easier by mechanization, it having been hard to move skilled workers.[72] In the 1970s the clothing industry declined like silkweaving in the 1860s because of foreign competition. It fought back with increasing mechanization, for example using lasers for cut-ting, and employing immigrants. By 1982 it was estimated that 95 per cent of the Bengalis in Tower Hamlets worked in the industry, often in conditions reminiscent of the sweating of the 1880s. The turnover of small firms continued and emphasis was placed on the fashion industry.[73] Nearly 40 clothing and fabric makers were listed in Bethnal Green in 1991, about half in new business centres, Green Heath in Three Colts Lane, Parmiter, no. 10 Hollybush Gardens, or nos. 244-54 Cambridge Heath Road.[74]

Footwear making in 1817 was represented by

54 Martin, 'Location of Ind.' 96; J. A. Schmiechen, *Sweated Ind. and Sweated Labor. Lond. Clothing Trades 1860-1914* (1984), 24-29.
55 Hall, *Inds. of Lond.* 40, 47, 49.
56 *4th Rep. Children's Employment Com.* H.C. [3548], p. xxxv (1865), xx.
57 *The Times*, 14 Feb. 1867, 5d.
58 Martin, 'Location of Ind.' 95-6; Schmiechen, *Sweated Inds.* 33, 42-3.
59 Martin, 'Location of Ind.' 97, figs. 13-14.
60 Booth, *Life and Labour*, i(4), 66-8.
61 *Census*, 1901-21; L.C.C. *Lond. Statistics*, xxiv. 72-3, 76-7.
62 C. Kerrigan, *Hist. Tower Hamlets* (1982), 32.
63 Booth, *Life and Labour*, ii(3), 10.

64 *The Times*, 16 Feb. 1916, 9f.
65 J. F. Bush, 'Labour politics and society in E. Lond. during First World War' (Lond. Univ. Ph.D. thesis, 1978), 25.
66 Martin, 'Location of Ind.' 106.
67 *New Lond. Life and Labour*, ii. 252-5, 260, 344-5, 348.
68 Forshaw and Abercrombie, *County of Lond. Plan* (1943), 88.
69 Simpson 'Comparative Study', 102-17, 135, 139.
70 Hall, *Inds. of Lond.* 40, 47, 49.
71 Simpson, 'Comparative Study', 105-6, 110-11, 116-17, 138-9; *P.O. Dir. Lond.* (1959, 1964, 1975).
72 Martin, 'Location of Ind.' 123, 125.
73 G.L.C. *The East Lond. File* (1982), 18, 29; Kerrigan, *Hist. Tower Hamlets*, 32.
74 Thomson, *Dir. E. Lond.* (1991-2).

two curriers and leather cutters, a bootmaker's, a ladies' shoe manufacturer, and a boot warehouse in Bethnal Green Road and a bootmaker in Dog Row.[75] By the end of the 1820s there were at least 26 bootmakers, half of them in Bethnal Green Road.[76] Shoemaking was suggested for parish paupers in 1827 and in 1833[77] and by 1851 was widespread, especially in the former silkweaving districts.[78] There were fewer specialists than in furniture or clothing, workers being described as boot- or shoe-makers, binders, closers or, more rarely, repairers; a leather cutter, cordwainer, and clogmaker were also recorded. One bootmaker, in Goulden Place, Old Bethnal Green Road, employed 10 men[79] and there was a shoe manufacturer in King's Row, Cambridge Road,[80] but most manufacture was on the chamber system whereby a family's products were hawked by the man. Some chamber masters prospered and opened warehouses for shoes made by others. Fierce competition, partly from the Northampton factories, drove down wages and led to great poverty. Mayhew told of one Bethnal Green shoemaker, originally a weaver, who lived with 15 people in a damp kitchen where he worked from 5.0 a.m. to midnight.[81]

By 1861 3,573 people were employed in the footwear industry.[82] Women and children provided cheap labour, as in 1865 when boys were employed as nailers by riveters.[83] Women often made the upper parts of shoes at home and took them by basket to the warehouse.[84] In 1860 Hackney Road and Bethnal Green Road were the centres of the trade although there were bootmakers in the east, notably around Globe Road and Green Street.[85] From the mid 1860s mechanization hastened the growth of the sweating system, by which each stage of production was contracted out from the warehouse and which reached its zenith c. 1900 with Jewish immigrants supplying further cheap labour.[86] By 1872 the industry had spread east of Cambridge Road to the canal and beyond, although Hackney Road remained the centre and there were local concentrations like Victoria Park Square.[87] Sweating in the 1880s brought irregular employment, long hours, specialization, widespread use of women and children, and outwork. Upper-making was usually carried on at home; the rivetting of boots, largely for working-class children, was concentrated in the east while the sewing of uppers ('sew-round') was done by groups, often Jews, women and children, mainly in the west.[88] There were 74 shoemakers in the Nichol in 1890.[89]

A strike against outwork in 1890 forced the manufacturers to have all lasting and finishing done on their own premises by their own workers.[90] Mechanization reduced the workforce by nearly 30 per cent, mainly men, between 1891 and 1911. There were 2,596 men and 1,659 women bootmakers in 1901, when there were more wholesalers and fewer individual craftsmen, although premises were distributed much as in 1872.[91]

In 1930 25 boot and shoe firms employed 241 outworkers.[92] In 1938 only one of the many workshops in Teesdale Street made shoes[93] but a former glass factory in Treadway Street had become a shoe works.[94] By 1951 premises had dwindled to seven wholesale shoemakers, two slipper makers, and a few retail shoemakers, employing a total of 648 workers (50 of whom were repairers).[95] Firms were still concentrated along Bethnal Green Road.[96] Larger ones tended to leave, including the British United Shoe Machinery Co., which moved its warehouse and servicing depot from Bethnal Green Road to Hackney in 1956.[97] Six addresses in that road were connected with shoe manufacture in 1964, three of them belonging to the Agombar family, boot dealers and makers. The other three were for a repairer, a dealer, and a maker of baby shoes. Eight more firms were scattered throughout the borough and included two in Vyner Street on the northern border, one of which (M. Rubin & Sons) had a factory at no. 30 stretching to Wadeson Street along Mowlem Street.[98] By 1975 those three streets contained six of the eight manufacturers (one of them still M. Rubin's) and one wholesaler left in the borough. Bethnal Green Road had lost all connexion with shoes except for a repairer and some retailers.[99] In 1991 a single small manufacturer was listed, at a unit at no. 272 Hackney Road.[1]

The paper and printing industry was also based mainly on small firms and developed during the early 19th century. Although many local boys (and at least one girl) were apprenticed to London printers and bookbinders in the 18th,[2] they do not appear to have returned to their parish to work. The Hands were a family of paper-stainers in Old Nichol Street c. 1749–65.[3] By 1828 Hackney Road had two paperhanging manufacturers and one of two

75 *Johnstone's Lond. Com. Dir.* (1817).
76 *Pigot's Lond. & Provincial Com. Dir.* (1828–9).
77 Vestry mins. 1823–8, 31 Jan. 1827; ibid. 1831–3, p. 281.
78 Rest of para. based on census: P.R.O., HO 107/1539–42.
79 P.R.O., HO 107/1539/21/1/31, p. 38.
80 Ibid. HO 107/1540/21/2/12, p. 8.
81 *Unknown Mayhew*, ed. Thompson and Yeo, 239, 241, 257, 262–4, 273.
82 *E. Lond. Papers*, v(1), 6–7.
83 *4th Rep. Children's Employment Com.*, p. xxxv.
84 *E. Lond. Papers*, v(1), 16.
85 Ibid. 8–9.
86 Ibid. 18–19.
87 Martin, 'Location of Ind.' 301, fig. 31; *P.O. Dir. Lond.* (1879).
88 Booth, *Life and Labour*, i(4), 92, 96, 112, 117.
89 L.C.C. *Housing Question in Lond.* [1900], 191.
90 Booth, *Life and Labour*, i(4), 136.
91 *Census*, 1901; *New Lond. Life and Labour*, ii. 353, 355,

359; *E. Lond. Papers*, v(1), 10; Bush, 'Labour politics and society in E. Lond.' 27.
92 *New Lond. Life and Labour*, ii. 384.
93 Simpson, 'Comparative Study', 138.
94 O.S. Map 5 ft., Lond. VII. 38 (1938 edn.); Old O.S. Map 51 (1914).
95 *E. Lond. Papers*, v(1), 6–7, 11.
96 *P.O. Dir. Lond.* (1952).
97 Martin, 'Location of Ind.' 306.
98 *P.O. Dir. Lond.* (1964); O.S. Map, 1:2,500, TQ 3483 (1955 edn.).
99 *P.O. Dir. Lond.* (1975).
1 Thomson, *Dir. E. Lond.* (1991–2).
2 McKenzie, *Stationers' Co. Apprentices 1701–1800*, 130, 165, 167, 186, 223, 308, 335, 389.
3 Ibid. 146, 156. Wallpaper was rapidly replacing wainscotting: Mortimer, *Universal Director* (1763), s.v. Paperhanging.

printers, the other being in Church Street (Bethnal Green Road).[4] Paper mills near Wellington Road in 1831[5] were probably for the manufacture of printing paper mentioned in 1849.[6] By 1834 a third paperhanging manufacturer was in Hackney Road and a fourth, Arnold Bening & Son, a Shoreditch papermaker's, in Elizabeth Street. There were a bookbinder in Tyssen Street, two print block cutters, one for paperstainers in Cheshire Street and another in Cambridge Road, and four printers.[7] The focus had shifted by 1851[8] to Cambridge Road, which had a paperstainer, three bookbinders, and (in Patriot Row) a printer. Many inmates of the neighbouring Jewish Converts Institute were classified as printers, bookbinders, and compositors.[9] Bethnal Green Road housed a paperhanging manufacturer, a bookbinder, and three printers, Hackney Road a printer, and Nelson Street a type founder. The industry, with some who worked from home, included pocket book makers, book folders, paper makers and marblers, compositors, a manufacturer of printing ink in Northampton Street, and a porter in an envelope factory.

There was a paper bag factory at the Octagon, Somerford Street, in 1872[10] and D. Cullen built a paper factory in Chisendale Road in 1882.[11] By 1901 the industry employed 5,146 people, 1,714 of them in paper making, 1,279 in printing, and 985 as bookbinders.[12] Manufacture was mainly of bags, made up in the home or in small workshops near Victoria Park by women.[13] The workforce grew to 5,439 in 1911 but then declined, to 3,657 in 1921.[14] In 1927 there were manufacturers in Wharf Road, off Pritchard's Road, and in Kerbela and Fuller streets, and at least ten printers, two of them in Hackney Road and two in Bethnal Green Road.[15] Most firms were short lived. Among the longer lasting were Walkden & Wetherall, printers from Glasgow established in 1888, bombed during both world wars but surviving at nos. 7–9 Old Nichol Street in 1967.[16] Baruch Weinburg, who founded a Yiddish daily paper, in 1915 moved his printing business from Bethnal Green Road to no. 175 Brick Lane; it moved to no. 73 (in Spitalfields) in 1937 and was still flourishing in 1987.[17] By 1938 there were only 27 printing and paper factories, employing 274 people.

Firms in 1955 included some large ones, especially bookbinders near the canal, and several printers south of Bethnal Green Road.[18] They suffered like others in the clearances, Webster printing works in St. Matthew's Row, for example, making way for the Granby Street scheme in 1966.[19] Papermaking had disappeared by 1975, although there were still 20 printers then and nearly 30, mostly very small firms, by 1991. They included Samuel Frankel in Old Nichol Street, having moved from Globe Road (1927) and Bethnal Green Road (1975).[20]

Among many manufactures by 1817 were coaches, pianos, umbrellas, soap, and various metals.[21] Sanderson Turner Sturtevant, a tallow chandler in 1788,[22] who later developed the area on Snow estate, leased a soaphouse in Rose and Mount streets in 1806[23] and made soap at no. 42 Church Street (Bethnal Green Road) in 1817. His factory had passed to Richard Sturtevant and Charles Turner by 1832 and to Charles Croft, tallow chandler, by 1851[24] when there was another soap manufacturer in Gloucester Street[25] and a candle factory belonged to William Palmer & Co. in Green Street.[26] By the 1870s there was a large candle, soap, and match factory north of Three Colts Lane and west of Coventry Street[27] and a candle factory in Victoria works between the canal and Victoria Park cemetery.[28]

Edward Tann of Minerva Terrace, Hackney Road, iron chest maker, was in 1814 already occupying land at the junction of Hackney Road and Harvey (later Hope then Treadway) Street[29] on which by 1846 George Tann had a factory.[30] In 1851 it was run by Edward Tann, iron safe manufacturer, with 24 men.[31] It was John Tann's in 1883 and still a safe factory in 1893[32] but had become a glass works by 1914.[33] There were several tinplate workers and two pewter manufacturers in Bethnal Green Road in 1817,[34] an iron foundry in Cock Lane (Boundary Street) c. 1827,[35] and two tinyards in Helen's Place on the east side of the green in 1836 and 1848.[36] Between 1850 and 1863 the foundry was taken over by John Keeves, whose descendant's large tinplate works in 1890 was the only factory to survive the clearing of the Nichol. Crowden & Keeves were wholesale hardware manufacturers by 1934 and brush makers by 1952.[37] Iron

4 *Pigot's Lond. & Provincial Com. Dir.* (1828–9).
5 G.L.R.O., THCS/62.
6 Lewis, *Topog. Dict. Eng.* (1849), i. 224–5.
7 *Pigot's Nat. Lond. & Provincial Com. Dir.* (1832–4); map in *Rep. Com. San. Condition of Labouring Pop.*
8 *P.O. Dir. Lond.* (1851); P.R.O., HO 107/1539–42.
9 P.R.O., HO 107/1540/21/2/20, p. 34.
10 Old O.S. Map Lond. 51 (1872).
11 G.L.R.O., MBW 1711 (26).
12 *Census*, 1901.
13 Booth, *Life and Labour*, ii(2), 267.
14 *Census*, 1911–21.
15 *P.O. Dir. Lond.* (1927).
16 V. Leff and G. H. Blunden, *Story of Tower Hamlets* (1967), 151.
17 *Spitalfields News*, June 1987, p. 5.
18 Martin, 'Location of Ind.' fig. 23.
19 G.L.C. *Mins.* (1966), 447.
20 *P.O. Dir. Lond.* (1927, 1975); Thomson, *Dir. E. Lond.* (1991–2).
21 *Johnstone's Lond. Com. Dir.* (1817).

22 T.H.L.H.L., TH/654.
23 M.L.R. 1807/6/359.
24 *Pigot's Nat. Lond. and Provincial Com. Dir.* (1832–4); *P.O. Dir. Lond.* (1851).
25 P.R.O., HO 107/1540/21/2/1, p. 1.
26 Ibid. 2, p. 1; 5, p. 10; 6, p. 11, 29; 7, p. 30; *P.O. Dir. Lond.* (1851).
27 Old O.S. Map Lond. 51 (1872).
28 O. S. Map 1/2,500, Lond. LII (1873 edn.).
29 M.L.R. 1814/4/24. The firm's acct. bk. 1829–60 was deposited in T.H.L.H.L.: *E. Lond. Rec.* xvii [p. 49].
30 G.L.R.O., THCS/520–1; Old O.S. Map Lond. 51 (1872).
31 P.R.O., HO 107/1539/21/1/31, p.1.
32 G.L.R.O., MBW 1721 (27).
33 Old O.S. Maps Lond. 51 (1893, 1914).
34 *Johnstone's Lond. Com. Dir.* (1817).
35 G.L.R.O., O/102/3.
36 Ibid. THCS 447; Gavin, *San. Ramblings*, 13; *P.O. Dir. Lond.* (1850).
37 *P.O. Dir. Lond.* (1863, 1879, 1902, 1934, 1952); L.C.C. *Opening of Boundary St. Area* [1900], 6 and maps.

foundries existed in Ann Street before 1850,[38] in Foster Street in 1851,[39] and in Hollybush Gardens in 1872,[40] where one was rebuilt or joined by another in 1883.[41] By 1851 metal-workers included those working with wire, zinc, copper, tinplate, and ironplate, beside brass and iron founders and moulders.[42] John Law, a goldbeater, employed 26 men in 1851,[43] probably at nos. 5 and 7 Old Ford Road before he conveyed the site in 1882 to Colman's.[44] Other factories included Trotway iron works in Punderson's Gardens in 1876,[45] Maughan geyser factory at the junction of Gloucester Street and Cambridge Road in 1878,[46] and the engineering firm of J. J. Lane in Cranbrook Street in 1894,[47] which expanded in 1914 and 1915.[48] Booth stated that there were 4,528 metalworkers in Bethnal Green (772 blacksmiths, 1,074 other workers in iron and steel, 1,617 workers in other metals, and 1,065 engine- and machine-makers).[49] A different classification listed 1,838 working in metals and machines in 1901 (besides 8 professional engineers and 112 makers of electrical apparatus), 2,022 in 'metals, machines and conveyances' in 1911, and 1,922 metal and 271 electrical workers in 1921.[50] By 1938 there were 86 engineering firms employing 485 people but metal working was not described.[51] Lane's large Phoenix works survived to the 1950s[52] but made way for the Cranbrook estate. In 1955 many, mostly small, firms made metal goods, including furniture or springs. Small firms were mainly in the western part of the borough and larger ones in the east, among them an engineering firm on the canal and others around Bethnal Green Road.[53] In 1975 Bethnal Green Road had makers of gaskets and scales, a radio engineer, and electrical contractors[54] but by 1991 only one metal manufacturer was listed,[55] together with four general, a mechanical, and three electrical engineers.

Noxious industries, uncontrolled, included horse boiling in Digby Street and near Dog Row in 1829,[56] catgut manufacture in Hares-marsh in 1831,[57] bladder drying near Three Colts Lane, tripe boiling in Boundary Street, and the processing of manure in Charles Street in 1848.[58]

By 1851 products included combs, spectacles, surgical instruments,[59] barges, guns[60] and gunpowder,[61] tobacco and matches, chemicals, glass, and brushes. There was a match manufacturer in Orange Street in 1840.[62] Workers in 1851 included matchmakers, tobacco strippers and a clerk in a tobacco factory, tobacco pipe makers and trimmers, and cigar makers, mostly in the west and south of the parish.[63] Many, especially makers of matches and match boxes, worked at home for firms outside Bethnal Green, but Letchford Buildings (later Allen & Hanbury) housed a match factory before 1874.[64] In 1901 892 people, mostly women, worked with tobacco,[65] which was later classified with food and drink.

Food firms established during the 1870s included Liebig's Malted Food Co. with a factory in Royal Victor Place by 1871,[66] Robertson's, which built a ginger beer factory in Bethnal Green Road in 1873,[67] and Davis, a vinegar manufacturer, which built a warehouse in Tyssen Street in 1874.[68] Messrs. Colman, the Norwich mustard manufacturers, had starch works on the north side of the green by the mid 1870s when they built warehouses there.[69] They were leased nos. 5 and 7 Old Ford Road in 1882 with permission to demolish,[70] acquired no. 13 Old Ford Road in 1897,[71] and made further alterations in 1899 and 1906.[72] The company left when it sold the site to the M.B. in 1923.[73] The Natural Food Co. (later Allinson's Bread Co.) acquired Cyclone mills in Cambridge Road, north of Patriot Square, in 1892,[74] made alterations in 1914 and 1917,[75] and closed between 1964 and 1975.[76] F. A. Bovill manufactured sauces and pickles in Derbyshire Street by 1928 and closed between 1944 and 1952.[77]

Food, drink, and tobacco provided employment for 6,125 people in 1911 but only

38 Guildhall MS. 6020/10.
39 P.R.O., HO 107/1541/21/3/7, p. 1.
40 Old O.S. Map Lond. 51 (1872).
41 G.L.R.O., MBW 1721 (27).
42 P.R.O., HO 107/1539–42.
43 Ibid. HO 107/1540/21/2/20, p.10.
44 T.H.L.H.L., TH/7956. For Colman's, below.
45 G.L.R.O., MBW 1659 (24). Closed by 1882: ibid. 1711 (27).
46 G.L.R.O., MBW 1675 (25).
47 Ibid. AR/BA/4/46 (5).
48 Ibid. AR/BA/4/269 (4); 384 (5).
49 Booth, *Life and Labour*, ii(1), 408.
50 *Census*, 1901–21.
51 Forshaw and Abercrombie, *County of Lond. Plan*, 88.
52 *P.O. Dir. Lond.* (1952); O.S. Map 1/2,500, TQ 3583 (1950 edn.).
53 Martin, 'Location of Ind.', figs. 16–18.
54 *P.O. Dir. Lond.* (1975).
55 Arts Metal Crafts Ltd. in Chance St.: Thomson, *Dir. E. Lond.* (1991–2).
56 Vestry mins. 1828–31, p. 153.
57 G.L.R.O., THCS/62.
58 Gavin, *San. Ramblings*, 20, 27, 46.

59 P.R.O., HO 107/1539/21/1/1, pp. 4, 19, 45.
60 Ibid. HO 107/1540/21/2/22, p. 20; 11, pp. p, 16.
61 Wal. Macklin employed 16 men in Mapes St.: ibid. HO 107/1541/21/3/9a, p. 80.
62 Jas. Brewerton, congreve and lucifer mfr: T.H.L.H.L., TH/2292.
63 P.R.O., HO 107/1539–42.
64 D. Chapman-Huston and E.C. Cripps, *Through a City Archway, The Story of Allen and Hanbury's, 1715–1954* (1954), 178.
65 *Census*, 1901.
66 G.L.R.O., MBW 1621 (23).
67 Ibid. 1636 (23).
68 Ibid. 1643 (23).
69 Ibid. 1651 (23); 1659 (23).
70 T.H.L.H.L., TH/7956.
71 Ibid. TH/7956, 7959.
72 G.L.R.O., AR/BA/4/89 (5); 150 (4).
73 For York Hall and baths: T.H.L.H.L., TH/6947; *The Times*, 18 Jan. 1924, 21a.
74 Leff and Blunden, *Story of Tower Hamlets*, 107.
75 G.L.R.O., AR/BA/4/269 (5); 309 (4).
76 *P.O. Dir. Lond.* (1964, 1975).
77 T.H.L.H.L., TH/8351 (boxes 1, 3).

1,886 in 1921, possibly because the 1921 census introduced a new category of warehousemen, storekeepers, and packers, of whom there were 2,434.[78] There were 101 factories employing 1,674 people in 1938.[79] They included 36 bakery and confectionery firms, 16 firms connected with meat and sausages, one producer of jellied eels, and four breweries. By 1958 there were five jellied eel firms but only 19 bakers and confectioners, five meat and sausage firms, and three breweries, while there had been a marked decline in tobacco.[80]

Chemical firms, apart from the dye factory at the green and white lead works in Hollybush Gardens, included William T. Hunt, druggists who had a warehouse and factory in Victoria Park Square in 1848.[81] The most important was Allen & Hanbury,[82] pharmaceutical and manufacturing chemists who had originated in an apothecary's shop off Lombard Street in 1715 and expanded under its eponymous Quakers beyond the City. They secured part of Letchford Buildings in Three Colts Lane in 1874, enlarging their warehouse in 1881.[83] In the 1880s Cornelius Hanbury (II), himself a surgeon, began making surgical instruments in a small workshop and forge at Bethnal Green. A factory for the instruments was built alongside the existing premises in 1904 and given an extra floor after fire damage in 1906. When the underlease expired in 1907, Hanbury was leased the whole premises, to which he transferred all his manufacturing and wholesale work. A new factory was built in 1922[84] after the premises were bombed in 1918. Bombed again in 1940, the firm acquired neighbouring bombed sites with a frontage on Cambridge Road for a brick and concrete building to house the engineering and surgical departments, although much of its manufacturing was transferred to Ware (Herts.). The company merged with Glaxo Group Ltd. in 1958 and moved the manufacture of surgical instruments to Portsmouth in 1963, leaving the Bethnal Green premises purely administrative from 1967 until 1982 when the site closed completely.[85] There were 855 people employed in chemicals and soap in 1911[86] and 24 chemical factories employing 738 people in 1938.[87] One

was the chemical works at Young's Wharf and another perhaps Cordova works where gum was processed.[88]

A glass manufacturer in Brick Lane,[89] a glassmaker in Three Colts Lane,[90] a glassdrop cutter in Virginia Row,[91] and many glassblowers and cutters around the Nichol were recorded in 1851.[92] A small glass industry in the late 19th century in part made beads for export to Africa;[93] although it had dwindled, there were 457 employed in a 'small works' industry of glass and earthenware c. 1903.[94] Firms included the London Glass Works in Minerva Street in 1880,[95] and glassworks in Somerford Street in 1887,[96] in Old Bethnal Green Road in 1889,[97] and at no. 34 Matilda Street in 1897.[98] In 1902 both Minerva Street and Old Bethnal Green Road housed bottle manufacturers,[99] the latter, James Anderson & Sons, surviving in 1927.[1] Morey and Holmes had a bottle factory in Jersey Street in the 1920s.[2] Monk & Brown, glass bevellers, had a factory behind no. 17 Old Ford Road by 1924 and until 1964 or later.[3] There were eight firms of bevellers in 1952,[4] six by 1964, together with two glass manufacturers, a glass cutter, four glass merchants, and two bottle merchants. Five glass firms survived until 1975, although only Dorell Glass Co. in Marian Place was a manufacturer.[5]

A brush manufacturer employed 10 men near Cheshire Street[6] and there were several brushmakers in the Nichol in 1851.[7] G. B. Kent & Co. had a factory in Robinson Road by 1876 when it added a warehouse, rebuilding the factory in 1877.[8] Still a brush factory in 1942,[9] it made bed springs by 1950.[10] Bethnal Green c. 1903 had 1,312 people employed in brush- and comb-making and was one of three places where brushmakers lived near most of the brush factories in London.[11] There were 16 in Bethnal Green in 1902, five in 1934 and 1964, and three by 1975. Mason Pearson Bros., at nos. 1–8 Royal Victor Place, survived from 1902, but had moved to Stratford by 1991.[12]

Industry had spread from the brickfields and weavers' houses of the west and south-west to reach Cambridge Road and the green by

78 Census, 1911–21.
79 Forshaw and Abercrombie, County of Lond. Plan, 88.
80 Simpson, 'Comparative Study', 142, 144–5.
81 G.L.R.O., MR/UP 340.
82 Para. based on Chapman-Huston and Cripps, Through a City Archway, passim and pp. 178 sqq.
83 Builder, 16 Apr. 1881, 494.
84 G.L.R.O., AR/BA/4/331 (4a).
85 Inf. from Glaxo Pharmaceuticals U.K. Ltd.
86 L.C.C. Lond. Statistics, xxiv. 72–7.
87 Forshaw and Abercrombie, County of Lond. Plan, 88.
88 O.S. Map 5', Lond. VII. 49 (1938 edn.).
89 P.R.O., HO 107/1542/21/4/17, p. 1.
90 Ibid. HO 107/1541/21/3/5, p. 1.
91 Ibid. HO 107/1539/21/1/9, p. 1.
92 Ibid. HO 107/1539/21/1/3, p. 1; 4, p. 12; 5, p. 1; 11, p. 22.
93 V.C.H. Mdx. ii. 157.
94 Booth, Life and Labour, ii(2), 97, 368.
95 G.L.R.O., MBW 1692 (27).
96 Ibid. MBW 1757 (27).
97 Ibid. AR/BA/4/4 (27).

98 Ibid. AR/BA/4/71 (6).
99 P.O. Dir. Lond. (1902).
1 Ibid. (1927).
2 Ibid.; G.L.R.O., AR/BA/4/437 (3).
3 Robinson and Chesshyre, The Green, 20; O.S. Map 1/2,500, TQ 3583 (1950 edn.); P.O. Dir. Lond. (1964, 1975).
4 P.O. Dir. Lond. (1952).
5 Ibid. (1964, 1975).
6 P.R.O., HO 107/1542/21/4/8, p. 45; 16, p. 1.
7 Ibid. HO 107/1539/21/1/1, p. 43; 3, p. 1; 4, p. 1, 12; 5, p. 32; 7, p. 17.
8 Ibid. LRRO 1/2344; G.L.R.O., MBW 1659 (23); 1667 (23); Old O.S. Map Lond. 52 (1894).
9 O.S. Map 5', Lond. VII. 38 (1938 edn.); P.O. Dir. Lond. (1942).
10 O.S. Map 1/2,500, TQ 3583 (1950 edn.).
11 The others were Bermondsey and Hackney: Booth, Life and Labour, ii(2), 181, 368.
12 P.O. Dir. Lond. (1902, 1934, 1964, 1975); Thomson, Dir. E. Lond. (1991/2).

1817.[13] It was carried on mostly within houses, sometimes in adjacent workshops and, in a few cases from the late 18th century, in purpose-built factories and warehouses. Between 1826[14] and 1836 two wharves were built on the canal and industrial premises included two dye-houses, four breweries, a ropeground, limeworks, two stoneyards, a dustyard, two tinyards, two timberyards, saw mills, four warehouses, and five factories.[15] There were at least eight factories by 1846 and one warehouse belonging to the Eastern Counties Railway.[16] Factories went up along the canal and also along the railways,[17] whose arches accommodated workshops.[18] In the relatively empty area east of Cambridge Road, Victoria works was built between the canal and cemetery by 1854[19] and there were workshops at the back of houses in Bonner's Fields c. 1857.[20]

Industrial development quickened in the 1870s. Applications were made in 1871 to build 34 warehouses, seven of them east of Cambridge Road,[21] and between 1872 and 1876 for another 97.[22] Workshops and factories, though fewer, were steadily built, including some in Royal Victor Place along the Hertford canal in the early 1880s.[23] In 1882 Green Street needed widening because of traffic congestion caused by the new factories.[24] In 1892 the medical officer of health believed that the north and south districts of Bethnal Green would soon become one vast factory and warehouse.[25] Old Ford Road in the east at about the same time was crowded with women taking matchboxes to Bryant & May's factory in Bow, with men taking boot uppers to factories, rolls of silk cloth to warehouses, or suitings to tailors, and with barrows laden with goods made at home; most homes had workshops and outworkers.[26]

Many employees worked for firms elsewhere, Bethnal Green in 1908 possessing nearly half as many more workers than could be employed in the borough. It had a large number of working women: 80 per cent of those aged 15–25, who were mostly unmarried, 22 per cent of married women, and 50 per cent of widows in 1911.[27] The proportion of people working outside the borough increased to 58 per

cent by 1921, only 17,388 people working within it and 15,084 elsewhere in the East End.[28] Some of the worst workshops were closed during the 1920s under Labour local and national governments[29] and there was a tendency towards larger planned premises, especially during the 1930s.[30] The threat to industry from clearance schemes was instanced in 1936, when one for the area around the northern part of Cambridge Road proposed removing many of its 63 factories to reduce industry by a third.[31] Only 8 firms, however, left the borough between 1932 and 1938. There were 1,746 factories employing 15,945 people in 1938, but more people left the borough for work.[32]

Reduced by bombing, there were 975 factories in 1947. A quarter (246) of them had more than 10 workers but they accounted for nearly 80 per cent (9,078) of the factory workforce of 11,476.[33] By 1951 68 per cent of the working population was employed outside Bethnal Green, albeit mainly in neighbouring boroughs. Although all the old industries had declined, some of the largest factories like Allen & Hanbury's and Mann's and Truman's breweries remained. There were hundreds of small manufacturers, many using premises damaged or vacant in the course of rebuilding schemes, and there was no shortage of work.[34] There were still 859 factories employing 11,337 workers in 1954.[35]

Changes came when rebuilding schemes proved only too successful in disentangling factories from housing, and in reducing the total amount of industry. By the late 1970s the number of factories had fallen by 44 per cent and their loss, with its concomitant unemployment, was 'disastrous'.[36] Attempting to reintroduce industry, the L.B. scheduled vacant sites in 1982[37] and offered grants and loans to firms in industrial improvement areas in 1984.[38] Several sites scheduled in 1986 for light industrial units[39] were rescheduled in 1988 for 'business'.[40] By the early 1990s there were light industrial units, often in groups like Huntingdon industrial units in Bethnal Green Road, GLEB industrial estate in Ebor Street, Parmiter Street industrial estate, or Greenearth

13 Johnstone's Lond. Com. Dir. (1817).
14 Cruchley's New Plan. (1826).
15 G.L.R.O., THCS 446–7.
16 Ibid. THCS 520–1.
17 e.g. three along rly. by 1863: G.L.R.O., MR/UP 671.
18 e.g. several blt. 1874: G.L.R.O., MBW 1643 (23).
19 P.R.O., MR/1480; LRRO 1/2117.
20 Ibid. LRRO 1/2111.
21 G.L.R.O., MBW 1621 (23).
22 Ibid. MBW 1628 (23); 1636 (23); 1643 (23); 1651 (23); 1659 (23, 24).
23 Ibid. MBW 1692 (26); 1702 (26).
24 Edwards, Lond. Street Improvements, 87.
25 Quoted in G. Stedman Jones, 'Social Consequences of Casual Labour Problem in Lond. 1860–90' (Oxford Univ. D.Phil. thesis, 1970), 240.
26 E. Lond. Rec. iv. 30.
27 Schmiechen, Sweated Inds. 58, 68, 70.
28 M. Young and P. Willmott, Family and Kinship in E. Lond. (1962), 91; J. A. Gillespie, 'Economic and Political Change in E. End of Lond. during 1920s' (Cambridge Univ.

Ph.D. thesis, 1984), 14.
29 Gillespie, 'Econ. and Political Change', 325; below, local govt. (local govt. 1900–65).
30 Gillespie, 'Econ. and Political Change', 224; G.L.R.O., AR/BA/4/585(3), 606(3), 628(3), 650(3), 672(3).
31 G.L.R.O., CL/TP/1/27.
32 Forshaw and Abercrombie, County of Lond. Plan, 93, 160–1.
33 L.C.C. Lond. Statistics. N.S. i. 163.
34 Young and Willmott, Family and Kinship, 89–91, 95.
35 L.C.C. Lond. Statistics, N.S. i. 163. The figure of 1,486 factories given for 1956 presumably inc. workshops not defined as factories elsewhere: ibid. N.S. iii. 146–7.
36 A. Coleman, 'Land Use in Tower Hamlets' (TS. Rep. for 2nd Land Utilization Survey, T.H.L.H.L., Pamphlet 720).
37 Tower Hamlets L.B. Planning Dept. Vacant Sites Survey, 1982 (T.H.L.H.L., Pamphlet 720.3).
38 Tower Hamlets L.B. Planning Handbk. [1984], 15.
39 Tower Hamlets Boro. Plan (1986).
40 Tower Hamlets L.B. Proposed Draft Alterations to Boro. Plan Proposals, 1988.

business centre off Three Colts Lane. One large employer, Albion brewery, was replaced by a large retailer, Sainsbury's. Many old factories and workshops remained, often amidst dereliction, and although most of the firms were new, the industries were mainly old: clothes, furniture, printing, and leather goods. Encouragement of the arts was an innovation, with antiques, restoration, and garden pottery in Columbia Road and Ezra Street, and studios in Chisenhale Road, Mowlem Street, Winkley Street, and Columbia Road.

SHOPS AND MARKETS. In the 18th century occupations included those of baker, chandler, and pawnbroker.[41] Shops existed by the early 19th century along Bethnal Green, Cambridge, and Hackney roads and there were corner shops, mostly selling groceries, throughout the parish.[42] Shopkeepers, chiefly along the main roads, formed the most prosperous residents in the surveys of the late 1880s and early 1930s.[43] A more popular form of retailing, however, was the street market of hawkers and costermongers. In 1833 36 inhabitants of Church Street (Bethnal Green Road) protested at stalls selling fish and fruit 'before our houses', especially on Sundays, and attracting crowds using bad language.[44] The twinfold objection, Sabbatarian and to undesirable elements, was reiterated well into the 20th century, never with much effect. The main street markets were in Brick Lane, Club Row, and Sclater Street, and Bethnal Green Road, and chiefly for fruit and vegetables. In 1838 a feature of the Monday and Tuesday morning markets was the hiring of children by weavers.[45] There were c. 100 costermongers in the mid 19th century who lived mostly near the markets and formed the core of its vivid street culture. Sunday markets flourished because Saturday was pay night and any money left over from the public house was spent by women on Sunday dinner.[46]

The most determined effort to wean Bethnal Green from its Sunday street markets was made by Miss (later Baroness) Angela Burdett-Coutts, who in 1866 obtained an Act[47] to establish a market next to the new model dwellings in Columbia Square and to make street improvements for access.[48] She commissioned Henry Ashley Darbishire to design a market on a 2-a. site, with the intention of providing work for builders and visual beauty for the poor, besides sanitary conditions and reasonable rents for sellers of foodstuffs and other articles.[49] Columbia Market was planned as an open quadrangle bordered by a large assembly hall and blocks of shops surmounted by galleries and residences for City clerks and dealers.[50] There was provision for 36 shops, with 673 spaces in the galleries and quadrangle for third- and fourth-class dealers. It was built to resemble a cathedral in a high Gothic style of the most expensive materials, teak, granite, and Irish marble, and entered through wrought-iron gates.[51] It was described on its opening in 1869 as 'greater than les Halles'[52] and c. 1950 as ' a structure as proud as any Flemish Guildhall of the prosperous Late Middle Ages'.[53]

Run by a committee more familiar with charities than markets, the project had failed within a year, shunned by the local population which preferred its street stalls and sabotaged by dealers in existing markets. In 1870 it reopened to sell fish brought from East Anglia on the Eastern Counties Railway. The quadrangle was roofed over and 110 stalls were provided rent-free, 20 to wholesalers, the rest to middlemen or retailers.[54] The baroness made the second of several applications for Acts to improve communications[55] but the project was again frustrated by commercial greed, when the fishing industry found that its produce would fetch more in Billingsgate. Management of the market was transferred to the City of London in 1871 but there were only 41 market tenants in 1872 and the corporation handed it back in 1874. An arrangement was made with railway companies in 1875 and Columbia Meat Co. was established in 1877 but had failed by 1878 when the market was closed. Reopened in 1884 and in 1891 'more successful than formerly',[56] it was by 1898 disused except for a small wholesale potato trade and a shop occupied by a cabinet maker.[57] It was acquired by the L.C.C. in 1915 and after the failure of an attempt by demobilized servicemen to have it reopened in 1919,[58] it was used as workshops in 1925,[59] a shelter during the

41 Vestry mins. 1747–81.
42 *Johnstone's Lond. Com. Dir.* (1817); *Pigot's Nat. Lond. & Provincial Dir.* (1832–4).
43 Above, settlement and building 1876–1914; building 1915–45.
44 Vestry mins. 1831–3, 2 Oct. 1833. At least one objector was himself a cheesemonger and as most shops in Bethnal Green Road were 'actively trading' on a Sunday in 1834, the protest was probably self interested: *The Times*, 11 Nov. 1834, 1e.
45 *Rep. Asst. Commrs. on Handloom Weavers*, pt. II, p. 234.
46 H. Mayhew, *Lond. Lab. and the Lond. Poor*, i. 10–11, 47.
47 29 & 30 Vic. c. 11 (Local Act).
48 Acct. of Columbia Mkt. based on *Guildhall Miscellany*, ii. 353–66.
49 29 & 30 Vic. c. 11 (Local Act).

50 *Builder*. 20 Feb. 1869, 146–7 (Guildhall Libr., Print Rm., B3/COL).
51 Gateposts survived 1993.
52 *The Times*, 29 Apr. 1869, 5e.
53 Pevsner, *Lond.* ii. 72.
54 *Illus. Lond. News*, 5 Mar. 1870 (Guildhall Libr., Print Rm., B3/COL).
55 G.L.R.O., MR/UP 1055; MBW 2621, vol. 16, no. 2. The third was in 1884: ibid. MR/UP 1475; MBW 2649, vol. 34, nos. 1 and 2.
56 H. B. Wheatley, *Lond. Past and Present*, i (1891), 446.
57 G. L. Gomme, *Lond. in Reign of Victoria* (1898), 114–15.
58 *The Times*, 26 Sept. 1919, 7c.
59 Bethnal Green Mus. *Cat. of drawings and prints relating to Hackney and Bethnal Green* (1925), 23.

Second World War when it was bombed,[60] the headquarters of a polytechnic, an L.C.C. nursery school,[61] and a store. The decision taken in 1958 to replace 'easily the most spectacular piece of design in Bethnal Green'[62] with council flats has been denounced as 'sterile'[63] and 'one of the most serious losses of Victorian architecture'.[64]

The traditional street market flourished throughout the fluctuating fortunes of Columbia Market. There were still 126 hawkers and 23 costermongers living on the Nichol redevelopment site in 1890.[65] In 1893 there were 83 stalls in Brick Lane south of Bethnal Green Road, of which 33 sold fruit and vegetables, 16 meat and eggs, 12 fish, 7 clothing, and 5 furniture;[66] there were 131 stalls in Bethnal Green Road, 28 in Hackney Road, and 63 in Green Street, which served the eastern side of the parish. By 1901 there were 206 in Brick Lane, 136 in Bethnal Green Road, 34 in Hackney Road, and 90 in Green Street.[67] Late 19th-century reminiscences commented on the ubiquitous hawkers and a reliance on prepared food from cook, pie, and coffee shops, as so many women worked and lacked facilities for cooking. Locally grown plants were sold on Sunday mornings in Hart's Lane (Barnet Grove) until rebuilding when the plant and flower market was transferred to Columbia Road,[68] which by c. 1900 was one of the largest flower markets in London. There was also a Sunday pets' market in Sclater Street.[69] In spite of attempts in 1888,[70] 1906,[71] and 1911[72] to suppress the Sunday markets, the costermonger supplanted the weaver as the quintessential figure of Bethnal Green,[73] and Bethnal Green Road was 'the typical wide East End market street', lined with hawkers' barrows.[74]

Licences were issued for 1,141 stalls in 1930–1, 127 for the southern part of Brick Lane, 222 for Bethnal Green Road, and 130 for Green Street, and, for the Sunday markets, 439 for the pet and 223 for the flower market. Hackney Road had apparently ceased to house stalls,[75] the pet market had spread to Hare and Cygnet streets and Club Row, and the flower market to the northern part of Brick Lane and Virginia Road. The Sunday market in Hare Street specialized in wireless and tools.[76] Little had changed by 1950[77] but in 1959 stalls were choking the streets and the council built an open market off Roman Road (Green Street) as part of its Cranbrook scheme. Traders showed the same reluctance to leave the streets as those offered Columbia Market had done.[78] By 1986 there had been many shop closures but district shopping centres remained in Bethnal Green Road and shopping parades in Columbia Road and Brick Lane. Weekday markets, mostly for food, remained in Brick Lane, Bethnal Green Road, and Roman Road and Sunday markets, mostly not for food, in Columbia Road and between Brick Lane and Sclater and Cheshire streets.[79] There was alarm in 1994 that higher rents would lead to the closure of the markets.

LOCAL GOVERNMENT

MANORIAL AND EARLY PARISH GOVERNMENT. Bethnal Green lay wholly within the manor of Stepney of which it was a recognized locality by 1405.[80] A constable recorded for the hamlet from the beginning of the 17th century[81] had probably existed long before, together with a headborough, recorded from 1616.[82] By 1640 Bethnal Green had a constable, two headboroughs, and an aleconner.[83] The officers, elected at the October view of frankpledge, might be rejected at the sessions, as were an elected constable in 1615[84] and a headborough in 1678.[85] A poundkeeper in 1642[86] possibly looked after the manorial pound depicted at the southern tip of the hamlet in 1703.[87] In 1732 there were for Bethnal Green one constable and seven headboroughs.[88] The number of headboroughs increased to 14 and, by 1816, to 28.[89]

The vestry clerk's reference in 1816 to books from 1627 'when the parish became a parish' was erroneous[90] although Bethnal Green had some experience of a measure of self government before it became a parish in 1743. It had joint auditors with Mile End in 1586,[91] joint churchwardens in 1589,[92] and a joint churchwarden,

60 M. Ashworth, *Oxford Ho. in Bethnal Green.*
61 Bethnal Green M.B. *Official Guide* (1950), 43.
62 Pevsner, *Lond.* ii. 72.
63 H. Hobhouse, *Lost Lond.* (1971), 185.
64 R. Dixon and S. Muthesius, *Victorian Architecture* (1978), 119.
65 L.C.C. *Housing Question in Lond.* [1900], 191.
66 Booth, *Life and Labour*, ii(3), 263.
67 *New Lond. Life and Labour*, iii. 320; above, plate 44.
68 *E. Lond. Rec.* iv. 31–3, 35.
69 Booth, *Life and Labour*, iii(2), 98, 246.
70 *The Times*, 23 Oct. 1888, 3e.
71 Ibid. 22 Sept. 1906, 13b.
72 Ibid. 12 July 1911, 12e.
73 W. Besant, *Survey of Lond.* ix (1911), 614–15.
74 *The Times*, 16 Feb. 1914, 9f.
75 *New Lond. Life and Labour*, iii. 320.
76 Ibid. 294–5.
77 Bethnal Green M.B. *Official Guide* (1950), 103.
78 *The Times*, 10 Apr. 1959, 6a.
79 *Tower Hamlets Boro. Plan* (1986), 51, 56, 163.
80 Guildhall MS. 25370; above, Stepney, local govt. (manorial govt.)
81 Cal. Mdx. Sess. Bks. i. 223; ii. 103 et seq.
82 *Mdx. Sess. Rec.* iii. 251.
83 B.L. Eg. MS. 3006, f. 57v.
84 *Mdx. Sess. Rec.* ii. 291.
85 Cal. Mdx. Sess. Bks. v. 170.
86 B.L. Add. MS. 22253, f. 15v.
87 Gascoyne, *Map.*
88 Co. of Par. Clerks, *New Remarks of Lond.*(1732), 194.
89 *Rep. from Cttee. on State of Police in Metropolis*, H.C. 510, p. 167 (1816) v.
90 Ibid. p. 181.
91 *Mem. Stepney Par.*, p. xi.
92 Ibid. p. x.

sidesman, and three auditors in 1600.[93] Upper and lower churchwardens in 1656[94] presumably foreshadowed churchwardens for each locality. In 1676 an order for the inhabitants of Bethnal Green to be taxed was addressed to the churchwardens and overseers of the poor.[95] Bethnal Green had its own overseer by 1677[96] but William Malin, described as constable in 1684,[97] was 'gardianus' of Bethnal Green at a visitation in 1685.[98] Highway surveyors existed by 1654[99] and there were two in 1671 and 1732.[1] A beadle was first mentioned in 1684. [2]

Officers' reimbursement was often ordered by the magistrates through the churchwarden, who might tax the inhabitants accordingly.[3] In 1684 Bethnal Green's constable, overseer, two headboroughs, and beadle refused to suppress conventicles and the beadle was set in the pillory.[4] The same beadle in 1690 was given the existing staff of office, surmounted by a medallion figuring the blind beggar of Bethnal Green and his dog.[5] Bethnal Green had its own scavenger by 1733.[6] The hamlet dealt with settlement disputes from the 1670s,[7] produced its own petition about the weavers' distress in 1697,[8] levied poor rates by 1728, and kept overseers' accounts by 1729.[9] It became a separate parish because of the need for a new church[10] rather than because it felt hampered by any connexion with Stepney.

PARISH GOVERNMENT FROM 1743 TO 1836.

In spite of opposition on financial grounds,[11] an Act in 1743 gave Bethnal Green its own church and vestry. Those who paid 4s. a month for poor relief qualified for the vestry,[12] from 1763 those renting at more than £15 a year.[13] The church was consecrated in 1746[14] and minutes of vestry meetings were kept from 1747.[15] Meetings, normally in the vestry room at the church, were initially once a month, dwindling by the 1780s and 1800s to c. 10 a year but increasing by 1820 to 25. On 23 March 1787, 'not one vestryman came'.[16] By contrast in 1816 all public vestry meetings were said to have adjourned to the churchyard 'where the mob is'[17] and on 23 March 1818 over 1,000 attenders caused the meeting to be held in the church.[18]

Rowdy meetings were allegedly the reason[19] for the introduction of a select vestry under an Act of 1823.[20] The 100 vestrymen were to be the rector and parish officers, the 30 governors of the poor, and 60 resident householders rated at more than £15. The Act named the first 60; the resident male rated householders were to elect 10 replacements yearly. By 1830 c. 2,000 could vote, c. 600 having done so at the last election by ballot.[21] There were 30 meetings in 1830, with attendances of between 14 and 104 but averaging 38.[22]

The vestry was never the sole local authority. Trustees were set up by an Act of 1738[23] with power to appoint surveyors, remove trees and gravel, and take tolls for certain roads. Cleaning, lighting, and watching, with powers to appoint scavengers and watchmen, direct the parish officers, and levy rates, were vested in another set of trustees under an Act of 1751.[24] The vestry could elect the trustees from those possessing a freehold or copyhold estate of £8 a year or leasehold estate of £12, or who were rateable at 2s. 6d. a month.

The Act of 1743[25] named the archbishop of Canterbury, the bishop of London, the principal of Brasenose College, Oxford, the rector of Stepney, and prominent local figures[26] as trustees for building the church. They could co-opt their successors and could levy rates and choose two collectors from 12 nominees at the Easter vestry. In 1746 another 14 trustees were named and they were empowered to raise £1,000 by an additional rate to pay off debts contracted on poor relief.[27] Trustees for the poor were made permanent in 1763 by an Act[28] setting up 20 'substantial' persons as governors of the poor for the 'better disposition' of money raised from the poor rate. The full vestry still set the rate and nominated the governors at Easter. In 1784 it resolved that governors must be vestrymen of three years residence.[29] The governors, by then numbering 32, were retained in an Act regulating local government in 1813[30] and in the Act of 1823,[31] whereby 30 were to be chosen from those men with property worth £80 a year. In 1830 c. 150–200 people took part in the election[32] but none of the three governors elected as replacements in 1831 was resident.[33]

93 Ibid. p. 36.   94 Ibid. pp. 217–18.
95 Cal. Mdx. Sess., Bks. v. 103.
96 Cases in Ct. of Arches 1660–1913 (Brit. Rec. Soc. lxxxv), 155, no. 3678.
97 Cal. Mdx. Sess. Bks. vii. 64; Mdx. County. Rec. iv. 241–2.
98 Guildhall MS. 9537/20, p. 80.
99 Cal. Mdx. Sess. Bks. ii. 97.
1 Ibid. ii. 130, 137; Co. of Par. Clerks, New Remarks of Lond. 194
2 Cal. Mdx. Sess. Bks. vii. 64; Mdx. County Rec. iv. 242
3 e.g. 1676: Cal. Mdx. Sess. Bks. v. 103; 1694 and 1695: Mdx. County. Rec. Sess. Bks. 1689–1709, 118–26. In 1711 Stepney was to reimburse Bethnal Green's churchwarden: Cal. Mdx. Sess. Bks. x. 71.
4 Cal. Mdx. Sess. Bks. vii. 64; Mdx. County Rec. iv. 241–2.
5 Freshfield, Communion Plate, pl. III and p. 1.
6 E. G. Dowdell, Hundred Years of Quarter Sess. 1660–1760 (1932), 114 n.
7 Cal. Mdx. Sess. Bks. v. 159; xiii. 85–6; Mdx. County. Rec. Sess. Bks. 1689–1709, 176, 180.
8 MSS. of H.L. N.S. ii. 509–10.
9 Recs. in T.H.L.H.L.
10 Lambeth Pal. Libr., MS. 2712, ff. 182–3; below, church.
11 C.J. xxiv. 448.
12 16 Geo. II, c. 28.
13 3 Geo. III, c. 40.
14 Guildhall MS. 953½0, pt. 1, f. 102v.
15 Vestry mins. 1747–81, pp. 1–2. Subsection based on vestry mins. in T.H.L.H.L.
16 Vestry mins. 1782–1813, p. 59.
17 Rep. Cttee. on Police in Metropolis, 154.
18 Vestry mins. 1813–21, ff. 98v.–99.
19 Rep. Com. Poor Laws, H.C. 44, p. 83 (1834), viii, app. B2.
20 4 Geo. IV, c. 21 (Local and Personal).
21 Rep. of Sel. Cttee. on Sel. Vestries, 1830, H.C. 25, pp. 673 sqq. (1830), iv.
22 Vestry mins. 1828–31.
23 11 Geo. II, c. 29.
24 24 Geo. II, c. 26.
25 16 Geo. II, c. 28.
26 e.g. the earl of Jersey, Sir. Edw. Gould, Bailey Heath, Ebenezer Mussell, and Sam. Tyssen.
27 19 Geo. II, c. 15.
28 3 Geo. III, c. 40.
29 Vestry mins. 1782–1813, p. 21.
30 53 Geo. III, c. 113 (Local and Personal).
31 4 Geo. IV, c. 21 (Local and Personal).
32 Rep. Cttee. on Sel. Vestries, 1830, 673 sqq.
33 Vestry mins. 1831–3, p. 24.

Elections took place at Easter of the trustees and most of the parish officers: a constable, two churchwardens (designated Upper and Renter), 'two or more overseers',[34] an aleconner until the office was discontinued in 1833,[35] an engineer by 1760,[36] and, from 1796, an inspector of slaughter houses, specified in 1800 as for horses.[37] The vestry elected two scavengers in 1748[38] before the office became the perquisite of the lighting and watching trustees. It also drew up lists for the trustees for the poor to choose rate collectors and, at the September vestry,[39] for the justices to choose surveyors of the highway. Other offices, such as that of sexton or treasurer to the poor rate[40], were filled on vacancy although some, like that of beadle and vestry clerk (below), were in theory annual.[41] There were usually two beadles, upper and lower, whose salary was doubled to £8 in 1749 and who were paid £20 and £16 respectively in 1751.[42]

The Act of 1743[43] provided for a parish clerk who was to be a member of the Company of Parish Clerks of London and pay the clerk of Stepney £12 a a year in compensation. The first was succeeded in 1749 by his son,[44] who was dismissed in 1762 for altering the baptismal register and was replaced by Philip James May,[45] 'as wet a dog as ever you smoked a pipe with',[46] who from 1767 to his death in 1789 was also vestry clerk.[47] The vestry in 1747 had appointed a vestry clerk at 40 guineas a year to keep the ledgers of the scavengers', church, and poor rates[48] and, presumably, the minutes. The salary was raised to £60 in 1774,[49] £300 in 1819,[50] and £400 by 1830. The last figure, business having increased, was intended to pay for two or three under-clerks and the rent of offices.[51] P. J. May was succeeded by James May who, in spite of Joseph Merceron's proposal in 1791 that the vestry clerk should be excused the poor rate,[52] gave evidence against Merceron in 1816.[53] At Easter 1820 the firm of May, Norton & May, whose most vigorous partner appears to have been James May the younger, was challenged over the provision of a vestry clerk, by Robert Brutton, Merceron's son-in-law.[54] Each faction claimed victory and for a year there were two vestry clerks and two sets of minutes[55] until the

next election confirmed Brutton as clerk, an office he occupied until after 1857,[56] in spite of May's continuing challenges.

To deal with the growth of population, two rating divisions were formed by 1760, one for the densely populated west and south and one for the rest of the parish.[57] By 1803 there were four divisions,[58] by 1810 named Green, Church, Town, and Hackney Road.[59] They survived the creation in 1832 of 20 districts, each with a committee to visit the outdoor poor.[60] The divisions each had a rate collector and overseer from 1818.[61] Extra officers were appointed as needed, including an overseer in 1807 for business connected with the militia at £20 a year,[62] and a fifth surveyor in 1831 at £40 to assist four who were to act as police collectors on a poundage basis.[63] Committees of the vestry often assisted the overseers or dealt with particular problems: turnpikes in 1752,[64] a watchhouse in the churchyard in 1754,[65] church repairs in 1787,[66] the rating of new houses in 1788,[67] and the choice of a lecturer in 1792.[68]

One former headborough served as churchwarden and overseer from 1816 to 1818,[69] but many parishioners tried to avoid office. Fines for avoidance were laid down in 1754: 10 guineas for renter churchwarden, 8 for constable, 6 for overseer, 4 for headborough, 3 for upper churchwarden, and £21 for all elected offices.[70] New rates were made in 1800 when the fine to avoid all offices, including collectorships of the scavengers' and watching rates, was £31 10s.[71] Prosecutions of prospective headboroughs, whose office was particularly unpopular, illustrate the overlap between manorial and parish government: it was the vestry clerk who reported the default and the vestry which instituted the indictment for refusing to attend the court leet where headboroughs were sworn in.[72] Sextons were dismissed for misbehaviour,[73] which in the 1820s included collusion in graverobbing.[74] The churchwarden in 1788 signed only with a mark.[75] A collector of the rates was imprisoned for embezzlement in 1775,[76] another was dismissed in 1811,[77] and another absconded in 1832.[78]

The vestry was given power to appoint eight

34 Ibid. 1782–1813, p. 247.
35 Ibid. 1831–3, p. 335.
36 Ibid. 1747–81, p. 161.
37 Ibid. 1782–1813, pp. 77, 323.
38 Ibid. 1747–81, p. 14.
39 When the constable chaired the vestry under 13 Geo. III, c. 78.
40 e.g. in 1769: Vestry mins. 1747–81, p. 278.
41 *Rep. Com Poor Laws*, H.C. 44, p. 83k (1834), ix, app. B2.
42 Ibid. p. 107a (1834), ii; Vestry mins. 1747–81, pp. 25–26, 55.
43 16 Geo. II, c. 28.
44 Vestry mins. 1747–81, p. 29.
45 Ibid. p. 196.
46 *The Times*, 18 Sept. 1788, 1c.
47 Vestry mins. 1747–81, p. 255; 1782-1813, p. 95.
48 Ibid. 1747–81, pp. 1–2.
49 Ibid. p. 335.
50 Ibid. 1813–21, pp. 122v., 144.
51 *Rep. Cttee. on Sel. Vestries, 1830*, 677.
52 Vestry mins. 1782–1813, p. 133.
53 *Rep. Cttee. on Police in Metropolis*, 162.
54 Vestry mins. 1813–21, ff. 156v.–62v.
55 Vestry mins. 1813–21 written by May, last entry 28 Mar. 1821; 1820–3 written by Brutton, beginning 4 May 1820.

56 *Metropolitan Drainage*, H.C. 233, p. 257 (1857- Sess. 2), xxxvi.
57 T.H.L.H.L., BG/202. See also BG/261–2.
58 Vestry mins. 1782–1813, p. 289.
59 Ibid. p. 365.
60 Ibid. 1831–3, p. 108.
61 Ibid. 1813–21, ff. 100, 148v.
62 Ibid. 1782–1813, p. 323.
63 Presumably collectors of the new police rate, allowed 5 per cent of the receipts: Vestry mins. 1831–3, pp. 18, 20.
64 Ibid. 1747–81, p. 67.
65 Ibid. p. 85.   66 Ibid. 1782–1813, p. 59.
67 Ibid. p. 79.
68 Ibid. p. 148.
69 *Rep. Com. Poor Laws*, H.C. 44, p. 112a (1834), ii, app. A3.
70 *Vestry mins.* 1747–81, p. 94.
71 Ibid. 1782–1813, p. 255.
72 e.g. in 1775 when two Huguenots tried to avoid office as foreigners: vestry mins. 1747–81, p. 347; in 1827 when 20 failed to attend when summoned: ibid. 1823–8, 4 May 1827.
73 Vestry mins. 1747–81, p. 41.
74 Below, pub svces. (pub. order).
75 Vestry mins. 1747–81, p. 77.
76 Ibid. pp. 358–9.
77 Ibid. 1782–1813, p. 382.
78 Ibid. 1831–3, p. 242.

commissioners of the court of requests for Tower Hamlets, established by an Act of 1750.[79] They were more substantial than the parish officers, as were the various trustees and most committee members, and from 1751 included Ebenezer Mussell,[80] who dominated parish government until his death in 1764.[81] David Wilmot and James Merceron, a pawnbroker from Brick Lane,[82] were prominent on committees and trustees for twenty years. Wilmot was parish treasurer until 1787.[83] He was displaced by Joseph Merceron[84] (1764–1839, possibly James's son),[85] already head of a committee to receive church rates,[86] who initiated reform[87] and who may have inspired a campaign of 1788 in *The Times* and at the Michaelmas vestry against his predecessor and other leading vestrymen.[88] Merceron became a member of all the vestry committees, of other local bodies,[89] in 1795 a magistrate,[90] and a property owner, by 1834 one of the chief landlords in the parish,[91] with a large fortune perhaps attributable to his control of parish funds and public and private trusts.[92] In 1804 he resigned as treasurer when the vestry resolved to audit his accounts, particularly those for £12,165 voted by parliament in 1800 for relief of the parish, but resumed office after securing a vote of thanks.[93]

From 1811[94] Merceron was in almost continuous conflict with the rector Joshua King until the latter's withdrawal from residence after 1823.[95] The quarrel, which split parish and vestry into two factions, was apparently started by Merceron's frustrating King's appointment as a J.P.[96] King successfully agitated for an Act of 1813 to increase the rector's salary and modify the management of the poor rates, but the attorney general dropped an indictment of Merceron for altering rate books. Following further agitation in 1814–17, and the publication in 1817 of a parliamentary report into metropolitan policing, King's party induced Laurence Gwynne, a resi-

dent magistrate, to bring proceedings against Merceron[97] which led to his conviction in 1818 of misappropriation of funds and of licensing public houses used for debauchery.[98] At Easter 1818 the vestry replaced Merceron as treasurer by the Bank of England and elected new parish officers and governors of the poor.[99] Thereafter King's relentless hostility to Merceron's supporters antagonized Gwynne and others.[1] Merceron's party made counter-allegations of corruption in 1819.[2] Continuing strife at vestry meetings, eventually leading to violence which in 1823 had to be suppressed by the reading of the Riot Act,[3] gave Merceron's party a pretext for an Act of 1823 to establish a select vestry.[4] After King's withdrawal Merceron was again chairing vestry committees in 1826[5] and held other parish and local offices in 1827 × 1830[6] but was not reinstated as a magistrate.[7]

RATES TO 1836. Although Robert Brutton considered that the change to a select vestry exchanged 'anarchy' for 'perfect tranquillity',[8] there were complaints that the select vestry withheld accounts from inspection and manipulated rate assessments.[9] As early as 1759 landholders had protested that they did not hold as much land as they were charged for. The vestry's promise to take measures[10] probably produced the surviving parish map of 1760.[11] To tackle evasion and especially the increasing numbers of tenemented houses which paid no rates, it was resolved in 1760 to charge poor rates on all occupiers of houses let at more than £6 a year.[12] For 1763 the poor rates were said to bring in £1,300–£1,400, 'much increased of late years', at a time when about a third of all houses were occupied by distressed weavers.[13] The Act of 1763 charged the owners rates ranging from a third of the rent of houses valued under £5 to three-quarters of houses valued at more than £15.[14] Despite relative prosperity after the passing

79 Smith, *Hist. E, Land.* 69; 23 Geo II, c. 30.
80 Vestry mins. 1747–81, p. 52.
81 Ibid. pp. 45, 198. For Mussell, above, the Green; estates (Pyotts).
82 Vestry mins. 1747–81, p. 259.
83 Ibid. pp. 224, 269, 299, 392; 1782–1813, p. 69. For Wilmot, above, settlement and building to 1836.
84 Ibid. 1782–1813, p. 69.
85 Joseph died aged 75: *Gent. Mag.* cix (2), 211; tablet in ch. Jas. had married Ann Mason in 1760: G.L.R.O., X25/10, no. 043.
86 Vestry mins. 1782–1813, pp. 63, 66–67.
87 Ibid. 73, 77.
88 *The Times*, 29 May 1788, 3c; 12 Sept. 2d; 27 Sept. 3c; 30 Sept. 1b; 2 Oct. 1d.
89 Vestry mins. 1782–1813, p.112; S. and B. Webb, *Eng. Local Govt., Par. and County* (1906), 81.
90 G.L.R.O., MJP/Q4, p. 75.
91 T.H.L.H.L., TH/2896, 2898; *Rep. Cttee. on Police in Metropolis*, 164, 166, 186, 513; M.L.R. 1808/5/256; G.L.R.O., MR/PLT 5024–5; ibid. MA/DC/8; ibid. M93/52, pp. 228–9; 54, pp. 24 sqq.; 60, pp. 16, 361; 63, p. 504; 64, pp. 654–5; 65, p. 508; *Rep. Com. Poor Laws*, H.C. 44, p. 111a (1834), ii, app. A3.
92 *Gent. Mag* cix. (2), 211; *Rep. Cttee. on Police in Metropolis*, 181, 207; Webb, *Eng. Local Govt.* 84.
93 Webb, *Eng. Local Govt.* 34; vestry mins. 1782–1813, pp. 294, 297.
94 Above, social; below, parish church.
95 BNC, Bethnal Green 3, letter by King 27 May 1823; below, parish church.

96 Timmings, whom Merceron favoured as a J.P., was described by King as a former alehouse-keeper, 'extremely ignorant'. Possibly he was the bldr. Wm. Timmins: *Rep. Cttee. on Police in Metropolis*, 151–2.
97 Vestry mins. 1813–21, ff. 44v.-5., 70v.-1, 73–4v., 146; *Rep. Cttee on Police in Metropolis*, 151 sqq., 162 sqq., 185 sqq., 207.
98 *The Times*, 18 May 1818, 3c.; 25 May, 3e; 2 June, 3e; 4 June, 3e; vestry mins. 1813–12, pp. 109–11.
99 Permanent officers like the beadle, also Merceron supporters, remained: *The Times*, 18 May, 3e; vestry mins. 1813–21, ff. 98v.-100.
1 Vestry mins. 1813–21, ff. 111v., 114, 140v., 162v.; *Trial for conspiracy to defraud poor rate funds of Bethnal Green at King's Bench*, 28 May 1819.
2 Vestry mins. 1813–21. f. 144.
3 Ibid. f. 158v.; 1820–3, pp. 165, 349.
4 Vestry mins. 1820–3, pp. 339–40; 4 Geo IV, c. 21 (Local and Personal); BNC, Bethnal Green 3, letter by King 25 Apr. 1823.
5 Vestry mins. 1823–8, 7 Sept. 1826.
6 Ibid 17 Apr 1827, 8 Apr. 1828; 1828–31, pp. 239, 242; 1831–3, p. 13; *Rep. Cttee. on Sel. Vestries, 1830*, 677.
7 *Rep. Cttee. on Sel. Vestries, 1830*, 673.
8 *Rep. Com. Poor Laws*, H.C. 44, p. 83 (1834), viii, app. B2.
9 *Rep. Cttee. on Sel. Vestries, 1830*, 673.
10 Vestry mins. 1747–81, p. 154.
11 T.H.L.H.L., Map no. 301.
12 Vestry mins. 1747–81, p. 164.
13 *C.J.* xxix. 446.
14 3 Geo. III, c. 40.

of the Spitalfields Act of 1773,[15] rates were high, 5s. 6d. in the £ in 1777 and 1782[16] and 6s. in 1786.[17] In the year ending Easter 1776 the poor rate raised £3,292, of which £2,825 was spent on the poor and £12 on the rent of the workhouse.[18] From 1783 to 1785 the average sum raised was £2,741 a year, of which £2,688 was spent on the poor and £26 on entertainment.[19] The figures suggest great exaggeration in a charge of extravagance.[20] By 1788 the rate was 5s. for houses rented at more than £20[21] and 5s. remained usual until c. 1810, calculated to raise £4,500.[22]

In 1803 5s. was only nominal, since the rate could vary between 1s. 8d. and 5s. In the year ending Easter 1803 it raised £3,300, of which £3,154 was spent on the workhouse and £265 on out-relief; total expenditure was £3,484, illustrating Bethnal Green's accumulating debt.[23] The rapid growth of building allowed the yield to reach £9,029 in the year to Easter 1813, of which £6,675 was spent on the poor.[24] Grievances about rating were among the strongest motives for the Act of 1813. It was estimated that 769 houses were not assessed and defaulters averaged 2,300 a year, so that two-thirds of the inhabitants bore the whole burden of the poor. The Act therefore directed that landlords of tenements let at less than £14 a year or monthly or weekly should compound, the rent-taker being deemed the owner.[25] The result was to reduce the rate from 5s. 9d. to 2s. 6d.[26] and for 1813–14 to raise the yield to £13,626, of which £9,288 was spent on the poor.[27] Merceron was defended in 1817 on the grounds that the poverty of three-quarters of the population, the numbers in the workhouse, and the weekly expenditure on the outdoor poor made it a wonder that the rates and the parish's debt were not higher.[28] As treasurer and governors of the poor he and his supporters, the landlords of small tenements, were in turn accused of manipulating the rating system:[29] a reduction by £20 of the rates on Merceron's and his supporter William Platt's houses in 1819 was soon rescinded by the opposition.[30] When Merceron was ousted in 1818 a survey and new ledgers were ordered[31] and the annual rate raised £10,551.[32] As he regained control, the amount

declined and the annual rate of 3s. 3d., levied quarterly, in 1820[33] raised only £908 while the debt mounted.[34] By 1823 payments were badly in arrears.[35]

The amount raised was £9,085 in 1824,[36] when the repeal of the Spitalfields Acts led to more pauperization.[37] Higher assessments in 1827 and 1828 at £20,000[38] raised only £14,246 and £15,766[39] and as distress increased, the resources and sympathy of ratepayers decreased. In 1828 a vestry committee remarked that houses might be unequally rated or not rated at all. Its warning of more discord was met by the vestry's referral to another committee which included at least two of Merceron's supporters.[40] Demands during the year to see the accounts arose from a perception of mismanagement.[41] A report in 1829 recorded complaints by landlords of compounded houses about empty houses and bad tenants; it recommended rackrenting and that compounded houses should be rated at half to three-quarters of their annual value.[42] However great the need, it was felt that 1s. 3d. a quarter was the maximum that could be demanded.[43] By 1834 it was said that hardly one shopkeeper in five paid his rates and that two thirds of the tenements were owned by people who compounded and let them out monthly or weekly; if rates were increased, the owners would leave, as several had already done, leaving whole streets untenanted.[44] The vestry resorted to subscriptions, appeals to the government,[45] and borrowing, falling more deeply into debt until in September 1829 four treasurers resigned on the grounds of ill health.[46] Expenditure reached £22,428 in 1832[47] and £25,046 in 1835.[48]

POOR RELIEF TO 1836. The poor received indoor and outdoor relief from the parish until 1929, when responsibility passed to the L.C.C. There was a workhouse in Jorey's house on the east side of the green by 1751, when a churchwarden and overseer were directed to give the inmates bread each month.[49] In 1757 the vestry farmed them out at 2s. 4d. a head a week, allowing for a daily diet of 2 pints of beer and 1 lb. of bread together with 4 oz. of cheese, 2 oz. of butter, 7 oz. of meat or ¾ lb. of suet dumpling and broth

15 Above, settlement and building to 1836.
16 Vestry mins. 1747–81, p. 375; 1782–1813, p. 4.
17 Ibid. 1782–1813, p. 47.
18 *Abstract of Returns by Overseers*, 1777 (3265) (H.C. Sess. Papers of 18th cent., ed. S. Lambert, xxxi), p. 101.
19 Ibid. *1787* (3999) (H.C. Sess. papers of 18th cent., ed. S. Lambert, lx), p. 143.
20 *The Times*, 12 Sept. 1788, 2d; 13 Sept. 2a.
21 Ibid. 18 Sept. 1788, 2d.
22 Vestry mins. 1782–1813, pp. 133, 248, 317, 362. It was 4s. 6d. in 1793: ibid. p. 169.
23 *Poor Law Abstract*, H.C. 175, pp. 298–9 (1803–4), xiii.
24 Ibid. H.C. 82, pp. 264–5 (1818), xiii.
25 53 Geo. III, c. 113 (Local and Personal); BNC, Second Ser. [Tower], 148, printed notice 1813.
26 BNC, Bethnal Green 3, letter by King 12 Mar. 1823.
27 *Poor Law Abstract*, H.C. 82, pp. 264–5 (1818), xiii.
28 Vestry mins. 1813–21, f. 86.
29 *Rep. Com. Poor Laws*, H.C. 44, p. 112a (1834), ii, app. A3.
30 Vestry Mins. 1813–21, f. 140–v.
31 Ibid. f. 104v.
32 *Rep. Sel. Cttee. on Poor Rate Rets*, H.C. 556, app. (1822), v.
33 Vestry mins. 1813–21, ff. 156v., 167, 176, 186v.

34 Ibid. f. 317; *Rep. Sel. Cttee. on Poor Rate Rets*. H.C. 556, app. (1822), v.
35 Vestry mins. 1820–3, p. 337.
36 *Rep. Sel. Cttee. on Poor Rate Rets*. H.C. 334, Suppl. app., p. 171 (1825), iv.
37 Above, settlement and bldg. to 1836.
38 *Rep. Cttee. on Sel. Vestries, 1830*, 673.
39 *Money expended for Relief of Poor*, H.C. 83, p. 343 (1830–1), xi.
40 Vestry mins. 1823–8, 20 Feb. 1828.
41 *Rep. Cttee. on Sel. Vestries, 1830*, 673 sqq.
42 Vestry mins. 1828–31, p. 142.
43 Ibid. pp. 58–60; *Rep. Com. Poor Laws*, H.C. 44, p. 108a (1834), ii, app. A3.
44 *Rep. Com Poor Laws*, H.C. 44, p. 108a (1834), iii, app. A.
45 *Poor Law Com. 3rd Ann. Rep*. H.C. 546, p. 84 (1837), xxxi, app. B.
46 Vestry mins. 1828–31, p. 174.
47 *Money expended for Relief of Poor*, H.C. 444, p. 114 (1835), xlvii.
48 *Ret. relating to Poor Rates in Metropolitan Dist*. H.C. 208, p. 5 (1857–8), xlix(i).
49 Vestry mins. 1747–81, p. 53; T.H.L.H.L., B.G./256; map no. 301.

or pottage. The contractor was to have the use of the workhouse, subject to inspection by a standing committee.[50] The arrangement ended in 1759 when the renter churchwarden was to pay both the workhouse and the casual poor, assisted by a committee.[51] Farming, at 2s. 5d. a head, began again in 1760, the contractor to teach the workhouse children to read.[52] The new contractor left in 1761 and the first contractor and his wife were employed as salaried master and mistress of the workhouse.[53]

The Act of 1763 empowered the new governors of the poor to raise £2,000 by annuities charged on the rates and to acquire property for a workhouse. The children were to be educated, the idle corrected, and the able bodied given work by master weavers.[54] A site was leased at the eastern end and on the south side of Hare Street,[55] where a new workhouse to hold 400[56] was completed by the end of 1766.[57]

The food allowance was reduced in 1768 to 2 oz. of cheese or 1 oz. of butter and 14 oz. of bread.[58] In 1774 a local weaver, James Hill, was appointed master at a salary of £15 a year or £10 with 1s. 6d. in the £ from the labour of the poor;[59] in 1778 he was allowed 2s. in the £.[60] The governors reduced the allowance of his successor, Cordell, in 1782 to 1s. 6d., but were overruled by the vestry.[61] On Cordell's death in 1801 George Hopwood and his wife replaced him at a salary of £20 a year.[62]

In 1778 inability to open windows at the workhouse was prejudicial to health[63] and in 1782 only hogs for the benefit of the poor were to be kept there.[64] Inmates numbered 450 in 1795[65] and nearly 500 in 1801.[66] An extension was built on the south side to house four sick wards in 1802.[67] Some 332 people were relieved in the workhouse in 1803.[68]

The master Thomas Nichols (d. 1820) was succeeded by his assistant James Martin (d. 1827), who was paid £30 a year and followed briefly by his widow.[69] In 1822 a vestry committee concluded that orphan boys, with the sanction of the governors, had been flogged, put on the treadwheel, and had half their heads shaved.[70] Mismanagement was alleged in 1823, particularly in the supply and consumption of goods.[71]

In 1826 increasing distress led to the acquisition of more of Great Haresmarsh behind the

workhouse, containing a large brick house and outbuildings 'easily convertible to parish use'.[72] A new master was appointed in 1827, paid at 2s. in the £ on all work performed by paupers in and out of the workhouse. A committee suggested employment other than silkweaving for the inmates: the manufacture of sheeting and 'camblets' for those accustomed to weaving and shoemaking and slop work[73] for the others.[74] Some five months later there was satisfaction with the management of the workhouse, where an average of 807 inmates cost 3s. 6d. a head a week.[75] By 1831, however, familiar complaints were heard. Expenditure had reached 3s. 10d. in 1830 because of higher food prices and consumption. Income from labour had fallen, because of lack of work, low wages, and a 'degree of deception' practised on the master through the poundage system.[76] In 1833 Thomas Stevens offered to teach various crafts, including shoemaking and making workmen's apparel, but he had difficulty in making some of the paupers work.[77] Poundage was replaced by a salary for the master in 1834 because the inmates had little work.[78] Overcrowding was such that in October 1831 there were 99 boys to 14 beds, each bed accommodating six and the rest sleeping on the floor; children were dying from lack of air or disease caused by rubbish in the back yard. There were 1,044 inmates in February 1832, crowded 3–5 to a bed[79] and producing 'indecent scenes'.[80] In 1834 the 900 inmates each received 1 lb. or 14 oz. of bread, together with 'meat etc.', but £8,000 was owed to victuallers, who would no longer supply. Some infant poor were cared for in Edmonton and Ilford (Essex), by nurses supervised by the overseers and guardians for 4s. a week a head.[81]

Outdoor relief, in the form of weekly doles, fluctuated with the silk industry. In 1755 the parish officers were directed to enquire into lodging houses and illegal settlement[82] and in 1788 the decline of the industry was blamed for the high rates.[83] Distress was much worse by 1800, when parliament voted £12,165 to Bethnal Green, to be used mostly in weekly instalments.[84] The parish petitioned parliament against altering the Corn Laws in 1815 and against introducing income tax in 1816, pleading the state of the industry and that the measures threatened further suffering.[85] One of the complaints against Merceron in 1816 was that,

50 Vestry mins. 1747–81, pp. 132–3, 137–9.
51 Ibid. p. 154.
52 Ibid. pp. 165–7.
53 Ibid. p. 182.
54 Ibid. p. 198; 3 Geo. III, c. 40.
55 On Great Haresmarsh est.: M.L.R. 1766/3/98; Horwood, *Plan* (1792–9).
56 *Abstract of Rets. of Overseers, 1777* (3265) (H.C. Sess. Papers of 18th cent., ed. S. Lambert, xxxi), p. 101.
57 Vestry mins. 1747–81, pp. 246–7.
58 Ibid. p. 260.
59 Ibid. p. 330.   60 Ibid. p. 396.
61 Ibid. 1782–1813, pp. 5–7.
62 Ibid. pp. 262–3.
63 Ibid. 1747–81, p. 387.
64 Ibid. 1782–1813, p. 6.
65 Lysons, *Environs,* ii. 37.
66 Vestry mins. 1782–1813, pp. 265, 271.
67 G.L.R.O., MR/B/R5 (1802 no. 63).
68 *Poor Law Abstract,* H.C. 175, pp. 298–9 (1803–4), xiii.
69 Vestry mins. 1813–21, p. 180; 1823–8, 27 Dec. 1826,

31 Jan. 1827.
70 Ibid. 1820–3, pp. 254, 265.
71 *Rep. Com Poor Laws,* H.C. 44, p. 113a (1834), ii, app. A3.
72 Vestry mins. 1823–8, pp. 180, 202; M.L.R. 1826/5/286; 1842/2/252; T.H.L.H.L., TH/2344.
73 Ready made clothing for army and navy.
74 Vestry mins. 1823–8, 31 Jan. 1827.
75 Ibid. 27 June 1827.
76 Ibid. 1831–3, pp. 5–11.
77 Ibid. pp. 281, 315.
78 Ibid. 1833–7, 31 Mar. 1834.
79 Ibid. 1831–3, p. 43; *Rep. Com. Poor Laws,* H.C. 44, p. 113a (1834), ii, app. A.
80 Vestry mins. 1831–3, p. 366.
81 *Rep. Com. Poor Laws,* H.C. 44, p. 108a (1834), ii, app. A3; p. 83g (1834), viii, app. B2.
82 Vestry mins. 1747–81, p. 109.
83 *The Times,* 2 Oct. 1788, 1d.
84 Webb, *Eng. Local Govt.* 84; *Rep. Cttee. on Police in Metropolis,* 154.
85 Vestry mins. 1813–21, ff. 55, 66v.

as treasurer, he had compelled the overseers to use their own money or leave the poor unrelieved.[86]

After the repeal of the Spitalfields Acts there were proposals for petitioning the government and the committee of the houseless poor in 1826[87] and the parish, in financial crisis by 1827, began to borrow on bonds.[88] National compassion for the weavers raised £30,000 by subscription in 1825–6 and £10,000 in 1829, whose recipients included casual applicants from elsewhere.[89] Five members of a committee set up in 1826 were to visit the applicants in each of the four parish divisions[90] and a visiting overseer was employed in 1829.[91] So many were the applicants, however, that an unemployed native silkweaver could not be distinguished from an outsider. By 1834[92] 6,000–7,000 were receiving from 6d. to 1s. 6d. a week, many of them from Spitalfields or farther afield, attracted by cheap housing. In 1834 it was estimated that nonparishioners, an eighth of them Irish, formed a third of the applicants. Demands became more aggressive, it being common for gangs to besiege the shop of the overseer, usually a tradesman. By 1834 there was a core of about 150 young people of 'bad character, thieves and prostitutes', who demanded relief and spent it mostly on gin. Parochial attempts at control were undermined by magistrates who ordered relief indiscriminately. Attempts were made in 1828 to make the 'lazy and abandoned' break stones[93] but in 1832 numbers had to be restricted because they were too riotous. A site fronting White and Manchester streets was supplied by Thomas Stone in 1832 as a stone breaking yard, to supply to 'Mr. McAdam for roads', but it proved a loss to the parish. Poor physique made Bethnal Green's inhabitants unsuitable as labourers, while men who were given tools for a trade merely sold or pawned them before again demanding relief.

Claimants, an average of 2,500 a year, steadily increased from 1826[94] and in January 1832 reached 6,000 in one week.[95] In that spring huge sums were said to be spent while thousands of paupers besieged the committee room and overseers' houses.[96] Although the amount paid to individuals was reduced,[97] growing numbers caused heavy expense to the parish. There was alarm that some people fraudulently obtained relief from each overseer but remedies such as payment by ticket were not adopted.[98] In the last full week of April 1836, 4,909 received outdoor relief.[99]

LOCAL GOVERNMENT FROM 1836 TO 1900. From 1836, under the Poor Law Act of 1834, until 1929[1] Bethnal Green was a poor law union, managed by a board of guardians, 20 in 1836,[2] 24 by 1875,[3] elected for the four wards. The board met weekly and employed a master and mistress of the workhouse and a board clerk, who in 1857 was Robert Brutton, also vestry clerk.[4] By 1875 its staff included an assistant clerk, a treasurer, three relieving and two assistant officers, a pay clerk, three vaccination officers, and six district medical officers. Workhouse staff also included a chaplain and medical officer and there were teachers, a chaplain, and a medical officer for children sent to Leytonstone (Essex).[5]

The board introduced the new system successfully, although there was jealousy between it and another authority, presumably the select vestry, which still levied the other rates.[6] Spending on the poor dropped to £9,126 in 1836 but in 1837 the guardians were criticized for failing to combat fraudulent dependency and the workhouse was found to be totally unfitted.[7] Recipients of outrelief dropped to 1,384 in April 1838.[8] The poor rate for 1840–1 was 2s. 9d. in the £[9] and for 1840 total expenditure from the poor rate was £15,684, of which £10,368 was spent on relief.[10] Rates of 4s. 4d. raised £20,628 in 1843.[11] Expenditure rose to £16,415 in 1845, £24,217 in 1855 and £29,014 in 1857 with an increasing proportion, reaching 75 per cent, for relief.[12] At the end of 1867 there were 3,151 recipients of outdoor relief.[13] In that year a mass refusal in Bethnal Green to pay rates probably helped to change a system whereby the highest rates were paid in areas least able to afford them. The Metropolitan Poor Act transferred much of the expense to a common fund to which each union contributed according to its rateable value.[14] Relative prosperity during the 1870s deteriorated and by early 1883 there were 1,000 outdoor poor, 300 more than in the previous year. The vestry raised the rates to 6s. 4d. which included general and sewer rates beside 10d. a quarter poor rate.[15] Both outdoor and indoor relief reportedly doubled between 1878 and 1895.[16]

86 Ibid. f. 73.
87 Vestry mins. 1823–8, 22, 27 Dec. 1826.
88 Ibid. 31 Jan. 1827; 1828–31, p. 113.
89 Poor Law Com. 3rd Rep. H.C. 546, pp. 84 sqq. (1837), xxxi, app. B.
90 Vestry mins. 1823–8, 4 Oct. 1826.
91 Ibid. 1828–31, p. 114.
92 Rest of para. based on Rep. Com Poor Laws, H.C. 44, pp. 95a, 97a, 106a, 113a (1834), ii, app. A3; pp. 83 f–k (1834), viii, ix, app. B2.
93 Vestry mins. 1828–31, p. 44.
94 Rep. Com Poor Laws. H.C. 44, p. 83h (1834), ix, app. B2.
95 Vestry mins. 1831–3, p. 92.
96 Ibid. p. 136.
97 Rep. Com Poor Laws. H.C. 44, p. 109a (1834), ii, app. A3.
98 Ibid. 113a; Vestry mins. 1831–3, p. 315.
99 Rep. from Asst. Com. on Handloom Weavers, pt. II (43-I), H.C. p. 252 (1840), xxiii.
1 19 Geo. V, c. 17.
2 Poor Law Com. 2nd Rep.. H.C. 595, pp. 306, 533 (1836), xxix(1).
3 Local Govt. Dir. (1875).
4 P.O. Dir. Lond. (1857).
5 Local Govt. Dir. (1875).
6 Poor Law Com. 2nd Rep. 308, 310.
7 Poor Law Com. 3rd Rep. 87, app. B.
8 Rep. from Asst. Com. on Handloom Weavers, pt. II (43-I), H.C. p. 252 (1840), xxiii.
9 2nd Rep. Sel. Cttee. on Metropolitan Local Govt. H.C. 452, p. 269 (1866), xiii.
10 Ret. relating to Poor Rates in Metropolitan Dist. H.C. 208, p. 5 (1857–8), xlix(1).
11 Parochial and Boro. Rates, H.C. 635, p. 287 (1844), xlii.
12 Poor Rates, H.C. 208, p. 5 (1857–8), xlix(1).
13 The Times, 28 Jan. 1868, 4c.
14 G. Stedman Jones, 'Social Consequences of Casual Labour Problem in Lond. 1860–90, with ref. to E. End' (Oxf. Univ. D. Phil. thesis, 1970), 34, 348–9.
15 The Times, 5 Jan. 1883, 4f.
16 Booth, Life and Labour,. iii(2), 103.

The workhouse had 800 inmates in November 1841, with some pauper children and old people accommodated in Norwood (Surr.) and Bromley (Kent).[17] A new workhouse for 1,014 was built on Sotheby land in the north of the parish by October 1842.[18] Vagrants remained a problem, 1,561 being admitted in 1848 and 1,620 in 1849.[19] There were 700 paupers, mostly former weavers, and a master and mistress and a schoolmaster and schoolmistress in the workhouse in 1851,[20] 762 inmates at Christmas 1852, and 1,082 in the new year.[21] In March 1866 there were 1,392 inmates, half of them sick.[22] During the year 180 children were sent to Mitcham (Surr.)[23] but from 1869 the workhouse school was in Leytonstone.[24] At the end of 1867 the workhouse was overcrowded by 200 and sick children were sent to Margate infirmary.[25] From 1868 to 1871 expenditure was authorized on a school, porter's lodge, and infirmary for 200 children, 438 men, and 88 women.[26] Building took place in 1871, when there were 2,200 inmates.[27] In 1875 the workhouse, with room for 1,500, was one of the largest in London; 909–1,086 were in residence at any one time.[28] Numbers rose to 1,254–1,522 from 1884 to 1886; that they were 'always more than the accommodation' suggests stricter standards of overcrowding than in 1875.[29] A declared aim of those who wanted to build on the green in 1889 was to erect a workhouse infirmary.[30] Additions were made to the workhouse in 1890,[31] an iron classroom was built in 1894,[32] committee rooms were altered in 1895,[33] and in 1897 a new infirmary was built in Cambridge Road.[34]

Criticized in 1837, the guardians installed a more abstemious regime in 1842. It was alleged that inmates were treated as prisoners, fed inadaquately, and beaten.[35] Inquiries were held in 1861, in response to a rape, and in 1863, 1864, 1866 and 1872, in response to deaths. [36] There was criticism of the workhouse school in 1869 and, by clergy, of the treatment of the poor in 1874.[37]

In 1843 an Act[38] set up a board of 60 commissioners for paving, lighting, and cleaning Bethnal Green and the parts of Old Cock Lane and York Street in Shoreditch. The commissioners, to be elected by those paying rents of £80, had to be resident and rated at more than £20, to serve for six years, and to elect their successors. They could levy rates and raise money by bonds, mortgages, and annuities, and supervised the clerks and officers, including scavengers of the previous trustees. Their clerk was Robert Brutton.[39] By 1852 the commissioners also employed a surveyor, a gas inspector and messenger and four collectors at a combined salary (including the clerk's) of just under £600 a year. In the year 1852–3 their income was £12,421 and expenditure £12,191 but they were already £30,450 in debt.[40]

Emphasis shifted from relieving the unemployed to such problems as sewerage, drainage, and housing. Inaction was in the interest of the governing class, mostly tradesmen or tenement owners, while the multiplicity of authorities also led to inefficiency. Reports of 1838[41] and 1842[42] blamed lack of effective government for the high incidence of illness. In 1848 Hector Gavin thanked the district health officers but castigated the authorities for neglect and for obstucting his investigation.[43] The confusion caused by overlapping authorities was illustrated in 1848 when filth beside the canal at Pritchard's Road, the alleged cause of typhus and many fevers, was blamed on the parish officers but the board of guardians was petitioned rather than the vestry or paving commissioners.[44] Dilatoriness in dealing with cholera in 1848 and 1849 provoked a special order from the General Board of Health but the guardians still took the minimum measures; the only recommendation adopted was the appointment of an inspector of nuisances.[45] When cholera returned during the 1850s the authorities 'promised everything but did nothing'[46] and tried to exclude from the post of medical officer of health all doctors who 'ran about stink hunting' and produced troublesome reports.[47]

The Metropolis Local Management Act, 1855,[48] set up the Metropolitan Board of Works to provide major sewers, drainage, and public works. Members were to be elected by the vestries every three years, with Bethnal Green

[17] *The Times*, 6 Nov. 1841, 5a.
[18] Ibid. 19 Oct. 1842, 3b; *Rep. to Gen. Bd. of Health on Metropolitan Workhos.* H.C. 133, pp. 827–9 (1850), xxi.
[19] H. Mayhew, *Lond. Lab. and Lond. Poor*, iii. 395.
[20] P.R.O., HO 107/1540/21/2/23, f. 669.
[21] *Lond. City Mission Mag.* xix. 102.
[22] *The Times*, 8 Mar. 1866, 12d.
[23] *V.C.H. Mdx.* i. 229.
[24] *The Times*, 1 Jan. 1869, 9d. Sch. still used in 1902: *P.O. Dir. Lond.* (1902).
[25] *The Times*, 28 Jan. 1868, 4c.
[26] *Ret. of Expenditure on Bldgs. for Paupers*, H.C. 86, p. 111 (1876), lxiii.
[27] G.L.R.O., MBW 1621 (23); *The Times*, 16 Jan. 1872, 5f.
[28] *Lond. City Mission Mag.* xli. 8.
[29] *Accn. in Metropolitan Workhos.* 741.
[30] *The Times*, 11 Sept. 1889, 12d.
[31] G.L.R.O., AR/BA/4/13, no. 26.
[32] Ibid. 46, no. 5.
[33] Ibid. 55, no. 5.
[34] Ibid. 71, no. 5; Booth, *Life and Labour*, iii (2), 103; below, pub. svces. (medical).
[35] *The Times*, 19 Oct. 1842, 3b; 24 Nov. 5e; 9 Nov. 1844, 5b; 12 Nov. 5d; 16 Nov. 5d. Much the same regime was in use in 1849: *Rep. to Gen. Bd. of Health on Metropolitan*

Workhos. H.C. 133, pp. 827–9 (1850), xxi.
[36] C. Bermant, *Point of Arrival* (1975), 79–81; J. Hollingshead, *Ragged Lond.* (1861), 195–6, 198; *The Times*, 15 Dec. 1863, 12e; 6 May 1864, 9f; 11 Jan. 1866, 9f; 12 Jan. 5f; 15 Jan. 12e; 17 Jan. 5e; 18 Jan. 10e; 16 Jan. 1872, 5f.
[37] *The Times*, 1 Jan. 1869, 9d; 8 Jan. 1874, 5e; 21 Jan. 7e.
[38] 6 & 7 Vic. c. 34 (Local and Personal).
[39] G.L.R.O., MR/UTJ/1.
[40] *Ret. on Paving, Cleansing and Lighting Metropolitan Dists.* H.C. 127, p. 161 (1854–5), liii.
[41] *Poor Law Com. 4th Rep.* H.C. 147, pp. 62 sqq. (1837–8), xxviii, app. A.
[42] *Rep. Poor Law Com. on San. Condition of Labouring Pop.* H.L. pp. 159–60 (1842), xxvi.
[43] Gavin, *San. Ramblings*, 3–5, 14; *E. Lond Papers*, viii(2), 110–18.
[44] *The Times*, 28 Nov. 1848, 8e; above, building 1837–75.
[45] The bd. recommended 2 inspectors and 6 other measures: *Rep. of Bd. of Health on Cholera* [1273], H.C. pp. 133 sqq. (1850), xxi; H. Jephson, *San. Evolution of Lond.* (1907), 46–48.
[46] Jephson, *San. Evolution*, 74.
[47] S. King, 'Formation and development of slums: E. Lond. in second half of 19th cent.' (Lond. Univ. Ph.D. thesis, 1981), 121.
[48] 18 & 19 Vic. c. 120; *Nineteenth Cent.* cxlv. 373.

initially electing one member. A parish vestry replaced the select vestry or the riotous open vestry and the paving, lighting, and watering trustees. Bethnal Green had 48 vestrymen, residents rated at more than £40 (9 each for East and North wards, 15 each for West and South Wards).[49] A third of them and the auditors were to be elected annually from the ratepayers, and the chairman, if not 'authorized by law or custom', was also to be elected. The vestry replaced the highway surveyors and the paving trustees, levied rates, and was responsible for parish sewerage and paving and compelling owners to provide house-drains and water closets. It was to publish reports, appoint medical officers, inspectors of nuisances and other officials, and execute the Nuisance Removals Acts.

A 'town hall' to serve both the vestry and the guardians had been begun in 1851 in Church Row,[50] with money borrowed for the purpose.[51] It was of brick with a stuccoed front and the vestry built a red-brick extension to the south in 1867.[52]

The new vestrymen resembled the old, in that their main aim was to keep down expenditure. Their staff was too small and badly supervised: in 1861 the enforcement of the Common Lodging Houses Act, to combat overcrowding, was dependent on the conscientiousness of local inspectors and was virtually ignored in Bethnal Green.[53] In 1863, following an outcry after deaths from contaminated water, a police report concluded that the tenements were neglected by their owners, who included several vestry members and who ought to provide proper sanitation.[54] The vestry then enlarged the nuisance removal committee, ordered that houses along the main sewer should be drained into it, and appointed a second inspector of nuisances.[55] A builder and surveyor from Hackney Road was made chief inspector of nuisances and new sewers were planned.[56] By 1864 the vestry employed 15 officers: the two inspectors of nuisances or sanitary inspectors, a clerk, a medical officer, a chief surveyor and a surveyor of the highways, a surveyors' clerk, an inspector of scavengers, a townhall keeper, a messenger, and five rate collectors. The collectors were paid a commission and the combined annual wages of the rest totalled £1,050.[57] The sewer rate in 1859, and the rates in general in 1865, were mortgaged.[58]

Acts to alleviate housing conditions were still largely ignored. The medical officer explained in 1867 that the Public Health Act of 1866 was unworkable because of high rents, scarcity of employment, and new taxes which had forced tenants to let out lodgings and thereby increased overcrowding.[59] The Torrens Act of 1868, which provided for the demolition of unfit houses on payment of compensation, similarly threatened more overcrowding. It was usually not enforced, as the medical officer reported in 1883, since vestries were largely composed of landlords. Neighbouring parishes like Hackney, by enforcing the legislation, merely displaced their own poor, who moved into Bethnal Green.[60] The vestry made no use of Acts in the 1870s and 1880s to facilitate slum clearance, maintaining, for example in 1883 that they were unnecessary[61] and that action could be taken when the long leases fell in; meanwhile leaseholders exploited the 'fag end of the lease' by subdividing.[62] The sanitary committee in 1883 declined to act over the old Nichol slums because, as one vestryman admitted, it seemed afraid of offending the owners.[63] At an inquiry ordered by the Home Secretary in 1887 Bethnal Green vestry was criticized for not applying the existing law, for an inadequate staff, and for acting only after complaints. The sanitary staff was much as it had been 20 years previously. Apart from pointing out such work as had been done (without mentioning that some, the reconstruction along Bethnal Green Road, was that of the M.B.W.), the vestrymen blamed the poor for their habits and, with more justification, stressed that theirs was a poor parish with high rates. Landlords rated at under £20 were allowed 25 per cent discount on the rates and of 18,493 rated houses 14,411 (78 per cent) qualified for the discount.[64]

Private charity tried to make up for the parish's weak response in the 1860s and 1870s, with the work of the denominations and of Baroness Burdett-Coutts and the beginnings of the model dwellings movement.[65] In 1868 the out-relief committee criticized a host of charitable organizations for destroying self-reliance and encouraging vagrants from outside.[66] More practical was the Employment and Relief Association, formed by gentry connected with Bethnal Green, which included Mrs. and Miss Merceron, to raise subscriptions to pay the unemployed for clearing the streets and stone breaking and to provide soup kitchens.[67] In 1869 the various charities were consolidated into the Bethnal Green Charity Organisation Society with an office in Bethnal Green Road, the rector as chairman, Sir T. F. Buxton, Bt., as treasurer, and a committee of local clergy. Welcomed as an intermediary by the guardians and supported by 11 organizations, 15 churches, and several chapels, the society raised subscriptions and dealt with individual cases, referring some to charities and others to the authorities. Although it lasted until 1948,[68] it could not cope

49 *Lond. Gaz.* 20 Oct. 1855, pp. 3881–2.
50 P.R.O., HO 107/1542/21/4/4, f. 63, p. 27; G.L.R.O., MBO/DS/G12, H12.
51 G.L.R.O., MR/UTJ/7/26.
52 Bethnal Green M.B. *Official Guide* [1921], 42.
53 Hollingshead, *Ragged Lond.* 199.
54 *The Times,* 6 Nov. 1863, 9f; Bermant, *Point of Arrival,* 83.
55 *The Times,* 27 Nov. 1863, 10c.
56 Ibid. 11 Dec. 1863, 4f.
57 *Ret. of Property and Officers,* H.C. 379, p. 47 (1864), I.
58 T.H.L.H.L., TH/2261–2.
59 Quoted in Jephson, *San. Evolution,* 202.
60 Stedman Jones, 'Casual Labour in Lond.' 269–72;

King, 'Formation of slums', 110.
61 Jephson, *San. Evolution,* 303.
62 *The Times,* 20 Oct. 1887, 3d; Jones, 'Casual Labour in Lond.' 300–1, 304–5.
63 *E. Lond. Papers,* xiii. 26.
64 *The Times,* 23 Sept. 1887, 5f; 13 Oct. 11e; 20 Oct. 3d; 7 Nov. 4c; 8 Nov. 12b.
65 Above, building 1837–75.
66 *The Times,* 28 Jan. 1868, 4c.
67 Ibid. 16 Dec. 1867, 12f; 25 Dec. 10c; 1 Jan. 1868, 10f; 6 Jan. 9d.
68 G.L.R.O., A/FWA/C/B2/1–79; Jones, 'Casual Labour in Lond.', 358–62.

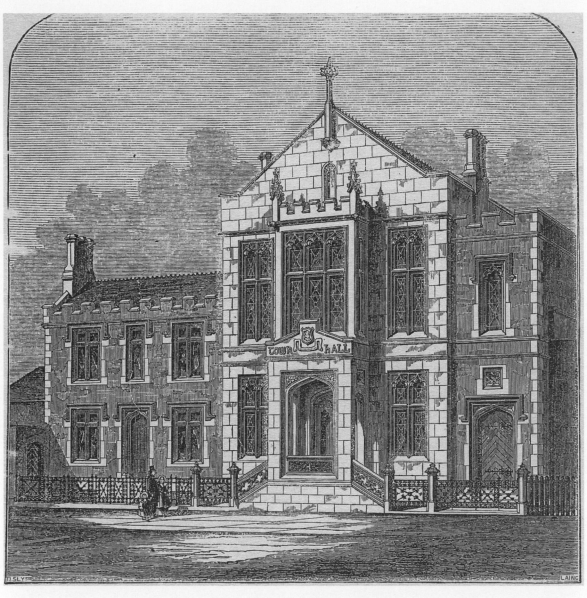

FIG. 25. OLD TOWN HALL IN 1852

with the rising poverty and its associated problems, nor could organizations of the 1880s like the university settlement movement.[69]

As early as 1834 the vestry clerk had seen salvation for Bethnal Green only in union with other parishes, not its immediate and almost equally poor neighbours but in the City and west London.[70] The Metropolitan Common Fund brought some resources from outside, for indoor relief.[71] A greater step was the replacement of the M.B.W. in 1888 by the L.C.C. and a consolidating Act in 1890 which enabled the latter to tackle large-scale slum clearance, beginning with the Nichol.[72] The Local Government Act, 1894, changed the qualifications of guardians and vestrymen, thereby weakening the landlord's grip.[73]

The parish still had four wards, governed by a vestry of 3 ex-officio and 57 elected members.[74] A former vestryman and guardian reported that they formed 'quite a different class' by 1898 but that, although they had inherited bad traditions and heavy arrears, they had appointed extra inspectors (by then five) and given them and the medical officer a freer hand.[75] The new guardians were praised for more careful administration, reducing the amount of out-relief.[76]

LOCAL GOVERNMENT FROM 1900 TO 1965. In 1900 Bethnal Green became a metropolitan borough under the London Government Act, 1899.[77] It was divided into East and South wards

69   Below, Anglican missions.
70   *Rep. Com. Poor Laws*, H.C. 44, p. 83 (1834), viii, app. B2.
71   J. A. Gillespie, 'Econ. and Political Change in E. End of Lond. during 1920s' (Cambridge Univ. Ph. D. thesis, 1984), 382.
72   H. Quigley and I. Goldie, *Housing and Slum Clearance*

in Lond. (1934), 52, 54–56; above, bldg. 1876–1914.
73   Jones, 'Casual Labour in Lond.', 460.
74   Gomme, *Lond. in Reign of Victoria*, 198.
75   *Lond. City Mission Mag.* lxiii. 65 sqq.; Jephson, *San. Evolution*, 383.
76   Booth, *Life and Labour.* iii(2), 103.
77   62 & 63 Vic. c. 14.

with 9 councillors each, and West and North, with 6 each.[78] A fifth ward, Central, was created in 1952, when each ward was allotted 6 councillors.[79] The council was headed by a mayor and five aldermen. It assumed some of the powers of the L.C.C. and was financed from a general rate, levied and collected like the poor rate which it replaced, together with any 'sewer' or lighting rates.

There were nine council committees by 1902:[80] survey, finance, works, public health and housing, law and general purposes, baths and washhouses, electricity, assessment, and records, besides special committees for departments and scavenging and for dusting. The department of the town clerk[81] employed a deputy town clerk, an assistant, and a junior clerk; that of the borough treasurer, divided between rating and bookkeeping, employed three rating clerks and five collectors, two bookkeepers, and a general and junior clerk; that of the borough surveyor employed three clerks and a draughtsman; the public health department had a medical officer,[82] eleven sanitary inspectors, three clerks, and a general assistant.[83] There was also a hall keeper and a superintendent and matron at the public baths. Municipal employees totalled 52 clerical and 334 other staff by 1909.[84] By the 1920s the public health department included, besides the medical officer, analyst, and seven sanitary inspectors, two food inspectors, ten health visitors, a chief clerk, and eight assistants. Among its other staff were disinfectors, a mortuary keeper, and, on a temporary basis, six part-time medical officers and a midwife.[85] There were 11 sanitary inspectors and 13 women health visitors in 1934,[86] and 9 public health inspectors in the early 1960s.[87]

After the move in 1889 to replace the town hall was defeated,[88] the vestry and the M.B. remained in Church Row, except the public health department, which was at no. 2 Paradise Row.[89] In 1908 the council acquired a site on the corner of Cambridge Road and Patriot Square, where a new town hall, was opened in 1910.[90] Designed by Percy Robinson and W. Alban Jones to include a tower and statues by Henry Poole, it has been termed Early Renaissance[91] or flamboyant Edwardian Baroque[92] with a 'pompous façade'.[93] A 3-storeyed 'weakly neo-classical' extension was built to the east in 1936–9.[94]

There were council elections every three years. The municipal electorate was at first confined to those owning or occupying premises as a tenant, excluding lodgers, the young living with their parents, and women. It rose from 14.4 per cent of the population in 1901 to 33.7 per cent in 1919 and 38.8 per cent in 1928.[95] The turnout varied from 45.5 per cent in 1937 and 42 per cent in 1903 to 20.5 per cent in 1956 and 24.4 per cent in 1962. [96]

Progressives, mostly small tradesmen, were dominant from 1900 to 1919.[97] Only four councillors lived outside the borough in 1902,[98] when they included two surgeons, four publicans, two butchers, a printer, a painter, a chemist, a tobacconist, a grocer, a corndealer, a photographer, a dairyman, an oilman, a brick and tile merchant, a sawmiller, a bootmaker, and a fretcutter.[99] Some later called themselves Liberals, among them Garnham Edmonds of Edmonds & Mears tripe dressers, a councillor in 1902,[1] religious and social worker and for long chairman of the Liberal Association, mayor in 1907,[2] member of the L.C.C. 1910–22,[3] and M.P. in 1922.[4] Of more proletarian origin was W. J. Lewis, born near Boundary Street in 1868, employed aged eleven in the book trade, influenced by Oxford House, secretary of the University club debating society, a trade union organizer and Liberal election agent, mayor in 1913,[5] and resident as an adult in St. Peter Street, close to where he was born.[6] A.J.S. (Tom) Brooks (d. 1954), a chimney sweep who lived for 40 years in Brick Lane, was a vestryman for six years, Liberal councillor for 28, and thrice mayor.[7]

Ratepayers, organized into associations by the 1890s,[8] lost their early importance as local government ceased to rely solely on the rates[9] and as a wider franchise brought in radical Jewish workers who had become naturalized.[10] The overwhelmingly working-class electorate did not vote solidly for the Progressives or, later, the Labour party, as sectional interests favoured parties of the right whether Municipal Reformers, Conservatives, or Fascists. Some casual poor, who lived mainly by cadging, were

78   Bethnal Green M.B. *Rep. of Procs. of Council* (1903), 3–4.
79   *Lond. Statistics*, N.S. i. 19.
80   Para. based on Bethnal Green M.B. *Rep. of Procs. of Council* (1903), 4–7.
81   Rob. Voss the yr., whose namesake had been one of the vestry clerks in 1857: *Metropolitan Drainage*, H.C. 223, p. 257 (1857-Sess. 2), xxxvi.
82   Geo. Bate, who had held the office under the vestry at least since 1883: *The Times*, 3 Nov. 1883, 10*f*.
83   Also a public analyst, based in Paddington.
84   *Municipal Year Bk.* (1909), 959.
85   Bethnal Green M.B. *Brief Acct. of Pub. Health Activities of Boro. Council* [1925], 3.
86   L.C.C. *Lond. Statistics*, xxxix. 79.
87   L.C.C. *Statistics of Metropolitan Boros.* (1960–1, 1962–3).
88   Robinson and Chesshyre, *The Green*, 9.
89   *Municipal Year Bk.* (1909), 225.
90   *The Times*, 16 Sept. 1908, 10*a*; 24 Sept. 1909, 10*c*; 2 Nov. 1910, 5*b*; G.L.R.O., AR/BA/4/190, no. 4.
91   Bethnal Green M.B. *Official Guide* [1921], 42 sqq.
92   Pevsner, *Lond.* ii. 69.
93   P. Marcan, *An East End Dir.* (1979), 106.
94   Pevsner, *Lond.* ii. 69; Bethnal Green M.B. *Official*

Guide (1950), 34–36; *The Times*, 18 July 1939, 11*g*.
95   L.C.C. *Lond. Statistics*, xvi. 20; Gillespie, 'Econ. and Political Change', 375, 377.
96   L.C.C. *Lond. Statistics*, xvi. 20; xxv. 27; xxx. 21; xxxix. 24; N.S. i 19; L.C.C. *Statistics of Metropolitan Boros.* (1937–8, 1952–3, 1955–6, 1960–1, 1962–3).
97   P. Thompson, *Socialists, Liberals and Labour, 1885–1914* (1967), 183, 313; *The Times*, 2 Nov. 1906, 7*f*; 3 Nov. 5*a*; 1 Nov. 1912, 10*a*, 2 Nov., 11*a*; 4 Nov. 1919, 14*a*.
98   Bethnal Green M.B. *Rep. of Procs. of Council* (1903), 3–4.
99   *P.O. Dir. Lond.* (1902).
1   Classified as butcher, above.
2   *The Times*, 11 Nov. 1907, 12*e*.
3   W. E. Jackson, *Achievement. Short Hist. of L.C.C.* (1965), App. II.
4   *The Times*, 2 Nov. 1922, 14*a*; 16 Nov. 7*c*.
5   Ibid. 17 Feb. 1914, 7*f*; M. McLeod, *Class and Religion in late Victorian City* (1974), 120 n.
6   *Municipal Year Bk.* (1909), 225.
7   Samuel, *E. End Underworld*, 264, 343 n.
8   T.H.L.H.L., TH/8258.
9   Gillespie, 'Econ. and Political Change', pp. x, xiii, 367, 373; *The Times*, 31 Oct. 1921, 14*e*; 21 July 1924, 18*e*.
10   *Jewish East End 1840–1939*, ed. A. Newman (1981), 256.

said to support the Conservatives from whom they received gifts.[11] Conservatives championed public houses, whereas the Liberals closed several in 1911.[12] Tom Brooks favoured temperance and was responsible for removing the Sunday market from the northern part of Brick Lane.[13] Cabmen and costermongers, organized in the Coster-mongers' Union, opposed teetotalism, traffic regulations in 1902, and Sunday closing in 1905.[14] Sunday trading had a long tradition and had generally been tolerated in spite of protests,[15] although in 1888 the vestry had tried to stop it[16] and in 1906 the M.B. had achieved more success.[17] In 1911 a clause in the Shops Bill for the M.B. to allow Sunday morning trading dismayed its mainly Liberal opponents, among them the rector, the head of Oxford House, and the chairmen of the board of guardians and the Public Welfare Association.[18]

Socialists, in the first years of the 20th century part of the Progressive alliance, began to organize during its second decade[19] and triumphed with 24 seats to the Progressives' 6 in 1919.[20] From 1919 to 1928 Bethnal Green was governed by an alliance of Labour and Communists. Joe Vaughan, London's first Labour councillor, was elected in 1914,[21] thrice mayor of Bethnal Green[22] and a parliamentary candidate in 1922 when accused of flaunting himself as a Communist.[23] Samuel Elsbury campaigned to enforce trade unionism as part of a Communist strategy;[24] he and his wife were both councillors, as were several couples on both sides of the political spectrum throughout the 1920s and 1930s.[25]

The guardians retained prime responsibility for the poor until 1929. In 1902, they included five who lived outside the borough, two women, and the vicar of St. James the Less. They employed five clerks, a collector, a settlement officer, seven relieving officers, five district medical officers, vaccinators, and staff at the workhouse, the infirmary, and the schools in Leytonstone.[26] The board was generally control-led by the Progressives and followed a policy of refusing relief outside the workhouse.[27] The workhouse held 1,161 inmates and 39 officials in 1901.[28] The respective numbers of those relieved outside and inside the workhouse were 479 and 2,603 on 1 July 1904, 533 and 2,683 on 1 January 1905,[29] and 372 and 2,862 on 1 January 1915.[30] The victory of the Poplar councillors led to a

sharp rise in able-bodied pauperism throughout East London in 1922, although Bethnal Green was one of the last areas to succumb 'to the general wave of Proletarianism'.[31] On January 1922 the figures for outdoor and indoor relief were 5,487 and 2,074[32] and in 1929 they were 7,524 and 2,151.[33]

The increase in outdoor relief did not represent changes among the guardians, whose election did not follow the council's. In 1925 their moderation was contrasted with the left-wing council's extremism. The board was drawn from the three political parties and included social workers, clergy of several denominations, the president of the Jewish synagogue, and the head of Oxford House,[34] M. R. Seymour, a Municipal Reformer and mayor in 1927.[35] Another active clergyman was Stewart Headlam.[36]

The borough sent two representatives to the L.C.C.:[37] Progressives predominated from 1889 to 1925, Labour from 1925 to 1928, Liberals from 1928 to 1934, and Labour from 1934 to 1946; from 1946 to 1949 North East Bethnal Green was Labour and South West Liberal. From 1949 the whole borough sent three representatives, all Labour except for Sir Percy Harris, Bt., 1949–52, a Liberal who had represented South West Bethnal Green 1907–34 and 1946–9.

The Labour-Communist coalition aroused the enmity both of the guardians and of the L.C.C. by calling for unrestricted out-relief[38] and by financial irresponsibility and political indisci-pline, particularly angering Herbert Morrison, chairman of the Labour Party on the L.C.C.[39] Although the new Labour M.B. in 1919 had inherited a mechanization programme for street cleaning from its predecessors, it paid its remaining 75 casual labourers weekly instead of hourly, introduced holiday and sick pay, and in 1921 put many casual labourers on the permanent work force.[40] By 1923 the council was threatened with legal action by the London auditor for overspending on wages.[41] In 1925 and 1927 it refused to accept uniforms from workshops that had not been approved by the unions,[42] and in 1926 Elsbury demanded a minimum wage and trade union clauses in municipal contracts.[43] By 1928 'illegal payments' had reached £28,000, mostly for paying equal wages to women and extra for Sunday work. An attempted reduction in line with the auditor's

11 Samuel, *E. End Underworld*, 30.
12 Ibid. 265.
13 Ibid. 264, 343 n.
14 Ibid. 290 n.
15 Above, econ. hist. (ind.).
16 *The Times*, 23 Oct. 1888, 3*e*.
17 Ibid. 22 Sept. 1906, 13*b*.
18 Ibid. 12 July 1911, 12*e*.
19 J. F. Bush, 'Labour Politics and Society in E. End during First World War' (Lond. Univ. Ph. D. thesis, 1978), 50, 53.
20 *The Times*, 4 Nov. 1919, 14*a*.
21 Thompson, *Socialists, Liberals and Labour*, 183 n.
22 *Tower Hamlets News*, N.S. i(4), Oct. 1972, p. 3.
23 *The Times*, 2 Nov. 1922, 14*a*.
24 Gillespie, 'Econ. and Political Change', 339.
25 *The Times*, 4 Nov. 1925, 9*a*; 3 Nov. 1928, 7*a*; 3 Nov. 1931, 12*d*; 3 Nov. 1934, 7*a*; 3 Nov. 1937, 19*a*; *Municipal Year Bk.* (1939), 1237.
26 Bethnal Green M.B. *Rep. of Procs. of Council* (1903), 7–9.
27 Thompson, *Socialists, Liberals and Labour*, 183.

28 *Census*, 1901.
29 L.C.C. *Lond. Statistics*, xvi. 74–6.
30 Ibid. xxvi. 70, 72.
31 S. and B. Webb, *Eng. Loc. Govt. Eng. Poor Law Hist* (1927), pt. ii, 903–4.
32 L.C.C. *Lond. Statistics*, xxviii. 62.
33 Ibid. xxxiv. 54.
34 *The Times*, 31 Mar. 1925, 16*f*; J. Bush, *Behind the Lines: E. Lond. Lab. 1914–19* (1984), 215–16.
35 *The Times*, 4 Nov. 1925, 9*a*; *Oxford Ho. In Bethnal Green,1884–1948*(1948), 80–1; M. Ashworth, *Oxford Ho. in Bethnal Green*, 29.
36 Below, parish church.
37 Para. based on W. E. Jackson, *Achievement. Short Hist. of L.C.C.* (1965), App. II.
38 Gillespie, 'Econ. and Political Change', 418.
39 *The Times*, 9 Oct. 1928, 13*a*; 31 Oct. 14*e*.
40 Gillespie, 'Econ. and Political Change', 76.
41 *The Times*, 31 July 1923, 4*d*.
42 Gillespie, 'Econ. and Political Change', 338.
43 Ibid. 77.

demands, led to scenes reminiscent of Merceron's years, with public protests and the singing of the Red Flag.[44] There was more controversy over council housing, first introduced by the left-wing M.B., especially when a scheme was named after Lenin.[45] To refute charges of corruption, race discrimination, and maladministration, the M.B. called for a public inquiry in 1927 and a councillor resigned.[46]

Rating, among the highest in London at 15s. 8d. in the £ in 1925–6 and 17s. in 1928–9, was the main issue in 1928 when all 30 seats were lost to the Liberals and Progressives.[47] The Communists continued to make noisy protests [48] but when Labour regained all 30 seats in 1934 it did not include Vaughan, Elsbury, or any other Communist or Worker candidate.[49] Elsbury was back in 1937 under the label of Labour.[50] Labour won all borough council seats after 1934, although in 1937 it faced new opponents in the Fascists. Anti-alienism in the 20th century had favoured some Conservative parliamentary candidates but had not been embodied in a separate party. A branch of the British Union of Fascists opened in Bethnal Green and put up candidates in the 1937 L.C.C. and borough elections.[51] Revived as the Union Movement, it contested South ward in 1949, Central and East wards in 1956, and North ward in 1962.[52]

Unemployment and bad housing continued to preoccupy the M.B. throughout the 1930s, whatever its political complexion. In 1930 the council considered a scheme of sewer reconstruction to give work to 450 men[53] but by the beginning of 1931 some 5,000 men and 1,000 women were unemployed.[54] In 1933 it sought government help[55] and in 1936 it again considered sewer reconstruction for some 500 unemployed.[56] Clearance and rebuilding re-emerged after 1945 as the M.B.'s most pressing problem.[57] Since Labour held every seat, any conflict was between various wards seeking priority for their own clearance.[58]

LOCAL GOVERNMENT AFTER 1965. In 1965, under the London Government Act of 1963, Bethnal Green M.B. merged with Poplar and Stepney into Tower Hamlets L.B.[59] It retained its five wards, North, South, East, West, and Central, each with three councillors,[60] until 1978, when it was covered by the new wards of Weavers, St. Peters, and St. James and by parts of Holy Trinity, Grove, and Park. St. James and Park wards had two councillors each, the other wards three.[61] Government was by the mainstream Labour party but the average turnout in Bethnal Green wards in 1974 was less than 19.0 per cent,[62] revealing a public apathy which aided the rise both of the far Left and of the Liberals.[63] The Liberals won 7 seats,

LONDON BOROUGH OF TOWER HAMLETS. *Argent on a base wavy argent and azure, a lymphad sail furled sable pennon and flying gules; on a chief azure between fire tongs and a weaver's shuttle a pale argent charged with a sprig of mulberry fructed proper* [Granted 1965]

FIG. 26

including all those for Park and Grove wards, in 1978,[64] 18 in 1982, and, as the Alliance (with the Social Democrats), gained control of Tower Hamlets council with 25 Liberal and 1 Social Democrat seats in 1986.[65] Tower Hamlets L.B. was then decentralized into seven neighbourhoods, governed by neighbourhood standing committees of ward councillors with their own resources. Most of Bethnal Green M.B. was contained in the neighbourhoods of Bethnal Green and Globe Town, with the eastern edge included in Bow neighbourhood.[66] The Liberal-Democrat alliance increased its lead to 30 seats in 1990 but lost control to Labour in 1994.[67]

PARLIAMENTARY REPRESENTATION[68]

BETHNAL GREEN, previously part of Hackney parliamentary constituency, was divided between the two constituencies of Bethnal Green North East and South West under the Redistribution of Seats Act of 1885.[69] They were combined from 1950 to 1973 in a single Bethnal Green constituency, which from 1974 was combined with Bow[70] and from 1982 with Stepney.[71] Bethnal Green North East was held by the trade unionist George Howell for the

44 *The Times*, 30 June 1928, 11c; 28 Sept. 16d.
45 Above, bldg. 1915–45.
46 *The Times*, 19 Sept. 1927, 9d; 23 Sept. 12a.
47 Ibid. 9 Oct. 1928, 13a; 3 Nov. 7a, 12a. The Progressives retained all 30 seats in 1931: ibid. 3 Nov. 1931, 12d.
48 *The Times*, 3 Dec. 1928, 16c; 7 Dec. 10e.
49 Ibid. 3 Nov. 1934, 7a, 13a.
50 Ibid. 3 Nov. 1937, 19a; *Oxford Ho.* 90.
51 *Lond. Jnl.* viii. 7, 12–13.
52 Ibid. 14–15.
53 *The Times*, 23 Sept. 1930, 9g.
54 Ibid. 13 Aug. 1931, 7f.
55 Ibid. 14 Feb. 1933, 7g.
56 Ibid. 3 Dec. 1936, 11g.
57 Ibid. 3 Nov. 1945, 2c; for housing, above, bldg. after 1945.
58 D. V. Donnion, V. Chapman and others, *Social Policy and Admin.* 60.
59 *The Times*, 14 Sept. 1963, 8a.

60 *Tower Hamlets News*, N.S. 3(2), June 1974, p. 5.
61 Ibid. 6(4), Oct. 1977, pp. 4–5.
62 Ibid., N.S. 3(2), June 1974, p. 5.
63 *The Times*, 1 Aug. 1984, 12b.
64 *Tower Hamlets News*, N.S. 7(2), June 1978, p. 4.
65 *The Times*, 10 May 1986, 10b.
66 *Municipal Year Bk.* (1987), 819; A. Cunningham and H. Watton, *Glimpses of Globe Town* (1988).
67 *The Times*, 5 May 1990, 5g; *Whitaker's Almanack* (1994, 1995).
68 Except where otherwise stated, inf. on elections, M.P.s, and voting percentages from F. W. S. Craig, *Brit. Parl. Election Results, 1832–85; 1885–1918; 1918–49; 1950–73; 1974–83*.
69 48 & 49 Vic. c. 23, 6th schedule.
70 F. W. S. Craig, *Boundaries of Parl. Constituencies* (1972), 173–5. From 1955 Bethnal Green constituency included part of Hackney M.B.: ibid. 49.
71 *The Times*, 14 May 1983, 4a.

Liberal or 'Radical' party[72] from 1885 to 1895 and by the Indian lawyer M. M. (later Sir Mancherjee) Bhownagree as a Conservative from 1895 to 1905.[73] It reverted to the Liberals under Sir Edwin Cornwall, Bt., chairman of the L.C.C., from 1906 to 1922 and under the former mayor, G. Edmonds, for a further year. Labour held it from 1923 to 1929, the Liberal Nathan (later Baron) Churt, a solicitor, from 1929 to 1933,[74] and Labour thereafter. E. H. Pickersgill held Bethnal Green South West for the Liberals from 1885 to 1900 and from 1906 to 1911. S. Forde Ridley, the Conservative member between 1900 and 1906, was supported by the Costermongers' Union and by voters alarmed at Jewish immigration.[75] The Independent Labour party contested a byelection in 1911 but lack of trade union backing was probably responsible for its low vote.[76] The Liberals won in 1911, the Conservatives in 1914, and the Liberals again in 1922, when the Communist candidate Joe Vaughan obtained 32 per cent of the vote. In 1924 Vaughan's share was 41 per cent and the Liberals'

42 per cent. Percy Harris (later Sir Percy, Bt.) held the seat for the Liberals from 1922 to 1945 when it passed to P. Holman for Labour, who held Bethnal Green's single seat from 1950 to 1966. Bethnal Green has remained Labour, Ian Mikardo being the M.P. from 1974 to 1983 and Peter Shore thereafter.[77] Communists put up candidates in 1929, 1931, and 1950 and the National Front in 1945, 1974, and 1979 from 1984 to 1986 there were attempts by the far Left to oust Shore.[78]

Although higher than at borough elections, the turnout at parliamentary elections was usually less than 70 per cent of the electorate and slightly lower in Bethnal Green South West than in Bethnal Green North East. The figures were 83 per cent in North East and 80 per cent in South West in January 1910 and 83.5 per cent at a byelection in South West in 1914. The lowest, in 1918 after a considerable widening of the franchise, were 31 per cent in North East and 41.6 per cent in South West. For the single constituency the highest turnout was 77 per cent in 1950 and the lowest 50.4 per cent in 1970.

PUBLIC SERVICES

WATER SUPPLY. Until the 19th century Bethnal Green relied on springs or wells. There was a conduit and lead pipes in Conduit close, part of Pyotts on the east side of Cambridge Heath, by 1601.[79] According to an 18th-century owner, the close contained a spring dedicated to St. Winifred in 1160 within a Gothic building from which copper pipes led to neighbouring villages and a monastery.[80] The building may have been erected by the Austin Friars to whom Richard II granted in 1394 land with a spring on Cambridge Heath, with permission to enclose it and bring water by conduit to their house in London.[81] In 1760 the 'conduit' was marked in the north of Conduit close.[82] The spring was sealed and the Gothic building pulled down when 'Bow water was laid into Bethnal Green', presumably in 1807.[83]

Simcock's or Sincook's well in the Great Hyde, mentioned c. 1399,[84] supplied the hospital of St. Mary without Bishopsgate before the Dissolution[85] and was there in the 1570s.[86] It may have been a well found in Old Nichol Street during work on the Boundary Street estate in the 1890s.[87]

By 1547 a well and conduit were 'of common use to the inhabitants' on the waste on the east side of the green, in front of the later

Kirby's Castle. Enclosed with a brick wall, it was apparently the main village well until 1652 or later.[88]

Another 'spring or conduit head', in Markhams field on the west side of Cambridge Road, was granted in 1567 to William Paulet, marquess of Winchester, with the right to lay pipes to his house in London, formerly of the Austin Friars to whom the watercourse was said to have belonged.[89] The conduit, mentioned in 1652[90] and marked in 1703 as the 'High Fountain' in the south-west corner of Sebrights, was too far from Cambridge Heath to have been the alleged spring of 1394.[91]

In 1723 a lessee of part of Bishop's Hall found plentiful springs and installed a well and pump,[92] although presumably there had been a supply at the manor house from the Middle Ages. A 27-ft. deep well, found in the garden of St. James the Less Vicarage,[93] may have served the farm buildings east of Bishop's Hall.

In 1807 Bethnal Green was among those parishes which, 'become very populous', did not have a sufficient supply of good water. An Act then set up the East London Water Co. and empowered it to draw upon the Lea and build waterworks and reservoirs at Old Ford.[94] In 1811 Bethnal Green village and its vicinity were said to be

[72] Bennett, 'East End Newspaper Opinion', 231; *The Times*, 11 Jan. 1906, 10f.
[73] *The Daily Telegraph*, 30 Apr. 1992.
[74] Samuel, *E. End Underworld*, 343.
[75] *The Times*, 2 Jan. 1906, 4f; 16 Jan. 11c; Bennett, 'East End Newspaper Opinion', 52.
[76] *The Times*, 21 July 1911, 7f; 25 July, 13b; 31 July, 8e; Bush, 'Labour politics and society in E. Lond.' 53.
[77] *The Times*, 14 May 1983, 4a.
[78] Ibid. 1 Aug. 1984, 12b; 7 Mar. 1985, 10a; 25 May 1985, 2d; 20 Jan. 1986, 2h
[79] B.L. Add. Ch. 39410; above, estates (Pyotts). 'Conduit' seems to have applied to the well or springhead rather than the channel.
[80] John Gretton, quoted in D. Hughson, *Lond., Brit. Metropolis* (1811), iv. 444–5.

[81] P.R.O. C 143/425, no. 24.
[82] T.H.L.H.L., Map no. 301.
[83] Hughson, *Lond., Brit. Metropolis*, iv. 445. For 'Bow water', below s.v. E. Lond. Water Co.
[84] P.R.O., SC 6/1139/21.
[85] *L. & P. Hen. VIII*, xvii, p.637.
[86] P.R.O., E 178/2986.
[87] L.C.C. *Opening of Boundary St. Area* (1900), 6.
[88] G.L.R.O., M93/158, ff. 22–23; Guildhall MS. 9171/223, f. 273v.; P.R.O., REQ 2/200/29.
[89] Lysons, *Environs*, iii. 418.
[90] G.L.R.O., M93/158, f. 10.
[91] Gascoyne, *Map*; above, estates (Sebright).
[92] Northants. R.O., X 1074 (xiii), Memo. 1723.
[93] *Tower Hamlets News, N.S.* i (3) Aug. 1972, p. 4.
[94] 47 Geo. III (Sess. 2), c. lxxii (Local and Personal).

properly supplied.[95] The company was laying large pipes in the parish to connect with its main reservoir at Old Ford in 1827[96] but it could not keep pace with the spread of building. By 1848 the water was said to be generally good but it was supplied only thrice a week for two hours at a time and many houses were not connected. Wells and standpipes, serving older houses, were often contaminated.[97]

An investigation in 1863 occasioned by the deaths of 12 children in Hollybush Gardens revealed that all but 3 out of 222 houses relied on a static tank and defective pump. Nichol Street had no supply.[98] Cholera in 1866 was associated with contamination by sewage from the Lea.[99] By 1867 the East London Co. supplied northern Bethnal Green from Lea Bridge and the rest of the parish from Old Ford works. Newer streets were supplied continuously and others for about 30 minutes a day.[1] In 1875 the company promised a constant supply to parts of Bethnal Green[2] but there were still streets with no water for their W.C.s in 1887.[3] The company was taken over by the Metropolitan Water Board in 1904.[4]

SEWERAGE. Drainage ditches or common sewers were recorded by 1660 near Kirby's Castle,[5] by the 1670s next to Shoreditch cemetery,[6] and by 1703 as forming the boundary between Bethnal Green and Mile End New Town.[7] Called Spitalfields sewer, the last was the responsibility of Tower Hamlets commission of sewers, to which Bethnal Green was assessed by 1723.[8] Until 1815 houses were supposed to discharge sewage only into cesspools.[9] A cat-gut manufacturer was presented in 1831 for polluting the sewer in Haresmarsh, presumably the main Spitalfields sewer.[10] Although the growth of building overburdened the existing system, the vestry opposed the commissioners' proposals for new sewers in 1826 because of the alarming expense.[11]

Fever around Lamb's Fields was attributed in 1838 to an area of stagnant water covering 700 ft. by 300 ft. and encircled by an open ditch into which the privies of North Street drained.[12] A gutter in the centre of Virginia Row received all the waste from the Nichol and Nova Scotia: in

1846 the London City Mission abandoned the Nichol after all its missionaries had succumbed to disease caused by the absence of sewers.[13] A detailed report in 1848[14] castigated Tower Hamlets commission of sewers and found that there were fewer than 8 miles of sewerage in the parish. Besides the old Spitalfields sewer and an ancient sewer along the east side of the green, part of which was open, there was a west–east sewer flowing into them from Shoreditch church along Castle and Virginia streets, Wellington Row, and Old Bethnal Green Road, and also east–west sewerage from Bonner's Fields and Green Street. Other sewers formed short stretches but there were none along Bethnal Green Road, Brick Lane, parts of Hackney Road, or the western and most densely built-up part of Cambridge Road. In 1847 house drainage into sewers was made compulsory[15] but in 1848 only 9 per cent of streets and courts were listed as sewered. In 1850 only 12 houses were connected to a sewer which had been laid a few years earlier between Pollard Row and Shoreditch church. Cesspools were seldom cleared and one open privy could serve 50 people.[16] In Town district only two houses had water closets.

The Metropolitan commission of sewers replaced Tower Hamlets commission in 1847[17] and contracted out the construction of sewers from 1851,[18] including brick sewers for the rest of Hackney Road and Cambridge Road in 1853.[19] Sewers were supplied to the Nichol in 1854–5[20] although houses were still not connected to them in 1863.[21] The Metropolis Local Management Act of 1855[22] divided responsibility between the vestry and the M.B.W., whose main middle-level intercepting sewer along Bethnal Green Road and Green Street was built between 1861 and 1864.[23] The board contracted for over a mile of brick sewer and the reconstruction of existing sewers in southern Bethnal Green in 1867.[24] The vestry by 1857 had effected a great improvement with many houses connected, the open sewer behind Hackney Road arched in, and the ditch in Lamb's Fields replaced by a pipe.[25] In 1863 Bethnal Green had 44 miles of streets, of which 30 miles were drained by the vestry, including 17 miles constructed since 1856. The surveyor's plan to drain every street awaited completion of the main intercepting sewer.[26] A contract for stoneware pipes was given at the end of 1863 to

95 Hughson, Lond., Brit. Metropolis, iv. 444.
96 Vestry mins. 1823–8, 22 Sept. 1827.
97 Gavin, San. Ramblings, 88, 92; Rep. of Bd. of Health on Cholera [1275], H.C., App. B, pp. 402 sqq. (1850), xxi.
98 The Times, 6 Nov. 1863, 9f; C. Bermant, Point of Arrival (1975), 83.
99 Rep. of Cttee. on Water Supply [4169], H.C. p. 168 (1868–9), xxxiii.
98 The Times, 6 Nov. 1863, 9f; C. Bermant, Point of Arrival (1975), 83.
99 Rep. of Cttee. on Water Supply [4169], H.C. p. 168 (1868–9), xxxiii.
1 9th Rep. of Medical Officer of Privy Council [3949], H.C. pp. 296–300, 307.
2 Ann. Rep. of M.B.W. H.C. 246, p. 41 (1875), lxiv.
3 The Times, 23 Sept. 1887, 5f.
4 H. W. Dickinson, Water Supply of Gtr. Lond. (1954), 95.
5 G.L.R.O., M93/3, p. 80.
6 Ibid. 7, p. 168; 8, p. 133.   7 Gascoyne, Map.
8 G.L.R.O., THCS 130, 250.
9 L.C.C. Main Drainage of Lond. (1909), 1.
10 G.L.R.O., THCS/62.

11 Vestry Mins. 1823–8, 7 Sept. 1826.
12 Rep. by Dr. Southwood Smith, chief physician of Lond. fever hosp.: Poor Law Com. 4th Rep. H.C. 147,p. 63 (1837–8), xxviii, app. A.
13 Lond. City Mission Mag. xi. 33.
14 Gavin, San. Ramblings, 7, 14–18, 31–34, 40–1, 53–5, 63–4, 84, map.
15 L.C.C. Main Drainage of Lond. (1909), 1.
16 Rep. of Bd. of Health on Cholera [1275], H.C. App. B, pp. 402 sqq. (1850), xxi.
17 L.C.C. Main Drainage of Lond. (1909), 1.
18 G.L.R.O., MCS 204/5/55.
19 Ibid. MCS 210/11/96.
20 Ibid. MCS 337.
21 The Times, 6 Nov. 1863, 9f.
22 18 & 19 Vic. c. 120.
23 L.C.C. Main Drainage of Lond. (1909), 1–2, map; (1930), 30; Ann. Rep. of M.B.W. H.C. 18, p. 61 (1866), lix.
24 Ann. Rep. of M.B.W. H.C. 34, p. 587 (1867), lviii.
25 First Ann. Rep. of M.O.H. in Bethnal Green (1857), 8.
26 The Times, 27 Nov. 1863, 10c.

Cole & Son for 48 undrained streets.[27] By 1872 'almost all houses' had been drained, mostly at the owners' cost, and between 1856 and 1872 13½ miles of pipe and 2½ miles of brick sewers had been laid.[28] By 1887 another three miles had been built by the vestry,[29] which was castigated in 1898 for leaving a defective sewer open for a fortnight.[30]

For storm relief between 1881 and 1884 the M.B.W. built the high-level and Ratcliff relief sewer along the line of Cambridge Road and from 1921 to 1928 its successor, the L.C.C., built the North-Eastern relief sewer from Hackney Road across Bethnal Green Road to Whitechapel Road and beyond.[31] In the 1930s the M.B. considered reconstructing the sewers to relieve unemployment.[32]

MEDICAL SERVICES. Among the earliest officers of the new parish were a woman searcher, appointed in 1749,[33] and a surgeon and apothecary for the workhouse, whose replacement in 1753 was to be paid £20 a year, to live in the parish, and to attend all 'except broken limbs, midwifery and persons who are foul'.[34] In 1790 the appointment of searchers was disputed between the vestry and the J.P.s.[35] Two women searchers were listed as parish officers in 1800,[36] but parish midwives were mentioned only when accused of incompetence in 1831[37] and of drunkenness in 1832.[38] In 1793 the office of surgeon and apothecary was held by a firm (Gilson & Bliss)[39] and from 1812 it was held by Frederick Agar, from 1817 assisted by his son.[40] A Frederick Agar still held the office in 1849.[41] Agar asked for salary increases in 1825 and 1831, claiming that in 1830 he had 2,000 tickets to attend the outdoor sick besides those in the workhouse and that he had to buy drugs himself.[42]

In 1818 the vestry paid 10 guineas to the fever hospital at Battle Bridge for the care of its sick poor.[43] In 1827 it opposed the building of a new lunatic asylum for the metropolis on the ground of expense.[44] There were many cases of fever, probably cholera, especially in the workhouse, in 1831[45] when the vestry temporarily accepted the government's advice to establish a local board of health, which in November was actively clearing 'nuisances', the breeding ground of cholera.[46] The vestry allocated £160 a year for the duties of surgeon and apothecary and, in addition to Agar, employed a doctor for the outdoor poor of Green and Hackney Road divisions and another for

Church and Town divisions.[47] The board spent most of the £2000 granted by the government for a cholera hospital, which was never built, a balance of £100 being used before 1859, supposedly during one of the later cholera outbreaks.[48]

Cholera returned in 1837-8 and in the quarter ending Lady Day 1838 the three doctors attended 521 cases and sent 26 to the London Fever hospital. There had been 2,084 cases of 'fever' in the parish in 1837 and it was recognized that in many parts sickness was always present because of bad drainage and sewerage.[49] In 1841 poorly drained houses in Bethnal Green Road and Cambridge Road were sometimes flooded to 2 ft. It was said that effective drainage might have prevented the 1,700 cases of fever 'arising from miasma' treated by the parish surgeon alone in 1838.[50] A death from cholera at a sweep's house by the canal near Pritchard's Road in 1848 was directly attributable to an immense dunghill; filth along the banks, condemned by 13 local doctors but left through the 'supineness or wilful neglect of the parish officers', was the alleged cause of typhus, scarlatina, and other fevers.[51] In the year ending October 1847 the five medical officers of health (recte district medical officers), attended 1,590 cases of zymotic disease, 119 of them fatal; 560 were cases of diarrhoea and 532 of 'typhus'. The average age of death was 26.6, having been 25.8 in 1839. More than a quarter of deaths were from epidemic disease, mostly of young children.[52]

Gavin's survey, published in 1848, conclusively linked the physical environment, for which he overworked such adjectives as filthy and abominable, with disease: 'typhus' from open privies and livestock in Paradise Row,[53] epidemics in the Nichol and Greengate Gardens,[54] and rheumatism and respiratory illness in the damp houses between Bethnal Green Road and Three Colts Lane[55] or in the oldest, south-west, part of the parish.[56] Cholera struck immediately after the report, causing 27 deaths in 1848 and a further 752 in 1849, mostly in Hackney Road and Town districts and including 211 in the Nichol in 16 days. Two fever wards in the workhouse received cases from the parish at large but the Board of Health found facilities 'totally inadequate'. It ordered the immediate appointment of an assistant for Agar, four medical visitors, nurses, two inspectors of nuisances, and lime washers; there should be more beds in the infirmary and full-time dispensaries

27 Ibid. 11 Dec. 1863, 4f.
28 Rets. from Vestries on Improvements since 1855, H.C. 298, pp. 16–17 (1872), xlix.
29 The Times, 8 Nov. 1887, 12b.
30 Ibid. 23 Nov. 1898, 7f.
31 L.C.C. Main Drainage of Lond. (1930), 30, map.
32 The Times, 23 Sept. 1930, 9g; 3 Dec. 1936, 11g.
33 Vestry mins. 1747–81, p. 27.
34 Ibid. p. 81.
35 Ibid. 1782–1813, p. 119.
36 Ibid. p. 247.
37 Ibid. 1828–31, p. 428.
38 Ibid. 1831–3, p. 98.
39 Ibid. 1782–1813, p. 167.
40 Ibid. 1813–21, f. 88v.; 1831–3, p. 42.
41 Rep. to Gen. Bd. of Health on Metropolitan Workhos. H.C. 133, pp. 827–9 (1850), xxi.
42 Vestry mins. 1831–3, p. 42.
43 Ibid. 1813–21, f. 111; M. D. George, Lond. Life in

18th Cent. (1925), 85.
44 Vestry mins. 1823–8, 28 Mar. 1827.
45 Ibid. 1828–31, 29 June 1831.
46 Ibid. 1831–3, pp. 47, 50–1.
47 Ibid. pp. 65–66, 81.
48 Endowed Chars. Lond. (1897), 13–15, 51.
49 Poor Law Com. 4th Rep. H.C. 147, pp. 62 sqq. (1837–8), xxviii, app. A; Rep. Poor Law Com. on San. Conditions of Labouring Poor, H.L. pp. 159 sqq. and map facing p. 160 (1842), xxvi; Rep. on San. Condition of Labouring Pop. by Edwin Chadwick, 1842, ed. M. W. Flinn, 8–10, 34.
50 The Times, 16 Dec. 1841, 7e.
51 Ibid. 25 Nov. 1848, 8f; 28 Nov. 8e.
52 Gavin, San. Ramblings, 94–6, 103, 105.
53 Ibid. 8.
54 Ibid. 42–3.
55 Ibid. 18.
56 Ibid. 34.

in each affected locality.[57] After five days the parish appointed one medical officer and one inspector of nuisances, ignoring the other instructions.[58] Gavin, however, as medical superintendent of the district, began visiting and reduced the mortality by 43 per cent in the worst area; 4,845 people received free medical relief in 54 days.[59]

The cholera outbreak of 1849 was the worst, with a death-rate of 90 for 10,000 inhabitants compared with 50 in 1832–3. It returned in 1854 when the death-rate was 20 and again in 1866 when it was 60.4.[60] Of the 3,824 deaths in 1866, 614 were from cholera and 181 from diarrhoea.[61] Although their causes were pointed out, there remained no hospital other than the workhouse. The five district medical officers provided free medicine and vaccination, treating 5,026 poor outside the workhouse, sick from all causes, in 1856-7.[62] Infant mortality was particularly high: deaths of children under 5 were 52 per cent in 1858, 60 per cent in 1862, 56 per cent in 1869–70, 51.5 per cent in 1896, and 49.7 per cent in 1898. An additional threat, according to the medical officer in 1893, was the 'colossal ignorance of working-class women on the subject of infant feeding'.[63]

In 1884 chest disease and rheumatism were common around Hague Street due to the damp caused by dilapidation and by laundering and sleeping in the same room.[64] Disease was still especially prevalent in the overcrowded Nichol in 1891.[65] In 1916 a council committee recommended the establishment of a tuberculosis dispensary in an agreement with the City of London Chest hospital. The M.B.'s provision for mothers and babies consisted of an inadequate shelter at no. 3 St. James's Road in 1917, when it was resolved to appoint, temporarily, a 'lady M.D.' as assistant medical officer of health with responsibility for maternity and child welfare, and to rent no. 505 Hackney Road for 3 years as a centre. Similar centres were then being contemplated by King Edward Institution, Spitalfields, in Green Street and by Queen's Children's hospital.[66] The council had agreed with the chest hospital to employ a tuberculosis health visitor and operate a dispensary with two medical officers by 1925, when it employed several visitors and ran welfare centres for mothers and infants. The main centre, with a dispensary and a planned dental clinic, was in Cornwall Road; another centre was in rented premises at Thornton hall in Mount Street. The

council also employed a midwife and wanted a municipal maternity home and day nursery in the borough. It had convalescent homes in Berkshire and Buckinghamshire. Home nursing was provided by Shoreditch and Bethnal Green Nursing Association.[67] St. James the Less medical mission and dispensary existed in St. James's Road in 1935.[68] The infant welfare centre in Cornwall Avenue (formerly Road) survived in 1950.[69] Bethnal Green health centre was built in Florida Street under the L.B.'s plan of 1986.[70]

Bethnal House lunatic asylum[71] opened as a private madhouse in Kirby's Castle between its lease to Matthew Wright in 1726[72] and the escape of Alexander Cruden (d. 1770), compiler of a biblical concordance, who sued Wright for false imprisonment, in 1738.[73] The building, extended and by 1777 stuccoed and called the White House, in 1800 was purchased by Thomas Warburton, who already owned a more select asylum in Hackney. Like other private asylums, Warburton's housed paupers paid for by their parish. It had 300 inmates, costing 9s. 6d.–10s. a head a week, in 1815[74] and 933, of whom 654 were paupers, in 1829-1830. By 1831 Warburton had built the Red House for men, the White House thereafter being for women only. Abuses were reported[75] although the presence of two resident medical officers after 1828 led to some improvement. The Red House was enlarged and the White House was rebuilt in the 1840s. Bethnal Green asylum housed 614 people, 558 of them inmates, in 1851.[76] It had 410 beds in 1892,[77] a new block for men from 1896, and 203 inmates and 60 staff in 1901.[78] The asylum closed in 1920.[79]

The epidemic of 1849 led to the opening in 1850 of Queen Adelaide's dispensary[80] with a resident medical officer in Warner Place.[81] In 1865 its trustees, led by the Revd. E.F. Coke, acquired a site at the corner of Pollard Row and William Street,[82] where a dispensary was built in 1866 in a Renaissance style, with an elaborate tower and cupola.[83] In 1868 Coke appealed for funds to aid the vast numbers of sick.[84] In 1889 the dispensary dealt with 6,656 medical and surgical cases and 3,248 dental cases.[85] It ceased to be a dispensary when it was registered as Queen Adelaide's charity in 1961 and governed by a scheme in 1963 to apply the income for the benefit of the sick poor of Bethnal Green.[86] The building was a nurses' home for Queen Elizabeth's Children's

57 *Rep. of Bd. of Health on Cholera* [1273], H.C. pp. 133 sqq. (1850), xxi; [1275], H.C. App. B, pp. 402 sqq. (1850), xxi; H.C. 133, pp. 827–9 (1850), xxi.
58 H. Jephson, *San. Evolution of Lond.* (1907), 47–48.
59 *Rep. of Bd. of Health on Cholera* [1273], H.C. pp. 133 sqq. (1850), xxi.
60 *9th Rep. of Med. Officer of Privy Council.* [3949], H.C. p. 339 (1867), xxxvii.   61 Ibid. p. 341.
62 *Ret. of Particulars of Unions, Parishes*, H.C. 230, p. 90 (1857-8), xlix(1).
63 Jephson, *San. Evolution*, 120, 138, 219, 393.
64 *Lond. City Mission Mag.* xlix 85.
65 *The Times*, 11 Mar. 1891, 3f.
66 G.L.R.O., Acc. 1844/B13/2.
67 Bethnal Green M.B. *Brief Acct. of Pub. Health Activities of Boro. Council.* [1925], 7, 10–13, 15, 18, 20–21.
68 *P.O. Dir. Lond.* (1935).
69 Bethnal Green M.B. *Tenants Handbk.* [1950], 25.
70 *Tower Hamlets Boro. Plan*, 1986.

71 Para based on Robinson and Chesshyre, *The Green*, 11 sqq.
72 M.L.R. 1727/4/12. And see estates (Kirby's Castle).
73 Hist. MSS. Com. 72 Laing II, p. 351; *D.N.B.*
74 *V.C.H. Mdx.* x.111; S. and B. Webb, *Eng. Local Govt., Poor Law*, pt. 1 (1927), 301.
75 K. Jones, *Hist. of Mental Health Svce.* (1972), 83–4, 101–12.   76 P.R.O., Ho 107/1540/21/2/[25], f. 696.
77 *Kelly's Lond. Medical Dir.* (1892), 328.
78 *Census*, 1901.
79 Above, building 1914-45.
80 *Kelly's Lond. Medical Dir.* (1892), 315.
81 P.R.O., HO 107/1541/21/3/17, f. 520.
82 Ibid C 54/16454 mm. 20–25; C.C.C. files, St. Jas. the Gt.(R. Pringle, 'St. James the Gt. par. hist to 1976', pamphlet).
83 Datestone; *Endowed Chars. Lond.* (1897), 57.
84 *The Times*, 3 Aug. 1868, 10f.
85 *Kelly's Lond. Medical Dir.* (1892), 315.
86 Char. Com. no. 232981.

hospital in the 1970s[87] but was derelict by the end of the 1980s.

The City of London Chest hospital[88] originated in a dispensary opened in 1848 on the site of Broad Street station by a committee of mostly Quaker businessmen. In 1849 they rented 4 a. next to Victoria Park, including Bishop's Hall and its associated buildings, which were demolished. In 1851 Prince Albert laid the foundation stone of a three-storeyed red-brick building with stone dressings and a central bell tower by Frederick Ordish, which opened as a consumption hospital in 1855.[89] A chapel was added in 1858,[90] and there were considerable rebuilding and enlargement in 1881[91] and further alterations in 1891,[92] 1899,[93] and 1928 when a surgical block and X-ray department were added.[94] The hospital had 164 beds, 1,200 in-patients and 56,000 out-patients in 1892[95] and 103 inmates and 46 staff in 1901.[96] Renamed the City of London Hospital for Diseases of the Heart and Lungs by 1923, it had 177 beds in 1931, more than half of them for the tubercular cases.[97] Bombing destroyed the chapel and one hospital wing in 1940 and in 1950 there were 135 beds and 5,727 new out-patients.[98] An out-patient extension and a teaching centre were added in 1975, a block containing wards and laboratories in 1983, and a new library in 1986.[99]

Two hospitals grew out of the epidemic of 1866. The vicar of St. Philip's, whose parish included the Nichol, appealed for help from the Mildmay Deaconesses. A fund in memory of the founder William Pennefather was used to establish a medical mission with a doctor and dispensary in a cottage in Turville Street in the heart of the slums in 1874. A disused warehouse nearby opened in 1877 as Mildmay Mission hospital[1] with three 10-bedded wards, for men, women, and children respectively, staffed by a doctor, three nurses, and five deaconesses as probationer nurses. It was demolished in the Boundary Street clearance scheme and in 1890 the foundation stone was laid of a hospital in Austin Street,[2] which opened as a five-storeyed red-brick building with 50 beds in 1892. It had 35 inmates and 30 'officials' in 1901.[3] It was extended in 1926 and 1938, damaged in 1944, and extended again in 1965,[4] bringing the total of beds to 72. Jacob Home and Sir Graham Rowlandson House opened for staff in 1977 and 1979 respectively. The hospital closed in 1984.[5]

Queen Elizabeth Children's hospital (originally North Eastern hospital, renamed Queen's in 1908), owed its origins to the same epidemic.[6] In 1867 two Quaker sisters, Mary Elizabeth and Ellen Phillips, rented a house in Virginia Row as a dispensary for women and children. In 1868 it was transferred to no. 125 Hackney Road, where 12 cots were provided and treatment was restricted to children. In 1870 the sisters purchased the freehold of no. 327 Hackney Road and began raising funds and charging 2d. for out-patients and 2s. 6d. a week for in-patients. In 1892 the hospital had 63 beds, 600 in-patients, and 15,282 out-patients.[7] A large gift by John Horniman started a building fund in 1893 and led to the opening of a building mainly fronting Goldsmith's Row, then in Shoreditch, with 134 beds. Boundary changes in 1899 brought the hospital wholly within Bethnal Green.[8] In 1901 it had 58 inmates and 26 'officials'.[9] Ear, nose, and throat and skin departments were started in 1910 and an isolation ward was built in 1911 on the site of nos. 331–5 Hackney Road.[10] Work expanded to rickets and anaemia, widespread diseases of poverty. Two annexes were built in 1918,[11] a new operating theatre followed in 1922,[12] and nos. 337–9 Hackney Road were converted into a dental clinic and staff accommodation in 1934;[13] a new out-patient department was opened in 1938 and casualty, pathology, and X-ray departments were opened in 1939. Bombed in 1940,[14] the hospital was amalgamated in 1942 with Princess Elizabeth of York Children's hospital in Shadwell as the Queen Elizabeth hospital for children. It had 157 beds and an average of 7,843 new out-patients in 1950.[15] Charles Hayward research building, by Lyons Israel Ellis, John McCain, and J. Jarvis & Sons, a concrete and glass tower 'slipped over' existing buildings, opened in 1972.[16] The hospital had 133 beds in 1993.[17]

Accommodation for the sick in the workhouse was inadequate long before the first attempts to acquire part of the Poor's Lands for an infirmary in 1889.[18] The guardians in 1895 bought the site of the Episcopal Jews' chapel and its associated buildings,[19] where they built Bethnal Green infirmary or hospital, three-storeyed and of red brick with stone dressings,[20] in 1900. It consisted of a central administrative block with three double ward blocks to the west. It had 619 inmates and 117 officials in 1901.[21] Additions

87 Pringle, 'St. James the Gt.'
88 Based on C. Poulsen, *Victoria Park* (1976), 67–9.
89 G. F. Vale, *Old Bethnal Green* (1934), 83; P.R.O., LRRO 1/2116, no. 37; B. Adams, *Lond. Illustrated 1604–1851* (1983), 500; A. Cunningham and H. Watton, *Glimpses of Globe Town* (1988), 28.
90 P.R.O., LRRO 1/2127.
91 G.L.R.O., MBW 1702, no. 26.
92 Ibid. AR/BA4/22, no. 26.   93 Ibid. 89, no. 5.
94 Cunningham and Watton, *Glimpses of Globe Town*, 28.
95 *Kelly's Lond. Medical Dir.* (1892), 302.
96 *Census*, 1901.
97 *Hosps. Year Bk.* (1931).
98 Ibid. (1950–1), pp. 323, 736.
99 Cunningham and Watton, *Glimpses of Globe Town*, 28.
1 Para. based on P. Thompson, *No Bronze Statue* (1982); Mildmay Mission Hosp., *The Mildmay* (1963) (T.H.L.H.L., 621.33, pamphlet); H.J. Cooke, *Mildmay, Story of first Deaconess Institution* (1982), 158–62.
2 P.R.O., C 54/19730, mm. 29–31.

3 *Census*, 1901.   4 *The Times*, 28 Oct. 1965, 14b.
5 Ibid. 26 Apr. 1984, 4f; *P.O. Dir. Lond.* (1979–80).
6 Para. based on *Brit. Medical Jnl.* 23 Dec. 1967, 733–5.
7 *Kelly's Lond. Medical Dir.* (1892), 313.
8 G.L.R.O., (L.C.C.)/CL/LOC/2/10, VII, 37.
9 *Census*, 1901.
10 G.L.R.O., AR/BA4/221, no. 5.
11 Ibid. 319, no. 5.
12 Ibid. 377, no. 3.   13 Ibid. 585, no. 3.
14 Vale, *Bethnal Green's Ordeal, 1939–45*, 4.
15 *Hosps. Year Bk.* (1950–1), 156.
16 *Modern Bldgs. in Lond.* ed. C. McKean and T. Jestico (1976), 52.
17 *Hosps. Year Bk.* (1985), 388.
18 *The Times*, 11 Sept. 1889, 12d.
19 C.C.C., Clarke, Demol. Chs., Jews' Chap., Palestine Pl.; below, churches (Episcopal Jews' chapel).
20 Rest of para. based on G.L.R.O., (L.C.C.)/CL/ESTAB/2/85.
21 *Census*, 1901.

included receiving wards in 1926, an extra floor on the central block in 1927,[22] and an operating theatre in 1929. The hospital, which still used the workhouse for extra room, had 650 beds in 1931.[23] It was bombed[24] and by 1950 was a general or acute hospital with 315 beds and 7,477 new out-patients.[25] Between 1978 and 1985 it was reclassified as geriatric and the beds were reduced to 199.[26] It closed in 1988[27] and was later demolished.

Under the National Health Act of 1948 Bethnal Green's hospitals were grouped under the Central group management committee of the North East Metropolitan region.[28] In 1966 the Central group amalgamated with Stepney group to form the East London hospital management committee.[29] Between 1970 and 1978 control passed to Tower Hamlets health authority.[30] By 1993 the only remaining hospitals, Queen Elizabeth Children's and the London Chest, were classified as Special Health Authorities, run by governors directly responsible to the Minister of Health.[31]

An old parish mortuary, possibly in Turville Street,[32] by 1879 was 'a standing local disgrace'. Despite ratepayers' reluctance to spend money, a protracted ecclesiastical suit reaffirmed the vestry's right to provide a new mortuary in St. Matthew's churchyard. Built by A. S. Judd of York Street, Globe Road, of Luton grey bricks mixed with Portland stone to plans by the vestry's surveyor, it opened in 1880[33] and was in use in 1902.[34] Alterations were made to the Turville Street mortuary in 1884.[35]

BURIAL GROUNDS. Although Bethnal Green never had a municipal cemetery, burial grounds were unusually numerous. To cope with the demand on Stepney's churchyard during the plague of 1665, a burial ground was enclosed on manorial waste north of Mile End Road and west of Dog Lane and the bishop licensed the parish clerk to bury parishioners there.[36] In 1670 it was described as west of the sewer[37] depicted in 1703 as running through the middle of Simkins Gardens,[38] which had replaced it after 1673.[39] A Jewish burial ground existed from 1761 to 1858 in North Street, not far from the plague burial ground.[40]

St. Matthew's churchyard (2 a.) was consecrated as a burial ground in 1746[41] but by 1819 was inadequate. The vestry stipulated that burial vaults should be included under the new National school built on part of the churchyard and finished by 1820, when 17 vaults could each hold 20 bodies.[42] In 1826 the vestry stopped the bringing of 'boxes or cases of bones' from St. Katharine's and other London churches to St. Matthew's churchyard,[43] where c. 50,000 had been buried by 1848.[44] In the cholera epidemic of 1849 the vaults contained 96 coffins piled up like 'bales of goods' and the common graves of cholera victims were a cause of sickness.[45] Burials in St. Matthew's churchyard and vaults were discontinued from 1853[46] and in the vaults under St. John's from 1856.[47] The churches of St. Peter, St. Bartholomew, and St. James the Less had burial grounds of c. 1 a. or less which were restricted from 1853 and closed in 1855.[48]

The Congregational Gibraltar (1792) and the Baptist Providence (1835) chapels, both in the north-western part of Bethnal Green, had burial grounds which were in use in 1848[49] but the first (c. ¾ a.) was closed in 1855.[50]

As a private speculation c. 4 a. of unconsecrated ground in Peel Grove, called Cambridge Heath or North East London cemetery or Kildy's ground after the owner or undertaker, opened c. 1840[51] with a resident superintendent.[52] It rapidly became overcrowded, especially in the cholera epidemic, and was used by the parish authorities. Some 20,000 corpses, buried six deep, were interred before its closure in 1855.

A private company opened Victoria Park cemetery in 1845 on 11½ a. of the Butler estate near the Regent's canal.[53] In 1846 a superintendent's house and a small mortuary chapel by Arthur Ashpitel were built by its entrance at the western end.[54] By 1856 burials were at the rate of 130 every Sunday and there were complaints about the cemetery, which was never consecrated.[55] After closure in 1876 the neglected ground was used by ruffians for gambling.[56] The Disused Burial Grounds Act, 1884,[57] prevented building on the site, which in 1885 became a recreation ground.

PARKS AND OTHER OPEN SPACES. Bethnal Green's largest open space was the 217-a. Victoria Park, started in 1842 and opened in 1845, which lay mostly in Hackney.[58]

22 G.L.R.O., AR/BA/4/437, no. 3.
23 Hosps. Year Bk. (1931), 362.
24 Vale, Bethnal Green's Ordeal, 1939–45, 4.
25 Hosps. Year Bk. (1950–1).
26 Ibid. (1978, 1985).
27 Inf. from E. Lond. & The City Health Authority, 1994.
28 Hosps. Year Bk. (1950–1), 145.
29 Ibid. (1970), 140.
30 Ibid. (1978).   31 Ibid. (1993).
32 G.L.R.O., MBW 1730, no. 27.
33 Ibid. MBW 1684, no. 26; The Times, 8 Nov. 1887, 12b; Builder, 13 Dec. 1879, 1389; 19 June 1880, 777.
34 Bethnal Green M.B. Rep. of Procs. of Council. (1903), 12.
35 G.L.R.O., MBW 1730, no. 27.
36 Ibid. M93/5, H. 100d.-101d; N. G. Brett-James, Growth of Stuart Lond. (1935), 194; Mems. Stepney Par. 107, 113.
37 G.L.R.O., M93/166.   38 Gascoyne, Map.
39 Lysons, Environs, iii. 446–8.
40 Below, Judaism.
41 B. Holmes, Lond. Burial Grounds (1896), 294.
42 Vestry mins. 1813–21, ff. 121, 144.

43 Ibid. 1823–8, 4 Oct. 1826.
44 Gavin, San. Ramblings, 86.
45 Rep. of Bd. of Health on Cholera [1275], H.C. App. B, p. 40 (1850), xxi.
46 Lond. Gaz. 9 Aug. 1853, p. 2184.
47 Ibid. 25 May 1855, pp. 2007–8.
48 Ibid. 25 Oct. 1853, pp. 2867–8; 29 Nov. 1853, p. 3470; 17 Nov. 1854, pp. 3513–14; Holmes, Lond. Burial Grounds, 294.
49 Gavin, San. Ramblings, 85–6.
50 Lond. Gaz. 3 Jan. 1854, pp. 4–5; Holmes, Lond. Burial Grounds, 295.
51 Based on Jephson, San. Evolution, 310; The Times, 21 Nov. 1928, 11b.
52 P.R.O., HO 107/1540/21/2/20, f. 583, p. 8.
53 Based on Holmes, Lond. Burial Grounds, 202, 235; J. J. Sexby, Municipal Pks. of Lond. (1898), 571–2.
54 G.L.R.O., MBO/506, f. 274; O.S. Map 1/2,500, Lond. XXVIII (1876 edn. but surveyed 1870).
55 Ann. Rep. of M.O.H. in Bethnal Green (1857), 13.
56 For map and list of tombstones: G.L.R.O., O/190/1–2; view c. 1850: Bethnal Green Mus., Cat. of Drawings and Prints relating to Hackney and Bethnal Green (1925), 48.
57 47 & 48 Vic. c. 72.
58 V.C.H. Mdx. x. 114.

The Poor's Lands in the centre of the green, acquired in 1678 chiefly to prevent building, for 200 years were leased as farmland and not accessible to the public.[59] When Bethnal Green Museum[60] was built on the northern section in 1868, the 2½ a. surrounding it were conveyed to the Science and Art Department for a public garden. Responsibility passed to the M.B.W. under the London Parks and Works Act, 1887.[61] In 1888 the Metropolitan Public Gardens Association proposed that the Museum garden be extended to the 6½ a. of Poor's Land south of Green Street, at the same time as the land was requested for public buildings. Pressed by the association, the Commons Preservation Society, and 'passionate enthusiasm among the poor',[62] the trustees in 1891 conveyed the whole 6½ a. to the L.C.C., which laid it out with shrubberies and a gymnasium as Bethnal Green Gardens.

Several closed burial grounds became public gardens. In 1883 the vestry considered a request by the rector to lay out St. Matthew's churchyard as an open space. Despite the bad state of St. Bartholomew's churchyard there were objections to what was seen as an attempted revival of the church rate and no further action was taken by the local authorities.[63] In 1884 the Metropolitan Public Gardens Association agreed to maintain St. Bartholomew's churchyard as a garden,[64] for which responsibility had passed by 1896 to the L.C.C. The Kyrle Society laid out gardens in St. Peter's churchyard which were maintained by the vicar.[65] In 1897 the rector agreed that the Metropolitan Public Gardens Association should lay out St. Matthew's churchyard, transferring the freehold to the vestry and in 1903 to the L.C.C.[66]

The association's most important acquisition in Bethnal Green was Victoria Park cemetery, whose freehold the Revd. Y. B. M. Butler agreed to hand over in 1891. It was conveyed to the L.C.C. and in 1894 reconveyed to the association which had carried out the conversion.[67] The tombstones were set against the wall and the converted cemetery opened in 1894 as Meath Gardens, named after the association's chairman.[68]

The L.C.C. came to be responsible for most of Bethnal Green's open space:[69] 77 a. of Victoria Park, 9½ a. of Meath gardens, 9 a. of Bethnal Green and Museum gardens, St. Bartholomew's churchyard (0.7 a.), St. Matthew's churchyard (1.8 a.), and Boundary Street gardens (0.8 a.), part of the Boundary Street scheme, opened in 1899. The M.B. opened gardens, all of less than

½ a., in Ion Square in 1895, at the Triangle, Columbia Road, in 1913, in Craft School memorial gardens in Globe Road in 1926, and in Pelter Street playground in 1928. Under the Transfer of Powers (London) Order, 1933, Boundary Street gardens and the two churchyards were transferred to the M.B.

In 1954 Bethnal Green had just over 100 a. with public access, which, for a reduced population, were still considered 60 a. too little.[70] The building of high-rise flats cleared more land, one of the largest areas being Weavers' Fields south of Bethnal Green Road, which was extended by the G.L.C. in 1965,[71] and others including Shacklewell Street open space, from 1973.[72] Tower Hamlets refused, on financial grounds, to accept the G.L.C.'s parks in 1969.[73] By the late 1970s there was much open space, mostly around housing estates and along the canal, although improvement was needed, especially in the planting of trees.[74] In 1985 the area west of Grove Road was cleared as part of a scheme for a canalside park from Victoria Park to Limehouse.[75]

PUBLIC ORDER. Policing, before the creation of the metropolitan police in 1829, was the responsibility of an elected constable, assisted by headboroughs.[76] In 1676 Bethnal Green hamlet was ordered to reimburse its constable, who had paid for a 'very needful' stocks and whipping post.[77]

Night watchmen by 1652 could shelter in a 10-ft. square watchhouse, 'lately built' at the inhabitants' expense on the waste near St. George's chapel.[78] In 1681 a watch of 14 men was organized[79] and in 1685 money from the Poor's Lands was spent on 'setting up the monument and four dials upon the watchhouse'.[80] The principal watchhouse was centrally situated, at the crossroads of Cambridge Road with Bethnal Green Road and Green Street. A second watchhouse stood at the junction of Bethnal Green Road and Brick Lane by 1694.[81] By 1746 the western watchhouse had apparently disappeared and the central one had been moved to just north of the madhouse (Kirby's Castle).[82] In 1748 the vestry decided to rebuild, using the fines paid by those excused from office.[83] The watchhouse was of brick in 1792[84] and was rebuilt on the Poor's Lands (probably the same site) in 1797.[85]

A second police authority consisted of the trustees set up by the Act of 1751,[86] which was

59 Section based on Sexby, *Municipal Pks.* 250–4; G.L.R.O., LCC/CL/CER/3/1; Allgood, *Hist. Bethnal Green*, 292 sqq.; above, the Green.
60 For museum, above, building 1837–175.
61 *Ann. Rep. of M.B.W.* H.C. 159, p. 580 (1888), lxxxvii.
62 *The Times*, 6 Nov. 1890, 4f; L.C.C. *Ann. Rep.* (1890), 55.
63 *The Times*, 24 Sept. 1883, 4f.
64 G.L.R.O., P72/BAT/68.
65 Holmes, *Lond. Burial Grounds*, 233, 294.
66 Ibid. 240, 294; L.C.C. *Lond. Statistics*, xxxix. 173; Old O.S. Map Lond. 51 (1914).   67 Guildhall MS. 21670/40.
68 Rose, *E. End of Lond.* 249.
69 Para. based upon L.C.C. *Lond. Statistics*, xxxix. 170–3.
70 L.C.C. *Lond. Statistics*, N.S. i (1945–54), 154.
71 G.L.C. *Mins.* (1964–5), p. 499.
72 *Tower Hamlets News*, N.S. 2(5), Dec. 1973.
73 G.L.C. *Mins.* (1969), 515.

74 A. Coleman, 'Land Use in Tower Hamlets' (TS. *c.* 1978, Rep. for 2nd Land Utilization Survey, T.H.L.H.L. Pamphlet 720).
75 C.C.C. file, St. Barnabas, Circular 22 Oct. 1985; *Tower Hamlets Boro. Plan* (1986), p. 172.
76 Above, local govt. (manorial govt.).
77 Cal. Mdx. Sess. Bks. v. 103.
78 G.L.R.O., M93/158, f. 24.
79 Cal. Mdx. Sess. Bks. vi. 92–93.
80 Allgood, *Hist. Bethnal Green*, 297.
81 C.L.R.O. Assess. Box 43, MS. 22; G.L.R.O., M93/132, f. 200; Gascoyne, *Map*.
82 Rocque, *Plan of Lond.* (1746).
83 Vestry mins. 1747–81, p. 19.
84 M.L.R. 1792/6/108.
85 Robinson and Chesshyre, *The Green*, 6.
86 24 Geo. II, c. 26.

designed, *inter alia*, to regulate the nightly watch and bedels. The trustees could direct the constable, who was to attend nightly with the headboroughs, to 'prevent mischiefs', detain wrongdoers in the watchhouse, and observe the watchmen; they could also levy rates and decide on the number of watchmen. The watch had apparently lapsed by 1780 when, following 'outrages' (presumably the Gordon riots), the vestry considered employing eight men to patrol at night.[87] In 1788, however, there were few watchmen and those were said to be always asleep.[88]

In 1754 the trustees and vestry jointly decided to build a watchhouse in the churchyard to curb body-snatching.[89] In 1792 a watchbox was set up in the churchyard, a watchman appointed at 10s.6d. a week, and a reward offered for the apprehension of grave robbers.[90] A patrol was appointed for the churchyard in 1804[91] and collusion with body snatchers was alleged against the gravedigger in 1821[92] and the sexton, gravedigger, and day watchman in 1826, when two 'old and leading offenders' were imprisoned.[93] In 1831 two local men murdered an Italian boy in the Nova Scotia area to sell his body for dissection.[94]

In 1816 the rector complained of the disorders connived at by Joseph Merceron and of the state of the police.[95] The vestry clerk James May, who was also clerk to the trustees, persuaded them to double the number of headboroughs to 28 in an apparently futile attempt to stop bull-running and dog fighting.[96] With the same object, 100 'sober householders' were sworn in as special constables in 1819.[97] In 1826 the activities of the ruffians denominated Bullock Hunters compelled the vestry to ask the Home Secretary for help.[98] Gangs of 500–600 met nightly in a brickfield in Spicer Street to cook food stolen from shops which had not put up their shutters early enough; they ambushed animals going to Smithfield and Barnet markets and drove them to the marshes, robbing anyone whom they met. Sir Robert Peel accordingly stationed 40 men throughout the parish and sent a horse patrol, whose arrests deterred the gang.[99] By 1828 the watch trust employed an elected constable and 28 headboroughs, 38 volunteer special constables and, as paid officers, a combined night beadle and inspector of watchmen, four horsemen, 49

watchmen, and 13 'sparemen'.[1] They, together with the watch trust, were replaced in 1829 by the metropolitan police.[2] Enthusiasm for Peel in 1826, when the Home Office had financed the police operation, contrasted with opposition in 1830, when a police rate of 4d. in the £ had been set to raise £1,300.[3] In 1834 the police were said to give little help to the overseers threatened by aggressive claimants.[4]

A police station for H division stood on the south side of Bethnal Green Road, almost opposite Turville Street, by 1870.[5] It was on land acquired by the M.B.W. at the western end of Bethnal Green Road in 1872 and was replaced by a station at the eastern end of the road, at the junction with Ainsley Street, by 1879.[6] In 1902 it was the headquarters of J division.[7] A new station at the rear of the fire centre behind Victoria Park Square was planned in 1986[8] but by 1988 the site had been rescheduled for housing.[9] In response to racial violence a second police station opened in 1976 in Brick Lane, to which 14 extra officers were allotted in 1987.[10]

FIRE ENGINES. In 1749 the beadle was granted £2 a year to look after a fire engine.[11] A separate engineer was elected to the office by 1760.[12] The watchhouse planned for the churchyard in 1754 was to have an adjoining engine house.[13] In 1775 the parish provided fire ladders which could be borrowed at a charge depending on their size.[14] In 1820 more than one engine was repaired[15] but in 1828 the duties of engineer were combined with those of night beadle and inspector of watchmen.[16] By the 1860s there was one person specially appointed to look after the engines, of which there were two, both 'in an efficient state'.[17]

The parish maintained its engine house in Bethnal Green Road, west of Squirries Street, until 1867 when it became a fire brigade station under the M.B.W.[18] By 1886 the building was inadequate and road widening made available a site at the north-west corner of Green Street and Globe Road, where in 1889 a station opened with accommodation on the eastern side of Globe Road for an officer and six men and, on the

87 Vestry mins. 1747–81, p. 410.
88 *The Times*, 18 Sept. 1788, 1c.
89 Vestry mins, 1747–81, pp. 85, 87.
90 Ibid. 1782–1813, p. 149.
91 Ibid. p. 291.
92 Ibid. 1813–21, f. 193v.
93 Ibid. 1823–8, 29 Mar., 26 Oct. 1826.
94 *The Times*, 3 Dec. 1831, 3a; above, building 1837-75.
95 *Rep. from Cttee. on State of Police in Metropolis*, H.C. 510, p. 151 (1816), v.
96 Ibid. p. 167.
97 *Morning Advertiser*, 12 Apr. 1819, quoted in S. and B. Webb, *Eng. Local Govt., Par. and County* (1906), 87–88.
98 Vestry mins. 1823–8, 7 Sept. 1826.
99 *The Times*, 19 Sept. 1826, 3f; 20 Sept. 3f.
1 *Rep. of Sel. Cttee. on Police of Metropolis*, H.C. 533, p. 352 (1828), vi.
2 10 Geo. IV, c. 44; *Rep. of Sel. Cttee. on Sel. Vestries, 1830*, H.C. 25, pp. 677 sqq. (1830), iv.
3 Vestry mins. 1828–31, pp. 231, 310.
4 *Rep. Com. Poor Laws*, H.C. 44 p. 106a (1834), ii, App. A., pt. 3.

5 G.L.R.O., MBW 2573; Old O.S. Map Lond. 51 (1872).
6 G.L.R.O., MR/UP 1397; *P.O. Dir. Lond..* (1879); the old police station was sold in 1884: *Ann. Rep. of M.B.W.* H.C. 186, p. 844 (1884–5), lxvii.
7 Bethnal Green M.B. *Rep. of Procs. of Council* (1903), 12.
8 *Tower Hamlets Boro. Plan* (1986), p. 179.
9 Tower Hamlets L.B. *Proposed Draft Alterations to Boro. Plan Proposals, 1988*, no. 115.
10 *Spitalfields News*, Oct. 1987, p. 3.
11 Vestry mins. 1747–81, p. 33.
12 Ibid. p. 161.
13 Ibid. p. 87.
14 Ibid. p. 348.
15 Ibid. 1813–21, f. 167.
16 *Rep. of Sel. Cttee. on Police of Metropolis*, H.C. 533, p. 352 (1828), vi.
17 *Rets. of Fire Engines (Metropolis)*, H.C. 322, p. 25 (1864), l.
18 No. 72 in 1867, no. 283 in 1886: *Ann. Rep. of M.B.W.* H.C. 34, pp. 41–42 (1867), lviii; ibid. H.C. 45, p. 33 (1867-8), lviii.

western side of Chester Place, for two horses.[19] The neighbouring no. 4 Chester Place was acquired in 1898 and the station was enlarged in 1907;[20] a drill tower was erected in 1912.[21] Plans to re-build[22] were delayed by the Second World War but revived in 1961[23] and a new station was built farther west, on the corner of Roman Road (Green Street) and Victoria Park Square, in 1966-7.[24] The old station survives as a Buddhist centre.[25]

GAS, ELECTRICITY, AND LIGHTING.

The Acts of 1751, 1813, and 1843 included provision for lighting. The first empowered the trustees to decide on the lamps.[26] There was at least one 'lighter of lamps' by 1768[27] but the existence of only a few lamps, serving for two or three hours in the winter, was cited in 1788 as a symptom of poor parish government.[28] Gas was presumably available by 1828, when the vestry discussed lighting St. John's church.[29] The building was to be heated with it in 1831,[30] by which time the parish was 'lighted with gas'.[31] The Act of 1843 allowed the imposition of a rate and empowered new commissioners to light the streets, 'saving the rights of the Independent Gas Light & Coke Co.'[32] The main supplier, however, was the Imperial Gas Co. to which £460 was paid in the first year, compared with £63 to the 'Incorporated Gas Co.'.[33] The parish had 648 public lamps and a gas inspection by 1854.[34] In 1855 responsibility for lighting passed to the vestry. The Imperial Gas Co. soon built gasholders on part of the Pritchard estate[35] and c. 1870 it added another gasholder, designed by its engineer, Joseph Clark, in a frame of 24 cast iron columns.[36] Between 1856 and 1872 150 street lamps were added and in 1871 the parish paid £3,475 to the gas companies for lighting.[37] The Imperial Gas Co. was merged in 1887 into the Gas Light & Coke Co., which in 1905-6 supplied all Bethnal Green except a small western part which was supplied by the Commercial Co.[38] By the Gas Act, 1948, the companies were superseded by the Gas Council's North Thames Board. The Gas Act, 1972, replaced the Gas Council with the British Gas Corporation, which was privatized in 1986 as British Gas Plc and included Bethnal Green as its North Thames district.[39] North Sea gas had made the gasholders next to the Regents Union canal redundant by c. 1978[40] but they remained in 1993.

The vestry undertook to supply electricity under an Act of 1899[41] but Bethnal Green was the only M.B. in north-east London still without it in 1903.[42] The M.B. acquired a site by 1905,[43] began to prepare a scheme in 1911,[44] laid cables in 1914,[45] and started supplies in 1916.[46] Applications to build substations were made for New Tyssen Street in 1915,[47] for Digby Street in 1916,[48] for St. Andrew's Street in 1927,[49] and for Vivian Road in 1936.[50] In 1937 the L.C.C. applied to build Electrical Transformer House in Waterloo Road.[51] In 1947 responsibility passed to London Electricity Board.[52] By the Electricity Act, 1989, the board was replaced by London Electricity Plc, which included Bethnal Green in its North Thames area.[53]

PUBLIC LIBRARIES.

A library in the church was to be locked by the vestry clerk in 1812, after books had been taken out of it 'improperly',[54] and was included in repairs in 1820.[55] After a failure to secure the adoption of the Public Libraries Act in 1875, Bethnal Green Free library was founded by the Christian Community in 1876. Initially in cramped rooms in London Street, it relied entirely on voluntary support, which included a gift from the Prince of Wales. In 1881 the library moved to the community's memorial hall in London Street and by 1882 it had been given c. 7,000 volumes. The library, an unsuccessful contender for a site on the Poor's Lands in 1888, survived until 1934.[56]

The borough adopted the Public Libraries Acts in 1912 and, after a delay caused by the war, opened a temporary library at nos. 1 and 3 Old Ford Road, on the corner with Cambridge Road, in 1919, the last of the libraries assisted by Andrew Carnegie.[57] In 1922 the first permanent public library opened in the newest part of the vacated Bethnal House asylum[58] with a red-brick neo-classical extension by the borough surveyor, A. E. Darby. Branch libraries opened

[19] Plaque, 1888, on bldg.; G.L.R.O., (LCC)/CL/FB/55; MISC. P/51/1-5.
[20] G.L.R.O., (LCC)/Cl/FB/55; AR/BA4/162, no. 4.
[21] Ibid. AR/BA4/235, no. 4.
[22] Ibid. (LCC)/CL/FB/55.
[23] Ibid. CL/HIG/2/163.
[24] G.L.C. Mins. (1966), p. 145.
[25] Below, Buddhism.
[26] 24 Geo. II, c. 26.
[27] Vestry mins. 1747-81, p. 263.
[28] The Times, 12 Sept. 1788, 2d; 13 Sept. 2a; 18 Sept. 1c.
[29] Vestry mins. 1828-31, p. 40.
[30] Ibid. 1831-3, pp. 58, 60.
[31] Lewis, Topog. Dict. Eng. (1831), i. 152.
[32] 6 & 7 Vic. c. 34 (Local and Personal).
[33] G.L.R.O., MR/UTJ/1.
[34] Rets. on Paving, Cleansing and Lighting Metropolitan Dists. H.C. 127, p. 161 (1854-5), liii.
[35] Stanford, Map of Lond. (1862-5 edn.); above, building 1837-75.
[36] Guildhall Print Rm., B3/P (Cutting, ? Illus. Lond. News, n.d.).
[37] Rets. from Vestries on Improvements since 1855, H.C. 298, pp. 601-2 (1872), xlix.
[38] L.C.C. Lond. Statistics, xvi. 375.

[39] Ibid. N.S. i. 194; Whitaker's Almanack (1995); British Telecom. Phone Bk. (1995), map.
[40] Coleman, 'Land Use in Tower Hamlets' (T.H.L.H.L. Pamphlet 720).
[41] 62 & 63 Vic. c. 140 (Local Act).
[42] E. Lond. Advertiser, 24 Oct. 1903, quoted in Robb, Working-Class Anti-Semite, 196.
[43] L.C.C. Lond. Statistics, xvi. 381.
[44] The Times, 23 Oct. 1911, 11c.
[45] L.C.C. Lond. Statistics, xxv. 435.
[46] Ibid. xxx. 285.
[47] G.L.R.O., AR/BA4/284 no. 5.
[48] Ibid. 297 no. 4.
[49] Ibid. 451 no. 3.   [50] Ibid. 628 no. 3.
[51] Ibid. 650 no. 3.
[52] L.C.C. Lond. Statistics, N.S. i map.
[53] Whitaker's Almanack (1995); Phone Bk. (1995).
[54] Vestry mins. 1782-1813, p. 408.
[55] Ibid. 1820-3, p. 26.
[56] The Times, 10 Apr. 1878, 11e; 19 May 1880, 10c; 24 Dec. 1882, 6c; Vale, Old Bethnal Green, 57; below, prot. nonconf. (Christian Community).
[57] T.H.L.H.L., TH/8327; E. Lond. Papers, ii (1), 31; The Times, 4 Oct. 1912, 8f; 18 Feb. 1913, 10e; 27 June, 6c.
[58] The Times, 4 Feb. 1922, 13c.

in 1935 in the disused coroner's court in Church (later St. Matthew's) Row, and in 1937 in a former shop at the corner of Roman and Vivian roads. The latter, bombed in 1940 and closed in 1942, was rebuilt on the same site, no. 369 Roman Road, in 1949.[59] A public library in Ravenscroft Street on Dorset estate opened in 1959.[60] and a music library was established in Mayfield House, the council estate opened in Cambridge Heath Road in 1964.[61] By 1990 the libraries were divided among the neighbourhoods: Bethnal Green library, still in its original buildings, in Globe Town, Roman Road in Bow, and Dorset in Bethnal Green.[62]

PUBLIC BATHS. The vestry adopted the Baths Act in 1895[63] and in 1898 built baths and washhouses in Cheshire Street.[64] In 1923 the M.B. purchased the site of Colman's starch factory, nos. 5–13, at the western end of Old Ford Road, where in 1929 the duke and duchess of York opened York Hall, public baths and a hall in a neo-Georgian red-brick building with stone dressings by A.E. Darby; it contained two swimming pools, Turkish, vapour, and electric baths, and washhouses.[65] The first-class swimming bath was converted into an assembly hall c. 1950[66] and Kenneth Wakeford, Jerram & Harris built a large new pool in 1965–7, the washhouses becoming a bar and kitchen and the remaining swimming pool a public hall.[67] Cheshire Street baths were derelict by 1988.

THE PARISH CHURCH

St. Dunstan's church, Stepney, served Bethnal Green until 1743. A domestic chapel existed from 1243 at Bishop's Hall, where a marriage was licensed in 1593.[68] There may have been a hermitage associated with the Austin Friars, who were granted land and a spring at Cambridge Heath in 1394,[69] and a chaplain dated his will from Bethnal Green in 1432.[70] He may have served St. George's chapel, which existed by 1512[71] and which, with its attached house, may have been the hermitage that stood near Bishop's Hall in the 1520s,[72] though bequests suggest that the chapel was used by villagers in the early 16th century.[73] In 1547 the bishop of London leased the 'chapel and messuage under one roof' on Bethnal green to Sir Ralph Warren for 99 years.[74] When the term expired the inhabitants used the chapel: sermons were preached there twice on Sunday and once on Tuesday. In 1652 the copyholders, with the steward's permission, had lately inclosed it and they asked for it to be settled 'to the same pious use'.[75] At the Restoration the owners of the manor appear to have reasserted their claim to it. In 1670 the lady of the manor leased to John Bumpstead the house with the adjoining chapel, 'anciently used for a preaching place'.[76] In the 1680s it was used as a school.[77] When the Poor's Land was set up in the 1690s the trustees were to meet at the chapel or chapel-house.[78] It was depicted in 1703[79] and Edward Barsham, a London goldsmith, in 1713 mortgaged what was still called St. George's chapel and house,[80] but it was decayed in 1716 and 'turned into houses' by 1720.[81]

A plaque dated 1553 on the house and extant Tudor brickwork in the cellar suggest that it was rebuilt by Sir Ralph Warren, his widow, or tenants.[82] Probably after 1647 the inhabitants repaired the chapel, to which a cottage was attached at the western end. The house was repaired either shortly before 1670, or by John Bumpstead before 1693.[83] That reconstruction is probably responsible for most of the existing building, which is either of the mid[84] or the later 17th century.[85] Edward Barsham may have carried out alterations dated by plaque to 1705 and possibly including new windows, stairs, and attic doors.[86] In the 1990s the building was known as Netteswell House.

Plate dating from 1635 and 1681 and given to the new church in 1746 may have come from St. George's chapel.[87]

In 1650 it was proposed to divide Stepney into four parishes, one of them to include Bethnal Green and another Cock Lane and Stepney Rents.[88] In 1711, after a petition by 36 leading

59 *Thirty Years Libr. Svce. in Bethnal Green, 1919–49*, ed. G. F. Vale (1949), unpag.; Bethnal Green M.B. *Tenants Handbk.* [1950], 34; Marcan, *E. End Dir.* (1979), 106.

60 *The Times*, 10 Apr. 1959, 6a; Marcan, *E. End Dir.* (1979), 106.

61 *Hackney Gaz.* 2 Oct. 1964 (T.H.L.H.L., 331.2).

62 C. Batt and A. Scott, *Dir. of Lond. Pub. Librs.* (1990).

63 Thompson, *Socialists, Liberals and Labour, 1885–1914*, 183.

64 G.L.R.O., AR/BA 4/80, no. 6.

65 T.H.L.H.L., TH/6947; *The Times*, 18 Jan. 1924, 21a; 6 Nov. 1929, 19d; Robinson and Chesshyre, *The Green*, 20; *Municipal Yr. Bk.* (1939), 1237.

66 Bethnal Green M.B. *Tenants Handbk.* [1950], 33.

67 *Tower Hamlets News*, 1(2), July 1965, p. 10; 3(2), June 1967, p. 22; Cunningham and Watton, *Glimpses of Globe Town*, 20.

68 Above, Stepney (man.); *Marriage Regs. of St. Dunstan's Stepney*, ed. T. Colyer-Fergusson (1898), i. 30.

69 P.R.O., C143/425, no. 24; above, pub. svces.

70 Guildhall MS. 9171/3, f. 299v.

71 *L. & P. Hen. VIII*, ii (2), p. 1453.

72 P.R.O., C 1/728/11. A close lay 'between the manor [house] and the hermitage'.

73 Guildhall MS. 9171/9, f. 162v.

74 G.L.R.O., M93/158, f. 24.

75 Guildhall MS. 9531/12, f. 123

76 P.R.O., C 10/512/66.

77 Below, educ. (private schs.).

78 Identified as St. George's by its position 'near the watchhouse': H. G. C. Allgood, *Hist. of Bethnal Green* (1894), 301.

79 Gascoyne, *Map*.

80 M.L.R. 1713/5/96.

81 G. Barnes, *Stepney Chs.* (1967), 15; Stow, *Survey*, ii. 47. Earlier edns. of Stow make no reference to it.

82 *Bricks and Mortar. Some Important Bldgs. in Tower Hamlets*, ed. H. Ward, D. Keeling, H. Cooke, B. Nurse and B. Jackson, no. 7.

83 P.R.O., C 10/512/66.

84 Pevsner, *Lond.* ii. 70; *Bricks and Mortar*, no. 7.

85 Hist. Mon. Com. *E. Lond.* 9.

86 Pevsner, *Lond.* ii. 70; Hist. Mon. Com. *E. Lond.* 9.

87 Hist. Mon. Com. *E. Lond.* 8.

88 *Home Counties Mag.* iii. 221–3.

inhabitants, the Commissioners for Building Fifty New Churches agreed that Bethnal Green should be a parish with its own church. A site was found in the most populated part, in Harefield east of Brick lane, and plans were drawn up for a church in the style of the 4th century, 'the purest times of Christianity', with room for the charity school and a parsonage, but negotiations with Thomas Sclater, the putative owner, lapsed in 1716.[89] Another petition in 1724 complained that inhabitants had to attend Shoreditch parish church or Sir George Wheler's tabernacle in Spitalfields, 'an annual charge' and an incitement to dissent.[90] The commissioners purchased 2+ a. east of the Harefields site from Charles White in 1725 but again nothing was done, in spite of five petitions between 1725 and 1738,[91] possibly because Stepney resisted the loss of offerings and garden pennies, estimated in 1727 at £169 a year from 4,219 communicants in Bethnal Green and Mile End New Town.[92] Presumably convinced that the lack of a church had led to dissoluteness among the young and poor and to an exodus of 'the better sort', the commissioners finally agreed to a Bill; yet more convincing was the inhabitants' readiness to pay for the building. In 1743 an Act made Bethnal Green a separate rectory, the advowson and great tithes to remain with Brasenose College, Oxford, the surplice fees to go to the new rector, and small tithes, garden pennies, Easter offerings, and burial fees to the churchwardens, who were to pay the rector £130 a year.[93]

In 1843 the advowson was exchanged by Brasenose for that of Weeley (Essex), the property of the bishop of London, by that time patron of most of the district churches in Bethnal Green. He first exercised it on the death of the incumbent rector in 1861 and remained the patron in 1995.[94]

In 1812 the rector sought an increase in salary, commensurate with the dues raised in his name.[95] King's remuneration became an issue in his struggle with Joseph Merceron, some of whose supporters for long refused on principle to pay the rector's salary,[96] despite the passing

in 1813 of an Act which secured £400 a year for the rector from dues such as those for tolling bells or for burials but not from the poor rates.[97] In 1845 a further Act[98] replaced small tithes, garden pennies, and Easter offerings by a fixed composition rate, of which £400 a year was for the rector and the rest for maintaining worship and repairing the churches of St. Matthew and St. John. The composition was abolished in 1898 when the vestry agreed to pay £20,000 to the Ecclesiastical Commissioners, who would pay £2,000 to the Incorporated Church Building Society for the fabric of the two churches and, from the rest, pay £350 a year to the rector and £190 for the salaries of church officials.[99]

A 'house for the minister' was planned in 1746[1] and, although not marked on maps until the 1790s,[2] existed by 1767;[3] its repair was discussed in 1789.[4] The Rectory was east of the churchyard and in 1823 the rector Joshua King purchased a strip to the east to prevent those 'wanting to incommode the incumbent' from building cottages and privies up to the garden wall.[5] A new Rectory was built in 1905, a plain but substantial building of red brick.[6]

All the rectors appointed by Brasenose were fellows of the college, mostly absentees and pluralists who retained the benefice for life.[7] The second rector was present for part of the 1750s.[8] Almost a century was covered by the incumbencies of William Loxham, 1766–1809 and Joshua King, 1809–61. Loxham, thought never to have set foot in the parish, was, according to King, driven out after less than six months by the aggressive system which dominated Bethnal Green.[9] King, a 'fine portly man', 'strong Tory', and sportsman,[10] started as a young campaigner against Merceron's faction[11] but in 1821 he became rector of Woodchurch (Ches.), a wealthier and less populous parish,[12] where he decided to reside from 1823.[13] For a few years he returned in May or June, possibly to chair vestry meetings,[14] but his interest in Bethnal Green narrowed to the rights, mostly financial, of the rectory and his letters became increasingly intemperate, both with regard to the bishop and to the young curates of the new

89 E. G. W. Bill, *Queen Anne Chs.* (1979), 39; *Commissions for Bldg. Fifty New Chs.*, ed. M. H. Port (Lond. Rec. Soc. xxiii), 5, 7, 35, 41, 43–4, 48–9, 146, 151, 155, 162; Lambeth Pal. Libr. MSS. 2712, f. 179; 2750/16.

90 Lambeth Pal. Libr. MS. 2712, ff. 182–3.

91 Ibid. MS. 2728, f. 7; Bill, *Queen Anne Chs.* 18, 39–40, 48, 105; *Com. for Bldg. Fifty New Chs.*, ed. Port, 114, 117–19, 129–30, 144.

92 Lambeth Pal. Libr. MS. 2713, ff. 234–5.

93 Ibid. MS. 2728, ff. 5–6; *C.J.* xxiv. 369; 16 Geo II, c. 28.

94 BNC, B12, letters 386, 545; *Brasenose Quartercentenary Monographs*, vi. 51; Hennessy, *Novum Rep.* 414; *Crockford* (1995–6).

95 BNC, Second Ser. [Tower] 148, letter from Joshua King 16 May 1812; vestry mins. 1782–1813, pp. 385–7.

96 BNC, Bethnal Green 3, letter to R. Heber, M.P., c. 1823; 1823: vestry mins. 1823–8, pp. 25–9.

97 53 Geo. III, c. 113 (Local and Personal).

98 8 & 9 Vic. c. 180 (Local and Personal); E. C. Rayner, *Story of the Christian Community 1685–1909* (1909) (T.H.L.H.L. 226.3).

99 61 & 62 Vic. c. 13 (Local Act).

1 Guildhall MS. 9531/20, pt. 1, f. 102v.

2 Horwood, *Plan.* (1792–9).

3 Lambeth Pal. Libr., Fulham papers, Osbaldeston 5, ff. 40–1.

4 Vestry mins. 1782–1813, p. 107.

5 BNC, Bethnal Green 3, letters from King 29 Mar., 5 May 1823; Bethnal Green 9–10.

6 C.C.C. files, St. Mat., TS. hist.; G.L.R.O., AR/BA/4/108, no. 6; Bethnal Green M.B. *Official Guide* [1921], 74.

7 Hennessy, *Novum Rep.* 414; *Alumni Oxon.* i. 167, 341; ii. 796; iii. 878; *Brasenose Coll. Reg. 1509–1909* (Oxf. Hist. Soc. lv), ii. 68; Guildhall MS. 9557, f. 42.

8 G.L.R.O., P72/MTW/37.

9 BNC, Bethnal Green 3, letter to R. Heber c. 1823; K. Leech, P. J. E. Eyre and J. Oldland, *Hist. Par. and Ch of St. Mat. and St. Jas, Bethnal Green* (pamphlet, 1984).

10 *Trans. Hist. Soc. Lancs. & Ches.* N.S xvii. 154.

11 Above, local govt. (par. govt. 1743–1836).

12 BNC, Bethnal Green 3, letter to Heber c. 1823. In 1859 Woodchurch (pop. 920) valued at £827 and St. Mat., Bethnal Green (pop. 7,961) at £614: *Clergy List* (1859).

13 BNC, Bethnal Green 3, letters by King 25 Apr., 27 May, 4 Nov. 1823.

14 G.L.R.O., P72/MTW/92.

district churches, whose insubordination he attributed to the philanthropist William Cotton (d.1866).[15]

Timothy Gibson (d. 1864), assistant curate from 1842,[16] was presented as rector in 1861 in response to popular demand. A non-graduate who was awarded a Lambeth D.D., Gibson had presided over the creation of the ten district churches and shown sympathy for the poor.[17] He was followed by Septimus Cox Holmes Hansard, 1864–95, an Oxford M.A. and High Church Socialist, a friend of F. D. Maurice and active in attending the cholera victims in 1866, when he was assisted by Edward Pusey. Hansard introduced a daily Eucharist and the reservation of the sacrament, campaigned for Bethnal Green Museum and a free library, and was sympathetic to trade unions. He was, however, autocratic, lived in some style and, like King, aroused hostility in local church and education officials.[18] Such hostility probably explains why in 1898 St. Matthew's was said to have been neglected for a long time before the incumbency of Arthur Foley Winnington-Ingram, 1895–7.[19] Winnington-Ingram (d.1946), later bishop of Stepney and then of London, had been head of Oxford House since 1888 and stimulated mission and social activities.[20] Attendances increased dramatically and the High Church tradition was intensified under Christopher Bedford (from 1981), to such an extent that wholesale conversion to Roman Catholicism was initiated after the passing of the Priests (Ordination of Women) Measure in 1993. The church was used for both Anglican and Roman Catholic services in 1996.[21]

Curates assumed importance from the rector's absenteeism. There was probably a lecturer and assistant curate from the foundation of the parish. An unendowed lecturer, Joseph Cookson from 1749 to 1791, gave the afternoon sermon on Sundays.[22] Appointment by the parish rather than by the rector was one of King's grievances.[23] An assistant curate, recorded in 1766,[24] was paid £45 a year in 1773[25] and £60 a year in 1810, and lived in the parsonage,[26] although in 1785 the vestry protested that it had no resident clergy.[27] In 1789 there was a conflict between churchgoers and allegedly more casual attenders over the appointment of a curate, the rector having promised to consult the parish.[28] King paid £40 a year for an occasional assistant in 1812[29] and in his later absence the curates John Mayne and Timothy Gibson occupied the parsonage.[30] Bishop Blomfield, who objected to non-residence, wished for a second assistant curate in 1832 but King maintained that Mayne was not overworked. The curate had accepted additional posts as afternoon lecturer, chaplain at the asylum, and private schoolmaster,[31] probably needing to supplement his pittance from the rector. Gibson, senior curate and lecturer from 1842, made appeals for the destitute, earning their affection and the wrath of other local ministers.[32] The most notable curate was Stewart Headlam, 1873–8, who shared S.C.H. Hansard's Christian Socialism, lived in working men's flats, joined radical clubs, and in 1877 started the parish guild of St. Matthew. He also organized debates, one with Charles Bradlaugh, and later became a member of the School Board for London and afterwards of the L.C.C. An associate of Bernard Shaw and the Fabians, his views proved too strong even for Hansard, who in 1877 dismissed him after the bishop's wrath was aroused by the publication of Headlam's lecture supporting the theatre.[33] From 1873 there were usually two assistant curates and from the 1890s to 1939 often three or four, especially during the period of close association with Oxford House.[34] Their duties, running clubs and dealing with applications for material help, were largely those of social workers.[35] In 1962 the curate, a declared anti-capitalist, was actively involved in a campaign against increased rent.[36]

By 1767 services were held twice on Sundays, twice on weekdays, and on all holidays; the sacrament was given once a month,[37] to c. 50 communicants between 1778 and 1810.[38] The organ was provided with a blower by the workhouse at 2s. 6d. a quarter.[39] In 1827 there were prayers and two sermons on Sunday and prayers on Wednesday and Friday. The sacrament was administered on the first Sunday in the month and at the great festivals.[40] Morning and evening Sunday services were fully choral by 1866, with the litany and a sermon on Sunday afternoons and Wednesday evenings and at the great

15 BNC, Second Ser. [Tower] 148, letters from King 17 Feb., 4 Oct. 1832; BNC, B12, letters from King 1843.
16 P.R.O., HO 129/21/4/1/1.
17 C.C.C. files, St. Mat., TS. hist.; *The Times*, 17 Feb. 1860, 5c.
18 C.C.C. files, St. Mat., TS. hist.; Leech and others, *Hist. St. Mat.*; Hennessy, *Novum Rep.* 414; F. G. Bettany, *Stewart Headlam* (1926), 35–6; H. P. Liddon, *Life of E. B. Pusey* (1897), iv. 142–4; J. Reeves, *Recollections of a Sch. Attendance Officer* (1913), 20.
19 Booth, *Life and Lab.* iii(2), 77.
20 M. Ashworth, *Oxford Ho. in Bethnal Green*, 10; Leech and others, *Hist. St. Mat.*; D.N.B. For Oxford Ho., below, Anglican missions.
21 *Daily Telegraph*, 19 Apr. 1993, 4; 18 July 1994, 7; inf. from chwdn.
22 Lambeth Pal. Libr., Fulham Papers, Lowth 5, ff. 386–9; Randolph 14, f. 65; Vestry mins. 1747–81, p. 31; 1782–1813, pp. 143, 148.
23 BNC, Bethnal Green 3, letter from King 2 Dec. 1822.
24 Guildhall MS. 9537/40.
25 Ibid. MS. 9557, f. 42.
26 Lambeth Pal. Libr., Fulham Papers, Osbaldeston 5,

ff. 40–1; Randolph 11/21.
27 Vestry mins. 1782–1813, p. 30.
28 Ibid. p. 97.
29 BNC, Bethnal Green 3, letter from King 2 Dec. 1822.
30 Ibid. B12, letter from King 5 June 1843; P.R.O., HO 129/21/4/1/1.
31 BNC, Second Ser. [Tower] 148, letter from King 17 Feb. 1832.
32 *The Times*, 15 Feb. 1860, 11a; 17 Feb. 5c.
33 Bettany, *Stewart Headlam*, 34–48, 79–81, 145, 148–9, 157; W. S. Smith, *The Lond. Heretics, 1870–1914* (1967), 181–3.
34 G.L.R.O., P72/MTW/137/1; below Anglican missions.
35 G.L.R.O., MTW/140.
36 *Daily Worker*, 6 July 1962 (G.L.R.O., P72/MTW/141/1).
37 Lambeth Pal. Libr., Fulham Papers, Osbaldeston 5, ff. 40–1.
38 Ibid. Lowth 5, ff. 386–9; Porteus 28/57; Randolph 11/21; Guildhall MS. 9557, f. 42.
39 Vestry mins. 1782–1813, p. 33.
40 BNC, Second Ser. [Tower] 148, reply to questions by Com. for Bldg. Chs. 7 May 1827.

festivals. Holy Communion twice on Sunday mornings and on saints' days had been added by 1881.[41]

The church accommodated 1,200 in 1816, when it and was 'overflowing',[42] and 2,000 by 1838.[43] All sittings were free in 1851, when 560 adults and 400 children attended in the morning and 650 adults and 380 children in the afternoon. There was no evening service and Gibson explained that, while attendance had suffered from the building of the district churches, it had improved since 1842.[44] In 1886 worshippers numbered 378 in the morning and 896 in the evening,[45] making St. Matthew's the best attended church in Bethnal Green. It was no longer so in 1903, with 421 in the morning and 261 in the evening.[46]

The parish guild of St. Matthew, founded by Stewart Headlam in 1877, promoted the Eucharist and by 1890 had 200 members, 70 of them clergy. Its other aims being political and social, its battles with secularists made it a pioneer of Christian Socialism. Membership reached 364 in the 1890s but by 1909 Headlam thought that the guild had become only another socialist debating society and dissolved it.[47] St. Matthew's mission at no. 203 Bethnal Green Road, formerly the nonconformist Hope Town mission, existed by c. 1898 and was taken over by Oxford House in 1924.[48] A parish hall, built south of the Rectory in 1904, housed St. Matthew's club, formed c. 1901, by the 1920s.[49]

The church of ST. MATTHEW, in St. Matthew's (formerly Church) Row, was begun in 1743 and consecrated in 1746.[50] George Dance the elder designed a 'neat, commodious edifice' of brick with stone dressings,[51] with two tiers of round-headed windows and a short, square, western tower.[52] Substantial repairs, largely to the roof, were undertaken in 1787[53] and in 1795 the communion table was within a recess at the east end, with galleries on the other three sides.[54] The Society for Promoting the Building of Churches granted £350, which was unspent in 1824 when a faculty was granted for an iron gallery on three sides.[55] Fire destroyed the interior in 1859, although the books and plate were saved.[56] A rate was levied to rebuild but,

after strikes and arguments between the architect T. E. Knightley and the local committee, it was not until 1861 that the church was reopened with a cupola added to the tower.[57] An elaborate choir-screen was among High Church furnishings added from the later 19th century.[58] The interior was severely damaged by bombing in 1940 and a temporary church, built within the old one and designed by A. Wontner Smith and Harold Jones, was dedicated in 1954, when the Tuscan portal of the west end was restored and the cupola removed. In 1957 Antony Lewis of Tapper & Lewis reconstructed the church according to Dance's designs except for the east window and the arrangement of the interior. The altar was placed in the body of the church with vestries and a Lady chapel in a gallery at the east end. A striking boat-shaped font by Lewis was placed at the west end and stained glass from St. Philip's was installed in the south-west crèche. The church was reconsecrated in 1961 and renovated in 1984.[59] Its fittings in 1996 included some introduced for Roman Catholic worship.[60]

Most plate was given in 1746 and included a silver flagon and cup of 1635, a cover paten datemarked 1681, and a beadle's staff dated 1690. A large silver paten on a foot dated from 1717 and mid 18th-century plate included a paten, a cup and cover, and six pewter plates.[61]

CHURCH EXTENSION. Apart perhaps from the French Protestant church, classified as Anglican in 1778 and 1810,[62] St. Matthew's remained the only Church of England place of worship until 1814, when the Episcopal Jews' chapel opened. Although the Church Building Commissioners had £1,000,000 to spend in populous parishes,[63] the vestry in 1819 expressed alarm at the possible cost of two intended churches, in north-west and east Bethnal Green.[64] By 1822 the commissioners had decided on a single church but it was not until 1828 that St. John's was consecrated and 1837 that a district was assigned to it after opposition from Joshua King.[65]

In 1836 Bishop Blomfield launched his scheme for 50 new churches but by 1839 he had raised much less than he had hoped. Persuaded either

[41] Mackeson's (1866, 1881).
[42] Rep. Sel. Cttee. on Educ. of Lower Orders in Metropolis, H.C. 495, pp. 231–4 (1816), iv.
[43] Lond. City Mission Mag. iii. 53.
[44] P.R.O., HO 129/21/4/1/1.
[45] Brit. Weekly, 12 Nov. 1886. Figures are for Harvest Sun.
[46] Mudie-Smith, Rel. Life, 55, 286.
[47] Bethany, Stewart Headlam, 79–81; Smith, Lond. Heretics, 182–4.
[48] P.O. Dir. Lond. (1892–3, 1898–1929); G.L.R.O., P72/MTW/140; Booth, Life and Lab. iii (2), 108; above, social.
[49] P.R.O., J1 8/20, no. 698; Leech and others, Hist. St. Mat. 8; Ashworth, Oxford Ho. map.
[50] Guildhall MS. 9531/20, pt. 1, f. 102v.; Leech and others, Hist. St. Mat. 4.
[51] B. Lambert, Hist. and Survey of Lond. and Environs (1806), iv. 80.
[52] Hughson, Lond., Brit. Metropolis (1811), iv. 443 (illus.); W. Maitland, Hist. Lond. (1756), ii, illus. facing p. 1363; Pevsner, Lond. ii. 67; above, plate 39.
[53] Vestry mins. 1782–1813, p. 58.
[54] Lysons, Environs, ii. 33.

[55] Vestry mins. 1823–8, 103, 109; Guildhall MS. 19224/475; G.L.R.O., P72/MTW/153.
[56] Illus. News of the World, 24 Dec. 1859 (B.M. Potter Colln. xxv. 30).
[57] G.L.R.O., P72/MTW/154; Leech and others, Hist. St. Mat. 1, 6.
[58] Bethnal Green M.B. Official Guide [1921], 74.
[59] Leech and others, Hist. St. Mat. 8; Hist. Par. and Ch. of St. Mat. rev. J. Oldland (1989); Guildhall MS. 19224/475 (TS. notes on ch.); G.L.R.O., P72/MTW/162/1; E. and W. Young, Old Lond. Chs.; Pevsner, Lond. ii. 67.
[60] Inf. from chwdn.
[61] Hist. Mon. Com. E. Lond. 8; Freshfield, Communion Plate, 1; Pevsner, Lond. ii. 67.
[62] Lambeth Pal. Libr., Fulham papers, Lowth 5, ff. 386–9; Randolph 13, ff. 125–6.
[63] B. I. Coleman, 'Anglican Ch. Extension and Related Movements c. 1800–60 with special ref. to Lond.' (Cambridge Univ. Ph. D. thesis, 1968), 43, 46–7.
[64] Vestry mins. 1813–21, f. 118.
[65] BNC, Bethnal Green 3, letter from King 2 Dec. 1822; Second Ser. [Tower] 148, letters from bp. of Lond. 28 Dec. 1830, from King 17 Feb. 1832, reply by King to Com. 7 May 1827.

by William Cotton or Bryan King, incumbent of St. John's, he decided to concentrate on Bethnal Green.[66] A committee, with Bryan King as secretary and Cotton as treasurer, issued appeals pleading the parish's spiritual destitution and planned ten churches, dedicated to the apostles, each with its parsonage and school. Landowners including Capt. Sotheby gave sites and money was solicited from such local figures as the Mercerons, Sir Thomas Fowell Buxton, and Robert Hanbury and from City businessmen and institutions, largely through sermons given by the bishop. Meanwhile two or three houses in the centre of the parish were hired for curates and the old French Protestant church in St. John Street and Friar's Mount school in the Nichol were fitted up as temporary churches in 1840.[67]

The foundation stone of the first church, St. Peter's, was laid in 1840, when jeering crowds loosed an ox at the ceremony.[68] By 1843 four churches (St. Peter's, St. Andrew's, St. Philip's, and St. James the Less's) had been consecrated and assigned chapelry districts under curates nominated by the rector and paid by the Ecclesiastical Commissioners.[69] Districts were assigned to the remaining six churches in 1844,[70] although the last, St. Thomas's, was not consecrated until 1850. By 1853 Bethnal Green had 12 churches with 11 parsonages, 10 schools, 22 clergymen, 129 district visitors, and 244 Sunday school teachers.[71] Accommodation for Anglicans increased from 4,900 seats in 1838[72] to 14,851 by 1851, when 11,751 attendances were recorded, compared with 11,799 at non-conformist chapels.[73]

Local anti-clericalism, compounded of radicalism, dissent, and 'infidelity', softened. In 1841 it had been difficult to find a single communicant to act as churchwarden of Blomfield's first church but by 1846 there were 100 communicants in each district. When the last foundation stone was laid in 1849, the procession was received by a sympathetic crowd and within a decade congregations were numbered in hundreds, if not thousands. Dissenting tradition, however, probably lay behind a continuing distrust of such Puseyite practices as preaching in surplices.[74] By 1851 clothing clubs, maternity charities, provident institutions, and a dispensary had been established[75] and by 1858 moral conditions

in St. Peter's were said to be better than 10 years earlier.[76] The new churches brought educated leadership, schools, and some social relief, although Blomfield's vision of civilizing the slums failed.[77] It was later admitted that larger, better endowed parishes with chapels of ease would have been more effective than the numerous districts,[78] for which it proved hard to find suitable incumbents, partly because local hoped-for funds failed to materialize and the clergy spent too much time on appeals.[79] By 1858 it was clear that the schools would not produce a generation of churchgoers.[80] Local clergy despaired at the poverty and irreligion, even if the 'mental torture' and fear of 'Christianity's dissolution' expressed by the incumbent of St. Andrew's, was extreme.[81]

The clergy became almost exclusively missioners and social workers, who were overwhelmed by work despite the help of visitors, usually middle-class women from outside the parish. New districts were formed: St. Paul's (1865) and Holy Trinity (1866) in the overcrowded west and St. Barnabas's (1870) in the most recently settled east. The principal benefactor, William Cotton, died in 1866.[82] There was some absenteeism among the clergy, debate about how to combat pauperism,[83] and notoriety at the 'Red church' (St. James the Great), where waival of marriage fees led to farcical scenes. In 1883 the curate-in-charge of St. Peter's attributed the 'deadness' in the church to incumbents being 'broken down'.[84]

In the later 19th century and up to 1914 energetic clergymen, beginning with Hansard and Headlam at St. Matthew's, were aided by a nationwide interest in the East End in bringing about a revival. It was manifested in ritualism, in more numerous curates, and in the opening of institutes, missions, and university settlements. Communicants so multiplied that in 1909 Winnington-Ingram, then bishop of London, contrasted the emptiness of all but two churches 20 years ago with the present where 'the nets were breaking' with the numbers.[85] Census figures concealed the increase by omitting afternoon services, some of the most successful, whereas 1886 figures were taken on Harvest Sunday.[86] Anglican attendances for 1886 were 7,399[87] and for 1903 7,992.[88] From 13 per cent of the population in 1851 Anglican congregations

66 *Third Rep. Metropolis Chs. Fund*, 19 June 1839 (BNC, Second Ser. [Tower] 148).
67 B.L. Add. MS. 40427, f. 396; *Spiritual Destitution of Bethnal Green*, 7 Aug. 1840 (BNC, Second Ser. [Tower] 148); *Final Rep. Metropolis Chs. Fund*, 1836–54 (Guildhall Libr.); *The Times*, 18 July 1839, 5d; 7 Nov. 3c; 31 Dec. 5c; 24 Mar. 1840, 6d; 12 May 1840, 5e; 21 June 1841, 3f; *Cal. of Papers of Sir Thos. Fowell Buxton 1786–1845*, ed. P. M. Pugh (L. & I. Soc., Special Ser. xiii), xviii. 120, 128, 148.
68 *Final Rep. Metropolis Chs. Fund*, 53; A. Blomfield, *Memoir of Chas. Jas. Blomfield, Bp. of Lond.* (1863), 244.
69 *Lond. Gaz.* 16 June 1843, pp. 2016 sqq.; 20 June 1843, pp. 2067–71.
70 Ibid. 3 June 1844, pp. 1891–4.
71 Blomfield, *Memoir*, 242.
72 *Lond. City Mission Mag.* iii. 53–4.
73 *Census, Rel. Worship* [1690], H.C. p. 7 (1852–3), lxxxix. Pop. 90,193 (1851): *Census*, 1851. Attendance total for 3 Sun. svces., some people attending more than one. Figs. not given for St. Bart. and St. Thos. but inc. Episcopal Jews' chapel.
74 *Rep. Sel. Cttee. on Divine Worship in Metropolis*, H.C. 387,

pp. 6–7, 15 (1857–8), ix; *Final Rep. Metropolis Chs. Fund*, 71.
75 *Final Rep. Metropolis Chs. Fund*, 87.
76 Lambeth Pal. Libr., Fulham Papers, Tait 440/11.
77 O. Chadwick, *Victorian Ch.* (1970), i. 331.
78 Blomfield, *Memoir*, 228.
79 BNC, B12, letter from Blomfield 24 July 1843; *Rep. Cttee. on Worship in Metropolis*, p. 12.
80 Blomfield, *Memoir*, 247.
81 Lambeth Pal. Libr., Fulham Papers, Tait 440/6–18, espec. 12.
82 *D.N.B.*
83 *The Times*, 15 Feb. 1860, 11a; 17 Feb. 5c; 8 Jan. 1874, 5e; 21 Jan. 7e.
84 H. McLeod, *Class and Religion in Late Victorian City* (1974), 105; below.
85 Ibid. 109.
86 Mudie-Smith, *Rel. Life*, 286.
87 Booth, *Lond. Life and Lab.* i (1), table. Pop. 1881: 126,961: *Census*, 1881.
88 Mudie-Smith, *Rel. Life*, 55. Pop. 1901: 129,680: *Census*, 1901.

fell to 5.8 per cent in 1886 and rose to 6.0 per cent in 1903.

Thereafter, with few exceptions, there was a decline in activities and congregations, hastened by rival social attractions, a falling population, and non-Christian immigration. The Episcopal Jews' chapel closed in 1895 and Holy Trinity in 1926. Most churches suffered bomb damage and in 1951 the Church Commissioners drew up a Scheme to reduce Bethnal Green's parishes from 14 to eight. St. Philip's, St. Paul's, and St. Matthias's, small western parishes which had been cleared

of slums, were united with St. Matthew's; St. Thomas's was united with St. Peter's, St. James the Great's with St. Jude's, and St. Simon Zelotes's (already united with St. Anthony's, Globe Rd.) with St. John's; adjustmestments were made to other parish boundaries.[89] Supplementary Schemes confirmed the plans for the first group, delayed by the restoration of St. Matthew's church in 1954,[90] and added St. Andrew's to St. Matthew's in 1958.[91] St. Bartholomew's was added to St. John's in 1978[92] and St. James the Great's with St. Jude's to St. Matthew's in 1984.[93]

LIST OF CHURCHES

Inf. about patrons and clergy is taken from *Clergy List*, *Crockford*, and *Lond. Dioc. Year Bk.* (various edns.); inf. about svces. is from Lambeth Pal. Libr., Fulham Papers, Tait 440 (for 1858), *Mackeson's Guide* (1866, 1871, 1899), and H. W. Harris and M. Bryant, *The Churches and Lond.* [1914], 381. Attendance figs. 1886 are from *Brit. Weekly*, 12 Nov. 1886, 1903 from Mudie-Smith *Rel. Life*, 55. Liturgical directions are used in all architectural descriptions. Illus. of churches in T. Roberts, *Housing and Ministry. An Experiment in Use of Ch. Land* (1975); photographs in N.M.R. and T.H.L.H.L. The following additional abbreviations are used: a.a., average attendance; aft., afternoon; asst., assistant; consecr., consecrated; demol., demolished; Eccl. Com., Ecclesiastical Commissioners; H.C., Holy Communion; min., minister; mtg., meeting; Q.A.B., Queen Anne's Bounty; R., rector; svce., service; temp., temporarily, temporary; V., vicar.

EPISCOPAL JEWS' CHAPEL, Palestine Pl. Lond. Soc. for Promoting Christianity among Jews, founded 1809 with earliest centres in Spitalfields and Ely Pl.,[94] acquired 99-yr. lease of site between Cambridge Rd. and Russia Lane, part of Bishop's Hall farm, 1811,[95] where bldgs. erected and chapel licensed 1814. No endowment but pew rents raised *c*. £170 p.a. 1851. Patron trustees of soc. Min.'s ho. at no. 1 Palestine Pl.[96] Chapel for 1,200[97] central bldg. of group inc. boys' and girls' boarding schs., institution (founded 1831) where converts learnt trades,[98] and missionaries' college.[99] Attendance 1851:[1] 400 adults and 100 children a.m., 50 adults and 100 children aft., 400 adults and 100 children p.m.; 1886: 378

a.m., 277 p.m. Svces. partly choral by 1881, thrice on Sun., once on Wed.; H.C. twice a month, after a.m. and p.m. svces. Aft. svce. and, by 1890s, weekday H.C. in Hebrew. Well attended lectures in chapel after p.m. svce.[2] Bldg. of brick in classical style by Chas. Augustus Busby and Geo. Maliphant 1814.[3] Demol. for Bethnal Green hosp. 1895 although bell turret survived on nurses' quarters and font and wall monuments taken to Christ Ch., Spitalfields.[4]

HOLY TRINITY, Shoreditch. Dist. assigned from St. Phil. Bethnal Green, and St. Leonard, Shoreditch, 1866. Benefice united with St. Leonard 1926.[5] Patron Crown alternating with bp. Benefice valued at £200 p.a. 1871.[6] Endowed by Eccl. Com. with £100 p.a. 1889 and £60 1891.[7] Svces. in hay loft over stable,[8] presumably in mission at junction of Club Row and Sclater St., where all seats free, partly choral with surplices worn by 1871; 6 svces., inc. 2 H.C., on Sun., 2 daily svces., 3 sermons a week, and H.C. on holy days by 1871.[9] Attendance 1886: 41 a.m., 50 p.m. Art. Osborne Montgomery Jay, inspiration for Morrison's *Child of the Jago*, V. 1886–1921.[10] With grant from Bp. of Lond.'s Fund and help from Magdalen Coll., Oxf., whose missioner he had been in Stepney, Jay secured site in Orange Ct., Old Nichol St. 1888, where complex of bldgs. opened 1889: classrooms, club room, hall, and gymnasium, with ch. above. Adjoining property to E. acquired 'by generosity of Miss Schuster' and model lodging ho., Trinity Chambers, built there. Ho. to W. acquired when clearance mooted 1894 and additional aisle and side chapel built there 1895.[11] From 1880s 1 or 2 asst. curates. Rich

89 *Lond. Gaz.* 23 Nov. 1951, p. 6124; G.L.R.O., P72/ BAT/39/1–6; 0/42/1, 14/1–6.

90 *Lond. Gaz.* 2 July 1954, p. 3896; Guildhall MS. 19224/475.

91 Guildhall MS. 19224/475; G.L.R.O., P72/MTW/146/1–2.

92 Guildhall MS. 19224/201.

93 C.C.C. files, St. Jas. the Gt. pastoral scheme 1984.

94 T. D. Halsted, *Our Missions: Hist. of Lond. Soc. for Promoting Christianity among Jews* (1866), 33–4.

95 P.R.O., C 54/19906, mm. 1–8.

96 Ibid. HO 129/21/2/1/1.

97 *Lond. City Mission Mag.* iii. 53–4.

98 Called Operative Jewish Converts Institution and occupied by 10 men and 2 women in 1851: P.R.O., HO 107/1540/ 21/2/20, f. 583; *Jewish Intelligence*, Jan. 1894, advert. inside cover. For schs., below, educ. (pub. schs.).

99 Halsted, *Our Missions*, 37, 68; C. Bermant, *Point of Arrival* (1975), 219.

1 P.R.O., HO 129/21/2/1/1.

2 Halsted, *Our Missions*, 67, 74; *Jewish Intelligence* (1892), 62.

3 Guildhall Pr. B3, Palestine Pl.; Bethnal Green Mus., *Cat. of Drawings relating to Bethnal Green* (1925), 45, no. 125; Colvin, *Brit. Architects*, 175; J. Dugdale, *New Brit. Traveller* (1819), iii. 473; *Jewish Intelligence*, N.S. ix, illus. on cover; above, plate 40.

4 C.C.C. Clarke, Demol. Chs., Jews' Chap., Palestine Pl.

5 *Lond. Gaz.* 10 July 1866, pp. 3924–6; 4 June 1926, pp. 3641–4; Guildhall MS. 19224/122; *Census*, 1871; G.L.R.O., P72/TR1/1/1–4.

6 *Mackeson's Guide.* (1871).

7 Guildhall MS. 19224/122.

8 A. O. Jay, *A Story of Shoreditch* (1896), 6.

9 *Mackeson's Guide.* (1871); G.L.R.O., MR/UP 953, 1011.

10 A. Morrison, *A Child of the Jago* (1982 edn.), 23–4.

11 Hennessy, *Novum Rep.* 399; Jay, *Story of Shoreditch*, 30–1, 70, 86, 89, 107; Guildhall MS. 19224/122; G.L.R.O., MBW 1766, no. 27; AR/BA/4/55, no. 6.

social life with men's club of 500 members, women's bible class, Sun. and ragged schs.[12] Svces. fully choral and High Ch. by 1889; 8 svces., inc. 3 H.C. on Sun., 4 on weekdays. Large red-brick ch. consecr. 1889. After union with St. Leonard's, ch. used by 'Hebrew Christians'.[13] Became hostel 1938 and conversion to factory refused 1939.[14] Bombed in Second World War.[15]

ST. ANDREW, Viaduct St. Dist. S. of Bethnal Green Rd. and W. of Cambridge Rd. assigned 1843.[16] Patron bp. Grants from Metropolis Ch. trustees 1843 and Q. A. B. 1854. Endowed by Eccl. Com. with £224 p.a. 1843, £50 p.a. 1869, and by Q. A. B. with £50 p.a. 1853.[17] Gross income £296, with £100 paid to curate by Pastoral Aid Soc., c. 1858 but incumbent called for ch. rates and better endowment, partly for Nat. schs.[18] Large Gothic Vicarage built between 1858 and 1873,[19] where bad sanitation led to typhoid 1884.[20] Chas. Kirton, V. 1864–1904, ill from 1884, when curates-in-charge inc. Geo. Wyndham Hamilton Knight-Bruce 1884–6, promoter of Oxford Ho. and later bp. of Mashonaland,[21] and Herb. V. S. Eck. 1897–1902, supporter of Charity Organisation Soc.[22] Usually 2 or 3 curates from 1880s, 6 in 1894. Ch. had 900 free sittings 1851, when attendance 160 adults and 130 Sun. sch. children a.m., 165 adults and 24 Sun. sch. children p.m.[23] Attendance 1886: 144 a.m., 242 p.m.; 1903: 180 a.m., 349 p.m. Three Sun. svces. 1858, a.a. 60–80 a.m., c. 30 aft., 100–150 p.m.; svce. on Wed. and monthly H.C. with a.a. c. 30 communicants.[24] Aft. svce. dropped by 1866 and fully choral svces. introduced 1880s; H.C. on Sun. and saints' days and 2 daily svces by 1889. Aided by Metropolitan Dist. Visiting Soc. and scripture reader who held mtgs. 1858; ch. supported libr. and bible classes.[25] By 1890s charitable income said to be flowing in and ch. ran mission in Cambridge Rd.[26] Brick bldg. in 'vague Italian Romanesque' style by Thos. Hen. Wyatt and David Brandon 1841: 3-sided apse, tower and stone turret at end of N. aisle.[27] Demol. after par. united with St. Mat. 1958[28]

ST. BARNABAS, Grove Rd. Originated as St. Luke's mission run by St. Simon Zelotes 1865.[29] Dist. assigned from St. Jas. the Less and St.

Simon Zelotes 1870.[30] Patron V. of St. Jas. the Less for first turn, then bp., from 1904 dean and chapter of Canterbury. Eccl. Com. granted £200 p.a. 1871;[31] benefice valued at £300 1881.[32] Large brick Vicarage S. of Roman Rd. built 1876.[33] Geo. Barnes, V. 1870–1902, also president of Sion college 1887 and rural dean of Spitalfields 1898–1901.[34] Svces. fully choral by 1881; 4 svces., inc. 2 H.C., on Sun. and 1 each weekday. Ch. had 700 free seats. Attendance 1886: 123 a.m., 188 p.m.; 1903: 67 a.m., 212 p.m. Asst. curate from 1882, 3 in 1911. Most active period before 1914 saw Nat. sch. in Lanfranc Rd. rebuilt as St. Barnabas institute and ch. hall 1906. Faculty granted to fit N. end of W. aisle as chapel for daily svces. 1908. Institute used for svces. 1942–56. Living suspended 1967, part of Bow team ministry 1968. Union with St. Paul, Old Ford, proposed 1975 but after local protests priest-in-charge appointed for independent par. 1976. By 1985 laity maintained ch. financially, visited all homes 3 times a year, and used ch. as mtg. place of numerous clubs.[35] Bldg., not oriented, former Bapt. chapel[36] of yellow brick with bands of red and black in Gothic style by Wm. Wigginton 1865, consecr. for Ch. of Eng. 1870: broad chancel, nave, W. gallery, octagonal NW. tower with spire. After war damage, steeple removed 1947. Ch. rebuilt by J. A. Lewis, retaining tower and N. and S. walls without arcades, 1956–7.[37]

ST. BARTHOLOMEW, Essex (later Buckhurst) St. Dist. assigned 1844 from St. Mat. 1844. Patron bp.,[38] from 1884 corp. of Lond.[39] Endowed by Eccl. Com. with £150 p.a. 1844, £80 p.a. 1864, and by Q. A. B. with £50 p.a. from of St. Cath. Coleman (Lond.) 1847. Apportioned part of income of St. Peter upon Cornhill (Lond.) 1885, varied 1916.[40] Income from St. Cath. extinguished by capital payment 1949.[41] Gothic parsonage built N. of ch.[42] Ch. had 950 free sittings 1858, when attendence 300 a.m., 100 aft., 500 p.m.[43] Attendance 1886: 120 a.m., 155 p.m.; 1903: 92 a.m., 118 p.m. Three svces. on Sun. with sermons Thurs. evg. and saints' days 1858; H.C. on alternate Sun. with a.a. 40 communicants and c. 130 at Easter.[44] Only a.m. and aft. Sun.

12 Jay, *Story of Shoreditch*, 59–60, 71; below, educ.
13 Bethnal Green M.B. *Official Guide* [1938].
14 G.L.R.O., AR/BA/4/672, no. 3; 694, no. 3.
15 Guildhall MS. 19224/122; R. Samuel, *East End Underworld* (1981), 2.
16 *Lond. Gaz.* 20 June 1843, pp. 2068–71.
17 Ibid. 16 June 1843, pp. 2016 sqq.; 3 Oct. 1843, p. 3220; 9 Aug. 1853, pp. 2168–70; 16 Apr. 1869, p. 2303; Hodgson, *Queen Anne's Bounty*, pp. lxxxix–xc.
18 Guildhall MS. 9561, no. 24.
19 Lambeth Pal. Libr., Fulham Papers, Tait 440/12; O.S. Map 1/2,500, Lond. XXVII (1873 edn.).
20 Guildhall MS. 19224/161.
21 G.L.R.O., P72/MTW/137/1; *D.N.B.*
22 McLeod, *Class and Rel. in Late Vic. City*, 112.
23 P.R.O., HO 129/21/3/1/3.
24 Guildhall MS. 9561, no. 24; Lambeth Pal. Libr., Fulham Papers, Tait 440/12.
25 Lambeth Pal. Libr., Fulham Papers, Tait 440/12.
26 Booth, *Life and Lab.* iii(2), 84, 107. Below, Anglican missions (St. Fras. of Assisi).
27 Guildhall MS. 19224/161; *Ecclesiologist*, i. 195–6; Pevsner, *Lond.* ii. 67; C.C.C. files, St. And.
28 Guildhall MS. 19224/475; G.L.R.O., P72/MTW/146/1–2.
29 Hennessy, *Novum Rep.* 415; C.C.C. file, St. Barnabas

(J. Mercer, Hist. of St. Barn. 1985); below, St. Simon Zelotes.
30 *Lond. Gaz.* 29 Nov. 1870, p. 5405; Guildhall MS. 19224/191.
31 *Lond. Gaz.* 15 Aug. 1871, pp. 3595–6.
32 *Clergy List* (1881).
33 *Lond. Gaz.* 18 Dec. 1874, p. 6278; C.C.C. files, St. Barnabas, circular 1985; G.L.R.O., MBW 1659, no. 23.
34 C.C.C. files, St. Barnabas (Mercer, Hist. St. Barn.).
35 G.L.R.O., AR/BA/4/150, no. 4; C.C.C. files, St. Barnabas (Mercer, Hist. St. Barn.; reps. on par. c. 1985).
36 Below, prot. nonconf. (Bapts.).
37 C.C.C. Clarke, xv. 156; C.C.C. files, St. Barnabas (Mercer, Hist. St. Barn.; circular, 1985; photos. of ch.); Clarke, *Lond. Chs.* 163; above, plate 41.
38 *Lond. Gaz.* 3 June 1844, pp. 1891–4.
39 Ibid. 15 Aug. 1884, p. 3672–3.
40 Ibid. 3 June 1844, pp. 1891–4; 15 June 1847, pp. 2175–8; 15 June 1864, pp. 3051–3; 10 Mar. 1885, p. 1076; 11 July 1916, pp. 6846–8; Hodgson, *Queen Anne's Bounty*, pp. lxxxix–xc.
41 G.L.R.O., P72/BAT/63/2–3.
42 Ibid. 64; P.R.O., HO 129/21/2/1/5; Guildhall MS. 19224/201.
43 P.R.O., HO 129/21/2/1/5; Guildhall MS. 9561.
44 *Rep. Cttee. on Worship in Metropolis*, 387, pp. 23 sqq.

FIG. 27. ST BARTHOLOMEW'S CHURCH C. 1840

svce. 1866. Alf. Ric. Clemens, V. 1886–1932,[45] introduced partly choral svces., H.C. every Sun., Thurs., and saints' days by 1889; 200 communicants on roll c. 1891.[46] Sung Eucharist every Sun. by 1906;[47] rood screen and other High Ch. fittings during first two decades of 20th cent.[48] Three clergy, dist. visitors, missionary assoc., maternity and provident socs. from early 1850s.[49] Two asst. curates, paid respectively £100 p.a. by City merchant and £65 p.a. by Additional Curates Soc., besides lay scripture reader, paid £70 by Scripture Readers' Assoc., and presumably unpaid women dist. visitors, c. 1858.[50] John Drummond MacGachen, V. 1861–86, apparently had no asst. curate but generally at least 1 until 1920s.[51] Helpers, inc. from univ. settlements, associated in 32 ch. activities c. 1891. Mission work inc. preaching from pulpit attached to exterior of ch., street svces., and attempted mission at 'Tiger's Corner';[52] mission ho., temp. occupied by founders of St. Margaret's Ho., 1892;[53] hall hired at no. 34 Tent St. from 1897,[54] replaced by St. Martin's mission 1899 and by par. hall N. of ch. 1934.[55] Bldg. of stock brick with stone dressings in Early Eng. style,

accommodating 1,058, by Wm. Railton, on site acquired 1841, consecr. 1844: chancel, transepts, aisled and clerestoried nave, SW. unfinished tower, W. gallery.[56] Alterations 1887;[57] bomb damage 1941 when svces. held in hall[58] until ch. reopened 1955.[59] Presentation suspended 1971 and par. united with St. John and St. Simon Zelotes under team mins., with V. at St. Barts. parsonage, under pastoral scheme 1978. Ch. closed and appropriated to residential use under Ch. Com. Scheme 1983;[60] converted into flats, Steeple Court, by 1996.

ST. JAMES THE GREAT, Bethnal Green Rd. Dist. assigned 1844. Patron bp. Endowed by Eccl. Com. with £150 p.a. 1844, £35 p.a. 1869, and by Q.A.B. with £25 p.a. 1853 and £2,400 consols 1856.[61] Parsonage built adjoining E. end of ch. 1842.[62] Attendance 1851: 160 adults and 200 children a.m. 30 adults and 80 children aft., 300 adults and 40 children p.m.;[63] 1886: 55 a.m., 56 p.m.; 1903: 133 a.m., 254 p.m.; a.a. 1967: 100–150 a.m.[64] Two full svces., occasional Sun. aft. svce., and monthly H.C. with a.a. 5–20 communicants 1858.[65] Three svces. on weekdays by 1889. Edw. Fras. Coke, V. 1852–97, raised money for poor by advertising in Times, helped found Queen Adelaide's dispensary, and offered marriages for fee of 7d.[66] Ensuing rowdy scenes as couples, many very young, married in batches aroused hostility of fellow clergymen, as did Coke's attitude to poor; grant for curate stopped, but Coke raised funds by appeal and, except 1856–62, par. never without asst. curate.[67] Aided by visiting soc. and young Sun. sch. teachers 1858, when ch. had libr. though not much used.[68] V. later resident outside par., when fabric neglected and ch. 'almost empty'. Reformation began under asst. curate Geo. M. Stüppell, 1885–92, who ended cheap weddings.[69] Fred. Gibson Wix, V. 1897–9, former curate of St. Thos., restored fabric and introduced High Ch. practices, provoking clashes at reopening of ch. 1898.[70] Royal Com. on Eccl. Discipline investigated H.C. 1904, when stations of cross featured.[71] New side chapel for daily svces. 1906.[72] Fred. A. Iremonger, V. 1912–16, introduced simplified svce. in place of evensong, daily office 1913, and daily Eucharist 1914. Requiem masses during war.[73] Incense first used 1917,

45 Hennessy, Novum Rep. 415; The Times, 6 May 1932, 17 f.
46 Lambeth Pal. Libr., Fulham Papers, F. Temple papers, Appeal for St. Bart.[c. 1891].
47 G.L.R.O., P72/BAT/119.
48 C.C.C. files, St. Bart. (paper, 1976).
49 Final Rep. Metropolis Chs. Fund, 103.
50 Rep. Cttee. on Worship in Metropolis, pp. 23–34.
51 G.L.R.O., P72/MTW/137/3.
52 Lambeth Pal. Libr., Fulham papers, F. Temple papers, Appeal for St. Bart. [c. 1891].
53 K. B. Beauman, St. Marg.'s Ho. Brief Hist. 1889–1989, 3.
54 G.L.R.O., P72/BAT/89.
55 G.L.R.O., P72/BAT/100/1,4; AR/BA/4/585, no. 3; O.S. Map 1/2,500, TQ 3582 (1966 edn.); below, Anglican missions.
56 M.L.R. 1842/2/369–70; Clarke, Lond. Chs. 162–3; Colvin, Brit. Architects, 670; C.C.C. files, St. Bart. (paper, 1976; photos.; 19th-cent. illus.); Guildhall Pr. B3/BAR; M. H. Port, Six Hundred New Chs. (1961), 150–1.
57 G.L.R.O., MBW 1757, no. 27.
58 Ibid. P72/BAT/64.
59 Clarke, Lond. Chs. 162–3.
60 G.L.R.O.,   P72/BAT/73/1–2;   Guildhall   MS.

19224/201; Lond. Gaz. 14 Feb. 1978, p. 1955; 28 June 1983, p. 8525; C.C.C. files, Bethnal Green chs., letter 1985.
61 Lond. Gaz. 3 June 1844, pp. 1891–4; 9 Aug. 1853, pp. 2168–70; 16 Apr. 1869, p. 2303; Hodgson, Queen Anne's Bounty, pp. lxxxix–xc.
62 Guildhall MS. 9561, no. 26; Ecclesiologist, i. 195; G.L.R.O., P72/JSG/118 (newspaper cutting 4 June 1844).
63 P.R.O., HO 129/21/3/1/1.
64 G.L.R.O., P72/JSG/118/7.
65 Lambeth Pal. Libr., Fulham Papers, Tait 440/15.
66 C.C.C. files, St. Jas. the Gt. (R. Pringle, 'St. Jas. the Gt. Par. Hist. to 1976'.); The Times, 15 Feb. 1860, 11a; 3 Aug. 1868, 10f.
67 G.L.R.O., P72/JSG/111, f. 4d; A. White, Problems of a Great City (1886), 36–9.
68 Lambeth Pal. Libr., Fulham Papers, Tait 440/15.
69 Spectator, 5 Feb. 1887 (cutting in G.L.R.O., P72/JSG/118); G.L.R.O., P72/JSG/111, f. 4d. Marriages reduced from 1890: ibid. P72/JSG/65.
70 Pringle, 'St. Jas. the Gt.'; The Times, 16 Mar. 1899, 10c.
71 G.L.R.O., P72/JSG/118 (letter by Royal Com. 1904).
72 Ibid. (Ann. Rep. 1907).
73 Ibid. JSG/111, ff. 3d, 16, 35; Pringle, 'St. Jas. the Gt.'.

Guild of the Altar pledging members to weekly communion, formed 1918, reservation of sacrament from 1923, confessions by 1929, Corpus Christi celebrated 1930.[74] Financial difficulties lessened under Iremonger, aided by 3 curates and members of Oxford Ho., of which he was head.[75] Assistance from Sisters of Soc. of St. Marg. from St. Saviour's priory, Haggerston, by 1965, withdrawn 1975.[76] Mission svces. in connexion with Church Army 1902;[77] used hall in Florida St. by 1913, rebuilt as Florida hall 1922 and as club 1956.[78] Ch. supported range of clubs, inc. choral soc. 1920;[79] prison visiting a high priority of priest-in-charge 1967.[80] Cost of ch. and parsonage met by Geo. Harrold, 'medical man', and sister.[81] Bldg., called 'Red ch.' because first in E. End built of red brick,[82] in Early Eng. style, with 1,153 free sittings by Edw. Blore on site acquired 1840, consecr. 1844: short sanctuary, N. and S. transepts, narrow aisled nave; 'poor' bell turret[83] at W. angle of S. transept; galleries, inc. W. organ gallery on iron pillars. Gallery removed, ch. reroofed, and chancel added 1897–8. Iron chancel screen erected and S. transept made into side chapel 1906. Site scheduled for development as social club 1975–6 when interior of ch. rearranged.[84] Par. united with St. Jude under Scheme of 1951.[85] Presentation of V. suspended 1956 and R. of St. Mat. made priest-in-charge with asst. curate at St. Jas. Vicarage. Curate made priest-in-charge 1962–9, when par. united with St. Mat. and St. Peter under team mins. Presentation suspended 1972 and priest-in-charge appointed until 1984, when St. Jas. the Great with St. Jude united with St. Mat.[86] Ch. and Vicarage converted into flats, St. Jas. Court, by 1996.

ST. JAMES THE LESS, St. James's Rd. (later Ave.). Dist. assigned from St. Mat. 1843.[87] Patron bp., from 1903 Church Pastoral Aid Soc. Patronage Trust.[88] Endowed by Eccl. Com. with £150 p.a. 1843 and by Q. A. B. with £50 p.a. 1853;[89] grants of £70 p.a. 1866 and £60 p.a. for asst. curate 1903. Grey-brick parsonage built N. of ch. by 1846.[90] Attendance 1851: 100 a.m., 30 p.m.;[91] 1886: 282 a.m., 298 p.m.; 1903: 377 a.m., 1,322 p.m. Two svces. on Sun., one on Wed. and monthly H.C. with a.a. c. 50 communicants 1858.[92] Partly choral Sun. p.m. svces. from 1880s and weekly H.C. by 1903;[93] a.a. communicants at Easter 26 in 1897, 915 in 1914, 79 in 1919,

FIG. 28. ST. JAMES THE LESS'S CHURCH C. 1840

217 in 1939, 110 in 1946, 74 in 1964.[94] Aided by curate and visitors 1858, when ch. ran bible class and provident soc.[95] Usually one asst. curate but 6 under John E. Watts-Ditchfield, V. 1897–1914 and later bp. of Chelmsford.[96] Watts-Ditchfield,[97] arriving when par. in 'state of spiritual torpor', was former Wes. preacher and 'notable example of the successful evangelical clergyman'. Promoted range of activities, inc. men's Sun. aft. svce.,[98] using brass band and inviting men from public hos. Churchyard converted into recreation ground and I sch. into medical mission and dispensary. Open-air svces. at corner of Green and Bonner streets. Mission svces. at no. 78 Cranbrook Rd. 1899–1901, when replaced by former nonconf. chapel in Sidney St. where attendance 1903: 16 a.m., 124 p.m.; also in working men's hostel, converted from 3 hos. in Ames St., purchased 1901; attendance 1903: 79 p.m. Anonymous donor financed refurbishment of ch. and schs. and range of new par.

74 G.L.R.O., P72/JSG/111, ff. 27, 35, 43d; 111/36; 118; Pringle, 'St. Jas. the Gt.'.
75 Pringle, 'St. Jas. the Gt.'; G.L.R.O., P72/JSG/118 (Ann. Rep. 1907).
76 Pringle, 'St. Jas. the Gt.'; G.L.R.O., P72/JSG/118/18.
77 G.L.R.O., P72/JSG/118 (leaflet 1902).
78 Ibid. (Ann. Rep. 1922); 111, f. 16; Pringle, 'St. Jas. the Gt.'.
79 G.L.R.O., P72/JSG/116.
80 Ibid. 118/7, 35.
81 BNC, B12, letter from bp. of Lond. 22 May 1843; Rep. Cttee. on Worship in Metropolis, p. 5. Not Blomfield's own siblings, pace G.L.R.O., P72/JSG/111, f. 2d.
82 Guildhall MS. 19224/29; P.R.O., HO 129/21/3/1/1. Pevsner (Lond. ii. 67), confusing St. Jas. the Gt. and the Less, gives Vulliamy as architect.
83 Ecclesiologist, i. 195.
84 Pringle, 'St. Jas. the Gt.'; G.L.R.O., P72/JSG/111, f. 2d; Clarke, Lond. Chs. 162, pl. 128; Colvin, Brit. Architects, 119; C.C.C. files, St. Jas. the Gt. (rep. on ch. 1983); The Times, 13 July 1906, 3e.

85 G.L.R.O., P72/BAT/39/1–2, 5.
86 Pringle, 'St. Jas. the Gt.'; Guildhall MS. 19224/295; C.C.C. files, St. Jas. the Gt. (pastoral scheme 1984).
87 Lond. Gaz. 20 June 1843, pp. 2068–71.
88 Guildhall MS. 19224/297.
89 Lond. Gaz. 16 June 1843, p. 2018; 9 Aug. 1853, pp. 2168–70; Hodgson, Queen Anne's Bounty, p. lxxxix.
90 Guildhall MS. 19224/297.
91 P.R.O., HO 129/21/2/1/3.
92 Lambeth Pal. Libr., Fulham Papers, Tait 440/16.
93 St. Jas. the Less, Par. Mag. July 1903 (T.H.L.H.L. 225.5).
94 E. N. Gowing, John Edwin Watts-Ditchfield, (1926), 71; G.L.R.O., P72/JSL/39.
95 Lambeth Pal. Libr., Fulham Papers, Tait 440/16.
96 St. Jas. the Less, Par. Mag. July 1903; Feb. 1914 (T.H.L.H.L. 225.5).
97 Based on Gowing, Watts-Ditchfield; Mudie-Smith, Rel. Life, 39, 55; A. Ronald, The World his Stage, Story of Clarence May (1972), 41.
98 Mudie-Smith, Rel. Life, 286.

bldgs., opened 1901.[99] Inc. St. James's Rd. where attendance 1903: 80 p.m., and St. James's hall, Sewardstone Rd., where accommodation for 1,000 and attendance 1903: 169 a.m., 179 p.m. Ridley Ho. opened 1904 for asst. curates. Watts-Ditchfield also assisted by 6–8 women, one of them a nurse.[1] Numbers fell after his resignation, men's svce. being replaced by children's 1930.[2] Only 2 asst. clergy by 1919 but tradition continued with Lond. City Missionary and woman ch. worker after Second World War.[3] Sidney (later Longman) St. mission chapel survived until Second World War and Ames St. hostel in 1919.[4] Hall converted to flats for asst. clergy by 1959.[5] Bldg. of yellow, red, and white brick and stone in Romanesque style, with 488 pews and 645 free seats, by Lewis Vulliamy on part of Bonner's Hall est. acquired 1841, consecr. 1842:[6] shallow semicircular apse, wide aisled nave with galleries; criticized for W. pediment and 'pretending wheel window' and for square SW tower with spire 'of very great pretension'.[7] Altered 1908,[8] damaged 1940; temp. ch. dedicated 1951.[9] Ch. rebuilt by J. A. Lewis, preserving N. and S. walls, chancel arch, and tower, and reconsecrated 1961.[10] Par. united with St Mark, Old Ford, which was closed 1973.

ST. JOHN, Cambridge (Heath) Rd. Chapel of ease to St. Mat. 1828. Dist. E. of Cambridge Rd. assigned 1837.[11] Patron Brasenose Coll., Oxf., from 1844 bp.[12] All pew rents, except £20 p.a. for clerk, assigned to perpetual curate 1828 but reduced to £170 by 1842.[13] Endowed by Q. A. B. with £150 p.a. from St. Cath. Coleman, 1847, with £1,191 consols 1849, and £387 stock 1854.[14] Gross income £400 c. 1858, of which pew rents c. £150 and surplice fees c. £75.[15] Falling pew rents led to Eccl. Com. grants 1869 and 1880 but value of living only £270 by 1881.[16] Vicarage built on former Poor's Land E. of ch. 1852,[17] enlarged by G.M. Hills 1879 and damaged by bombing 1941; St. Simon Zelotes's Vicarage used from 1951 until replaced by no. 30 Victoria Pk. Sq. 1975.[18] Early incumbents were fellows

of Brasenose Coll. Probably Low. Ch., with 'mean, uncovered altar table'1831. Bryan King, perpetual curate 1837–42, nephew of R. Joshua King but ritualist and promoter of Blomfield's scheme; difficulty in appointing successor from Brasenose because vestry refused finance from ch. rate.[19] Three Sun. and 2 weekday svces. with 4 sermons a week and monthly H.C. with c. 80 communicants 1858; also p.m. svce., a.a. 50–80, during week in schoolroom.[20] Svces. partly choral by 1866, fully by 1871, with Anglican and Gregorian music and altar lights by 1889. Five Sun. svces. by 1914. Attendance 1851: 700 adults and 380 children a.m., 50 adults and 12 children aft., 1,300 adults and 100 children p.m.;[21] a.a. 1858: 1,000 a.m. and p.m. Sun., 50 weekdays.[22] Attendance 1886, under 'well known High Churchman'[23] Hen. B. Bromby, V. 1885–92, 536 a.m., 625 p.m.; 1903: 101 a.m., 211 p.m. Head of Episcopal Jews' chapel acted as B. King's curate 1841.[24] Curate, paid £90 by Curates Pastoral Aid Soc., by incumbent, and by subscriptions, from 1857. Usually 1, in 1890s 3, asst. curates. Also scripture reader and 24 women visitors 1858, when ch. supported provident soc., libr., and bible class.[25] Hugh Huleatt, V. 1879–85 and superintendent of Lond. City Mission dist., opened mission in Peel Grove 1881 and held open-air svces. 1883; parochial mission woman employed 1889.[26] Bldg. of brick with stone dressings, seating 2,000, inc. 1,200 free, on Poor's Land acquired by Com. for New Chs., by Sir John Soane 1826–8:[27] chancel, E. vestries, aisled nave with round-headed windows, and W. galleries; W. tower with cupola a 'monstrous excrescence' and 'object of low wit and vulgar abuse'. Combination of massive rectangular W. façade with small tower considered typical of architect but marred by com.'s budget.[28] Restored after fire 1870 by Wm. Mundy but 'clumsiest tracery' in windows spoiled Grecian style of original.[29] Chancel extended by G. F. Bodley 1888.[30] Altered 1892,[31] damaged 1941, svces. held in crypt.[32] Under Scheme of 1951,

99 Souvenir of opening of new par. bldgs. 1901 (T.H.L.H.L. 225.5 pamphlet).
1 St. Jas. the Less, *Par. Mag.* July 1903, Feb. 1914 (T.H.L.H.L. 225.5).
2 G.L.R.O., P72/JSL/39.
3 St. Jas. the Less, *Par. Mag.* June 1919, Jan. 1948, Apr. 1952 (T.H.L.H.L. 225.5); *Lond. City Mission Mag.* cv.
4 St. Jas. the Less, *Monthly Mag.* July 1919 (T.H.L.H.L. 225.5); *P.O. Dir. Lond..* (1929, 1939, 1951).
5 *The Gateway*, Sept. 1959 (C.C.C. files, St. Jas. the Less).
6 M.L.R. 1842/2/368; Guildhall MS. 19224/297; Port, *Six Hundred New Chs.* 150–1; Colvin, *Brit. Architects*, 858; St. Jas. the Gt., above.
7 *Ecclesiologist*, i (1842), 196; Lewis, *Topog. Dict. Eng.* (1849), 225; C.C.C. files, St. Jas. the Less (photos. 1944).
8 G.L.R.O., AR/BA/4/176, no. 4.
9 *The Times*, 19 Feb. 1951, 8b.
10 Clarke, *Lond. Chs.* 162; P. Marcan, *An East End Dir.* (1979), 107.
11 *Lond. Gaz.* 31 Mar. 1837, p. 876.
12 Ibid. 3 June 1844, p. 1892; Hennessy, *Novum Rep.* 416.
13 Guildhall MS. 19224/304; BNC, Second Ser. [Tower] 148, letter from Bryan King 4 Jan. 1842.
14 *Lond. Gaz.* 15 June 1847, pp. 2175–8; Hodgson, *Queen Anne's Bounty*, pp. lxxxix–xc.
15 *Rep. Cttee. on Worship in Metropolis*, p. 596; Guildhall MS. 9561, no. 22.
16 *Lond. Gaz.* 19 Feb. 1869, p. 851; 12 Mar. 1880, pp. 2022–3.
17 Guildhall MS. 19224/304; G.L.R.O., DC/PH/6/1–2, 29.

18 Guildhall MS. 19224/304; G.L.R.O., DC/PH/6/29; *Crockford* (1969–70, 1980–1).
19 Hennessy, *Novum Rep.* 416; *Brasenose Coll. Reg. 1509–1909*, i. 465, 492; *Gent. Mag.* ci (1), 106–8; C.C.C. files:, St. John (TS. hist. 1828–1978); BNC., B12, letters 1842–3.
20 Lambeth Pal. Libr., Fulham Papers, Tait 440/7.
21 P.R.O., HO 129/21/2/1/2.
22 Lambeth Pal. Libr., Fulham Papers, Tait 440/7.
23 Mudie-Smith, *Rel. Life*, 286.
24 BNC, Second Ser. [Tower] 148, letter from principal 23 Aug. 1841.
25 Lambeth Pal. Libr., Fulham Papers, Tait 440/7.
26 *Lond. City Mission Mag.* xlviii. 55; TS. hist. 1828–1978; *Mackeson's Guide.* (1889).
27 Guildhall MS. 19224/304; TS. hist. 1828–1978; Port, *Six Hundred New Chs.* 31, 47, 134–5; *Lond. Gaz.* 31 Mar. 1837, p. 876.
28 J. Summerson, *Georgian Lond.* (1945), 206; A. Service, *Architects of Lond.* (1973), 89, illus. 79; Pevsner, *Lond.* ii. 68; *Archit. of Lond.* 371; Port, *Six hundred New Chs.* 47; *Gent. Mag.* ci (1), 106–8; BNC, Second Ser. [Tower] 148, letter from vestry clerk 30 July 1827; above, plate 43.
29 Clarke, *Lond. Chs.* 161; Lewis, *Topog. Dict. Eng.* (1831), 152; plaque in vestibule.
30 *The Times*, 21 Feb. 1889, 9f; G.L.R.O., MBW 1757, no. 26.
31 G.L.R.O., AR/BA/4/31, no. 23.
32 TS. hist. 1828–1978; H. P. Clunn, *The Face of Lond.* (1951), 290.

FIG. 29. ST JOHN'S CHURCH C. 1840

N. part of par. united with St. Jas. the Less and rest with St. Simon Zelotes with St. Ant. to form par. of St. John with St. Simon.[33] Under Scheme of 1978, united with St. Bart. to form St. John with St. Bart. St. John's remained par. ch., after 1978 run by team ministry of R., chosen by Patronage Board and resident in St. John's parsonage, and V., chosen by bp. and R. and resident at St. Bartholomew's parsonage.[34]

ST. JUDE, Old Bethnal Green Rd. Dist. assigned from St. Mat. 1844. Patron bp. Endowed by Eccl. Com. with £150 p.a. 1844, £80 p.a. 1863, and by Q. A. B. with £50 p.a. from St. Cath. Coleman 1847.[35] Parsonage built S. of ch.[36] Attendance 1851: 500 adults and 250 children a.m., 700 p.m.;[37] a.a. c. 1858: 300 a.m., 400 p.m.;[38] attendance 1886: 175 a.m., 197 p.m.; 1903: 126 a.m., 279 p.m. Programme of svces. 'very scanty' 1848.[39] Two Sun. svces. with sermons, one during week, and monthly H.C. with c. 65 communicants 1858;[40] H.C. still monthly 1889 but weekly by 1897; Easter communicants 37 in 1892, 90 in 1900.[41] City Missionary scripture reader and women visitors but no curate 1858, when ch. supported young men's assoc., provident soc., and libr.[42] Usually 1 and, after grant by E.

Lond. Church Fund 1898–1908, 2 asst. curates. Alf. Strügnell, V. 1868–97, later often left curate in sole charge. Wilfred Davies, curate 1892–6, raised money for repair of ch. and schs.[43] and for institute and iron bldg. and soup kitchen in St. Jude's St. and Old Bethnal Green Rd.[44] Mission svces. at institute 1914;[45] open-air svces. in George Gdns. and Punderson's Gdns. Ch., helped by Oxford Ho., supported brigades, temperance and bible classes, wide range of clubs, and penny bank; country holidays for mothers and children.[46] Bldg. of yellow brick and stone in 'German Romanesque' style, seating 1,110 inc. 300 free, by Hen. Clutton on site acquired 1842, consecr. 1846: apsidal chancel, transepts, barrel roofed and clerestoried nave with N. and S. galleries, 2 towers with short spires in W. angle of transepts. Criticized for cold from lack of chimneys and for echo 1858. Restored 1869, altered six times 1878–1931, damaged by bombing 1940, and later demol.[47] Par. united with St. Jas. the Great under Scheme of 1951.[48]

ST. MATTHIAS, Hare (later Cheshire) St. Dist. assigned from SW. part of St. Mat. 1844. Patron bp. Endowed by Eccl. Com. with £150 p.a.

33 G.L.R.O., P72/BAT/39/1, 6.
34 Guildhall MS. 19224/304.
35 *Lond. Gaz.* 3 June 1844, pp. 1891–4; 15 June 1847, pp. 2175–8; *16th Rep. Eccl. Com.* [3273], H.C. p. 115 (1864), xviii; Hodgson, *Queen Anne's Bounty*, pp. lxxxix–xc.
36 Guildhall MS. 9561, no. 29; OS. Map 1/2,500, Lond. XXVII (1873 edn.).
37 P.R.O., HO 129/21/3/1/2.
38 Guildhall MS. 9561, no. 29.
39 *Ecclesiologist*, viii. 317–18.
40 Lambeth Pal. Libr., Fulham Papers, Tait 440/9.
41 G.L.R.O., P72/JUD/50.

42 Lambeth Pal. Libr., Fulham Papers, Tait 440/9.
43 G.L.R.O., P72/JUD/50; ibid. MTW/137/5.
44 Ibid. AR/BA/4/63, no. 6.
45 Harris and Bryant, *Chs. and Lond.* 381.
46 G.L.R.O., P72/JUD/50.
47 Ibid. C/72/187; Guildhall MS. 19224/353; P.R.O., HO 129/21/3/1/2; C.C.C. Clarke, Demol. Chs.; *Gent. Mag.* cxvii (2), 173; *Ecclesiologist*, viii. 317–18; G.L.R.O., MBO/506, f. 47; ibid. MBW 1676, no. 26; Lambeth Pal. Libr., Fulham Papers, Tait 440/9.
48 Guildhall MS. 19224/353.

1844, £50 p.a. 1864, and by Q. A. B. with £50 p.a. from St. Cath. Coleman 1847.[49] Incumbent allowed £25 p.a. to rent ho. 1857, but refused to live in unhealthy dist.[50] Site N. of Bethnal Green Rd., next to Gibraltar Walk, for parsonage blt. to design by Wm. White 1881, but V. still non-resident. 1889.[51] Attendance 1851: 150 adults and 300 children a.m., 400 p.m.;[52] a.a. 500–600 Sun. p.m. in summer, 800 winter but 'comparatively thin' a.m. c. 1858; attendance 1886: 103 a.m., 317 p.m.; 1903: 115 a.m., 163 p.m. Three Sun. svces., one weekday, and H.C. twice a month after p.m. svce. with a.a. 120–30 communicants c. 1858.[53] Svces. partly choral by 1866. Four Sun. svces. by 1914. First incumbent, 'energetic and popular', took poor for country excursions. Throughout 1850s close association with Lond. City Mission, which supplied 2 missionaries;[54] assisted by 2 curates, 2 lay scripture readers, and 2 men and 9 women visitors c. 1858. Curates held 3 svces. a week in schoolroom and readers held cottage lectures and bible classes. Ch. supported young men's class, provident soc., and libr.[55] Later usually 1 or no asst. curate. V. established industrial sch. 1868;[56] V.'s 'painstaking' work noted 1898.[57] Bldg. of yellow brick with stone dressings in 'Byzantine' or Romanesque style, seating 1,300 free, by T.H. Wyatt and D. Brandon 1846–8: apsidal sanctuary, short chancel, aisled and clerestoried nave, W. gallery, octagonal SW tower with spire.[58] St. Matthias's par. united with St. Mat. 1954 and ch. demol. 1957.[59]

ST. PAUL, Virginia Row. Dist. assigned from St. Matthias and St. Thos. 1865. First incumbent appointed by perpetual curate of St. Matthias and second by abp. of Canterbury by lapse; patron thereafter bp., from 1896/1900 dean and chapter of Canterbury.[60] Endowed by Eccl. Com. with £200 p.a. 1866.[61] Grant 1883 for parsonage built in Gosset St. 1899.[62] Attendance 1886: 34 a.m., 105 p.m.; 1903: 136 a.m., 201 p.m. Three Sun. svces., one weekday, H.C. twice a month 1889. First V. former curate of St. Matthias,[63] third former dissenting min. and curate of St. Simon Zelotes and St. Phil.[64] V. commended for conscientiousness 1898.[65] Among poorest benefices, with one and often no asst. curate.[66] Institute built in Gosset St. 1896.[67] High Ch. V., R. C. Jones, attracted more than 1,000 to Sun. p.m. svces. c. 1936.[68] Bldg. of stock brick with bands of red and black, seating 900, by Wm. Wigginton 1863–4: chancel, aisled nave, NE. tower. Damaged by bombing and demol. when par. united with St. Mat. 1951.[69]

ST. PETER, St. Peter's St. (later Ave.). Dist. assigned from St. Mat. 1843. Patron bp., from 1889/92 corp. of Lond.[70] Endowed by Eccl. Com. with £150 p.a. 1843, £50 p.a. 1865, and by Q. A. B. with £50 p.a. from St. Cath. Coleman 1847.[71] Parsonage built by Vulliamy at same time as ch. but in poor repair 1858.[72] Three Sun. svces. with large congregations, 30–40 at H.C., and regular attendants at twice daily prayers 1842.[73] Attendance 1851: 510 a.m., 90 aft., 610 p.m.;[74] a.a. c. 1858: 300 a.m., 70 aft., 250 p.m.;[75] attendance 1886: 286 a.m., 284 p.m.; 1903: 79 a.m., 140 p.m. Three Sun. svces. and 2 sermons, 2 daily svces, and H.C. twice a month 1858.[76] Partly choral by 1866, fully from 1880s when weekly H.C. By 1908 202 Easter communicants, H.C. twice on Sun., once choral, and once during week.[77] Daily office 1911.[78] John Graham Packer, V. 1841–73, bullied free thinker Chas. Bradlaugh (d.1891), in 1840s a Sun. sch. teacher at St. Peter's, and perhaps drove him out of Ch.[79] Par. supported libr. and was assisted by visiting soc. connected with metropolitan soc. 1858.[80] V. non-resident by 1870, when curate at parsonage.[81] Edw. Hyndman Beckles, V. 1873–1902 and bp. of Sierra Leone, lived in Suss. while G. H. Woolley, curate 1887–1903 and father of archaeologist Sir Leonard, found parsonage too small and lived in schoolmaster's ho. and part of sch. Wm. Hen. Maynard, V. 1903–30, raised funds to restore ch., extend Vicarage, and inaugurate many clubs and missions.[82] Mission svces. at St.

[49] Lond. Gaz. 3 June 1844, pp. 1891–4; 15 June 1847, pp. 2175–8; 15 June 1864, pp. 3051–3; Hodgson, Queen Anne's Bounty, pp. lxxxix–xc.
[50] Rep. Cttee. on Worship in Metropolis, p. 35, where min. J. Colbourne wrongly identified as incumbent of St. Mat.
[51] Guildhall MS. 19224/494; Lond. Gaz. 10 June 1881, p. 2966; Builder, 4 Feb. 1882, 150.
[52] P.R.O., HO 129/21/4/1/2.
[53] Rep. Cttee. on Worship in Metropolis, pp. 36, 39–40.
[54] Ibid. pp. 40–41; Lond. City Mission Mag. xvii. 66; xix 88.
[55] Rep. Cttee. on Worship in Metropolis, pp. 36, 41–3; Lambeth Pal. Libr., Fulham Papers, Tait 440/10.
[56] The Times, 14 Feb. 1867, 5d; 5 Jan. 1868, 10f.
[57] Booth, Life and Lab. iii(2), 77.
[58] Guildhall MS. 19224/494; 27th Ann. Rep. Com. for Bldg. New Chs. H.C. 693, p. 225 (1847), xxxiii; 1st Rep. Eccl. Com. H.C. 35, p. 240 (1846), xxiv; P.R.O., HO 129/21/4/1/2; Illus. Lond. News, 26 Feb. 1848, 122; Ecclesiologist, viii. 392–3; Lewis, Topog. Dict. Eng. (1849), i. 225; Pevsner, Lond. ii. 68; C.C.C. files, St. Matthias (photos.).
[59] Lond. Gaz. 2 July 1954, p. 3896; Guildhall MS. 19224/494; C.C.C. files, Bethnal Green chs., letter 3 Sept. 1985.
[60] Lond. Gaz. 1 Dec. 1865, pp. 6394–5; Guildhall MS. 19224/572; Hennessy, Novum Rep. 417.
[61] Lond. Gaz. 10 Aug. 1866, pp. 4467–8.
[62] Ibid. 15 June 1883, p. 3100; Guildhall MS. 19224/572; G.L.R.O., AR/BA/4/89, no 6.

[63] The Times, 29 Oct. 1863, 9f.
[64] Hennessy, Novum Rep. 417.
[65] Booth, Life and Lab. iii(2), 77.
[66] G.L.R.O., P72/MTW/137/6.
[67] Ibid. AR/BA/4/63, no. 6; Guildhall MS. 19224/572.
[68] Samuel, E. End Underworld, 343, n. 7, quoting The Star, 31 Mar. 1936.
[69] The Times, 29 Oct. 1863, 9f; C.C.C. Clarke. xv. 156; G.L.R.O., P72/BAT/39/1, 3.
[70] Lond. Gaz. 20 June 1843, pp. 208–71; Guildhall MS. 9561.
[71] Lond. Gaz. 16 June 1843, pp. 2016 sqq.; 15 June 1847, pp. 2175–8; 8 Aug. 1865, p. 3879; Hodgson, Queen Anne's Bounty, pp. lxxxix–xc.
[72] Guildhall MS. 19224/600; Lambeth Pal. Libr., Fulham Papers, Tait 440/11; Colvin, Brit. Architects, 858.
[73] Final Rep. Metropolis Chs. Fund, 61.
[74] P.R.O., HO 129/21/1/1/2.
[75] Guildhall MS. 9561, no. 23.
[76] Lambeth Pal. Libr., Fulham Papers, Tait 440/11.
[77] C.C.C. files, St. Peter (TS. Story of St. Peter's ch. 1980).
[78] G.L.R.O., P72/PET/30–1.
[79] H. B. Bonner, Chas. Bradlaugh (1894), i. 8, 12–15.
[80] Lambeth Pal. Libr., Fulham Papers, Tait 440/11.
[81] P.O. Dir. Lond. (1869, 1870).
[82] Hennessy, Novum Rep. 417; C.C.C. files, St. Peter (TS. Story of St. Peter's ch. 1980); G.L.R.O., P72/MTW/137/7.

Peter's schs. 1903 when attendance 101 p.m.
Nos. 40–42 St. Peter's St., inc. mission room
formerly used by Mildmay Trust, leased 1903
until par. hall and institute built on site of nos.
50–2 Warner Pl. 1912, where svces. held 1914.[83]
Asst. curate paid £80 p.a. by Additional Curates
Soc. 1858.[84] Usually 1 curate, sometimes 2 or
more, especially in late 19th cent.[85] Bldg., first
of Blomfield's chs., of flint, stone, and stock
brick in Romanesque style with 472 pews and
658 free seats, by Lewis Vulliamy 1840–1: sanctuary, large nave, W. porch beneath square
tower with octagonal lantern and spire.[86] In
bad repair c. 1858,[87] altered 1891,[88] restored,
with galleries removed and NE. vestry added,
1905; SE. choir vestry by E. T. Dunn. 1911.
Damaged by bombing 1941 and svces. held in
former sch. until ch. reconsecr. 1955.[89] Scheme
of 1951 united par. with St. Thos. and part of
St. Jude in new par. centred on St. Peter's.[90]
Served by visiting clergy, V. of St. Jas. the
Great, and Church Army 1963–72, then by
priest-in-charge, made V. 1978.[91] Church hall,
of red brick with stone dressings and in Tudor
style, built 1912, survived in Warner place in
1996.

St. Philip, Friar's Mount (later Swanfield St.).
'Clergyman' appointed 1842 and dist. assigned
from St. Mat. 1843. Patron bp. Endowed by
Eccl. Com. with £150 p.a. and £74 1843,
£64 p.a. 1863, and by Q. A. B. with £50 1853;[92]
Further £50 p.a. after closure of Holy Trinity
1926.[93] Parsonage built S. of ch. 1862.[94]
Attendance 1851: 130 adults and 200 children
a.m., 300 adults and 120 children p.m.;[95] 1886:
121 a.m., 245 p.m.; 1903: 122 a.m., 116 p.m. Two
Sun. svces., litany twice weekly, and a.a. 40
communicants 1858.[96] By 1889 H.C. twice a
month and 2 weekday svces.; 4 Sun. svces. by
1914. Poorest par., as 'the Nichol', where clergy
mainly concerned with material distress.
Geo. Alstone, incumbent 1842–51, declined fees
for baptisms;[97] Jas. Trevitt, 1851–72, exposed
conditions in letters to press.[98] Asst. curate paid
£80 by Additional Curates Soc. 1858, when 3
curates needed and want of funds 'oppressive'.[99]
Metropolitan Dist. Visiting Soc. paid £80 p.a. to

FIG. 30. St Simon Zelotes's church in 1850

support 40 visitors 1861, when ch. ran several
schs., socs., and library.[1] From 1870 usually 1 and
sometimes no asst. curate, especially after 1918.[2]
Ch. said c. 1898 to dispense indiscriminate
charity and work 'confined to children'.[3] Par.
room, later boys' club, built N. of ch. 1902.[4]
Bldg. of stock brick with red mouldings and
stone dressings in Romanesque style, seating
1,100 free, by T. L. Walker 1841–2: shallow
chancel, nave, twin short W. towers and low
spires.[5] Under Scheme of 1954 par. united with
St. Mat. Ch. then used as ch. furniture store
until demol. 1966.[6]

St. Simon Zelotes, Morpeth St.[7] Dist.
assigned from St. John and St. Jas. the Less
1844. Patron bp. Endowed by Eccl. Com. with
£150 p.a. 1844 and £50 1865 and by Q. A. B.
with £50 p.a. 1853.[8] Parsonage, to S., built at

83 TS. Story of St. Peter's; G.L.R.O., P72/PET/21–26;
AR/BA/4/235, no. 5.
84 Lambeth Pal. Libr., Fulham Papers, Tait 440/11.
85 G.L.R.O., P72/MTW/137/7.
86 *Final Rep. Metropolis Chs. Fund*, App. IV, 53;
Guildhall MS. 19224/600; Port, *Six Hundred New Chs.*
152–3; Colvin, *Brit. Architects*, 858; Pevsner, *Lond.* ii. 68;
Clarke, *Lond. Chs.* 161–2; *Ecclesiologist*, i. 196–7; above,
plate 42.
87 Guildhall MS. 9561, no. 23.
88 G.L.R.O., AR/BA/4/22, no. 27.
89 Ibid. P72/PET/28–31, 34–36; TS. Story of St. Peter's.
90 *Lond. Gaz.* 23 Nov. 1951, p. 6124; G.L.R.O.,
P72/BAT/39/1, 4.
91 Guildhall MS. 19224/600; TS. Story of St. Peter's.
92 *Final Rep. Metropolis Chs. Fund*, App. IV, 61; *Lond.
Gaz.* 16 June 1843, pp. 2016 sqq.; 20 June 1843, pp. 2068–71;
3 Oct. 1843, p. 3220; 9 Aug. 1853, pp. 2168–70; *16th Rep.
Eccl. Com.* [3273], H.C. p. 115 (1864), xviii; Hodgson, *Queen
Anne's Bounty*, pp. lxxxix–xc.
93 *Lond. Gaz.* 4 July 1926, pp. 3641–4.
94 G.L.R.O., P72/PH1/51.
95 P.R.O., HO 129/21/4/1/5.
96 Lambeth Pal. Libr., Fulham Papers, Tait 440/17.

97 BNC, B12, letters from R. 1843.
98 e.g. *The Times*, 17 Feb. 1853, 5*f*.
99 Guildhall MS. 9561, no. 28; Lambeth Pal. Libr.,
Fulham Papers, Tait 440/17.
1 Lambeth Pal. Libr., Fulham papers, Tait 440/17; J.
Hollingshead, *Ragged Lond. in 1861* (1861), 71, 82–85. Pop.
in par. greatest (11,397) in 1861 before creation of Holy
Trinity, Shoreditch: *Census*, 1861, 1871.
2 G.L.R.O., P72/MTW/137/8.
3 Booth, *Life and Lab.* iii (2), 75.
4 G.L.R.O., AR/BA/4/117, no. 5; ibid. P72/MTW/147/3;
O.S. Map 1/500, TQ. 338.2 (1964 edn.).
5 C.C.C. Clarke, Demol. Chs., St. Phil.; Guildhall MS.
19224/618; *Lond. Gaz.* 20 June 1843, pp. 2068–71; Pevsner,
Lond. ii. 68; Lewis, *Topog. Dict. Eng.* (1849), 225.
6 *Lond. Gaz.* 2 July 1954, p. 3896; G.L.R.O.,
P72/BAT/39/1–3; C.C.C. file, Bethnal Green chs., letter 3
Sept. 1985.
7 Site of ch., parsonage, and sch. enclosed by Morpeth,
Knottisford, and William (Warley) streets and Cemetery
(Bullard's) Pl.: O.S. Map 1/2,500, Lond. XXVIII (1873 edn).
8 *Lond. Gaz.* 3 June 1844, pp. 1891–4; 9 Aug. 1853, pp.
2168–70; 8 Aug. 1865, pp. 3877–9; Hodgson, *Queen Anne's
Bounty*, pp. lxxxix–xc.

same time as ch.[9] Attendance 1851: 99 adults and 94 children a.m., 150 adults and 17 children p.m.;[10] 1886: 109 a.m., 159 p.m.; 1903: 183 a.m., 216 p.m. Two Sun. svces., occasional aft. svce. in schoolroom, and monthly H.C. with a.a. 15–32 communicants 1858.[11] Three, partly choral, Sun. svces. and daily svce. 1881. Weekly H.C. by 1914. Incumbent[12] usually assisted by curate, paid £80 p.a. and by scripture reader and 9 visitors from Metropolitan Visiting Assoc. 1858, when ch. supported provident soc. and par. libr.[13] Three curates before the First World War. Mission in Surat St. c. 1898 and par. bldgs. erected in Warley St. 1907.[14] Bldg. in Transitional Gothic style, seating 933 free, by Ben. Ferrey, on site acquired 1840, consecr. 1847: chancel, aisled and clerestoried nave, W. galleries, belfry, and small tower.[15] Large window cut in W. wall 1912.[16] Damaged by bombing 1943–4 and later demol.[17] Par. united with St. Ant., Stepney, 1936 and, under Scheme of 1951, with St. John, Bethnal Green.[18] Parsonage served combined benefice until 1975.[19]

ST. THOMAS, Baroness Rd. Dist. assigned from St. Mat. 1844. Patron bp. Endowed by Eccl. Com. with £150 p.a. 1844, £75 p.a. 1864, £25 p.a. 1865, and by Q. A. B. with £50 from St. Cath. Coleman 1847.[20] Annual grants from St. Paul, Hampstead, 1900–5.[21] Parsonage, to NE., built at same time as ch.[22] a.a. c. 1858: 150 a.m., 200 p.m.;[23] attendance 1886: 140 a.m., 220 p.m.; 1903: 156 a.m., 194 p.m. Three svces. with 2 sermons on Sun., 1 on Fri., and monthly H.C. with a.a. 40–50 communicants 1858.[24] Svces. fully choral with altar lights by 1881, when H.C. every Sun. and once on weekdays and 2 daily svces.; 5 Sun. svces. by 1914. Two asst. curates, paid respectively £100 by Church Pastoral Soc. and £80 by Curates Pastoral Aid Soc., and 11 women and 2 or 3 men visitors and 60–70 Sun. sch. teachers c. 1857.[25] After loss of a curate, incumbent complained of too few clergy 1858;[26] thereafter usually 1 asst. curate until 1930s.[27] Mission svces. in institute in Baroness Rd. c. 1914. Bldg. of Kentish rag in Early Eng. style, with 480 free sittings and 300 sittings for children, by Lewis Vulliamy on site in Nova

Scotia Gdns. given by owners 1848 and financed by Wm. Cotton as memorial to son, consecr. 1850: short apsidal chancel, aisled nave, SW. tower. Altered 1892, restored 1909, damaged during Second World War, and demol. 1954.[28] Under Scheme of 1951 par. united with St. Peter.[29]

ANGLICAN MISSIONS. ALL SAINTS, Vyner St. Maria Pope of Kensington gave land behind no. 244 Cambridge Rd. to Christ Ch., S. Hackney, 1888.[30] Site nearby, at junction of Vyner and Mowlem streets, where mission ch. built at her expense 1894–5, sold by Maria Pope to trustees (inc. V. of Christ Ch.) appointed by bp. 1896. Premises inc. gym, club room, classrooms, and chapel seating 300. Attendance 1903: 30 a.m., 27 p.m. Bldg. of red brick and stone dressings, by J. E. K. and J. P. Cutts, used as mission c. 1914 but converted to workshop 1926 and later used as shoe factory.[31]

PETLEY HALL, Chilton St. Site on W. side opposite St. Matthias ch., with mission ho. and other bldgs. erected 1886, conveyed by C. R. C. Petley to Bp. of Lond.'s Fund for mission 1887.[32] Listed as place of worship c. 1898, mission hall 1910, and par. room of St. Matthias 1938.[33]

ST. FRANCIS OF ASSISI, Cambridge Rd. Former Birkbeck sch. (closed 1884) on. W. side opened as St. And.'s hall 1888. Clubroom and offices on lower floor, halls above. Attendance 1903: 34 p.m. Dilapidated by 1914 and reconstructed by Austin Durst 1919. Reopened as ch. of St. Francis of Assisi 1920 and used as mission until destroyed in war.[34]

ST. MARTIN, Somerford St. Mission hall on site at corner of Somerford and Tapp streets, leased by Hilda Barry of St. Margaret's Ho. to St. Bart's par. 1899.[35] By 1927 owned by Lond. Diocesan Fund, which conveyed it to parochial ch. council of St. Bart. Always run as mission from St. Bart. with curate as priest-in-charge, aided by mission women 1906. Attendance 1903: 69 p.m.; Sun. sch. and p.m. mission svce. each Sun. 1906.[36] Large red-brick bldg. with Bath stone dressings 1898–99.[37] Sold to L.C.C. 1934 when St. Bart. built new

9 G.L.R.O., MBO/DS/12/B.
10 P.R.O., HO 129/21/2/1/4.
11 Lambeth Pal. Libr., Fulham Papers, Tait 440/18.
12 For incumbents, Hennessy, *Novum Rep.* 418.
13 G.L.R.O., P72/MTW/137/9; Lambeth Palace Libr., Fulham Papers, Tait 440/18.
14 Booth, *Life and Lab.* iii (1), 72; G.L.R.O., AR/BA/4/162, no. 4.
15 Guildhall MS. 19224/640; P.R.O., HO 129/21/2/1/4; C.C.C. Clarke, Demol. Chs., St. Simon Zelotes (illus.); *Ecclesiologist*, viii. 318–19.
16 G.L.R.O., AR/BA/4/235, no. 4.
17 Ibid. note in cal. to P72/SIM/1–14.
18 Guildhall MS. 19224/640; G.L.R.O., P72/BAT/39/1–2, 4; *Lond. Gaz.* 23 Nov. 1951, p. 6124.
19 O.S. Map 1/500, TQ 3582 (1966 edn.); above, St. John.
20 *Lond. Gaz.* 3 June 1844, pp. 1891–4; 15 June 1847, pp. 2175–8; 15 June 1864, pp. 3051–3; 10 Oct. 1865, pp. 4775–8; Hodgson, *Queen Anne's Bounty*, pp. lxxxix–xc.
21 C.C.C. Clarke, Demol. Chs., St. Thos.
22 Guildhall MS. 19224/658.
23 Ibid. 9561, no. 32.
24 Lambeth Pal. Libr., Fulham papers, Tait 440/13.
25 *Rep. Cttee. on Worship in Metropolis*, pp. 47–9.

26 Guildhall MS. 9561, no. 32.
27 G.L.R.O., P72/MTW/137/10.
28 Ibid. MBO/DS/12E; ibid. AR/BA/4/31, no. 24; Guildhall MS. 19224/658; *D.N.B.*; *Rep. Cttee. on Worship in Metropolis*, p. 5; C.C.C. Clarke, Demol. Chs., St. Thos.; Pevsner, *Lond.* ii. 68; P.R.O., HO 129/21/1/1/1.
29 *Lond. Gaz.* 23 Nov. 1951, p. 6124; G.L.R.O., P72/BAT/39/1–2; Guildhall MS. 19224/658.
30 P.R.O., C 54/19268, mm. 1–3; G.L.R.O., MBW 1776, no. 26.
31 P.R.O., C 54/20115, mm. 25–30; C.C.C., Clarke, Demol. Chs., All Saints mission; G.L.R.O., AR/BA/4/437, no. 3.
32 P.R.O., C 54/19352, mm. 14–16; *Builder*, 30 Jan. 1886, 221.
33 Booth, *Life and Lab.* iii (2), 108; *Bacon's New Atlas of Lond. and Suburbs* (1910), sheet 47; O.S. Map 1/500, Lond. VII. 47 (1938 edn.).
34 C.C.C. Clarke, Demol. Chs., St. Fras. of Assisi, mission; Robinson and Chesshyre, *The Green*, 29; *P.O. Dir. Lond.* (1886–1929).
35 G.L.R.O., AR/BA/4/80, no. 6; ibid. P72/BAT/90.
36 Ibid. P72/BAT/99/1, 119.
37 *Eastern Argus*, 30 Apr. 1898 (T.H.L.H.L. Cuttings file 226.1); C.C.C. Clarke, Demol. Chs., St. Martin's mission ch.

par. hall.[38] Closed by 1939 and destroyed in war.[39]

UNIVERSITY SETTLEMENTS. OXFORD HOUSE,[40] Derbyshire St. Founded 1884 by group led by warden of Keble Coll., Oxf., alarmed at undenom. nature of recently opened Toynbee Hall. Conceived as settlement for Anglican graduates to provide religious, social, and educational svces. for East End and to acquire practical experience, especially if they intended to take holy orders. G. W. H. Knight-Bruce,[41] curate of St. And.'s, offered Nat. sch. next to ch., converted into clubroom and for 2 residents. More rooms rented in ho. until large red-brick bldg. by Sir Art. Blomfield erected in Derbyshire St. 1891.[42] Provided clubs for men and boys, dispensary, workshops, lectures, reading rooms, and legal advice. Mission svces. in large iron Oxford hall, built behind no. 17 Victoria Park Sq. 1887,[43] at chapel belonging to Webbe institute, founded 1888, and in chs.[44] By 1899 eight Bethnal Green pars. receiving help, especially in visiting and running clubs, from Oxford Ho. and 7 clergy former residents. Heads of Oxford Ho. inc. A. F. Winnington-Ingram (1889–97) and B. R. Wilson (1897–1901), successive R.s under whom Rectory housed members of Ho., and Fred. A. Iremonger (1911–6), also V. of St. Jas. the Great.[45] Often resented as rival by local clergy, especially after First World War. Oxf. institutions provided 68 per cent. of finance 1885, 9 per cent. 1914. Women residents and club members from 1937; first married head of ho. 1938. After 1945 local element dominant and mainly a community centre, financial difficulties bringing temp. closure 1969. Reopened but no longer residential and religious dimension almost entirely lost. Housed Lesbian and Gay Christian Movement 1992.[46]

RIDLEY HOUSE,[47] St. James's Rd. Univ. settlement by evangelical wing of Ch. of Eng. linked with Ridley Hall, Camb. and Wycliffe Hall, Oxf., opened next to St. Jas. the Less ch. 1904. V., J. E. Watts-Ditchfield, first warden. Housed candidates for holy orders,[48] under supervision of V. and, for shorter periods, other univ. men and outside clergy interested in East End. Social and medical svces. provided but emphasis on spiritual appeal.

ST. MARGARET'S HOUSE,[49] 21 Old Ford Rd. Women's branch of Oxford Ho. founded 1889, run by cttee. of Oxf. women and alumnae of Cheltenham Ladies' Coll. Opened Mayfield

Ho., nos. 1–3 Old Ford Rd., providing for women svces. similar to those of Oxford Ho.[50] Oxf. group moved to St. Bart.'s mission ho. 1892 and leased no. 4 Victoria Park Sq., which opened as St. Margaret's Ho. 1893. Leased University Ho. at no. 17 Victoria Park Sq. 1895. Both replaced by no. 21 Old Ford Rd., purchased from Female Guardians Assoc. 1900, where chapel by Paul Waterhouse opened 1904.[51] By 1912 residents active in 6 pars., running schs. and social and welfare organizations. Recognized as training centre for ch. workers 1922 and for social workers 1929. Involved with Citizens' Advice Bureau 1939–89. No. 19 Old Ford Rd. acquired 1946 and association with local govt. strengthened after war. Cozy club, claimed as first old age pensioners' club in Lond., started 1936, became day centre for pensioners 1957. Youth clubs declined until 1962 when community svce. volunteers established. Formal connexion with Oxford Ho. severed 1966 and other groups housed from 1970s, inc. Newpin (parent and infant network), Tower Hamlets Vietnamese Families Assoc., and work centre and social club for elderly. Financial difficulties brought proposal to sell no. 19 Old Ford Rd. 1989. Still resident Christian settlement 1990.

ST. HILDA'S EAST,[52] 18 Club Row. Settlement left at Mayfield Ho. after foundation of St. Margaret's Ho. built hall and residence at no. 3 Old Nichol St., in new Boundary Street est., which opened as St. Hilda's East 1898.[53] Contained chapel and carried out parochial and non-parochial work inc. help with nursery schs. and social clubs and for unemployed. Bldg. opposite, no. 18 Club Row, on site of Nichol ragged sch. and mission, purchased 1944. Reconstructed after bomb damage as Bruce hall, opened 1950. Bldg. in Old Nichol St. had 15 residents, mostly social science students, c. 1950, by which time Anglican connexion much attenuated; men admitted from 1950.[54] Bldg. given up 1964 and later used by Cheshire Foundation as mental health hostel. Club Row bldg. used for young and old people's social activities and new day centre opened 1968. Increasing involvement of local community. Immigration caused friction with vandalizing of youth club bldgs., leading to closure of youth section by I.L.E.A. 1973. Rebuilt 1977. Club Row club opened 1975, with bar by 1981 which was later closed to attract Muslims. No specific religious connexion 1990, rebuilt 1994.[55]

38 G.L.R.O., P72/BAT/100/1, 4.
39 C.C.C. Clarke, Demol. Chs., St. Martin's; P.O. Dir. Lond.. (1936–51).
40 Based on Oxford Ho. in Bethnal Green, 1884–1948 (1948); M. Ashworth, Oxford Ho. in Bethnal Green (c. 1987).
41 D.N.B; above, St. And.
42 Datestone.
43 G.L.R.O., MBW 1757, no. 26; E. Lond. Mag. v (1), Dec. 1890.
44 Universities and the Social Problem, ed. J. M. Knapp (1985 reprint of 1895), 33 sqq.
45 Pringle, 'St. Jas. the Gt.'; Harris and Bryant, Churches and Lond. 271–2.
46 Yellow Pages, Lond. E. 1992/3.

47 Based on 'Roads from the Univ. Which shall I take'? [1906] (T.H.L.H.L. pamphlet 225.5).
48 Described as 'clergy ho.': G.L.R.O. AR/BA/4/133, no. 4.
49 Based on K. B. Beauman, St. Marg.'s Ho. Brief Hist.: 1889–1989 (1989); St. Marg.'s Ho., Ann. Rep. 1988–9.
50 Universities and Social Problem, ed. Knapp, 120 sqq.; Robinson and Chesshyre, The Green, 20–1.
51 G.L.R.O., AR/BA/4/133, no. 4.
52 Based on M. Rendel and E. Kyle, St. Hilda's East, Cent. of Community Svce. 1889–1989 (1989).
53 Robinson and Chesshyre, The Green, 22; G.L.R.O., AR/BA/4/71, no. 6.
54 G.L.R.O., A/FWA/C/A61/3/31.
55 Inf. from director; Mr. C.O. O'Brien (Bldgs. of Eng.).

ROMAN CATHOLICISM

A CORNISH recusant, Richard Tremayne, was living in Bethnal Green when he was indicted in 1588.[56] John Howe, a tenant of Bishop's Hall, was absent from church in 1640[57] but suspicions that Sir Balthazar Gerbier was harbouring priests in 1642 proved unfounded.[58] Fifteen recusants were listed in 1678 and 1689.[59] One, a weaver in Nichol Street, was also listed in 1706[60] and another weaver, who lived in Hare Street, was a recusant c. 1717.[61] Four men, none long-term residents, and a woman were returned as papists in 1767.[62] In 1778 there were a few papists but 'none of any note' and in 1810 'very few if any'.[63] There were English Roman Catholics in the area in the 1830s and 1840s[64] and four families of 'avowed Romanists' in St. John's parish in 1858.[65] Although Bethnal Green lay outside the area of Irish settlement, some proselytizing emanated from communities to the south. In the mid 19th century Sisters of Charity tended destitute families in Bethnal Green.[66] The Marists in Spitalfields opened a school in Parliament Street in 1869.[67]

The first permanent Roman Catholic church served late 19th-century Polish and Lithuanian refugees, who settled near their Jewish compatriots and learnt tailoring and cabinet making from them.[68]

Religious orders moved from Mile End Road, where they ran a Polish mission, to open a Polish and Lithuanian church in 1896. The Assumptionists, originally a French order, opened a chapel in 1902,[69] when the local Protestant Alliance, already alarmed at Anglican ritualism, unsuccessfully took out a summons against the Roman Catholics.[70] Roman Catholic attendances of 729 were, however, less than 4 per cent of the total in 1903.[71] The Missionaries of the Divine Love, who ran the Polish church, had left by 1905 and the Sisters of the Holy Family of Nazareth, the other Polish order, by 1910. Two churches opened in 1912, a Lithuanian church in the Oval and Our Lady of the Assumption in Victoria Park Square, served by the Assumptionists. Other religious orders were the Sisters of the Christian Retreat in Victoria Park c. 1927–1941, the Marian Fathers

at the Lithuanian church from 1931, and the Canonesses of St. Augustine from 1982.[72] The churches and other institutions are described below.

The abbreviation reg. denotes registration for worship. Attendance figs. 1903 are from Mudie-Smith, *Rel. Life*, 57.

ST. JOSEPH AND ST. CASIMIR Polish and Lithuanian ch., run by Missionaries of Divine Love, reg. at no. 184A Cambridge Rd. 1896.[73] Attendance 1903: 252 a.m., 96 p.m. Moved to corner of Cambridge Rd. and Patriot Sq. where reg. as St. Mary and St. Casimir chapel 1905. Moved to Shadwell 1906.[74]

ST. CASIMIR Lithuanian ch. opened in St. Geo.-in-the-East 1902,[75] moved to the Oval, off Hackney Rd. where ch. reg. 1912.[76] Average attendance c. 1926: 200–250. Served by Marian fathers since 1931. Bldg. in vaguely Italian style, though capitals 'Egyptian', by Benedict Williamson 1911:. inc. accommodation for clergy and social centre for parishioners opened 1974.[77]

Augustinians of the Assumption, concerned mainly with educ., invited from France by Cardinal Manning 1901 and opened chapel of OUR LADY OF THE ASSUMPTION in North Passage, Green St., near Globe Rd. 1902.[78] Attendance 1903: 197 a.m., 79 p.m. Moved to vacated Polish and Lithuanian chapel at no. 184A Cambridge Rd. 1905.[79] Gift of Florence Cottrell-Dormer, in memory of husband, for new ch. and priory as headquarters of order on NE. side of Victoria Park Sq., on site of Park Congreg. chapel, 1912. Assumptionists opened sch. 1925. Bldg. of stock brick and stone in Gothic style by Edw. Goldie: shallow apse, high chancel, large nave, cloistered aisles.[80]

Sch. chapel in Parliament St. used for pub. worship 1903, attendance 105 a.m., and 1934.[81]

St. Patrick's hall in Cranbrook St. reg. 1905–6.[82]

Missionaries of the Divine Love, from Polish mission in Mile End Rd., at no. 184A Cambridge Rd. 1896–1905.[83]

Sisters of the Holy Family of Nazareth, Polish order devoted to sick and poor, moved from Mile End Rd. to no. 14 Patriot Sq. 1897, to no.

[56] *Recusants in Exchequer Pipe Rolls 1581–92* (Cath. Rec. Soc. lxxi), 175; *Miscellanea XII* (Cath. Rec. Soc. xxii), 123.
[57] *Mdx. County Rec.* iii. 153.
[58] *E. Lond. Papers*, x(1), 24. For Gerbier, below, educ. (private schs.).
[59] Hist. MSS. Com. 17, *MSS. of H.L.* i. 59 (*11th Rep.* pt. 2, p. 59); ii. 10 (*12th Rep.* pt. 6, p. 10).
[60] Guildhall MS. 9800/2.
[61] G.L.R.O., MR/RR 26/15.
[62] *Rets. of Papists 1767*, ii (Cath. Rec. Soc., Occas. Publs. no. 2, 1989), 135.
[63] Lambeth Pal. Libr., Fulham Papers, Lowth 5; Randolph 11/21.
[64] T.H.L.H.L., TH/8362/1.
[65] Lambeth Pal. Libr., Fulham Papers, Tait 440/7.
[66] *Studies in Lond. Hist. presented to P. E. Jones*, ed. A. G. J. Hollaender and W. Kellaway (1969), 433.
[67] Below, educ. (pub. schs.).
[68] Inf. from R. of St. Casimir's Lithuanian ch.
[69] Below.
[70] Booth, *Life and Lab.* iii (2), 82; Robinson and

Chesshyre, *The Green*, 24.
[71] Mudie-Smith, *Rel. Life*, 58.
[72] Below.
[73] G.R.O. Worship Reg. no. 35628; G.L.R.O., AR/BA/4/71, no. 5; *Cath. Dir.* (1900–2).
[74] G.R.O. Worship Reg. nos. 40868, 41629; *Cath. Dir.* (1905).
[75] G.R.O. Worship Reg. no. 39107.
[76] Ibid. no. 45202; G.L.R.O., AR/BA/4/221, no. 5.
[77] A. Rottmann, *Lond. Cath. Chs.* (1926), 206–7; T.H.L.H.L., Cuttings file 226.6; inf. from rector 1991.
[78] P.F. Anson, *Religious Orders of Gt. Britain and Irel.*(1949), 18–22; G.R.O. Worship Reg. no. 38855.
[79] G.R.O. Worship Reg. no. 41068.
[80] Ibid. no. 45266; G.L.R.O., AR/BA/4/251, no. 4; Rottmann, *Lond. Cath. Chs.* 188–9, 191; Robinson and Chesshyre, *The Green*, 24; C.C.C. Clarke, xv. 155; *The Times*, 24 June 1912, 3d; below, educ. (pub. schs.).
[81] *Cath. Dir.* (1934).
[82] G.R.O. Worship Reg. no. 41142.
[83] *Cath. Dir.* (1896–1905).

1 Old Ford Rd. 1899, where ran rescue home for *c.* 50 boys, and to no. 37 Approach Rd. in Victoria Pk. by 1905. Left before 1910.[84]

Sisters of the Christian Retreat, French order specializing in educ., maintained St. Teresa's convent at no. 106 Sewardstone Rd. *c.* 1927–41.[85]

Congregation of Our Lady (Canonesses of St. Augustine), originally French order specializing in educ., moved into council property in Burnham est., Globe Rd. 1982. Moved to nos. 38 and 44 Stafford Cripps Ho., Globe Rd., 1984 and gave up no. 38 1990.[86]

PROTESTANT NONCONFORMITY

THE first dissenting congregation was either that of an Independent meeting house from 1669[87] or one using the formerly Anglican St. George's chapel and associated with the dissenters' academy at Bishop's Hall.[88] Early ministers included Francis Bampfield, John Hodges, a Congregationalist, and Thomas Lye, a Presbyterian, all licensed in 1672. Bampfield (d. 1684), an ejected vicar, organized a Seventh-Day Baptist chapel in his house in Bethnal Green in 1676.[89] Lye died at Bethnal Green in 1684 and Hodges was still a minister there in 1690.[90] In 1684 the officials of Bethnal Green were punished for refusing to reveal conventicles, of which there were 'great numbers in private houses'.[91] George Fox often stayed with a friend in Bethnal Green in 1685–6.[92] There was a meeting house on the western side of Bethnal Green, at which Thomas Brand was the preacher, in 1689.[93]

The Huguenot église de St. Jean, Spitalfields, had been established on the north side of St. John Street by 1687 and probably by 1682. It was opened by English nonconformists who allowed the Huguenots to use it outside regular service times. As the native congregation declined, it became a wholly French chapel, using the liturgy of the French Reformed Church.[94] Two French meeting houses in Bethnal Green were reported in 1711.[95]

The house of Nicholas Humfrey on the green was certified for Independent meetings in 1713[96] although it is not clear whether it served the congregation of 1669. A meeting house was 'near finished' in 1724[97] and a house in 'The Way leading from Castle Street to Virginia Row' was used as a meeting house in 1728.[98] There were meeting houses in 1732[99] including, presumably, at least one for Independents and two for Huguenots, those in St. John Street and others from

1721 to *c.* 1740 at Swanfields in Slaughter (Sclater) Street, who may also have met in Cock Lane. The St. John Street chapel was rebuilt in 1765 and used regularly until 1821 and occasionally until 1827.[1] It was connected with the Sunday School Tract Society in the 1820s[2] and accommodated 450 in 1838.[3]

A Presbyterian meeting house, in 1795 on the green,[4] was recorded from 1711. Several dissenters 'under the denomination of Presbyterian' had a meeting house with a licensed teacher in 1778. It may have been Bethnal Green Independent chapel,[5] which was so described in the 1780s.[6]

John Wesley preached at Bonner's Hall, where he had stayed in 1754, in 1755–7 and in the parish church in 1775, 1785, and 1788. He also visited the 'French church in Spitalfields',[7] gave advice in 1772 to 'La Communauté Chrétienne', whose members became closely associated with the Methodists,[8] and mentioned his visit in 1777 to 'those of our society who lived in Bethnal Green' in terrible poverty.[9] Methodists were 'increasing daily' under enthusiastic preachers' in 1778[10] and were 'very numerous' in the 1780s.[11] In 1810 they were said to be most prevalent among the 'lower class' with five meeting houses, each with resident licensed teachers besides preachers who visited the workhouse.[12] In 1811 three Methodist meeting houses were noted, one of which had been said in 1808 to be the principal London station of the Kilhamites or New Methodist Connexion.[13] No registration for worship since 1792 had been for Methodists and if the three meeting houses were registered earlier it was probably as Protestant or Independent. Middlesex chapel, certainly Methodist by 1811, was registered in 1797 as Independent.

The Christian Community, having discarded

84 Ibid. (1896–1910); Anson, *Rel. Orders*, 289.
85 *Cath. Dir.* (1926–42); Anson, *Rel. Orders*, 237–8.
86 *Cath. Dir.* (1984–90); inf. from Sister Jennifer Dines, Congreg. of Our Lady.
87 Below, this section (Congs.).
88 Guildhall MS. 9537/20, p. 12; below, educ. (private schs.).
89 A.C. Underwood, *Hist. Eng. Bapts.* (1947), 114.
90 *Calamy Revised*, 26, 270, 332; *Cal. S.P. Dom.* 1672, 676.
91 Cal. Mdx. Sess. Bks. vii. 59 sqq.
92 *Jnl. of Geo. Fox*, ed. N. Penney (1911), ii. 419, 434.
93 Cal. Mdx. Sess. Bks. viii. 100.
94 *Proc. Huguenot Soc. of Lond.* viii. 23–4; *E. Lond. Papers*, xiii(2), 76; C L.R.O., Box 43, MS. 22; W. Morgan, *Survey of Lond. and Westm.* (1682).
95 *C.J.* xvi. 542.
96 Cal. Mdx. Sess. Bks. x. 148.
97 Lambeth Pal. Libr., MS. 2712, ff. 182–3.
98 M.L.R. 1728/2/140.
99 Co. of Par. Clerks, *New Remarks of Lond.* (1732), 195.
1 *Procs. Huguenot Soc. of Lond.* viii. 23, 53; *Reg. of ch.*

of *St. Jean Spitalfields* (Hug. Soc. xxxix), pp. xi–xiv; *E. Lond. Papers*, xiii(2), 76, 86–7.
2 G.L.R.O., Acc. 2330/86/1.
3 *Lond. City Mission Mag.* iii. 53–4.
4 Lysons, *Environs*, ii. 37.
5 *C.J.* xi. 542; W. Maitland, *Hist. Lond.* (1739), 516–17; ibid (1756), i. 1189–90; ibid (1775), i. 1189–90; Lambeth Pal. Libr., Fulham Papers, Lowth S, ff. 386–9. No Ind. chapel listed for Bethnal Green although continuous hist. of chapel testified by reg.: below, Congs.
6 Guildhall MS. 9557, ff. 42.
7 *John Wesley's Jnl.* ed. N. Curnock (1938), iv. 101, 126, 187, 193; vi. 83; vii. 126, 420.
8 E.C. Rayner, *Story of the Christian Community, 1685–1909* (1909) (T.H.L.H.L. 226.3).
9 *Wesley's Jnl.* vi. 136.
10 Lambeth Pal. Libr., Fulham Papers, Lowth 5, ff. 386–9.
11 Guildhall MS. 9557, f. 42.
12 Lambeth Pal. Libr., Fulham Papers, Randolph 11/21.
13 Lysons, *Environs*, Suppl. 101; W. Wilson, *Hist. Dissenting Chs. in Lond.* (1808), ii. 561.

its French name, published its rules in 1800 and 1816. It preached outdoors in summer and hired rooms in winter, holding Sunday schools and meetings under leaders approved by the Methodists at City Road. Among Methodist chapels originating in these cottage meetings were Globe Road and Hart's Lane. In 1819 the Community broke with the Wesleyan City Circuit when its preachers refused to acknowledge the Circuit's exclusive control of Globe Road chapel.[14]

There were secessions and regroupings among all nonconformists in the later 18th and early 19th century. Of the 95 meeting places registered for worship[15] between 1792 and 1850, 9 were for Methodists, 9 for Baptists, 36 for Independents, 2 for Unitarians, 4 for Calvinists, 3 for Independent Calvinists, 1 each for the Christian Society, Universalists, Latter-day Saints, and Protestants of the Catholic Apostolic Church, 21 for 'Protestants', and 7 were not designated. Most meeting places were short lived and in private houses. A few were forerunners of the chapels whose histories are given below.

The largest denomination was Independent, whose meetings usually developed into Congregational chapels. Returns of worship made presumably by the Anglican incumbent in 1810 classified the French church, with 550 places, as Anglican and calculated that there were 1,650 places in six nonconformist chapels, although he was confused as to their denominations.[16] A survey of all accommodation for worship made by the London City Mission in 1838[17] found that 6,610 (recte 6,910) places were for nonconformists. Of these 3,950 (57 per cent) belonged to 11 Independent chapels, of which 9 became Congregational[18] and 2 Baptist chapels.[19] Four Baptist chapels[20] had 1,100 places (16 per cent), 4 Methodist chapels[21] had 810, one Unitarian had 300, and St. John Street, for which no denomination was given, had 450. An unidentified missionary chapel accommodated 300.

Independents in 1851[22] still had the largest proportion of the accommodation (7,762), although it had fallen to 52 per cent. Their attendances were by far the highest, 7,789 at 14 places of worship[23] amounting to 73 per cent of the nonconformist total of 10,642. Baptists had 21 per cent of the accommodation at their 6 places.[24] Methodists had increased to 17 per cent

of the accommodation and 19 per cent (2,033) of the attendance at their 4 chapels.[25] There was one chapel for Unitarians and one for Lady Huntingdon's Connexion,[26] besides two 'mixed and undefined' chapels, presumably the Calvinistic (later Baptist) Hephzibah and Zehovah in Thorold Square, described as 'various Christian denominations'.[27] In 1858 the Anglican clergy of 12 Bethnal Green parishes listed as dissenting places of worship 7 for Independents, 4 for Baptists, 3 for Wesleyans, 2 for Primitive and one for Reforming Methodists, 2 rooms for Plymouth Brethren, one for 'Ranters' and 6 undescribed. Mormons from just outside St. John's parish were said to be active and there was some open-air preaching by dissenters but 'infidelity' was much more prevalent than dissent.[28]

In 1886[29] a census confined to the larger chapels found a total accommodation of 11,000 and a combined morning and evening attendance of 9,885. Congregationalists provided less than 40 per cent (3,918) of the attendance at 4 chapels.[30] Baptists, with 42 per cent (4,157) attendances at 5 chapels,[31] had overtaken them mainly because of the dominance of Shoreditch tabernacle. Methodists had 18 per cent (1,806) of the attendance at 3 chapels.[32]

A much more comprehensive census in 1903[33] gave a nonconformist attendance of 11,975, c. 9 per cent of the population. Baptists and Congregationalists each had c. 30 per cent of the attendance: 3,683 at 6 Baptist chapels and 4 missions, and 3,608 at 4 Congregationalist chapels and 4 missions. Methodists had 20 per cent (2,402) at 4 chapels and 2 missions. The Unitarians still had one chapel and others included Quakers, with 5 per cent, Salvation Army, and Brethren. Some 11 per cent attended 'other services', mostly undenominational missions.

The many small, short lived groups of the early 19th century gave way to fewer moderately sized chapels belonging mainly to the regular denominations.[34] In 1838 the largest chapel (Bethnal Green Congregational) held 800 and 15 of the 22 chapels held 100–400 each. In 1851 of the 23 chapels for which accommodation figures are available, 15 held 100–300 each but four had room for more than 600, of which one (Adelphi) held 950 and one (Bethnal Green Congregational) 1,200. Most chapels were run

14 Rayner, *Christian Community*.
15 P.R.O., RG 31/3; Guildhall MSS. 9580/1–9.
16 Lambeth Pal. Libr., Fulham Papers, Randolph 13, ff. 125-6.
17 *Lond. City Mission Mag.* iii. 53–4.
18 i.e. Bethnal Green, Gibraltar, Virginia, Ebenezer, Tent St., Abbey, Hare St., Zion, and Shalom.
19 i.e. Hephzibah and Claremont St.
20 i.e. Squirries St., Providence, Wolverley St., and Bethel.
21 i.e. Middlesex, Hart's La., Hare St. schoolroom (all Wes.), and New York St. (New Connexion).
22 *Census, Religious Worship, 1851* [1690], H.C. p. 7 (1852–3), lxxxix. Figs. for a.m.,. aft., and evg. are amalgamated and inc. people who may have attended more than one svce. There is a discrepancy between the figs. in the printed summary (above) and those in the returns.
23 Returns exist for 7 Ind. chapels (Tent St., Zion, Shalom, Thomas St., Short St., Adelphi, Gascoigne Pl.), 3 Cong. (Bethnal Green, Gibraltar, and Virginia), and 1 Cong.

Ind. (Ebenezer).
24 Returns exist for Squirries St., Providence, Claremont, and Ann's Pl. (all Bapt.), and Trinity (Particular Bapt.).
25 Returns for Mdx., Hart's La., and Collingwood St. (Wes.) and Cooper's Gdns. (Prim. Meths.).
26 Sydney St.
27 Below, undenom. missions.
28 Lambeth Pal. Libr., Fulham Papers, Tait 440/6-18.
29 *British Weekly*, 12 Nov. 1886.
30 Bethnal Green, Sydney St., Adelphi, and Victoria Park.
31 Shoreditch tabernacle, Hope, Shalom, Grove Rd., and Bethnal Green Rd.
32 Mdx., Cooper's Gdns. Memorial, and Victoria Pk.
33 Mudie-Smith, *Rel. Life*, 55–8.
34 Para. based on lists of individual chs. below and on H. McLeod, *Class and Religion in the late Victorian City* (1974), 106.

by local trustees, composed of weavers and other small craftsmen. Some had wealthier supporters like Robert Gammon, a coal merchant of Wilmot Square who was a trustee of Bethnal Green Congregational chapel and Abbey mission. Most wealthy patrons lived just outside the parish, like the silk merchants and manufacturers of Spitalfields and Hackney. The most notable was the silk manufacturer Jonathan Duthoit, who was behind most of the religious and educational activity in the Nichol district. Several large chapels were built in the 1860s and 1870s, especially in the more middle-class Victoria Park. The trustees of the 2,000-seat Victoria Park Congregational chapel (opened 1869) included two trimming manufacturers and John David Link, merchant, of Victoria Park Road; James Link, presumably a relative, gave it £5,000. By c. 1890 such people were migrating to Essex and the decline of weaving and growth of apathy led to the closure of the smaller chapels. As early as 1857 it was said that when a district became poor the dissenters could no longer maintain themselves.[35]

The emphasis shifted to missions, mostly funded from outside and often by supporters who had recently moved out.[36] The depravity and poverty of Bethnal Green had excited comment since the early 19th century and there had been missionary activity from the days of the Sunday School Tract movement and the Unitarian Domestic Mission, whose pioneering social work has been claimed as the precursor of the later settlement movement. The missionary movement received stimulus with the publication of the *Bitter Cry of Outcast London* in 1883. There was some concern about ritualism in Anglican churches[37] but most missionaries were not interested in dogma; missions were rarely confined to one denomination and there was co-operation between the churches on such questions as temperance, gambling, Sabbath breaking, and 'purity propaganda'.[38] More attention was given to secularism and political radicalism. In the 1850s the late London City Mission began open-air meetings as a challenge to the radicals in 'a noted wicked place', Club Row and Hare Street.[39] Bonner's Fields, once filled with 'infidel crowds', was by 1862 the venue of 'preachers of the gospel'.[40] Appeals for funds stressed that Christian principles should be inculcated to support order and the rights of property.[41]

Other missionaries sought the transformation of the slums and became increasingly involved in social work,[42] especially as public education largely superseded the ragged schools, so closely associated with missions, after 1870. Besides the missionary preacher there was a band of often female voluntary workers who visited the

poor and who ran homes, Sunday schools, and hospitals. Among the earliest were women appointed in 1828 by the Sunday School Tract Society to collect money and distribute tracts but 'not to be considered members of the committee'.[43] Later deaconesses and sisterhoods were employed, by the Mildmay Mission, Bonner Methodist Home, and Shoreditch Baptist tabernacle.

In spite of the effort, most observers saw the smaller missions as failures, if measured by attendances at services.[44] Several established chapels reorganized themselves as missions, often directed, like the Union Congregational chapel from Islington or the Unitarian mission from Hampstead, from outside.[45] The most successful chapels were usually the largest, with a powerful preacher, a team of helpers, and many associated activities. Examples were the Baptists' Shoreditch tabernacle under William Cuff and Middlesex chapel, reorganized in 1888 as the Hackney Road branch of the Wesleyan Missionary society.[46]

The most flourishing chapels nonetheless declined during the 20th century. Of the 24 chapels and missions belonging to the main three denominations in 1903, some 9 had closed by 1914, another 7 by 1939, and 5 by 1960. Those which were rebuilt after bomb damage were on a much smaller scale. No compensating growth came from new denominations: although there were several short lived Salvation Army and some Jehovah's Witness halls, the groups were small. Most of the missions died out. The decline, attributed partly to Jewish immigration in the late 19th century, has probably been hastened by more recent non-Christian arrivals. The natives of Bethnal Green were always reluctant to attend services and the social attractions of the larger chapels finally failed to compete with commercial alternatives.

The following abbreviations are used: accn., accommodation; aft., afternoon; amalg., amalgamated; Bapt., Baptist; Cong., Congregationalist; evg., evening; Ind., Independent; mtg. ho., meeting house; Meth., Methodist; min., minister; Prim., Primitive; Prot., Protestant; reg., registered; undenom., undenominational; Utd. Ref., United Reformed; Wes., Wesleyan. Attendance figs. 1838 from *Lond. City Mission Mag.* iii. 53–4; figs. 1886 from *Brit. Weekly*, 19 Nov. 1886; figs. 1903 from Mudie-Smith, *Rel. Life*, 55–7.

CONGREGATIONALISTS. Congregationalism in Bethnal Green traditionally dated from 1662 but more correctly 1669 when Ind. mtg. ho. 'lately fitted'.[47] Continuous line of mins. from Dan. Evans 1690 and registers from 1704.[48]

35 *Rep. Cttee. on Worship in Metropolis*, p.12.
36 *Trans. Cong. Hist. Soc.* xx. 33.
37 *Lond. City Mission Mag.* xv. 165; xvii. 49, 66; xlii. 94.
38 H. W. Harris and M. Bryant, *The Churches and Lond.* [1914], 79.
39 *Lond. City Mission Mag.* xxvi. 24–5.
40 Ibid. xxvii. 45, 48.
41 Ibid. xli. 2.
42 K. S. Inglis, *Churches and the Working Classes in Victorian Eng.* (1963), 63–100.
43 G.L.R.O., Acc. 2330/86/1.

44 Booth, *Life and Lab.* iii(1), 37; iii(2), 72–3, 80–1, 85; Mudie-Smith, *Rel. Life*, 31, 33.
45 Booth, *Life and Lab.* iii(2), 80.
46 McLeod, *Class and Religion*, 106, 117; K. Heasman, *Evangelicals in Action* (1962), 30, 54.
47 *Orig. Recs. of Early Nonconf.* ed. G. L. Turner, i. 89. Para. based on J. Avery, 'Bethnal Green Cong. Ch., Brief Hist.' (c. 1910) (T.H.L.H.L. TS. pamphlet 226.4).
48 Bethnal Green Ind. Chap. Reg. of Bapts. 1704–55, transcribed by J. Capewell (1979) (T.H.L.H.L. pamphlet 226.4).

Mins. inc. Hebrew scholar Dr. John Walker, *c.* 1755–70,[49] succeeded by asst. John Kello, 1771–1827. Chapel benefited from charity under wills of John Welch 1748 and John Dorsett 1762.[50] Mtg. ho., mentioned 1689[51] and 1694,[52] probably dissenters' mtg. ho. on W. side of green 1766[53] and Kello's chapel on W. side of Cambridge Rd. next Green Man, with accn. for 300 in 1810[54] and by 1818 'decayed'. New chapel built and reg. 1819 at corner of Bath (later Birkbeck) St.;[55] accn. for 800 in 1838. Under Josiah Viney, 1843–57, members, called Calvinistic Inds., built larger chapel and school-rooms between Bethnal Green Rd. and Pott St. 1849.[56] Bldg., called BETHNAL GREEN chapel, of Kentish rag and Bath stone in Gothic style with spire by John Tarring,[57] seating 1,200 inc. 400 free in 1851. Attendance 1851: 557 a.m., 745 p.m.;[58] 1886: 323 a.m., 567 p.m.; 1903: 88 a.m., 205 p.m. Membership 150 in 1910, 70 in 1939.[59] Close 19th-cent. connexion with Lond. City Mission.[60] Chapel after bombing reopened with 200 sittings 1954.[61] Utd. Ref. Ch. from 1965.[62] Part of premises rented 1985 to Robt. Kemble Christian Institute, founded 1982 under will of Utd. Ref. Ch. min to promote radical Christian activities.[63]

GIBRALTAR chapel, Gibraltar Pl. off Bethnal Green Rd., dated by Congs. to 1792[64] but possibly originated 1760.[65] Inds. reg. no. 1 Gibraltar Fields 1793 and chapel in Gibraltar Field 1798.[66] Simple rectangular bldg. in 1796.[67] Incorrectly listed as Meth., accommo-dated 200 in 1810[68] and 600 in 1838; 264 free sittings 1851, when attendance 80 a.m., 130 p.m.[69] Rebuilt 1871 to seat 578[70] but closed to Congs. *c.* 1877 although min. Jas. Brown lived there until death 1881.[71]

In late 18th cent. Inds. used various premises. No. 4 Green St. reg. 1792.[72] Min. Wm. Brittain

reg. ho. in Castle Ct., Castle St., 1793[73] and no. 2 'near the New Rd.' 1794;[74] Jas. Turner reg. hos. in Anchor St.[75] and Green St. 1795.[76] Ho. belonging to magistrate John Wilmot on N. side of Wilmot Sq. reg. 1795.[77]

VIRGINIA chapel, Virginia Row. Built 1819 on site of no. 10 or no. 14.[78] First was home of min. Thos. Wheeler, reg. 1798[79] and, when belonging to Ric. Saunders, City draper and min. of Mile End New Town, reg. by Prots. 1814;[80] second was shop also used as Sun. sch., reg. by Saunders 1815.[81] Accn. for 150 in 1838. Hen. Althans, Ind. min. by 1825, resigned to Jos. Massingham, sec. of Lond. City Mission, 1849.[82] Bldg. had 180 sittings inc. 72 free 1851, when attendance 80 a.m., 20 aft., 90 p.m.[83] Taken over by Wes. 1856–7.[84]

Hos. reg. by Inds. in early 19th cent. inc. ho. at Friar's Mount under min. Thos. Hemmans 1805[85] and no. 95 Church St. and no. 120 Brick Lane 1806,[86] possibly identifiable with 'Meth.' Brick Lane mtg. ho. with accn. for *c.* 150 1810.[87] Jos. Phillips, who had founded Gibraltar chapel, reg. no. 67 Mount St., in possession of Lazarus Soc., 1808.[88] Other mtg. hos. were reg. at no. 99 Hare St. 1809[89] and no. 5 Bethnal Green Rd. 1811.[90]

EBENEZER or PARK chapel, built on site of Aldgate Ho. at NE corner of green 1811,[91] originated in Ind. Calvinists or Inds. under min. Robt. Langford who reg. no. 5 Norwell Pl., Bethnal Green Rd., 1808[92] and John Shegog's ho. 1811.[93] Accn. for 650 in 1838 and had 560 sittings inc. 66 free 1851, when attendance 203 a.m., 299 p.m. with bible class of 20.[94] Reg. again when premises assigned to new trustees 1854[95] but closed 1876.[96]

TENT STREET off North St., chapel said to have been built for Inds. 1811. Accn. for 200 in 1838 and for 150 free in 1851, when attendance 20

49 Lysons, *Environs.* Suppl. (1811), 101; T.H.L.H.L., TH/8230/1.
50 *Endowed Chars. Lond.* (1897), 8, 65.
51 Cal. Mdx. Sess. Bks. viii. 100.
52 C.L.R.O., Box 43, MS. 22.
53 T.H.L.H.L., TH/2330-4
54 Lambeth Pal. Libr., Fulham Papers, Randolph 13, ff. 125-6.
55 P.R.O., C 54/9752, mm. 21-24; ibid. RG 31/3/1133; Guildhall MS. 9580/5; Robinson and Chesshyre, *The Green*, 28-9; T.H.L.H.L., R.B. Schnebbelie, View of hos. facing lower part of Bethnal Green, 1819.
56 P.R.O., C 54/13855, mm. 52-66.
57 *Cong. Year Bk.* (1850), 194, 197.
58 P.R.O., HO 129/21/2/1/8.
59 *Cong. Year Bk.* (1910, 1919, 1926, 1939).
60 Below.
61 *Cong. Year Bk.* (1960); *E.L.A.* 2 Mar. 1962 (T.H.L.H.L. Cuttings file 226.4).
62 G.R.O. Worship Reg. no. 70027.
63 Inf. from Praxis; above, social.
64 *Cong. Year Bk.* (1875).
65 G.F. Vale and S. Snaith, *Bygone Bethnal Green* (1948), 45.
66 P.R.O., RG 31/3/343, 457; Guildhall MS. 9580/1, pp. 51, 170.
67 B.M. Crace Colln. Portf. xxxiii, no. 60. Date in *Cat. of Crace Colln.* ed. J. G. Crace (1878).
68 Lambeth Pal. Libr., Fulham Papers, Randolph 13, ff. 125-6.
69 P.R.O., HO 129/21/1/1/9.
70 *Boro. of Hackney Dir.* (1872).
71 *P.O. Dir Lond..* (1876, 1879); *Cong. Year Bk.* (1875-9, 1895).
72 P.R.O., RG 31/3/321; Guildhall MS. 9580/1, p. 29.

73 P.R.O., RG 31/3/344; Guildhall MS. 9580/1, p. 53.
74 P.R.O., RG 31/3/352; Guildhall MS. 9580/1, p. 61.
75 P.R.O., RG 31/3/371; Guildhall MS. 9580/1, p. 83.
76 P.R.O., RG 31/3/384; Guildhall MS. 9580/1, p. 96.
77 P.R.O., RG 31/3/385; Guildhall MS. 9580/1, p. 96.
78 G.L.R.O., MR/PLT 5064.
79 P.R.O., RG 31/3/448; Guildhall MS. 9580/1, p. 160.
80 P.R.O., RG 31/3/875; Guildhall MS. 9580/4; G. Morgan, *Hist. 50 years work of Abbey St. Sun. Schs.* (1890) (T.H.L.H.L. 226.4), 5.
81 P.R.O., RG 31/3/921; Guildhall MS. 9580/4; Morgan, op. cit. 5.   82 Morgan, op. cit. 4, 6-7.
83 P.R.O., HO 129/21/1/1/10.
84 *Cong. Year Bk.* (1855-6, 1860); *P.O. Dir. Lond..* (1857); below, Meths.
85 P.R.O., RG 31/3/609; Guildhall MS. 9580/2, p. 44.
86 P.R.O., RG 31/3/649, 653; Guildhall MS. 9580/3. John Gibbons appears in both regs.
87 Lambeth Pal. Libr., Fulham Papers, Randolph 13, ff. 125-6.
88 P.R.O., RG 31/3/692; Guildhall MS. 9580/3.
89 P.R.O., RG 31/3/719; Guildhall MS. 9580/3.
90 P.R.O., RG 31/3/773; Guildhall MS. 9580/3.
91 Guildhall MS. 9580/3; P.R.O., C 54/9753, mm. 36-39; *Cruchley's New Plan* (1826).
92 P.R.O., RG 31/3/678; Guildhall MS. 9580/3.
93 P.R.O., RG 31/3/789. In 1817 John Shegog lived at no. 1 Spittal St., off Spicer St. in Mile End New Town, which he reg. for 'Christian believers': Guildhall MS. 9580/4.
94 P.R.O., HO 129/21/2/1/7.
95 G.R.O. Worship Reg. no. 1638; P.R.O., C 54/14548, mm. 56-9.
96 Letter from United Ref. Ch. Hist. Soc. (T.H.L.H.L. Cuttings file 226.4); *Cong. Year Bk.* (1875, 1880).

a.m., 40 p.m.[97] Closed by 1867 when probably taken over by Prim. Meths.[98]

ABBEY, later ESSEX STREET, mission originated in Calvinists[99] under min. Geo. Evans, who reg. outho. of John Mandeno at no. 11 Hollybush Pl. as mtg. ho. and Sun. sch. 1812[1] although congregation possibly existed by 1800.[2] Robt. Gammon built Sun. sch. and mission in his gdn. at no. 7 Wilmot Sq., reg. as Abbey Sun. sch., named after nearby Abbey Pl., 1828.[3] Listed as Ind. mtg. ho. accommodating 150 in 1838. Enlarged for 300 c. 1840.[4] Gammon, deacon at Wycliffe Ind. chapel in Mile End, built 2 rooms in gdn. of adjoining ho. after lease expired 1856 and was replaced by Geo. Kelsey 1865. Svces. by Lond. City Missionary from 1848 until departure because of lack of funds c. 1867. Renamed Essex (later Blythe) St. schs. and mission 1867 and another missionary briefly engaged but connexion with Mission severed when Sun. sch. cttee. tried to establish own chapel. Former missionary from Hackney held svces. until 1871, when svces. Bapt. (below). Cttee. asked Stamford Hill Cong. chap. to supervise schs. and mission 1873. Appointed former Lond. City Missioner, Jas. T. Bennett, min. of Old Zion chap., with which mission merged.[5] Sun. sch. work continued until amalg. with Abbey St. 1888.[6]

Inds. reg. no. 8 Vincent St. 1813,[7] no. 1 Albion St., Duke St.,[8] no. 32 Bacon St. 1818,[9] and no. 39 Old Nichol St. 1820.[10]

IMMANUEL chapel, so called 1831,[11] on N. side of Hare St.,[12] newly erected and reg. for Prots. 1820.[13] Accn. for 350 by 1838, when Cong., but apparently closed 1849.[14]

ZION chapel, on S. side of Old Bethnal Green Rd., built 1836[15] and reg. 1837[16] by Thos. Geo. Williams, Ind. min. of High St. Hoxton and later of Northampton Pl., Hackney Rd., who had reg. no. 6 Teale St. 1829.[17] Bldg. had 120 sittings inc. 80 free in 1838; also in 1851, when attendance 40 a.m., 100 p.m. and nos. had fallen after opening of 10 Anglican chs.[18] Closed 1865/9,

when used by congregation later at Mansford St. (below).[19]

Inds. reg. no. 2 Clare St. near Cambridge Rd.,[20] no. 2 Sebright Rd. (recte St.) off Hackney Rd.,[21] no. 14 Green St.,[22] and no. 14 East St., Twig Folly,[23] 1830, no. 5 Golden Pl., Bethnal Green Rd.,[24] no. 5 North Side of the green,[25] and no. 6 South Pavement 1834,[26] and ho. in Pritchard's Rd. off Hackney Rd. 1835.[27]

SHALOM chapel, in New Grove near the Oval, N. of Hackney Rd., built by Calvinistic Inds. or Congs. 1836.[28] Accn. for 350 in 1838 and for 300 inc. 50 free 1851, when average attendance 150 a.m., 200 p.m.[29] Cong. 1855[30] and depicted as such c. 1873[31] but Bapt. by 1865 and possibly by 1856.[32]

ZION chapel and ragged sch., Thomas St. (Passage), North St. built 1842 by T.G. Williams, founder of earlier Zion chapel (above). Bldg. had 100 free sittings in 1851, when attendance 16 a.m., 6 p.m., but was mainly Sun. sch. with 100 scholars a.m., 138 aft., 30 p.m.[33] Although sch. probably closed in 1860s, mission hall survived in 1894.[34]

NICHOL STREET mission originated in mission started by Jonathan Duthoit, a deacon in Union chap., Highbury, 1836. Duthoit opened and initially supported small chapel formed from 2 hos. in Short St. c 1843.[35] 'Tolerably large room' for Sun. sch. and svces. by lay preachers under Lond. City Mission. Accn. for 100–120 free, on sch. benches 1851, when attendance 15 a.m., 50 p.m. Mission, although unsectarian, regarded as station of Cong. Union chapel[36] and itself often called Union chapel.[37] Bldg. condemned 1860 and sch. and mission room built at NE. corner of Old Nichol St. and Nichol Row 1861.[38] Run by Union chapel alone after missionary killed by drunk; connexion with Lond. City Mission re-established 1871[39] but bldgs. completed 1879 reg. for Congs. 1880. Accn. for 1,400 children and 550 adults 1913.[40] Vigorous ch. life inc. mothers' mtgs., young men's club, and free breakfasts for children in winter.[41] Attendance

97 P.R.O., HO 129/21/2/1/9. No record of reg.
98 Below, Meths.
99 Para. based on Morgan, *Abbey St. Sun. Schs.* 75–86.
1 P.R.O., RG 31/3/828; Guildhall MS. 9580/4.
2 Chapel in Bethnal Green Rd.: G.L.R.O., MR/PLT 5024.
3 P.R.O., RG 31/3/1605. Sch. fronting rd. called successively Mary's Row, John's Pl., Essex St., Blythe St.
4 P.R.O., C 54/12505, mm. 56–8.
5 Below, Mansford St. Cong. chapel.
6 Below, educ. (pub. schs., Abbey St.). Abbey St. Sun. sch. was separate, geographically and institutionally, from Abbey Sun. sch.
7 P.R.O., RG 31/3/861; Guildhall MS. 9580/4.
8 P.R.O., RG 31/3/1082; Guildhall MS. 9580/4.
9 P.R.O., RG 31/3/1102; Guildhall MS. 9580/5. John Gibbons was assoc. with this reg.
10 P.R.O., RG 31/3/1200; Guildhall MS. 9580/5.
11 Ibid. 62, G.L.R.O. THCS 62.
12 Ibid. THCS 446.
13 P.R.O., RG 31/3/1181; Guildhall MS. 9580/5.
14 *Cong. Year Bk.* (1848, 1849).
15 P.R.O., HO 129/21/2/1/10; *Cassell's Map of Lond. and Suburbs* (c. 1861–2); T.H.L.H.L.,TH/1565.
16 P.R.O., RG 31/3/1933; Guildhall MS. 9580/7, p. 253.
17 P.R.O., RG 31/3/1648; Guildhall MS 9580/6, p. 260.
18 P.R.O., HO 129/21/2/1/10.
19 *Cong. Year Bk.* (1865, 1870); A. Mearns, *Guide to Cong. Chs. of Lond.* (1882), 5.
20 P.R.O., RG 31/3/1661; Guildhall MS. 9580/6, p. 272.
21 P.R.O., RG 31/3/1685; Guildhall MS. 9580/6, p. 305.

22 P.R.O., RG 31/3/1686; Guildhall MS. 9580/6, p. 306.
23 P.R.O., RG 31/3/1687; Guildhall MS. 9580/6, p. 307.
24 P.R.O., RG 31/3/1827; Guildhall MS. 9580/7, p. 139.
25 P.R.O., RG 31/3/1828; Guildhall MS. 9580/7, p. 140.
26 P.R.O., RG 31/3/1834; Guildhall MS. 9580/7, p. 146.
27 P.R.O., RG 31/3/1873; Guildhall MS. 9580/7, p. 185.
28 P.R.O., C 54/13106, mm. 30–34; RG 31/3/1897; Guildhall MS. 9580/7, p. 214.
29 P.R.O., HO 129/21/1/1/6.
30 *Cong. Year Bk.* (1855–6).
31 O.S. Map 1/2,500, Lond. XXVII (1873 edn.).
32 Below, Bapts.
33 P.R.O., RG 31/3/2139; HO 129/21/3/1/5; Guildhall MS. 9580/8, p. 149. Below, educ. (pub. schs., North St. ragged schs.).
34 O.S. Map 1/500, Lond. VII. 58 (1894 edn.).
35 Para. based on *Nichol St. Mission, 'The Nichol' 1836–1936* (1936) (T.H.L.H.L. pamphlet 226.4). Short St. ran between Half and Old Nichol sts., with chapel at NE. corner: G.L.R.O., O/102/3; *Ragged Sch. Union Mag.* (1858).
36 P.R.O., HO 129/21/1/1/8; *V.C.H. Mdx.* viii. 104.
37 G.R.O. Worship Reg. nos. 10299, 25122.
38 P.R.O., C 54/16175, mm. 11–19; below, educ.)pub. schs., Nichol St. Ragged sch.).
39 *Lond. City Mission Mag.* xxxvi. 139.
40 J. Reeves, *Recollections of a Sch. Attendence Officer* (1913), 47.
41 G.R.O. Worship Reg. no. 25122; *Illus. Lond. News*, 17 Apr. 1886, 405; *Union Chapel, Story of 100 Years, 1799–1899* (1899), 48–54.

1903: 20 a.m., 95 p.m. Attendance, mostly children, at Old Nichol St. schs., classified as Cong. mission, 55 a.m., 555 p.m. Twenty members at mission in 1939,[42] when closed as dangerous structure.[43]

SYDNEY STREET chapel dated origins to group under Revd. Josiah Viney at schoolroom in Bonner St. 1844. Moved to Morpeth St. 1845 and Sydney St., Globe Town, 1850,[44] where chapel existed in 1831.[45] As Countess of Huntingdon's Connexion, occupied 'very poor bldg.' with 200 free sittings in 1851, when attendance 63 a.m., 128 p.m. Worshipers entirely 'working people' and inc. most of women at industrial home in Homerton, to which min. Ben. Woodyard was attached.[46] Chapel reg. for Inds. 1861[47] and again when rebuilt for 370 in 1865.[48] By will proved 1880, Sam. Yates left £500 to be invested for min.[49] Attendance 1886: 162 a.m., 187 p.m. Closed 1901.[50]

ADELPHI chapel between nos. 352 and 354 Hackney Rd., built 1845 by W. Woodhouse, min. of closed Adelphi Cong. chapel in Strand (Westm.), after reading of work of Abbey St. Sun. sch.[51] Accn. for 950 inc. 370 free in 1851, when attendance 850 a.m., 950 p.m.[52] Bldg. remodelled 1871[53] with 'atrocious columns' in W. windows and thick Corinthian front columns, 'exhibiting the nonconformist tradition shattered by Victorian showiness'.[54] Attendance 1886: 271 a.m., 570 p.m.; 1903: 228 a.m., 446 p.m. Declined under homesick min. from Yorks. and closed 1909, when chapel became cinema.[55]

GASCOIGNE PLACE, off Crab Tree Row, schoolroom used as Ind. preaching station by British Mission by 1851. Free seating for 180 with standing for 250 in 1851, when attendance 45 p.m.; Sun. sch. a.m. and p.m.[56] Reg. for Inds. 1854 and described as mission ch. in 1870 but closed 1872.[57]

ALBION grammar sch. in Oxford St., W. side of Cambridge Rd., reg. for Ind. worship 1853.[58]

MORPETH STREET, Cong. chapel built 1857.[59]

VICTORIA PARK Cong. ch. was reg. 1865 at iron ch. opened 1864 by group called Free Meths. formed 1862 at Peel Grove hall.[60] New bldg. at SW. junction of Approach and Bonner rds., of red brick with stone dressings in Lombardic style, seating 2,000, by W. F. Poulton 1869: campanile, iron gallery.[61] Highest Cong. attendance in Bethnal Green 1886, when 885 a.m., 953 p.m., and in 1903, when 412 a.m., 625 p.m. Vigorous ch. life inc. Sun. schs. at Victoria hall and Twig Folly, free concerts, and work among poor, missions, and ragged schs.[62] Labour leader Ben. Tillett (d. 1943), was librarian in 1880s.[63] Membership 397 in 1910, 309 in 1919, 190 in 1926, and 70 in 1939.[64] Bldg. damaged 1940 and closed 1953. Site acquired by neighbouring Parmiter's sch.[65]

MANSFORD STREET chapel originated in group around Lond. City Missioner Jas. T. Bennett in Satchwell St. British sch. 1868. Met in vacated Old Zion chapel, listed as Durham (later Teesdale) St., 1869–80.[66] Leased site between Mansford and Blythe streets 1880, where chapel built and reg. 1881.[67] Divisions led to sale 1884 to Lond. Cong. Union, which supplied min. (R. Mackey), who left after 8 months with other seceders. Having no regular pastor, chapel dissolved 1886 although Sun. sch. continued until sale to Unitarians 1888.[68]

VICTORIA HALL, Approach Rd., built by Victoria Park Cong. ch. on site to S. acquired 1870, reg. 1877.[69] Bldg. in 'mixed Lombardic style', seating 900–1,000, by Woodman of Notting Hill; inc. 2 schoolrooms and libr.[70] Cong. mission in 1903, when attendance 100 a.m., 484 p.m. Damaged 1940 and closed 1953, site being sold to Parmiter's sch.[71]

SATCHWELL STREET British sch. used for Ind. worship 1871.[72]

VICTORIA (PARK) hall, so called 1895, had formerly been United Meth. Free chapel in Bonner Lane (St.).[73] Cong. mission in 1903, when attendance 23 a.m., 70 p.m.

POTT STREET premises of former Bethnal Green Chap. British sch. used as Cong. mission 1903, when attendance, mostly Sun. sch., 52 a.m., 150 p.m. Still in use 1914.[74]

TWIG FOLLY mission, at N. junction of Bonner and Hartley streets,[75] housed mission and Sun. sch. associated with Victoria Park Cong. ch. c. 1910 to c. 1926.[76]

42 *Cong. Year Bk.* (1939).
43 Samuel, *E. End Underworld*, 286–7 and n.
44 Mearns, *Guide to Cong. Chs.* 5, no. 15.
45 G.L.R.O., THCS/62.
46 P.R.O., HO 129/21/2/1/14.
47 G.R.O. Worship Reg. no. 11402.
48 Ibid. no. 16915; *Boro. of Hackney Dir.* (1872).
49 *Endowed Chars. Lond.* (1897), 68
50 Letter from United Ref. Ch. Hist. Soc. 1977 (T.H.L.H.L. Cuttings file 226.4).
51 Morgan, *Abbey St. Sun. Schs.*; Mearns, *Guide to Cong. Chs.* 20, no. 101; P.R.O., RG 31/3/2260; Guildhall MS. 9580/8, p. 270.
52 P.R.O., HO 129/21/1/1/5.
53 *Boro. of Hackney Dir.* (1872).
54 Pevsner, *Lond.* ii. 70.
55 McLeod, *Class and Religion*, 107; G.L.R.O., AR/BA/4/206, no. 5; above, social.
56 P.R.O., HO 129/21/1/1/7; Stanford, *Map of Lond.* (1862–5).
57 G.R.O. Worship Reg. no. 5917; *Cong. Year Bk.* (1856, 1870); below, educ. (pub. schs., Gascoigne Pl.).
58 G.R.O. Worship Reg. no. 1074; *Ret. of Chs., Chapels, Bldgs. Reg. for Worship*, H.C. 401, no. 1074 (1882), 1.
59 *Builder*, 6 June 1857, 329.

60 Mearns, *Guide to Cong. Chs.* 42, no. 227; G.R.O. Worship Reg. no. 16706.
61 P.R.O., C 54/18116, mm. 33–9; *Cong. Year Bk.* (1868), 337; (1869), 316–7; *The Times*, 14 Apr. 1869, 5a.
62 Harris and Bryant, *Chs. and Lond.* 169, 331 sqq.
63 J. Schneer, *Ben. Tillett. Portrait of a Labour Leader* (1982), 24.
64 *Cong. Year Bk.* (1910, 1919, 1926, 1939).
65 M. J. Fletcher, *Hist Parmiter's Foundation* (1971), 39; letter from United Ref. Ch. Hist. Soc. 1977 (T.H.L.H.L. Cuttings file 226.4).
66 Mearns, *Guide to Cong. Chs.* 5; *Cong. Year Bks.* (1875, 1880, 1886); Morgan, *Abbey St. Sun. Schs.* 83–5.
67 P.R.O., C 54/20642, mm. 8–12.
68 Morgan, op. cit. 86; below, Unitarians.
69 P.R.O., C 54/17287, m. 32; G.R.O. Worship Reg. no. 23580.
70 *Builder*, 12 May 1877, 489.
71 Fletcher, *Parmiter's Foundation*, 39.
72 P.R.O., ED 3/11, no. 264.
73 O.S. Map 1/500, Lond. VII. 39 (1895 edn.).
74 Harris and Bryant, *Chs. and Lond.* 382; below, educ. (pub. schs., Bethnal Green chapel British).
75 O.S. Map 1/500, Lond. VII. 39 (1895, 1938 edns.).
76 *Cong. Year Bk.* (1910, 1919, 1926); Harris and Bryant, *Chs. and Lond.* 382.

BAPTISTS. Under min. Geo. Gray, Bapts. reg. no. 5 St. John St. near Brick Lane 1809[77] and others reg. no. 27 Club Row, at SW. corner of par., 1814;[78] Particular Bapts. reg. tenement at entrance of Pitt St., on S. side of Bethnal Green Rd. 1824.[79]

SQUIRRIES STREET chapel built by dissenting group under W. Woodland and reg. for Prots. 1819,[80] after Wes. Circuit had dissolved Christian Community and claimed exclusive control over Globe Rd. chapel. Perhaps rebuilt 1823,[81] Bapt. by 1827.[82] Accn. for 250 in 1838 and 224 inc. 40 free in 1851, when attendance 40 aft., 200 evg.[83] Membership 70 in 1868,[84] when sch. started.[85] Reorganized as mission 1871 but apparently closed by 1883.[86]

PROVIDENCE chapel, later SHOREDITCH TABERNACLE, originated in group associated with ragged sch. in Shoreditch which worshipped nearby 1832 and chose 'Calvinistic' Jas. Smith (d. 1838), as min. 1833.[87] Moved to Providence hall, Worship St., 1833 and acquired site in Austin St. 1835 for new Providence chapel for Particular or Calvinistic Bapts.[88] New school-room for Sun. sch. 1844. Bldg. in simple classical style with pedimented front[89] seated 600 inc. 300 free 1838 and 1851, when attendance 148 a.m., 152 p.m.[90] Membership 130 in 1837, 200 in 1844, 320 in 1865, and 461 in 1875.[91] Seceders formed Union chapel in Cumberland St., Shoreditch, 1839, where joined by others 1855. Wm. Cuff, pastor from 1872 and unlike most of congregation not a Strict Bapt., established open-air mission, other mission halls, and schs. Adjoining property purchased 1860 and 1877,[92] where Shoreditch Tabernacle, in classical style and seating 2,000, built 1879; adjoining equally large Sun. sch. built 1890. Enormous cost,[93] despite fund raising by Chas. Spurgeon, who had preached at Providence chapel years before, incurred prolonged debt.[94] Cuff became president of Bapt. Union in 1910 and remained min. until 1917. Chapel had Bethnal Green's largest nonconf. attendance: 1886: 1,033 a.m., 1,468 p.m.; 1903: 546 a.m., 1,220 p.m. By c. 1900 early supporters had moved away and congregation exclusively working-class. Social work increasingly important, aided by many lay workers (300 c. 1898)[95] and by deaconesses from 1918. Membership 941 in 1900, 336 by 1935.[96] Bldg. neglected by 1928, when sale narrowly averted, damaged by bombing 1944, and demolished 1960. New brick chapel in modern style, seating 250, opened 1963.[97] Run mainly by deaconess and visiting preachers, membership dropping to 61 in 1987–8,[98] but later fall in evg. attendance offset by higher attendance a.m., especially of Nigerians and Afro-Caribbeans.

HEPHZIBAH chapel, later MARNHAM hall, no. 1 Darling Pl., at junction with Cambridge Rd. on S. boundary, reg. for Inds. 1836.[99] Accn. for 300 in 1838. Calvinistic or evangelical Bapt. in 1851, when bldg. seated 240 inc. 60 free and attendance 200 a.m., 240 p.m.[1] Membership 58 in 1858, when well attended, but apparently closed c. 1872.[2] Reopened as Bapt. mission, called Marnham hall, by E. Lond. tabernacle (Stepney) 1876.[3] Attendance 1903: 58 p.m. Used by Lond. City Mission 1904–18 and closed by 1938.[4]

CLAREMONT STREET, S. of Hackney Rd., chapel reg. for Inds. 1836.[5] Accn. for 280 in 1838. Bapt. by 1848[6] and seated 250 inc. 150 free in 1851, when attendance 30 a.m., 45 p.m.[7] Poor attendance c. 1858.[8] Membership 30 in 1872. Closed by 1875.[9]

WOLVERLEY STREET Bapt. chapel accommodated 150 in 1838.

BETHEL Bapt. chapel, Austin St., accommodated 100 in 1838, although not reg. until 1840. Passed to Latter-Day Saints 1843.[10] May have existed earlier as Bethel chapel, Meth. and accommodating 150 in 1810[11] and belonging to Seventh-Day Bapts. 1851-4 when 1675 given as foundation,[12] probably claiming descent from Fras. Brampfield.[13] Was mainstream Bapt. chapel called Austin St., Virginia Row, 1862-76. Membership 60 in 1872.[14] Later became mission of Shoreditch tabernacle and attended in 1903 by 29 p.m.

ANN'S PLACE, off Pritchard's Rd., infants' schoolroom reg. for Bapts. 1839.[15] New infants' and Sun. sch., presumably on same site, reg.

77 Guildhall MS. 9580/3.
78 Ibid. 4; P.R.O., RG 31/3/895.
79 P.R.O., RG 31/3/1410; Guildhall MS. 9580/5.
80 E.C. Rayner, *Story of the Christian Community, 1685–1909* (T.H.L.H.L. 226.3); P.R.O., RG 31/3/1145; Guildhall MS. 9580/5.
81 P.R.O., HO 129/21/2/1/13.
82 W.T. Whitley, *Bapts. of Lond.* (1928) 157; *Bapt. Manual* (1850); *Cassell's Map of Lond.* (c. 1861–2).
83 P.R.O., HO 129/21/2/1/13.
84 *Bapt. Handbk.* (1868).
85 P.R.O., ED 3/11, no. 449.
86 Whitley, *Bapts. of Lond.* 157; *Boro. of Hackney Dir.* (1872).
87 Para. based on D.V. Evans, '*More light, more power*' (1985) (T.H.L.H.L. pamphlet 226.2).
88 P.R.O., C 54/11454, mm. 7–11.
89 Illus. in T.H.L.H.L. Cuttings File 226.2.
90 P.R.O., HO 129/21/1/1/13.
91 *Bapt. Handbk.* (1865, 1875).
92 P.R.O., C 54/15580, mm. 2–9; C 54/18378, mm. 8–10; *Endowed Chars. Lond.* (1897), 65–6.
93 G.R.O. Worship Reg. no. 24834; *Bapt. Handbk.* (1877), 441; (1890), 367.
94 *Shoreditch Tabernacle* (1945) (T.H.L.H.L. pamphlet 226.2).
95 Booth, *Life and Lab.* iii (2), 81.
96 *Bapt. Handbk.* (1900, 1935).

97 G.R.O. Worship Reg. no. 69359.
98 *Bapt. Handbk.* (1987–8).
99 P.R.O., RG 31/3/1898; Guildhall MS. 9580/7, p. 215; G.L.R.O., THCS 447 (1836): as Mile End Corner N., chapel.
1 P.R.O., HO 129/21/2/1/12; *Bapt. Manual* (1854); *Cassell's Map of Lond.* (c. 1861–2).
2 *Bapt. Manual* (1858); Whitley, *Bapts. of Lond.* 184, 196; Guildhall MS. 9561, no. 27.
3 Whitley, *Bapts. of Lond.* 218.
4 Below, Lond. City Mission; Harris and Bryant, *Chs. and Lond.* 381; O.S. Maps 1/500, Lond. VII, 58 (1894, 1913, 1938 eans).
5 P.R.O., RG 31/3/1881; Guildhall MS. 9580/7, p. 195.
6 *Bapt. Handbk.* (1865). Whitley, *Bapts. of Lond.* 206, claims chapel founded in 1847 but there is no reg.
7 P.R.O., HO 129/21/1/1/12.
8 Guildhall MS. 9561 no. 29.
9 *Bapt. Handbk.* (1872, 1875).
10 Guildhall MS. 9580/8, pp. 57, 179.
11 Lambeth Pal. Libr., Fulham Papers, Randolph 13, ff. 125–6.
12 *Bapt. Manual* (1851–4).
13 Above, prot. nonconf. (intro.).
14 Whitley, *Bapts. of London* 191 *Bapt. Handbk.* (1865, 1872, 1875).
15 P.R.O., RG 31/3/2037; Guildhall MS. 9580/8, p. 46.

1840.[16] Attendance 1851: 70 p.m., all free sittings.[17] By 1871 dist. missionary held Sun. and Tues. evg. svces. at sch.[18] Bldg. enlarged to 200 seats 1881–2.[19] As Ames (sic) Pl. Bapt. mission, attendance, mostly children, 1903: 339 a.m., 159 p.m. Closed c. 1909.[20]

POLLARD ROW, N. of Bethnal Green Rd., room reg. for bapts. by Jesse Hobson of Stepney Coll., who also reg. Ann's Pl. (above), 1839.[21]

WILLIAMS PLACE, room reg. for Bapts. by another member of Stepney Coll. 1840.[22]

TRINITY chapel and schs., Peel Grove, reg. but not yet so named by Bapts. 1848.[23] Many seceded when Tim. Appleford appointed min. 1850 and Trinity chapel said to belong to Particular Bapts. or Calvinists 1851. Bldg. seated 313 inc. 122 free in 1851, when attendance 40 a.m., 150 p.m.[24] Evangelical Bapt. 1851–8[25] but used later by other groups.[26]

ZOAR meeting, no. 1 Peel Terr., Old Ford Rd., reg. by particular Bapts., perhaps descended from original group, 1866– 95.[27]

MORPETH STREET, Bapt. chapel 1849–56. Min. from 1851 was Tim. Appleford, previously at Peel Grove.[28]

HOPE chapel, between Norton and Type streets, reg. 1859 by Strict Calvinistic Bapts. on site leased 1854 by Bapts. who had begun preaching at Twig Folly 1851.[29] Membership 33 in 1855, 82 in 1868, and 120 in 1872 when bldg., originally seating 150, enlarged for 250. Attendance 1886: 122 a.m., 105 p.m.; 1903: 88 a.m., 90 p.m. Membership fell to 98 in 1910 and 43 in 1925.[30] Closed 1935/8.[31]

HART'S LANE, Bapt. chapel opened by one of dissident groups from Providence chapel 1854, probably in former Wes. chapel. Closed by 1863.[32]

THE OVAL, vacated Cong. Shalom chapel taken over by Bapts. from Squirries St. 1856[33] and reg. 1872,[34] when membership 100.[35] Attendance 1886: 77 a.m., 86 p.m.; 1903: 23 a.m., 54 p.m. Closed 1908.[36] Later housed industrial mission (below) and Lithuanian Rom. Cath. ch. (above).

UNION church, at corner of Grove and Esmond (later Roman) rds., taken over by congregation under Allan Curr, who preached at Peel Grove

hall 1865. Gothic bldg. described by C.H. Spurgeon, who preached there, as more fit for mass ho. than a Bapt. chapel. Curr left within year to become Presbyterian min., selling bldg. to Lond. Bapt. Assoc. which appointed pastor 1867 and sold bldg. to Ch. of Eng. to become St. Barnabas ch.

GROVE ROAD or VICTORIA PARK chapel, replacing Union ch. on site to N., reg. for Particular Bapts. 1872. Bldg. of yellow brick with stone dressings in Italianate style, seating 800 and with large schoolroom in basement,[37] by Chas. Gray, Searle & Son 1869. Attendance 1886: 403 a.m., 433 p.m.; 1903: 284 a.m., 432 p.m. Membership 416 in 1890, 330 in 1910, 179 in 1925, 66 in 1955, and 43 in 1987,[38] but one of few chapels surviving 1988.

ZION chapel, Matilda Rd. off Old Bethnal Green Rd., 1866–80.[39]

ESSEX STREET mission sch., off Bethnal Green Rd., used as Bapt. chapel on Sun. 1871.[40]

PRESTON STREET, Victoria Park, off Green St., chapel seating 70 from 1872 to c. 1900/3.[41]

BETHNAL GREEN ROAD chapel reg. 1882[42] in new bldg. at W. end where 17th-cent. Glasshouse Memorial Bapt. ch. had moved 1881.[43] Belonged to General Bapt. Assoc. and General Bapt. Assembly and seated 850. Membership 288 in 1885.[44] Attendance 1886: 188 a.m., 242 p.m.; 1903: 16 a.m., 23 p.m. falling nos. attributed to Jewish immigration. Sec. of Lond. Bapt. Assoc. assumed pastorate, cancelled reg. 1905, and leased chapel as synagogue. Freehold sold to Jews 1927.[45]

GIBRALTAR PLACE, former Cong. Gibraltar chapel reopened as Bapt. mission seating 500 and connected with Shoreditch Tabernacle 1883.[46] Attendance 1903: 127 p.m. Apparently called Nichol St. from c. 1915 and closed 1920.[47]

SHACKLEWELL STREET sch., associated with Gibraltar chapel, used as Bapt. mission by Shoreditch Tabernacle before reg. as Shoreditch Tabernacle mission chapel 1906. Attendance 1903: 32 a.m., 163 p.m. Closed by 1925.[48]

GREEN STREET, no. 222 reg. as mission hall 1901–76.[49]

16 P.R.O., RG 31/3/2080; Guildhall MS. 9580/8, p. 90.
17 P.R.O., HO 129/21/1/1/11.
18 Ibid. ED 3/11, no. 152.
19 Bapt. Handbk. (1885); below, educ. (pub. schs., Ann's Pl.).
20 Whitley, Bapts. of Lond. 228, 267; Bapt. Handbk. (1909, 1910).
21 P.R.O., RG 31/3/2039.
22 Ibid. RG 31/3/2053; Guildhall MS. 9580/8, p. 63.
23 Stanford, Map of Lond. (1862–5); P.R.O., RG 31/3/2291; Guildhall MS. 9580/8, p. 300.
24 P.R.O., HO 129/21/2/1/11.
25 Whitley, Bapts. of Lond. 176; Bapt. Manual (1854, 1857, 1858).
26 Below, undenom. missions.
27 G.R.O. Worship Reg. no. 17453.
28 Whitley, Bapts. of Lond. 173.
29 G.R.O. Worship Reg. no. 8716; P.R.O., C 54/15102, mm. 14–18; Whitley, Bapt. of Lond. 180.
30 Whitley, Bapts. of Lond. 268; Bapt. Manual (1858); Bapt. Handbk. (1868, 1872, 1910, 1925); G.L.R.O., MBW 1621, no. 23.
31 Bapt. Handbk. (1935, 1944–6); Bethnal Green M.B. Official Guide. [1930, 1938].
32 Whitley, Bapts. of Lond. 165, 181; Bapt. Manual (1854, 1862–3).

33 Whitley, Bapts. of Lond. 185–6. Listed from 1862: Bapt. Handbk. (1862).
34 G.R.O. Worship Reg. no. 21048.
35 Bapt. Handbk. (1872).
36 Whitley, Bapts. of Lond. 185–6.
37 Ibid. 267; E. Lond. Observer, 18 Dec. 1869 (T.H.L.H.L. Cuttings file 226.2); Bapt. Handbk. (1870), 228–9; G.R.O. Worship Reg. no. 20687; C.C.C. files, St. Barnabas.
38 Bapt. Handbk. (1890, 1910, 1925, 1955, 1987–8).
39 Whitley, Bapts. of Lond. 199.
40 P.R.O., ED 3/11, no. 193; above, Congs. (Abbey St.)
41 Bapt. Handbk. (1885, 1890, 1900, 1910).
42 G.R.O. Worship reg. no. 26096.
43 D. Monkcom and R. Whitfield, Three Hund. Yrs. of Bapt. Witness 1680–1980. Glasshouse Mem. Ch. (T.H.L.H.L. 226.2).
44 Bapt. Handbk. (1885).
45 Monkcom and Whitfield, op. cit.; G.R.O. Worship Reg. no. 26096.
46 Whitley, Bapts. of Lond. 229; Evans, 'More light, more power'; Bapt. Handbk. (1885).
47 Bapt. Handbk. (1900, 1910, 1912, 1915, 1920, 1921).
48 Whitley, Bapts. of Lond. 229; G.R.O., Worship Reg. no. 41877.
49 G.R.O. Worship Reg. no. 38453.

CHURCH ROW, old town hall reg. 1911–25.[50]

TENT STREET, mission hall reg. for strict and Particular Bapts. 1934–54.[51]

METHODISTS. MIDDLESEX chapel in Middlesex Terr. on SE. side of Hackney Rd. reg. for Inds. 1797 by min. John Jefferies,[52] who leased site 1798. Described as Wes. Meth. from 1811.[53] Accn. for 400 in 1838 but 'small and dilapidated' 1841 when new chapel founded on same site. Bldg., with galleries added 1847,[54] reg. 1854;[55] seated 820 inc. 200 free in 1851, when attendance 310 a.m., 504 p.m.[56] Attendance 1886: 232 a.m., 383 p.m.; 1903: 239 a.m., 471 p.m. Run as Shoreditch Meth. mission from 1888 and 'overflowing with energy' 1898. Large nos. at svces. enlivened by brass band. Also held cottage mtgs. and provided medical and legal advice.[57] Closed 1955.[58]

HART'S LANE, chapel on W. side off Bethnal Green Rd. built c. 1817 by Wes., who had reg. bldg. in Wilmot Sq. 1815.[59] Accn. for 160 in 1838 and seated 120 inc. 40 free in 1851, when attendance 29 a.m.,[60] 55 p.m. Apparently passed to Bapts. by 1854.

WEAVER STREET, Sun. sch. 'lately erected' on boundary with Spitalfields reg. by unspecified group 1818.[61] Associated with Wes. Tract Soc.,[62] it may have developed into Lion chapel in same street, reg. for Wes. 1824[63] and apparently closed by 1838.

NO. 4 PERSEVERANCE TERRACE, Church St., reg. by 'Arminian Methodists late in connexion with Wesley' 1819.[64] Their min. Tim. Gibson reg. ho. in Spitalfields for 'Calvinistic Inds.' 1821.[65]

GLOBE ROAD, Mile End, Wes. chapel next to later rly. line opened 1819 and taken over by Dr. T.B. Stephenson of Children's Home as mission hall named after Gen. Gordon 1885.[66] Transferred to Bethnal Green by boundary changes 1900. Attendance 1903: 66 a.m., 118 p.m. Remained Meth. mission until sold to Salvation Army 1959.[67]

COOPER'S GARDENS, off Hackney Rd., chapel reg. for Prots. 1820 by group[68] which built Hare St. chapel (above, Congs.). Acquired and probably rebuilt by Prim. Meths. 1835[69] but not listed 1838.[70] Seated 250 inc. 106 free in 1851, when attendance 180 a.m., 190 aft., 300 p.m.; 'crowded to excess' Sun. evgs., with simultaneous svce. in schoolroom.[71] New bldg. 1852,[72] reg. 1853.[73] 'Fairly attended' c. 1858.[74] Plot acquired at corner of Hackney Rd. and the Oval 1877,[75] where new Cooper's Gdns. Memorial ch. reg. 1879.[76] Attendance 1886: 85 a.m., 95 p.m.; 1903: 57 a.m., 61 p.m. Closed 1919.[77]

COLLINGWOOD STREET Sun. sch., behind Shoreditch ch. and supposedly built 1821, may have originated in room in Castle Ct., reg. for Meths. under min. Thos. Crossley 1821.[78] Reg. by Prots. 1832[79] and by Wes. 1838 but not listed 1838.[80] Wes. preaching 'now discontinued' in 1851[81] but bldg., retained mainly as Sun. sch., used for Wes. svces. on weekday evgs. in 1871.[82]

HARE STREET Sun. sch. (c. 1821), associated with Wes. Tract Soc.,[83] accommodated 200 for Wes. worship 1838.

Hos. reg. by Wes. in early 19th cent. inc. ho. and wareho. at no. 6 Spicer St. 1824,[84] no. 11 Kittisford Pl., Hackney Rd., 1832,[85] and no. 36 Anchor St. 1845.[86] Ind. Meths. reg. chapel in King St. off Hackney Rd. 1835.[87] New Connexion had room in New York St. accommodating 50 in 1838. Prim. Meths. reg. room in Three Colts Lane off Cambridge Rd. 1855–95.[88]

VIRGINIA ROW chapel, formerly Ind., was listed as Wes. 1857–75.[89]

PEEL GROVE chapel built for Free Meths. 1862[90] but members left to form Victoria Park Cong. chapel 1865.[91]

BONNER LANE (later St.), ground N. of Twig Folly British boys' sch. leased 1863 for United Meth. Free chapel,[92] which existed 1872[93] and was probably 'Prim. Meth.' chapel attended by young Geo. Lansbury, where pastor vividly described torments of hell.[94] Had become Victoria hall by 1895[95] and may have housed so-called Cripples' ch. in Bonner St., described as Wes. mission 1903, when attendance 46 p.m.

50 Ibid. no. 44782.   51 Ibid. no. 55381.
52 P.R.O., RG 31/3/420; Guildhall MS. 9580/1, p. 133; Home Counties Mag. xi. 293–8.
53 P.R.O., C 54/9292, mm. 6–12; G.L.R.O., Acc. 2330/57/1.
54 G.L.R.O., Acc. 2330/57/1.
55 G.R.O. Worship Reg. no. 3399.
56 P.R.O., HO 129/21/1/1/3.
57 G.L.R.O., Acc. 2330/57/1; N/M/23/1–12; Booth, Life and Lab. iii(2), 80.
58 G.R.O. Worship Reg. no. 3399; G.L.R.O., N/M/23/7.
59 P.R.O., RG 31/3/942; Guildhall MS. 9580/4.
60 P.R.O., HO 129/21/2/1/6; G.L.R.O., THCS 447, 521; below, Christian Community.
61 Guildhall MS. 9580/5. Weaver St. Sun. sch. was assoc. with Wes. by 1821: G.L.R.O., Acc. 2330/86/1.
62 G.L.R.O., Acc. 2330/86/1.
63 P.R.O., RG 31/3/1417; Guildhall MS. 9580/5.
64 P.R.O., RG 31/3/1128; Guildhall MS. 9580/5.
65 Guildhall MS. 9580/5.
66 H.M. Twixt Aldgate Pump and Poplar: Story of Fifty Years' Adventure in E. Lond. (1935), 72; G.R.O. Worship Reg. no. 29288.
67 B. Guy, Gordon Hall (1985) (T.H.L.H.L. 226.3 pamphlet); G.R.O. Worship Reg. no. 29288; P.O. Dir. Lond. (1950, 1960).
68 P.R.O., RG 31/3/1183; Guildhall MS. 9580/5.
69 P.R.O., C 54/13037, mm. 26–32.
70 Lond. City Mission Mag. iii. 53–4.
71 P.R.O., HO 129/21/1/1/4.
72 G.L.R.O., MBO/DS/H12 (surveyors' rets. 1852).
73 G.R.O. Worship Reg. no. 1358.
74 Guildhall MS. 9561 no. 32.
75 P.R.O., C 54/18007, mm. 11–14.
76 G.R.O. Worship Reg. no. 24783; G.L.R.O., MBW 1676, no. 26.   77 P.O. Dir Lond. (1919–20).
78 P.R.O., HO 129/21/1/(blank); ibid. RG 31/3/1257; Guildhall MS. 9580/5. Castle Ct. lay between Old Castle St. and Collingwood St.: O.S. Map 1/2,500, Lond. XXVII (1873 edn.).
79 P.R.O., RG 31/3/1756; Guildhall MS. 9580/7, p. 66.
80 P.R.O., RG 31/3/2000; Guildhall MS. 9580/8, p. 9; Lond. City Mission Mag. iii. 53–4.
81 P.R.O., HO 129/21/1/(blank).
82 Ibid. ED 3/11, no. 260.
83 G.L.R.O., Acc. 2330/86/1; below, educ. (pub. schs., Hare St.)
84 P.R.O., RG 31/3/1402; Guildhall MS. 9580/5.
85 P.R.O., RG 31/3/1776; Guildhall MS. 9580/7, p.86.
86 P.R.O., RG 31/3/2218; Guildhall MS. 9580/8, p. 228.
87 P.R.O., RG 31/3/1858; Guildhall MS. 9580/7, p. 170.
88 G.R.O. Worship Reg. no. 6539.
89 P.O. Dir Lond.. (1856, 1857, 1875, 1876); above, Congs.
90 Builder, 13 Dec. 1862, 900.
91 Above, Congs.
92 P.R.O., C 54/16128, mm. 22–25.
93 Boro. of Hackney Dir. (1872); O.S. Map 1/2,500, Lond. XXVIII (1873 edn.).
94 R. Postgate, Life of Geo. Lansbury (1951), 8.
95 O.S. Map 1/500, Lond. VII. 39 (1895 edn.); above, Congs.

VICTORIA PARK church was established by Bethnal Green Meth. Circuit, formed 1864 from Spitalfields, which rented Peel Grove hall for svces. 1865. Site at NE. junction of Approach and Bonner rds. acquired 1867,[96] where ch. opened and reg. for Wes. 1868.[97] Bldg. in classical style with pediment and massive Corinthian pillars, seating 1,000 and largest Meth. ch. in Bethnal Green.[98] Attendance 1886: 479 a.m., 532 p.m. Closely associated with adjacent Children's Home, whose founder Thos. Bowman Stephenson was its min. and from 1893 superintendent of Victoria Park circuit, which replaced Bethnal Green circuit. Ch. not listed 1903 and declined after Children's Home moved 1913.[99] Bldg. closed 1928, but reopened as Bethnal Green Central hall, serving East End Mission, 1929, with brutal concrete façade labelled 'the Church of the Happy Welcome' cloaking pediment.[1] Damaged 1941 and demolished, worshippers using former Twig Folly mission premises (below).[2] Plain brick chapel seating 150, with 4 classrooms for 442, opened on site 1959.[3]

TENT STREET, off North (later Brady) St., mtgs. of Prim. Meths. c. 1867–77[4] probably at former Ind. chapel later used as mission hall.

TWIG FOLLY British sch., junction of Bonner and Hartley streets, used by Lond. City Mission from c. 1860[5] and for unsectarian Sun. evg. svces. 1871.[6] Wes. mission 1903, when attendance 86 a.m., 298 p.m. Still Wes.[7] but apparently also used by Congs. 1914.[8] Served worshippers from bombed Victoria Park Meth. ch. 1942–59.[9]

DRIFFIELD ROAD, Prim. Meth. chapel on W. side reg. as in St. Mary Stratford (at Bow) 1878. Transferred to Bethnal Green by boundary changes 1900.[10] Extended 1935[11] and closed c. 1951.[12]

No. 66 RAVENSCROFT STREET, off Hackney Rd., reg. by Meth. Army 1883–95.[13]

CHILDREN'S HOME chapel, Bonner Rd., reg. for Wes. 1886.[14] Attendance, mostly children, 1903: 515 a.m., 445 p.m. Closed 1913.[15]

UNITARIANS. SPICER STREET, ho. on Spitalfields border reg. 1832 by Unitarians[16] who built Domestic Mission chapel and sch. in same street, reg. 1837.[17] Accn. for 300 in 1838. All sittings free and missionary acknowledged no 'peculiar dogmas'. Attendance 1851: 70–100 p.m. and 155 Sun. sch. a.m., 175 Sun. sch. aft.[18] Described by incumbent of St. Matthias as 'rather influential... liberally supported by wealthy individual from West End' 1857.[19] Primarily a Brit. sch. but Sun. evg. svces. still held 1871.[20] Mission apparently closed with schs. 1884, Unitarians moving to Mansford St.[21]

MANSFORD STREET, former Cong. chapel bought by Lond. Dist. Unitarian Soc., reg. as mission 1889.[22] Attendance 1903: 39 a.m., 82 p.m. Membership 97 in 1906, when new bldgs. added in neighbouring Blythe St. for associated clubs;[23] extended 1911.[24] Average attendance 1947: 36.[25] Nos. fell when area redeveloped in 1960s.[26] Mission reconstructed as Chalice foundation 1985 and bldgs. restored by 1989 for community centre and activities inc. Church Action with Unemployment and Rathbone Soc. Chapel converted to Garrett centre and manse to small residential settlement.[27]

CAMBRIDGE hall, no. 365 Cambridge Rd., was Unitarian 1890.[28]

BRETHREN. No. 22 GLOBE STREET (later part of Globe rd.) reg. by Christian Brethren as Twig Folly mtg. 1859–76.[29]

GLOBE ROAD, bldg. reg. by Plymouth Brethren, who in 1858 had occupied 2 small rooms in St. Simon Zelotes par., 1861–76.[30]

SCLATER STREET, iron room behind G.E.R. station used by Brethren 1876–93.[31]

No. 117 COVENTRY STREET, gospel hall used by Brethren 1893–c. 1905.[32] Attendance, mostly children, 1903: 81 p.m.

No. 55 BETHNAL GREEN ROAD reg. by Brethren 1909–54.[33]

CHRISTIAN COMMUNITY.[34] After severing its Meth. connexion c. 1819, community held open-air svces. in Bonner's Fields and, often with other groups, met in Cheapside (Lond.) and Shoreditch. Used mission room in Menotti St. 1872[35] and opened Christian Community Memorial hall, commemorating centenary of

96 *E.L.A.* 21 June 1968 (T.H.L.H.L. Cuttings file 226.3).
97 G.R.O. Worship Reg. no. 18460.
98 Unidentified cuttings (T.H.L.H.L. Cuttings file 226.3).
99 A.A. Jacka, *Story of Children's Home, 1869–1969* (1969), 9, 11, 18; *Twixt Aldgate Pump and Poplar*, 127.
1 *Meth. Recorder* (1929) and other cuttings (T.H.L.H.L. Cuttings file 226.3).
2 *E.L.A.* 21 June 1968 (T.H.L.H.L. Cuttings file 226.3); R.G. Burnett, *These my brethren. Story of Lond. E. End Mission* (1946), 20.
3 Meth. Ch. Dept. for Chapel Affairs, *Statistical Returns* (1972–3), 7; G.R.O. Worship Reg. no. 67551.
4 *P.O. Dir Lond..* (1867–77); T.H.L.H.L., TH/7514.
5 *Lond. City Mission Mag.* xli. 9.
6 P.R.O., ED 3/11, no. 211.
7 Harris and Bryant, *Chs. and Lond.* 382.
8 Above, Congs.
9 G.R.O. Worship Reg. no. 60050.
10 Ibid. no. 24345.
11 G.L.R.O., AR/BA/4/606, no. 3.
12 O.S. Map 1/2,500, TQ 3683 (1950 edn.); *P.O. Dir Lond..* (1947, 1952).
13 G.R.O. Worship reg. no. 27038.
14 Ibid. no. 29275.   15 Ibid. no. 43681.
16 P.R.O., RG 31/3/1769; Guildhall MS. 9580/7, p. 79.
17 P.R.O., RG 31/3/1936; Guildhall MS. 9580/7, p. 257.

18 P.R.O., HO 129/21/4/1/4.
19 *Rep. Cttee. on Worship in Metropolis*, p. 44.
20 P.R.O., ED 3/11, no. 267.
21 Mansford St. Ch. and Mission, *Ann. Rep.* (1912) (T.H.L.H.L. 226.13); below, educ. (pub. schs., Abbey St.).
22 Mansford St. Ch. and Mission, *Ann. Rep.* (1912); G.R.O. Worship Reg. no. 31623.
23 Mansford St. Ch. and Mission, *Cal. and Monthly Messenger* (1906) (T.H.L.H.L. 226.13).
24 G.L.R.O., AR/BA/4/221, no. 5.
25 Mansford St. Ch. and Mission, *Ann. Rep.* (1947) (T.H.L.H.L. 226.13).
26 Mansford St. Unitarian Ch. *Newsletter*, 1964–82 (T.H.L.H.L. 226.13).
27 *Hackney Gaz.* 6 Sept. 1985; 22 Mar. 1986 (T.H.L.H.L. 226.13); inf. from M. Bracey, Chalice Foundation.
28 *P.O. Dir Lond.* (1890).
29 G.R.O. Worship Reg. no. 8803.
30 Lambeth Pal. Libr., Fulham Papers, Tait 440/18; G.R.O. Worship reg. no. 11725.
31 *P.O. Dir Lond..* (1876–93).
32 Ibid. (1893–1905).
33 G.R.O. Worship Reg. nos. 43926, 45292.
34 Para. based on Rayner, *Story of Christian Community*. For early hist., above.
35 *Boro. of Hackney Dir.* (1872).

reorganization, 1875.[36] Acquired site at junction of London (later Dunbridge) St. with Mapes St., bought by Ind. min. Wm. Tyler of Hanbury St. (Spitalfields) ch., 1878.[37] Bldg. in Gothic style, seating 700, used for religious mtgs., Sun. sch., men's club, and lectures and closely associated with Lond. City Mission.[38] Extended by free libr., inc. books given by royalty, 1881. Attendance 1903: 3 a.m., 79 p.m. Libr. closed 1934 and memorial hall 1949. Headquarters of Community moved to Good Shepherd mission, Three Colts Lane, and after 1973 to Romford (Essex).[39]

SALVATION ARMY. First headquarters in old wool store in Three Colts Lane,[40] although no. 198 Three Colts Lane reg. as barracks only 1893–5,[41] whereas first hall was under rly. arch in Bethnal Green Rd. by 1890.[42] No. 245 Brick Lane, barracks reg. 1890–5.[43] No. 45 Brady Lane, barracks reg. 1894–1900.[44] No. 86 Sclater St., barracks reg. c. 1898–1907;[45] attendance 1903: 6 a.m., 20 p.m. Tent St., barracks reg. c. 1898–1907;[46] attendance 1903: 14 a.m., 13 p.m. No. 1 Parmiter St., mission hall reg. 1898–1903.[47] No. 374 Hackney Rd., Cambridge Heath outpost reg. c. 1898–1925;[48] attendance 1903: 11 a.m. 20 p.m. No. 343 Bethnal Green Rd., citadel and institute reg. 1908–33; reg. again as hall 1933–54.[49] No. 58 Russia Lane, ground floor room reg. as hall 1925–8; replaced by hall at no. 40 Tagg St. 1928–54.[50] Goodwill Centre in Warley St. and hostel in Roman Rd., near Bonner St., in use c. 1950.[51] Gordon hall, Globe Rd., acquired from Meths. (above) 1959; rebuilt and reg. as Sigsworth hall after local Army Worker Alice Sigsworth 1960.[52]

SOCIETY OF FRIENDS (QUAKERS). Mission hall at junction of Barnet Grove and Ivimey St. reg. 1892.[53] Attendance, mostly children, 1903: 236 a.m., 398 p.m. Closed 1956.[54]

PRESBYTERIANS. Presbyterian Jewish mission from Whitechapel Rd. moved to new built mission ho. at nos. 207–11 Cambridge Rd. 1913.[55] Closed c. 1946.[56]

JEHOVAH'S WITNESSES. KINGDOM HALL, no. 195 Roman Rd., reg. for International Bible Students Organisation 1942–54, presumably belonged to Jehovah's Witnesses.[57]

KINGDOM HALL, no. 184 Grove Rd., where premises had been reg. 1972, built with accn. for 250 by Jehovah's Witnesses 1974.[58]

UNDENOMINATIONAL MISSIONS. LONDON CITY MISSION, undenom. Prot. mission founded 1835 and often closely associated with existing chs. Each dist. had missioner, usually drawn from lower classes, supervised by min. or prominent layman. Work inc. preaching and holding svces., Sun. and ragged schs., visiting, clubs, medical assistance, and soup kitchens. Four dists. in Bethnal Green by 1838: Cambridge Rd., North St., Quaker St., and Wilmot Sq.[59] One of first probably Wilmot Sq., associated with Abbey Sun. sch. and Robt. Gammon, supervisor 1847.[60] Cambridge Rd. originated in Christian Instruction Soc., established with 20 visitors and Lond. City Missioner 1838; links with Bethnal Green Cong. chapel, where mtgs. held and whose min. was supervisor.[61]

Appeal launched to support 42 missionaries in Spitalfields and Bethnal Green W. of Cambridge Rd. 1843.[62] Bethnal Green had 15 missionaries, mostly in crowded W. and S. but inc. Globe Lane and Twig Folly, E. of Cambridge Rd. 1846.[63] Eleven missionaries in 1850; little progress over 8 years reported 1852.[64] Thirteen missionaries, one each supported by Suffolk Auxiliary, Clifton Ladies' Assoc., and Jonathan Duthoit, 1854. Other contributions made by brewers Truman, Hanbury, Buxton & Co., by min. of Bethnal Green Cong. chapel, and by other silk manufacturers.[65] E. Counties Rly. provided premises rent free.[66] Still 13 missionaries 1875 and 2 more 1876 after appeal, little money being raised locally.[67] Missionaries at Shaftesbury and Marnham halls until First World War and probably beyond.[68] One, associated with V. of St. Jas. the Less, still working 1950.[69]

Mtg. places, usually short lived, inc. Brick Lane from 1848,[70] where at no. 160 attendance 1903 was 23 p.m., Anchor St. ragged sch. 1849–72,[71] no. 1 Castle St. c. 1855–c. 1862,[72] Cudworth ragged sch. 1859–72 with svces. for adults 3 times a week c. 1870,[73] and Twig Folly British sch. c. 1860–c. 1871.[74] Schoolroom and mission

36 G.R.O. Worship Reg. no. 22608; G.L.R.O., MBW 1643, no. 23.　　37 P.R.O., C 54/8164.
38 Lond. City Mission Mag. lii. 43, 52.
39 The Star, Mar./Apr. 1969 (T.H.L.H.L. Cuttings file 226.3); Christian Community, Ann. Rep. (1973) (T.H.L.H.L. 226.3); Christian Community. Abridged Hist. and Handbk. (n.d.) (T.H.L.H.L. 226.3 pamphlet).
40 V. Leff and G. H. Blunden, Story of Tower Hamlets (1967), 65.　　41 G.R.O. Worship Reg. no. 33915.
42 Leff and Blunden, op. cit. 65; P.O. Dir. Lond.. (1890).
43 G.R.O. Worship Reg. no. 32198.
44 Ibid. no. 34609.
45 Ibid. no. 37102; Booth, Life and Lab. iii(2), 109.
46 Booth, op. cit. 107; G.R.O. Worship Reg. no. 38078.
47 G.R.O. Worship Reg. no. 36639.
48 Ibid. no. 38792; Booth, op. cit. 109.
49 G.R.O. Worship Reg. nos. 43078, 54759.
50 Ibid. nos. 49655, 51278.
51 Bethnal Green M.B. Official Guide [1950], 78–9.
52 G.R.O. Worship Reg. no. 68033; B. Guy, Gordon Hall (1985) (T.H.L.H.L. 226.3 pamphlet); inf. from Tower Hamlets L.B. (1986).
53 G.R.O. Worship Reg. no. 33436.
54 P.O. Dir. Lond. (1956, 1957).

55 G.R.O. Worship Reg. nos. 23435, 45912; G.L.R.O., AR/BA/4/252, no. 5.
56 P.O. Dir. Lond. (1945, 1947).
57 G.R.O. Worship Reg. no. 60024.
58 Ibid. no. 72894; E.L.A. 7 June 1974 (T.H.L.H.L. Cuttings file 226.13); P.O. Dir. Lond. (1980).
59 Lond. City Mission Mag. iii. 173.
60 Ibid. xii. pp. xvi–xvii; Ragged Sch. Mag. vi. 95; above, Congs.
61 Lond. City Mission Mag. iii. 173; iv. 176.
62 Ibid. viii. 165–6.
63 Ibid. xi. 33; xii. pp. xvi–xvii.
64 Ibid. xv. 165; xvii. 49.　　　　65 Ibid. xix. 86.
66 i.e. ho. in Anchor St.: ibid. xv. 167.
67 Ibid. xli. 2–3.
68 Ibid. lxxiv. 85–6; lxxviii. 10–13. 20th-cent. mags. less useful than earlier edns.
69 Lond. City Mission Mag. cv. 3.
70 Ibid. xiv. 89; Booth, Life and Lab. iii(2), 108.
71 Below, educ. (pub. schs., Anchor ragged).
72 Lond. City Mission Mag. xxvii. 63–4.
73 Ibid. xxvii. 59–60; P.R.O., ED 7/80; below, educ. (pub. schs., Cudworth ragged).
74 P.R.O., ED 3/11, no. 211; Lond. City Mission Mag. xli. 9.

station in George St., W. of Cambridge Rd., opened by missioner of Punderson's Gdns. dist. *c.* 1863, where weekly evg. cottage mtgs. had average attendance 1865 of 60–70.[75] Probably identifiable with Albion sch., at no. 7 George St., bldg. owned by Lond. City Mission superintendent (Josiah Goodman), which housed svces. 1871.[76] Mission had ho. at no. 26 Blythe St.[77] and opened station in former shop in Gibraltar Walk 1872.[78] Other stations at former Cong. and Meth. chapel in Tent St. 1880–92[79] and in Columbia Rd. 1882–95.[80] Lond. City Mission's Shaftesbury hall, built in Gosset St. 1885 although reg. only 1930, survived until 1950s.[81] Attendance 1903: 15 a.m., 67 p.m. Other mission halls reg. at no. 224 Hackney Rd. 1892,[82] in Old Bethnal Green Rd. *c.* 1893–1898,[83] and at Marnham hall in Darling Row 1904–18, where Mission held Sun. evg. svces.[84]

MILDMAY MISSION, similarly evangelistic,[85] came to Bethnal Green when founder Revd. Wm. Pennefather offered help of deaconesses to V. of St. Phil. during cholera outbreak 1866. From ho. in Friar's Mount they opened invalid kitchen and offered 1*d.* dinners,[86] moving to larger premises in Little Bacon St. 1871 for mtgs. and classes.[87] Former police station in Church St. (W. end of Bethnal Green Rd. opposite Turville St.), acquired 1884[88] and converted into mission ho. and men's lodging ho., with accn. for deaconesses and soup kitchen. Replaced by mission halls in Cross St. and Sweetapple Sq. by 1903, where attendances 84 p.m. and 72 p.m. Other activities inc. lads' institute, mothers' mtgs., sewing classes for factory girls, and mission to Jews.[89] Medical mission opened 1874 and gospel svces. held weekly at hosp. opened in Turville Street 1877.[90]

BETHNAL GREEN MEDICAL MISSION was opened as Home of Industry[91] in Commercial St. 1866 by Annie Macpherson (d. 1904), who moved it to purpose-built home designed by Geo. Baines at no. 29 Bethnal Green Rd. 1887.[92] Activities inc. distributing bibles, medical assistance, working among women, training missionaries, and running large Sun. sch.,[93] where attendance,

mostly children, 1903 was 530 p.m. Emigration of many children to Canada disrupted by war and finally discontinued 1925. After home in Bethnal Green Rd. closed 1916,[94] work carried on from training home in Hackney until site acquired at no. 305 Cambridge Rd. 1925. Medical work, started under Miss Macpherson's doctor nephew 1901, increasingly important and led to renaming 1926. Reg. as undenom. mission 1930. New bldg. opened on same site 1955[95] and survived 1990.

OTHER MISSIONS. Trinity chapel, Peel Grove, reg. for Bapts. 1848[96] but part of bldg. let to 'socialists' and rest to Particular Bapts. and Sun. sch. 1851.[97] New sch. chapel reg. by members of Ch. of Eng. [98] and Sun. evg. svces. introduced 1859. Bldg. also used by young men's association, by Bible and book soc. based on Soc. for the Diffusion of Pure Literature among the People, and for evg. classes and Sun. lectures.[99] Run in 1860s by temperance movement,[1] which let it to Wes., Congs., and Bapts.[2] As Anglican mission, called St. Thos. mission ho. in 1870s.[3] Connected with Ragged School Union, as Ashley mission hall, from 1880.[4] Attendance, mostly children, 1903: 57 a.m., 48 p.m. Survived as lecture hall until destroyed in Second World War.[5]

Good Shepherd sch. and mission[6] in large workshop, probably nos. 75 and 76 railway arches near North St., opened by Sun. sch. teachers from closed St. And. and reg. for nonconfs. 1855.[7] Mission moved three times before new bldg. erected in Mapes St. 1866. After bldg. destroyed by extensions to G.E.R., cottages in Wilmot St. temp. housed Good Shepherd British sch., Sun. sch., and Sun. evg. mission svces. 1871.[8] Permanent sch. and mission opened at corner of Three Colts La. and Wilmot St. 1871. Amalg. with Abbey St. sch. under Ragged Sch. Union (later Shaftesbury Soc.) 1894 but still used for mission svces.[9] Attendance 1903: 73 a.m., 265 p.m. Amalg. with King Edward Institute 1933,[10] premises enlarged 1934, and reg. as King Edw. Institute and Good Shepherd mission by 'Christians' 1939.[11] In 1990 still non-denominational

75 *Lond. City Mission Mag.* xxx. 208, 213.
76 Ibid. xlvi. 207; P.R.O., ED 3/11, no. 182; above, Congs.
77 *Boro. of Hackney Dir.* (1872).
78 *Lond. City Mission Mag.* xxxviii. 174; xl. 159.
79 *P.O. Dir. Lond.* (1880–93).
80 G.R.O. Worship Reg. no. 26636.
81 Ibid. no. 52386; G.L.R.O., MBW 1739 no. 27; *P.O. Dir. Lond.* (1890–1955); Samuel, *E. End Underworld*, 296 n; *Lond. City Mission Mag.* lxxiv. 85–6.
82 G.R.O. Worship Reg. no. 33335; Booth, *Life and Lab.* iii(2), 109; G.L.R.O., CL/LOC/2/10. Not listed 1903 although reg. not cancelled until 1906.
83 *Lond. City Mission Mag.* lxiii. 71; Old O.S. Map Lond. 51 (1893).
84 *Lond. City Misssion Mag.* lxxviii. 13; *P.O. Dir. Lond.* (1904–19). For hall before 1903, see Bapts. (Hephzibah chapel).
85 Based on H. J. Cooke, *Mildmay, Story of First Deaconess Institution* (1892), 94–110; *V.C.H. Mdx.* viii. 115–16.
86 K. J. Heasman, 'Influence of Evangelicals upon Voluntary Charitable Institutions in second half of 19th cent.' (Lond. Univ. Ph. D. thesis, 1959), 680.
87 Samuel, *E. End Underworld*, 287 n; G.L.R.O., MR/UP 953.
88 G.L.R.O., MBW 1730 no. 27; O.S. Map 1/2,500, Lond. XXVII (1873 edn).
89 Cooke, *Mildmay*, 175–8.
90 Ibid. 158–62; L.C.C. *Opening of Boundary St. Area* (1900), map of area before rebldg.

91 Para. based on *A Clean Thing out of an Unclean. Short Hist. Bethnal Green Medical Mission 1866–1966* (pamphlet).
92 *P.O. Dir. Lond.* (1887); *Builder*, 20 Aug. 1887, 287; 17 Dec. 1887, 838.
93 Booth, *Life and Lab.* iii(2), 73.
94 *P.O. Dir. Lond.* (1916–17).
95 G.R.O. Worship Reg. nos. 52368, 65172.
96 P.R.O., RG 31/3/2291; above, Bapts.
97 Ibid. HO 129/21/2/1/11.
98 G.R.O. Worship Reg. no. 8739.
99 *Illus. Lond. News*, 16 Apr. 1859, 385; below, educ. (pub. schs., Trinity).
1 Morgan, *Abbey. St. Sun. Schs.* 22.
2 Above.
3 O.S. Map 1/2,500, Lond. XXVIII (1873 edn.); *P.O. Dir. Lond.* (1875–6).
4 *P.O. Dir. Lond.* (1880 et seq.); Harris and Bryant, *Churches and Lond.* 382.
5 *P.O. Dir. Lond.* (1932, 1939, 1945); O.S. Map 1/500, Lond. VII. 38 (1938); O.S. Map 1/2,500, 51/3583 (1950 edn.).
6 Based on *Good Shepherd Mission* (1988) (T.H.L.H.L. Cuttings file 226.13).
7 G.R.O. Worship Reg. no. 6453.
8 P.R.O., ED 3/11, no. 183; ED 4/30.
9 Ragged Sch. and Mission Union, *In His Name* (1894), 95.
10 King Edw. Institution, *100th Ann. Rep.* (1944–5) (T.H.L.H.L. pamphlet 226.13).
11 G.R.O. Worship Reg. no. 58975.

mission belonging to Shaftesbury Soc., offering Sun. svces., Sun. sch., bible study and youth clubs founded 1980 in association with evangelical Anglican ch. of St. Helen, Bishopsgate (Lond.).[12] Also housed Christian Community 1949–74[13] and from 1983 Pentecostal Bibleway ch. founded in Weavers' Field sch. and housed in former St. Jas. the Gt. ch. 1979–83.[14]

Abbey Street British[15] and Sun. schs. used for Lond. City Mission mtgs. 1881.[16] Sold to Ragged Sch. Union 1891[17] and used by missionary for svces., bible classes, and associated activities 1892.[18] Amalg. with Good Shepherd mission 1894.[19]

King Edward Mission and Institute, founded as ragged sch. and mission by Dr. Tyler in King Edward St., Spitalfields, 1845, used hall at corner of Tent St. and North (Brady) St. 1909–34. Site housed successively from 1811 Congs., Prim. Meths., gospel mission (1878–9), Lond. City Mission, Salvation Army, and after 1934, when King Edw. mission merged with Good Shepherd mission, Particular Bapts.[20]

Zehovah (or Jehovah) in Thorold Sq. N. of Bethnal Green Rd. built 1844. Lower part of bldg. used for sch. and worship by 'various Christian denominations' 1851, when 48 free sittings; attendance 22 aft., 20 evg. Census return signed by agent for Christian Soc. of Operative Silkweavers.[21] Bldg. disappeared in redevelopment 1872 and new chapel built at no. 204 Bethnal Green Rd. on site leased to pastor by 1874, when congregation 42.[22] Sun. sch. built at no. 203 Bethnal Green Rd. 1879,[23] where chapel and schoolrooms survived 1899.[24] Christian Industrial Mission occupied former Bapt. Shalom chap. in the Oval 1909–11.[25]

London Open Air Gospel Mission and Free Gospel Ch., which preached at markets and factories, reg. no. 7 St. Jude's St. 1853.[26]

Unsectarian gospel mission in large workshop at no. 43 Old Castle St. opened by Wm. Jarvis 1867. Adjoining ho. acquired and 'commodious' hall for religious and other mtgs. on Sun. and most evgs. built 1869. Apparently unsuccessful appeal claimed that closure would leave c. 40,000 adults without ch. or chapel accn. 1871.[27]

Bible Defence Association reg. no. 304 Hackney Rd. as Amicable hall 1869–95.[28]

Unsectarian gospel mission hall reg. at no. 69 Green St. 1876–95.[29]

The Hon. Mr. Ashley's mission operated from no. 31 Gloucester St., Cambridge Heath, in 1871.[30]

Mission hall existed at corner of Squirries St. and South (Florida) St. c. 1871–2.[31]

Christian Mission met in Hart's Lane, probably in former Wes. and Bapt. chapel, 1872[32] and reg. people's halls at no. 121 Brick Lane and under rly. at E. end of Bethnal Green Rd. 1876– 95.[33]

People's Gospel Mission reg. no. 244 Hackney Rd. 1887–95.[34]

Mission hall erected in Hart's Lane 1885.[35]

Young Men's Christian Mission reg. former Unitarian no. 365 Cambridge Rd. as Emmanuel hall 1891–5.[36] Y.M.C.A. reg. Cambridge club, no. 128 Cambridge Rd. 1899–1906 and no. 17 Victoria Park Sq. 1905–25.[37]

Parmiter St. mission existed 1892–7.[38]

League of Charity mission ho., nos. 31 and 33 Church St., existed 1902–14.[39]

Lighthouse Mission, unsectarian, reg. at no. 13 Winchester St. 1929.[40]

Christian Tulipeans reg. Tulip hall, no. 20 Victoria Park Sq., 1940–1.[41]

JUDAISM

SEPHARDI worshippers at Bevis Marks synagogue (Lond.) rented houses in Bethnal Green from the early 18th century.[42] They included Jacob Alvares in the 'Great House' before 1728[43] and the *hazan* or chief rabbi Moses Cohen d'Azevedo (d. 1784) in 1760. Aldgate House was leased by Israel Levin Salomons in 1765 and by Abraham de Mattos Mocatta of the bullion-broking family in 1769. The boxer Daniel Mendoza (d. 1836) lived from 1788 at no. 3 Paradise Row, while Ephraim

Lopez Pereira, Baron D'Aguilar (d. 1802), a wealthy but eccentric miser, pastured cattle at Bethnal Green and stored furniture in houses there.[44] Among the few Ashkenazim were Jospa ben Jacob Buchtel, who organized services in a *minyan* at his house in Bethnal Green in 1747, provoking fears that it might come to rival the Great Synagogue.[45] The western portion of Old Ford Lane was named Jews' Walk by 1779[46] and a statement in 1788 that the inhabitants of

[12] Inf. from administrator, Good Shepherd Mission.
[13] Above.
[14] Inf. from pastor, Bibleway ch.
[15] Below, educ.
[16] *Lond. City Mission Mag.* xlvi. 206, 208. (pub. schs., Abbey Str.).
[17] P.R.O., ED 21/345.
[18] Abbey St. Sun. and Ragged Schs. Mission and Institute, *52nd Ann. Rep.* (1892) (T.H.L.H.L. pamphlet 226.1).
[19] Above.
[20] Above; *King Edw. Institution. 100th Ann. Rep.* (1944–5) (T.H.L.H.L. pamphlet 226.13); *P.O. Dir. Lond.* (1878 and later edns.).
[21] P.R.O., HO 129/21/3/1/10.
[22] Ibid. C 54/17662, mm. 1–6; G.L.R.O., A/FWA/C/B2/1; above, building 1837–75.
[23] G.L.R.O., MBW 1684, no. 26.
[24] *P.O. Dir. Lond.* (1899).
[25] Ibid. (1908–12).
[26] G.R.O. Worship Reg. no. 957; K. Heasman, *Evangelicals in Action* (1962), 32.
[27] *Ragged Sch. Union Mag.* (1869), 96, 150–2; P.R.O.,

ED 3/11, no. 262; *The Times*, 22 Dec. 1871, 10c.
[28] G.R.O. Worship Reg. no. 19340.
[29] Ibid. no. 23033.
[30] G.L.R.O., A/FWA/C/B2/1.
[31] Ibid.; Old O.S. Map Lond. 51 (1872).
[32] *Boro. of Hackney Dir.* (1872).
[33] G.R.O. Worship Reg. no. 22627–8.
[34] Ibid. no. 30536.
[35] *Builder*, 26 Dec. 1885, 920.
[36] G.R.O, Worship Reg. no. 32653; above, Unitarians.
[37] G.R.O. Worship Reg. nos. 37329, 41358.
[38] Ibid. no. 33083; Booth, *Life and Lab.* iii(1), 71.
[39] Samuel, *E. End Underworld*, 290 n; *P.O. Dir. Lond.* (1903).
[40] G.R.O. Worship Reg. no. 52011.
[41] Ibid. nos. 59107, 59168.
[42] Section based on *Jewish Hist. Soc Trans.* xxx. 78–9.
[43] M.L.R. 1728/5/241.
[44] Vale, *Old Bethnal Green*, 95; A. M. Hyamson, *Sephardim of Eng.* (1951), 31, 102–3.
[45] C. Roth, *The Great Syn.* (1950), 68.
[46] Ibid. 154; Horwood, *Plan* (1792–9).

Bethnal Green were 'mostly French Jews',[47] while exaggerated, reflected Huguenot numbers and the importance of Jews.

In the late 18th century the Sephardi merchants, like other wealthy Londoners, began to abandon the large houses round the green. Jews of a lower class, both Sephardi and Ashkenazi, moved into the areas bordering Mile End and Spitalfields. In 1761 the Ashkenazi New Synagogue acquired a burial ground west of Ducking Pond Lane, on the boundary with Mile End, where the Great Synagogue bought the freehold in 1795. The cemetery, called successively North Street and Brady Street, was closed in 1858[48] and maintained throughout by Jews who occupied a house on the site.[49] About 1783 Isaac Mendes Furtado, who was among rioters ejected for over-exuberance at the celebration of Purim, built a terrace on the east side of Dog Row, which he called Purim Place.[50] By the 1840s Jews were being married there at no. 7.[51] A little to the north, on the east side of Cambridge Road in Queen's Row,[52] a Jews' asylum existed from 1820[53] and possibly from 1800[54] but had closed by 1832.[55]

Jews lived in Bethnal Green throughout the 19th century, some with Anglicized names,[56] a few of them merchants but most of them small tradesmen or hawkers.[57] Large-scale immigration came towards the end, with the pogroms of Ashkenazim in Russia and Poland, and spread from Whitechapel into south-west Bethnal Green and the new Boundary Street estate where in 1899 some 75–95 per cent of the population was Jewish.[58] In the population as a whole, however, the foreign-born formed only 3.5 per cent in 1901, rising to a peak of 6.3 per cent in 1911. Although Jews settled in other districts and never formed more than a small minority,[59] their concentration around Brick Lane lay behind the growth of anti-semitism in the 1930s. After dispersal during the Second World War, their numbers never recovered. Most early immigrants attended tiny synagogues in private homes in Spitalfields and Whitechapel[60] and a few were later established in south-west Bethnal Green. The Federation of Synagogues claimed the foundation of Rosiner synagogue from 1901, Bethnal Green Great synagogue from 1905, and the Glory of Israel synagogue from 1910. Two Independent synagogues, in Teesdale and Hare streets claimed foundation in 1901. There was only one synagogue, in Globe Road from 1928, in the eastern part of the borough. Half had closed by the 1950s, two survived until the 1980s, and one until 1990.

The following abbreviations are used: Fed., federation; reg., registered; syn., synagogue.

Nos. 68–70 TEESDALE STREET claimed to have been established as Independent congregation 1901,[61] although not reg. until 1927.[62] Sole syn. listed in Bethnal Green 1990.[63] Closed by 1991.

UNITED WORKMAN'S or WLODOWA SYNAGOGUE, claiming establishment as Independent congregation 1901[64] or 1914,[65] reg. at no. 21 Hare St. 1919.[66] Bldg. closed as unsafe soon after 1987, when membership was 180.[67]

ROSINER SYNAGOGUE, no. 13 Buxton St., claimed foundation by Fed. of Syn. 1901 and reg. 1912–64; probably closed before 1964.[68]

BETHNAL GREEN GREAT SYNAGOGUE, member of Fed. of Syn., was built on site of Bapt. chapel at no. 13 Bethnal Green Rd. by Lewis Solomon, reg. 1905, and opened officially with 250 members 1906.[69] After damage by bombing[70] svces. at nos. 2 and 4 Chance St. from 1941 until rebldg. 1956 and reg. again at nos. 11–15 (odd) Bethnal Green Rd 1960.[71] Absorbed Princelet St. syn., Spitalfields, 1970.[72] Membership 360 in 1984 but poor attendance led to closure 1985.[73]

GLORY OF ISRAEL SYNAGOGUE, member of Fed. of Syn., was reg. 1910–54 behind no. 10 Code St. near Brick Lane.[74]

GREEN STREET SYNAGOGUE was reg. at no. 223 Globe Rd. 1928–54; probably closed before 1954.[75]

BUDDHISM

FRIENDS of Western Buddhist Order[76] were leased former fire station at corner of Roman and Globe rds. by G.L.C. 1975, where Lond. Buddhist Centre and Sukhavati reg. as two shrine rooms 1976.[77] Shrine room at no. 119 Roman Rd., initially called Sukhavati Meditation Centre and later Golgonooza, reg. 1977.[78] Another community opened at no. 95 Bishop's Way.

47 *The Times*, 12 Sept. 1788, 2d; 18 Sept. 1788, 1c; 27 Sept. 1788, 1b.
48 Roth, *Gt. Syn.* 177; *Lond. Gaz.* 11 May 1858, p.2352.
49 e.g. G.L.R.O., THCS 446; P.R.O., HO 1541/3/6, f. 144.
50 Hyamson, *Sephardim*, 197; G.L.R.O., C/93/1538.
51 T.H.L.H.L., TH/8362/1.
52 *Bowles's New Pocket Plan of Lond. and Westm.* (1783).
53 G.L.R.O., MR/PLT 5065.
54 Perhaps the unlocated Jews' home in Bethnal Green rated in 1800: G.L.R.O., MR/PLT 5024.
55 Vestry mins. 1831–3, p. 205.
56 e.g. Phillips and Martin.
57 T.H.L.H.L., TH/8362/1.
58 C. Russell and H. S. Lewis, *The Jew in Lond.* (1900), map at back; *The Jewish E. End 1840–1939*, ed. A. Newman (1981), 30–5.   59 *Census*, 1901–51.
60 H. Blacker, *Just Like It Was* (1974), 21, 71.
61 *Jewish Year Bk.* (1953 et seq.). Existed by 1914: Harris and Bryant, *Chs. and Lond.* 382.
62 G.R.O. Worship Reg. no. 50967.
63 *Jewish Year Bk.* (1990).
64 *Jewish Chron.* 24 Apr. 1987 (T.H.L.H.L. cuttings file 226.7).
65 *Jewish Year Bk.* (1953 et seq.). Not listed in Harris and Bryant, *Chs. and Lond.* [1914], 382.
66 G.R.O. Worship Reg. no. 47489.
67 Bethnal Green M.B. *Official Guide* [1950], 79; *Jewish Chron.* 24 Apr. 1987.
68 *Jewish Year Bk.* (1953 et seq.); G.R.O. Worship Reg. no. 45403; Harris and Bryant, *Chs. and Lond.* 382.
69 *Jewish Year Bk.* (1906–7), 46; G.R.O. Worship Reg. no. 41317; Bethnal Green M.B. *Official Guide* [1921], 81.
70 Bethnal Green M.B. *Official Guide* [1950], 79.
71 G.R.O. Worship Reg. nos. 59870, 67758.
72 T.H.L.H.L., note in cat. for TH/8262.
73 *Jewish Chron.* 31 Aug. 1984; *E.L.A.* 5 July 1985 (T.H.L.H.L., Cuttings file 226.7).
74 G.R.O. Worship Reg. no. 44359; Harris and Bryant, *Chs. and Lond.* 382.
75 G.R.O. Worship Reg. no. 51279; Bethnal Green M.B. *Official Guide* [1938]. Not in ibid. [1950].
76 Section based on *Lond. Buddhist Centre* (prospectus) (T.H.L.H.L., pamphlet 226.13).
77 G.R.O. Worship Reg. no. 74286.
78 Ibid. no. 74617.

EDUCATION

THOMAS Parmiter in his will proved 1682[79] hoped that St. George's chapel could be obtained as a schoolhouse for the poor of Bethnal Green.[80] It was, however, apparently used only for the dissenting academy at Bishop's Hall[81] and the first public school was Parmiter's, built in St. John Street in 1722. In 1765, when Parmiter's was educating 30 boys, a parochial charity school was founded for 30 girls. By c. 1800 the two schools taught c. 130 children.

Sunday schools, which taught reading and sometimes writing, were associated with the spread of Dissent from the early 19th century. Some of the earliest, although unrecorded, may have been opened by the Christian Community.[82] The Sunday School Union was founded in 1803[83] and Friar's Mount, allegedly the first Methodist Sunday school in London, may have opened in 1802;[84] the Sunday School Tract Society was instituted there in 1806.[85] William Hale in 1806 observed that several Sunday schools had been lately established around Spitalfields, with a pleasing effect on morals.[86] By 1810 Bethnal Green possessed a large Sunday school attended by several hundred children, three Methodist Sunday schools at their respective chapels attended by 200, a Sunday school belonging to Protestant dissenters attended by 40, and a charity school for 10 children also belonging to Protestant dissenters.[87] Other Sunday schools included the Poor Child's, opened for c. 80–100 children by John Mandeno in a garden shed in 1812,[88] and one associated with Independents, opened soon afterwards in Virginia Row. In 1814 Henry Althans moved to Bethnal Green where he founded the East London Auxiliary to the Sunday School Union and became involved in several nonconformist Sunday schools.[89]

The London Society for Promoting Christianity among the Jews, an Anglican body, included schools among its new institutions in Bethnal Green in 1813, although it was not listed by the rector in 1816.[90] He recorded two schools 'under the Establishment', Parmiter's and the Parochial charity school, the workhouse, where a pauper schoolmaster taught the children to read but the education was 'very bad', and Spitalfields British school in Spicer Street which, although beyond the boundary, taught some Bethnal Green children.[91] There were no Anglican Sunday schools but Methodist and dissenters' Sunday schools were attended by some Anglicans. A total of 2,535 children were receiving some education in 1816, 130 of them at the two day schools and the others at 11 Sunday schools, two of them Methodist (Friar's Mount and Middlesex) and the rest also dissenters'. Three of the schools were connected with Congregational chapels (Virginia Row, Bethnal Green, and Gibraltar) and Wilmot Square and Mandeno's were precursors of the largely Congregational Abbey Sunday school. There were two Sunday schools in Globefields, one of them connected with the Calvinist minister George Evans. The Revd. William Shenton opened a nonconformist Sunday school at no. 3 Darling Place between 1804 and 1816. The last Sunday school, for girls only, was in Church Street.[92] By 1818[93] there were 9 Methodist Sunday schools with 2,600 children, two endowed (charity) schools with 120, and three unendowed day schools with 135 (the London Orphan asylum, the Jews' chapel, and Mr. Kello's).[94]

The Society for the Education of the Poor of Bethnal Green in the principles of the Established Church was formed at a vestry chaired by the rector in 1818. Appealing for funds, it blamed lack of education for the 'demoralization of the lower orders', the profanation of Sunday, and the 'tumultuous assemblies' of young people.[95] As a result the first National school, St. Matthew's, opened in 1819.

The British and Foreign Schools Society, founded in 1808, opened an important school in Spitalfields in 1812 but in 1816 it was only half full because parents could not afford 1d. a week and children were set to work in silk manufacturing when very young.[96] Sunday schools therefore had a major role but they, too, were constantly in difficulties. Some of the early Methodist Sunday schools could pay neither rent nor the interest on loans and many schools closed. The Sunday School Tract Society lapsed, to be refounded in 1821 under the patronage of T. F. Buxton.[97] In 1833[98] no Sunday schools were recorded for the Methodists; there were three Church of England (Friar's Mount, the Episcopal Jews' chapel, and one started in 1829), two Independent, one Calvinist, and one Protestant dissenters'. Of the combined day and Sunday schools, two were departments of St. Matthew's National School and three were Lancasterian (probably Hackney Road, Twig Folly, and Abbey). Thirty schools were listed,[99] attended by 5,612; two thirds of schooling took place on Sundays.

79 Below, charities. Introductory account of educ. based on accounts of individual schs. below.
80 P.R.O., PROB 11/369 (P.C.C. 48 Cottle), ff. 371–2v.
81 Below, private schs. and colleges.
82 Rayner, Story of Christian Community.
83 K. Heasman, Evangelicals in Action (1962), 16.
84 G. F. Vale, Old Bethnal Green (1934), 130.
85 G.L.R.O., Acc. 2330/86/1.
86 W. Hale, Letter to Sam. Whitbread . . . Observations on Poor of Spitalfields (1806), 26.
87 Lambeth Pal. Libr., Fulham Papers, Randolph 11/21.
88 Morgan, Abbey St. Sun. Schs. 75, 77.
89 Ibid. 4–7; Rep. from Sel. Cttee. on Educ. of Lower Orders in Metropolis, H.C. 427, pp. 53, 73 (1816), iv.

90 Rep. from Sel. Cttee. on Educ. of Lower Orders in Metropolis, H.C. 495, pp. 231 sqq. (1816), iv.
91 Ibid. p. 188.
92 Ibid. H.C. 469, p. 123 (1816), iv.
93 Educ. of Poor Digest, 551, 562.
94 Kello was min. of Bethnal Green Cong. chapel.
95 B.L. Add. MS. 38275, ff. 42–45.
96 Rep. from Sel. Cttee. on Educ. of Lower Orders in Metropolis, H.C. 427, p. 85 (1816), iv; ibid. H.C. 469, pp. 114, 122 (1816), iv; ibid. H.C. 495, p. 231 (1816), iv.
97 G.L.R.O., Acc. 2330/86/1; ibid. N/M/14/1; B.L., Add. MS. 40413, f. 211.
98 Educ. Enq. Abstract, 85–6.
99 Depts. were often listed as separate schs.

The total number of educated children was smaller, since, for example, Twig Folly district day pupils usually also attended on Sunday. In Twig Folly *c.* 45 per cent received some education at the British school, a small infants' school, three or four private day schools, and five or six dame schools.[1]

The British and Foreign Schools Society, which had one school in Bethnal Green (Hackney Road) from 1819, opened several during the 1830s and 1840s. In 1835 an attempt 'to pre-empt the dissenters' and open a second National school, connected with St. John's church (opened in 1828), was frustrated by the controversy between the rector and Joseph Merceron.[2] The situation was transformed by Bishop Blomfield's decision to found 10 district churches, each with its own National school. By 1843[3] eight National schools provided 2,463 day-school places, attended by 1,780 children, and two Church infants' schools provided another 138 places, attended by 90, in addition to the 170 places, all filled, provided by the older Anglican charity schools. The list omitted St. Bartholomew's National, which was being built, and the Episcopal Jews' school, which included children from outside the parish. Five British schools provided 1,659 places attended by 1,327 children and three other infants' schools provided 375 places, attended by 320. Of *c.* 14,000 children aged 5–14 in Bethnal Green, 4,820 received daily instruction, the rest presumably being taught in dame schools of which there were 2,109 in the combined districts of Bethnal Green and Spitalfields. There were 23 Sunday schools teaching 5,167 children in the same area. By 1846 ten parishes had National schools, mostly both as day and Sunday schools and, together with infants' and charity schools, Church schools in Bethnal Green were attended by 4,812 pupils.[4] At the end of the 1850s William Cotton reported a school in every parish save one (probably St. James the Less), where the incumbent would not allow schools to be built lest they entail him in expense.[5]

The pence placed National and British schools beyond the reach of many. The incumbent of St. Bartholomew's explained in 1853 that, besides the National school, there was an infants' school attended long after infancy by the children of hawkers, labourers, and costermongers because it charged half as much, and a free ragged school for the children of casual labourers.[6]

As the Methodist Sunday school movement declined, new organizations, which in part grew out of it, sought to serve the very poor. The London City Mission, founded in 1835,[7] opened schools largely run by missioners and voluntary teachers. Most of them joined the Ragged School Union which was established in 1844.[8] They were often part of a group including place of worship, mission, day, Sunday, and infants' schools, and social centre, the schools themselves receiving grants from the British and Foreign Schools Society, the Ragged School Union, and the London City Mission. Abbey Street, one of the largest British schools, also supported Sunday schools, evening classes, a library, and a reading room. Under the patronage of Charles Buxton, by 1857 it had more than 12 separate educational agencies with more than 6,000 registered pupils.[9]

In 1851 there were 3,519 Sunday attendances at nonconformist, mainly Congregational, chapels and Sunday schools and 3,236 at Anglican churches.[10] Some 6,000 children were taught in Anglican, mainly National, schools and Sunday schools by 1858.[11]

By 1871 when the school board for London assumed responsibility for public education, all 15 parishes had National Schools with a total day roll of 5,655 and average attendance of 4,383. There were seven British schools with a total day roll of 8,522 and average attendance of 6,668, the figures distorted by those for the Good Shepherd schools (6,442 and 4,961). One British school, Satchwell Street, was classified as private.[12] Five ragged schools had a total of 1,250 on the roll and an attendance of 922; a sixth, Cranbrook Street, was classified as private. Approach Road Wesleyan school and the private Christian Orphanage, Methodist Children's Home, and St. Matthias's nursery schools, with a combined roll of 285 and average attendance of 237, also had denominational links. There was one Roman Catholic public school (Parliament Street), opened in 1869, which had an average attendance of 263. The private St. Matthew's German and English school, with an average attendance of 39, had no apparent religious connexion. Surprisingly, in view of the area's strong radical atheist tradition, only Birkbeck school was avowedly non-Christian. A total of 16,644 children were enrolled and an average of 12,955 attended 36 schools.[13]

The board was leased two British schools, one ragged school, and one National school while erecting its own buildings. By 1887 there were 14 board schools, mostly standing out above the terraces, with accommodation for 16,537 children. Eight National schools accommodated 4,054 and three other schools, Approach Road Wesleyan, Bonner Road Children's Home, and Parliament Street Roman Catholic, accommodated 1,002.[14] The L.C.C.'s education committee in 1904 took over 20 board schools, accommodating 25,083.[15]

[1] *Rep. Sel. Cttee. on Educ.* H.C. 465, pp. 271–4 (1835), vii.
[2] BNC, Second Ser. [Tower],148, letters from Revd. G. Casson 4 July, 11 Aug. 1835.
[3] *Lond. City Mission Mag.* viii. 174–7.
[4] Nat. Soc. *Inquiry,1846–7,* Mdx. 2–3.
[5] *Rep. from Sel. Cttee. of H.L. on Deficiency of Divine Worship in Metropolis,* H.C. 387, p. 11 (1857–8), ix.
[6] *Final Rep. Metropolis Chs. Fund, 1836–54,* App. IV, pp. 97–100.
[7] Above, prot. nonconf. (undemon. missions).
[8] A. M. Babler, 'Educ. of the Destitute: study of Lond. Ragged Schs. 1844–74' (N. Illinois Univ. Ph.D. thesis, 1978), 23, 25.

[9] *Educational Record,* iii. 220.
[10] P.R.O., HO 129/21.
[11] Lambeth Pal. Libr., Fulham Papers, Tait 440/6–18. No returns for St. Paul's and no numbers given for St. Matthias's; total for the other pars. is 5,784 and excludes evg. schs.
[12] All the so-called private schs. provided some free places.
[13] G.L.R.O., SBL 1518 (tables of elem. schs. 1871).
[14] *Rep. Educ. Cttee. of Council, 1887* [C. 547-I], H.C. p. 663 (1888), xxxviii.
[15] *Final Rep. of Sch. Bd. for Lond.* (1904); L.C.C. *Lond. Statistics,* xvi. 264.

It maintained the National schools, the Wesleyan school, and the Roman Catholic school but the Children's Home refused its help and closed in 1913. As the population began to fall schools were reorganized and accommodation was reduced, although new schools were still built. By 1919[16] the L.C.C. had 24 schools, including one former National and the Wesleyan school which it had taken over, and accommodation for 24,949; six Church of England schools could accommodate 2,796 and one Roman Catholic school 189. By 1932[17] there were 22 council schools accommodating 19,033, six Church of England schools accommodating 2,585, and two Roman Catholic schools accommodating 493.

The only secondary school in 1904 was Parmiter's.[18] A central school, Morpeth Street, opened in 1910 and a second, Mansford Street, was created out of its senior department in 1911. Between 1927 and 1932 most council schools were reorganized into junior, senior, and infants' departments.

The closure of several older schools gave rise in 1933 to a Board of Education Scheme[19] grouping the educational portions of Greenwood's, Inman's, Robertson's, Jane Thomas's, and the Bread charities with the endowments of the Parochical school. Thirteen trustees, the rector and representatives of the L.C.C. and M. B., were to apply the income, then £350 a year, for the benefit of the remaining Church schools. The combinaton, entitled Bethnal Green Educational charities under a Charity Commission Scheme of 1978,[20] had an income of £3,659 in 1993.[21]

Despite heavy bomb damage and the evacuation of children, 22 schools accommodating c. 9,000 were open in 1944.[22] The London school plan of 1947 allowed for 18 council primary schools and six voluntary primary schools in Bethnal Green, which by 1951 had 15 council primary and four voluntary primary schools. The most radical proposals were for reorganizing secondary education on comprehensive lines. Nine schools, including two outside the borough, were to be combined in three newly built schools. New buildings were also planned for the voluntary Parmiter's and St. Jude's schools. In the event one school amalgamated with another outside the borough to create Bowbrook in 1956, although using the existing buildings, and two more amalgamated in 1959 to create Daneford comprehensive, which acquired new buildings in 1965. Bowbrook closed in 1975 and St. Jude's secondary school in 1977. Parmiter's moved out of the control of the I.L.E.A., the L.C.C.'s successor, in 1981. By 1988 four secondary and fifteen primary schools survived to serve the smaller population.

Under the Local Government Act, 1963, Bethnal Green became part of Division 5 of the I.L.E.A.[23] On the abolition of the I.L.E.A. in 1990 responsibility for education passed to Tower Hamlets L.B.

Public schools.[24] Except where otherwise stated, basic historical information and figures of accommodation and average attendance have been taken from: files on Church of England schools at the National Society; National Society, *Inquiry,1846–7*, Mdx.2–3; National Society, *Annual Reps.* (1820– 44); British and Foreign Schools Society, *Reps.* (1812–82); Ragged School Union, *Annual Reps.* (1847–56); *Ragged School Union Magazine* (1849–70); P.R.O., ED 3/11; ED 7/74, 80; ED 14/8; *Educ. Enq. Abstract*, H.C. 62, pp. 85–86 (1835), xlii; *Mins. of Educ. Cttee. of Council,1846* [866], H.C. (1847), xlv; *1849* [1215], H.C. (1850), xliii; *1851–2* [1480], H.C. (1852), xl; *1856–7* [2237], H.C. (1857 Sess. 2), xxxiii; *Rep. of Educ. Cttee. of Council,1865–6* [3666], H.C. (1866), xxvii; *1870* [C. 406], H.C. (1871), xxii; *1887* [C. 547-I], H.C. (1888), xxxviii; *1893–4* [C. 7437-I], H.C. (1894), xxix; *Schs. transferred to Sch. Bds.* H.C. 253 (1875), lviii; *Schs. receiving Bldg. Grants* [Cd. 1336], H.C. (1902), lxxviii; *Return of Non-Provided Schs.* H.C. 178-XXXIII (1906), lxxxviii; *Bd. of Educ., List 21, 1908–38* (H.M.S.O.); L.C.C. *Educ. Svce. Particulars* (1909–10 and later edns.); L.C.C. (I.L.E.A. from 1965), *Educ. Svce. Inf.* (1937 and later edns.). Building alterations from Dist. Surveyors' Returns (G.L.R.O, MBW and AR/BA/4).

The following abbreviations are used: a.a., average attendance; accn., accommodation; amalg., amalgamation; B, boy, boys; Bapt., Baptist; bd., board; Brit., British; C.E., Church of England; Cong., Congregational; demol., demolished; dept., department; evg., evening; G, girl, girls; I, infant, infants; Ind., Independent; J, JB, JG, JM, junior, junior boys, girls, mixed; M, mixed; Meth., Methodist; mod., modern; Nat., National; parl., parliamentary; perm., permanent; R.C., Roman Catholic; reorg., reorganized; roll, numbers on roll; S, SB, SG, SM, senior, senior boys, girls, mixed; S.B.L., School Board for London; sch., school; sec., secondary; Sun., Sunday; temp., temporarily, temporary; V., vicar; vol., voluntary; Wes., Wesleyan. The word 'school' is to be understood after each named entry. Separate departments are indicated by commas: B, G, I; JM, I.

ABBEY,[25] Abbey Pl., Wilmot Sq., or Essex St. Sun. sch. built 1828 by Robt. Gammon of no. 7 Wilmot Sq. at end of gdn., bounded N. by Abbey Pl. and E. by narrow street called successively Mary's Row, John's Pl., Essex St., and Blythe St. Named after the ho., once known as the Abbey.[26] Connected with Brit. and Foreign Schs. Soc. by 1833, when supported by sch. pence and roll 120 B, but described as Nat. 1837.[27] Enlarged for 300 c. 1841 when leased to Gammon and other trustees for children of labouring classes, for sch. teacher, Sun. sch., or other

16 *Bd. of Educ., List 21*, 1919.   17 Ibid. *1932*.
18 L.C.C. *Lond. Statistics*, xvi (1905–6), 293.
19 G.L.R.O., P72/MTW/23515.; below, charities.
20 G.L.R.O., P72/MTW/235/7; Char. Com. no. 312296.
21 Char. Com. no. 3 2296.
22 G.L.R.O., L.C.C. Educ. Officer'a Dept., Elem.Schs. open 1944.
23 *Ann. Abstract of Gtr. Lond. Statistics* (1967).
24 Private schs. are treated separately below.
25 Para. based on G. Morgan, *Hist. 50 years work of Abbey St. Sun. Schs.* (1890), 77 sqq.
26 P.R.O., RG 31/3/1605; M.L.R. 1842/1/671; above, settlement and bldg., the Centre.
27 P.R.O., C 54/12505, mm. 56–58.

charitable purposes connected with C.E. but links also with Inds. and Lond. City Mission. Absorbed Poor Child's Sun. sch. and used small adjoining ho. as I sch., where roll 1843 220 I.[28] Additions for older children *c.* 1856. Free evg. sch. for G under Gammon's successor. Renamed Essex St. 1867, Blythe St. 1871. One room used for Sun. and day sch., roll 1871: 51 B, 55 G; a.a. 41 B, 33 G, but mostly I; financed by sch. pence, instruction basic, 'books wretched'. Connexion with Lond. City Mission severed 1871 and replaced by supervision of Cong. ch. at Stamford Hill. Union with Satchwell St. Sun. sch. 1873 and Sun. classes later divided between Blythe St., Satchwell St., and Zion chapel. Lease expired 1878, when day sch. moved to Wolverley St. (q.v.). Sun. sch. used new bldg. in Mansford St. 1880–8, then moved to Abbey St. Sun. sch.

ABBEY STREET.[29] Spitalfields and Bethnal Green Brit. Soc. built sch. on site between Abbey and Ramsey streets purchased 1838 and conveyed to trustees 1842.[30] Day sch. opened 1839 and Sun. sch. (successor of that associated with Virginia Ind. chapel) opened 1840. Rapid turnover of children although schs. 'well conducted'. Improvements 1843, 1851, 1857.[31] Day sch. a.a. 1840: 430 B, 160 G. a.a. 1857: 400 B, 205 G, 201 I. Model Sun. sch. visited by French statesman François Guizot, a.a. 1857: 600 and 32 teachers.[32] a.a. 1867: 721 and 50 teachers. Day sch. accn. for 373 B, 216 G, 206 I in 1871, when financed by parl. grant, sch. pence, and subscriptions.[33] Additions 1872. Accn. 1879: 979 B,G,I. a.a. 1882: 217 B, 205 G, 136 I. Day sch. transferred to S.B.L. 1883 and replaced Hague (q.v.). 1884.[34] Part of Sun. sch. united with Hope St. (Spitalfields) ragged sch. 1884, rest under cttee. becoming sole tenants of premises. Evg. Sun. sch. a.a. 1888: 375, with 22 teachers. By Char. Com. Order 1892 constituted a charity to advance educ. in Bethnal Green and Spitalfields by payments and exhibitions.[35] Site sold to S.B.L. 1894[36] and proceeds invested. As Abbey St. Educ. Foundation, governed by Scheme 1913, made grants in 1993.[37]

ADELPHI CHAPEL BRIT., Gloucester St., Hackney Rd. Revd. W. Woodhouse persuaded by Althans to settle in Bethnal Green after visit to Abbey St. Sunday sch.[38] Missionary sch. with 30 pupils supplied with schoolroom, teachers, and funds from Woodhouse's new Adelphi chapel by 1849.[39] Three-storeyed sch. built 1853 as day and Sun. sch. although also used by chapel.[40] Financed by parl. grant and sch. pence, a.a. 1855: 204 B, 160 G. Enlarged 1868.[41] Roll 1871: 289 B, 283 G. Subsequently Sun. sch. only.[42]

ALBION, No. 7 George St., Old Bethnal Green Rd. Day and Sun. sch. opened by Lond. City Mission 1863, a.a. 30 weekday: 45 Sun.[43] Free night sch. in room also used for Sun. sch. and worship 1871, when roll 18 B, 17 G.

ANCHOR RAGGED, No. 22 Sclater St. Opened 1849 by Lond. City Mission in large ho. in Anchor (later Sclater) St. rented at nominal sum from Eastern Counties Rly.[44] Accn. 1850: 180; roll: 60 Sun. a.m. and p.m., 112 Sun. evg., 65 B, 60 G, 7 adults weekday evg., with 10 vol. teachers and 1 paid teacher. Roll 1856: 86 B, 91 G, 43 I. Scheme to extend premises 1858 apparently unsuccessful and Sun. evg. sch. closed 1866. Room for I beneath room for 'juvenals', itself beneath room for svces., the whole dilapidated 1871. Most children aged under 9 and many left to enter match trade; roll 1871: 69 B, 41 G day, 36 B, 21 G, evg. Probably soon closed.

ANN'S PLACE BRIT. Opened by 1839 in room and probably built as day and Sun. sch. for I by Bapts. E. of Pritchard's Rd.[45] Improvements 1845. Financed by parl. grants and sch. pence 1871, when accn. 181 I, roll 85 I. 'Inefficient in instruction' when S.B.L. leased it and replaced day sch. by Pritchard's Road (q.v.). Continued as Sun. sch.[46] under Char. Com. Scheme 1909.[47]

APPROACH ROAD TEMPORARY, Victoria Pk. Opened 1859 as Approach Rd. Wes. in bldg. attached to chapel at corner of Approach and Bonner rds. Accn. 1871: 333 B & G on first floor, 191 I on ground floor; roll 139 B, 45 G, 104 I. Financed by parl. grant, collections, subscriptions, and sch. pence. Accn. reduced 1907 and 1908 to 156 M, 100 I. a.a. 1906–7: 170 M, 75 I. Transferred to S.B.L. 1913 and closed 1927.

APPROACH ROAD WES., see Approach Road temp.

BACON STREET RAGGED, see St. Philip's ragged.

BARNET STREET BD., see Columbia primary.

BETHNAL GREEN CHAPEL BRIT. Kello, minister of Cong. chapel at corner of Cambridge Rd. and Bath St., had sch. for 12 G 1818.[48] Roll 1833: 30 G, of whom 12 clothed and educ. by subscription, rest paid sch. pence. Sch. behind chapel built or rebuilt *c.* 1835 when grant made towards new sch. for 250;[49] a.a. 1840: 84 G; 1846: 132 G. Closed and conveyed to Birkbeck schs. 1849, when new Cong. chap. opened at junction of Bethnal Green Rd. and Pott St. with sch. for 400 I underneath;[50] a.a. 1857: 220 I; 1861: 175 I. Connexion with Brit. and Foreign Schs. Soc. apparently severed 1862. Managed by cttee. associated with chapel and financed by sch. pence until 1870, when run as private sch. by mistress. Sch. 'wretched' 1871, when a.a. 89 I.

28   *Lond. City Mission Mag.* viii. 175.
29   Para. based on Morgan, *Abbey St. Sun. Schs.*
30   *Endowed Chars. Lond.* (1897), 36; G.L.R.O., Y/SP/72/1.
31   P.R.O., ED 21/345, no. 4164.
32   *Educational Record*, iii (1857).
33   G.L.R.O., SBL 1518, no. 256.
34   Ibid. SBL 678, pp. 245 sqq.
35   *Endowed Chars. Lond.* (1897), 36–8; P.R.O., ED 21/345.
36   P.R.O., HO 45/9868; below, special schs.
37   Char. Com. file no. 312430.
38   Morgan, *Abbey St. Sunday Schs.* 11.
39   *Lond. City Mission Mag.* xiv. 89. For chapel, above, prot. nonconf. (Congs.).
40   P.R.O., C 54/14592, mm. 7–10.

41   T.H.L.H.L., Cuttings file 226.2 (corresp. between J. Avery and G. F. Vale 1932).
42   Old O.S. Map Lond. 51 (1893).
43   *Lond. City Mission Mag.* xxx. 208, 213.
44   Ibid.. xv. 167; *Cassell's Map of Lond.* (*c.* 1861–2).
45   P.R.O., C 54/12474, mm. 14–17; ibid. RG 31/3/2080, 2037; above, prot. nonconf. (Bapts.).
46   G.L.R.O., CL/LOC/2/10, Map VII. 38.
47   Char. Com. file no. 312280.
48   *Educ. of Poor Digest*, 551; above, prot. nonconf. (Congs.).
49   *Ret. of Grants to Nat. Soc. and Brit. and Foreign Soc. 1834–7*, p. 356, H.C. 395 (1837–8), xxxviii.
50   P.R.O., C 54/13855, mm. 52–66; *Cong. Year Bk.* (1850), 194, 197.

S.B.L. agreed to hire premises 1872 but never opened.[51]

BETHNAL GREEN GOSPEL MISSION RAGGED, 42–43 Old Castle St. (later Virginia Rd.). Wm. Jarvis, evangelist, opened mission 1867 in large workshop at no. 43, inc. night sch. for adults, soon also attended by children and followed by free day sch. Also Sunday sch. with 100—150 children by 1869, when adjoining house leased and new room behind with accn. for 500 opened. Roll 1871: 260 B day, 40 B evg. Day sch., overcrowded and 'inefficient in instruction' closed 1871[52] but used as temp. sch. by S.B.L. 1872–3.[53]

BIRDCAGE WALK. Received grant from Ragged Sch. Union 1849.

BIRKBECK, Cambridge Rd. Opened 1849 in vacated Bethnal Green Chapel Brit. sch. and Cong. chapel at corner of Cambridge Rd. and Bath (later Birkbeck) St.[54] One of four schs. named after Geo. Birkbeck founded by City philanthropist Wm. Ellis for children of 'small tradesmen and others of moderate means', and particularly to improve character of educ. available.[55] Wide curriculum inc. natural sciences, algebra, mechanics, French, and book keeping; said by Anglican source 1853 to provide 'first rate intellectual education but where Bible is absolutely excluded'.[56] Site and bldgs. secured to trustees 1865.[57] Accn. 1871: 212 B, 85 G; a.a. 181 B, 82 G. Bldgs. then large and well fitted and instruction 'above average', although B discipline 'indifferent'. Sch. pence, already 6d. – 9d., increased when schs. raised to higher grade and after foundations by S.B.L. Schs. became too expensive and closed 1884. Premises sold under Char. Com. Order and sum invested for other Birkbeck schs.[58]

BLYTHE STREET., see Abbey.

BONNER LANE BD., see Twig Folly Brit.

BONNER PRIMARY. Built as Bonner Street bd. on site of former Twig Folly Brit. G. sch. 1875 in Queen Anne style by Edw. Robt. Robson and John Jas. Stevenson.[59] Opened 1876 for 261 B, 261 G, 292 I on three floors.[60] Additions 1881. a.a. 1887: 728 B, G, I; 1906–7: 241 B, 237 G, 269 I. Alterations 1895, 1902, 1903. Remodelled 1914–15 for 240 B, 240 G, 279 I.[61] Reorg. 1930 for 479 JG, 270 I.[62] a.a. 1932: 378 JG, 217 I. After return from evacuation, roll 1944: 336 M & I. Reorg. for JM & I 1945 and renamed Bonner primary 1949.[63] Roll 1988: 371 JM & I.[64]

BONNER ROAD CHILDREN'S HOME, Victoria Pk. Moved from Lambeth, where founded by Thos. Bowman Stephenson, 1871,[65] when bldgs. rented by Wes. for orphanage and sch. Accn. 1871: 154 B & G; a.a. 33 B, 2 G. Sch. then 'inefficient in instruction' but improved by 1872 when larger premises built in Bonner Rd. behind private hos. New schoolrooms completed 1877, when application made to become pub. elementary sch. Parl. grant 1887. Accn. 1887: 239; a.a. 150. Alterations 1896 and enlargement 1902. Decided against transfer to L.C.C. 1905.[66] Accn. 1908: 319 M; a.a. 175 M. Closed 1913.

BONNER STREET BD., see Bonner primary.

BOWBROOK SEC. Formed 1956 by amalg. of Cranbrook sec. with Bow sch., Wright's Rd. (Bow) as G. sch. providing general and commercial subjects and dressmaking. Upper sch. in Cranbrook bldgs. and lower in Wright's Rd.[67] Cranbrook bldgs. remodelled as annexe for art, needlework, and commercial subjects by 1971.[68] Closed 1975 and pupils moved to Central Foundation G sch. (Bow).[69]

BUTLER STREET BRIT. Opened 1840 for 160 G in hired rooms in Butler St., presumably off Green St. Probably replaced by Twig Folly schs.(q.v.).

CAMBRIDGE HEATH, see Mowlem primary

CASTLE STREET BRIT., see Gascoigne Place Brit.

CASTLE STREET RAGGED. Lond. City Mission opened first Sun. then weekday ragged sch. in room at no. 1 Castle St. 1856. Roll 1857: weekday 60, Sun. 30 a.m., 70 p.m. with 6 vol. teachers and one paid teacher. a.a. by 1862: 80, Sun. 140, evg. (2 nights a week) 40. Assistance from Ragged Church and Chapel Union, Ragged Sch. Union, and Sun. Sch. Union.[70] Apparently closed between 1868[71] and 1871.[72]

CHILDREN'S HOME, see Bonner Road Children's Home.

CHISENHALE PRIMARY, Victoria Pk. Opened by S.B.L. 1893 between Chisenhale, Vivian, and Auckland (later Zealand) rds. for 240 B, 240 G, 320 I.[73] Additions 1902 for 344 B, 288 G, 296 I. a.a. 1908: 273 B, 260 G, 352 I. Reorg. 1931 for 240 JB, 200 JG, 239 I. a.a. 1932: 239 JB, 203 JG, 205 I. Roll 1944: 240 M & I.[74] By 1951 JM & I, inc. nursery class.[75] Roll 1988: 267 JM & I.[76]

CHRISTIAN ORPHANAGE, Grove Rd., Victoria Pk. Founded by 1867 by Revd. Hen. Lance for

51 G.L.R.O., SBL 1527 (list of temp. schs. provided by Bd. 1885).
52 *The Times*, 22 Dec. 1871, 10c.
53 G.L.R.O., SBL 1527 (list of temp. schs. 1885).
54 Robinson and Chesshyre, *The Green*, 29.
55 P.R.O., C 54/16415, mm. 2–10; *Endowed Chars. Lond.* (1904), 22 sqq.; *V.C.H. Mdx.* i. 256.
56 *Bethnal Green Chs. and Schs. Fund* [1854] (pamphlet in Guildhall Libr.).
57 P.R.O., C 54/16415. mm. 2–10.
58 *Endowed Chars. Lond.* (1904), 22 sqq.
59 G. Stamp and C. Amery, *Victorian Bldgs. of Lond. 1837–87* (1980), 130–1.
60 G.L.R.O., SBL 659, pp. 19 sqq.
61 W. Wilford, *Bonner Schs. 1876–1976* (pamphlet in T.H.L.H.L.).
62 P.R.O., ED 21/34516.
63 Wilford, *Bonner Schs.*; G.L.R.O., L.C.C. Educ. Officer's Dept., Elem. Schs. open 1944.
64 Inf. from I.L.E.A.

65 K. J. Heasman, 'Influence of Evangelicals upon Vol. Charitable Institutions in Second Half of 19th cent.' (Lond. Univ. Ph. D. Thesis, 1959), 697.
66 P.R.O., ED 30/52, no. 29833.
67 *Educ. Authorities Dir.* (1960); G.L.R.O., EO/DIV 5/BBK/LB/1–2; L.C.C. Sec. Schs. in Bethnal Green. (1965).
68 I.L.E.A. Sec. Schs. in Tower Hamlets, Div. 5 (1971).
69 Ibid. (1974); *Reorganisation of ILEA schs.* Sept. 1973–Jan. 1984.
70 *Lond. City Mission Mag.* xxvii. 63–4.
71 E. A. G. Clark, 'Ragged Sch. Union Educ. of Lond. Poor' (Lond. Univ. M.A. thesis, 1967), 299.
72 Not listed in G.L.R.O. SBL 1518 (tables of elem. schs.).
73 G.L.R.O., SBL 1527, p. 50.
74 Ibid., L.C.C. Educ. Officer's Dept., Elem. Schs. open 1944.
75 *Gtr. Lond. & Essex Newspapers Ltd.* 29 Sept. 1978 (T.H.L.H.L., cuttings file, Bethnal Green Educ.).
76 Inf. from I.L.E.A.

children of cholera victims. Roll 1868: 20.[77] 23 G boarded, clothed, and taught free 1871, when supported by vol. contributions, but hired bldg. insufficient and closure expected.

CHURCH ROW NAT., see St. Matthew's Nat.

CLAREMONT STREET BD., see Teesdale primary.

CLUB ROW, see Holy Trinity Nat.

COLLINGWOOD STREET RAGGED. Opened as Sun. sch. before 1832,[78] possibly when bldg. associated with Wes. erected 1821.[79] Ragged sch. in bldg. behind Shoreditch ch. belonging to Wes. Sun. Sch. cttee. by 1854, when roll 40 B, 40 G, weekday evg., 150 Sun. evg. with 11 vol. teachers. Roll 1871: 84 B, 116 G weekday, 59 B evg. Inspector found 54 small children crowded into two rooms and completely ignorant, teacher inefficient, and strong smell from factory. Subsequently run as ragged sch. by V. of St. Philip's.[80]

COLUMBIA MARKET MISSION, No. 15 Virginia Row. C.E. Sun. and evg. sch. for 'rough boys' aged 7–19 in home for 24 messengers and shoeblacks financed by Baroness Burdett-Coutts. Accn. 1871: 49, roll 150, a.a. 40–50.

COLUMBIA MARKET NURSERY, Columbia Rd. Site acquired by S.B.L. 1915[81] and sch. for 150 opened 1930. After evacuation during war, reopened for children aged 2–5.[82] Roll 1975: 81.[83] Housed in new wooden hut by 1988.[84]

COLUMBIA PRIMARY, Columbia Rd. Opened 1875 as Barnet St. bd. between Barnet St. (later Columbia Rd.), Ravenscroft St., and James (later Ezra) St.[85] for 245 B, 237 G, 266 I. Enlarged 1879, 1881, and 1893. Renamed Columbia Rd. 1888.[86] Accn. 1908: 458 B, 458 G, 463 I; a.a. 415 B, 405 G, 437 I. Reorg. 1931 for 355 JB, 453 JG, 390 I, a.a. 339 JB, 337 JG, 338 I. Roll 1944: 600 M & I. Reorg. by 1951 as Columbia primary for JM, I. Roll 1988: 338.[87]

COOPER'S GARDENS TEMP. BD. Opened 1879 for 174 G & I in leased bldg. attached to cottages belonging to Baroness Burdett-Coutts.[88] I dept. closed 1883 and rest of sch. 1887, when a.a. 123 M. Children moved to New Castle St. bd.[89]

CRANBROOK. Opened 1881 as Cranbrook Rd. bd. in bldg. by E. R. Robson for 480 B, 480 G, 638 I on 3 floors near canal in Twig Folly dist. a.a. 1887: 1,321 B, G, I.[90] Remodelled 1899. Accn. 1908: 261 B, 261 G, 314 I; a.a. 241 B, 237 G, 269 I. Reorg. 1930 for 388 SB, 389 SG, 373 I. a.a. 1932: 204 SB, 151 SG, 268 I. Renamed Cranbrook Terrace 1938.[91] Roll 1944: 572 M &

I.[92] After war reorg. into Cranbrook primary with JM & I depts. and Cranbrook sec. for SB until 1951 and for SG until 1956. Primary sch. closed and sec. amalg. with Bow sch. to form Bowbrook sec. (q.v.) 1956.[93]

CRANBROOK SEC., see Cranbrook.

CRANBROOK STREET RAGGED. Opened by 1870 on rented first floor of no. 39 also used for worship and evg. sch. Managed by C.E. cttee. but sch. undenominational. Free sch., roll 1871: 74 B, 39 G; a.a. 70 B, 35 G. Praised for work but premises unsuitable and probably soon closed.

CRANBROOK TERRACE, see Cranbrook.

CUDWORTH RAGGED. Opened 1859 by managers of North St. ragged schs. (q.v.) at junction of Cudworth St. with Burton (Collingwood) St.[94] in leased room over warehouse as day, Sun., and evg. sch. for 262 'children of the lowest class'. Teacher worked as shoemaker in evgs.; financed by vol. contributions and grants by Ragged Sch. Union and, from 1863, by Brit. and Foreign Schs. Soc. Day roll 1871: 105 B, 79 G; a.a. 88 B, 66 G. Closed after 1872.

CUMBERLAND PLACE RAGGED, see North St. ragged.

DANEFORD, Gosset St. Comprehensive M sch. formed 1959 by amalg. of Daniel sec. with Mansford. sec. Initially lower sch. in Daniel bldgs. and upper in Mansford. Daniel bd. sch. adapted and 3 blocks built 1961–5 to designs of Armstrong & MacManus. Opened 1965 as comprehensive sec. for 975 B.[95] Roll 1988: 554 B.[96]

DANIEL SEC. Opened by S.B.L. 1900 in new bldgs. between Daniel, Gosset, and Orange (later Satchwell) streets. Accn. 1908: 353 B, 353 G, 378 I; a.a. 314 B, 315 G, 375 I. Reorg. 1931 for 422 SB, 422 SG, 438 I. a.a. 1932: 362 SB, 354 SG, 385 I. Roll 1944: 610 M & I.[97] After war reorg. as sec. sch. for SB, SG, from 1955 for SM.[98] Amalg. with Mansford sec. to form Daneford 1959.

DOMESTIC MISSION BRIT., Spicer St. Chapel and sch. on N. side of street within Bethnal Green opened by Lond. Domestic Missionary Soc. 1837 and conveyed to trustees 1839.[99] Connected with Unitarians but undenominational. Roll 1843: 150.[1] Sun. sch. a.a. 1851: 775.[2] Brit. sch. by 1856.[3] Financed by parl. grant and sch. pence, described by V. of St. Matthias 1858 as large I sch. belonging to Unitarians.[4] Day sch. a.a. 1858:

[77] Heasman, 'Influence of Evangelicals', 696; *P.O. Dir Lond.* (1870).
[78] P.R.O., RG 31/3/1756.
[79] Ibid. 2000; ibid. HO 129/21/1/unnumbered; above, prot. nonconf. (Meths.).
[80] J. Reeves, *Recollections of Sch. Attendance Officer* (1913), 157.
[81] P.R.O., ED 14/62.
[82] *Educ. Authorities Dir.* (1945); L.C.C. *Sch. Plan* (1947), 111.
[83] Tower Hamlets L. B. *Boro. Plan Topic Paper no. 5: Educ.*, Nov. 1976, 86.
[84] Personal observation.
[85] *Builder.* 30 May 1874, 470.
[86] G.L.R.O., SBL 659, pp. 3 sqq.; SBL 1527, pp. 50 sqq.
[87] Inf. from I.L.E.A.
[88] G.L.R.O., SBL 1527 (index of sites 1903).
[89] Ibid. (list of bd. schs. 1896); SBL 678, pp. 267 sqq.
[90] Ibid. SBL 1527, pp. 50 sqq.; R. Ringshall, M. Miles, F. Kelsall, *Urban Sch. Bldgs. for Educ. in Lond. 1870–1980* (1983), 22.
[91] G.L.R.O., L.C.C. schs. file, Name changes.
[92] Ibid. L.C.C. Educ. Officer's Dept., Elem. Schs. open 1944.
[93] G.L.R.O., EO/DIV 5/CRA 1/LB/5; BBK/LB/1–2.
[94] Not Collingwood St. near Shoreditch ch., above; *Cassell's Map of Lond.* (c. 1861–2).
[95] *Educ. Authorities Dir.* (1960); I.L.E.A. *Sec. Schs. in Tower Hamlets* (1971, 1980); *Hackney Gaz.* 2 Feb. 1965; *Bethnal Green Civic News*, no. 8, July 1964 (T.II.L.II.L., Cuttings file, Bethnal Green Educ.); L.C.C. *Daneford Sch. Ceremonial Opening of New Bldgs.* (1965).
[96] Inf. from I.L.E.A.
[97] G.L.R.O., L.C.C. Educ. Officer's Dept., Elem. Schs. open 1944.
[98] Ibid. EO/DIV 5/DAN 1/LB/7.
[99] P.R.O., RG 31/3/1936; ibid. C 54/12076, mm. 51–56.
[1] *Lond. City Mission Mag.* viii. 175.
[2] P.R.O., HO 129/21/4/1.
[3] *P.O. Dir Lond.* (1856).
[4] *Rep. Sel. Cttee. on Worship in Metropolis*, p.35, H.C. 387 (1857–8), ix.

60 G, 60 I. a.a. 1871: 123 B, 67 G, 108 I.[5] Accn.
1879: 372 B, G, I. Closed for B 1883, for G, I
1884.[6]

EBENEZER. I day sch., roll 1843: 105; a.a. 100.[7]

EPISCOPAL JEWS', Palestine Pl. Duke of Kent
laid foundation stone for schs. and chapel for
Lond. Soc. for Promoting Christianity among
Jews 1813.[8] B sch., with salaried master and
mistress, to N. of chapel and G sch., with salaried
matron and mistress, to S. Children boarded,
clothed, and financed by vol. contributions. B
apprenticed at age of 14, G put out for svce. at
16. Roll 1819: 71 B & G.[9] Roll 1835: 35 B, 45
G. C.E. Sun. sch. started 1818 in bldg. to N. in
Gloucester (later Parmiter) St., leased 1829 as I
and adult sch.[10] Roll 1835: 220 B, 244 G. Roll
1846: week day 50 B, 50 G, 96 I, Sun. 45 B, 84
G. Alterations to G sch. 1878, to Gloucester St.
sch. 1884. Accn. 1892: 100 B, G; a.a. 42 B, 25
G. Closed 1895.[11]

ESSEX STREET, see Abbey.

FRIAR'S MOUNT.[12] First Meth. Sun. sch. in
Lond. opened 1802 in purpose-built, rented
bldg.[13] Roll 1810: 294 B, 318 G, but 'great want
of discipline'. Roll 1820: 388 B, 403 G. Closed
1820 by Meth. Sun. Sch. Soc. in protest at high
rent and temp. transferred to ho. adjoining
chapel in Church St., Spitalfields. Reopened
1821 by local Sun. sch. cttee., which tried to
buy premises 1824, but probably closed as
Meth. Sun. sch. 1829. Bldg. also housed sch. of
industry run by cttee. of ladies and appointed
mistress 1811–17. Also housed B day sch. from
1817, initially probably connected to Brit. and
Foreign Schs. Soc. Roll 1835: 70 B, financed by
subscriptions and school pence with salaried
master. C.E. Sun. sch. had 324 B, 339 G, with
35 vol. teachers. Bldg. to be used for Anglican
worship 1840 until new chs. built.[14] B day sch.
apparently survived 1849.[15]

FRIAR'S MOUNT MISSION, No. 11 Little Bacon
St., Brick Lane. Free evg. sch. with accn. for 49
G aged over 12 in room also used for C.E.
mission svces. leased to Revd. W. Pennefather
1870.[16] Roll 1871: 30 G; a.a. 20.

GASCOIGNE PLACE BRIT., Castle St. Built 1841
with parl. grant for 200 B, 200 G. Grants 1842,
1850, 1854, 1861, mostly for improvements, inc.
new bldg. 1850.[17] Probably owned by Baroness
Burdett-Coutts and also used for worship by
Inds. 1854.[18] Financed by sch. pence. a.a. 1849:
170 B, 96 G. a.a. 1857: 167 B, 246 G. Bldg.
demol. for Columbia Market developments 1872

and sch. moved to new bldg. in Church St., Mile
End New Town.[19]

GLOBE PRIMARY, Welwyn St. Built as Globe
Terrace bd. 1874 for 342 B, 343 G, 415 I on 3 floors
between Globe St. (Rd.), Gauber St., and Park
(later Welwyn) St. Enlarged 1885 for additional
120 B, 120 G, 160 I.[20] a.a. 1887: 1,281 B, G, I.
Remodelled 1900 and 1904 and renamed Globe
Rd. 1911. Reorg. 1930 for 666 JB, 402 I. a.a.
1932: 437 JB, 294 I. Bombed in Second World
War. Roll 1944: 480 M & I.[21] Reopened as Globe
primary for JM & I, although briefly, c. 1951,
called Pilgrim.[22] Roll 1988: 294 JM & I.[23]

GOOD SHEPHERD BRIT. Opened 1866 for 120
M in Mape St. Ejected by Gt. Eastern Rly. and
temp. used two cottages in Wilmot St. 1871,
when roll 126 I, a.a. 117 I. Financed by sch.
pence. New sch. for 400 I built with parl. grant
at corner of Wilmot St. and Three Colts Lane
1871. S.B.L. hired premises until completion of
its Wilmot sch. (q.v.) 1873.[24] Amalg. with Abbey
St. 1894 as Good Shepherd and Abbey St. Sun.
and ragged schs. which still flourished 1898.[25]

GOSPEL MISSION RAGGED, see Bethnal Green
Gospel Mission ragged.

GREENCOAT, see Parochial Charity.

GREY COAT, see Parmiter's.

HACKNEY ROAD BRIT.[26] Sun. sch. in Middlesex
chapel adopted by Meth. Sun. Sch. Soc. 1812.
Roll 1816: 110 B, 90 G.[27] Separate bldg. erected
behind chapel 1817. Roll 1823: 119 B, 107 G.
Brit. day sch. for G under auspices of N.E.
Lond. Auxiliary opened in leased premises and
partly financed by sch. pence. Roll 1820: 146 G.
Chapel with Brit. sch. in rear conveyed 1827 to
trustees, who purchased freehold 1840.[28] After
1824 day sch. became B sch. a.a. 1833: 240 B. a.a.
1840: 312 B. New day sch. built in Weymouth
Terr. (Shoreditch) when chapel rebuilt 1841.
Sun. sch. continued at chapel, a.a. 1851: 156
a.m., 50 p.m.[29]

HACKNEY ROAD (PROVIDENCE CHAPEL). Sun.
sch. formed part of Bapt. chapel built 1835 near
Austin St. New schoolroom built 1844.[30] Roll
1851: 72 a.m.[31] Day sch. opened by 1860. Roll
1871: 119 B, taught wide range of subjects inc.
book keeping. Sch., clean and with 'good tone',
financed by sch. pence. Presumably Sun. sch.
only by 1891, when large schoolroom and 10
classrooms for 1,500 belonged to Shoreditch
Tabernacle as Providence chapel's successor.[32]

HAGUE PRIMARY. Opened 1883 as Hague St.
bd. between Hague, Cross (later Kelsey), and

5 G.L.R.O., SBL 1518, no. 267.
6 P.O. Dir. Lond. (1883, 1884).
7 Lond. City Mission Mag. viii. 175.
8 Jewish Hist. Soc. Trans. xix. 113; above, list of chs;
above, plate 40.
9 Educ. of Poor Digest, 551.
10 P.R.O., C 54/10959, mm. 5–8; O.S. Map 1/2,500,
Lond. XXVIII (1873 edn.).
11 P.O. Dir. Lond. (1895, 1896).
12 Based on G.L.R.O., N/M/14/1–2; ibid. Acc. 2330/86/1.
13 G. F. Vale, Old Bethnal Green (1934), 30.
14 Final Rep. of Metropolis Chs. Fund, 1836–1854, App.
IV, p. 52.
15 Lewis, Topog. Dict. Eng. (1849), i. 225.
16 G.L.R.O., MR/UP 953, 1011.
17 Cassell's Map of Lond. (c. 1861–2); G.L.R.O.,
MBO/DS/12A; Y/SP/72/3.
18 G.R.O. Worship Reg. no. 5917.
19 Rep. Educ. Cttee. of Council 1872 [C. 812], p. 663, H.C.

(1873), xxiv; Builder, 22 July 1871, 566–7; 16 Dec. 1871, 992.
20 G.L.R.O., SBL 1527, pp. 50 sqq.
21 Ibid., L.C.C. Educ. Officer's file, Elem. Schs. open (1944).
22 E. Lond. Argus, 18 Oct. 1974 (T.H.L.H.L. Cuttings
file, Bethnal Green Educ.).
23 Inf. from I.L.E.A.
24 G.L.R.O., SBL 1527 (index of sites 1903).
25 Ragged Sch. & Mission Union, In His Name (1894),
95; Good Shepherd and Abbey St. Sun. and Ragged Sch.
Ann. Rep. (1897, 1898) (T.H.L.H.L.).
26 Based on G.L.R.O., N/M/14/1–2; ibid. Acc. 2330/56, 57/1.
27 Rep. from Sel. Cttee. on Educ. of Lower Orders in
Metropolis, p. 123, H.C. 469 (1816), iv.
28 P.R.O., C 54/12278, mm. 18–24.
29 Ibid. HO 129/21/1/1/3.
30 D. V. Evans, 'More Light, More Power' (1985) (T.H.L.H.L.,
pamphlet 226.2); above, prot. nonconf. (Bapts.).
31 P.R.O., HO 129/21/1/1/13.
32 Bapt. Handbk. (1877), 441; (1890), 367.

Mapes streets for 360 B, 360 G, 469 I.[33] Free from 1891. Roll 1884: 949 B, G, I.[34] a.a. 1887: 876 B, G, I. a.a. 1908: 348 B, 308 G, 402 I. Reorg. 1930 for 440 SB, 330 I. a.a. 1932: 435 SB, 330 I. Roll 1944: 405 M & I.[35] After war reorg. as primary sch. for JM & I. Moved to former Wilmot sec. site probably c. 1965. Roll 1996: 226.[36] Hague bd. bldg. later housed Weavers' Field special sch. (q.v.).

HARE STREET. Built c. 1821 at corner of Hare and Hereford streets by Spitalfields Sun. Sch. Subscription Soc. to educate children of labouring poor of Bethnal Green and Spitalfields in C.E., although associated during 1820s with Wes. Tract Soc. No formal link with Ragged Sch. Union, but trustees inc. Sam. Hoare, Buxton fam., and other supporters.[37] Possibly same as Hare St. day and I sch. for 80 children, supported by sch. pence and subscriptions and connected with Calvinists 1835. Housed Calvinist adult sch. 1838.[38] By 1851 schoolho. uninhabited but I schoolmistress, resident at no. 17 Hereford St., may have had some connexion with sch.[39]

HOLY TRINITY NAT., Club Row. Opened 1864 for I in ground floor room at junction with Anchor St. a.a. 1865: 42 I. Enlarged for 159 I by 1871 when day and Sun. schs. financed by parl. grant and sch. pence, evg. sch. free. Roll 1871: 123 I day, 61 I evg.; a.a. 82 I day, 37 I evg.[40] Taught natural hist., drawing, needlework, and drill besides basic subjects. Closed 1878 during road alterations.[41]

JOHN BARTLETT PRIMARY, see Olga primary.

LANCE'S CHRISTIAN HOME FOR ORPHAN AND NEGLECTED GIRLS, see Christian Orphanage.

LAWDALE PRIMARY, Mansford St. Formed 1975 by amalg. of Lawrence primary with Teesdale primary JM in former Lawrence bldgs., I in new bldg. in Old Bethnal Green Rd.[42] Roll 1988: 253 JM, 256 I.[43]

LAWRENCE PRIMARY, Mansford St. Opened 1883 as Mansford St. bd. for 420 B, 420 G, 560 I between Mansford St. on E. and Old Bethnal Green Rd. on N.[44] a.a. 1887: 1,076. Renamed Lawrence by 1905.[45] a.a. 1908: 338 B, 329 G, 391 I. Reorg. 1931 for 280 JB, 280 JG, 288 I. a.a. 1932: 227 JB, 221 JG, 239 I. Accn. 1940: 572 JB, 322 I. Roll 1944: 506 M & I.[46] After war reorg. for JB, I, with nursery class by 1964. Amalg. with Teesdale primary 1975 to form Lawdale primary (above).

LONDON ORPHAN ASYLUM, Hackney Rd. Sch.

existed by 1819, when roll 52 B & G,[47] although said in 1835 to have been established 1827 for I. a.a. 1835: 67 I. Supported by subscriptions and donations. Bldg., on S. side of rd. near James Pl., apparently housed Maritime Penitent Female Refuge by 1836.[48]

LONDON STREET (MISSION). Existed by 1854 as North St. Rly. Arches ragged sch., with 3 paid and 24 vol. teachers for 35 B, 130 I in day sch., 95 B, 80 G on weekday evgs., and 189 on Sun. Named New North St. 1856 when 'for a number of years these schs. successful'. As London St. (Mission)[49] served as temp. S.B.L. sch. 1876–80 with accn. for 227 B, 184 G in 2 schoolrooms and 2 classrooms in leased bldg. Partly financed by sch. pence.[50] Replaced by Somerford St. bd.[51]

MANSFORD SEC. Opened 1896 as SM section of Mansford St. bd. between Mansford St. on W. and Old Bethnal Green Rd. on S. for 210 SB, 210 SG.[52] a.a. 1908: 319 SM. Reorg. as higher elem. sch. 1906 and as central sch. 1911.[53] a.a. 1932: 353 SM. After war reorg. as Mansford Sec. Commercial and Technical sch. for SB until amalg. with Daniel sec. to form Daneford (q.v.) 1959.

MANSFORD STREET BD., see Lawrence primary.

MANSFORD STREET CENTRAL, see Mansford sec.

MANSFORD STREET SUN., see Abbey.

MIDDLESEX CHAPEL SUN., see Hackney Road Brit.

MORPETH SEC. Opened 1910 as Morpeth St. Central by S.B.L. for 320 M between rly., Morpeth St., and Portman Pl.[54] a.a. 1912: 287 M. a.a. 1932: 280 SM. Roll 1944: 231 M.[55] After war provided general, technical, and commercial courses for SM on larger site inc. bldgs. of former Portman Pl. sch. (q.v.). Acquired former John Scurr sch., Wessex St. (Mile End), as annexe by 1964. Roll 1970: 750 SM.[56] Block containing workshops, gymnasium, libr., and hall added to existing 3 bldgs. 1974.[57] Roll 1988: 969 SM.[58]

MORPETH STREET BRIT. Existed by 1847 when Lond. City Mission applied to use it. Mission opened adult free sch. there 1848, when 160 taught reading and writing on 2 evgs. a week.[59] Brit. sch. survived 1850.[60]

MOWLEM PRIMARY, Cambridge Heath. Opened 1887 as Mowlem St. bd. for 360 B, 360 G, 466 I between Mowlem and Lyte streets.[61] a.a. 1893: 1,058 B, G, I. Enlarged 1898 and altered 1902

33 P.R.O., C 54/18859, mm. 3–6; G.L.R.O., SBL 659, pp. 563 sqq.
34 Notes from S.B.L. mins. & reps. (T.H.L.H.L., Cuttings file, Bethnal Green Educ.).
35 G.L.R.O., L.C.C. Educ. Officer's Dept., Elem. Schs. open 1944.
36 Inf. from head teacher.
37 P.R.O., C 54/10118, mm. 5–9; G.L.R.O., Acc. 2330/86/1; A. M. Babler, 'Educ. of the Destitute: study of Lond. Ragged Schs. 1844–74' (N. Illinois Univ. Ph. D. thesis, 1978) (copy in G.L.R.O. libr.).
38 Pigot & Co.'s Lond. Dir. (1838).
39 P.R.O., HO 107/1542/21/4/5, ff. 91 sqq.
40 G.L.R.O., SBL 1518.
41 P.O. Dir. Lond. (1877, 1878); Reeves, Recollections of Sch. Attendance Officer, 51.
42 Reorganisation of ILEA Schs. Sept. 1973–Jan. 1984.
43 Inf. from I.L.E.A.
44 G.L.R.O., SBL 659, pp. 579 sqq.
45 T.H.L.H.L., BG 179.
46 G.L.R.O., L.C.C. Educ. Officer's Dept., Elem. Schs.

open 1944.
47 Educ. of Poor Digest, 551.
48 Robson's Lond. Dir. (1833, 1836).
49 London St. led off Upper North St., parallel with rly.: Stanford, Map of Lond. (1862–5).
50 G.L.R.O., SBL 677, p. 473 sqq.; ibid. SBL 1527 (list of temp. schs. 1885).
51 G.L.R.O., EO/DIV 5/LON/LB/1–2.
52 Ibid. SBL 1527, pp. 50 sqq.
53 P.R.O., ED 20/70, no. 29366.
54 L.C.C. Municipal Map of Lond. (1930).
55 G.L.R.O., L.C.C. Educ. Officer's Dept., Elem. Schs. open 1944.
56 Educ. Authorities Dir. (1970).
57 E. L. A. 20 Sept. 1974 (T.H.L.H.L., Cuttings file, Bethnal Green Educ.); I.L.E.A. Changing Schs. at Eleven: Sec. Schs. in City of Lond., Tower Hamlets (1986), 16.
58 Inf. from I.L.E.A.
59 Lond. City Mission Mag. xiii. 57.
60 G.L.R.O., MC/R3, no. 299.
61 Ibid. SBL 1527, pp. 50 sqq.

for 410 B, 410 G, 466 I. a.a. 1908: 356 B, 359 G, 348 I. Reorg. 1930 for 315 SB, 315 SG, 357 I. a.a. 1932: 193 SB, 194 SG, 208 I. Roll 1944: 395 M & I.[62] After war reorg. for JM & I, with nursery class by 1964. New single-storeyed bldg. for 280 opened 1971.[63] Roll 1988: 209 JM & I.[64]

NATIONAL CHILDREN'S HOME, see Bonner Road Children's Home.

NEW CASTLE STREET BD., see Virginia primary.

NEW NORTH STREET RAGGED, see London Street (Mission).

NICHOL STREET BD., see Rochelle Street.

NICHOL STREET RAGGED.[65] Jonathan Duthoit, active in humanitarian work in dist. from 1836, started Sun. sch. in small room in New Nichol St. Developed 1849 into day sch. supported by

100 B, 77 G; Sun. 202 a.m., 351 p.m., 304 evg., with 3 paid and 30 vol. teachers. By 1855 40 teachers, of whom 32 from Islington. Sch. 'overflowing with children', although few remained long. Inc. nursery from 1856 and occupied 17 rooms, attended by c. 1,000 children and 300 adults, by 1860 but closed as unsafe. Trustees, min. and members of Islington Union chapel acquired site at corner of Old Nichol Street and Nichol Row 1863.[66] New sch. completed 1866. a.a. 1871: day 100 B, 130 G, 90 I, evg. 150 B, 125 G. Used by S.B.L. as temp. Old Nichol St. bd. 1872–9 until Rochelle St. opened, and 1884–8 before children transferred to New Castle St. Accn. 1878: 339 B, 342 G, 356 I. Also used for free ragged sch. on four weekday evgs. and Sun.,[67]

FIG. 31. NEW NICHOL STREET RAGGED SCHOOL IN 1858

Lond. City Mission. Joined Ragged Sch. Union 1850, when accn. 90, roll 100 I weekday, 50 Sun., with 12 vol. teachers and one paid teacher. Numbers grew in spite of ruffians' opposition until missioner c. 1852 converted 3 houses into one room and by 1854, helped by Islington Union chapel and £100 donation, built room with gallery for 170 I over yard. a.a. 1854: weekday 119 B & G, 112 I, evg.

where roll by 1886 was 1,800, with 120 vol. teachers.[68] Ragged sch. still attended by c. 600 on Sun. evg. 1898.[69] Bldg. continued as Sun. sch. and mission centre until closed as unsafe 1939.[70]

NORTH STREET RAGGED. Name given to several ragged schs. in very poor dist. bordering Whitechapel. Originated in 'commodious schoolho.' erected 1842 in Thames Pl. at own expense by

62 Ibid. L.C.C. Educ. Officer's Dept., Elem. Schs. open 1944.
63 *E. L. A.* 9 Apr. 1971; *ILEA Contact*, vol. 4, issue 5, 16 May 1975 (T.H.L.H.L., Cuttings file, Bethnal Green Educ.).
64 Inf. from I.L.E.A.
65 Based on *Union Chapel. Story of 100 years 1799–1899* (1899); *Nichol St. Mission, 'The Nichol' 1836–1936* (1936)

(T.H.L.H.L. 226.4, pamphlet).
66 P.R.O., C 54/16175, mm. 11–19.
67 G.L.R.O., SBL 677, pp. 293 sqq.; ibid. EO/DIV 5/NIC/LB/1–2; ROC/LB/4.
68 *Illus. Lond. News*, 17 Apr. 1886, 405.
69 L.C.C. *Opening of Boundary St. Area* (1900), maps; Booth, *Life and Lab.* iii (2), 72.
70 R. Samuel, *E. End Underworld.* (1981), 286–7 n.

Cong. min. Williams and reg. as Zion chapel and Sun. sch.[71] Later attempt to hold Sun. and weekday ragged sch. in room offered by poor woman broken up by ruffians. Local cttee. formed 1848 which, aided by Ragged Sch. Union, opened I sch. in Thomas Pl. 1849. Accn. 1850: 200; roll: weekday 120 I, evg. 50 B, 45 G; Sun. 180 I; also 45 G in industrial classes; 2 paid and 5 vol. teachers. Assistance also given for ragged schs. opened 1850 in neighbouring cottages: Cumberland Pl., accn. 60, roll Sun. 24 a.m., 60 p.m. with 8 vol. teachers; Pleasant Pl., accn. 100, roll weekday 30 B, 45 G, 30 I, Sun. 117, industrial classes 20 G, with one paid and 8 vol. teachers. Cumberland Pl., available only on Sun., replaced 1852 by premises adjoining those in Pleasant Pl., which were thrown into one sch. a.a. 1852: weekday 180, Sun. 150. North St. schs. joint accn. 1858: 500; a.a.: weekday 300, Sun. evg. 45. Adopted by Brit. and Foreign Schs. Soc. 1859–65, then probably closed.

NORTH STREET RAILWAY ARCHES RAGGED, see London Street (Mission).

NOVA SCOTIA GARDENS NAT. Sch. established 1858 in iron bldg. owned by Baroness Burdett-Coutts who, with archdeacon of Kensington, managed and largely financed it. Parl. grant. Probably sch. at corner of Crabtree Row and Columbia Sq. c. 1862.[72] a.a. 1865: 247. Closed by 1870 and partly replaced by Columbia Market Mission (q.v.).

OAKEY STREET BRIT. Roll 1843: 71.[73]

OAKLANDS, Old Bethnal Green Rd. Opened as sec. M on site of St. Bernard's R.C. sec. 1991. New arts bldg. on opposite side of road, linked by bridge. Roll 1994: 450 SM. [74]

OLD CASTLE STREET RAGGED, see Bethnal Green Gospel Mission ragged.

OLD NICHOL STREET BD., see Nichol Street ragged.

OLD ZION, see Zion, Old Bethnal Green Rd.

OLGA PRIMARY. Opened by 1874 as Olga St. bd. for 324 B, 325 G, 418 I between Olga St. and Arbery Rd. Enlarged 1881. Accn. 1887: 1,455 B, G, I; a.a. 1,374 B, G, I. Improved 1898.[75] Remodelled 1931 for 333 SB, 380 SG, 462 I. a.a. 1932: 263 SB, 284 SG, 338 I. Reorg. c. 1935 for 427 I. a.a. 1936: 213 I. Roll 1944: 500.[76] After war reorg. for JM, I, briefly called John Bartlett primary but by 1951 Olga primary. Inc. nursery class by 1964. Bldg. replaced by single-storeyed open-plan sch., designed by Anne Webb and housing nursery, evg. institute, and play centre, opened fronting Lanfranc Rd. 1982. Roll 1988: 208 JMI. Accn. already inadequate 1989.[77]

OUR LADY OF THE ASSUMPTION R.C. PRIMARY. Opened 1925 as Priory Hall R.C. temp. sch. by Augustinians of Assumption next to priory in Victoria Park Sq. Perm. premises opened and reorg. 1926. Accn. 1927: 304 M & I; a.a. 153 M & I. Called Our Lady of the Assumption by 1930.[78] Roll 1944: 100 M & I.[79] Vol. assisted after war. Roll 1954: 94 JB, 100 JG, 29 SB, 33 SG.[80] Reorg. 1955 as JM & I on new site in Bonner Rd. Reorg. as I 1964/70.[81] Roll 1988: 155 I.[82]

PARLIAMENT STREET R.C., see St. Patrick's R.C.

PARMITER'S.[83] Thos. Parmiter by will proved 1682 left property to found almshos. and sch. with master, elected by trustees, to teach 10 poor children to read, write and 'such other knowledge as they should be capable of being taught in the English tongue'.[84] Chancery accordingly ordered lands to be mortgaged 1705. Almshouses and sch. built on site at E. end of St. John St., leased at peppercorn rent, 1722. Additional gifts inc. £5 a year rent charge towards children's clothing by Edw. Mayhew (1726). From 1787 children given shoes, stockings, and books.[85] By 1809 uniform of dark (probably grey)[86] Yorkshire cloth. Master paid £1 p.a. for each B, aged 10–14, resident of Bethnal Green and C.E. Roll 1723: 10 B; 1730: 30 B; 1790: 40 B; 1792: 50 B; 1819: 60 B. Music master 1768–1809. Also called Grey Coat sch. 1818. Curriculum 1819 reading, writing, arithmetic, and religious instruction. New almshos. and schoolho. built in Gloucester (later Parmiter) St. 1839.[87] Roll 1846: 70 B. Trustees purchased site 1871 in Approach Rd., where T. Chatfeild Clarke designed 'handsome Gothic structure' for 250 B. Old sch. closed 1885 and used for almshos. New sch. opened 1887 with 118 B. Char. Com. Scheme of 1884 allotted ⅔ income to sch., removed residential qualification, and established 6 co-optative governors and 6 appointed by vestry, S.B.L., and Bethnal Green Museum.[88] L.C.C., which made grants from 1889, replaced co-optative members 1894.[89] Roll 1894: 311 B aged 7–16. Art room adapted for additional classrooms;[90] further alterations 1897, 1906. Listed as efficient sec. sch. 1908.[91] Bd. of Educ. Scheme 1913 established separate sch. branch of Parmiter's charity with 15 governors, 6 co-optative and 9 appointed by L.C.C., Bethnal Green M.B., and Oxf. and Lond. univs. Sch. to provide 40 free places for B from public elem. schs. in Bethnal Green.[92] Scholarships and exhibitions provided under will of Thos. Hen. Rippin, dated 1927.[93] Sch. evacuated 1939–43, granted vol. aided grammar sch. status 1951. Roll 1952: 480 B.

71 P.R.O., RG 31/3/2139.
72 Stanford, *Map of Lond.* (1862–5).
73 *Lond. City Mission Mag.* viii. 175.
74 Inf. from Oaklands sch.
75 G.L.R.O., SBL 659, pp. 273 sqq.; 1527, pp. 50 sqq.
76 Ibid. L.C.C. Educ. Officer's Dept., Elem. Schs. open 1944.
77 *E. L. A.* 9 July 1982 (T.H.L.H.L., Cuttings file, Bethnal Green Educ.); Ringshall, Miles, Kelsall, *Urban Sch. Bldgs. in Lond.* 162; inf. from I.L.E.A. and head teacher.
78 *Cath. Dir.* (1931).
79 G.L.R.O., L.C.C. Educ. Officer's Dept., Elem. Schs. open 1944.
80 *Cath. Schs. in Eng. & Wales* (1954).
81 *P.O. Dir. Lond.* (1970).   82 Inf. from I.L.E.A.

83 Para. based on M. J. Fletcher, *Hist. Parmiter's Foundation* (1971); *1st Rep. Com. Char. for Educ. of Poor*, pp. 186–7, 322–5, H.C. 83 (1819), X–A; below, charities.
84 P.R.O., PROB 11/369 (P.C.C. 48 Cottle), ff. 371–2v.
85 Lysons, *Environs*, ii. 35.
86 Vestry mins. 1813–21, f. 100.
87 Photo. in Fletcher, *Parmiter's Foundation*, 18; G.L.R.O., Cat. to Acc. 1844.
88 G.L.R.O., Acc. 1844/A1/3/1–2.
89 Ibid. 4/1–2.
90 *Endowed Chars. Lond.* (1897), 20–2.
91 *List of Sec. Schs. Recognised as Efficient* [Cd. 4374], pp. 304–5, H.C. (1908), lxxxiii.
92 G.L.R.O., Acc. 1844/A1/7/1–13.
93 Ibid. C 10/8.

Acquired premises of bombed Cong. chapel where science block built 1962 and gymnasium 1968. Roll 1969: 500 B. Roll 1980: 530 B.[94] Rejected proposed amalg. into comprehensive system and 1981 moved to Watford (Herts.). Bldgs. taken over by Raine's Foundation (q.v.).[95]

PAROCHIAL CHARITY (GREENCOAT), Church Row. Founded 1763 by vol. subscription for educ. and clothing of 30 G, and, from 1765, 10 B.[96] Roll 1810: 30 B, 30 G;[97] 1816: 35 B, 35 G; 1835: 45 B, 45 G; 1846: 80 B, 80 G. Taught reading, writing, accounts, and sewing 1816.[98] Financed by sermons, vol. contributions, sch. pence, and rent charge of £4 4s. left by Fras. Newham (d. 1809), but mostly by dividends from gift by Jas. Le Grew (1778) or bequests under wills of Jas. Limborough (or Linborough), Mic. Le Mounier (1783), Geo. Leeds (1785), Peter Debeze (1791), Revd. Cornelius Winter (1808), Eliz. Pontier (n.d.), Hen. Staveley (1816), Thos. Stanfield (1826), and Jas. Geo. Greenwood (1837).[99] Margaretta Brown's Gift (1830) left the residue on £1,400 consols for bibles and prayer books for Parochial sch., amounting to £18 p.a. in 1861 and, by 1920s, no longer spent on religious books.[1] 'Suitable bldg.' with ho. for master and mistress erected at junction of Church St. (later Bethnal Green Rd.) and Gibraltar Walk by 1813.[2] Three-storeyed sch. for 200 built on same site 1845.[3] Road improvements necessitated move to bldg. belonging to St. And.'s ch. 1879 and then to empty St. Mat.'s Nat. sch. in Church Row. Bldgs. repaired and, by agreement with rector, also used for St. Matthew's Sun. and evg. schs. Geo. Robertson's educational charity transferred to Parochial sch. after closure of St. Mat.'s Nat. sch.[4] and children from Parochial sch. received scholarships from Sam. Butler's apprenticing char. 1889–93.[5] Roll 1894: 80 B, 70 G.[6] Closed 1930.[7] Funds applied to 6 remaining C.E. schs. under Bd. of Educ. Scheme 1933.[8]

PILGRIM PRIMARY, see Globe primary.

PLEASANT PLACE RAGGED, see North Street ragged.

PORTMAN PLACE, Globe Rd. Opened by S.B.L. 1878 for 365 B, 355 G, 452 I, largely from Bethnal Green although site in Mile End until boundary changes of 1900. Accn. 1884 for additional 120 B, 120 G, 150 I. New 3-storeyed block 1896 for 414 JMI, with drawing room, laboratory, cookery and manual training centres, and special sch. Accn. 1908: 435 B, 435 G, 408 JM, 494 I. Reorg. 1927/30 for 314 SG, 389 JB,

307 JG, 498 I. Closed 1947/51 and site taken for adjoining Morpeth sec. (q.v.).[9]

PRINCE'S COURT, Tyssen St. Housed Sun. sch. 1818.[10] I day sch. in unsecured room 1846. Roll 1846: 115 B, 115 G, with one paid teacher and 21 vol. teachers. Also evg. sch., roll 1846: 14 B, 46 G. Possibly run as ragged sch. by V. of St. Matthias 1858.[11]

PRIORY HALL R.C., see Our Lady of the Assumption primary.

PRITCHARD'S ROAD. Erected by S.B.L. next to Ann's Place Brit. sch. for 195 B, 189 G 1875 and 270 I 1878. Enlarged 1881[12] and altered 1890, 1897. Accn. 1908: 315 B, 275 G, 296 I; a.a. 274 B, 265 G, 294 I. Remodelled 1909 and 1927. Accn. 1932: 516 SG, 312 I; a.a. 352 SG, 231 I. Closed during Second World War.[13]

PROVIDENCE CHAPEL, see Hackney Rd. (Providence Chapel).

RACHEL KEELING NURSERY, Bullard's Pl., Morpeth St. Opened 1962 in purpose-built sch. under block of flats. Roll 1989: 100.[14]

RAINE'S FOUNDATION C.E. Vol. aided Raine's Foundation grammar sch. (dating from c. 1719)[15] in Arbour Sq., Mile End, amalg. 1977 with St. Jude's C.E. sec. into Raine's Foundation C.E. comprehensive for 750 SM. Lower sch. in St. Jude's bldg. in Old Bethnal Green Rd., upper at Arbour Sq. until move to vacated Parmiter sch. in Approach Rd. 1981. New science block 1985. Roll 1988: 840 SM.[16]

ROCHELLE STREET. Opened 1879 as Shoreditch Nichol St. bd. in new bldg. for 312 B, 312 G, 363 I to replace Nichol St. ragged.[17] Rebuilt as tall, red-brick and stone bldg. under Boundary St. scheme 1898, when renamed after new Rochelle St.[18] Accn. 1908: 270 B, 270 G, 363 I; a.a. 241 B, 250 G, 284 I. Accn. for I reduced to 294 in 1909. Reorg. 1929 for 228 JB, 200 JG, 190 I. 'Almost entirely Jewish' 1930. Alumni inc. Louis and Bernard Grade and Chas. Clore.[19] I dept. closed 1933.[20] Closed during Second World War and later reopened as special sch. (below).

ROYAL VICTORIA PARK, see Twig Folly Brit.

ST. ANDREW'S NAT. Originated c. 1841 as Sun. sch. in private ho. Day sch. for 200 B, 120 G, 75 I opened 1842 next to ch. on corner of St. And. St. with Teale St. Grants from parl., Nat. Soc., and Bethnal Green Fund.[21] Roll 1843: 279.[22] Premises conveyed to Nat. Soc. 1845.[23] V. sole manager. I closed by 1846, when roll 141 B, 110 G and 'much life, intelligence and good work in sch.'. I reopened by 1852 but in financial

94 *Educ. Authorities Dir.* (1980).
95 I.L.E.A. *Planning for 1980* (1972), 17–18, 20–21; *Reorg. of ILEA Schs.* Sept. 1973–Jan. 1984; G.L.R.O., Cat. to Acc. 1844.
96 *Rep. Com. Char. for Educ of Poor*, pp. 75–76, H.C. 547, (1819), x–B.
97 Lambeth Pal. Libr., Fulham Papers, Randolph 11/21.
98 *Rep. from Sel. Cttee. on Educ. of Poor of Metropolis*, p. 318, H.C. 495 (1816), iv.
99 Lysons, *Environs*, ii. 36; *Endowed Chars. Lond.* (1897), 7–8, 14–15, 38–42; T.H.L.H.L., TH/2255.
1 *Endowed Chars. Lond.* (1897), 12–15, 50–1, 72.
2 J. N. Brewer, *Beauties of Eng. & Wales*, x(4), 281; *Regency A to Z.*
3 G.L.R.O., MBO/DS/A/12; MBO/505, f. 169.
4 *Endowed Chars. Lond.* (1897), 14–15, 55.
5 Ibid. 33–5.
6 Ibid. 38–42; Old O.S. Map Lond. 51 (1872).
7 *P.O. Dir. Lond.* (1930, 1931).

8 G.L.R.O., P72/MTW/233, 234/5, 9.
9 P.R.O., ED 21/11282.
10 G.L.R.O., MR/PLT 5061.
11 *Rep. Sel. Cttee. on Worship in Metropolis*, 35.
12 G.L.R.O., SBL 659, pp. 289 sqq.; SBL 1527, p. 50 sqq.
13 *P.O. Dir. Lond.* (1942, 1949).
14 Inf. from head teacher.
15 For early hist., *V.C.H. Mdx.* i. 312–14.
16 T.H.L.H.L., Cuttings 820.1; *Educ. Authorities Dir.* (1988); inf. from head teacher.
17 G.L.R.O., SBL 1527, pp. 50 sqq.
18 Ibid. 661, pp. 205 sqq.
19 H. Davies, *The Grades* (1981), 19.
20 G.L.R.O., EO/DIV 5/ROC/LB/2–3, 5.
21 *Ret. of Sums Expended for Educ. 1840–2*, p. 550, H.C. 444 (1843), xl.
22 *Lond. City Mission Mag.* viii. 175.
23 P.R.O., C 54/13192, mm. 17–19.

difficulties. Sch. closed 1867 but reopened by 1871, when financed by sch. pence. Roll 1871: 93 B, 116 G; a.a. 60 B, 103 G; I taught in Vicarage. Teaching poor and sch. probably soon finally closed.[24] Bldg. offered to Oxford Ho. 1884.[25]

St. Anne's R.C. sec., Wood Close. Founded by Marists 1955 as vol. aided SM, linked with existing primary sch. in Underwood Rd. (Stepney). Became separate sch., named St. Gregory's 1959 and amalg. to form St. Bernard's R.C. sec. 1965.[26]

St. Barnabas's Nat. (formerly St. Luke's), Gernon Rd., Roman Rd. Founded 1866 for 252 I in Gothic bldg. on corner with Lawfranc Rd. also used as mission ch.; teacher's ho. to E.[27] Financed by grants from parl., Nat. Soc., and Bp. of Lond.'s Fund and by sch. pence.[28] Roll 1871: 244; a.a. 166. 'Cannot be looked on as permanent' by S.B.L. 1879. Roll 1905: 165; a.a. 137. Closed 1905 and bldgs. converted to ch. institute.[29]

St. Bartholomew's C.E., Coventry St. Founded as Sun. and day sch. in temp. premises 1841:a.a. 70 B, 40 G, 30 I. Schs. blt. 1842 with parl. and Nat. Soc. grants for 200 B, 120 G, 75 I, S. of ch. between Suffolk (later Coventry) St. and Essex (later Buckhurst) St. Schs. and teachers' hos. conveyed to Nat. Soc. 1844.[30] Roll 1846: weekday 75 B, 53 G; Sun. 74 B, 93 G; 34 B, 34 G attended both, with paid master and mistress and 11 vol. teachers in 2 schoolrooms. I sch. roll 1846: weekday 46 B, 47 G; Sun. 28 B, 29 G who also attended day sch., with one paid mistress in one schoolroom. V. reported 1852 that B and G schs. were attended by children of artisans who paid 2d.–4d. a week to be taught book keeping, history, geography, and English besides the elements. I sch., 'crammed to suffocation', was attended by children of lower classes who paid 1d.–2d. Bldgs., consisting of teachers' ho. flanked by single-storeyed B sch. and G & I sch., converted 1853 into sch., sometimes called upper sch., for 340 B, G. New I sch., sometimes called elementary sch., built N. of ch. at corner of Suffolk and Newport (later Cudworth) streets 1853, enlarged 1858 for 310 I.[31] Roll 1858: 130 B, 100 G, 200 I.[32] Roll 1871: 240 B, 184 G, 239 I, when financed by sch. pence, subscriptions and parl. and Nat. Soc. grants and managed by V. Offered to S.B.L. 1874[33] but continued as vol. sch. Accn. 1879: 644 B, G, I. a.a. 1906: 292 B & G, 234 I. a.a. 1932: 210 M, 121 I. Both schs. bombed and not reopened.[34]

St. Bernard's R.C. sec. Comprehensive sch. for SB, formed 1965 by amalg. of St. Bernard's R.C. of Damien St. (Stepney) with Johnson St. B (Stepney) and St. Gregory's SM. Upper sch. in former St. Gregory's premises in Wood Close and middle sch. in former Daneford premises in Mansford St.[35] Roll 1970: 660 B. Roll 1988: 650 B.[36] Amalg. with St Phil. Howard into Blessed John Roche sec. 1991 and site used for Oaklands (q.v.). [37]

St. Gregory's R.C., see St. Anne's R.C. sec.

St. James the Great Nat., Bethnal Green Rd. Day and Sun. schs. for 200 B, 112 G, 86 I built 1842 with grants by parl., Nat. Soc., and Bethnal Green Churches' Fund.[38] Single-storeyed Gothic teacher's ho. flanked by B sch. and by G & I sch., N. of church on corner of Pollard Row and Ann (later Florida) St., conveyed to Nat. Soc. 1848.[39] Financed by sch. pence, subscriptions, and incumbent and attended 1846 by children of 'respectable weavers'. Roll 1846: 100 B, 104 G, 120 I, in 3 schoolrooms with paid master and two mistresses and 19 vol. teachers. Bldgs. unsatisfactory and parl. withdrew financial aid 1858.[40] Endowed, possibly in 1843, with £1,106 stock by Thos. Churchman Harrold, which produced £33 in 1861.[41] Closed 1866 but reopened by 1871, when 'dark, dirty and inefficient'. Roll 1871: 140; a.a. 64 B, 55 G.[42] Still Nat. sch. 1885 but by 1893[43] Sun. schs. only, which received dividends of Harrold's charity.[44]

St. James the Less Nat., St. James's Rd. and Sewardstone Rd., Victoria Pk. Built 1858 for 141 I on ground floor and 168 G above, with adjoining teacher's ho., in St. James's Rd. and conveyed to incumbent and churchwardens 1859. a.a. 1860: 40 B, 40 G, 80 I.[45] Sch. for 270 B built in ecclesiastical style with grant from Nat. Soc. 1861 next to teacher's ho. in Sewardstone Rd.[46] Financed by parl. grant and sch. pence. Attended 1868–70 by Geo. Lansbury.[47] Roll 1871: 293 B, 144 G, 164 I. In disrepair by late 1898. G & I sch. converted under Char. Com. Scheme 1900 into parochial bldgs., inc. 5 classrooms for day and Sun. schs. but probably used only for Sun. sch. B sch. sold under Scheme 1908 to L.C.C.[48]

St. John the Baptist R.C. primary, Bonner Rd. Moved 1968 from Hackney Road to new bldgs. next to Our Lady of the Assumption R.C. I sch.[49] Roll 1988: 217 JM.[50]

24 G.L.R.O., SBL 1518.
25 *The Oxford Ho. in Bethnal Green 1884–1948.*
26 *E.L.A.* 1 Jan. 1971 (T.H.L.H.L., Cuttings file, Bethnal Green Educ.); L.C.C. *Sec. Schs. in Bethnal Green Div. 5* (1965).
27 O.S. Map 1/2,500, Lond. XXVIII (1873 edn.).
28 G.L.R.O., SBL 1518; ibid. Y/SP/72/10; Guildhall MS. 19224/191.
29 P.R.O., ED 21/346; L.C.C. *Lond. Statistics,* xvi.
30 *Final Rep. Metropolis Chs. Fund,* 1836–54, App. IV, 61, 97; P.R.O., C 54/13100, mm. 4–5.
31 P.R.O., C 54/15164, mm. 18–19; G.L.R.O., Y/SP/72/5.
32 Lambeth Pal. Libr., Fulham papers, Tait 440/14.
33 P.R.O. ED 4/31.
34 Guildhall MS. 19224/201.
35 *E.L.A.* 1 Jan. 1971 (T.H.L.H.L., Cuttings file, Bethnal Green Educ.); L.C.C. *Sec. Schs. in Bethnal Green.* Div. 5 (1965); Tower Hamlets L. B. *Boro. Plan Topic Paper no. 5: Educ.* Nov. 1976, 89.

36 *Educ. Authorities Dir.* (1970, 1988).
37 Inf. from Oaklands sch.
38 *Ret. of Sums Expended for Educ. 1840–2,* p. 532, H.C. 444 (1843), xl.
39 P.R.O., C 54/13637, mm. 53–55; G.L.R.O., Y/SP/72/5.
40 Lambeth Pal. Libr., Fulham Papers, Tait 440/15.
41 *Endowed Chars. Lond.* (1897), 14–15, 61–2; G.L.R.O., A/FWA/C/B2/1.
42 G.L.R.O., SBL 1518.
43 *P.O. Dir. Lond.* (1885); Old O.S. Map Lond. 51 (1893).
44 *Endowed Chars. Lond.* (1897), 61–62.
45 P.R.O., C 54/15407, mm. 31–5; G.L.R.O., Y/SP/72/7.
46 G.L.R.O., Y/SP/72/6.
47 R. Postgate, *Life of Geo. Lansbury* (1951), 9.
48 E. N. Gowing, *John Edwin Watts-Ditchfield* (1926), 41–48; below, Sewardstone Rd. temp.
49 *V.C.H.Mdx.* x. 156; *ILEA Contact,* 20 Sept. 1974 (T.H.L.H.L., Cuttings file, Bethnal Green Educ.).
50 Inf. from I.L.E.A.

ST. JOHN C.E. PRIMARY, Peel Grove. Sch. for 600 opened 1843 on site acquired 1841 on W. side of Peel Grove, with parl. grant and subscriptions, after failure to obtain part of Poor's Land on green. Gothic bldg. with adjacent B and G depts. and teacher's ho. adjoining at back.[51] Roll 1843: 390; a.a. 220.[52] Financed also by Nat. Soc. grants and sch. pence and managed by trustees. Roll 1846: weekday 110 B, 86 G; Sun. 46 B, 92 G, besides 30 B, 48 G on both weekdays and Sun., in 2 schoolrooms with paid master and mistress and 33 vol. teachers. Alleged lack of discipline and poor instructions. Teacher's ho. converted into classrooms, I dept. blt. adjoining B dept., and detached teacher's ho. blt. to S. 1860.[53] Roll 1858: 170 B, 106 G, 112 I. Roll 1871: 119 B, 54 G, 93 I. a.a. 1887: 203; 1893: 387. Bldgs. condemned by Educ. Dept. 1897 and new bldg. for 700 opened 1900.[54] a.a. 1908: 385 M, 226 I. a.a. 1932: 339 M, 200 I. After war vol. assisted C.E. M & I, reorg. 1954 as JM & I. Roll 1988: 197.[55]

ST. JOHN STREET. Opened by 1827 as Sun. sch. associated with mainly Wes. Spitalfields Sun. Sch. Tract Soc. in former Huguenot chapel.[56] By 1835 housed day sch., roll 35 B, 35 G, of whom 12 paid for by Lond. French Ch. Soc., rest by parents. Sun. sch. taken over by St. Matthias C.E. by 1846, when 44 B, 43 G paid sch. pence. Day sch. taken over by St. Matthias Nat. 1850 but still used as Sun. sch. 1863 and demol. for rly.[57]

ST. JUDE'S C.E. SEC., Old Bethnal Green Rd. Opened by 1846 as Sun. sch. in old chapel. Roll 1846: 109 B, 107 G, financed by incumbent and with 22 vol. teachers. Day sch. for 452 B, G, I and adjoining teachers' ho. in yellow brick built E. of church 1846 with parl. grant and conveyed to Nat. Soc. 1848.[58] B. sch., a.a. 78, in difficulties and master dismissed for 'gross misbehaviour' 1852. Older children attended only a few days a week. Roll 1858: 100 B, 50 G, 120 I, all supported by vol. contributions.[59] Roll 1871: 149 B, 110 G, 120 I.[60] Alterations 1875. Accn. 1878: 144 B, 85 G, 168 I. After 'many years of temp. non-existence', new bldg. opened 1895[61] and reorg. for 108 G, 146 I. Accn. 1932: 264 JG & I; a.a. 175. Under Lond. Plan 1947,[62] reorg. in new bldg. on same site as vol. assisted C.E. Sec. M 1959.[63] Amalg. with Raine's Foundation 1977 and bldgs. used for lower sch.[64]

ST. LUKE'S NAT., see St. Barnabas's Nat.

ST. MATTHEW'S GERMAN AND ENGLISH, No. 1 Halliford Terr., Grove Rd., Victoria Pk. Day,

Sun., and evg. sch. where by 1870 Theodor Winkley or Winckler of Leipzig Univ. and wife taught the elements and German. Some free pupils, others paid sch. pence. a.a. 1871: 24 B, 15 G day, 9 G evg. Closed soon afterwards amid rumours of murder.

ST. MATTHEW'S NAT., Church Row. Nat. sch. opened 1819 by rector, with aid from bp. of Lond. and Soc. for Educ. of Poor in Principles of Established Ch. and from tithe rate, in temp. premises in Wilmot Sq. for 120. Nat. Soc. built sch. on NW. corner of churchyard with burial vaults underneath 1819. Roll 1820: weekday 304 B, 106 G; Sun. 109 B, 92 G; also evg. sch. Financed by parl. grants, Nat. Soc., local subscriptions, Geo. Robertson's charity (1862), and sch. pence.[65] Roll 1848: 275 B in upper room with master, 135 G in lower room with mistress. Suffered stench of corpses on one side, slaughter house on other.[66] Master absconded 1854. Roll 1858: 350 B, G, 120 I.[67] Roll 1871: 294 B, 286 G & I. Bldgs. altered 1859, conveyed to rector and churchwardens for sch. 1860, in disrepair by 1879. Closed after rector refused use to S.B.L., and later occupied by Parochial Charity sch.[68] Sun. sch. beneficiary of Margaretta Brown Educ. Fund.[69]

ST. MATTHIAS C.E. PRIMARY, Granby St. Opened by 1843 when roll 629.[70] By 1844 Sun. and Nat. day sch. for 112 B, 112 G in 2 unsecured rooms. Roll 1846: weekday and Sun. 58 B, 117 G; Sun. 87 B, 77 G, with paid master and mistress. Parish also ran I day sch. in Prince's Ct. and Sun. sch. in St. John St., probably in former French chapel acquired by Nat. Soc. 1850. First floor used as St. Matthias Nat. B. sch. and ground floor as teacher's ho. until demol. 1871.[71] Site in Hare St. next to ch. conveyed for G & I sch. and teacher's ho. 1851.[72] Parl. grant 1852, when 'much overcrowded'.[73] Financed by parl. grants, vol. contributions, and sch. pence. Roll 1871: 145 B, 225 G & I.[74] Single-storeyed sch. for 300 B, 200 G blt. at corner of Granby St. with Oakley St. 1871, when Hare St. converted for I only.[75] Accn. 1879: 773 B, G, I. Alterations 1894, when schs. free.[76] a.a. 1906: 375 B, G, 203 I. a.a. 1932: 142 B, 117 G, 92 I. After evacuation temp. reopened 1944 in Wood Close (Hare St.) premises.[77] Reopened as vol. assisted JM & I in Granby St. bldgs. 1953. Roll 1988: 103 JM & I.[78]

ST. PATRICK'S R.C., Parliament St., Cambridge Rd. Built 1869 by St. Anne's Spitalfields R.C. church and opened as Parliament (later

51 *Return of Sums Expended for Educ. 1840–2*, p. 532; P.R.O., C 54/15296, mm. 33–7; G.L.R.O., Y/SP/72/8.
52 *Lond. City Mission Mag.* viii. 175.
53 G.L.R.O., Y/SP/72/8.
54 Opening of St. John's New Bldg. (T.H.L.H.L., Cuttings file, Bethnal Green Educ.); *The Times*, 29 May 1899, 10*b*.
55 Inf. from I.L.E.A.
56 G.L.R.O., Acc. 2330/86/1.
57 Ibid. MR/UP 671.
58 Ibid. Y/SP/72/9; ibid. MBO/505, f. 678; P.R.O., C 54/13730, mm. 27–9; *Ecclesiologist*, viii (N.S. vi, 1848), 317–18.
59 Lambeth Pal. Libr., Fulham papers, Tait 440/9.
60 G.L.R.O., SBL 1518.
61 Ibid. P72/JUD/50.
62 L.C.C. *Lond. Sch. Plan* (1947), 117.
63 *The Times*, 29 Oct. 1959, 14*b*; I.L.E.A. *Sec. Schs. in Tower Hamlets*, Div. 5 (1971).
64 I.L.E.A. *Sec. Schs. in Tower Hamlets* (1980); *Educ.*

Authorities Dir. (1988).
65 B.L. Add. MS. 38275, ff. 42–3; vestry mins. 1813–21, ff. 121, 123v., 144; 1820–3, f. 259; *Endowed Chars. Lond.* (1897), 55–56.
66 Gavin, *San. Ramblings*, 72–74.
67 Lambeth Pal. Libr., Fulham papers, Tait 440/6.
68 G.L.R.O., Y/SP/72/11.
69 Char. Com. file no. 312306; above, Parochial Charity sch.
70 *Lond. City Mission Mag.* viii. 175.
71 P.R.O., C 54/14139, mm. 41 sqq.; G.L.R.O., Y/SP/72/12.
72 P.R.O., C 54/14344, mm. 20–24; G.L.R.O., Y/SP/72/12.
73 *Mins. of Educ. Cttee. of Council, 1854* [1926], p. 197, H.C. (1854–5), xlii; *Lond. City Mission Mag.* xvii. 67.
74 G.L.R.O., SBL 1518.
75 Ibid. Y/SP/72/12.
76 *Endowed Chars. Lond.* (1897), 62.
77 G.L.R.O., EO/DIV 5/ST MAT/LB/4.
78 Inf. from I.L.E.A. and headmaster.

Witan) St. R.C. Financed by parl. grant, vol. contributions, and sch. pence. Roll 1871: 29 B, 85 G, 116 I; 'a very nice sch.'. Accn. 1879: 163 B, G, I. Alterations 1895. Roll 1908: 95 G, 94 I; a.a. 91 G, 85 I. Renamed St. Patrick's 1936.[79] After war vol. assisted M & I sch., at Stewart Headlam sch. in Tapp St. until move 1953 to Buxton St., Mile End New Town.

St. Paul's Nat., No. 11 Gosset St. Opened 1851 in ho. belonging to V. and churchwardens with I on ground floor and G above. Financed by sch. pence, vol. contributions, parl. and Nat. Soc. grants. Roll 1871: 164; a.a. 155 G & I.[80] Adjoining property conveyed, subject to lease, in trust for schs. 1870 and 1871. New bldg. for 168 I 1873. Accn. 1878: 170 G. Day sch. closed c. 1884 although Sun. sch. continued. By 1892 income from trust augmented V.'s income.[81] Property vested in official trustees by Char. Com. Scheme 1896.[82] Bldgs. hired by S.B.L. but given up by 1903.[83]

St. Peter's C.E., St. Peter's Ave. (formerly St. Peter St.), Hackney Rd. Opened by 1842 as Nat. day and Sun. sch. in temp. bldg. for 70.[84] Roll 1844: 84 B, 31 G. Room for B enlarged 1845. Roll 1846: weekday and Sun. 74 B, 27 G; Sun. 29 B, 12 G, in 2 'virtually secured' schoolrooms with paid master and mistress and 11 vol. teachers. Accn. inadequate and new sch. 1851 near ch. with parl. grant and contributions, especially from relatives of dead curate. Accn. 1851: 245 B, 130 G, 133 I. Financed by vol. contributions and sch. pence.[85] Roll 1858: 120 B, 45 G, 109 I.[86] Roll 1871: 126 B, 56 G, 82 I. Application to Nat. Soc. for more accn. 1873 sought conversion of G & I schs. for 200 I, move by G to B sch. and extension for 300 B. Extension, also to be used as mission room, built on adjacent site 1875.[87] Accn. 1878: 225 B, 172 G, 172 I. Bldgs. condemned by inspector 1881 and B & G schs. abandoned 1886. a.a. 1887: 57 I. Nat. Soc. asked for grant to convert ground floor, then a club room, for M sch. and to add I classroom. M sch. opened 1891 and improved with anonymous benefaction 1894.[88] a.a. 1898: 203 M, 180 I. Vol. contributions saved sch. from condemnation by L.C.C. 1907[89] Reorg. 1931 for 246 JM, 222 I. a.a. 1932: 162 JM, 110 I. Evacuated during Second World War and not reopened. Bldg. let for industry before demol. in 1960s.

St. Philip's C.E., Swanfield (formerly Mount) St. Opened by 1843 in Friar's Mount[90] as day and Sun. sch. in hired ho. a.a. 1844: 48 B, 48 G. Sites on E. side of Mount St., N. and S. of ch. for B and G & I schs., with accn. for 536

conveyed to Nat. Soc. 1852.[91] Financed by parl. and Nat. Soc. grants and sch. pence. Roll 1858: 110 B, 100 G, 250 I.[92] Roll 1871: 170 B, 170 G, 101 I. Classroom added 1877 and sch. efficient in 1870s.[93] a.a. 1887: 405. a.a. 1893: 267. By 1899 G sch. closed, B sch. became M; heavy debt and incompetent staff. Alterations 1901 and 1902. Always in poor dist., by 1922 'swamped by Jews', sch. drew children from wider area as other C.E. schs. closed. Reorg. 1931 for 231 JM & I. a.a. 1932: 161. Closed during Second World War.[94]

St. Philip's Ragged, no. 32 Bacon St. Opened by 1855 as C.E. ragged sch. by V. of St. Phil. Roll 1855: weekday 80; Sun. 40 a.m., 60 p.m. with one paid teacher and 2 vol. teachers. In large old ho. at corner of Anchor (Sclater) St. and Club Row, later Holy Trinity Nat. sch., in early 1860s.[95] At no. 32 Bacon St. by 1871, when 80 B, 85 G, all but five aged under 9, taught free in large room on third floor; badly furnished and instruction poor. Open 1872 but probably soon closed.[96]

St. Simon Zelotes Nat., Bullard St. and Morpeth St. Opened 1841 as St. Jas. the Less Nat. Sun. and day sch. for 140 G and 100 I on ground floor and 200 B on first floor in plain bldg. adjoining teacher's ho. in Twig Folly. Financed by grants from parl. and Nat. Soc. and private subscriptions.[97] Site at corner of Bullard St. and William (later Warley) St. conveyed to Nat. Soc. 1843.[98] Roll 1846: weekday 38 I in I schoolroom; weekday and Sun. 67 B, 40 G in 2 schoolrooms; Sun. 100 B, 80 G, with paid master and mistress and 13 vol. teachers; schs. attached to new dist. of St. Simon Zelotes. Chapel and schoolroom 'once an infidel lecture hall', in Knottisford St. off Morpeth St., leased 1855 to V. and churchwardens and later housed I.[99] Roll 1858: 116 B, 66 G, 171 I.[1] Roll 1871: 229 B, 92 G, 206 I. Financed by sch. pence. I sch. a 'tumbledown barn sort of mission hall' 1875. Both schs. transferred to S.B.L. 1877 and closed 1881.[2] B & G sch. housed Warley St. temp. bd. 1884–5 and I sch. St. Simon Zelotes temp. bd. 1895–7.[3] Teacher's ho. occupied by ladies' mission 1905.[4]

St. Thomas's Nat., Westminster St., Columbia Market. Opened by 1843 as Sun. and day sch. for 75 B, 75 G in large hired room in Gascoigne Pl.[5] Roll 1846: weekday and Sun. 72 B, 24 G; Sun. 9 B, 5 G, in one schoolroom with paid master and 2 vol. teachers. New sch. blt. 1847 for 110 G, 165 I on ground and 225 B on first floor of plain bldg. in Westminster St., W. of ch.

79 P.R.O., ED 21/52824 no. 12908.
80 G.L.R.O., SBL 1518, no. 252.
81 *Endowed Chars. Lond.* (1897), 63–4.
82 G.L.R.O., P72/MTW/202/21.
83 Ibid. SBL 1527 (index of sites 1903).
84 *Final Rep. Metropolis Chs. Fund*, App. IV, p. 61.
85 Ibid. 106; *Mins. of Educ. Cttee. of Council, 1854* [1926], p. 197, H.C. (1854–6), xlii; P.R.O., C 54/14245, mm. 37–41; G.L.R.O., MBO/DS/G12; *Builder*, 28 Dec. 1850, 622.
86 Lambeth Pal. Libr., Fulham Papers, Tait 440/11.
87 P.R.O., C 54/17730, m. 44.   88 G.L.R.O., P72/PET/81.
89 *The Times*, 16 Mar. 1907, 14a; 24 Sept. 1907, 3f.
90 *Lond. City Mission Mag.* viii. 175.
91 P.R.O., C 54/14375, mm. 49–53; *Final Rep. Metropolis Chs. Fund*, App. IV, 108.
92 Lambeth Pal. Libr., Fulham Papers, Tait 440/17.
93 Reeves, *Recollections of Sch. Attendance Officer*, 57.

94 *P.O. Dir. Lond.* (1942, 1945); L.C.C. *Lond. Sch. Plan* (1947), 109.
95 *Cassell's Map of Lond.* (c. 1861–2); Hollingshead, *Ragged Lond. in 1861*, 83; Reeves, *Recollections of Sch. Attendance Officer*, 57.
96 *Hackney Dir.* (1872), s.v. Bacon St.
97 *Ret. of Sums Expended for Educ. 1840–2*, 552; G.L.R.O., Y/SP/72/13.
98 P.R.O., C 54/12924, mm. 12–13.
99 Ibid. 14852, mm. 44–50; G.L.R.O., Y/SP/72/14; *Lond. City Mission Mag.* xxvii. 55; Stanford, *Map of Lond.* (1862–5).
1 Lambeth Pal. Libr., Fulham Papers, Tait 440/18.
2 Wilford, *Bonner Schs.*; P.R.O., ED 4/32–33; G.L.R.O., SBL 677, pp. 555 sqq.
3 G.L.R.O., SBL 1527, (list of temp. schs. 1896, 1898).
4 T.H.L.H.L., BG 179.
5 *Lond. City Mission Mag.* viii. 175.

conveyed to Nat. Soc. 1851. Financed by grants from parl. and Nat. Soc., vol. contributions, and sch. pence. Improvements 1858 and 1866.[6] Roll 1858: 90 B, 60 G, 110 I.[7] Roll 1871: 90 B, 81 G, 228 I.[8] a.a. 1875: 425 M & I. Supposedly closed as day sch. 1876 but accn. given 1878 as 80 B, 84 G, 94 I and V. referred 1882 to proposed reopening. Gymnasium rebuilt 1906. Continued as Sun. sch. until 1919 or later.

SATCHWELL STREET BRIT. Opened 1859 as Sun. sch. under supervision of Cong. minister Geo. Kelsey with 60 children in Orange St. dist. of Lond. City Mission. Day sch. for 130 M opened 1862, when a.a. 130.[9] Mission sch. associated with Cong. and Brit. and Foreign Schs. Soc., financed by sch. pence. Roll 1871: 43 B, 39 G; a.a. 20 B, 30 G, mostly I. Bldg. condemned 1871. Probably replaced by Turin St. bd. Sun. sch. united with Blythe St. (Abbey) Sun. sch. 1873.[10]

SEWARDSTONE ROAD TEMP. Opened 1911 by L.C.C. in former St. James the Less B sch. for 675 SM, JM, I. a.a. 1912: 564. Reorg. 1930 for 320 JM, 141 I. a.a. 1932: 442. Closed 1940.

SHOREDITCH NICHOL STREET BD., see Rochelle Street.

SOMERFORD STREET BD., see Stewart Headlam primary.

SQUIRRIES STREET MISSION HALL.[11] Opened as Bapt. Sun. sch., a.a. 70,[12] and possibly day sch. by 1851, when schoolmistress resident in street.[13] Day sch. by 1868. Day and evg. schs. given up by 1871, when 20 G taught free on Sun. Closed 1871.

STEWART HEADLAM PRIMARY, Somerford St. Designed by E. R. Robson and opened 1881 as Somerford St. bd. for 1,643 B, G, I between Somerford (originally Summerford) and Tapp streets.[14] a.a. 1887: 998 B, G, I. Accn. 1908: 465 B, 465 G, 616 I; a.a. 411 B, 388 G, 358 I. First L.C.C. day nursery opened 1917.[15] Renamed Stewart Headlam 1925.[16] Reorg. 1930 for 392 JB, 392 JG, 457 I. a.a. 1932: 372 JB, 374 JG, 373 I. Roll 1944: 394 M & I.[17] After war reorg for JM & I and absorbed Wilmot primary 1955/8. Roll 1988: 310 JM & I.[18]

SUMMERFORD STREET BD., see Stewart Headlam primary.

TEALE STREET. I and day sch. built by 'benevolent individual' 1825. a.a. 70–90 and financed by subscriptions and sch. pence 1835.

TEESDALE PRIMARY, Teesdale St. Opened by 1873 as Claremont St. bd. for 257 B, 273 G, 289 I in Claremont St. New bldg. called Teesdale

St. bd. opened 1878 for 409 B, 387 G, 416 I at junction of Claremont and Teesdale streets. a.a. 1887: 1,093 B, G, I. Improvements 1899.[19] Accn. 1908: 358 B, 348 G, 449 I; a.a. 310 B, 334 G, 393 I. Remodelled 1909. Reorg. 1931 for 304 JB, 297 JG, 290 I. a.a. 1932: 268 JB, 178 JG, 241 I. Roll 1944: 656 M & I.[20] After war reorg. as Teesdale primary, with nursery class by 1964. Amalg. with Lawrence primary 1975 to form Lawdale primary.

THOMAS PLACE RAGGED, see North Street ragged.

THOROLD SQUARE. Lower part of ho. used for Zehovah chapel and I sch. 1851.[21]

TRINITY, Peel Grove. Sun. sch. started 1846 by Theodore Habershon in NE. part of Bethnal Green moved by 1851 to Trinity chapel, a.a. 60 a.m., 70 p.m. Nos. rose and new schs., under patronage of earl of Shaftesbury and financed by vol. subscriptions and collections, built in Gothic style on E. side of Peel Grove 1859. Roll Sun. 400, with 30 vol. teachers; weekday evg. classes.[22] Sun. and day schs. c. 1861.[23] Called Ashley mission from 1880 and connected with Ragged Sch. Union 1903.[24]

TURIN STREET. Opened 1875 E. of Turin St. and designed by Bodley & Garner, winners of S.B.L. competition, for 466 B, 468 G, 697 I in adjoining bldgs., for B & G and for I.[25] a.a. 1887: 1,424 B, G, I. Remodelled 1903. Accn. 1908: 284 B, 284 G, 423 I; a.a. 263 B, 265 G, 354 I. B and G depts. closed 1927, I 1929.

TURK STREET. Roll 1843: 50.[26]

TURVILLE STREET BRIT. Opened 1839 in hired rooms at no. 43. Roll 1843: 60. Probably replaced by other Nichol schs.[27]

TWIG[28] FOLLY BRIT. Opened 1830 as Lancasterian schs. for 120 B and 80 G in adjacent bldgs. in Sidney St. Financed by sch. pence but rooms 'almost untenantable'.[29] Sch. for 250 B built with parl. and Brit. and Foreign Schs. Soc. grants on W. side of Bonner Lane and conveyed to trustees 1837. a.a. 1838: 120 B.[30] G sch. opened in Green Pl., William St., by 1840, when a.a. 80. Singlestoreyed G sch. built S. of B sch. 1849.[31] As Royal Victoria Park sch., partly financed by sch. pence, a.a. 1850: 186 B, 150 G. Accn. 1871: 285 B but roll only 60 due to illness and death of teacher; accn. in leased G sch. 153; a.a. 170 B sch. housed Bonner Lane temp. bd. 1874–6 and 1878–80[32] and subsequently used as Cong. Sun. sch.[33] G sch. replaced by Bonner St. bd., later Bonner primary.

TWIG FOLLY RAGGED. Opened c. 1849 for 70

6 P.R.O., C 54/14191, mm. 18–22; G.L.R.O., Y/SP/72/15.
7 Lambeth Pal. Libr., Fulham Papers, Tait 440/13.
8 G.L.R.O., SBL 1518.
9 Lond. City Mission Mag. xxvii. 60–62.
10 Above, Abbey.
11 Old O.S. Map Lond. 51 (1872).
12 P.R.O., HO 129/21/2/1/13.
13 Ibid. HO 107/1541/21/3/15, f. 443.
14 G.L.R.O., SBL 659, pp. 451 sqq.; Builder, 12 Apr. 1879, 414.   15 The Times, 19 July 1917, 8f.
16 G.L.R.O., L.C.C. Schs., file on name changes.
17 Ibid. L.C.C. Educ. Officer's Dept., Elem. Schs. open 1944.
18 Inf. from I.L.E.A.
19 G.L.R.O., SBL 1527, pp. 50 sqq.
20 Ibid. L.C.C. Educ. Officer's Dept., Elem. Schs. open 1944.
21 P.R.O., HO 129/21/3/1/10.

22 Ibid. HO. 129/21/2/1/11; Illus. Lond. News, 16 Apr. 1859, 385; Morgan, Abbey St. Sun. Schs.
23 Cassell's Map of Lond.. (c. 1861–2).
24 Mudie-Smith, Rel. Life, 57; above, prot. nonconf. (undenom. missions).
25 G.L.R.O., SBL 659, pp. 369 sqq.; G. Stamp and C. Amery, Victorian Bldgs. of Lond. 1837–87 (1980), 130.
26 Lond. City Mission Mag. viii. 175.
27 Ibid.
28 Or Twigg.
29 Rep. Sel. Cttee. on Educ. pp. 271–4, H.C. 465 (1835), vii.
30 P.R.O., C 54/11657, mm. 1–4; Rep. Sel. Cttee. on Educ. pp. 609–14, H.C. 589 (1837), vi.
31 G.L.R.O., MBO/DS/E/12; Cassell's Map of Lond. (c. 1861–2).
32 G.L.R.O., SBL 1527 (list of temp. schs. 1885).
33 Old O.S. Map Lond. 52 (1894).

on 4 evgs. a week with 12 vol. teachers. Roll 1849: 45 B, 50 G. Accn. by 1850: 120. Roll by 1851: 30 B, 30 G with one paid teacher and 8 vol. teachers. Listed as active 1854 but not thereafter.

VICTORIA PARK Chisenhale Road, see Chisenhale primary.

VICTORIA PARK COLLEGE INSTITUTE, Albert (later Waterloo) Rd. Opened 1851 by incumbent of St. Jas. the Less for children of 'intermediate class', professionals of limited income, clerks, and tradesmen. C.E. sch. managed by dist. chs.[34] Bldg. needing repair 1861 and sold 1862, probably to become commercial, non-Anglican sch.[35]

VIRGINIA PRIMARY, Virginia Rd. Opened 1875 as New Castle St. bd. for 156 B, 161 G, 270 I. Enlarged and reorg. 1887 for 210 B, 260 G in old bldg. and 360 JM, 469 I in new bldg.[36] a.a. 1887: 541. Renamed Virginia Rd. 1899 as part of Boundary St. rebuilding scheme.[37] By 1901 many Jewish children. a.a. 1908: 204 B, 225 G, 299 JM, 373 I. JM dept. closed 1913. Reorg. 1932 for 464 SM, 323 I; a.a. 274 SM, 189 I; 'almost entirely Jewish'. Roll 1944: 330 M & I.[38] After war reorg. as primary sch. Special English teaching needed; turnover of 15 supply teachers in 3 months 1968.[39] Roll 1988: 228 JM & I.[40]

VIRGINIA ROW RAGGED. Opened 1856 with roll 100 I day, 35 B, 59 G evg., and one paid teacher.

WARLEY STREET BD., see St. Simon Zelotes Nat.

WILMOT. Opened 1873 as Wilmot St. bd. for 542 B, 472 G, 686 I in bldg. designed by Giles & Gough on site bought from Industrial Dwellings Co. on E. side of street. Damaged by rioting B 1877.[41] a.a. 1887: 1,426 B, G, I. Alterations 1887, 1901, 1904, 1905. Accn. 1908: 465 B, 456 G, 616 I; a.a. 429 B, 426 G, 454 I. Reorg. 1930 for 352 SG, 406 I; a.a. 1932: 268 SG, 240 I, when rebuilt[42] I dept. closed 1936. Roll 1944: 398 M & I.[43] After war reorg. as Wilmot primary for I and Wilmot sec. for SG. Primary sch. amalg. with Stewart Headlam 1955/8. Wilmot sec. closed 1965.[44]

WOLVERLEY STREET. Opened by S.B.L. 1877 for 355 B, 355 G, 414 I E. of Wolverley St. Enlarged 1887 for additional 48 I.[45] a.a. 1887: 971 B, G, I. a.a. 1908: 316 B, 303 G, 331 I. Alterations 1895, 1897, 1912. Remodelled 1916 for 272 B, 272 G, 324 I. Reorg. 1931 for 320 SB, 280 SG, 261 I. a.a. 1932: 233 SB, 227 SG, 204 I. Closed during Second World War and not reopened.

WOOD CLOSE PRIMARY. Plan for bd. sch. in Wood Close 1894 opposed by neighbouring schs. New free sch. between Wood Close, Hare (later Cheshire) St., and St. Matthew's Row opened 1901 for 242 B, 242 G, 244 I.[46] a.a. 1908: 218 B, 204 G, 238 I. Reorg. 1929 for 400 JM, 218 I. a.a. 1932: 359 JM, 189 I; 'almost entirely Jewish'. Shared premises with St. Matthias primary by 1944, when joint roll 396 M & I.[47] Closed when St. Matthias moved to Granby St. 1953, premises being occupied by St. Anne's R.C. sec.[48]

ZION (OLD), Old Bethnal Green Rd. Chapel blt. 1836 by Ind. min. Thos. G. Williams[49] housed 'charity sch.' by 1846.[50] Sun. and I day schs. 1851, when roll 100 a.m., 150 p.m.[51] After closure of chapel 1865/9, bldg. used for overflow of Abbey Sun. sch.[52]

ZION, Thomas Street (Passage), see North Street ragged.

Special schools. ABBEY STREET. Opened 1896 for 80, by 1909 for an additional 20, mentally deficient children. Closed 1927.

BEATRICE TATE, St. Jude's Rd. Begun as vol. enterprise in temp. bldgs. in Bethnal Green Gdns. New bldg. for handicapped children aged 6–16, between St. Jude's Rd. and Poyster St., authorized 1967.[53] Opened 1970 as Junior Training Centre by Social Svces. Dept. of Tower Hamlets L.B. Transferred to I.L.E.A. 1971 as M sch. for educationally subnormal. Roll 1989: 82.[54]

CRANBROOK ROAD. Dept. for myopic children at bd. sch. 1920–4.[55]

DANIEL STREET. Opened 1900 as temp. centre for mentally defective children in bd. sch. Single-storeyed bldg. with 4 classrooms for 90 children built 1901 adjoining bd. sch. Roll 1921: 81. Roll 1929: 58.[56] Closed 1929 and children transferred to Mowlem St. and Hoxton Ho., Osborn Pl. (Whitechapel).[57] Reopened 1929 for 45 partially sighted children. Roll 1938: 32.[58] Scheduled for closure 1947 and gone by 1951.[59]

MANSFORD STREET. Opened 1901 for 40 physically defective children in 2 classrooms in bd. sch. previously used as centre for deaf. Closed 1914 and children transferred to Tollit St., Mile End.[60]

MOWLEM STREET. Opened 1908 in single-storeyed brick bldg. with hall and 4 classrooms for 90 mentally deficient children. By 1921 JM only, roll 93.[61] Roll 1933: 64. Closed 1935.[62] Reopened 1941 for partially sighted but closed by 1951.[63]

ROCHELLE PRIMARY, Arnold Circus. L.C.C. in 1947 planned sch. for deaf in new and enlarged

34 P.R.O., C 54/14417, mm. 37–41; G.L.R.O., E/COT/1560; Stanford, *Map of Lond.* (1862–5).
35 G.L.R.O., E/COT/1561.
36 Ibid. SBL 659, pp. 211 sqq; Stanford, *Map of Lond.* (1891).
37 Above, bldg. 1876–1914.
38 G.L.R.O., L.C.C. Educ. Officer's Dept., Elem. Schs. open 1944.
39 *The Times*, 27 July 1968, 3a.
40 Inf. from I.L.E.A.
41 G.L.R.O., SBL 659, pp. 401 sqq.; *The Metropolitan*, 2 Aug. 1873 (T.H.L.H.L., Cuttings file, Bethnal Green Educ.).
42 G.L.R.O., EO/DIV 5/WIL/LB/2–6.
43 Ibid. L.C.C. Educ. Officer's Dept., Elem. Schs. open 1944.
44 L.C.C. *Sec. Schs. in Bethnal Green, County of Lond. Div. 5.*
45 G.L.R.O., SBL 1527, pp. 50 sqq.
46 Ibid.

47 Ibid. L.C.C. Educ. Officer's Dept., Elem. Schs. open 1944.
48 T.H.L.H.L., TH/8434/7.
49 Above, prot. nonconf. (Congs.).
50 G.L.R.O., THCS 521.
51 P.R.O., HO 129/21/2/1/10.   52 Above, Abbey.
53 *Tower Hamlets News*, 3(2), June 1967, p. 21.
54 Inf. from head teacher 1989.
55 G.L.R.O., EO/DIV 5/CRA 1/LB/13.
56 P.R.O., ED 32/78, no. 29028.
57 Ibid. ED 32/501.
58 Ibid. ED 32/502, no. 28845.
59 *Educ. Authorities Dir.* (1945); L.C.C. *Lond. Sch. Plan* (1947), 189.
60 P.R.O., ED 32/79, no. 29137.
61 Ibid. ED 32/80, no. 29482.
62 Ibid. ED 32/504, no. 29482.
63 Ibid. ED 32/503, no. 30484.

bldg. on site of former bd. sch.[64] Instead prim. sch. for educationally subnormal opened by 1951 and closed 1976.[65]

SOMERFORD STREET. Opened 1882 for 40 deaf children as classroom in bd. sch. Closed 1909/18.

VIRGINIA ROAD. Opened as New Castle St. special 1893.[66] Was room at bd. sch., used for mentally defective children but needed for ordinary sch., 1900.[67] Closed by 1909.

WEAVERS' FIELD, Mape Street. Opened 1965/70 for M maladjusted children aged 5–16 in former Hague primary sch. Roll 1989: 52.[68]

WOOD CLOSE. There were depts. for 25 mentally defective and 25 physically defective children at council sch. before 1941, when temp. suspended. Finally closed by 1945.[69]

Adult and technical education. A school of industry, run by women, was housed in Friar's Mount school in 1811.[70] The Sunday schools established by the East London Auxiliary to the Sunday School Union by 1816 taught reading and, on weekday evenings, writing to pupils who included adults.[71] An adult school existed at Hare Street by 1819.[72] St. Matthew's, Bethnal Green's first National school, included evening classes in 1820.[73] Only two parishes, St. James the Great and St. Matthias, ran evening schools in 1846, St. James's with 13 pupils and St. Matthias's two schools (one at Prince's Court) with 92 pupils.[74] By 1858 St. James the Great had an evening school in winter for 150 children and one for 20 adults and St. Matthias ran one for adults; St. Matthias ran an industrial school in Thomas Street off Brick Lane in 1892.[75] Five other parishes in 1858 ran evening schools and St. Bartholomew's reported that it had provided one for four winters with little success. St. John's was for 20 women and St. Philip's included classes and reading for adults. Many ragged schools ran evening classes, needed particularly in districts where both adults and children worked in the day-time.[76]

A total of 3,115 people were enrolled and an average of 1,568 attended evening schools in 1871. Of these 648 were enrolled and 463 attended schools run by 8 parishes; 662 were enrolled and 479 attended 2 British Schools, all but 30 of them the large Good Shepherd schools. The still bigger Nichol Street ragged school had an evening roll of 1,200, although only 275 usually attended; 270 were enrolled and 148 attended

four other ragged schools and the remainder belonged to 5 other schools.[77]

The education provided by evening schools shifted after the Education Act of 1870 led to the replacement of simple teaching of the elements by continuation classes. Stewart Headlam, the local school board representative, headed a campaign for continuation classes at board schools,[78] where they existed at Wilmot Street by 1882,[79] Cooper's Gardens by 1887,[80] Globe Terrace by 1890,[81] Columbia Road by 1896,[82] Somerford Street (a women's evening institute) by 1899,[83] Chisenhale Road by 1904,[84] and Bonner and Mowlem streets, Portman Place, Daniel, Lawrence, Mansford, and Rochelle streets and Wood Close by 1909. Classes were also held at Oxford House by 1909.[85] There were 1,673 evening scholars in 1904.[86] In 1918 there were six evening institutes:[87] Rochelle Street for men, Daniel Street, Somerford Street, Olga Street (probably opened in 1914),[88] and Lawrence for women, the last described as a junior commercial institute. Mansford Street was a junior technical institute and the Cordwainers' technical college at no. 42 Bethnal Green Road from 1879/1902 to 1923 provided day and evening classes in footwear manufacture and fancy leather goods. The Craft School occupied nos. 137–41 Globe Road from 1879/1902 to 1905/12.[89]

By 1930 there were five evening institutes: Daniel Street and Olga Street for women, Mansford Street as a junior commercial and technical institute, Stewart Headlam at Portman Place with a branch at Pritchard's Road as a junior men's institute, and Bethnal Green's men's institute at no. 229 Bethnal Green Road, long a social club.[90] As the host schools closed and merged, the institutes contracted, Pritchard's Road closing during the war and Portman Place soon afterwards. Mansford Street housed a junior commercial and technical section until the school closed in 1965 after which, tenanted by a branch of St. Bernard's R.C. school, it functioned as an evening branch of Bethnal Green College for Further Education which had its headquarters in Jubilee Street, Stepney, and provided general, technical, and commercial courses.[91] Bethnal Green women's institute survived in 1955 but apparently not in 1964.[92] Daniel Street was replaced in 1965 by Daneford, which was used as a branch of Bethnal Green Institute.[93] By 1966 the latter, classed as

64 L.C.C. *Lond. Sch. Plan* (1947), 190.
65 *Reorganisation of ILEA Schs.* Sept. 1973–Jan. 1984.
66 G.L.R.O., EO/DIV 5/NEW/LB/6.
67 P.R.O., ED 32/78, no. 29028.
68 *Educ. Authorities Dir.* (1970, 1980); inf. from head teacher (1989); above, Hague sch.
69 P.R.O., ED 32/503; ED 32/505, no. 30482; ED 32/506, no. 30483; *Educ. Authorities Dir.* (1945).
70 G.L.R.O., N/M/14/1.
71 *Rep. from Sel. Cttee. on Educ. of Lower Orders in Metropolis,* H.C. 427, pp. 53–56 (1816), iv.
72 G.L.R.O., MR/PLT 5063.
73 Nat. Soc. *Ann. Rep.* (1820), 193.
74 Nat. Soc. *Inquiry, 1846–7,* Mdx. 2–3.
75 *Boro. of Hackney Dir.* (1872).
76 Lambeth Pal. Libr., Fulham Papers, Tait 440/6–18.
77 G.L.R.O., SBL 1518.
78 C. Kerrigan, *Hist. of Tower Hamlets* (1982), 59.
79 G.L.R.O., EO/DIV 5/WIL/LB/7.
80 *Rep. Educ. Cttee. of Council, 1887* [C. 547-I], H.C. p.

663 (1888), xxxviii.
81 G.L.R.O., EO/DIV 5/GLO/LB/9.
82 Ibid. COL/LB/2.
83 Ibid. SOM/LB/7.
84 *Sch. Bd. for Lond. 1870–1904, Final Rep.* (1904), map, p. 32.
85 L.C.C. *Educ. Svce. Partics.* (1909–10), 224.
86 L.C.C. *Lond. Statistics,* xvi. 299.
87 L.C.C. *Educ. Svce. Partics.* (1918–19), 175.
88 Olga St. Women's Institute 1914–29 (MS. in T.H.L.H.L. 822.3, pamphlet).
89 L.C.C. *Educ. Svce. Partics.* (1918–19), 196; *P.O. Dir. Lond.* (1879, 1902, 1905, 1912, 1923, 1924).
90 L.C.C. *Educ. Svce. Partics.* (1930–1), 176, 195; above, social.
91 I.L.E.A. *Bethnal Green College for Further Educ. 1965–6* (T.H.L.H.L. 822.3).
92 L.C.C. *Educ. Svce. Inf.* (1955, 1964).
93 L.C.C. *Daneford Sch. Ceremonial Opening of New Bldgs.* 1965 (pamphlet in G.L.R.O.).

an adult evening educational institute, had branches in Turin and Buckfast streets, and in Haggerston and Shoreditch, and provided courses at 17 other places, former University settlements, old people's homes, clubs, and halls.[94] By 1974 it had branches at Daneford, Morpeth, and Olga schools.[95]

Other adult institutes included one for community studies at no. 18 Victoria Park Square from 1959 to 1988/92, when it was replaced by the Open College of the Arts,[96] and an urban studies centre on the site of St. Simon Zelotes Vicarage in Morpeth Street from 1983.[97]

Private schools. There may have been a Roman Catholic school for girls in Bethnal Green before the Civil War.[98] A schoolmistress Mrs. Green, who was not a Roman Catholic, lived near the green in 1642 and accused Balthazar Gerbier of harbouring papist priests. Gerbier himself opened an academy at his house on the west side of the green in 1649 where, as an alternative to sending sons abroad, he offered languages, history, philosophy, mathematics, geography, cosmography, military architecture, and the 'art of well-speaking'. He also gave public lectures, several of which were printed. The academy closed, probably for financial reasons, in 1650.[99]

Shortly afterwards Bishop's Hall housed a dissenting academy. William Walker, a schoolmaster there in 1653,[1] may have been William *ludimagister* at Bishop's Hall, who 'taught school and carried his scholars to conventicles' in 1673.[2] Thomas Walton, an ejected minister presented for the same offence,[3] lived in Bethnal Green from 1671 or earlier until 1674 when his assessment for hearth tax suggests he had charge of all Bishop's Hall.[4] One of his pupils, to whom he taught the classics, was the biographer Edmund Calamy (1671–1732).[5] By the late 1680s when St. George's chapel served as a schoolhouse 'for the use of Bishop's Hall',[6] the academy was conducted by the Presbyterian Thomas Brand (d. 1691), assisted by John Kerr (d. 1708), another Presbyterian, who succeeded Brand until John Short took over in 1692, when Kerr went to Leyden for five years. Short became a Congregational minister in Cannon Street (Lond.) in 1698 but the academy probably continued under Kerr until 1708 or later. Samuel Palmer (d. 1724), author of *Defence of the Dissenters' Education* in answer to Samuel Wesley, described his education at Bishop's Hall *c.* 1700. The course covered logic, rhetoric, metaphysics, ethics, natural philosophy, the classics, Hebrew, and Jewish antiquities, besides theology.[7]

Samuel Morland, dissenter and classical scholar, kept a school at Bethnal Green where the mathematician William Jones (1675–1749) was a tutor.[8] In 1694 Mrs. Palfryman kept a boarding school and Mr. Haines a grammar school in Bethnal Green.[9] A 'considerable boarding school' providing an intensive Latin course was kept *c.* 1698 by the lexicographer Robert Ainsworth (d. 1743).[10]

With the decline in dissenting academies and a changing social composition, the number and quality of private schools diminished. Before 1816 the daughter of Joseph Merceron attended a dame school run by Charlotte Cowdery.[11] Proximity to Hackney, noted for its private schools, probably accounted for the many early 19th-century schools in Hackney Road and Cambridge Heath. T. W. H. Askey ran College House in Hackney Road in 1822[12] and eight out of seven gentlemen's and 14 ladies' academies in Bethnal Green were in Hackney Road or Cambridge Road in 1828. Two of the boys' and six of the girls' schools (one a preparatory school) took boarders. There was also a dancing academy in Camden Row and a 'drawing master in landscape' in Church Street (Bethnal Green Road).[13] The curate established a private school *c.* 1832.[14] Only one of the schools of 1828 survived until 1851, Ann Miller's in St. Matthew's Place, Hackney Road, with 14 girl boarders.[15] In 1851 some 87 teachers of public and private schools were living in the parish.[16] Ten private schools (four boys', three girls', and three unspecified) were listed for 1855 and seven for 1863 and 1872.[17] Most were short lived. Among the exceptions were no. 120 Cambridge Road, established in 1843, a middle class school providing a 'mercantile education' for 90 pupils under the Revd. W. Bradford in 1872,[18] Henry W. Rolfe's school at no. 252 Bethnal Green Road from 1845 to the 1880s,[19] where 12 boys boarded in 1851,[20] and Albion Academy or Grammar School, sometimes called Knight's school after its headmaster George Knight, in Oxford Street off Cambridge

94 I.L.E.A. *Bethnal Green Institute prospectus, 1966–7* (T.H.L.H.L. 822.3).

95 I.L.E.A. *Educ. Svce. Inf.* (1974).

96 *P.O. Dir. Lond.* (1958, 1959, 1988).

97 Ibid. (1982, 1983, 1990).

98 *V.C.H. Mdx.* i. 254.

99 Ibid. 242; *E. Lond. Papers*, x(1), 19–34; Lysons, *Environs*, ii. 31; *A Wicked and Inhumane Plot of Nich. Parney etc.* (1642, Thomason Tract); *To All Fathers of Noble Families and Lovers of Vertue* (prospectus n.d.).

1 P.R.O., PROB 11/233, f. 177v. (P.C.C. 23 Alchin, will of John Wheatley).

2 Guildhall MS. 9537/20, p. 12.

3 *Calamy Revised*, 509.

4 G.L.R.O., MR/TH 16, f. 22; MR/TH 46.

5 *Calamy Revised*, 509.

6 P.R.O., C 10/512/66.

7 *Freedom after Ejection*, ed. A. Gordon (1917), 214, 221, 296, 351; *Trans. Cong. Hist. Soc.* vi. 20–4; J. W. Ashley Smith, *Birth of Modern Educ.* (1954), 72–5; I. Parker, *Dissenting Acads. in Eng.* (1914), 55 n, 60, 140.

8 *V.C.H. Mdx.* i. 245–6; Lysons, *Environs*, ii. 32.

9 Adverts. in J. Houghton's *Colln.* 29 June 1694, quoted in A. S. Turberville, *Eng. Men and Manners in 18th Cent.* (1926), 162.

10 *D.N.B.*; *V.C.H. Mdx.* i. 245–6.

11 *Rep. from Cttee. on State of Police in Metropolis*, H.C. 510, p. 204 (1816), v.

12 E. J. Greenberg, 'Contribution by Private Acads. in first half of 19th cent. to Modern Curriculum and Methods' (Lond. Univ. M.A. thesis, 1953), App. I.

13 *Boarding Schs. and Lond. Masters' Dir.* (1828); *Pigot's New Com. Dir.* (1827–8).

14 BNC, Second Ser. [Tower] 148, letter from rector 17 Feb. 1832).

15 P.R.O., HO 107/1539/21/1/28, f. 617, p. 19.

16 Based on ibid. HO 107/1539–42.

17 *P.O. Dir. Lond.* (1855, 1863); *Boro. of Hackney Dir.* (1872).

18 F. S. de Carteret-Bisson, *Our Schs. and Colleges* (1872), 260; *Boro. of Hackney Dir.* (1872).

19 *P.O. Dir. Lond.* (1844, 1845, 1879, 1890).

20 P.R.O., HO 107/1541/21/3/2, f. 28, p. 3.

Road from 1851 or earlier to 1882 and possibly 1893.[21]

In 1871 there were 83 adventure schools teaching 1,921 children.[22] They included the Collegiate school at no. 50 Roman Road[23] and Wellington House preparatory school in Wellington Row, each with 85 pupils. Yelf's school in Elwin Street off Hackney Road had 55, mostly infants, Mrs. Mary Stillwell's infants' school in Orange Street had 50,[24] the East London Grammar school at no. 463 Bethnal Green Road had 45 'of the tradesmen class', and Mrs. Camp's school at no. 24 Warner Place off Hackney Road had 40. Most schools, at least 50 being infants', were very small and were condemned either for their premises, often back rooms or cellars, or for poor teachers. Dame schools, whether in the 1830s[25] or 1870s, were generally used for baby-minding and were 'in no sense educational'.[26] The schools charged between 2d. and 9d. a week for each child, generally 2d. – 4d. for infants and more for older children. Although found throughout the parish, schools were clustered most thickly in East ward, where 32 took 711 pupils.

Eight of the 13 private schools listed in 1879 lay east of Cambridge Road. The East London Grammar school, condemned in 1871, survived until 1902, then one of only three private schools listed for Bethnal Green. Another was Miss Millicent Gee's preparatory school at no. 37 Approach Road.[27] Miss Mabel Gee ran Ingleside House school with 80 pupils at no. 22 Approach Road from c. 1927 until between 1952 and 1958, apparently as the only private school.[28]

Gatehouse school, opened in Sewardstone Road in 1948 as an independent school for the handicapped,[29] was classified in 1994 as an independent secondary school with a roll of 300 mixed pupils aged 2–18.[30]

CHARITIES FOR THE POOR

As a hamlet of Stepney parish Bethnal Green was a beneficiary of early Stepney charities,[31] including Prisca Coburn's (1701) and Dame Sarah Pritchard's (1718), and shared in Fuller's, Bowry's, and Pemel's almshouses,[32] the last of which, at 'Dog Corner' in 1732, were in Bethnal Green.[33] Also in Bethnal Green were the nonparochial Fisher's almshouses for widows of ships' commanders, built in 1711 on the western side and southern end of Dog Row.[34] They were absorbed by Trinity almshouses, which stood just outside the boundaries but took over property within them.[35]

Bethnal Green's combined annual income from charities averaged £650 in 1818–37, £1,203 in 1861–76, and £5,804 in 1894–1904. Of the last, more than half, £2,961, was spent on education,[36] £1,359 on almshouses and pensions, £278 distributed in money and £209 in kind, £187 for medical uses,[37] £113 for church and £302 for nonconformist purposes, and £36 for apprentices.[38] Bethnal Green Parish Charities was formed by amalgamating the charities of Mary Baker, Robertson, Greenwood, Truss, Fontaneau, Mary Bowry, and Henry Merceron in 1978.[39] In 1994, together with the Poor's Land charity, they were jointly administered by trustees appointed by Tower Hamlets L.B., the rector, and up to 6 appointed under governing instruments. Reinvestment of capital had doubled income since c. 1979. In 1994 23 pensions and 24 £10 Christmas payments were paid out of the joint charities.[40]

Almshouse charities. Parmiter's almshouses commemorated Thomas Parmiter, probably from a Suffolk family;[41] he or his father was a merchant tailor, who lived in Bethnal Green with his wife Ann in 1651.[42] The purchasers of the green in 1678[43] considered, in a draft agreement of 1681, using the rents to build and maintain four almshouses on the waste. One of the group, apparently acting as treasurer or 'town clerk', was Parmiter,[44] who by will proved 1682 left lands in Suffolk to be used, after the death of his widow Elizabeth (d. 1702), to build and endow a school and six almshouses 'on the waste of Bethnal Green'.[45] In 1705 Chancery ordered the lands to be mortgaged to build the school and almshouses, the trustees to be 10 inhabitants of Bethnal Green appointed at the general vestry. In 1720 they leased a site at the eastern end of St. John Street from Elizabeth Carter for 600 years at a peppercorn rent, where a school and almshouses were opened in 1722. Further gifts included a rent charge of £10 from Elizabeth Carter and another payable by the Dyers' Co. and granted in 1720 by William Lee. In 1732

21 Ibid. HO 107/1540/21/2/11, f. 307, p. 53; G.L.R.O., M93/150; G.R.O. Worship Reg. no. 1074; *Ret. of Churches, Chapels, Bldgs. Reg. for Worship*, H.C. 401, no. 1074 (1882), 1.
22 Para. based on P.R.O., ED 3/11.
23 P.R.O., ED 3/11, nos. 233, 274, 280.
24 Ibid. ED 3/11, nos. 270, 205, 159.
25 *Lond. City Mission Mag.* ii. 183; *Rep. of Sel. Cttee. on Educ.* H.C. 589, pp. 609–14 (1837–8), vi.
26 Reeves, *Recollections of Sch. Attendance Officer*, 29.
27 P.R.O., ED 3/11, no. 205; *P.O. Dir. Lond.* (1879, 1902).
28 P.R.O., ED 15/23; *P.O. Dir. Lond.* (1927, 1934, 1952, 1958).
29 Marcan, *E. End Dir.* 40.
30 *Educ. Authorities Dir.* (1994).
31 Section based on *Endowed Chars. Lond.* (1897), 3–68.
32 Above, Stepney, charities.
33 Co. of Par. Clerks, *New Remarks of Lond.* (1732), 196.

34 Ibid.; Lysons, *Environs*, ii. 36.
35 G.L.R.O., C93/1530–1, 1533–4.
36 Above, educ.
37 Probably Queen Adelaide's char., above, pub. svces.
38 L.C.C. *Lond. Statistics*, xvi. 62.
39 G.L.R.O., P72/MTW/232/1.
40 Inf. from clerk to trustees, Bethnal Green Par. Chars.
41 *Ship-Money Ret. for Suff. 1639–40*, ed. V. B. Redstone (1904), 31, 187, 200, 212; W. A. Copinger, *County of Suff.* iv. (1904), 290.
42 P.R.O., C 7/323/121.
43 Above, Bethnal Green village; below, distributive chars., Poor's Land.
44 G.L.R.O., A/PLC/VI/2, nos. 11, 15, 20; Co. of Par. Clerks, *New Remarks of Lond.* 195.
45 P.R.O., PROB 11/369 (P.C.C. 48 Cottle), ff. 371–2v. Acct. of Parmiter's char. based on M. J. Fletcher, *Hist. Parmiter's Foundation* (1971); *1st Rep. Com. Char. for Educ. of Poor*, H.C. 83, pp. 196–7, App. pp. 322–5 (1819), x-A.

the charity was said to have been founded by the donations of the town clerk and beadle of Bethnal Green.[46] If the first was Parmiter, the second was probably Lee, churchwarden and overseer in 1703.[47]

In 1723 the trustees bought 4½ a. of waste at Cambridge Heath,[48] which by 1786 produced £25 a year of the charity's total revenue of £102[49] and in 1819, after building had begun, £225 out of a total income of £338, which included £12 from £400 stock purchased out of savings. By 1863 £928 stock yielded nearly £63 out of a total income of nearly £400. The bulk of the income was always applied to the school. The six almsmen, Anglican parishioners, received £2 10s. a year each in 1732,[50] £5 by 1763, and £10 by 1809. Coal, worth 15 guineas a year, was also given to the almsmen by 1819.

In 1838 the site in St. John Street was sold to the G.E.R. and land was leased in Gloucester (later Parmiter) Street where a new school and three almshouses on either side, of yellow brick and designed by Sir William Tite, were built in 1839.[51] In 1891, after the school had again moved, its buildings were adapted for two more almspeople; by 1894 the inmates were 6 married couples and two widowers.

Further bequests included £500 stock left by the treasurer Peter Renvoize (d. 1841). In 1870 the G.E.R. bought much of the Cambridge Heath property, the proceeds being invested until in 1893 part was used to purchase a freehold estate in Lewisham (Kent).[52] In 1884 a Charity Commission Scheme allotted ⅔ of the income to the school and ⅓ to the almshouses.[53] By 1894 the gross income was £3,505, of which £1,262 was for the almshouses.[54]

In 1913, under Schemes of the Charity Commissioners and the Board of Education,[55] the school became a separate foundation.[56] The almshouses were combined with the Widows' fund into Parmiter's Almshouse and Pension charity.[57] Its assets were the almshouse site, ⅓ of Parmiter's income, and the Widows' fund.[58] Parmiter's Estate was set up to administer the assets of the two charities.[59]

Thomas Henry Rippin by will dated 1927 left £500 to Parmiter's school and £600 to the almshouse charity.[60] The almshouses were bombed in 1945 and their site was sold in 1959 to the L.C.C., the proceeds augmenting the pensions.[61] In 1952 the almshouse trust absorbed Bethnal Green Philanthropic Pension society (below). The estate and almshouse charities were registered in 1961 and 1963 respectively and, although amended in 1993 and 1992, continued to provide pensions and annuities.[62]

Spitalfields almshouses,[63] adjoining the early Parmiter's almshouses, owed their existence to William Lee, the dyer and benefactor of Parmiter's. In accordance with an agreement with the Dyers' Co., which held mortgaged property in Thames Street from him, Lee by will dated 1720 left £300 for his nephew John Ham to build 6 almshouses for the company. Ham leased land in St. John Street from Elizabeth Carter on the same terms as Parmiter's in 1721, building the almshouses and assigning the trust to the Dyers' Co. In 1732 the inmates were 6 dyers' widows, each of whom received 6s. a quarter, together with 6s. for coal at Christmas, financed by Dyers' Co. subscriptions.[64] Another 4 almshouses had been built and endowed with an estate in Leytonstone (Essex) by 1739 by John Peck, a trustee for the new Bethnal Green parish in 1743, for the widows of freemen of the company who had lived in Bethnal Green. By 1795, however, the almshouses had 'no farther connection' with the parish.[65] They closed with Parmiter's in 1838 and moved to Islington in 1840–1.[66]

George Crump almshouses were founded after Miss Mary Edith Crump, by will proved 1925, left money for a house to accommodate one or two old people resident in St. Matthew's parish. No. 61 Hereford Street was bought under a Scheme of 1933 and used as an almshouse until compulsorily purchased by the G.L.C. in 1966. Administered with Mary Bowry's charity from 1933, the proceeds were distributed as pensions, from 1978 as part of Bethnal Green parish charities.[67] In 1994 the income of Crump's charity, £903, was distributed to two pensioners and £18, the income from Bowry's charity, was paid to a seaman's widow.[68]

Distributive charities. The Poor's Land or Green Lands[69] was the name given to the charity and its endowment formally founded in 1690 but originating in the purchase of 11½ a. of waste in the centre of the hamlet from the lady of the manor in 1678. Although the primary object was to restrict building, a secondary motive was the 'yearly relief of the poor'. The 11½ a. were turned into three closes and let as farmland on 21-year leases from 1678. At first the profits augmented the contributions of the original purchasers but after Parmiter's bequest made the suggested building of almshouses unnecessary,[70] it was decided to spend the rent money on coal and doles. From 1685 the first yearly distribution of coal and £12 in money was made to 24 poor families. That application was established by deed of 1690. Trustees were to be co-opted

46 Co. of Par. Clerks, *New Remarks of Lond.* 195.
47 P.R.O., C 5/588/64.
48 M.L.R. 1723/1/14–15.
49 *Abstract of Ret. of Char. Donations for Poor, 1786–8,* H.C. 511, pp. 776–7 (1816), xvi.
50 Co. of Par. Clerks, *New Remarks of Lond.* 195.
51 Illus. in Fletcher, *Parmiter's Foundation,* 18.
52 G.L.R.O., Acc. 1844/A1/2.
53 Ibid. Acc. 1844/A1/3.
54 L.C.C. *Lond. Statistics,* xvi. 67.
55 G.L.R.O., Acc. 1844/A1/7/1–3.
56 Char. Com. no. 312704.
57 Ibid. no. 215087.
58 G.L.R.O., Acc. 1844/A1/8/1–2.
59 Char. Com. no. 215086.   60 G.L.R.O., C10/8.
61 Ibid. Acc. 1844. Notes accompanying rec. deposited 1983.
62 Char. Com. nos. 215086–7.
63 Para. based on *6th Rep. Com. Char.* H.C. 12, p. 253 (1822), ix.
64 Co. of Par. Clerks, *New Remarks of Lond.* 196.
65 Lysons, *Environs,* ii. 36.
66 *V.C.H. Mdx.* viii. 42.
67 G.L.R.O., P72/MTW/225–30.
68 Inf. from clerk to trustees, Bethnal Green Par. Chars.
69 Acct. of Poor's Land based on Allgood, *Hist. Bethnal Green,* 290–336; Robinson and Chesshyre, *The Green,* 6–10; above, estates.
70 Above.

and building on the land was forbidden. Income was £38 in 1768, although £42 was spent on coal for 65 people,[71] and £59 by 1820.[72] In 1822 Joseph Merceron accused a fellow trustee, who was a supporter of the rector, of being the sole supplier of coal. Some stock was sold in 1831 to finance repairs to the fencing around the Poor's Land. In 1825 and 1849 part of the land was sold to the Ecclesiastical Commissioners and the money invested.[73] By 1834 the total income was £154, of which £19 was dividends. By 1857 the income of £172 was distributed in coal and pensions to some 100 recipients, mostly residing around the green.[74] In 1868 £2,000 from the sale of the northern close for Bethnal Green Museum was invested,[75] enabling payments to be made to 190 recipients.

Between 1889 and 1890 the Charity Commission drew up three schemes as disputes raged over the direction of the charity and especially over whether any of the Poor's Land should be sold as sites for admittedly worthy causes. Under the last Scheme, established in 1891 by a suit in Chancery, there were to be 12 trustees, representing the four wards and chosen from residents or local businessmen; they could sell a small part and grant the rest to the L.C.C. for a recreation ground, the income to be applied as pensions or in other ways for the poor. Most of the land was conveyed in 1893 to the L.C.C.[76] and by 1896 the resulting stock yielded £307 a year, paid in 20 weekly pensions. The charity was registered in 1961 and in 1994 an income of £277 was applied in £20 pensions.[77]

John George Fabry, carver of Bloomsbury, by will proved 1794 left dividends for six old weavers and six weavers' widows of Christ Church, Spitalfields, and Bethnal Green parishes, with preference for any named Fabry or Ovington. In 1797 Chancery settled an endowment of £548 on the charity, to be administered by the churchwardens of the parishes. In 1799 each recipient received 7s. 1¼d.[78] Bethnal Green's share of the dividends was £7 14s. 1d. in 1819 and £8 4s. 7d. in 1857[79] but no distribution was made in 1890–4.

The Bread charity originated in subscriptions raised before 1817 to provide bread for children of the Parochial Charity school who attended St. Matthew's church. By 1817 the fund consisted of £120 in consols and £50 in annuities. In 1818 one of the three trustees, George Seaman Inman, gave £66 13s. 4d. consols to provide £2 a year for a sermon by the rector in aid of the charity. Benefactions were received throughout the 19th century, including £200 from Joseph Merceron (1840) and £388 from other members of his family. The income reached £38 in 1857[80] and £88 by 1893. In 1933 it was merged in

Greencoat and other Bethnal Green Educational charities.[81]

Bethnal Green Philanthropic Pension society[82] was founded by subscribers in 1822 to make weekly grants to the aged. Its income was £478 in 1870, distributed in weekly half crowns to 41 pensioners.[83] The fund was augmented in 1874 by the bequest of William Cluff of £500 consols and by 1894 consisted of £4,235 in government securities. The society purchased property in Hackney in 1906 and in Islington in 1914, which was sold during the 1930s and 1940s. Responsibility for the fund was allotted by a Scheme of 1952 to the trustees of Parmiter's Almshouse and Pension charity.

Margaret Vaughan by will proved 1836 left the interest on £6,000 for clothing and other needs of unemployed mechanics and weavers in Spitalfields. In 1843 Chancery decreed that Miss Vaughan's Spitalfields charity was to benefit the parishes of Christ Church Spitalfields, Mile End New Town, St. Leonard Shoreditch, and Bethnal Green. In 1893 Bethnal Green received £47 which was distributed in money, coal, food, clothing, and blankets throughout the civil parish. The charity, registered in 1971, had an income of £799 in 1992.[84]

James George Greenwood by will proved 1837 left money to apprentice pupils of the Parochial Charity school and the interest on £1,300 stock to provide coal before Christmas for the poor in the western half of Bethnal Green. The coal charity received £39 a year in 1861 and £36, given in coal to 61 people, in 1893. The apprenticing part, called Greenwood's gift, was merged with other educational charities in 1933.[85] The coal portion was jointly administered with Mary Baker's charity from 1978.[86] Its income of £64 was distributed in £10 doles in 1994.[87]

George Fournier by will proved 1841 left the dividends on £4,447 as doles of £10–£15 to industrious parishioners, to be paid by the minister and officers of St. Matthew's parish. The yield was £133 in 1861 and £119, distributed to 12 people by the vestry, in 1894.

Alexander Truss by will proved 1851 left the dividends from the residue of his personal estate to be distributed in charity, one third in £5 doles to widows in St. Matthew's parish yearly. In 1864 Bethnal Green was allocated £11,207 stock, which by 1894 yielded £45 a year, paid to unrelieved elderly widows. A Scheme of 1884 vested the Bethnal Green portion in the rector and three other trustees. From 1978 it was administered with the other Bethnal Green Parish charities.[88] In 1994 the £82 income was distributed in £10 pensions.[89]

The Widows' fund originated in the bequest of Jemima Margaret Thomas by will proved

71 G.L.R.O., A/PLC/IV/1.
72 *Charitable Donations I*, H.C. 28, p. 79 (1820), vi.
73 Above, list of churches (St. John).
74 G.L.R.O., A/FWA/C/B2/1.
75 Above, building 1837–1875.
76 Above, pub. svces. (open spaces).
77 Char. Com. no. 241422; inf from clerk to trustees, Bethnal Green Par. Chars.
78 Vestry mins. 1782–1813, p. 237.
79 G.L.R.O., A/FWA/C/B2/1.
80 Ibid.

81 Ibid. P72/MTW/234/5; Char. Com. no. 312296. Above, educ.
82 G.L.R.O., Acc. 1844/E1–9.
83 Ibid. A/FWA/C/B2/1.
84 Char. Com. no. 262480.
85 Ibid. no. 312296; above, educ.
86 G.L.R.O., P72/MTW/208.
87 Inf. from clerk to trustees, Bethnal Green Par. Chars.
88 G.L.R.O., P72/MTW/212/1.
89 Inf. from clerk to trustees, Bethnal Green Par. Chars.

1854 of £200 consols to the trustees of Parmiter's charity, the income to go to widows forced to leave the almshouses on the death of their husbands. Additions were made of £100 stock by Henry Merceron's will in 1864 and of £100 consols by Jane Thomas's will in 1892. Three widows benefited in 1894. A Scheme of 1913 merged the fund with Parmiter's Almshouse charity.[90]

George Robertson in 1862 vested property in Mile End Old Town in the rector and others, to use half for St. Matthew's National school[91] and half for parishioners at the rector's discretion. The second part was governed by an instrument of 1897 and registered in 1966 as the Eleemosynary charity of George Robertson; money was distributed annually among parishioners chosen by the rector but payments were no longer made in 1994.[92]

Nehemiah Robson by will proved 1863 left the dividends from £100 consols to be distributed in money, bread, coal, or clothing in St. Matthew's parish on St. Thomas's day by the rector and churchwardens. Dividends of £2 9s. 4d. were paid out in 1864 but were irregular.

Robert Leverington by will proved 1865 left the dividends from £1,333 6s. 8d. stock to 40 'honest and industrious' poor of St. Matthew's parish, chosen at the vestry. The rector and parish officers were to distribute the money in winter. In 1894 £36 13s. 4d. was distributed in £1 pensions.

Mrs. Esther Doe by will proved 1871 left annuities of up to £10 for unmarried women, with preference for those living in Bethnal Green and Whitechapel. The income was £236 in 1991.[93]

Mary Baker by will proved 1872 left £5,000 annuities to the rector and parish officers of Bethnal Green in trust to distribute the dividends in £5 yearly doles to industrious parishioners who had not received parish relief for two years. The income was £137 10s. in 1894 and £250 in 1992.[94] From 1978 it was administered with other Bethnal Green Parish charities.[95]

The Hastelow Pension fund was founded by the will proved 1892 of Henry Hastelow. He left a house in Clapton to be sold, the proceeds to be paid by Bethnal Green Philanthropic Pension society to 8 pensioners in weekly doles of 2s. 6d. The society paid out £346 received from trustees in 1892.

Louisa Fontaneau (d. 1893) left £1,495 for an annual distribution in bread and coal for the parishioners of St. Matthew's. Income was £41 in 1894. From 1978 it was administered with other Bethnal Green parish charities.[96] In 1994 the income was £192, distributed in £10 doles.[97]

Jane Wood by will proved 1904 left money to relieve poor members of Approach Road Methodist chapel. Governed by a scheme of 1980, its income in 1993 was £10.[98]

The Alfred Ewin trust, governed by a deed of 1910, provided assistance to 'deserving persons' in Bethnal Green M.B. It was registered in 1961.[99]

Miss Emily Searley Long by will proved 1912 founded a charity for women and children of St. Matthew's parish. It was registered in 1966 and amended in 1989 but had lapsed by 1994.[1]

Nathan Dell's charity, governed by a Scheme of 1951 and registered in 1966, provided money for the poor of the Congregational chapel in Bethnal Green Road. The income in 1994 was £31,379.[2]

Bethnal Green Old People's Trust fund was instituted in 1970 to relieve aged residents in the former Bethnal Green M.B. The income in 1992 was £2,011.[3]

The Immigrant Welfare and Legal Advisory Services was set up in 1988 and registered in 1991 to advance education and relieve poverty among immigrants and refugees, especially through legal and other advice. The income was £21,389 in 1994.[4]

90 G.L.R.O., Acc. 1844/A1/8/1–2; above, almshouse charities.
91 Above, educ. (pub. schs.).
92 Char. Com. no. 248002.
93 Ibid. no. 207627.
94 Ibid. no. 210858.
95 G.L.R.O., P72/MTW/217–21.
96 Ibid. 222/1; 232/1.
97 Inf. from clerk to trustees, Bethnal Green Par. Chars.
98 Char. Com. no. 247943.
99 Ibid. no. 222058.
1   Ibid. no. 248758.
2   Ibid. no. 249214.
3   Ibid. no. 261607.
4   Ibid. no. 1001435.

INDEX

NOTE. An italic page number denotes a map or figure on that page. A page number preceded by the letters *pl.* refers to one of the plates between pages 138 and 139.

Buildings, streets, and localities are in Bethnal Green except where otherwise stated. The municipal ownership of housing estates, so described to distinguish them from landed estates, is indicated by the abbreviations G.L.C., L.C.C., M.B., or T.H., all other housing estates being company owned or private. M.E.N.T. denotes Mile End New Town, M.E.O.T. Mile End Old Town.

Bissaker, Mrs., 69, 81
Bitter Cry of Outcast London, 230
Black Bull P.H., Bethnal green, 147
Black Bull P.H., Thomas St., 153
Black Ditch, the, 7
Black Dog P.H., Bethnal Green Rd., 154
Black Eagle brewery, *see* Truman's brewery
Black Prince, *see* Edw., Prince of Wales
Blackett:
  Thos. (d. 1701), 161
    wid. of, *see* Naylor
  Thos., s. of Thos., 161
Blacktop, Edw., 120
Blackwall, in Poplar, 3, 11, *14*, *16*, 18–19, 55, 63, 65, 69, 71, 74, 81
  coach svces., 10
  omnibus svces., 10
  shipbuilding, 18
Blackwall tunnel, 11
Blackwell, Ric., 21, 24–5
Blackwood Ho. (L.C.C.), flats in Collingwood housing est., 133
Bladen:
  Martin, 165
  Frances, *see* Foche
Blake:
  Ann, *see* Todd
  Humph., 24, 158
  Jas., auctioneer and developer, 101, 112
  Rob., 158
Blanche, John, 36
Blancmuster, *see* Wm. de, and Alice his w., 33
Blashill, T., architect, 131
Blenheim Rd., *see* Zealand Rd.
Blethenale (Bethnal Green), 18, 64
Blienhale (Bethnal Green), tenement, 29
Blind Beggar of Bethnal Green, legend of, 87, 91–2, 165, 191
  statue of, 138
Blind Beggar P.H. in Bethnal Green village, 97, 99, 147, 149, 166
Blind Beggar P.H., Whitechapel Rd., 146
Blind Beggar's Ho., *see* Kirby's Castle
Blisset (later New York) St., 117, 236
Blissett (Blisset):
  Revd. Geo., 166
  Jos. (d. c. 1708), 99, 166, 179
  Jos. (fl. 1748), 166
  Sar. (née ? Coling or Haynes), w. of Jos. (d. c. 1708), 166
  fam., 114, 166
  ——, 93
Blida, 91, 95
Blithenhal, *see* Reimund of Blithenhal
Blithehale, Blithenhale, Blythenhale, 91, 95; *and see* Bethnal Green
Blomfield:
  Sir Art., architect, 226
  Chas. Jas., bp. of Lond., 124–5, 214–15, 243
Bloomsbury, in Holborn, 262
Blore, Edw., architect, 220
Blue Anchor Lane, *see* Russia Lane
Blue Anchor P.H., in Chance St., 152
Blue Anchor P.H., in Russia Lane, 117, 174
Blund:
  Lettice, w. of Wm., 32, 39, 60
  Sim., 27
  Wm., 32, 39, 60
Blunt:
  S., 22
  Wm., 181
Blythe (formerly Essex) St., 129, 132, 139, 183, 233, 237, 239, 245, 256
Blythenhale Ho. (T.H.), flats in St. Peter's housing est., 139
Board of Education Scheme, 244, 251–2, 261
Board of Health, 205

Bodley, G. F., architect, 221
Bodley & Garner, architects, 256
body snatching, 210
Bogays:
  Felicia, *see* Frebarn
  John, potter, 49, 63
  John, s. of John, 49
Bohun:
  Humph. de, earl of Hereford and Essex, 37, 59, 60
  Joan (de Bathonia), w. of John de, 41
  John de, 41
  and see Bine
Bokelton:
  Cath., *see* Falk
  Marg., *see* Mitton
  Phil., 26
  Rog., 26
Bokkemad, near Old Ford, 34
Bold Defiance, 148, 178
Bolemad, in Old Ford, 30, 42
Bolyfan mill, *see* Bullivant mill
Bond, Ben., 110
Bondfield (Marg.) Ho. (M.B.), flats, later part of Lakeview (T.H.) housing est., 136, 140 *n*, *143*
bondmen, 6
Bond's Pl., Cambridge Heath, 110, 180
Bonner:
  Edm., bp. of Lond., 23, 117
  Solomon, 177
Bonner Hall, *see* Bishop's Hall
Bonner Lane, N. of Old Ford Lane, *see* St. James's Ave.
Bonner Lane (later St.), S. of Old Ford Lane, 123, 175, 233, 236, 246, 256
Bonner Methodist Home, 230, 243, 246
Bonner Rd., 122–3, 135, 233, 237, 243, 245–6, 251, 253
Bonner St., *96*, 118–19, 130, 138–9, 140 *n*, 220, 233, 237, 246, 258
Bonner's Fields, 122–3, 149, 157, 188, 204, 230, 237
bookbinding, 185
Boon:
  Chas., 161
  Steph., 161
  Thos., 161
  fam., 101, 161
Booth, Chas., social reformer, 129, 132, 186
Booth, Ledeboer & Pinckheard, architects, 138
Border's gdn., 173
Boreham St., 129, 140
Borough:
  Jane, w. of Wm., wid. of Thos., Lord Wentworth, 45, 52
  Mary, dau. of Wm., *see* Moore
  Wm., 18, 45, 51–2
Borough, the (Southwark), 127
Borough of Bethnal Green Working Men's club, 150
Borton, R., bldr., 121
Bothe, John, 63
Bothelelcroft (unlocated), 36
Botulph, John, 57
Boucher P.H., 148 *n*
Boult (Adrian) Ho. (T.H.), flats, part of Mansford housing est., 139 *n*
Boundary St. (formerly Cock Lane), 127–9, 131, 162, 185–6, 200, *pl.* 32
Boundary St. gdns., 209
Boundary St. (L.C.C.) housing est. (or scheme), 127–8, 131–2, 138, 140, *143*, 144, 146, 162, 168, 207, 209, 226, 241, 252, 257, *pl.* 33
Bourne, David, 38
Bourne's (or Baker's Arms) Gdns., 121, 175 *n*
Bovill, F. A., 186
Bow, *see* Stratford Bow
Bow creek, *8*, 11
Bow neighbourhood, 144, 146, 202, 212
Bow Rd., in Stratford Bow, *8*, 9, 38, 85, 124

Bow team ministry, 218
Bowen:
  Wm., bldr., 122
  W. S., bldr., 124
Bowes:
  Martin, 161
  Paul, 161
Bowes est. (or land), part of St. Paul's est., *93*, *119*, 161
Bowle, John, 63
bowling, bowling greens, 24, 114, 150, 153
Bowman, Chris., daus. of, 166
Bowry, Mary, 85, 260
Bowry's almshos., in Bromley, 69, 85, 260–1, *pl.* 13
Bowyer:
  Dan., bldr., 97
  Fras., 32
  John of Histon (Cambs.), 32
  John (? another), 32
  Thos., 32
  Thos. (? another), 32
  Sir Wm., ld. mayor of Lond., 32
Box, Gillian, wid. of Hen., 43
boxing, 153–4; *and see* Mendoza
Bradbury:
  Hen., bldr., 121
  Hen., gdner., 174
Bradfield (M.E.O.T. and/or Stratford Bow), *14*, 32
Bradford, Revd. W., 259
Bradlaugh, Chas., freethinker, 149–50, 214, 223
Bradley Ho.(M.B.), flats in Claredale housing est., 137
Bradshaw, Wm., 110, 118, 167
Brady (formerly North) St., 130, 132–4, 138, 150, 238
Brady St. Bldgs., Stepney M.B., 141 *n*, *pl.* 35
Brady's Bldgs., Hart Lane, 129, 141
Braemar St., 137
Brailey, Wm., carpenter, 114
Braintree (Essex), 179
Brampfield, Fras., 234
Bramston (or Brampston):
  Hugh, 62
  John (d. 1504), 62
  John, mercer, 62
  Rog., 165
Brand, Thos., 228, 259
Brandon, David, architect, 218, 223
Brasenose Coll., Oxford Univ., 70–2, 76, 213, 221
  principal of, 191; *and see* Cawley
  fellows of, 213, 221
Brayne, John, 40
Breedon, Wm., carpenter and bldr., 107
Brembre:
  Idonea, w. of Nic., 47
  Nic., 47
Brendmill (Burnt mill) hill, Wapping-Stepney, *14*, 59
Brendwood, John de, 30–1, 42
Brethren, 229, **237**
Brett:
  Mary, 160
  Wm., 63
Brewerton, Jas., 186 *n*
brewhouses and brewing, 39, 59, 61, 99, 100, 103, 147, 179–80, 187–9; *and see* Albion brewery; Truman's brewery; White Hart brewery; Wiltshire brewery
Brice of Shadwell (and of Stepney and Hecham), 15, 27–8, 33–4, 36, 59, 161
  w. Cath., dau. of Salomon, 27–8
  grds. of, *see* Ralph
Brice of Stepney, *see* Brice of Shadwell
brick and tile making, 24, 41, 56–7, 62–3, 87, 92, 103–4, 107, 110, 112, 114–15, 118, 125, 169, 171, 175–7, 210

burial grounds:
  plague cem., 102
  and see Bethnal Green, burial
    grounds; Jews, Sephardim
Burnham (M.B.) housing est., 134, 140
  n, 143, 144–5, 228
Burnham (Bernham) Sq., 100
Burnham St., 134
Burns Ho. (M.B.), flats in Bethnal
  Green housing est., 134
Burnside St., 124
Burroughs, Jeremy, 75
Burt (Thos.) Ho. (T.H.), flats in
  Mansford housing est., 139 *n*
Burton:
  Alesia, w. of John, 25
  John, 25
  Wm., 25
  Wm., & Sons, dye manufacturers,
    181
Burton & Garraway, merchants, 181
Burton field, 167
Burton (later Collingwood) St., 247
Busby:
  Chas. Augustus, architect, 217
  Edw. Sclater, 160
  Eliz. (King), w. of Hen., 160
  Hen., 107, 160
  Marg., *see* Butcher
Busby St., 129, 181
Butcher:
  Edw. Augustus, 160
  Marg. (Busby), w. of Edw. Augustus,
    160
Butcher Row, in Radcliff, 9
Butler:
  Chas. Salisbury, 157–8
  John, 118, 157
  Revd. John Banks Meek, 158, 209
  Sam., 85, 252
Butler est., 208
Butler (M.B.) housing est., 134, 140 *n,*
  143, 144
Butler St., 246, *pl.* 30
Butt, Jas., 118
Buxton:
  Chas., 243
  Sir Thos. Fowell, Bt., 198, 216, 242
  fam., 249
Buxton (formerly Spicer) St. (Bethnal
  Green and M.E.N.T.), 241, 255
Byde:
  John, 157
  Thos. Plumer, 163
  Sir Thos., 104, 157, 167
  fam., 104
Byde est., 94, 104–5, 107–8, 127, 131,
  156, 172
Byford, John, 174
Bythewater:
  Joan, w. of John, 49
  John, 49

cabinet making, 129, 132, 181–2, 189,
  227; *and see* furniture making
Cable St. (formerly Hachestreet, *q.v.*),
  in Whitechapel, St. Geo.-
  in-the-East, and Shadwell, 7, 9, 58,
  146
Cade, Jack, 17
Cadell Close, 139, 140 *n*
Cage:
  Cornelius, 52
  Eliz., 52
Calais, 63; *and see* Staple of Calais,
  merchants of
Calamy, Edm., biographer, 259
Calder, Wm., gdner., 174
Calvert Ave., 131
Calvin St., *see* Nichol St., Old
Cambridge:
  John of, 41, 62
  Maud (Ewell), w. of Steph. of, 41
  Steph. of, 41, 62
Cambridge club, 150, 240
Cambridge Circus (or Cres.), in

Cambridge Heath, 110, *111,* 129,
  130
Cambridge Heath (Camprichesheth,
  Colmrichehath), 3, 9, 36, 54, 87,
  90–1, 95, *96,* **109–12,** 117, 123,
  162–3, 169, 171, 176, 181–2, 203,
  212, 259, 261
  chap., 110
  turnpike, *pl.* 22
Cambridge Heath (or North East
  London) cemetery (or Kildy's
  ground), 208
Cambridge Heath est., in Cambridge
  Heath, 110, *111,* 121, 130–1, 156,
  165–6
Cambridge Heath (formerly Lenin)
  (M.B.) housing est., 132, 134, 140
  n, 143, 145, 202
Cambridge Heath mission, 150
Cambridge Heath (formerly
  Cambridge) Rd., 7, 9, 29, 36, 42–3,
  56, 62, 66, 84, 87–90, 94–5, 97–101,
  103, 109–12, 120, 122, 128–9,
  132–6, 138–9, 147, 149–50, 152–5,
  161–3, 169–71, 173–5, 180–9, 197,
  200, 203–5, 209, 211–12, 217–18,
  221, 225, 227, 231, 237–40, 245–6,
  259–60, *pls.* 16, 28
Cambridge Pl., in Cambridge Heath,
  109, *111*
Cambridge Rd., *see* Cambridge Heath
  Rd.
Cambridge Row, Cambridge Heath,
  174
Cambridge St., off Bethnal Green Rd.,
  117
Cambridge Univ., *see* Clare Hall
Cambridgeshire, *see* Catley
Camden Gdns., 126, 175
Camden Row, 114, 259
Camden St., 117
Camp, Mrs., 260
Campbell:
  Ann (Hamilton), w. of Jas., 159
  Jas., 159
Campbell (Jas.) Ho. (M.B.), flats in
  Approach Rd. housing est., 137
Camprichesheth, *see* Cambridge Heath
Canada, emigration to, 239
canals and canal transport, 11, 157–8,
  177
Cannock, Thos., 51
Cannon, Geo., bldr., 129
Canon, Wm., 61
Canonbury man. (Islington), 19
Canrobert St., 121, 129, 139, 164
Canterbury, John of, *see* John of
  Canterbury
Canterbury:
  abp. of, 73, 77, 191, 223; *and see*
    Cranmer; Dunstan
  archdeacon of, *see* Chichele
  dean and chapter of, 218, 223
Carden;
  Bridget, wid. of Wm., 38
  Wm., 38
Careswyesham (? location), 27
Carewe:
  Marg., wid., *see* Chedworth
  Thos., 44
Carey:
  Alan, 31
  Anne, w. of Alan, 31
Carlisle, bp. of, Treasurer, 20
Carlisle St., 115
Carlo, Seth, 155
Carnaby:
  Mary, w. of Wal., 161
  Wal., 161
Carnegie, And., 211
Carnell (Cardnall):
  Abraham, 107, 175
  Edw., cowkeeper and brickmaster,
    93, 112, 175
  Edw., saddler, 158, 175, 176
  Sam., 158

Caroline St., 112, *113*
Caron, Noel de, Dutch ambassador,
  100, 165, 172
Carson, Wal., 122
Carter:
  Ansell, 160
  Eliz., 160, 260–1
  Geo., 160
  Geo., of Hackney, 160
  John, 104, 160
  Kath., 171
  fam., 104
Carter est., *see* Hare Marsh demesne
  est.
Carter St., *105,* 108, 180
Carter St., another, 122
Carter's Rents, 94, 108, 160, 177
Cartwright, Ric., 20
Cartwright (John) Ho. (T.H.), flats in
  Mansford housing est., 139 *n*
Casket St., 138, 140
Caslon, Wm., 92
Caslon (Wm.) Ho. (T.H.), flats in
  Patriot Sq. housing est., 139 *n*
Cass est., *119,* 122, *156,* 167, 171, 174
Cassuns:
  John, 45
  John, s. of John, 45
Castello (atte Castle):
  Joan, w. of John de, 25
  John de, 25
  Nic. de, 25
Castle Ct., Castle St., 231, 236
Castle (later Old Castle) St. (later
  Virginia Rd.), 92, 94, *96,* 104–8,
  113, 147, 167, 172, 177, 204, 228,
  238, 240, 246, 250–1,
Castle St., New, 108, 247, 250, 257–8
Caswell, John, 168
Catchfield, Claxton, bldr., 112
Catesby, Rob., 91
(Ca?)tesplace (? location), 33
Catherine, dau. of Salomon, m. 1 Brice
  of Shadwell, 2 Adam le Despenser,
  27, 59
Catherine St., *see* Winkley St.
Catley (Cambs.), 160
Catling, Jas., bldr., 120
Caton, John, bldr., 118
Caunton, John, 62
Causdell (Cansdell), Wm., bldr., 92,
  110, 112
Causton:
  Christian, w. of Wm. of, 60
  Eve, w. of John of, wid. of Sim. of
    Abingdon, 30
  John of, 30
  Pet., 99
  Wm. of, 60
Cawley, Dr. Ralph, rector of Stepney,
  later principal of Brasenose Coll.,
  72, 76
Cecil:
  Eliz., dau. of Wm., Lord Burghley,
    20
  Ric., 51
  Wm., Lord Burghley, 20
  Wm., Lord Roos, 51
Cely:
  Geo., merchant of Staple, 63
  Marg., see ships
Cemetery Pl., *see* Bullard's Pl.
Central (undergrd. rly.) line, 13
Centre St., in Cambridge Heath, 110,
  130, 175
Chadwick, Edwin, 124–5
chalk mills, 18
Chalker:
  Jeremy, 160, 168 *n,* 169
  Laurence, 161, 168 *n*
Chamberlain:
  Wm. the, *see* William the chamber-
    lain
  Maj. ——, 94
Chambers:
  Geo., bldr., 130

A HISTORY OF MIDDLESEX

Fountain St., 130
Four Per Cent Dwellings Co., 128, 130
  housing est., see Mocatta Ho.
Fournier, Geo., 262
Fourteen Acre, the, 175
Fox:
  Geo., Quaker, 228
  Maj. Geo. Malcolm, 159
  Marion Jane (Mills), w. of Maj. Geo.
    Malcolm, 159
Fox St., 101
Foxes Lane, in Shadwell, 29, 68
France, 227; and see Poitou
Francis, Adam, see Fraunceys
Frankel, Sam., 185
frankpledge, views of, 20, 25, 37, 63–4,
  190
Fraunceys (Francis):
  Adam, 28, 30–2
  Adam, the younger, 32
  Agnes, wid. of Adam, 32
  Hugh le, see Hugh
  Maud, see Montagu
Frazier, Alex., 70
Frebarn:
  Felicia, w. of John, 49
  John, 49
Freeman:
  Hen., 35
  Wm., 70
freemen and freehold, 6, 9, 13, 15, 17,
  19–20, 38, 92, 191
freehold estates in Bethnal Green, 156,
  161–4, 175
Fremantle Ho. (L.C.C.), flats in
  Collingwood housing est., 133 n
French Reformed Church, 228
Frere, John, vicar of Stepney and rector
  of St. Swithun (Lond.), 73
Friar's Mount, 109, 121, 216, 231, 239,
  242, 248, 255, 258; and see Mount
  St.
Friendly Artisans, the, 149
Friendly soc., the, 148
Frink, Dame Elis., sculptor, 138
Fry, Drew, Drake & Lasdun,
  architects, 137; and see Lasdun
Fryer, Jas., 109
Fryes (or Fryers) field, 170
Fulham:
  man., 56
  man. ho., 22
  omnibus svce., 10
  rector, see Heynes
Fuller:
  Fras., bldr., 101
  Jane, wid. of John, m. 2 Sir Thos.
    Mansell, 23, 84
  John, 'judge', 23, 57, 84, 117
Fuller St., 105–6, 182, 185
Fuller's almshos., 69, 83–4, 260, pl. 14
fulling mills, 37, 58, 60
Fullmore Close (Foulmere) est., 87,
  102, 103, 121, 156, 166, 174
Furby, Geo., ironmonger, 122
furniture making, 128, 181–2, 189
Furseheath, 14
Furtado, Isaac Mendes, 241
Fytche:
  Ann, wid. of Sir Thos., 159
  Sir Comport, Bt., 159
  Sir Thos., Bt., 159

Gabell, Wm., 174
Gadbury, Thos., bldr., 122
Gadenne, John, carpenter and bldr.,
  108–9
Gale's Gdns., 120, 131, 138, 143, 174–5
Gale's Gdns. (G.L.C.) housing est.,
  138, 143
Galeysfield (Waleysfield), later London
  field, in M.E.O.T., 14, 30, 35
gallows, 63, 65
Galton, ——, bldr., 103
gambling, 153
Game, Rob., 36

Gammon, Rob., 230, 232, 238, 244
gardens, gardeners and nurseries, 52,
  55, 58, 106, 108, 112, 120, 129,
  148, 167–71, 172–5; and see
  Allport's nursery; Austin's gdn.;
  Beasley's gdn.; Border's gdn.;
  Bourne's gdn.; Brown's gdn.;
  Camden Gdns.; Chapman's gdn.;
  Cooper's Gdns.; Duthie's nursery;
  Edger's gdn.; Edith Gdns.; Gale's
  Gdns.; George Gdns.; Goodwell's
  gdns.; Greengate Gdns.;
  Hambleton's gdn.; Hollybush
  Gdns.; Kemp's Gdn.; Lamb
  Gdns.; Long Mead gdn.; Nova
  Scotia Gdns.; Pain's gdn.; Penn's
  gdn. or nursery; Preston's gdn.;
  Punderson's Gdns.; Russia Lane
  nursery; Satchwell's gdn.;
  Saunderson's gdns.; Sharp's gdn.;
  Simkins Gdns.; Smart's gdn.;
  Weatherhead's Gdns.; Whisker's
  gdns.
Gardiner, John, 114
Gardner:
  John, 124, 169, 174
  Jos. (Hardwoods), timber merchants,
    182
  fam., 124
Gardner's Rd., 124
Garlik, mess. by Stepney chyd., 17 n
Garner Passage, 164
Garnett, Hen., Jesuit, 81
Garrett, fam., 177
Garrett St., 180
Gas Acts, 1948 and 1972, 211
Gas Council, 211
Gas Light & Coke Co., 211
Gascoigne (or Gascoyne):
  Harriet, see Child
  Joel, 95
  Pet., 109
  Wm., 108, 159
Wm., s. of Wm., 159
Gascoigne est., see Fitches est.
Gascoigne Pl. (formerly Crabtree
  Lane), 130, 233, 248, 255
Gascoyne, see Gascoigne
gasworks, 11, 158
Gatehouse, the, mansion (M.E.O.T.),
  45
Gates, Sir John, chancellor of duchy of
  Lancaster, 91
Gatyn:
  Maud, w. of Thos., see Aleyn
  Thos., 33
Gauber (or Gawber) St., 130, 248
Gavill, Rob., 108
Gavin, Dr. Hector, 125, 197, 205–6
Geary:
  Eliz (Tracy), w. of John, 42
  John, 42
Gee:
  Jonathan, carpenter and bldr., 107
  Miss Mabel, 260
  Miss Millicent, 260
General Baptist Assembly, 235
General Baptist Assoc., 235
General Improvement Areas, 141
Geoffrey, s. of Osbert (? Trentemars),
  29; and see Trentemars
Geoffrey, s. of Susan (Trentemars), 29;
  and see Trentemars
George, Prince of Wales, Prince
  Regent, 153
George field, 115, 176
George Gdns., 120, 175, 222
George P.H., Old Bethnal Green Rd.,
  114, 147
George St., off Old Bethnal Green Rd.,
  98–9, 239, 245
George St., on Hare Marsh est., 94,
  104, 131, 178
George St., on Tyssen est., 108, 122
George St., Little, off Cambridge
  Heath Rd., 100

George Walk, 129
George's Pl., Old Ford Rd., 118, 123
G.E.R., see Great Eastern Rly.
Gerard of Old Ford, s. of, see Edm.
Gerbier, Sir Balthazar, 94 and n, 100,
  147, 227, 259
Germany, 127; and see Leipzig
Gernon Rd., 124, 253
Gerrard:
  Alice, see Elliott
  Edw., 38
Gervis, Sir Geo. Wm. Tapps, Bt., see
  Tapps
Ghyepe (or Yepe or Waterlader), John
  le, 36
Gibbons, Wm., leatherseller, 50
Gibraltar Bldgs., Gibraltar Gdns., 127
Gibraltar Field, 108, 231
Gibraltar Pl., off Bethnal Green Rd.,
  231, 235
Gibraltar P.H., Gibraltar Wk., 107–8,
  148, 170
Gibraltar (or Lord's) Wk., 109, 112,
  113, 115, 131, 137, 145, 148, 170
  n, 223, 239, 252
Gibson:
  Avice, wid. of Nic., see Knyvett
  Nic. (d. 1540), sheriff of London, 83
  Tim., rector of Bethnal Green, 214
  Tim., Meth. min., 236
Gibson's almshos., 83
Gibson's schs., 83
Gift Fund of the Grand Council of the
  Knights of Burgundy, 148
Gilbert, s. of Emma de la Milaunde
  (Mile End), 32
Gilbert, Lewis, licencee, 148 n
Giles & Gough, architects, 257
Giles Row, 183
Gill, Ann (Dormer), 164
Gillingham, Rog., 95 n
Gillingham (Kent), man. of, 35
Gillman (formerly Wolverley) St., 164
Gilnest, Hugh, 35
Gilson & Bliss, 205
Gisby, Mic., bldr., 175
Gisors:
  John (II) (d. 1296), 41
  John (III), 41–3, 46
  Marg., granddau. of John (III), see Burcestre
  Margery (Ewell), w. of John (II), 41
Gittings, Edw., 21, 25
Gladstone Radical or Working Men's
  club, 150
Glasgow, 185
glass ind., 187
Glaxo Group Ltd., 187
G.L.C., see Greater London Council
GLEB ind. est., Ebor St., 188
Glemham:
  Dr. Hen., 20–1, 24
  Sir Thos., 20
Globe Alley, Wapping, 82
Globe Cottage, 117, 119
Globe Hall, 117
Globe Pl., 98
Globe Rd. (formerly Back Lane,
  Thieving Lane, Globe Lane or
  St.), 88, 93–100, 118–20, 130, 134,
  136, 139–40, 145, 147, 152, 157,
  166 n, 180, 184–5, 210, 227–9, 234,
  236–8, 241, 248, 258
Globe Terr., 248, 258
Globe Town, 88, 96, 117–18, 139, 233
Globe Town neighbourhood, 90,
  144–6, 153, 202, 212
Globe Wharf, Mile End Rd., 177
Globefields, 242
Gloucester:
  Maud, w. of Wm. de, see Trentemars
  Ric. of, alderman, 30
  Ric., s. of Ric. of, 30
  Wal. of, see Crepyn
  Wm. de, 31
Gloucester, Humph., duke of, see
  Plantagenet

276

Poorefield, in Stepney and Hackney, 32
Pope:
　Anne, w. of Sir Wm., 20
　John, 37, 39, 161
　Maria, 163, 225
　Mic. (d. by 1808), 161–2
　Mic. (d. by 1848), 163
　Sir Wm., Bt., 20
　fam., 115
Poplar, in Stepney, 2–5, 15, 17–18,
　29–30, 33, 38, 44, 47, 58, 61, 63–5,
　67–9, 71, 80–2, 84–6, 118, 135
　Blackwall, q.v.
　chap., 75
　ch. and par. of All Sts., 75
　Isle of Dogs, q.v.
　Leamouth, q.v.
　man., 15, 20, 27, 32–3, **37–8**, 42, 52,
　　59–60
　　copyhold, 38
　　ct., 38, 44
　　freehold of, 47
　　man. ho., *14, 16*, 18, 38
　　tenants, 26, 38
　marshes in, 21; *and see* East Marsh;
　　Stepney Marsh
　metropolitan boro. (M.B.), 3, 201–2
　Millwall, q.v.
　pop., 18
　tram svces., 11
Poplar High (formerly Poplar) St., in
　Poplar, 10, *16*, 18, 38
Poplar marsh, *see* Stepney marsh
Poplar Ruridecanal Conference, 134
Poplar (later Poplar High) St., in
　Poplar, *14*, 58
Port of London Authority, 12
Portland Pl., White St., 176
Portman Pl., Globe Rd., in Mile End,
　later in Bethnal Green, 139, 140 n,
　249, 252, 258
Portsmouth (Hants), 63, 187
Potter:
　Cecily, w. of Wm. (fl. *c.* 1350), 49
　John (d. 1388), 91
　John, cordwainer (fl. 1405), 45
　John (fl. 1681), 81
　Thos., 110
　Wm. (fl. *c.* 1350), 49, 55
　Wm. (fl. 1380), 58
　Wm., priest (fl. 1487), 61
　Wm. (fl. 1653), 21
　fam., 91
Potters ferry, 11
Potter's Row, in Cambridge Heath, 110
Potts, Ann, 101
Potts (Pott) St., 101, 133–4, 153, 231,
　233, 245
Poulton, W. F., architect, 233
Pountfreit, man. of, *see* Pomfret
Pountfreyt, adv. of chap. of, *see*
　Pomfret, chap.
Povey:
　John, 172
　Pet., 172
Powell, ——, dyer, 178
Powis, Lord, *see* Grey
Powle, Sir Stephen, 45
Poyster St., 257
Pratt, Edw., 97
Praxis, 153
Preedy, John, bldr., 121
'prefabs', 135
Presbyterians, 82, 228, 235, **238**, 259
Preston:
　John (fl. 1672), 32, 169
　John (fl. 1703), 168
　John (fl. 1763), 170
　Thos., 70
　Thos., radical, 149
Preston St., Victoria Pk., 235
Preston's gdn., 104, 172
Prestonian soc., 149
Price:
　A. W., bldr., 130
　Jas., bldr., 118

John, bldr., 107, 114
　Thos., 92
Prickard, Mr., *see* Pritchard
Priestley (Jos.) Ho. (T.H.), flats in
　Mansford housing est., 139 n
Priests (Ordination of Women) Act,
　1993, 214
Primitive Methodists, *see* Methodists
Primrose St., 98, 101
Prince of Wales, *see* Edw.; Geo.
Prince of Wales P.H., 122, 154 n
Prince Regent, *see* Geo., Prince of
　Wales
Prince's Ct., Tyssen St., 252, 254, 258
Prince's Pl., 129
Prince's ('Coomb', later Chambord)
　St., 108–9, 129
Prince's Terr., Bonner Rd., 123
Princelet St., Spitalfields, 241
Princess Elizabeth of York children's
　hosp., in Shadwell, 207
printing, 184–5, 189
Prison (later Old Prison) Ho.,
　Whitechapel High St., 66
Pritchard:
　And. (fl. 1789), 110, 112, 176
　And. (fl. 1889), 163
　Clive Fleetwood, 163
　Ion, 121 n
　John, publican (fl. *c.* 1730), 112
　John, tilemaker (fl. 1790), 112
　Dame Sarah, 86, 260
　fam., 121, 163, 176
Pritchard est., 211
Pritchard Ho. (L.C.C.), flats in
　Pritchard's housing est., 134
Pritchard's (Pritchard) (L.C.C.)
　housing est., 134, 140, *143*
Pritchard's Rd. (formerly Ann's Pl.),
　110, 121, 133–4, 141, 164, 174,
　197, 205, 232, 234, 245, 252, 258
Privy Council, 11
Proby, Edw., 94
Progressive party, 200–2
Prospect Pl. (or Row), Russia La., 110
Protestant Alliance, 227
Protestant Refugees from High and
　Low Normandy, soc. of, 148
Providence Pl., 100
Prusons Island, in Ratcliff, 68
Pryour, John, 49
Public Health Act, 1866, 198
Public Libraries Act, 1875, 211
Public Welfare Assoc., 201
Pulley, Jon., 177
Pulteney:
　Sir John, mayor of Lond., 18, 37,
　　59–60
　John de (? another), 33
　Marg., w. of Sir John, m. 2 Sir Nic.
　　Lovayne, 37
　Marg., w. of Sir Wm., prob. m. 2 Sir
　　John Pekbrugge, 37–8
　Rob., *see* Owen
　Sir Wm., 37–8, 60
Pulteney's Inn, *see* London, City,
　Pulteney's Inn in
Punderson, Capt. Jon., 100
Punderson's Gdns., 100–1, 120, 129,
　133, 171, 174, 176, 186, 222, 239
Punderson's Pl., 100, 120, 180
Punderson's St., 98, *116*
Purim Pl., Dog Row, 103, 241
Pusey, Edw., 214
Puteaux Ho. (M.B.), flats in Cranbrook
　housing est., 138 n
Pye, Dame Hester, 100
Pyke, John, 91
Pynchepole, Rog., 31
Pyott:
　Ann, *see* Gubbs
　Ann, *see* Righton
　Blanch, *see* Hinckley
　Caroline, *see* Malie
　Chas., 163
　Jane, w. of Wm., *see* Christmas

John, s. of Ric., 163
John (d. 1689), 163
John (d. by 1734), 163
Pyarea, w. of Ric., 163
Ric., grocer (d. 1620), 163–4
Ric. of Streethay, s. of Ric., 163, 166
　and n
Ric. (d. 1747), 163
Rob., 163
Susan, *see* Cockram
Wm. (d. 1643), 163, 166 n
Wm., s. of Ric. of Streethay, 163, 166
　and n
fam., 163
Pyotts (Pyott, Piot) est., *93*, 95, 97–8,
　100, 110, *111*, 118, *119*, 120, 130,
　156, 157, **163–4**, 169, 203
　mansion ho., *see* Corner, later
　　Aldgate Ho.

Quaker St., 238
Quakers, *see* Society of Friends
Queen Adelaide P.H., 101
Queen Adelaide's charity, 206
Queen Adelaide's dispensary, in
　Warner Pl., 206, 219
Queen Anne's Bounty, 71, 218, 220–5
Queen Elizabeth's Children's (formerly
　North Eastern, later Queen's)
　hosp., 206–8
Queen Margaret Flats, St. Jude's Rd.,
　135, *143*
Queen St., near Hackney Rd., 112, 114
Queen's Bldgs., Gosset St., 127, 129,
　141
Queen's Children's hosp., *see* Queen
　Elizabeth's Children's hosp.
Queen's Head, in Mile End, 32
Queen's Own Light Infantry
　Regiment, Tower Hamlets militia,
　120, 154
Queen's Pl., near Hackney Rd., 126
Queen's (or Charlotte) Row,
　Cambridge Rd., 103, 241
Quilter St., 126
Quiltotex Ltd., 146
Quinn, Thos., bldr., 129
Quinn Sq., 129, 132, 139

Racine, Jas., dyer, 178
racism, 146, 152, 210; *and see*
　anti-semitism
Radford, Rob., 86
Radical club, 149, 214
radicalism, 148–50, 216, 230
Ragged Church and Chapel Union, 246
Ragged London, 125
Ragged School Union (later
　Shaftesbury Soc.), 239–40, 243,
　246–7, 249–51, 256
Railton, Wm., architect, 219
Ralph of the marsh, 27
Ralph the clerk, 15, 19, 26–7, 32, 36, 52
　s. of, *see* Ralph; Rob.
　est. of, 26–7
Ralph, grds. of Brice of Stepney, 36
Ralph, s. of Ralph the clerk, 27–8
Ram Alley, 104, 148
Ramesey, John de, 34
Ramsey St., 115, 130, 245
Ranwell West (T.H.) housing est., 144
Rapley Pl., 137
Ratcliff:
　Alice, wid. of Edm., 42
　Alice, dau. of Hugh, *see* Shakerley
　Edm., 33, 42, 62
　Hugh, 42
Ratcliff, in Stepney, 2–5, 15–19, 23, 42,
　48–9, 61, 63, 65, 67–9, 75–6, 80–1,
　83–6
　almshos., 83–4
　char., 83
　ch. of St. Jas., 84
　chwdn. of, 86
　fire at, 84
　pop., 18

INDEX

portionist of, 71–2
shipbldg., 17
Ratcliff Cross, in Ratcliff, 6, 9, 13, 65, 82
Ratcliff Highway (formerly Shadwell St.), in Shadwell and Wapping, 5, 9, 29, 41, 58, 68, *pl. 2*; *and see* Broad St.
Ratcliff St., in Ratcliff, 68
Ratcliff Wall, in Ratcliff, 68
Rathbone (Wm.) Ho. (T.H.), flats in Mansford housing est., 139 n
Rathbone Soc., 237
Ravenscroft, Jas., 24, 158–9
Ravenscroft St., 114, 130, 134, 137, 139, 182, 212, 237, 247
Raymond, Thos., 23
Rayner, Edw., 122
Raynesford, Sir John, 61
Reason (Reyson, *q.v.*):
  Ric., 95 n
  fam., 95 n
Recoches, Louis, 45
Red Cock, Spitalfields, 24
Red Bull P.H., near Stepney ch., 17
Red Cow est., 92, *105*, 106–7, 122, 127, 129, 131, *156*, **160**
  Red Cow (or Milkho.), 106, *156*, 160, 170, 173
Red Cow La., *96*, 102–3, 174
Red Cross P.H., Hare St., 149, 154 and n
Red Flag, singing of the, 202
Red Ho., asylum, 101, 121, 165, 206
Red Lion farm, M.E.O.T. and Whitechapel, 40
Red Lion inn, M.E.O.T. and Whitechapel, 40
Red Maid La., Wapping, 82
Redclyf, the, 9
Redclyff (Ratcliff), 9
Redding, demesne close, 61
Rede, John le, 44
Redene, in Ratcliff, *14*
Redistribution of Seats Act, 1885, 202
Redmill Ho. (L.C.C.), flats in Collingwood housing est., 136
Regent's canal, 8, 11, 89, *96*, *111*, 122–3, 132, 136, 176, 181–2, 185, 197, 205, 208–9, 211, *pl. 6*
  dock, *see* Limehouse basin
  wharves, 124, 177, 188
Reimund of Blithenhal (Bethnal Green), 15
Renvoize, Pet., 94, 261
Repton club, 152–3
Repton Sch. (Derbys.), 152
Resurrectionists, 112
Revocation of the Edict of Nantes, 92, 177
Reymond, Wm., 95 n
Reymund, 95 n
Reymund, s. of Aluric, 28
Reymund, s. of, *see* Adam
Reynolds:
  Edm., 179
  G. W. M., 136 n
  John, bldr., 103
Reynolds Ho. (M.B.), flats, later part of Approach housing est., 136, *143*
Reyson:
  John the older (fl. 1362), 55
  John the younger (fl. 1362), 55
  John (d. 1421), 163
  and see Reason
Rhodes:
  Wm. (d. 1843), 176
  Wm., file maker, 180–1
Rich:
  Sir Edm., 51
  Eliz., wid. of Rob., 51
  Rob., Baron, 51
Richard II, 17, 203
Richard Aynolf, 34
Richard, s. of Wm. Picton, 28
Richard Fitzneal, bp. of Lon., 28, 59

Richard of Hecham, 28, 36
Richard, the bp. of Lond.'s beadle, 29, 59
Richard, s. of Ric. of Gloucester, *see* Gloucester, Ric. of
Richards:
  Blanche (Pelter), w. of Morgan, 39
  Morgan, skinner, 39
  Wm., 39
Richardson:
  Chas., 39
  Jon, 104, 162, 172
  Sarah, wid. of Chas., 39
  Thos. (fl. 1647), 39
  Thos., clothworker (fl. 1706), 106
  fam., 161
Richardson's gdn., 172–3
Richborough Castle (Kent), 164
Rider:
  Priscilla, w. of Sir Wm., 165
  Thos., 95 n, 162, 165
  Wm., haberdasher, 91, 165
  Wm., bricklayer, 108
  Sir Wm., hemp merchant, 165
Ridge:
  John, 123, 171, 176
  Sam., farmer and brickmaker, 110, 118, 169, 176
  est. of, 171
Ridley:
  Nic., bp. of Lond., 20, 70
  S. Forde, M.P., 203
Ridley Hall, Cambridge, 226
Ridley Hall, university settlement, St. James's Rd., 221, 226
Righton, Ann (Pyott), w. of ——, 163
Riley, Wm., bldr., 121
Riot Act, 193
riots, 19, 147–8, 178, 193; *and see* Gordon riots
Rippin:
  John, bricklayer and bldr., 107
  Thos. Hen., 251, 261
Ripple, Salomon de, 36, 47
Rising Sun, Green St., 64
Risley, Sir John, 32
Rissemad, near Old Ford, 34
ritualism, *see* High Church practices
Robert (? de Barton), dean of St. Paul's cath., 29–30
Robert de Tessunt (or Teffunt), s. of, *see* John
Robert le Coner, 34
Robert le Cutiller, 19
Robert of Aleford (? Old Ford), 28
Robert Fafiton, 19, 45
Robert le Messag', 28
Robert, s. of Bernard of Stepney, 27, 32, 37
Robert, s. of Chedric, 32
Robert, s. of Ralph the clerk, 27, 36
  his wid., *see* Maud
Robert, s. of Roscelin, 19
Robert, s. of Terricus, 32
Robert Turneboet', 28
Robert St., *113*, 115, *116*
Roberts:
  Patrick, 166
  Ted, vicar of St. Jas. the Less, 145
Roberts (Ted) Ho., flats for elderly, 145
Robertson, Geo., 252, 254, 260, 263
Robertson's ginger beer factory, 186
Robesard, Sir John, 45
Robinson:
  Ann, wid. of Wm., m. 2 Fras. Howell, 157
  Ann, dau. of Wm., *see* Sotheby
  Humfry, 164
  Sir John, lieutenant of Tower Hamlets, 82
  Percy, architect, 200
  Wm., 21, 24, 155, 157
Robinson Rd., 122–3, 139, 140 n, 187
Robinson's Charity est., *119*, 122, 157, 169, 171

Robson:
  Edw. Rob., architect, 246–7, 256
  John, bldr., 123, 176
  Nehemiah, 263
Rochelle St., 250, 252, 258
Roebuck P.H., Hackney Rd., 149
Rodland, s. of Bernard, 27
Roger, s. of, *see* Peter
Roger the sheriff, 45
Roger, vicar of Stepney, 36, 70
Roger Dowley Ct., 145
Rogers:
  Sgt. Maurice, V.C., 136
  Thos., 124
Rogers (M.B.) housing est., 136, 140–1, *143*, 144, 181
Rogue La., *156*, 159, 162; *and see* Bethnal Green Rd.; Old Bethnal Green Rd.; Pollard Row
Rogueswell common (M.E.O.T.), 9, 48
Rolfe, Hen. W., 259
Rolliston:
  Rob., 48
  ——, 48
Roman Catholicism, 76, 214, 227, 235
  convents, 228
  schs., 227, 243–4, 251, 253–4, 257–9
  and see Augustinians of the Assumption; Charity, Sisters of; Christian Retreat, Sisters of the; Congregation of Our Lady (Canonesses of St. Augustine); Divine Love, Missionaries of the; Holy Family of Nazareth, Sisters of the; Marian Fathers; Marists
Roman Rd. (formerly Claremont, Esmond and Bridge Rds. and Green St. *q.v.*), 7, 88, 124, 136–9, 145, 155, 157, 162, 182, 190, 212, 218, 235, 238, 241, 260
Romford (Essex), 182, 238
  coach svces. from, 11
  rly. svces. from, 90
Romney marsh (Kent), 6
Ronan Point flats (West Ham, Essex), 139, 140
Rondeau, John, 177
Rooff, J. & R., bldrs., 139
Rooke:
  John the elder (fl. 1471), 41
  John (? another, fl. 1494), 41
  Thos., 62
Roos, Lord, *see* Cecil
Ropemakers field, in Shadwell, 29
ropemaking, 18, 180, 188
Ropley St., 134
Roscelin, s. of, *see* Robert
Rose La., Spitalfields, 10, 24, 82
Rose St., 106, 109, 185
Rosemary La. (formerly Hachestreet, *q.v.*) in Whitechapel, St. George-in-the-East, Shadwell and Ratcliff, 7, 9, 65; *and see* Cable St. and Brook St.
Rosery, the, flats in Stepney, 72
Rothschild, fam., 128
Rotheley, Wm., 26
Rotherhithe (Surr.), 11
  tunnel, 11
Rothleys mill, in Stratford Bow, 60
Rous, John le, 41
Row, Dame Alice, wid. of Capt. Jas. Cook, 84
Rowe, Hen., 168
Rowlandson, Thos., 154
Rowlandson (Sir Graham) Ho. (T.H.), flats, part of Dorset housing est., *143*, 207
Rowley, R. J., bldr., 134
Rowley Bros., bldrs., 133, 139
Royal Adelaide Provident institution, 150
Royal Commission on Ecclesiastical Discipline, 219
Royal Contract Estates, 38
Royal Horse Guards, 183

289

Warley (formerly William) St., 137, 224–5, 238, 257

Warn, ——, bldr., 108

Warner:
Eliz, dau. of Rob., *see* Green
John, 179
Nowell, 11
Rob., 33

Warner & Ramm, Messrs., 179

Warner Pl., off Hackney Rd., 114, 121, 139, 149, 206, 224, 260

Warren:
Joan, w. of Sir Ralph, 75, 163, 212
Joan, dau. of Sir Ralph, *see* Cromwell
Sir Ralph, mayor of Lond., 23, 37, 56, 75, 161, 163, 212
Sir Ric., 163

Warren, the, *156*

Warris, Thos., 62

Waryn:
Joan (Huscarl), w. of Wm., 33
Ric., 25
Rog., 25
Wm., 33

Washington Ho., Wapping, 81

Water La., *see* Three Colts La.

Waterhouse, Paul, architect, 226

Waterlader, *see* Ghyepe

Waterloo Ho., formerly workho., 134

Waterloo housing est., *see* Wellington housing est.

Waterloo (formerly Albert) Rd., 122–3, 211, 257

Waterloo Town, 115

Waterlow, Sir Sydney, Bt., 126

Waterlow (M.B.) housing est., 126, 138, 140, *143*, 144, 146, *pl.* 37; *and see* Improved Industrial Dwellings Co.

Wates (London), bldr., 138–9

Watford (Herts.), 252

Watson:
Eliz. (Kirby), w. of John, 164
John, 164–5, 172
——, bldr., 108

Watts, Mary, *see* Goodman

Watts-Ditchfield, John E., vicar of St. Jas. the Less, later bp. of Chelmsford, 220–1, 226

Wear St., 139

Wearing:
Edw. Bird, 167
Hen. Fred., 167

Weatherhead's Gdns., 109, 175–6

Weaver Ho. (M.B.) housing est., 134, 140, *143*

Weaver St., 107, 122, 177–8, 236

Weavers' Fields (Field), 137, 209, 240

weaving, weavers, *see* silkweaving

Webb:
Anne, architect, 251
Jas., 182

Webb (Beatrice) Ho. (M.B.), flats, later part of Lakeview housing est., 136, 140 *n*, *143*

Webbe, H.B., 152

Webbe institute, 152–3, 226

Webster, Arth., 35

Webster printing works, St. Matthew's Row, 185

Wedgwood Ho. (M.B.), flats in Greenways housing est., 137

Weeley (Essex), adv. of, 213

Weinberg, Baruch, 155, 185

Welch:
Hester, 76
John, 231

Weld, Lady Frances, 20

Wellclose Sq. (in St. Geo.-in-the-East and Whitechapel), 7

Wellington:
Alice, w. of John, 49
John, 49

Wellington (formerly Waterloo) (L.C.C.) housing est., 134–6, 140, 146, 153

Wellington Pl. (later Royston St.), 123

Wellington Pl., off Old Bethnal Green Rd., *113*, 114, 121

Wellington pond, 175

Wellington Row (or St.), off Virginia Row, 115, 204, 260

Wellington St., off Globe Rd., *see* Cyprus St.

Wellington St., Waterloo Town, 115

Wells:
Ant., 114, 175
John, bldr., 107

Welsh, John, bricklayer and bldr., 104

Welwyn (formerly Park) St., 248

Wendover:
Agnes, w. of Mic., 51
John, 41–2, 62
Mic., 51

Wennington St., 124

Wentworth:
Anne, wid. of Hen. and w. of Sir Wm. Pope, 20
Anne, dau. of Thos., earl of Cleveland, *see* Lovelace
Henrietta Maria, Baroness Wentworth, 21–3
Hen., Lord Wentworth, 10, 20, 45, 53, 99, 101
Jane, wid. of Thos., Lord Wentworth, *see* Borough
Martha, Baroness Wentworth, w. of Sir Hen. Johnson, 66
Philadelphia, Lady Wentworth, w. of Thos. (d. 1665), 21–3, 25, 66, 70–2, 102, 157–8
ho. of, *pl.* 9
Thos., Baron Wentworth (d. 1551), 20, 70
Thos., Lord Wentworth (d. 1584), 20, 42, 49, 51, 101, 164
Thos., Lord Wentworth, later earl of Cleveland (d. 1667), 20–1, 23–5, 51, 53, 57, 66, 70, 72, 84, 100–1, 155, 157–9
Thos., Lord Wentworth (d. 1665), 20–1
Wm., 20

Wentworth, barony of, 22

Wentworth St., Spitalfields, 24, 65

Wesley:
John, 228
Sam., 259

Wesleyan Missionary soc., 230

Wesleyan Sunday Sch. cttee., 247

Wesleyan Tract Soc., 236, 249

Wesleyans, *see* Methodists

Wessex St. (M.E.O.T.), 153, 249

West, Eliz., 168

West St., off Bethnal Green Rd., *116*, 176

West St., in Cambridge Heath, 110

West St., off Green St., 118, *119*

West End of London, 183

West Ham (Essex), 3, 34, 55, 60; *and see* 'Hamme'

West Heath, in Mile End and Bethnal Green, 102

West India docks, in Poplar, 10–11

West India Docks Co., 10

West Tilbury (Essex), 25

Westbrook Ho., flats in East End Dwellings, later Victoria Park Sq. (or Charlwood) housing est., 140

Westbury St., Spitalfields, 82

Westheath, Mile End, *14*, 51

Westheye:
Aubrey, w. of John, 32
John, 32

Westmacott, Ric., 81

Westminster, 17, 82, 124, 159; *and see* St. Clement Danes; Strand

Westminster abbey:
abbey and abbots, 27
chamberlain, 60
dean and chapter of, 60

Westminster Hall, 66

Westminster St., *see* Baroness Rd.

Weston, Rob., 162

Westover St., *see* Temple St.

Westwall. in Poplar, *14*, 15, 18

Wete marsh, the, in Poplar, 57

Weymouth Terr., Shoreditch, 248

Whaley, ——, *93*

Wharf Cottage, Park Terr., 123, 177

Wharf Rd., 121, 185

Wheatsheaf P.H., on Bethnal green , 97, 147, 165

Wheeler, Thos., 231

Wheeler (Wheler) St., in Bethnal Green and Spitalfields, 87, 104, 147

Wheler (Wheeler), Sir Geo., 75

Wheler est., in Spitalfields, 104

Wheler's chap., tabernacle, *see* Spitalfields, Wheler's chap.

Whetecroft (? M.E.O.T.), 43

Whiltenbury, Jos., 110

Whisker's gdns., 120, 175

Whitby St., *see* York St., Lt.

White:
Chas. (d. 1754), 160, 213
Chas. (fl. 1771), 160
John, 160
Martha (Wightwick), w. of Chas., 160
Miles, 177
Thos., 160
Wm., leatherseller (fl. 1517), 50
Wm. (fl. 1754), 160
Wm., brickmaker, 176
Wm., architect, 223
fam., 115

White Bros., 182

White Bear P.H., in Dog Row, 101, 147

White Cock P.H., Spitalfields, 24

White Hart brewery, Sugar Loaf Wk., 100, 180

White Hart Pl., 120

White Hart P.H., Bethnal Green Rd., 114

White Hart P.H., in Ratcliff, 9, *14*

White Hart St., *see* White Horse St.

White Horse (later Three Colts) farm and inn, *see* Mewes

White Horse La., 49, 58, 72; *and see* Commercial Rd. East

White Horse P.H., Hare St., 149

White Horse (or White Hart) St., in Ratcliff, 9, 33, 49, 68; *and see* Clevestreet

White Ho., *see* Kirby's Castle

White Lion St., Spitalfields, 75

White Roding (Essex), 86

White St., 115, 122, 176, 196

White's Passage, *see* Thomas Passage

Whitechapel (St. Mary Matfelon), formerly in Stepney, 2–6, 10, 13, 17, 20, 27, 30, 33, 35–6, 39–41, 43, 46–7, 62, 64–6, 77, 91, 97, 103, 122, 127, 146, 154–5, 162, 175, 183, 241, 263
adv., 21–2
boundaries, 17
chap. (ch.), 17, 36, 58, 64, 70, 73
dock, 39
Homefield, *q.v.*
par. of, *16*, 67, 73, 83
rlys., 12
rectory, 21
vicarage, 73
wharf, 39

Whitechapel field, in Whitechapel, *14*, 43

Whitechapel High St. (formerly Algatestreet) in Whitechapel, 9, 15, 17–18, 29–30, 66

Whitechapel La. (? later Brick La.), in Whitechapel and Spitalfields, 6

Whitechapel Rd., in Whitechapel, 9, 54, 56–8, 62, 81, 85, *93*, 130, 155, 180, 205, 238

Whitman Ho. (M.B.), flats in Bethnal Green housing est., 134

CORRIGENDA TO VOLUMES V AND X

Earlier lists of corrigenda will be found in Volumes I and III - X.

Vol V,   page 251*b*,   line 8, *for* 'began with a chapel' *read* 'existed by 1845; a second chapel, also'

"   "   251,   note 10, delete full point and add '; P. Charters, *Brief History of Meths. in Ponders End* (1993), 45, which contains additional inf. on other chapels.'

Vol X,   page 32*a*,   line 14, *for* '1878' *read* '1876'

"   "   122*a*,   line 8 from end, *for* 'Wgs.' *read* 'Figs.'

"   "   128,   note 30, *for* 'Rottman' *read* 'Rottmann'

"   "   129,   notes 34, 39, 43, 47, *for* 'Rottman' *read* 'Rottmann'

"   "   161,   note 96, *for* 'v' *read* 'viii'

"   Illus. no. 62, underline, *for* '1857' *read* '1875'